ABC

CW00557658

With the ABC
Thumb Index at
this page you place
the letter you want at
the German-En-
glish-German
dictionary.

You place your thumb on the
letter you want at the edge of
this page, then flick through the
dictionary till you come to the
appropriate pages in the German-English or English-German section.

Left-handed people should use
the ABC Thumb Index at the
end of the book.

A
F
G
H
I
J
K
L
M
N
O
P
Q
R
S
T
U
V
W
Z

Langenscheidt

Pocket German Dictionary

German – English
English – German

includes new German spelling

edited by the
Langenscheidt editorial staff

Langenscheidt

New York · Berlin · Munich · Vienna · Zurich

Neither the presence nor the absence of a
designation indicating that any entered word
constitutes a trademark should be regarded as
affecting the legal status thereof.

This dictionary uses the standardised German
spelling system as of 2006.

10010 (98084)

Contents

Preface

This new dictionary of English and German is a tool with more than 55,000 references for those who work with these languages at beginner's or intermediate level.

Languages are in a constant process of change. Therefore many words which have entered German and English in the last few years have been included in the vocabulary, e.g. *abgasfrei, Blog, chatten, DVD-Player, Handynummer, Kanzlerin, Lauschangriff, SMS, Vogelgrippe; blog, cell (phone), chat, coach class, digital camera, Internet access, low-calorie, snowboarding, text message.*

The easy-to-read, clearly laid out typography with all the headwords in blue makes for good readability and allows the user to find words and expressions and their translations more quickly. The **new German spelling** has been used and detailed notes for the user have been included.

The A–Z part of this dictionary contains many important German and English proper names and abbreviations. Another feature is the special quick-reference sections listing the States of Germany and Austria and the Cantons of Switzerland, German weights and measures, examples of German declension and conjugation and alphabetical lists of German and English irregular verbs.

Designed for the widest possible variety of uses, this dictionary will be of great value to students, teachers and tourists, and will find a place in home and office libraries alike.

How to use this dictionary

This dictionary endeavors to do everything it can to help you find the words and translations you are looking for as quickly and as easily as possible.

To enable you to get the most out of your dictionary, you will be shown exactly where and how to find the information that will help you choose the right translation in every situation – whether at school or at home, in your profession, when writing letters, or in everyday conversation.

1. German and English headwords

1.1 When you are looking for a particular word it is important to know that the dictionary entries are arranged in strict **alphabetical order:**

> Aal – ab
> beugen – biegen
> hay – haze

In the German-English section the letters **ä**, **ö** and **ü** are treated on the same basis as **a**, **o** and **u**. **ß** is treated as **ss**.

1.2 Besides the headwords and their derivatives and compounds, the past tense and past participle of irregular German verbs are also given as individual entries in alphabetical order in the German-English section, e.g. **ging, gegangen.**

1.3 Many German and English proper names and abbreviations are included in the vocabulary.

1.4 How then do you go about finding a particular word? Take a look at the words in bold print at the top of each page. These are the so-called **catchwords** and they serve as a guide to tracing your word as quickly as possible. The catchword on the top left gives you the first headword on the left-hand page, while the one on the top right gives you the last word on the right-hand page, e.g.

> **Griechenland – gut**

1.5 What about entries comprising hyphenated expressions or two or more words, such as **DVD-Player, left-handed** or **mass media?** Expressions of this kind are treated in the same way as single words and thus appear in strict alphabetical order. Should you be unable to find a compound in the dictionary, just break it down into its components and look these up separately. In this way the meaning of many compound expressions can be derived indirectly.

When using the dictionary you will notice many 'word families', or groups of words stemming from a common root, which have been collated within one article in order to save space:

> Einkaufs... – ~bummel – ~preis – ~wagen – ~zentrum
> amend – amendment – amends

2. Spelling

2.1 Where American and British spelling of a word differs, the American spelling is given first as in

> center, *Br* centre
> center (*Br* centre) forward
> dialog, *Br* dialogue
> analy|ze, *Br* -se etc.

or in the English-German section as a separate headword, e.g. **theater, defense** etc.

A 'u' or an 'l' in parentheses in a word also indicates variant spellings:

> colo(u)red means: American **colored**, British **coloured**
> travel(l)er means: American **traveler**, British **traveller**

2.2 Word division in a German word is possible after each syllable, e.g.

> ein-hül-len, Zu-cker, ba-cken, tes-ten

In the English-German section the centered dots within a headword indicate syllabification breaks.

3. The different typefaces and their functions

3.1 **Bold type** is used for the German and English headwords and for Arabic numerals separating different parts of speech (nouns, transitive and intransitive verbs, adjectives and adverbs etc.) and different grammatical forms of a word:

> **bieten 1.** *v/t* ... **2.** *v/i* ...
> **hängen 1.** *v/i* (*irr, ge-, h*) hang (**an** *dat* on...); **2.** *v/t* (*ge-, h*) hang (**an** *acc* on)
> **feed 1.** Futter *n* ; ... **2.** *v/t* füttern

3.2 *Italics* are used for

a) grammatical and other abbreviations: *v/t, v/i, adj, adv, appr, fig* etc.
b) gender labels (masculine, feminine and neuter): *m, f, n*
c) grammatical references in brackets in the German-English section
d) any additional information preceding or following a translation (including dative or accusative objects):

> **knacken** *v/t and v/i* ... *twig*: snap; *fire, radio*: crackle
> **Etikett** *n* ... label (*a. fig*)
> **Gedanke** *m* (*-n; -n*) ...
> **geben** (*irr, ge-, h*) ...
> **befolgen** ... follow, take (*advice*); observe (*rule etc*)
> **file** ... *Briefe etc* ablegen
> **labored** schwerfällig (*style etc*); mühsam (*breathing etc*)

3.3 **_Boldface italics_** are used for phraseology etc., notes on German grammar and prepositions taken by the headword:

> **Lage** *f* ... **_in der ~ sein zu_** *inf* be able to *inf*
> **BLZ** ... **_abbr of Bankleitzahl_**
> **abheben** (*irr,* **_heben_**, *sep, -ge-, h*)
> **abfahren** ... (*irr,* **_fahren_**, *sep, -ge-, sein*) leave, depart (*both:* **_nach_** for)
> **line** ... **_hold the ~_** TEL bleiben Sie am Apparat
> **agree** ... sich einigen (**_on_** über *acc*)

3.4 Normal type is used for translations of the headwords.

4. Pronunciation

When you have found the headword you are looking for in the German-English section, you will notice that very often this word is followed by certain symbols enclosed in square brackets. This is the phonetic transcription of the word, which tells you how it is pronounced. And one phonetic alphabet has come to be used internationally, namely that of the International Phonetic Association. This phonetic system is known by the abbreviation **IPA.** The symbols used in this dictionary are listed in the following tables on page 9 and 10.

4.1 The length of vowels is indicated by [ː] following the vowel symbol.

4.1.1 Stress is indicated by ['] or [ˌ] preceding the stressed syllable. ['] stands for strong stress, [ˌ] for weak stress:

> Kabel ['kaːbəl] – Kabine [kaˈbiːnə]
> 'nachsehen – Be'sitz – beˈsprechen
> Jusˈtizminisˌterium – Miˈnisterpräsiˌdent

4.1.2 The glottal stop [ʔ] is the forced stop between one word or syllable and a following one beginning with a vowel, as in

> Analphabet [anʔalfaˈbeːt]
> beeindrucken [bəˈʔaindrʊkən]

4.2 No transcription of compounds is given if the parts appear as separate entries. Each individual part should be looked up, as with

> 'Blumenbeet (= **Blume** and **Beet**)

4.3 Guide to pronunciation for the German-English section

A. Vowels

[a] as in French *carte*: **Mann** [man]

[aː] as in *father*: **Wagen** ['vaːgən]

[e] as in *bed*: **Tenor** [te'noːɐ]

[eː] resembles the first sound in English [eɪ]: **Weg** [veːk]

[ə] unstressed e as in *ago*: **Bitte** ['bɪtə]

[ɛ] as in *fair*: **männlich** ['mɛnlɪç], **Geld** [gɛlt]

[ɛː] same sound but long: **zählen** ['tsɛːlən]

[ɪ] as in *it*: **Wind** [vɪnt]

[i] short, otherwise like [iː]: **Kapital** [kapi'taːl]

[iː] long, as in *meet*: **Vieh** [fiː]

[ɔ] as in *long*: **Ort** [ɔrt]

[o] as in *molest*: **Moral** [mo'raːl]

[oː] resembles the English sound in *go* [gəʊ] but without the [ʊ]: **Boot** [boːt]

[øː] as in French *feu*. The sound may be

acquired by saying [e] through closely rounded lips: **schön** [ʃøːn]

[ø] same sound but short: **ökumenisch** [økuˈmeːnɪʃ]

[œ] as in French *neuf*. The sound resembles the English vowel in *her*. Lips, however, must be well rounded as for [ɒ]: **öffnen** ['œfnən]

[ʊ] as in *book*: **Mutter** ['mʊtɐ]

[u] short, otherwise like [uː]: **Musik** [mu'ziːk]

[uː] long, as in *boot*: **Uhr** [uːɐ]

[ʏ] short, opener than [yː]: **Hütte** ['hʏtə]

[y] almost like the French u as in *sur*. It may be acquired by saying [ɪ] through fairly closely rounded lips: **Büro** [by'roː]

[yː] same sound but long: **führen** ['fyːrən]

B. Diphthongs

[aɪ] as in *like*: **Mai** [maɪ]

[aʊ] as in *mouse*: **Maus** [maʊs]

[ɔʏ] as in *boy*: **Beute** ['bɔʏtə], **Läufer** ['lɔʏfɐ]

C. Consonants

[b] as in *better*: **besser** ['bɛsɐ]

[d] as in *dance*: **du** [duː]

[f] as in *find*: **finden** ['fɪndən], **Vater** ['faːtɐ], **Philosoph** [filo'zoːf]

[g] as in *gold*: **Gold** [gɔlt]

[ʒ] as in *measure*: **Genie** [ʒe'niː]

[h] as in *house* but not aspirated: **Haus** [haʊs]

[ç] an approximation to this sound may be acquired by assuming the mouth-configuration for [ɪ] and emitting a strong current of breath: **Licht** [lɪçt], **Mönch** [mœnç], **lustig** ['lʊstɪç]

[x] as in Scottish *loch*, Whereas [ç] is pronounced at the front of the

mouth, [x] is pronounced in the throat: **Loch** [lɔx]

[j] as in *year*: **ja** [jaː]

[k] as in *kick*: **keck** [kɛk], **Tag** [taːk], **Chronik** ['kroːnɪk], **Café** [ka'feː]

[l] as in *lump*. Pronounced like English initial "clear l": **lassen** ['lasən]

[m] as in *mouse*: **Maus** [maʊs]

[n] as in *not*: **nein** [naɪn]

[ŋ] as in *sing*, *drink*: **singen** ['zɪŋən], **trinken** ['trɪŋkən]

[p] as in *pass*: **Pass** [pas], **Trieb** [triːp], **obgleich** [ɔp'glaɪç]

[r] as in *rot*. There are two pronunciations: the frontal or lingual r: **rot** [roːt] and the uvular r [ʁ] (unknown in the

English language): **Mauer** ['mauɐ]

[s] as in *miss*. Unvoiced when final, doubled, or next a voiceless consonant: **Glas** [glaːs], **Masse** ['masə], **Mast** [mast], **nass** [nas]

[z] as in *zero*. S voiced when initial in a word or syllable: **Sohn** [zoːn], **Rose** ['roːzə]

[ʃ] as in *ship*: **Schiff** [ʃɪf], **Charme**

[ʃarm], **Spiel** [ʃpiːl], **Stein** [ʃtain]

[t] as in *tea*: **Tee** [teː], **Thron** [troːn], **Stadt** [ʃtat], **Bad** [baːt], **Findling** ['fɪntlɪŋ], **Wind** [vɪnt]

[v] as in *vast*: **Vase** ['vaːze], **Winter** ['vɪntɐ]

[ã, ẽ, õ] are nasalized vowels. Examples: **Ensemble** [ãˈsãːbəl], **Terrain** [teˈrɛ̃ː], **Bonbon** [bõˈbõː]

4.3.1 Phonetic changes in plurals

singular		plural		example
-g	[-k]	-ge	[-gə]	Flug – Flüge
-d	[-t]	-de	[-də]	Grund – Gründe, Abend – Abende
-b	[-p]	-be	[-bə]	Stab – Stäbe
-s	[-s]	-se	[-zə]	Los – Lose
-ch	[-x]	-che	[-çə]	Bach – Bäche
-iv	[-iːf]	-ive	[-iːvə]	Stativ – Stative

4.3.2 The German alphabet

a [aː], b [beː], c [tseː], d [deː], e [eː], f [ɛf], g [geː], h [haː], i [iː], j [jɔt], k [kaː], l [ɛl], m [ɛm], n [ɛn], o [oː], p [peː], q [kuː], r [ɛr], s [ɛs], t [teː], u [uː], v [fau], w [veː], x [ɪks], y ['ʏpsilɔn], z [tsɛt]

4.3.3 List of suffixes

The German suffixes are not transcribed unless they are parts of headwords.

-bar	[-baːɐ]	-isch	[-ɪʃ]
-chen	[-çən]	-ist	[-ɪst]
-d	[-t]	-keit	[-kait]
-de	[-də]	-lich	[-lɪç]
-ei	[-ai]	-ling	[-lɪŋ]
-en	[-ən]	-losigkeit	[-loːzɪçkait]
-end	[-ənt]	-nis	[-nɪs]
-er	[-ɐ]	-sal	[-zaːl]
-haft	[-haft]	-sam	[-zaːm]
-heit	[-hait]	-schaft	[-ʃaft]
-icht	[-ɪçt]	-sieren	[-ziːrən]
-ie	[-iː]	-ste	[-stə]
-ieren	[-iːrən]	-tät	[-tɛːt]
-ig	[-ɪç]	-tum	[-tuːm]
-ik	[-ɪk]	-ung	[-ʊŋ]
-in	[-ɪn]	-ungs-	[-ʊŋs-]
		-wärts	[-vɛrts]

5. The tilde (~)

5.1 A symbol you will repeatedly come across in the dictionary articles is the so-called tilde (~), which serves as a replacement mark. For reasons of space, related words are often combined in groups with the help of the tilde. In these cases, the tilde represents either the complete headword or that part of the word up to a vertical line (|):

> **Ski** ... **~fahrer(in)** (= *Skifahrer, Skifahrerin*)
> **Ess|löffel** ... **~stäbchen** (= *Essstäbchen*)
> **jet** ... ~ **engine** (= *jet engine*)
> **natural| resources** ... ~ **science** (= *natural science*)

5.2 In the case of the phrases in boldface italics, the tilde represents the headword immediately preceding, which itself may also have been formed with the help of a tilde:

> **kommen** ... *zu spät* ~ (= *kommen*)
> **ange|bracht** ... *~gossen* ... *wie* ~ (= *angegossen*) *sitzen*
> **foreign** ... ~ (= *foreign*) *affairs*
> **break** ... *take a* ~ (= *break*)

6. Abbreviations of grammatical terms and subject areas are designed to help the user choose the appropriate headword or translation of a word.

Words which are predominantly used in British English are marked by the abbreviation *Br*:

> **Bürgersteig** *m* sidewalk, *Br* pavement
> **girl guide** *Br* Pfadfinderin *f*

List of abbreviations

a.	*also*, auch	GASTR	*gastronomy*, Kochkunst
abbr	*abbreviation*, Abkürzung	*gen*	*genitive (case)*, Genitiv
acc	*accusative (case)*, Akkusativ	GEOGR	*geography*, Geografie
adj	*adjective*, Adjektiv	GEOL	*geology*, Geologie
adv	*adverb*, Adverb	*ger*	*gerund*, Gerundium
AGR	*agriculture*, Landwirtschaft	GR	*grammar*, Grammatik
Am	*American English*, amerikanisches Englisch		
		h	*haben*, have
ANAT	*anatomy*, Anatomie	*hist*	*historically*, historisch
appr	*approximately*, etwa	HIST	*history*, Geschichte
ARCH	*architecture*, Architektur	HUMOR	*humorous*, humorvoll
art	*article*, Artikel		
ASTR	*astrology*, Astrologie; *astronomy*, Astronomie	*impers*	*impersonal*, unpersönlich
		indef	*indefinite*, unbestimmt
attr	*attributively*, attributiv	*inf*	*infinitive (mood)*, Infinitiv
AVIAT	*aviation*, Luftfahrt	*int*	*interjection*, Interjektion
		interr	*interrogative*, fragend
BIOL	*biology*, Biologie	*irr*	*irregular*, unregelmäßig
BOT	*botany*, Botanik	IT	*information technology*, Informationstechnologie
Br	*British English*, britisches Englisch		
		j-m	*jemandem*, to someone
CHEM	*chemistry*, Chemie	*j-n*	*jemanden*, someone
cj	*conjunction*, Konjunktion	*j-s*	*jemandes*, someone's
coll	*collectively*, als Sammelwort	JUR	*jurisprudence*, Recht
comp	*comparative*, Komparativ		
contp	*contemptuously*, verächtlich	LING	*linguistics*, Sprachwissenschaft
cpds	*compounds*, Zusammensetzungen	*lit*	*literary*, nur in der Schriftsprache vorkommend
dat	*dative (case)*, Dativ	*m*	*masculine*, männlich
		MAR	*maritime term*, Schifffahrt
ECON	*economy*, Wirtschaft	MATH	*mathematics*, Mathematik
e-e	*a(n)*, eine	*m-e*	*my*, meine
e.g.	*for example*, zum Beispiel	MED	*medicine*, Medizin
ELECTR	*electrical engineering*, Elektrotechnik	METEOR	*meteorology*, Meteorologie
		MIL	*military term*, militärisch
e-m	*einem*, to a(n)	MOT	*motoring*, Kraftfahrwesen
e-n	*einen*, a(n)	*m-r*	*meiner*, of my, to my
e-r	*einer*, of a(n), to a(n)	*mst*	*mostly*, *usually*, meistens
e-s	*eines*, of a(n)	MUS	*music*, Musik
esp.	*especially*, besonders		
et., et.	etwas, *something*	*n*	*neuter*, sächlich
etc	*et cetera, and so on*, usw., und so weiter	*neg!*	*negative, usually considered offensive*, kann als beleidigend empfunden werden
F	*colloquial*, umgangssprachlich	*nom*	*nominative (case)*, Nominativ
f	*feminine*, weiblich	*num*	*numeral*, Zahlwort
fig	*figuratively*, übertragen		

OPT	*optics*, Optik	*s-m*	*seinem*, to his, to one's
o.s., *o.s.*	*oneself*, sich	*s-n*	*seinen*, his, one's
		s.o., *s.o.*	*someone*, jemand(en)
PAINT	*painting*, Malerei	SPORT	*sports*, Sport
PARL	*parliamentary term*, parlamen-	*s-r*	*seiner*, of his, of one's, to his, to
	tarischer Ausdruck		one's
pass	*passive voice*, Passiv	*s-s*	*seines*, of his, of one's
PED	*pedagogy*, Schulwesen	s.th., *s.th.*	*something*, etwas
pers	*personal*, persönlich	*su*	*substantive*, Substantiv
PHARM	*pharmacy*, Pharmazie	*subj*	*subjunctive* (*mood*), Konjunk-
PHIL	*philosophy*, Philosophie		tiv
PHOT	*photography*, Fotografie	*sup*	*superlative*, Superlativ
PHYS	*physics*, Physik		
pl	*plural*, Plural	TECH	*technology*, Technik
POET	*poetry*, Dichtung	TEL	*telephony*, Telefon;
POL	*politics*, Politik		*telecommunications*, Telekom-
poss	*possessive*, besitzanzeigend		munikation
POST	*post and telecommunications*,	THEA	*theater*, Theater
	Postwesen	TV	*television*, Fernsehen
pp	*past participle*, Partizip Perfekt		
pred	*predicative*, prädikativ	u., *u.*	*und*, and
pres	*present*, Präsens	UNIV	*university*, Hochschulwesen
pres p	*present participle*, Partizip Prä-		
	sens	V	*vulgar*, vulgär, unanständig
pret	*preterit(e)*, Präteritum	*v/aux*	*auxiliary verb*, Hilfsverb
PRINT	*printing*, Druckwesen	*vb*	*verb*, Verb
pron	*pronoun*, Pronomen	VET	*veterinary medicine*, Veterinär-
prp	*preposition*, Präposition		medizin, Tiermedizin
PSYCH	*psychology*, Psychologie	*v/i*	*intransitive verb*, intransitives
			Verb
RAIL	*railroad, railway*, Eisenbahn	*v/refl*	*reflexive verb*, reflexives Verb
refl	*reflexive*, reflexiv	*v/t*	*transitive verb*, transitives Verb
REL	*religion*, Religion		
RHET	*rhetoric*, Rhetorik	ZO	*zoology*, Zoologie
s-e	*seine*, his, one's	→	*see, refer to*, siehe
sep	*separable*, abtrennbar		
sg	*singular*, Singular	®	*registered trademark*, eingetra-
sl	*slang*, Slang		gene Marke

7. Translations and phraseology

After the boldface headword in the German-English section, the phonetic transcription of this word, its part of speech label, and its grammar, we finally come to the most important part of the entry: **the translation(s).**

7.1 It is quite rare for a headword to be given just one translation. Usually a word will have several related translations, which are separated by a **comma.**

7.2 Different senses of a word are indicated by

a) **semicolons:**

> **Fest** ... celebration; party; REL festival
> **balance** ... Waage *f*; Gleichgewicht *n*

b) italics for **definitions:**

> **Läufer** ... runner (*a . carpet*); *chess*: bishop
> **call** ... Berufung *f* (**to** in *ein Amt*; auf *einen Lehrstuhl*)
> **cake** ... Tafel *f Schokolade*, Stück *n Seife*

c) **abbreviations** of subject areas:

> **Bug** *m* ... MAR bow; AVIAT nose
> **Gespräch** *n* talk (*a*. POL); ... TEL call
> **daisy** BOT Gänseblümchen *n*
> **duck** ... ZO Ente *f*

7.2.1 Where a word has fundamentally different meanings, it very often appears as two or more separate entries distinguished by **exponents** or raised figures:

> **betreten**[1] *v/t* ... step on; enter
> **betreten**[2] *adj* embarrassed
> **Bauer**[1] *m* ... farmer
> **Bauer**[2] *n, m* ... (bird)cage
> **chap**[1] ... Riss *m*
> **chap**[2] ... *Br* F Bursche *m*

This does not apply to senses which have directly evolved from the primary meaning of the word.

7.3 When a headword can be several different parts of speech, these are distinguished by boldface **Arabic numerals** (see also the section on p.7, paragraph 3.1 concerning the different typefaces):

geräuschlos	1. *adj* noiseless (*adjective*) 2. without a sound (*adverb*)
work	1. Arbeit *f* (*noun*) 2. *v/i* arbeiten (*verb*)
green	1. grün (*adjective*) 2. Grün *n* (*noun*)

7.3.1 In the German-English section boldface Arabic numerals are also used to distinguish between transitive, intransitive and reflexive verbs (if this affects their translation) and to show that where there is a change of meaning a verb may be differently conjugated:

> **fahren** (*irr, ge-*) **1.** *v/i* (*sein*) go; *bus etc*: run; ... **2.** *v/t* (*h*) drive (*car etc*) ...

If grammatical indications come before the subdivision they refer to all translations that follow:

> **bauen** (*ge-, h*) **1.** *v/t* build ...; **2.** *fig v/i*: ~ **auf** ...

7.3.2 Boldface Arabic numerals are also used to indicate the different meanings of nouns which can occur in more than one gender and to show that where there is a change of meaning a noun may be differently inflected:

> **Halfter 1.** *m, n* (*-s; -*) halter; **2.** *n* (*-s; -*), *f* (*-; -n*) holster

7.4 Illustrative phrases in boldface italics are generally given within the respective categories of the dictionary article:

> **baden 1.** *v/i* ... ~ **gehen** go swimming; **2.** *v/t* ...
> **good 1.** ... *real* ~ F echt gut (= *adjective*); **2.** ... **for** ~ für immer (= *noun*)

8. Grammatical references

Knowing what to do with the grammatical information available in the dictionary will enable the user to get the most out of this dictionary.

8.1 verbs (see the list of irregular German verbs on page 654).

Verbs have been treated in the following ways:

a) **bändigen** *v/t* (*ge-, h*)

The past participle of this word is formed by means of the prefix *ge-* and the auxiliary verb *haben*: **er hat gebändigt.**

b) **abfassen** *v/t* (*sep*, *-ge-*, *h*)

In conjugation the prefix *ab* must be separated from the primary verb *fassen*: **sie fasst ab**; **sie hat abgefasst**.

c) **finden** *v/t* (*irr*, *ge-*, *h*)

irr following a verb means that it is an irregular verb. The principal parts of this particular word can be found as an individual headword in the main part of the German-English section and in the list of irregular German verbs on page 654: **sie fand**; **sie hat gefunden**.

d) **abfallen** *v/i* (*irr*, **fallen**, *sep*, *-ge-*, *sein*)

A reference such as *irr*, **fallen** indicates that the compound word **abfallen** is conjugated in exactly the same way as the primary verb **fallen** as given in the list of irregular German verbs on page 654: **er fiel ab**; **er ist abgefallen**.

e) **senden** *v/t* ([*irr*,] *ge-*, *h*)

The square brackets indicate that **senden** can be treated as a regular or an irregular verb: **sie sandte** or **sie sendete**; **sie hat gesandt** or **sie hat gesendet**.

8.2 nouns

The inflectional forms (*genitive singular*, *nominative plural*) follow immediately after the indication of gender. No forms are given for compounds if the parts appear as separate headwords.

The horizontal stroke replaces the part of the word which remains unchanged in the inflection:

Affäre *f* (-; *-n*)
Keks *m*, *n* (*-es*; *-e*)
Bau *m* (*-[e]s*; *Bauten*)
Blatt *n* (*-[e]s*; *Blätter* ['blɛtɐ])

The inflectional forms of German nouns ending in **-in** are given in the following ways:

Ärztin *f* (-; *-nen*)
Chemiker(in) (*-s*; *-/-*; *-nen*) = **Chemiker** *m* (*-s*; *-*) and **Chemikerin** *f* (-; *-nen*)

8.3 Prepositions

If, for instance, a headword (verb, adjective or noun) is governed by certain prepositions, these are given in boldface italics and in brackets together with their English or German translations and placed next to the appropriate translation. If the German or English preposition is the same for all or several translations, it is given only once before or after the first translation and then also applies to the translations which follow it:

> **abrücken** ... **1.** v/t (h) move away (***von*** from)
> **befestigen** v/t (*no -ge-, h*) fasten (***an*** dat to), fix (to), attach (to)
> **dissent** ... **2.** anderer Meinung sein (***from*** als)
> **dissimilar** (***to***) unähnlich (*dat*); verschieden (von)

With German prepositions which can take the dative or the accusative, the case is given in brackets:

> **fürchten** ... **sich ~** ... be afraid (***vor*** dat of)
> **bauen** ... **~ auf** (*acc*) rely *or* count on

We hope that this somewhat lengthy introduction has shown you that this dictionary contains a great deal more than simple one-to-one translations, and that you are now well-equipped to make the most of all it has to offer.

GERMAN – ENGLISH

A

à [a] *prp* **5 Karten ~ 20 Euro** 5 tickets at 20 euros each *or* a piece

Aal [a:l] *m* (-[e]s; -e) zo eel

aalen ['a:lən] *v/refl* (ge-, h) **sich in der Sonne ~** bask in the sun

'aal'glatt *fig adj* (as) slippery as an eel

Aas [a:s] *n* (-[e]s) *no pl* carrion; F *contp pl* **Äser** beast, *sl* bastard

'Aasgeier *m* zo vulture (*a. fig*)

ab [ap] *prp and adv:* **München ~ 13.55** departure from Munich (at) 1.55; **~ 7 Uhr** from 7 o'clock (on); **~ morgen (1. März)** starting tomorrow (March 1st); **von jetzt ~** from now on; **~ und zu** now and then; **ein Film ~ 18** an X (-rated) film; **ein Knopf ist ~** a button has come off

'abarbeiten *v/t* (sep, -ge-, h) work out *or* off (*debts*); **sich ~** wear o.s. out

Abart ['apʔart] *f* (-; -en) variety

abartig ['apʔartıç] *adj* abnormal

Abb. *abbr of* **Abbildung** fig., illustration

'Abbau *m* (-[e]s; *no pl*) mining; TECH dismantling; *fig* overcoming (*of prejudices etc*); reduction (*of expenditure, staff etc*); **'abbauen** *v/t* (sep, -ge-, h) mine; TECH dismantle; *fig* overcome (*prejudices etc*); reduce (*expenditure, staff etc*); **sich ~** BIOL break down

'abbeißen *v/t* (irr, **beißen**, sep, -ge-, h) bite off

'abbeizen *v/t* (sep, -ge-, h) remove *old paint etc* with corrosives

'abbekommen *v/t* (irr, **kommen**, sep, no -ge-, h) get off; **s-n Teil** *or* **et. ~** get one's share; **et. ~** *fig* get hurt, get damaged

'abberufen *v/t* (irr, **rufen**, sep, no -ge-, h), **'Abberufung** *f* recall

'abbestellen *v/t* (sep, no -ge-, h) cancel one's subscription (*or* order) for

'Abbestellung *f* cancellation

'abbiegen *v/i* (irr, **biegen**, sep, -ge-, sein) turn (off); **nach rechts (links) ~** turn right (left)

'abbilden *v/t* (sep, -ge-, h) show, depict

'Abbildung *f* (-; -en) picture, illustration

'Abbitte *f apology; **j-m ~ leisten wegen** apologize to s.o. for

'abblasen F *v/t* (irr, **blasen**, sep, -ge-, h)

call off, cancel

'abblättern *v/i* (sep, -ge-, sein) paint etc: flake off

'abblenden 1. *v/t* (sep, -ge-, h) dim **2.** *v/i* MOT dim (*Br* dip) the headlights

'Abblendlicht *n* MOT dimmed (*Br* dipped) headlights *pl*, low beam

'abbrechen *v/t* (irr, **brechen**, sep, -ge-) **1.** *v/t* (h) break off (*a. fig*); pull down, demolish (*building etc*); strike (*camp, tent*) **2.** *v/i* (sein) break off; (h) *fig* stop; **'abbremsen** *v/t* (sep, -ge-, h) slow down; **'abbrennen** *v/t* (irr, **brennen**, sep, -ge-) **1.** *v/i* (sein) burn down **2.** *v/t* (h) burn down (*building etc*); let *or* set off (*fireworks*); **'abbringen** *v/t* (irr, **bringen**, sep, -ge-, h) **j-n von e-r Sache ~** talk s.o. out of (doing) s.th.; **j-n vom Thema ~** get s.o. off a subject

'Abbruch *m* (-[e]s; *no pl*) breaking off; demolition; **'abbruchreif** *adj* derelict, due for demolition

'abbuchen *v/t* (sep, -ge-, h) debit (**von** to); **'Abbuchung** *f* debit

'abbürsten *v/t* (sep, -ge-, h) brush off (*dust etc*); brush (*coat etc*)

Abc [a:be:'tse:] *n* (-; *no pl*) ABC, alphabet; **ABC-Waffen** *pl* MIL nuclear, biological and chemical weapons

'abdanken *v/i* (sep, -ge-, h) resign; *king etc*: abdicate; **'Abdankung** *f* (-; -en) resignation; abdication

'abdecken *v/t* (sep, -ge-, h) uncover; untile (*roof*); unroof (*house*); clear (*the table*); ECON cover (up)

'abdichten *v/t* (sep, -ge-, h) TECH seal

'abdrängen *v/t* (sep, -ge-, h) push aside

'abdrehen 1. *v/t* (sep, -ge-, h) turn *or* switch off (*light, water etc*) **2.** *v/i* (*a. sein*) *ship, plane:* change one's course

'Abdruck *m* print, mark

'abdrucken *v/t* (sep, -ge-, h) print

'abdrücken (sep, -ge-, h) **1.** *v/t* fire (*gun*) **2.** *v/i* pull the trigger

Abend ['a:bənt] *m* (-s; -e) evening; **am ~** in the evening, at night; **heute ~** tonight; **morgen (gestern) ~** tomorrow (last) night; **→ bunt, essen**; **~brot** *n* (-[e]s; *no pl*), **~essen** *n* supper, dinner, *Br a.* high tea; **~kasse** *f* THEA *etc* box office; **~kleid** n evening dress or gown; **~kurs** m evening classes pl

'Abendland n (-[e]s; no pl) West, Occident; 'abendländisch ['a:bəntlɛndɪʃ] adj Western, Occidental

'Abendmahl n (-[e]s; no pl) the (Holy) Communion, the Lord's Supper; **das ~ empfangen** receive Communion

abends ['a:bənts] adv in the evening, at night; **dienstags ~** (on) Tuesday evenings

'Abendschule f evening classes pl, night school

Abenteuer ['a:bəntɔʏɐ] n (-s; -) adventure (a. in cpds …ferien, …spielplatz) 'abenteuerlich adj adventurous; fig risky; fantastic

Abenteurer ['a:bəntɔʏɐ] m (-s; -) adventurer; 'Abenteurerin ['a:bəntɔʏrərɪn] f (-; -nen) adventuress

aber ['a:bɐ] cj and adv but; **oder ~** or else; **~, ~!** now then!; **~ nein!** not at all!

'Aberglaube m superstition

abergläubisch ['a:bɐglɔʏbɪʃ] adj superstitious

'aberkennen v/t (irr, kennen, sep, no -ge-, h) **j-m et. ~** deprive s.o. of s.th. (a. JUR); 'Aberkennung f (-; -en) deprivation (a. JUR)

abermalig ['a:bɐma:lɪç] adj repeated

abermals ['a:bɐma:ls] adv once more or again

'aber'tausend adj: **tausende und ~e** thousands upon thousands

'abfahren (irr, fahren, sep, -ge-) **1.** v/i (sein) leave, depart (both: **nach** for); F **(voll) ~ auf** (acc) really go for **2.** v/t (h) carry or cart away

'Abfahrt f departure (**nach** for), start (for); skiing: descent

'Abfahrts|lauf m downhill skiing (or race); **~zeit** f (time of) departure

'Abfall m waste, refuse, garbage, trash, Br a. rubbish; **~beseitigung** f waste disposal; **~eimer** m → **Mülleimer**

'abfallen v/i (irr, fallen, sep, -ge-, sein) fall (off); terrain: slope (down); fig fall away (**von** from); esp POL secede (from); **vom Glauben~** renounce one's faith; **~ gegen** compare badly with

'abfällig **1.** adj derogatory **2.** adv: **~ von j-m sprechen** run s.o. down

'Abfallpro,dukt n waste product

'abfälschen v/t (sep, -ge-, h) SPORT deflect; 'abfangen v/t (irr, **fangen**, sep, -ge-, h) catch, intercept; MOT, AVIAT right; 'abfärben v/i (sep, -ge-, h) color etc: run, material: a. bleed; fig **~ auf** (acc) rub off on; 'abfassen v/t (sep, -ge-, h) compose, word, write

'abfertigen v/t (sep, -ge-, h) dispatch; customs: clear; serve (customers); check in (passengers etc); **j-n kurz ~** be short with s.o.; 'Abfertigung f dispatch; clearance; check-in

'abfeuern v/t (sep, -ge-, h) fire (off); launch (rocket)

'abfinden v/t (irr, **finden**, sep, -ge-, h) ECON pay off (creditor); buy out (partner); compensate; **sich mit e-r Sache~** put up with s.th.; 'Abfindung f (-; -en) ECON satisfaction; compensation

'abflachen v/t and v/refl (sep, -ge-, h) flatten; 'abflauen v/i (sep, -ge-, sein) wind etc: drop (a. fig); 'abfliegen v/i (irr, **fliegen**, sep, -ge-, sein) AVIAT leave, depart; 'abfließen v/i (irr, **fließen**, sep, -ge-, sein) flow off, drain (off or away)

'Abflug m AVIAT departure

'Abfluss m (-es; Abflüsse) no pl flowing off; TECH drain

'Abflussrohr n wastepipe, drain(pipe)

'abfragen v/t (sep, -ge-, h) quiz or question s.o. (**über** acc about), test s.o. orally

'Abfuhr ['apfu:ɐ] f (-; -en) removal; **j-m e-e ~ erteilen** rebuff (F SPORT lick) s.o.

'abführen (sep, -ge-, h) **1.** v/t lead or take away; ECON pay (over) (**an** acc to); **2.** v/i MED move one's bowels; act as a laxative; 'abführend adj, 'Abführmittel n MED laxative

'abfüllen v/t (sep, -ge-, h) bottle; can

'Abgabe f (-; -n) no pl handing in; SPORT pass; ECON rate; duty

'abgabenfrei adj tax-free

'abgabenpflichtig adj dutiable

'Abgang m (-[e]s; Abgänge) no pl departure; Am graduation, Br school-leaving; THEA exit (a. fig); SPORT dismount; **Abgänger** ['apgɛŋɐ] m (-s; -) Am graduate, Br school-leaver

'Abgas n waste gas; pl emission(s pl); MOT exhaust fumes pl

'abgasfrei adj emission-free

'Abgasuntersuchung f MOT Am emission test, Br exhaust emission test

'abgearbeitet adj worn out

'**abgeben** v/t (irr, **geben**, sep, -ge-, h) leave (**bei** with); hand in; deposit (one's baggage etc), hand over (ticket etc) (**an** acc to); cast (vote); pass (ball); give off, emit (heat etc); make (offer, statement etc); **j-m et. ~ von** share s.th. with s.o.; **sich ~ mit** concern o.s. with s.th., associate with s.o.

'**abge|brannt** adj burnt down; F fig broke; **~brüht** fig adj hard-boiled; **~droschen** adj hackneyed; **~fahren** adj tires: worn out; **~griffen** adj worn; **~hackt** fig adj disjointed; **~hangen** adj: **gut ~es Fleisch** well-hung meat; **~härtet** adj hardened (**gegen** to)

'**abgehen** v/i (irr, **gehen**, sep, -ge-, sein) train etc: leave; mail, goods: get off; THEA go off (stage); button etc: come off; path etc: branch off; **von der Schule ~** leave school; **~ von** drop (plan etc); **von s-r Meinung ~** change one's mind or opinion; **ihm geht … ab** he lacks …; **gut ~** end well, pass off well

'**abge|hetzt**, **~kämpft** adj exhausted, worn out; **~kartet** ['apgəkartət] F adj: **~e Sache** put-up job; **~legen** adj remote, distant; **~macht** adj fixed; **~!** it's a deal!; **~magert** adj emaciated; **~neigt** adj: **e-r Sache ~ sein** be averse to s.th.; **ich wäre nicht ~, et. zu tun** I wouldn't mind doing s.th.; **~nutzt** adj worn out

Abgeordnete ['apgə°ɔrdnətə] m, f (-n; -n) Am representative, congress|man (-woman), Br Member of Parliament (abbr MP); '**Abgeordnetenhaus** n Am House of Representatives, Br House of Commons

'**abgepackt** adj prepack(ag)ed
'**abgeschieden** adj secluded
'**Abgeschiedenheit** f (-; no pl) seclusion

'**abge|schlossen** adj completed; **~e Wohnung** self-contained apartment (Br flat); **~sehen** adj: **~ von** aside (Br a. apart) from; **ganz ~ von** not to mention, let alone; **~spannt** adj exhausted, weary; **~standen** adj stale; **~storben** adj dead (tree etc); numb (leg etc); **~stumpft** adj insensitive, indifferent (**gegen** to); **~tragen**, **~wetzt** adj worn out; threadbare, shabby

abgewöhnen v/t (sep, -ge-, h) **j-m et. ~** make s.o. give up s.th.; **sich** (dat) **das**

Rauchen ~ stop or give up smoking
'**Abgott** m idol (a. fig); **abgöttisch** ['apgœtɪʃ] adv: **j-n ~ lieben** idolize s.o.

'**abgrasen** v/t (sep, -ge-, h) graze; fig scour

'**abgrenzen** v/t (sep, -ge-, h) mark off; delimit (**gegen** from)

'**Abgrund** m abyss, chasm, gulf (all a. fig); **am Rande des ~s** fig on the brink of disaster; '**abgrund'tief** adj abysmal

'**abgucken** v/t (sep, -ge-, h) **j-m et. ~** learn s.th. from (watching) s.o.; → **abschreiben**

'**Abguss** m cast
'**abhaben** F v/t (irr, **haben**, sep, -ge-, h) **willst du et. ~?** do you want some (of it)? '**abhacken** v/t (sep, -ge-, h) chop or cut off; '**abhaken** v/t (sep, -ge-, h) check (Br tick) off; F forget; '**abhalten** v/t (irr, **halten**, sep, -ge-, h) hold (meeting etc); **j-n von der Arbeit ~** keep s.o. from his work; **j-n davon ~, et. zu tun** keep s.o. from doing s.th.

'**abhandeln** v/t (sep, -ge-, h) treat (subject etc); **j-m et. ~** make a deal with s.o. for s.th.; '**Abhandlung** f treatise (**über** acc on)

'**Abhang** m slope
'**abhängen**[1] v/t (sep, -ge-, h) take down (picture etc); RAIL etc uncouple; F shake s.o. off

'**abhängen**[2] v/i (irr, **hängen**, sep, -ge-, h) **~ von** depend on; **das hängt davon ab** that depends

abhängig ['aphɛŋɪç] adj: **~ von** dependent on; a. addicted to drugs etc
'**Abhängigkeit** f (-; -en) dependence (**von** on); addiction (to)

'**abhärten** v/t (sep, -ge-, h) **sich ~** harden o.s. (**gegen** to)

'**abhauen** (irr, **hauen**, sep, -ge-) **1.** v/t (h) cut or chop off **2.** F v/i (sein) make off (**mit** with), run away (with); **hau ab!** beat it!, scram!

'**abheben** (irr, **heben**, sep, -ge-, h) **1.** v/t lift or take off; pick up (receiver); (with)draw (money); cut (cards); **sich ~** stand out (**von** among, from), fig a. contrast with **2.** v/t cut the cards; answer the phone; plane: take (esp rocket: lift) off

'**abheften** v/t (sep, -ge-, h) file
'**abheilen** v/i (sep, -ge-, sein) heal (up)
'**abhetzen** v/refl (sep, -ge-, h) wear o.s.

out

'**Abhilfe** f remedy; ~ **schaffen** take remedial measures

'**Abholdienst** m pickup service

'**abholen** v/t (sep, -ge-, h) pick up, collect; **j-n von der Bahn** ~ meet s.o. at the station; '**abholzen** v/t (sep, -ge-, h) fell, cut down (trees); deforest (area); '*abhorchen* (sep, -ge-, h) MED auscultate, sound; '**abhören** v/t (sep, -ge-, h) listen in on, tap (telephone conversation), F bug; → **abfragen**

'**Abhörgerät** n bugging device, F bug

Abitur [abi'tuːɐ] n (-s; -e) school-leaving examination (qualifying for university entrance)

'**abjagen** v/t (sep, -ge-, h) **j-m et.** ~ recover s.th. from s.o.; '**abkanzeln** F v/t (sep, -ge-, h) tell s.o. off; '**abkaufen** v/t (sep, -ge-, h) **j-m et.** ~ buy s.th. from s.o.

Abkehr ['apkeːɐ] f (-; no pl) break (**von** with); '**abkehren** v/refl (sep, -ge-, h) **sich** ~ **von** turn away from

'**abklingen** v/i (irr, klingen, sep, -ge-, sein) fade away; pain etc: ease off

'**abklopfen** v/t (sep, -ge-, h) MED sound

'**abknallen** F v/t (sep, -ge-, h) pick off

'**abknicken** v/t (sep, -ge-, h) snap or break off; bend

'**abkochen** v/t (sep, -ge-, h) boil

'**abkomman,dieren** v/t (sep, no -ge-, h) MIL detach (**zu** for)

'**abkommen** v/i (irr, kommen, sep, -ge-, sein) ~ **von** get off; drop (plan etc); **vom Thema** ~ stray from the point; → **Weg**

'**Abkommen** n (-s; -) agreement, treaty; **ein** ~ **schließen** make an agreement

Abkömmling ['apkœmlɪŋ] m (-s; -e) descendant

'**abkoppeln** v/t (sep, -ge-, h) uncouple (**von** from); undock (spacecraft)

'**abkratzen** (sep, -ge-) **1.** v/t (h) scrape off **2.** F v/i (sein) kick the bucket

'**abkühlen** v/t and v/refl (sep, -ge-, h) cool down (a. fig)

'**Abkühlung** f cooling

'**abkürzen** v/t (sep, -ge-, h) shorten; abbreviate; **den Weg** ~ take a short cut

'**Abkürzung** f abbreviation; short cut

'**abladen** v/t (irr, laden, sep, -ge-, h) unload; dump (waste etc)

'**Ablage** f (-; -n) no pl filing; filing tray; Swiss → **Zweigstelle**

'**ablagern** (sep, -ge-, h) **1.** v/t season

(wood); let wine age; GEOL etc deposit; **sich** ~ settle, be deposited **2.** v/i (a. sein) season; age; '**Ablagerung** f (-; -en) CHEM, GEOL deposit, sediment

'**ablassen** (irr, lassen, sep, -ge-, h) **1.** v/t drain off (liquid); let off (steam); drain (pond etc) **2.** v/i: **von et.** (**j-m**) ~ stop doing s.th. (leave s.o. alone)

'**Ablauf** m (-[e]s; Abläufe) course; process; order of events; no pl expiration, Br expiry; → **Abfluss**

'**ablaufen** (irr, laufen, sep, -ge-) **1.** v/i (sein) water etc: run off; performance etc: go, proceed; come to an end; period, passport etc: expire; time, record, tape: run out; clock: run down; **gut** ~ turn out well **2.** v/t (h) wear down

'**ablecken** v/t (sep, -ge-, h) lick (off)

'**ablegen** (sep, -ge-, h) **1.** v/t take off (clothes); file (letters etc); give up (habit etc); take (examination, oath); **abgelegte Kleider** cast-offs pl **2.** v/i take off one's (hat and) coat; MAR put out, sail

'**Ableger** m (-s; -) BOT layer; offshoot (a. fig)

'**ablehnen** v/t (sep, -ge-, h) refuse; turn down (application etc); PARL reject; object to; condemn; **~d** adj negative

'**Ablehnung** f (-; -en) refusal; rejection; objection (gen to)

'**ableiten** v/t (sep, -ge-, h) divert; LING, MATH derive (**aus** dat, **von** from) (a. fig)

'**Ableitung** f diversion; LING, MATH derivation (a. fig)

'**ablenken** v/t (sep, -ge-, h) divert (**von** from); soccer: turn away (ball); deflect (rays etc); **j-n von der Arbeit** ~ distract s.o. from his work; **er lässt sich leicht** ~ he is easily diverted

'**Ablenkung** f diversion

'**ablesen** v/t (irr, lesen, sep, -ge-, h) read

'**abliefern** v/t (sep, -ge-, h) deliver (**bei** to, at); hand over (to)

'**ablösbar** adj detachable; '**ablösen** v/t (sep, -ge-, h) detach; take off; take s.o.'s place, take over from s.o.; esp MIL relieve; replace; **sich** ~ take turns (driving etc); '**Ablösesumme** f SPORT transfer fee; '**Ablösung** f relief

'**abmachen** v/t (sep, -ge-, h) remove, take off; settle, arrange

'**Abmachung** f (-; -en) arrangement, agreement, deal

'**abmagern** v/i (sep, -ge-, sein) get thin

'**Abmagerung** f (-; -en) emaciation

'**Abmagerungskur** f slimming diet

'**abmähen** v/t (sep, -ge-, h) mow

'**abmalen** v/t (sep, -ge-, h) copy

'**Abmarsch** m (-[e]s; no pl) start; MIL marching off; '**abmar,schieren** v/i (sep, no -ge-, sein) start; MIL march off

'**abmelden** v/t (sep, -ge-, h) cancel the registration of (car etc); cancel s.o.'s membership (in a club etc); give notice of s.o.'s withdrawal (from school); **sich** ~ give notice of change of address; report off duty; '**Abmeldung** f notice of withdrawal; notice of change of address

'**abmessen** v/t (irr, **messen**, sep, -ge-, h) measure; '**Abmessung** f measurement; pl dimensions

'**abmon,tieren** v/t (sep, no -ge-, h) take off; take down; TECH dismantle

'**abmühen** v/refl (sep, -ge-, h) work very hard; try hard (to do s.th.); struggle (**mit** with)

'**abnagen** v/t (sep, -ge-, h) gnaw (at)

Abnahme ['apna:mə] f (-; -n) reduction, decrease; loss (a. of weight); ECON purchase; TECH acceptance

'**abnehmbar** adj removable

'**abnehmen** (irr, **nehmen**, sep, -ge-, h) **1.** v/t take off (a. MED); remove; pick up (receiver); TECH accept; ECON buy; **j-m et.** ~ take s.th. (away) from s.o. **2.** v/i decrease, diminish; lose weight; answer the phone; moon: wane

'**Abnehmer** m (-s; -) buyer; customer

'**Abneigung** f (**gegen**) dislike (of, for); aversion (to)

abnorm [ap'nɔrm] adj abnormal; exceptional, unusual; **Abnormität** [apnɔrmi'tɛːt] f (-; -en) abnormality

'**abnutzen**, '**abnützen** v/t and v/refl (sep, -ge-, h) wear out

'**Abnutzung**, '**Abnützung** f (-; no pl) wear (and tear) (a. fig)

Abonnement [abɔnə'maː] n (-s; -s) subscription (**auf** acc to); **Abonnent** [abɔ'nɛnt] m (-en; -en) subscriber; THEA season-ticket holder; **abonnieren** [abɔ'niːrən] v/t (no -ge-, h) subscribe to

Abordnung f (-; -en) delegation

Abort [a'bɔrt] m (-[e]s; -e) lavatory, toilet

'**abpassen** v/t (sep, -ge-, h) watch or wait for (s.o., s.th.); waylay s.o. (a. fig)

'**abpfeifen** v/t and v/i (irr, **pfeifen**, sep, -ge-, h) SPORT blow the final whistle; stop the game

'**abplagen** v/refl (sep, -ge-, h) struggle (**mit** with)

'**abprallen** v/i (sep, -ge-, sein) rebound, bounce (off); bullet: ricochet

'**abputzen** v/t (sep, -ge-, h) wipe off; clean

'**abraten** v/i (irr, **raten**, sep, -ge-, h) **j-m ~ von** advise or warn s.o. against

'**abräumen** v/t (sep, -ge-, h) clear away; clear (the table)

'**abrea,gieren** v/t (sep, no -ge-, h) work off (one's anger etc) (**an** dat on); **sich** ~ F let off steam

'**abrechnen** (sep, -ge-, h) **1.** v/t deduct, subtract; claim (expenses) **2.** v/i: **mit j-m ~** settle accounts (fig a. get even) with s.o.; '**Abrechnung** f settlement; F fig showdown

'**abreiben** v/t (irr, **reiben**, sep, -ge-, h) rub off; rub down (body); polish

'**Abreise** f departure (**nach** for)

'**abreisen** v/i (sep, -ge-, sein) depart, leave, start, set out (all: **nach** for)

'**Abreisetag** m day of departure

'**abreißen** (irr, **reißen**, sep, -ge-) **1.** v/t (h) tear or pull off; pull down (building) **2.** v/i (sein) break; button etc: come off

'**Abreiß,kalender** m tear-off calendar

'**abrichten** v/t (sep, -ge-, h) train (animal), a. break a horse in

'**abriegeln** v/t (sep, -ge-, h) block off, cordon off

'**Abriss** m (-es; -e) (no pl) demolition; outline, summary

'**abrollen** v/t (sep, -ge-, sein) and v/t (h) unroll (a. fig)

'**abrücken** (sep, -ge-) **1.** v/t (h) move away (**von** from); **2.** v/i (sein) draw away (**von** from); MIL march off

'**Abruf** m: **auf** ~ ECON on call

'**abrufen** v/t (irr, **rufen**, sep, -ge-, h) call away; IT recall, fetch, retrieve

'**abrunden** v/t (sep, -ge-, h) round (off)

'**abrupfen** v/t (sep, -ge-, h) pluck (off)

abrupt [ap'rʊpt] adj abrupt

'**abrüsten** v/i (sep, -ge-, h) MIL disarm

'**Abrüstung** f (-; no pl) MIL disarmament

'**abrutschen** v/i (sep, -ge-, sein) slide down; slip (off) (**von** from)

ABS

ABS [aːbeːˈʔɛs] → *Antiblockiersystem*

Absage [ˈʔapzaːɡə] *f* (-; -*n*) refusal; cancellation; '**absagen** (*sep*, -*ge*-, *h*) **1.** *v/t* call off, cancel (*event etc*) **2.** *v/i* call off; *j-m* ~ *a.* cancel one's appointment with s.o.; decline (the invitation)

'**absägen** *v/t* (*sep*, -*ge*-, *h*) saw off; F *fig* oust, sack *s.o.*

'**absahnen** F *v/i* (*sep*, -*ge*-, *h*) cash in

'**Absatz** *m* paragraph; ECON sales *pl*; *shoe*: heel; *stairs*: landing

'**abschaben** *v/t* (*sep*, -*ge*-, *h*) scrape off

'**abschaffen** *v/t* (*sep*, -*ge*-, *h*) do away with, abolish; repeal (*law*); put an end to (*abuses etc*); '**Abschaffung** *f* (-; *no pl*) abolition; repeal

'**abschalten** (*sep*, -*ge*-, *h*) **1.** *v/t* switch *or* turn off **2.** F *v/i* relax, switch off

'**abschätzen** *v/t* (*sep*, -*ge*-, *h*) estimate; assess; size up; '**abschätzig** [ˈapʃɛtsɪç] *adj* contemptuous; derogatory

'**Abschaum** *m* (-*s*; *no pl*) scum (*a. fig*)

'**Abscheu** *m* (-*s*; *no pl*) disgust (*vor*, *gegen* at, for); *e-n* ~ *haben vor* abhor, detest; ~ *erregend* → *abscheuerregend*; '**abscheuerregend** *adj* revolting, repulsive

ab'**scheulich** *adj* abominable, despicable (*a. person*), *a.* atrocious (*crime*)

'**abschicken** *v/t* (*sep*, -*ge*-, *h*) → *absenden*

'**abschieben** *fig v/t* (*irr*, *schieben*, *sep*, -*ge*-, *h*) push away; get rid of; deport; *et. auf j-n* ~ shove *s.th.* off on (to) *s.o.*

Abschied [ˈapʃiːt] *m* (-[*e*]*s*; -*e*) parting, farewell; ~ *nehmen* (*von*) say goodbye (to), take leave (of); *s-n* ~ *nehmen* resign, retire

'**Abschiedsfeier** *f* farewell party

'**Abschiedskuss** *m* goodbye kiss

'**abschießen** *v/t* (*irr*, *schießen*, *sep*, -*ge*-, *h*) shoot off (AVIAT down); launch (*rocket*); shoot, kill (*deer*); F pick *s.o.* off; *fig* oust; get rid of *s.o.*

'**abschirmen** *v/t* (*sep*, -*ge*-, *h*) shield (*gegen* from); *fig* protect (*gegen* against, from); '**Abschirmung** *f* (-; -*en*) shield, screen; *fig* protection

'**abschlachten** *v/t* (*sep*, -*ge*-, *h*) slaughter (*a. fig*)

'**Abschlag** *m* SPORT kickoff; ECON down payment; '**abschlagen** *v/t* (*irr*, *schlagen*, *sep*, -*ge*-, *h*) knock off; cut off (*head*); cut down (*tree*); refuse (*request*

etc), turn *s.th.* down

'**abschleifen** *v/t* (*irr*, *schleifen*, *sep*, -*ge*-, *h*) grind off; sand(paper), smooth

'**Abschleppdienst** *m* MOT emergency road (*Br* breakdown) service

'**abschleppen** *v/t* (*sep*, -*ge*-, *h*) MOT (*give s.o. a.*) tow; *police*: tow away

'**Abschlepp|seil** *n* towrope; ~*wagen* *m* *Am* tow truck, *Br* breakdown lorry

'**abschließen** (*irr*, *schließen*, *sep*, -*ge*-, *h*) **1.** *v/t* lock (up); close, finish; complete; take out (*insurance*); conclude (*research etc*); *e-n Handel* ~ strike a bargain; *sich* ~ shut o.s. off; → *Wette* **2.** *v/i* close, finish; ~**d 1.** *adj* concluding; final **2.** *adv*: ~ *sagte er* he concluded by saying

'**Abschluss** *m* conclusion, close; ~*prüfung* *f* final examination, finals *pl*, *esp Am a.* graduation; *s-e* ~ *machen* graduate (*an dat* from); ~*zeugnis* *n* *Am* diploma, *Br* school-leaving certificate

'**abschmecken** *v/t* (*sep*, -*ge*-, *h*) season

'**abschmieren** *v/t* (*sep*, -*ge*-, *h*) TECH lubricate, grease

'**abschminken** *v/t* (*sep*, -*ge*-, *h*) *sich* ~ remove one's make-up

'**abschnallen** *v/t* (*sep*, -*ge*-, *h*) undo; take off (*skis*); *sich* ~ MOT, AVIAT unfasten one's seat belt

'**abschneiden** (*irr*, *schneiden*, *sep*, -*ge*-, *h*) **1.** *v/t* cut (off) (*a. fig*); *j-m das Wort* ~ cut *s.o.* short **2.** *v/i*: *gut* ~ come off well

'**Abschnitt** *m* passage, section (*of book etc*); paragraph; MATH, BIOL segment; period (*of time*), stage (*of journey*), phase (*of development*); coupon, slip, stub (*of check etc*)

'**abschnittweise** *adv* section by section

'**abschrauben** *v/t* (*sep*, -*ge*-, *h*) unscrew

'**abschrecken** *v/t* (*sep*, -*ge*-, *h*) deter (*von* from); GASTR douse *eggs etc* with cold water; ~**d** *adj* deterrent; ~*es Beispiel* warning example

'**Abschreckung** *f* (-; -*en*) deterrence

'**abschreiben** *v/t* (*irr*, *schreiben*, *sep*, -*ge*-, *h*) copy; PED crib; ECON write off (*a.* F *fig*); '**Abschrift** *f* copy, duplicate

'**abschürfen** *v/t* (*sep*, -*ge*-, *h*) graze

'**Abschürfung** *f* (-; -*en*) abrasion

Abschuss *m* launch(ing) (*of rocket*); AVIAT shooting down, downing; kill;

absteigen A

~basis *f* MIL launching base

abschüssig ['apʃʏsɪç] *adj* sloping; steep

'**Abschussliste** F *f*: *auf der* ~ *stehen* be on the hit list

'**Abschussrampe** *f* MIL launching pad

'**abschütteln** *v/t* (*sep*, *-ge-*, *h*) shake off

'**abschwächen** *v/t* (*sep*, *-ge-*, *h*) lessen, diminish

'**abschweifen** *fig v/i* (*sep*, *-ge-*, *sein*) digress (*von* from)

'**Abschweifung** *f* (*-*; *-en*) digression

absehbar ['apzeːbaːɐ] *adj* foreseeable; *in* ~*er* (*auf* ~*e*) *Zeit* in the (for the) foreseeable future

'**absehen** *v/t* (*irr*, *sehen*, *sep*, *-ge-*, *h*) foresee; *es ist kein Ende abzusehen* there is no end in sight; *es abgesehen haben auf* (*acc*) be after; ~ *von* refrain from

'**abseilen** *v/refl* (*sep*, *-ge-*, *h*) descend by a rope, *Br a.* abseil; F make a getaway

abseits ['apzaɪts] *adv and prp* away *or* remote from

'**Abseitsfalle** *f* soccer: offside trap

'**abseitsstehen** *v/i* (*irr*, *stehen*, *sep*, *-ge-*, *h*) soccer: be offside; *fig* be left out

'**absenden** *v/t* ([*irr*, *senden*,] *sep*, *-ge-*, *h*) send (off), dispatch; mail, *esp Br* post (*letter etc*)

'**Absender** *m* (*-s*; *-*) sender

absetzbar ['apzɛtsbaːɐ] *adj*: *steuerlich* ~ deductible from tax

'**absetzen** (*sep*, *-ge-*, *h*) **1.** *v/t* take off (*hat*, *glasses etc*); set *or* put down (*bag etc*); drop (*passenger*); dismiss (*employee*); THEA, *film*: take off; deduct (*from tax*); depose (*king etc*); ECON sell; *sich* ~ CHEM, GEOL settle, be deposited **2.** *v/i*: *ohne abzusetzen* without stopping

'**Absetzung** *f* (*-*; *-en*) dismissal; deposition; THEA, *film*: withdrawal

'**Absicht** *f* (*-*; *-en*) intention; *mit* ~ on purpose; '**absichtlich** **1.** *adj* intentional **2.** *adv* on purpose

'**absitzen** (*irr*, *sitzen*, *sep*, *-ge-*) **1.** *v/i* (*sein*) dismount (*von* from); **2.** *v/t* (*h*) serve (*sentence*); F sit out (*play etc*)

absolut [apzoˈluːt] *adj* absolute

Absolvent [apzɔlˈvɛnt] *m* (*-en*; *-en*), **Absol'ventin** [apzɔlˈviːrən] *f* (*-*; *-nen*) graduate; ab-**solvieren** [apzɔlˈviːrən] *v/t* (*no -ge-*, *h*) attend (*school*); complete (*studies*);

graduate from (*college etc*)

'**absondern** *v/t* (*sep*, *-ge-*, *h*) separate; MED, BIOL secrete; *sich* ~ cut o.s. off (*von* from); '**Absonderung** *f* (*-*; *-en*) separation; MED, BIOL secretion

absorbieren [apzɔrˈbiːrən] *v/t* (*no -ge-*, *h*) absorb (*a. fig*)

'**abspeichern** *v/t* (*sep*, *-ge-*, *h*) IT store, save

abspenstig ['apʃpɛnstɪç] *adj*: *j-m die Freundin* ~ *machen* steal s.o.'s girlfriend

absperren *v/t* (*sep*, *-ge-*, *h*) lock; turn off (*water*, *gas etc*); block off (*road*); cordon off; '**Absperrung** *f* (*-*; *-en*) barrier; cordon

'**abspielen** *v/t* (*sep*, *-ge-*, *h*) play (*record etc*); SPORT pass (*the ball*); *sich* ~ happen, take place

'**Absprache** *f* agreement

'**absprechen** *v/t* (*irr*, *sprechen*, *sep*, *-ge-*, *h*) agree upon; arrange; *j-m die Fähigkeit etc* ~ dispute s.o.'s ability *etc*

'**abspringen** *v/i* (*irr*, *springen*, *sep*, *-ge-*, *sein*) jump off; AVIAT jump, bail out; *fig* back out (*von* of)

'**Absprung** *m* jump; SPORT take-off; *fig den* ~ *schaffen* make it

'**abspülen** *v/t* (*sep*, *-ge-*, *h*) rinse; wash up

abstammen *v/i* (*sep*, *no past participle*) be descended (*von* from); CHEM, LING derive; '**Abstammung** *f* (*-*; *no pl*) descent; derivation; '**Abstammungslehre** *f* theory of the origin of species

'**Abstand** *m* distance (*a. fig*); interval; ~ *halten* keep one's distance; *fig mit* ~ by far

abstatten ['apʃtatən] *v/t* (*sep*, *-ge-*, *h*) *j-m e-n Besuch* ~ pay a visit to s.o.

'**abstauben** *v/t* (*sep*, *-ge-*, *h*) dust; F *fig* sponge; swipe

'**Abstauber** F *m* (*-s*; *-*), '**Abstaubertor** *n* SPORT opportunist goal

'**abstechen** (*irr*, *stechen*, *sep*, *-ge-*, *h*) **1.** *v/t* stick (*pig etc*) **2.** *v/i* contrast (*von* with); '**Abstecher** *m* (*-s*; *-*) side-trip, excursion (*a. fig*)

'**abstecken** *v/t* (*sep*, *-ge-*, *h*) mark out

'**abstehen** *v/i* (*irr*, *stehen*, *sep*, *-ge-*, *h*) stick out, protrude; → **abgestanden**

'**absteigen** *v/i* (*irr*, *steigen*, *sep*, *-ge-*, *sein*) get off (*a horse etc*); climb down;

stay (*in dat* at); SPORT *Am* be moved down to a lower division, *Br* be relegated; 'Absteiger *m* (-s; -) SPORT *Br* relegated club

'abstellen *v/t* (*sep*, -ge-, *h*) put down; leave (*s.th. with s.o.*); turn off (*gas etc*); park (*car*); *fig* put an end to *s.th.*

'Abstellgleis *n* RAIL siding; *j-n aufs ~ schieben* F push s.o. aside

'Abstellraum *m* storeroom

'abstempeln *v/t* (*sep*, -ge-, *h*) stamp

'absterben *v/i* (*irr*, *sterben*, *sep*, -ge-, *sein*) die off; *limb*: go numb

Abstieg ['apʃtiːk] *m* (-[e]s; -e) descent; *fig* decline; SPORT *Br* relegation

'abstimmen *v/i* (*sep*, -ge-, *h*) vote (*über acc* on)

'Abstimmung *f* vote; *radio*: tuning

Abstinenzler [apsti'nɛntslɐ] *m* (-s; -) teetotal(l)er

'Abstoß *m* SPORT goal-kick

'abstoßen *v/t* (*irr*, *stoßen*, *sep*, -ge-, *h*) repel; MED reject; push off (*boat*); F get rid of *s.th.*; **~d** *fig adj* repulsive

abstrakt [ap'strakt] *adj* abstract

'abstreiten *v/t* (*irr*, *streiten*, *sep*, -ge-, *h*) deny

'Abstrich *m* MED smear; *pl* ECON cuts; *fig* reservations

'abstufen *v/t* (*sep*, -ge-, *h*) graduate; gradate (*colors*)

'abstumpfen (*sep*, -ge-) **1.** *v/t* (*h*) blunt, dull (*a. fig*) **2.** *fig v/i* (*sein*) become unfeeling

'Absturz *m*, 'abstürzen *v/i* (*sep*, -ge-, *sein*) fall; AVIAT, IT crash

'absuchen *v/t* (*sep*, -ge-, *h*) search (*nach* for)

absurd [ap'zurt] *adj* absurd, preposterous

Abszess [aps'tsɛs] *m* (-es; -e) MED abscess

Abt [apt] *m* (-[e]s; *Äbte* ['ɛptə]) REL abbot

'abtasten *v/t* (*sep*, -ge-, *h*) feel (for); MED palpate; frisk; TECH, IT scan

'abtauen *v/t* (*sep*, -ge-, *h*) defrost

Abtei [ap'taɪ] *f* (-; -en) REL abbey

Abteil [ap'taɪl] *n* (-[e]s; -e) RAIL compartment

'abteilen *v/t* (*sep*, -ge-, *h*) divide; ARCH partition off

Ab'teilung *f* (-; -en) department (*a.* ECON); ward (*of hospital*); MIL detachment; Ab'teilungsleiter *m* head of (a) department; *Am* floorwalker, *Br* shopwalker

Äbtissin [ɛp'tɪsɪn] *f* (-; -nen) REL abbess

'abtöten *v/t* (*sep*, -ge-, *h*) kill (*bacteria etc*); *fig* deaden (*feelings etc*)

'abtragen *v/t* (*irr*, *tragen*, *sep*, -ge-, *h*) wear out (*clothes*); clear away (*dishes etc*); pay off (*debt*)

'Abtrans,port *m* transportation

'abtreiben (*irr*, *treiben*, *sep*, -ge-) **1.** *v/t* MED (*h*) have an abortion; MAR, AVIAT (*sein*) be blown off course **2.** *v/t* (*h*) MED abort; 'Abtreibung *f* (-; -en) abortion; *e-e ~ vornehmen* perform an abortion

'abtrennen *v/t* (*sep*, -ge-, *h*) detach; separate; MED sever

'abtreten (*irr*, *treten*, *sep*, -ge-) **1.** *v/t* (*h*) wear down (*heels*); wipe (*one's feet*); *fig* give up (*an acc* to); **2.** *v/i* (*sein*) resign; THEA; exit; 'Abtreter *m* (-s; -) doormat

'abtrocknen (*sep*, -ge-, *h*) **1.** *v/t* dry; *sich ~* dry o.s. off **2.** *v/i* dry the dishes, *Br a.* dry up

abtrünnig ['aptrʏnɪç] *adj* unfaithful, disloyal; 'Abtrünnige ['aptrʏnɪgə] *m*, *f* (-n; -n) renegade, turncoat

abtun *v/t* (*irr*, *tun*, *sep*, -ge-, *h*) dismiss (*als* as), brush *s.o.*, *s.th.* aside

abwägen ['apvɛːgən] *v/t* (*irr*, *wägen*, *sep*, -ge-, *h*) weigh (*gegen* against)

'abwählen *v/t* (*sep*, -ge-, *h*) vote out

'abwälzen *v/t* (*sep*, -ge-, *h*) *et. auf j-n ~* shove s.th. off on (to) s.o.

'abwandeln *v/t* (*sep*, -ge-, *h*) vary, modify

'abwandern *v/i* (*sep*, -ge-, *sein*) migrate (*von* from; *nach* to); 'Abwanderung *f* migration

'Abwandlung *f* modification, variation

'Abwärme *f* TECH waste heat

Abwart ['apvart] *m* (-s; -e) *Swiss* → *Hausmeister*

'abwarten (*sep*, -ge-, *h*) **1.** *v/t* wait for, await **2.** *v/i* wait; *warten wir ab!* let's wait and see!; *wart nur ab!* just wait!

abwärts ['apvɛrts] *adv* down, downward(s)

Abwasch ['apvaʃ] *m* (-[e]s; *no pl*) *den ~ machen* do the washing-up

'abwaschbar *adj* washable

'abwaschen (*irr*, *waschen*, *sep*, -ge-, *h*) **1.** *v/t* wash off **2.** *v/i* do the dishes, *Br a.*

wash up

'**Abwaschwasser** *n* dishwater

'**Abwasser** *n* TECH waste water, sewage; **~aufbereitung** *f* TECH sewage treatment

'**abwechseln** *v/i* (*sep, -ge-, h*) alternate; **sich mit j-m ~** take turns (**bei et.** at [doing] s.th.); **~d** *adv* by turns

'**Abwechslung** *f* (-; -*en*) change; **zur ~** for a change; '**abwechslungsreich** *adj* varied; colo(u)rful

'**Abweg** *m*: **auf ~e geraten** go astray

abwegig ['apveːgɪç] *adj* absurd, unrealistic

'**Abwehr** *f* (-; *no pl*) defen|se, *Br* -ce (*a.* SPORT); warding off (*of blow etc*); save (*of ball*)

'**abwehren** *v/t* (*sep, -ge-, h*) ward off (*blow etc*); beat off; SPORT block

'**Abwehr|fehler** *m* SPORT defensive error; **~kräfte** *pl* MED resistance; **~spieler** *m* SPORT defender; **~stoffe** *pl* MED antibodies

'**abweichen** *v/i* (*irr,* **weichen***, sep, -ge-, sein*) deviate (**von** from); digress

'**Abweichung** *f* (-; -*en*) deviation

'**abweisen** *v/t* (*irr,* **weisen***, sep, -ge-, h*) turn away; rebuff; decline, turn down (*request, offer etc*); **~d** *adj* unfriendly

'**abwenden** *v/t* ([*irr,* **wenden**,] *sep, -ge-, h*) turn away (*a.* **sich ~**) (**von** from); avert (*tragedy etc*)

'**abwerfen** *v/t* (*irr,* **werfen***, sep, -ge-, h*) throw off; AVIAT drop; BOT shed (*leaves*); ECON yield (*profit*)

'**abwerten** *v/t* (*sep, -ge-, h*) ECON devalue; **~d** *fig adj* disparaging

'**Abwertung** *f* ECON devaluation

'**abwesend** *adj* absent

'**Abwesenheit** *f* (-; *no pl*) absence

abwickeln *v/t* (*sep, -ge-, h*) unwind; ECON handle; transact (*business*)

'**abwiegen** *v/t* (*irr,* **wiegen***, sep, -ge-, h*) weigh (out)

'**abwimmeln** F *v/t* (*sep, -ge-, h*) **j-n ~** get rid of s.o., give s.o. the elbow

'**abwischen** *v/t* (*sep, -ge-, h*) wipe (off)

'**Abwurf** *m* dropping; *soccer*: throw-out

'**abwürgen** F *v/t* (*sep, -ge-, h*) MOT stall; *fig* stifle; '**abzahlen** *v/t* (*sep, -ge-, h*) make *monthly etc* payments for; pay off; '**abzählen** *v/t* (*sep, -ge-, h*) count

'**Abzahlung** *f*: **et. auf ~ kaufen** *Am* buy s.th. on the instalment plan (*Br* on hire

purchase)

'**abzapfen** *v/t* (*sep, -ge-, h*) tap, draw off

'**Abzeichen** *n* badge; medal

'**abzeichnen** *v/t* (*sep, -ge-, h*) copy, draw; sign, initial; **sich ~** (*begin to*) show; stand out (**gegen** against)

'**Abziehbild** *n* *Am* decal, *Br* transfer

'**abziehen** (*irr,* **ziehen***, sep, -ge-*) **1.** *v/t* (*h*) take off, remove; MATH subtract; strip (*bed*); take out (*key*); **das Fell ~** skin **2.** *v/i* (*sein*) go away; MIL withdraw; *smoke*: escape; *storm, clouds*: move off

'**Abzug** *m* ECON deduction; discount; MIL withdrawal; PRINT copy; PHOT print; *gun*: trigger; TECH vent, outlet; cooker hood

abzüglich ['aptsyːklɪç] *prp* less, minus

'**abzweigen** (*sep, -ge-*) **1.** *v/t* (*h*) divert (*resources etc*) (**für** to); **2.** *v/i* (*sein*) *path etc*: branch off

'**Abzweigung** *f* (-; -*en*) junction

ach [ax] *int* oh!; **~ je!** oh dear!; **~ so!** I see; **~ was!** *surprised*: really?, *annoyed*: of course not!, nonsense!

Achse ['aksə] *f* (-; -*n*) TECH axle; MATH *etc* axis; F **auf ~ sein** be on the move

Achsel ['aksəl] *f* (-; -*n*) ANAT shoulder; **die ~n zucken** shrug one's shoulders

'**Achselhöhle** *f* ANAT armpit

'**Achsenbruch** *m* MOT broken axle

acht [axt] *adj* eight; **heute in ~ Tagen** a week from today, *esp Br* today week; (**heute**) **vor ~ Tagen** a week ago (today)

Acht *f*: **~ geben** → **achtgeben**; **außer ~ lassen** disregard; **sich in ~ nehmen** be careful, look *or* watch out (**vor** *dat* for)

achte ['axtə] *adj* eighth

'**achteckig** *adj* octagonal

Achtel ['axtəl] *n* (-*s*; -) eighth (part)

achten (*ge-, h*) **1.** *v/t* respect **2.** *v/i*: **~ auf** (*acc*) pay attention to; keep an eye on; watch; be careful with; **darauf ~**, **dass** see to it that

ächten ['ɛçtən] *v/t* (*ge-, h*) ban; *esp* HIST outlaw

Achter ['axtɐ] *m* (-*s*; -) *rowing*: eight

'**Achterbahn** *f* roller coaster

'**achtfach** *adj and adv* eightfold

achtgeben *v/i* (*irr,* **geben***, sep, -ge-, h*) be careful; pay attention (**auf** *acc* to); take care (**auf** *acc* of); **gib acht!** look *or* watch out!, be careful!

'**achtlos** *adj* careless, heedless

'**Achtung** *f* (-; *no pl*) respect (**vor** *dat*

for); **~!** look out!; MIL attention!; **~! ~!** attention please!; **~! Fertig! Los!** On your marks! Get set! Go!; **~ Stufe!** Am caution: step!, Br mind the step!

'**achtzehn** adj eighteen

'**achtzehnte** adj eighteenth

achtzig ['axtsɪç] adj eighty; **die ~er Jahre** the eighties; **~ste** adj eightieth

ächzen ['ɛçtsən] v/i (ge-, h) groan (**vor** dat with)

Acker ['akɐ] m (-s; Äcker ['ɛkɐ]) field; **~bau** m (-[e]s; no pl) agriculture; farming; **~ und Viehzucht** crop and stock farming; **~land** n (-[e]s; no pl) farmland

'**ackern** F v/i (ge-, h) slog (away)

Adapter [a'daptɐ] m (-s; -) TECH adapter

addieren [a'di:rən] v/t (no -ge-, h) add (up); **Addition** [adi'tsio:n] f (-; -en) addition, adding up

Adel ['a:dəl] m (-s; no pl) aristocracy

'**adeln** v/t (ge-, h) ennoble (a. fig); Br knight

Ader ['a:dɐ] f (-; -n) ANAT blood vessel, vein

Adjektiv ['atjɛkti:f] n (-s; -e) LING adjective

Adler ['a:dlɐ] m (-s; -) zo eagle

adlig ['a:dlɪç] adj noble; **Adlige** ['a:dlɪgə] m, f (-n; -n) noble|man (-woman)

Admiral [atmi'ra:l] m (-s; -e) MAR admiral

adoptieren [adɔp'ti:rən] v/t (no -ge-, h) adopt; **Adoptivkind** [adɔp'ti:fkɪnt] n adopted child

Adressbuch [a'drɛsbu:x] n directory

Adresse [a'drɛsə] f (-; -n) address

adressieren [adrɛ'si:rən] v/t (no -ge-, h) address (**an** acc to)

Advent [at'vɛnt] m (-[e]s; no pl) REL Advent; Advent Sunday

Ad'ventszeit f Christmas season

Adverb [at'vɛrp] n (-s; Adverbien [at'vɛrbiən]) LING adverb

Aerobic [ɛ'ro:bɪk] n (-s; no pl) aerobics

Affäre [a'fɛ:rə] f (-; -n) affair

Affe ['afə] m (-n; -n) zo monkey; ape

Affekt [a'fɛkt] m (-[e]s; -e) **im ~** in the heat of passion (a. JUR)

affektiert [afɛk'ti:ɐt] adj affected

Afrika ['a:frika] Africa; **Afrikaner** [afri'ka:nɐ] m (-s; -), **Afri'kanerin** [afri'ka:nərɪn] f (-; -nen), **afri'kanisch** adj African

After ['aftɐ] m (-s; -) ANAT anus

AG abbr of **Aktiengesellschaft** Am (stock) corporation, Br PLC, public limited company

Agent [a'gɛnt] m (-en; -en), **A'gentin** f (-; -nen) agent; POL (secret) agent

Agentur [agɛn'tu:ɐ] f (-; -en) agency

Aggression [agrɛ'sio:n] f (-; -en) aggression; **aggressiv** [agrɛ'si:f] adj aggressive; **Aggressivität** [agresivi'tɛ:t] f (-; no pl) aggressiveness

Agitator [agi'ta:tɔr] m (-s; -en [agita-'to:rən]) agitator

ah [a:] int ah!

äh [ɛ:] int er; disgusted: ugh!

aha [a'ha] int I see!, oh!

A'ha-Erlebnis n aha-experience

Ahn [a:n] m (-[e]s; -en; -en) ancestor, pl a. forefathers

ähneln ['ɛ:nəln] v/i (ge-, h) resemble, look like

ahnen ['a:nən] v/t (ge-, h) suspect; foresee, know

ähnlich ['ɛ:nlɪç] adj similar (dat to); **j-m ~ sehen** look like s.o.

'**Ähnlichkeit** f (-; -en) likeness, resemblance, similarity (**mit** to)

'**Ahnung** f (-; -en) presentiment, a. foreboding; notion, idea; **ich habe keine ~** I have no idea; '**ahnungslos** adj unsuspecting, innocent

Ahorn ['a:hɔrn] m (-s, -e) BOT maple

Ähre ['ɛ:rə] f (-; -n) BOT ear; spike

Aids [eɪdz] n (-; no pl) MED AIDS

'**Aids-Kranke** m, f MED AIDS victim or sufferer; **~test** m MED AIDS test

Airbag ['ɛəbæg] m (-s; -s) MOT airbag

Akademie [akade'mi:] f (-; -n) academy, college; **Akademiker(in)** [aka-'de:mikɐ, aka'de:mikərɪn] m(f) (-s; -/-; -nen) university graduate; **akademisch** [aka'de:mɪʃ] adj academic

akklimatisieren [aklimati'zi:rən] v/refl (no -ge-, h) acclimatize (**an** acc to)

Akkord [a'kɔrt] m (-[e]s; -e) MUS chord; **im ~** ECON by the piece or job; **~arbeit** f ECON piecework; **~arbeiter(in)** ECON pieceworker

Akkordeon [a'kɔrdeɔn] n (-s; -s) MUS accordion

Ak'kordlohn m ECON piece wages

Akku ['aku] F m (-s; -s), **Akkumulator** [akumu'la:tɔr] m (-s; -en [akumula-'to:rən]) TECH (storage) battery, Br a.

accumulator

Akkusativ['akuzati:f] *m* (*-s*; *-e*) LING accusative (case)

Akne ['aknə] *f* (*-*; *-n*) MED acne

Akrobat [akro'ba:t] *m* (*-en*; *-en*), **Akro-'batin** *f* (*-*; *-nen*) acrobat; **akro'batisch** *adj* acrobatic

Akt [akt] *m* (*-[e]s*; *-e*) act(ion); THEA act; PAINT, PHOT nude

Akte['aktə]*f*(*-*;*-n*) file; *pl.* files, records; **zu den ~n legen** file

'Akten|deckel *m* folder; **~koffer** *m* attaché case; **~ordner** *m* file; **~tasche** *f* briefcase; **~zeichen** *n* reference (number)

Aktie ['aktsiə] *f* (*-*; *-n*) ECON share, *esp Am* stock; **'Aktiengesellschaft** *f Am* corporation; *Br* joint-stock company

Aktion [ak'tsio:n] *f* (*-*; *-en*) campaign, drive; MIL *ect* operation; **in ~** in action

Aktionär [aktsio'nε:ɐ] *m* (*-s*; *-e*), **Aktio-'närin** *f* (*-*; *-nen*) ECON shareholder, *esp Am* stockholder

aktiv [ak'ti:f] *adj* active

Aktiv [ak'ti:f] *n* (*-s*; *no pl*) LING active voice; **aktivieren** *v/t* (*no -ge-*, *h*) activate; **Aktivist** [akti'vist] *m* (*-en*; *-en*) *esp* POL activist

Ak'tivurlaub *m* activity vacation

aktualisieren [aktuali'zi:rən] *v/t* (*no -ge-*, *h*) update

aktuell [aktu'εl] *adj* topical; current; up-to-date; TV, *radio*: **e-e ~e Sendung** a current affairs or news feature

Akupunktur [akupʊŋk'tu:ɐ] *f* (*-*; *-en*) MED acupuncture

Akustik [a'kʊstɪk] *f* (*-*; *no pl*) acoustics **a'kustisch** *adj* acoustic

akut [a'ku:t] *adj* urgent (*problem etc*); *a.* MED acute

Akzent [ak'tsεnt] *m* (*-[e]s*; *-e*) accent, stress (*a. fig*)

akzeptabel [aktsεp'ta:bəl] *adj* acceptable; reasonable (*price etc*)

akzeptieren [aktsεp'ti:rən] *v/t* (*no -ge-*, *h*) accept

Alarm [a'larm] *m* (*-[e]s*; *-e*) alarm; **~ schlagen** sound the alarm; **~anlage** *f* alarm system; **~bereitschaft** *f*: **in ~** on standby, on the alert

alarmieren [alar'mi:rən] *v/t* (*no -ge-*, *h*) call; alert; **~d** *adj* alarming

albern ['albɐn] *adj* silly, foolish

Album['albʊm]*n*(*-s*; *Alben* ['albən]) al-

bum (*a. record*)

Algebra['algəbra]*f*(*-*;*no pl*) MATH algebra

Algen ['algən] *pl* BOT algae; **~pest** *f* plague of algae, algal bloom

Alibi [a:libi] *n* (*-s*; *-s*) JUR alibi

Alimente [ali'mεntə] *pl* JUR alimony

Alkohol ['alkoho:l] *m* (*-s*; *no pl*) alcohol; **'alkoholfrei** *adj* nonalcoholic, soft; **Alkoholiker(in)** [alko'ho:likɐ, alko'ho:likərɪn] *m(f)* (*-s*; *-/-*; *-nen*) alcoholic; **alko'holischadj** alcoholic; **Alkoholismus** [alkoho'lɪsmʊs] *m* (*-*; *no pl*) alcoholism; **alkoholsüchtigadj** addicted to alcohol; **Alkoholtest** *m* alcohol test, *Br* breathalyser® test

All *n* (*-s*; *no pl*) universe; (outer) space

alle[¹'alə]*indefpron and adj* all; **~s (Be-liebige)** anything; **~ (Leute)** everybody; anybody; **~ beide** both of them; **wir ~** all of us; **~s in ~m** in all in all; **auf ~ Fälle** in any case; **~ drei Tage** every three days; → **Art, Gute, vor**;

alle²['alə]*F adj*: **~ sein** be all gone; **mein Geld ist ~** I'm out of money

Allee [a'le:] *f* (*-*; *-n*) avenue

allein[a'lain]*adj and adv* alone; lonely; by o.s.: **ganz ~** all alone; **er hat es ganz ~ gemacht** he did it all by himself; **~ stehend → alleinstehend**

Al'lein|erziehende *m*, *f* (*-n*; *-n*) single parent; **~gangm**: **im~** single-handedly, solo

alleinig [a'lainɪç] *adj* sole

Al'leinsein *n* (*-s*; *no pl*) loneliness

alleinstehend *adj* single

Allerbeste['alɐ'bεstə]: **der (die, das) ~** the best of all, the very best

allerdings ['alɐ'dɪŋs] *adv* however, though; **~f** certainly!, *esp Am* F sure!

'aller'erste *adj* very first

Allergie [alεr'gi:] *f* (*-*; *-n*) MED allergy (**gegen** to); **allergisch**[a'lεrgɪʃ]*adj* allergic (**gegen** to)

'aller'hand F *adj* a good deal (of); **das ist ja ~!** that's a bit much!

'Aller'heiligen *n* REL All Saints' Day

allerlei ['alɐ'lai] *adj* all kinds or sorts of

'aller'letzte *adj* last of all, very last; **~ 'liebst 1.** *adj* (most) lovely **2.** *adv*: **am ~en mögen** like best of all; **~'meiste** *adj* (by far the) most; **~'nächste** *adj* very next; **in ~r Zeit** in the very near future; **~'neu(e)ste** *adj* very latest

'Aller'seelen n REL All Souls' Day

allerseits ['alɛ'zaits] adv F: **Tag~!** hi, everybody!

'aller'wenigst adv: **am ~en** least of all

alles everything

allesamt ['alə'zamt] adv all together

'allge'mein 1. adj general; common; universal **2.** adv: **im Allgemeinen** in general, generally; **~ verständlich** intelligible (to all), popular

Allge'mein|arzt m, **Allge'meinärztin** f Br GP, Am family practitioner; **~bildung** f general education

'Allge'meinheit f (-; no pl) (general) public

allgemeinver'ständlich adj → **allgemein**

All'heilmittel n cure-all (a. fig)

Allianz [a'ljants] f (-; -en) alliance

Alligator [ali'gaːtoːɐ] m (-s; -en) alligator

Alliierte [ali'iːɐtə]: **die ~n** pl POL the Allies

'all|'jährlich adv every year; **~ stattfindend** annual; **~'mächtig** adj omnipotent; Almighty (God)

allmählich [al'mɛːlɪç] **1.** adj gradual **2.** adv gradually

'Allradantrieb m MOT four-wheel drive

allseitig ['alzaitɪç] adv: **~ interessiert sein** have all-round interests

Alltag m everyday life

'all|'täglich adj everyday; fig a. ordinary; **~'wissend** adj omniscient

'allzu adv (all) too; **~ viel** too much

Alm [alm] f (-; -en) alpine pasture, alp

Almosen ['almoːzən] n (-s; -) alms

'Alpdruck m (-[e]s; no pl) nightmare (a. fig)

Alphabet [alfa'beːt] n (-[e]s; -e) alphabet; **alpha'betisch** adj alphabetical

alpin [al'piːn] adj alpine

'Alptraum m nightmare (a. fig)

als [als] cj time: when; while; after comp: than; **~ ich ankam** when I arrived; **~ Kind (Geschenk)** as a child (present); **älter ~** older than; **~ ob** as if, as though; **nichts ~** nothing but

also ['alzo] cj so, therefore; F well, you know; **~ gut!** very well (then)!, all right (then)!; **~ doch** so ... after all; **du willst ~ gehen** etc? so you want to go etc?

alt [alt] adj old; HIST ancient; classical (language); **ein 12 Jahre ~er Junge** a twelve-year-old boy

Alt m (-s; no pl) MUS alto

Altar [al'taːɐ] m (-s; Altäre [al'tɛːrə]) REL altar

'Alte m, f (-n; -n) **der ~** the old man (a. fig); the boss; **die ~** the old woman (a. fig); **die ~n** pl the old

'Altenheim n → **Altersheim**

'Altenpfleger(in) geriatric nurse

Alter ['altɐ] n (-s; no pl) old age; **im ~ von ...** at the age of ...; **er ist in deinem ~** he's your age

älter ['ɛltɐ] adj older; **mein ~er Bruder** my elder brother; **ein ~er Herr** an elderly gentleman

altern v/i (ge-, sein) grow old, age

alternativ [altɛrna'tiːf] adj alternative; POL ecological, green; a. counter-culture (movement etc)

Alternative¹ [altɛrna'tiːvə] f (-; -n) alternative; option, choice

Alterna'tive² m, f (-n; -n) ecologist, member of the counterculture movement

'Alters|grenze f age limit; retirement age; **~heim** n old people's home; **~rente** f old-age pension; **~schwäche** f (-; no pl) infirmity; **an ~ sterben** die of old age; **~versorgung** f old age pension (scheme)

Altertum n (-s; no pl) antiquity

'Altglascon,tainer m Am glass recycling bin, Br bottle bank

'altklug adj precocious

'Altlasten f pl residual pollution

'Altme,tall n scrap (metal)

'altmodisch adj old-fashioned

'Altöl n waste oil

'Altpa,pier n waste paper

'altsprachlich adj: **~es Gymnasium** appr classical secondary school

'Altstadt f old town; **~sa,nierung** f town-cent|er (Br -re) rehabilitation

'Altwarenhändler m second-hand dealer

Alt'weibersommer m Indian summer; gossamer

Aluminium [alu'miːnjʊm] n (-s; no pl) alumin(i)um

am [am] prp at the (window etc); time: in the (morning etc); at the (weekend etc); on (Sunday etc); **~ 1. Mai** on May 1st; **~ Tage** during the day; **~ Himmel** in the sky; **~ meisten** most; **~ Leben** alive

Amateur [ama'tø:ɐ] m (-s; -e) amateur; **~funker** m radio amateur, F radio ham

Amboss ['ambɔs] m (-es; -e) anvil

ambulant [ambu'lant] adv: **~ behandelt werden** MED get outpatient treatment

Ambulanz [ambu'lants] f (-; -en) MED outpatients' department; MOT ambulance

Ameise ['a:maizə] f (-; -n) ZO ant

'Ameisenhaufen m ZO anthill

Amerika [a'me:rika] America

Amerikaner [ameri'ka:nɐ] m (-s; -), **Ameri'kanerin** [ameri'ka:nərɪn] f (-; -nen), **ameri'kanisch** adj American

Amnestie [amnɛs'ti:] f (-; -n), **amnes-'tieren** v/t (no -ge-, h) JUR amnesty

Amok ['a:mɔk] m: **~ laufen** run amok

Ampel ['ampəl] f (-; -n) traffic light(s)

Amphibie [am'fi:bjə] f (-; -n) ZO amphibian

Ampulle [am'pulə] f (-; -n) ampoule

Amputation [amputa'tsjo:n] f (-; -en) MED amputation; **amputieren** [ampu-'ti:rən] v/t (no -ge-, h) MED amputate

Amsel ['amzəl] f (-; -n) ZO blackbird

Amt [amt] n (-[e]s; Ämter ['ɛmtɐ]) office, department, esp Am bureau; position; duty, function; TEL exchange

'amtlich adj official

'Amts|arzt m medical examiner (Br officer); **~einführung** f inauguration; **~geheimnis** n official secret; **~ge-schäfte** pl official duties; **~zeichen** n TEL dial (Br dialling) tone; **~zeit** f term (of office)

Amulett [amu'lɛt] n (-[e]s; -e) amulet, (lucky) charm

amüsant [amy'zant] adj amusing, entertaining

amüsieren [amy'zi:rən] v/t (no -ge-, h) amuse; **sich ~** enjoy o.s., have a good time; **sich ~ über** (acc) laugh at

an [an] **1.** prp: **~ der Themse** (Küste, Wand) on the Thames (coast, wall); **~ s-m Schreibtisch** at his desk; **~ der Hand** by the hand; **~ der Arbeit** at work; **~ den Hausaufgaben sitzen** sit over one's homework; **et. schicken ~** (acc) send s.th. to; **sich lehnen ~** (acc) lean against; **~ die Tür** etc **klopfen** knock at the door etc; **~ e-m Sonntag-morgen** on a Sunday morning; **~ dem Tag, ...** on the day ...; **~ Weihnachten** etc at Christmas etc; → **Mangel, Stelle,**

sterben 2. adv on (a. light etc); **von jetzt (da, heute) ~** from now (that time, today) on; **München ~ 16.45** arrival Munich 4.45 p.m.

Anabolikum [ana'bo:likum] n (-s; -ka) PHARM anabolic steroid

analog [ana'lo:k] adj analogous

Ana'log... in cpds analog(ue) (computer etc)

Analphabet [an?alfa'be:t] m (-en; -en), **Analpha'betin** f(-; -nen) illiterate (person)

Analyse [ana'ly:zə] f (-; -n) analysis

analysieren [analy'zi:rən] v/t (no -ge-, h) analy|ze, Br -se

Ananas ['ananas] f(-; -, -se) BOT pineapple

Anarchie [anar'çi:] f (-; -n) anarchy

Anatomie [anato'mi:] f (-; -n) anatomy

anatomisch [ana'to:mɪʃ] adj anatomical

'anbahnen v/t (sep, -ge-, h) pave the way for; **sich ~** be developing; be impending

'Anbau m (-[e]s; -ten) AGR (no pl) cultivation; ARCH annex, extension

'anbauen v/t (sep, -ge-, h) AGR cultivate, grow; ARCH add (**an** acc to), build on

'anbehalten v/t (irr, halten, sep, no -ge-, h) keep on

an'bei adv ECON enclosed

'anbeißen (irr, beißen, sep, -ge-, h) **1.** v/t take a bite of **2.** v/i fish: bite; fig take the bait; **'anbellen** v/t (sep, -ge-, h) bark at; **'anbeten** v/t (sep, -ge-, h) adore, worship (a. fig)

'Anbetracht m: **in ~ (dessen, dass)** considering (that)

'anbetteln v/t (sep, -ge-, h) **j-n um et. ~** beg s.o. for s.th.; **anbiedern** ['anbi:dɐn] v/refl (sep, -ge-, h) curry favo(u)r (**bei** with); **'anbieten** v/t (irr, bieten, sep, -ge-, h) offer; **'anbinden** v/t (irr, binden, sep, -ge-, h) tie up; **~ an** (acc or dat) tie to

'Anblick m sight; **'anblicken** v/t (sep, -ge-, h) look at; glance at

'anbohren v/t (sep, -ge-, h) tap

'anbrechen (irr, brechen, sep, -ge-) **1.** v/t (h) break into (supplies); open **2.** v/i (sein) begin; day: break; night: fall

'anbrennen v/t (irr, brennen, sep, -ge-, sein) burn (a. ~ lassen)

'anbringen v/t (irr, bringen, sep, -ge-, h)

fix (*an dat* to)

'**Anbruch** *m* (-[*e*]*s*; *no pl*) beginning; *bei ~ der Nacht* at nightfall

'**anbrüllen** *v/t* (*sep*, -*ge*-, *h*) roar at

Andacht ['andaxt] *f* (-; -*en*) REL (*no pl*) devotion; service; prayers

andächtig ['andɛçtɪç] *adj* REL devout

'**andauern** *v/i* (*sep*, -*ge*-, *h*) continue, go on, last; **~d** *adj and adv* → *dauernd*

'**Andenken** *n* (-*s*; -) keepsake; souvenir (*both*: **an** *acc* of); *zum ~ an* (*acc*) in memory of

andere ['andərə] *adj and indef pron* other; different; *mit ~n Worten* in other words; *am ~n Morgen* the next morning; *et.* (*nichts*) *~s* s.th. (nothing) else; *nichts ~s als* nothing but; *die ~n* the others; *alle ~n* everybody else

andererseits ['andərə'zaɪts] *adv* on the other hand

ändern ['ɛndɐn] *v/t* (*ge*-, *h*) change; alter (*clothes*); *ich kann es nicht ~* I can't help it; *sich ~* change

'**andern|falls** *adv* otherwise

anders ['andɐs] *adv* different(ly); *jemand ~* somebody else; *~ werden* change; *~ sein* (*als*) be different (from); *es geht nicht ~* there is no other way; *~herum* **1.** *adv* the other way round **2.** F *adj* queer; *~wo(hin)* *adv* elsewhere

anderthalb ['andɐt'halp] *adj* one and a half

'**Änderung** *f* (-; -*en*) change; alteration

'**andeuten** *v/t* (*sep*, -*ge*-, *h*) hint (at); suggest; indicate; *j-m ~, dass* give s.o. a hint that

'**Andeutung** *f* (-; -*en*) hint, suggestion

'**Andrang** *m* (-[*e*]*s*; *no pl*) crush; ECON rush (*nach* for); run (*zu, nach* on)

'**andrehen** *v/t* (*sep*, -*ge*-, *h*) turn on; F *j-m et. ~* fob s.th. off on s.o.

'**androhen** *v/t* (*sep*, -*ge*-, *h*) *j-m et. ~* threaten s.o. with s.th.

'**aneignen** *v/refl* (*sep*, -*ge*-, *h*) acquire; *esp* JUR appropriate

anei'nander *adv tie etc* together; *~ denken* think of each other; *~geraten* *v/i* (*irr, geraten, sep, sein*) clash (*mit* with)

Anekdote [anɛk'doːtə] *f* (-; -*n*) anecdote

'**anekeln** *v/t* (*sep*, -*ge*-, *h*) disgust, sicken; *es ekelt mich an* it makes me sick

'**anerkannt** *adj* acknowledged, recognized

'**anerkennen** *v/t* (*irr, kennen, sep, no -ge*-, *h*) acknowledge, recognize; appreciate; *~d* *adj* appreciative

'**Anerkennung** *f* (-; -*en*) acknowledg(e)ment, recognition; appreciation

'**anfahren** (*irr, fahren, sep, -ge*-) **1.** *v/i* (*sein*) start **2.** *v/t* (*h*) deliver; MOT *etc* hit, *car etc: a.* run into; *fig j-n ~* jump on s.o.; '**Anfahrt** *f* journey, ride

'**Anfall** *m* MED fit, attack

'**anfallen** *v/t* (*irr, fallen, sep, -ge*-, *h*) attack, assault; *dog*: go for

'**anfällig** *adj* delicate; *~ für* susceptible to

'**Anfang** *m* beginning, start; *am ~* at the beginning; *~ Mai* early in May; *~ nächsten Jahres* early next year; *~ der neunziger Jahre* in the early nineties; *er ist ~ 20* he is in his early twenties; *von ~ an* from the beginning *or* start; '**anfangen** *v/t and v/i* (*irr, fangen, sep, -ge*-, *h*) begin, start; do; '**Anfänger** *m* (-*s*; -), '**Anfängerin** *f* (-; -*nen*) beginner

'**anfangs** *adv* at first

'**Anfangs|buchstabe** *m* initial (letter); *großer ~* capital (letter); *~stadium n*: *im ~* at an early stage

'**anfassen** *v/t* (*sep*, -*ge*-, *h*) touch; take (hold of); *sich ~* take each other by the hands; F *zum Anfassen* everyman's

'**anfechtbar** *adj* contestable; '**anfechten** *v/t* (*irr, fechten, sep, -ge*-, *h*) contest; '**Anfechtung** *f* (-; -*en*) contesting

'**anfertigen** *v/t* (*sep*, -*ge*-, *h*) make, manufacture

'**anfeuchten** *v/t* (*sep*, -*ge*-, *h*) moisten

'**anfeuern** *fig v/t* (*sep*, -*ge*-, *h*) cheer

'**anflehen** *v/t* (*sep*, -*ge*-, *h*) implore

'**anfliegen** *v/t* (*irr, fliegen, sep, -ge*-, *h*) AVIAT approach; fly (regularly) to

'**Anflug** *m* AVIAT approach; *fig* touch

'**anfordern** *v/t* (*sep*, -*ge*-, *h*) demand; request; '**Anforderung** *f* (-; -*en*) demand; request; *pl* requirements, qualifications

'**Anfrage** *f* (-; -*n*) inquiry

'**anfragen** *v/i* (*sep*, -*ge*-, *h*) inquire (*bei j-m nach et.* of s.o. about s.th.)

'**anfreunden** *v/refl* (*sep*, -*ge*-, *h*) make friends (*mit* with)

'**anfühlen** *v/refl* (*sep*, -*ge*-, *h*) feel; *es*

fühlt sich weich an it feels soft

'anführen v/t (*sep*, *-ge-*, *h*) lead; state; F fool; **'Anführer(in)** leader

'Anführungszeichen *pl* quotation marks, inverted commas

'Angabe f (-; *-n*) statement; indication; F big talk; *tennis*: service; *pl* information, data; TECH specifications

'angeben (*irr*, *geben*, *sep*, *-ge-*, *h*) **1.** v/t give, state; *customs*: declare; indicate; quote (*price*) **2.** v/i F *fig* brag, show off; *tennis*: serve; **'Angeber** F m (*-s*; -) braggart, show-off; **Angeberei** [ange:bə'rai] F f (-; *no pl*) bragging, showing off

angeblich ['ange:pliç] *adj* alleged; ~ *ist er ...* he is said to be ...

'angeboren *adj* innate, inborn; MED congenital

'Angebot n (*-[e]s*, *-e*) offer (*a.* ECON); ~ *und Nachfrage* supply and demand

ange|bracht *adj* appropriate; **~bunden** *adj*: *kurz* ~ curt; **~gossen** F *adj*: *wie* ~ *sitzen* fit like a glove; **~heitert** *adj* tipsy, Br *a.* (slightly) merry

'angehen (*irr*, *gehen*, *sep*, *-ge-*, *sein*) **1.** F v/i light etc: go on **2.** v/t concern; *das geht dich nichts an* that is none of your business; **~d** *adj* future; **~er Arzt** doctor-to-be

'angehören v/i (*sep*, *no -ge-*, *h*) belong to; **'Angehörige** m, f (*-n*; *-n*) relative; member; *die nächsten* **~n** the next of kin

'Angeklagte m, f (*-n*; *-n*) JUR defendant

'Angel ['aŋəl] f (-; *-n*) fishing tackle; TECH hinge

'Angelegenheit f (-; *-en*) matter, affair

angelehnt *adj* door etc: ajar

'angelernt *adj* semi-skilled (*worker*)

'Angelhaken m fishhook

'angeln (*-ge-*, *h*) **1.** v/i (*nach* for) fish, angle (*both a. fig*) **2.** v/t catch, hook

'Angelrute f fishing rod

Angelsachse ['aŋəlzaksə] m (*-n*; *-n*), **angelsächsisch** ['aŋəlzɛksiʃ] *adj* Anglo-Saxon

'Angelschein m fishing permit

'Angelschnur f fishing line

angemessen *adj* proper, suitable; just (*punishment*); reasonable (*price*)

angenehm *adj* pleasant, agreeable; **~!** pleased to meet you

'ange|nommen *cj* (let's) suppose, supposing; **~regt** *adj* animated; lively;

~schrieben *adj*: *bei j-m gut* (*schlecht*) **~ sein** be in s.o.'s good (bad) books; **~sehen** *adj* respected

'angesichts *prp* (*gen*) in view of

'Angestellte m, f (*-n*; *-n*) employee (*bei* with), *pl* the staff

'ange|tan *adj*: *ganz* ~ *sein von* be taken with; **~trunken** *adj* (slightly) drunk; *in* **~em Zustand** under the influence of alcohol; **~wandt** *adj* applied; **~wiesen** *adj*: ~ *auf* (*acc*) dependent (up)on

'angewöhnen v/t (*sep*, *no -ge-*, *h*) *sich* (*j-m*) ~, *et. zu tun* get (s.o.) used to doing s.th.; *sich das Rauchen* ~ take to smoking; **'Angewohnheit** f habit

Angina [aŋ'gi:na] f (-; *-nen*) MED tonsillitis

'angleichen v/t (*irr*, *gleichen*, *sep*, *-ge-*, *h*) adjust (*an acc* to)

Angler ['aŋlɐ] m (*-s*; -) angler

Anglist [aŋ'glɪst] m (*-en*; *-en*), **Anglistin** f (-; *-nen*) student of (*or* graduate in) English

'angreifen v/t (*irr*, *greifen*, *sep*, *-ge-*, *h*) attack (*a.* SPORT *and fig*); affect (*health etc*); touch (*supplies*)

'Angreifer m (*-s*; -) attacker, SPORT *a.* offensive player; *esp* POL aggressor

'angrenzend *adj* adjacent (*an acc* to)

'Angriff m attack (*a.* SPORT *and fig*); MIL assault, charge; *in* ~ *nehmen* set about

'angriffslustig *adj* aggressive

Angst [aŋst] f (-; *Ängste* ['ɛŋstə]) fear (*vor dat* of); ~ *haben* (*vor dat*) be afraid *or* scared (of); *j-m* ~ *einjagen* frighten *or* scare s.o.; (*hab*) *keine Angst!* don't be afraid!; **~hase** F m chicken

ängstigen ['ɛŋstɪgən] v/t (*ge-*, *h*) frighten, scare; *sich* ~ be afraid (*vor dat* of); be worried (*um* about)

ängstlich ['ɛŋstlɪç] *adj* timid, fearful; anxious

'anhaben F v/t (*irr*, *haben*, *sep*, *-ge-*, *h*) have on (*a. light etc*), *a.* wear, be wearing (*dress etc*)

'anhalten (*irr*, *halten*, *sep*, *-ge-*, *h*) **1.** v/t stop; *den Atem* ~ hold one's breath **2.** v/i stop; continue; **~d** *adj* continual

'Anhalter m (*-s*; -) hitchhiker; F *per* ~ *fahren* hitchhike

'Anhaltspunkt m clue

an'hand *prp* (*gen*) by means of

'Anhang m appendix; (*no pl*) relations;

'anhängen v/t (*sep*, *-ge-*, *h*) add; hang

up; RAIL, MOT couple (*an acc* to); '**Anhänger** *m* (-*s*; -) follower, supporter (*a.* SPORT); pendant; label, tag; MOT trailer; '**anhänglich** *adj* affectionate; *contp* clinging

'**anhäufen** *v/t and v/refl* (*sep*, -*ge*-, *h*) heap up, accumulate

'**Anhäufung** *f* (-; -*en*) accumulation

'**anheben** *v/t* (*irr, heben, sep*, -*ge*-, *h*) lift, raise (*a. price*); MOT jack up

'**anheften** *v/t* (*sep*, -*ge*-, *h*) attach, tack (*both*: *an acc* to)

'**Anhieb** *m*: *auf* ~ on the first try

'**anhimmeln** F *v/t* (*sep*, -*ge*-, *h*) idolize, worship

'**Anhöhe** *f* rise, hill, elevation

'**anhören** *v/t* (*sep*, -*ge*-, *h*) listen to; *mit* ~ overhear; *es hört sich ... an* it sounds ...; '**Anhörung** *f* (-; -*en*) hearing

animieren [ani'mi:rən] *v/t* (*no* -*ge*-, *h*) encourage; stimulate

'**ankämpfen** *v/i* (*sep*, -*ge*-, *h*) ~ *gegen* fight *s.th.*

'**Ankauf** *m* purchase

'**Anker** ['aŋkɐ] *m* (-*s*; -) MAR anchor; *vor- gehen* drop anchor

'**ankern** *v/i* (*ge*-, *h*) MAR anchor

'**anketten** *v/t* (*sep*, -*ge*-, *h*) chain up

'**Anklage** *f* (-; *no pl*) JUR accusation, charge (*a. fig*); '**anklagen** *v/t* (*sep*, -*ge*-, *h*) JUR accuse (*wegen* of), charge (with) (*both a. fig.*)

'**anklammern** *v/t* (*sep*, -*ge*-, *h*) clip *s.th.* on; *sich* ~ (*an acc*) cling (to)

Anklang *m*: ~ *finden* meet with approval

'**ankleben** *v/t* (*sep*, -*ge*-, *h*) stick on (*an dat or acc* to)

'**anklicken** *v/t* (*sep*, -*ge*-, *h*) IT click

'**anklopfen** *v/i* (*sep*, -*ge*-, *h*) knock (*an dat or acc* at)

'**anknipsen** *v/t* (*sep*, -*ge*-, *h*) switch on

'**anknüpfen** *v/t* (*sep*, -*ge*-, *h*) tie (*an acc* to); *fig* begin; *Beziehungen* ~ (*zu*) es- tablish contacts (with)

'**ankommen** *v/i* (*irr, kommen, sep*, -*ge*-, *sein*) arrive; *nicht gegen j-n* ~ be no match for *s.o.*; *es kommt (ganz) dar- auf an* it (all) depends; *es kommt dar- auf an, dass* what matters is; *darauf kommt es nicht an* that doesn't mat- ter; *es darauf ~ lassen* take a chance; *gut* ~ (*bei*) *fig* go down well (with)

'**ankündigen** *v/t* (*sep*, -*ge*-, *h*) announce;

advertise; '**Ankündigung** *f* announce- ment; advertisement

Ankunft ['ankʊnft] *f* (-; *no pl*) arrival

'**anlächeln**, '**anlachen** *v/t* (*sep*, -*ge*-, *h*) smile at

'**Anlage** *f* arrangement; facility; plant; TECH system; (stereo *etc*) set; ECON in- vestment; enclosure; *fig* gift; *fig* park, gardens; *sanitäre* ~*n* sanitary facilities

Anlass ['anlas] *m* (-*es*; *Anlässe* ['an- lɛsə]) occasion; cause

'**anlassen** *v/t* (*irr, lassen, sep*, -*ge*-, *h*) MOT start; F keep on, leave on (*a. light etc*); '**Anlasser** *m* (-*s*; -) MOT starter

anlässlich ['anlɛslɪç] *prp* (*gen*) on the occasion of

'**Anlauf** *m* SPORT run-up; *fig* start

'**anlaufen** (*irr, laufen, sep*, -*ge*-) **1.** *v/i* (*sein*) run up; *fig* start; *metal*: tarnish; *glasses etc*: steam up **2.** *v/t* (*h*) MAR call *or* touch at

'**anlegen** (*sep*, -*ge*-, *h*) **1.** *v/t* put on (*dress etc*); lay out (*garden etc*); build (*road etc*); invest (*money*); found (*town etc*); MED apply (*dressing etc*); lay in (*sup- plies*); *sich mit j-m* ~ pick a quarrel with s.o. **2.** *v/i* MAR land; moor; *es* ~ *auf* (*acc*) aim at; '**Anleger** *m* (-*s*; -) ECON inves- tor; MAR landing stage

'**anlehnen** *v/t* (*sep*, -*ge*-, *h*) lean (*an acc* against); leave *door etc* ajar; *sich* ~ *an* (*acc*) lean against, *fig* lean on *s.o.*

Anleihe ['anlaiə] *f* (-; -*n*) ECON loan

'**Anleitung** *f* (-; -*en*) guidance, instruc- tion; *written* instructions

'**Anliegen** *n* (-*s*; -) request; message (*of a film etc*)

Anlieger ['anli:gɐ] *m* (-*s*; -) resident

'**anlocken** *v/t* (*sep*, -*ge*-, *h*) attract, lure

'**anmachen** *v/t* (*sep*, -*ge*-, *h*) light (*fire etc*); turn on (*light etc*); dress (*salad*); F chat *s.o.* up; turn *s.o.* on

'**anmalen** *v/t* (*sep*, -*ge*-, *h*) paint

'**Anmarsch** *m*: *im* ~ on the way

anmaßen *v/t* (*sep*, -*ge*-, *h*) *sich* ~ as- sume; claim (*right*); *sich* ~, *et. zu tun* presume to do s.th.; ~*d adj* arrogant

'**anmelden** *v/t* (*sep*, -*ge*-, *h*) announce (*visitor*); register (*birth etc*); *customs*: declare; *sich* ~ enrol(l) (*for classes etc*); register (*at a hotel*); *sich* ~ *bei* make an appointment with (*doctor etc*)

'**Anmeldung** *f* announcement; registra- tion, enrol(l)ment 'anmerken v/t (sep, -ge-, h) j-m et. ~ notice s.th. in s.o.; **sich et.** (**nichts**) ~ **lassen** (not) let it show; 'Anmerkung f (-; -en) note; annotation, footnote

Anmut ['anmu:t] f (-; no pl) grace

'anmutig adj graceful

'annähen v/t (sep, -ge-, h) sew on (**an** acc to)

'annähernd adv approximately

'Annäherung f (-; -en) approach (**an** acc to); 'Annäherungsversuche pl advances, F pass

Annahme ['anna:mə] f (-; -n) (no pl) acceptance (a. fig); assumption

'annehmbar adj acceptable; reasonable (price etc); 'annehmen v/t (irr, **nehmen**, sep, -ge-, h) accept; suppose; adopt (child, name); take (ball); take on (color, look etc); **sich e-r Sache** or **j-s** ~ take care of s.th. or s.o.; 'Annehmlichkeiten pl comforts, amenities

Annonce [a'nɔ̃:sə] f (-; -n) advertisement

annullieren [anʊ'liːrən] v/t (no -ge-, h) annul; ECON cancel

anöden ['an'øːdən] F v/t (sep, -ge-, h) bore s.o. to death

anonym [ano'nyːm] adj anonymous

Anonymität [anonymi'tɛːt] f (-; no pl) anonymity

Anorak ['anorak] m (-s; -s) anorak

'anordnen v/t (sep, -ge-, h) arrange; give order(s), order; 'Anordnung f (-; -en) arrangement; direction, order

'anorganisch adj CHEM inorganic

'anpacken F (sep, -ge-, h) **1.** v/t tackle **2.** v/i: **mit ~** lend a hand

'anpassen v/t (sep, -ge-, h) adapt, adjust (both a. **sich** ~) (dat, **an** acc to)

'Anpassung f (-; -en) adaptation, adjustment

'anpassungsfähig adj adaptable

'Anpassungsfähigkeit f adaptability

'Anpfiff m SPORT starting whistle; F fig dressing-down

'anpflanzen v/t (sep, -ge-, h) cultivate, plant; 'Anpflanzung f cultivation

'anpöbeln ['anpøːbəln] v/t (sep, -ge-, h) accost; shout abuse at; anprangern ['anpraŋɐn] v/t (sep, -ge-, h) denounce; 'anpreisen v/t (irr, **preisen**, sep, -ge-, h) push; plug; 'anpro,bieren v/t (no -ge-, h) try on; 'anpumpen F v/t (sep, -ge-, h) touch

s.o. (**um** for); 'anraten v/t (irr, **raten**, sep, -ge-, h) advise; 'anrechnen v/t (sep, -ge-, h) charge; allow

'Anrecht n: **ein ~ haben auf** (acc) be entitled to

'Anrede f address; 'anreden v/t (sep, -ge-, h) address (**mit Namen** by name)

'anregen v/t (sep, -ge-, h) stimulate; suggest; ~**d** adj stimulating

'Anregung f stimulation; suggestion

'Anregungsmittel n PHARM stimulant

'Anreise f (Anfahrt) journey; (Ankunft) arrival

'anreisen v/i (sep, -ge-, sein) arrive

'Anreisetag m day of arrival

'Anreiz m incentive

'anrichten v/t (sep, -ge-, h) GASTR prepare, dress; cause, do (damage etc)

anrüchig ['anryçiç] adj disreputable

'Anruf m call (a. TEL.); ~**beantworter** m TEL answering machine

'anrufen v/t (irr, **rufen**, sep, -ge-, h) TEL call or ring up, phone

'anrühren v/t (sep, -ge-, h) touch; mix

'Ansage f announcement; 'ansagen v/t (sep, -ge-, h) announce; Ansager ['anzaːgɐ] m (-s; -), Ansagerin ['anzaːgərɪn] f (-; -nen) announcer

'ansammeln v/t and v/refl (sep, -ge-, h) accumulate; 'Ansammlung f collection, accumulation; crowd

'Ansatz m start (**zu** to); attempt (**zu** at); approach; TECH attachment; MATH set--up; pl first signs

'anschaffen v/t (sep, -ge-, h) get; **sich et.** ~ buy or get (o.s.) s.th.

'Anschaffung f (-; -en) purchase, buy

'anschauen v/t (sep, -ge-, h) → **ansehen**; 'anschaulich adj graphic (account etc); 'Anschauung f (-; -en) (von) view (of), opinion (about, of)

'Anschauungsmateri,al n PED visual aids

'Anschein m (-[e]s; no pl) appearance; **allem ~ nach** to all appearances; **den ~ erwecken, als** (**ob**) give the impression of ...; 'anscheinend adv apparently

'anschieben v/t (irr, **schieben**, sep, -ge-, h) give a push (a. MOT)

'Anschlag m attack; poster; bill, notice; typewriter: stroke; MUS, swimming: touch; **e-n ~ auf j-n verüben** make an attempt on s.o.'s life; ~**brett** n bulletin (esp Br notice) board

'**anschlagen** (*irr*, *schlagen*, *sep*, *-ge-*, *h*)
1. *v/t* post; MUS strike; chip (*cup etc*) **2.**
v/i dog: bark; take (effect) (*a.* MED);
swimming: touch the wall

'**anschließen** *v/t* (*irr*, *schließen*, *sep*,
-ge-, *h*) ELECTR, TECH connect; *sich ~*
follow; agree with; *sich j-m or e-r Sa-*
che ~ join s.o. or s.th.; *~d* **1.** *adj* following **2.** *adv* then, afterwards

'**Anschluss** *m* connection; *im ~ an* (*acc*)
following; *~ finden* (*bei*) make contact
or friends (with); *~ bekommen* TEL get
through

'**anschmiegen** *v/refl* (*sep*, *-ge-*, *h*) snuggle up (*an acc* to)

'**anschmiegsam** *adj* affectionate

'**anschnallen** *v/t* (*sep*, *-ge-*, *h*) strap on,
put on (*a.* ski); *sich ~* AVIAT, MOT fasten
one's seat belt; '**anschnauzen** F *v/t*
(*sep*, *-ge-*, *h*) tell s.o. off, *Am a.* bawl
s.o. out; '**anschneiden** *v/t* (*irr*, *schnei-*
den, *sep*, *-ge-*, *h*) cut; *fig* bring up;
'**anschrauben** *v/t* (*sep*, *-ge-*, *h*) screw
on (*an acc* to); '**anschreiben** *v/t* (*irr*,
schreiben, *sep*, *-ge-*, *h*) write on the
(black)board; *j-n ~* write to s.o.; (*et.*)
~ lassen buy (s.th.) on credit; → *ange-*
schrieben; '**anschreien** *v/t* (*irr*,
schreien, *sep*, *-ge-*, *h*) shout at

'**Anschrift** *f* address

'**Anschuldigung** *f* (*-*; *-en*) accusation

'**anschwellen** *v/i* (*irr*, *schwellen*, *sep*,
-ge-, *sein*) swell (*a.* fig);
'**anschwemmen** *v/t* (*sep*, *-ge-*, *h*) wash
ashore

'**ansehen** *v/t* (*irr*, *sehen*, *sep*, *-ge-*, *h*)
look at, have *or* take a look at; watch;
see (*all a.* **sich** [*dat*] **~**); *~ als* look upon
as; *et. mit ~* watch *or* witness s.th.; *man*
sieht ihm an, dass ... one can see that
...; '**Ansehen** *n* (*-s*; *no pl*) reputation

ansehnlich ['anze:nlɪç] *adj* considerable

'**anseilen** *v/t and v/refl* (*sep*, *-ge-*, *h*) rope

'**ansetzen** (*sep*, *-ge-*, *h*) **1.** *v/t* put (*an acc*
to); put on, add; fix, set (*date etc*); *Fett*
etc ~ put on weight *etc* **2.** *v/i*: *~ zu* prepare for (*landing etc*)

'**Ansicht** *f* (*-*; *-en*) view, *a.* opinion, *a.*
sight; *der ~ sein, dass* ... be of the
opinion that ...; *meiner ~ nach* in
my opinion; *zur ~* ECON on approval

'**Ansichts**|**karte** *f* picture postcard; *~sa-*
che *f* matter of opinion

'**anspannen** *v/t* (*sep*, *-ge-*, *h*) strain

'**Anspannung** *f* (*-*; *-en*) strain, exertion

'**anspielen** *v/i* (*sep*, *-ge-*, *h*) soccer: kick
off; *~ auf* (*acc*) allude to, hint at

'**Anspielung** *f* (*-*; *-en*) allusion, hint

'**anspitzen** *v/t* (*sep*, *-ge-*, *h*) sharpen

'**Ansporn** *m* (*-[e]s*; *no pl*) incentive

'**anspornen** *v/t* (*sep*, *-ge-*, *h*) encourage,
spur *s.o.* on

'**Ansprache** *f* address, speech; *e-e ~*
halten deliver an address

'**ansprechen** *v/t* (*irr*, *sprechen*, *sep*,
-ge-, *h*) address, speak to; *fig* appeal
to; *~d adj* attractive

'**Ansprechpartner** *m* s.o. to talk to, contact

'**anspringen** (*irr*, *springen*, *sep*, *-ge-*) **1.**
v/i (*sein*) engine: start **2.** *v/t* (*h*) jump
(up)on

'**anspritzen** *v/t* (*sep*, *-ge-*, *h*) spatter

'**Anspruch** *m* claim (*auf acc* to) (*a.* JUR);
~ haben auf (*acc*) be entitled to; *~ er-*
heben auf (*acc*) claim; *Zeit in ~ neh-*
men take up time

'**anspruchslos** *adj* modest; light, unde-
manding (*reading etc*); *contr* trivial

'**anspruchsvoll** *adj* demanding; sophisticated, refined (*tastes etc*)

Anstalt ['anʃtalt] *f* (*-*; *-en*) establishment, institution; mental hospital;
~en machen zu get ready for

'**Anstand** *m* (*-[e]s*; *no pl*) decency; manners; '**anständig** *adj* decent (*a.* fig)

'**anstandslos** *adv* unhesitatingly; without difficulty

'**anstarren** *v/t* (*sep*, *-ge-*, *h*) stare at

an'statt *prp* (*gen*) *and cj* instead of

'**anstechen** *v/t* (*irr*, *stechen*, *sep*, *-ge-*, *h*)
tap (*barrel*)

'**anstecken** *v/t* (*sep*, *-ge-*, *h*) stick on; put
on (*ring*); light; set fire to; MED infect;
sich bei j-m ~ MED catch s.th. from s.o.;
~d adj MED infectious, contagious,
catching (*all a.* fig)

'**Ansteckinadel** *f* pin, button

'**Ansteckung** *f* (*-*; *no pl*) MED infection,
contagion

'**anstehen** *v/i* (*irr*, *stehen*, *sep*, *-ge-*, *h*)
(*nach* for) stand in line, *Br* queue up

'**ansteigen** *v/i* (*irr*, *steigen*, *sep*, *-ge-*,
sein) rise

'**anstellen** *v/t* (*sep*, *-ge-*, *h*) engage, employ; TV etc: turn on; MOT start; F be up
to (*s.th. illegal etc*); make (*inquiries etc*);

sich ~ line up (*nach* for), Br queue up (for); F (make a) fuss

'**Anstellung** f job, position; *e-e* ~ *finden* find employment

Anstieg ['anʃtiːk] *m* (-[e]s; *no pl*) rise, increase

'**anstiften** v/t (*sep*, *-ge-*, *h*) incite

'**Anstifter** *m* instigator

'**Anstiftung** f incitement

'**anstimmen** v/t (*sep*, *-ge-*, *h*) MUS strike up

'**Anstoß** *m* soccer: kickoff; *fig* initiative, impulse; offen|se, Br -ce; ~ *erregen* give offense (*bei* to); ~ *nehmen an* take offense at; *den* ~ *zu et. geben* start s.th., initiate s.th.; '**anstoßen** (*irr*, *stoßen*, *sep*, *-ge-*) 1. v/t (*h*) nudge s.o. 2. v/i (*sein*) knock, bump; (*h*) clink glasses; ~ *auf* (*acc*) drink to s.o. or s.th.

anstößig ['anʃtøːsɪç] *adj* offensive

'**anstrahlen** v/t (*sep*, *-ge-*, *h*) illuminate; beam at s.o.

'**anstreichen** v/t (*irr*, *streichen*, *sep*, *-ge-*, *h*) paint; PED mark (*mistakes etc*)

'**Anstreicher** *m* (house)painter

'**anstrengen** v/refl (*sep*, *-ge-*, *h*) try (hard), make an effort; ~*d adj* strenuous, hard

'**Anstrengung** f (-; *-en*) exertion, strain; effort

'**Ansturm** *fig* *m* (-[e]s; *no pl*) rush (*auf acc* for)

'**Anteil** *m* share (*a.* ECON), portion; ~ *nehmen an* (*dat*) take an interest in; sympathize with; ~*nahme* ['antaɪlnaːmə] f (-; *no pl*) sympathy; interest

Antenne [an'tɛnə] f (-; *-n*) antenna, Br aerial

Anti..., **anti...** *in cpds* anti...

Anti|**alko**'**holiker** *m* teetotal(l)er; ~'**babypille** F f birth control pill, F the pill; ~'**biotikum** n MED antibiotic; ~**blo-**'**ckiersys,tem** n MOT anti-lock braking system

antik [an'tiːk] *adj* antique, HIST *a.* ancient; **An'tike** f (-; *no pl*) ancient world

'**Antikörper** *m* MED antibody

Antilope [anti'loːpə] f (-; *-n*) zo antelope

Antipathie [antipa'tiː] f (-; *-n*) antipathy

Antiquariat [antikva'rjaːt] n (-[e]s; *-e*) second-hand bookshop

antiquarisch [anti'kvaːrɪʃ] *adj and adv* second-hand

Antiquitäten [antikvi'tɛːtən] *pl* antiques; ~*laden m* antique shop

Antisemit [antize'miːt] *m* (-*en*; *-en*) anti-Semite; **antise**'**mitisch** *adj* anti-Semitic; **Antisemitismus** [antizemi-'tɪsmʊs] *m* (-; *no pl*) anti-Semitism

Antrag ['antraːk] *m* (-[e]s; *Anträge* ['antrɛːgə]) application; PARL motion; proposal; ~ *stellen auf* (*acc*) make an application for; PARL move for; ~*stel-ler(in)* ['antraːkʃtɛlɐ, 'antraːk-ʃtɛlərɪn] *m* (-*s*; *-/-*; *-nen*) applicant; PARL mover

'**antreiben** (*irr*, *treiben*, *sep*, *-ge-*) 1. v/t (*h*) TECH drive; urge s.o. (on) 2. v/i (*sein*) float ashore

'**antreten** (*irr*, *treten*, *sep*, *-ge-*) 1. v/t (*h*) enter upon (*office etc*); take up (*position*); set out on (*journey*) 2. v/i (*sein*) take one's place; MIL line up

'**Antrieb** *m* TECH drive (*a. fig*), propulsion; *fig* motive, impulse; *aus eige-nem* ~ of one's own accord

'**antun** v/t (*irr*, *tun*, *sep*, *-ge-*, *h*) *j-m et.* ~ do s.th. to s.o.; *sich et.* ~ lay hands on o.s.

Antwort ['antvɔrt] f (-; *-en*) answer (*auf acc* to), reply (to)

'**antworten** v/i (*ge-*, *h*) answer (*j-m* s.o., *auf et.* s.th.), reply (to s.o. or s.th.)

'**anvertrauen** v/t (*sep*, *no -ge-*, *h*) *j-m et.* ~ (en)trust s.o. with s.th.; confide s.th. to s.o.

'**anwachsen** v/i (*irr*, *wachsen*, *sep*, *-ge-*, *sein*) BOT take root; *fig* increase

Anwalt ['anvalt] *m* (-[e]s; *Anwälte* ['an-vɛltə]) → **Rechtsanwalt**

'**Anwärter** *m* candidate (*auf acc* for)

'**anweisen** v/t (*irr*, *weisen*, *sep*, *-ge-*, *h*) instruct; direct, order

'**Anweisung** f instruction; order

'**anwenden** v/t ([*irr*, *wenden*,] *sep*, *-ge-*, *h*) use; apply (*auf acc* to)

'**Anwendung** f use; application

'**anwerben** v/t (*irr*, *werben*, *sep*, *-ge-*, *h*) recruit (*a. fig*)

'**Anwesen** n (-*s*; -) estate; property

'**anwesend** *adj* present

'**Anwesenheit** f (-; *no pl*) presence; PED attendance; *die* ~ *feststellen* call the roll; '**Anwesenheitsliste** f attendance record (Br list)

anwidern ['anviːdɐn] v/t (*sep*, *-ge-*, *h*) make s.o. sick

'**Anzahl** f (-; *no pl*) number, quantity

'**anzahlen** v/t (sep, -ge-, h) pay on account; '**Anzahlung** f down payment

'**anzapfen** v/t (sep, -ge-, h) tap

'**Anzeichen** n symptom (a. MED), sign

Anzeige ['antsaigə] f (-; -n) advertisement; announcement; JUR information; IT display; TECH reading

'**anzeigen** v/t (sep, -ge-, h) announce; report to the police; TECH indicate, show

'**anziehen** v/t (irr, ziehen, sep, -ge-, h) put on (dress etc); dress s.o.; fig attract, draw; tighten (screw); pull (lever etc); **sich** ~ get dressed; dress;~**d** adj attractive

'**Anziehung** f (-; no pl), '**Anziehungskraft** f (-; no pl) PHYS attraction, fig a. appeal

'**Anzug** m suit

anzüglich ['antsy:klıç] adj suggestive (joke); personal, offensive (remark etc)

'**anzünden** v/t (sep, -ge-, h) light; set on fire

apart [a'part] adj striking

Apartment [a'partmənt] n (-s; -s) studio (apartment or Br flat)

apathisch [a'pa:tıʃ] adj apathetic

Apfel ['apfəl] m (-s; Äpfel ['ɛpfəl]) BOT apple; ~**mus** n GASTR apple sauce

Apfelsine [apfəl'zi:nə] f (-; -n) BOT orange

'**Apfelwein** m cider

Apostel [a'pɔstəl] m (-s; -) REL apostle

Apostroph [apo'strɔf] m (-s; -e) apostrophe

Apotheke [apo'te:kə] f (-; -n) pharmacy, drugstore, Br chemist's

Apotheker [apo'te:kɐ] m (-s; -), **Apo'thekerin** f (-; -nen) pharmacist, druggist, Br chemist

App. abbr of **Apparat** TEL ext., extension

Apparat [apa'ra:t] m (-[e]s; -e) apparatus; device; (tele)phone; radio; TV set; camera; POL etc machine(ry); **am** ~! TEL speaking!; **am** ~ **bleiben** TEL hold the line

Appell [a'pɛl] m (-s; -e) appeal (**an** acc to); MIL roll call

appellieren [apɛ'li:rən] v/i (no -ge-, h) (make an) appeal (**an** acc to)

Appetit [ape'ti:t] m (-[e]s; no pl) appetite (**auf** acc for); ~ **auf et. haben** feel like s.th.; **guten** ~! enjoy your meal!

appe'titanregend adj appetizing

Appe'tithappen m GASTR appetizer

appe'titlich adj appetizing, savo(u)ry, fig a. inviting

applaudieren [aplau'di:rən] v/i (no -ge-, h) applaud; **Applaus** [a'plaus] m (-es; no pl) applause

Aprikose [apri'ko:zə] f (-; -n) BOT apricot

April [a'prıl] m (-[s]; no pl) April; ~! ~! April fool!

Aqua|jogging ['akvadʒɔgıŋ] n (-s; no pl) SPORT aqua jogging; ~**planing** [akva'pla:nıŋ] n (-[s]; no pl) MOT hydroplaning, Br aquaplaning

Aquarell [akva'rɛl] n (-s; -e) watercolo(u)r

Aquarium [a'kva:rjum] n (-s; -ien) aquarium

Äquator [ɛ'kva:to:ɐ] m (-s; no pl) equator

Ära ['ɛːra] f (-; no pl) era

Araber ['arabɐ] m (-s; -), **Araberin** ['arabərın] f (-; -nen) Arab

arabisch [a'ra:bıʃ] adj Arabian; Arabic

Arbeit ['arbaıt] f (-; -en) work, ECON, POL a. labo(u)r; employment, job; PED test; scientific etc paper; workmanship; **bei der** ~ at work; **zur** ~ **gehen** or **fahren** go to work; **gute** ~ **leisten** make a good job of it; **sich an die** ~ **machen** set to work; '**arbeiten** v/i (ge-, h) work (**an** dat at, on)

'**Arbeiter** m (-s; -), '**Arbeiterin** f (-; -nen) worker

'**Arbeitgeber** m (-s; -) employer

'**Arbeitnehmer** m (-s; -) employee

'**Arbeits|agentur** f Am (un)employment agency, Br employment agency; ~**amt** n Am employment office, Br job centre; ~**blatt** n PED worksheet; ~**erlaubnis** f green card, Br work permit

'**arbeitsfähig** adj fit for work

'**Arbeits|gang** m TECH operation; ~**gemeinschaft** f work or study group; ~**gericht** n JUR labor court, Br industrial tribunal; ~**hose** f overalls; ~**kleidung** f working clothes; ~**kräfte** pl workers, labo(u)r

'**arbeitslos** adj unemployed, out of work; '**Arbeitslose** m, f (-n; -n) **die** ~**n** pl the unemployed

'**Arbeitslosengeld** n unemployment compensation (Br benefit); ~ **beziehen** F be on the dole

'**Arbeitslosigkeit** f (-; no pl) unemployment

'Arbeits|markt *m* labo(u)r market; **~mi,nister** *m Am* Secretary of Labor; *Br* Minister of Labour; **~niederlegung** *f* strike, walkout; **~pause** *f* break, intermission; **~platz** *m* workplace; job

'arbeitsscheu *adj* work-shy

'Arbeits|speicher *m* IT main memory; **~suche** *f*: **er ist auf ~** he is looking for a job; **~süchtige** *m, f* workaholic; **~tag** *m* workday

'arbeitsunfähig *adj* unfit for work; *permanently* disabled

'Arbeits|weise *f* method (of working); **~zeit** *f* (**gleitende** flexible) working hours; **~zeitverkürzung** *f* fewer working hours; **~zimmer** *n* study

Archäologe [arçεo'loːgə] *m* (-*n*; -*n*) arch(a)eologist;   **Archäologie** [arçεolo'giː] *f* (-; *no pl*) arch(a)eology; **Archäo'login** *f* (-; -*nen*) arch(a)eologist

Arche ['arçə] *f* (-; -*n*) ark; **die ~ Noah** Noah's ark

Architekt [arçi'tεkt] *m* (-*en*; -*en*), Archi'tektin *f* (-; -*nen*) architect; **architektonisch** [arçitεk'toːnɪʃ] *adj* architectural; **Architektur** [arçitεk'tuːɐ] *f* (-; -*en*) architecture

Archiv [ar'çiːf] *n* (-*s*; -*e*) archives; record office

Arena [a'reːna] *f* (-; -*nen*) ring

Ärger ['εrgɐ] *m* (-*s*; *no pl*) anger (**über** *acc* at); trouble; F *j-m ~ machen* cause s.o. trouble; **ärgerlich** *adj* angry (**über, auf** *acc* at *s.th.*; with *s.o.*); annoying; **ärgern** *v/t* (*ge-, h*) annoy; **sich ~** be annoyed (**über** *acc* at, about *s.th.*, with *s.o.*); 'Ärgernis *n* (-*ses*; -*se*) nuisance

arglos ['arkloːs] *adj* innocent

Argwohn ['arkvoːn] *m* (-[*e*]*s*; *no pl*) suspicion (**gegen** of)

argwöhnisch ['arkvøːnɪʃ] *adj* suspicious

Arie ['aːrjə] *f* (-; -*n*) MUS aria

Aristokratie [arɪstokra'tiː] *f* (-; -*n*) aristocracy

arm [arm] *adj* poor; **die Armen** the poor

Arm *m* (-[*e*]*s*; -*e*) ANAT arm; GEOGR branch; F *j-n auf den ~ nehmen* pull s.o.'s leg

Armaturen [arma'tuːrən] *pl* TECH instruments; (plumbing) fixtures; **~brett** *n* MOT dashboard

'Armband *n* bracelet

'Armbanduhr *f* wrist-watch

Armee [ar'meː] *f* (-; -*n*) MIL armed forces; army

Ärmel ['εrməl] *m* (-*s*; -) sleeve

ärmlich ['εrmlɪç] *adj* poor (*a. fig*); shabby

'Armreif(en) *m* bangle

'armselig *adj* wretched, miserable

Armut ['armuːt] *f* (-; *no pl*) poverty; **~ an** (*dat*) lack of

Aroma [a'roːma] *n* (-*s*; -*men*) flavo(u)r; aroma

Arrest [a'rεst] *m* (-[*e*]*s*; -*e*) PED detention; **~ bekommen** be kept in

arrogant [aro'gant] *adj* arrogant, conceited

Arsch [arʃ] V *m* (-*es*; *Ärsche* ['εrʃə]) ass, *Br* arse; **~loch** V *n* asshole, *Br* arsehole

Art [art] *f* (-; -*en*) way, manner; kind; sort; BIOL species; **auf diese ~** (in) this way; **e-e~ ...** a sort of ...; **Geräte aller~** all kinds or sorts of tools

'Artenschutz *m* protection of endangered species

Arterie [ar'teːrjə] *f* (-; -*n*) ANAT artery

Ar'terienverkalkung *f* MED arteriosclerosis

Arthritis [ar'triːtɪs] *f* (-; -*tiden*) MED arthritis

artig ['artɪç] *adj* good, well-behaved; **sei ~!** be good!, be a good boy (*or* girl)!

Artikel [ar'tiːkəl] *m* (-*s*; -) article

Artillerie [artɪləri'] *f* (-; *no pl*) MIL artillery

Artist [ar'tɪst] *m* (-*en*; -*en*), Ar'tistin *f* (-; -*nen*) acrobat, (circus) performer

Arznei [aːɐts'nai] *f* (-; -*en*), **~mittel** *n* medicine, drug

Arzt [aːɐtst] *m* (-*es*; *Ärzte* ['εːɐtstə]) doctor, physician; **Ärztin** ['εːɐtstɪn] *f* (-; -*nen*) (lady) doctor *or* physician

'ärztlich *adj* medical; **sich ~ behandeln lassen** undergo treatment

As [as] *n* (-; -) MUS A flat

Asbest [as'bεst] *m* (-[*e*]*s*; -*e*) asbestos

Asche ['aʃə] *f* (-; -*n*) ash(es)

'Aschen|bahn *f* SPORT cinder-track, MOT dirt track; **~becher** *m* ashtray

Ascher'mittwoch *m* Ash Wednesday

äsen ['εːzən] *v/i* (*ge-, h*) HUNT feed, browse

Asiat [a'zjaːt] *m* (-*en*; -*en*), Asi'atin *f* (-; -*nen*) Asian; **asi'atisch** *adj* Asian, Asiatic; **Asien** ['a:zjən] *n* (-*s*; *no pl*) Asia

Asket [as'ke:t] *m* (-*en*; -*en*), **as'ketisch** *adj* ascetic

'**asozial** *adj* antisocial

Asphalt [as'falt] *m* (-*s*; -*e*) asphalt

asphaltieren [asfal'ti:rən] *v/t* (*no -ge-*, *h*) (cover with) asphalt

Ass [as] *n* (-; -*e*) ace (*a.* tennis *and fig*)

aß [a:s] *pret of* **essen**

Assistent [asɪs'tɛnt] *m* (-*en*; -*en*), **Assis'tentin** *f* (-; -*nen*) assistant

Assis'tenzarzt *m Am* intern, *Br* houseman

Ast [ast] *m* (-*es*; *Äste* ['ɛstə] BOT branch

Astronaut [astro'naut] *m* (-*en*; -*en*), **Astro'nautin** *f* (-; -*nen*) astronaut

Astronom [astro'no:m] *m* (-*en*; -*en*) astronomer; **Astronomie** [astrono'mi:] *f* (-; *no pl*) astronomy

ASU ['a:zu] *abbr of* **Abgas-Sonder-Untersuchung** MOT *Am* emissions test, *Br* exhaust emission test

Asyl [a'zy:l] *n* (-*s*; -*e*) asylum; **Asylant** [azy'lant] *m* (-*en*; -*en*), **Asy'lantin** *f* (-; -*nen*) asylum seeker, (political) refugee

A'sylbewerber(in) asylum seeker; **~recht** *n* right of (political) asylum

Atelier [ate'lje:] *n* (-*s*; -*s*) studio

Atem ['a:təm] *m* (-*s*; *no pl*) breath; **außer** out of breath; (**tief**) **~ holen** take a (deep) breath; '**atemberaubend** *adj* breathtaking; '**Atemgerät** *n* MED respirator; '**atemlos** *adj* breathless; '**Atempause** *f* F breather; '**Atemzug** *m* breath

Äther ['ɛ:tɐ] *m* (-*s*; *no pl*) CHEM ether; *radio etc*: air

Athlet [at'le:t] *m* (-*en*; -*en*), **Ath'letin** *f* (-; -*nen*) SPORT athlete

ath'letisch *adj* athletic

Atlas ['atlas] *m* (-*ses*; -*se*, *Atlanten*) atlas

atmen ['a:tmən] *v/i and v/t* (*ge-*, *h*) breathe

Atmosphäre [atmo'sfɛ:rə] *f* (-; -*n*) atmosphere

'**Atmung** *f* (-; *no pl*) breathing, respiration

Atoll [a'tɔl] *n* (-*s*; -*e*) atoll

Atom [a'to:m] *n* (-*s*; -*e*) atom

A'tom... *in cpds* -*energie*, -*forschung*, -*kraft*, -*krieg*, -*müll*, -*rakete*, -*reaktor*, -*waffen etc* nuclear ...

atomar [ato'ma:ɐ] *adj* atomic, nuclear

A'tombombe *f* MIL atom(ic) bomb

A'tomkern *m* PHYS (atomic) nucleus

a'tomwaffenfrei *adj* nuclear-free

Attentat ['atənta:t] *n* (-[*e*]*s*; -*e*) assassination attempt, attempt on *s.o.'s* life; **Opfer e-s ~s werden** be assassinated

'**Attentäter** *m* (-*s*; -) assassin

Attest [a'tɛst] *n* (-[*e*]*s*; -*e*) (doctor's) certificate

Attraktion [atrak'tsjo:n] *f* (-; -*en*) attraction; **attraktiv** [atrak'ti:f] *adj* attractive

Attrappe [a'trapə] *f* (-; -*n*) dummy

Attribut [atri'bu:t] *n* (-[*e*]*s*; -*e*) LING attribute (*a. fig*)

ätzend ['ɛtsənt] *adj* corrosive, caustic (*a. fig*); F gross; **das ist echt ~** it's the pits

au [au] *int* ouch!; **~ fein!** oh, good!

Aubergine [obɐr'ʒi:nə] *f* (-; -*n*) BOT eggplant, *Br* aubergine

auch [aux] *cj* also, too, as well; **ich ~** so am (*or* do) I, F me too; **~ nicht** not ... either; **wenn ~** even if; **wo ~** (**immer**) wherever; **ist es ~ wahr?** is it really true?

Audienz [au'djɛnts] *f* (-; -*en*) audience (**bei** with)

auf [auf] *prp* (*dat and acc*) *and adv* on; in; at; open; up; **~ Seite 20** on page 20; **~ der Straße** (on *Br* in) the street; on the road; **~ der Welt** in the world; **~ See** at sea; **~ dem Lande** in the country; **~ dem Bahnhof** *etc* at the station *etc*; **~ Urlaub** on vacation; **die Uhr stellen ~** (*acc*) set the watch to; **~ deutsch** in German; **~ deinen Wunsch** at your request; **~ die Sekunde genau** to the second; **~ und ab** up and down

'**auflarbeiten** *v/t* (*sep*, -*ge*-, *h*) catch up on (*backlog*); refurbish; **~atmen** *v/i* (*sep*, -*ge*-, *h*) heave a sigh of relief

'**Aufbau** *m* (-[*e*]*s*; *no pl*) building (up); structure; '**aufbauen** *v/t* (*sep*, -*ge*-, *h*) build (up) (*a. fig*); set up; construct

'**aufbauschen** *v/t* (*sep*, -*ge*-, *h*) exaggerate; **~bekommen** *v/t* (*irr*, **kommen**, *sep*, *no -ge-*, *h*) get *door etc* open; be given (*a task etc*); **~bereiten** *v/t* (*sep*, *no -ge-*, *h*) process, clean, treat; **~bessern** *v/t* (*sep*, -*ge*-, *h*) raise (*salary etc*); **~bewahren** *v/t* (*sep*, *no -ge-*, *h*) keep; **~bieten** *v/t* (*irr*, **bieten**, *sep*, -*ge*-, *h*) muster; **~blasen** *v/t* (*irr*, **blasen**, *sep*,

-ge-, h) blow up; **~bleiben** v/i (irr, **bleiben**, sep, -ge-, sein) stay up; door etc: remain open; **~blenden** v/i (sep, -ge-, h) MOT turn the headlights up; **~blicken** v/i (sep, -ge-, h) look up (**zu** at) (a. fig); **~blitzen** v/i (sep, -ge-, h, sein) flash (a. fig)

aufbrausen v/i (sep, -ge-, sein) fly into a temper; **~d** adj irascible

aufbrechen (irr, **brechen**, sep, -ge-) **1.** v/t (h) break or force open **2.** v/i (sein) burst open; fig leave (**nach** for)

aufbringen v/t (irr, **bringen**, sep, -ge-, h) raise (money); muster (courage etc); start (fashion etc); → **aufgebracht**

Aufbruch m (-[e]s; no pl) departure, start

auf|brühen v/t (sep, -ge-, h) make; **~bürden** v/t (sep, -ge-, h) **j-m et. ~** burden s.o. with s.th.; **~decken** v/t (sep, -ge-, h) uncover; **~drängen** v/t (sep, -ge-, h) **j-m et. ~** force s.th. on s.o.; **sich j-m ~** impose on s.o.; **sich ~** fig suggest itself; **~drehen** F (sep, -ge-, h) **1.** v/t turn on **2.** v/i MOT step on the gas

aufdringlich adj obtrusive

Aufdruck m imprint; on stamps: overprint, surcharge

aufei'nander adv on top of each other; one after another; **~folgend** adj successive

Aufenthalt ['aufɛnthalt] m (-[e]s; -e) stay; RAIL stop

Aufenthalts|genehmigung f residence permit; **~raum** m lounge, recreation room

auferstehen v/i (irr, **stehen**, sep, no -ge-, sein) rise (from the dead)

Auferstehung f (-; -en) REL resurrection

aufessen v/t (irr, **essen**, sep, -ge-, h) eat up

auffahren v/i (irr, **fahren**, sep, -ge-, sein) crash (**auf** acc into); fig start up; **Auffahrt** f approach; driveway, Br drive; **Auffahrunfall** m MOT rear-end collision; pileup

auffallen v/i (irr, **fallen**, sep, -ge-, sein) attract attention; **j-m ~** strike s.o.

auffallend, **auffällig** adj striking; conspicuous; flashy (clothes)

auffangen v/t (irr, **fangen**, sep, -ge-, h) catch (a. fig)

auffassen v/t (sep, -ge-, h) understand

(**als** as)

Auffassung f view; interpretation

auffinden v/t (irr, **finden**, sep, -ge-, h) find, discover

auffordern v/t (sep, -ge-, h) **j-n ~**, **et. zu tun** ask (or tell) s.o. to do s.th.

Aufforderung f request; demand

auffrischen v/t (sep, -ge-, h) freshen up; brush up

aufführen v/t (sep, -ge-, h) THEA etc perform, present; state; **sich ~** behave

Aufführung f THEA etc performance; film: showing

Aufgabe f task, job; duty; PED task, assignment; MATH problem; fig surrender; **es sich zur ~ machen** make it one's business

Aufgang m staircase; AST rising

aufgeben (irr, **geben**, sep, -ge-, h) **1.** v/t give up; mail, send, Br post; check (baggage); PED set, give, assign (homework etc); ECON place (order etc) **2.** v/i give up or in

aufge|bracht adj furious; **~dreht** F adj excited; **~dunsen** ['aufgədunzən] adj puffed(-up)

aufgehen v/i (irr, **gehen**, sep, -ge-, sein) open; sun, dough etc: rise; MATH come out even; **in Flammen ~** go up in flames

aufge|hoben fig adj: **gut ~ sein bei** be in good hands with; **~legt** adj: **zu et. ~ sein** feel like (doing) s.th.; **gut (schlecht) ~** in a good (bad) mood; **~regt** adj excited; nervous; **~schlossen** fig adj open-minded; **~ für** open to; **~weckt** fig adj bright

aufgreifen v/t (irr, **greifen**, sep, -ge-, h) pick up

auf'grund (gen) because of

auf|haben F v/t (irr, **haben**, sep, -ge-, h) have on, wear; PED have homework etc to do; **~halten** v/t (irr, **halten**, sep, -ge-, h) stop, hold up (a. traffic, thief etc); keep open; **sich ~** (**bei j-m**) stay (with s.o.); **~hängen** v/t (sep, -ge-, h) hang (up); **j-n ~** hang s.o.; **~heben** v/t (irr, **heben**, sep, -ge-, h) pick up; keep; abolish (law etc); break up (meeting etc); **sich gegenseitig ~** neutralize each other; → **aufgehoben**

Aufheben n (-s; no pl) **viel ~s machen** make a fuss (**von** about)

auf|heitern v/t (sep, -ge-, h) cheer up;

sich ~ *weather*: clear up; ~**helfen** *v/i* (*irr*, **helfen**, *sep*, *-ge-*, *h*) help s.o. up; ~**hellen** *v/t and v/refl* (*sep*, *-ge-*, *h*) brighten; ~**hetzen** *v/t* (*sep*, *-ge-*, *h*) *j-n* ~ **gegen** set s.o. against; ~**holen** (*sep*, *-ge-*, *h*) **1.** *v/t* make up for **2.** *v/i* catch up (**gegen** with); ~**horchen** *v/i* (*sep*, *-ge-*, *h*) prick (up) one's ears: ~ *lassen* make *s.o.* sit up; ~**hören** *v/i* (*sep*, *-ge-*, *h*) stop, end, finish, quit; *mit et.* ~ stop (doing) s.th.; *hör(t) auf!* stop it!; ~**kau-fen** *v/t* (*sep*, *-ge-*, *h*) buy up

'**aufklären** *v/t* (*sep*, *-ge-*, *h*) clear up, *a.* solve (*crime*); *j-n* ~ *über* (*acc*) inform s.o. about; *j-n* (*sexuell*) ~ F tell s.o. the facts of life; '**Aufklärung** *f* (*-*; *no pl*) clearing up, solution; information; sex education; PHILOS Enlightenment; MIL reconnaissance

'**aufkleben** *v/t* (*sep*, *-ge-*, *h*) paste or stick on; '**Aufkleber** *m* (*-s*; *-*) sticker

'**aufknöpfen** *v/t* (*sep*, *-ge-*, *h*) unbutton

'**aufkommen** *v/i* (*irr*, **kommen**, *sep*, *-ge-*, *sein*) come up; come into fashion *or* use; *rumo(u)r etc*: arise; ~ **für** pay (for)

'**Aufladegerät** *n* charger

'**aufladen** *v/t* (*irr*, **laden**, *sep*, *-ge-*, *h*) load; ELECTR charge; (*prepaid card etc*) top up

'**Auflage** *f* edition; circulation

'**auf|lassen** F *v/t* (*irr*, **lassen**, *sep*, *-ge-*, *h*) leave *door etc* open; keep *one's hat etc* on; ~**lauern** *v/i* (*sep*, *-ge-*, *h*) *j-m* ~ waylay s.o.

'**Auflauf** *m* crowd; GASTR soufflé, pudding

'**auf|laufen** *v/i* (*irr*, **laufen**, *sep*, *-ge-*, *sein*) MAR run aground; ~**leben** *v/i* (*sep*, *-ge-*, *sein*) *a.* (**wieder**) ~ *lassen* revive; ~**legen** (*sep*, *-ge-*, *h*) **1.** *v/t* put on, lay on **2.** *v/i* TEL hang up

'**auflehnen** *v/t and v/refl* (*sep*, *-ge-*, *h*) lean (**auf** *acc* on); *sich* ~ rebel, revolt (**gegen** against); '**Auflehnung** *f* (*-*; *-en*) rebellion, revolt

'**auf|lesen** *v/t* (*irr*, **lesen**, *sep*, *-ge-*, *h*) pick up (*a. fig*); ~**leuchten** *v/i* (*sep*, *-ge-*, *h*) flash (up); ~**listen** *v/t* (*sep*, *-ge-*, *h*) list (*a.* IT); ~**lockern** *v/t* (*sep*, *-ge-*, *h*) loosen up; *fig* liven up

'**auflösen** *v/t* (*sep*, *-ge-*, *h*) dissolve; solve (*a.* MATH); disintegrate; '**Auflösung** *f* (dis)solution; disintegration

'**aufmachen** F *v/t* (*sep*, *-ge-*, *h*) open;

sich ~ set out; '**Aufmachung** *f* (*-*; *-en*) get-up

'**aufmerksam** *adj* attentive (**auf** *acc* to); thoughtful; *j-n* ~ **machen auf** (*acc*) call s.o.'s attention to

'**Aufmerksamkeit** *f* (*-*; *-en*) (*no pl*) attention; (*gift*) small present

'**aufmuntern** *v/t* (*sep*, *-ge-*, *h*) encourage; cheer up

Aufnahme ['aufna:mə] *f* (*-*; *-n*) taking up; reception (*a.* MED *etc*); admission; photo(graph); recording; *film*: shooting

'**aufnahmefähig** *adj* receptive (**für** of)

'**Aufnahme|gebühr** *f* admission fee; ~**prüfung** *f* entrance exam(ination)

'**aufnehmen** *v/t* (*irr*, **nehmen**, *sep*, *-ge-*, *h*) take up (*a. post etc*); pick up; put *s.o.* up; hold; take *s.th.* in; receive; PED *etc* admit; PHOT take a picture of; record; take (*the ball*); *es* ~ *mit* be a match for

'**aufpassen** *v/i* (*sep*, *-ge-*, *h*) pay attention; take care; ~ **auf** (*acc*) take care of, look after; keep an eye on; *pass auf!* look out!

'**Aufprall** *m* (*-[e]s*; *no pl*) impact

'**aufprallen** *v/i* (*sep*, *-ge-*, *sein*) ~ **auf** (*dat or acc*) hit

'**aufpumpen** *v/t* (*sep*, *-ge-*, *h*) pump up

'**aufputschen** *v/t* (*sep*, *-ge-*, *h*) pep up

'**Aufputschmittel** *n* PHARM stimulant, pep pill

'**auf|raffen** *v/refl* (*sep*, *-ge-*, *h*) *sich* ~ *zu* bring s.o. to do *s.th.*; ~**räumen** *v/t* (*sep*, *-ge-*, *h*) tidy up; clear

'**aufrecht** *adj and adv* upright (*a. fig*); ~**erhalten** *v/t* (*irr*, **halten**, *sep*, *no -ge-*, *h*) maintain, keep up

'**aufregen** *v/t* (*sep*, *-ge-*, *h*) excite, upset; *sich* ~ get excited *or* upset (**über** *acc* about); ~**d** *adj* exciting

'**Aufregung** *f* excitement; fuss

'**aufreiben** *v/t* (*irr*, **reiben**, *sep*, *-ge-*, *h*) wear down; ~**d** *adj* stressful

'**aufreißen** *v/t* (*irr*, **reißen**, *sep*, *-ge-*, *h*) tear open; fling *door etc* open; open *one's eyes* wide; F pick *s.o.* up

'**aufreizend** *adj* provocative

'**aufrichten** *v/t* (*sep*, *-ge-*, *h*) put up, raise; *sich* ~ straighten up; sit up

'**aufrichtig** *adj* sincere; frank

'**Aufrichtigkeit** *f* (*-*; *no pl*) sincerity; frankness

'**Aufriss** *m* (*-es*; *-e*) ARCH elevation

'aufrollen v/t and v/refl (sep, -ge-, h) roll up

'Aufruf m call; appeal (**zu** for)

'aufrufen v/t (irr, **rufen**, sep, -ge-, h) call on

Aufruhr ['aufruːɐ] m (-s; no pl) revolt; riot; turmoil; **'Aufrührer** m (-s; -) rebel; rioter; **aufrührerisch** ['aufryːrərɪʃ] adj rebellious

'aufrunden v/t (sep, -ge-, h) round off

'aufrüsten v/t and v/i (sep, -ge-, h) (re)arm; **'Aufrüstung** f (re)armament

'auf|rütteln fig v/t (sep, -ge-, h) shake up, rouse; **~sagen** v/t (sep, -ge-, h) say; a. recite (poem)

aufsässig ['aufzɛsɪç] adj rebellious

'Aufsatz m PED essay, Am a. theme; (newspaper etc) article; TECH top

'auf|saugen v/t (sep, -ge-, h) absorb (a. fig); **~scheuern** v/t (sep, -ge-, h) chafe; **~schichten** v/t (sep, -ge-, h) pile up; **~schieben** fig v/t (irr, **schieben**, sep, -ge-, h) put off, postpone; delay

'Aufschlag m impact; ECON extra charge; lapel; cuff, Br turnup; tennis: service; **'aufschlagen** (irr, **schlagen**, sep, -ge-, h) **1.** v/t open (book, eyes etc); pitch (tent); cut (one's knee etc); **Seite 3** ~ open at page 3 **2.** v/i tennis: serve; **auf dem Boden** ~ hit the ground

'auf|schließen v/t (irr, **schließen**, sep, -ge-, h) unlock, open; **~schlitzen** v/t (sep, -ge-, h) slit or rip open

'Aufschluss m information (**über** acc on)

'auf|schnappen F fig v/t (sep, -ge-, h) pick up; **~schneiden** (irr, **schneiden**, sep, -ge-, h) **1.** v/t cut open; GASTR cut up **2.** F fig v/i brag, boast, talk big

'Aufschnitt m (-[e]s; no pl) GASTR cold cuts, Br (slices of) cold meat

'auf|schnüren v/t (sep, -ge-, h) untie; unlace; **~schrauben** v/t (sep, -ge-, h) unscrew; **~schrecken** (sep, -ge-) **1.** v/t (h) startle **2.** v/i (sein) start (up)

'Aufschrei m yell; scream, outcry (a. fig)

'auf|schreiben v/t (irr, **schreiben**, sep, -ge-, h) write down; **~schreien** v/i (irr, **schreien**, sep, -ge-, h) cry out, scream

'Aufschrift f inscription

'Aufschub m postponement; delay; adjournment; respite

'Aufschwung m SPORT swing-up; esp ECON recovery, upswing; boom

'Aufsehen n (-s; no pl) **~ erregen** attract attention; cause a sensation; **~ erregend** → **aufsehenerregend**; **'aufsehenerregend** adj sensational

'Aufseher m (-s; -), **'Aufseherin** f (-; -nen) guard

'aufsetzen (sep, -ge-, h) **1.** v/t put on; draw up (letter etc); **sich ~** sit up **2.** v/i AVIAT touch down

'Aufsetzer m (-s; -) SPORT awkward bouncing ball

'Aufsicht f (-; no pl) supervision, control; **~ führen** PED etc be on (break) duty; proctor, Br invigilate

'Aufsichts|behörde f supervisory board; **~rat** m ECON board of directors; supervisory board

'auf|sitzen v/i (irr, **sitzen**, sep, -ge-, sein) mount; **~spannen** v/t (sep, -ge-, h) stretch; put up (umbrella); spread; **~sparen** v/t (sep, -ge-, h) save; **~sperren** v/t (sep, -ge-, h) unlock; F open wide; **~spielen** v/refl (sep, -ge-, h) show off; **sich ~ als** play; **~spießen** v/t (sep, -ge-, h) spear, skewer; animal: gore; **~springen** v/i (irr, **springen**, sep, -ge-, sein) jump up; door etc: fly open; lips etc: chap; **~spüren** v/t (sep, -ge-, h) track down; **~stacheln** v/t (sep, -ge-, h) goad (s.o. into doing s.th.); **~stampfen** v/i (sep, -ge-, h) stamp (one's foot)

'Aufstand m revolt, rebellion

'auf|stapeln v/t (sep, -ge-, h) pile up; **~stechen** v/t (irr, **stechen**, sep, -ge-, h) puncture, prick open; MED lance; **~stecken** v/t (sep, -ge-, h) put up (hair); F fig give up; **~stehen** v/i (irr, **stehen**, sep, -ge-, sein) get up, rise; **~steigen** v/i (irr, **steigen**, sep, -ge-, sein) rise (a. fig); get on (horse, bicycle); be promoted; SPORT Am a. be moved up to a higher division

'aufstellen v/t (sep, -ge-, h) set up, put up; post (guard); set (trap, record etc); nominate s.o.; draw up (table, list etc)

'Aufstellung f putting up; nomination; list; SPORT line-up

Aufstieg ['aufʃtiːk] m (-[e]s; -e) ascent, fig a. rise

'auf|stöbern fig v/t (sep, -ge-, h) ferret out; **~stoßen** (irr, **stoßen**, sep, -ge-,

h) 1. v/t push open **2.** v/i belch; ~stützen v/i/refl (sep, -ge-, h) lean (auf acc or dat on); ~suchen v/t (sep, -ge-, h) visit; see

'Auftakt m MUS upbeat; fig prelude

'auf|tanken v/t (sep, -ge-, h) fill up; MOT, AVIAT refuel; ~tauchen v/i (sep, -ge-, sein) appear; MAR surface; ~tauen v/t (sep, -ge-, h) thaw; GASTR defrost; ~teilen v/t (sep, -ge-, h) divide (up)

Auftrag ['auftra:k] m (-[e]s; Aufträge ['auftrɛ:gə]) instructions, order (a. ECON); MIL mission; im ~ von on behalf of; auftragen v/t (irr, tragen, sep, -ge-, h) serve (up) (food); apply (paint); j-m et. ~ ask (or tell) s.o. to do s.th; F dick ~ exaggerate; 'Auftraggeber m (-s; -) principal; customer

'auf|treffen v/i (irr, treffen, sep, -ge-, sein) strike, hit; ~treiben F v/t (irr, treiben, sep, -ge-, h) get hold of; raise (money); ~trennen v/t (sep, -ge-, h) undo (seam), cut open; ~treten v/i (irr, treten, sep, -ge-, sein) THEA etc appear (als as); behave, act; occur

'Auftreten n (-s; no pl) appearance; behavio(u)r; occurrence

'Auftrieb m (-[e]s; no pl) PHYS buoyancy (a. fig); AVIAT lift; fig impetus

'Auftritt m THEA entrance

'auf|tun v/t/refl (irr, tun, sep, -ge-, h) open (a. fig); abyss: yawn; ~türmen v/t (sep, -ge-, h) pile or heap up; sich ~ pile up; ~wachen v/i (sep, -ge-, sein) wake up; ~wachsen v/i (irr, wachsen, sep, -ge-, sein) grow up

Aufwand ['aufvant] m (-[e]s; no pl) expenditure (an dat of), a. expense; pomp

aufwändig ['aufvɛndɪç] adj costly; extravagant (lifestyle)

'aufwärmen v/t (sep, -ge-, h) warm up; F fig contp bring up

aufwärts ['aufvɛrts] adv upward(s); ~gehen v/i (irr, gehen, sep, -ge-, sein) fig improve

'auf|wecken v/t (sep, -ge-, h) wake (up); ~weichen v/t (sep, -ge-, h) soften; soak; ~weisen v/t (irr, weisen, sep, -ge-, h) show, have; ~wenden v/t ([irr, wenden,] sep, -ge-, h) spend (für on); Mühe ~ take pains

aufwendig → aufwändig

'aufwerfen v/t (irr, werfen, sep, -ge-, h)

raise (question etc)

'aufwerten v/t (sep, -ge-, h) ECON revalue; fig increase the value of

'Aufwertung f revaluation

'aufwickeln v/t and v/refl (sep, -ge-, h) wind up, roll up; put hair in curlers

aufwiegeln ['aufvi:gəln] v/t (sep, -ge-, h) stir up, incite, instigate

'aufwiegen v/t (irr, wiegen, sep, -ge-, h) make up for

Aufwiegler ['aufvi:glɐ] m (-s; -) agitator; instigator

'Aufwind m upwind; im ~ fig on the upswing

'auf|wirbeln v/t (sep, -ge-, h) whirl up; fig (viel) Staub ~ make (quite) a stir; ~wischen v/t (sep, -ge-, h) wipe up; ~wühlen fig v/t (sep, -ge-, h) stir, move

'aufzählen v/t (sep, -ge-, h) name (one by one), list; 'Aufzählung f enumeration, list

'aufzeichnen v/t (sep, -ge-, h) TV, radio etc: record, tape; draw; 'Aufzeichnung f recording; pl notes

'aufzeigen v/t (sep, -ge-, h) show; demonstrate; point out (mistake etc)

'aufziehen (irr, ziehen, sep, -ge-) 1. v/t (h) draw or pull up; (pull) open; bring up (child); wind (up) (clock); mount (photo etc); j-n ~ tease s.o. 2. v/i (sein) come up; 'Aufzug m elevator, Br lift; THEA act; F contp get-up

'aufzwingen v/t (irr, zwingen, sep, -ge-, h) j-m et. ~ force s.th. upon s.o.

Augapfel ['auk'apfəl] m ANAT eyeball

Auge ['augə] n (-s; -n) ANAT eye; ein blaues ~ a black eye; mit bloßem ~ with the naked eye; mit verbundenen ~n blindfold; in meinen ~n in my view; mit anderen ~n in a different light; aus den ~n verlieren lose sight of; ein ~ zudrücken turn a blind eye; unter vier ~n in private; F ins ~ gehen go wrong

'Augenarzt m eye specialist

'Augenblick m moment, instant

'augenblicklich 1. adj present; immediate; momentary 2. adv at present, at the moment; immediately

'Augen|braue f eyebrow; ~licht n (-[e]s; no pl) eyesight; ~lid n eyelid; ~maß n: ein gutes ~ a sure eye; nach dem ~ by the eye; ~merk n: sein ~ richten auf (acc) turn one's attention to, fig a. have in view; ~schein m (-s; no pl) appearance; **in ~ nehmen** examine, inspect; **~zeuge** m eyewitness

August [au'gʊst] m (-; no pl) August

Auktion [auk'tsjoːn] f (-; -en) auction

Auktionator [auktsjoˈnaːtoːɐ] m (-s; -en [auktsjonaˈtoːrən]) auctioneer

Aula ['aula] f (-; -s, Aulen) auditorium, Br (assembly) hall

aus [aus] prp (dat) and adv mst out of, from; of (silk etc); out of (spite etc); light etc: out, off; play etc: over, finished; SPORT out; **~ dem Fenster** etc out of the window etc; **~ München** from Munich; **~ Holz** (made) of wood; **~ Mitleid** out of pity; **~ Spaß** for fun; **~ Versehen** by mistake; **~ diesem Grunde** for this reason; **von hier~** from here; F **von mir ~** I don't care!; **~ der Mode** out of fashion; F **~ sein** be over; be out; **~ sein auf** (acc) be out for; be after (s.o.'s money etc); **die Schule (das Spiel) ist ~** school (the game) is over; **einl~** TECH on / off

Aus n: **im ~** ball: out of play

'aus|arbeiten v/t (sep, -ge-, h) work out; prepare; **~arten** v/i (sep, -ge-, sein) get out of hand; **~atmen** v/t and v/i (sep, -ge-, h) breathe out; **~baden** F v/t (sep, -ge-, h) **et. ~ müssen** take the rap for s.th.

'Ausbau m (-[e]s; no pl) extension; completion; removal; **'ausbauen** v/t (sep, -ge-, h) extend; complete; remove; improve; **'ausbaufähig** adj: **et. ist ~** there is potential for growth or development

'ausbessern v/t (sep, -ge-, h) mend, repair, F a. fix; **'Ausbesserung** f (-; -en) repair(ing)

'Ausbeute f (-; no pl) gain, profit; yield; **'ausbeuten** v/t (sep, -ge-, h) exploit (a. contp); **'Ausbeutung** f (-; no pl) exploitation

'ausbilden v/t (sep, -ge-, h) train, instruct; **j-n ~ zu** train s.o. to be

'Ausbilder m (-s; -) instructor

'Ausbildung f (-; -en) training, instruction

'ausbleiben v/i (irr, bleiben, sep, -ge-, sein) stay out; fail to come; **es konnte nicht ~** it was inevitable

'Ausblick m view (**auf** acc of); fig outlook (for)

'ausbrechen v/i (irr, brechen, sep, -ge-, sein) break out (a. fig); **in Tränen ~**

burst into tears; **'Ausbrecher** m (-s; -) escaped prisoner

'ausbreiten v/t (sep, -ge-, h) spread (out); **sich ~** spread; **'Ausbreitung** f (-; no pl) spreading

'ausbrennen v/t (irr, **brennen**, sep, -ge-, sein) burn out

'Ausbruch m escape, breakout; outbreak (of fire etc); eruption (of volcano); (out)burst (of resentment etc)

'ausbrüten v/t (sep, -ge-, h) hatch (a. fig)

'Ausdauer f perseverance, stamina, esp SPORT a. staying power; **'ausdauernd** adj persevering; SPORT tireless

'ausdehnen v/t and v/refl (sep, -ge-, h) stretch; fig expand, extend

'Ausdehnung f expansion; extension

'ausdenken v/t (irr, **denken**, sep, -ge-, h) think s.th. up; invent (a. fig)

'Ausdruck m expression, term; IT printout; **'ausdrucken** v/t (sep, -ge-, h) IT print out

'ausdrücken v/t (sep, -ge-, h) stub out (cigarette etc); fig express

ausdrücklich ['ausdrʏklɪç] adj express, explicit

'ausdrucks|los adj expressionless, blank; **~voll** adj expressive

'Ausdrucksweise f language, style

'Ausdünstung f (-; -en) exhalation; perspiration; odo(u)r

auseinander [ausˀaiˈnandɐ] adv apart; separate(d); **~bringen** v/t (irr, **bringen**, sep, -ge-, h) separate; **~gehen** v/i (irr, **gehen**, sep, -ge-, sein) part; meeting etc: break up; opinions etc: differ; married couple: separate; **~halten** v/t (irr, **halten**, sep, -ge-, h) tell apart; **~nehmen** v/t (irr, **nehmen**, sep, -ge-, h) take apart (a. fig); **~setzen** v/t (irr, **setzen**, sep, -ge-, h) explain; **sich ~ setzen mit** v/refl deal with; argue with s.o.

Auseinandersetzung f (-; -en) argument

'auserlesen adj choice, exquisite

'ausfahren (irr, **fahren**, sep, -ge-) **1.** v/i (sein) go for a drive or ride **2.** v/t (h) take s.o. out; AVIAT extend (landing gear); **'Ausfahrt** f drive, ride; MOT exit

'Ausfall m TECH, MOT, SPORT failure; loss

'ausfallen v/i (irr, **fallen**, sep, -ge-, sein) fall out; not take place, be cancelled; TECH, MOT break down, fail; **gut** etc **~** turn out well etc; **~ lassen** cancel;

die Schule fällt aus there is no school

'ausfallend, 'ausfällig *adj* insulting

'ausfertigen *v/t* (*sep, -ge-, h*) draw up (*contract etc*); make out (*check etc*)

'Ausfertigung *f* drawing up; copy; *in doppelter ~* in duplicate

'ausfindig *adj*: ~ *machen* find

ausflippen ['ausflɪpən] F *v/i* (*sep, -ge-, sein*) freak out

Ausflüchte ['ausflʏçtə] *pl* excuses

'Ausflug *m* trip, excursion, outing

Ausflügler ['ausflyːklɐ] *m* (*-s; -*) day tripper

'Ausfluss *m* TECH outlet; MED discharge

'aus|fragen *v/t* (*sep, -ge-, h*) question (*über acc* about); sound out; ~fransen *v/i* (*sep, -ge-, sein*) fray; ~fressen F *v/t* (*irr, fressen, sep, -ge-, h*) *et.* ~ be up to no good

Ausfuhr ['ausfuːɐ] *f* (*-; -en*) ECON export (*-ation*); 'ausführbar *adj* practicable; 'ausführen *v/t* (*sep, -ge-, h*) take *s.o.* out; carry out (*task etc*); ECON export; explain

ausführlich ['ausfyːɐlɪç] **1.** *adj* detailed; comprehensive **2.** *adv* in detail; 'Ausführlichkeit *f*: *in aller ~* in great detail

'Ausführung *f* execution, performance; type, model, design

'ausfüllen *v/t* (*sep, -ge-, h*) fill out (*Br in*) (*form*)

'Ausgabe *f* distribution; edition; expense; issue; IT output

'Ausgang *m* exit, way out; end; result, outcome; TECH, ELECTR output, outlet

'Ausgangs|punkt *m* starting point; ~sperre *f* POL curfew

'ausgeben *v/t* (*irr, geben, sep, -ge-, h*) give out; spend; end; *hair*: fall out; *money, supplies*: run out; *leer* ~ get nothing; ~ *von* start from *or* at; come from; *davon ~, dass* assume that; *ihm ging das Geld aus* he ran out of money

'ausge|kocht *fig adj* cunning; out-and--out (*villain etc*); ~lassen *fig adj* cheerful; hilarious; ~ *sein* in high spirits; ~macht *adj* agreed(-on); downright (*nonsense*); ~prägt *adj* marked, pronounced; ~rechnet *adv*: ~ *er* he of all people; ~ *heute* today of all days; ~schlossen *adj* out of the question; ~storben *adj* extinct; ~sucht *adj* select, choice; ~wachsen *adj* fullgrown; ~wogen *adj* (well-)balanced; ~zeichnet *adj* excellent

ausgiebig ['ausgiːbɪç] *adj* extensive, thorough; substantial (*meal*)

'ausgießen *v/t* (*irr, gießen, sep, -ge-, h*) pour out

'Ausgleich *m* (*-[e]s; no pl*) compensation; SPORT even score, *Br* equalization; *tennis*: deuce; 'ausgleichen *v/t and v/i* (*irr, gleichen, sep, -ge-, h*) compensate; equalize (*Br a.* SPORT); ECON balance; SPORT make the score even

'Ausgleichs|sport *m* remedial exercises; ~tor *n*, ~treffer *m* SPORT tying point, *Br* equalizer

'ausgraben *v/t* (*irr, graben, sep, -ge-, h*) dig out *or* up (*a. fig*)

'Ausgrabungen *pl* excavations

'ausgrenzen *v/t* (*sep, -ge-, h*) isolate

'Ausguss *m* (kitchen) sink

'aushalten (*irr, halten, sep, -ge-, h*) **1.** *v/t* bear, stand; keep (*mistress etc*); *nicht auszuhalten sein* be unbearable **2.** *v/i* hold out

aushändigen ['aushɛndɪgən] *v/t* (*sep, -ge-, h*) hand over

'Aushang *m* notice; bulletin

'aushängen *v/t* (*sep, -ge-, h*) hang out, put up; unhinge (*door*)

'aus|heben *v/t* (*irr, heben, sep, -ge-, h*) dig (*trench*); raid (*place etc*); ~helfen *v/i* (*irr, helfen, sep, -ge-, h*) help out

'Aushilfe *f* (temporary) help

'Aushilfs... *in cpds -kellner etc*: temporary

'aus|holen *v/i* (*sep, -ge-, h*) *zum Schlag ~* swing (to strike); *fig weit ~* go far back; ~horchen *v/t* (*sep, -ge-, h*) sound (*über acc* on); ~hungern *v/t* (*sep, -ge-, h*) starve out; ~kennen *v/refl* (*irr, kennen, sep, -ge-, h*) *sich ~* (*in dat*) know one's way (about); *fig* know a lot (about); ~klingen *v/i* (*irr, klingen, sep, -ge-, sein*) draw to a close; ~klopfen *v/t* (*sep, -ge-, h*) knock out; ~kommen *v/i* (*irr*, **kommen**, *sep*, *-ge-*, *sein*) get by; **~ mit** manage with *s.th.*; get along with *s.o.*

Auskunft ['auskʊnft] *f* (-; *Auskünfte* ['auskʏnftə]) information; (*no pl*) information desk; TEL inquiries

'aus|lachen *v/t* (*sep*, *-ge-*, *h*) laugh at (**wegen** for); **~laden** *v/t* (*irr*, **laden**, *sep*, *-ge-*, *h*) unload

'Auslage *f* window display; *pl* expenses

'Ausland *n* (-[*e*]*s*; *no pl*) **das ~** foreign countries; **ins ~, im ~** abroad

Ausländer ['auslɛndɐ] *m* (-*s*; -) foreigner; **~feindlichkeit** *f* hostility to foreigners, xenophobia

Ausländerin ['auslɛndərɪn] *f* (-; *-nen*) foreigner

ausländisch ['auslɛndɪʃ] *adj* foreign

'Auslands|gespräch *n* international call; **~korrespondent(in)** foreign correspondent

'aus|lassen *v/t* (*irr*, **lassen**, *sep*, *-ge-*, *h*) leave out; omit (**butter** *etc*); let out (*seam*); **s-n Zorn an j-m ~** take it out on *s.o.*; **sich~über** (*acc*) express o.s. on

'Auslassung *f* (-; *-en*) omission

'Auslassungszeichen *n* LING apostrophe

'Auslauf *m* room to move about; *dog*: exercise; '**auslaufen** *v/i* (*irr*, **laufen**, *sep*, *-ge-*, *sein*) MAR leave port; *pot etc*: leak; *liquid etc*: run out; '**Ausläufer** *m* METEOR ridge, trough; *pl* GEOGR foothills; 'Auslaufmo,dell *n* ECON close-out (*Br* phase-out) model

'aus|legen *v/t* (*sep*, *-ge-*, *h*) lay out; carpet; line (*with paper etc*); display (*goods*); interpret (*text etc*); advance (*money*)

'Auslegung *f* (-; *-en*) interpretation

'aus|leihen *v/t* (*irr*, **leihen**, *sep*, *-ge-*, *h*) lend (out), loan; **sich** (*dat*) **et. ~** borrow *s.th.*; **~lernen** *v/i* (*sep*, *-ge-*, *h*) complete one's training; **man lernt nie aus** we live and learn

'Auslese *f* choice, selection; *fig* pick

'aus|lesen *v/t* (*irr*, **lesen**, *sep*, *-ge-*, *h*) pick out, select; finish (*book etc*)

'aus|liefern *v/t* (*sep*, *-ge-*, *h*) hand *or* turn over, deliver (up); POL extradite; 'Auslieferung *f* delivery; extradition

'aus|liegen *v/i* (*irr*, **liegen**, *sep*, *-ge-*, *h*) be laid out; **~löschen** *v/t* (*sep*, *-ge-*, *h*) put out; *fig* wipe out; **~losen** *v/t* (*sep*, *-ge-*, *h*) draw (lots) for

'aus|lösen *v/t* (*sep*, *-ge-*, *h*) TECH release; ransom, redeem; cause, start, trigger *s.th.* off; 'Auslöser *m* (PHOT shutter) release; trigger

'aus|machen *v/t* (*sep*, *-ge-*, *h*) put out (*fire*); turn off (*light etc*); arrange (*date etc*); agree on (*price etc*); make up; amount to; settle (*dispute*); sight, spot; **macht es Ihnen et. aus (, wenn...)?** do you mind (if ...)?; **es macht mir nichts aus** I don't mind; **das macht (gar) nichts aus** that doesn't matter (at all)

'aus|malen *v/t* (*sep*, *-ge-*, *h*) paint; **sich et. ~** imagine *s.th.*

'Ausmaß *n* extent; *pl* proportions

aus|merzen ['ausmɛrtsən] *v/t* (*sep*, *-ge-*, *h*) eliminate; **~messen** *v/t* (*irr*, **messen**, *sep*, *-ge-*, *h*) measure

Ausnahme ['ausnaːmə] *f* (-; *-n*) exception; **~zustand** *m* POL state of emergency

'ausnahmslos *adv* without exception

'ausnahmsweise *adv* by way of exception; just this once

'aus|nehmen *v/t* (*irr*, **nehmen**, *sep*, *-ge-*, *h*) clean (*chicken etc*); except; F *contp* fleece *s.o.*; **~d** *adv* exceptionally

'aus|nutzen *v/t* (*sep*, *-ge-*, *h*) use; take advantage of (*a. contp*); exploit; **~packen** (*sep*, *-ge-*, *h*) **1.** *v/t* unpack **2.** F *v/i* talk; **~pfeifen** *v/t* (*irr*, **pfeifen**, *sep*, *-ge-*, *h*) boo, hiss; **~plaudern** *v/t* (*sep*, *-ge-*, *h*) blab out; **~plündern** *v/t* (*sep*, *-ge-*, *h*) plunder, rob; **~pro,bieren** *v/t* (*sep*, *no -ge-*, *h*) try out, test

'Auspuff *m* MOT exhaust; **~gase** *pl* MOT exhaust fumes; **~rohr** *n* MOT exhaust pipe; **~topf** *m* MOT muffler, *Br* silencer

'aus|quar,tieren *v/t* (*sep*, *no -ge-*, *h*) move out; **~ra,dieren** *v/t* (*sep*, *no -ge-*, *h*) erase; *fig* wipe out; **~ran,gieren** *v/t* (*sep*, *no -ge-*, *h*) discard; **~rauben** *v/t* (*sep*, *-ge-*, *h*) rob; **~räumen** *v/t* (*sep*, *-ge-*, *h*) empty; clear out (*room etc*); *fig* clear up (*doubt etc*); **~rechnen** *v/t* (*sep*, *-ge-*, *h*) work out

'Ausrede *f* excuse

'aus|reden (*sep*, *-ge-*, *h*) **1.** *v/i* finish speaking; **j-n ~ lassen** hear *s.o.* out **2.** *v/t*: **j-m et. ~** talk *s.o.* out of *s.th.*

'aus|reichen *v/i* (*sep*, *-ge-*, *h*) be enough; **~d** *adj* sufficient, enough; *grade*: (barely) passing, only average, weak, D

'Ausreise f departure; 'ausreisen v/i (sep, -ge-, sein) leave (a or one's country); 'Ausreisevisum n exit visa

'ausreißen (irr, **reißen**, sep, -ge-) **1.** v/t (h) pull or tear out **2.** F v/i (sein) run away; 'Ausreißer m ⟨-s; -⟩ runaway

'aus|renken v/t (sep, -ge-, h) MED dislocate; ~richten v/t (sep, -ge-, h) tell s.o. s.th.; deliver (message); accomplish; arrange (party etc); **richte ihr e-n Gruß von mir aus!** give her my regards!; **kann ich et. ~?** can I take a message

'ausrotten v/t (sep, -ge-, h) exterminate

'Ausrottung f ⟨-; -en⟩ extermination

'ausrücken v/i (sep, -ge-, sein) F run away; MIL march out

'Ausruf m cry, shout; 'ausrufen v/t (irr, **rufen**, sep, -ge-, h) cry, shout, exclaim; call out (name); POL proclaim; 'Ausrufung f ⟨-; -en⟩ POL proclamation; 'Ausrufungszeichen n LING exclamation mark

'ausruhen v/i, v/t and v/refl (sep, -ge-, h) rest

'ausrüsten v/t (sep, -ge-, h) equip; 'Ausrüstung f equipment

'ausrutschen v/i (sep, -ge-, sein) slip

'Aussage f statement; JUR evidence

'aussagen v/i (sep, -ge-, h) state, declare; JUR testify

ausschalten v/t (sep, -ge-, h) switch off; fig eliminate

'Ausschau f: ~ **halten nach** → 'ausschauen v/i (sep, -ge-, h) ~ **nach** look out for, watch out for

'ausscheiden (irr, **scheiden**, sep, -ge-) **1.** v/i (sein) be ruled out; SPORT etc drop out (**aus** dat of); retire (**aus** dat from office etc); ~ **aus** (dat) leave (a firm etc) **2.** v/t (h) eliminate; MED etc secrete, exude; 'Ausscheidung f elimination (a. SPORT); MED secretion

'Ausscheidungs... in cpds ...spiel etc: SPORT qualifying ...

'aus|schlachten fig v/t (sep, -ge-, h) salvage, Br a. cannibalize; contp exploit; ~schlafen v/t (**schlafen**, sep, -ge-, h) **1.** v/i sleep in **2.** v/t sleep off

'Ausschlag m rash; TECH deflection; **den ~ geben** decide it

'ausschlagen (irr, **schlagen**, sep, -ge-, h) **1.** v/t knock out (tooth etc); fig refuse, decline (offer etc) **2.** v/i horse: kick; BOT bud; TECH deflect

'ausschlaggebend adj decisive

'ausschließen v/t (irr, **schließen**, sep, -ge-, h) lock out; fig exclude; expel; SPORT disqualify

'ausschließlich adj exclusive

'Ausschluss m exclusion; expulsion; SPORT disqualification; **unter ~ der Öffentlichkeit** in closed session

'aus|schmücken v/t (sep, -ge-, h) decorate; fig embellish; ~schneiden v/t (irr, **schneiden**, sep, -ge-, h) cut out

'Ausschnitt m clothing: neck; (press) clipping (Br cutting); fig part; extract; **mit tiefem ~** low-necked

'ausschreiben v/t (irr, **schreiben**, sep, -ge-, h) write out (a. check etc); advertise (post etc); 'Ausschreibung f advertisement

'Ausschreitungen pl violence, riots

'Ausschuss m committee, board; TECH (no pl) refuse, waste, rejects

'aus|schütteln v/t (sep, -ge-, h) shake out; ~schütten v/t (sep, -ge-, h) pour out (a. fig); spill; ECON pay; **sich vor Lachen ~** split one's sides

'ausschweifend adj dissolute

'Ausschweifung f ⟨-; -en⟩ debauchery, excess

'aussehen v/i (irr, **sehen**, sep, -ge-, h) look; **krank** (**traurig**) ~ look ill (sad); ~ **wie** ... look like ...; **wie sieht er aus?** what does he look like? 'Aussehen n ⟨-s; no pl⟩ look(s), appearance

außen ['ausən] adv outside; **nach ~** (hin) outward(s); fig outwardly

'Außenbordmotor m outboard motor

aussenden v/t (irr, **senden**, sep, -ge-, h) send out

'Außen|dienst m field service; ~handel m foreign trade; ~minister m Am Secretary of State, Br Foreign Secretary; ~minis,terium n Am State Department, Br Foreign Office; ~poli,tik f foreign affairs; foreign policy

'außenpo,litisch adj foreign-policy

'Außenseite f outside

Außenseiter ['ausənzaitɐ] m ⟨-s; -⟩ outsider

'Außen|spiegel m MOT outside rearview mirror; ~stände pl ECON receivables; ~stelle f branch; ~stürmer m SPORT winger; ~welt f outside world

außer ['ausɐ] **1.** prp (dat) out of; aside

from, *Br* beside(s); except; **~ sich sein** be beside o.s. (**vor Freude** with joy); **alle ~ e-m** all but one; → **Betrieb, Gefahr 2.** *cj:* **~ dass** except that; **~ wenn** unless

'aus**serdem** *cj* besides, moreover

äußere ['ɔysərə] *adj* exterior, outer, outward; '**Äußere** *n* (-*n*; *no pl*) exterior, outside; (outward) appearance

'auß**ergewöhnlich** *adj* unusual

außerhalb *prp* (*gen*) *and adv* outside; out of; beyond

'auß**erirdisch** *adj* extraterrestrial

äußerlich *adj* external, outward

Äußerlichkeit *f* (-; -*en*) formality; minor detail

äußern ['ɔysən] *v/t* (*ge-*, *h*) utter, express; **sich ~** say s.th.; **sich ~ zu** *or* **über** (*acc*) express o.s. on

'auß**er'ordentlich** *adj* extraordinary

'auß**erplanmäßig** *adj* unscheduled

äußerst ['ɔysəst] **1.** *adj* outermost; *fig* extreme; **im ~en Fall** at (the) worst; at (the) most **2.** *adv* extremely

außer'stande *adj:* **~ sein** be unable

'**Äußerung** *f* (-; -*en*) utterance, remark

'aus**setzen** (*sep*, -*ge*-, *h*) **1.** *v/t* abandon; expose (*dat* to); **et. auszusetzen haben an** (*dat*) find fault with **2.** *v/i* stop, break off; MOT, TECH fail

'**Aussicht** *f* view (**auf** *acc* of); *fig* prospect (of), chance (**auf Erfolg** of success); '**aussichtslos** *adj* hopeless, desperate; '**Aussichtspunkt** *m* vantage point; '**aussichtsreich** *adj* promising; '**Aussichtsturm** *m* lookout tower

'**Aussiedler** *m* resettler, evacuee

'aus**sitzen** *v/t* (*irr*, *sitzen*, *sep*, -*ge*-, *h*) sit *s.th.* out

aussöhnen ['auszø:nən] *v/refl* (*sep*, -*ge*-, *h*) **sich ~** (**mit**) become reconciled (with), F make it up (with)

'**Aussöhnung** *f* (-; -*en*) reconciliation

'aus|**sor,tieren** *v/t* (*sep*, *no* -*ge*-, *h*) sort out; **~spannen** (*sep*, -*ge*-, *h*) **1.** *v/t* unharness **2.** *fig v/i* (take a) rest, relax

'aus**sperren** *v/t* (*sep*, -*ge*-, *h*) lock out (*a.* ECON); '**Aussperrung** *f* (-; -*en*) ECON lock-out

'aus|**spielen** (*sep*, -*ge*-, *h*) **1.** *v/t* play; **j-n gegen j-n ~** play s.o. off against s.o. **2.** *v/i card game:* lead; **er hat ausgespielt** *fig* he is done for; **~spio,nieren** *v/t* (*sep*, *no* -*ge*-, *h*) spy out

'**Aussprache** *f* pronunciation; discussion; *private* heart-to-heart (talk)

'aus**sprechen** *v/t* (*irr*, *sprechen*, *sep*, -*ge*-, *h*) pronounce; express; **sich ~ für** (**gegen**) speak for (against); **sich mit j-m gründlich ~** have a heart-to-heart talk with s.o.

'**Ausspruch** *m* saying; remark

'aus|**spucken** *v/i and v/t* (*sep*, -*ge*-, *h*) spit out; **~spülen** *v/t* (*sep*, -*ge*-, *h*) rinse

'**Ausstand** *m* strike, F walkout

'aus**statten** *v/t* (*sep*, -*ge*-, *h*) fit out, equip, furnish; '**Ausstatung** *f* (-; -*en*) equipment, furnishings; design

'aus|**stechen** *v/t* (*irr*, *stechen*, *sep*, -*ge*-, *h*) GASTR cut out (*a. fig*); put out (*eyes*); **~stehen** (*irr*, *stehen*, *sep*, -*ge*-, *h*) **1.** *v/t* stand, endure; F **ich kann ihn** (**es**) **nicht ~** I can't stand him (it) **2.** *v/i:* (**noch**) **~** be outstanding *or* overdue

'aus**steigen** *v/i* (*irr*, *steigen*, *sep*, -*ge*-, *sien*) get out (**aus** *dat* of); (*a.* **~ aus** *dat*) get off *a* bus, train; F *fig* drop out; '**Aussteiger** F *m* (-*s*; -) drop-out

'aus**stellen** *v/t* (*sep*, -*ge*-, *h*) exhibit, display, show; make out (*check etc*); issue (*passport*); '**Aussteller** *m* (-*s*; -) exhibitor; issuer; drawer (*of check*)

'**Ausstellung** *f* exhibition, show

'aus**sterben** *v/i* (*irr*, *sterben*, *sep*, -*ge*-, *sein*) die out, become extinct (*both a. fig*)

'**Aussteuer** *f* trousseau; dowry

'aus**steuern** *v/t* (*sep*, -*ge*-, *h*) ELECTR modulate; '**Aussteuerung** *f* ELECTR modulation; level control

Ausstieg ['aus\|ti:k] *m* (-[*e*]*s*; -*e*) exit; *fig* withdrawal (**aus** *dat* from)

'aus**stopfen** *v/t* (*sep*, -*ge*-, *h*) stuff; pad

'**Ausstoß** *m* TECH, PHYS discharge, ejection; ECON output

'aus**stoßen** *v/t* (*irr*, *stoßen*, *sep*, -*ge*-, *h*) TECH, PHYS give off, eject, emit; ECON turn out; give (*cry, sigh*); expel

'aus|**strahlen** *v/t* (*sep*, -*ge*-, *h*) radiate (*happiness etc*); TV, *radio:* broadcast, transmit; '**Ausstrahlung** *f* radiation; *fig* magnetism, charisma

'**Austausch** *m* (-[*e*]*s*; *no pl*) exchange

'**austauschbar** *adj* exchangeable

'austauschen v/t (sep, -ge-, h) exchange (**gegen** for)

'Austauschschüler(in) exchange student

'austeilen v/t (sep, -ge-, h) distribute, hand out; deal (out) (cards, blows)

Auster ['aʊstɐ] f (-; -n) zo oyster

'austragen v/t (irr, **tragen**, sep, -ge-, h) deliver (mail); settle (dispute etc); hold (contest etc); **das Kind ~** have the baby

'Austragungsort m SPORT venue

Australien [aʊs'tra:ljən] Australia

Australier [aʊs'tra:ljɐ] m (-s; -), Australierin [aʊs'tra:ljərɪn] f (-; -nen), aust'ralisch adj Australian

'austreiben v/t (irr, **treiben**, sep, -ge-, h) exorcise; F **j-m et. ~** cure s.o. of s.th.; ~**treten** (irr, **treten**, sep, -ge-) 1. v/t (h) tread or stamp out (fire); wear out (shoes) 2. v/i (sein) escape (**aus** dat from); F go to the bathroom (Br toilet); ~ **aus** (dat) leave (a club etc); resign from; ~**trinken** v/t (irr, **trinken**, sep, -ge-, h) drink up; empty

'Austritt m leaving; resignation; escape

'austrocknen v/t (sep, -ge-, h) and v/i (sein) dry up

'ausüben v/t (sep, -ge-, h) practi|ce, Br -se; hold (office); exercise (power etc); exert (pressure etc); 'Ausübung f (-; no pl) practice; exercise

'Ausverkauf m ECON (clearance) sale

'ausverkauft adj ECON, THEA sold out; **vor ~em Haus spielen** play to a full house

'Auswahl f choice, selection (both a. ECON); SPORT representative team

'auswählen v/t (sep, -ge-, h) choose, select

'Auswanderer m emigrant

'auswandern v/i (sep, -ge-, sein) emigrate; 'Auswanderung f emigration

auswärtig ['aʊsvɛrtɪç] adj out-of-town; POL foreign

'auswärts adv out of town

'Auswärtssieg m SPORT away victory; ~spiel n SPORT away game

'auswechseln v/t (sep, -ge-, h) exchange (**gegen** for); change (tire); replace; **A gegen B ~** SPORT substitute B for A; **wie ausgewechselt** (like) a different person; 'Auswechselspieler m SPORT substitute

'Ausweg m way out; 'ausweglos adj

hopeless; 'Ausweglosigkeit f (-; no pl) hopelessness

'ausweichen v/i (irr, **weichen**, sep, -ge-, sein) make way (dat for); fig avoid s.o.; evade (question); ~d adj evasive

'ausweinen v/refl (sep, -ge-, h) have a good cry

Ausweis ['aʊsvaɪs] m (-es; -e) identification (card); card

'ausweisen v/t (irr, **weisen**, sep, -ge-, h) expel; **sich ~** identify o.s.

'Ausweispapiere pl documents

'Ausweisung f (-; -en) expulsion

'ausweiten fig v/t (sep, -ge-, h) expand

'auswendig adv by heart; **et. ~ können** know s.th. by heart; **~ lernen** memorize; learn by heart

'auswerfen v/t (irr, **werfen**, sep, -ge-, h) throw out; cast (anchor); TECH eject

'auswerten v/t (sep, -ge-, h) evaluate, analyze, interpret, utilize, exploit; 'Auswertung f evaluation; utilization

'auswickeln v/t (sep, -ge-, h) unwrap

'auswirken v/refl (sep, -ge-, h) **sich ~ auf** (acc) affect; **sich positiv ~** have a favo(u)rable effect; 'Auswirkung f effect

'auswischen v/t (sep, -ge-, h) wipe out

'auswringen v/t (irr, **wringen**, sep, -ge-, h) wring out

'Auswuchs m (-es; Auswüchse ['aʊsvy:ksə]) excrescence; fig pl excesses

'aus|wuchten v/t (sep, -ge-, h) TECH balance; ~**zahlen** v/t (sep, -ge-, h) pay (out); pay s.o. off; **sich ~** pay; ~**zählen** v/t (sep, -ge-, h) count; boxing: count out

'Auszahlung f payment; paying off

'auszeichnen v/t (sep, -ge-, h) price, mark (out) (goods); **sich ~** distinguish o.s.; **j-n mit et. ~** award s.th. to s.o.; 'Auszeichnung f marking; fig distinction, hono(u)r; award; decoration

'ausziehen (irr, **ziehen**, sep, -ge-) 1. v/t (h) take off (coat etc); pull out (table etc); **sich ~** undress 2. v/i (sein) move out

'Auszubildende m, f (-n; -n) apprentice, trainee

'Auszug m move, removal; extract, excerpt; statement (of account)

authentisch [aʊ'tɛntɪʃ] adj authentic, genuine

Autismus [aʊ'tɪsmʊs] m PSYCH autism

autistisch [aʊ'tɪstɪʃ] adj PSYCH autistic

Auto ['auto] n (-s; -s) car, auto(mobile); (**mit dem**) ~ **fahren** drive, go by car

'**Autobahn** f Am expressway, Br motorway; ~**dreieck** n interchange; ~**gebühr** f toll; ~**kreuz** n interchange

Autobiogra'phie f autobiography

'**Auto|bombe** f car bomb; ~**bus** m → **Bus**; ~**fähre** f car ferry; ~**fahrer(in)** motorist, driver; ~**fahrt** f drive; ~**friedhof** F m car dump, auto junkyard

Autogramm [auto'gram] n autograph; ~**jäger** m autograph hunter

'**Auto|karte** f road map; ~**kino** n drive-in theater (Br cinema)

Automat [auto'ma:t] m (-en; -en) vending (Br a. slot) machine; TECH robot; → **Spielautomat**; **Automatik** [auto-'ma:tɪk] f (-; no pl) automatic (system or control); MOT automatic transmission; automatic; **Automation**

[automa'tsjo:n] f (-; no pl) automation; auto'matisch adj automatic

'**Auto|me,chaniker** m car mechanic

autonom [auto'no:m] adj autonomous

'**Autonummer** f license (Br licence) number

Autor ['auto:ɐ] m (-s; -en [au'to:rən]) author

'**Autorepa,turwerkstatt** f garage, car repair shop

Autorin [au'to:rɪn] f (-; -nen) author(ess)

autorisieren [autori'zi:rən] v/t (no -ge-, h) authorize; **autoritär** [autori'tɛ:ɐ] adj authoritarian; **Autorität** [autori'tɛ:t] f (-; -en) authority

'**Auto|tele,fon** n car phone; ~**vermietung** f car rental (Br hire) service; ~**waschanlage** f car wash

Axt [akst] f (-; **Äxte** ['ɛkstə]) ax(e)

B

Baby ['be:bi] n (-s; -s) baby; ~**bett** n crib, Br cot; ~**fläschchen** n baby's bottle; ~**nahrung** f baby food; ~**sitter(in)** babysitter; ~**sitz** m child seat; ~**wickelraum** m baby-changing room

Bach [bax] m (-[e]s; **Bäche** ['bɛçə]) brook, stream, Am a. creek

'**Backblech** n baking sheet

'**Backbord** n (-s; no pl) MAR port

Backe ['bakə] f (-; -n) ANAT cheek

backen v/t and v/i ([irr, **backen**,] -ge-, h) bake

'**Backenzahn** m ANAT molar (tooth)

Bäcker ['bɛkɐ] m (-s; -) baker; **beim** ~ at the baker's; **Bäckerei** [bɛkə'rai] f (-; -en) bakery, baker's (shop)

'**Back|form** f baking tin; ~**hendl** ['bak-hɛndl] Austrian n (-s; -n) fried chicken; ~**obst** n dried fruit; ~**ofen** m oven; ~**pflaume** f prune; ~**pulver** n baking powder; ~**stein** m brick

backte ['baktə] pret of **backen**

'**Backwaren** pl breads and pastries

Bad [ba:t] n (-[e]; **Bäder** ['bɛ:dɐ]) bath; swim; bathroom; → **Badeort**; **ein** ~ **nehmen** → **baden** 1

'**Bade|anstalt** f swimming pool, public baths; ~**anzug** m swimsuit; ~**hose** f

bathing trunks; ~**kappe** f bathing cap; ~**mantel** m bathrobe; ~**meister** m pool or bath attendant

baden ['ba:dən] (ge-, h) **1.** v/i bathe, take or have a bath; swim; ~ **gehen** go swimming **2.** v/t bathe (a. MED); Br a. bath

'**Bade|ort** m seaside (or health) resort; ~**sachen** Pl swimming things; ~**schaum** m bubble bath, bath foam; ~**tuch** n bath towel; ~**wanne** f bathtub; ~**zeug** n swimming gear; ~**zimmer** n bathroom

Badminton ['bɛtmɪntn] n (-; no pl) badminton

baff [baf] adj: F ~ **sein** be flabbergasted

Bagatelle [baga'tɛlə] f (-; -n) trifle

Baga'tellschaden m superficial damage

Bagger ['bagɐ] m (-s; -) TECH excavator; dredge(r); '**baggern** v/i (ge-, h) TECH excavate; dredge

Bahn [ba:n] f (-; -en) railroad, Br railway; train; way, path, course; SPORT track; **mit der** ~ by rail; ~ **frei!** make way!; cpds → a. **Eisenbahn**

'**bahnbrechend** adj epoch-making

BahnCard® [ba:n'ka:t] f (-; -s) rail card (allowing 50% or 25% reduction on

B

tickets)

'**Bahndamm** *m* railroad (*Br* railway) embankment

'**bahnen** *v/t* (*ge-, h*) **den Weg ~** clear the way (*dat for s.o. or s.th.*); **sich e-n Weg ~** force *or* work one's way

'**Bahn|hof** *m* (railroad, *Br* railway) station; ~**linie** *f* railroad (*Br* railway) line; ~**steig** ['baːnʃtaɪk] *m* (*-[e]s; -e*) platform; ~**übergang** *m* grade (*Br* level) crossing

Bahre ['baːrə] *f* (*-; -n*) stretcher; bier

Baisse ['bɛːsə] *f* (*-; -n*) ECON fall, slump

Bakterien [bak'teːrjən] *pl* MED bacteria, germs

balancieren [balaˈsiːrən] *v/t and v/i* (*no -ge-, h*) balance

bald [balt] *adv* soon; F almost, nearly; **so ~ wie möglich** as soon as possible

baldig ['baldɪç] *adj* speedy; ~**e Antwort** ECON early reply; **auf(ein) ~es Wiedersehen!** see you again soon!

balgen ['balgən] *v/refl* (*ge-, h*) scuffle (**um** for)

Balken ['balkən] *m* (*-s; -*) beam

Balkon ['balkɔn] *m* (*-s; -s, -e* [balˈkoːnə]) balcony; ~**tür** *f* French window

Ball [bal] *m* (*-[e]s; Bälle* ['bɛlə]) ball; dance; **am ~ sein** SPORT have the ball; **am ~ bleiben** *fig* stick to it

Ballade [baˈlaːdə] *f* (*-; -n*) ballad

Ballast ['balast] *m* (*-[e]s; no pl*) ballast, *fig a.* burden; ~**stoffe** *pl* MED roughage, bulk

ballen ['balən] *v/t* (*ge-, h*) clench (*fist*)

'**Ballen** *m* (*-s; -*) bale; ANAT ball

Ballett [baˈlɛt] *n* (*-[e]s; -e*) ballet

Ballon [baˈlɔŋ] *m* (*-s; -s, -e*) balloon

'**Ballungs|raum** *m*, ~**zentrum** *n* congested area, conurbation

Balsam ['balzaːm] *m* (*-s; no pl*) balm

Bambus ['bambʊs] *m* (*-ses, -; -se*) BOT bamboo; ~**rohr** *n* BOT bamboo (cane)

banal [baˈnaːl] *adj* banal, trite

Banane [baˈnaːnə] *f* (*-; -n*) BOT banana

Banause [baˈnauzə] *m* (*-n; -n*) philistine

band [bant] *pret of* **binden**

Band[1] *n* (*-[e]s; Bänder* ['bɛndɐ]) ribbon; tape; (*hat*) band; ANAT ligament, *fig* tie, link; **auf ~ aufnehmen** tape; **am laufenden ~** *fig* continuously

Band[2] *m* (*-[e]s; Bände* ['bɛndə]) volume

Bandage [banˈdaːʒə] *f* (*-; -n*) bandage

bandagieren [bandaˈʒiːrən] *v/t* (*no*

-ge-, h) bandage (up)

'**Bandbreite** *f* ELECTR bandwidth; *fig* range

Bande ['bandə] *f* (*-; -n*) gang; *billiards*: cushions; *ice hockey*: boards; *bowling*: gutter

'**Bänderriss** *m* MED torn ligament

bändigen ['bɛndɪgən] *v/t* (*ge-, h*) tame (*a. fig*); restrain, control (*children etc*)

Bandit [banˈdiːt] *m* (*-en; -en*) bandit, outlaw

'**Band|maß** *n* tape measure; ~**scheibe** *f* ANAT (intervertebral) disk (*Br* disc); ~**scheibenschaden** *m*, ~**scheibenvorfall** *m* MED slipped disk; ~**wurm** *m* ZO tapeworm

bange ['baŋə] *adj* afraid; anxious

'**Bange** *f*: **j-m ~ machen** frighten *or* scare *s.o.*; **keine ~!** (have) no fear!

'**bangen** *v/i* (*ge-, h*) be anxious *or* worried (**um** about)

Bank[1] [baŋk] *f* (*-; Bänke* ['bɛŋkə]) bench; **durch die ~** without exception; **auf die lange ~ schieben** put off

Bank[2] *f* (*-; -en*) bank; **auf der ~** in the bank

'**Bankangestellte** *m, f* bank clerk *or* employee

'**Bankauto,mat** *m* → **Geldautomat**

Bankett [baŋˈkɛt] *n* (*-[e]s; -e*) banquet

'**Bankgeschäfte** *pl* banking transactions

Bankier [baŋˈkjeː] *m* (*-s; -s*) banker

'**Bank|konto** *n* bank(ing) account; ~**leitzahl** *f* A.B.A. number, *Br* bank (sorting) code; ~**note** *f* bill, *Br* (bank) note; ~**raub** *m* bank robbery

bankrott [baŋˈkrɔt] *adj* ECON bankrupt

Bank'rott *m* (*-[e]s; -e*) ECON bankruptcy; **~ machen** go bankrupt

'**Bankverbindung** *f* account(s), account details

Bann [ban] *m* (*-[e]s; no pl*) ban; spell

'**bannen** *v/t* (*ge-, h*) ward off; (**wie**) **gebannt** spellbound

Banner ['banɐ] *n* (*-s; -*) banner (*a. fig*)

bar [baːɐ] *adj* (in) cash; **gegen ~** for cash

Bar *f* (*-; -s*) bar; nightclub

Bär [bɛːɐ] *m* (*-en; -en*) ZO bear

Baracke [baˈrakə] *f* (*-; -n*) hut; *contp* shack

Barbar [barˈbaːɐ] *m* (*-en; -en*) barbarian; **barbarisch** [barˈbaːrɪʃ] *adj* barbarous, *a.* atrocious (*crime etc*)

'**Bardame** f barmaid

'**barfuß** adj and adv barefoot

barg [bark] pret of **bergen**

'**Bargeld** n cash

'**bargeldlos** adj noncash

'**Barhocker** m bar stool

Bariton ['ba:riton] m (-s; -e ['ba:ri-
to:nə]) MUS baritone

Barkasse [bar'kasə] f (-; -n) MAR launch

barm'herzig adj merciful; charitable

Barm'herzigkeit f (-; no pl) mercy;
charity

'**Barmixer** m barman

Barometer [baro'me:tɐ] n (-s; -) barometer

Baron [ba'ro:n] m (-s; -e) baron

Ba'ronin f (-; -nen) baroness

Barren ['barən] m (-s; -) bar, ingot, a.
gold, silver bullion; SPORT parallel bars

Barriere [ba'rje:rə] f (-; -n) barrier

Barrikade [bari'ka:də] f (-; -n) barricade

barsch [barʃ] adj rough, gruff, brusque

Barsch m (-[e]s; -e) zo perch

'**Barscheck** m (negotiable) check, Br
open cheque

barst [barst] pret of **bersten**

Bart [ba:ɐt] m (-[e]s; Bärte ['bɛ:ɐtə])
beard; TECH bit; **sich e-n ~ wachsen
lassen** grow a beard

bärtig ['bɛ:ɐtɪç] adj bearded

'**Barzahlung** f cash payment

Basar [ba'za:ɐ] m (-s; -e) bazaar

Base ['ba:zə] f (-; -n) cousin; CHEM base

basieren [ba'zi:rən] v/i (no -ge-, h) ~ **auf**
(dat) be based on

Basis ['ba:zɪs] f (-; Basen) basis; MIL,
ARCH base

Baskenmütze ['baskənmytsə] f beret

Bass [bas] m (-es; Bässe ['bɛsə]) MUS
bass

Bassin [ba'sɛ̃:] n (-s; -s) basin; (swimming) pool

Bassist [ba'sɪst] m (-en; -en) MUS bass
singer or player

Bast [bast] m (-[e]s; -e) bast; HUNT velvet

Bastard ['bastart] m (-s; -e) BIOL hybrid;
mongrel; V bastard

basteln ['bastəln] (ge-, h) **1.** v/i make or
repair things o.s. **2.** v/t build, make

Bastler ['bastlɐ] m (-s; -) home handy-
man, do-it-yourselfer

bat [ba:t] pret of **bitten**

Batik ['ba:tɪk] m (-s; -en), f (-; -en) batik

Batist [ba'tɪst] m (-[e]s; -e) cambric

Batterie [batə'ri:] f (-; -n) ELECTR, MIL
battery

Bau [bau] m (-[e]s; Bauten) (no pl)
building, construction; build, frame;
building; zo (pl Baue) hole, den; **im
~** under construction; **~arbeiten** pl
construction work; road works; **~arbei-
ter** m construction worker; **~art** f style
(of construction); type, model

Bauch [baux] m (-[e]s; Bäuche ['bɔy-
çə]) belly (a. fig); ANAT abdomen; F
tummy

'**bauchig** adj bulgy

'**Bauch|landung** f AVIAT belly landing;
~redner m ventriloquist; **~schmerzen**
pl stomachache; **~tanz** m belly dancing

bauen ['bauən] (ge-, h) **1.** v/t build, construct, a. make (furniture etc) **2.** fig v/i: ~
auf (acc) rely or count on

Bauer¹ ['bauɐ] m (-n; -n) farmer; chess:
pawn

'**Bauer²** n, m (-s; -) (bird)cage

Bäuerin ['bɔyərɪn] f (-; -nen) farmer's
wife; farmer

bäuerlich ['bɔyərlɪç] adj rural; rustic

'**Bauern|fänger** contp m trickster, con-
man; **~haus** n farmhouse; **~hof** m
farm; **~möbel** pl rustic furniture

'**baufällig** adj dilapidated

'**Bau|firma** f builders and contractors;
~genehmigung f building permit;
~gerüst n scaffold(ing); **~herr** m owner; **~holz** n lumber, Br a. timber;
~inge,nieur m civil engineer; **~jahr** n
year of construction; **~ 1995** 1995 model; **~kasten** m box of building blocks
(Br bricks); TECH construction set;
kit; **~leiter** m building supervisor

'**baulich** adj structural

Baum [baum] m (-[e]s; Bäume
['bɔymə]) BOT tree

'**Baumarkt** m do-it-yourself superstore

baumeln ['bauməln] v/i (ge-, h) dangle,
swing; **mit den Beinen ~** dangle one's
legs

'**Baum|schule** f nursery; **~stamm** m
trunk; log; **~wolle** f cotton

'**Bau|plan** m architectural drawing;
blueprints; **~platz** m building site

Bausch [bauʃ] m (-[e]s; -e) wad, ball; **in
~ und Bogen** lock, stock and barrel

'**Bausparkasse** f building and loan association, Br building society

'**Bau|stein** m brick; (building) block; fig

B

element; **~stelle** f building site; MOT construction zone, Br roadworks; **~stil** m (architectural) style; **~stoff** m building material; **~techniker** m engineer; **~teil** n component (part), unit, module; **~unternehmer** m building contractor; **~vorschriften** pl building regulations; **~werk** n building; **~zaun** m hoarding; **~zeichner** m draftsman, Br draughtsman

Bayer ['baiɐ] m (-n; -n), **Bayerin** ['baiə-rɪn] f (-; -nen), **bay(e)risch** ['bai(ə)rɪʃ] adj Bavarian; **Bayern** ['baiɐn] Bavaria

Bazillus [ba'tsɪlus] m (-; -len) MED bacillus, germ

beabsichtigen [bə'ʔapzɪçtɪgən] v/t (no -ge-, h) intend, plan; **es war beabsichtigt** it was intentional

be'achten v/t (no -ge-, h) pay attention to; observe, follow (rule etc); **~ Sie, dass …** note that …; **nicht ~** take no notice of; disregard; **be'achtlich** adj remarkable; considerable

Be'achtung f (-; no pl) attention; consideration; observance

Beamte [bə'ʔamtə] m (-n; -n), **Be'amtin** f (-; -nen) official; (police etc) officer; civil servant

be'ängstigend adj alarming

beanspruchen [bə'ʔanʃpruxən] v/t (no -ge-, h) claim; take up (time etc); TECH stress; **Beanspruchung** f (-; -en) claim; TECH stress, strain (a. fig)

beanstanden [bə'ʔanʃtandən] v/t (no -ge-, h) complain about; object to

beantragen [bə'ʔantra:gən] v/t (no -ge-, h) apply for; JUR, PARL move (for); propose

be'antworten v/t (no -ge-, h) answer, reply to

be'arbeiten v/t (no -ge-, h) work; AGR till; hew (stone); process; be in charge of (a case etc); treat (subject); revise; THEA adapt (**nach** from); esp MUS arrange; F **j-n ~** work on s.o.

Be'arbeitung f (-; -en) working; revision; THEA adaptation; esp MUS arrangement; TECH processing, treatment

be'atmen v/t (no -ge-, h) MED give artificial respiration to s.o.

beaufsichtigen [bə'ʔaufzɪçtɪgən] v/t (no -ge-, h) supervise; look after; Be-'aufsichtigung f (-; -en) supervision;

looking after

be'auftragen v/t (no -ge-, h) commission; instruct; **~ mit** put s.o. in charge of; **Beauftragte** [bə'ʔauftra:ktə] m, f (-n; -n) agent; representative; commissioner

be'bauen v/t (no -ge-, h) build on; AGR cultivate

beben ['be:bən] v/i (ge-, h) shake, tremble; shiver (all: **vor** with); earth: quake

bebildern [bə'bɪldɐn] v/t (no -ge-, h) illustrate

Becher ['bɛçɐ] m (-s; -) cup, mug

Becken ['bɛkən] n (-s; -) basin, bowl; pool; ANAT pelvis; MUS cymbal(s)

bedacht [bə'daxt] adj: **darauf ~ sein zu** inf be anxious to inf

bedächtig [bə'dɛçtɪç] adj deliberate; measured

bedang [bə'daŋ] pret of **bedingen**

be'danken v/refl (no -ge-, h) **sich bei j-m für et. ~** thank s.o. for s.th.

Bedarf [bə'darf] m (-[e]s; no pl) need (**an** dat of), want (of); ECON demand (for); **bei ~** if necessary

Be'darfshaltestelle f request stop

bedauerlich [bə'dauɐlɪç] adj regrettable; **be'dauerlicher'weise** adv unfortunately

be'dauern v/t (no -ge-, h) feel or be sorry for s.o., pity s.o.; regret s.th.; Be-'dauern n (-s; no pl) regret (**über** at); **be'dauernswert** adj pitiable; deplorable

be'decken v/t (no -ge-, h) cover

be'deckt adj METEOR overcast

be'denken v/t (irr, **denken**, no -ge-, h) consider, think s.th. over; **Be'denken** pl doubts; scruples; objections

be'denkenlos adv unhesitatingly; without scruples

be'denklich adj doubtful; serious, critical; alarming

Be'denkzeit f: **e-e Stunde ~** one hour to think it over

be'deuten v/t (no -ge-, h) mean; **~d** adj important; considerable; distinguished

Be'deutung f (-; -en) meaning; importance; **be'deutungslos** adj insignificant; meaningless; **be'deutungsvoll** adj significant; meaningful

be'dienen (no -ge-, h) **1.** v/t serve, wait on s.o.; TECH operate, work; **sich ~** help o.s.; **~ Sie sich!** help yourself! **2.** v/i serve; wait (at table); *card games*: follow suit; Be'dienung *f* (-; -en) (*no pl*) service; waiter, waitress; shop assistant, clerk; TECH operation, control; Be-'dienungsanleitung *f* operating instructions

bedingen [bə'dɪŋən] v/t (*irr,*] *no ge-, h*) require; cause; imply, involve; be-'dingt *adj*: **~ durch** caused by, due to Be'dingung *f* (-; -en) condition; *pl* ECON terms; requirements; conditions; **unter einer ~** on one condition

be'dingungslos *adj* unconditional

be'drängen v/t (*no -ge-, h*) press (hard)

be'drohen v/t (*no -ge-, h*) threaten, menace; be'drohlich *adj* threatening; Be'drohung *f* threat, menace (*gen* to)

be'drücken v/t (*no -ge-, h*) depress, sadden

bedungen [bə'dʊŋən] *pp of* **bedingen**

Bedürfnis [bə'dyrfnɪs] *n* (-ses; -se) need, requirement (**für, nach** for); ~anstalt *f* comfort station, *Br* public convenience (*or* toilets)

be'dürftig *adj* needy, poor

be'eilen v/refl (*no -ge-, h*) hurry (up)

beeindrucken [bə'ʔaindrʊkən] v/t (*no -ge-, h*) impress

beeinflussen [bə'ʔainflʊsən] v/t (*no -ge-, h*) influence; affect

beeinträchtigen [bə'ʔaintrɛçtɪɡən] v/t (*no -ge-, h*) affect, impair

be'end(ig)en v/t (*no -ge-, h*) (bring to an) end, finish, conclude, close

beengen [bə'ɛŋən] v/t (*no -ge-, h*) make s.o. (feel) uncomfortable; be'engt *adj*: **~ wohnen** live in cramped quarters

be'erben v/t (*no -ge-, h*) **j-n ~** be s.o.'s heir

beerdigen [bə'ʔeːɐdɪɡən] v/t (*no -ge-, h*) bury; Be'erdigung *f* (-; -en) burial, funeral

Beere ['beːrə] *f* (-; -n) BOT berry; grape

Beet [beːt] *n* (-[e]s; -e) bed, patch

befähigen [bə'fɛːɪɡən] v/t (*no -ge-, h*) enable; qualify (**für, zu** for); be'fähigt *adj* (cap)able; **zu et. ~** fit *or* qualified for s.th.; Be'fähigung *f* (-; *no pl*) qualification(s), (cap)ability

befahl [bə'faːl] *pret of* **befehlen**

be'fahrbar *adj* passable, practicable; MAR navigable

be'fahren v/t (*irr,* **fahren,** *no -ge-,* h) drive *or* travel on; MAR navigate

be'fallen v/t (*irr,* **fallen,** *no -ge-,* h) attack, seize (*a. fig*)

be'fangen *adj* self-conscious; prejudiced, JUR *a.* bias(s)ed

Be'fangenheit *f* (-; *no pl*) self-consciousness; JUR bias, prejudice

be'fassen v/refl (*no -ge-,* h) **sich ~ mit** engage *or* occupy o.s. with; work on s.th.; deal with s.o., s.th.

Befehl [bə'feːl] *m* (-[e]s; -e) order; command (**über** *acc* of); be'fehlen v/t (*irr,* *no -ge-,* h) order; command

Be'fehlshaber *m* (-s; -) MIL commander

be'festigen v/t (*no -ge-,* h) fasten (**an** *dat* to), fix (to), attach (to); MIL fortify; Be'festigung *f* (-; -en) fixing, fastening; MIL fortification

be'feuchten v/t (*no -ge-,* h) moisten, damp

be'finden v/refl (*irr,* **finden,** *no -ge-,* h) be (situated); Be'finden *n* (-s; *no pl*) (state of) health

befohlen [bə'foːlən] *pp of* **befehlen**

be'folgen v/t (*no -ge-,* h) follow, take (advice); observe (rule etc); REL keep; Be'folgung *f* (-; *no pl*) following; observance

be'fördern v/t (*no -ge-,* h) carry, transport; haul, ship; promote (**zu** to); Be'förderung *f* (-; -en) (*no pl*) transport (-ation); shipment; promotion

be'fragen v/t (*no -ge-,* h) question, interview

be'freien v/t (*no -ge-,* h) free, liberate; rescue; exempt (**von** from); Be'freiung *f* (-; *no pl*) liberation; exemption

Befremden [bə'frɛmdən] *n* (-s; *no pl*) irritation, displeasure; be'fremdet *adj* irritated, displeased

befreunden [bə'frɔyndən] v/refl (*no -ge-,* h) **sich ~ mit** make friends with; *fig* warm to; be'freundet *adj* friendly; **~ sein** be friends

befriedigen [bə'friːdɪɡən] v/t (*no -ge-,* h) satisfy; **sich selbst ~** masturbate; ~d *adj* satisfactory; grade: fair

befriedigt [bə'friːdɪçt] *adj* satisfied, pleased

Be'friedigung *f* (-; *no pl*) satisfaction

be'fristet *adj* limited (**auf** *acc* to), temporary

be'fruchten v/t (no -ge-, h) BIOL fertilize, inseminate; Be'fruchtung f (-; -en) BIOL fertilization, insemination

Befugnis [bə'fu:knɪs] f (-; -se) authority; esp JUR competence; befugt [bə'fu:kt] adj authorized; competent

be'fühlen v/t (no -ge-, h) feel, touch

Be'fund m finding(s) (a. MED, JUR)

be'fürchten v/t (no -ge-, h) fear, be afraid of; suspect; Be'fürchtung f (-; -en) fear, suspicion

befürworten [bə'fy:ɛvɔrtən] v/t (no -ge-, h) advocate, speak or plead for; Be'fürworter m (-s; -) advocate

begabt [bə'ga:pt] adj gifted, talented Be'gabung f (-; -en) gift, talent(s)

begann [bə'gan] pret of **beginnen**

be'geben v/refl (irr, **geben**, no -ge-, h) **sich in Gefahr** ~ expose o.s. to danger

Be'gebenheit f (-; -en) incident, event

begegnen [bə'ge:gnən] v/i (no -ge-, sein) meet (a. fig **mit** with); **sich ~** meet

Be'gegnung f (-; -en) meeting, encounter (a. SPORT)

be'gehen v/t (irr, **gehen**, no -ge-, h) walk (on); celebrate (birthday etc); commit (crime); make (mistake); **ein Unrecht ~** do wrong

begehren [bə'ge:rən] v/t (no -ge-, h) desire; be'gehrenswert adj desirable

be'gehrlich adj desirous, covetous

begehrt [bə'ge:ɐt] adj (very) popular, (much) in demand

begeistern [bə'gaistən] v/t (no -ge-, h) fill with enthusiasm; carry away (audience); **sich ~ für** be enthusiastic about

be'geistert adj enthusiastic

Be'geisterung f (-; no pl) enthusiasm

Begierde [bə'gi:ɐdə] f (-; -n) desire (**nach** for), appetite (for)

be'gierig adj greedy; eager (**nach, auf** acc for; **zu** inf to inf)

be'gießen v/t (irr, **gießen**, no -ge-, h) water; GASTR baste; F fig celebrate s.th. (with a drink)

Beginn [bə'gin] m (-[e]s; no pl) beginning, start; **zu ~** at the beginning

be'ginnen v/t and v/i (irr, no -ge-, h) begin, start

beglaubigen [bə'glaubɪgən] v/t (no -ge-, h) attest, certify; Be'glaubigung f (-; -en) attestation, certification

be'gleichen v/t (irr, **gleichen**, no -ge-, h)

pay, settle

be'gleiten v/t (no -ge-, h) accompany (a. MUS **auf** dat on); **j-n nach Hause ~** see s.o. home; Be'gleiter(in) (-s; -/-; -nen) companion; MUS accompanist

Be'gleiterscheinung f concomitant; MED side effect; **~schreiben** n covering letter

Be'gleitung f (-; -en) company; esp MIL escort; MUS accompaniment

be'glückwünschen v/t (no -ge-, h) congratulate (**zu** on)

begnadigen [bə'gna:dɪgən] v/t (no -ge-, h), Be'gnadigung f (-; -en) JUR pardon; amnesty

begnügen [bə'gny:gən] v/refl (no -ge-, h) **sich ~ mit** be satisfied with; make do with

begonnen [bə'gɔnən] pp of **beginnen**

be'graben v/t (irr, **graben**, no -ge-, h) bury (a. fig); Be'gräbnis [bə'grɛ:pnɪs] n (-ses; -se) burial; funeral

begradigen [bə'gra:dɪgən] v/t (no -ge-, h) straighten

be'greifen v/t (irr, **greifen**, no -ge-, h) comprehend, understand

be'greiflich adj understandable

be'grenzen v/t (no -ge-, h) limit, restrict (**auf** acc to); be'grenzt adj limited

Be'griff m (-[e]s; -e) idea, notion; term (a. MATH); **im ~ sein zu** inf be about to inf; be'griffsstutzig contp adj F slow on the uptake

be'gründen v/t (no -ge-, h) give reasons for; be'gründet adj well-founded, justified; Be'gründung f (-; -en) reasons, arguments

be'grünen v/t (no -ge-, h) landscape

be'grüßen v/t (no -ge-, h) greet, welcome (a. fig); Be'grüßung f (-; -en) greeting, welcome

begünstigen [bə'gynstɪgən] v/t (no -ge-, h) favo(u)r

be'gutachten v/t (no -ge-, h) give an (expert's) opinion on; examine; **~ lassen** obtain expert opinion on

begütert [bə'gy:tɐt] adj wealthy

be'haart adj hairy

behäbig [bə'hɛ:bɪç] adj slow; portly

be'haftet adj: **mit Fehlern ~** flawed

behagen [bə'ha:gən] v/i (no -ge-, h) **j-m ~** please or suit s.o.; Be'hagen n (-s; no pl) pleasure, enjoyment; behaglich [bə'ha:klɪç] adj comfortable, cozy, snug

be'halten v/t (irr, **halten**, no -ge-, h) keep (fig **für sich** to o.s.); remember

Behälter [bəˈhɛltɐ] m (-s; -) container, receptacle

be'handeln v/t (no -ge-, h) handle; treat (a. MED); **sich (ärztlich) ~ lassen** undergo (medical) treatment

Be'handlung f (-; -en) handling; a. MED treatment

beharren [bəˈharən] v/i (no -ge-, h) insist (**auf** dat on)

be'harrlich adj persistent

behaupten [bəˈhauptən] v/t (no -ge-, h) claim; pretend; Be'hauptung f (-; -en) statement, claim

be'heben v/t (irr, **heben**, no -ge-, h) repair (damage etc)

be'heizen v/t (no -ge-, h) heat

be'helfen v/refl (irr, **helfen**, no -ge-, h) **sich ~ mit** make do with; **sich ~ ohne** do without

Be'helfs... in cpds mst temporary

beherbergen [bəˈhɛrbɛrgən] v/t (no -ge-, h) accommodate

be'herrschen v/t (no -ge-, h) rule (over), govern; ECON dominate, control; have (a good) command of (language); **sich ~** control o.s.; Be'herrschung f (-; no pl) command, control

beherzigen [bəˈhɛrtsɪgən] v/t (no -ge-, h) take to heart, mind

be'hilflich adj: **j-m ~ sein** help s.o. (**bei** with, in)

be'hindern v/t (no -ge-, h) hinder; obstruct (a. SPORT); be'hindert adj MED handicapped; disabled

Be'hinderung f (-; -en) obstruction; MED handicap

Behörde [bəˈhøːɐda] f (-; -n) authority, mst the authorities; board

be'hüten v/t (no -ge-, h) guard (**vor** dat from)

behutsam [bəˈhuːtzaːm] adj careful; gentle

bei [baɪ] prp (dat) near; at; with; by; time: during; at; ~ **München** near Munich; **wohnen** ~ stay (or live) with; ~ **mir** (**ihr**) at my (her) place; ~ **uns** (**zu Hause**) at home; **arbeiten** ~ work for; **e-e Stelle** ~ a job with; ~ **der Marine** in the navy; ~ **Familie Müller** at the Müllers'; ~ **Müller** c/o Müller; **ich habe kein Geld** ~ **mir** I have no money with

or on me; ~ **e-r Tasse Tee** over a cup of tea; **wir haben Englisch** ~ **Herrn X** we have Mr X for English; ~ **Licht** by light; ~ **Tag** during the day; ~ **Nacht** (**Sonnenaufgang**) at night (sunrise); ~ **s-r Geburt** at his birth; ~ **Regen** (**Gefahr**) in case of rain (danger); ~ **100 Grad** at a hundred degrees; → **Arbeit, beim, weit**

beibehalten v/t (irr, **halten**, sep, no -ge-, h) keep up, retain

beibringen v/t (irr, **bringen**, sep, no -ge-, h) teach; tell; inflict (dat on)

Beichte [ˈbaɪçtə] f (-; -n) REL confession

beichten v/t and v/i (ge-; h) REL confess (a. fig)

Beichtstuhl m REL confessional

beide [ˈbaɪdə] adj and pron both; **m-e** ~**n Brüder** my two brothers; **wir** ~ the two of us; both of us; **keiner von** ~**n** neither of them; **30** ~ tennis: 30 all

beiei'nander adv together

Beifahrer m front(-seat) passenger

Beifall m (-[e]s; no pl) applause; fig approval

Beifallssturm m (standing) ovation

beifügen v/t (sep, -ge-, h) enclose (dat with)

beige [beːʃ] adj beige

beigeben (irr, **geben**, sep, -ge-, h) **1.** v/t add **2.** F v/i: **klein** ~ knuckle under

Beigeschmack m smack (**von** of) (a. fig); ~**hilfe** f aid, allowance; JUR aiding and abetting

Beil [baɪl] n (-[e]s; -e) hatchet; ax(e)

Beilage f supplement; GASTR side dish; vegetables

beiläufig adj casual

beilegen v/t (sep, -ge-, h) add (dat to); enclose (with); settle (dispute)

Beilegung f (-; -en) settlement

Beileid n (-[e]s; no pl) condolence; **herzliches** ~ my deepest sympathy

beiliegen v/i (irr, **liegen**, sep, -ge-, h) be enclosed (dat with)

beim [baɪm] prp: ~ **Bäcker** at the baker's; ~ **Sprechen** etc while speaking etc; ~ **Spielen** at play; → a. **bei**

beimessen v/t (irr, **messen**, sep, -ge-, h) attach importance to (dat)

Bein [baɪn] n (-[e]s; -e) ANAT leg; bone

beinah(e) [ˈbaɪnaː(ə)] adv almost, nearly

Beinbruch m MED fracture of the leg

beipflichten v/i (sep, -ge-, h) agree (dat

B

with)

be'irren v/t (no -ge-, h) confuse

beisammen [bai'zamən] adv together

Bei'sammensein n: **geselliges ~** get-together

'Beischlaf m JUR sexual intercourse

bei'seite adv aside; **~schaffen** v/t (sep, -ge-, h) remove; liquidate s.o.

'beisetzen v/t (sep, -ge-, h) bury

'Beisetzung f (-; -en) funeral

'Beispiel n (-[e]s; -e) example; **zum ~** for example, for instance; **sich an j-m ein ~ nehmen** follow s.o.'s example

'beispiel|haft adj exemplary; **~los** adj unprecedented, unparalleled

'beispielsweise adv such as

beißen ['baisən] v/t and v/i (irr, -ge-, h) bite (a. fig); **sich ~** colors: clash; **~d** biting, pungent (both a. fig)

'Beistand m (-[e]s; no pl) assistance

'beistehen v/i (irr, stehen, sep, -ge-, h) **j-m ~** assist or help s.o.; **~steuern** v/t (sep, -ge-, h) contribute (**zu** to)

Beitrag ['baitra:k] m (-[e]s; Beiträge ['baitrɛːgə]) contribution; dues, Br subscription; 'beitragen v/t (irr, tragen, sep, -ge-, h) contribute (**zu** to)

'beitreten v/i (irr, treten, sep, -ge-, sein) join; 'Beitritt m (-[e]s; -e) joining

'Beiwagen m MOT sidecar

bei'zeiten adv early, in good time

beizen ['baitsən] v/t (ge-, h) stain (wood); pickle (meat)

bejahen [bə'ja:ən] v/t (no -ge-, h) answer in the affirmative, affirm; **~d** adj affirmative

bekannt [bə'kant] adj (well-)known; familiar; **et. ~ geben** announce s.th.; **j-n mit j-m ~ machen** introduce s.o. to s.o.; Be'kannte m, f (-n; -n) acquaintance, mst friend

be'kanntgeben v/t (irr, geben, sep, -ge-, h) →bekannt

be'kanntlich adv as you know

be'kanntmachen v/t (sep, -ge-, h) →bekannt; Be'kanntmachung f (-; -en) announcement

Be'kanntschaft f (-; -en) acquaintance

be'kehren v/t (no -ge-, h) convert

be'kennen v/t (irr, kennen, no -ge-, h) confess (a. REL); admit; **sich schuldig ~** JUR plead guilty; **sich ~ zu** profess

s.th.; claim responsibility for; Be'kennerbrief m letter claiming responsibility

Be'kenntnis n (-ses; -se) confession, REL a. denomination

be'klagen v/t (no -ge-, h) deplore; **sich ~** complain (**über** acc about)

be'klagenswert adj deplorable

be'kleben v/t (no -ge-, h) stick (or paste) on s.th.; **mit Etiketten ~** label s.th.

be'kleckern F v/t (no -ge-, h) stain; **sich ~ mit** spill s.th. over o.s.

Be'kleidung f (-; -en) clothing, clothes

be'kommen (irr, kommen, no -ge-) 1. v/t (h) get, receive; MED catch; be having (baby) 2. v/i (sein) **j-m (gut) ~** agree with s.o.; bekömmlich [bə'kœmlɪç] adj wholesome

be'kräftigen v/t (no -ge-, h) confirm

be'kreuzigen v/refl (no -ge-, h) cross o.s.

bekümmert [bə'kʏmɐt] adj worried

be'laden v/t (irr, laden, no -ge-, h) load, fig a. burden

Belag [bə'la:k] m (-[e]s; Beläge [bə-'lɛːgə]) covering; TECH coat(ing); MOT lining; (road) surface; MED fur; plaque; GASTR topping; spread; (sandwich) filling

be'lagern v/t (no -ge-, h) MIL besiege (a. fig); Be'lagerung f (-; -en) MIL siege

be'langlos adj irrelevant

be'lassen v/t (irr, lassen, no -ge-, h) leave; **es dabei ~** leave it at that

be'lastbar adj resistant to strain or stress; TECH loadable; be'lasten v/t (no -ge-, h) load; fig burden; JUR incriminate; pollute; damage; **j-s Konto ~ mit** charge s.th. to s.o.'s account

belästigen [bə'lɛstɪgən] v/t (no -ge-, h) molest; annoy; disturb, bother; Be'lästigung f (-; -en) molestation; annoyance; disturbance

Be'lastung f (-; -en) load (a. TECH); fig burden; strain; stress; JUR incrimination; pollution, contamination

Be'lastungszeuge m JUR witness for the prosecution

be'laufen v/refl (irr, laufen, no -ge-, h) **sich ~ auf** (acc) amount to

be'lauschen v/t (no -ge-, h) eavesdrop on

be'leben fig v/t (no -ge-, h) stimulate; **~d** adj stimulating

belebt [bə'le:pt] adj busy, crowded

Beleg [bə'le:k] *m* (-[e]s; -e) proof; receipt; document; **be'legen** *v/t* (*no -ge-*, *h*) cover; reserve (*seat*); prove; enrol(l) for, take (*classes*); GASTR put s.th. on; **den ersten** *etc* **Platz ~** SPORT take first *etc* place

Be'legschaft *f* (-; -en) staff

be'legt *adj* taken, occupied; *hotel etc*: full; TEL busy, *Br* engaged; MED coated; **~es Brot** sandwich

be'lehren *v/t* (*no -ge-*, *h*) teach, instruct, inform; **sich ~ lassen** take advice

beleidigen [bə'laidɪɡən] *v/t* (*no -ge-*, *h*) offend (*a. fig*), insult; **~d** *adj* offensive, insulting

Be'leidigung *f* (-; -en) offense, *Br* offence, insult

be'lesen *adj* well-read

be'leuchten *v/t* (*no -ge-*, *h*) light (up), illuminate (*a. fig*); *fig* throw light on

Be'leuchtung *f* (-; -en) light(ing); illumination

Belgien ['bɛlɡjən] Belgium; **Belgier** ['bɛlɡjɐ] *m* (-s; -), **Belgierin** ['bɛlɡjərɪn] *f* (-; -nen), '**belgisch** *adj* Belgian

be'lichten *v/t* (*no -ge-*, *h*) PHOT expose

Be'lichtungsmesser *m* PHOT exposure meter

Be'lieben *n*: **nach ~** at will

beliebig [bə'li:bɪç] *adj* any; optional; **jeder ~e** anyone

beliebt [bə'li:pt] *adj* popular (**bei** with)

Be'liebtheit *f* (-; *no pl*) popularity

be'liefern *v/t* (*no -ge-*, *h*) supply, furnish (**mit** with); **Be'lieferung** *f* supply

bellen ['bɛlən] *v/i* (*ge-*, *h*) bark (*a. fig*)

be'lohnen *v/t* (*no -ge-*, *h*) reward

Be'lohnung *f* (-; -en) reward; **zur ~** as a reward

be'lügen *v/t* (*irr*, **lügen**, *no -ge-*, *h*) **j-n ~** lie to s.o.

belustigen [bə'lustɪɡən] *v/t* (*no -ge-*, *h*) amuse; **belustigt** [bə'lustɪçt] *adj* amused; **Be'lustigung** *f* (-; -en) amusement

bemächtigen [bə'mɛçtɪɡən] *v/refl* (*no -ge-*, *h*) get hold of, seize

be'malen *v/t* (*no -ge-*, *h*) paint

bemängeln [bə'mɛŋəln] *v/t* (*no -ge-*, *h*) find fault with

bemannt [bə'mant] *adj* manned

be'merkbar *adj* noticeable; **sich ~ machen** draw attention to o.s.; begin to show; **be'merken** *v/t* (*no -ge-*, *h*) notice;

remark; **be'merkenswert** *adj* remarkable; **Be'merkung** *f* (-; -en) remark (**über** *acc* about)

be'mitleiden *v/t* (*no -ge-*, *h*) pity, feel sorry for; **be'mitleidenswert** *adj* pitiable

be'mühen *v/refl* (*no -ge-*, *h*) try (hard); **sich ~ um** try to get s.th.; try to help *s.o.*; **bitte, ~ Sie sich nicht!** please don't bother; **Be'mühung** *f* (-; -en) effort; **danke für Ihre ~en!** thank you for your trouble

be'muttern *v/t* (*no -ge-*, *h*) mother *s.o.*

be'nachbart *adj* neighbo(u)ring

benachrichtigen [bə'na:xrɪçtɪɡən] *v/t* (*no -ge-*, *h*) inform, notify

Be'nachrichtigung *f* (-; -en) information, notification

benachteiligen [bə'na:xtailɪɡən] *v/t* (*no -ge-*, *h*) place *s.o.* at a disadvantage; discriminate against *s.o.*; **benachteiligt** [bə'na:xtailɪçt] *adj* disadvantaged; **die Benachteiligten** the underprivileged; **Be'nachteiligung** *f* (-; -en) disadvantage; discrimination

be'nehmen *v/refl* (*irr*, **nehmen**, *no -ge-*, *h*) behave (o.s.); **Be'nehmen** *n* (-s; *no pl*) behavio(u)r; manners

be'neiden *v/t* (*no -ge-*, *h*) **j-n um et. ~** envy s.o. s.th.

be'neidenswert *adj* enviable

BENELUX [ben'neluks] *abbr of* **Belgien, Niederlande, Luxemburg** Belgium, the Netherlands and Luxembourg

be'nennen *v/t* (*irr*, **nennen**, *no -ge-*, *h*) name

Bengel ['bɛŋəl] *m* (-s; -) (little) rascal, urchin

benommen [bə'nɔmən] *adj* dazed, F dopey

be'noten *v/t* (*no -ge-*, *h*) grade, *Br* mark

be'nötigen *v/t* (*no -ge-*, *h*) need, want, require

be'nutzen *v/t* (*no -ge-*, *h*) use

Be'nutzer *m* (-s; -) user

be'nutzerfreundlich *adj* user-friendly

Be'nutzeroberfläche *f* IT user interface

Be'nutzung *f* use

Benzin [bɛn'tsi:n] *n* (-s; -e) gasoline, F gas, *Br* petrol

beobachten [bə'ʔo:baxtən] *v/t* (*no -ge-*, *h*) watch; observe

Be'obachter *m* (-s; -) observer

B

Be'obachtung f (-; -en) observation

be'pflanzen v/t (no -ge-, h) plant (**mit** with)

bequem [bə'kveːm] adj comfortable; easy; lazy; **be'quemen** v/refl (no -ge-, h) **sich ~ zu** inf bring o.s. to inf

Be'quemlichkeit f (-; -en) comfort; **alle ~en** all conveniences; (no pl) laziness

be'raten v/t (irr, **raten**, no -ge-, h) advise s.o.; debate, discuss s.th.; **sich ~** confer (**mit** j-m with s.o.; **über et.** on s.th.); Be'rater m (-s; -) adviser, consultant; Be'ratung f (-; -en) advice (a. MED); debate; consultation, conference; Be'ratungsstelle f counsel(l)ing center (Br centre)

be'rauben v/t (no -ge-, h) rob

be'rauschend adj intoxicating; F fig **nicht gerade ~!** not so hot!; be'rauscht fig adj: **~ von** drunk with

be'rechnen v/t (no -ge-, h) calculate; ECON charge (**zu** at); **~d** adj calculating

Be'rechnung f calculation (a. fig)

berechtigen [bə'rɛçtɪɡən] v/t: **j-n ~ zu** entitle (or authorize) s.o. to; berechtigt [bə'rɛçtɪçt] adj entitled (**zu** to); authorized (to); legitimate; Be'rechtigung f (-; no pl) right (**zu** to); authority

Beredsamkeit [bə'reːtzaːmkaɪt] f (-; no pl) eloquence

beredt [bə'reːt] adj eloquent (a. fig)

Be'reich m (-[e]s; -e) area; range; field

bereichern [bə'raɪçɐn] v/t (no -ge-, h) enrich; **sich ~** get rich (**an** dat on); Be'reicherung [bə'raɪçərʊŋ] f (-; no pl) enrichment

Be'reifung f (-; -en) (set of) tires (Br tyres)

be'reinigen v/t (no -ge-, h) settle

be'reisen v/t (no -ge-, h) tour; cover

bereit [bə'raɪt] adj ready, prepared; willing; **be'reiten** v/t (no -ge-, h) prepare; cause; **be'reithalten** v/t (irr, **halten**, sep, -ge-, h) have s.th. ready; **sich ~** stand by; **be'reits** adv already; Be'reitschaft f (-; no pl) readiness; **in ~** on standby; Be'reitschaftsdienst m: **~ haben** doctor etc: be on call; be'reitstellen v/t (sep, -ge-, h) provide; be'reitwillig adj ready, willing

be'reuen v/t (no -ge-, h) repent (of); regret

Berg [bɛrk] m (-[e]s; -e) mountain; **~e von** F loads of; **die Haare standen ihm zu ~e** his hair stood on end

berg'ab adv downhill (a. fig)

'Bergarbeiter m miner

berg'auf adv uphill

'Bergbahn f mountain railroad (Br railway); **~bau** m (-[e]s; no pl) mining

bergen ['bɛrɡən] v/t (irr, **ge-**, h) rescue, save s.o.; salvage s.th.; recover (body)

'Bergführer m mountain guide

bergig ['bɛrɡɪç] adj mountainous

'Bergkette f mountain range; **~mann** m (-[e]s; -leute) miner; **~rutsch** m landslide; **~schuhe** pl mountain(eering) boots; **~spitze** f (mountain) peak; **~steigen** n mountaineering, (mountain) climbing; **~steiger** m (-s; -) mountaineer, (mountain) climber

'Bergung f (-; -en) recovery; rescue

'Bergungsarbeiten pl rescue work; salvage operations

'Bergwacht f alpine rescue service

'Bergwerk n mine

Bericht [bə'rɪçt] m (-[e]s; -e) report (**über** acc on), account (of)

be'richten v/t and v/i (no -ge-, h) report (**über** acc on); **j-m et. ~** inform s.o. of s.th.; tell s.o. about s.th.

Be'richterstatter m (-s; -) reporter; correspondent; **~erstattung** f (-; -en) report(ing)

berichtigen [bə'rɪçtɪɡən] v/t (no -ge-, h) correct; Be'richtigung f (-; -en) correction

be'rieseln v/t (no -ge-, h) sprinkle

Bernstein ['bɛrnʃtaɪn] m (-s; no pl) amber

bersten ['bɛrstən] v/i (irr, -ge-, sein) burst (fig **vor** dat with)

berüchtigt [bə'rʏçtɪçt] adj notorious (**wegen** for)

berücksichtigen [bə'rʏkzɪçtɪɡən] v/t (no -ge-, h) take into consideration; **nicht ~** disregard

Be'rücksichtigung f: **unter ~** (gen) in consideration of

Be'ruf m (-[e]s; -e) job, occupation; trade; profession; be'rufen v/t (irr, **rufen**, no -ge-, h) appoint (**zu** [as] s.o.; to s.th.); **sich ~ auf** (acc) refer to

be'ruflich adj professional; **~ unterwegs** away on business

Be'rufs... in cpds ...sportler etc: professional ...;~**ausbildung** f vocational (or professional) training; ~**berater** m careers advisor; ~**beratung** f careers guidance; ~**bezeichnung** f job designation or title; ~**kleidung** f work clothes; ~**krankheit** f occupational disease; ~**schule** f vocational school

be'**rufstätig** adj: ~ **sein** (go to) work, have a job; Be'**rufstätige** m, f (-n; -n) working person, pl working people

Be'**rufsverkehr** m rush-hour traffic

Be'**rufung** f (-; -en) appointment (**zu** to); JUR appeal (**bei** to); **unter ~ auf** (acc) with reference to; on the grounds of

be'**ruhen** v/i (no -ge-, h) ~ **auf** (dat) be based on; et. **auf sich ~ lassen** let s.th. rest

beruhigen [bə'ru:ɪgən] v/t (no -ge-, h) quiet(en), calm, soothe; reassure s.o.; **sich ~** calm down; ~**d** adj reassuring; MED sedative

Be'**ruhigung** f (-; -en) calming (down); soothing; relief; Be'**ruhigungsmittel** n MED sedative; tranquil(l)izer

berühmt [bə'ry:mt] adj famous (**wegen** for); Be'**rühmtheit** f (-; -en) (no pl) fame; celebrity, star

be'**rühren** v/t (no -ge-, h) touch (a. fig); concern; Be'**rührung** f (-; -en) touch; **in ~ kommen** come into contact

Be'**rührungs|angst** f fear of contact; ~**punkt** m point of contact

besänftigen [bə'zɛnftɪgən] v/t (no -ge-, h) appease, calm, soothe

Be'**satzung** f (-; -en) AVIAT, MAR crew; MIL occupying forces

Be'**satzungs|macht** f MIL occupying power; ~**truppen** pl MIL occupying forces

be'**saufen** F v/refl (irr, **saufen**, no -ge-, h) get drunk, get bombed

be'**schädigen** v/t (no -ge-, h) damage

Be'**schädigung** f (-; -en) damage

be'**schaffen** v/t (no -ge-, h) provide, get; raise (money); Be'**schaffenheit** f (-; no pl) state, condition

beschäftigen [bə'ʃɛftɪgən] v/t (no -ge-, h) employ; keep s.o. busy; **sich ~** occupy o.s.; beschäftigt [bə'ʃɛftɪçt] adj busy, occupied; Be'**schäftigte** m, f (-n; -n) employed person, pl employed people; Be'**schäftigung** f (-; -en) employment; occupation

be'**schämen** v/t (no -ge-, h) shame s.o., make s.o. feel ashamed; ~**d** adj shameful; humiliating

be'**schämt** adj ashamed (**über** acc of)

be'**schatten** fig v/t (no -ge-, h) shadow, F tail

Bescheid [bə'ʃait] m (-[e]s; -e) answer; JUR decision; information (**über** acc on, about); **sagen Sie mir ~** let me know; (**gut**) ~ **wissen über** (acc) know all about

be'**scheiden** adj modest (a. fig); humble; Be'**scheidenheit** f (-; no pl) modesty

bescheinigen [bə'ʃainɪgən] v/t (no -ge-, h) certify

Be'**scheinigung** f (-; -en) (no pl) certification; certificate

be'**scheißen** V v/t (irr, **scheißen**, no -ge-, h) cheat; **j-n ~ um** do s.o. out of

be'**schenken** v/t (no -ge-, h) **j-n (reich)~** give s.o. (shower s.o. with) presents

Be'**scherung** f (-; -en) distribution of (Christmas) presents; F fig mess

be'**schichten** v/t (no -ge-, h) TECH coat

Be'**schichtung** f (-; -en) TECH coat

be'**schießen** v/t (irr, **schießen**, no -ge-, h) MIL fire or shoot at; bombard (a. PHYS), shell

be'**schimpfen** v/t (no -ge-, h) abuse, insult; swear at; Be'**schimpfung** f (-; -en) abuse, insult

be'**schissen** V adj lousy, rotten

Be'**schlag** m TECH metal fitting(s); **in ~ nehmen** monopolize s.o.; bag; occupy; be'**schlagen** (irr, **schlagen**, no -ge-) **1.** v/t (h) cover; TECH fit, mount; shoe (horse) **2.** v/i (sein) window etc: steam up **3.** adj steamed-up; fig well-versed (**auf**, **in** dat in)

Be'**schlagnahme** [bə'ʃla:kna:mə] f (-; -n) confiscation; be'**schlagnahmen** v/t (no -ge-, h) confiscate

beschleunigen [bə'ʃlɔynɪgən] v/t and v/i (no -ge-, h) accelerate, speed up; Be'**schleunigung** f (-; -en) acceleration

be'**schließen** v/t (irr, **schließen**, no -ge-, h) decide (on); pass (law); conclude; Be'**schluss** m decision

be'**schmieren** v/t (no -ge-, h) smear, soil; scrawl all over; cover wall etc with graffiti; spread (toast etc)

be'**schmutzen** v/t (no -ge-, h) soil (a.

B

fig), dirty

be'schneiden *v/t* (*irr,* **schneiden,** *no -ge-, h*) clip, cut (*a. fig*); prune; MED circumcise

be'schönigen [bəˈʃøːnɪɡən] *v/t* (*no -ge-, h*) gloss over

beschränken [bəˈʃrɛŋkən] *v/t* (*no -ge-, h*) confine, limit, restrict; **sich ~ auf** (*acc*) confine o.s. to; **be'schränkt** *adj* limited; *contp* dense; narrow-minded

Be'schränkung *f* (*-; -en*) limitation, restriction

be'schreiben *v/t* (*irr,* **schreiben,** *no -ge-, h*) describe; write on

Be'schreibung *f* (*-; -en*) description

be'schriften *v/t* (*no -ge-, h*) inscribe; mark (*goods*); Be'schriftung *f* (*-; -en*) inscription

beschuldigen [bəˈʃʊldɪɡən] *v/t* (*no -ge-, h*) blame; **j-n e-r Sache ~** accuse s.o. of s.th. (*a.* JUR); Be'schuldigung *f* (*-; -en*) accusation

be'schummeln F *v/t* (*no -ge-, h*) cheat

Be'schuss *m*: **unter ~** MIL under fire

be'schützen *v/t* (*no -ge-, h*) protect, shelter, guard (**vor** *dat* from)

Be'schützer *m* (*-s; -*) protector

Beschwerde [bəˈʃveːɐdə] *f* (*-; -n*) complaint (**über** *acc* about; **bei** to); *pl* MED complaints, trouble

beschweren [bəˈʃveːrən] *v/t* (*no -ge-, h*) weight *s.th.*; **sich ~** complain (**über** *acc* about; **bei** to)

be'schwerlich *adj* hard, arduous

beschwichtigen [bəˈʃvɪçtɪɡən] *v/t* (*no -ge-, h*) appease (*a.* POL), calm

be'schwindeln *v/t* (*no -ge-, h*) tell a fib *or* lie; cheat

beschwingt [bəˈʃvɪŋt] *adj* buoyant; MUS lively, swinging

beschwipst [bəˈʃvɪpst] F *adj* tipsy

be'schwören *v/t* (*irr,* **schwören,** *no -ge-, h*) swear to; implore; conjure up

beseitigen [bəˈzaɪtɪɡən] *v/t* (*no -ge-, h*) remove (*a. s.o.*), *a.* dispose of (*waste etc*); eliminate; POL liquidate

Be'seitigung *f* (*-; no pl*) removal; disposal; elimination

Besen ['beːzən] *m* (*-s; -*) broom

'Besenstiel *m* broomstick

besessen [bəˈzɛsən] *adj* obsessed (**von** by, with); **wie ~** like mad

be'setzen *v/t* (*no -ge-, h*) occupy (*a.* MIL); fill (*post etc*); THEA cast; trim; squat in; **be'setzt** *adj* occupied; *seat*: taken; *bus etc*: full up; TEL busy, *Br* engaged; Be'setztzeichen *n* TEL busy signal, *Br* engaged tone; Be'setzung *f* (*-; -en*) THEA cast; MIL occupation

besichtigen [bəˈzɪçtɪɡən] *v/t* (*no -ge-, h*) visit, see the sights of; inspect

Be'sichtigung *f* (*-; -en*) sightseeing; visit (*gen* to); inspection (of)

be'siedeln *v/t* (*no -ge-, h*) settle; colonize; populate; **be'siedelt** *adj*: **dicht** (**dünn**) ~ densely (sparsely) populated; Be'siedlung *f* (*-; -en*) settlement; colonization; population

be'siegeln *v/t* (*no -ge-, h*) seal

be'siegen *v/t* (*no -ge-, h*) defeat, beat; conquer (*a. fig*)

besinnen *v/refl* (*irr,* **sinnen,** *no -ge-, h*) remember; think (**auf** *acc* about); **sich anders ~** change one's mind

be'sinnlich *adj* contemplative

Be'sinnung *f* (*-; no pl*) MED consciousness; (**wieder**) **zur ~ kommen** MED come round; *fig* come to one's senses

be'sinnungslos *adj* MED unconscious

Be'sitz *m* (*-es; no pl*) possession; property; **~ ergreifen von** take possession of; be'sitzanzeigend *adj* LING possessive; be'sitzen *v/t* (*irr,* **sitzen,** *no -ge-, h*) possess, own; Be'sitzer *m* (*-s; -*) possessor, owner; **den ~ wechseln** change hands

besoffen [bəˈzɔfən] F *adj* drunk, plastered, stoned

be'sohlen [bəˈzoːlən] *v/t* (*no -ge-, h*) ~ **lassen** have (re)soled

Be'soldung *f* (*-; -en*) pay; salary

besondere [bəˈzɔndərə] *adj* special, particular; peculiar

Be'sonderheit *f* (*-; -en*) peculiarity

be'sonders *adv* especially, particularly; chiefly, mainly

be'sonnen *adj* prudent, level-headed

be'sorgen *v/t* (*no -ge-, h*) buy; → **erledigen**; Be'sorgnis [bəˈzɔrknɪs] *f* (*-; -se*) concern, alarm, anxiety (**über** *acc* about; at); **~ erregend → besorgniserregend**; be'sorgniserregend *adj* alarming; besorgt [bəˈzɔrkt] *adj* worried, concerned; Be'sorgung *f* (*-; -en*) **~en machen** go shopping

be'spielen *v/t* (*no -ge-, h*) make a recording on

be'spitzeln *v/t* (*no -ge-, h*) spy on *s.o.*

be'sprechen *v/t* (*irr,* **sprechen,** *no -ge-, h*) discuss, talk *s.th.* over; review (*book etc*); Be'sprechung *f* (-; *-en*) discussion, talk(s); meeting, conference; review

be'spritzen *v/t* (*no -ge-, h*) spatter

besser ['bɛsɐ] *adj and adv* better; **es ist ~, wir fragen ihn** we had better ask him; **immer ~** better and better; **es geht ihm ~** he is better; **oder ~ gesagt** or rather; **es ~ wissen** know better; **es ~ machen als** do better than; **~ ist ~** just to be on the safe side

'bessern *v/refl* (*ge-, h*) improve, get better; 'Besserung *f* (-; *no pl*) improvement; **auf dem Wege der ~** on the way to recovery; **gute ~!** get better soon

Besserwisser ['bɛsɐvɪsɐ] *m* (*-s;* -) F smart aleck

Be'stand *m* (*no pl*) (continued) existence; stock; **~ haben** last, be lasting

be'ständig *adj* constant, steady (*a. character*); settled; **...beständig** *in cpds* ...-resistant, ...proof

Be'standsaufnahme *f* ECON stocktaking (*a. fig*); **~ machen** take stock (*a. fig*)

Be'standteil *m* part, component

be'stärken *v/t* (*no -ge-, h*) confirm, strengthen, encourage (**in** *dat* in)

bestätigen [bə'ʃtɛːtɪɡən] *v/t* (*no -ge-, h*) confirm; certify; acknowledge (*receipt*); **sich ~** prove (to be) true; come true; **sich bestätigt fühlen** feel affirmed; Be'stätigung *f* (-; *-en*) confirmation; certificate; acknowledg(e)ment; letter of confirmation

bestatten [bə'ʃtatən] *v/t* (*no -ge-, h*) bury; Be'stattungsinsti,tut *n* funeral home, *Br* undertakers

be'stäuben *v/t* (*no -ge-, h*) dust; BOT pollinate

beste ['bɛstə] *adj and adv* best; **am ~n** best; **welches gefällt dir am ~n?** which one do you like best?; **am ~n nehmen Sie den Bus** it would be best to take a bus; Beste *m, f* (*-n;* -n), *n* (-n; *no pl*) the best; **das ~ geben** do one's best; **das ~ machen aus** make the best of; (*nur*) **zu deinem ~n** for your own good

be'stechen *v/t* (*irr,* **stechen,** *no -ge-, h*) bribe; fascinate (**durch** by)

be'stechlich *adj* corrupt

Be'stechung *f* (-; *-en*) bribery, corruption; Be'stechungsgeld *n* bribe

Besteck [bə'ʃtɛk] *n* (-[*e*]*s;* -e) (set of) knife, fork and spoon; cutlery

be'stehen (*irr,* **stehen,** *no -ge-, h*) **1.** *v/t* pass (*examination etc*) **2.** *v/i* be, exist; **~ auf** (*dat*) insist on; **~ aus** (**in**) (*dat*) consist of (in); **~ bleiben** last, survive

Be'stehen *n* (-s; *no pl*) existence

be'stehlen *v/t* (*irr,* **stehlen,** *no -ge-, h*) **j-n ~** steal s.o.'s money *etc*

be'steigen *v/t* (*irr,* **steigen,** *no -ge-, h*) climb; get on *a* bus *etc*; ascend (*the throne*)

be'stellen *v/t* (*no -ge-, h*) order; book (*room etc*); reserve (*seat etc*); call (*taxi*); give, send (*message etc*); AGR cultivate; **kann ich et. ~?** can I take a order?; **~ Sie ihm bitte, ...** please tell him ...

Be'stellschein *m* ECON order form

Be'stellung *f* (-; *-en*) booking; reservation; ECON order; **auf ~** to order

'bestenfalls *adv* at best

'bestens *adv* very well

bestialisch [bɛs'tjaːlɪʃ] *adj fig* bestial

Bestie ['bɛstjə] *f* (-; *-n*) beast, *fig a.* brute

be'stimmen *v/t* (*no -ge-, h*) determine, decide; define; choose, pick; **zu ~ haben** be in charge, F be the boss; **bestimmt für** meant for; **be'stimmt 1.** *adj* determined, firm; LING definite (*article*); **~e Dinge** certain things **2.** *adv* certainly; **ganz ~** definitely; **er ist ~ ...** he must be ...; Be'stimmung *f* (-; *-en*) regulation; destiny

Be'stimmungsort *m* destination

'Bestleistung *f* SPORT (personal) record

be'strafen *v/t* (*no -ge-, h*) punish

Be'strafung *f* (-; *-en*) punishment

be'strahlen *v/t* (*no -ge-, h*) irradiate (*a.* MED); Be'strahlung *f* (-; *-en*) irradiation; MED ray treatment, radiotherapy

be'streichen *v/t* (*irr,* **streichen,** *no -ge-, h*) spread; be'streiten *v/t* (*irr,* **streiten,** *no -ge-, h*) challenge; deny; pay for, finance; be'streuen *v/t* (*no -ge-, h*) sprinkle (**mit** with); be'stürmen *v/t* (*no -ge-, h*) urge; bombard

be'stürzt *adj* dismayed (**über** *acc* at); Be'stürzung *f* (-; *no pl*) consternation, dismay

Besuch [bə'zuːx] *m* (-[*e*]*s;* -e) visit (*gen, bei, in* *dat* to); call (*bei* on; *in* *dat* at); attendance (*gen* at); **~ haben** have company *or* guests; be'suchen *v/t*

B

(no -ge-, h) visit; call on, (go to) see; look *s.o.* up; attend (*meeting etc*); go to (*pub etc*); **Be'sucher(in)** (*-s; -/-; -nen*) visitor, guest; **Be'suchszeit** f visiting hours; **be'sucht** adj: **gut (schlecht)** ~ well (poorly) attended; much (little) frequented

betagt [bə'ta:kt] adj aged

be'tasten v/t (no -ge-, h) touch, feel

be'tätigen v/t (no -ge-, h) TECH operate; apply (*brake*); **sich** ~ be active

Be'tätigung f (-; -en) activity

betäuben [bə'tɔybən] v/t (no -ge-, h) stun (a. fig), daze; MED an(a)esthetize

Be'täubung f (-; -en) MED an(a)esthetization; an(a)esthesia; fig daze, stupor

Be'täubungsmittel n MED an(a)esthetic; narcotic

Bete ['be:tə] f (-; -) **rote** ~ BOT beet, Br beetroot

beteiligen [bə'tailıgən] v/t (no -ge-, h) **j-n** ~ give s.o. a share (**an** dat in); **sich** ~ take part (**an** dat, **bei** in), participate (in) (a. JUR); **beteiligt** [bə'tailıçt] adj concerned; ~ **sein an** (dat) be involved in; ECON have a share in; **Be'teiligung** f (-; -en) participation (a. JUR, ECON); involvement; share (a. ECON)

beten ['be:tən] v/i (ge-, h) pray (**um** for), say one's prayers; say grace

beteuern [bə'tɔyɐn] v/t (no -ge-, h) protest (*one's innocence etc*)

Beton [be'tɔŋ] m (-s; -s, -e [be'to:nə]) concrete

betonen [bə'to:nən] v/t (no -ge-, h) stress, fig a. emphasize

betonieren [beto'ni:rən] v/t (no -ge-, h) (cover with) concrete

Be'tonung f (-; -en) stress; fig emphasis

betören [bə'tø:rən] v/t (no -ge-, h) infatuate, bewitch

Betr. abbr of **betrifft** re

Betracht [bə'traxt] m: **in** ~ **ziehen** take into consideration; **nicht in** ~ **kommen** be out of the question

be'trachten v/t (no -ge-, h) look at, fig a. view; ~ **als** look upon or regard as, consider; **Be'trachter** m (-s; -) viewer

beträchtlich [bə'trεçtlıç] adj considerable

Be'trachtung f (-; -en) view; **bei näherer** ~ on closer inspection

Betrag [bə'tra:k] m (-[e]s; **Beträge** [bə-'trε:gə]) amount, sum; **be'tragen** (*irr*, **tragen**, no -ge-, h) **1.** v/t amount to **2.** v/refl behave (o.s.); **Be'tragen** n (-s; no pl) behavio(u)r, conduct

be'trauen v/t (no -ge-, h) entrust (**mit** with)

be'treffen v/t (irr, **treffen**, no -ge-, h) concern; refer to; **was ... betrifft** as for ..., as to ...; **betrifft** (abbr **Betr.**) re; ~**d** adj concerning; **die** ~**en Personen** etc the people etc concerned

be'treiben v/t (irr, **treiben**, no -ge-, h) operate, run; go in for (*sport etc*)

be'treten[1] v/t (irr, **treten**, no -ge-, h) step on; enter; **Betreten (des Rasens) verboten!** keep out! (keep off the grass!)

be'treten[2] adj embarrassed

betreuen [bə'trɔyən] v/t (no -ge-, h) look after, take care of; **Be'treuung** f (-; no pl) care (gen of, for)

Betrieb [bə'tri:p] m (-[e]s; -e) business, firm, company; (no pl) operation, running; (no pl) rush; **in** ~ **sein (setzen)** be in (put into) operation; **außer** ~ out of order; **im Geschäft war viel** ~ the shop was very busy

Be'triebs|anleitung f operating instructions; ~**berater** m business consultant; ~**ferien** pl company (Br a. works) holiday; ~**fest** n annual company fête; ~**kapi tal** n working capital; ~**klima** n working atmosphere; ~**kosten** pl operating costs; ~**leitung** f management; ~**rat** m works council

be'triebssicher adj safe to operate

Be'triebs|störung f TECH breakdown; ~**sys,tem** n IT operating system; ~**unfall** m industrial accident; ~**wirtschaft** f business administration

be'trinken v/refl (irr, **trinken**, no -ge-, h) get drunk

betroffen [bə'trɔfən] adj affected, concerned; dismayed, shocked; **Be'troffenheit** f (-; no pl) dismay, shock

betrübt [bə'try:pt] adj sad, grieved (**über** acc at)

Betrug [bə'tru:k] m (-[e]s; no pl) cheat; JUR fraud; deceit; **be'trügen** v/t (irr, **trügen**, no -ge-, h) deceive; cheat (**beim Kartenspiel** at cards); swindle, trick (**um et.** out of s.th.); be unfaithful to; **Be'trüger(in)** (-s; -/-; -nen) swindler, trickster

betrunken [bə'trʊŋkən] adj drunken; ~

sein be drunk

Be'trunkene *m, f (-n; -n)* drunk

Bett [bɛt] *n (-[e]s; -en)* bed; ***am ~*** at the bedside; ***ins ~ gehen*** (***bringen***) go (put) to bed; **~bezug** *m* comforter case, *Br* duvet cover; **~decke** *f* blanket; quilt

betteln ['bɛtəln] *v/i (ge-, h)* beg (***um*** for)

'Bettgestell *n* bedstead

bettlägerig ['bɛtlɛːgərɪç] *adj* bedridden

'Bettlaken *n* sheet

Bettler ['bɛtlɐ] *m (-s; -)* beggar

Bett|nässer ['bɛtnɛsɐ] *m (-s; -)* MED bed wetter; **~ruhe** *f* bed rest; ***j-m ~ verordnen*** tell s.o. to stay in bed; **~vorleger** *m* bedside rug; **~wäsche** *f* bed linen; **~zeug** *n* bedding, bedclothes

beugen ['bɔʏɡən] *v/t (ge-, h)* bend; LING inflect; ***sich ~*** (***vor*** *dat* to) bend, bow

Beule ['bɔʏlə] *f (-; -n)* MED bump; MOT dent

beunruhigen [bə'ʔʊnruːɪɡən] *v/t (no -ge-, h)* alarm, worry

beurlauben [bə'ʔuːɐlaʊbən] *v/t* give *s.o.* leave *or* time off; suspend; ***sich ~ lassen*** ask for leave; beurlaubt [bə-'ʔuːɐlaʊpt] *adj* on leave

be'urteilen *v/t (no -ge-, h)* judge (***nach*** by); rate; Be'urteilung *f (-; -en)* judg(e)-ment; evaluation

Beute ['bɔʏtə] *f (-; no pl)* booty, loot; ZO prey (*a. fig*); HUNT bag; *fig a.* victim

Beutel ['bɔʏtəl] *m (-s; -)* bag; pouch

bevölkern [bə'fœlkɐn] *v/t (no -ge-, h)* populate; dicht **~** ***besiedelt***; Be-'völkerung *f (-; -en)* population

bevollmächtigen [bə'fɔlmɛçtɪɡən] *v/t (no -ge-, h)* authorize

be'vor *cj* before

bevor|munden [bə'foːɐmʊndən] *v/t (no -ge-, h)* patronize; **~stehen** *v/i (irr,* **stehen,** *sep, -ge-, h)* be approaching; lie ahead; be imminent; ***j-m ~*** be in store for s.o., await s.o.

bevorzugen [bə'foːɐtsuːɡən] *v/t (no -ge-, h)* prefer; favo(u)r; Be-'vorzugung *f (-; -en)* preferential treatment

be'wachen *v/t (no -ge-, h)* guard, watch over; Be'wacher *m (-s; -)* guard; SPORT marker; Be'wachung *f (-; -en) no pl* guarding; SPORT marking; guard

bewaffnen [bə'vafnən] *v/t (no -ge-, h)* arm (*a. fig*); Be'waffnung *f (-; -en)* ar-

mament; arms

be'wahren *v/t (no -ge-, h)* keep; **~ vor** (*dat*) keep *or* save from

be'währen *v/refl (no -ge-, h)* prove successful; ***sich ~ als*** prove to be

bewährt [bə'vɛːɐt] *adj* (well-)tried, reliable; experienced; Be'währung *f (-; -en)* JUR probation

Be'währungs|frist *f* JUR (period of) probation; **~helfer** *m* JUR probation officer; **~probe** *f* (acid) test

bewaldet [bə'valdət] *adj* wooded, woody

bewältigen [bə'vɛltɪɡən] *v/t (no -ge-, h)* manage, cope with; cover (*distance*)

be'wandert *adj* (well-)versed (***in*** *dat* in)

be'wässern *v/t (no -ge-, h)* irrigate; Be-'wässerung *f (-; -en)* irrigation

bewegen [bə've:ɡən] *v/t and v/refl (no -ge-, h)* move (*a. fig*); ***nicht ~!*** don't move!; (*irr*) ***j-n zu et. ~*** get s.o. to do s.th.

Be'weggrund *m* motive

beweglich [bə've:klɪç] *adj* movable; agile; flexible; TECH moving (*parts*); Be'weglichkeit *f (-; no pl)* mobility; agility; be'wegt *adj* rough (*sea*); choked (*voice*); eventful (*life*); *fig* moved, touched; Be'wegung *f (-; -en)* movement (*a.* POL); motion (*a.* PHYS); exercise; *fig* emotion; ***in ~ setzen*** set in motion; Be-'wegungsfreiheit *f (-; no pl)* freedom of movement (*fig a.* of action); be-'wegungslos *adj* motionless

Beweis [bə'vais] *m (-es; -e)* proof (***für*** of); **~(e)** evidence (*esp* JUR)

be'weisen *v/t (irr,* **weisen,** *no -ge-, h)* prove; show

Be'weismittel *n* JUR (piece of) evidence

Be'weisstück *n* (piece of) evidence, JUR exhibit

be'wenden *v/i:* ***es dabei ~ lassen*** leave it at that

be'werben *v/refl (irr,* **werben,** *no -ge-, h)* ***sich ~ um*** apply for; Be'werber(in) *(-s; -/-; -nen)* applicant; Be'werbung *f (-; -en)* application; Be-'werbungsschreiben *n* (letter of) application

be'werten *v/t (no -ge-, h)* assess; judge; Be'wertung *f (-; -en)* assessment

bewilligen [bə'vɪlɪɡən] *v/t (no -ge-, h)* grant, allow; be'wirken *v/t (no -ge-,*

B

h) cause; **bewirten** [bə'vɪrtən] *v/t* (*no -ge-, h*) entertain

be'wirtschaften *v/t* (*no -ge-, h*) run; AGR farm; be'wirtschaftet *adj* open (to the public)

Be'wirtung *f* (-; -*en*) catering; service; hospitality

bewog [bə'vo:k] *pret of* **bewegen**

bewogen [bə'vo:gən] *pp of* **bewegen**

be'wohnen *v/t* (*no -ge-, h*) live in; inhabit; Be'wohner(in) (-*s*; -/-; -*nen*) inhabitant; occupant; be'wohnt *adj* inhabited; occupied

bewölken [bə'vœlkən] *v/refl* (*no -ge-, h*) METEOR cloud over (*a. fig*); be'wölkt *adj* METEOR cloudy, overcast

Be'wölkung *f* (-; *no pl*) METEOR clouds

Bewunderer [bə'vundərɐ] *m* (-*s*; -) admirer; be'wundern *v/t* (*no -ge-, h*) admire (*wegen* for); be'wundernswert *adj* admirable; Be'wunderung *f* (-; *no pl*) admiration

bewusst [bə'vʊst] *adj* conscious; intentional; *sich e-r Sache ~ sein* be conscious *or* aware of s.th., realize s.th.; *j-m et. ~ machen* make s.o. realize s.th.

be'wusstlos *adj* MED unconscious

be'wusstsein *n* (-*s*; *no pl*) MED consciousness; *bei ~* conscious

be'zahlen *v/t* (*no -ge-, h*) pay; pay for (*a. fig*); be'zahlt *adj*: *~er Urlaub* paid leave; *es macht sich ~* it pays; Be'zahlung *f* (-; *no pl*) payment; pay

be'zaubern *v/t* (*no -ge-, h*) charm; ~*d adj* charming, F sweet, darling

be'zeichnen *v/t* (*no -ge-, h*) ~ *als* call, describe as; ~*d adj* characteristic, typical (*für* of)

Be'zeichnung *f* (-; -*en*) name, term

be'zeugen *v/t* (*no -ge-, h*) JUR testify to

be'ziehen *v/t* (*irr, ziehen, no -ge-, h*) cover; put clean sheets on (*bed*); move into; receive; subscribe to (*paper etc*); ~ *auf* (*acc*) relate to; *sich ~* cloud over; *sich ~ auf* (*acc*) refer to; Be'ziehung *f* (-; -*en*) relation (*zu* to s.th.; with s.o.); connection (*zu* with); relationship; respect; ~*en haben* have connections

be'ziehungsweise *cj* respectively; or; or rather

Bezirk [bə'tsɪrk] *m* (-[*e*]*s*; -*e*) precinct,

Br *a.* district

Bezug [bə'tsu:k] *m* (-[*e*]*s*; *Bezüge* [bə-'tsy:gə]) cover(ing); case, slip; (*no pl*) ECON purchase; subscription (*gen* to); *pl* earnings; ~ *nehmen auf* (*acc*) refer to; *in ~ auf* (*acc*) → **bezüglich**

bezüglich [bə'tsy:klɪç] *prp* (*gen*) regarding, concerning

Be'zugsˌperˌson *f* PSYCH person to relate to, role model; ~*punkt* *m* reference point; ~*quelle* *f* source (of supply)

be'zwecken *v/t* (*no -ge-, h*) aim at, intend; be'zweifeln *v/t* (*no -ge-, h*) doubt, question; be'zwingen *v/t* (*irr, zwingen, no -ge-, h*) conquer, defeat

Bibel ['bi:bəl] *f* (-; -*n*) Bible

Biber ['bi:bɐ] *m* (-*s*; -) zo beaver

Bibliothek [biblio'te:k] *f* (-; -*en*) library

Bibliothekar [bibliote'ka:ɐ] *m* (-*s*; -*e*), Bibliothe'karin *f* (-; -*nen*) librarian

biblisch ['bi:blɪʃ] *adj* biblical

bieder ['bi:dɐ] *adj* honest; square

biegen ['bi:gən] *v/t* (*irr, ge-, h*) *and v/i* (*sein*) bend (*a. sich ~*), road: *a.* turn; *um die Ecke ~* turn (round) the corner

biegsam ['bi:kza:m] *adj* flexible

'Biegung *f* (-; -*en*) curve

Biene ['bi:nə] *f* (-; -*n*) zo bee

'Bienenˌkönigin *f* zo queen (bee); ~*korb* *m*, ~*stock* *m* (bee)hive; ~*wachs* *n* beeswax

Bier [bi:ɐ] *n* (-[*e*]*s*; -*e*) beer; *vom Faß* draft (Br draught) beer; ~*deckel* *m* coaster, beer mat; ~*krug* *m* beer mug, stein

Biest [bi:st] F *fig n* (-[*e*]*s*; -*er*) beast; (*kleines*) ~ brat, little devil, stinker

bieten ['bi:tən] (*irr, ge-, h*) **1.** *v/t* offer; *sich ~* present itself **2.** *v/i* auction: (make a) bid

Bigamie [biga'mi:] *f* (-; -*n*) bigamy

Bikini [bi'ki:ni] *m* (-*s*; -*s*) bikini

Bilanz [bi'lants] *f* (-; -*en*) ECON balance; *fig* result; ~ *ziehen aus* (*dat*) *fig* take stock of

Bild [bɪlt] *n* (-[*e*]*s*; -*er* ['bɪldɐ]) picture; image; *sich ein ~ machen von* get an idea of; ~*ausfall* *m* TV blackout; ~*bericht* *m* photo(graphic) essay (Br report)

bilden ['bɪldən] *v/t* (*ge-, h*) form (*a. sich ~*); shape; *fig* educate (*sich* o.s.); be, constitute

'Bilderbuch *n* picture book

'Bild|fläche f: F **auf der ~ erscheinen** (**von der ~ verschwinden**) appear on (disappear from) the scene

'Bildhauer m (-s; -), 'Bildhauerin f (-; -nen) sculptor

'bildlich adj graphic; figurative

'Bildnis n (-ses; -se) portrait

'Bildplatte f videodisk (Br -disc)

'Bildröhre f picture tube

'Bildschirm m TV screen, IT a. display, monitor; ~schoner m (-s; -) screen saver; ~text m videotext, Br viewdata

'bild'schön adj most beautiful

'Bildung f (-; -en) (no pl) education; formation

'Bildungs... in cpds ...chancen, ...reform, ...urlaub etc: educational...; ~lücke f gap in one's knowledge

'Bildunterschrift f caption

Billard ['bɪljart] n (-s; -e) billiards, pool; ~kugel f billiard ball; ~stock m cue

Billett [bɪl'jɛt] n (-[e]s; -e) Swiss ticket

billig ['bɪlɪç] adj cheap (a. contp), inexpensive

billigen ['bɪlɪɡən] v/t (ge-, h) approve of; 'Billigung f (-; no pl) approval

Billion [bɪl'joːn] f (-; -en) trillion

bimmeln ['bɪməln] F v/i (ge-, h) jingle, TEL ring

binär [bi'nɛːɐ] adj MATH, PHYS etc binary

Binde ['bɪndə] f (-; -n) bandage; sling; → **Damenbinde**; ~gewebe n ANAT connective tissue; ~glied n (connecting) link

'Bindehaut f ANAT conjunctiva; ~entzündung f MED conjunctivitis

binden (irr, ge-, h) **1.** v/t bind (a. book), tie (**an** acc to); make (wreath etc); knot (tie); **sich ~** bind or commit o.s. **2.** v/i bind

'Bindestrich m LING hyphen

'Bindewort n LING conjunction

'Bindfaden m ['bɪntfaːdən] m string

'Bindung f (-; -en) tie, link, bond; skiing: binding

Binnen|hafen m ['bɪnənhaːfən] m inland port; ~handel m domestic trade; ~markt m: **Europäischer ~** European single market; ~schifffahrt f inland navigation; ~verkehr m inland traffic or transport

Binse ['bɪnzə] f (-; -n) BOT rush

'Binsenweisheit f (-; -en) truism

Bio..., bio... [bio-] in cpds ...chemie,

...dynamisch, ...sphäre etc: bio...

Biografie, Biographie [biogra'fiː] f (-; -n) biography

bio'grafisch, bio'graphisch adj biographic(al)

Bioladen ['biːolaːdən] m health food shop or store

Biologe [bio'loːɡə] m (-n; -n) biologist

Biologie [biolo'giː] f (-; no pl) biology

Bio'login f (-; -nen) biologist

biologisch [bio'loːɡɪʃ] adj biological; AGR organic; **~ abbaubar** biodegradable

'Biorhythmus m biorhythms

Biotechnik f (-; no pl) biotechnology

Biotop [bio'toːp] n (-s; -e) biotope

Birke ['bɪrkə] f (-; -n) birch (tree)

Birne ['bɪrnə] f (-; -n) BOT pear; ELECTR (light) bulb

bis [bɪs] prp (acc) and adv and cj time: till, until, (up) to; space: (up) to, as far as; **von ... ~ ...** from ... to ...; **~ auf** (acc) except; **~ zu** up to; **~ später!** see you later!; **~ jetzt** up to now, so far; **~ Montag** by Monday; **zwei ~ drei** two or three; **wie weit ist es ~ ...?** how far is it to ...?

Bischof ['bɪʃɔf] m (-s; Bischöfe ['bɪʃœfə]) REL bishop

bisexuell [bizɛ'ksuɛl] adj bisexual

bis'her adv up to now, so far; **wie ~** as before

bisherig [bɪs'heːrɪç] adj previous

Biskuit [bɪs'kviːt] n (-[e]s; -e) sponge cake (mix)

biss [bɪs] pret of **beißen**

Biss m (-es; -e) bite (a. fig)

bisschen ['bɪsçən] adj and adv: **ein ~** a little, a (little) bit (of); **nicht ein ~** not in the least

Bissen ['bɪsən] m (-s; -) bite; **keinen ~** not a thing

bissig ['bɪsɪç] adj fig cutting; **ein ~er Hund** a dog that bites; **Vorsicht, ~er Hund!** beware of the dog!

Bistum ['bɪstuːm] n (-s; Bistümer ['bɪstyːmɐ]) REL bishopric, diocese

bis'weilen adv at times, now and then

Bit [bɪt] n (-[s]; -[s]) IT bit

bitte ['bɪtə] adv please; **~ nicht!** please don't!; **~ (schön)!** that's all right, not at all, you're welcome; here you are; (**wie**) **~?** pardon?; **~ sehr?** can I help you?; 'Bitte f (-; -n) request (**um** for);

B

ich habe e-e ~ (an dich) I have a favo(u)r to ask you; **'bitten** v/t (irr, ge-, h) **j-n um et. ~** ask s.o. for s.th.; **darf ich..?** may I have (the pleasure of) this dance?; → **Erlaubnis**

bitter ['bɪtɐ] adj bitter (a. fig), a. biting (cold); **~'kalt** adj bitterly cold

blähen ['blɛːən] v/refl (ge-, h) swell

'Blähungen pl MED flatulence, Br a. wind

blamabel [bla'maːbəl] adj embarrassing; **Blamage** [bla'maːʒə] f (-; -n) disgrace, shame; **blamieren** [bla'miːrən] v/t (no -ge-, h) **j-n ~** make s.o. look like a fool; **sich ~** make a fool of o.s.

blank [blaŋk] adj shining, shiny, bright; polished; F broke

Blanko... ['blaŋko] in cpds ECON blank

Bläschen ['blɛːsçən] n (-s; -) MED vesicle, small blister

Blase ['blaːzə] f (-; -n) bubble; ANAT bladder; MED blister

'Blasebalg m (pair of) bellows

'blasen v/t (irr, ge-, h) blow (a. MUS)

'Blas|instru, ment n MUS wind instrument; **~ka,pelle** f brass band; **~rohr** n blowpipe

blass [blas] adj pale (vor with); **~ werden** turn pale; **Blässe** ['blɛsə] f (-; no pl) paleness, pallor

Blatt [blat] n (-[e]s; Blätter ['blɛtɐ]) BOT leaf; piece, sheet (a. MUS); (news)paper; card games: hand; **blättern** ['blɛtɐn] v/i (ge-, h) **~ in** (dat) leaf through

'Blätterteig m puff pastry

blau [blau] adj blue; F loaded, stoned; **~es Auge** black eye; **~er Fleck** bruise; **Fahrt ins Blaue** mystery tour

blauäugig ['blauɔygɪç] adj blue-eyed; fig starry-eyed

'Blaubeere f BOT blueberry, Br bilberry

'blaugrau adj bluish-gray (Br -grey)

bläulich ['blɔylɪç] adj bluish

'Blaulicht n (-[e]s; -er) flashing light(s)

'blaumachen F v/i (sep, -ge-, h) stay away from work or school

'Blausäure f CHEM prussic acid

Blech [blɛç] n (-[e]s; -e) sheet metal; in cpds ...dach, ...löffel etc: tin ...; ...instrument: MUS brass ...

'Blech|büchse, ~dose f can, Br a. tin

'blechen F v/t and v/i (ge-, h) shell out

'Blechschaden m MOT bodywork damage

Blei [blai] n (-[e]s; -e) lead; **aus ~** leaden

Bleibe ['blaibə] f (-; -n) place to stay

'bleiben v/i (irr, ge-, sein) stay, remain; **~ bei** stick to; F **et. ~ lassen** not do s.th.; **lass das ~!** stop that!; **das wirst du schön ~ lassen!** you'll do nothing of the sort!; → **Apparat, ruhig**; **~d** adj lasting, permanent

'bleibenlassen v/i → **bleiben**

bleich [blaiç] adj pale (vor from with)

'bleichen v/t ([sn]; ge-, h) bleach

bleiern ['blaiɐn] adj lead(en fig)

'bleifrei adj MOT unleaded

'Bleistift m pencil; **~spitzer** m pencil sharpener

Blende ['blɛndə] f (-; -n) blind; PHOT aperture; **(bei) ~ 8** (at) f-8

'blenden v/t (ge-, h) blind, dazzle (both a. fig); **~d** adj dazzling (a. fig); brilliant; **~ aussehen** look great

'blendfrei adj OPT antiglare

blich [blɪç] pret of **bleichen**

Blick [blɪk] m (-[e]s; -e) look (auf acc at); view (of); **flüchtiger ~** glance; **auf den ersten ~** at first sight; **'blicken** v/i (ge-, h) look, glance (both: auf acc, nach at)

'Blickfang m eye-catcher

'Blickfeld n field of vision

blieb [bliːp] pret of **bleiben**

blies [bliːs] pret of **blasen**

blind [blɪnt] adj blind (a. fig gegen, für to; vor with); dull (mirror etc); **~er Alarm** false alarm; **~er Passagier** stowaway; **auf e-m Auge ~** blind in one eye; **ein Blinder** a blind man; **e-e Blinde** a blind woman; **die Blinden** the blind

'Blinddarm m ANAT appendix; **~entzündung** f MED appendicitis; **~operati,on** f MED appendectomy

Blinden|hund ['blɪndənhʊnt] m seeing eye (Br guide) dog; **~schrift** f braille

Blindgänger ['blɪntgɛŋɐ] m (-s; -) MIL dud

'Blindheit f (-; no pl) blindness

blindlings ['blɪntlɪŋs] adv blindly

'Blindschleiche f ZO blindworm

blinken ['blɪŋkən] v/i (ge-, h) sparkle, shine; twinkle; flash (a signal); MOT indicate; **Blinker** ['blɪŋkɐ] m (-s; -) MOT turn signal, Br indicator

blinzeln ['blɪntsəln] v/i (ge-, h) blink (one's eyes)

Blitz [blɪts] m (-es; -e) (flash of) lightning; PHOT flash; ~ableiter m (-s; -) lightning conductor

'blitzen v/i (ge-, h) flash; **es blitzt** it's lightening

'Blitz|gerät n PHOT (electronic) flash; ~lampe f PHOT flashbulb; flash cube; ~licht n (-[e]s; -er) PHOT flash(light); ~schlag m lightning stroke

'blitz'schnell adj and adv like a flash; attr split-second

Block [blɔk] m (-[e]s; Blöcke ['blœkə]) block; POL, ECON bloc; (writing) pad

Blockade [blɔ'kaːdə] f (-; -n) MAR, MIL blockade

'Blockflöte f recorder

'Blockhaus n log cabin

blockieren [blɔ'kiːrən] v/t and v/i (no -ge-, h) block; MOT lock

'Blockschrift f block letters

blöde ['bløːdə] F adj silly, stupid

'blödeln v/i (ge-, h) fool or clown around

Blödheit ['bløːthait] f (-; no pl) stupidity

'Blödsinn F m (-[e]s; no pl) rubbish, nonsense

'blödsinnig F adj stupid, idiotic

Blog [blɔk] m, n (-s; -s) blog

blöken ['bløːkən] v/i (ge-, h) ZO bleat

blond [blɔnt] adj blond, fair

Blondine [blɔn'diːnə] f (-; -n) blonde

bloß [bloːs] **1.** adj bare; naked (eye); mere; ~ **legen** v/t (sep, -ge-, h) lay bare, expose **2.** adv only, just, merely

Blöße ['bløːsə] f (-; -n) nakedness; **sich e-e ~ geben** lay o.s. open to attack or criticism

'bloß|legen v/t → **bloß**; ~stellen v/t (sep, -ge-, h) expose, compromise, unmask; **sich** ~ compromise o.s.

blühen ['blyːən] v/i (ge-, h) (be in) bloom; (be in) blossom; fig flourish

Blume ['bluːmə] f (-; -n) flower; GASTR bouquet; head, froth

'Blumen|beet n flowerbed; ~händler m florist; ~kohl m BOT cauliflower; ~laden m flower shop, florist's; ~strauß m bunch of flowers; bouquet; ~topf m flowerpot; ~vase f vase

Bluse ['bluːzə] f (-; -n) blouse

Blut [bluːt] n (-[e]s; no pl) blood

'blutarm adj MED an(a)emic (a. fig)

'Blut|armut f MED an(a)emia; ~bad n massacre; ~bahn f ANAT bloodstream; ~bank f (-; -en) MED blood bank

'blutbefleckt adj bloodstained

'Blut|bild n MED blood count; ~blase f MED blood blister; ~druck m MED blood pressure

Blüte ['blyːtə] f (-; -n) flower; bloom (a. fig); blossom; fig height, heyday; **in** (**voller**) ~ in (full) bloom

'Blutegel m ZO leech

'bluten v/i (ge-, h) bleed (**aus** dat from)

'Blüten|blatt n petal; ~staub m pollen

Bluter ['bluːtɐ] m (-s; -) MED h(a)emophiliac

'Blut|erguss m bruise; MED h(a)ematoma; ~gefäß n ANAT blood vessel; ~gerinnsel n MED blood clot; ~gruppe f MED blood group; ~hund m ZO bloodhound

'blutig adj bloody; ~er Anfänger rank beginner, F greenhorn

'Blut|körperchen n MED blood corpuscle; ~kreislauf m MED (blood) circulation; ~lache f pool of blood

'blutleer adj bloodless

'Blutprobe f MED blood test

blutrünstig ['bluːtrynstɪç] adj bloodthirsty, gory

'Blutschande f JUR incest

'Blutspender m blood donor

'Blutsverwandte m, f blood relation

'Blutübertragung f MED blood transfusion

'Blutung f (-; -en) MED bleeding, h(a)emorrhage

'blutunterlaufen adj bloodshot

'Blut|vergießen n (-s; no pl) bloodshed; ~vergiftung f MED blood poisoning; ~wurst f black sausage (Br pudding)

BLZ [beːɛl'tsɛt] abbr of **Bankleitzahl** A.B.A. number, Br bank (sorting) code

Bö [bøː] f (-; -en) gust, squall

Bob [bɔp] m (-s; -s) bob(sled); ~bahn f bob run; ~fahrer m bobber

Bock [bɔk] m (-[e]s; Böcke ['bœkə]) ZO buck; he-goat, billy-goat; ram; SPORT buck; F **e-n ~ schießen** (make a) blunder; F **keinen** (or **null**) ~ **auf et. haben** have zero interest in s.th.

'bocken v/i (ge-, h) buck; sulk

'bockig adj obstinate; sulky

'Bockspringen n leapfrog

Boden ['boːdən] m (-s; Böden ['bøːdən]) ground; AGR soil; bottom; floor; attic

B

'Boden|perso,nal n AVIAT ground crew; ~schätze pl mineral resources; ~stati,on f AVIAT ground control; ~turnen n floor exercises

Body ['bɔdi] m (-s; -s) bodysuit

bog [boːk] pret of **biegen**

Bogen ['boːgən] m (-s; Bögen ['bøːgən]) bend, curve; MATH arc; ARCH arch; skiing: turn; bow; sheet; ~schießen n archery; ~schütze m archer

Bohle ['boːlə] f (-; -n) plank

Bohne ['boːnə] f (-; -n) BOT bean; **grüne ~n** green (Br a. French) beans

'Bohnenstange f beanpole (a. F)

bohnern ['boːnɐn] v/t (ge-, h) polish, wax; 'Bohnerwachs n floor polish

bohren ['boːrən] v/t (ge-, h) bore, drill (a. dentist); ~d fig adj piercing (look); insistent (questions etc)

Bohrer ['boːrɐ] m (-s; -) TECH drill

'Bohr|insel f oil rig; ~loch n borehole, well(head); ~ma,schine f (electric) drill; ~turm m derrick

'Bohrung f (-; -en) drilling; bore

Boje ['boːjə] f (-; -n) MAR buoy

Bolzen ['bɔltsən] m (-s; -) TECH bolt

bombardieren [bɔmbar'diːrən] v/t (no -ge-, h) bomb; fig bombard

Bombe ['bɔmbə] f (-; -n) bomb; fig bombshell

'Bomben|angriff m air raid; ~anschlag m bomb attack; ~erfolg F m roaring success; THEA etc smash hit; ~geschäft F n super deal

'Bombenleger m (-s; -) bomber

'bombensicher adj bombproof

Bomber ['bɔmbɐ] F m (-s; -) MIL bomber (a. SPORT)

Bon [bɔŋ] m (-s; -s) coupon, voucher

Bonbon [bɔŋ'bɔŋ] m, n (-s; -s) candy, Br sweet

Boot [boːt] n (-[e]s; -e) boat

'Bootsmann m (-[e]s; -leute) boatswain

Bord[1] [bɔrt] n (-[e]s; -e) shelf

Bord[2] m: an ~ AVIAT, MAR on board; **über ~** MAR overboard; **von ~ gehen** MAR disembark

'Bordkarte f AVIAT boarding pass

Bordstein m curb, Br kerb

borgen ['bɔrgən] v/t (ge-, h) borrow; **sich et. von j-m ~** borrow s.th. from s.o.; **j-m et. ~** lend s.th. to s.o.

Borke ['bɔrkə] f (-; -n) BOT bark

borniert [bɔr'niːɐt] adj narrow-minded

Börse ['bœrzə] f (-; -n) ECON stock exchange

'Börsen|bericht m market report; ~kurs m quotation; ~makler m stockbroker; ~speku,lant m stock-jobber

Borste ['bɔrstə] f (-; -n) bristle

'borstig adj bristly

Borte ['bɔrtə] f (-; -n) border; braid, lace

bösartig ['bøːsartɪç] adj vicious; MED malignant

Böschung ['bœʃʊŋ] f (-; -en) slope, bank; RAIL embankment

böse ['bøːzə] adj bad, evil, wicked; angry (**über** acc about; **auf j-n** with s.o.), mad (**auf** acc at); **er meint es nicht ~** he means no harm

'Böse n (-n; no pl) (the) evil

'Bösewicht m (-[e]s; -er) villain

boshaft ['boːshaft] adj malicious

Bosheit ['boːshait] f (-; no pl) malice

'böswillig adj malicious, JUR a. wil(l)ful

bot [boːt] pret of **bieten**

Botanik [bo'taːnɪk] f (-; no pl) botany

Bo'taniker m (-s; -) botanist

bo'tanisch adj botanical

Bote ['boːtə] m (-n; -n) messenger

'Botengang m errand; **Botengänge machen** run errands

Botschaft ['boːtʃaft] f (-; -en) message; POL embassy

'Botschafter m (-s; -) POL ambassador (**in** dat to); 'Botschafterin f (-; -nen) POL ambassadress (**in** dat to)

Bottich ['bɔtɪç] m (-s; -e) tub, vat

Bouillon [bul'jɔŋ] f (-; -s) consommé, bouillon, broth

Boulevard|blatt [bulə'vaːɐblat] n, ~zeitung f tabloid

Bowle ['boːlə] f (-; -n) (cold) punch; bowl

boxen ['bɔksən] (ge-, h) 1. v/i box 2. v/t punch; 'Boxen n (-s; no pl) boxing; Boxer ['bɔksɐ] m (-s; -) boxer

'Box|handschuh m boxing glove; ~kampf m boxing match, fight; ~sport m boxing

Boykott [bɔy'kɔt] m (-[e]s; -e), boykottieren [bɔykɔ'tiːrən] v/t (no -ge-, h) boycott

brach [braːx] pret of **brechen**

brachliegend adj AGR fallow

brachte ['braxtə] pret of **bringen**

Branche ['brã:ʃə] f (-; -n) ECON line (of business); **'Branchenverzeichnis** n TEL yellow pages

Brand [brant] m (-[e]s; **Brände** ['brendə]) fire; **in ~ geraten** catch fire; **in ~ stecken** set fire to; **~blase** f MED blister

branden ['brandən] v/i (ge-, sein) surge (**gegen** against)

'Brand|fleck m burn; **~mal** n brand

'brandmarken fig v/t (ge-, h) brand, stigmatize

'Brand|mauer f fire wall; **~stätte** f, **~stelle** f scene of fire; **~stifter** m arsonist; **~stiftung** f arson

Brandung f (-; no pl) surf, surge, breakers

'Brandwunde f MED burn; scald

brannte ['brantə] pret of **brennen**

'Branntwein m brandy, spirits

braten ['bra:tən] v/t (irr, ge-, h) roast; grill, broil; fry; **am Spieß ~** roast on a spit, barbecue

'Braten (-s; -) roast (meat); joint; **~fett** n dripping; **~soße** f gravy

'Brat|fisch m fried fish; **~huhn** n roast chicken; **~kar,toffeln** pl fried potatoes; **~ofen** m oven; **~pfanne** f frying pan

Bratsche ['bra:tʃə] f (-; -n) MUS viola

'Bratwurst f grilled sausage

Brauch [braux] m (-[e]s; **Bräuche** ['brɔʏçə]) custom; habit, practice

'brauchbar adj useful

'brauchen v/t (ge-, h) need; require; take (time); use; **wie lange wird er ~?** how long will it take him?; **du brauchst es nur zu sagen** just say the word; **ihr braucht es nicht zu tun** you don't have to do it; **er hätte nicht zu kommen ~** he need not have come

brauen ['brauən] v/t (ge-, h) brew

Brauerei [brauə'rai] f (-; -en) brewery

braun [braun] adj brown; (sun)tanned; **~ werden** (get a) tan

Bräune ['brɔʏnə] f (-; no pl) (sun)tan

'bräunen (ge-, h) **1.** v/t brown, tan **2.** v/i (get a) tan

'Braunkohle f brown coal, lignite

'bräunlich adj brownish

Brause ['brauzə] f (-; -n) shower; → **Limonade**; **'brausen** v/i (ge-, h) roar; (sein) rush; (h) → **duschen**

Braut [braut] f (-; **Bräute** ['brɔʏtə]) bride; fiancée; **Bräutigam** ['brɔʏtɪ-**B**gam] m (-s; -e) (bride)groom; fiancé

'Braut|jungfer f bridesmaid; **~kleid** n wedding-dress; **~paar** n bride and (bride)groom; engaged couple

brav [bra:f] adj good; honest; **sei(d) ~!** be good!

BRD [be:?ɛr'de:] abbr of **Bundesrepublik Deutschland** FRG, Federal Republic of Germany

brechen ['breçən] (irr, ge-) **1.** v/t (h) break (a. fig); MED vomit; **sich ~** OPT be refracted; **sich den Arm ~** break one's arm **2.** v/i (h) MED vomit; F throw up, Br a. be sick; **mit j-m ~** break with s.o; **~d voll** crammed, packed; (sein) break, get broken, fracture

'Brechreiz m MED nausea

'Brechstange f crowbar

'Brechung f (-; -en) OPT refraction

Brei [brai] m (-[e]s; -e) pulp, mash; pap; porridge; pudding

'breiig adj pulpy, mushy

breit [brait] adj wide; broad (a. fig)

'breitbeinig adj with legs (wide) apart

Breite ['braitə] f (-; -n) width, breadth; ASTR, GEOGR latitude

'breiten v/t (ge-, h) spread

'Breiten|grad m degree of latitude; **~kreis** m parallel (of latitude)

breitmachen v/refl (sep, ge-, h): **sich ~** F spread o.s., take up room

'Breitwand f film: wide screen

Bremsbelag ['brɛmsbəla:k] m brake lining

Bremse ['brɛmzə] f (-; -n) TECH brake; ZO gadfly; **'bremsen** (ge-, h) **1.** v/i MOT brake, put on the brake(s); slow down **2.** v/t MOT brake; fig curb

'Brems|licht n (-[e]s; -er) MOT stop light; **~pe,dal** n MOT brake pedal; **~spur** f MOT skid marks; **~weg** m MOT stopping distance

'brennbar adj combustible; (in)flammable; **brennen** ['brɛnən] (irr, ge-, h) **1.** v/t burn; distil(l) (whisky etc); bake (bricks) **2.** v/i burn; be on fire; wound, eyes: smart, burn; F **darauf ~ zu** inf be dying to inf; **es brennt!** fire!; **Brenner** ['brɛnɐ] m (-s; -) burner

Brenn|holz n firewood; **~materi,al** n fuel; **~nessel** f BOT (stinging) nettle; **~punkt** m focus, focal point; **~spiritus** m methylated spirit; **~stab** m TECH fuel rod; **~stoff** m fuel

B

brenzlig ['brɛntslɪç] *adj* burnt; *fig* hot

Bresche ['brɛʃə] *f* (-; -n) breach (*a. fig*), gap

Brett [brɛt] *n* (-[e]s; -er) board

'**Bretterzaun** *m* wooden fence

'**Brettspiel** *n* board game

Brezel ['breːtsəl] *f* (-; -n) pretzel

Brief [briːf] *m* (-[e]s; -e) letter; ~**beschwerer** *m* (-s; -) paperweight; ~**bogen** *m* sheet of (note)paper; ~**freund(in)** pen pal (*Br* friend); ~**kasten** *m* mailbox, *Br* letterbox

'**brieflich** *adj and adv* by letter

'**Brief|marke** *f* (postage) stamp; ~**markensammlung** *f* stamp collection; ~**öffner** *m* letter opener, *Br* paper knife; ~**pa,pier** *n* stationery; ~**tasche** *f* wallet; ~**taube** *f* zo carrier pigeon; ~**träger(in)** (-s; -/-; -nen) mailman (mailwoman), *Br* postman (postwoman); ~**umschlag** *m* envelope; ~**wahl** *f* postal vote; ~**wechsel** *m* correspondence

briet [briːt] *pret of* **braten**

Brikett [bri'kɛt] *n* (-s; -s) briquet(te)

brillant [brɪl'jant] *adj* brilliant

Bril'lant *m* (-en; -en) (cut) diamond

Bril'lantring *m* diamond ring

Brille ['brɪlə] *f* (-; -n) (pair of) glasses, spectacles; goggles; toilet seat

'**Brillen|etui** *n* eyeglass (*Br* spectacle) case; ~**träger(in)** (-s; -/-; -nen) ~ **sein** wear glasses

bringen ['brɪŋən] *v/t* (*irr, ge-, h*) bring; take; cause; make (*sacrifice*); yield (*profit*); *j-n nach Hause* ~ see (*or* take) s.o. home; *in Ordnung* ~ put in order; *das bringt mich auf e-e Idee* that gives me an idea; *j-n dazu* ~, *et. zu tun* get s.o. to do s.th.; *et. mit sich* ~ involve s.th.; *j-n um et.* ~ deprive s.o. of s.th.; *j-n zum Lachen* ~ make s.o. laugh; *j-n wieder zu sich* ~ bring s.o. round; *es zu et. (nichts)* ~ go far (get nowhere); F *es* ~ make it; *das bringt nichts* it's no use

Brise ['briːzə] *f* (-; -n) breeze

Brite ['brɪtə] *m* (-n; -n), '**Britin** *f* (-; -nen) Briton; *die Briten pl* the British

'**britisch** *adj* British

bröckeln ['brœkəln] *v/i* (*ge-, h, sein*) crumble

Brocken ['brɔkən] *m* (-s; -) piece; lump; rock; GASTR chunk; morsel; *ein paar* ~

Englisch a few scraps of English; F *ein harter* ~ a hard nut to crack

Brombeere ['brɔmbeːrə] *f* BOT blackberry

Bronchitis [brɔn'çiːtɪs] *f* (-; -tiden [brɔnçi'tiːdən]) MED bronchitis

Bronze ['brõːsə] *f* (-; -n) bronze; ~**zeit** *f* (-; *no pl*) HIST Bronze Age

Brosche ['brɔʃə] *f* (-; -n) brooch, pin

broschiert [brɔ'ʃiːrt] *adj* paperback

Broschüre [brɔ'ʃyːrə] *f* (-; -n) pamphlet; brochure

Brot [broːt] *n* (-[e]s; -e) bread; sandwich; *ein (Laib)* ~ a loaf (of bread); *e-e Scheibe* ~ a slice of bread; *sein* ~ *verdienen* earn one's living

Brötchen ['brøːtçən] *n* (-s; -) roll

'**Brot|rinde** *f* crust; ~**(schneide)maschine** *f* bread cutter

Bruch [brux] *m* (-[e]s; *Brüche* ['bryçə]) break; MED fracture; hernia; MATH fraction; GEOL fault; *fig* breach (*of promise etc*); JUR violation; *zu* ~ *gehen* be wrecked; ~**bude** F *f* dump, hovel

brüchig ['bryçɪç] *adj* brittle

'**Bruch|landung** *f* AVIAT crash landing; ~**rechnung** *f* MATH fractional arithmetic, F fractions

'**bruchsicher** *adj* breakproof

'**Bruch|strich** *m* MATH fraction bar; ~**stück** *n* fragment; ~**teil** *m* fraction; *im* ~ *e-r Sekunde* in a split second; ~**zahl** *f* MATH fraction(al) number

Brücke ['brykə] *f* (-; -n) bridge (*a. SPORT*); rug; '**Brückenpfeiler** *m* pier

Bruder ['bruːdɐ] *m* (-s; *Brüder* ['bryːdɐ]) brother (*a. REL*); ~**krieg** *m* civil war

brüderlich ['bryːdɐlɪç] **1.** *adj* brotherly **2.** *adv:* ~ *teilen* share and share alike

'**Brüderlichkeit** *f* (-; *no pl*) brotherhood

'**Brüderschaft** *f:* ~ *trinken* agree to use the familiar 'du' form of address

Brühe ['bryːə] *f* (-; -n) broth; stock; F dishwater; slops; F filthy water, bilge

'**Brühwürfel** *m* beef cube

brüllen ['brylən] *v/i* (*ge-, h*) roar (*vor Lachen* with laughter); zo bellow; F bawl; ~**des Gelächter** roars of laughter

brummen ['brumən] *v/i* (*ge-, h*) growl; zo hum, buzz (*a. engine etc*); head: be buzzing; '**brummig** *adj* grumpy

brünett [bry'nɛt] *adj* brunette, dark-haired

Brunnen ['brunən] *m* (-s; -) well, spring,

fountain

Brunstzeit ['brʊnsttsait] f ZO rutting season

Brust [brʊst] f (-; *Brüste* ['brʏstə]) ANAT (*no pl*) chest; breast(s), bosom; ~**bein** n ANAT breastbone; ~**beutel** m neck pouch, Br money bag

brüsten ['brʏstən] v/refl (ge-, h) boast, brag (*mit* a)

'**Brust|kasten** m, ~**korb** m ANAT chest, thorax; ~**schwimmen** n breaststroke

'**Brüstung** f (-; -en) parapet

'**Brustwarze** f ANAT nipple

Brut [bruːt] f (-; -en) ZO brooding; brood (*a.* F), hatch; fry

brutal [bru'taːl] adj brutal; **Brutalität** [brutali'tɛːt] f (-; -en) brutality

'**Brutapparat** m ZO incubator

brüten ['bryːtən] v/i (ge-, h) ZO brood, sit (on eggs); ~ *über* (dat) fig brood over

'**Brutkasten** m MED incubator

brutto ['brʊto] adv ECON gross

'**Brutto|einkommen** n ECON gross earnings; ~**sozi,alpro,dukt** n ECON gross national product

Bube ['buːbə] m (-n; -n) boy, lad; *card game:* knave, jack

Buch [buːx] n (-[e]s; *Bücher* ['byːçɐ]) book; ~**binder** m (-s; -) (book)binder; ~**drucker** m printer; ~**druckerei** f print shop, Br printing office

Buche ['buːxə] f (-; -n) BOT beech

'**buchen** v/t (ge-, h) book; ECON enter

Bücherbord ['byːçɐbɔrt] n bookshelf

Bücherei [byːçə'rai] f (-; -en) library

'**Bücherre,gal** n bookshelf

'**Bücherschrank** m bookcase

'**Buch|fink** m ZO chaffinch; ~**halter(in)** bookkeeper; ~**haltung** f (-; *no pl*) bookkeeping; ~**händler(in)** bookseller; ~**handlung** f bookstore, Br bookshop; ~**macher** m bookmaker

Büchse ['bʏksə] f (-; -n) can, Br tin; box; rifle

'**Büchsen|fleisch** n canned (Br tinned) meat; ~**öffner** m can (Br tin) opener

Buchstabe ['buːxʃtaːbə] m (-n; -n) letter; *großer* (*kleiner*) ~ capital (small) letter; **buchstabieren** [buːxʃta'biːrən] v/t (no -ge-, h) spell; **buchstäblich** ['buːxʃtɛːplɪç] adv literally

'**Buchstütze** f bookend

Bucht [bʊxt] f (-; -en) bay, creek, inlet

'**Buchung** f (-; -en) booking; ECON entry

Buckel ['bʊkəl] m (-s; -) hump, hunch; *e-n* ~ *machen* hump or hunch one's back

bücken ['bʏkən] v/refl (ge-, h) bend (down), stoop

bucklig ['bʊklɪç] adj hunchbacked

Bucklige ['bʊklɪgə] m, f (-n; -n) hunchback

Bückling ['bʏklɪŋ] m (-s; -e) smoked herring, Br kipper

Buddhismus [bʊ'dɪsmʊs] m (-; *no pl*) Buddhism; **Buddhist** [bʊ'dɪst] m (-en; -en), **bud'dhistisch** adj Buddhist

Bude ['buːdə] f (-; -n) stall, booth; hut; F pad, Br digs; *contp* shack, dump, hole

Budget [by'dʒeː] n (-s; -s) budget

Büfett [by'fɛt] n (-[e]s; -s, -e) counter, bar, buffet; sideboard, cupboard; *kaltes* ~ GASTR cold buffet (meal)

Büffel ['bʏfəl] m (-s; -) ZO buffalo

'**büffeln** F v/i (ge-, h) grind, cram, swot

Bug [buːk] m (-[e]s; -e) MAR bow; AVIAT nose; ZO, GASTR shoulder

Bügel ['byːgəl] m (-s; -) hanger; bow; ~**brett** n ironing board; ~**eisen** n iron; ~**falte** f crease

'**bügelfrei** adj no(n)-iron

'**bügeln** v/t (ge-, h) iron, press

buh [buː] int boo

buhen ['buːən] v/i (ge-, h) boo

Bühne ['byːnə] f (-; -n) stage, fig a. scene

'**Bühnen|bild** n (stage) set(ting); ~**bildner(in)** m (-s; -/-; -nen) stage designer

'**Buhrufe** pl boos

Bullauge ['bʊlaugə] n MAR porthole

'**Bulldogge** f ZO bulldog

Bulle ['bʊlə] m (-n; -n) ZO bull (*a. fig*); F *contp* cop, pl the fuzz

Bummel ['bʊməl] F m (-s; -) stroll;

Bummelei [bʊmə'lai] f (-; *no pl*) F *contp* dawdling; slackness; '**bummeln** F v/i (ge-, sein) stroll, saunter; (ge-, h) *contp* dawdle; ECON go slow; '**Bummelstreik** m ECON slowdown, Br go-slow (strike); **Bummler** ['bʊmlɐ] F m (-s; -) stroller; *contp* dawdler, slowpoke, Br slowcoach

bumsen ['bʊmzən] v/i *and* v/t (ge-, h) F → **krachen**; V screw

Bund¹ [bʊnt] m (-[e]s; *Bünde* ['bʏndə]) union, federation, alliance; association; (waist)band; *der* ~ POL the Federal Government; F → **Bundeswehr**

B

Bund² *n* (-[*e*]*s*; -*e*) bundle; bunch

Bündel ['byndəl] *n* (-*s*; -) bundle

'**bündeln** *v/t* (*ge*-, *h*) bundle (up)

Bundes... ['bundəs-] *in cpds* Federal ...; German ...; **~bahn** *f* Federal Railroad(s); **~genosse** *m* ally; **~kanzler**(**in**) Federal Chancellor; **~land** *n appr* (federal) state, Land; **~liga** *f* SPORT First Division; **~präsi,dent** *m* Federal President; **~rat** *m* Bundesrat, Upper House of German Parliament; **~repu,blik** *f* Federal Republic; **~staat** *m* federal state; confederation; **~straße** *f* Federal Highway; **~tag** *m* (-[*e*]*s*; *no pl*) Bundestag, Lower House of German Parliament; **~trainer** *m* coach of the (German) national team; **~verfassungsgericht** *n* Federal Constitutional Court, *Am appr* Supreme Court; **~wehr** *f* (-; *no pl*) MIL (German Federal) Armed Forces

bündig ['byndıç] *adj* TECH flush; **kurz und ~** terse(ly); point-blank

Bündnis ['byntnıs] *n* (-*ses*; -*se*) alliance

Bunker ['bʊŋkɐ] *m* (-*s*; -) air-raid shelter, bunker

bunt [bʊnt] *adj* colo(u)red; multicolo(u)red; colo(u)rful (*a. fig*); varied; **~er Abend** evening of entertainment; F **mir wird's zu ~** that's all I can take

'**Buntstift** *m* colo(u)red pencil, crayon

Bürde ['byrdə] *f* (-; -*n*) burden (**für j-n** to s.o.)

Burg [bʊrk] *f* (-; -*en*) castle

Bürge ['byrgə] *m* (-*n*; -*n*) JUR guarantor (*a. fig*); '**bürgen** *v/i* (*ge*-, *h*) **für j-n ~** JUR stand surety for s.o.; **für et. ~** guarantee s.th.

Bürger ['byrgɐ] *m* (-*s*; -), '**Bürgerin** *f* (-; -*nen*) citizen; **~initia,tive** *f* (citizen's *or* local) action group; **~krieg** *m* civil war

'**bürgerlich** *adj* civil; middle-class; *esp contp* bourgeois; **~e Küche** home cooking; '**Bürgerliche** *m, f* (-*n*; -*n*) commoner

'**Bürger|meister** *m* mayor; **~rechte** *pl* civil rights; **~steig** ['byrgɐʃtaik] *m* (-[*e*]*s*; -*e*) sidewalk, *Br* pavement

'**Bürgschaft** *f* (-; -*en*) JUR surety; bail

Büro [by'ro:] *n* (-*s*; -*s*) office; **~ange-stellte** *m, f* (-*n*; -*n*) clerk, office worker; **~klammer** *f* (paper) clip

Bürokrat [byro'kra:t] *m* (-*en*; -*en*) bureaucrat; **Bürokratie** [byrokra'ti:] *f* (-; -*n*) bureaucracy; *contp* red tape

Bü'rostunden *pl* office hours

Bursche ['bʊrʃə] *m* (-*n*; -*n*) fellow, guy

burschikos [bʊrʃi'ko:s] *adj* (tom)boyish, pert

Bürste ['byrstə] *f* (-; -*n*) brush

'**bürsten** *v/t* (*ge*-, *h*) brush

'**Bürstenschnitt** *m* crew cut

Bus [bʊs] *m* (-*ses*; -*se*) bus; coach

Busch [bʊʃ] *m* (-[*e*]*s*; **Büsche** ['byʃə]) BOT bush, shrub

Büschel ['byʃəl] *n* (-*s*; -) bunch; tuft

'**buschig** *adj* bushy

Busen ['bu:zən] *m* (-*s*; -) ANAT bosom, ,breast(s)

'**Busfahrer** *m* bus driver

'**Bushaltestelle** *f* bus stop

Bussard ['busart] *m* (-*s*; -*e*) ZO buzzard

Buße ['bu:sə] *f* (-; -*n*) REL penance; repentance; **~ tun** do penance

büßen ['by:sən] *v/t* (*ge*-, *h*) pay *or* suffer for *s.th.*; REL repent

'**Bußgeld** *n* fine, penalty

'**Bußtag** *m* REL day of repentance

Büste ['by:stə] *f* (-; -*n*) bust

'**Büstenhalter** *m* bra

Butter ['bʊtɐ] *f* (-; *no pl*) butter; **~blume** *f* BOT buttercup; **~brot** *n* (slice *or* piece of) bread and butter; F **für ein ~** for a song; **~brotpa,pier** *n* greaseproof paper; **~dose** *f* butter dish; **~milch** *f* buttermilk

b.w. *abbr of* **bitte wenden** PTO, please turn over

bzw. *abbr of* **beziehungsweise** resp., respectively

C

C abbr of **Celsius** C, Celsius, centigrade

ca. abbr of **circa** approx., approximately

Café [ka'feː] n (-s; -s) café, coffee house

Cafeteria [kafeˈtriːa] f (-; -s or -ien) cafeteria

campen ['kɛmpən] v/i (ge-, h) camp

Camper ['kɛmpɐ] m (-s; -) camper

Camping... ['kɛmpɪŋ-] in cpds ...**bett,** ...**tisch** etc camp ...; ~**bus** m camper (van Br); ~**platz** m campground, Br campsite

Cappuccino [kapuˈtʃiːno] m (-[s]; [s]) cappuccino

Casino [kaˈziːno] n → **Kasino**

Catcher ['kɛtʃɐ] m (-s; -) wrestler

C'D [tseːˈdeː] f (-; -s) CD, compact disk (Br disc); **C'D-Brenner** m CD burner, CD writer; **C'D-Player** m CD player; **CD-'ROM** CD-ROM; **CD-'ROM-Laufwerk** n CD-ROM drive; **C'D-Spieler** m CD player

Cellist [tʃɛˈlɪst] m (-en; -en), **Cel'listin** f (-; -nen) MUS cellist

Cello ['tʃɛlo] n (-s; -s, Celli) MUS Cello

Celsius ['tsɛlzjʊs] **5 Grad** ~ (abbr **5° C**) five degrees centigrade or Celsius

Cembalo ['tʃɛmbalo] n (-s; -s, -li) MUS harpsichord

Champagner® [ʃamˈpanjɐ] m (-s; -) champagne

Champignon ['ʃampɪnjɔn] m (-s; -s) BOT mushroom

Chance ['ʃãːsə] f (-; -n) chance; **die ~n stehen gleich (3 zu 1)** the odds are even (three to one); **'Chancengleichheit** f equal opportunities

Chaos ['kaːɔs] n (-; no pl) chaos

Chaot [kaˈoːt] m (-en; -en) chaotic person; POL anarchist, pl a. lunatic fringe **cha'otisch** adj chaotic

Charakter [kaˈraktɐ] m (-s; -e [karak-ˈteːrə]) character, nature; **charakterisieren** [karakteriˈziːrən] v/t (no -ge-, h) characterize, describe (**als** as); **charakteristisch** [karakteˈrɪstɪʃ] adj characteristic, typical (**für** of); **Charakterzug** m trait

charmant [ʃarˈmant] adj charming

Charme [ʃarm] m (-s; no pl) charm

Charterflug ['tʃartɐfluːk] m (-[e]s; -flüge) charter flight

chartern ['tʃartɐn] v/t (ge-, h) charter

Chassis [ʃaˈsiː] n (-; -) TECH chassis

Chat [tʃɛt] m (-s; -s) IT chat

chatten ['tʃɛtən] v/t (ge-, h) IT chat

Chauffeur [ʃɔˈføːɐ] m (-s; -e) chauffeur, driver

Chauvi ['ʃoːvi] m (-s; -s) F male chauvinist (pig)

Chauvinismus [ʃoviˈnɪsmʊs] m (-; no pl) chauvinism, POL a. jingoism

checken ['tʃɛkən] v/t (ge-, h) check; F (understand) get

Chef [ʃɛf] m (-s; -s) head, chief, F boss; ~**arzt** m medical director, Br senior consultant; ~**sekreˌtärin** f executive secretary

Chemie [çeˈmiː] f (-; no pl) chemistry; ~**faser** f synthetic fiber (Br fibre)

Chemikalien [çemiˈkaːljən] pl chemicals; **Chemiker(in)** ['çeːmikɐ, 'çeːmikərɪn] m(f) (-s; -/-; -nen) (analytical) chemist; **chemisch** ['çeːmɪʃ] adj chemical; ~**e Reinigung** dry cleaning

Chemothera'pie [çemoteraˈpiː] f MED chemotherapy

Chiffre ['ʃɪfrə] f (-; -n) code, cipher; box (number); **chiffrieren** [ʃɪˈfriːrən] v/t (no -ge-, h) (en)code

China ['çiːna] China; **Chinese** [çiˈneːzə] m (-n; -n), **Chi'nesin** f (-; -nen), **chi'nesisch** adj Chinese

Chinin [çiˈniːn] n (-s; no pl) PHARM quinine

Chip [tʃɪp] m (-s; -s) a. IT chip; GASTR pl chips, Br crisps

Chirurg [çiˈrʊrk] m (-en; -en) surgeon

Chirurgie [çirʊrˈgiː] f (-; -n) surgery

Chirurgin [çiˈrʊrgɪn] f (-; -nen) surgeon

chirurgisch [çiˈrʊrgɪʃ] adj surgical

Chlor [kloːɐ] n (-s; no pl) CHEM chlorine

chloren ['kloːrən] v/t (ge-, h) chlorinate

Cholera ['koːlera] f (-; no pl) MED cholera; **cholerisch** [koˈleːrɪʃ] adj choleric

Cholesterin [çolesteˈriːn] n (-s; no pl) MED cholesterol

Chor [koːɐ] m (-[e]s; Chöre ['køːrə]) MUS choir (a. ARCH); **im** ~ in chorus

Choral [koˈraːl] m (-s; Chorale [ko-

'reːlə]) MUS, REL chorale, hymn

Christ [krɪst] m (-en; -en) REL Christian; **~baum** m Christmas tree

'**Christenheit: die ~** REL Christendom

'**Christentum** n (-s; no pl) REL Christianity

Christin ['krɪstɪn] f (-; -nen) REL Christian

'**Christkind** n Infant Jesus; Father Christmas, Santa Claus

'**christlich** adj REL Christian

Christus ['krɪstʊs] REL Christ; **vor ~** B.C.; **nach ~** A.D.

Chrom [kroːm] n (-s; no pl) chrome, CHEM a. chromium

Chromosom [kromo'zoːm] n (-s; -en) BIOL chromosome

Chronik ['kroːnɪk] f (-; -en) chronicle

chronisch ['kroːnɪʃ] adj MED chronic

chronologisch [krono'loːgɪʃ] adj chronological

circa → zirka

City ['sɪtɪ] f (-; -s) downtown, (city) center, Br centre

Clique ['klɪkə] f (-; -n) F group, set; contp clique

Clou [kluː] F m (-s; -s) highlight, climax;

der ~ daran the whole point of it

Compact Disc, Compact Disk ['kɔmpæktdɪsk] f (-; -s) compact disk (Br disc)

Computer [kɔm'pjuːtɐ] m (-s; -) computer; **~ausdruck** m computer printout

com'putergesteuert adj computer-controlled; **~gestützt** adj computer-aided

Com'putergrafik f computer graphics

computerisieren [kɔmpjutəri'ziːrən] v/t (no -ge-, h) computerize

Com'puterspiel n computer game; **~virus** m computer virus

Conférencier [kõ.fera.'sjeː] m (-s; -s) master of ceremonies, F emcee, MC, Br compère

Cord etc **→ Kord** etc

Couch [kautʃ] f (-; -s) couch

Coupé [ku'peː] n (-s; -s) MOT coupé

Coupon → Kupon

Cousin [ku'zɛː] m (-s; -s), **Cousine** [ku'ziːnə] f (-; -n) cousin

Creme [kreːm] f (-; -s) cream (a. fig)

Curry ['kari] m (-s; -s) curry powder

Cursor ['kɜːsə] m (-s; -s) IT cursor

D

da [daː] **1.** adv space: there; here; time: then, at that time; **~ drüben (draußen, hinten)** over (out, back) there; **von ~ aus** from there; **das ... ~** that ... (over there); **~ kommt er** here he comes; **~ bin ich** here I am; **~ sein** be there; exist; **ist noch ... ~?** is any ... left?; **noch nie ~ gewesen** unprecedented; **er ist gleich wieder ~** he'll be right back; **von ~ an** or **ab** from then on **2.** cj as, since, because

'**dabehalten** v/t (irr, **halten**, sep, no -ge-, h) keep; **j-n ~** keep s.o. in

dabei [daˈbai] adv here, present; near or close by; at the same time; included with it; **~ sein** be there; take part; be in on it; **ich bin ~!** count me in!; **er ist gerade ~ zu gehen** he's just leaving; **es ist nichts ~** there's nothing to it; there's no harm in it; **was ist schon ~?** (so) what of it?; **lassen wir es ~!**

let's leave it at that!; **~bleiben** v/i (irr, **bleiben**, sep, -ge-, sein) stick to it; **~haben** F v/t (irr, **haben**, sep, -ge-, h) have with (or on) one

'**dableiben** v/i (irr, **bleiben**, sep, -ge-, sein) stay

Dach [dax] n (-[e]s; Dächer ['dɛçɐ]) roof

'**Dach|boden** m attic; **~decker** ['daxdɛkɐ] m (-s; -) roofer; **~fenster** n dormer window; **~gepäckträger** m MOT roof-rack

'**Dachgeschoss** n, '**Dachgeschoß** Austrian n attic; **~wohnung** f loft apartment, Br attic flat

'**Dach|kammer** f garret; **~luke** f skylight; **~pappe** f roofing felt; **~rinne** f gutter

Dachs [daks] m (-es; -e) ZO badger

'**Dachstuhl** m roof framework

dachte ['daxtə] pret of **denken**

'**Dachter,rasse** f roof terrace

'**Dachverband** *m* ECON *etc* umbrella organization

Dackel ['dakəl] *m* (-s; -) ZO dachshund

'**dadurch** *adv and cj* this *or* that way; for this reason, so; ~, **dass** due to the fact that

dafür [da'fy:ɐ] *adv* for it, for that; instead; in return, in exchange; ~ **sein** be in favo(u)r of it; **er kann nichts ~** it is not his fault; ~ **sorgen, dass** see to it that

da'gegen *adv and cj* against it; however, on the other hand; ~ **sein** be against (*or* opposed to) it; **haben Sie et. ~, dass ich …?** do you mind if I …?; **wenn Sie nichts ~ haben** if you don't mind; **… ist nichts ~** … can't compare

da'heim *adv* at home

'**daher** *adv and cj* from there; that's why

da'hin *adv* there, to that place; gone, past; **bis ~** till then; up to there

da'hinten *adv* back there

da'hinter *adv* behind it; **es steckt nichts ~** there is nothing to it; F ~ **kommen** find out (about it)

da'lassen F *v/t* (*irr*, **lassen**, *sep*, *-ge-*, *h*) leave behind

damalig ['da:ma:lɪç] *adj* then

damals ['da:ma:ls] *adv* then, at that time

Dame ['da:mə] *f* (-; -n) lady; partner; *cards, chess:* queen; *checkers, Br* draughts

'**Damen…** *in cpds* ladies' …; SPORT women's …; ~**binde** *f* sanitary napkin (*Br* towel)

'**damenhaft** *adj* ladylike

'**Damen|toi,lette/lette** *f* ladies' room (*Br* toilet), *the* ladies; ~**wahl** *f* ladies' choice

damit 1. ['da:mɪt] *adv* with it *or* that; by it, with it; **was will er ~ sagen?** what's he trying to say?; **wie steht es ~?** how about it?; ~ **einverstanden sein** have no objections **2.** [da'mɪt] *cj* so that; in order to *inf*; ~ **nicht** so as not to *inf*

Damm [dam] *m* (-[e]s; **Dämme** ['dɛmə]) dam; embankment

dämmerig ['dɛmərɪç] *adj* dim

'**Dämmerlicht** *n* (-[e]s; *no pl*) twilight

dämmern ['dɛmɐn] *v/i* (*ge-*, *h*) dawn (*a.* F *j-m* on s.o.); get dark *or* dusky

'**Dämmerung** *f* (-; *-en*) dusk; dawn

Dämon ['dɛ:mɔn] *m* (-s; *-en* [dɛ-'mo:nən]) demon; **dämonisch** [dɛ-'mo:nɪʃ] *adj* demoniac(al)

Dampf [dampf] *m* (-[e]s; **Dämpfe** ['dɛmpfə]) steam; PHYS vapo(u)r

'**dampfen** *v/i* (*ge-*, *h and sein*) steam

dämpfen ['dɛmpfən] *v/t* (*ge-*, *h*) deaden; muffle (*voice*); soften (*light, sound, blow*); GASTR steam, stew; steam-iron; *fig* put a damper on; curb (*a.* ECON)

Dampfer ['dampfɐ] *m* (-s; -) steamer, steamship

'**Dampf|kochtopf** *m* pressure cooker; ~**ma,schine** *f* steam engine; ~**schiff** *n* steamer, steamship

da'nach *adv* after it *or* that; afterwards; for it; according to it; **ich fragte ihn ~** I asked him about it; F **mir ist nicht ~** I don't feel like it

Däne ['dɛ:nə] *m* (-n; -n) Dane

da'neben *adv* next to it, beside it; besides, as well, at the same time; beside the mark; ~**benehmen** F *v/refl* (*irr*, **nehmen**, *sep*, *no -ge-*, *h*) step out of line; ~**gehen** F *v/i* (*irr*, **gehen**, *sep*, *-ge-*, *sien*) miss (the target); F misfire

'**Dänemark** Denmark

Dänin ['dɛ:nɪn] *f* (-; *-nen*) Danish woman *or* girl; '**dänisch** *adj* Danish

dank [daŋk] *prp* (*gen*) thanks to

Dank *m* (-[e]s; *no pl*) thanks; **Gott sei ~!** thank God!; **vielen ~!** many thanks!

'**dankbar** *adj* grateful (*j-m* to s.o.); rewarding (*task etc*)

'**Dankbarkeit** *f* (-; *no pl*) gratitude

'**danken** *v/i* (*ge-*, *h*) thank (*j-m für et.* s.o. for s.th.); **danke (schön)** thank you (very much); (**nein,**) **danke** no, thank you; **nichts zu ~** not at all

dann [dan] *adv* then; ~ **und wann** (every) now and then

daran [da'ran] *adv* on it; *die, think etc* of it; *believe etc* in it; *suffer etc* from it; → **liegen**

darauf [da'rauf] *adv* on (top of) it; after (that); *listen, drink etc* to it; *proud etc* of it; *wait etc* for it; **am Tage ~** the day after; **zwei Jahre ~** two years later; ~ **kommt es an** that's what matters

darauf'hin *adv* after that; as a result

daraus [da'raus] *adv* from (*or* out of) it; **was ist ~ geworden?** what has become of it?; ~ **wird nichts!** F nothing doing!

Darbietung ['da:ɐbi:tʊŋ] *f* (-; *-en*) presentation; performance

darin [da'rɪn] *adv* in it; ['da:rɪn] in that

darlegen ['daːʁleːgən] v/t (sep, -ge-, h) explain, set out

Darlehen ['daːʁleːən] n (-s; -) loan; **ein~ geben** grant a loan

Darm [darm] m (-[e]s; Därme ['dɛrmə]) ANAT bowel(s), intestine(s); GASTR skin; **~grippe** f MED intestinal flu

darstellen ['daːʁʃtɛlən] v/t (sep, -ge-, h) represent, show, depict; describe; **'Darsteller(in** (-s; -/-; -nen) THEA performer, actor (actress); **'Darstellung** f (-; -en) representation; description; account; portrayal

darüber [da'ryːbɐ] adv over or above it; across it; in the meantime; **write, talk etc about it**; **... und ~ ...** and more; **~ werden Jahre vergehen** that will take years

darum [da'rom] adv and cj (a)round it; because of it, that's why; **~ bitten** ask for it; → **gehen**

darunter [da'rontɐ] adv under or below it, underneath; among them; including; **... und ~ ...** and less; **was verstehst du ~?** what do you understand by it?

das [das] → **der**

'Dasein n (-s; no pl) life, existence

dass [das] cj that; so (that); **es sei denn, ~** unless; **nicht ~ ich wüsste** not that I know of

'dastehen v/i (irr, **stehen**, sep, -ge-, h) stand (there)

Datei [da'tai] f (-; -en) IT file; **~verwaltung** f IT file management

Daten ['daːtən] pl data (a. IT), facts; particulars; **~bank** f (-; -en) database, data bank; **~schutz** m JUR data protection; **~speicher** m data memory or storage; **~träger** m data medium or carrier; **~übertragung** f data transfer; **~verarbeitung** f data processing

datieren [da'tiːrən] v/t and v/i (no -ge-, h) date

Dativ ['daːtiːf] m (-s; -e) dative (case)

Dattel ['datəl] f (-; -n) BOT date

Datum ['daːtom] n (-s; Daten ['daːtən]) date; **welches ~ haben wir heute?** what's the date today?

Dauer ['daʊɐ] f (-; no pl) duration; continuance; **auf die ~** in the long run; **für die ~ von** for a period or term of; **von ~ sein** last; **~arbeitslosigkeit** f long-term unemployment; **~auftrag** m ECON

standing order; **~geschwindigkeit** f MOT etc cruising speed

'dauerhaft adj lasting; durable

'Dauer|karte f season ticket; **~lauf** m SPORT jogging; **im ~** at a jog; **~lutscher** m lollipop

dauern v/i (ge-, h) last, take; → **lange**

'Dauerwelle f permanent, Br perm

Daumen ['daʊmən] m (-s; -) ANAT thumb; F **j-m den ~ halten** keep one's fingers crossed (for s.o.); **am ~ lutschen** suck one's thumb

Daunen ['daʊnən] pl down

'Daunendecke f eiderdown

da'von adv (away) from it; by it; about it; away; of it or them; **et. ~ haben** get s.th. out of it; **das kommt ~!** there you are!, that will teach you!; **~kommen** v/i (irr, **kommen**, sep, -ge-, sein) escape, get away; **~laufen** v/i (irr, **laufen**, sep, -ge-, sein) run away

da'vor adv before it; in front of it; **be afraid, warn s.o. etc** of it

da'zu adv for it, for that purpose; in addition; **noch ~** into the bargain; **~ ist es da** that's what it's there for; **Salat ~?** a salad with it?; → **kommen, Lust**; **~gehören** v/i (sep, no -ge-, h) belong to it, be part of it; **~gehörig** adj belonging to it; **~kommen** v/i (irr, **kommen**, sep, -ge-, sein) join s.o.; be added

da'zwischen adv between (them); in between; among them; **~kommen** v/i (irr, **kommen**, sep, -ge-, sein) intervene, happen; **wenn nichts dazwischenkommt** if all goes well

DB [deː'beː] abbr of **Deutsche Bahn** German Rail

dealen ['diːlən] v/i (ge-, h) F push drugs

Dealer ['diːlɐ] m (-s; -) drug dealer, F pusher

Debatte [de'batə] f (-; -n) debate

debattieren [deba'tiːrən] v/i (no -ge-, h) debate (**über** acc on)

Debüt [de'byː] n (-s; -s) debut; **sein ~ geben** make your debut

dechiffrieren [deʃɪ'friːrən] v/t (no -ge-, h) decipher, decode

Deck [dɛk] n (-[e]s; -s) MAR deck

Decke ['dɛkə] f (-; -n) blanket; quilt; ARCH ceiling

Deckel ['dɛkəl] m (-s; -) lid, cover, top

'decken v/t and v/i (ge-, h) cover (a. ZO, SPORT a. mark; **sich ~ (mit)** coincide (with); → **Tisch**

'**Deckung** f (-; no pl) cover; boxing: guard; **in ~ gehen** take cover

defekt [de'fɛkt] adj defective, faulty; TECH out of order; **De'fekt** m (-[e]s; -e) defect, fault

defensiv [defɛn'siːf] adj, **Defensive** [defɛn'ziːvə] f (-; no pl) defensive

definieren [defi'niːrən] v/t (no -ge-, h) define; **Definition** [defini'tsjoːn] f (-; -en) definition

Defizit ['deːfitsɪt] n (-s; -e) deficit; deficiency

Degen ['deːgən] m (-s; -) sword; fencing: épée

degradieren [degra'diːrən] v/t (no -ge-, h) degrade (a. fig)

dehnbar ['deːnbaːɐ] adj flexible, elastic (a. fig); **dehnen** ['deːnən] v/t (ge-, h) stretch (a. fig)

Deich [daiç] m (-[e]s; -e) dike

Deichsel ['daiksəl] f (-; -n) pole, shaft

dein [dain] poss pron your; **~er, ~e, ~e(s)** yours; **deinerseits** ['dainɐ'zaits] adv on your part; **deines'gleichen** ['dainəsglaiçən] pron contp the likes of you; **deinetwegen** ['dainət've:gən] adv for your sake; because of you

Dekan [de'kaːn] m (-s; -e), **De'kanin** f (-; -nen) REL, UNIV dean

Deklination [deklina'tsjoːn] f (-; -en) LING declension; **deklinieren** [dekli-'niːrən] v/t (no -ge-, h) decline

Dekolleté [dekɔl'teː] n (-s; -s) low neckline

Dekorateur [dekora'toːɐ] m (-s; -e), **Dekora'teurin** f (-; -nen) decorator; window dresser; **Dekoration** [dekora-'tsjoːn] f (-; -en) decoration; (window) display; THEA scenery; **dekorativ** [dekora'tiːf] adj decorative; **dekorieren** [deko'riːrən] v/t (no -ge-, h) decorate; dress

Delfin → **Delphin**

delikat [deli'kaːt] adj delicious, exquisite; fig delicate, ticklish

Delikatesse [delika'tesə] f (-; -n) delicacy; **Delika'tessenladen** m delicatessen, F deli

Delphin [dɛl'fiːn] m (-s; -e) ZO dolphin

Dementi [de'mɛnti] n (-s; -s) (official) denial; **dementieren** [demɛn'tiːrən] v/t (no -ge-, h) deny (officially)

dementsprechend, **demgemäß**

['deːmgəmεːs] adv accordingly

'**demnach** adv according to that

'**demnächst** adv shortly, before long

Demo ['deːmo] F f (-; -s) demo

Demokrat [demo'kraːt] m (-en; -en) democrat; **Demokratie** [demokra'tiː] f (-; -n) democracy; **Demo'kratin** f (-; -nen) democrat; **demo'kratisch** adj democratic

demolieren [demo'liːrən] v/t (no -ge-, h) demolish, wreck

Demonstrant [demɔn'strant] m (-en; -en), **Demon'strantin** f (-; -nen) demonstrator; **Demonstration** [demɔnstra'tsjoːn] f (-; -en) demonstration; **demonstrieren** [demɔn-'striːrən] v/t and v/i (no -ge-, h) demonstrate

demontieren [demɔn'tiːrən] v/t (no -ge-, h) dismantle

demoralisieren [demorali'ziːrən] v/t (no -ge-, h) demoralize

Demoskopie [demosko'piː] f (-; -n) public opinion research

Demut ['deːmuːt] f (-; no pl) humility, humbleness; **demütig** ['deːmyːtɪç] adj humble; **demütigen** ['deːmyːtɪgən] v/t (ge-, h) humiliate; '**Demütigung** f (-; -en) humiliation

denkbar ['dɛŋkbaːɐ] **1.** adj conceivable **2.** adv: **~ einfach** most simple

denken ['dɛŋkən] v/t and v/i (irr, ge-, h) think (**an** acc, **über** acc of, about); **daran ~ (zu** inf) remember (to inf)

'**Denkfabrik** f think tank

'**Denkmal** n monument; memorial

'**denkwürdig** adj memorable

denn [dɛn] cj and adv for, because; **es sei ~, dass** unless; **mehr ~ je** more than ever; **dennoch** ['dɛnnɔx] cj yet, still, nevertheless

Denunziant [denʊn'tsjant] m (-en; -en) informer; **denunzieren** [denʊn-'tsiːrən] v/t (no -ge-, h) inform on or against

Deodorant [de'ʔodo'rant] n (-s; -e, -s) deodorant

Deponie [depo'niː] f (-; -n) dump, waste disposal site

deponieren [depo'niːrən] v/t (no -ge-, h) deposit, leave

Depot [de'poː] n (-s; -s) depot (a. MIL); Swiss: deposit

Depression [depre'sjoːn] f (-; -en) depression (*a.* ECON)

depressiv [deprɛ'si:f] *adj* depressive

deprimieren [depri'mi:rən] *v/t* (*no -ge-, h*) depress; **~d** *adj* depressing

deprimiert [depri'mi:ɐt] *adj* depressed

der [de:ɐ], **die** [di:], **das** [das] **1.** *art* the **2.** *dem pron* that, this; he, she, it; **die** *pl* these, those, they **3.** *rel pron* who, which, that; '**derartig 1.** *adv* so (much); like that **2.** *adj* such (as this)

derb [dɛrp] *adj* coarse; tough, sturdy

'**dergleichen** *dem pron:* **nichts ~** nothing of the kind

derjenige ['de:ɐˌje:nɪgə], **diejenige** ['di:je:nɪgə], **dasjenige** ['dasje:nɪgə] *dem pron* the one; **diejenigen** *pl* the ones, those

dermaßen ['de:ɐˈma:sən] *adv* so (much), like that

Dermatologe [dɛrmato'lo:gə] *m* (*-n; -n*), **Dermato'login** *f* (*-; -nen*) dermatologist **derselbe** [dɛr'zɛlbə], **dieselbe** [di:'zɛlbə], **dasselbe** [das'zɛlbə] *dem pron* the same

Deserteur [dezɛr'tø:ɐ] *m* (*-s; -e*) MIL deserter; **desertieren** [dezɛr'ti:rən] *v/i* (*no -ge-, sein*) MIL desert

deshalb ['dɛs'halp] *cj and adv* therefore, for that reason, that is why, so

Desinfektionsmittel [dɛsˀɪnfɛk'tsjo:nsmɪtəl] *n* MED disinfectant

desinfizieren [dɛsˀɪnfi'tsi:rən] *v/t* (*no -ge-, h*) MED disinfect

'**Desinteresse** *n* (*-s; no pl*) indifference

'**desinteresˌsiert** *adj* uninterested, indifferent

destillieren [dɛstɪ'li:rən] *v/t* (*no -ge-, h*) distil(l)

desto ['dɛsto] *cj and adv* → **je**

'**desˈwegen** *cj and adv* → **deshalb**

Detail [de'tai] *n* (*-s; -s*) detail

detailliert [deta'ji:ɐt] *adj* detailed

Detektiv [detɛk'ti:f] *m* (*-s; -e*) detective

deuten ['dɔytən] (*ge-, h*) **1.** *v/t* interpret **2.** *v/i:* **~ auf** (*acc*) point at

'**deutlich** *adj* clear, distinct, plain

deutsch [dɔytʃ] *adj* German; **auf Deutsch** in German

'**Deutsche** *m, f* (*-n; -n*) German

'**Deutschland** Germany

Devise [de'vi:zə] *f* (*-; -n*) motto

De'visen *pl* ECON foreign currency

Dezember [de'tsɛmbɐ] *m* (*-[s]; -*) December

---

dezent [de'tsɛnt] *adj* discreet, unobtrusive; conservative (*clothes etc*); soft (*music etc*)

Dezimal... [detsi'ma:l-] MATH *in cpds* **...bruch, ...system** *etc:* decimal ...; **~stelle** *f* MATH decimal (place)

DGB [de:ge:'be:] *abbr of* **Deutscher Gewerkschaftsbund** Federation of German Trade Unions

d. h. *abbr of* **das heißt** i. e., that is

Dia ['di:a] *n* (*-s; -s*) PHOT slide

Diagnose [dia'gno:zə] *f* (*-; -n*) diagnosis

diagonal [diago'na:l] *adj*, **Diago'nale** *f* (*-; -n*) diagonal

Dialekt [dia'lɛkt] *m* (*-[e]s; -e*) dialect

Dialog [dia'lo:k] *m* (*-[e]s; -e*) dialog, *Br* dialogue

Diamant [dia'mant] *m* (*-en; -en*) diamond

'**Diaproˌjektor** *m* slide projector

Diät [di'ɛ:t] *f* (*-; -en*) diet; **e-e ~ machen** (**Diät leben**) be on (keep to) a diet

Di'äten *pl* PARL allowance

dich [dɪç] *pers pron* you; **~ (selbst)** yourself

dicht [dɪçt] **1.** *adj* dense, *a.* thick (*fog*); heavy (*traffic*); F closed, shut **2.** *adv:* **~ an** (*dat*) *or* **bei** close to

'**dichten** *v/t and v/i* (*ge-, h*) write (poetry); **Dichter(in)** ['dɪçtɐ, 'dɪçtərɪn] *m(f)* (*-s; -/-; -nen*) poet; writer; **dichterisch** ['dɪçtərɪʃ] *adj* poetic; **~e Freiheit** poetic licen|se, *Br* -ce

'**dichthalten** F *v/i* (*irr*, **halten**, *sep, -ge-, h*) keep mum

'**Dichtung**¹ *f* (*-; -en*) TECH seal(ing)

'**Dichtung**² *f* (*-; -en*) poetry

dick [dɪk] *adj* thick; fat; **es macht ~** it's fattening

'**Dicke** *f* (*-; -n*) thickness; fatness;

'**dickfellig** F *adj* thick-skinned

'**dickflüssig** *adj* thick; TECH viscous

Dickicht ['dɪkɪçt] *n* (*-[e]s; -e*) thicket

'**Dick|kopf** *m* stubborn *or* pig-headed person; **~milch** *f* soured milk

Dieb [di:p] *m* (*-[e]s; -e* ['di:bə]), **Diebin** ['di:bɪn] *f* (*-; -nen*) thief

diebisch ['di:bɪʃ] *adj* thievish; *fig* malicious (*glee etc*)

Diebstahl ['di:pʃta:l] *m* (*-[e]s; -stähle* ['di:pʃtɛ:lə]) theft; JUR *mst* larceny

Diele ['di:lə] *f* (*-; -n*) board, plank; hallway, *Br a.* hall

dienen ['di:nən] *v/i* (*ge-, h*) serve (**j-m**

s.o.; **als** as); Diener ['diːnɐ] *m* (-s; -) servant; *fig* bow (**vor** *dat* to)

Dienst [diːnst] *m* (-[e]s; -e) service; work; **~ haben** be on duty; **im (außer) ~** on (off) duty; **~ tuend** on duty; **~... in** *cpds ...wagen, ...wohnung etc*: official ..., company ..., business ...

'**Dienstag** *m* (-[e]s; -e) Tuesday

'**Dienstalter** *n* seniority, length of service

'**dienstbereit** *adj* on duty

'**diensteifrig** *adj* (*contp* over-)eager

'**Dienstgrad** *m* grade, rank (*a.* MIL)

'**Dienstleistung** *f* service

'**dienstlich** *adj* official

'**Dienstreise** *f* business trip

'**Dienststunden** *pl* office hours

'**Dienstweg** *m* official channels

dies [diːs], **dieser** ['diːzɐ], **diese** ['diːzə], **dieses** ['diːzəs] *dem pron* this; this one; **diese** *pl* these

diesig ['diːzɪç] *adj* hazy, misty

diesjährig ['diːsjɛːrɪç] *adj* this year's

'**diesmal** *adv* this time

diesseits ['diːszaits] *prp* (*gen*) on this side of; '**Diesseits** *n* (-; *no pl*) this life *or* world

Dietrich ['diːtrɪç] *m* (-s; -e) TECH picklock, skeleton key

Differenz [dɪfə'rɛnts] *f* (-; -en) difference; disagreement

differenzieren [dɪfərɛn'tsiːrən] *v/i* (*no -ge-*, *h*) distinguish

Digital... [digi'taːl] *in cpds ...anzeige, ...uhr etc*: digital ...

Diktat [dɪk'taːt] *n* (-[e]s; -e) dictation; **Diktator** [dɪk'taːtoːɐ] *m* (-s; -en [dɪkta'toːrən]) dictator; **diktatorisch** [dɪkta'toːrɪʃ] *adj* dictatorial; **Diktatur** [dɪkta'tuːɐ] *f* (-; -en) dictatorship; **diktieren** [dɪk'tiːrən] *v/t and v/i* (*no -ge-*, *h*) dictate

Dik'tiergerät *n* Dictaphone®

Dilettant [dilɛ'tant] *m* (-en; -en) amateur; **dilet'tantisch** *adj* amateurish

DIN® [diːn] *abbr of* **Deutsches Institut für Normung** German Institute for Standardization

Ding [dɪŋ] *n* (-[e]s; -e) thing; **vor allen ~en** above all; **F ein ~ drehen** pull a job

'**Dings(bums)** *m, f, n*, **Dingsda** *m, f, n* thingamajig, whatchamacallit

Dinosaurier [dino'zaurjɐ] *m* (-s; -) ZO dinosaur

Dioxid ['diːʔɔksyːt] *n* (-s; -e) CHEM dioxide

Dioxin [diɔ'ksiːn] *n* (-s; -e) CHEM dioxin

Diphtherie [dɪfte'riː] *f* (-; -n) MED diphtheria

Diplom [di'ploːm] *n* (-s; -e) diploma, degree; **~... in** *cpds ...ingenieur etc*: qualified ..., graduate ...

Diplomat [diplo'maːt] *m* (-en; -en) diplomat; **Diplomatie** [diploma'tiː] *f* (-; *no pl*) diplomacy; **Diplo'matin** *f* (-; -nen) diplomat; **diplo'matisch** *adj* diplomatic (*a. fig*)

dir [diːɐ] *pers pron* (to) you; **~ (selbst)** yourself

direkt [di'rɛkt] **1.** *adj* direct; TV live **2.** *adv* direct; TV live; *fig* directly, right; TV live; **~ gegenüber (von)** right across

Direktion [dirɛk'tsjoːn] *f* (-; -en) management

Direktor [di'rɛktoːɐ] *m* (-s; -en [dirɛk'toːrən]) director, manager; PED principal, *Br* headmaster; **Direktorin** [dirɛk'toːrɪn] (-; -nen) director, manager; PED principal, *Br* headmistress

Di'rektübertragung *f* TV live transmission *or* broadcast

Dirigent [diri'gɛnt] *m* (-en; -en) conductor; **dirigieren** [diri'giːrən] *v/t and v/i* (*no -ge-*, *h*) MUS conduct; *fig* direct

Dirne ['dɪrnə] *f* (-; -n) prostitute, whore

Discman® ['dɪsmən] *m* (-s; -men) portable CD player, Discman®

Disharmonie [dɪsharmo'niː] *f* MUS dissonance (*a. fig*); **dishar'monisch** *adj* MUS discordant

Diskette [dɪs'kɛtə] *f* (-; -n) diskette, floppy (disk); **Dis'kettenlaufwerk** *n* disk drive

Disko ['dɪsko] *f* (-; -s) disco

Diskont [dɪs'kɔnt] *m* (-s; -e) ECON discount

Diskothek [dɪsko'teːk] (-; -en) disco, discotheque

diskret [dɪs'kreːt] *adj* discreet; **Diskretion** [dɪskre'tsjoːn] *f* (-; *no pl*) discretion

diskriminieren [dɪskrimi'niːrən] *v/t* (*no -ge-*, *h*) discriminate against

Diskrimi'nierung *f* (-; -en) discrimination (**von** against)

Diskussion [dɪsku'sjoːn] *f* (-; -en) discussion, debate

Diskussi'ons|leiter *m* (panel) chair-

man; **~runde** f, **~teilnehmer** pl panel
Diskuswerfen ['dɪskʊsvɛrfən] n (-s; no pl) SPORT discus throwing
diskutieren [dɪsku'tiːrən] v/t and v/i (no -ge-, h) discuss
Disqualifikati'on f SPORT disqualification (**wegen** for); **disqualifi'zieren** v/t (no -ge-, h) SPORT disqualify
Dissident [dɪsi'dɛnt] m (-en; -en), **Dissi'dentin** f (-; -nen) POL dissident
Distanz [dɪs'tants] f (-; -en) distance
distanzieren [dɪstan'tsiːrən] v/refl (no -ge-, h) distance o.s. (**von** from)
Distel ['dɪstəl] f (-; -n) BOT thistle
Distrikt [dɪs'trɪkt] m (-[e]s; -e) district
Disziplin [dɪstsi'pliːn] f (-; -en) (no pl) discipline; SPORT event; **diszipliniert** [dɪstsipli'niːɐt] adj disciplined
divers [di'vɛrs] adj various; several
Dividende [divi'dɛndə] f (-; -n) ECON dividend
dividieren [divi'diːrən] v/t (no -ge-, h) MATH divide (**durch** by)
Division [divi'zjoːn] f (-; -en) MATH, MIL division
DJH [deːjɔt'haː] abbr of **Deutsches Jugendherbergswerk** German Youth Hostel Association
DM [deː'ɛm] abbr of **Deutsche Mark** hist (former monetary unit of Germany) German mark(s)
doch [dɔx] cj and adv but, however, yet; **kommst du nicht (mit)? - ~!** aren't you coming? - (oh) yes, I am!; **ich war es nicht - ~!** I didn't do it - yes, you did!; **er kam also ~?** so he did come after all?; **du kommst ~?** you're coming, aren't you?; **kommen Sie ~ herein!** do come in!; **wenn ~ ...!** if only ...!
Docht [dɔxt] m (-[e]s; -e) wick
Dock [dɔk] n (-s; -s) MAR dock
Dogge ['dɔgə] f (-; -n) ZO mastiff; Great Dane
Dogma ['dɔgma] n (-s; Dogmen ['dɔgmən]) dogma; **dogmatisch** [dɔg'maːtɪʃ] adj dogmatic
Dohle ['doːlə] f (-; -n) ZO (jack)daw
Doktor ['dɔktoːɐ] m (-s; -en [dɔk'toːrən]) doctor; UNIV doctor's degree; **~arbeit** f UNIV (doctoral or PhD) thesis
Dokument [doku'mɛnt] n (-[e]s; -e) document
Dokumentar... [dokumɛn'taːɐ-] in cpds ...**spiel** etc: documentary ...; **~film**

m documentary (film)
Dolch [dɔlç] m (-[e]s; -e) dagger
Dollar ['dɔlar] m (-[s]; -s) dollar
dolmetschen ['dɔlmɛtʃən] v/i interpret; '**Dolmetscher(in)** (-s; -/-; -nen) interpreter
Dom [doːm] m (-[e]s; -e) cathedral
dominierend [domi'niːrənt] adj (pre-)dominant
Dompteur [dɔmp'tøːɐ] m (-s; -e), **Dompteuse** [dɔmp'tøːzə] f (-; -n) animal tamer or trainer
Donner ['dɔnɐ] m (-s; no pl) thunder
'**donnern** v/i (ge-, h) thunder (a. fig)
'**Donnerstag** m (-[e]s; -e) Thursday
'**Donnerwetter** F n (-s; -) dressing-down; **~!** wow!
doof [doːf] F adj stupid, dumb
Doppel ['dɔpəl] n (-s; -) duplicate; tennis etc: doubles; **~... in** cpds ...**bett**, ...**zimmer** etc: double ...
Doppeldecker ['dɔpəldɛkɐ] m (-s; -) AVIAT biplane; MOT double-decker (bus)
Doppelgänger ['dɔpəlgɛŋɐ] m (-s; -) double, look-alike
'**Doppelhaus** n duplex, Br of semis; **~hälfte** f semidetached (house)
'**Doppel|pass** m soccer: wall pass; **~punkt** m LING colon; **~stecker** m ELECTR two-way adapter
doppelt adj double; **~ so viel** (**wie**) twice as much (as)
'**Doppelverdiener** pl two-income family
Dorf [dɔrf] n (-[e]s; Dörfer ['dœrfɐ]) village; **~bewohner** m villager
Dorn [dɔrn] m (-[e]s; -en) BOT thorn (a. fig); TECH tongue; spike
'**dornig** adj thorny (a. fig)
Dorsch [dɔrʃ] m (-[e]s; -e) ZO cod(fish)
dort [dɔrt] adv there
'**dorther** adv from there
'**dorthin** adv there
Dose ['doːzə] f (-; -n) can, Br a. tin
'**Dosen...** in cpds canned, Br a. tinned
dösen ['døːzən] F v/i (ge-, h) doze
'**Dosenöffner** m can (Br tin) opener
Dosis ['doːzɪs] f (-; Dosen) MED dose
Dotter ['dɔtɐ] m, n (-s; -) yolk
Double ['duːbəl] n (-s; -s) film: stunt man (or woman)
Dozent [do'tsɛnt] m (-en; -en), **Do'zentin** f (-; -nen) (university) lecturer, assistant professor

Dr. *abbr of* **Doktor** Dr., Doctor

Drache ['draxə] *m* (*-n*; *-n*) dragon

'Drachen *m* (*-s*; *-*) kite; SPORT hang glider; **e-n ~ steigen lassen** fly a kite; **~fliegen** *n* SPORT hang gliding

Draht [dra:t] *m* (*-[e]s*; *Drähte* ['drɛ:tə]) wire; F **auf ~ sein** be on the ball

drahtig ['dra:tɪç] *fig adj* wiry

'drahtlos *adj* wireless

'Drahtseil *n* TECH cable; *circus*: tightrope; **~bahn** *f* cable railway

'Drahtzieher *fig m* (*-s*; *-*) wirepuller

drall [dral] *adj* buxom, strapping

Drall *m* (*-[e]s*; *no pl*) twist, spin

Drama ['dra:ma] *n* (*-s*; *Dramen*) drama

Dramatiker [dra'ma:tikɐ] *m* (*-s*; *-*) dramatist, playwright

dra'matisch *adj* dramatic

dran [dran] F *adv* → **daran**; **du bist ~** it's your turn; *fig* you're in for it

drang [draŋ] *pret of* **dringen**

Drang *m* (*-[e]s*; *no pl*) urge, drive (**nach** for)

drängeln ['drɛŋəln] F *v/t and v/i* (*ge-*, *h*) push, shove

drängen ['drɛŋən] *v/t and v/i* (*ge-*, *h*) push, shove; **j-n zu et. ~** press *or* urge s.o. to do s.th.; **sich ~** press; force one's way; **~d** *adj* pressing

'drankommen F *v/i* (*irr*, **kommen**, *sep*, *-ge-*, *sein*) have one's turn; **als erster ~ be** first

drastisch ['drastɪʃ] *adj* drastic

drauf [drauf] F *adv* → **darauf**; **~ und dran sein, et. zu tun** be just about to do s.th.; **'Draufgänger** ['draufgɛŋɐ] *m* (*-s*; *-*) daredevil

draus [draus] F *adv* → **daraus**

draußen ['drausən] *adv* outside; outdoors; **da ~** out there; **bleib(t) ~!** keep out!

drechseln ['drɛksəln] *v/t* (*ge-*, *h*) turn (on a lathe)

Drechsler ['drɛkslɐ] *m* (*-s*; *-*) turner

Dreck [drɛk] F *m* (*-[e]s*; *no pl*) dirt; filth (*a. fig*); mud; *fig* trash; **dreckig** ['drɛkɪç] F *adj* dirty; filthy (*both a. fig*)

Dreh|arbeiten ['dre:arbaitən] *pl film*: shooting; **~bank** *f* (*-*; *-bänke*) TECH lathe; **'drehbar** *adj* revolving, rotating

'Drehbuch *n film*: script

drehen ['dre:ən] *v/t* (*ge-*, *h*) turn; *film*: shoot; roll; **sich ~** turn, rotate; spin; **sich ~ um** *fig* be about; → **Ding**

Dreher ['dre:ɐ] *m* (*-s*; *-*) TECH turner

'Dreh|kreuz *n* turnstile; **~orgel** *f* barrel organ; **~ort** *m film*: location; **~strom** *m* ELECTR three-phase current; **~stuhl** *m* swivel chair; **~tür** *f* revolving door

'Drehung *f* (*-*; *-en*) turn; rotation

'Drehzahl *f* TECH (number of) revolutions; **~messer** *m* MOT rev(olution) counter

drei [drai] *adj* three

Drei *f* (*-*; *-en*) three; *grade*: fair, C

'drei|beinig *adj* three-legged; **~dimensio,nal** *adj* three-dimensional

'Dreieck *n* (*-[e]s*; *-e*) triangle

'dreieckig *adj* triangular

dreierlei ['draiɐlai] *adj* three kinds of

'dreifach *adj* threefold, triple

'Drei|gang... TECH *in cpds* three-speed ...; **~kampf** *m* SPORT triathlon; **~rad** *n* tricycle; **~satz** *m* (*-es*; *no pl*) MATH rule of three; **~sprung** *m* (*-[e]s*; *no pl*) SPORT triple jump

dreißig ['draisɪç] *adj* thirty

'dreißigste *adj* thirtieth

dreist [draist] *adj* brazen, impertinent

dreistufig ['draiʃtu:fɪç] *adj* three-stage

dreizehn(te) *adj* thirteen(th)

Dresche ['drɛʃə] F *f* (*-*; *no pl*) thrashing

'dreschen *v/t and v/i* (*irr*, *ge-*, *h*) AGR thresh; thrash; **'Dreschma,schine** *f* AGR threshing machine

dressieren [drɛ'si:rən] *v/t* (*no -ge-*, *h*) train

Dressman ['drɛsmən] *m* (*-s*; *-men*) male model

Dressur [drɛ'su:ɐ] *f* (*-*; *-en*) training; act; **~reiten** *n* dressage

dribbeln ['drɪbəln] *v/i* (*ge-*, *h*), **Dribbling** *n* (*-s*; *-s*) SPORT dribble

drillen ['drɪlən] *v/t* (*ge-*, *h*) MIL drill (*a. fig*)

Drillinge ['drɪlɪŋə] *pl* triplets

drin [drɪn] F *adv* → **darin**; **das ist nicht ~!** no way!

dringen ['drɪŋən] *v/i* (*irr*, *ge-*, *h*) **~ auf** (*acc*) insist on; **~ aus** come from; **~ durch** force one's way through, penetrate, pierce; **~ in** (*acc*) penetrate into; **darauf~**, **dass** urge that; **~d** *adj* urgent, pressing; strong (*suspicion etc*)

drinnen ['drɪnən] F *adv* inside; indoors

dritte ['drɪtə] *adj* third; **wir sind zu dritt** there are three of us; **die Dritte Welt** the Third World; **'Drittel** (*-s*; *-*) third;

'**drittens** *adv* thirdly; '**Dritte-Welt-La-den** *m* third world shop

Droge ['dro:gə] *f* (-; -*n*) drug

'**drogenabhängig** *adj* addicted to drugs; **~ sein** be a drug addict

'**Drogen|abhängige** *m*, *f* (-*n*; -*n*) drug addict; **~missbrauch** *m* drug abuse

'**drogensüchtig** → **drogenabhängig**

'**Drogentote** *m*, *f* drug victim

Drogerie [drogə'ri:] *f* (-; -*n*) drugstore, *Br* chemist's (shop)

Drogist [dro'gɪst] *m* (-*en*; -*en*), **Dro-'gistin** *f* (-; -*nen*) chemist

drohen ['dro:ən] *v/i* (*ge-, h*) threaten, menace

dröhnen ['drø:nən] *v/i* (*ge-, h*) roar

'**Drohung** *f* (-; -*en*) threat (**gegen** to)

drollig ['drɔlɪç] *adj* funny, droll

Dromedar [dromə'da:ɐ] *n* (-*s*; -*e*) ZO dromedary

drosch [drɔʃ] *pret of* **dreschen**

Drossel ['drɔsəl] *f* (-; -*n*) ZO thrush

'**drosseln** *v/t* (*ge-, h*) TECH throttle

drüben ['dry:bən] *adv* over there (*a. fig*)

drüber ['dry:bɐ] F *adv* → **darüber, drunter**

Druck [drʊk] *m* (-[*e*]*s*; -*e*) pressure; printing; print

'**Druckbuchstabe** *m* block letter

Drückeberger ['drʏkəbɛrgɐ] F *m* (-*s*; -) shirker

'**drucken** *v/t* (*ge-, h*) print; **et. ~ lassen** have s.th. printed *or* published

drücken ['drʏkən] (*ge-, h*) **1.** *v/t* press; push; *fig* force down; **j-m die Hand ~** shake hands with s.o. **2.** *v/i* pinch **3.** *v/refl*: **sich vor et. ~** shirk (doing) s.th.; **~d** *adj* heavy, oppressive

Drucker ['drʊkɐ] *m* (-*s*; -) printer (*a.* IT)

Drücker ['drʏkɐ] *m* (-*s*; -) latch; trigger; F hawker

Druckerei [drʊkə'raɪ] *f* (-; -*en*) printers

'**Druck|fehler** *m* misprint; **~kammer** *f* pressurized cabin; **~knopf** *m* snap fastener, *Br* press stud; TECH (push) button; **~luft** *f* TECH compressed air; **~sache** *f* printed (*or* second-class) matter; **~schrift** *f* block letters; **~taste** *f* TECH push button

drunter ['drʊntɐ] F *adv* → **darunter**; **es ging ~ und drüber** it was absolutely chaotic

Drüse ['dry:zə] *f* (-; -*n*) ANAT gland

Dschungel ['dʒʊŋəl] *m* (-*s*; -) jungle (*a.*

fig)

Dschunke ['dʒʊŋkə] *f* (-; -*n*) MAR junk

du [du:] *pers pron* you

Dübel ['dy:bəl] *m* (-*s*; -), '**dübeln** *v/t* (*ge-, h*) TECH dowel

ducken ['dʊkən] *v/refl* (*ge-, h*) duck; *fig* cringe (**vor** *dat* before); crouch

Duckmäuser ['dʊkmɔʏzɐ] *m* (-*s*; -) coward; yes-man

Dudelsack ['du:dəlzak] *m* MUS bagpipes

Duell [du'ɛl] *n* (-*s*; -*e*) duel; **duellieren** [duɛ'li:rən] *v/refl* (*no -ge-, h*) fight a duel

Duett [du'ɛt] *n* (-[*e*]*s*; -*e*) MUS duet

Duft [dʊft] *m* (-[*e*]*s*; **Düfte** ['dʏftə]) scent, fragrance, smell (**nach** of); '**duften** *v/i* (*ge-, h*) smell (**nach** of); '**duftend** *adj* fragrant; '**duftig** *adj* dainty

dulden ['dʊldən] *v/t* (*ge-, h*) tolerate, put up with; suffer

duldsam ['dʊltza:m] *adj* tolerant

dumm [dʊm] *adj* stupid, F dumb

'**Dummheit** *f* (-; -*en*) (*no pl*) stupidity, ignorance; stupid *or* foolish thing

'**Dummkopf** *m contp* fool, blockhead

dumpf [dʊmpf] *adj* dull; *fig* vague

Düne ['dy:nə] *f* (-; -*n*) (sand) dune

Dung [dʊŋ] *m* (-[*e*]*s*; *no pl*) dung, manure

düngen ['dʏŋən] *v/t* (*ge-, h*) fertilize; manure; **Dünger** ['dʏŋɐ] *m* (-*s*; -) fertilizer; manure

dunkel ['dʊŋkəl] *adj* dark (*a. fig*)

'**Dunkelheit** *f* (-; *no pl*) dark(ness)

'**Dunkel|kammer** *f* PHOT darkroom; **~ziffer** *f* number of unreported cases

dünn [dʏn] *adj* thin; weak (*coffee etc*)

Dunst [dʊnst] *m* (-[*e*]*s*; **Dünste** ['dʏnstə]) haze, mist; CHEM vapo(u)r; **dünsten** ['dʏnstən] *v/t* (*ge-, h*) GASTR stew, braise; '**dunstig** *adj* hazy, misty

Duplikat [dupli'ka:t] *n* (-[*e*]*s*; -*e*) duplicate; copy

Dur [du:ɐ] *n* (-; *no pl*) MUS major (key)

durch [dʊrç] *prp* (*acc*) *and adv* through; across; MATH divided by; GASTR (well) done; **~ j-n (et.)** by s.o. (s.th.); **~ und ~** through and through

'**durcharbeiten** (*sep, -ge-, h*) **1.** *v/t* study thoroughly; **sich ~ durch** work (one's way) through a *text etc* **2.** *v/i* work without a break

'durch'aus *adv* absolutely, quite; **~ nicht** by no means

'durchblättern *v/t* (*sep*, *-ge-*, *h*) leaf *or* thumb through

'Durchblick *fig m* grasp of *s.th.*

'durchblicken *v/i* (*sep*, *-ge-*, *h*) look through; **~ lassen** give to understand; **ich blicke (da) nicht durch** I don't get it

durch'bohren *v/t* (*no -ge-*, *h*) pierce; perforate

'durchbraten *v/t* (*irr*, **braten**, *sep*, *-ge-*, *h*) roast thoroughly

'durchbrechen[1] (*irr*, **brechen**, *sep*, *-ge-*) **1.** *v/t* (*h*) break (in two) **2.** *v/i* (*sein*) break through *or* apart

durch'brechen[2] *v/t* (*irr*, **brechen**, *no -ge-*, *h*) break through

'durch|brennen *v/i* (*irr*, **brennen**, *sep*, *-ge-*, *sein*) ELECTR blow; *reactor:* melt down; F run away

'durchbringen *v/t* (*irr*, **bringen**, *sep*, *-ge-*, *h*) get (MED pull) *s.o.* through; go through *one's money*; support (*family*)

'Durchbruch *m* breakthrough (*a. fig*)

durch'dacht *adj* (well) thought-out

'durchdrehen (*sep*, *-ge-*, *h*) **1.** *v/i wheels:* spin; F *fig* crack up, flip **2.** *v/t* GASTR grind, *Br* mince

'durchdringend *adj* piercing

durchei'nander *adv* confused; (in) a mess; **~bringen** *v/t* (*irr*, **bringen**, *sep*, *-ge-*, *h*) confuse, mix up; mess up; **Durchei'nander** *n* (*-s*; *no pl*) confusion, mess

durch'fahren[1] *v/t* (*irr*, **fahren**, *no -ge-*, *h*) go (*or* pass, drive) through

'durchfahren[2] *v/i* (*irr*, **fahren**, *sep*, *-ge-*, *sein*) go (*or* pass, drive) through

'Durchfahrt *f* passage; **~ verboten** no thoroughfare

'Durchfall *m* MED diarrh(o)ea

'durch|fallen *v/i* (*irr*, **fallen**, *sep*, *-ge-*, *sein*) fall through; fail, F flunk (*test etc*); F be a flop; **j-n ~ lassen** fail (F flunk) s.o.; **~fragen** *v/refl* (*sep*, *-ge-*, *h*) ask one's way (**nach, zu** to)

'durchführbar *adj* practicable, feasible

'durchführen *v/t* (*sep*, *-ge-*, *h*) carry out, do

'Durchgang *m* passage

'Durchgangs... *in cpds* ...*verkehr etc*: through ...; ...*lager etc*: transit ...

'durchgebraten *adj* well done

'durchgehen (*irr*, **gehen**, *sep*, *-ge-*, *sein*) **1.** *v/i* go through (*a.* RAIL *and* PARL); *fig* run away (**mit** with); *horse:* bolt **2.** *v/t* go *or* look through; **~ lassen** tolerate; **~d** *adj* continuous; **~er Zug** through train; **~ geöffnet** open all day

'durchgreifen *fig v/i* (*irr*, **greifen**, *sep*, *-ge-*, *h*) take drastic measures; **~d** *adj* drastic; radical

'durchhalten (*irr*, **halten**, *sep*, *-ge-*, *h*) **1.** *v/t* keep up **2.** *v/i* hold out

'durchhängen *v/i* (*irr*, **hängen**, *sep*, *-ge-*, *h*) sag; F have a low

'durchkämpfen *v/t* (*sep*, *-ge-*, *h*) fight out; **sich ~** fight one's way through

'durchkommen *v/i* (*irr*, **kommen**, *sep*, *-ge-*, *sein*) come through (*a.* MED); get through; get along; get away (**mit e-r Lüge** *etc* with a lie *etc*)

durch'kreuzen *v/t* (*no -ge-*, *h*) cross, thwart

'durchlassen *v/t* (*irr*, **lassen**, *sep*, *-ge-*, *h*) let pass, let through

'durchlässig *adj* permeable (**für** to)

'durch|laufen[1] (*irr*, **laufen**, *sep*, *-ge-*) **1.** *v/i* (*sein*) run through **2.** *v/t* (*h*) wear through

durch'laufen[2] *v/t* (*irr*, **laufen**, *no -ge-*, *h*) pass through

'Durchlauferhitzer *m* (*-s*; *-*) (instant) water heater, *Br a.* geyser

'durchlesen *v/t* (*irr*, **lesen**, *sep*, *-ge-*, *h*) read through

'durch|leuchten *v/t* (*no -ge-*, *h*) MED X-ray; *fig* screen; **~löchern** [durç-ˈlœçən] *v/t* (*no -ge-*, *h*) perforate, make holes in

'durchmachen F *v/t* (*sep*, *-ge-*, *h*) go through; **viel ~** suffer a lot; **die Nacht ~** make a night of it

'Durchmesser *m* (*-s*; *-*) diameter

durch'nässen *v/t* (*no -ge-*, *h*) soak

'durchnehmen *v/t* (*irr*, **nehmen**, *sep*, *-ge-*, *h*) PED do, deal with

'durchpausen *v/t* (*sep*, *-ge-*, *h*) trace

durch'queren *v/t* (*no -ge-*, *h*) cross

'Durchreiche *f* (*-*; *-n*) hatch

'Durchreise *f:* **ich bin nur auf der ~** I'm only passing through; 'durchreisen *v/i* (*sep*, *-ge-*, *sein*) travel through

'Durchreisevisum *n* transit visa

'durch|reißen (*irr*, **reißen**, *sep*, *-ge-*) **1.** *v/t* (*h*) tear (in two) **2.** *v/i* (*sein*) tear, break; **~ringen** v/refl (irr, **ringen**, sep, -ge-, h) **sich ~, et. zu tun** bring o.s. to do s.th.

'**Durchsage** f announcement

durch'**schauen** v/t (no -ge-, h) see through s.o. or s.th.

'**durchscheinen** v/i (irr, **scheinen**, sep, -ge-, h) shine through; **~d** adj transparent

'**durchscheuern** v/t (sep, -ge-, h) chafe; wear through

'**durchschlafen** v/i (irr, **schlafen**, sep, -ge-, h) sleep through

'**Durchschlag** m (carbon) copy

durch'**schlagen**[1] v/t (irr, **schlagen**, no -ge-, h) cut in two; **bullet** etc: go through, pierce

'**durchschlagen**[2] (irr, **schlagen**, sep, -ge-) **1.** v/refl (h): **sich ~ nach** make one's way to **2.** v/i (sein) come through (a. fig); **~d** adj sweeping; effective

'**Durch**|**schlagpa**,**pier** n carbon paper; **~schlagskraft** fig f force, impact

'**durchschneiden** v/t (irr, **schneiden**, sep, -ge-, h) cut (through)

'**Durchschnitt** m average; **im** (**über, unter dem**) **~** on an (above, below) average; **im ~ betragen** (**verdienen** etc) average

'**durchschnittlich 1.** adj average; ordinary **2.** adv on an average

'**Durchschnitts...** in cpds average ...

'**Durchschrift** f (carbon) copy

'**durch**|**sehen** v/t (irr, **sehen**, sep, -ge-, h) look or go through; check; **~setzen** v/t (sep, -ge-, h) put (or push) s.th. through; **s-n Kopf ~** have one's way; **sich ~** get one's way; be successful; **sich ~ können** have authority (**bei** over)

durch'**setzt** adj: **~ mit** interspersed with

'**durchsichtig** adj transparent (a. fig); clear; see-through

'**durchsickern** v/i (sep, -ge-, sein) seep through; fig leak out

'**durchstarten** v/i (sep, -ge-, sein) AVIAT climb and reaccelerate

durch'**stechen** v/t (irr, **stechen**, no -ge-, h) pierce

'**durch**|**stecken** v/t (sep, -ge-, h) stick through; **~stehen** v/t (irr, **stehen**, sep, -ge-, h) go through

durch'**stoßen** v/t (irr, **stoßen**, no -ge-, h) break through

'**durchstreichen** v/t (irr, **streichen**, sep, -ge-, h) cross out

durch'**suchen** v/t (no -ge-, h) search, F frisk; **Durch**'**suchung** f (-; -en) search; **Durch**'**suchungsbefehl** m search warrant

durch'**trieben** [dʊrç'triːbən] adj cunning, sly; **~'wachsen** adj GASTR streaky

'**Durchwahl** f (-; no pl) TEL direct dial-(l)ing; '**durchwählen** v/i (sep, -ge-, h) TEL dial direct

durchweg ['dʊrçvɛk] adv without exception

durch'**weicht** adj soaked, drenched

durch'**wühlen** v/t (no -ge-, h) rummage through

'**durch**|**zählen** v/t (sep, -ge-, h) count off (Br up); **~ziehen** (irr, **ziehen**, sep, -ge-) **1.** v/i (sein) pass through **2.** v/t (h) pull s.th. through; fig carry s.th. through (to the end)

durch'**zucken** v/t (no -ge-, h) flash through

'**Durchzug** m (-[e]s; no pl) draft, Br draught

dürfen ['dʏrfən] **1.** v/aux (irr, no -ge-, h) be allowed or permitted to inf; **darf ich gehen?** may I go?; **ja(**, **du darfst**) yes, you may; **du darfst nicht** you must not, you aren't allowed to; **dürfte ich ...?** could I ...?; **das dürfte genügen** that should be enough **2.** v/i (irr, ge-, h) **er darf (nicht)** he is (not) allowed to inf

durfte ['dʊrftə] pret of **dürfen**

dürftig ['dʏrftɪç] adj poor; scanty

dürr [dʏr] adj dry; barren, arid; skinny

Dürre ['dʏrə] f (-; -n) drought; (no pl) barrenness

Durst [dʊrst] m (-[e]s; no pl) thirst (**auf** acc for); **~ haben** be thirsty

durstig adj thirsty

Dusche ['dʊʃə] f (-; -n) shower

'**duschen** v/refl and v/i (ge-, h) have or take a shower

Düse ['dyːzə] f (-; -n) TECH nozzle; jet

'**düsen** F v/i (ge-, sein) jet

'**Düsen**|**antrieb** m jet propulsion; **mit ~** jet-propelled; **~flugzeug** n jet (plane); **~jäger** m MIL jet fighter; **~triebwerk** n jet engine

düster ['dyːstɐ] adj dark, gloomy (both a. fig); dim (light); fig dismal

Dutzend ['dʊtsənt] n (-s; -e) dozen

'**dutzendweise** adv by the dozen

duzen ['du:tsən] *v/t* (*ge-, h*) use the familiar 'du' with s.o.; **sich ~** be on 'du' terms

DVD [de:fau'de:] *abbr of Digital Versatile Disk* DVD; **~-Player** *m* (*-s; -*) DVD player; **~-Rekorder** *m* (*-s; -*) DVD recorder

Dynamik [dy'na:mɪk] *f* (*-; no pl*) PHYS dynamics; *fig* dynamism

dy'namisch *adj* dynamic

Dynamit [dyna'mi:t] *n* (*-s; no pl*) dynamite

Dynamo [dy'an:mo] *m* (*-s; -s*) ELECTR dynamo, generator

D-Zug ['de:tsu:k] *m* express train

E

'Edelmetall *n* precious metal

'Edelstahl *m* stainless steel

'Edelstein *n* precious stone; gem

EDV [e:de:'fau] *abbr of Elektronische Datenverarbeitung* electronic data processing

Efeu ['e:fɔy] *m* (*-s; no pl*) BOT ivy

Effekt [ɛ'fɛkt] *m* (*-[e]s; -e*) effect

effektiv [ɛfɛk'ti:f] **1.** *adjective* effective **2.** *adv* actually; Effektivität [ɛfɛkti'tɛ:t] *f* (*-; no pl*) effectiveness

ef'fektvoll *adj* effective, striking

Effet [ɛ'fe:] *m* (*-s; -s*) SPORT spin

EG [e:'ge:] *hist abbr of Europäische Gemeinschaft* EC, European Community

egal [e'ga:l] *F adj:* **~ ob (warum, wer** *etc*) no matter if (why, who, *etc*); **das ist ~** it doesn't matter; **das ist mir ~** I don't care, it's all the same to me

Egge ['ɛgə] *f* (*-; -n*), 'eggen *v/t* (*ge-, h*) AGR harrow

Egoismus [ego'ɪsmus] *m* (*-; no pl*) ego(t)ism; Egoist(in) [ego'ɪst(ɪn)] (*-en; -en/-; -nen*) ego(t)ist; ego'istisch *adj* selfish, ego(t)istic(al)

ehe ['e:ə] *cj* before; **nicht ~** not until

Ehe ['e:ə] *f* (*-; -n*) marriage (*mit* to); **~beratung** *f* marriage counseling (*Br* guidance)

'Ehe|bruch *m* adultery; **~frau** *f* wife; **~leute** *pl* married couple

'ehelich *adj* conjugal; JUR legitimate

ehemalig ['e:əma:lɪç] *adj* former, ex-...

ehemals ['e:əma:ls] *adv* formerly

'Ehemann *m* husband

'Ehepaar *n* (married) couple

eher ['e:ɐ] *adv* earlier, sooner; **je ~, desto lieber** the sooner the better; **nicht ~ als** not until *or* before

Ebbe ['ɛbə] *f* (*-; -n*) ebb, low tide

eben ['e:bən] **1.** *adj* even; flat; MATH plane; **zu ~er Erde** (*Br* ground) floor **2.** *adv* just; **an ~ dem Tag** on that very day; **so ist es ~** that's the way it is; **gerade ~ so** *or* **noch** just barely

'Ebenbild *n* image

ebenbürtig ['e:bənbyrtɪç] *adj:* **j-m ~ sein** be a match for s.o., be s.o.'s equal

Ebene ['e:bənə] *f* (*-; -n*) GEOGR plain; MATH plane; *fig* level

'ebenerdig *adj and adv* at street level; on the first (*Br* ground) floor

'ebenfalls *adv* as well, too

'Ebenholz *n* ebony

'Ebenmaß *n* (*-es; no pl*) symmetry; harmony; regularity; 'ebenmäßig *adj* symmetrical; harmonious; regular

'ebenso *adv and cj* just as; as well; **~ wie** in the same way as; **~ gern, ~ gut** just as well; **~ sehr, ~ viel** just as much; **~ wenig** just as little *or* few

Eber ['e:bɐ] *m* (*-s; -*) ZO boar

ebnen ['e:bnən] *v/t* (*ge-, h*) even, level; *fig* smooth

Echo ['ɛço] *n* (*-s; -s*) echo; *fig* response

echt [ɛçt] *adj* genuine (*a. fig*), real; true; pure; fast (*color*); authentic; F **~ gut** real good; 'Echtheit *f* (*-; no pl*) genuineness; authenticity

Eckball ['ɛkbal] *m* SPORT corner (kick)

Ecke ['ɛkə] *f* (*-; -n*) corner; edge; SPORT **lange (kurze) ~** far (near) corner; → **Eckball**; eckig ['ɛkɪç] *adj* square, angular; *fig* awkward

'Eckzahn *m* canine tooth

Economyclass [i'kɔnəmikla:s] *f* (*-; no pl*) coach (class)

edel ['e:dəl] *adj* noble; MIN precious

'**Ehering** *m* wedding ring

ehrbar ['e:ɐbaːɐ] *adj* respectable

Ehre ['e:rə] *f* (-; -*n*) hono(u)r; **zu ~n (von)** in hono(u)r of

ehren *v/t* (*ge-*, *h*) hono(u)r; respect

'**ehrenamtlich** *adj* honorary

'**Ehren|bürger** *m* honorary citizen; ~**doktor** *m* UNIV honorary doctor; ~**gast** *m* guest of hono(u)r; ~**kodex** *m* code of hono(u)r; ~**mann** *m* man of hono(u)r; ~**mitglied** *n* honorary member; ~**platz** *m* place of hono(u)r; ~**rechte** *pl* civil rights; ~**rettung** *f* rehabilitation

'**ehrenrührig** *adj* defamatory

'**Ehren|runde** *f* *esp* SPORT lap of hono(u)r; ~**sache** *f* point of hono(u)r; ~**tor** *n*, ~**treffer** *m* SPORT consolation goal

'**ehrenwert** *adj* hono(u)rable

'**Ehrenwort** *n* (-[*e*]*s*; -*e*) word of hono(u)r; F ~*!* cross my heart!

ehrerbietig ['e:ɐˀe:ɐbiːtɪç] *adj* respectful

Ehrfurcht ['e:ɐfʊrçt] *f* (-; *no pl*) respect (**vor** *dat* for); awe (of); ~ **gebietend** awe-inspiring, awesome; **ehrfürchtig** ['e:ɐfʏrçtɪç] *adj* respectful

'**Ehrgefühl** *n* (-[*e*]*s*; *no pl*) sense of hono(u)r

'**Ehrgeiz** *m* ambition; '**ehrgeizig** *adj* ambitious

'**ehrlich** *adj* honest; frank; fair; '**Ehrlichkeit** *f* (-; *no pl*) honesty; fairness

Ehrung *f* (-; -*en*) hono(u)r(ing)

'**ehrwürdig** *adj* venerable

Ei [ai] *n* (-[*e*]*s*; *Eier* ['aiɐ]) egg; V *pl* balls

Eiche ['aiçə] *f* (-; -*n*) oak(-tree)

Eichel ['aiçəl] *f* (-; -*n*) BOT acorn; *card games*: club(s); ANAT glans (penis)

eichen ['aiçən] *v/t* (*ge-*, *h*) ga(u)ge

Eichhörnchen ['aiçhœrnçən] *n* (-*s*; -) zo squirrel

Eid [ait] *m* (-[*e*]*s*; -*e*) oath; **e-n ~ ablegen** take an oath

Eidechse ['aidɛksə] *f* (-; -*n*) zo lizard

eidesstattlich ['aidəsʃtatlɪç] *adj*: ~*e* **Erklärung** JUR statutory declaration

'**Eidotter** *m*, *n* (egg) yolk

'**Eier|becher** *m* eggcup; ~**kuchen** *m* pancake; ~**li,kör** *m* eggnog; ~**schale** *f* eggshell; ~**stock** *m* ANAT ovary; ~**uhr** *f* egg timer

Eifer ['aifɐ] *m* (-*s*; *no pl*) zeal, eagerness; **glühender ~** ardo(u)r

'**Eifersucht** *f* (-; *no pl*) jealousy

'**eifersüchtig** *adj* jealous (**auf** *acc* of)

eifrig *adj* eager, zealous; ardent

'**Eigelb** *n* (-[*e*]*s*; -*e*) (egg) yolk

eigen ['aigən] *adj* own, of one's own; peculiar; particular, F fussy; ...**eigen** *in cpds* staatseigen *etc*: ...-owned

'**Eigenart** *f* peculiarity

'**eigenartig** *adj* peculiar; strange

'**Eigenbedarf** *m* personal needs

'**Eigengewicht** *n* dead weight

eigenhändig ['aigənhɛndɪç] **1.** *adj* personal **2.** *adv* personally, with one's own hands

'**Eigen|heim** *n* home (of one's own); ~**liebe** *f* self-love; ~**lob** *n* self-praise

'**eigenmächtig** *adj* arbitrary

'**Eigenname** *m* proper noun

'**Eigennutz** *m* (-*es*; *no pl*) self-interest

eigennützig ['aigənnytsɪç] *adj* selfish

'**eigens** *adv* (e)specially, expressly

'**Eigenschaft** *f* (-; -*en*) quality; TECH, PHYS, CHEM property; **in s-r ~ als** in his capacity as; '**Eigenschaftswort** *n* (-[*e*]*s*; -*wörter*) LING adjective

'**Eigensinn** *m* (-[*e*]*s*; *no pl*) stubbornness; '**eigensinnig** *adj* stubborn, obstinate

eigentlich ['aigəntlɪç] **1.** *adj* actual, true, real; exact **2.** *adv* actually, really; originally

'**Eigentor** *n* SPORT own goal (*a. fig*)

'**Eigentum** *n* (-[*e*]*s*; *no pl*) property

Eigentümer ['aigənty:mɐ] *m* (-*s*; -), '**Eigentümerin** *f* (-; -*nen*) owner, proprietor (proprietress)

eigentümlich ['aigənty:mlɪç] *adj* peculiar; strange, odd; '**Eigentümlichkeit** *f* (-; -*en*) peculiarity

'**Eigentumswohnung** *f* condominium, F condo, *Br* owner-occupied flat

'**eigenwillig** *adj* wil(l)ful; individual, original (*style etc*)

eignen ['aignən] *v/refl* (*ge-*, *h*) **sich ~ für** be suited *or* fit for; '**Eignung** *f* (-; *no pl*) suitability; aptitude; qualification

'**Eignungs|prüfung** *f*, ~**test** *m* aptitude test

'**Eil|bote** ['ailboːtə] *m*: **durch ~n** by special delivery; ~**brief** *m* special delivery (*Br* express) letter

Eile ['ailə] *f* (-; *no pl*) haste, hurry; '**eilen**

v/i (*ge-*, *sein*) hurry, hasten, rush; (*ge-*, *h*) be urgent; '**eilig** *adj* hurried, hasty; urgent; *es ~ haben* be in a hurry

Eimer ['aimɐ] *m* (*-s*; *-*) bucket, pail

ein [ain] **1.** *adj* one **2.** *indef art a*, an **3.** *adv:* "**einlaus**" "on / off"; *~ und aus gehen* come and go; *nicht mehr ~ noch aus wissen* be at one's wits' end

einander [ai'nandɐ] *pron* each other, one another

'**einarbeiten** *v/t* (*sep*, *-ge-*, *h*) train, acquaint *s.o.* with his work, F break *s.o.* in; *sich ~* work o.s. in

'**einarmig** ['ainarmɪç] *adj* one-armed

einäschern ['ain'ɛʃɐn] *v/t* (*sep*, *-ge-*, *h*) cremate; **Einäscherung** ['ain'ɛʃərʊŋ] *f* (*-*; *-en*) cremation

'**einatmen** *v/t* (*sep*, *-ge-*, *h*) inhale, breathe

einäugig ['ainʔɔygɪç] *adj* one-eyed

'**Einbahnstraße** *f* one-way street

einbalsamieren ['ainbalzami:rən] *v/t* (*no -ge-*, *h*) embalm

'**Einband** *m* (*-[e]s*; *-bände*) binding, cover

'**Einbau** *m* (*-[e]s*; *-bauten*) installation, fitting; *~... in cpds ...möbel etc:* built-in ...; '**einbauen** *v/t* (*sep*, *-ge-*, *h*) build in, install(l), fit

'**einberufen** *v/t* (*irr*, **rufen**, *sep*, *no -ge-*, *h*) MIL draft, Br call up; call (*meeting etc*); '**Einberufung** *f* (*-*; *-en*) MIL draft, Br call-up

'**ein|beziehen** *v/t* (*irr*, **ziehen**, *sep*, *no -ge-*, *h*) include; *~biegen* *v/i* (*irr*, **biegen**, *sep*, *-ge-*, *sein*) turn (*in acc* into)

'**einbilden** *v/refl* (*sep*, *-ge-*, *h*) imagine; *sich et. ~ auf* (*acc*) be conceited about

'**Einbildung** *f* (*-*; *no pl*) imagination, fancy; conceit

'**einblenden** *v/t* (*sep*, *-ge-*, *h*) TV fade in

'**Einblick** *m* insight (*in acc* into)

'**einbrechen** *v/i* (*irr*, **brechen**, *sep*, *-ge-*, *sein*) collapse; *winter:* set in; *~ in* (*acc*) break into, burgle; fall through (the ice); '**Einbrecher** *m* (*-s*; *-*) burglar

'**einbringen** *v/t* (*irr*, **bringen**, *sep*, *-ge-*, *h*) bring in; yield (*profit etc*)

'**Einbruch** *m* burglary; *bei ~ der Nacht* at nightfall

'**einbürgern** ['ainbyrgɐn] *v/t* (*sep*, *-ge-*, *h*) naturalize; *sich ~ fig* come into use; '**Einbürgerung** *f* (*-*; *-en*) naturalization

'**Einbuße** *f* (*-*; *-n*) loss

'**einbüßen** *v/t* (*sep*, *-ge-*, *h*) lose

eindämmen *v/t* (*sep*, *-ge-*, *h*) dam (up), *fig a.* get under control

'**eindecken** *fig v/t* (*sep*, *-ge-*, *h*) provide (*mit* with)

'**eindeutig** ['aindɔytɪç] *adj* clear

'**eindrehen** *v/t* (*sep*, *-ge-*, *h*) put *hair* in curlers

'**eindringen** *v/i* (*irr*, **dringen**, *sep*, *-ge-*, *sein*) *~ in* (*acc*) enter (*a. fig*); force one's way into; MIL invade; '**eindringlich** *adj* urgent; '**Eindringling** *m* (*-s*; *-e*) intruder; MIL invader

'**Eindruck** *m* impression; '**eindrücken** *v/t* (*sep*, *-ge-*, *h*) break *or* push in

'**eindrucksvoll** *adj* impressive

einelig ['ainʔaitɡ] *adj* identical (*twins*)

einein'halb *adj* one and a half

einengen ['ainʔɛŋən] *v/t* (*sep*, *-ge-*, *h*) confine, restrict

einer ['ainɐ], **eine** ['ainə], **ein(e)s** ['ain(ə)s] *indef pron* one

'**Einer** *m* (*-s*; *-*) MATH unit; *rowing:* single sculls

einerlei ['ainɐ'lai] *adj:* *ganz ~* all the same; *~ ob* no matter if; '**Einer'lei** *n:* *das tägliche ~* the daily grind *or* rut

'**einer'seits** *adv* on the one hand

'**einfach** *adj* simple; easy; plain; one-way (Br single) (*ticket*)

'**Einfachheit** *f* (*-*; *no pl*) simplicity

einfädeln ['ainfɛːdəln] *v/t* (*sep*, *-ge-*, *h*) thread; F start, set afoot; MOT merge

'**einfahren** (*irr*, **fahren**, *sep*, *-ge-*) **1.** *v/t* (*h*) MOT run in; bring in (*harvest*) **2.** *v/i* (*sein*) come in, RAIL *a.* pull in

'**Einfahrt** *f* entrance, way in

'**Einfall** *m* idea; MIL invasion

'**einfallen** *v/i* (*irr*, **fallen**, *sep*, *-ge-*, *sein*) fall in; collapse; MUS join in; *~ in* (*acc*) MIL invade; *ihm fiel ein, dass* it came to his mind that; *mir fällt nichts ein* I have no ideas; *es fällt mir nicht ein* I can't think of it; *dabei fällt mir ein* that reminds me; *was fällt dir ein?* what's the idea?

einfältig ['ainfɛltɪç] *adj* simple-minded; stupid

'**Einfa'milienhaus** *n* detached house

'**einfarbig** *adj* solid-colored, Br self-coloured

'**ein|fassen** *v/t* (*sep*, *-ge-*, *h*) border; *~fetten* *v/t* (*sep*, *-ge-*, *h*) grease; *~finden* *v/refl* (*irr*, **finden**, *sep*, *-ge-*, *h*) appear, arrive; **~flechten** *fig v/t* (*irr*, **flechten**, *sep*, *-ge-*, *h*) work in; **~fliegen** *v/t* (*irr*, **fliegen**, *sep*, *-ge-*, *h*) fly in; **~fließen** *v/i* (*irr*, **fließen**, *sep*, *-ge-*, *sein*) *fig et.* **~ lassen** slip s.th. in; **~flößen** *v/t* (*sep*, *-ge-*, *h*) pour (*j-m* into s.o.'s mouth); *fig* fill with (*awe etc*)

'**Einfluss** *fig m* influence

'**einflussreich** *adj* influential

einförmig ['aɪnfœrmɪç] *adj* uniform

'**einfrieren** (*irr*, **frieren**, *sep*, *-ge-*) **1.** *v/i* (*sein*) freeze (in) **2.** *v/t* (*h*) freeze (*a. fig*)

'**einfügen** *v/t* (*sep*, *-ge-*, *h*) put in; fit in; *fig* insert; **sich ~** fit in; adjust (o.s.) (*in acc* to); '**Einfügetaste** *f* IT insert key

einfühlsam ['aɪnfyːlzaːm] *adj* sympathetic; '**Einfühlungsvermögen** *n* (*-s*; *no pl*) empathy

Einfuhr ['aɪnfuːɐ] *f* (*-*; *-en*) ECON (*no pl*) importation; import

'**einführen** *v/t* (*sep*, *-ge-*, *h*) introduce; instal(l); ECON import

'**Einfuhrstopp** *m* ECON import ban

'**Einführung** *f* (*-*; *-en*) introduction

'**Einführungs...** *in cpds* ...kurs, ...preis *etc*: introductory ...

'**Eingabe** *f* petition; IT input; **~taste** *f* IT enter *or* return key

'**Eingang** *m* entrance; ECON arrival; receipt; '**eingängig** *adj* catchy (*tune etc*)

'**eingangs** *adv* at the beginning

'**eingeben** *v/t* (*irr*, **geben**, *sep*, *-ge-*, *h*) MED administer (*dat* to); IT feed, enter

'**eingebildet** *adj* imaginary; conceited (**auf** *acc* of)

'**Eingeborene** *m*, *f* (*-n*; *-n*) native

'**Eingebung** *f* (*-*; *-en*) inspiration; impulse

'**eingefallen** *adj* sunken, hollow

'**eingefleischt** *adj* confirmed

'**eingehen** (*irr*, **gehen**, *sep*, *-ge-*, *sein*) **1.** *v/i* ECON come in, arrive; BOT, ZO die; *fabric*: shrink; **~ auf** (*acc*) agree to; go into (*detail*); listen to *s.o.* **2.** *v/t* enter into (*a contract etc*); make (*a bet*); take (*a risk etc*); **~d** *adj* thorough; detailed

'**eingemacht** *adj* preserved

eingemeinden ['aɪnɡəmaɪndən] *v/t* (*sep*, *no -ge-*, *h*) incorporate (*in acc* into)

'**einge|nommen** *adj* partial (**für** to); prejudiced (**gegen** against); **von sich ~** full of o.s.; **~schlossen** *adj* locked in; trapped; ECON included; **~schnappt**

F *adj* in a huff; **~schrieben** *adj* registered; **~spielt** *adj*: (**gut**) **aufeinander ~ sein** work well together, be a good team; **~stellt** *adj*: **~ auf** (*acc*) prepared for; **~ gegen** opposed to

Eingeweide ['aɪnɡəvaɪdə] *pl* ANAT intestines, guts

'**Eingeweihte** *m*, *f* (*-n*; *-n*) insider

'**eingewöhnen** *v/refl* (*sep*, *no -ge-*, *h*) **sich ~ in** (*acc*) get used to, settle in

'**eingießen** *v/t* (*irr*, **gießen**, *sep*, *-ge-*, *h*) pour

eingleisig ['aɪnɡlaɪzɪç] *adj* single-track

'**eingliedern** *v/t* (*sep*, *-ge-*, *h*) integrate

'**Eingliederung** *f* integration

'**ein|graben** *v/t* (*irr*, **graben**, *sep*, *-ge-*, *h*) bury; **~gra,vieren** *v/t* (*sep*, *no -ge-*, *h*) engrave

'**eingreifen** *v/i* (*irr*, **greifen**, *sep*, *-ge-*, *h*) step in, interfere; '**Eingriff** *m* intervention, interference; MED operation

'**einhaken** *v/t* (*sep*, *-ge-*, *h*) hook in; **sich ~** link arms, take s.o.'s arm

'**Einhalt** *m*: **~ gebieten** put a stop (*dat* to); '**einhalten** *v/t* (*irr*, **halten**, *sep*, *-ge-*, *h*) keep

'**einhängen** (*sep*, *-ge-*, *h*) **1.** *v/t* hang in; TEL hang up (*receiver*); **sich ~ → einhaken 2.** *v/i* TEL hang up

'**einheimisch** *adj* native, local; ECON home, domestic; '**Einheimische** *m*, *f* (*-n*; *-n*) local, native

'**Einheit** *f* (*-*; *-en*) unit; POL unity

'**einheitlich** *adj* uniform; homogeneous

'**Einheits...** *in cpds* ...preis *etc*: standard

einhellig ['aɪnhɛlɪç] *adj* unanimous

'**einholen** *v/t* (*sep*, *-ge-*, *h*) catch up with (*a. fig*); make up for *lost time*; make (*inquiries*) (**über** *acc* about); seek (*advice*) (**bei** from); ask for *permission etc*; strike (*sail*); **~ gehen** go shopping

'**Einhorn** *n* MYTH unicorn

'**einhüllen** *v/t* (*sep*, *-ge-*, *h*) wrap (up); *fig* shroud

einig ['aɪnɪç] *adj*: **sich ~ sein** agree; **sich nicht ~ sein** disagree, differ

einige ['aɪnɪɡə] *indef pron* some, a few, several

einigen ['aɪnɪɡən] *v/t* (*ge-*, *h*) **sich ~ über** (*acc*) agree on

einigermaßen ['aɪnɪɡə'maːsən] *adv* quite, fairly; not too bad

'**einiges** *indef pron* some, something; quite a lot

'**Einigkeit** f (-; no pl) unity; agreement

'**Einigung** f (-; -en) agreement, settlement; POL unification

'**einjagen** v/t (sep, -ge-, h) **j-m e-n Schrecken~** give s.o. a fright, frighten or scare s.o.

einjährig ['ainjɛːrɪç] adj one-year-old; **~e Pflanze** annual

'**einkalku,lieren** v/t (no -ge-, h) take into account, allow for

'**Einkauf** m purchase; **Einkäufe machen → einkaufen** 2; '**einkaufen** (sep, -ge-, h) **1.** v/t buy, ECON a. purchase **2.** v/i go shopping

'**Einkaufs...** in cpds shopping ...; **~bummel** m shopping spree; **~preis** m ECON purchase price; **~wagen** m grocery or shopping cart, Br (supermarket) trolley; **~zentrum** n (shopping mall, Br shopping centre

'**ein|kehren** v/i (sep, -ge-, sein) stop (**in** dat at); **~klammern** v/t (sep, -ge-, h) put in brackets

'**Einklang** m (-[e]s; no pl) MUS unison; fig harmony

'**ein|kleiden** v/t (sep, -ge-, h) clothe (a. fig); **~klemmen** v/t (sep, -ge-, h) squeeze, jam; **eingeklemmt sein** be stuck, be jammed; **~kochen** (sep, -ge-) **1.** v/t (h) preserve **2.** v/i (sein) boil down

'**Einkommen** n (-s; -) income; **~steuererklärung** f income-tax return

'**einkreisen** v/t (sep, -ge-, h) encircle, surround

Einkünfte ['ainkʏnftə] pl income

'**einladen** v/t (irr, **laden**, sep, -ge-, h) invite; load; **~d** adj inviting

'**Einladung** f (-; -en) invitation

'**Einlage** f (-; -n) ECON investment; MED arch support; THEA, MUS interlude

Einlass ['ainlas] m (-es; no pl) admission, admittance; '**einlassen** v/t (irr, **lassen**, sep, -ge-, h) let in; run (a bath); **sich ~ auf** (acc) get involved in; let o.s. in for; agree to; **sich mit j-m ~** get involved with s.o.

'**Einlauf** m SPORT finish; MED enema

'**einlaufen** (irr, **laufen**, sep, -ge-) **1.** v/i (sein) come in (a. SPORT): water: run in; MAR enter port; fabric: shrink **2.** v/t (h) break new shoes in; **sich ~** warm up

'**einleben** v/refl (sep, -ge-, h) settle in

'**einlegen** v/t (sep, -ge-, h) put in; set (hair); GASTR pickle; MOT change into

'**Einlegesohle** f insole

'**einleiten** v/t (sep, -ge-, h) start; introduce; MED induce; TECH dump, discharge (sewage); **~d** adj introductory

'**Einleitung** f introduction

'**ein|lenken** v/i (sep, -ge-, h) come round; **~leuchten** v/i (sep, -ge-, h) be evident, be obvious; **das leuchtet mir (nicht) ein** that makes (doesn't make) sense to me; **~liefern** v/t (sep, -ge-, h) take (**ins Gefängnis** to prison; **in die Klinik** to [the] hospital); **~lösen** v/t (sep, -ge-, h) redeem; cash (check); **~machen** v/t (sep, -ge-, h) preserve

'**einmal** adv once; some or one day, sometime; **auf~** suddenly; at the same time, at once; **noch ~** once more or again; **noch ~ so ... (wie)** twice as ... (as); **es war ~** once (upon a time) there was; **haben Sie schon ~ ...?** have you ever ...?; **schon ~ dort gewesen sein** have been there before; **nicht ~** not even

'**Einmal...** in cpds disposable ...

Einmal'eins n (-; no pl) multiplication table

einmalig ['ainmaːlɪç] adj single; fig unique; F fabulous

'**Einmann...** in cpds one-man ...

'**Einmarsch** m entry; MIL invasion

'**einmar,schieren** v/i (no -ge-, sein) march in; **~ in** (acc) MIL invade

'**einmischen** v/refl (sep, -ge-, h) meddle (**in** acc in, with), interfere (with)

'**Einmündung** f junction

einmütig ['ainmyːtɪç] adj unanimous

'**Einmütigkeit** f (-; no pl) unanimity

Einnahmen ['ainaːmən] pl takings, receipts; '**einnehmen** v/t (irr, **nehmen**, sep, -ge-, h) take (a. MIL); earn, make; '**einnehmend** adj engaging

'**einnicken** v/i (sep, -ge-, sein) doze off

'**einnisten** v/refl (sep, -ge-, h) **sich bei j-m ~** park o.s. on s.o.

Einöde f (-; -n) desert, wilderness

'**ein|ordnen** v/t (sep, -ge-, h) put in its proper place; file; **sich ~** MOT get in lane; **~packen** v/t (sep, -ge-, h) pack (up); wrap up; **~parken** v/t and v/i (sep, -ge-, h) park (between two cars); **~pferchen** v/t (sep, -ge-, h) pen in; coop up; **~pflanzen** v/t (sep, -ge-, h) plant; fig implant (a. MED); **~planen** v/t (sep, -ge-, h) allow for; **~prägen** v/t (sep, -ge-, h) impress; **sich et. ~** keep s.th. in mind; memorize s.th.; **~quartieren** F v/t (no -ge-, h) put s.o. up (**bei j-m** at s.o.'s place); **sich ~ bei** (dat) move in with; **~rahmen** v/t (sep, -ge-, h) frame; **~räumen** v/t (sep, -ge-, h) put away; furnish; fig grant, concede; **~reden** (sep, -ge-, h) **1.** v/t: **j-m et.~** talk s.o. into (believing) s.th. **2.** v/i: **auf j-n~** keep on at s.o.; **~reiben** v/t (irr, **reiben**, sep, -ge-, h) rub; **~reichen** v/t (sep, -ge-, h) hand or send in; **~reihen** v/t (sep, -ge-, h) place (among); **sich ~** take one's place

einreihig ['ainraiiç] adj single-breasted

'Einreise f entry (a. in cpds)

'einreisen v/i (sep, -ge-, sein) enter (**in ein Land** a country)

'ein|reißen (irr, **reißen**, sep, -ge-) **1.** v/t (h) tear; pull down **2.** v/i (sein) tear; fig spread; **~renken** v/t (sep, -ge-, h) MED set; fig straighten out

'einrichten v/t (sep, -ge-, h) furnish; establish; arrange; **sich ~ auf** (acc) prepare for; **'Einrichtung** f (-; -en) furnishings; fittings; TECH installation(s), facilities; institution, facility

'einrücken (sep, -ge-) **1.** v/i (sein) MIL join the forces; march in **2.** v/t (h) PRINT indent

eins [ains] pron and adj one; one thing; **es ist alles ~** it's all the same (thing) **Eins** f (-; -en) one; grade: excellent, A

einsam ['ainza:m] adj lonely, lonesome; solitary; **'Einsamkeit** f (-; no pl) loneliness; solitude

'einsammeln v/t (sep, -ge-, h) collect

'Einsatz m TECH inset, insert; stake(s) (a. fig); MUS entry; fig effort(s), zeal; use, employment; MIL action, mission; deployment; **im ~** in action; **unter ~ des Lebens** at the risk of one's life

'einsatz|bereit adj ready for action; **~freudig** adj dynamic, zealous

'einschalten v/t (sep, -ge-, h) ELECTR switch or turn on; call s.o. in; **sich ~** step in; **'Einschaltquote** f TV rating

'ein|schärfen v/t (sep, -ge-, h) urge (**j-m et.** s.o. to do s.th.); **~schätzen** v/t (sep, -ge-, h) estimate; judge, rate; **falsch ~** misjudge; **~schenken** v/t (sep, -ge-, h) pour (out); **~schicken** v/t (sep, -ge-, h)

send in; **~schieben** v/t (irr, **schieben**, sep, -ge-, h) slip in; insert

einschl. abbr of **einschließlich** incl., including

'ein|schlafen v/i (irr, **schlafen**, sep, -ge-, sein) fall asleep, go to sleep; **~schläfern** ['ainʃlɛ:fɐn] v/t (sep, -ge-, h) put to sleep

'Einschlag m strike, impact; fig touch

'einschlagen (irr, **schlagen**, sep, -ge-, h) **1.** v/t knock in (or out); break (in), smash; wrap up; take (road etc); turn (wheels); → **Laufbahn 2.** v/i lightning etc: strike; fig be a success

einschlägig ['ainʃlɛ:gɪç] adj relevant

'ein|schleusen fig v/t (sep, -ge-, h) infiltrate (**in** acc into); **~schließen** (irr, **schließen**, sep, -ge-, h) lock in or up; enclose; MIL surround, encircle; fig include; **~schließlich** prp (gen) including, ... included; **~schmeicheln** v/refl (sep, -ge-, h) **sich ~ bei** ingratiate o.s. with; **~schnappen** v/i (sep, -ge-, sein) snap shut; fig go into a huff; → **eingeschnappt**

'einschneidend fig adj drastic; far-reaching; **'Einschnitt** m cut; notch; fig break

'einschränken v/t (sep, -ge-, h) restrict, reduce (both: **auf** acc to); cut down on; **sich ~** economize; **'Einschränkung** f (-; -en) restriction, reduction, cut; **ohne ~** without reservation

'Einschreibebrief m registered letter

'einschreiben v/t (irr, **schreiben**, sep, -ge-, h) enter; book; enrol(l) (a. MIL); **(sich) ~ lassen (für)** enrol(l) (o.s.) (for)

'einschreiten fig v/i (irr, **schreiten**, sep, -ge-, sein) step in, intervene; **~ (gegen)** take (legal) measures (against)

'einschüchtern v/t (sep, -ge-, h) intimidate; bully; **'Einschüchterung** f (-; -en) intimidation

'einschulen v/t (sep, -ge-, h) **eingeschult werden** start school

'Einschuss m bullet hole

'einschweißen v/t (sep, -ge-, h) shrink-wrap

'einsegnen v/t (sep, -ge-, h) REL consecrate; confirm; **'Einsegnung** f (-; -en) REL consecration; confirmation

'einsehen v/t (irr, **sehen**, sep, -ge-, h) see, realize; **das sehe ich nicht ein!** I don't see why!; **'Einsehen** n: **ein ~ ha-**

ben show some understanding

'**einseifen** v/t (sep, -ge-, h) soap; lather; F fig **j-n ~** take s.o. for a ride

'**einseitig** ['ainzaitɪç] adj one-sided; MED, POL, JUR unilateral

'**einsenden** v/t (irr, **senden**,] sep, -ge-, h) send in; '**Einsendeschluss** m closing date (for entries)

'**einsetzen** (sep, -ge-, h) **1.** v/t put in, insert; appoint; use, employ; TECH put into service; ECON invest, stake; bet; risk; **sich ~** try hard, make an effort; **sich ~ für** stand up for **2.** v/i set in, start

'**Einsicht** f (-; -en) insight; (no pl) understanding; **zur ~ kommen** listen to reason; **~ nehmen in** (acc) take a look at; '**einsichtig** adj understanding; reasonable

'**Einsiedler** m (-s; -) hermit

'**einsilbig** ['ainzılbıç] adj monosyllabic; fig taciturn

'**ein|spannen** v/t (sep, -ge-, h) harness; TECH clamp, fix; F rope s.o. in; **~sparen** v/t (sep, -ge-, h) save, economize on; **~sperren** v/t (sep, -ge-, h) lock or shut up; **~spielen** v/t (sep, -ge-, h) bring in; **sich ~** warm up; fig get going; → **eingespielt**

'**Einspielergebnisse** pl film: box office returns

'**einspringen** v/i (irr, **springen**, sep, -ge-, sein) **für j-n ~** take s.o.'s place

'**Einspritz...** in cpds MOT fuel-injection

'**Einspruch** m objection (a. JUR), protest; POL veto; appeal

'**einspurig** ['ainʃpu:rıç] adj RAIL single-track; MOT single-lane

'**einst** [ainst] adv once, at one time

'**Einstand** m start; tennis: deuce

'**ein|stecken** v/t (sep, -ge-, h) pocket (a. fig); ELECTR plug in; mail, post; fig take; **~stehen** v/i (irr, **stehen**, sep, -ge-, h) **~ für** stand up for; **~steigen** v/i (irr, **steigen**, sep, -ge-, sein) get in; get on (bus etc); **alles ~!** RAIL all aboard!; **~stellen** v/t (sep, -ge-, h) engage, employ, hire; give up; stop; SPORT equal; TECH adjust (**auf** acc to); radio: tune in (to); OPT, PHOT focus (on); **die Arbeit ~** (go on) strike, walk out; **das Feuer ~** MIL cease fire; **sich ~ auf** (acc) adjust to; be prepared for

'**Einstellung** f attitude (**zu** towards); employment; cessation; TECH adjust-

ment; OPT, PHOT focus(s)ing; film: take

'**Einstellungsgespräch** n interview

Einstieg ['ainʃtiːk] m (-[e]s; -e) entrance, entry (a. POL, ECON)

'**Einstiegsdroge** f gateway drug

'**einstig** ['ainstıç] adj former, one-time

'**einstimmen** v/i (sep, -ge-, h) MUS join in

einstimmig ['ainʃtımıç] adj unanimous

'**einstöckig** ['ainʃtœkıç] adj one-storied, Br one-storey(ed)

'**ein|stu,dieren** v/t (no -ge-, h) THEA rehearse; **~stufen** v/t (sep, -ge-, h) grade, rate

'**einstufig** ['ainʃtu:fıç] adj single-stage

'**Einstufungsprüfung** f placement test

'**Einsturz** m, '**einstürzen** v/i (sep, -ge-, sein) collapse

'**einstweilen** adv for the present

einstweilig ['ainstvailıç] adj temporary

'**ein|tauschen** v/t (sep, -ge-, h) exchange (**gegen** for); **~teilen** v/t (sep, -ge-, h) divide (**in** acc into); organize

einteilig ['aintailıç] adj one-piece

'**Einteilung** f (-; -en) division; organization; arrangement

eintönig ['aintø:nıç] adj monotonous

'**Eintönigkeit** f (-; no pl) monotony

'**Eintopf** m GASTR stew

'**Eintracht** f (-; no pl) harmony, unity

'**einträchtig** adj harmonious, peaceful

Eintrag ['aintra:k] m (-[e]s; Einträge ['aintrε:gə]) entry (a. ECON), registration; '**eintragen** v/t (irr, **tragen**, sep, -ge-, h) enter (**in** acc in); register (**bei** with); enrol(l) (with); fig earn; **sich ~** register, hotel: a. check in

einträglich ['aintrε:klıç] adj profitable

'**ein|treffen** v/i (irr, **treffen**, sep, -ge-, sein) arrive; happen; come true; **~treiben** fig v/t (irr, **treiben**, sep, -ge-, h) collect; **~treten** v/i (irr, **treten**, sep, -ge-) **1.** v/i (sein) enter; happen, take place; **~ für** stand up for, support; **~ in** (acc) join (club etc) **2.** v/t (h) kick in (door etc); **sich et. ~** run s.th. into one's foot

'**Eintritt** m entry; admission; **~ frei!** admission free!; **~ verboten!** keep out!

'**Eintritts|geld** n entrance or admission (fee); **~karte** f (admission) ticket

'**einüben** v/t (sep, -ge-, h) practise; rehearse

'**einverstanden** adj: **~ sein** agree (**mit** to); **~!** agreed!; '**Einverständnis** n (-ses; no pl) agreement

E

Einwand ['ainvant] *m* (-[e]s; *Einwände* ['ainvɛndə]) objection (**gegen** to)

'**Einwanderer** *m*, '**Einwanderin** *f* immigrant; '**einwandern** *v/t* (*sep*, -*ge*-, *sein*) immigrate; '**Einwanderung** *f* immigration

'**einwandfrei** *adj* perfect, faultless

einwärts ['ainvɛrts] *adv* inward(s)

'**Einweg...** *...rasierer, ...spritze etc*: disposable; ~**flasche** *f* non-returnable bottle; ~**packung** *f* throwaway pack

'**einweichen** *v/t* (*sep*, -*ge*-, *h*) soak

'**einweihen** *v/t* (*sep*, -*ge*-, *h*) dedicate, *Br* inaugurate: *j-n* ~ *in* (*acc*) *F* let s.o. in on; '**Einweihung** *f* (-; -*en*) dedication, *Br* inauguration

'**einweisen** *v/t* (*irr*, **weisen**, *sep*, -*ge*-, *h*) *j-n* ~ *in* (*acc*) send (*esp* JUR commit) s.o. to; instruct s.o. in, brief s.o. in

'**einwenden** *v/t* ([*irr*, **wenden**,] *sep*, -*ge*-, *h*) object (**gegen** to)

'**Einwendung** *f* (-; -*en*) objection

'**einwerfen** *v/t* (*irr*, **werfen**, *sep*, -*ge*-, *h*) throw in (*a. fig*, SPORT *a. v/i*); break (*window*); mail, *Br* post; insert (*coin*)

'**einwickeln** *v/t* (*sep*, -*ge*-, *h*) wrap (up); *F* take *s.o.* in

'**Einwickelpa|pier** *n* wrapping-paper

einwilligen ['ainvilign̩] *v/i* (*sep*, -*ge*-, *h*) consent (**in** *acc* to), agree (to)

'**Einwilligung** *f* (-; -*en*) consent (**in** *acc* to), agreement

'**einwirken** *v/i* (*sep*, -*ge*-, *h*) ~ **auf** (*acc*) act (up)on; *fig* work on *s.o.*

'**Einwirkung** *f* effect, influence

Einwohner ['ainvoːnɐ] *m* (-*s*; -), '**Einwohnerin** *f* (-; -*nen*) inhabitant; '**Einwohnermeldeamt** *n* registration office

'**Einwurf** *m* slot; SPORT throw-in

'**Einzahl** *f* (-; *no pl*) LING singular

'**einzahlen** *v/t* (*sep*, -*ge*-, *h*) pay in

'**Einzahlung** *f* payment, deposit

einzäunen ['aintsɔynən] *v/t* (*sep*, -*ge*-, *h*) fence in

Einzel ['aintsəl] *n* (-*s*; -) *tennis*: singles

'**Einzel...** *in cpds ...bett, ...zimmer etc*: single ...; ~**fall** *m* special case; ~**gänger** ['aintsəlgɛŋɐ] *m* (-*s*; -) *F* loner; ~**haft** *f* solitary confinement; ~**handel** *m* retail trade; ~**händler** *m* retailer; ~**haus** *n* detached house

'**Einzelheit** *f* (-; -*en*) detail

'**einzeln** *adj* single; odd (*shoe etc*); **Ein-**

zelne *pl* several, some; **der Einzelne** the individual; ~ **eintreten** enter one at a time; ~ **angeben** specify; **im Einzelnen** in detail; **jeder Einzelne** each and every one

'**einziehen** (*irr*, **ziehen**, *sep*, -*ge*-) **1.** *v/t* (*h*) draw in; *esp* TECH retract; duck; strike (*sail etc*); MIL draft, *Br* call up; confiscate; withdraw (*license etc*); make (*inquiries*) **2.** *v/i* (*sein*) move in; march in; soak in

einzig ['aintsɪç] *adj* only; single; **kein Einziger ...** not a single ...; **das Einzige** the only thing; **der** (**die**) **Einzige** the only one; ~**artig** *adj* unique, singular

'**Einzug** *m* moving in; entry

Eis [ais] *n* (-*es*; *no pl*) ice; GASTR ice cream; ~ **am Stiel** ice lolly; ~**bahn** *f* skating rink; ~**bär** *m* ZO polar bear; ~**becher** *m* sundae; ~**bein** *n* GASTR (pickled) pork knuckles; ~**berg** *m* iceberg; ~**brecher** *m* (-*s*; -) MAR icebreaker; ~**diele** *f* ice-cream parlo(u)r

Eisen ['aizən] *n* (-*s*; -) iron

'**Eisenbahn** *f* railroad, *Br* railway; train set; **Eisenbahner** ['aizənbaːnɐ] *m* (-*s*; -) railroadman, *Br* railwayman

'**Eisenbahnwagen** *m* (railroad) car, *Br* coach, railway carriage

'**Eisen|erz** *n* iron ore; ~**gießerei** *f* iron foundry; ~**hütte** *f* TECH ironworks

'**Eisenwaren** *pl* hardware, ironware; ~**handlung** *f* hardware store, *Br* ironmonger's

eisern ['aizɐn] *adj* iron (*a. fig*), of iron

'**eisgekühlt** *adj* iced

'**Eishockey** *n* hockey, *Br* ice hockey

eisig ['aizɪç] *adj* icy (*a. fig*)

'**eis|kalt** *adj* ice-cold

'**Eiskunst|lauf** *m* (-[e]s; *no pl*) figure skating; ~**läufer(in)** figure skater

'**Eis|meer** *n* polar sea; ~**re|vue** *f* ice show; ~**schnelllauf** *m* speed skating; ~**scholle** *f* ice floe; ~**verkäufer** *m* iceman; ~**würfel** *m* ice cube; ~**zapfen** *m* icicle; ~**zeit** *f* (-; *no pl*) GEOL ice age

eitel ['aitəl] *adj* vain; '**Eitelkeit** *f* (-; *no pl*) vanity

Eiter ['aitɐ] *m* (-*s*; *no pl*) MED pus

'**Eiterbeule** *f* MED abscess, boil

'**eitern** *v/i* (*ge*-, *h*) MED fester

eitrig ['aitrɪç] *adj* MED purulent, festering

'**Eiweiß** *n* (-*es*; *no pl*) white of egg; BIOL

protein
'eiweiß|arm adj low in protein, low-protein; **~reich** adj rich in protein, high-protein

'Eizelle f BIOL egg cell, ovum

Ekel ['e:kəl] **1.** m (-s; no pl) disgust (*vor* dat at), loathing (for); **~ erregend → ekelhaft 2.** F n (-s; -) beast; ekelerregend adj → **ekelhaft**

'ekelhaft, **'ek(e)lig** adj sickening, disgusting, repulsive

'ekeln v/refl and v/impers (ge-, h) **ich ekle mich davor** it makes me sick

Ekstase [ɛk'staːzə] f (-; -n) ecstasy

Elan [e'laːn] m (-s; no pl) vigo(u)r

elastisch [e'lastɪʃ] adj elastic, flexible

Elch [ɛlç] m (-[e]s; -e) ZO elk; moose

Elefant [ele'fant] m (-en; -en) ZO elephant; **Ele'fantenhochzeit** F f ECON jumbo merger

elegant [ele'gant] adj elegant

Eleganz [ele'gants] f (-; no pl) elegance

Elektriker [e'lɛktrɪkɐ] m (-s; -) electrician; **elektrisch** [e'lɛktrɪʃ] adj electrical; electric; **elektrisieren** [elɛktri-'ziːrən] v/t (no -ge-, h) electrify

Elektrizität [elɛktritsi'tɛːt] f (-; no pl) electricity; **Elektrizi'tätswerk** n (electric) power station

Elektrogerät [e'lɛktrogərɛːt] n electric appliance

Elektronik [elɛk'troːnɪk] f (-; no pl) electronics; electronic system; **elektronisch** [elɛk-'troːnɪʃ] adj electronic

E'lektrora¸sierer m (-s; -) electric razor

Elektro|'technik f electrical engineering; **~'techniker** m electrical engineer

Element [ele'mɛnt] n (-[e]s; -e) element; **elementar** [elemɛn'taːɐ] adj elementary

elend ['eːlɛnt] adj miserable

Elend n (-s; no pl) misery

'Elendsviertel n slum

elf [ɛlf] adj eleven

Elf f (-; -en) eleven; soccer: team

Elfe ['ɛlfə] f (-; -n) elf, fairy

'Elfenbein n ivory

Elf'meter m (-s; -) soccer: penalty; **~punkt** m penalty spot; **~schießen** n penalty shoot-out

'elfte adj eleventh

Elite [e'liːtə] f (-; -n) elite

Ellbogen ['ɛlboːgən] m ANAT elbow

Elster ['ɛlstɐ] f (-; -n) ZO magpie

elterlich ['ɛltɐlɪç] adj parental

Eltern ['ɛltɐn] pl parents

'Elternhaus n (one's parents') home

'elternlos adj orphan(ed)

'Eltern|teil m parent; **~vertretung** f appr Parent-Teacher Association; **~zeit** f parental leave

Email [e'mai] n (-s; -s), **Emaille** [e-'maljə] f (-; -n) enamel

Emanzipation [emantsipa'tsjoːn] f (-; -en) emancipation; women's lib (-eration); **emanzipieren** [emantsi-'piːrən] v/refl (no -ge-, h) become emancipated

Embargo [ɛm'bargo] n (-s; -s) ECON embargo

Embolie [ɛmbo'liː] f (-; -n) MED embolism

Embryo ['ɛmbryo] m (-s; -en [ɛmbry-'oːnən]) BIOL embryo

Emigrant [emi'grant] m (-en; -en), **Emi'grantin** f (-; -nen) emigrant, esp POL refugee; **Emigration** [emigra'tsjoːn] f (-; -en) emigration; **in der ~** in exile; **emigrieren** [emi'griːrən] v/i (no -ge-, sein) emigrate

Emission [emi'sjoːn] f (-; -en) PHYS emission; ECON issue

empfahl [ɛm'pfaːl] pret of **empfehlen**

Empfang [ɛm'pfaŋ] m (-[e]s; Empfänge [ɛm'pfɛŋə]) reception (a. radio, hotel); welcome; receipt (**nach, bei** on)

emp'fangen v/t (irr, **fangen**, no -ge-, h) receive; welcome; **Emp'fänger(in)** (-s; -/-; -nen) receiver (m a. radio); addressee

emp'fänglich adj susceptible (**für** to)

Empfängnis [ɛm'pfɛŋnɪs] f (-; no pl) MED conception; **~verhütung** f MED contraception; birth control

Emp'fangs|bescheinigung f receipt; **~dame** f receptionist

empfehlen [ɛm'pfeːlən] v/t (irr, no -ge-, h) recommend; **emp'fehlenswert** adj advisable; **Emp'fehlung** f (-; -en) recommendation

empfinden [ɛm'pfɪndən] v/t (irr, **finden**, no -ge-, h) feel (**als** ... to be ...); **empfindlich** [ɛm'pfɪntlɪç] adj sensitive (**für, gegen** to) (a. PHOT, CHEM); tender, delicate; touchy; irritable (a. MED); severe (*punishment etc*); **~e Stelle** sore spot

Emp'findlichkeit f (-; -en) sensitivity;

PHOT speed; delicacy; touchiness

empfindsam [ɛmˈpfɪntzaːm] *adj* sensitive

Emp'findung *f* (-; -en) sensation; perception; feeling, emotion

empfohlen [ɛmˈpfoːlən] *pp of* **empfehlen**

empor [ɛmˈpoːɐ] *adv* up, upward(s)

empören [ɛmˈpøːrən] *v/t* (*no* -ge-, *h*) outrage; shock; **sich ~** (**über** *acc*) be outraged *or* shocked (at); **~d** *adj* shocking, outrageous

Emporkömmling [ɛmˈpoːɐkœmlɪŋ] *contp m* (-s; -e) upstart

empört [ɛmˈpøːɐt] *adj* indignant (**über** *acc* at), shocked (at); **Em'pörung** *f* (-; *no pl*) indignation

Ende [ˈɛndə] *n* (-s; *no pl*) end; *film:* ending; **am ~** at the end; in the end, finally; **zu ~** over; *time:* up; **zu ~ gehen** come to an end; **zu ~ lesen** finish reading; **er ist ~ zwanzig** he is in his late twenties; **~ Mai** at the end of May; **~ der achtziger Jahre** in the late eighties; *mitae:* **~!** over!; **'enden** *v/i* (ge-, *h*) (come to an) end; stop, finish; F **~ als** end up as

'Endergebnis *n* final result

'endgültig *adj* final, definitive

Endlagerung [ˈɛntlaːgərʊŋ] *f* final disposal (*of radioactive waste*)

'endlich *adv* finally, at last

'endlos *adj* endless

'End|runde *f,* **~spiel** *n* SPORT final(s); **~spurt** *m* SPORT final spurt (*a. fig*); **~stati,on** *f* RAIL terminus, terminal; **~summe** *f* (sum) total

'Endung *f* (-; -en) LING ending

Energie [enɛrˈgiː] *f* (-; -n) energy; TECH, ELECTR power; **~sparen** *n* energy saving, conservation of energy

ener'giebewusst *adj* energy-conscious

Ener'giekrise *f* energy crisis

Ener'giequelle *f* source of energy; **~versorgung** *f* power supply

energisch [eˈnɛrgɪʃ] *adj* energetic, vigorous

eng [ɛŋ] *adj* narrow; tight; cramped; *fig* close; **~ beieinander** close(ly) together

Engagement [aˌgaʒəˈmaː:] *n* (-s; -s) THEA *etc* engagement; POL commitment; **engagieren** [aˌgaˈʒiːrən] *v/t* (*no* -ge-, *h*) engage; **sich ~ für** be very involved in; **engagiert** [aˌgaˈʒiːɐt] *adj*

involved, committed

Enge [ˈɛŋə] *f* (-; *no pl*) narrowness; cramped conditions; **in die ~ treiben** drive into a corner

Engel [ˈɛŋəl] *m* (-s; -) angel

'England England; **Engländer** [ˈɛŋlɛndɐ] *m* (-s; -) Englishman; **die ~** *pl* the English; **Engländerin** [ˈɛŋlɛndərɪn] *f* (-; -nen) Englishwoman

'englisch *adj* English; **auf Englisch** in English

'Englischunterricht *m* English lesson(s) *or* class(es); teaching of English

'Engpass *m* bottleneck (*a. fig*)

engstirnig [ˈɛŋʃtɪrnɪç] *adj* narrow-minded

Enkel [ˈɛŋkəl] *m* (-s; -) grandchild; grandson

'Enkelin *f* (-; -nen) granddaughter

enorm [eˈnɔrm] *adj* enormous; F terrific

Ensemble [aˈsaˑ:bl] *n* (-s; -s) THEA company; cast

entarten [ɛntˈʔaːɐtən] *v/i* (*no* -ge-, *sein*), **ent'artet** *adj* degenerate; **Ent'artung** *f* (-; -en) degeneration

entbehren [ɛntˈbeːrən] *v/t* (*no* -ge-, *h*) do without; spare; miss; **entbehrlich** [ɛntˈbeːrlɪç] *adj* dispensable; superfluous; **Ent'behrung** *f* (-; -en) want, privation

ent'binden (*irr*, **binden**, *no* -ge-, *h*) **1.** *v/i* MED have the baby **2.** *v/t:* **j-n ~ von** *fig* relieve s.o. of; **entbunden werden von** MED give birth to

Ent'bindung *f* (-; -en) MED delivery

Ent'bindungsstati,on *f* MED maternity ward

entblößen [ɛntˈbløːsən] *v/t* (*no* -ge-, *h*) bare, uncover

ent'decken *v/t* (*no* -ge-, *h*) discover

Ent'decker *m* (-s; -), **Ent'deckerin** *f* (-; -nen) discoverer

Ent'deckung *f* (-; -en) discovery

Ente [ˈɛntə] *f* (-; -n) ZO duck; F *fig* hoax

ent'ehren *v/t* (*no* -ge-, *h*) dishono(u)r

enteignen [ɛntˈʔaignən] *v/t* (*no* -ge-, *h*) expropriate; dispossess *s.o.*

Ent'eignung *f* (-; -en) expropriation; dispossession

ent'erben *v/t* (*no* -ge-, *h*) disinherit

entern [ˈɛntɐn] *v/t* (ge-, *h*) MAR board

ent|fachen [ɛntˈfaxən] *v/t* (*no* -ge-, *h*) kindle, *fig a.* rouse; **~fallen** *v/i* (*irr*, **fallen**, *no* -ge-, *sein*) be cancelled; **~ auf**

(*acc*) fall to s.o. ('s share); **es ist mir ~** it has slipped my memory; **~falten** *v/t* (*no -ge-, h*) unfold; *fig* develop; **sich ~** unfold; *fig* develop (**zu** into)

entfernen [ɛntˈfɛrnən] *v/t* (*no -ge-, h*) remove (*a. fig*); **sich ~** leave; **ent'fernt** *adj* distant (*a. fig*); **weit** (**zehn Meilen**) **~** far (10 miles) away; **Ent'fernung** *f* (*-; -en*) distance; removal

Ent'fernungsmesser *m* (*-s; -*) PHOT range finder

ent'flammbar *adj* (in)flammable

entfremden [ɛntˈfrɛmdən] *v/t* (*no -ge-, h*) estrange (*dat* from); **Ent'fremdung** *f* (*-; -en*) estrangement, alienation

ent'führen *v/t* (*no -ge-, h*) kidnap; AVIAT hijack; **Ent'führer** *m* (*-s; -*) kidnapper; AVIAT hijacker; **Ent'führung** *f* (*-; -en*) kidnapping; AVIAT hijacking

ent'gegen *prp* (*dat*) and *adv* contrary to; toward(s); **~gehen** *v/i* (*irr*, **gehen**, *sep, -ge-, sein*) go to meet

ent'gegengesetzt *adj* opposite

ent'gegenkommen *v/i* (*irr*, **kommen**, *sep, -ge-, sein*) come to meet; *fig* **j-m ~** meet s.o. halfway; **~d** *fig adj* obliging

ent'gegen|nehmen *v/t* (*irr*, **nehmen**, *sep, -ge-, h*) accept, receive; **~sehen** *v/i* (*irr*, **sehen**, *sep, -ge-, h*) await; look forward to *s.th.*; **~setzen** *v/t* (*sep, -ge-, h*) **j-m Widerstand ~** put up resistance to s.o.; **~treten** *v/i* (*irr*, **treten**, *sep, -ge-, sein*) walk towards; oppose; face

entgegnen [ɛntˈɡeːɡnən] *v/i* (*no -ge-, h*) reply, answer; retort

Ent'gegnung *f* (*-; -en*) reply; retort

ent'gehen *v/i* (*irr*, **gehen**, *no -ge-, sein*) escape; miss

entgeistert [ɛntˈɡaistɐt] *adj* aghast

Entgelt [ɛntˈɡɛlt] *n* (*-[e]s; -e*) remuneration; fee

ent|giften [ɛntˈɡɪftən] *v/t* (*no -ge-, h*) decontaminate; **~gleisen** [ɛntˈɡlaizən] *v/i* (*no -ge-, sein*) RAIL be derailed; *fig* blunder; **~'gleiten** *fig v/i* (*irr*, **gleiten**, *no -ge-, sein*) get out of control; **~gräten** [ɛntˈɡrɛːtən] *v/t* (*no -ge-, h*) bone, fil(l)et

ent'halten *v/t* (*irr*, **halten**, *no -ge-, h*) contain, hold; include; **sich ~** (*gen*) abstain *or* refrain from; **ent'haltsam** *adj* abstinent; moderate; **Ent'haltsamkeit** *f* (*-; no pl*) abstinence; moderation

Ent'haltung *f* (*-; -en*) abstention

ent'härten *v/t* (*no -ge-, h*) soften

enthaupten [ɛntˈhauptən] *v/t* (*no -ge-, h*) behead, decapitate

ent'hüllen *v/t* (*no -ge-, h*) uncover; unveil; *fig* reveal, disclose; **Ent'hüllung** *f* (*-; -en*) unveiling; *fig* revelation, disclosure

Enthusiasmus [ɛntuˈʒjasmʊs] *m* (*-; no pl*) enthusiasm; **Enthusiast(in)** [ɛntu-ˈʒjast(-ɪn)] (*-en, -en/-; -nen*) enthusiast; *film*, SPORT F fan; **enthusi'astisch** *adj* enthusiastic

ent|'kleiden *v/t* and *v/refl* (*no -ge-, h*) undress, strip; **~'kommen** *v/i* (*irr*, **kommen**, *no -ge-, sein*) escape (*dat* from); **~'korken** *v/t* (*no -ge-, h*) uncork

entkräften [ɛntˈkrɛftən] *v/t* (*no -ge-, h*) weaken (*a. fig*); **Ent'kräftung** *f* (*-; -en*) weakening, exhaustion

ent|'laden *v/t* (*irr*, **laden**, *no -ge-, h*) unload; *esp* ELECTR discharge; **sich ~** *esp* ELECTR discharge; *fig* explode

Ent'ladung *f* (*-; -en*) unloading; *esp* ELECTR discharge; *fig* explosion

ent'lang *prp* (*dat*) and *adv* along; **hier~, bitte!** this way, please!; **die Straße** *etc* **~** along the street *etc*

entlarven [ɛntˈlarfən] *v/t* (*no -ge-, h*) unmask, expose

ent'lassen *v/t* (*irr*, **lassen**, *no -ge-, h*) dismiss, F fire, give *s.o.* the sack; MED discharge; JUR release

Ent'lassung *f* (*-; -en*) dismissal; MED discharge; JUR release

ent'lasten *v/t* (*no -ge-, h*) relieve *s.o.* of some of his work; JUR exonerate, clear *s.o.* of a charge; **den Verkehr ~** relieve the traffic congestion; **Ent'lastung** *f* (*-; -en*) relief; JUR exoneration

Ent'lastungszeuge *m* JUR witness for the defense (*Br* defence)

ent'laufen *v/i* (*irr*, **laufen**, *no -ge-, sein*) run away (*dat* from)

ent'legen *adj* remote, distant

ent|'locken *v/t* (*no -ge-, h*) draw, elicit (*dat* from); **~'lohnen** *v/t* (*no -ge-, h*) pay (off); **~'lüften** *v/t* (*no -ge-, h*) ventilate; **~machten** [ɛntˈmaxtən] *v/t* (*no -ge-, h*) deprive *s.o.* of his power; **~militarisieren** [ɛntmilitari'ziːrən] *v/t* (*no -ge-, h*) demilitarize; **~mündigen** [ɛnt-ˈmʏndɪɡən] *v/t* (*no -ge-, h*) JUR place under disability; **~mutigen** [ɛnt-ˈmuːtɪɡən] *v/t* (*no -ge-, h*) discourage;

~'nehmen v/t (irr, **nehmen**, no -ge-, h) take (dat from); ~ aus (with-)draw from; fig gather or learn from; ~'puppen v/refl (no -ge-, h) sich ~ als turn out to be; ~'rahmen v/t (no -ge-, h) skim; ~'reißen v/t (irr, **reißen**, no -ge-, h) snatch (away) (dat from); ~'rinnen v/i (irr, **rinnen**, no -ge-, sein) escape (dat from); ~'rollen v/t (no -ge-, h) unroll

ent'rüsten v/t (no -ge-, h) fill with indignation; **sich** ~ become indignant (**über** acc at s.th., with s.o.); ent'rüstet adj indignant (**über** acc at s.th., with s.o.); Ent'rüstung f (-; -en) indignation

Entsafter [ɛnt'zaftɐ] m (-s; -) juice extractor

ent'salzen v/t (no -ge-, h) desalinize

ent'schädigen v/t (no -ge-, h) compensate; Ent'schädigung f (-; -en) compensation

ent'schärfen v/t (no -ge-, h) defuse (a. fig)

ent'scheiden v/t and v/i and v/refl (irr, **scheiden**, no -ge-, h) decide (**für** on, in favo[u]r of; **gegen** against); settle; **er kann sich nicht** ~ he can't make up his mind; ~d adj decisive; crucial Ent'scheidung f (-; -en) decision

entschieden [ɛnt'ʃiːdən] adj decided, determined, resolute; ~ dafür strongly in favo(u)r of it; Ent'schiedenheit f (-; no pl) determination

ent'schließen v/refl (irr, **schließen**, no -ge-, h) decide, determine, make up one's mind; Ent'schließung f (-; -en) POL resolution

entschlossen [ɛnt'ʃlɔsən] adj determined, resolute; Ent'schlossenheit f (-; no pl) determination, resoluteness

Ent'schluss m decision, resolution

entschlüsseln [ɛnt'ʃlʏsəln] v/t (no -ge-, h) decipher, decode

entschuldigen [ɛnt'ʃʊldɪgən] v/t (no -ge-, h) excuse; **sich** ~ apologize (**bei** to; **für** for); excuse o.s.; ~ **Sie!** (I'm) sorry!; excuse me!; Ent'schuldigung f (-; -en) excuse; apology; **um** ~ **bitten** apologize; ~! (I'm) sorry!; excuse me!

ent'setzen v/t (no -ge-, h) shock; horrify; Ent'setzen n (-s; no pl) horror; terror; ent'setzlich adj horrible, dreadful, terrible; atrocious; ent'setzt adj shocked; horrified

ent'sichern v/t (no -ge-, h) release the safety catch of; ~'sinnen v/refl (irr, **sinnen**, no -ge-, h) remember, recall

ent'sorgen v/t (no -ge-, h) dispose of

Ent'sorgung f (-; -en) (waste) disposal

ent'spannen v/t and v/refl (no -ge-, h) relax; **sich** ~ a. take it easy; fig ease (up); ent'spannt adj relaxed

Ent'spannung f (-; -en) relaxation; POL détente

ent'spiegelt adj OPT non-glare

ent'sprechen v/i (irr, **sprechen**, no -ge-, h) correspond to; answer to a description; meet (requirements etc); ~d adj corresponding (dat to); appropriate

Ent'sprechung f (-; -en) equivalent

ent'springen v/i (irr, **springen**, no -ge-, sein) river: rise

entstehen v/i (irr, **stehen**, no -ge-, sein) come into being; arise; emerge, develop; ~ aus originate from

Ent'stehung f (-; -en) origin

ent'stellen v/t (no -ge-, h) disfigure, deform; fig distort; Ent'stellung f (-; -en) disfigurement, deformation, distortion (a. fig)

entstört [ɛnt'ʃtøːɐt] adj ELECTR interference-free

ent'täuschen v/t (no -ge-, h) disappoint; Ent'täuschung f (-; -en) disappointment

entwaffnen [ɛnt'vafnən] v/t (no -ge-, h) disarm

Ent'warnung f all clear (signal)

ent'wässern v/t (no -ge-, h) drain; Ent'wässerung f (-; -en) drainage; CHEM dehydration

'entweder cj: ~ ... **oder** either ... or

ent'weichen v/i (irr, **weichen**, no -ge-, sein) escape (aus from); ~'weihen v/t (no -ge-, h) desecrate; ~'wenden v/t (no -ge-, h) pilfer, steal; ~'werfen v/t (irr, **werfen**, no -ge-, h) design; draw up

ent'werten v/t (no -ge-, h) lower the value of (a. fig); cancel; Ent'wertung f (-; -en) devaluation; cancellation

ent'wickeln v/t and v/refl (no -ge-, h) develop (a. PHOT) (**zu** into); Ent'wicklung f (-; -en) development, BIOL a. evolution; adolescence, age of puberty

Ent'wicklungs|helfer m, ~helferin f POL, ECON development aid volunteer; Peace Corps volunteer, Br VSO work-

er; ~hilfe f development aid; ~land n
POL developing country

ent'wirren [ɛnt'vɪrən] v/t (no -ge-, h)
disentangle (a. fig); ~'wischen v/i (no
-ge-, sein) get away

ent'würdigend adj degrading

Ent'wurf m outline, (rough) draft, plan;
design; sketch

ent|'wurzeln v/t (no -ge-, h) uproot; ~-
'ziehen v/t (irr, ziehen, no -ge-, h) take
away (dat from); revoke (license etc);
deprive of (rights etc; CHEM extract;
sich j-m (e-r Sache) ~ evade s.o. (s.th.)

Ent'ziehungs|anstalt f substance (Br
drug) abuse clinic; ~kur f detoxi(fi)-
cation (treatment), a. F drying out

entziffern [ɛnt'tsɪfɐn] v/t (no -ge-, h) decipher, make out

ent'zücken v/t (no -ge-, h) charm, delight; Ent'zücken n (-s; no pl) delight;
ent'zückend adj delightful, charming,
F sweet; ent'zückt adj delighted (über
acc, von at, with)

Ent'zug m withdrawal; revocation

Ent'zugserscheinung f MED withdrawal symptom

entzündbar [ɛnt'tsʏntbaːɐ] adj (in-)
flammable; ent'zünden v/refl (no
-ge-, h) catch fire; MED become in-
flamed; Ent'zündung f (-; -en) MED in-
flammation

ent'zwei adv in two, to pieces

Enzyklopädie [ɛntsyklopɛ'diː] f (-; -n)
encyclop(a)edia

Epidemie [epide'miː] f (-; -n) MED epidemic (disease)

Epilog [epi'loːk] m (-[e]s; -e [epi'loːgə])
epilog, Br epilogue

episch ['eːpɪʃ] adj epic

Episode [epi'zoːdə] f (-; -n) episode

Epoche [e'pɔxə] f (-; -n) epoch, period,
era

Epos ['eːpɔs] n (-; Epen ['eːpən]) epic
(poem)

er [eːɐ] pers pron he; it

Er'achten n: meines ~s in my opinion

Erbanlage ['ɛrp²anlaːgə] f BIOL genes,
genetic code

erbarmen [ɛɐ'barmən] v/refl (no -ge-, h)
sich j-s ~ take pity on s.o.

erbärmlich [ɛɐ'bɛrmlɪç] adj pitiful, pitiable; miserable; mean

er'barmungslos adj pitiless, merciless

er'bauen v/t (no -ge-, h) build, con-

struct; Er'bauer m (-s; -) builder, con-
structor

er'baulich adj edifying; Er'bauung fig f
(-; -en) edification, uplift

Erbe ['ɛrbə] 1. m (-n; -n) heir 2. n (-s; no
pl) inheritance, heritage

erben ['ɛrbən] v/t (ge-, h) inherit

erbeuten [ɛɐ'bɔytən] v/t (no -ge-, h) MIL
capture; thief: get away with

'Erbfaktor m BIOL gene

Erbin ['ɛrbɪn] f (-; -nen) heir, heiress

er'bitten v/t (irr, bitten, no -ge-, h) ask
for, request

erbittert [ɛɐ'bɪtɐt] adj fierce, furious

'Erbkrankheit f MED hereditary disease

erblich ['ɛrplɪç] adj hereditary

er'blicken v/t (no -ge-, h) see, catch sight
of

erblinden [ɛɐ'blɪndən] v/i (no -ge-, sein)
go blind

er'brechen v/t and v/refl (irr, brechen,
no -ge-, h) MED vomit

Erbschaft ['ɛrpʃaft] f (-; -en) inheritance, heritage

Erbse ['ɛrpsə] f (-; -n) BOT pea; (grüne)
~n green peas

'Erbstück n heirloom

Erd|apfel ['eːɐtapfəl] Austrian m pota-
to; ~ball m (-[e]s; no pl) globe; ~beben
n (-s; -) earthquake; ~beere f BOT straw-
berry; ~boden m earth, ground

Erde ['eːɐdə] f (-; -n) (no pl) earth;
ground, soil; → eben; 'erden v/t (ge-,
h) ELECTR earth, ground

erdenklich ['eːɐ'dɛŋklɪç] adj imaginable

Erd|gas ['eːɐtgaːs] n natural gas; ~ge-
schoss n, ~geschoß Austrian n first
(Br ground) floor

er'dichten v/t (no -ge-, h) invent, make
up; er'dichtet adj invented, made-up

erdig ['eːɐdɪç] adj earthy

'Erd|klumpen m clod, lump of earth;
~kruste f earth's crust; ~kugel f globe;
~kunde f (-; no pl) geography; ~leitung
f ELECTR ground (Br earth) connection;
underground pipe(line); ~nuss f BOT
peanut; ~öl n (mineral) oil, petroleum;
~reich n ground, earth

erdreisten [ɛɐ'draɪstən] v/refl (no -ge-,
h) F have the nerve

er'drosseln v/t (no -ge-, h) throttle

er'drücken v/t (no -ge-, h) crush (to
death); ~d fig adj overwhelming

'Erd|rutsch m (-[e]s; -e) landslide (a.

POL); **~teil** *m* GEOGR continent

er'**dulden** *v/t* (*no* -ge-, *h*) suffer, endure

'**Erdumlaufbahn** *f* earth orbit

'**Erdung** *f* (-; -en) ELECTR grounding, *Br* earthing

'**Erdwärme** *f* GEOL geothermal energy

er'**eifern** *v/refl* (*no* -ge-, *h*) get excited

ereignen [ɛɐ'ʔaignən] *v/refl* (*no* -ge-, *h*) happen, occur; **Ereignis** [ɛɐ'ʔaignɪs] *n* (-ses; -se) event, occurrence

er'**eignisreich** *adj* eventful

Erektion [erɛk'tsjoːn] *f* (-; -en) erection

Eremit [ere'miːt] *m* (-en; -en) hermit, anchorite

er'**fahren**[1] *v/t* (*irr*, **fahren**, *no* -ge-, *h*) hear; learn; experience

er'**fahren**[2] *adj* experienced

Er'fahrung *f* (-; -en) (work) experience

Er'fahrungsaustausch *m* exchange of experience; er'**fahrungsgemäß** *adv* as experience shows

er'**fassen** *v/t* (*no* -ge-, *h*) grasp; record, register; cover, include; IT collect

er'**finden** *v/t* (*irr*, **finden**, *no* -ge-, *h*) invent; **Er'finder(in)** (-s; -/-; -nen) inventor; **erfinderisch** [ɛɐ'fɪndərɪʃ] *adj* inventive; **Er'findung** *f* (-;-en) invention; **Er'findungskraft** *f* (-; *no pl*) inventiveness

Erfolg [ɛɐ'fɔlk] *m* (-[e]s; -e) success; result; **viel ~!** good luck!; **~ versprechend** promising; er'**folgen** *v/i* (*no* -ge-, *sein*) happen, take place; er'**folglos** *adj* unsuccessful; futile; **Er'folglosigkeit** *f* (-; *no pl*) lack of success; er'**folgreich** *adj* successful; **Er'folgserlebnis** *n* sense of achievement

erforderlich [ɛɐ'fɔrdəlɪç] *adj* necessary, required; er'**fordern** *v/t* (*no* -ge-, *h*) require, demand; **Erfordernis** [ɛɐ'fɔrdənɪs] *n* (-ses; -se) requirement, demand

er'**forschen** *v/t* (*no* -ge-, *h*) explore; investigate, study; **Er'forscher** *m* explorer; **Er'forschung** *f* exploration

er'**freuen** *v/t* (*no* -ge-, *h*) please

erfreulich [ɛɐ'frɔylɪç] *adj* pleasing, pleasant; gratifying

er'**freut** *adj* pleased (**über** *acc* at, about); **sehr ~!** pleased to meet you

er'**frieren** *v/i* (*irr*, **frieren**, *no* -ge-, *sein*) freeze to death; **Er'frierung** *f* (-; -en) MED frostbite

er'**frischen** *v/t and v/refl* (*no* -ge-, *h*) re-

fresh (o.s.); **~d** *adj* refreshing

Er'frischung *f* (-; -en) refreshment

erfroren [ɛɐ'froːrən] *adj* frostbitten; BOT killed by frost

er'**füllen** *fig v/t* (*no* -ge-, *h*) fulfil(l); keep (*promise etc*); serve (*purpose etc*); meet (*requirements etc*); **~ mit** fill with; **sich ~** be fulfilled, come true; **Er'füllung** *f* (-; -en) fulfil(l)ment; **in ~ gehen** come true

ergänzen [ɛɐ'gɛntsən] *v/t* (*no* -ge-, *h*) complement (**einander** each other); supplement, add; **~d** *adj* complementary, supplementary

Er'gänzung *f* (-; -en) completion; supplement, addition

ergattern [ɛɐ'gatən] F *v/t* (*no* -ge-, *h*) (manage to) get hold of

er'**geben** (*irr*, **geben**, *no* -ge-, *h*) **1.** *v/t* amount *or* come to **2.** *v/refl* surrender; *fig* arise; **sich ~ aus** result from; **sich ~ in** (*acc*) resign o.s. to

Er'gebenheit *f* (-; *no pl*) devotion

Ergebnis [ɛɐ'geːpnɪs] *n* (-ses; -se) result, SPORT *a.* score; outcome

er'**gebnislos** *adj* without result

er'**gehen** *v/i* (*irr*, **gehen**, *no* -ge-, *sein*) order *etc*: be issued (**an** *acc* to); **wie ist es dir ergangen?** how did things go with you?; **et. über sich ~ lassen** (patiently) endure s.th.

ergiebig [ɛɐ'giːbɪç] *adj* productive, rich; **Er'giebigkeit** *f* (-; *no pl*) (high) yield; productiveness

er'**gießen** *v/refl* (*irr*, **gießen**, *no* -ge-, *h*) **sich ~ über** (*acc*) pour down on

er'**grauen** *v/i* (*no* -ge-, *sein*) turn gray (*Br* grey)

er'**greifen** *v/t* (*irr*, **greifen**, *no* -ge-, *h*) seize, grasp, take hold of; take (*measures etc*); take up; *fig* move, touch

ergriffen [ɛɐ'grɪfən] *fig adj* moved

Er'griffenheit *f* (-; *no pl*) emotion

er'**gründen** *v/t* (*no* -ge-, *h*) find out, fathom

er'**haben** *adj* raised, elevated; *fig* sublime; **~ sein über** (*acc*) be above

er'**halten**[1] *v/t* (*irr*, **halten**, *no* -ge-, *h*) get, receive; keep, preserve; protect; support, maintain (*life etc*)

er'**halten**[2] *adj*: **gut ~** in good condition

erhältlich [ɛɐ'hɛltlɪç] *adj* obtainable, available

Er'haltung *f* (-; *no pl*) preservation; upkeep

er'hängen v/t (no -ge-, h) hang (**sich** o.s.)

er'heben v/t (irr, **heben**, no -ge-, h) raise (a. voice), lift; **sich ~** rise up (**gegen** against)

erheblich [ɛɐˈheːplɪç] adj considerable

Er'hebung f (-; -en) survey; revolt

erheitern [ɛɐˈhaɪtɐn] v/t (no -ge-, h) cheer up, amuse; **erhellen** [ɛɐˈhɛlən] v/t (no -ge-, h) light up; fig throw light upon; **erhitzen** [ɛɐˈhɪtsən] v/t (no -ge-, h) heat; **sich ~** get hot; **er'hoffen** v/t (no -ge-, h) hope for

erhöhen [ɛɐˈhøːən] v/t (no -ge-, h) raise; increase; **Er'höhung** f (-; -en) increase

er'holen v/refl (no -ge-, h) recover; relax, rest; **erholsam** [ɛɐˈhoːlzaːm] adj restful, relaxing; **Er'holung** f (-; no pl) recovery; relaxation

Er'holungsheim n rest home

erinnern [ɛɐˈʔɪnɐn] v/t (no -ge-, h) **j-n ~ an** (acc) remind s.o. of; **sich ~ an** (acc) remember, recall; **Erinnerung** [ɛɐˈʔɪnərʊŋ] f (-; -en) memory (**an** acc of); remembrance, souvenir; keepsake; **zur ~ an** (acc) in memory of

erkalten [ɛɐˈkaltən] v/i (no -ge-, sein) cool down (a. fig)

erkälten [ɛɐˈkɛltən] v/refl (no -ge-, h) **sich ~** catch (a) cold; (**stark**) **erkältet sein** have a (bad) cold; **Er'kältung** f (-; -en) cold

erkennbar [ɛɐˈkɛnbaːɐ] adj recognizable; **er'kennen** v/t (irr, **kennen**, no -ge-, h) recognize (**an** dat by), know (by); see, realize; **er'kenntlich** adj: **sich** (**j-m**) **~ zeigen** show (s.o.) one's gratitude; **Er'kenntnis** f (-; -se) realization; discovery; pl findings

Er'kennungs|dienst m (police) records department; **~melo¦die** f signature tune; **~zeichen** n badge; AVIAT markings

Erker [ˈɛrkɐ] m (-s; -) ARCH bay; **~fenster** n ARCH bay window

er'klären v/t (no -ge-, h) explain (**j-m** to s.o.); declare; **j-n** (offiziell) **für ... ~** pronounce s.o. ...; **~d** adj explanatory

erklärlich [ɛɐˈklɛːɐlɪç] adj explainable; **er'klärt** adj declared; **Er'klärung** f (-; -en) explanation; declaration; definition; **e-e ~ abgeben** make a statement

er'klingen v/i (irr, **klingen**, no -ge-, sein)

(re)sound, ring (out)

erkranken [ɛɐˈkraŋkən] v/i (no -ge-, sein) fall ill, get sick; **~ an** (dat) get; **Er'krankung** f (-; -en) illness, sickness

erkunden [ɛɐˈkʊndən] v/t (no -ge-, h) explore

erkundigen [ɛɐˈkʊndɪgən] v/refl (no -ge-, h) inquire (**nach** about s.th.; after s.o.); make inquiries (about); **sich** (**bei j-m**) **nach dem Weg ~** ask (s.o.) the way; **Er'kundigung** f (-; -en) inquiry

Er'kundung f (-; -en) exploration; MIL reconnaissance

Erlagschein [ɛɐˈlaːkʃaɪn] Austrian m money-order form

er'lahmen v/i (no -ge-, sein) flag

Erlass [ɛɐˈlas] m (-es; -e) decree; JUR remission; certain kind; **er'lassen** v/t (irr, **lassen**, no -ge-, h) issue; enact (bill etc); **j-m et. ~** release s.o. from s.th.

erlauben [ɛɐˈlaʊbən] v/t (no -ge-, h) allow, permit; **sich et. ~** permit o.s. (or dare) to do s.th.; treat o.s. to s.th.

Erlaubnis [ɛɐˈlaʊpnɪs] f (-; no pl) permission; authority; **um ~ bitten** ask s.o.'s permission; **~schein** m permit

erläutern [ɛɐˈlɔɪtɐn] v/t (no -ge-, h) explain, illustrate; **Er'läuterung** f (-; -en) explanation; annotation

Erle [ˈɛrlə] f (-; -n) BOT alder

er'leben v/t (no -ge-, h) experience; go through; see; have; **das werden wir nicht mehr ~** we won't live to see that

Erlebnis [ɛɐˈleːpnɪs] n (-ses; -se) experience; adventure

er'lebnisreich adj eventful

erledigen [ɛɐˈleːdɪgən] v/t (no -ge-, h) take care of, do, handle; settle; F finish s.o. (a. SPORT); do s.o. in; **erledigt** [ɛɐˈleːdɪçt] adj finished, settled; F worn out; F **der ist ~!** he is done for

Er'ledigung f (-; -en) (no pl) settlement; pl things to do, shopping

er'legen v/t (no -ge-, h) HUNT shoot

erleichtern [ɛɐˈlaɪçtɐn] v/t (no -ge-, h) ease, relieve; **er'leichtert** adj relieved; **Erleichterung** [ɛɐˈlaɪçtərʊŋ] f (-; no pl) relief (**über** acc at)

er'leiden v/t (irr, **leiden**, no -ge-, h) suffer

er'lesen adj choice, select

er'leuchten v/t (no -ge-, h) illuminate

er'liegen v/i (irr, **liegen**, no -ge-, sein) succumb to

Er'liegen *n*: **zum ~ kommen** (**bringen**) come (bring) to a standstill

erlogen [ɛɐˈloːɡən] *adj* false; **~ sein** be a lie

Erlös [ɛɐˈløːs] *m* (-es; -e) proceeds; profit(s)

erlosch [ɛɐˈlɔʃ] *pret of* **erlöschen**

erloschen [ɛɐˈlɔʃən] **1.** *pp of* **erlöschen** **2.** *adj* extinct (*volcano*)

er'löschen *v/i* (*irr, no -ge-, sein*) go out; *fig* die; JUR lapse, expire

er'lösen *v/t* (*no -ge-, h*) deliver, free (*both*: **von** from); **Erlöser** [ɛɐˈløːzɐ] *m* (-s; *no pl*) REL Savio(u)r; **Er'lösung** *f* (-; *no pl*) REL salvation; relief

ermächtigen [ɛɐˈmɛçtɪɡən] *v/t* (*no -ge-, h*) authorize; **Er'mächtigung** *f* (-; -en) authorization; authority

er'mahnen *v/t* (*no -ge-, h*) admonish; reprove, warn (*a.* SPORT)

Er'mahnung *f* (-; -en) admonition; warning; *esp* SPORT (first) caution

Er'mangelung *f*: **in ~** (*gen*) for want of

ermäßigt [ɛɐˈmɛːsɪçt] *adj* reduced, cut; **Er'mäßigung** *f* (-; -en) reduction, cut

er'messen *v/t* (*irr*, **messen**, *no -ge-, h*) assess; judge; **Er'messen** *n* (-s; *no pl*) discretion; **nach eigenem ~** at one's own discretion

er'mitteln (*no -ge-, h*) **1.** *v/t* find out; determine **2.** *v/i esp* JUR investigate; **Er'mittlung** *f* (-; -en) finding; JUR investigation

er'möglichen *v/t* (*no -ge-, h*) make possible

er'morden *v/t* (*no -ge-, h*) murder; *esp* POL assassinate; **Er'mordung** *f* (-; -en) murder; *esp* POL assassination

ermüden [ɛɐˈmyːdən] (*no -ge-*) **1.** *v/t* (*h*) tire, fatigue **2.** *v/i* (*sein*) tire, get tired, fatigue (*a.* TECH); **Er'müdung** *f* (-; *no pl*) fatigue, tiredness

er'muntern [ɛɐˈmʊntɐn] *v/t* (*no -ge-, h*) encourage; stimulate; **Er'munterung** *f* (-; -en) encouragement; incentive

ermutigen [ɛɐˈmuːtɪɡən] *v/t* (*no -ge-, h*) encourage; **~d** *adj* encouraging

Er'mutigung *f* (-; -en) encouragement

er'nähren *v/t* (*no -ge-, h*) feed; support (*family etc*); **sich ~ von** live on; **Er'nährer** *m* (-s; -) breadwinner, supporter; **Er'nährung** *f* (-; *no pl*) nutrition, food, diet

er'nennen *v/t* (*irr*, **nennen**, *no -ge-, h*) *j-n ~ zu* appoint s.o. (to be)

Er'nennung *f* (-; -en) appointment

erneuern [ɛɐˈnɔyɐn] *v/t* (*no -ge-, h*) renew; **Er'neuerung** *f* (-; -en) renewal

er'neut 1. *adj* renewed **2.** *adv* once more

erniedrigen [ɛɐˈniːdrɪɡən] *v/t* (*no -ge-, h*) humiliate; **sich ~** degrade o.s.

Er'niedrigung *f* (-; -en) humiliation

ernst [ɛrnst] *adj* serious, earnest; **~ nehmen** take *s.o. or s.th.* seriously

Ernst *m* (-es; *no pl*) seriousness, earnest; **im ~**(?) seriously(?); **ist das dein ~?** are you serious?

'ernsthaft, 'ernstlich *adj* serious

Ernte ['ɛrntə] *f* (-; -n) harvest; crop(s)

'Erntedankfest *n* Thanksgiving (Day), *Br* harvest festival

'ernten *v/t* (*ge-, h*) harvest, reap (*a. fig*)

er'nüchtern *v/t* (*no -ge-, h*) sober, *fig a.* disillusion; **Er'nüchterung** *f* (-; -en) sobering up; *fig* disillusionment

Eroberer [ɛɐˈʔoːbərɐ] *m* (-s; -) conqueror; **erobern** [ɛɐˈʔoːbɐn] *v/t* (*no -ge-, h*) conquer; **Er'oberung** *f* (-; -en) conquest (*a. fig*)

er'öffnen *v/t* (*no -ge-, h*) open; inaugurate; disclose *s.th.* (**j-m** to s.o.)

Er'öffnung *f* (-; -en) opening; inauguration; disclosure

erörtern [ɛɐˈʔœrtɐn] *v/t* (*no -ge-, h*) discuss; **Er'örterung** *f* (-; -en) discussion

Erotik [eˈroːtɪk] *f* (-; *no pl*) eroticism

erotisch [eˈroːtɪʃ] *adj* erotic

er'pressen *v/t* (*no -ge-, h*) blackmail; extort; **Er'presser(in)** *(-s; -/-; -nen)* blackmailer; **Er'pressung** *f* (-; -en) blackmail(ing); extortion

er'proben *v/t* (*no -ge-, h*) try, test

er'raten *v/t* (*irr*, **raten**, *no -ge-, h*) guess

er'rechnen *v/t* (*no -ge-, h*) calculate, work *s.th.* out

erregbar [ɛɐˈreːkbaɐ] *adj* excitable; irritable

er'regen *v/t* (*no -ge-, h*) excite, *sexually: a.* arouse; *fig* rouse; cause; **sich ~** get excited; **~d** *adj* exciting, thrilling

Er'reger *m* (-s; -) MED germ, virus

Er'regung *f* (-; -en) excitement

erreichbar [ɛɐˈraiçbaɐ] *adj* within reach (*a. fig*); available; **leicht ~** within easy reach; **nicht ~** out of reach; not available; **er'reichen** *v/t* (*no -ge-, h*) reach; catch (*train etc*); **es ~, dass ...** succeed in *doing s.th.*; **et. ~** get somewhere; **telefonisch zu ~ sein** have a (*Br* be on the) phone

er'**richten** *v/t* (*no -ge-, h*) put up, erect; *fig* found, *esp* ECON set up

Er'**richtung** *f* (-; -en) erection; *fig* establishment

er'**ringen** *v/t* (*irr, ringen, no -ge-, h*) win, gain; achieve

er'**röten** *v/i* (*no -ge-, sein*) blush

Errungenschaft [ɛɐ'rʊŋənʃaft] *f* (-; -en) achievement; **m-e neueste ~** my latest acquisition

Ersatz [ɛɐ'zats] *m* (-es; *no pl*) replacement; substitute; surrogate; compensation; damages; **als ~ für** in exchange for; ~**dienst** *m → Zivildienst;* ~**mann** *m* (-[e]s; -leute) substitute (*a.* SPORT); ~**mine** *f* refill; ~**reifen** *m* MOT spare tire (*Br* tyre); ~**spieler** *m* SPORT substitute; ~**teil** *n* TECH spare part

er'**schaffen** *v/t* (*irr, schaffen, no -ge-, h*) create

er'**schallen** *v/i* ([*irr, schallen,*] *no -ge-, sein*) (re)sound, ring (out)

er'**scheinen** *v/i* (*irr, scheinen, no -ge-, sein*) appear, F turn up; be published; **Er'scheinen** *n* (-s; *no pl*) appearance; publication; **Er'scheinung** *f* (-; -en) appearance; apparition; phenomenon

er'**schießen** *v/t* (*irr, schießen, no -ge-, h*) shoot (dead); **erschlaffen** [ɛɐ-'ʃlafən] *v/i* (*no -ge-, sein*) go limp; *fig* weaken; er'**schlagen** *v/t* (*irr, schlagen, no -ge-, h*) kill; er'**schließen** *v/t* (*irr, schließen, no -ge-, h*) open up; develop

erschollen [ɛɐ'ʃɔlən] *pp of* **erschallen**

er'**schöpfen** *v/t* (*no -ge-, h*) exhaust; er-'**schöpft** *adj* exhausted

Er'**schöpfung** *f* (-; *no pl*) exhaustion

erschrak [ɛɐ'ʃraːk] *pret of* **erschrecken** 2

er'**schrecken** 1. *v/t* (*no -ge-, h*) frighten, scare 2. *v/i* (*irr, no -ge-, sein*) be frightened (**über** *acc* at); ~**d** *adj* alarming; terrible

erschrocken [ɛɐ'ʃrɔkən] *pp of* **erschrecken** 2

erschüttern [ɛɐ'ʃʏtən] *v/t* (*no -ge-, h*) shake; *fig a.* shock; *fig* move

Er'**schütterung** *f* (-; -en) shock (*a. fig*); TECH vibration

er'**schweren** [ɛɐ'ʃveːrən] *v/t* (*no -ge-, h*) make more difficult; aggravate

er'**schwindeln** *v/t* (*no -ge-, h*) obtain *s.th.* by fraud; (*sich*) *et. von j-m* ~ swindle s.o. out of s.th.

er'**schwingen** *v/t* (*irr, schwingen, no -ge-, h*) afford; er'**schwinglich** *adj* within one's means, affordable; reasonable (*price*)

er'**sehen** *v/t* (*irr, sehen, no -ge-, h*) see, learn, gather (*all:* **aus** from)

ersetzbar [ɛɐ'zɛtsbaːɐ] *adj* replaceable; reparable; er'**setzen** *v/t* (*no -ge-, h*) replace (**durch** by); compensate for; *j-m et.* ~ reimburse s.o. for s.th.

er'**sichtlich** *adj* evident, obvious

er'**sparen** *v/t* (*no -ge-, h*) save; *j-m et.* ~ spare s.o. s.th.

Ersparnisse [ɛɐ'ʃpaːɐnɪsə] *pl* savings

erst [eːɐst] *adv* first; at first; *jetzt* (*gestern*) only now (yesterday); ~ **nächste Woche** not before *or* until next week; **es ist ~ neun Uhr** it's only nine o'clock; **eben ~** just (now); ~ **recht** all the more; ~ **recht nicht** even less; → **einmal**

er'**starren** *v/i* (*no -ge-, sein*) stiffen; *fig* freeze; er'**starrt** *adj* stiff; numb

erstatten [ɛɐ'ʃtatən] *v/t* (*no -ge-, h*) refund, reimburse (*j-m et.* s.o. for s.th.); **Bericht** ~ (give a) report (**über** *acc* on); **Anzeige** ~ report to the police

'**Erstaufführung** *f* THEA first night *or* performance, premiere, *film: a.* first run

er'**staunen** *v/t* (*no -ge-, h*) surprise, astonish; **Er'staunen** *n* (-s; *no pl*) surprise, astonishment; **in ~** (**ver**)**setzen** astonish; er'**staunlich** *adj* surprising, astonishing; er'**staunt** *adj* astonished

'**Erstausgabe** *f* first edition

'**erst** *adj* first; any old

'**erste** *adj* first; **auf den ~n Blick** at first sight; **fürs Erste** for the time being; **als Erste(r)** first; **zum ~n Male** for the first time; **am Ersten** on the first

er'**stechen** *v/t* (*irr, stechen, no -ge-, h*) stab

'**erstens** *adv* first(ly), in the first place

'**Erstere**: **der** (**die, das**) ~ the former

er'**sticken** *v/t* (*no -ge-, h*) *and v/i* (*sein*) choke, suffocate; **Er'stickung** *f* (-; *no pl*) suffocation

erst|klassig ['eːɐstklasɪç] *adj* first--class, F *a.* super; ~**malig** ['eːɐstmaːlɪç] *adj* first; ~**mals** ['eːɐstmaːls] *adv* for the first time

er'streben v/t (no -ge-, h) strive after

er'strebenswert adj desirable

er'strecken v/refl (no -ge-, h) extend, stretch (**bis, auf** acc to; **über** acc over); **sich ~ über** (acc) a. cover

'Erstschlag m MIL first strike

er'suchen v/t (no -ge-, h) request

er'tappen v/t (no -ge-, h) catch; → **Tat**

er'tönen v/i (no -ge-, sein) (re)sound

Ertrag [ɛɐ'traːk] m (-[e]s; Erträge [ɛɐ-'trɛːgə]) AGR yield, produce, TECH a. output; ECON proceeds, returns

er'tragen v/t (irr, **tragen**, no -ge-, h) bear, endure; stand

erträglich [ɛɐ'trɛːklɪç] adj bearable, tolerable

er'tränken v/t (no -ge-, h) drown

er'trinken v/i (irr, **trinken**, no -ge-, sein) drown

erübrigen [ɛɐ'ʔyːbrɪgən] v/t (no -ge-, h) spare; **sich ~** be unnecessary

Erw. abbr of **Erwachsene(r)** adult(s)

er'wachen v/i (no -ge-, sein) wake (up); esp fig awake, awaken

er'wachsen¹ v/i (irr, **wachsen**, no -ge-, sein) arise (**aus** from)

er'wachsen² adj grown-up, adult

Er'wachsene m, f (-n; -n) adult; **nur für ~!** adults only! Er'wachsenenbildung f adult education

erwägen [ɛɐ'vɛːgən] v/t (irr, **wägen**, no -ge-, h) consider, think s.th. over; Er-'wägung f (-; -en) consideration; **in ~ ziehen** take into consideration

erwähnen [ɛɐ'vɛːnən] v/t (no -ge-, h) mention; Er'wähnung f (-; -en) mention(ing)

er'wärmen v/t and v/refl (no -ge-, h) warm (up); fig **sich ~ für** warm to Er'wärmung f (-; -en) warming up; **der Erdatmosphäre** global warming

er'warten v/t (no -ge-, h) expect; wait for, await; Er'wartung f (-; -en) expectation, anticipation

er'wartungsvoll adj and adv full of expectation, expectant(ly)

er'wecken fig v/t (no -ge-, h) awaken; arouse; → **Anschein**

er'weisen v/t (irr, **weisen**, no -ge-, h) do (service etc); show (respect etc); **sich ~ als** prove to be

erweitern [ɛɐ'vaitən] v/t and v/refl (no -ge-, h) extend, enlarge; esp ECON ex-

pand; Er'weiterung f (-; -en) extension, enlargement, expansion

Erwerb [ɛɐ'vɛrp] m (-[e]s; -e) acquisition; purchase; income; er'werben v/t (irr, **werben**, no -ge-, h) acquire (a. fig); purchase

er'werbs|los adj unemployed; **~tätig** adj (gainfully) employed, working; **~unfähig** adj unable to work Er'werbung f (-; -en) acquisition; purchase

erwidern [ɛɐ'viːdən] v/t (no -ge-, h) reply, answer; return (visit etc) Er'widerung f (-; -en) reply, answer; return

er'wischen v/t (no -ge-, h) catch, get; **ihn hat's erwischt** he's had it

er'wünscht adj desired; desirable; welcome

er'würgen v/t (no -ge-, h) strangle

Erz [eːrts] n (-es; -e) ore

er'zählen v/t (no -ge-, h) tell; narrate; **man hat mir erzählt** I was told Er'zähler m (-s; -), Er'zählerin f (-; -nen) narrator

Er'zählung f (-; -en) (short) story, tale 'Erzbischof m REL archbishop

'Erzbistum n REL archbishopric

'Erzengel m REL archangel

er'zeugen v/t (no -ge-, h) ECON produce (a. fig); TECH make, manufacture; ELECTR generate; fig cause, create; Er-'zeuger m (-s; -) ECON producer; Er-'zeugnis n (-ses; -se) ECON product (a. fig); Er'zeugung f (-; -en) ECON production

er'ziehen v/t (irr, **ziehen**, no -ge-, h) bring up, raise; educate; **j-n zu et. ~** teach s.o. to be or to do s.th.

Erzieher [ɛɐ'tsiːə] m (-s; -), Erzieherin [ɛɐ'tsiːərɪn] f (-; -nen) educator; teacher; (qualified) kindergarten teacher; er'zieherisch adj educational, pedagogic(al); Er'ziehung f (-; no pl) upbringing; education

Er'ziehungs|anstalt f reform (Br approved) school; **~berechtigte m, f** (-n; -n) parent or guardian; **~wesen n** (-s; no pl) educational system

er'zielen v/t (no -ge-, h) achieve; SPORT score

erzogen [ɛɐ'tsoːgən] adj: **gut ~ sein** be well-bred; **schlecht ~ sein** be ill-bred er'zwingen v/t (irr, **zwingen**, no -ge-, h) (en)force

es [ɛs] *pers pron* it; he; she; **~ gibt** there is, there are; **ich bin ~** it's me; **ich hoffe ~** I hope so; **ich kann ~** I can (do it)

Esche ['ɛʃə] *f* (-; -*n*) BOT ash (tree)

Esel ['eːzəl] *m* (-*s*; -) zo donkey, ass (*a.* F)

'Eselsbrücke *f* mnemonic

'Eselsohr *fig n* dog-ear

Eskorte [ɛs'kɔrtə] *f* (-; -*n*) MIL escort, MAR *a.* convoy

essbar ['ɛsbaːɐ] *adj* eatable; edible

essen ['ɛsən] *v/t and v/i* (*irr, ge-, h*) eat; **zu Mittag ~** (have) lunch; **zu Abend ~** have supper (*or* dinner); **~ gehen** eat *or* dine out; **'Essen** *n* (-*s*; -) food; meal; dish; dinner

'Essensˌmarke *f* meal ticket; **~zeit** *f* lunchtime; dinner *or* supper time

Essig ['ɛsɪç] *m* (-*s*; -*e*) vinegar

'Essiggurke *f* pickled gherkin, pickle

Essˌlöffel *m* tablespoon; **~stäbchen** *pl* chopsticks; **~tisch** *m* dining table; **~zimmer** *n* dining room

Estrich ['ɛstrɪç] *m* (-*s*; -*e*) ARCH flooring, subfloor; *Swiss:* loft, attic, garret

etablieren [eta'bliːrən] *v/refl* (*no -ge-, h*) establish o.s.

Etage [e'taːʒə] *f* (-; -*n*) floor, stor(e)y; **auf der ersten ~** on the second (*Br* first) floor; **E'tagenbett** *n* bunk bed

Etappe [e'tapə] *f* (-; -*n*) stage, SPORT *a.* leg

Etat [e'taː] *m* (-*s*; -*s*) budget

Ethik ['eːtɪk] *f* (-; *no pl*) ethics

ethisch ['eːtɪʃ] *adj* ethical

ethnisch ['ɛtnɪʃ] *adj* ethnic

Etikett [eti'kɛt] *n* (-[*e*]*s*; -*e*[*n*]) label (*a. fig*); (price) tag; **Eti'kette** *f* (-; -*n*) etiquette; **etikettieren** [etikɛ'tiːrən] *v/t* (*no -ge-, h*) label

etliche ['ɛtlɪçə] *indef pron* several, quite a few

Etui [ɛt'viː] *n* (-*s*; -*s*) case

etwa ['ɛtva] *adv* about, around; perhaps, by any chance; **nicht ~, dass** not that; **etwaig** ['ɛtvaɪç] *adj* any

etwas ['ɛtvas] **1.** *indef pron* something; anything **2.** *adj* some; any **3.** *adv* a little, somewhat

EU [eː'uː] *abbr of* **Europäische Union** EU, European Union

euch [ɔyç] *pers pron* you; **~ (selbst)** yourselves; **euer** ['ɔyɐ] *poss pron* your; **der (die, das) Eu(e)re** yours

Eule ['ɔylə] *f* (-; -*n*) zo owl; **~n nach Athen tragen** carry coals to Newcastle

euresgleichen ['ɔyrəs'glaɪçən] *pron* people like you, F *contp* the likes of you

Euro…['ɔyro] *in cpds* …*cheque etc*: Euro…

Europa [ɔy'roːpa] Europe; **~…** *in cpds* European; **Europäer** [ɔyro'pɛːɐ] *m* (-*s*; -), **Europäerin** [ɔyro'pɛːərɪn] *f* (-; -*nen*), **euro'päisch** *adj* European; **Europäische Gemeinschaft** European Community

Euter ['ɔytɐ] *n* (-*s*; -) udder

ev. *abbr of* **evangelisch** Prot., Protestant

evakuieren [evaku'iːrən] *v/t* (*no -ge-, h*) evacuate

evangelisch [evaŋ'geːlɪʃ] *adj* REL Protestant; **~lutherisch** Lutheran

Evangelium [evaŋ'geːljʊm] *n* (-*s*; -*lien*) Gospel

eventuell [evɛntu'ɛl] **1.** *adj* possible **2.** *adv* possibly, perhaps

evtl. *abbr of* **eventuell** poss., possibly

ewig ['eːvɪç] *adj* eternal; F constant, endless; **auf ~** for ever; **'Ewigkeit** *f* (-; *no pl*) eternity; F **eine ~** (for) ages

exakt [ɛ'ksakt] *adj* exact, precise

Ex'aktheit *f* (-; *no pl*) exactness, precision

Examen [ɛ'ksaːmən] *n* (-*s*; *Examina* [ɛ'ksaːmina]) exam, examination

Exekutive [ɛkseku'tiːvə] *f* (-; -*n*) POL executive (power)

Exemplar [ɛksɛm'plaːɐ] *n* (-*s*; -*e*) specimen; copy

exerzieren [ɛksɛr'tsiːrən] *v/i* (*no -ge-, h*) MIL drill

Exil [ɛ'ksiːl] *n* (-*s*; -*e*) exile

Existenz [ɛksɪs'tɛnts] *f* (-; -*en*) existence; living, livelihood; **~kampf** *m* struggle for survival; **~minimum** *n* subsistence level

existieren [ɛksɪs'tiːrən] *v/i* (*no -ge-, h*) exist; live (**von** on)

exklusiv [ɛksklu'ziːf] *adj* exclusive, select

exotisch [ɛ'ksoːtɪʃ] *adj* exotic

Expansion [ɛkspan'zjoːn] *f* (-; -*en*) expansion

Expedition [ɛkspedi'tsjoːn] *f* (-; -*en*) expedition

Experiment [ɛksperi'mɛnt] *n* (-[*e*]*s*; -*e*), **experimentieren** [ɛksperimɛn'tiːrən]

E

v/i (*no -ge-, h*) experiment

Experte [ɛks'pɛrtə] *m* (*-n; -n*), **Ex'pertin** *f* (*-; -nen*) expert (*für* on)

explodieren [ɛksplo'di:rən] *v/i* (*no -ge-, sein*) explode (*a. fig*), burst; **Explosion** [ɛksplo'zjo:n] *f* (*-; -en*) explosion (*a. fig*); **explosiv** [ɛksplo'zi:f] *adj* explosive

Export [ɛks'pɔrt] *m* (*-[e]s; -e*) (*no pl*) export(ation); exports

exportieren [ɛkspɔr'ti:rən] *v/t* (*no -ge-, h*) export

Express [ɛks'prɛs] *m* (*-es; no pl*) RAIL express; **per ~** by special delivery, *Br* express

extra ['ɛkstra] *adv* extra; separately; F on purpose; **~ für dich** especially for you

Extra *n* (*-s; -s*), **~blatt** *n* extra

Extrakt [ɛks'trakt] *m* (*-[e]s; -e*) extract

extravagant [ɛkstrava'gant] *adj* flamboyant

extrem [ɛks'tre:m] *adj*, **Ex'trem** *n* (*-s; -e*) extreme; **Extremist(in)** [ɛkstre'mɪst(ɪn)] (*-en; -en/-; -nen*), **extre'mistisch** *adj* extremist, ultra

Exzellenz [ɛkstsɛ'lɛnts] *f* (*-; -en*) Excellency

exzentrisch [ɛks'tsɛntrɪʃ] *adj* eccentric

Exzess [ɛks'tsɛs] *m* (*-ses; -se*) excess

F

Fa. *abbr of* **Firma** firm; Messrs.

Fabel ['fa:bəl] *f* (*-; -n*) fable (*a. fig*)

'fabelhaft *adj* fantastic, wonderful

Fabrik [fa'bri:k] *f* (*-; -en*) factory, works, shop; **Fabrikant** [fabri'kant] *m* (*-en; -en*) factory owner; manufacturer

Fa'brikarbeiter *m* factory worker

Fabrikat [fabri'ka:t] *n* (*-[e]s; -e*) make, brand; product

Fabrikation [fabrika'tsjo:n] *f* (*-; -en*) manufacturing, production

Fabrikati'onsfehler *m* flaw

Fa'brik|besitzer *m* factory owner; **~ware** *f* manufactured product(s)

Fach [fax] *n* (*-[e]s; Fächer* ['fɛçɐ]) compartment; pigeonhole; shelf; PED, UNIV subject; → **Fachgebiet**; (*field of*) specialized knowledge

Fächer ['fɛçɐ] *m* (*-s; -*) fan

'Fach|frau *f* expert; **~gebiet** *n* line, field; trade, business; **~geschäft** *n* dealer (specializing in …); **~hochschule** *f* *appr* (*technial*) college, *esp Br* polytechnic; **~kenntnisse** *pl* specialized knowledge

'fachkundig *adj* competent, expert

'fachlich *adj* professional, specialized

'Fach|litera,tur *f* specialized literature; **~mann** *m* (*-[e]s; -leute*) expert

fachmännisch ['faxmɛnɪʃ] *adj* expert

'Fachschule *f* technical school *or* college

fachsimpeln ['faxzɪmpəln] *v/i* (*ge-, h*) talk shop

'Fach|werk *n* framework; **~werkhaus** *n* half-timbered house; **~zeitschrift** *f* (professional *or* specialist) journal

Fackel ['fakəl] *f* (*-; -n*) torch; **~zug** *m* torchlight procession

fade ['fa:də] *adj* GASTR tasteless, flat; stale; *fig* dull, boring

Faden ['fa:dən] *m* (*-s; Fäden* ['fɛ:dən]) thread (*a. fig*); **'fadenscheinig** *adj* threadbare; *fig* flimsy (*excuse etc*)

fähig ['fɛ:ɪç] *adj* capable (*zu* of [*doing*] *s.th.*), able (*to do s.th.*); **'Fähigkeit** *f* (*-; -en*) (cap)ability; talent, gift

fahl [fa:l] *adj* pale; ashen (*face*)

fahnden ['fa:ndən] *v/i* (*ge-, h*) search (*nach* for); **'Fahndung** *f* (*-; -en*) search; **'Fahndungsliste** *f* wanted list

Fahne ['fa:nə] *f* (*-; -n*) flag; *mst fig* banner; F **e-e ~ haben** reek of alcohol

'Fahnen|flucht *f* (*-; no pl*) MIL desertion; **~stange** *f* flagpole, flagstaff

Fahrbahn ['fa:rba:n] *f* road(way), pavement; MOT lane

'fahrbar *adj* mobile

Fähre ['fɛ:rə] *f* (*-; -n*) ferry(boat)

fahren ['fa:rən] (*irr, ge-*) **1.** *v/i* (*sein*) go; *bus etc*: run; leave; MOT drive; ride; **mit dem Auto** (*Zug, Bus etc*) **~** go by car (train, bus *etc*); **über e-e Brücke** *etc*

~ cross a bridge *etc*; **mit der Hand über et.** ~ run one's hand over s.th.; **was ist denn in dich gefahren?** what's got into you? **2.** *v/t* (*h*) drive (*car etc*); ride (*bicycle etc*); carry

Fahrer ['fa:rɐ] *m* (*-s*; *-*) driver; ~**flucht** *f* hit-and-run offense (*Br* offence)

'**Fahrerin** *f* (*-*; *-nen*) driver

Fahr|gast ['fa:rɡast] *m* passenger; ~**geld** *n* fare; ~**gelegenheit** *f* means of transport(ation); ~**gemeinschaft** *f* car pool; ~**gestell** *n* MOT chassis; AVIAT → **Fahrwerk**; ~**karte** *f* ticket

'**Fahrkarten|automat, mat** *m* ticket machine; ~**entwerter** *m* (*-s*; *-*) ticket-cancel(l)ing machine; ~**schalter** *m* ticket window

'**fahrlässig** *adj* careless, reckless (*a.* JUR); **grob** ~ grossly negligent

'**Fahrlehrer** *m* driving instructor

'**Fahrplan** *m* timetable, schedule

'**fahrplanmäßig 1.** *adj* scheduled **2.** *adv* according to schedule; on time

'**Fahr|preis** *m* fare; ~**prüfung** *f* driving test; ~**rad** *n* bicycle, F bike; ~**schein** *m* ticket; ~**schule** *f* driving school; ~**schüler** *m* MOT student driver, *Br* learner (driver); PED non-local student; ~**stuhl** *m* elevator, *Br* lift; ~**stunde** *f* driving lesson

Fahrt [fa:rt] *f* (*-*; *-en*) ride, MOT *a.* drive; trip, journey, MAR voyage, cruise; speed (*a.* MOT); **in voller** ~ at full speed

Fährte ['fɛ:rtə] *f* (*-*; *-n*) track (*a.* fig)

'**Fahrtenschreiber** *m* MOT tachograph

'**Fahrwasser** *n* MAR fairway

'**Fahrwerk** *n* AVIAT landing gear

'**Fahrzeug** *n* (*-[e]s*; *-e*) vehicle

Fairness ['fɛ:rnɪs] *f* (*; no pl*) fair play

Faktor ['fakto:ɐ] *m* (*-s*; *-en* [fak'to:rən]) factor

Fakultät [fakʊl'tɛ:t] *f* (*-*; *-en*) UNIV faculty, department

Falke ['falkə] *m* (*-n*; *-n*) ZO hawk, falcon

Fall [fal] *m* (*-[e]s*; *Fälle* ['fɛlə]) fall; LING, JUR, MED case; **auf jeden** ~ in any case; **auf keinen** ~ on no account; **für den** ~, **dass ...** in case ...; **gesetzt den** ~, **dass** suppose (that); **zu** ~ **bringen** fig defeat

Falle ['falə] *f* (*-*; *-n*) trap (*a.* fig)

fallen ['falən] *v/i* (irr, ge-, sein) fall (*a.* rain etc), drop; ~ **lassen** drop (*a.* fig); MIL be killed (in action); **ein Tor fiel** SPORT a goal was scored

fällen ['fɛlən] *v/t* (ge-, h) fell, cut down (tree); JUR pass (sentence); make (a decision etc)

'**fallenlassen** ['faləlasən] *v/i* (irr, **fallen**, no ge-, h) fig drop

fällig ['fɛlɪç] adj due; payable

'**Fall|obst** *n* windfall; ~**rückzieher** *m* soccer: overhead kick

falls [fals] cj if, in case; ~ **nicht** unless

'**Fallschirm** *m* parachute; ~**jäger** *m* MIL paratrooper; ~**springen** *n* MIL parachuting; ~**springen** *n* SPORT skydiving; ~**springer** *m* MIL parachutist; SPORT skydiver

'**Falltür** *f* trapdoor

falsch [falʃ] adj and adv wrong; false (*a.* fig); forged; ~ **gehen** watch: be wrong; **et.** ~ **aussprechen (schreiben, verstehen)** mispronounce (misspell, misunderstand etc) s.th.; ~ **verbunden!** TEL sorry, wrong number

fälschen ['fɛlʃən] *v/t* (ge-, h) forge, fake; counterfeit; '**Fälscher** *m* (*-s*; *-*) forger

'**Falsch|geld** *n* counterfeit or false money; ~**spieler** *m* cheat

'**Fälschung** *f* (*-*; *-en*) forgery; counterfeit; '**fälschungssicher** adj forgery-proof

Falt... ['falt-] in cpds ...bett, ...boot etc: folding ...; **Falte** ['faltə] *f* (*-*; *-n*) fold; wrinkle; pleat; crease; '**falten** *v/t* (ge-, h) fold; '**Faltenrock** *m* pleated skirt

Falter ['faltɐ] *m* (*-s*; *-*) ZO butterfly

faltig ['faltɪç] adj wrinkled

familiär [fami'ljɛ:r] adj personal; informal; ~**e Probleme** family problems

Familie [fa'mi:ljə] *f* (*-*; *-n*) family (*a.* ZO, BOT)

Fa'milien|angelegenheit *f* family affair; ~**anschluss** *m*: ~ **haben** live as one of the family; ~**name** *m* family (or last) name, surname; ~**packung** *f* family size (package); ~**planung** *f* family planning; ~**stand** *m* marital status; ~**vater** *m* family man

Fanatiker [fa'na:tikɐ] *m* (*-s*; *-*), **Fa'natikerin** *f* (*-*; *-nen*), **fa'natisch** adj fanatic; **Fanatismus** [fana'tɪsmʊs] *m* (*-*; *no pl*) fanaticism

fand [fant] pret of **finden**

Fang [faŋ] *m* (*-[e]s*; *Fänge* ['fɛŋə]) catch (*a.* fig); '**fangen** *v/t* (irr, ge-, h) catch (*a.* fig); **sich wieder** ~ get a grip on o.s. again; **Fangen spielen** play tag (*Br* catch); '**Fangzahn** m zo fang

Fantasie [fanta'zi:] f (-; -n) imagination; fantasy; fancy; **fanta'sielos** adj unimaginative; **fanta'sieren** v/i (no -ge-, h) daydream; MED be delirious; F talk nonsense; **fanta'sievoll** adj imaginative; **Fantast** [fan'tast] m (-en; -en) dreamer; **fan'tastisch** adj fantastic, F a. great, terrific

Farbband ['farpbant] n (typewriter) ribbon

Farbe ['farbə] f (-; -n) colo(u)r; paint; complexion; tan; *card games*: suit

'**farbecht** adj colo(u)r-fast

färben ['fɛrbən] v/t (ge-, h) dye; *esp fig* colo(u)r; **sich rot ~** turn red; → **abfärben**

'**farben|blind** adj colo(u)r-blind; **~froh**, **~prächtig** adj colo(u)rful

'**Farb|fernsehen** n colo(u)r television; **~fernseher** m colo(u)r TV set; **~film** m colo(u)r film; **~foto** n colo(u)r photo

farbig ['farbɪç] adj colo(u)red; stained (*glass*); *fig* colo(u)rful; **Farbige** ['farbɪgə] m, f (-n; -n) → **Schwarze**

'**Farbkasten** m paintbox

'**farblos** adj colo(u)rless (a. fig)

'**Farbstift** m colo(u)red pencil, crayon

'**Farbstoff** m dye; GASTR colo(u)ring

'**Farbton** m shade, tint

'**Färbung** f (-; -en) colo(u)ring; hue

Farnkraut ['farnkraut] n BOT fern

Fasan [fa'za:n] m (-[e]s; -e[n]) zo pheasant

Faschismus [fa'ʃɪsmʊs] m (-; no pl) POL fascism; **Faschist** [fa'ʃɪst] m (-en; -en), **fa'schistisch** adj POL fascist

faseln ['fa:zəln] F v/i (ge-, h) drivel

Faser ['fa:zɐ] f (-; -n) fiber, Br fibre; grain; **faserig** ['fa:zərɪç] adj fibrous; '**fasern** v/i (ge-, h) fray

Fass [fas] n (-es; Fässer ['fɛsɐ]) cask, barrel; **vom ~** on tap

Fassade [fa'sa:də] f (-; -n) ARCH facade, front (a. fig)

'**Fassbier** n draft (Br draught) beer

fassen ['fasən] (ge-, h) **1.** v/t take hold of, grasp; seize; catch (*criminal*); hold, take; set (*jewels*); fig grasp, understand; pluck up (*courage*); make (a *decision*); **sich ~** compose o.s.; **sich kurz ~** be brief; **es ist nicht zu ~** that's incredible **2.** v/i: **~ nach** reach for

'**Fassung** f (-; -en) setting; frame (*of*

glasses); ELECTR socket; draft(ing); wording, version; (*no pl*) composure; **die ~ verlieren** lose one's composure; **j-n aus der ~ bringen** put s.o. out

'**fassungslos** adj stunned; speechless

'**Fassungsvermögen** n capacity

fast [fast] adv almost, nearly; **~ nie** (**nichts**) hardly ever (anything)

fasten ['fastən] v/i (ge-, h) fast

'**Fastenzeit** f REL Lent

'**Fastnacht** f → **Karneval**

fatal [fa'ta:l] adj unfortunate; awkward; disastrous

fauchen ['fauxən] v/i (ge-, h) zo hiss

faul [faul] adj rotten, bad, GASTR a. spoiled; fig lazy; F fishy; **~e Ausrede** lame excuse; '**faulen** v/i (ge-, h, sein) rot, go bad; decay

faulenzen ['faulɛntsən] v/i (ge-, h) laze, loaf (about); **Faulenzer(in)** ['faulɛntsɐ, 'faulɛntsərɪn] (-s; -/-; -nen) lazybones; *contp* loafer

'**Faulheit** f (-; no pl) laziness

faulig ['faulɪç] adj rotten

Fäulnis ['fɔylnɪs] f (-; no pl) rottenness, decay (a. fig)

'**Faulpelz** F m → **Faulenzer**

'**Faultier** n zo sloth

Faust [faust] f (-; Fäuste ['fɔystə]) fist; **auf eigene ~** on one's own initiative; **~handschuh** m mitten; **~regel** f (**als ~** as a) rule of thumb; **~schlag** m punch

Favorit [favo'ri:t] m (-en; -en), **Favo'ritin** f (-; -nen) favo(u)rite

Fax [faks] n (-; -[e]) fax; fax machine

faxen ['faksən] v/i and v/t (ge-, h) fax, send a fax (to)

'**Faxgerät** n fax machine

FCKW [eftse:ka:'ve:] abbr of **Fluorchlorkohlenwasserstoff** chlorofluorocarbon, CFC

Feber ['fe:bɐ] Austrian m (-s; -), **Februar** ['fe:brua:ɐ] m (-s; -e) February

fechten ['fɛçtən] v/i (irr, ge-, h) SPORT fence; fig fight; '**Fechten** (-s; no pl) SPORT fencing; **Fechter(in)** ['fɛçtɐ, 'fɛçtərɪn] m(f) (-s; -/-; -nen) SPORT fencer

Feder ['fe:dɐ] f (-; -n) feather; plume; nib; TECH spring; **~ball** m SPORT badminton; shuttlecock; **~bett** n comforter, Br duvet; **~gewicht** n SPORT featherweight; **~halter** m penholder

'**feder'leicht** adj (as) light as a feather

Federmäppchen ['fe:dɐmɛpçən] n (-s; -) pencil case

federn (ge-, h) **1.** v/i be springy **2.** v/t TECH spring; **~d** adj springy, elastic

Federstrich m stroke of the pen

Federung ['fe:dərʊŋ] f (-; -en) springs; MOT suspension; **e-e gute ~ haben** be well sprung

Federzeichnung f pen-and-ink drawing

Fee [fe:] f (-; -n) fairy

fegen ['fe:gən] v/t (ge-, h) and fig v/i (sein) sweep

fehl [fe:l] adj: **~ am Platze** out of place

Fehlbetrag m deficit

fehlen v/i (ge-, h) be missing; be absent; **ihm fehlt (es an)** ... he is lacking ...; **du fehlst uns** we miss you; **was dir fehlt, ist ...** what you need is ...; **was fehlt Ihnen?** what's wrong with you?

Fehler ['fe:lɐ] m (-s; -) mistake; fault; TECH a. defect, flaw; IT error

fehlerfrei adj faultless, flawless

fehlerhaft adj faulty; full of mistakes; TECH defective

Fehlermeldung f IT error message

Fehl|ernährung f malnutrition; **~ge-burt** f MED miscarriage; **~griff** m mistake; wrong choice

Fehlschlag m failure; **fehlschlagen** v/i (irr, schlagen, sep, -ge-, sein) fail

Fehl|start m false start; **~tritt** m slip; fig lapse; **~zündung** f MOT backfire (a. **~ haben**)

Feier ['faiɐ] f (-; -n) celebration; party

Feierabend m end of a day's work; closing time; evening (at home); **~ machen** finish (work), F knock off; **nach ~** after work

feierlich adj solemn; festive

Feierlichkeit f (-; -en) (no pl) solemnity; ceremony

feiern v/t and v/i (ge-, h) celebrate; have a party

Feiertag m holiday; **gesetzlicher ~** public (or legal, Br a. bank) holiday

feig [faik], **feige** ['faigə] adj cowardly; **~ sein** be a coward

Feige ['faigə] f (-; -n) BOT fig

Feigheit f (-; no pl) cowardice

Feigling m (-s; -e) coward

Feile ['failə] f (-; -n), **feilen** v/t and v/i (ge-, h) file

feilschen ['failʃən] v/i (ge-, h) haggle (**um** about, over)

fein [fain] adj fine; choice, excellent; keen (ear); delicate; distinguished, F posh; **~!** good!, okay!

Feind [faint] m (-[e]s; -e ['faində]) enemy (a. fig); **~bild** n enemy image

Feindin ['faindn] f (-; -nen) enemy

feindlich adj hostile; MIL enemy

Feindschaft f (-; no pl) hostility

feindselig adj hostile (**gegen** to)

Feindseligkeit f (-; no pl) hostility

feinfühlig ['fainfy:lɪç] adj sensitive

Feingefühl n (-[e]s; no pl) sensitiveness

Feinheit f (-; -en) (no pl) fineness; keenness; delicacy; pl niceties

Fein|kostgeschäft n delicatessen; **~me,chaniker** m precision mechanic

Feinschmecker m (-s; -) gourmet

feist [faist] adj fat, stout

Feld [fɛlt] n (-[e]s; -er ['fɛldɐ]) field (a. fig); chess: square; **~arbeit** f AGR work in the fields; fieldwork; **~bett** n cot, Br camp bed; **~flasche** f water bottle, canteen; **~lerche** f ZO skylark; **~marschall** m MIL field marshal

Feldstecher ['fɛltʃtɛçɐ] m (-s; -) field glasses

Feldwebel ['fɛltve:bəl] m (-s; -) MIL sergeant

Feldzug m MIL campaign (a. fig)

Felge ['fɛlgə] f (-; -n) rim; SPORT circle

Fell [fɛl] n (-[e]s; -e) ZO coat; skin, fur

Fels [fɛls] m (-en; -en) rock

Felsbrocken m boulder

Felsen ['fɛlzən] m (-s; -) rock

felsig ['fɛlzɪç] adj rocky

Felsspalte f crevice

Felsvorsprung m ledge

feminin [femi'ni:n] adj feminine (a. LING); contp effeminate; **Femininum** [femi'ni:nʊm] m (-; no pl) feminism; **Feministin** [femi'nɪstn] f (-; -nen), **femi'nistisch** adj feminist

Fenchel ['fɛnçəl] m (-s; no pl) BOT fennel

Fenster ['fɛnstɐ] n (-s; -) window; **~bank** f (-; -bänke), **~brett** n windowsill; **~flügel** m casement; **~laden** m shutter; **~rahmen** m window frame; **~scheibe** f (window)pane

Ferien ['fe:rjən] pl vacation, esp Br holiday(s pl); **~ haben** be on vacation; **~haus** n vacation home, cottage; **~la-**

ger *n* summer camp; **~wohnung** *f* vacation rental, *Br* holiday apartment

Ferkel ['fɛrkəl] *n* (-s; -) zo piglet; F pig

fern [fɛrn] *adj and adv* far(away), far-off, distant; **von ~** from a distance

'**Fernamt** *n* telephone exchange

'**Fernbedienung** *f* remote control

'**fernbleiben** *v/i* (*irr,* **bleiben***, sep, -ge-, sein*) stay away (*dat* from)

Ferne ['fɛrnə] *f* (-; *no pl*) distance; **aus der ~** from a distance

'**ferner** ['fɛrnɐ] *adv* further(more); in addition, also

'**Fern|fahrer** *m* long-haul truck driver, F trucker, *Br* long-distance lorry driver; **~gespräch** *n* TEL long-distance call

'**ferngesteuert** *adj* remote-controlled; MIL guided (*missile etc*)

'**Fernglas** *n* binoculars

'**fernhalten** *v/t* (*irr,* **halten***, sep, -ge-, h*) keep away (**von** from)

Fern|heizung *f* district heating; **~kurs** *m* correspondence course; **~laster** F *m* (-s; -) MOT longhaul truck, *Br* long-distance lorry; **~lenkung** *f* remote control; **~licht** *n* MOT full (*or* high) beam

'**fernliegen** *v/i* (*irr,* **liegen***, sep, -ge-, h*): **es liegt mir fern zu** far be it from me to

'**Fernmelde|satellit** *m* communications satellite; **~technik** *f*, **~wesen** *n* (-s; *no pl*) telecommunications

'**Fern|rohr** *n* telescope; **~schreiben** *n*, **~schreiber** *m* telex

'**fernsehen** *v/i* (*irr,* **sehen***, sep, -ge-, h*) watch television; '**Fernsehen** *n* (-s; *no pl*) television (**im** on); '**Fernseher** F *m* (-s; -) TV (set); TV viewer

'**Fernseh|schirm** *m* (TV) screen; **~sendung** *f* TV program(me)

'**Fernsteuerung** *f* remote control

'**Fernverkehr** *m* long-distance traffic

Ferse ['fɛrzə] *f* (-; -*n*) ANAT heel (*a. fig*)

fertig ['fɛrtɪç] *adj* ready; finished; **~ bringen** manage; *iro* be capable of; **~ machen** finish (*a.* F *s.o.*); get *s.th.* ready; F give *s.o.* hell, do *s.o.* in; **sich ~ machen** get ready; (**mit et.**) **~ sein** have finished (*s.th.*); **mit et. ~ werden** cope with *a problem etc*; F **völlig ~** dead beat

'**fertigbringen** *v/t* (*irr,* **bringen***, sep, -ge-, h*) → **fertig**

'**Fertig|gericht** *n* ready(-to-serve) meal; **~haus** *n* prefabricated house, F prefab

'**Fertigkeit** *f* (-; -*en*) skill

'**fertigmachen** *v/t* (*irr,* **bringen***, sep, -ge-, h*) → **fertig**

'**Fertigstellung** *f* (-; *no pl*) completion

'**fertigwerden** *v/t* (*irr,* **bringen***, sep, -ge-, sein*) → **fertig**

fesch [fɛʃ] *Austrian adj* smart, chic

Fessel ['fɛsəl] *f* (-; -*n*) shackle (*a. fig*); ANAT ankle; '**fesseln** *v/t* (*ge-, h*) bind, tie (up); *fig* fascinate

fest [fɛst] *adj* firm (*a. fig*); solid; fast; *fig* fixed (*state etc*); sound (*sleep*); steady (*girlfriend etc*); **~ schlafen** be fast asleep

Fest *n* (-[*e*]*s*; -*e*) celebration; party; REL festival, feast; → **froh**

'**festbinden** *v/t* (*irr,* **binden***, sep, -ge-, h*) fasten, tie (**an** *dat* to)

'**Festessen** *n* banquet, feast

'**festfahren** *v/refl* (*irr,* **fahren***, sep, -ge-, h*) get stuck

'**Festhalle** *f* (festival) hall

'**festhalten** (*irr,* **halten***, sep, -ge-, h*) **1.** *v/i:* **~ an** (*dat*) stick to **2.** *v/t* hold on to; hold *s.o.* or *s.th.* tight; **sich ~ an** (*dat*) hold on to

'**festigen** ['fɛstɪgən] *v/t* (*ge-, h*) strengthen; **sich ~** grow firm *or* strong

Festigkeit ['fɛstɪçkaɪt] *f* (-; *no pl*) firmness; strength

'**Festland** *n* mainland; *the* Continent

'**festlegen** *v/t* (*sep, -ge-, h*) fix, set; **sich ~ auf** (*acc*) commit o.s. to *s.th.*

'**festlich** *adj* festive

'**festmachen** *v/t* (*sep, -ge-, h*) fasten, fix (**an** *dat* to); MAR moor; ECON fix

Festnahme ['fɛstnaːmə] *f* (-; -*n*), '**festnehmen** *v/t* (*irr,* **nehmen***, sep, -ge-, h*) arrest

'**Festplatte** *f* IT hard disk

'**fest|schrauben** *v/t* (*sep, -ge-, h*) screw (on) tight; **~setzen** *v/t* (*sep, -ge-, h*) fix; **~sitzen** *v/i* (*irr,* **sitzen***, sep, -ge-, h*) be stuck; be (left) stranded

'**Festspiele** *pl* festival

'**feststehen** *v/i* (*irr,* **stehen***, sep, -ge-, h*) be certain; *date etc*: be fixed; **~d** *adj* established (*fact etc*); set (*phrase etc*)

'**feststellen** *v/t* (*sep, -ge-, h*) find (out); establish; see, notice; state; TECH lock, arrest; '**Feststellung** *f* (-; -*en*) finding(s); realization; statement

'**Festtag** *m* holiday; REL religious holiday; F red-letter day

Festung *f* (-; -*en*) fortress

'**Festzug** m procession

fett [fɛt] adj fat (a. fig); PRINT bold; **~ge-druckt** boldface, in bold type (or print); **Fett** n (-[e]s; -e) fat; dripping; shorten-ing; TECH grease; '**fettarm** adj low-fat, pred low in fat; '**Fettfleck** m grease spot; '**fettig** ['fɛtɪç] adj greasy

'**Fettnäpfchen** n: **ins ~ treten** put one's foot in it

Fetzen ['fɛtsən] m (-s; -) shred; rag; scrap (of paper etc)

feucht [fɔʏçt] adj moist, damp; humid

Feuchtigkeit ['fɔʏçtɪçkaɪt] f (-; no pl) moisture; dampness; humidity

feudal [fɔʏ'daːl] adj POL feudal; F posh, Br swish

Feuer ['fɔʏɐ] n (-s; -) fire (a. fig); **j-m ~ geben** give s.o. a light; **~ fangen** catch fire; fig fall for s.o.; **~a,larm** m fire alarm; **~bestattung** f cremation

'**feuerfest** adj fireproof, fire-resistant

'**Feuergefahr** f danger of fire

'**feuergefährlich** adj inflammable

'**Feuer|leiter** f fire escape; **~löscher** ['fɔʏɐlœʃɐ] m (-s; -) fire extinguisher; **~melder** ['fɔʏɐmɛldɐ] m (-s; -) fire alarm

feuern ['fɔʏɐn] v/i and v/t (ge-, h) fire (a. F s.o.)

'**feuer'rot** adj blazing red; crimson

'**Feuer|schiff** n lightship; **~stein** m flint; **~wache** f fire station; **~waffe** f firearm, gun; **~wehr** f (-; -en) fire brigade (or de-partment); fire truck (Br engine); **~wehrmann** m (-[e]s, -männer, -leute) fireman, fire fighter; **~werk** n fire-works; **~werkskörper** m firework, fire-cracker; **~zeug** n (cigarette) lighter

feurig ['fɔʏrɪç] adj fiery, ardent

Fiasko ['fjasko] n (-s; -s) fiasco, (com-plete) failure

Fibel ['fiːbəl] f (-; -n) primer, first reader

Fiber ['fiːbɐ] f fiber, Br fibre; **~glas** n fi-berglass, Br fibreglass

Fichte ['fɪçtə] f (-; -n) BOT spruce, F mst pine or fir (tree)

ficken ['fɪkən] V v/i and v/t (ge-, h) fuck

Fieber ['fiːbɐ] n (-s; no pl) MED temper-ature, fever (a. fig); **~ haben** (**messen**) have a (take s.o.'s) temperature; **~ sen-kend** MED antipyretic

'**fieberhaft** adj MED feverish (a. fig)

'**fiebern** v/i (ge-, h) MED have or run a temperature; **~ nach** fig crave for

'**Fieberthermo,meter** n fever (Br clini-cal) thermometer

fiel [fiːl] pret of **fallen**

fies [fiːs] F adj mean, nasty

Figur [fi'guːɐ] f (-; -en) figure

Filet [fi'leː] n (-s; -s) GASTR fil(l)et

Filiale [fi'ljaːlə] f (-; -n) branch

Film [fɪlm] m (-[e]s; -e) film; movie, esp Br (motion) picture; the movies, Br the cinema; **~aufnahme** f filming, shoot-ing; take, shot

filmen ['fɪlmən] (ge-, h) **1.** v/t film, shoot **2.** v/i make a film

'**Film|gesellschaft** f motion-picture (Br film) company; **~kamera** f mo-tion-picture (Br film) camera; **~kas-sette** f film magazine, cartridge; **~pro-jektor** m film (or movie) projector; **~regis,seur** m film director; **~schauspieler(in)** film (or screen, movie) actor (actress); **~studio** n film studio(s); **~the,ater** n → **Kino**; **~verleih** m film distributors; **~vorführer** m (-s; -) projectionist

Filter ['fɪltɐ] m, esp TECH n (-s; -) filter

'**Filterkaffee** m filter coffee

'**filtern** v/t (ge-, h) filter

'**Filterziga,rette** f filter(-tipped) ciga-rette, filter tip

Filz [fɪlts] m (-es; -e) felt; F POL corrup-tion, sleaze; '**filzen** F v/t (ge-, h) frisk

'**Filz|schreiber** ['fɪltsʃraɪbɐ] m (-s; -), **~stift** m felt(-tipped) pen

Finale [fi'naːlə] n (-s; -) finale; SPORT fi-nal(s)

Finanzamt ['finants'?amt] n tax office; Internal (Br Inland) Revenue; **~beam-te** m tax officer

Finanzen [fi'nantsən] pl finances

finanziell [finan'tsjɛl] adj financial

finanzieren [finan'tsiːrən] v/t (no -ge-, h) finance

Fi'nanz|mi,nister m minister of fi-nance; Secretary of the Treasury, Br Chancellor of the Exchequer; **~mi,nis-terium** n ministry of finance; Treasury Department, Br Treasury; **~wesen** n (-s; no pl) finance

Findelkind ['fɪndəlkɪnt] n JUR found-ling

finden v/t (irr, ge-, h) find; think, believe; **ich finde ihn nett** I think he's nice; **wie ~ Sie ...?** how do you like ...?; **~ Sie (nicht)?** do (don't) you think so?;

das wird sich ~ we'll see
Finder ['fɪndɐ] *m* (-s; -) finder
'Finderlohn *m* finder's reward
findig ['fɪndɪç] *adj* clever
fing [fɪŋ] *pret of* **fangen**
Finger ['fɪŋɐ] *m* (-s; -) ANAT finger; ~abdruckm fingerprint; ~fertigkeit*f* (-; no *pl*) manual skill; ~hut *m* thimble; BOT foxglove; ~nagel *m* ANAT fingernail; ~spitze *f* fingertip; ~spitzengefühl *n* (-[e]s; no *pl*) sure instinct; tact
fingiert [fɪŋ'giːɐt] *adj* faked; fictitious
Fink [fɪŋk] *m* (-en; -en) ZO finch
Finne ['fɪnə] *m* (-n; -n), Finnin ['fɪnɪn] *f* (-; -nen) Finn; 'finnisch *adj* Finnish
Finnland ['fɪnlant] Finland
finster ['fɪnstɐ] *adj* dark, gloomy; *fig* grim; shady
'Finsternis *f* (-; -se) darkness, gloom
Finte ['fɪntə] *f* (-; -n) trick; SPORT feint
Firma ['fɪrma] *f* (-; -men) firm, company
firmen ['fɪrmən] *v/t* (ge-, h) REL confirm
'Firmung *f* (-; -en) REL confirmation
First [fɪrst] *m* (-[e]s; -e) ARCH ridge
Fisch [fɪʃ] *m* (-[e]s; -e) ZO fish; *pl* ASTR Pisces; **er ist (ein) ~** he's (a) Pisces
'Fischdampfer *m* trawler
fischen ['fɪʃən] *v/t and v/i* (ge-, h) fish
Fischer ['fɪʃɐ] *m* (-s; -) fisherman; ~... *in cpds* ...boot, ...dorf *etc*: fishing ...
Fischerei [fɪʃə'raɪ] *f* (-; no *pl*) fishing
'Fisch|fang *m* (-[e]s; no *pl*) fishing; ~gräte *f* fishbone; ~grätenmuster *n* herring-bone (pattern); ~gründe *pl* fishing grounds; ~händler *m* fish dealer, *esp Br* fishmonger; ~kutter *m* smack; ~laich *m* spawn; ~stäbchen *n* GASTR fish stick (*Br* finger); ~zucht *f* fish farming; ~zug *m* catch, haul (*both a. fig*)
Fisole [fi'zoːlə] *Austrian f* (-; -n) BOT string bean
Fistel ['fɪstəl] *f* (-; -n) MED fistula
'Fistelstimme *f* falsetto
fit [fɪt] *adj* fit; **sich ~ halten** keep fit
'Fitness *f* (-; no *pl*) fitness; ~center *n* health club, fitness center, gym
fix [fɪks] *adj* ECON fixed; F quick; F smart, bright; F **~ und fertig sein** be dead beat; be a nervous wreck; **~e Idee** PSYCH obsession
fixen ['fɪksən] F *v/i* (ge-, h) shoot, fix; be a junkie; Fixer ['fɪksɐ] F *m* (-s; -) junkie, mainliner

fixieren [fɪ'ksiːrən] *v/t* (*no -ge-, h*) fix (*a.* PHOT); stare at *s.o.*
'Fixstern *m* ASTR fixed star
FKK [ɛfkaː'kaː] *abbr of* **Freikörperkultur** nudism
FK'K-Strand *m* nudist beach
flach [flax] *adj* flat; level, even, plane; *fig* shallow
Fläche ['flɛçə] *f* (-; -n) surface (*a.* MATH); area (*a.* MATH); expanse, space
'flächendeckend *adj* exhaustive
'Flächen|inhalt *m* MATH (surface) area; ~maß *n* square *or* surface measure
'Flachland *n* (-[e]s; no *pl*) lowland, plain
Flachs [flaks] *m* (-es; no *pl*) BOT flax
flackern ['flakɐn] *v/i* (ge-, h) flicker
Fladenbrot ['flaːdənbroːt] *n* round flat bread (*or* loaf)
Flagge ['flagə] *f* (-; -n) flag
'flaggen *v/i* (ge-, h) fly a flag *or* flags
Flak [flak] *f* (-; -) MIL anti-aircraft gun
Flamme ['flamə] *f* (-; -n) flame (*a. fig*)
Flanell [fla'nɛl] *m* (-s; -e) flannel
Flanke ['flaŋkə] *f* (-; -n) flank, side; *soccer:* cross; SPORT flank vault
flankieren [flaŋ'kiːrən] *v/t* (*no -ge-, h*) flank
Flasche ['flaʃə] *f* (-; -n) bottle; baby's bottle; F *contp* dead loss
'Flaschen|bier *n* bottled beer; ~hals *m* neck of a bottle; ~öffner *m* bottle opener; ~pfand *n* (bottle) deposit; ~zug *m* TECH block and tackle, pulley
flatterhaft ['flatɐhaft] *adj* fickle, flighty
flattern ['flatɐn] *v/i* (ge-, sein) flutter; TECH (h) wobble
flau [flau] *adj* queasy; *fig* flat; ECON slack
Flaum [flaum] *m* (-[e]s; no *pl*) down, fluff, fuzz
Flausch [flauʃ] *m* (-es; -e) fleece
flauschig ['flauʃɪç] *adj* fleecy, fluffy
Flausen ['flauzən] F *pl* (funny) ideas
Flaute ['flautə] *f* (-; -n) MAR calm; ECON slack period
Flechte ['flɛçtə] *f* (-; -n) plait, braid; BOT, MED lichen; 'flechten *v/t* (*irr, ge-, h*) plait, braid (*hair*); weave (*basket*)
Fleck [flɛk] *m* (-[e]s; -e) stain, mark; speck; dot; blot(ch); *fig* place, spot; patch; **blauer ~** bruise: **vom ~ weg** on the spot; **nicht vom ~ kommen** not get anywhere; 'Flecken *m* → **Fleck**

'**Fleckenentferner** *m* stain remover

'**fleckenlos** *adj* spotless (*a. fig*)

fleckig [ˈflɛkɪç] *adj* spotted; stained

Fledermaus [ˈfleːdɐmaus] *f* zo bat

Flegel [ˈfleːgəl] *m* (-s; -) lout, boor

'**flegelhaft** *adj* loutish

'**Flegeljahre** *pl* awkward age

'**flegeln** F *contp v/refl* (ge-, h) lounge

flehen [ˈfleːən] *v/i* (ge-, h) beg; pray (**um** for); **flehentlich** [ˈfleːəntlɪç] *adj* imploring, entreating

Fleisch [flaiʃ] *n* (-[e]s; *no pl*) flesh (*a. fig*); GASTR meat; **~ fressend → fleischfressend**; **~brühe** *f* (meat) broth, consommé

Fleischer [ˈflaiʃɐ] *m* (-s; -) butcher

Fleischerei [flaiʃəˈrai] *f* (-; -en) butcher's (shop)

'**fleischfressend** *adj* BOT, ZO carnivorous

Fleischhauer [ˈflaiʃhaʊɐ] *Austrian m* (-s; -) butcher

fleischig [ˈflaiʃɪç] *adj* fleshy

'**Fleisch|klößchen** *n* (-s; -) meatball; **~kon,serven** *pl* canned (*Br* tinned) meat

'**fleischlos** *adj* meatless

'**Fleischwolf** *m* meat grinder, *Br* mincer

Fleiß [flais] *m* (-es; *no pl*) diligence, hard work; **fleißig** [ˈflaisɪç] *adj* diligent, hard-working; **~ sein** work hard

fletschen [ˈflɛtʃən] *v/t* (ge-, h) bare

flexibel [flɛˈksiːbəl] *adj* flexible

Flexibilität [flɛksibiliˈtɛːt] *f* (-; *no pl*) flexibility

flicken [ˈflɪkən] *v/t* (ge-, h) mend, repair, *a. fig* patch (up); '**Flicken** *m* (-s; -) patch; '**Flickwerk** *n* patchwork (*a. fig*); '**Flickzeug** *n* TECH repair kit

Flieder [ˈfliːdɐ] *m* (-s; -) BOT lilac

Fliege [ˈfliːgə] *f* (-; -n) ZO fly; bow tie

'**fliegen** *v/i* (*irr*, ge-, *sein*) *and v/t* (h) fly (*a.* **~ lassen**); F fall; F be fired, F get the sack; be kicked out *of school*; F **~ auf** (*acc*) really go for; F **in die Luft ~** blow up

'**Fliegen** *n* (-s; *no pl*) flying; aviation

'**Fliegen|fänger** *m* flypaper; **~fenster** *n* flyscreen; **~gewicht** *n* SPORT flyweight; **~gitter** *n* wire mesh (screen); **~klatsche** *f* flyswatter; **~pilz** *m* BOT fly agaric

Flieger [ˈfliːgɐ] *m* (-s; -) MIL airman; F plane; *cycling*: sprinter; **~a,larm** *m* air-raid warning

fliehen [ˈfliːən] *v/i* (*irr*, ge-, *sein*) flee, run away (*both*: **vor** *dat* from)

'**Fliehkraft** *f* PHYS centrifugal force

Fliese [ˈfliːzə] *f* (-; -n), '**fliesen** *v/t* (ge-, h) tile; '**Fliesenleger** *m* (-s; -) tiler

Fließband [ˈfliːsbant] *n* (-[e]s; *-bänder*) TECH assembly line; conveyor belt

fließen [ˈfliːsən] *v/i* (*irr*, ge-, *sein*) flow (*a. fig*); run; **~d1.** *adj* flowing; running; LING fluent **2.** *adv*: **er spricht ~ Englisch** he speaks English fluently *or* fluent English

'**Fließheck** *n* MOT fastback

flimmern [ˈflɪmɐn] *v/i* (ge-, h) shimmer; *film*: flicker

flink [flɪŋk] *adj* quick, nimble

Flinte [ˈflɪntə] *f* (-; -n) shotgun; F gun

Flipper [ˈflɪpɐ] F *m* (-s; -) pinball machine; '**flippern** *v/i* (ge-, h) play pinball

Flirt [flœrt] *m* (-s; -s) flirtation

flirten [ˈflœrtən] *v/i* (ge-, h) flirt

'**Flittchen** [ˈflɪtçən] F *n* (-s; -) floozie

Flitter [ˈflɪtɐ] *m* (-s; -) tinsel (*a. fig*), spangles; **~wochen** *pl* honeymoon

flitzen [ˈflɪtsən] F *v/i* (ge-, *sein*) flit, whizz, shoot

flocht [flɔxt] *pret of* **flechten**

Flocke [ˈflɔkə] *f* (-; -n) flake

flockig [ˈflɔkɪç] *adj* fluffy, flaky

flog [floːk] *pret of* **fliegen**

floh [floː] *pret of* **fliehen**

Floh *m* (-[e]s; *Flöhe* [ˈfløːə]) zo flea

'**Flohmarkt** *m* flea market

Florett [floˈrɛt] *n* (-[e]s; -e) foil

florieren [floˈriːrən] *v/i* (*no* ge-, h) flourish, prosper

Floskel [ˈflɔskəl] *f* (-; -n) empty *or* cliché(d) phrase

floss [flɔs] *pret of* **fließen**

Floß [floːs] *n* (-es; *Flöße* [ˈfløːsə]) raft, float

Flosse [ˈflɔsə] *f* (-; -n) zo fin, *a.* SPORT flipper

Flöte [ˈfløːtə] *f* (-; -n) MUS flute; recorder

flott [flɔt] *adj* brisk (*pace*); F smart, chic; MAR afloat

Flotte [ˈflɔtə] *f* (-; -n) MAR fleet; navy

'**Flottenstützpunkt** *m* MIL naval base

Fluch [fluːx] *m* (-[e]s; *Flüche* [ˈflyːçə]) curse; swear word; **fluchen** [ˈfluːxən] *v/i* (ge-, h) swear, curse

Flucht [fluːxt] *f* (-; -en) flight (**vor** *dat* from); escape, getaway (**aus** *dat* from)

'**fluchtartig** *adv* hastily

'Fluchtauto n getaway car

flüchten ['flʏçtən] v/i (ge-, sein) flee (**nach, zu** to), run away; escape, get away; **flüchtig** ['flʏçtɪç] adj quick; superficial; careless; fugitive, *criminal etc*: on the run, at large; **~er Blick** glance; **~er Eindruck** glimpse

'Flüchtigkeitsfehler m slip

Flüchtling ['flʏçtlɪŋ] m fugitive; POL refugee

'Flüchtlingslager n refugee camp

Flug [fluːk] m (-[e]s; Flüge ['flyːgə]) flight; **im ~(e)** rapidly, quickly; **~abwehra,kanone** f MIL anti-aircraft missile; **~bahn** f trajectory; **~ball** m tennis: volley; **~begleiter(in)** flight attendant; **~blatt** n handbill, leaflet; **~dienst** m air service

Flügel ['flyːgəl] m (-s; -) ZO wing (a. SPORT); TECH blade; windmill: sail; MUS grand piano; **~mutter** f TECH wing nut; **~schraube** f TECH thumb screw; **~stürmer** m SPORT wing forward; **~tür** f folding door

'Fluggast m (air) passenger

flügge ['flʏgə] adj full-fledged

'Flug|gesellschaft f airline; **~hafen** m airport; **~linie** f air route; → **Fluggesellschaft**; **~lotse** m air traffic controller; **~nummer** f flight number; **~plan** m flight schedule; **~platz** m airfield, airport; **~schein** m (flight) ticket; **~schreiber** m (-s; -) flight recorder, black box; **~sicherung** f air traffic control; **~ticket** n (flight) ticket; **~verbindung** f flight connection; **~verkehr** m air traffic; **~zeit** f flying time

'Flugzeug n (-[e]s; -e) (air)plane, aircraft, Br a. aeroplane; **mit dem ~** by air or plane; **~absturz** m air or plane crash; **~entführung** f hijacking, skyjacking; **~halle** f hangar; **~träger** m MAR MIL aircraft carrier

Flunder ['flʊndɐ] f (-; -n) ZO flounder

flunkern ['flʊŋkɐn] v/i (ge-, h) fib; brag

Fluor ['fluːoːɐ] n (-s; no pl) CHEM fluorine; fluoride

'Fluorchlorkohlenwasserstoff m CHEM chlorofluorocarbon, CFC

Flur [fluːɐ] m (-[e]s; -e) hall; corridor

Fluss [flʊs] m (-es; Flüsse ['flʏsə]) river; stream; **im ~** fig in (a state of) flux

fluss'abwärts adv downstream

fluss'aufwärts adv upstream

'Flussbett n river bed

flüssig ['flʏsɪç] adj liquid; melted; fig fluent; ECON available; **'Flüssigkeit** f (-; -en) liquid; (no pl) liquidity; fig fluency; **'Flüssigkris,tallanzeige** f liquid crystal display, LCD; **'Flüssigseife** f liquid soap

'Fluss|lauf m course of a river; **~pferd** n zo hippopotamus, F hippo; **~ufer** n riverbank, riverside

flüstern ['flʏstɐn] v/i and v/t (ge-, h) whisper

Flut [fluːt] f (-; -en) flood (a. fig); high tide; **es ist ~** the tide is in; **~licht** n floodlights; **~welle** f tidal wave

focht [fɔxt] pret of **fechten**

Fohlen ['foːlən] n (-s; -) ZO foal; colt; filly

Föhn[1] [føːn] m (-[e]s; -e) hairdrier

Föhn[2] m (-[e]s; -e) METEOR foehn, föhn

föhnen ['føːnən] v/t (ge-, h) blow-dry

Folge ['fɔlgə] f (-; -n) result, consequence; effect; succession; order; series; TV etc: sequel, episode; aftermath; MED aftereffect

folgen ['fɔlgən] v/i (ge-, sein) follow; obey; **hieraus folgt, dass** from this it follows that; **wie folgt** as follows; **~d** adj following, subsequent

folgendermaßen ['fɔlgəndɐ'maːsən] adv as follows

'folgenschwer adj momentous

'folgerichtig adj logical; consistent

folgern ['fɔlgɐn] v/t (ge-, h) conclude (**aus** from); **Folgerung** ['fɔlgəruŋ] f (-; -en) conclusion

folglich ['fɔlklɪç] cj consequently, thus, therefore

folgsam ['fɔlkzaːm] adj obedient

Folie ['foːljə] f (-; -n) foil; transparency

Folter ['fɔltɐ] f (-; -n) torture; **auf die ~ spannen** tantalize; **foltern** v/t (ge-, h) torture, fig a. torment

Fön® m → **Föhn**[1]

Fonds [fɔ̃ː] m (-; -) ECON fund

fönen v/t → **föhnen**

Fontäne [fɔn'tɛːnə] f (-; -n) jet, spout; gush

Förder|band ['fœrdɐbant] n TECH conveyor belt; **~korb** m mining: cage

fordern ['fɔrdɐn] v/t (ge-, h) demand, esp JUR a. claim; ECON ask, charge

fördern ['fœrdɐn] v/t (ge-, h) promote; support (a. UNIV), sponsor; PED tutor, provide remedial classes for; TECH mine

Forderung ['fɔrdərʊŋ] f (-; -en) demand; claim (a. JUR); ECON charge

Förderung ['fœrdərʊŋ] f (-; -en) promotion, advancement; support, sponsorship; UNIV etc: grant; PED tutoring, remedial classes; TECH mining

Forelle [fo'rɛlə] f (-; -n) ZO trout

Form [fɔrm] f (-; -en) form, shape, SPORT a. condition; TECH mo(u)ld; **gut in ~** in great form; **formal** [fɔr'maːl] adj formal; **Formalität** [fɔrmaliˈtɛːt] f (-; -en) formality

Format [fɔr'maːt] n (-[e]s; -e) size; format; fig caliber, Br calibre

formatieren [fɔrmaˈtiːrən] v/t (no -ge-, h) IT format; **Forma'tierung** f (-; -en) IT formatting

Formel ['fɔrməl] f (-; -n) formula

formell [fɔr'mɛl] adj formal

formen ['fɔrmən] v/t (ge-, h) shape, form; fig mo(u)ld

Formfehler m irregularity

formieren [fɔr'miːrən] v/t and v/refl (no -ge-, h) form (up)

förmlich ['fœrmlɪç] **1.** adj formal; fig regular **2.** adv formally; fig literally

formlos adj shapeless; fig informal

formschön adj well-designed

Formular [fɔrmuˈlaːr] n (-s; -e) form, blank

formulieren [fɔrmuˈliːrən] v/t (no -ge-, h) word, phrase; formulate; express

Formu'lierung f (-; -en) wording, phrasing; formulation; expression, phrase

forsch [fɔrʃ] adj dashing

forschen ['fɔrʃən] v/i (ge-, h) research, do research; **~ nach** search for

Forscher ['fɔrʃɐ] m (-s; -), **'Forscherin** f (-; -nen) explorer; (research) scientist; **Forschung** ['fɔrʃʊŋ] f (-; -en) research (work)

Forst [fɔrst] m (-[e]s; -e[n]) forest

Förster ['fœrstɐ] m (-s; -) forester; forest ranger

'Forstwirtschaft f (-; no pl) forestry

fort [fɔrt] adv off, away; gone; missing

Fort [foːɐ] n (-s; -s) MIL fort

'fortbestehen v/i (irr, **stehen**, sep, no -ge-, h) continue

'fortbewegen v/refl (sep, no -ge-, h) move; **'Fortbewegung** f moving; (loco)motion

'Fortbildung f (-, no pl) further education or training

'fort|**fahren** v/i (irr, **fahren**, sep, -ge-) (sein) leave, go away, MOT a. drive off; (h) continue, go or keep on (**et. zu tun** doing s.th.); **~führen** v/t (sep, -ge-, h) continue, carry on; **~gehen** v/i (irr, **gehen**, sep, -ge-, sein) go away, leave

'fortgeschritten adj advanced

'fortlaufend adj consecutive, successive

'fort|**pflanzen** v/refl (sep, -ge-, h) BIOL reproduce; fig spread; **'Fortpflanzung** f BIOL reproduction

'fortschreiten v/i (irr, **schreiten**, sep, -ge-, sein) advance, proceed, progress; **~d** adj progressive

'Fortschritt m progress

'fortschrittlich adj progressive

'fortsetzen v/t (sep, -ge-, h) continue, go on with; **'Fortsetzung** f (-; -en) continuation; film etc: sequel; **~ folgt** to be continued; **'Fortsetzungsro**,**man** m serialized novel

'fortwährend adj continual, constant

fossil [fɔ'siːl] adj, **Fos'sil** n (-s; -ien) GEOL fossil (a. fig F)

Foto ['foːto] n (-s; -s) photo(graph); **ein ~ machen (von)** take a photo (of)

'Fotoalbum n photo album

'Fotoappa,**rat** m camera

Fotograf [foto'graːf] m (-en; -en) photographer; **Fotografie** [fotograˈfiː] f (-; -n) (no pl) photography; photograph, picture; **fotografieren** [fotograˈfiːrən] v/t and v/i (no -ge-, h) take a photo(graph) or picture (of); **sich ~ lassen** have one's picture taken; **Foto**'**grafin** f (-; -nen) photographer

'Fotohandy n camera phone

Fotoko'pie f photocopy; **fotoko'pieren** v/t (no -ge-, h) (photo)copy

'Fotomo,**dell** n model

'Fotozelle f photoelectric cell

Fotze ['fɔtsə] V f (-; -n) cunt

Foul [faul] n (-s; -s) SPORT foul; **foulen** ['faulən] v/t and v/i (ge-, h) SPORT foul

Foyer [foaˈjeː] n (-s; -s) foyer, lobby, lounge

Fr. abbr of **Frau** Mrs, Ms

Fracht [fraxt] f (-; -en) freight, load, MAR, AVIAT a. cargo; ECON freight, Br carriage; **~brief** m RAIL bill of lading (a. MAR), Br consignment note

Frachter ['fraxtɐ] m (-s; -) MAR freighter

Frack [frak] m (-[e]s; *Fräcke* ['frɛkə]) tails, tailcoat

Frage ['fraːɡə] f (-; -n) question; *e-e ~ stellen* ask a question; → *infrage*

'**Fragebogen** n question(n)aire

'**fragen** v/t and v/i (ge-, h) ask (*nach* for; *wegen* about); *nach dem Weg (der Zeit) ~* ask the way (time); *sich ~* wonder

'**Frage|wort** n LING interrogative; *~zeichen* n LING question mark

fraglich ['fraːklɪç] adj doubtful, uncertain; ... in question

fraglos ['fraːkloːs] adv undoubtedly, unquestionably

Fragment [fraˈɡmɛnt] n (-[e]s; -e) fragment

fragwürdig ['fraːkvʏrdɪç] adj dubious, F shady

Fraktion [frakˈtsjoːn] f (-; -en) (parliamentary) group *or* party

'**Frakti'onsführer** m PARL floor leader, Br chief whip

Franc [fraˑ] m (-; -s), **Franken** ['fraŋkən] m (-; -) franc

frankieren [fraŋˈkiːrən] v/t (no -ge-, h) stamp; frank

Frankreich ['fraŋkraiç] France

Franse ['franzə] f (-; -n) fringe

fransig ['franzɪç] adj frayed

Franzose [franˈtsoːzə] m (-n; -n) Frenchman; *die ~n pl* the French

Französin [franˈtsøːzɪn] f (-; -nen) Frenchwoman

französisch [franˈtsøːzɪʃ] adj French

fraß [fraːs] pret of *fressen*

Fraß F contp m (-es; no pl) muck

Fratze ['fratsə] f (-; -n) grimace

Frau [frau] f (-; -en) woman; wife; *~ X* Mrs (*or* Ms) X

Frauchen ['frauçən] n mistress (*of dog*)

'**Frauen|arzt** m, *~ärztin* f gyn(a)ecologist; *~bewegung* f: *die ~* POL women's lib(eration)

'**frauenfeindlich** adj sexist

'**Frauen|haus** n women's shelter (Br refuge); *~klinik* f gyn(a)ecological hospital; *~rechtlerin* ['frauənrɛçtlərɪn] f (-; -nen) feminist

Fräulein ['frɔɪlain] n (-s; -) Miss

'**fraulich** adj womanly, feminine

frech [frɛç] adj sassy, Br cheeky

'**Frechheit** f (-; no pl) F Br cheek

Freeclimbing ['friːklaimiŋ] n (-s; no pl) free climbing

frei [frai] adj free (*von* from, of); independent; freelance; vacant; candid, frank; SPORT unmarked; *ein ~er Tag* a day off; *morgen haben wir ~* there is no school tomorrow; *im Freien* outdoors; → *Fuß*; *sich ~ machen* undress; *sich ~ machen von* free o.s. from; → a. **freibekommen**, **freigeben**, **freihaben**; *~ halten* keep clear (*exit*), → **freihalten**

'**Freibad** n open-air swimming-pool

'**freibekommen** v/t (irr, *kommen*, sep, no -ge-, h) get a day etc off

'**freiberuflich** adj freelance, self-employed

'**Freiexem,plar** n free copy

'**Freigabe** f (-; no pl) release

'**freigeben** (irr, *geben*, sep, -ge-, h) **1.** v/t release; *e-n Tag etc ~* give a day etc off **2.** v/i: *j-m ~* give s.o. time off

freigebig ['fraigeːbɪç] adj generous

'**Freigepäck** n AVIAT baggage allowance

'**freihaben** F v/i (irr, *haben*, sep, -ge-, h) have a day off (Br a. a holiday)

'**Freihafen** m free port

'**freihalten** v/t (irr, *halten*, sep, -ge-, h) keep, save (*seat etc*); treat (*s.o.*)

'**Frei|handel** m free trade; *~handelszone* f free trade area

freihändig ['fraihɛndɪç] adv with no hands

'**Freiheit** f (-; -en) freedom, liberty; *sich ~en herausnehmen gegen* take liberties with

'**Freiheitsstrafe** f JUR prison sentence

'**Freikarte** f free ticket

'**freikaufen** v/t (sep, -ge-, h) ransom

'**Freikörperkul,tur** f (-; no pl) nudism

'**freilassen** v/t (irr, *lassen*, sep, -ge-, h) release, set free; '**Freilassung** f (-; -en) release

'**Freilauf** m freewheel (a. *im ~ fahren*)

'**freilich** adv indeed, of course

'**Freilicht-** ... in cpds open-air ...

'**freimachen** v/t (sep, -ge-, h) post: stamp; *sich ~* undress; *sich ~ von* free o.s. from; → *frei*; → *Oberkörper*

'**Freimaurer** m freemason

freimütig ['fraimyːtɪç] adj candid, frank

'**freischaffend** adj freelance

'**freischwimmen** v/refl (irr, *schwimmen*, sep, -ge-, h) pass a 15-minute swimming test

'**Freisprechanlage** f hands-free kit

'**freisprechen** v/t (irr, **sprechen**, sep, -ge-, h) esp REL absolve (**von** from); JUR acquit (of); '**Freispruch** m JUR acquittal

'**Freistaat** m POL free state

'**frei|stehen** v/i (irr, **stehen**, sep, -ge-, h) be unoccupied; SPORT be unmarked; **es steht dir frei zu** inf you are free to inf; ~**stellen** v/t (sep, -ge-, h) **j-n** ~ exempt s.o. (**von** from) (a. MIL.); **j-m et.** ~ leave s.th. (up) to s.o.

'**Frei|stil** m freestyle; ~**stoß** m soccer: free kick; ~**stunde** f PED free period; ~**tag** m Friday; ~**tod** m suicide; ~**treppe** f outdoor stairs; ~**wild** fig n fair game

'**freiwillig** adj voluntary; **sich** ~ **melden** volunteer (**zu** for); **Freiwillige** ['frai-viligə] m, f (-n; -n) volunteer

'**Freizeit** f free or leisure time; ~**gestaltung** f leisure-time activities; ~**kleidung** f leisurewear; ~**park** m amusement park; ~**zentrum** n leisure center (Br centre)

'**freizügig** adj permissive; film etc: explicit

fremd [frɛmt] adj strange; foreign; unknown; **ich bin auch** ~ **hier** I'm a stranger here myself; '**fremdartig** adj strange, exotic; **Fremde** ['frɛmdə] m, f (-n; -n) stranger, foreigner

'**Fremden|führer** m, **~führerin** f (-; -nen) (tourist) guide; ~**hass** m xenophobia; ~**legion** f Foreign Legion; ~**verkehr** m tourism; ~**verkehrsbü,ro** n tourist office; ~**zimmer** n guest room; ~ (**zu vermieten**) rooms to let

'**fremdgehen** F v/i (irr, **gehen**, sep, -ge-, sein) be unfaithful (to one's wife or husband), play around

'**Fremd|körper** m MED foreign body; fig alien element; ~**sprache** f foreign language; ~**sprachensekre,tärin** f bilingual secretary

'**fremd|sprachig**, ~**sprachlich** adj foreign-language

'**Fremdwort** n (-[e]s; -wörter) foreign word

Frequenz [fre'kvɛnts] f (-; -en) PHYS frequency

Fresse ['frɛsə] V f (-; -n) big (fat) mouth

'**fressen** v/t (irr, ge-, h) ZO eat, feed on; F gobble (up); fig devour

Freude ['frɔydə] f (-; -n) joy, delight; pleasure; ~ **haben an** (dat) take pleasure in

'**Freuden|geschrei** n shouts of joy, cheers; ~**haus** F n brothel; ~**tränen** pl tears of joy

'**freudestrahlend** adj radiant (with joy)

'**freudig** ['frɔydɪç] adj joyful, cheerful; happy (event etc)

'**freudlos** ['frɔytloːs] adj joyless, cheerless

freuen ['frɔyən] v/t (ge-, h) **es freut mich, dass** I'm glad or pleased (that); **sich** ~ **über** (acc) be pleased or glad about; **sich** ~ **auf** (acc) look forward to

Freund [frɔynt] m (-[e]s; -e ['frɔyndə]) friend; boyfriend; **Freundin** ['frɔyndɪn] f (-; -nen) friend; girlfriend

'**freundlich** adj friendly, kind, nice; fig cheerful (room etc); '**Freundlichkeit** f (-; no pl) friendliness, kindness

'**Freundschaft** f (-; -en) friendship; ~ **schließen** make friends

'**freundschaftlich** adj friendly

'**Freundschaftsspiel** n SPORT friendly (game)

Frevel ['freːfəl] m (-s; -) outrage (**an** dat, **gegen** on)

Frieden ['friːdən] m (-s; no pl) peace; **im** ~ in peacetime; **lass mich in** ~**!** leave me alone!

'**Friedens|bewegung** f peace movement; ~**forschung** f peace studies; ~**verhandlungen** pl peace negotiations or talks; ~**vertrag** m peace treaty

'**friedfertig** ['friːtfɛrtɪç] adj peaceable

'**Friedhof** m cemetery, graveyard

'**friedlich** adj peaceful

'**friedliebend** adj peace-loving

frieren ['friːrən] v/i (irr, ge-, h) freeze; **ich friere** I am or feel cold; I'm freezing

Fries [friːs] m (-es; -e) ARCH frieze

Frikadelle [frika'dɛlə] f (-; -n) meatball

frisch [frɪʃ] adj fresh; clean (shirt etc); ~ **gestrichen!** wet (or fresh) paint!

Frische ['frɪʃə] f (-; no pl) freshness

'**Frischhalte|beutel** m polythene bag; ~**folie** f plastic wrap, Br. cling film

Friseur [fri'zøːr] m (-s; -e) hairdresser; barber; ~**sa,lon** m hairdresser's (shop), barber's shop

Friseuse [fri'zøːzə] f (-; -n) hairdresser

frisieren [fri'ziːrən] v/t (no -ge-, h) do s.o.'s hair; F MOT soup up

Frisör etc → **Friseur** etc

Frist [frɪst] f (-; -en) (fixed) period of time; deadline; extension (a. ECON)

fristen ['frɪstən] v/t (ge-, h) **sein Dasein** ~ scrape a living

'fristlos adj without notice

Frisur [fri'zu:ɐ] f (-; -en) hairstyle, hairdo

Fritten ['frɪtən] F pl fries, Br chips; frittieren [fri'ti:rən] v/t (no -ge-, h) deep fry

frivol [fri'vo:l] adj frivolous; suggestive

froh [fro:] adj glad (**über** acc about); cheerful; happy; ~**es Fest!** happy holiday!; Merry Christmas!

fröhlich ['frø:lıç] adj cheerful, happy; merry; 'Fröhlichkeit f (-; no pl) cheerfulness, merriment

fromm [frɔm] adj pious, devout; meek; steady (horse); ~**er Wunsch** pious hope

Frömmigkeit ['frœmıçkait] f (-; no pl) religiousness, piety

Fronleichnam [fro:n'laiçna:m] m (-[e]s; no pl) REL Corpus Christi

Front [frɔnt] f (-; -en) front (a. fig), ARCH a. face, MIL a. line; **in ~ liegen** SPORT be ahead

frontal [frɔn'ta:l] adj MOT head-on

Fron'talzusammenstoß m MOT head--on collision

'Frontantrieb m MOT front-wheel drive

fror [fro:ɐ] pret of **frieren**

Frosch [frɔʃ] m (-[e]s; Frösche ['frœʃə]) zo frog; ~**mann** m frogman; ~**perspektive** f worm's-eye view

Frost [frɔst] m (-[e]s; Fröste ['frœstə]) frost; ~**beule** f chilblain

frösteln ['frœstəln] v/i (ge-, h) feel chilly, shiver (a. fig)

'frostig adj frosty, fig a. chilly

'Frostschutzmittel n MOT antifreeze

Frottee [frɔ'te:] n, m (-[s]; -s) terry (-cloth); frottieren [frɔ'ti:rən] v/t (no -ge-, h) rub down

Frucht [frʊxt] f (-; Früchte ['frʏçtə]) BOT fruit (a. fig); 'fruchtbar adj BIOL fertile, esp fig a. fruitful; 'Fruchtbarkeit f (-; no pl) fertility; fig fruitfulness

'fruchtlos adj fruitless, futile

'Fruchtsaft m fruit juice

früh [fry:] adj and adv early; **zu ~ kommen** be early; ~ **genug** soon enough; **heute** (**morgen**) ~ this (tomorrow)

morning; 'Frühaufsteher m (-s; -) early riser (F bird); Frühe ['fry:ə] f: **in aller** ~ (very) early in the morning

früher ['fry:ɐ] **1.** adj former; previous **2.** adv in former times, at one time; ~ **oder später** sooner or later; **ich habe ~** (**einmal**) ... I used to ...

'frühestens adv at the earliest

'Früh|geburt f MED premature birth; premature baby; ~**jahr** n spring; ~**jahrsputz** m spring cleaning

früh'morgens adv early in the morning

'frühreif adj precocious

'Frühstück n breakfast (**zum** for)

'frühstücken v/i (ge-, h) (have) breakfast

Frust [frʊst] m F (-[e]s; no pl) frustration

Frustration [frʊstra'tsjo:n] f (-; -en) frustration; frustrieren [frʊs'tri:rən] v/t (no -ge-, h) frustrate

frz. abbr of **französisch** Fr., French

Fuchs [fʊks] m (-es; Füchse ['fʏksə]) zo fox (a. fig); sorrel; ~**jagd** f foxhunt(ing); ~**schwanz** m TECH handsaw

'fuchs'teufels'wild F adj hopping mad

fuchteln ['fʊxtəln] v/i (ge-, h) ~ **mit** wave s.th. around

Fuge ['fu:gə] f (-; -n) TECH joint; MUS fugue

fügen ['fy:gən] v/t/refl (ge-, h) submit (**in** acc, dat to s.th.)

fühlbar ['fy:lba:ɐ] fig adj noticeable; considerable; fühlen ['fy:lən] v/t and v/i and v/refl (ge-, h) feel, fig a. sense; **sich wohl ~** → **wohlfühlen**

Fühler ['fy:lɐ] m (-s; -) zo feeler (a. fig)

fuhr [fu:ɐ] pret of **fahren**

führen ['fy:rən] (ge-, h) **1.** v/t lead; guide; take; run, manage; ECON sell, deal in; keep (account, books etc); have (a talk etc); bear (name etc); MIL command; **j-n ~ durch** show s.o. round; **sich ~** conduct o.s. **2.** v/i lead (**zu** to, a. fig), SPORT a. be leading, be ahead; ~**d** adj leading

Führer ['fy:rɐ] m (-s; -) leader (a. pol.); guide; head, chief; guide(book)

'Führerschein m MOT driver's license, Br driving licence

'Führung f (-; -en) (no pl) leadership, control; ECON management; (guided) tour; **gute ~** good conduct; **in ~ gehen** (**sein**) SPORT take (be in) the lead;

'Führungszeugnis *n* certificate of (good) conduct

Fuhrunternehmen ['fuːɐˈʔʊntɐneːmən] *n* trucking company, *Br* haulage contractors

'Fuhrwerk *n* horse-drawn vehicle

Fülle ['fʏlə] *f* (-; *no pl*) crush; *fig* wealth, abundance; GASTR body

'füllen *v/t and v/refl* (*ge-*, *h*) fill (*a.* MED), stuff (*a.* GASTR)

Füller ['fʏlɐ] *m* (*-s*; -), 'Füllfederhalter *m* fountain pen

füllig ['fʏlɪç] *adj* stout, portly

'Füllung *f* (-; *-en*) filling (*a.* MED), stuffing (*a.* GASTR)

fummeln ['fʊməln] F *v/i* (*ge-*, *h*) fiddle, tinker (*both*: **an** *dat* with); F grope

Fund [fʊnt] *m* (-[*e*]*s*; *-e* ['fʊndə]) discovery; find

Fundament [fʊndaˈmɛnt] *n* (-[*e*]*s*; *-e*) ARCH foundation(s), *fig* basis

Fundamentalist [fʊndamɛntaˈlɪst] *m* (*-en*; *-en*) fundamentalist

'Fundbü,ro *n* lost and found (office), *Br* lost-property office

'Fundgrube *fig f* treasure trove

Fundi ['fʊndi] F *m* (*-s*; *-s*) POL radical Green

fundiert [fʊnˈdiːɐt] *adj* well-founded (*argument etc*); sound (*knowledge*)

fünf [fʏnf] *adj* five; *grade*: F, N, *Br* fail, poor, E; 'Fünfeck *n* (-[*e*]*s*; *-e*) pentagon; 'fünffach *adj* fivefold

'Fünfkampf *m* SPORT pentathlon

'Fünflinge *pl* quintuplets

'fünfte *adj* fifth; 'Fünftel *n* (*-s*; -) fifth

'fünftens *adv* fifth(ly), in the fifth place

'fünfzehn(te) *adj* fifteen(th)

fünfzig ['fʏnftsɪç] *adj* fifty

'fünfzigste *adj* fiftieth

fungieren [fʊŋˈɡiːrən] *v/i* (*no -ge-*, *h*) ~ **als** act as, function as

Funk [fʊŋk] *m* (*-s*; *no pl*) radio; *über or durch* ~ by radio

'Funkama,teur *m* radio ham

Funke ['fʊŋkə] *m* (*-n*; *-n*) spark; *fig a.* glimmer; funkeln ['fʊŋkəln] *v/i* (*ge-*, *h*) sparkle, glitter; 'twinkle

'funken *v/t* (*ge-*, *h*) radio, transmit

Funker ['fʊŋkɐ] *m* (*-s*; -) radio operator

'Funk|gerät *n* radio set; ~haus *n* broadcasting center (*Br* centre); ~sig,nal *n* radio signal; ~spruch *m* radio message; ~stati,on *f* radio station; ~streife

f (radio) patrol car; ~tele,fon *n* cellular phone

Funktion [fʊŋkˈtsjoːn] *f* (-; *-en*) function; Funktionär [fʊŋktsjoˈnɛːɐ] *m* (*-s*; *-e*) functionary, official (*a.* SPORT); funktionieren [fʊŋktsjoˈniːrən] *v/i* (*no -ge-*, *h*) work

'Funkturm *m* radio tower

'Funkverkehr *m* radio communication

für [fyːɐ] *prp* (*acc*) for; in favo(u)r of; on behalf of; ~ *immer* forever; *Tag* ~ *Tag* day by day; *Wort* ~ *Wort* word by word; *jeder* ~ *sich* everyone by himself; *was* ~ *...?* what (kind *or* sort of) ...?; *das Für und Wider* the pros and cons

Furche ['fʊrçə] *f* (-; *-n*) furrow; rut

Furcht [fʊrçt] *f* (-; *no pl*) fear, dread (*both*: *vor* *dat* of); *aus* ~ for fear (that); ~ *erregend* → *furchterregend*

'furchtbar *adj* terrible, awful

fürchten ['fʏrçtən] *v/t and v/i* (*ge-*, *h*) fear, be afraid of; dread; ~ *um* fear for; *sich* ~ be scared; be afraid (*vor dat* of); *ich fürchte, ...* I'm afraid ...

fürchterlich ['fʏrçtɐlɪç] → *furchtbar*

'furcht|erregend *adj* frightening; ~los *adj* fearless; ~sam *adj* timid

füreiˈnander *adv* for each other

Furnier [fʊrˈniːɐ] *n* (-[*e*]*s*; *-e*), furnieren [fʊrˈniːrən] *v/t* (*no -ge-*, *h*) veneer

'Fürsorge *f* (-; *no pl*) care; *öffentliche* ~ (public) welfare (work); ~empfänger *m* social security beneficiary

fürsorglich ['fyːɐzɔrklɪç] *adj* considerate

'Für|sprache *f* intercession (*für* for; *bei* with); ~sprech *m* (-[*e*]*s*; *-e*) *Swiss*: lawyer; ~sprecher(in) *f* advocate (*a. fig*)

Fürst [fʏrst] *m* (*-en*; *-en*) prince

'Fürstentum *n* (*-s*; *-tümer* ['fʏrstəntyːmɐ]) principality

'Fürstin *f* (-; *-nen*) princess

'fürstlich *adj* princely (*a. fig*)

Furt [fʊrt] *f* (-; *-en*) ford

Furunkel [fuˈrʊŋkəl] *m* (*-s*; -) MED boil, furuncle

'Fürwort *n* (-[*e*]*s*; *-wörter*) LING pronoun

Furz [fʊrts] *m* (*-es*; *-e*), 'furzen *v/i* (*ge-*, *h*) fart

Fusion [fuˈzjoːn] *f* (-; *-en*) ECON merger, amalgamation

fusionieren [fuzjoˈniːrən] *v/i* (*no -ge-*, *h*) ECON merge, amalgamate

Fuß [fuːs] *m* (*-es*; *Füße*) ANAT

foot; stand; stem; **zu~** on foot; **zu~ gehen** walk; **gut zu~ sein** be a good walker; **~ fassen** become established; **auf freiem ~** at large

'**Fußball** m (no pl) soccer, Br football; soccer ball, Br football

Fußballer ['fuːsbalɐ] m (-s; -) footballer

'**Fußball|feld** n football field; **~rowdy** m (football) hooligan; **~spiel** n soccer or football match; **~spieler(in)** football player, footballer; **~toto** n football pools

'**Fußboden** m floor; flooring; **~heizung** f underfloor heating

'**Fußbremse** f MOT footbrake

Fussel ['fusəl] f (-; -n), m (-s; -[n]) piece of lint (Br fluff); pl lint, Br fluff; '**fusselig** ['fusəliç] adj linty, Br covered in fluff; '**fusseln** v/i (ge-, h) shed a lot of lint (Br fluff), F mo(u)lt

Fußgänger ['fuːsgɛŋɐ] m (-s; -), '**Fußgängerin** f (-; -nen) pedestrian; '**Fußgängerzone** f (pedestrian or shopping) mall, Br pedestrian precinct

'**Fußgeher** Austrian m → **Fußgänger**

'**Fuß|gelenk** n ANAT ankle; **~matte** f doormat; **~note** f footnote; **~pflege** f pedicure; MED podiatry, Br. chiropody; **~pfleger(in)** podiatrist, Br chiropodist; **~pilz** m MED athlete's foot; **~sohle** f ANAT sole (of the foot); **~spur** f footprint; track; **~stapfen** pl: **in j-s ~ treten** follow in s.o.'s footsteps; **~tritt** m kick; **~weg** m foothpath; **e-e Stunde ~** an hour's walk

Futter¹ ['fotɐ] n (-s; no pl) AGR feed, fodder, food

Futter² n (-s; -) lining

Futteral [fotəˈraːl] n (-s; -e) case; cover

füttern¹ ['fytɐn] v/t (ge-, h) AGR feed

füttern² v/t (ge-, h) line

'**Futternapf** m (feeding) bowl

Fütterung ['fytərʊŋ] f (-; -en) feeding (time)

Futur [fuˈtuːɐ] n (-s; -e) future (a. LING)

G

gab [gaːp] pret of **geben**

Gabe ['gaːbə] f (-; -n) gift, present; MED dose; fig talent, gift; **milde ~** alms

Gabel ['gaːbəl] f (-; -n) fork; TEL cradle

'**gabeln** v/refl (ge-, h) fork, branch

Gabelstapler ['gaːbəlˌʃtaːplɐ] m (-s; -) TECH fork-lift (truck)

Gabelung ['gaːbəlʊŋ] f (-; -en) fork(ing)

gackern ['gakɐn] v/i (ge-, h) cluck, cackle (a. fig)

gaffen ['gafən] v/i (ge-, h) gawk, gawp, F rubberneck; **Gaffer** ['gafɐ] m (-s; -) F rubberneck(er), Br nosy parker

Gage ['gaːʒə] f (-; -n) fee

gähnen ['gɛːnən] v/i (ge-, h) yawn

Gala ['gaːla] f (-; -s) gala

galant [gaˈlant] adj gallant, courteous

Galeere [gaˈleːrə] f (-; -n) MAR galley

Galerie [galəˈriː] f (-; -n) gallery

Galgen ['galgən] m (-s; -) gallows; **~frist** f reprieve; **~humor** m gallows humo(u)r; **~vogel** F m crook

Galle ['galə] f (-; -n) ANAT gall; bile

'**Gallen|blase** f ANAT gall bladder; **~stein** m MED gallstone

Gallert ['galɛt] n (-[es]; -e), **Gallerte** [gaˈlɛtə] f (-; -n) jelly

Galopp [gaˈlɔp] m (-s; -s, -e) gallop

galoppieren [galɔˈpiːrən] v/i (no -ge-, sein) gallop

galt [galt] pret of **gelten**

gammeln ['gaməln] F v/i (ge-, h) loaf (about), bum around; **Gammler(in)** ['gamlɐ, 'gamlərɪn] m(f) F (-s; -/-; -nen) loafer, bum

Gämse ['gɛmzə] f (-; -n) ZO chamois

gang [gaŋ] adj: **~ und gäbe** nothing unusual, (quite) usual

Gang [gaŋ] m (-[e]s; **Gänge** ['gɛŋə]) walk, gait, way s.o. walks; ARCH passage, a. AVIAT etc aisle; corridor; MOT gear; GASTR course; **et. in ~ bringen** get s.th. going, start s.th.; **in ~ kommen** get started; **im ~(e) sein** be (going) on, be in progress; **in vollem ~(e)** in full swing

gängeln ['gɛŋəln] v/t (ge-, h) lead s.o. by the nose

gängig ['gɛŋɪç] adj current; ECON sal(e)able

'Gangschaltung f MOT gears
Ganove [ga'no:və] F m (-n; -n) crook
Gans [gans] f (-; Gänse ['gɛnzə]) zo goose
Gänse|blümchen ['gɛnzəbly:mçən] n BOT daisy; **~braten** m roast goose; **~haut** f (-; no pl) gooseflesh; **dabei kriege ich e-e ~** F it gives me the creeps; very; quite, rather, fairly; **~marsch** m (-[e]s; no pl) single or Indian file
Gänserich ['gɛnzərɪç] m (-s; -e) zo gander
ganz [gants] **1.** adj whole, entire, total; F undamaged; full (hour etc); **den ~en Tag** all day; **die ~e Zeit** all the time; **auf der ~en Welt** all over the world; **sein ~es Geld** all his money **2.** adv completely, totally; very; quite, rather, fairly; **~ allein** all by oneself; **~ aus Holz** etc all wood etc; **~ und gar** completely, totally; **~ und gar nicht** not at all, by no means; **~ wie du willst** just as you like; **nicht ~** not quite; → **voll**
Ganze ['gantsə] n (-n; no pl) whole; **das ~** the whole thing; **im ~n** in all, altogether; **im großen und ~n** on the whole; **aufs ~ gehen** go all out
gänzlich ['gɛntslɪç] adv completely, entirely
'Ganztags|beschäftigung f full-time job; **~schule** f all-day school(ing)
gar [ga:ɐ] **1.** adj GASTR done **2.** adv: **~ nicht** not at all; **~ nichts** nothing at all; **~ zu ...** (a bit) too ...
Garage [ga'ra:ʒə] f (-; -n) garage
Garantie [garan'ti:] f (-; -n) guarantee, esp ECON warranty; **garantieren** [garan'ti:rən] v/t and v/i (no -ge-, h) guarantee (**für et.** s.th.)
Garbe ['garbə] f (-; -n) AGR sheaf
Garde ['gardə] f (-; -n) guard; MIL (the) Guards
Garderobe [gardə'ro:bə] f (-; -n) (no pl) wardrobe, clothes; checkroom, Br cloakroom; THEA dressing room
Garde'roben|frau f checkroom (Br cloakroom) attendant; **~marke** f coat check (Br cloakroom) ticket; **~ständer** m coat stand or rack
Gardine [gar'di:nə] f (-; -n) curtain
Gar'dinenstange f curtain rod
gären ['gɛ:rən] v/i ([irr], ge-, h, sein) ferment, work
Garn [garn] n (-[e]s; -e) yarn; thread;

cotton
Garnele [gar'ne:lə] f (-; -n) zo shrimp; prawn
garnieren [gar'ni:rən] v/t (no -ge-, h) garnish (a. fig)
Garnison [garni'zo:n] f (-; -en) MIL garrison, post
Garnitur [garni'tu:ɐ] f (-, -en) set; suite
Garten ['gartən] m (-s; Gärten ['gɛr-tən]) garden; **~arbeit** f gardening; **~bau** m (-[e]s; no pl) horticulture; **~erde** f (garden) mo(u)ld; **~fest** n garden party; **~geräte** pl gardening tools; **~haus** n summerhouse; **~lo,kal** n beer garden; outdoor restaurant; **~schere** f pruning shears; **~stadt** f garden city; **~zwerg** m (garden) gnome
Gärtner ['gɛrtnɐ] m (-s; -) gardener
Gärtnerei [gɛrtnə'rai] f (-; -en) truck farm, Br market garden
'Gärtnerin f (-; -nen) gardener
Gärung ['gɛ:rʊŋ] f (-; -en) fermentation
Gas [ga:s] n (-es; -e ['ga:zə]) gas; **~ geben** MOT accelerate, F step on the gas
gasförmig ['ga:sfœrmɪç] adj gaseous
'Gas|hahn m gas valve (or cock, Br tap); **~heizung** f gas heating; **~herd** m gas cooker or stove; **~kammer** f gas chamber; **~la,terne** f gas (street) lamp; **~leitung** f gas main; **~maske** f gas mask; **~ofen** m gas stove; **~pe,dal** n MOT gas pedal, Br accelerator pedal
Gasse ['gasə] f (-; -n) lane, alley
Gast [gast] m (-[e]s; Gäste ['gɛstə]) guest; visitor; customer
'Gastarbeiter m, 'Gastarbeiterin f foreign worker
Gästebuch ['gɛstəbu:x] n visitors' book
'gastfreundlich adj hospitable
'Gastfreundschaft f hospitality
Gastgeber ['gastge:bɐ] m (-s; -) host
Gastgeberin ['gastge:bərɪn] f (-; -nen) hostess
'Gast|haus n, **~hof** m restaurant, inn
gastieren [gas'ti:rən] v/i (no -ge-, h) give performances; THEA guest, give a guest performance
'gastlich adj hospitable
'Gast|mannschaft f SPORT visiting team; **~spiel** n THEA guest performance; **~stätte** f restaurant; **~stube** f taproom; restaurant; **~wirt** m landlord;

~wirtschaft f restaurant, inn

'Gaswerk n TECH gasworks

'Gaszähler m TECH gas meter

Gatte ['gatə] m (-n; -n) husband

Gatter ['gatə] n (-s; -) fence; gate

Gattin ['gatɪn] f (-; -nen) wife

Gattung ['gatʊŋ] f (-; -en) type, class, sort; BIOL genus; species

GAU [gau] (ABBR of **größter anzunehmender Unfall**) m (-[s]; no pl) worst case scenario, Br maximum credible accident, MCA

Gaul [gaul] m (-[e]s; **Gäule** ['gɔylə]) nag

Gaumen ['gaumən] m (-s; -) ANAT palate

Gauner ['gaunə] m (-s; -), **'Gaunerin** f (-; -nen) F crook

Gaze ['ga:zə] f (-; -n) gauze

Gazelle [ga'tsɛlə] f (-; -n) ZO gazelle

geb. abbr of **geboren** b., born

Gebäck [gə'bɛk] n (-[e]s; -e) pastry; cookies, Br biscuits

ge'backen pp of **backen**

Gebälk [gə'bɛlk] n (-[e]s; -e) timberwork, beams

gebar [gə'ba:ɐ] pret of **gebären**

Gebärde [gə'bɛ:ɐdə] f (-; -n) gesture

ge'bärden v/refl (no -ge-, h) behave, act (**wie** like)

gebären [gə'bɛ:rən] v/t (irr, no -ge-, h) give birth to; **Gebärmutter** [gə-'bɛ:ɐmutɐ] f ANAT uterus, womb

Gebäude [gə'bɔydə] n (-s; -) building, structure

Ge'beine pl bones, mortal remains

geben ['ge:bən] v/t (irr, ge-, h) give (**j-m et.** s.o. s.th.); hand, pass; deal (**cards**); make; **sich ~** pass; get better; **von sich ~** utter, let out; **j-m die Schuld ~** blame s.o.; **es gibt** there is, there are; **was gibt es?** what's up?; what's for **lunch** etc?; TV etc what's on?; **das gibt's nicht** that can't be true; that's out

Gebet [gə'be:t] n (-[e]s; -e) prayer

ge'beten pp of **bitten**

Gebiet [gə'bi:t] n (-[e]s; -e) region, area; esp POL territory; fig field

ge'bieterisch adj imperious

ge'bietsweise adv regionally; **~ Regen** local showers

Gebilde [gə'bɪldə] n (-s; -) thing, object

gebildet [gə'bɪldət] adj educated

Gebirge [gə'bɪrgə] n (-s; -) mountains

gebirgig [gə'bɪrgɪç] adj mountainous

Ge'birgs|bewohner m mountain-

-dweller; ~zug m mountain range

Ge'biss n (-es; -e) (set of) teeth; (set of) false teeth, denture(s)

ge'bissen pp of **beißen**

Gebläse [gə'blɛ:zə] n (-s; -) TECH blower, (MOT air) fan

ge'blasen pp of **blasen**

geblichen [gə'blɪçən] pp of **bleichen**

geblieben [gə'bli:bən] pp of **bleiben**

geblümt [gə'bly:mt] adj floral

gebogen [gə'bo:gən] 1. pp of **biegen** 2. adj bent, curved

geboren [gə'bo:rən] 1. pp of **gebären** 2. adj born; **~e Smith** née Smith; **ich bin am ... ~** I was born on the ...

geborgen [gə'bɔrgən] 1. pp of **bergen** 2. adj safe, secure; **Ge'borgenheit** f (-; no pl) safety, security

geborsten [gə'bɔrstən] pp of **bersten**

Gebot [gə'bo:t] n (-[e]s; -e) REL commandment; fig rule; necessity; auction etc: bid

geboten [gə'bo:tən] pp of **bieten**

gebracht [gə'braxt] pp of **bringen**

gebrannt [gə'brant] pp of **brennen**

ge'braten pp of **braten**

Ge'brauch m (-[e]s; no pl) use; application; **ge'brauchen** v/t (no -ge-, h) use; employ; **gut (nicht) zu ~ sein** be useful (useless); **ich könnte ... ~** I could do with ...; **gebräuchlich** [gə'brɔyçlɪç] adj in use; common, usual; current

Ge'brauchsanweisung f directions or instructions for use

ge'brauchsfertig adj ready for use; instant (coffee etc)

Ge'brauchsgrafiker m commercial artist

ge'braucht adj used, ECON a. second-hand

Ge'brauchtwagen m MOT used or second-hand car; **~händler** m used car dealer

Ge'brechen n (-s; -) defect, handicap

gebrechlich [gə'brɛçlɪç] adj frail; infirm; **Ge'brechlichkeit** f (-; no pl) frailty; infirmity

gebrochen [gə'brɔxən] pp of **brechen**

Ge'brüder pl brothers

Gebrüll [gə'bryl] n (-[e]s; no pl) roar (-ing)

Gebühr [gə'by:ɐ] f (-; -en) charge (a. TEL), fee; postage; due; **gebührend** [gə'by:rənt] adj due; proper ge'bühren|frei *adj* free of charge; TEL toll-free; *Br* nonchargeable;~**pflichtig** *adj* chargeable; ~**e Straße** toll road; ~**e Verwarnung** fine

gebunden [gəˈbʊndən] **1.** *pp of* **binden 2.** *adj* bound, *fig a.* tied

Geburt [gəˈbuːɐt] *f* (-; -en) birth

Ge'burten|kon,trolle *f*, ~**regelung** *f* birth control

ge'burten|schwach *adj* low-birthrate; ~**stark** *adj*: ~**e Jahrgänge** baby boom

Ge'burtenziffer *f* birthrate

gebürtig [gəˈbʏrtɪç] *adj* by birth

Ge'burts|anzeige *f* birth announcement;~**datum** *n* date of birth;~**fehler** *m* congenital defect;~**helfer(in)** obstetrician;~**jahr** *n* year of birth;~**land** *n* native country; ~**ort** *m* birthplace; ~**tag** *m* birthday;~**tagsfeier** *f* birthday party; ~**tagskind** *n* birthday boy (*or* girl);~**urkunde** *f* birth certificate

Gebüsch [gəˈbʏʃ] *n* (-[e]s; -e) bushes, shrubbery

gedacht [gəˈdaxt] *pp of* **denken**

Gedächtnis [gəˈdɛçtnɪs] *n* (-ses; -se) memory; *aus dem* ~ from memory; *zum* ~ *an* (*acc*) in memory (*or* commemoration) of; *im* ~ *behalten* keep in mind, remember;~**lücke** *f* memory lapse; ~**schwund** *m* MED amnesia; blackout;~**stütze** *f* memory aid

Gedanke [gəˈdaŋkə] *m* (-n; -n) thought; idea; *was für ein* ~*!* what an idea!; *in* ~*n* absorbed in thought; absent-minded; *sich* ~*n machen über* (*acc*) think about; be worried *or* concerned about; *j-s* ~*n lesen* read s.o.'s mind

Ge'danken|austausch *m* exchange of ideas;~**gang** *m* train of thought

ge'dankenlos *adj* thoughtless

Ge'danken|strich *m* dash; ~**übertragung** *f* telepathy

Gedeck [gəˈdɛk] *n* (-[e]s; -e) cover; *ein* ~ *auflegen* set a place

gedeihen [gəˈdaiən] *v/i* (*irr, no -ge-, sein*) thrive, prosper; grow; flourish

ge'denken *v/i* (*irr, denken, no -ge-, h*) (*gen*) think of; commemorate; mention

Ge'denk|feier [gəˈdɛŋkfaiɐ] *f* commemoration; ~**mi,nute** *f*: *e-e* ~ a moment's (*Br* minute's) silence;~**stätte** *f*,~**stein** *m* memorial;~**tafel** *f* plaque

Gedicht [gəˈdɪçt] *n* (-[e]s; -e) poem

gediegen [gəˈdiːgən] *adj* solid; tasteful

gedieh [gəˈdiː] *pret of* **gedeihen**

gediehen [gəˈdiːən] *pp of* **gedeihen**

Gedränge [gəˈdrɛŋə] *n* (-s; -) crowd, F crush; ge'drängt *fig adj* concise

gedroschen [gəˈdrɔʃən] *pp of* **dreschen**

ge'drückt *fig adj* depressed

gedrungen [gəˈdrʊŋən] **1.** *pp of* **dringen 2.** *adj* squat, stocky; thickset

Geduld [gəˈdʊlt] *f* (-; *no pl*) patience; ge'dulden *v/refl* (*no -ge-, h*) wait (patiently); geduldig [gəˈdʊldɪç] *adj* patient; Ge'duldspiel *n* puzzle (*a. fig*)

gedurft [gəˈdʊrft] *pp of* **dürfen**

geehrt [gəˈʔeːɐt] *adj* hono(u)red; *Sehr* ~*er Herr N.* Dear Mr N.

geeignet [gəˈʔaignət] *adj* suitable; suited, qualified; right

Gefahr [gəˈfaːɐ] *f* (-; -en) danger; threat; risk; *auf eigene* ~ at one's own risk; *außer* ~ out of danger, safe

gefährden [gəˈfɛːɐdən] *v/t* (*no -ge-, h*) endanger; risk, jeopardize

ge'fahren *pp of* **fahren**

gefährlich [gəˈfɛːɐlɪç] *adj* dangerous; risky

ge'fahrlos *adj* without risk, safe

Gefährte [gəˈfɛːɐtə] *m* (-n; -n), Ge'fährtin *f* (-; -nen) companion

Gefälle [gəˈfɛlə] *n* (-s; -) fall, slope, descent; gradient (*a.* PHYS)

ge'fallen **1.** *pp of* **fallen 2.** *v/i* (*irr, fallen, no -ge-, h*) please; *es gefällt mir* (*nicht*) I (don't) like it; *wie gefällt dir ...?* how do you like it ...?; *sich et.* ~ *lassen* put up with s.th.

Ge'fallen[1] *m* (-s; -) favo(u)r; *j-n um e-n* ~ *bitten* ask a favo(u)r of s.o.

Ge'fallen[2] *n*: ~ *finden an* (*dat*) enjoy, like

ge'fällig *adj* pleasant, agreeable; obliging, kind; *j-m* ~ *sein* do s.o. a favo(u)r

Ge'fälligkeit *f* (-; -en) (*no pl*) kindness; favo(u)r

ge'fangen **1.** *pp of* **fangen 2.** *adj* captive; imprisoned; ~ *halten* keep s.o. prisoner; ~ *nehmen* take s.o. prisoner; *fig* captivate; Ge'fangene *m*, *f* (-n; -n) prisoner; convict; Ge'fangennahme *f* (-; *no pl*) capture; Ge'fangenschaft *f* (-; *no pl*) captivity, imprisonment; *in* ~ *sein* be a prisoner of war

Gefängnis [gəˈfɛŋnɪs] *n* (-ses; -se) prison, jail, *Br a.* gaol; *ins* ~ *kommen* go to jail *or* prison; **~di,rektor** *m* governor, warden; **~strafe** *f* (sentence *or* term of) imprisonment; **~wärter** *m* prison guard

Gefäß [gə'fɛːs] *n* (-es; -e) vessel (*a.* ANAT), container

gefasst [gə'fast] *adj* composed; **~ auf** (*acc*) prepared for

Gefecht [gə'fɛçt] *n* (-[e]s; -e) MIL combat, action

gefedert [gə'feːdət] *adj:* **gut ~ sein** MOT have good suspension

gefeit [gə'fait] *adj:* **~ gegen** immune to

Gefieder [gə'fiːdɐ] *n* (-s; -) ZO plumage, feathers

geflochten [gə'flɔxtən] *pp of* **flechten**

geflogen [gə'floːgən] *pp of* **fliegen**

geflohen [gə'floːən] *pp of* **fliehen**

geflossen [gə'flɔsən] *pp of* **fließen**

Ge'flügel *n* (-s; *no pl*) poultry

ge'flügelt *adj:* **~es Wort** saying

gefochten [gə'fɔxtən] *pp of* **fechten**

Ge'folge *n* (-s; -) entourage, retinue, train; **Gefolgschaft** [gə'fɔlkʃaft] *f* (-; -en) followers

gefragt [gə'fraːkt] *adj* in demand, popular

gefräßig [gə'frɛːsiç] *adj* greedy, voracious

Gefreite [gə'fraitə] *m* (-n; -n) MIL private first class, *Br* lance corporal

ge'fressen *pp of* **fressen**

ge'frieren *v/i* (*irr*, **frieren**, *no* -ge-, *sein*) freeze

Gefrierfach [gə'friːɐfax] *n* freezer, freezing compartment

ge'friergetrocknet *adj* freeze-dried

Ge'frier|punkt *m* freezing point; **~truhe** *f* freezer, deep-freeze

gefroren [gə'froːrən] *pp of* **frieren**

Ge'frorene *Austrian n* (-n; *no pl*) ice cream

Gefüge [gə'fyːgə] *n* (-s; -) structure, texture

gefügig [gə'fyːgiç] *adj* pliant

Ge'fügigkeit *f* (-; *no pl*) pliancy

Gefühl [gə'fyːl] *n* (-[e]s; -e) feeling; sense; sensation; emotion; **ge'fühllos** *adj* insensible, numb; unfeeling, heartless; **ge'fühlsbetont** *adj* (highly) emotional; **ge'fühlvoll** *adj* (full of) feeling; tender; sentimental

gefunden [gə'fundən] *pp of* **finden**

gegangen [gə'gaŋən] *pp of* **gehen**

gegeben [gə'geːbən] *pp of* **geben**

gegen ['geːgən] *prp* (*acc*) against, JUR, SPORT *a.* versus; about, around; (in return) for; MED *etc* for; compared with

'Gegen... *in cpds* **...aktion, ...angriff, ...argument, ...frage** *etc:* counter-...; **~besuch** *m* return visit

Gegend ['geːgənt] *f* (-; -en) region, area; countryside; neighbo(u)rhood

gegenei'nander *adv* against one another *or* each other

'Gegen|fahrbahn *f* MOT opposite *or* oncoming lane; **~gewicht** *n* counterweight; **ein ~ bilden zu et.** counterbalance s.th.; **~kandi,dat** *m* rival candidate; **~leistung** *f* quid pro quo; **als ~** in return; **~licht** *n* (-[e]s; *no pl*) PHOT back light; **im** *or* **bei ~** against the light; **~maßnahme** *f* countermeasure; **~mittel** *n* MED antidote (*a. fig*); **~par,tei** *f* other side; POL opposition; SPORT opposite side; **~richtung** *f* opposite direction

'Gegensatz *m* contrast; opposite; **im ~ zu** in contrast to *or* with; **gegensätzlich** ['geːgənzɛtsliç] *adj* contrary, opposite

'Gegenseite *f* opposite side

gegenseitig ['geːgənzaitiç] *adj* mutual

'Gegenseitigkeit *f:* **auf ~ beruhen** be mutual

'Gegen|spieler *m*, **~spielerin** *f* SPORT opponent (*a. fig*); **~sprechanlage** *f* intercom (system)

'Gegenstand *m* object (*a. fig*); *fig* subject; **gegenständlich** ['geːgənʃtɛntliç] *adj* *art:* representational; **'gegenstandslos** *adj* invalid; irrelevant; *art:* abstract, nonrepresentational

'Gegen|stimme *f* PARL vote against, no; **nur drei ~n** only three noes; **~stück** *n* counterpart

'Gegenteil *n* opposite; **im ~** on the contrary; **'gegenteilig** *adj* contrary, opposite

gegen'über *adv and prp* (*dat*) opposite; *fig* to, toward(s); compared with

Gegen'über *n* (-s; -) person opposite; neighbo(u)r across the street

gegen'überstehen *v/i* (*irr*, **stehen**, *sep*, -ge-, *h*) face, be faced with

Gegen'überstellung *f* confrontation

'Gegenverkehr *m* oncoming traffic

Gegenwart ['ge:gənvart] *f* (-; *no pl*) present (time); presence; LING present (tense)

gegenwärtig ['ge:gənvɛrtɪç] **1.** *adj* present, current **2.** *adv* at present

Gegen|wehr ['ge:gənve:ɐ] *f* (-; *no pl*) resistance; ~wert *m* equivalent (value); ~wind *m* head wind

'**gegenzeichnen** *v/t* (*sep*, -*ge*-, *h*) countersign

'**Gegenzug** *m* countermove; RAIL train coming from the opposite direction

gegessen [gə'gɛsən] *pp of* **essen**

geglichen [gə'glɪçən] *pp of* **gleichen**

geglitten [gə'glɪtən] *pp of* **gleiten**

geglommen [gə'glɔmən] *pp of* **glimmen**

Gegner ['ge:gnɐ] *m* (-*s*; -), '**Gegnerin** *f* (-; -*nen*) opponent (*a.* SPORT), adversary; MIL enemy

'**gegnerisch** *adj* opposing; MIL (of the) enemy, hostile

'**Gegnerschaft** *f* (-; -*en*) opposition

gegolten [gə'gɔltən] *pp of* **gelten**

gegoren [gə'go:rən] *pp of* **gären**

gegossen [gə'gɔsən] *pp of* **gießen**

ge'graben *pp of* **graben**

gegriffen [gə'grɪfən] *pp of* **greifen**

gehabt [gə'ha:pt] *pp of* **haben**

Gehackte [gə'haktə] *n* → **Hackfleisch**

Gehalt [gə'halt] **1.** *m* (-[*e*]*s*; -*e*) content **2.** *n* (-[*e*]*s*; *Gehälter* [gə'hɛltɐ]) salary

ge'halten *pp of* **halten**

Ge'halts|empfänger *m* salaried employee; ~erhöhung *f* raise, *Br* increase *or* rise in salary

ge'haltvoll *adj* substantial; nutritious

gehangen [gə'haŋən] *pp of* **hängen** 1

gehässig [gə'hɛsɪç] *adj* malicious, spiteful; **Ge'hässigkeit** *f* (-; *no pl*) malice, spite(fulness)

ge'hauen *pp of* **hauen**

Gehäuse [gə'hɔyzə] *n* (-*s*; -) case, box; TECH casing; ZO shell; BOT core

Gehege [gə'he:gə] *n* (-*s*; -) enclosure

geheim [gə'haim] *adj* secret; **et.** ~ **halten** keep s.th. (a) secret

Ge'heim|a,gent *m* secret agent; ~dienst *m* secret service

Geheimnis [gə'haimnɪs] *n* (-*ses*; -*se*) secret; mystery

ge'heimnisvoll *adj* mysterious

Ge'heim|nummer *f* TEL unlisted (*Br* ex-directory) number; ~poli,zei *f* secret

police; ~schrift *f* code, cipher

ge'heißen *pp of* **heißen**

gehemmt [gə'hɛmt] *adj* inhibited, self--conscious

gehen ['ge:ən] *v/i* (*irr*, *ge*-, *sein*) go; walk; leave; TECH work (*a.* fig); ECON sell; fig last; **einkaufen** (**schwimmen**) ~ go shopping (swimming); ~ **wir!** let's go!; **wie geht es dir** (**Ihnen**)? how are you?; **es geht mir gut** (**schlecht**) I'm fine (not feeling well); ~ **in** (*acc*) go into; ~ **nach** *road etc*: lead to; *window etc*: face; fig go *or* judge by; **das geht nicht** that's impossible; **das geht schon** that's o.k.; **es geht nichts über** (*acc*) … there is nothing like …; **worum geht es?** what is it about?; **darum geht es** (**nicht**) that's (not) the point; **sich** ~ **lassen** let o.s. go

'**gehenlassen** *v/refl* (*irr*, **lassen**, *sep*, *no* -*ge*-, *h*) → **gehen**

geheuer [gə'hɔyɐ] *adj*: **nicht** (**ganz**) ~ eerie, creepy, F fishy

Geheul [gə'hɔyl] *n* (-[*e*]*s*; *no pl*) howling

Ge'hirn *n* (-[*e*]*s*; -*e*) ANAT brain(s); ~er-schütterung *f* MED concussion (of the brain); ~schlag *m* MED (cerebral) apoplexy; ~wäsche *f* brainwashing

gehoben [gə'ho:bən] **1.** *pp of* **heben** **2.** *adj* elevated; high(er); ~*e* **Stimmung** high spirits

Gehöft [gə'hœft] *n* (-[*e*]*s*; -*e*) farm (-stead)

geholfen [gə'hɔlfən] *pp of* **helfen**

Gehölz [gə'hœlts] *n* (-*es*; -*e*) wood, coppice, copse

Gehör [gə'hø:ɐ] *n* (-[*e*]*s*; -*e*) (sense of) hearing; ear; **nach dem** ~ by ear; **sich** ~ **verschaffen** make o.s. heard

ge'horchen *v/i* (*no* -*ge*-, *h*) obey; **nicht** ~ disobey

ge'hören *v/i* (*no* -*ge*-, *h*) belong (*dat or* **zu** to); **gehört dir das?** is this yours?; **es gehört sich** (**nicht**) it is proper *or* right (not done); **das gehört nicht hierher** that's not to the point

ge'hörig **1.** *adj* due, proper; necessary; decent; **zu et.** ~ belonging to s.th. **2.** *adv* properly, thoroughly

ge'hörlos *adj* deaf; **die Gehörlosen** the deaf

gehorsam [gə'ho:rza:m] *adj* obedient; **Ge'horsam** *m* (-*s*; *no pl*) obedience

'**Gehsteig** *m*, '**Gehweg** *m* sidewalk, *Br*

pavement

Geier ['gaiɐ] *m* (-s; -) zo vulture, buzzard

Geige ['gaigə] *f* (-; -n) MUS violin, F fiddle; (*auf der*) ~ *spielen* play (on) the violin

'Geigen|bogen *m* MUS (violin) bow; ~kasten *m* MUS violin case

'Geiger ['gaigɐ] *m* (-s; -), Geigerin ['gaigərɪn] *f* (-; -nen) MUS violinist

'Geigerzähler *m* PHYS Geiger counter

geil [gail] *adj* V hot, horny; *contp* lecherous, lewd; BOT rank; F awesome, Br brill, ace

Geisel ['gaizəl] *f* (-; -n) hostage; ~nehmer ['gaizəlneːmɐ] *m* (-s; -) kidnap(p)er

Geißel ['gaisəl] *fig f* (-; -n) scourge

Geist [gaist] *m* (-[e]s; -er) (*no pl*) spirit; soul; mind; intellect; wit; ghost; *der Heilige* ~ REL the Holy Ghost *or* Spirit

Geister|bahn ['gaistɐbaːn] *f* tunnel of horror, Br ghost train; ~fahrer F *m* MOT wrong-way driver

'geisterhaft *adj* ghostly

'geistesabwesend *adj* absent-minded

'Geistes|arbeiter *m* brainworker; ~blitz *m* brainstorm, Br brainwave

'Geistesgegenwart *f* presence of mind; 'geistesgegenwärtig *adj* alert; quick-witted

'geistesgestört *adj* mentally disturbed, deranged

'geisteskrank *adj* mentally ill

'Geisteskrankheit *f* mental illness

'geistesschwach *adj* feeble-minded

'Geisteswissenschaften *pl* the arts, *the* humanities

'Geisteszustand *m* mental state

geistig ['gaistɪç] *adj* mental; intellectual; spiritual; ~ *behindert* mentally handicapped

'geistlich *adj* religious; spiritual; ecclesiastical; clerical; 'Geistliche *m* (-n; -n) clergyman; priest; minister; *die* ~*n* the clergy

'geistlos *adj* trivial, inane, silly

'geistreich, 'geistvoll *adj* witty, clever

Geiz [gaits] *m* (-es; *no pl*) stinginess

'Geizhals *m* miser, niggard

geizig ['gaitsɪç] *adj* stingy, miserly

Ge'jammer F *n* (-s; *no pl*) wailing, complaining

gekannt [gə'kant] *pp of* **kennen**

Gekläff [gə'klɛf] F *n* (-[e]s; *no pl*) yapping

Geklapper [gə'klapɐ] F *n* (-s; *no pl*) clatter(ing)

Geklimper F *n* (-s; *no pl*) tinkling

geklungen [gə'kluŋən] *pp of* **klingen**

gekniffen [gə'knɪfən] *pp of* **kneifen**

ge'kommen *pp of* **kommen**

gekonnt [gə'kɔnt] **1.** *pp of* **können 2.** *adj* masterly

gekränkt [gə'krɛŋkt] *adj* hurt, offended

Gekritzel [gə'krɪtsəl] *contp n* (-s; *no pl*) scrawl, scribble

gekrochen [gə'krɔxən] *pp of* **kriechen**

gekünstelt [gə'kynstəlt] *adj* affected; artificial

Gelächter [gə'lɛçtɐ] *n* (-s; *no pl*) laughter

ge'laden *pp of* **laden**

Ge'lage *n* (-s; -) feast; carouse

Gelände [gə'lɛndə] *n* (-s; -) area, country, ground; site; *auf dem* ~ on the premises; ~... *in cpds* ...*lauf,* ...*ritt,* ...*wagen etc:* cross-country ...

Geländer [gə'lɛndɐ] *n* (-s; -) banisters; handrail, rail(ing); parapet

ge'lang *pret of* **gelingen**

ge'langen *v/i* (*no -ge-, sein*) ~ *an* (acc) *or nach* reach, arrive at, get *or* come to; ~ *in* (acc) get *or* come into; *fig zu et.* ~ gain *or* win *or* achieve s.th.

ge'lassen 1. *pp of* **lassen 2.** *adj* calm, composed, cool

Gelatine [ʒela'tiːnə] *f* (-; *no pl*) gelatin(e)

ge'laufen *pp of* **laufen**

ge'läufig *adj* common, current; familiar

gelaunt [gə'launt] *adj*: *schlecht (gut)* ~ *sein* be in a bad (good) mood

gelb [gɛlp] *adj* yellow

'gelblich *adj* yellowish

'Gelbsucht *f* (-; *no pl*) MED jaundice

Geld [gɛlt] *n* (-[e]s; -er [ˈgɛldɐ]) money; *zu* ~ *machen* turn into cash

'Geld|angelegenheiten *pl* money *or* financial matters *or* affairs; ~anlage *f* investment; ~ausgabe *f* expense; ~automat *m* automatic teller machine, ATM, autoteller, Br cash dispenser; ~beutel *m*, ~börse *f* purse; ~buße *f* fine, penalty; ~geber(in) [ˈgɛltgeːbɐ, ˈgɛltgeːbərɪn] (-s; -/-; -nen) financial backer; investor '**geldgierig** *adj* greedy for money

'**Geld|knappheit** *f*, **~mangel** *m* lack of money; ECON (financial) stringency; **~mittel** *pl* funds, means, resources; **~schein** *m* bill, *Br* (bank)note; **~schrank** *m* safe; **~sendung** *f* remittance; **~strafe** *f* fine; **~stück** *n* coin; **~verlegenheit** *f* financial embarrassment; **~verschwendung** *f* waste of money; **~waschanlage** *f* money laundering scheme; **~wechsel** *m* exchange of money; **~wechselautomat** *m*, **~wechsler** ['gɛltvɛkslə] *m* (-s; -) change machine

Gelee [ʒe'le:] *n*, *m* (-s; -s) jelly; gel

ge'legen 1. *pp of* **liegen 2.** *adj* situated, located; *fig* convenient, opportune; **Ge'legenheit** *f* (-; -en) occasion; opportunity, chance; **bei ~** on occasion

Ge'legenheits|arbeit *f* casual *or* odd job; **~arbeiter** *m* casual labo(u)rer, odd-job man; **~kauf** *m* bargain

gelegentlich [gə'le:gəntlɪç] *adv* occasionally

gelehrig [gə'le:rɪç] *adj* docile

Gelehrsamkeit [gə'le:ɐza:mkait] *f* (-; *no pl*) learning; **gelehrt** [gə'le:ɐt] *adj* learned; **Ge'lehrte** *m*, *f* (-*n*; -*n*) scholar, learned man *or* woman

Geleise [gə'laizə] *n* → **Gleis**

Geleit [gə'lait] *n* (-[e]s; -e) escort

ge'leiten *v/t* (*no -ge-*, *h*) accompany, conduct, escort

Ge'leitzug *m* MAR, MIL convoy

Gelenk [gə'lɛŋk] *n* (-[e]s; -e) ANAT, TECH joint; **ge'lenkig** *adj* flexible (*a. TECH*); lithe, supple

gelernt [gə'lɛrnt] *adj* skilled, trained

ge'lesen *pp of* **lesen**

geliebt [gə'li:pt] *adj* (be)loved, dear

Ge'liebte 1. *m* (-*n*; -*n*) lover **2.** *f* (-*n*; -*n*) mistress

geliehen [gə'li:ən] *pp of* **leihen**

gelingen [gə'lɪŋən] *v/i* (*irr, no -ge-, sein*) succeed, manage; turn out well; **es gelang mir, et. zu tun** I succeeded in doing (I managed to do) s.th.; **Ge'lingen** *n* (-s; *no pl*) success; **gutes ~!** good luck!

gelitten [gə'lɪtən] *pp of* **leiden**

gelogen [gə'lo:gən] *pp of* **lügen**

gelten ['gɛltən] *v/i and v/t* (*irr, ge-*, *h*) be worth; *fig* count for; be valid; SPORT count; ECON be effective; **~ für** apply

to; **~ als** be regarded *or* looked upon as, be considered *or* supposed to be; **~ lassen** accept (*als* as); **~d** *adj* accepted; **~ machen** assert; **s-n Einfluss** (*bei j-m*) **~ machen** bring one's influence to bear (on s.o.)

'**Geltung** *f* (-; *no pl*) prestige; weight; **zur ~ kommen** show to advantage

'**Geltungsbedürfnis** *n* (-ses; *no pl*) need for recognition

Gelübde [gə'lʏpdə] *n* (-s; -) vow

gelungen [gə'lʊŋən] **1.** *pp of* **gelingen 2.** *adj* successful, a success

gemächlich [gə'mɛ:çlɪç] *adj* leisurely

ge'mahlen *pp of* **mahlen**

Gemälde [gə'mɛ:ldə] *n* (-s; -) painting, picture; **~gale,rie** *f* art (*or* picture) gallery

gemäß [gə'mɛːs] *prp* (*dat*) according to

gemäßigt [gə'mɛːsɪçt] *adj* moderate; temperate (*climate etc*)

gemein [gə'main] *adj* mean; dirty, filthy (*joke etc*); BOT, ZO common

Gemeinde [gə'maində] *f* (-; -n) POL municipality; local government; REL parish; congregation; **~rat** *m* (member of the) city (*Br* local) council; **~rätin** [gə-'maindɛ:rtɪn] *f* (-; -nen) member of the city (*Br* local) council; **~steuern** *pl* local taxes, *Br* (local) rates

ge'meingefährlich *adj*: **~er Mensch** public enemy

Ge'meinheit *f* (-; -en) (*no pl*) meanness; mean thing (to do *or* say), F dirty trick

gemeinnützig [gə'mainnʏtsɪç] *adj* nonprofit, *Br* non-profitmaking

Ge'meinplatz *m* commonplace

ge'meinsam 1. *adj* common, joint; mutual **2.** *adv* together

Ge'meinschaft *f* (-; -en) community

Ge'meinschafts|arbeit *f* teamwork; **~kunde** *f* (-; *no pl*) PED social studies; **~produkti,on** *f* coproduction; **~raum** *m* recreation room, lounge

Ge'meinsinn *m* (-[e]s; *no pl*) public spirit; (sense of) solidarity

ge'meinverständlich *adj* popular

Ge'meinwohl *n* public welfare

Gemetzel [gə'mɛtsəl] *n* (-s; -) slaughter, massacre

gemieden [gə'mi:dən] *pp of* **meiden**

Gemisch [gə'mɪʃ] n (-[e]s; -e) mixture (a. CHEM)

gemocht [gə'mɔxt] pp of **mögen**

gemolken [gə'mɔlkən] pp of **melken**

Gemse → **Gämse**

Gemurmel [gə'mʊrməl] n (-s; no pl) murmur, mutter

Gemüse [gə'my:zə] n (-s; -) vegetable(s); greens; ~händler m greengrocer('s)

gemusst [gə'mʊst] pp of **müssen**

Gemüt [gə'my:t] n (-[e]s; -er) mind, soul; heart; nature, mentality

ge'mütlich adj comfortable, snug, cozy, Br cosy; peaceful, pleasant, relaxed; **mach es dir ~** make yourself at home; **Ge'mütlichkeit** f (-; no pl) snugness, coziness, Br cosiness; cozy (Br cosy) or relaxed atmosphere

Ge'mütsbewegung f emotion

ge'mütskrank adj emotionally disturbed

Ge'mütszustand m state of mind

Gen [ge:n] n (-s; -e) BIOL gene

genannt [gə'nant] pp of **nennen**

genas [gə'na:s] pret of **genesen** 1

genau [gə'nau] 1. adj exact, precise, accurate; careful, close; strict; **Genaueres** further details 2. adv: ~ **um 10 Uhr** at 10 o'clock sharp; ~ **der** ... that very ...; ~ **zuhören** listen closely; **es ~ nehmen (mit et.)** be particular (about s.th.); **Ge'nauigkeit** f (-; no pl) accuracy, precision, exactness

ge'nauso adv → **ebenso**

genehmigen [gə'ne:mɪgən] v/t (no -ge-, h) permit, allow; approve

Ge'nehmigung f (-; -en) permission; approval; permit; licen|se, Br -ce

geneigt [gə'naikt] adj inclined (zu to)

General [genə'ra:l] m (-s; Generäle [genə'rɛ:lə]) MIL general; ~di,rektor m ECON president, Br chairman; ~konsul m consul general; ~konsu,lat n consulate general; ~probe f THEA dress rehearsal; ~sekre,tär m secretary-general; ~stab m MIL general staff; ~streik m general strike; ~versammlung f general meeting; ~vertreter m ECON sole agent

Generation [genəra'tsjo:n] f (-; -en) generation; **Generati'onenkon,flikt** m generation gap

Generator [genə'ra:to:ɐ] m (-s; -en

[genəra'to:rən]) ELECTR generator

generell [genə'rɛl] adj general, universal

genesen [gə'ne:zən] 1. v/i (irr, no -ge-, sein) recover (**von** from), get well 2. pp of **genesen** 1

Ge'nesung f (-; no pl) recovery

Genetik [ge'ne:tɪk] f (-; no pl) BIOL genetics; **ge'netisch** adj BIOL genetic; ~**er Fingerabdruck** genetic fingerprint

genial [ge'nja:l] adj brilliant, of genius

Genialität [genjali'tɛ:t] f (-; no pl) genius

Genick [gə'nɪk] n (-[e]s; -e) ANAT (back or nape of the) neck

Genie [ʒe'ni:] n (-s; -s) genius

genieren [ʒe'ni:rən] v/refl (no -ge-, h) be embarrassed

genießen [gə'ni:sən] v/t (irr, no -ge-, h) enjoy

Genießer [gə'ni:sɐ] m (-s; -) gourmet

Genitiv ['ge:niti:f] m (-s; -e) LING genitive or possessive (case)

genommen [gə'nɔmən] pp of **nehmen**

genormt [gə'nɔrmt] adj standardized

genoss [gə'nɔs] pret of **genießen**

Genosse [gə'nɔsə] m (-n; -n) POL comrade; F pal, buddy, Br mate

genossen [gə'nɔsən] pp of **genießen**

Ge'nossenschaft f (-; -en) cooperative

Ge'nossin f (-; -nen) POL comrade

'Gentechnik f, **'Gentechnolo,gie** f genetic engineering

genug [gə'nu:k] adj enough, sufficient

Genüge [gə'ny:gə] f: **zur ~** (well) enough, sufficiently

ge'nügen v/i (no -ge-, h) be enough, be sufficient; **das genügt** that will do; ~**d** adj enough, sufficient; plenty of

genügsam [gə'ny:kza:m] adj easily satisfied; frugal; modest; **Ge'nügsamkeit** f (-; no pl) modesty; frugality

Ge'nugtuung f (-; no pl) satisfaction

Genus ['ge:nʊs] n (-; Genera ['ge:nəra]) LING gender

Genuss [gə'nʊs] m (-es; Genüsse [gə'nʏsə]) pleasure; (no pl) consumption; **ein ~** a real treat; food: a. delicious; ~**mittel** n excise item, Br (semi-)luxury

Geografie, Geographie [geogra'fi:] f (-; no pl) geography; **geografisch, geographisch** [geo'gra:fɪʃ] adj geographic(al)

Geologe [geo'lo:gə] m (-n; -n) geologist; **Geologie** [geolo'gi:] f (-; no pl) geology; **Geo'login** f (-; -nen) geologist; **geologisch** [geo'lo:gɪʃ] adj geologic(al)

Geometrie [geome'tri:] f (-; no pl) geometry; **geometrisch** [geo'me:trɪʃ] adj geometric(al)

Gepäck [gə'pɛk] n (-[e]s; no pl) baggage, luggage; **~ablage** f baggage (or luggage) rack; **~aufbewahrung** f baggage room, Br left-luggage office; **~kon,trolle** f baggage check, Br luggage inspection; **~schalter** m baggage (or luggage) counter; **~schein** m baggage check, Br luggage ticket; **~träger** m porter; bicycle: carrier

gepanzert [gə'pantsɐt] adj MOT armo(u)red

Gepard ['ge:part] m (-s; -e) zo cheetah

gepfiffen [gə'pfɪfən] pp of **pfeifen**

gepflegt [gə'pfle:kt] adj well-groomed, neat; fig cultivated

Gepflogenheit [gə'pflo:gənhait] f (-; -en) habit, custom

Geplapper [gə'plapɐ] F n (-s; no pl) babbling, chatter(ing)

Geplauder [gə'plaudɐ] n (-s; no pl) chat (-ting)

Gepolter [gə'pɔltɐ] n (-s; no pl) rumble

gepriesen [gə'pri:zən] pp of **preisen**

Gequassel [gə'kvasəl] F n (-s; no pl), **Gequatsche** [gə'kvatʃə] F n (-s; no pl) blather, blabber

gequollen [gə'kvɔlən] pp of **quellen**

gerade [gə'ra:də] 1. adj straight (a. fig); even (number); direct; upright, erect (posture); 2. adv just; **nicht ~** not exactly; **das ist es ja ~!** that's just it!; **~ deshalb** that's just why; **~ rechtzeitig** just in time; **warum ~ ich?** why me of all people?; **da wir ~ von ... sprechen** speaking of ...; **Ge'rade** f (-n; -n) MATH (straight) line; SPORT straight; **linke** (**rechte**) **~** boxing: straight left (right)

gerade'aus adv straight on or ahead; **~he'raus** adj straightforward, frank

ge'radestehen v/i (irr, stehen, sep, -ge-, h) stand straight; **~ für** answer for

ge'radewegs adv straight, directly

ge'radezu adv simply

gerannt [gə'rant] pp of **rennen**

Gerät [gə'rɛ:t] n (-[e]s; -e) device; F gadget; appliance; (kitchen) utensil;

radio, TV set; coll, a. SPORT etc equipment; SPORT apparatus; TECH tool; instrument

ge'raten 1. pp of **raten** 2. v/i (irr, **raten**, no -ge-, **sein**) turn out (**gut** well); **~ an** (acc) come across; **~ in** (acc) get into; **in Brand ~** catch fire

Ge'räteturnen n apparatus gymnastics

ge'ratewohl n: **aufs ~** at random

geräumig [gə'rɔymɪç] adj spacious, roomy

Geräusch [gə'rɔyʃ] n (-[e]s; -e) sound, noise; **ge'räuschlos 1.** adj noiseless (a. TECH); **2.** adv without a sound; **ge'räuschvoll** adv noisy

gerben ['gɛrbən] v/t (ge-, h) tan

Gerberei [gɛrbə'rai] f (-; -en) tannery

Ge'recht adj just, fair; (j-m, e-r Sache) **~ werden** do justice to; meet (demands etc); **Ge'rechtigkeit** f (-; no pl) justice

Ge'rede F n (-s; no pl) talk; gossip

gereizt [gə'raitst] adj irritable

Ge'reiztheit f (-; no pl) irritability

Gericht[1] [gə'rɪçt] n (-[e]s; -e) GASTR dish

Ge'richt[2] n (-[e]s; -e) JUR court; **vor ~ stehen** (**stellen**) stand (bring to) trial; **vor ~ gehen** go to court

ge'richtlich adj JUR judicial, legal

Ge'richtsbarkeit f (-; no pl) JUR jurisdiction

Ge'richts|gebäude n JUR law court(s), courthouse; **~hof** m JUR law court; **~medi,zin** f JUR forensic medicine; **~saal** m JUR courtroom; **~verfahren** n JUR lawsuit; **~verhandlung** f JUR hearing; trial; **~vollzieher** [gə'rɪçtsfɔltsi:ɐ] m (-s; -) JUR marshal, Br bailiff

gerieben [gə'ri:bən] pp of **reiben**

gering [gə'rɪŋ] adj little, small; slight, minor; low; **~ schätzen** think little of

ge'ringfügig adj slight, minor; petty

ge'ring|schätzen v/t (sep, -ge-, h) → **gering**; **~schätzig** [gə'rɪŋʃɛtsɪç] adj contemptuous

ge'ringst adv least; **nicht im Geringsten** not in the least

ge'rinnen v/i (irr, **rinnen**, no -ge-, **sein**) coagulate; curdle; clot

Ge'rippe n (-s; -) skeleton (a. fig); TECH framework

gerissen [gə'rɪsən] **1.** pp of **reißen 2.** F adj cunning, smart

geritten [gə'rɪtən] pp of **reiten**

germanisch [gɛr'maːnɪʃ] *adj* Germanic; **Germanist(in)** [gɛrmaˈnɪst(ɪn)] (-*en*; -*en*/-; -*nen*) student of (*or* graduate in) German

gern [gɛrn] *adv* willingly, gladly; *et.* (*sehr*) ~ *tun* like (love) to do s.th. *or* doing s.th.; *ich möchte* ~ I'd like (to); ~ *geschehen!* not at all, (you're) welcome

gernhaben *v/t* (*irr*, *haben*, *sep*, -*ge*-, *h*) like, be fond of.

gerochen [gəˈrɔxən] *pp of* **riechen**

Geröll [gəˈrœl] *n* (-[*e*]*s*; -*e*) scree; boulders

geronnen [gəˈrɔnən] *pp of* **rinnen**

Gerste ['gɛrstə] *f* (-; -*n*) BOT barley 'Gerstenkorn *n* MED sty(e)

Gerte ['gɛrtə] *f* (-; -*n*) switch, rod, twig

Geruch [gəˈrux] *m* (-[*e*]*s*; *Gerüche* [gəˈryçə]) smell; odo(u)r; scent

ge'ruchlos *adj* odo(u)rless

Ge'ruchssinn *m* (sense of) smell

Gerücht [gəˈrʏçt] *n* (-[*e*]*s*; -*e*) rumo(u)r

ge'rufen *pp of* **rufen**

gerührt [gəˈryːɐt] *adj* touched, moved

Gerümpel [gəˈrʏmpəl] *n* (-*s*; *no pl*) lumber, junk

Gerundium [geˈrʊndiʊm] *n* (-*s*; -*ien*) LING gerund

gerungen [gəˈrʊŋən] *pp of* **ringen**

Gerüst [gəˈrʏst] *n* (-[*e*]*s*; -*e*) frame (-work); scaffold(ing); stage

ge'salzen *pp of* **salzen**

gesamt [gəˈzamt] *adj* whole, entire, total, all

Ge'samt... *in cpds* ...*ergebnis etc: mst* total ...; ~*ausgabe* *f* complete edition; ~*schule* *f* comprehensive school

gesandt [gəˈzant] *pp of* **senden**

Gesandte [gəˈzantə] *m*, *f* (-*n*; -*n*) POL envoy; **Ge'sandtschaft** *f* (-; -*en*) legation, mission

Gesang [gəˈzaŋ] *m* (-[*e*]*s*; *Gesänge* [gəˈzɛŋə]) singing; song; voice; ~*buch* *n* REL hymn book; ~(*s*)*lehrer(in)* singing teacher; ~*verein* *m* choral society, glee club

Gesäß [gəˈzɛːs] *n* (-*es*; -*e*) ANAT buttocks, bottom

ge'schaffen *pp of* **schaffen**[1]

Geschäft [gəˈʃɛft] *n* (-[*e*]*s*; -*e*) business; store, *Br* shop; bargain

ge'schäftig *adj* busy, active

Ge'schäftigkeit *f* (-; *no pl*) activity

ge'schäftlich 1. *adj* business ...; commercial **2.** *adv* on business

Ge'schäfts|brief *m* business letter; ~*frau* *f* businesswoman; ~*freund* *m* business friend; ~*führer(in)* managing director; (*of shop*) manager; ~*inhaber(in)* proprietor; ~*leitung* *f* executive board; ~*mann* *m* businessman

ge'schäftsmäßig *adj* businesslike

Ge'schäfts|ordnung *f* PARL standing orders; rules (of procedure); ~*partner(in)* (business) partner; ~*räume* *pl* (business) premises; ~*reise* *f* business trip; ~*schluss* *m* closing time; *nach* ~ *a.* after business hours; ~*stelle* *f* office; ~*straße* *f* shopping street

ge'schäftstüchtig *adj* efficient, smart

Ge'schäfts|verbindung *f* business connection; ~*viertel* *n* commercial district; downtown; ~*zeit* *f* office *or* business hours; ~*zweig* *m* branch *or* line (of business)

geschah [gəˈʃaː] *pret of* **geschehen**

geschehen [gəˈʃeːən] **1.** *v/i* (*irr*, *no* -*ge*-, *sein*) happen, occur, take place; be done; *es geschieht ihm recht* it serves him right **2.** *pp of* **geschehen** 1

gescheit [gəˈʃaɪt] *adj* clever, bright, F brainy

Geschenk [gəˈʃɛŋk] *n* (-[*e*]*s*; -*e*) present, gift; ~*gutschein* *m* gift voucher; ~*packung* *f* gift box; ~*papier* *n* gift wrap

Geschichte [gəˈʃɪçtə] *f* (-; -*n*) story; (*no pl*) history; F business, thing

ge'schichtlich *adj* historical

Ge'schichts|schreiber *m* (-*s*; -), ~*wissenschaftler* *m* historian

Geschick [gəˈʃɪk] *n* (-[*e*]*s*; -*e*) fate, destiny; → **Ge'schicklichkeit** *f* (-; *no pl*) skill; dexterity; **ge'schickt** *adj* skil(l)-ful, skilled; dext(e)rous; clever

geschieden [gəˈʃiːdən] **1.** *pp of* **scheiden 2.** *adj* divorced, *marriage*: dissolved

geschienen [gəˈʃiːnən] *pp of* **scheinen**

Geschirr [gəˈʃɪr] *n* (-[*e*]*s*; -*e*) dishes, china; (*no pl*) kitchen utensils, pots and pans, crockery; harness; ~ *spülen* wash *or* do the dishes

Ge'schirrspüler *m* (-*s*; -) dishwasher

geschissen [gəˈʃɪsən] *pp of* **scheißen**

ge'schlafen *pp of* **schlafen**

ge'schlagen *pp of* **schlagen**

Geschlecht [gə'ʃlɛçt] *n* (-[e]s; -er) (*no pl*) sex; kind, species; family, line(age); generation; LING gender

Ge'schlechts|krankheit *f* MED sexually transmitted disease, venereal disease; ~teile *pl* genitals; ~trieb *m* sexual instinct *or* urge; ~verkehr *m* (sexual) intercourse; ~wort *n* LING article

geschlichen [gə'ʃlɪçən] *pp of* **schleichen**

geschliffen [gə'ʃlɪfən] **1.** *pp of* **schleifen²** **2.** *adj* cut; *fig* polished

geschlossen [gə'ʃlɔsən] **1.** *pp of* **schließen** **2.** *adj* closed

geschlungen [gə'ʃlʊŋən] *pp of* **schlingen**

Geschmack [gə'ʃmak] *m* (-[e]s; Geschmäcke [gə'ʃmɛkə]) taste (*a. fig*); flavo(u)r; ~ **finden an** (*dat*) develop a taste for; **ge'schmacklos** *adj. fig* tasteless; **Ge'schmacklosigkeit** *f* (-; *no pl*) tastelessness; **Ge'schmack(s)-sache** *f* matter of taste; **ge-'schmackvoll** *adj* tasteful, in good taste

geschmeidig [gə'ʃmaidɪç] *adj* supple, pliant

geschmissen [gə'ʃmɪsən] *pp of* **schmeißen**

geschmolzen [gə'ʃmɔltsən] *pp of* **schmelzen**

geschnitten [gə'ʃnɪtən] *pp of* **schneiden**

geschoben [gə'ʃoːbən] *pp of* **schieben**

Geschöpf [gə'ʃœpf] *n* (-[e]s; -e) creature

geschoren [gə'ʃoːrən] *pp of* **scheren**

Geschoss [gə'ʃɔs] *n* (-es; -e), Geschoß [gə'ʃoːs] *Austrian n* (-es; -e) projectile, missile; stor(e)y, floor

ge'schossen *pp of* **schießen**

Ge'schrei F *n* (-s; *no pl*) shouting, yelling; screams; crying; *fig* fuss

geschrieben [gə'ʃriːbən] *pp of* **schreiben**

geschrie(e)n [gə'ʃriː(ə)n] *pp of* **schreien**

geschritten [gə'ʃrɪtən] *pp of* **schreiten**

geschunden [gə'ʃʊndən] *pp of* **schinden**

Geschütz [gə'ʃʏts] *n* (-es; -e) MIL gun, cannon

Geschwader [gə'ʃvaːdɐ] *n* (-s; -) MIL MAR squadron; AVIAT group, *Br* wing

Geschwätz [gə'ʃvɛts] F *n* (-es; *no pl*) chatter, babble; gossip; *fig* nonsense; **ge'schwätzig** *adj* talkative; gossipy

geschweige [gə'ʃvaigə] *cj*: ~ (**denn**) let alone

geschwiegen [gə'ʃviːgən] *pp of* **schweigen**

geschwind [gə'ʃvɪnt] *adj* quick, swift

Geschwindigkeit [gə'ʃvɪndɪçkait] *f* (-; -en) speed; fastness, quickness; PHYS velocity; **mit e-r ~ von ...** at a speed *or* rate of ...

Ge'schwindigkeits|begrenzung *f* speed limit; ~überschreitung *f* MOT speeding

Geschwister [gə'ʃvɪstɐ] *pl* brother(s) and sister(s); JUR siblings

geschwollen [gə'ʃvɔlən] **1.** *pp of* **schwellen** **1 2.** *adj* MED swollen; *fig* bombastic, pretentious, pompous

geschwommen [gə'ʃvɔmən] *pp of* **schwimmen**

geschworen [gə'ʃvoːrən] *pp of* **schwören**; **Ge'schworene** *m, f* (-n; -n) member of a jury; **die ~n** the jury

Geschwulst [gə'ʃvʊlst] *f* (-; Geschwülste [gə'ʃvʏlstə]) MED growth, tumo(u)r

geschwunden [gə'ʃvʊndən] *pp of* **schwinden**

geschwungen [gə'ʃvʊŋən] *pp of* **schwingen**

Geschwür [gə'ʃvyːɐ] *n* (-s; -e) MED abscess, ulcer

ge'sehen *pp of* **sehen**

Geselchte [gə'zɛlçtə] *Austrian n* (-n; *no pl*) GASTR smoked meat

Geselle [gə'zɛlə] *m* (-n; -n) journeyman

ge'sellen *v/refl* (*no -ge-, h*) **sich zu j-m ~** join s.o.

ge'sellig *adj* sociable; ZO *etc* social; **~es Beisammensein** get-together

Ge'sellin *f* (-; -nen) trained woman *hairdresser etc*, journeywoman

Gesellschaft [gə'zɛlʃaft] *f* (-; -en) society; company; party; ECON company, corporation; **j-m ~ leisten** keep s.o. company

ge'sellschaftlich *adj* social

Ge'sellschafts-... *in cpds* ...kritik, ...ordnung *etc*: social ...; ~spiel *n* parlo(u)r game; ~tanz *m* ballroom dance

gesessen [gə'zɛsən] *pp of* **sitzen**

Gesetz [gə'zɛts] *n* (-es; -e) JUR law; act;

G

~buch *n* JUR code (of law); **~entwurf** *m* PARL bill

ge'setzgebend *adj* JUR legislative

Ge'setzgeber *m* (-s; -) JUR legislator

Ge'setzgebung *f* (-; -en) JUR legislation

ge'setzlich 1. *adj* legal; lawful **2.** *adv:* **~ geschützt** JUR patented, registered

ge'setzlos *adj* lawless

ge'setzmäßig *adj* legal, lawful

gesetzt [gə'zɛtst] **1.** *adj* staid, dignified; mature (*age*) **2.** *cj:* **~ den Fall(, dass)** ... supposing (that)

ge'setzwidrig *adj* illegal, unlawful

Gesicht [gə'zɪçt] *n* (-[e]s; -er) face; **zu ~ bekommen** catch sight of

Ge'sichts|ausdruck *m* look, expression; **~creme** *f* face cream; **~farbe** *f* complexion; **~punkt** *m* point of view, aspect, angle; **~wasser** *n* toner; **~zug** *m* feature

Gesindel [gə'zɪndəl] *n* (-s; *no pl*) trash, *the* riff-raff

gesinnt [gə'zɪnt] *adj* minded; **j-m feindlich ~ sein** be ill-disposed towards s.o.

Ge'sinnung *f* (-; -en) mind; attitude; POL conviction(s)

ge'sinnungslos *adj* unprincipled

ge'sinnungstreu *adj* loyal

Ge'sinnungswechsel *m* about-face, *Br* about-turn

gesittet [gə'zɪtət] *adj* civilized, well-mannered

gesoffen [gə'zɔfən] *pp of* **saufen**

gesogen [gə'zo:gən] *pp of* **saugen**

gesotten [gə'zɔtən] *pp of* **sieden**

gespalten [gə'ʃpaltən] *pp of* **spalten**

Gespann [gə'ʃpan] *n* (-[e]s; -e) team (*a. fig*)

gespannt [gə'ʃpant] *adj* tense (*a. fig*); **~ sein auf** (*acc*) be anxious to see; **ich bin ~, ob (wie)** I wonder if (how)

Gespenst [gə'ʃpɛnst] *n* (-[e]s; -er) ghost, apparition, *esp fig* specter, *Br* spectre

ge'spenstisch *adj* ghostly, F spooky

gespie(e)n [gə'ʃpi:(ə)n] *pp of* **speien**

Gespinst [gə'ʃpɪnst] *n* (-[e]s; -e) web, tissue (*both a. fig*)

gesponnen [gə'ʃpɔnən] *pp of* **spinnen**

Gespött [gə'ʃpœt] *n* (-[e]s; *no pl*) mockery, ridicule; **j-n zum ~ machen** make a laughingstock of s.o.

Gespräch [gə'ʃprɛːç] *n* (-[e]s; -e) talk (*a. POL*), conversation; TEL call

ge'sprächig *adj* talkative

gesprochen [gə'ʃprɔxən] *pp of* **sprechen**

gesprossen [gə'ʃprɔsən] *pp of* **sprießen**

gesprungen [gə'ʃprʊŋən] *pp of* **springen**

Gespür [gə'ʃpy:ɐ] *n* (-s; *no pl*) flair, nose

Gestalt [gə'ʃtalt] *f* (-; -en) shape, form; figure; **ge'stalten** *v/t* (*no -ge-, h*) arrange; design; **Ge'staltung** *f* (-; -en) arrangement; design; decoration

gestanden [gə'ʃtandən] *pp of* **stehen**

ge'ständig *adj:* **~ sein** confess; have confessed

Geständnis [gə'ʃtɛntnɪs] *n* (-ses; -se) confession (*a. fig*)

Gestank [gə'ʃtaŋk] *m* (-[e]s; *no pl*) stench, stink

gestatten [gə'ʃtatən] *v/t* (*no -ge-, h*) allow, permit

Geste ['gɛstə] *f* (-; -n) gesture (*a. fig*)

ge'stehen *v/t and v/i* (*irr*, **stehen**, *no -ge-, h*) confess

Gestein *n* (-[e]s; -e) rock, stone

Gestell [gə'ʃtɛl] *n* (-[e]s; -e) stand, base, pedestal; shelves; frame

gestern ['gɛstɐn] *adv* yesterday; **~ Abend** last night

gestiegen [gə'ʃti:gən] *pp of* **steigen**

gestochen [gə'ʃtɔxən] *pp of* **stechen**

gestohlen [gə'ʃto:lən] *pp of* **stehlen**

gestorben [gə'ʃtɔrbən] *pp of* **sterben**

ge'stoßen *pp of* **stoßen**

gestreift [gə'ʃtraift] *adj* striped

gestrichen [gə'ʃtrɪçən] *pp of* **streichen**

gestrig ['gɛstrɪç] *adj* yesterday's, of yesterday

gestritten [gə'ʃtrɪtən] *pp of* **streiten**

Gestrüpp [gə'ʃtrʏp] *n* (-[e]s; -e) brushwood, undergrowth; *fig* jungle, maze

gestunken [gə'ʃtʊŋkən] *pp of* **stinken**

Gestüt [gə'ʃty:t] *n* (-[e]s; -e) stud

Gesuch [gə'zu:x] *n* (-[e]s; -e) application, request

gesund [gə'zʊnt] *adj* healthy; healthful, *fig a.* sound; **~er Menschenverstand** common sense; **(wieder) ~ werden** get well (again), recover; **Ge'sundheit** *f* (-; *no pl*) health; **auf j-s ~ trinken** drink to s.o.'s health; **~!** bless you!; **ge'sundheitlich 1.** *adj:* **~er Zustand** state of health; **aus ~en Grün-**

den for health reasons **2.** adv: **~ geht es ihm gut** he is in good health

Ge'sundheitsamt n Public Health Department (Br Office)

ge'sundheitsschädlich adj bad for one's health

Ge'sundheits|zeugnis n health certificate; **~zustand** m state of health

gesungen [gə'zʊŋən] pp of **singen**

gesunken [gə'zʊŋkən] pp of **sinken**

getan [gə'taːn] pp of **tun**

Getöse [gə'tøːzə] n (-s; no pl) din, (deafening) noise

ge'tragen pp of **tragen**

Getränk [gə'trɛŋk] n (-[e]s; -e) drink, beverage; **Ge'tränkeauto,mat** m drinks machine

Getreide [gə'traidə] n (-s; -) cereals, grain, Br a. corn; **~ernte** f grain harvest (or crop)

ge'treten pp of **treten**

Getriebe [gə'triːbə] n (-s; -) MOT transmission

ge'trieben [gə'triːbən] pp of **treiben**

getroffen [gə'trɔfən] pp of **treffen**

getrogen [gə'troːgən] pp of **trügen**

getrost [gə'troːst] adv safely

getrunken [gə'trʊŋkən] pp of **trinken**

Getue [gə'tuːə] F n (-s; no pl) fuss

Getümmel [gə'tʏməl] n (-s; -) turmoil

Gewächs [gə'vɛks] n (-es; -e) plant; MED growth

ge'wachsen 1. pp of **wachsen**[1] **2.** fig adj: **j-m ~ sein** be a match for s.o.; **e-r Sache ~ sein** be equal to s.th., be able to cope with s.th.

Ge'wächshaus n greenhouse, hothouse

gewagt [gə'vaːkt] adj daring; fig risqué

gewählt [gə'vɛːlt] adj refined

Gewähr [gə'vɛːr] f: **~ übernehmen (für)** guarantee; **ge'währen** v/t (no -ge-, h) grant, allow; **ge'währleisten** v/t (no -ge-, h) guarantee

Gewahrsam [gə'vaːrzaːm] m: **et. (j-n) in ~ nehmen** take s.th. in safekeeping (s.o. into custody)

Gewalt [gə'valt] f (-; -en) (no pl) force, violence; power; **mit ~** by force; **höhere ~** act of God; **häusliche ~** domestic violence; **in s-e ~ bringen** seize by force; **die ~ verlieren über** (acc) lose control over; **~herrschaft** f tyranny

ge'waltig adj powerful, mighty; enormous

ge'waltlos adj nonviolent; **Ge'waltlosigkeit** f (-; no pl) nonviolence

ge'waltsam 1. adj violent **2.** adv by force; **~ öffnen** force open

ge'walttätig adj violent

Ge'walttätigkeit f (-; -en) (no pl) violence; act of violence

Ge'waltverbrechen n crime of violence

Gewand [gə'vant] n (-[e]s; Gewänder [gə'vɛndə]) robe, gown; REL vestment

gewandt [gə'vant] **1.** pp of **wenden** (v/refl) **2.** adj nimble; skil(l)ful; clever

Ge'wandtheit f (-; no pl) nimbleness; skill; ease

gewann [gə'van] pret of **gewinnen**

ge'waschen pp of **waschen**

Gewässer [gə'vɛsə] n (-s; -) body of water; pl waters

Gewebe [gə'veːbə] n (-s; -) fabric; BIOL tissue

Gewehr [gə'veːr] n (-[e]s; -e) rifle, shotgun; **~kolben** m (rifle) butt; **~lauf** m (rifle or gun) barrel

Geweih [gə'vai] n (-[e]s; -e) ZO antlers, horns

Gewerbe [gə'vɛrbə] n (-s; -) trade, business; **~schein** m trade licen|se, Br -ce

gewerblich [gə'vɛrplɪç] adj commercial, industrial; **gewerbsmäßig** [gə'vɛrpsmɛːsɪç] adj professional

Gewerkschaft [gə'vɛrkʃaft] f (-; -en) labor union, Br (trade) union

Ge'werkschaft(l)er m (-s; -), **Ge'werkschaft(l)erin** f (-; -nen) labor (Br trade) unionist; **ge'werkschaftlich** adj, **Ge'werkschafts...** in cpds labor (Br trade) union ...

ge'wesen pp of **sein**[1]

gewichen [gə'vɪçən] pp of **weichen**

Gewicht [gə'vɪçt] n (-[e]s; -e) weight; importance; **~ legen auf** (acc) stress

gewiesen [gə'viːzən] pp of **weisen**

gewillt [gə'vɪlt] adj willing, ready

Gewimmel [gə'vɪməl] n (-s; no pl) throng

Gewinde [gə'vɪndə] n (-s; -) TECH thread; **ein ~ bohren in** (acc) tap

Gewinn [gə'vɪn] m (-[e]s; -e) ECON profit (a. fig) gain(s); prize; winnings; **~bringend → gewinnbringend**

ge'winnbringend adj profitable

ge'winnen v/t and v/i (irr, no -ge-, h)

win; gain; **~d** *fig adj* winning, engaging

Gewinner [gə'vɪnɐ] *m (-s; -)*, **Ge'winnerin** *f (-; -nen)* winner

Ge'winnzahl *f* winning number

Gewirr [gə'vɪr] *n (-[e]s; no pl)* tangle; maze

gewiss [gə'vɪs] **1.** *adj* certain **2.** *adv* certainly

Ge'wissen *n (-s; -)* conscience

ge'wissenhaft *adj* conscientious

ge'wissenlos *adj* unscrupulous

Ge'wissens|bisse *pl* pricks *or* pangs of conscience; **~frage** *f* question of conscience; **~gründe** *pl*: **aus ~n** for reasons of conscience

Ge'wissheit *f (-; no pl)* certainty; **mit ~** know *etc* for certain *or* sure

Gewitter [gə'vɪtɐ] *n (-s; -)* thunderstorm; **~regen** *m* thundershower; **~wolke** *f* thundercloud

gewoben [gə'voːbən] *pp of* **weben**

gewogen [gə'voːgən] *pp of* **wiegen¹** and **wägen**

gewöhnen [gə'vøːnən] *v/t and v/refl (no -ge-, h)* **sich (j-n) ~ an** *(acc)* get (s.o.) used to; **Gewohnheit** [gə'voːnhait] *f (-; -en)* habit (**et. zu tun** of doing s.th.); **ge'wohnheitsmäßig** *adj* habitual

gewöhnlich [gə'vøːnlɪç] *adj* common, ordinary, usual; *vulgar*, F common

gewohnt [gə'voːnt] *adj* usual; **et. (zu tun) ~ sein** be used *or* accustomed to (doing) s.th.

Gewölbe [gə'vœlbə] *n (-s; -)* vault

gewölbt [gə'vœlpt] *adj* arched

gewonnen [gə'vɔnən] *pp of* **gewinnen**

geworben [gə'vɔrbən] *pp of* **werben**

geworden [gə'vɔrdən] *pp of* **werden**

geworfen [gə'vɔrfən] *pp of* **werfen**

gewrungen [gə'vrʊŋən] *pp of* **wringen**

Gewühl [gə'vyːl] *n (-[e]s; no pl)* crowd, crush

gewunden [gə'vʊndən] **1.** *pp of* **winden 2.** *adj* winding

Gewürz [gə'vʏrts] *n (-es; -e)* spice; **~gurke** *f* pickle(d gherkin)

gewusst [gə'vʊst] *pp of* **wissen**

gezackt [gə'tsakt] *adj* jagged, serrated

Ge'zeiten *pl* tide(s)

Gezeter [gə'tseːtɐ] *contp n (-s; no pl)* (shrill) clamo(u)r; nagging

geziert [gə'tsiːrt] *adj* affected

gezogen [gə'tsoːgən] *pp of* **ziehen**

Gezwitscher [gə'tsvɪtʃɐ] *n (-s; no pl)* chirp(ing), twitter(ing)

gezwungen [gə'tsvʊŋən] **1.** *pp of* **zwingen 2.** *adj* forced, unnatural

Gicht [gɪçt] *f (-; no pl)* MED gout

Giebel [giːbəl] *m (-s; -)* gable

Gier [giːɐ] *f (-; no pl)* greed(iness) (**nach** for); **gierig** ['giːrɪç] *adj* greedy (**nach, auf** *acc* for, after)

gießen ['giːsən] *v/t and v/i (irr, ge-, h)* pour; TECH cast; water

Gieße'rei *f (-; -en)* TECH foundry

'Gießkanne *f* watering pot (*Br* can)

Gift [gɪft] *n (-[e]s; -e)* poison, ZO *a.* venom *(a. fig)*; **'giftig** *adj* poisonous; venomous *(a. fig)*; poisoned; MED toxic

'Gift|müll *m* toxic waste; **~mülldepo,nie** *f* toxic waste dump; **~schlange** *f* ZO poisonous *or* venomous snake; **~stoff** *m* poisonous *or* toxic substance; pollutant; **~zahn** *m* ZO poison fang

Gigant [gi'gant] *m (-en; -en)* giant

gi'gantisch *adj* gigantic

ging [gɪŋ] *pret of* **gehen**

Gipfel ['gɪpfəl] *m (-s; -)* top, peak, summit, *fig a.* height; **~konfe,renz** *f* POL summit (meeting *or* conference)

'gipfeln *v/i (ge-, h)* culminate (**in** *dat* in)

Gips [gɪps] *m (-es; -e)* plaster (of Paris); **in ~** MED in (a) plaster (cast); **~abdruck** *m*, **~abguss** *m* plaster cast

'gipsen *v/t (ge-, h)* plaster (a. F MED)

'Gipsverband *m* MED plaster cast

Giraffe [gi'rafə] *f (-; -n)* ZO giraffe

Girlande [gɪr'landə] *f (-; -n)* garland, festoon

Girokonto ['ʒiːrokɔnto] *n* checking (*or* current) account; postal check (*Br* giro) account

Gischt [gɪʃt] *m (-[e]s; -e), f (-; -en)* (sea) spray, spindrift

Gitarre [gi'tarə] *f (-; -n)* MUS guitar

Gitarrist [gita'rɪst] *m (-en; -en)* guitarist

Gitter ['gɪtɐ] *n (-s; -)* lattice; grating; F **hinter ~n (sitzen)** (be) behind bars

'Gitterbett *n* crib, *Br* cot

'Gitterfenster *n* latticed (window)

Glanz [glants] *m (-es; no pl)* shine, gloss *(a.* TECH*)*, luster, *Br* lustre, brilliance *(a. fig)*; *fig* splendo(u)r, glamo(u)r

glänzen ['glɛntsən] *v/i (ge-, h)* shine, gleam; glitter, glisten; **~d** *adj* shining, shiny, bright; PHOT glossy; *fig* brilliant, excellent

Gletscherspalte

'**Glanz|leistung** f brilliant achievement; ~**zeit** f heyday

Glas [glaːs] n (-es; Gläser ['glɛːzə]) glass

Glaser ['glaːzɐ] m (-s; -) glazier

gläsern ['glɛːzɐn] adj (of) glass

'**Glas|faser** f, ~**fiber** f glass fiber (Br fibre); ~**hütte** f TECH glassworks

glasieren [gla'ziːrən] v/t (no -ge-, h) glaze; GASTR ice, frost

glasig ['glaːzɪç] adj glassy

'**glasklar** adj crystal-clear (a. fig)

'**Glasscheibe** f (glass) pane

Glasur [gla'zuːɐ] f (-; -en) glaze; GASTR icing

glatt [glat] adj smooth (a. fig); slippery; fig clear; **Glätte** ['glɛtə] f (-; no pl) smoothness (a. fig); slipperiness

'**Glatteis** n (glare, BR black) ice; **es herrscht ~** the roads are icy; F **j-n aufs ~ führen** mislead s.o.

glätten ['glɛtən] v/t (ge-, h) smooth; Swiss: → **bügeln**

'**glattgehen** v/i (irr, sep, -ge-, sein) F work (out well), go (off) well

Glatze ['glatsə] f (-; -n) bald head; **e-e ~ haben** be bald

Glaube ['glaubə] m (-ns; no pl) belief, esp REL faith (both: **an** acc in)

glauben v/t and v/i (ge-, h) believe; think, guess; ~ **an** (acc) believe in (a. REL)

'**Glaubens|bekenntnis** n REL creed, profession or confession of faith; ~**leh-re** f, ~**satz** m dogma, doctrine

glaubhaft ['glauphaft] adj credible, plausible

gläubig ['glɔybɪç] adj religious; devout; **die Gläubigen** the faithful

Gläubiger ['glɔybɪgɐ] m (-s; -), '**Gläubigerin** f (-; -nen) ECON creditor

'**glaubwürdig** adj credible; reliable

gleich [glaɪç] **1.** adj same; equal (right etc); **auf die ~e Art** (in) the same way; **zur ~en Zeit** at the same time; **das ist mir ~** it's all the same to me; **ganz ~, wann** etc no matter when etc; **das Gleiche** the same; (**ist**) **~ ...** MATH equals ..., is ...; ~ **bleibend** → **gleichbleibend**; ~ **gesinnt** like-minded; ~ **lautend** → **gleichlautend 2.** adv equally, alike; at once, right away; in a moment or minute; ~ **groß** (**alt**) of the same size (age); ~ **nach** (**neben**) right after (next to); ~ **gegenüber** just oppo-

site or across the street; **es ist ~ 5 Uhr** it's almost 5 o'clock; ~ **aussehen** (**gekleidet sein**) look (be dressed) alike; **bis ~!** see you soon or later!; **gleichaltrig** ['glaɪçˀaltrɪç] adj (of) the same age

'**gleichberechtigt** adj equal, having equal rights; '**Gleichberechtigung** f (-; no pl) equal rights

'**gleichbleibend** adj constant, steady

'**gleichen** v/i (irr, ge-, h) (dat) be or look like

'**gleichfalls** adv also, likewise; **danke, ~!** (thanks,) the same to you

gleichförmig ['glaɪçfœrmɪç] adj uniform

'**Gleichgewicht** n (-[e]s; no pl) balance (a. fig)

'**gleichgültig** adj indifferent (**gegen** to); careless; **das (er) ist mir ~** I don't care (for him); '**Gleichgültigkeit** f (-; no pl) indifference

'**Gleichheit** f (-; no pl) equality

'**gleichkommen** v/i (irr, kommen, sep, -ge-, sein) **e-r Sache** ~ amount to s.th.; **j-m ~** equal s.o. (**an** dat in)

'**gleichlautend** adj identical

'**gleichmäßig** adj regular; constant; even

gleichnamig ['glaɪçnaːmɪç] adj of the same name

'**Gleichnis** n (-ses; -se) parable

'**gleichsam** adv as it were, so to speak

'**gleichseitig** ['glaɪçzaɪtɪç] adj MATH equilateral

'**gleich|setzen**, ~**stellen** v/t (sep, -ge-, h) equate (dat to, with); put s.o. on an equal footing (with)

'**Gleichstrom** m ELECTR direct current

'**Gleichung** f (-; -en) MATH equation

'**gleichwertig** adj equally good; **j-m ~ sein** be a match for s.o. (a. SPORT)

'**gleichzeitig** adj simultaneous; **beide ~** both at the same time

Gleis [glaɪs] n (-es; -e) RAIL rail(s), track(s), line; platform, gate

gleiten ['glaɪtən] v/i (irr, ge-, sein) glide, slide; ~**d** adj: ~**e Arbeitszeit** flexible working hours, flextime, Br a. flexi-time

'**Gleitflug** m glide

'**Gleitschirm|fliegen** n paragliding; ~**flieger** m paraglider

Gletscher ['glɛtʃɐ] m (-s; -) glacier; ~**spalte** f crevasse

glich [glıç] *pret of* **gleichen**
Glied [gliːt] *n* (-es; Glieder ['gliːdɐ])
ANAT limb; penis; TECH link
gliedern ['gliːdɐn] *v/t* (*ge-*, *h*) structure;
divide (**in** *acc* into)
Gliederung ['gliːdərʊŋ] *f* (-; -en) structure, arrangement; outline
'Gliedmaßen *pl* ANAT limbs, extremities
glimmen ['glɪmən] *v/i* (*[irr.]*, *ge-*, *h*) glow;
smo(u)lder
'Glimmstängel F *m* (-s; -) cigarette, *Br*
sl fag
glimpflich ['glɪmpflɪç] **1.** *adj* lenient,
mild **2.** *adv*: **~ davonkommen** get off
lightly
glitschig ['glɪtʃɪç] *adj* slippery
glitt [glɪt] *pret of* **gleiten**
glitzern ['glɪtsɐn] *v/i* (*ge-*, *h*) glitter,
sparkle, glint
global [gloˈbaːl] *adj* global
Globus ['gloːbʊs] *m* (-[ses]; -se) globe
Glocke ['glɔkə] *f* (-; -n) bell
'Glocken|blume *f* bluebell; **~spiel** *n*
chimes; **~turm** *m* bell tower, belfry
glomm [glɔm] *pret of* **glimmen**
glorreich ['gloːʁraıç] *adj* glorious
Glotze ['glɔtsə] F *f* (-; -n) TV the tube, *Br*
goggle box; 'glotzen F *v/i* (*ge-*, *h*) goggle, gape, stare
Glück [glʏk] *n* (-[e]s; *no pl*) (good) luck,
fortune; happiness; **~ haben** be lucky;
zum ~ fortunately; **viel ~!** good luck!
Glucke ['glʊkə] *f* (-; -n) ZO sitting hen;
fig hen
gluckern ['glʊkɐn] *v/i* (*ge-*, *h*) gurgle
'glücklich *adj* happy; **~er Zufall** lucky
chance
'glücklicher'weise *adv* fortunately
'Glücks|bringer *m* (-s; -) lucky charm;
~fall *m* lucky chance; **~pfennig** *m*
lucky penny; **~pilz** *m* lucky fellow;
~spiel *n* game of chance; *coll* gambling; **~spieler** *m* gambler; **~tag** *m*
lucky day
'glückstrahlend *adj* radiant
'Glückwunsch *m* congratulations;
herzlichen ~! congratulations!; happy
birthday!
Glühbirne ['glyːbɪrnə] *f* ELECTR light
bulb
glühen ['glyːən] *v/i* (*ge-*, *h*) glow (*a. fig*)
glühend ['glyːənt] *adj* glowing; red-hot
(*iron*); *fig* burning; **~ heiß** blazing hot
'Glühwein *m* mulled wine

Glut [gluːt] *f* (-; -en) (glowing) fire; em-
bers; live coals; *fig* ardo(u)r
'Gluthitze *f* blazing heat
GmbH [geːʔɛmbeːˈhaː] *abbr of* **Gesellschaft mit beschränkter Haftung** private limited liability company
Gnade ['gnaːdə] *f* (-; -n) mercy, *esp* REL
a. grace; favo(u)r
'Gnaden|frist *f* reprieve; **~gesuch** *n* JUR
petition for mercy
'gnadenlos *adj* merciless
gnädig ['gnɛːdɪç] *adj* gracious; *esp* REL
merciful
Gold [gɔlt] *n* (-[e]s; *no pl*) gold; **~barren**
m gold bar *or* ingot; *coll* bullion
golden ['gɔldən] *adj* gold; *fig* golden
'Goldfisch *m* ZO goldfish
'goldgelb *adj* golden (yellow)
'Gold|gräber ['gɔltgrɛːbɐ] *m* (-s; -) gold
digger; **~grube** *fig f* goldmine, bonanza
goldig ['gɔldɪç] *adj* sweet, lovely, cute
'Gold|mine *f* goldmine; **~münze** *f* gold
coin; **~schmied** *m* goldsmith; **~stück** *n*
gold coin
Golf[1] [gɔlf] *m* (-[e]s; -e) GEOGR gulf
Golf[2] *n* (-s; *no pl*) SPORT golf; **~platz** *m*
golf course; **~schläger** *m* golf club;
~spieler *m* golfer
Gondel ['gɔndəl] *f* (-; -n) gondola; cabin
Gong [gɔŋ] *m* (-s; -s) gong
gönnen ['gœnən] *v/t* (*ge-*, *h*) *j-m et.* ~ not
(be)grudge s.o. s.th.; *j-m et. nicht* ~
(be)grudge s.o. s.th.; *sich et.* ~ allow
o.s. s.th., treat o.s. to s.th.
gönnerhaft ['gœnɐhaft] *adj* patronizing
gor [goːɐ] *pret of* **gären**
Gorilla [goˈrɪla] *m* (-s; -s) ZO gorilla
goss [gɔs] *pret of* **gießen**
Gosse ['gɔsə] *f* (-; -n) gutter (*a. fig*)
Gotik ['goːtɪk] *f* (-; *no pl*) ARCH Gothic
style *or* period; 'gotisch *adj* Gothic
Gott [gɔt] *m* (-[e]s; Götter ['gœtɐ]) REL
God, Lord; MYTH god; **~ sei Dank!**(!)
thank God(!); **um ~es Willen!** for
heaven's sake!; 'gottgeben *adj* resigned (to the will of God)
'Gottesdienst *m* REL (divine) service
gottesfürchtig ['gɔtəsfʏrçtɪç] *adj* god-
-fearing
'Gottes|lästerer ['gɔtəslɛstərə] *m* (-s; -)
blasphemer; 'Gotteslästerung *f* (-;
-en) blasphemy
'Gottheit *f* (-; -en) deity, divinity
Göttin ['gœtɪn] *f* (-; -nen) goddess

'göttlich ['gœtlıç] *adj* divine

gott'lob *int* thank God *or* goodness!

'gottlos *adj* godless, wicked

'gottverlassen F *adj* godforsaken

'Gottvertrauen *n* trust in God

Götze ['gœtsə] *m* (-n; -n), **'Götzenbild** *n* idol

Gouverneur [guvɛr'nøːɐ] *m* (-s; -e) governor

Grab [graːp] *n* (-[e]s; *Gräber* ['grɛːbɐ]) grave; tomb

graben ['graːbən] *v/t and v/i* (*irr*, *ge*, *h*) dig, zo *a.* burrow; **'Graben** *m* (-s; *Gräben* ['grɛːbən]) ditch; MIL trench

'Grab|mal *n* monument; tomb; ~**rede** *f* funeral address; ~**schrift** *f* epitaph; ~**stätte** *f* burial place; grave, tomb; ~**stein** *m* tombstone, gravestone

Grad [graːt] *m* (-[e]s; -e) degree; MIL *etc* rank, grade; **15 ~ Kälte** 15 degrees below zero; ~**einteilung** *f* graduation

graduell [gra'duɛl] *adj* in degree

Graf [graːf] *m* (-en; -en) count, *Br* earl

Graffiti [gra'fiːti] *pl* graffiti

Grafik ['graːfɪk] *f* (-; -en) (*no pl*) graphic arts; print; MATH, TECH graph, diagram; (*no pl*) art(work), illustrations; (*no pl*) IT graphics

'Grafiker *m* (-s; -), **'Grafikerin** *f* (-; -nen) graphic artist

Gräfin ['grɛːfɪn] *f* (-; -nen) countess

grafisch ['graːfɪʃ] *adj* graphic

Grafologie *f* → **Graphologie**

'Grafschaft *f* (-; -en) county

Gramm [gram] *n* (-s; -e) gram

Grammatik [gra'matɪk] *f* (-; -en) grammar; **gram'matisch** *adj* grammatical

Granat [gra'naːt] *m* (-[e]s; -e) MIN garnet

Gra'nate *f* (-; -n) MIL shell

Gra'nat|splitter *m* MIL shell splinter; ~**werfer** *m* MIL mortar

grandios [gran'djoːs] *adj* magnificent, grand

Granit [gra'niːt] *m* (-s; -e) granite

Graphik *f etc* → **Grafik** *etc*

Graphologie [grafolo'giː] *f* (-; *no pl*) graphology

Gras [graːs] *n* (-es; *Gräser* ['grɛːzɐ]) grass; **grasen** ['graːzən] *v/i* (*ge*, *h*) graze; **'Grashalm** *m* blade of grass

grassieren [gra'siːrən] *v/i* (*no* -*ge*-, *h*) rage, be rife

grässlich ['grɛslıç] *adj* hideous, atrocious

Gräte ['grɛːtə] *f* (-; -n) (fish)bone

Gratifikation [gratifika'tsjoːn] *f* (-; -en) gratuity, bonus

gratis ['graːtɪs] *adv* free (of charge)

Grätsche ['grɛːtʃə] *f* (-; -n), **'grätschen** *v/i* (*ge*, *h*) straddle; *soccer*: stride tackle

Gratulant [gratu'lant] *m* (-en; -en), **Gratu'lantin** *f* (-; -nen) congratulator; **Gratulation** [gratula'tsjoːn] *f* (-; -en) congratulation; **gratulieren** [gratu'liːrən] *v/i* (*no* -*ge*-, *h*) congratulate (*j-m zu et.* s.o. on s.th.); *j-m zum Geburtstag ~* wish s.o. many happy returns (of the day)

grau [grau] *adj* gray, *Br* grey

'Graubrot *n* rye bread

Gräuel ['grɔyəl] *m* (-s; -) horror

'Gräueltat *f* atrocity

'grauen *v/i* (*ge*, *h*) **mir graut es vor** (*dat*) I dread (the thought of)

'Grauen *n* (-s; -) horror

'grauenhaft, **'grauenvoll** *adj* horrible, horrifying

Graupel ['graupəl] *f* (-; -n) sleet, soft hail

grausam ['grauzaːm] *adj* cruel

'Grausamkeit *f* (-; -en) cruelty

grausig ['grauzıç] *adj* → **grauenhaft**

'Grauzone *f* fig gray (*Br* grey) area

gravieren [gra'viːrən] *v/t* (*no* -*ge*-, *h*) engrave; ~**d** *adj* serious

Gravur [gra'vuːɐ] *f* (-; -en) engraving

Grazie ['graːtsjə] *f* (-; *no pl*) grace

graziös [gra'tsjøːs] *adj* graceful

greifen ['graifən] (*irr*, *ge*, *h*) **1.** *v/t* seize, grasp, grab, take *or* catch hold of **2.** *v/i* *fig* take effect; ~ *nach* reach for; grasp at

Greis [grais] *m* (-es; -e) (very) old man; **greisenhaft** ['graizənhaft] *adj* senile (*a.* MED); **Greisin** ['graizɪn] *f* (-; -nen) (very) old woman

grell [grɛl] *adj* glaring; shrill

Grenze ['grɛntsə] *f* (-; -n) border; boundary; *fig* limit; **'grenzen** *v/i* (*ge*, *h*) ~ *an* (*acc*) border on

'grenzenlos *adj* boundless

'Grenz|fall *m* borderline case; ~**land** *n* borderland, frontier; ~**linie** *f* borderline, POL demarcation line; ~**stein** *m* boundary stone; ~**übergang** *m* frontier crossing (point), checkpoint

Greuel *m* → **Gräuel**

Grieche ['griːçə] *m* (-n; -n) Greek;

'**Griechenland** Greece; '**Griechin** f (-; -nen), '**griechisch** adj Greek

Grieß [gri:s] m (-es; -e) semolina

griff [grɪf] pret of **greifen**

Griff m (-[e]s; -e) grip, grasp; handle

'**griffbereit** adj at hand, handy

Grill [grɪl] m (-s; -s) grill

Grille ['grɪlə] f (-; -n) zo cricket

'**grillen** v/t (ge-, h) grill, barbecue

Grimasse [gri'masə] f (-; -n) grimace; **~n schneiden** pull faces

grimmig ['grɪmɪç] adj grim

grinsen ['grɪnzən] v/i (ge-, h) grin (**über** acc at); **höhnisch** or **spöttisch ~** (**über** acc) sneer (at); '**Grinsen** n (-s; no pl) grin; **höhnisches** or **spöttisches ~** sneer

Grippe ['grɪpə] f (-; -n) MED influenza, F flu

Grips [grɪps] F m (-es; no pl) brains

grob [gro:p] **1.** adj coarse (a. fig); fig gross; crude; rude; rough **2.** adv: **~ geschätzt** at a rough estimate

'**Grobheit** f (-; no pl) coarseness; roughness; rudeness

grölen ['grø:lən] F v/t and v/i (ge-, h) bawl

Groll [grɔl] m (-[e]s; no pl) grudge, ill will; '**grollen** v/i (ge-, h) **j-m ~** bear s.o. a grudge

Groschen ['grɔʃən] m (-s; -) hist (former monetary unit of Austria) groschen; F ten-pfennig piece, ten pfennigs

groß [gro:s] adj big; large (a. family); tall; grown-up; F big (brother etc); fig great (a. fun, trouble, pain etc); capital (letter); **~es Geld** bills, Br notes; **~e Ferien** summer vacation, Br summer holiday(s); **Groß und Klein** young and old; **im Großen und Ganzen** on the whole; F **~ in et. sein** be great at (doing) s.th.; **wie ~ ist es?** what size is it?; **wie ~ bist du?** how tall are you?

'**großartig** adj great, F a. terrific

'**Großaufnahme** f film: close-up

Größe ['grø:sə] f (-; -n) size; height; esp MATH quantity; fig greatness; celebrity

'**Großeltern** pl grandparents

'**großen'teils** adv to a large or great extent, largely

'**Größenwahn** m megalomania (a. fig)

'**Groß|fa‚milie** f extended family; **~händel** m ECON wholesale (trade); **~händ**-

ler m ECON wholesale dealer, wholesaler; **~handlung** f ECON wholesale business; **~indus‚trie** f big industry; big business; **~industri‚elle** m big industrialist, F tycoon; **~macht** f POL great power; **~markt** m ECON hypermarket; wholesale market; **~maul** F n braggart; **~mutter** f grandmother; **~raum** m conurbation, metropolitan area; **der ~ München** Greater Munich, the Greater Munich area; **~raumflugzeug** n wide-bodied jet

'**großschreiben** v/t (irr, schreiben, sep, -ge-, h) capitalize; '**Großschreibung** f (use of) capitalization

großsprecherisch ['gro:sʃprɛçərɪʃ] adj boastful

großspurig ['gro:sʃpu:rɪç] adj arrogant

'**Großstadt** f big city; '**großstädtisch** adj of or in a big city, urban

'**größten'teils** adv mostly, mainly

'**großtun** v/i (irr, tun, sep, -ge-, h) show off; **sich mit et. ~** brag about s.th.

'**Großvater** m grandfather

'**Großverdiener** m (-s; -) big earner

'**Großwild** n big game

'**großziehen** v/t (irr, ziehen, sep, -ge-, h) raise, rear; bring up

'**großzügig** adj generous, liberal; ... on a large scale; spacious

'**Großzügigkeit** f (-; no pl) generosity, liberality; spaciousness

grotesk [gro'tɛsk] adj grotesque

Grotte ['grɔtə] f (-; -n) grotto

grub [gru:p] pret of **graben**

Grübchen ['gry:pçən] n (-s; -) dimple

Grube ['gru:bə] f (-; -n) pit; mine

Grübelei [gry:bə'lai] f (-; -en) pondering, musing

grübeln ['gry:bəln] v/i (ge-, h) ponder, muse (**über** acc on, over)

Gruft [gruft] f (-; Grüfte ['gryftə]) tomb, vault

grün [gry:n] adj green; **Grün** n (-s; -) green; **im ~en** in the country

'**Grünanlage** f park

Grund [grunt] m (-[e]s; Gründe ['gryndə]) reason; cause; ground, AGR a. soil; bottom; **~ und Boden** property, land; **aus diesem ~e** for this reason; **von ~ auf** entirely; **im ~e** (**genommen**) actually, basically; → **aufgrund**; → **zugrunde**

'**Grund...** in cpds ...bedeutung, ...be-

dingung, ...regel, ...prinzip, ...wort-
schatz etc: *mst* basic ...;~**begriffe** *pl* ba-
sics, fundamentals; ~**besitz** *m* property, land; ~**besitzer** *m* landowner
gründen ['gryndən] *v/t* (*ge-, h*) found (*a.*
family), set up, establish; **sich ~ auf**
(*dat*) be based *or* founded on
Gründer ['gryndɐ] *m* (*-s; -*), '**Gründerin**
f (*-; -nen*) founder
'**grund**'**falsch** *adj* absolutely wrong
'**Grund|fläche** *f* MATH base; ARCH area;
~**gedanke** *m* basic idea; ~**geschwin-**
digkeit *f* AVIAT ground speed; ~**gesetz**
n POL Basic (Constitutional) Law (for
the Federal Republic of Germany);
~**lage** *f* foundation, *fig a.* basis; *pl* (basic) essentials
'**grundlegend** *adj* fundamental, basic
gründlich ['gryntlɪç] *adj* thorough
'**Grundlinie** *f* tennis etc: base line
'**grundlos** *adj* groundless, unfounded
'**Grundmauer** *f* foundation
Grün'**donnerstag** *m* REL Maundy *or*
Holy Thursday
'**Grund|rechnungsart** *f* MATH basic ar-
ithmetical operation; ~**riss** *m* ARCH
ground plan; ~**satz** *m* principle
grundsätzlich ['gruntzetslɪç] **1.** *adj*
fundamental **2.** *adv:* **ich bin~ dagegen**
I am against it on principle
'**Grund|schule** *f* elementary (*or* grade)
school, *Br* primary (*or* junior) school;
~**stein** *m* ARCH foundation stone; *fig*
foundations; ~**stück** *n* plot (of land),
lot; (building) site; premises; ~**stücks-**
makler *m* realtor, *Br* real estate agent
'**Gründung** *f* (*-; -en*) foundation, establishment, setting up
'**grundver**'**schieden** *adj* totally different
'**Grund|wasser** *n* ground water; ~**zahl** *f*
cardinal number; ~**zug** *m* main feature, characteristic
Grüne ['gry:nə] *m, f* (*-n; -n*) POL Green
'**Grünfläche** *f* green space
'**grünlich** *adj* greenish
'**Grünspan** *m* (*-[e]s; no pl*) verdigris
grunzen ['gruntsən] *v/i and v/t* (*ge-, h*)
grunt
Gruppe ['grupə] *f* (*-; -n*) group
'**Gruppenreise** *f* group tour
gruppieren [gru'pi:rən] *v/t* (*no -ge-, h*)
group, arrange in groups; **sich ~** form
groups

Grusel... ['gru:zəl-] *in cpds* ...**film** etc:
horror ...; '**gruselig** *adj* eerie, creepy,
spine-chilling; '**gruseln** *v/t and v/refl*
(*ge-, h*) **es gruselt mich** F it gives me
the creeps
Gruß [gru:s] *m* (*-es; Grüße* ['gry:sə])
greeting(s); MIL salute; **viele Grüße**
an (*acc*) ... give my regards (*or* love)
to ...; **mit freundlichen Grüßen** yours
sincerely; **herzliche Grüße** best wish-
es; love
grüßen ['gry:sən] *v/t* (*ge-, h*) greet, F say
hello to; MIL salute; **~ Sie ihn von mir**
give my regards (*or* love) to him
gucken ['gukən] *v/i* (*ge-, h*) look
'**Guckloch** *n* peephole
Güggeli ['gy:gəli] *n* (*-s; -*) Swiss chicken
gültig ['gyltɪç] *adj* valid; current
'**Gültigkeit** *f* (*-; no pl*) validity; *s-e* ~ **ver-**
lieren expire
Gummi ['gumi] *m, n* (*-s; -[s]*) rubber;
~**band** *n* (*-[e]s; -bänder*) rubber (*esp*
Br a. elastic) band; ~**bärchen** *pl* gum-
my bears; ~**baum** *m* BOT rubber tree;
rubber plant
gummieren [gu'mi:rən] *v/t* (*no -ge-, h*)
gum
'**Gummi|knüppel** *m* truncheon; ~**stie-**
fel *m* rubber boot, *esp Br* wellington
(boot); ~**zug** *m* elastic
Gunst [gunst] *f* (*-; no pl*) favo(u)r, good-
will; → **zugunsten**
günstig ['gynstɪç] *adj* favo(u)rable (**für**
to); convenient; **im ~sten Fall** at best;
~e Gelegenheit chance
Gurgel ['gurgəl] *f* (*-; -n*) throat; *j-m an*
die **~ springen** fly at s.o.'s throat;
'**gurgeln** *v/i* (*ge-, h*) MED gargle
Gurke ['gurkə] *f* (*-; -n*) BOT cucumber
gurren ['gurən] *v/i* (*ge-, h*) ZO coo
Gurt [gurt] *m* (*-[e]s; -e*) belt (*a.* MOT and
AVIAT); strap
Gürtel ['gyrtəl] *m* (*-s; -*) belt; ~**reifen** *m*
MOT radial (tire, *Br* tyre)
GUS [gus, ge:?u:'?ɛs] *abbr of* **Gemein-**
schaft Unabhängiger Staaten CIS,
Commonwealth of Independent States
Guss [gus] *m* (*-es; Güsse* ['gysə]) downpour; TECH casting; GASTR icing; *fig* **aus**
e-m ~ of a piece; '**Gusseisen** *n* cast
iron; '**gusseisern** *adj* cast-iron
gut [gu:t] **1.** *adj* good; fine; **ganz ~** not
bad; **also ~!** all right (then)!; **schon**
~! never mind!; (**wieder**) **~ werden**

come right (again), be all right; **~e Reise!** have a nice trip!; **sei bitte so ~ und ...** would you be so good as to or good enough to ...; **in et. ~ sein** be good at (doing) s.th. **2.** adv well; **look, taste** etc good; **du hast es ~** you are lucky; **es ist ~ möglich** it may well be; **es gefällt mir ~** I (do) like it; **~ gebaut** well-built; **~ gelaunt** in a good mood; **~ gemacht!** well done!; **mach's ~!** take care (of yourself)!; **~ gehen** go (off) well, work out well or all right; **wenn alles ~ geht** if nothing goes wrong; **mir geht es ~** I'm (doing) well; **Gut n** (-[e]s; Güter ['gy:tɐ]) estate; pl goods

'Gutachten n (-s; -) (expert) opinion; certificate; **Gutachter** ['gu:ʔaxtɐ] m (-s; -) expert

'gutartig adj good-natured; MED benign

Gutdünken ['gu:tdyŋkən] n: **nach ~** at one's discretion

Gute ['gu:tə] n (-n; no pl) good; **~s tun** do good; **alles ~!** all the best!, good luck!

Güte ['gy:tə] f (-; no pl) goodness, kindness; ECON quality; F **meine ~!** good gracious!

Güter|bahnhof ['gy:tɐba:nho:f] m freight depot, Br goods station; **~gemeinschaft** f JUR community of property; **~trennung** f JUR separation of property; **~verkehr** m freight (Br goods) traffic; **~wagen** m freight car, Br goods wag(g)on; **~zug** m freight (Br goods) train

'gutgläubig adj credulous

'Guthaben n (-s; -) ECON credit (balance)

'gutheißen v/t (irr, **heißen**, sep, -ge-, h) approve (of)

'gutherzig adj kind(-hearted)

gütig ['gy:tɪç] adj good, kind(ly)

gütlich ['gy:tlɪç] adv: **sich ~ einigen** come to an amicable settlement

'gutmachen v/t (sep, -ge-, h) make up for, repay

gutmütig ['gu:tmy:tɪç] adj good-natured

'Gutmütigkeit f (-; no pl) good nature

'Gutsbesitzer m, **'Gutsbesitzerin** f (-; -nen) estate owner

'Gutschein m coupon, esp Br voucher

'gutschreiben v/t (irr, **schreiben**, sep, -ge-, h) **j-m et. ~** credit s.th. to s.o.'s account; **'Gutschrift** f credit

'Gutshaus n manor (house)

'Gutshof m estate, manor

'gutstehen v/refl (irr, **stehen**, sep, -ge-, h): **sich ~** be well off; F **sich gut mit j-m stehen → stehen**

'Gutsverwalter m steward, manager

'gutwillig adj willing

Gymnasium [gym'na:zjum] n (-s; -ien) high school, Br appr grammar school

Gymnastik [gym'nastɪk] f (-; no pl) exercises, gymnastics; **gym'nastisch** adj: **~e Übungen** physical exercises

Gynäkologe [gyneko'lo:gə] m (-n; -n), **Gynäko'login** f (-; -nen) MED gyn(a)ecologist

H

Haar [ha:ɐ] n (-[e]s; -e ['ha:rə]) hair; **sich die ~e kämmen (schneiden lassen)** comb one's hair (have one's hair cut); **sich aufs ~ gleichen** look absolutely identical; **um ein ~** by a hair's breadth

'Haarausfall m loss of hair

'Haarbürste f hairbrush

haaren ['ha:rən] v/i and v/refl (ge-, h) ZO lose its hair; fur: shed hairs

'Haaresbreite f: **um ~** by a hair's breadth

'haarfein adj (as) fine as a hair

'Haarfestiger m (-s; -) setting lotion

'Haargefäß n ANAT capillary (vessel)

'haargenau F adv precisely; **(stimmt) ~!** dead right!

haarig ['ha:rɪç] adj hairy

'haarklein F adv to the last detail

'Haar|klemme f bobby pin, Br hair clip; **~nadel** f hairpin; **~nadelkurve** f hairpin bend; **~netz** n hair-net

'haarscharf F adv by a hair's breadth

'Haar|schnitt m haircut; **~spalterei** f (-; no pl) hair-splitting; **~spange** f barrette, Br (hair) slide; **~spray** m, n hairspray

'**haarsträubend** *adj* hair-raising

'**Haar**|**teil** *n* hairpiece; **~trockner** *m* hair dryer; **~wäsche** *f,* **~waschmittel** *n* shampoo; **~wasser** *n* hair tonic; **~wuchs** *m,* **haben** **~ haben** have a lot of hair; **~wuchsmittel** *n* hair restorer

haben ['ha:bən] *v/t (irr, ge-, h)* have (got); **Hunger ~** be hungry; **Durst ~** be thirsty; **Ferien (Urlaub) ~** be on vacation (*Br* holiday); **er hat Geburtstag** it's his birthday; **welche Farbe hat ...?** what colo(u)r is ...?; **zu ~ sein** be available; F **sich ~** make a fuss; F **was hast du?** what's the matter with you?; F **da~ wir's!** there we are!; → **Datum**

'**Haben** *n (-s; no pl)* ECON credit

Habgier ['ha:pgi:ɐ] *f* greed(iness)

'**habgierig** *adj* greedy

Habicht ['ha:bɪçt] *m (-s; -e)* ZO hawk

'**Habseligkeiten** *pl* belongings

Hacke ['hakə] *f (-; -n)* AGR hoe; (pick-)axe; ANAT heel; '**hacken** *v/t (ge-, h)* chop; AGR hoe; ZO peck

'**Hackentrick** *m* soccer: backheeler

Hacker ['hakɐ] *m (-s; -)* IT hacker

'**Hack**|**fleisch** *n* ground (*Br* minced) meat; **~ordnung** *f* ZO pecking order

Hafen ['ha:fən] *m (-s; Häfen* ['hɛ:fən]) harbo(u)r, port; **~arbeiter** *m* docker, longshoreman; **~stadt** *f* (sea)port

Hafer ['ha:fɐ] *m (-s; -)* BOT oats; **~brei** *m* oatmeal, *Br* porridge; **~flocken** *pl* (rolled) oats; **~schleim** *m* gruel

Haft [haft] *f (-; no pl)* JUR confinement, imprisonment; **in ~** under arrest

'**haftbar** *adj* responsible, JUR liable

'**Haftbefehl** *m* JUR warrant of arrest

haften *v/i (ge-, h)* stick, adhere (**an** *dat* to); **~ für** JUR answer for, be liable for

Häftling ['hɛftlɪŋ] *m (-s; -e)* prisoner, convict

'**Haftpflicht** *f* JUR liability; **~versicherung** *f* liability insurance; MOT third party insurance

Haftung *f (-; -en)* responsibility, JUR liability; **mit beschränkter ~** limited

Hagel ['ha:gəl] *m (-s; no pl)* hail, *fig a.* shower, volley; '**Hagelkorn** *n* hailstone; '**hageln** *v/i (ge-, h)* hail (*a. fig*); '**Hagelschauer** *m* hail shower

hager ['ha:gɐ] *adj* lean, gaunt, haggard

Hahn [ha:n] *m (-[e]s; Hähne* ['hɛ:nə]) ZO

cock, rooster; TECH (water) tap, faucet

Hähnchen ['hɛ:nçən] *n (-s; -)* ZO chicken

'**Hahnenkamm** *m* ZO cockscomb

Hai [hai] *m (-[e]s; -e),* **~fisch** *m* ZO shark

häkeln ['hɛ:kəln] *v/t and v/i (ge-, h)* crochet

Haken ['ha:kən] *m (-s; -)* hook (*a. boxing*), peg; check, *Br* tick; F snag, catch

'**Hakenkreuz** *n* swastika

halb [halp] *adj and adv* half; **e-e ~e Stunde** half an hour; **ein ~es Pfund** half a pound; **zum ~en Preis** at half-price; **auf ~em Wege (entgegenkommen)** (meet) halfway; **~ so viel** half as much; F **(mit j-m) halbe-halbe machen** go halves *or* fifty-fifty (with s.o.); **~ gar** GASTR underdone

'**Halbbruder** *m* half-brother

'**Halbdunkel** *n* semi-darkness

Halbe ['halbə] *f (-n; -)* pint (of beer)

'**halbfett** *adj* GASTR medium-fat; PRINT semi-bold

'**Halbfi**,**nale** *n* SPORT semifinal

'**Halbgott** *m* demigod

'**halbherzig** *adj* half-hearted

halbieren [hal'bi:rən] *v/t (no -ge-, h)* halve; MATH bisect

'**Halbinsel** *f* peninsula

'**Halbjahr** *n* six months; **halbjährig** ['halpjɛ:rɪç] *adj* six-month; '**halbjährlich 1.** *adj* half-yearly **2.** *adv* half-yearly, twice a year

'**Halbkreis** *m* semicircle

'**Halbkugel** *f* hemisphere

'**halblaut 1.** *adj* low, subdued **2.** *adv* in an undertone

'**Halbleiter** *m* ELECTR semiconductor

'**halbmast** *adv* (at) half-mast

'**Halb**|**mond** *m* half-moon, crescent; **~pensi**,**on** *f (-; no pl) esp Br* half board; **~schlaf** *m* doze; **~schuh** *m* (low) shoe; **~schwester** *f* half-sister

'**halbtags** *adv*: **~ arbeiten** work part-time; '**Halbtagsarbeit** *f (-; no pl)* part-time job; '**Halbtagskraft** *f* part-time worker, F part-timer

halbwegs ['halpve:ks] *adv* reasonably

Halbwüchsige ['halpvy:ksɪgə] *m, f (-n; -n)* adolescent

'**Halbzeit** *f* SPORT half (time); **~stand** *m* SPORT half-time score

Halde ['haldə] *f (-; -n)* slope; dump

half [half] *pret of* **helfen**

Hälfte ['hɛlftə] *f* (-; -n) half; **die ~ von** half of

Halfter ['halftɐ] **1.** *m, n* (-s; -) halter **2.** *n* (-s; -), *f* (-; -n) holster

Halle ['halə] *f* (-; -n) hall; lounge; **in der ~** SPORT *etc* indoors

'**hallen** *v/i* (ge-, h) resound, reverberate

'**Hallenbad** *n* indoor swimming pool

'**Hallensport** *m* indoor sports

Halm [halm] *m* (-[e]s; -e) BOT blade; ha(u)lm, stalk; straw

Hals [hals] *m* (-es; *Hälse* ['hɛlzə]) ANAT neck; throat; **~ über Kopf** helter-skelter; F **sich vom ~ schaffen** get rid of; F **es hängt mir zum ~ (e)** (he)**raus** I'm fed up with it; *fig* **bis zum ~** up to one's neck;**~band** *n* (-[e]s; -bänder) necklace; collar; **~entzündung** *f* MED sore throat; **~kette** *f* necklace; **~schmerzen** *pl:* **~ haben** have a sore throat

halsstarrig ['halsʃtarɪç] *adj* stubborn, obstinate

'**Halstuch** *n* neckerchief; scarf

Halt *m* (-[e]s; -e, -s) (*no pl*) hold; support (*a. fig*); *fig* stability; stop

halt [halt] *int* stop!, MIL halt!

'**haltbar** *adj* durable; GASTR not perishable; *fig* tenable; **~ bis ...** best before ...

'**Haltbarkeitsdatum** *n* best-by (*or* best-before) date

halten ['haltən] (*irr*, ge-, h) **1.** *v/t* hold; keep (*animal, promise etc*); make (*speech*); give (*lecture*); take (*Br a. in*) *a paper etc*; SPORT save; **~ für** regard as; (mis)take for; **viel** (**wenig**) **~ von** think highly (little) of; **sich ~** last; GASTR keep; **sich gut ~** *fig* do well; **sich ~ an** (*acc*) keep to **2.** *v/i* hold, last; stop, halt; *ice:* bear; *rope etc:* hold; **~ zu** stand by, F stick to; **Halter(in)** ['haltɐ, 'haltərɪn] *m(f)* (-s; -/-; -nen) owner; TECH holder

'**Haltestelle** *f* stop, RAIL *a.* station

'**Halteverbot** *n* MOT no stopping (area)

'**haltlos** *adj* unsteady; *fig* baseless

'**haltmachen** *v/i* (*sep*, -ge-, h) stop; *fig* **vor nichts ~** stop at nothing

'**Haltung** *f* (-; -en) posture; *fig* attitude (**zu** towards)

hämisch ['hɛːmɪʃ] *adj* malicious, sneering

Hammel ['haməl] *m* (-s; -) ZO wether

'**Hammelfleisch** *n* GASTR mutton

Hammer ['hamɐ] *m* (-s; *Hämmer* ['hɛmɐ]) hammer (*a.* SPORT); **hämmern** ['hɛmɐn] *v/t and v/i* (ge-, h) hammer

Hämorrhoiden, **Hämorriden** [hɛmɔro-'iːdən] *pl* MED h(a)emorrhoids, F *Br* piles

Hampelmann ['hampəlman] *m* jumping jack

Hamster ['hamstɐ] *m* (-s; -) ZO hamster

'**hamstern** *v/t and v/i* (ge-, h) hoard

Hand [hant] *f* (-; *Hände* ['hɛndə]) hand; **von ~, mit der ~** by hand; **an ~ von** (*or* **gen**) by means of; **zur ~** at hand; **aus erster** (**zweiter**) **~** first-hand (second-hand); **an die ~ nehmen** take by the hand; **sich die ~ geben** shake hands; **aus der ~ legen** lay aside; **~ breit** → **handbreit**; **~ voll** → **handvoll**; **Hände hoch** (**weg**)! hands up (off)!; **~arbeit** *f* (*no pl*) manual labo(u)r; needlework; **es ist ~** it is handmade; **~ball** *m* SPORT (European) handball; **~betrieb** *m* TECH manual operation; **~breit** *f* (-; -) man's breadth; **~bremse** *f* MOT handbrake; **~buch** *n* manual, handbook

Händedruck ['hɛndədrʊk] *m* (-[e]s; -drücke) handshake

Handel ['handəl] *m* (-s; *no pl*) commerce, business; trade; market; transaction, deal, bargain; **~ treiben** ECON trade (**mit** with *s.o.*); '**handeln** *v/i* (ge-, h) act, take action; bargain (**um** for), haggle (over); **mit j-m** ECON trade with *s.o.*; **~ mit** deal in; **~ von** deal with, be about; **es handelt sich um** it concerns, it is about; it is a matter of

'**Handels**|**abkommen** *n* trade agreement; **~bank** *f* (-; -banken) commercial bank; **~bi**|**lanz** *f* balance of trade

'**handelseinig** *adj:* **~ werden** come to terms

'**Handels**|**gesellschaft** *f* (trading) company; **~kammer** *f* chamber of commerce; **~schiff** *n* merchant ship; **~schule** *f* commercial school; **~vertreter** *m* (traveling) salesman, *Br* sales representative; **~ware** *f* commodity, merchandise

'**Hand**|**feger** ['hantfeːgɐ] *m* (-s; -) handbrush; **~fertigkeit** *f* manual skill

'**handfest** *adj* solid

'**Handfläche** *f* ANAT palm

'**handgearbeitet** *adj* handmade

'Hand|gelenk n ANAT wrist; **~gepäck** n hand baggage (Br luggage); **~gra.nate** f MIL hand grenade

handgreiflich ['hantgraiflıç] adj: **~ werden** turn violent, get tough

'handhaben v/t (ge-, h) handle, manage; TECH operate

Händler ['hɛndlɐ] m (-s; -), **'Händlerin** f (-; -nen) dealer, trader

'handlich adj handy, manageable

Handlung ['handlʊŋ] f (-; -en) act, action; film etc: story, plot

'Handlungs|reisende m sales representative, travel(l)ing salesman; **~weise** f behavio(u)r

'Hand|rücken m ANAT back of the hand; **~schellen** pl handcuffs; **j-m ~ anlegen** handcuff s.o.; **~schlag** m' handshake; **~schrift** f hand(writing)

'handschriftlich adj handwritten

'Hand|schuh m glove; **~spiel** n soccer: hand ball; **~stand** m handstand; **~tasche** f handbag, purse; **~tuch** n towel; **~voll** f handful; **~wagen** m handcart; **~werk** n craft, trade

Handwerker ['hantvɛrkɐ] m (-s; -) craftsman; workman

'Handwerkszeug n (kit of) tools

'Handwurzel f ANAT wrist

Handy ['hɛndi] n (-s; -s) Br mobile (phone), Am cell (phone); **~nummer** f Br mobile number, Am cell phone number

Hanf [hanf] m (-es; no pl) BOT hemp; cannabis

Hang [haŋ] m (-[e]s; Hänge ['hɛŋə]) slope; (no pl) fig inclination (**zu** for), tendency (towards)

Hänge|brücke ['hɛŋəbrʏkə] f suspension bridge; **~lampe** f hanging lamp; **~matte** f hammock

hängen ['hɛŋən] **1.** v/i (irr, ge-, h) hang (**an** dat on the wall etc; from the ceiling etc); **~ bleiben** get stuck (a. fig); **~ bleiben an** (dat) get caught on; **~ an** (dat) be fond of; be devoted to; **alles, woran ich hänge** everything that is dear to me **2.** v/t (ge-, h) hang (**an** acc on); **~bleiben** v/i (irr, bleiben, sep, -ge-, sein) fig get stuck; → **hängen**

hänseln ['hɛnzəln] v/t (ge-, h) tease (**wegen** about)

Hanswurst [hans'vʊrst] m (-[e]s; -e) fool, clown

Hantel ['hantəl] f (-; -n) dumbbell

hantieren [han'tiːrən] v/i (no -ge-, h) **~ mit** handle; **~ an** (dat) fiddle about with

Happen ['hapən] m (-s; -) morsel, bite; snack

Hardware ['haːdwɛə] f (-; -s) IT hardware

Harfe ['harfə] f (-; -n) MUS harp

Harfenist [harfə'nıst] m (-en; -en), **Harfe'nistin** f (-; -nen) MUS harpist

Harke ['harkə] f (-; -n), **'harken** v/t (ge-, h) rake

harmlos ['harmloːs] adj harmless

Harmonie [harmo'niː] f (-; -n) harmony (a. MUS); **harmo'nieren** v/i (no -ge-, h) harmonize (**mit** with); **harmonisch** [har'moːnıʃ] adj harmonious

Harn [harn] m (-[e]s; -e) MED urine

'Harnblase f ANAT (urinary) bladder

'Harnröhre f ANAT urethra

Harpune [har'puːnə] f (-; -n) harpoon

harpunieren [harpu'niːrən] v/t (no -ge-, h) harpoon

hart [hart] **1.** adj hard, F a. tough; SPORT rough; severe; **~ gekocht** hard-boiled **2.** adv hard

Härte ['hɛrtə] f (-; -n) hardness; toughness; roughness; severity; esp JUR hardship; **~fall** m case of hardship

'härten v/t (ge-, h) harden

'Hartfaserplatte f hardboard

'Hartgeld n coin(s)

hartgesotten ['hartgəzɔtən] adj hard-boiled

'hartherzig adj hard-hearted

hartnäckig ['hartnɛkıç] adj stubborn, obstinate; persistent

Harz [haːɐts] n (-es; -e) resin; rosin

harzig adj resinous

Hasch [haʃ] F n (-s; no pl) hash

haschen F v/i (ge-, h) smoke hash

Haschisch ['haʃıʃ] n (-[s]; no pl) hashish

Hase ['haːzə] m (-n; -n) zo hare

Haselmaus ['haːzəlmaus] f zo dormouse

'Haselnuss f BOT hazelnut

'Hasenscharte f MED harelip

Hass [has] m (-es; no pl) hatred, hate (**auf** acc, **gegen** of, for)

hassen ['hasən] v/t (ge-, h) hate

hässlich ['hɛslıç] adj ugly, fig a. nasty

Hast [hast] f (-; no pl) hurry, haste; rush

hasten ['hastən] v/i (ge-, sein) hurry,

hasten, rush

'hastig adj hasty, hurried

hätscheln ['hɛːtʃəln] v/t (ge-, h) fondle; *contp* pamper

hatte ['hatə] *pret of* **haben**

Haube ['haubə] f (-; -n) bonnet (a. Br MOT); cap; ZO crest; MOT hood

Hauch [haux] m (-[e]s; -e) breath; whiff; fig touch, trace; **hauchen** ['hauxən] v/t (ge-, h) breathe

hauen F v/t (irr,] ge-, h) hit, beat, thrash; TECH hew; **sich ~** (have a) fight

Haufen ['haufən] m (-s; -) heap, pile (both a. F); F crowd; **häufen** ['hɔyfən] v/t (ge-, h) heap (up), pile (up); **sich ~** fig become more frequent, be on the increase; **häufig** ['hɔyfiç] **1.** adj frequent **2.** adv frequently, often

Haupt [haupt] n (-[e]s; Häupter ['hɔyptɐ]) head, fig a. leader; **~bahnhof** m main or central station; **~beschäftigung** f chief occupation; **~bestandteil** m chief ingredient; **~darsteller(in)** leading actor (actress), lead

Häuptelsalat ['hɔyptəlzalaːt] Austrian m BOT lettuce

Haupt|fach n UNIV major, Br main subject; **~film** m feature (film); **~gericht** n GASTR main course; **~gewinn** m first prize; **~grund** m main reason; **~leitung** f TECH main

Häuptling ['hɔyptliŋ] m (-s; -e) chief

Haupt|mann m (-[e]s; -leute) MIL captain; **~menü** n IT main menu; **~merkmal** n chief characteristic; **~person** F f center (Br centre) of attention; **~quartier** n headquarters; **~rolle** f THEA lead(ing part)

Hauptsache f main thing or point

hauptsächlich adj main, chief, principal

Haupt|satz m LING main clause; **~sendezeit** f TV prime time, Br peak time (or viewing hours); **~speicher** m IT main memory; **~stadt** f capital; **~straße** f main street; main road; **~verkehrsstraße** f arterial road; **~verkehrszeit** f rush or peak hour(s); **~versammlung** f general meeting; **~wohnsitz** m main place of residence; **~wort** n (-[e]s; -wörter) LING noun

Haus [haus] n (-es; Häuser ['hɔyzɐ]) house; building; **zu ~e** at home, in; **nach ~e kommen** (**bringen**) come or

get (take) home; **~angestellte** m, f domestic (servant); **~apotheke** f medicine cabinet; **~arbeit** f housework; **~arzt** m, **~ärztin** f family doctor; **~aufgaben** pl PED homework, assignment; **s-e ~ machen** a. fig do one's homework; **~bar** f cocktail cabinet; **~besetzer** m (-s; -) squatter; **~besetzung** f squatting; **~besitzer** m house owner; **~einweihung** f house-warming (party)

hausen ['hauzən] v/i (ge-, h) live; fig play havoc

'Haus|flur m (entrance) hall, hallway

'Hausfrau f housewife

'Hausfriedensbruch m JUR trespass

'hausgemacht adj homemade

'Haushalt m (-[e]s; -e) household; PARL budget; (**j-m**) **den ~ führen** keep house (for s.o.); **Haushälterin** ['haushɛltərin] f (-; -nen) housekeeper

'Haushalts|geld n housekeeping money; **~plan** m PARL budget; **~waren** pl household articles

'Haus|herr m head of the household; host; **~herrin** f lady of the house; hostess

'haushoch adj huge; crushing (defeat etc)

hausieren [hau'ziːrən] v/i (no -ge-, h) peddle, hawk (**mit et.** s.th.) (a. fig); **Hausierer** m (-s; -) pedlar, hawker

häuslich ['hɔyslɪç] adj domestic; home-loving

'Haus|mädchen n (house)maid; **~mann** m house husband; **~mannskost** f plain fare; **~meister** m caretaker, janitor; **~mittel** n household remedy; **~ordnung** f house rules; **~rat** m (-[e]s; no pl) household effects; **~schlüssel** m front-door key; **~schuh** m slipper

Hausse ['hoːs(ə)] f (-; -n) ECON rise, boom

'Haus|suchung f (-; -en) house search; **~tier** n domestic animal; **~tür** f front door; **~verwaltung** f property management; **~wirt** m landlord; **~wirtin** f landlady; **~wirtschaft** f (-; no pl) housekeeping; **~wirtschaftslehre** f domestic science, home economics; **~wirtschaftsschule** f domestic science (or home economics) school

Haut [haut] f (-; Häute ['hɔytə]) skin; complexion; **bis auf die ~ durchnässt**

soaked to the skin; ~**abschürfung** f MED abrasion; ~**arzt** m, ~**ärztin** f dermatologist; ~**ausschlag** m MED rash

'**hauteng** adj skin-tight

'**Haut**|**farbe** f colo(u)r of the skin; complexion; ~**krankheit** f skin disease; ~**pflege** f skin care; ~**schere** f cuticle scissors

Hbf. abbr of **Hauptbahnhof** cent. sta., central station

H-Bombe ['haːbɔmbə] f MIL H-bomb

Hebamme ['heːpʔamə] f (-; -n) midwife

Hebebühne ['heːbəbyːnə] f MOT car hoist

Hebel ['heːbəl] m (-s; -) TECH lever

heben ['heːbən] v/t (irr, ge-, h) lift, raise (a. fig); heave; hoist; fig a. improve; **sich** ~ rise, go up

Hecht [hɛçt] m (-[e]s; -e) ZO pike

'**hechten** v/i (ge-, sein) dive (**nach** for); SPORT do a long-fly

Heck [hɛk] n (-[e]s; -e) MAR stern; AVIAT tail; MOT rear

Hecke ['hɛkə] f (-; -n) BOT hedge

'**Heckenrose** f BOT dogrose

'**Heckenschütze** m MIL sniper

'**Heckscheibe** f MOT rear window

Heer [heːɐ] n (-[e]s; -e) MIL army, fig a. host

Hefe ['heːfə] f (-; -n) yeast

Heft [hɛft] n (-[e]s; -e) notebook; exercise book; booklet; issue, number

'**heften** ['hɛftən] v/t (ge-, h) fix, fasten, attach (**an** acc to); pin (to); tack, baste; stitch

'**Hefter** ['hɛftɐ] m (-s; -) stapler; file

'**heftig** ['hɛftɪç] adj violent, fierce; heavy

'**Heftklammer** f staple

'**Heftpflaster** n bandage, Band Aid®, Br (adhesive or sticking) plaster

hehl [heːl] n: **kein** ~ **aus et. machen** make no secret of s.th.

'**Hehler** ['heːlɐ] m (-s; -) JUR receiver of stolen goods, sl fence

Hehlerei [heːlə'raɪ] f (-; -en) JUR receiving stolen goods

'**Heide**[1] ['haɪdə] m (-n; -n) REL heathen

'**Heide**[2] f (-; -n) heath(land)

'**Heidekraut** n (-[e]s; no pl) BOT heather, heath

'**Heiden**|**angst** F f: **e-e** ~ **haben** be scared stiff; ~**geld** F n: **ein** ~ a fortune; ~**lärm** F m: **ein** ~ a hell of a noise; ~**spaß** F m: **e-n** ~ **haben** have a ball

'**Heidentum** n (-s; no pl) REL heathenism; '**Heidin** ['haɪdɪn] f (-; -nen), '**heidnisch** ['haɪdnɪʃ] adj REL heathen

heikel ['haɪkəl] adj delicate, tricky; tender; F fussy

heil [haɪl] adj safe, unhurt; undamaged, whole, intact; **Heil** n (-s; no pl) REL grace

Heiland ['haɪlant] m (-[e]s; no pl) REL Savio(u)r, Redeemer

'**Heilbad** n health resort, spa

'**heilbar** adj curable

heilen ['haɪlən] **1.** v/t (ge-, h) cure **2.** v/i (ge-, sein) heal (up)

'**Heilgym**'**nastik** f physiotherapy

heilig ['haɪlɪç] adj REL holy; sacred (a. fig)

Heilig'**abend** m Christmas Eve

'**Heilige** ['haɪlɪgə] m, f (-n; -n) REL saint

'**heiligen** ['haɪlɪgən] v/t (ge-, h) REL sanctify (a. fig), hallow

'**heiligsprechen** v/t (irr, **sprechen**, sep, -ge-, h) canonize

'**Heiligtum** n (-s; -tümer ['haɪlɪçtyːmɐ]) REL sanctuary, shrine

'**Heilkraft** f healing or curative power; '**heilkräftig** adj curative

'**Heilkraut** n BOT medicinal herb

'**heillos** fig adj utter, hopeless

'**Heil**|**mittel** n remedy, cure (both a. fig); ~**praktiker**(**in**) ['haɪlpraktikɐ, 'haɪlpraktikərɪn] (-s; -/-; -nen) non-medical practitioner; ~**quelle** f (medicinal) mineral spring

'**heilsam** fig adj salutary

'**Heilsar**'**mee** f Salvation Army

'**Heilung** f (-; -en) cure; healing

heim [haɪm] adv home

Heim n (-[e]s; -e) (no pl) home; hostel; **Heim...** in cpds ...**mannschaft**, ...**sieg**, ...**spiel** etc: home

Heimat ['haɪmaːt] f (-; no pl) home; home country; home town; **in der** (**meiner**) ~ at home; '**heimatlos** adj homeless; '**Heimatstadt** f home town; '**Heimatvertriebene** m, f expellee

'**heimisch** ['haɪmɪʃ] adj home, domestic; BOT, ZO etc native; fig homelike, hom(e)y; **sich** ~ **fühlen** feel at home

'**Heimkehr** ['haɪmkeːɐ] f (-; no pl) return (home); '**heimkehren** v/i (sep, -ge-, sein) return home, come back

'**heimlich** adj secret; '**Heimlichkeit** f (-;

-en *(no pl)* secrecy; *pl* secrets

'**Heimreise** *f* journey home

'**heimsuchen** *v/t* (*sep*, -ge-, *h*) strike

'**heimtückisch** *adj* insidious (*a.* MED); treacherous

heimwärts ['haimverts] *adv* homeward(s)

'**Heimweg** *m* way home

'**Heimweh** *n* (-s; *no pl*) homesickness; ~ **haben** be homesick

'**Heimwerker** ['haimverkɐ] *m* (-s; -) do--it-yourselfer

Heirat ['hairaːt] *f* (-; -en) marriage

heiraten ['hairaːtən] *v/t and v/i* (ge-, *h*) marry, get married (to)

'**Heirats|antrag** *m* proposal (of marriage); *j-m e-n* ~ *machen* propose to s.o.; ~**schwindler** *m* marriage impostor; ~**vermittler(in)** (-s; -/-; -nen) marriage broker; ~**vermittlung** *f* marriage bureau

heiser ['haizɐ] *adj* hoarse, husky

'**Heiserkeit** *f*(-; *no pl*) hoarseness, huskiness

heiß [hais] *adj* hot, *fig a.* passionate, ardent; *mir ist* ~ I am *or* feel hot

heißen ['haisən] *v/i* (*irr*, ge-, *h*) be called; mean; *wie* ~ *Sie?* what's your name?; *wie heißt das?* what do you call this?; *was heißt ... auf Englisch?* what is ... in English?; *es heißt im Text* it says in the text; *das heißt* that is (*abbr d. h.* i. e.)

heiter ['haitɐ] *adj* cheerful; humorous (*film etc*); METEOR fair; *fig aus* ~**em Himmel** out of the blue; '**Heiterkeit** *f* (-; *no pl*) cheerfulness; amusement

heizbar ['haitsbaːɐ] *adj* heated; **heizen** ['haitsən] *v/t and v/i* (ge-, *h*) heat; *mit Kohlen* ~ burn coal; '**Heizer** ['haitsɐ] *m* (-s; -) MAR, RAIL stoker

'**Heiz|kessel** *m* boiler; ~**kissen** *n* electric cushion; ~**körper** *m* radiator; ~**kraftwerk** *n* thermal power-station; ~**materi,al** *n* fuel; ~**öl** *n* fuel oil

'**Heizung** *f* (-; -en) heating

Held [hɛlt] *m* (-en; -en) ['hɛldən] hero

heldenhaft ['hɛldənhaft] *adj* heroic

'**Heldentat** *f* heroic deed

'**Heldentum** *n* (-s; *no pl*) heroism

Heldin ['hɛldɪn] *f* (-; -nen) heroine

helfen ['hɛlfən] *v/i* (*irr*, ge-, *h*) help, aid; assist; *j-m bei et.* ~ help s.o. with *or* in (doing) s.th.; ~ *gegen* MED *etc* be good

for; *er weiß sich zu* ~ he can manage; *es hilft nichts* it's no use

Helfer ['hɛlfɐ] *m* (-s; -), '**Helferin** *f* (-; -nen) helper, assistant

'**Helfershelfer** *contp m* accomplice

hell [hɛl] *adj* bright (*light, flame etc*); light (*color etc*); light-colo(u)red (*dress etc*); clear (*voice etc*); pale (*beer*); *fig* bright, clever; *es wird schon* ~ it's getting light already; ~**blau** *adj* light blue; ~**blond** *adj* very fair; ~**hörig** *adj* quick of hearing; ARCH poorly soundproofed; ~ *werden* prick up one's ears

'**Hellseher** *m* (-s; -), '**Hellseherin** *f* (-; -nen) clairvoyant

Helm [hɛlm] *m* (-[e]s; -e) helmet

Hemd [hɛmt] *n* (-[e]s; -en ['hɛmdən]) shirt; vest; ~**bluse** *f* shirt; ~**blusenkleid** *n* shirtwaist, *Br* shirt-waister

Hemisphäre [hemi'sfɛːrə] *f* (-; -n) hemisphere

hemmen ['hɛmən] *v/t* (ge-, *h*) check, stop; hamper; '**Hemmung** *f* (-; -en) PSYCH inhibition; scruple

'**hemmungslos** *adj* unrestrained; unscrupulous

Hengst [hɛŋst] *m* (-[e]s; -e) zo stallion

Henkel ['hɛŋkəl] *m* (-s; -) handle

Henker ['hɛŋkɐ] *m* (-s; -) hangman, executioner

Henne ['hɛnə] *f* (-; -n) zo hen

her [heːɐ] *adv* here; *das ist lange* ~ that was a long time ago

herab [hɛ'rap] *adv* down; ~**lassen** *fig v/refl* (*irr, lassen, sep*, -ge-, *h*) condescend; ~**lassend** *adj* condescending; ~**sehen** *fig v/i* (*irr, sehen, sep*, -ge-*h*) ~ *auf* (*acc*) look down upon; ~**setzen** *v/t* (*sep*, -ge-, *h*) reduce; *fig* disparage

heran [hɛ'ran] *adv* close, near; ~ *an* (*acc*) up *or* near to; ~**gehen** *v/i* (*irr, gehen, sep*, -ge-, *sein*) ~ *an* (*acc*) walk up to *fig* set about a task *etc*; ~**kommen** *v/i* (*irr, kommen, sep*, -ge-, *sein*) come near (*a. fig*); ~**wachsen** *v/i* (*irr, wachsen, sep*, -ge-, *sein*) grow (up) (*zu* into

He'ranwachsende *m, f* (-n; -n) adolescent

he'ranwinken *v/t* (*sep*, -ge-, *h*) hail (*taxi etc*)

herauf [hɛ'rauf] *adv* up (here); upstairs; ~**beschwören** *v/t* (*irr, schwören, sep, no -ge-, h*) call up; bring on, provoke

heraus [hɛ'raus] *adv* out; *fig aus (da*

... ~ out of ...; **zum Fenster** ~ out of the window; ~ **mit der Sprache!** speak out!, out with it!; ~**bekommen** *v/t* (*irr,* **kommen,** *sep, no -ge-, h*) get out; get back (*change*); *fig* find out; ~**bringen** *v/t* (*irr,* **bringen,** *sep, -ge-, h*) bring out; PRINT publish; THEA stage; *fig* find out; ~**finden** (*irr,* **finden,** *sep, -ge-, h*) **1.** *v/t* find; *fig* find out, discover **2.** *v/i* find one's way out

He'rausforderer *m* (*-s; -*) challenger; he'rausfordern *v/t* (*sep, -ge-, h*) challenge; provoke, F ask for it; He'rausforderung *f* challenge; provocation

he'rausgeben *v/t* (*irr,* **geben,** *sep, -ge-, h*) give back; give up; issue; give change (**auf** *acc* for); He'rausgeber(in) [he'rausge:bɐ, he'rausge:bərɪn] *m(f)* (*-s; -/-; -nen*) publisher

he'raus|kommen *v/i* (*irr,* **kommen,** *sep, -ge-, sein*) come out; *book:* be published; *stamps:* be issued; ~ **aus** get out of; F **groß** ~ be a great success; ~**nehmen** *v/t* (*irr,* **nehmen,** *sep, -ge-, h*) take out; SPORT take *s.o.* off the team; *fig* **sich et.** ~ take liberties, go too far; ~**putzen** *v/t and v/refl* (*sep, -ge-, h*) spruce (o.s.) up; ~**reden** *v/refl* (*sep, -ge-, h*) make excuses; talk one's way out; ~**stellen** *v/t* (*sep, -ge-, h*) put out; *fig* emphasize; **sich** ~ **als** turn out *or* prove to be; ~**strecken** *v/t* (*sep, -ge-, h*) stick out; ~**suchen** *v/t* (*sep, -ge-, h*) pick out; **j-m et.** ~ find *s.o. s.th.*

herb [hɛrp] *adj* tart; dry (*wine etc*); *fig* harsh; bitter

her'bei *adv* up, over, here; ~**eilen** *v/i* (*sep, -ge-, sein*) come running up; ~**führen** *fig v/t* (*sep, -ge-, h*) cause, bring about

Herberge ['hɛrbergə] *f* (*-; -n*) inn; lodging; hostel

Herbst [hɛrpst] *m* (*-[e]s; -e*) fall, autumn

Herd [he:ɐt] *m* (*-[e]s; -e* ['he:ɐdə]) cooker, stove; *fig* center, *Br* centre; MED focus, seat

Herde ['he:ɐdə] *f* (*-; -n*) ZO herd (*a. fig contp*); flock (*of sheep, geese etc*)

herein [hɛ'raɪn] *adv* in (here); ~**! come in!; ~**brechen** *v/i* (*irr,* **brechen,** *sep, -ge-, sein*) night: fall; ~ **über** (*acc*) befall

---

s.o.; ~**fallen** F *v/i* (*irr,* **fallen,** *sep, -ge-, sein*) be taken in (**auf** *acc* by); ~**legen** F *v/t* (*sep, -ge-, h*) take *s.o.* in

'herfallen *v/i* (*irr,* **fallen,** *sep, -ge-, sein*) ~ **über** (*acc*) attack (*a. fig*)

'Hergang *m:* **j-m den** ~ **schildern** tell *s.o.* what happened

'hergeben *v/t* (*irr,* **geben,** *sep, -ge-, h*) give up, part with; **sich** ~ **zu** lend o.s. to

Hering ['he:rɪŋ] *m* (*-s; -e*) ZO herring

'herkommen *v/i* (*irr,* **kommen,** *sep, -ge-, sein*) come (here); ~ **von** come from, *fig a.* be caused by

herkömmlich ['he:ɐkœmlɪç] *adj* conventional (*a.* MIL)

Herkunft ['he:ɐkʊnft] *f* (*-; no pl*) origin; birth, descent

heroisch [he'ro:ɪʃ] *adj* heroic

Herr [hɛr] *m* (*-n; -en*) gentleman; master; REL *the* Lord; ~ **Brown** Mr Brown; ~ **der Lage** master of the situation

'Herren|bekleidung *f* menswear; ~**doppel** *n tennis:* men's doubles; ~**einzel** *n tennis:* men's singles

'herrenlos *adj* abandoned; stray (*dog*)

'Herrentoi,lette *f* men's restroom (*Br* toilet *or* lavatory)

'herrichten *v/t* (*sep, -ge-, h*) get ready, F fix

herrisch ['hɛrɪʃ] *adj* imperious

herrlich ['hɛrlɪç] *adj* marvel(l)ous, wonderful, F fantastic; 'Herrlichkeit *f* (*-; -en*) glory

'Herrschaft *f* (*-; no pl*) rule, power, control (*a. fig*) (**über** *acc* over); **die** ~ **verlieren über** (*acc*) lose control of

herrschen ['hɛrʃən] *v/i* (*ge-*) h) rule; **es herrschte** ... there was ...; 'Herrscher(in) ['hɛrʃɐ, 'hɛrʃərɪn] *m(f)* (*-s; -/-; -nen*) ruler; sovereign, monarch; 'herrschsüchtig *adj* domineering, F bossy

'herrühren *v/i* (*sep, -ge-, h*) ~ **von** come from, be due to

'herstellen *v/t* (*sep, -ge-, h*) make, produce; *fig* establish; 'Herstellung *f* (*-; no pl*) production; *fig* establishment; 'Herstellungskosten *pl* production cost(s)

herüber [hɛ'ry:bɐ] *adv* over (here), across

herum [hɛ'rʊm] *adv* (a)round; F **anders** ~ the other way round; ~**führen** *v/t* (*sep, -ge-, h*) **j-n** (**in der Stadt** *etc*) ~ show *s.o.*

(a)round (the town *etc*); ~**kommen** F *v/i* (*irr*, **kommen**, *sep*, *-ge-*, *sein*) (*weit or viel*) ~ get around; **um et. ~** *fig* get (a)round s.th.; ~**kriegen** F *v/t* (*sep*, *-ge-*, *h*) *j-n zu et. ~* get s.o. round to (do)ing s.th.; ~**lungern** F *v/i* (*sep*, *-ge-*, *h*) loaf *or* hang around; ~**reichen** *v/t* (*sep*, *-ge-*, *h*) pass *or* hand round; ~**sprechen** *v/refl* (*irr*, **sprechen**, *sep*, *-ge-*, *h*) get around; ~**treiben** F *v/refl* (*irr*, **treiben**, *sep*, *-ge-*, *h*) gad *or* knock about

He'**rumtreiber** F *m* (*-s*; *-*), He'**rumtreiberin** F *f* (*-*; *-nen*) tramp, loafer

herunter [hɛ'rʊntɐ] *adv* down; downstairs; ~**gekommen** *adj* run-down; seedy, shabby; ~**hauen** F *v/t* (*sep*, *-ge-*, *h*) *j-m e-e ~* smack *or* slap s.o. ('s face); ~**machen** F *v/t* (*sep*, *-ge-*, *h*) run *s.o. or* s.th. down; ~**spielen** F *v/t* (*sep*, *-ge-*, *h*) play *s.th.* down

hervor [hɛɐ'foːɐ] *adv* out of *or* from, forth; ~**bringen** *v/t* (*irr*, **bringen**, *sep*, *-ge-*, *h*) bring out, produce (*a. fig*); yield; utter; ~**gehen** *v/i* (*irr*, **gehen**, *sep*, *-ge-*, *sein*) ~ **aus** (*dat*) follow from; *als Sieger* ~ come out victorious; ~**heben** *v/t* (*irr*, **heben**, *sep*, *-ge-*, *h*) stress, emphasize; ~**ragend** *adj* outstanding, excellent, superior; prominent, eminent; ~**rufen** *v/t* (*irr*, **rufen**, *sep*, *-ge-*, *h*) cause, bring about; create; ~**stechend** *adj* striking; ~**tretend** *adj* prominent; protruding, bulging; ~**tun** *v/refl* (*irr*, **tun**, *sep*, *-ge-*, *h*) distinguish o.s. (*als* as)

Herz [hɛrts] *n* (*-ens*; *-en*) ANAT heart (*a. fig*); *cards*: heart(s); *j-m das ~ brechen* break s.o.'s heart; *sich ein ~ fassen* take heart; *mit ganzem ~en* wholeheartedly; *schweren ~ens* with a heavy heart; *sich et. zu ~en nehmen* take s.th. to heart; *es nicht übers ~ bringen zu inf* not have the heart to *inf*; *et. auf dem ~en haben* have s.th. on one's mind; *ins ~ schließen* take to one's heart; ~**anfall** *m* heart attack; 'Herzens|**lust** *f*: *nach ~* to one's heart's content; ~**wunsch** *m* heart's desire, dearest wish

'Herz**fehler** *m* cardiac defect
'herz**haft** *adj* hearty; savo(u)ry
'herz**ig** *adj* sweet, lovely, cute
'Herz|**in,farkt** *m* MED cardiac infarct

(-ion), F *mst* heart attack, coronary; ~**klopfen** *n* (*-s*; *no pl*) palpitation; *er hatte ~* (*vor dat*) his heart was throbbing (with)

'herz**krank** *adj* suffering from (a) heart disease

'herz**lich 1.** *adj* cordial, hearty; warm, friendly **2.** *adv*: ~ **gern** with pleasure

'herz**los** *adj* heartless

Herzog ['hɛrtsoːk] *m* (*-s*; *Herzöge* ['hɛrtsøːgə]) duke; Herzogin ['hɛrtsoːɡɪn] *f* (*-*; *-nen*) duchess

'Herz|**schlag** *m* heartbeat; MED heart failure; ~**schrittmacher** *m* MED (cardiac) pacemaker; ~**transplanti,ati,on** *f* MED heart transplant

'herz**zerreißend** *adj* heart-rending

heterosexuell [heterozɛksu'ɛl] *adj* heterosexual

Hetze ['hɛtsə] *f* (*-*; *no pl*) hurry, rush; POL *etc* agitation, campaign(ing) (*gegen* against); '**hetzen 1.** *v/t* (*ge-*, *h*) rush; *zo* hunt, chase; *e-n Hund auf j-n ~* set a dog on s.o. **2.** *v/i* (*ge-*, *sein*) hurry, rush; (*ge-*, *h*) POL *etc* agitate (*gegen* against); '**hetzerisch** *adj* inflammatory; 'Hetz**jagd** *f* hunt(ing), chase (*a. fig*); *fig* rush; 'Hetz**kam,pagne** *f* POL smear campaign

Heu [hɔy] *n* (*-[e]s*; *no pl*) hay
'Heu**boden** *m* hayloft

Heuchelei [hɔyçə'lai] *f* (*-*; *-en*) hypocrisy; cant; 'heucheln *v/i and* *v/t* (*ge-*, *h*) feign, simulate; Heuchler(in) ['hɔyçlɐ (-lərɪn)] (*-s*; *-/-*; *-nen*) hypocrite; 'heuchlerisch ['hɔyçlərɪʃ] *adj* hypocritical

heuer ['hɔyɐ] *Austrian adv* this year
Heuer ['hɔyɐ] *f* (*-*; *-n*) MAR pay; 'heuern *v/t* (*ge-*, *h*) hire, MAR *a.* sign on
heulen ['hɔylən] *v/i* (*ge-*, *h*) howl; F *contp* bawl; MOT roar; *siren*: whine
'Heuschnupfen *m* MED hay fever
'Heuschrecke *f* (*-*; *-n*) ZO grasshopper; locust

heute ['hɔytə] *adv* today; ~ *Abend* this evening, tonight; ~ *früh*, ~ *Morgen* this morning; ~ *in acht Tagen* a week from now; ~ *vor acht Tagen* a week ago today; heutig ['hɔytɪç] *adj* today's; of today, present(-day); 'heutzutage *adv* nowadays, these days

Hexe ['hɛksə] *f* (*-*; *-n*) witch (*a. fig*); *alte ~* (old) hag; 'hexen *v/i* (*ge-*, *h*) practice witchcraft; F work miracles

'Hexen|kessel *m* inferno; **~schuss** *m* (*-es*; *no pl*) MED lumbago

hieb [hi:p] *pret of* **hauen**

Hieb [hi:p] *m* (*-[e]s*; *-e* ['hi:bə]) blow, stroke; punch; lash, cut; *pl* beating; thrashing

hielt [hi:lt] *pret of* **halten**

hier [hi:ɐ] *adv* here, in this place; present; **~ entlang!** this way!

hieran ['hi:'ran] *adv* from *or* in this; **hierauf** ['hi:'rauf] *adv* on it *or* this; after this, then; **hieraus** ['hi:'raus] *adv* from *or* out of this; **'hier'bei** *adv* here, in this case; on this occasion; **'hier'durch** *adv* by this, hereby, this way; **'hier'für** *adv* for this; **'hier'her** *adv* (over) here, this way; **bis~** so far; **hierin** ['hi:'rɪn] *adv* in this; **'hier'mit** *adv* with this; **'hier'nach** *adv* after this; according to this; **hierüber** ['hi:'ry:bɐ] *adv* about this (subject); among these; **hierunter** ['hi:'rʊntɐ] *adv* under this; among these; *understand etc* by this *or* that; **'hier'von** *adv* of *or* from this; **'hier'zu** *adv* for this; to this

hiesig ['hi:zɪç] *adj* local; **ein Hiesiger** one of the locals

hieß [hi:s] *pret of* **heißen**

Hilfe ['hɪlfə] *f* (*-; -n*) help; aid (*a.* ECON), assistance (*a.* MED), relief (**für** to); **Erste ~** first aid; **um ~ rufen** cry for help; **~!** help!; → **mithilfe**; **~me,nü** *n* IT help menu; **~ruf** *m* call (*or* cry) for help; **~stellung** *f* support (*a. fig*)

'hilf|los *adj* helpless; **~reich** *adj* helpful

'Hilfsakti,on *f* relief action

'Hilfsarbeiter *m*, **'Hilfsarbeiterin** *f* unskilled worker

'hilfsbedürftig *adj* needy

'hilfsbereit *adj* helpful, ready to help; **'Hilfsbereitschaft** *f* (*-; no pl*) readiness to help, helpfulness

'Hilfs|mittel *n* aid, TECH *a.* device; **~organisati,on** *f* relief organization; **~verb** *n* LING auxiliary (verb)

Himbeere ['hɪmbe:rə] *f* BOT raspberry

Himmel ['hɪməl] *m* (*-s; -*) sky; REL heaven (*a. fig*); **um ~s willen** for Heaven's sake; → **heiter**

'Himmelfahrt REL Ascension (Day)

'Himmels|körper *m* AST celestial body; **~richtung** *f* direction; cardinal point

himmlisch ['hɪmlɪʃ] *adj* heavenly, *fig a.* marvel(l)ous

hin [hɪn] **1.** *adv* there; **bis~ zu** as far as; **noch lange ~** still a long way off; **auf s-e Bitte** (**s-n Rat**) **~** at his request (advice); **~ und her** to and fro, back and forth; **~ und wieder** now and then; **~ und zurück** there and back; RAIL round trip, round-trip ticket, *esp Br* return (ticket) **2.** F *pred adj* ruined; done for; gone

hi'nab *adv* → **hinunter**

'hinarbeiten *v/i* (*sep, -ge-, h*) **~ auf** (*acc*) work towards

hi'nauf *adv* up (there); upstairs; **die Straße** *etc* **~** up the street *etc*; **~gehen** *v/i* (*irr, gehen, sep, -ge-, sein*) go up, *fig a.* rise

hi'naus *adv* out; **aus ... ~** out of ...; **in** (*acc*) **... ~** out into ...; **~ (mit dir)!** (get) out!, out you go!; **~gehen** *v/i* (*irr, gehen, sep, -ge-, sein*) go out (side); **~ über** (*acc*) go beyond; **~ auf** (*acc*) window *etc*: look out onto; **~laufen** *v/i* (*irr, laufen, sep, -ge-, sein*) run out (side); **~ auf** (*acc*) come *or* amount to; **~schieben** *v/t* (*irr, schieben, sep, -ge-, h*) put off, postpone; **~stellen** *v/t* (*sep, -ge-, h*) SPORT send *s.o.* off (the field); **~werfen** *v/t* (*irr, werfen, sep, -ge-, h*) throw out (**aus** of), *fig a.* kick out; (give *s.o.* the) sack, fire; **~wollen** *v/i* (*irr, sep, -ge-, h*) **~ auf** (*acc*) aim (*or* drive *or* get) at; **hoch ~** aim high

'Hinblick *m*: **im ~ auf** (*acc*) in view of, with regard to

'hinbringen *v/t* (*irr, bringen, sep, -ge-, h*) take there

hinderlich ['hɪndɐlɪç] *adj* hindering, impeding; **j-m ~ sein** be in s.o.'s way

hindern ['hɪndɐn] *v/t* (*ge-, h*) hinder, hamper; **~ an** (*dat*) prevent from

Hindernis ['hɪndɐnɪs] *n* (*-ses; -se*) obstacle (*a. fig*); **~rennen** *n* steeplechase

Hindu ['hɪndu] *m* (*-[s]; -[s]*) Hindu

Hinduismus [hɪndu'ɪsmʊs] *m* (*-; no pl*) hinduism

hin'durch *adv* through; **das ganze Jahr** *etc* **~** throughout the year *etc*

hi'nein *adv* in; **~ mit dir!** in you go!; **~gehen** *v/i* (*irr, gehen, sep, -ge-, sein*) go in; **~ in** (*acc*) go into

'hinfallen *v/i* (*irr, fallen, sep, -ge-, sein*) fall (down)

'hinfällig *adj* frail, infirm; invalid

hing [hɪŋ] *pret of* **hängen** 1

H

'**Hingabe** f (-; no pl) devotion (**an** acc to); '**hingeben** v/t (irr, **geben**, sep, -ge-, h) give (up); **sich ~** (dat) give o.s. to; devote o.s. to

'**hinhalten** v/t (irr, **halten**, sep, -ge-, h) hold out; **j-n ~** put s.o. off

hinken ['hɪŋkən] v/i (ge-, h) (walk with a) limp; (ge-, sein) limp

'**hin|kommen** v/i (irr, **kommen**, sep, -ge-, sein) get there; **~kriegen** F v/t (sep, -ge-, h) manage

'**hinlänglich** adj sufficient

'**hin|legen** v/t (sep, -ge-, h) lay or put down; **sich ~** lie down; **~nehmen** v/t (irr, **nehmen**, sep, -ge-, h) put up with

'**hinreißen** v/t (irr, **reißen**, sep, -ge-, h) carry away; **~d** adj entrancing; breathtaking

'**hinrichten** v/t (sep, -ge-, h) execute; '**Hinrichtung** f (-; -en) execution

'**hinsetzen** v/t (sep, -ge-, h) set or put down; **sich ~** sit down

'**Hinsicht** f (-; no pl) respect; **in gewisser ~** in a way; '**hinsichtlich** prp (gen) with respect or regard to

'**Hinspiel** n SPORT first leg

'**hinstellen** v/t (sep, -ge-, h) put (down); **~ als** make s.o. or s.th. appear to be

hinten ['hɪntən] adv at the back; MOT in the back; **von ~** from behind

hinter ['hɪntə] prp (dat) behind

'**Hinter...** in cpds **...achse**, **...eingang**, **...rad** etc: rear ...; **~bein** n hind leg

Hinterbliebenen [hɪntə'bliːbənən] pl the bereaved; esp JUR surviving dependents

hinterei'nander adv one after the other; **dreimal ~** three times in a row

'**Hintergedanke** m ulterior motive

hinter'gehen v/t (irr, **gehen**, no -ge-, h) deceive

'**Hintergrund** m background (a. fig)

'**Hinterhalt** m ambush; **hinterhältig** ['hɪntəhɛltɪç] adj insidious, underhand(ed)

'**Hinterhaus** n rear building

hinter'her adv behind, after; afterwards

'**Hinterhof** m backyard

'**Hinterkopf** m back of the head

hinter'lassen v/t (irr, **lassen**, no -ge-, h) leave (behind); **Hinter'lassenschaft** f (-; -en) property (left), estate

hinter'legen v/t (no -ge-, h) deposit (**bei** with)

'**Hinterlist** f deceit(fulness); (underhanded) trick; '**hinterlistig** adj deceitful; underhand(ed)

'**Hintermann** m person (car etc) behind (one); fig mst pl person behind the scenes, brain(s), mastermind

'**Hintern** F m (-s; -) bottom, backside, behind, Br bum

hinterrücks ['hɪntəryks] adv from behind

'**Hinter|seite** f back; **~teil** F n → **Hintern**; **~treppe** f back stairs; **~tür** f back door

hinter'ziehen v/t (irr, **ziehen**, no -ge-, h) evade (taxes)

'**Hinterzimmer** n back room

hi'nüber adv over, across; **~ sein** F be ruined; GASTR be spoilt

hi'nunter adv down; downstairs; **die Straße ~** down the road

Hinweg ['hɪnveːk] m way there

hinweg [hɪn'vɛk] adv: **über** (acc) ... **~** over ...; **~kommen** v/i (irr, **kommen** sep, -ge-, sein) **~ über** (acc) get over; **~sehen** v/i (irr, **sehen**, sep, -ge-, h) **~ über** (acc) ignore; **~setzen** v/refl (sep, -ge-, h) **sich ~ über** (acc) ignore, disregard

Hinweis ['hɪnvaɪs] m (-es; -e) reference (**auf** acc to); hint, tip (as to, regarding); indication (of), clue (as to); '**hinweisen** (irr, **weisen**, sep, -ge-, h) **1.** v/t: **j-n ~ auf** (acc) draw or call s.o.'s attention to **2.** v/i: **~ auf** (acc) point at or to, indicate; fig point out, indicate; hint at

'**Hinweis|schild** n, **~tafel** f sign, notice

'**hin|werfen** v/t (irr, **werfen**, sep, -ge-, h) throw down; **~ziehen** v/refl (irr, **ziehen**, sep, -ge-, h) extend (**bis zu** to), stretch (to); drag on

hin'zu|fügen v/t (sep, -ge-, h) add (**zu** to) (a. fig); **~kommen** v/i (irr, **kommen**, sep, -ge-, sein) be added; **hinzu kommt, dass** add to this ..., and what is more, ...; **~ziehen** v/t (irr, **ziehen**, sep, -ge-, h) call in, consult

Hirn [hɪrn] n (-[e]s; -e) ANAT brain; fig brain(s), mind; **~gespinst** n fantasy

Hirsch [hɪrʃ] m (-[e]s; -e) zo stag; **~geweih** n zo antlers; **~kuh** f zo hind

Hirse ['hɪrzə] f (-; -n) BOT millet

Hirte ['hɪrtə] m (-n; -n) herdsman; shepherd (a. fig)

hissen ['hɪsən] v/t (ge-, h) hoist

Historiker [hɪsˈtoːrikɐ] m (-s; -), **Historikerin** f (-; -nen) historian; **historisch** adj historical; historic (event etc)

Hitliste [ˈhɪtlɪstə] f top 40 etc, charts

Hitze [ˈhɪtsə] f (-; no pl) heat

Hitzewelle f heat wave

hitzig adj hot-tempered, peppery; heated (debate etc)

Hitzkopf m hothead

Hitzschlag m MED heatstroke

HIV|-negativ [haːʔiːfauˈneːgatiːf] adj MED HIV negative; **~positiv** adj MED HIV positive; **~Positive** m, f (-n; -n) MED HIV carrier

H-Milch [ˈhaːmɪlç] f Br long-life milk

hob [hoːp] pret of **heben**

Hobby [ˈhɔbi] n (-s; -s) hobby

Hobby... in cpds amateur ...

Hobel [ˈhoːbəl] m (-s; -) TECH plane

Hobelbank f (-; -bänke) TECH carpenter's bench

hobeln v/t (ge-, h) TECH plane

hoch [hoːx] adj and adv high; tall; fig heavy (fine etc); distinguished (guest); great, old (age); deep (snow); **10 ~ 4** MATH 10 to the power of 4; **3000 Meter ~ fly** etc at an altitude of 3,000 meters; **in hohem Maße** highly, greatly; **~ verschuldet** heavily in debt; F **das ist mir zu ~** that's above me

Hoch n (-s; -s) METEOR high (a. fig)

Hochachtung f (deep) respect (**vor** dat for); **hochachtungsvoll** adv Yours sincerely

Hoch|bau m (-[e]s; no pl) **Hoch- und Tiefbau** structural and civil engineering; **~betrieb** F m (-[e]s; no pl) rush

hochdeutsch adj High or standard German

Hoch|druck m high pressure (a. fig); **~ebene** f plateau, tableland; **~form** f: **in ~** in top form or shape; **~fre‚quenz** f ELECTR high frequency; **~gebirge** n high mountains; **~genuss** m real treat

hochgezüchtet adj ZO, TECH highbred, TECH a. sophisticated; MOT tuned up, F souped up

hochhackig [ˈhoːxhakɪç] adj high-heeled

Hoch|haus n high rise, tower block; **~konjunk‚tur** f ECON boom; **~land** n highlands; **~leistungs...** in cpds ...sport etc: high-performance ...

Hochmut m arrogance; **hochmütig** [ˈhoːxmyːtɪç] adj arrogant

Hochofen m TECH blast furnace

hochpro‚zentig adj high-proof

Hoch|rechnung f projection; POL computer prediction; **~sai‚son** f peak (or height of the) season; **~schulab‚schluss** m degree; **~schulausbildung** f higher education; **~schule** f university; college; academy; **~seefischerei** f deep-sea fishing; **~sommer** m midsummer; **~spannung** f ELECTR high tension (a. fig) or voltage; **~sprung** m SPORT high jump

höchst [høːçst] **1.** adj highest, fig a. supreme; extreme **2.** adv highly, most, extremely; **Höchst...** in cpds mst maximum ..., top ...

Hochstapler [ˈhoːxʃtaːplɐ] m (-s; -), **Hochstaplerin** f (-; -nen) impostor, swindler

höchstens adv at (the) most, at best

Höchst|form f SPORT top form or shape; **~geschwindigkeit** f top speed (**mit** at); speed limit; **~leistung** f SPORT record (performance); TECH maximum output; **~maß** n maximum (**an** dat of)

höchstwahr‚scheinlich adv most likely or probably

Hochtechnolo‚gie f high technology, hi tech

hochtrabend adj pompous

Hochverrat m high treason

Hochwasser n high tide; flood

hochwertig [ˈhoːxveːɐtɪç] adj high-grade, high-quality

Hochzeit [ˈhɔxtsait] f (-; -en) wedding

Hochzeits... in cpds ...geschenk, ...kleid, ...tag etc: wedding ...; **~reise** f honeymoon

Hocke [ˈhɔkə] f (-; -n) crouch, squat

hocken v/i (ge-, h) squat, crouch; F sit

Hocker [ˈhɔkɐ] m (-s; -) stool

Höcker [ˈhœkɐ] m (-s; -) ZO hump

Hockey [ˈhɔki] n (-s; no pl) SPORT field hockey, Br hockey

Hoden [ˈhoːdən] m (-s; -) ANAT testicle

Hof [hoːf] m (-[e]s; Höfe [ˈhøːfə]) yard; AGR farm; court(yard); court; **~dame** f lady-in-waiting

hoffen [ˈhɔfən] v/i and v/t (ge-, h) hope (**auf** acc for); trust (in); **das Beste ~** hope for the best; **ich hoffe es** I hope so; **ich hoffe nicht, ich will es nicht ~** I

H

hope not; **'hoffentlich** *adv* I hope, let's hope, hopefully; **'Hoffnung** *f* (-; *-en*) hope (*auf acc* of); **sich ~en machen** have hopes; **die ~ aufgeben** lose hope

'hoffnungslos *adj* hopeless

'hoffnungsvoll *adj* hopeful; promising

höflich ['hø:flɪç] *adj* polite, courteous (*zu* to); **'Höflichkeit** *f* (-; *no pl*) politeness, courtesy

Höhe ['hø:ə] *f* (-; *-n*) height; AVIAT, MATH, ASTR, GEOGR altitude; peak (*a. fig*); *fig* amount; level; extent (*of damage etc*); MUS pitch; **auf gleicher ~ mit** on a level with; **in die ~** up; F **ich bin nicht ganz auf der ~** I'm not feeling up to the mark

Hoheit ['ho:haɪt] *f* (-; *no pl*) POL sovereignty; Highness

'Hoheits|gebiet *n* territory; **~gewässer** *pl* territorial waters; **~zeichen** *n* national emblem

'Höhen|luft *f* mountain air; **~messer** *m* altimeter; **~ruder** *n* AVIAT elevator; **~sonne®** *f* MED ultraviolet lamp, sunlamp; **~zug** *m* mountain chain

'Höhepunkt *m* climax, culmination, height, peak; highlight

hohl [ho:l] *adj* hollow (*a. fig*)

Höhle ['hø:lə] *f* (-; *-n*) cave, cavern; ZO hole, burrow; den, lair

'Hohl|maß *n* measure of capacity; **~raum** *m* hollow, cavity; **~spiegel** *m* concave mirror

Hohn [ho:n] *m* (-[*e*]*s*; *no pl*) derision, scorn; **'Hohngelächter** *n* jeering laughter; **höhnisch** ['hø:nɪʃ] *adj* derisive, scornful; **~es Lächeln** sneer

holen ['ho:lən] *v/t* (*ge-, h*) (go and) get, fetch, go for; draw (*breath*); call (*s.o., the police etc*); **~ lassen** send for; **sich ~** catch, get (*a cold etc*); seek (*advice*)

Holland ['hɔlant] Holland, *the* Netherlands; **Holländer** ['hɔlɛndɐ] *m* (-*s*; -) Dutchman; **Hol'länderin** ['hɔlɛndərɪn] *f* (-; *-nen*) Dutchwoman; **'holländisch** *adj* Dutch

Hölle ['hœlə] *f* (-; *no pl*) hell; **'Höllenlärm** F *m* a hell of a noise

Holler ['hɔlɐ] *Austrian m* (-*s*; -) BOT elder

höllisch ['hœlɪʃ] *adj* infernal, F hellish

holperig ['hɔlpərɪç] *adj* bumpy (*a. fig*), rough, uneven; *fig* clumsy (*style etc*)

holpern ['hɔlpɐn] *v/i* (*ge-, sein*) jolt, bump; *fig* be bumpy

Holunder [ho'lʊndɐ] *m* (-*s*; -) BOT elder

Holz [hɔlts] *n* (-*es*; *Hölzer* ['hœltsɐ]) wood; lumber, *Br a.* timber; **aus ~** (made) of wood, wooden; **~ hacken** chop wood; **~blasinstru,ment** *n* MUS woodwind (instrument)

hölzern ['hœltsɐn] *adj* wooden, *fig a.* clumsy

'Holz|fäller ['hɔltsfɛlɐ] *m* (-*s*; -) woodcutter, lumberjack; **~hammer** *m* mallet; *fig* sledgehammer

holzig ['hɔltsɪç] *adj* woody; stringy

'Holz|kohle *f* charcoal; **~schnitt** *m* woodcut; **~schnitzer** *m* wood carver; **~schuh** *m* clog; **~weg** *fig m*: **auf dem ~ sein** be barking up the wrong tree; **~wolle** *f* wood shavings, excelsior; **~wurm** *m* ZO woodworm

homöopathisch [homøo'pa:tɪʃ] *adj* hom(o)eopathic

homosexuell [homoze'ksuɛl] *adj* homosexual

Honig ['ho:nɪç] *m* (-*s*; -*e*) honey

'Honigwabe *f* honeycomb

Honorar [hono'ra:ɐ] *n* (-*s*; -*e*) fee

honorieren [hono'ri:rən] *v/t* (*no -ge-, h*) pay (a fee to); *fig* appreciate, reward

Hopfen ['hɔpfən] *m* (-*s*; -) BOT hop; *brewing:* hops

hoppla ['hɔpla] *int* (wh)oops!

hopsen ['hɔpsən] F *v/i* (*ge-, sein*) hop, jump

Hörappa,rat ['hø:ɐ'apara:t] *m* hearing aid

hörbar ['hø:ɐba:ɐ] *adj* audible

horchen ['hɔrçən] *v/i* (*ge-, h*) listen (*auf acc* to); eavesdrop; **Horcher** ['hɔrçɐ] *m* (-*s*; -) eavesdropper

Horde ['hɔrdə] *f* (-; *-n*) horde (*a. zo*), *contp a.* mob, gang

hören ['hø:rən] *v/i and v/t* (*ge-, h*) hear; listen to; obey, listen; **~ auf** (*acc*) listen to; **von j-m ~** hear from (*or* of, about) *s.o.*; **er hört schwer** his hearing is bad; **hör(t) mal!** listen!; look (here)!; **nun** *or also* **hör(t) mal!** wait a minute!, now look *or* listen here!; **Hörer** ['hø:rɐ] *m* (-*s*; -) listener; TEL receiver; **'Hörerin** ['hø:rərɪn] *f* (-; *-nen*) listener

'Hör|fehler ['hø:ɐfɛlɐ] *m* MED hearing defect; **~gerät** *n* hearing aid

hörig ['hø:rɪç] *adj*: **j-m ~ sein** be s.o.'s slave

Horizont [hori'tsɔnt] *m* (-[*e*]*s*; -*e*) horizon (*a. fig*); **s-n ~ erweitern** broaden one's mind; **das geht über meinen ~** that's beyond me; **horizontal** [horitsɔn'taːl] *adj* horizontal

Hormon [hɔr'moːn] *n* (*-s; -e*) hormone

Horn [hɔrn] *n* (*-[e]s; Hörner* ['hœrnɐ]) horn; **~haut** *f* horny skin, callus(es); ANAT cornea

Hornisse [hɔr'nɪsə] *f* (*-; -n*) ZO hornet

Horoskop [horo'skoːp] *n* (*-s; -e*) horoscope

Hör|rohr ['høːrroːrə] *n* MED stethoscope; **~saal** *m* lecture hall, auditorium; **~spiel** *n* radio play; **~weite** *f*: **in (au-ßer) ~** within (out of) earshot

Höschen ['høːsçən] *n* (*-s; -*) panties

Hose ['hoːzə] *f* (*-; -n*) (**e-e ~ zu rup-fen haben** a pair of) pants, *Br* trousers; slacks; shorts

'**Hosen|anzug** *m* pants (*Br* trouser) suit; **~schlitz** *m* fly; **~tasche** *f* trouser pocket; **~träger** *pl* (a pair of) suspenders *or Br* braces

Hospital [hɔspi'taːl] *n* (*-s; -täler* [hɔspi-'tɛːlɐ]) hospital

Hostie ['hɔstjə] *f* (*-; -n*) REL host

Hotel [ho'tɛl] *n* (*-s; -s*) hotel; **~di.rektor** *m* hotel manager; **~fach** (*-[e]s; no pl*) hotel business; **~zimmer** *n* hotel room

HP *abbr of* **Halbpension** half-board

Hr(n). *abbr of* **Herrn** Mr

Hubraum ['huːpraum] *m* MOT cubic capacity

hübsch [hypʃ] *adj* pretty, nice (-looking), cute; *fig* nice, lovely

Hubschrauber ['huːpʃraubɐ] *m* (*-s; -*) helicopter; **~landeplatz** *m* heliport

Huf [huːf] *m* (*-[e]s; -e*) ZO hoof

Hufeisen *n* horseshoe

Hüfte ['hyftə] *f* (*-; -n*) ANAT hip

'**Hüftgelenk** *n* ANAT hip joint

'**Hüftgürtel** *m* girdle

Hügel ['hyːgəl] *m* (*-s; -*) hill; '**hügelig** *adj* hilly; '**Hügelland** *n* downs

Huhn [huːn] *n* (*-[e]s; Hühner* ['hyːnɐ]) ZO chicken; hen; **Hühnchen** ['hyːnçən] *n* (*-s; -*) chicken; *F* **mit j-m ein ~ zu rup-fen haben** have a bone to pick with s.o.

Hühner|auge *n* MED corn; **~brühe** *f* chicken broth; **~ei** *n* hen's egg; **~farm** *f* poultry *or* chicken farm; **~hof** *m* poultry *or* chicken yard; **~leiter** *f* chicken ladder; **~stall** *m* henhouse

'**huldigen** ['hʊldɪgən] *v/i* (*ge-, h*) pay homage to; *fig* indulge in

Hülle ['hylə] *f* (*-; -n*) cover(ing), wrap (-ping); jacket, *Br* sleeve; sheath; **in ~ und Fülle** in abundance; '**hüllen** *v/t* (*ge-, h*) **~ in** (*acc*) wrap (up) in, cover in

Hülse ['hylzə] *f* (*-; -n*) BOT pod; husk; TECH case; '**Hülsenfrüchte** *pl* pulse

human [hu'maːn] *adj* humane

humanitär [humani'tɛːr] *adj* humanitarian; **Humanität** [humani'tɛːt] *f* (*-; no pl*) humanity

Hummel ['hʊməl] *f* (*-; -n*) ZO bumblebee

Hummer ['hʊmɐ] *m* (*-s; -*) ZO lobster

Humor [hu'moːr] *m* (*-s; no pl*) hu-mo(u)r; (**keinen**) **~ haben** have a (no) sense of humo(u)r; **Humorist** [humo'rɪst] *m* (*-en; -en*) humorist; **humo'ristisch, hu'morvoll** *adj* hu-morous

humpeln ['hʊmpəln] *v/i* (*ge-, h*) hobble; (*ge-, sein*) limp

Hund [hʊnt] *m* (*-[e]s; -e*) ZO dog

Hunde|hütte ['hʊndəhytə] *f* doghouse, *Br* kennel; **~kuchen** *m* dog biscuit; **~leine** *f* lead, leash

'**hunde|müde** *adj* dog-tired

hundert ['hʊndɐt] *adj a or* one hundred; **zu hunderten** by the hundreds

'**hundertfach** *adj* hundredfold

Hundert'jahrfeier *f* centenary, centen-nial; **hundertjährig** ['hʊndɐtjɛːrɪç] *adj* a hundred years old; a hundred years of

'**hundertste** *adj* hundredth

Hündin ['hʊndɪn] *f* (*-; -nen*) ZO bitch

hündisch ['hʊndɪʃ] *adj* doglike, slavish

Hüne ['hyːnə] *m* (*-n; -n*) giant

'**Hünengrab** *n* dolmen

Hunger ['hʊŋɐ] *m* (*-s; no pl*) hunger; **~ bekommen** get hungry; **~ haben** be hungry; **vor ~ sterben** die of starva-tion, starve to death

'**Hungerlohn** *m* starvation wages

'**hungern** *v/i* (*ge-, h*) go hungry, starve

'**Hungersnot** *f* famine

'**Hungerstreik** *m* hunger strike

'**Hungertod** *m* (death from) starvation

hungrig ['hʊŋrɪç] *adj* hungry (**nach, auf** *acc*)

Hupe ['huːpə] *f* (*-; -n*) MOT horn

'**hupen** *v/i* (*ge-, h*) MOT sound one's horn, hoot, honk

hüpfen ['hypfən] *v/i* (*ge, sein*) hop, skip; *ball etc*: bounce

Hürde ['hyrdə] *f* (*-; -n*) hurdle, *fig a.* ob-

stacle; zo fold, pen
'Hürdenlauf *m* SPORT hurdles
'Hürdenläufer *m*, **'Hürdenläuferin** *f*
SPORT hurdler
Hure ['huːrə] *f* (-; -n) whore, prostitute
huschen ['huʃən] *v/i* (ge-, sein) flit, dart
hüsteln ['hyːstəln] *v/i* (ge-, h) cough
slightly; **iro** hem; **husten** ['huːstən]
v/i (ge-, h), **Husten** (-s; *no pl*) cough
'Husten|bon,bon *m, n* cough drop;
~saft *m* PHARM cough syrup
Hut¹ [huːt] *m* (-[e]s; *Hüte* ['hyːtə]) hat;
den ~ aufsetzen (*abnehmen*) put on
(take off) one's hat
Hut² *f*: **auf der ~ sein** be on one's guard
(**vor** *dat* against)
hüten ['hyːtən] *v/t* (ge-, h) guard, protect, watch over; zo herd, mind; look
after; **das Bett~** be confined to (one's)
bed; **sich ~ vor** (*dat*) beware of; **sich ~,
et. zu tun** be careful not to do s.th.
'Hutkrempe *f* (hat) brim
hutschen ['hutʃən] *Austrian v/t and v/i*
→ **schaukeln**
Hütte ['hytə] *f* (-; -n) hut; *contp* shack;

cottage, cabin; mountain hut; TECH
ironworks
Hyäne ['hyːɛnə] *f* (-; -n) zo hy(a)ena
Hyazinthe [hya'tsɪntə] *f* (-; -n) BOT hya-
cinth
Hydrant [hy'drant] *m* (-en; -en) hydrant
hydraulisch [hy'draulɪʃ] *adj* hydraulic
Hydrokultur ['hyːdrokultuːɐ] *f* hydro-
ponics
Hygiene [hy'gjeːnə] *f* (-; *no pl*) hygiene
hygienisch [hy'gjeːnɪʃ] *adj* hygienic
Hypnose [hyp'noːzə] *f* (-; -n) hypnosis;
Hypnotiseur [hypnoti'zøːɐ] *m* (-s; -e)
hypnotist; **hypnotisieren** [hypnoti-
'ziːrən] *v/t* (*no -ge-, h*) hypnotize
Hypotenuse [hypote'nuːzə] *f* (-; -n)
MATH hypotenuse
Hypothek [hypo'teːk] *f* (-; -en) ECON
mortgage; **e-e ~ aufnehmen** take out
a mortgage
Hypothese [hypo'teːzə] *f* (-; -n) hypoth-
esis, supposition; **hypothetisch** [hypo-
'teːtɪʃ] *adj* hypothetical
Hysterie [hyste'riː] *f* (-; -n) hysteria
hysterisch [hys'teːrɪʃ] *adj* hysterical

I

i. A. *abbr of* **im Auftrag** p. p., per proc-
uration
ICE® [iːtseː'ʔeː] *abbr of* **Intercityex-
presszug** intercity express (train)
ich [ɪç] *pers pron* I; **~ selbst** (I) myself; **~
bin's** it's me
ideal [ide'aːl] *adj*, **Ideal** *n* (-s; -e) ideal;
Idealismus [idea'lɪsmʊs] *m* (-; *no pl*)
idealism; **Idea'list(in)** (-en; -en/-;
-nen) idealist
Idee [i'deː] *f* (-; -n) idea
identifizieren [identifi'tsiːrən] *v/t* (*no
-ge-, h*) identify; **sich ~ mit** identify
with; **identisch** [i'dentɪʃ] *adj* identical
Identitätskarte [identi'teːtskartə] *Austrian f* identity card
Ideologe [ideo'loːgə] *m* (-n; -n) ideolo-
gist; **Ideologie** [ideolo'giː] *f* (-; -n) ide-
ology; **ideo'logisch** *adj* ideological
idiomatisch [idio'maːtɪʃ] *adj* LING idio-
matic; **~er Ausdruck** idiom
Idiot [i'djoːt] *m* (-en; -en) idiot
Idi'otenhügel F *m skiing*: nursery slope

idi'otisch *adj* idiotic
Idol [i'doːl] *n* (-s; -e) idol
Idyll [i'dyl] *n* (-s; -e), **I'dylle** *f* (-; -n)
idyll(l); **i'dyllisch** *adj* idyllic
Igel ['iːgəl] *m* (-s; -s) zo hedgehog
Iglu ['iːglu] *m* (-s; -s) igloo
ignorieren [ɪgno'riːrən] *v/t* (*no -ge-, h*)
ignore, disregard
i. H. *abbr of* **im Hause** on the premises
ihr [iːɐ] *poss pron* her; *pl* their; **Ihr** your
ihrerseits ['iːɐzaits] *adv* on her (*pl*
their) part; **ihresgleichen** ['iːɐsglai-
çən] *indef pron* her (*pl* their) equals
people like herself (*pl* themselves); **ih-
retwegen** ['iːɐtveːgən] *adv* for her (*pl*
their) sake
Ikone [i'koːnə] *f* (-; -n) icon
illegal ['ɪlegaːl] *adj* JUR illegal
illegitim [ɪlegi'tiːm] *adj* JUR illegitimate
Illusion [ɪlu'zjoːn] *f* (-; -en) illusion
illusorisch [ɪlu'zoːrɪʃ] *adj* illusory
Illustration [ɪlʊstra'tsjoːn] *f* (-; -en) illustration; **illustrieren** [ɪlʊs'triːrən]

v/t (no -ge-, h) illustrate; **Illustrierte** [ɪlus'triːetə] *f (-n; -n)* magazine

im [ɪm] *prep* in the; ~ **Bett** in bed; ~ **Kino** *etc* at the cinema *etc*; ~ **Erdgeschoss** on the first (*Br* ground) floor; ~ **Mai** in May; ~ **Jahre 1997** in (the year) 1997; ~ **Stehen** (while) standing up; → **in**

imaginär [imagi'nɛːɐ] *adj* imaginary

Imbiss ['ɪmbɪs] *m (-es; -e)* snack

'Imbissstube *f* snack bar

imitieren [imi'tiːrən] *v/t (no -ge-, h)* imitate

Imker ['ɪmkɐ] *m (-s; -)* beekeeper

immatrikulieren [ɪmatriku'liːrən] *v/t and v/refl (no -ge-, h)* UNIV enrol(l), register

immer ['ɪmɐ] *adv* always, all the time; ~ **mehr** more and more; ~ **wieder** again and again; **für** ~ for ever, for good

'Immergrün *n* BOT evergreen

'immer'hin *adv* after all

'immer'zu *adv* all the time, constantly

Immigrant [imi'grant] *m (-en; -en)*, **Immi'grantin** *f (-; -nen)* immigrant

Immissionen [ɪmɪ'sjoːnən] *pl* (harmful effects of) noise, pollutants *etc*

Immobilien [ɪmo'biːliən] *pl* real estate; ~**makler** *m* realtor, real estate agent

immun [ɪ'muːn] *adj* immune (**gegen** to, against, from); ~ **machen** → **immunisieren** [imuni'ziːrən] *v/t (no -ge-, h)* immunize; **Immunität** [imuni'tɛːt] *f (-; no pl)* immunity; **Im'munschwäche** *f (-; -n)* MED immunodeficiency; **Im'munsystem** *n (-s; -e)* MED immune system

Imperativ ['ɪmperatiːf] *m (-s; -e)* LING imperative (mood)

Imperfekt ['ɪmperfɛkt] *n (-s; -e)* LING past (tense)

Imperialismus [ɪmperja'lɪsmʊs] *m (-; no pl)* imperialism; **Imperialist** [ɪmperja'lɪst] *m (-en; -en)*, **imperia-'listisch** *adj* imperialist

impfen ['ɪmpfən] *v/t (ge-, h)* MED vaccinate

'Impfpass *m* MED vaccination card; ~**schein** *m* MED vaccination certificate; ~**stoff** *m* MED vaccine, serum

'Impfung *f (-; -en)* MED vaccination

imponieren [ɪmpo'niːrən] *v/i (no -ge-, h) j-m* ~ impress s.o.

Import [ɪm'pɔrt] *m (-[e]s; -e)* ECON import(ation); **Importeur** [ɪmpɔr'tøːɐ] *m (-s; -e)* ECON importer; **importieren** [ɪmpɔr'tiːrən] *v/t (no -ge-, h)* ECON import

imposant [ɪmpo'zant] *adj* impressive, imposing

imprägnieren [ɪmprɛ'gniːrən] *v/t (no -ge-, h)*, **imprägniert** [ɪmprɛ'gniːɐt] *adj* waterproof

improvisieren [ɪmprovi'ziːrən] *v/t and v/i (no -ge-, h)* improvise

Impuls [ɪm'pʊls] *m (-es; -e)* impulse; stimulus

impulsiv [ɪmpʊl'ziːf] *adj* impulsive

imstande [ɪm'ʃtandə] *adj:* ~ **sein zu** *inf* be capable of *ger*

in [ɪn] *prp (dat and acc)* **1.** in, at; within, inside; into, in; **überall** ~ all over; ~ **der Stadt** in town; ~ **der Schule** at school; ~ **die Schule** to school; ~**s Kino** to the cinema; ~**s Bett** to bed; **warst du schon mal** ~ ...? have you ever been to ...?; → **im 2.** in, at; during; ~ **dieser** (**der nächsten**) **Woche** this (next) week; ~ **diesem Alter** (**Augenblick**) at this age (moment); ~ **der Nacht** at night; **heute** ~ **acht Tagen** a week from now; **heute** ~ **e-m Jahr** this time next year; → **im 3.** in, at; (*dat*) **gut sein** ~ (*dat*) be good at; ~ **Eile** in a hurry; ~ **Behandlung** (**Reparatur**) under treatment (repair); ~**s Deutsche** into German; → **im 4.** F ~ **sein** be in

'Inbegriff *m* epitome

'inbegriffen *adj* ECON included

in'dem *cj* while, as; by *doing s.th.*

Inder ['ɪndɐ] *m (-s; -)*, **Inderin** ['ɪndərɪn] *f (-; -nen)* Indian

Indian ['ɪndja:n] *Austrian m (-s; -e)* ZO turkey (cock)

Indianer [ɪn'dja:nɐ] *m (-s; -)*, **Indianerin** [ɪn'dja:nərɪn] *f (-; -nen)* Native American, (American) Indian

Indien ['ɪndjən] India

Indikativ ['ɪndikati:f] *m (-s; -e)* LING indicative (mood)

indirekt ['ɪndirɛkt] *adj* indirect, LING *a.* reported

indisch ['ɪndɪʃ] *adj* Indian

indiskret ['ɪndɪskreːt] *adj* indiscreet

Indiskretion [ɪndɪskre'tsjoːn] *f (-; -en)* indiscretion

indiskutabel [ɪndɪsku'taːbəl] *adj* out of the question

individuell [ɪndivi'duɛl] *adj*, **Individuum** [ɪndi'viːduʊm] *n* (-s; -en) individual

indiz [ɪn'diːts] *n* (-es; -ien) indication, sign; *pl* JUR circumstantial evidence

industrialisieren [ɪndʊstriali'ziːrən] *v/t* (*no* -ge-, h) industrialize; **Industriali'sierung** *f* (-; *no pl*) industrialization

Industrie [ɪndʊs'triː] *f* (-; -n) industry

Indus'triegebiet *n* industrial area

industriell [ɪndʊstri'ɛl] *adj* industrial

Industri'elle *m* (-n; -n) industrialist

inei'nander *adv* into one another; **~ verliebt** in love with each other; **~greifen** *v/i* (*irr*, **greifen**, *sep*, -ge-, h) TECH interlock (*a. fig*)

Infanterie [ɪnfantə'riː] *f* (-; -n) MIL infantry; **Infanterist** ['ɪnfantərɪst] *m* (-en; -en) MIL infantryman

Infektion [ɪnfɛk'tsjoːn] *f* (-; -en) MED infection; **Infekti'onskrankheit** *f* infectious disease

Infinitiv ['ɪnfinitiːf] *m* (-s; -e) LING infinitive (mood)

infizieren [ɪnfi'tsiːrən] *v/t* (*no* -ge-, h) MED infect

Inflation [ɪnfla'tsjoːn] *f* (-; -en) inflation

in'folge *prp* (*gen*) owing to, due to

infolge'dessen *adv* consequently

Informatik [ɪnfɔr'maːtɪk] *f* (-; *no pl*) computer science; **Infor'matiker(in)** [ɪnfɔr'maːtikɐ, ɪnfɔr'maːtikərɪn] *m(f)* (-s; -/-; -nen) computer scientist

Information [ɪnfɔrma'tsjoːn] *f* (-; -en) information; **die neuesten ~en** the latest information

informieren [ɪnfɔr'miːrən] *v/t* (*no* -ge-, h) inform; **falsch ~** misinform

in'frage: ~ stellen question; put in jeopardy; **~ kommen** be possible (*person*: eligible); **nicht ~ kommen** be out of the question

infrarot ['ɪnfraroːt] *adj* PHYS infrared

Infrastruk'tur *f* infrastructure

Ing. *abbr of* **Ingenieur** eng., engineer

Ingenieur [ɪnʒe'njøːɐ] *m* (-s; -e), **Inge'nieurin** [ɪnʒe'njøːrɪn] *f* (-; -nen) engineer

Ingwer ['ɪŋvɐ] *m* (-s; *no pl*) ginger

Inhaber ['ɪnhaːbɐ] *m* (-s; -), **'Inhaberin** *f* (-; -nen) owner, proprietor (proprietress); holder

Inhalt ['ɪnhalt] *m* (-[e]s; -e) contents; volume, capacity; *fig* meaning

'Inhalts|angabe *f* summary; **~verzeichnis** *n* table of contents

Initiative [initsja'tiːvə] *f* (-; -n) initiative; **die ~ ergreifen** take the initiative

inklusive [ɪnklu'ziːvə] *prp* ECON including

inkonsequent ['ɪnkɔnzekvɛnt] *adj* inconsistent

In-'Kraft-Treten *n* (-s; *no pl*) coming into force, taking effect

'Inland *n* (-[e]s; *no pl*) home (country); **~flug** *m* domestic (*or* internal) flight

inländisch ['ɪnlɛndɪʃ] *adj* domestic, home, inland

Inlett ['ɪnlɛt] *n* (-[e]s; -e) ticking

in'mitten *prp* (*gen*) in the middle of

innen ['ɪnən] *adv* inside; **nach ~** inwards

'Innen|archi,tekt *m*, **~archi,tektin** *f* interior designer; **~architek,tur** *f* interior design; **~mi,nister(in)** minister of the interior; Secretary of the Interior, *Br* Home Secretary; **~minis,terium** *n* ministry of the interior; Department of the Interior, *Br* Home Office; **~politik** *f* domestic politics

'innenpo,litisch *adj* domestic, internal

'Innenseite *f*: **auf der ~** (on the) inside

'Innenstadt *f* downtown, (city *or* town) center *or Br* centre

inner ['ɪnɐ] *adj* inside; *fig* inner; MED, POL internal; **Innere** ['ɪnərə] *n* (-n; *no pl*) interior, inside

Innereien [ɪnə'raiən] *pl* GASTR offal

'innerhalb *prp* (*gen*) within

'innerlich *adj* internal (*a.* MED)

innert ['ɪnɐt] *Swiss prp* (*gen or dat*) with in

innig ['ɪnɪç] *adj* tender, affectionate

Innung ['ɪnʊŋ] *f* (-; -en) guild

inoffiziell *adj* unofficial

ins [ɪns] → *in*

Insasse ['ɪnzasə] *m* (-n; -n) inmate; MOT passenger; **'Insassenversicherung** *f* MOT passenger insurance; **'Insassin** *f* (-; -nen) inmate; MOT passenger

insbe'sondere *adv* (e)specially

Inschrift *f* inscription, legend

Insekt [ɪn'zɛkt] *n* (-s; -en) ZO insect, bug

In'sektenstich *m* insect bite

Insel ['ɪnzəl] *f* (-; -n) island

'Inselbewohner *m* islander

Inserat [ɪnze'raːt] *n* (-[e]s; -e) advertisement, F ad; **inserieren** [ɪnze'riːrən] *v/t* *and v/i (no -ge-, h)* advertise

insge'heim *adv* secretly

insge'samt *adv* altogether, in all

inso'fern 1. *adv* as far as that goes **2.** *cj:* **~ als** in so far as

Inspektion [ɪnspɛk'tsjoːn] *f (-; -en)* inspection; MOT service

Inspektor [ɪn'spɛktoːɐ] *m (-s; -en* [ɪnspɛk'toːrən]), **Inspek'torin** *f (-; -nen)* inspector

inspizieren [ɪnspi'tsiːrən] *v/t (no -ge-, h)* inspect

Installateur [ɪnstala'tøːɐ] *m (-s; -e)* plumber; (gas *or* electrical) fitter

installieren [ɪnsta'liːrən] *v/t (no -ge-, h)* put in, fit, instal(l)

instand [ɪn'ʃtant] *adv:* **~ halten** keep in good condition *or* repair; TECH maintain; **~ setzen** repair

In'standhaltung *f (-; no pl)* maintenance

'inständig *adv:* **j-n ~ bitten** implore s.o.

In'standsetzung *f (-; -en)* repair

Instanz [ɪn'stants] *f (-; -en)* authority; JUR instance

Instinkt [ɪn'stɪŋkt] *m (-[e]s; -e)* instinct

instinktiv [ɪnstɪŋk'tiːf] *adv* instinctively

Institut [ɪnsti'tuːt] *n (-[e]s; -e)* institute

Institution [ɪnstitu'tsjoːn] *f (-; -en)* institution

Instrument [ɪnstru'mɛnt] *n (-[e]s; -e)* instrument

inszenieren [ɪnstse'niːrən] *v/t (no -ge-, h)* (put on) stage; *film:* direct; *fig* stage

Insze'nierung *f (-; -en)* production

intellektuell [ɪntɛlɛk'tuɛl] *adj,* **Intellektu'elle** *m, f (-n; -n)* intellectual, F highbrow

intelligent [ɪnteli'gɛnt] *adj* intelligent

Intelligenz [ɪnteli'gɛnts] *f (-; -en)* intelligence; **~quoti,ent** *m* I.Q.

Intendant [ɪntɛn'dant] *m (-en; -en),* **Inten'dantin** *f (-; -nen)* THEA *etc* director

intensiv [ɪntɛn'ziːf] *adj* intensive; intense; **Inten'sivkurs** *m* crash course

interessant [ɪntərɛ'sant] *adj* interesting; **Interesse** [ɪntə'rɛsə] *n (-s; -n)* interest (**an** *dat,* **für** in)

Inte'ressengebiet *n* field of interest

Interessent [ɪntərɛ'sɛnt] *m (-en; -en),* **Interes'sentin** *f (-; -nen)* interested person; ECON prospect, *Br* prospective buyer

interessieren [ɪntərɛ'siːrən] *v/t (no -ge-, h)* interest (**für** in); **sich ~ für** take an interest in; be interested in

intern [ɪn'tɛrn] *adj* internal

Internat [ɪntɐ'naːt] *n (-[e]s; -e)* boarding school

internatio'nal [ɪntɐnatsjo'naːl] *adj* international

Internet ['ɪntɐnɛt] *n (-[s]; no pl)* Internet

Internist [ɪntɐ'nɪst] *m (-en; -en),* **Inter'nistin** *f (-; -nen)* MED internist

Interpretation [ɪntɐpreta'tsjoːn] *f (-; -en)* interpretation; analysis

interpretieren [ɪntɐpre'tiːrən] *v/t (no -ge-, h)* interpret, ana|lyze, *Br* -lyse

Interpunktion [ɪntɐpuŋk'tsjoːn] *f (-; no pl)* punctuation

Intervall [ɪntɐ'val] *n (-[e]s; -e)* interval

intervenieren [ɪntɐve'niːrən] *v/i (no -ge-, h)* intervene

Interview ['ɪntɐvjuː] *n (-s; -s),* **interviewen** [ɪntɐ'vjuːən] *v/t (no -ge-, h)* interview

intim [ɪn'tiːm] *adj* intimate (**mit** with) (*a.* sexually); **Intimität** [ɪntimi'tɛːt] *f (-; no pl)* intimacy; **In'timsphäre** *f* privacy

intolerant ['ɪntolerant] *adj* intolerant (**gegen** of); **Intoleranz** ['ɪntolerants] *f (-; no pl)* intolerance

intransitiv ['ɪntranzitiːf] *adj* LING intransitive

Intrige [ɪn'triːgə] *f (-; -n)* intrigue, scheme, plot; **intrigieren** [ɪntri'giːrən] *v/i (no -ge-, h)* (plot and) scheme

Invalide [ɪnva'liːdə] *m (-n; -n)* invalid; **Inva'lidenrente** *f* disability pension

Invalidität [ɪnvalidi'tɛːt] *f (-; no pl)* disablement, disability

Inventar [ɪnvɛn'taːɐ] *n (-s; -e)* inventory, stock

Inventur [ɪnvɛn'tuːɐ] *f (-; -en)* ECON stocktaking; **~ machen** take stock

investieren [ɪnvɛs'tiːrən] *v/t (no -ge-, h)* ECON invest (*a. fig*); **Investition** [ɪnvɛsti'tsjoːn] *f (-; -en)* ECON investment

inwiefern [ɪnvi'fɛrn] *cj and adv* in what respect *or* way

inwie'weit *cj and adv* to what extent

'Inzucht *f* inbreeding

in'zwischen *adv* meanwhile, in the meantime; by now

irdisch ['ɪrdɪʃ] *adj* earthly, worldly

Ire ['iːrə] *m* (-*n*; -*n*) Irishman; *pl* the Irish

irgend ['ɪrgənt] *adv in cpds*: some...; any...; **wenn ~ möglich** if at all possible; **wenn du ~ kannst** if you possibly can; F **~ so ein** ... some ...;**~'ein(e)** *indef pron* some(one); any(one); **~'ein(e)s** *indef pron* some; any;**~etwas** something; anything;**~jemand** someone, somebody; anyone, anybody; **~'wann** *adv* sometime (or other); (at) any time;**~'wie** *adv* somehow (or other);**~'wo** *adv* somewhere; anywhere

Irin ['iːrɪn] *f* (-; -nen) Irishwoman;**irisch** ['iːrɪʃ] *adj* Irish;**Irland** ['ɪrlant] Ireland

Ironie [iro'niː] *f* (-; *no pl*) irony

ironisch [i'roːnɪʃ] *adj* ironic(al)

irre ['ɪrə] *adj* mad, crazy, insane; confused; F super, terrific

'Irre *m, f* (-*n*; -*n*) madman (madwoman), lunatic; **wie ein ~r** like mad *or* a madman

'irreführen *v/t* (*sep*, -*ge*-, *h*) mislead, lead astray;**~d** *adj* misleading

'irre|gehen *v/i* (*irr*, *gehen*, *sep*, -*ge*-, *sein*) go astray, *fig a.* be wrong;**~ma-chen** *v/t* (*sep*, -*ge*-, *h*) confuse

irren ['ɪrən] **1.** *v/refl* (*ge*-, *h*) be wrong, be mistaken; **sich ~** be wrong; **sich in et. ~** get s.th. wrong **2.** *v/i* (*ge*-, *sein*) wander, stray, err

irritieren [ɪri'tiːrən] *v/t* (*no* -*ge*-, *h*) irritate; F confuse

'Irrlicht *n* (-[*e*]*s*; -*er*) will-o'-the-wisp

'Irrsinn *m* (-[*e*]*s*; *no pl*) madness

'irrsinnig *adj* insane, mad; F terrific

Irrtum ['ɪrtuːm] *m* (-*s*; *Irrtümer* ['ɪrtyːmɐ]) error, mistake; **im ~ sein** be mistaken;**'irrtümlich** *adv* by mistake

Ischias ['ɪʃjas] *m, n, f* (-; *no pl*) MED sciatica

Islam [ɪs'laːm] *m* (-[*s*]; *no pl*) Islam

Island ['iːslant] Iceland

Isländer ['iːslɛndɐ] *m* (-*s*; -),**'Isländerin** ['iːslɛndərɪn] *f* (-; -nen) Icelander

'isländisch *adj* Icelandic

Isolierband [izo'liːɐbant] *n* (-[*e*]*s*; -*bän-der*) insulating tape; **isolieren** [izo-'liːrən] *v/t* (*no* -*ge*-, *h*) isolate; ELECTR, TECH insulate; **Iso'lierstati₀on** *f* MED isolation ward;**Iso'lierung** *f* (-; -*en*) isolation; ELECTR, TECH insulation

Israel ['ɪsraeːl] Israel

Israeli [ɪsra'eːli] *m* (-[*s*]; -[*s*]), *f* (-; -[*s*]),**israelisch** [ɪsra'eːlɪʃ] *adj* Israeli

Italien [i'taːljən] Italy; **Italiener** [ita-'ljeːnɐ] *m* (-*s*; -),**Itali'enerin** [ita-'ljeːnərɪn] *f* (-; -nen),**itali'enisch** *adj* Italian

J

ja [jaː] *adv* yes, F aye, yeah; PARL yea, aye; **wenn ~** if so; **da ist er ~!** well, there he is!; **ich sagte es Ihnen ~** I told you so; **ich bin ~ (schließlich)** ... after all, I am ...; **tut es 'ja nicht!** don't you dare do it!; **sei 'ja vorsichtig!** do be careful!; **vergessen Sie es 'ja nicht!** be sure not to forget it!; **~, weißt du nicht?** why, don't you know?; **du kommst doch, ~?** you're coming, aren't you?

Jacht [jaxt] *f* (-; -*en*) MAR yacht

Jacke ['jakə] *f* (-; -*n*) jacket; coat

Jackett [ʒa'kɛt] *n* (-*s*; -*s*) jacket, coat

Jagd [jaːkt] *f* (-; -*en*) hunt(ing) (*a. fig*); shoot(ing); *fig* chase; → **Jagdrevier**; **auf (die) ~ gehen** go hunting *or* shoot-ing; **~ machen auf** (*acc*) hunt (for); *a.* chase *s.o.*;**~aufseher** *m* gamekeeper;**~flugzeug** *n* MIL fighter (plane);**~hund**

m ZO hound;**~hütte** *f* (hunting) lodge;**~re₀vier** *n* hunting ground;**~schein** *m* hunting *or* shooting licen|se, *Br* -*ce*

jagen ['jaːgən] *v/t and v/i* (*ge*-, *h*) hunt; shoot; *fig* race, dash; hunt, chase; **j-n aus dem Haus** *etc* ~ drive *or* chase s.o. out of the house *etc*

Jäger ['jɛːgɐ] *m* (-*s*; -) hunter, hunts-man

Jaguar ['jaːguaːɐ] *m* (-*s*; -*e*) ZO jaguar

jäh [jɛː] *adj* sudden; steep

Jahr [jaːɐ] *n* (-[*e*]*s*; -*e* ['jaːrə]) year; **ein drei viertel ~** nine months; **einmal im ~** once a year; **im ~e 1995** in (the year) 1995; **ein 10 ~e altes Auto** a ten--year-old car; **mit 18 ~en, im Alter von 18 ~en** at (the age of) eighteen; **heute vor e-m ~** a year ago today; **die 80er-Jahre** the eighties

jahr'aus adv: ~, **jahrein** year in, year out; year after year

'**Jahrbuch** n yearbook, annual

jahrelang ['ja:rəlaŋ] **1.** adj longstanding, (many) years of **2.** adv for (many) years

Jahres... ['ja:rəs-] in cpds ...bericht, ...bilanz, ...einkommen etc: annual ...;~anfang m beginning of the year; ~ende n end of the year;~tag m anniversary;~wechsel m turn of the year; ~zahl f date, year;~zeit f season, time of (the) year

'**Jahrgang** m age group; PED year, class (*1995* of '95); GASTR vintage

Jahr'hundert n (-s; -e) century;~wende f turn of the century

jährlich ['jɛːrlɪç] **1.** adj annual, yearly **2.** adv every year, yearly, once a year

'**Jahrmarkt** m fair

Jahr'tausend n (-s; -e) millennium

Jahr'zehnt n (-[e]s; -e) decade

'**Jähzorn** m violent (fit of) temper

'**jähzornig** adj hot-tempered

Jalousie [ʒaluˈziː] f (-; -n) (venetian) blind

Jammer ['jamɐ] m (-s; no pl) misery; **es ist ein~** it is a pity;**jämmerlich** ['jɛmɐ-lɪç] adj miserable, wretched; pitiful, sorry; **~ versagen** fail miserably; '**jammern** v/i (ge-, h) moan, lament (**über** acc over, about); complain (of, about);**jammer'schade** adj: **es ist ~, dass** it's a crying shame that

Janker ['jaŋkɐ] m (-s; -) Austrian jacket

Jänner ['jɛnɐ] Austrian m (-s; -), **Janu-ar** ['janua:ɐ] m (-[s]; -e) January

Japan ['ja:pan] Japan; **Japaner** [ja-'pa:nɐ] m (-s; -), **Ja'panerin** [ja-'pa:nərɪn] f (-; -nen), **ja'panisch** adj Japanese

Jargon [ʒarˈɡõː] m (-s; -s) jargon; slang

'**Jastimme** f PARL aye, yea

jäten ['jɛːtən] v/t (ge-, h) weed

Jauche ['jauxə] f (-; -n) liquid manure

jauchzen ['jauxtsən] v/i (ge-, h) shout for or with joy; exult, rejoice

Jause ['jauzə] Austrian f (-; -n) snack

ja'wohl adv (that's) right, (yes,) indeed

je [je:] adv and cj ever; each; per; **der beste Film, den ich ~ gesehen habe** the best film I have ever seen; **~ zwei** (**Pfund**) two (pounds) each; **drei Euro ~ Kilo** three euros per kilo; **~ nach Grö-**ße (**Geschmack**) according to size (taste); **~ nachdem**(, **wie**) it depends (on how); **~ ..., desto ...** the ... the ...

Jeans [dʒiːnz] pl, a. f (-; -) (**e-e ~** a pair of) jeans;~jacke f denim jacket

jede ['je:də],**jeder** ['je:dɐ],**jedes** ['je:-dəs] indef pron every; any; each; either; **jeder weiß** (**das**) everybody knows; **du kannst jeden fragen** (you can) ask anyone; **jeder von uns** (**euch**) each of us (you); **jeder, der** whoever; **jeden zweiten Tag** every other day; **je-den Augenblick** any moment now; **je-des Mal** every time; **jedes Mal wenn** whenever

'**jeden'falls** adv in any case, anyhow

'**jedermann** indef pron everyone, everybody

'**jeder'zeit** adv any time, always

je'doch cj however

je'her adv: **von ~** always

jemals ['je:ma:ls] adv ever

jemand ['je:mant] indef pron someone, somebody; anyone, anybody

jene ['je:nə],**jener** ['je:nɐ],**jenes** ['je:-nəs] dem pron that (one); pl those; **dies und jenes** this and that

jenseitig ['je:nzaitɪç] adj opposite

jenseits ['je:nzaits] adv and prp (gen) on the other side (of), beyond (a. fig)

'**Jenseits** n (-; no pl) next world, hereafter

jetzig ['jɛtsɪç] adj present; existing

jetzt [jɛtst] adv now, at present; **bis ~** up to now, so far; **erst ~** only now; **~ gleich** right now or away; **von ~ an** from now on

jeweilig ['je:ˈvailɪç] adj respective

jeweils ['je:ˈvails] adv each; at a time

Jh. abbr of **Jahrhundert** cent., century

Jochbein ['jɔxbain] n ANAT cheekbone

Jockei ['dʒɔkə] m (-s; -s) jockey

Jod [jo:t] n (-[e]s; no pl) CHEM iodine

jodeln ['jo:dəln] v/i (ge-, h) yodel

Joga → **Yoga**

joggen ['dʒɔɡən] v/i (ge-, h) jog

Jogger ['dʒɔɡɐ] m (-s; -) jogger

Jogging ['dʒɔɡɪŋ] n (-s; no pl) jogging; ~anzug m tracksuit;~hose f tracksuit trousers

Joghurt , Jogurt ['jo:gurt] m, n (-[s]; -[s]) yog(h)urt, yoghourt

Johannisbeere [joˈhanɪsbeːrə] f: **rote~** redcurrant; **schwarze ~** blackcurrant

johlen ['jo:lən] v/i (ge-, h) howl, yell

Jolle ['jɔlə] f (-; -n) MAR dinghy

Jongleur [ʒɔ-'gløːɐ] m (-s; -e) juggler

jonglieren [ʒɔ-'gliːrən] v/t and v/i (no -ge-, h) juggle

Joule [dʒuːl] n (-[s]; -) PHYS joule

Journalismus [ʒʊrna'lɪsmʊs] m (-; no pl) journalism; **Journalist(in)** [ʒʊrna-'lɪst(ɪn)] (-en; -en/-; -nen) journalist

jr. → **jun.**

Jubel ['juːbəl] m (-s; no pl) cheering, cheers; rejoicing; **jubeln** v/i (ge-, h) cheer, shout for joy; rejoice

Jubiläum [jubi'lɛːʊm] n (-s; -läen) anniversary; **50-jähriges ~** fiftieth anniversary, (golden) jubilee

jucken ['jʊkən] v/t and v/i (ge-, h) itch; **es juckt mich am ...** my ... itches

Jude ['juːdə] m (-n; -n) Jewish person; **er ist ~** he is Jewish; **Jüdin** ['jyːdɪn] f (-; -nen) Jewish woman or girl; **sie ist ~** she is Jewish; **jüdisch** ['jyːdɪʃ] adj Jewish

Judo ['juːdo] n (-[s]; no pl) SPORT judo

Jugend ['juːgənt] f (-; no pl) youth; **die ~** young people; **~amt** n youth welfare office; **~arbeitslosigkeit** f youth unemployment

jugendfrei adj: **~er Film** G(-rated) (Br U(-rated)) film; **nicht ~** X-rated

Jugendfürsorge f youth welfare; **~gericht** n JUR juvenile court; **~herberge** f youth hostel; **~klub** m youth club; **~kriminalität** f juvenile delinquency

jugendlich adj youthful, young

Jugendliche m, f (-n; -n) young person, m a. youth, JUR a. juvenile

Jugendstil m (-s; no pl) Art Nouveau; **~strafanstalt** f detention center (Br centre), reformatory; **~verbot** n for adults only; → **jugendfrei**; **~zentrum** n youth center (Br centre)

Juli ['juːli] m (-[s]; -s) July

Jumbojet ['jumbojet] m jumbo (jet)

jun. abbr of **junior** Jun., jun., Jnr., Jr., junior

jung [jʊŋ] adj young

Junge[1] ['jʊŋə] m (-n; -n) boy; lad; cards: jack, knave

Junge[2] n (-n; -n) zo young; puppy; kitten; cub; **~ bekommen** or **werfen** have young

jungenhaft adj boyish

Jungenstreich m boyish prank

jünger ['jyŋɐ] adj younger

Jünger m (-s; -) REL disciple (a. fig)

Jungfern|fahrt f MAR maiden voyage; **~flug** m AVIAT maiden flight

Jungfrau f virgin; ASTR Virgo; **er ist ~** he's (a) Virgo; **~geselle** m bachelor, single (man); **~gesellin** f bachelor girl, single (woman); esp Br spinster

jüngste ['jyŋstə] adj youngest; fig latest; **in ~r Zeit** lately, recently; **das Jüngste Gericht** the Last Judg(e)-ment; **der Jüngste Tag** Doomsday

Juni ['juːni] m (-[s]; -s) June

junior ['juːnjoːɐ] adj, **Junior** m (-s; -en [ju'njoːrən]), **Junior|in** f (-; -nen) junior (a. SPORT)

Jupe [ʒyːp] Swiss m (-s; -s) skirt

Jura ['juːra]: **~ studieren** study (the) law

juridisch [ju'riːdɪʃ] Austrian → **juristisch**; **Jurist(in)** [ju'rɪst(ɪn)] (-en; -en/-; -nen) lawyer; law student; **ju'ristisch** adj legal

Jurorenkomitee [ju'roːrənkomiteː] Austrian n → **Jury**

Jury [ʒy'riː] f (-; -s) jury

justieren [jʊs'tiːrən] v/t (no -ge-, h) TECH adjust, set

Justiz [jʊs'tiːts] f (-; no pl) (administration of) justice, (the) law; **~beamte** m judicial officer; **~irrtum** m error of justice; **~minister** m minister of justice; Attorney General, Br Lord Chancellor; **~ministerium** n ministry of justice; Department of Justice

Jute ['juːtə] f (-; no pl) jute

Juwel [ju'veːl] m, n (-s; -en) jewel, gem (both a. fig); pl jewel(le)ry

Juwelier [juve'liːɐ] m (-s; -e) jewel(l)er

K

Kabarett [kaba'rɛt] n (-s; -s) (political) revue

Kabel ['ka:bəl] n (-s; -) cable

Kabelfernsehen n cable TV

Kabeljau ['ka:bəljau] m (-s; -e, -s) zo cod(fish)

Kabine [ka'bi:nə] f (-; -n) cabin; cubicle; SPORT dressing room; TECH car; TEL etc booth; **Ka'binenbahn** f cable railway

Kabinett [kabi'nɛt] n (-s; -e) POL cabinet

Kabis ['ka:bɪs] Swiss m (no pl) green cabbage

Kabriolett [kabrio'lɛt] n (-s; -s) MOT convertible

Kachel ['kaxəl] f (-; -n), **'kacheln** v/t (ge-, h) tile; **'Kachelofen** m tiled stove

Kadaver [ka'da:vɐ] m (-s; -) carcass

Kadett [ka'dɛt] m (-en; -en) MIL cadet

Käfer ['kɛ:fɐ] m (-s; -) zo beetle, bug

Kaffee ['kafe] m (-s; -s) coffee; **~ kochen** make coffee; **~ mit Milch** white coffee; **~auto, mat** m coffee machine; **~bohne** f coffee bean; **~haus** [ka-'fe:haus] Austrian n café, coffee house; **~kanne** f coffee pot; **~ma,schine** f coffeemaker; **~mühle** f coffee grinder

Käfig ['kɛ:fɪç] m (-s; -e) cage (a. fig)

kahl [ka:l] adj bald; fig bare (rock, wall etc); barren, bleak (landscape)

Kahn [ka:n] m (-[e]s; Kähne ['kɛ:nə]) boat; barge

Kai [kai] m (-s; -s) quay, wharf

Kaiser ['kaizɐ] m (-s; -) emperor

Kaiserin ['kaizərɪn] f (-; -nen) empress

'Kaiserreich n empire

Kajüte [ka'jy:tə] f (-; -n) MAR cabin

Kakao [ka'kau] m (-s; -s) cocoa; (hot) chocolate; chocolate milk

Kaktee [kak'te:] f (-; -n), **Kaktus** ['kak-tus] m (-; -Kakteen) BOT cactus

Kalb [kalp] n (-[e]s; Kälber ['kɛlbɐ]) zo calf; **kalben** ['kalbən] v/i (ge-, h) calve

'Kalbfleisch n veal

Kalbs | **braten** m roast veal; **~schnitzel** n veal cutlet; escalope (of veal)

Kaldaunen [kal'daunən] pl GASTR tripe

Kalender [ka'lɛndɐ] m (-s; -) calendar; **~jahr** n calendar year

Kali ['ka:li] n (-s; no pl) CHEM potash

Kaliber [ka'li:bɐ] m (-s; -) caliber, Br cal-ibre (a. fig)

Kalk [kalk] m (-[e]s; -e) lime; GEOL lime-stone, chalk; MED calcium; **'kalken** v/t (ge-, h) whitewash; AGR lime; **'kalkig** adj limy; **'Kalkstein** m limestone

Kalorie [kalo'ri:] f (-; -n) calorie

kalo'rien | **arm** adj, **~redu,ziert** adj low--calorie, low in calories; **~reich** adj high-calorie, high or rich in calories

kalt [kalt] adj cold; **mir ist ~** I'm cold; **es (mir) wird ~** it's (I'm) getting cold; **~ bleiben** fig keep (one's) cool; **das lässt mich kalt** that leaves me cold

kaltblütig ['kaltbly:tɪç] **1.** adj cold--blooded (a. fig) **2.** adv in cold blood

Kälte ['kɛltə] f (-; no pl) cold; fig cold-ness; **vor ~ zittern** shiver with cold; **fünf Grad ~** five degrees below zero; **~einbruch** m cold snap; **~grad** m de-gree below zero; **~peri,ode** f cold spell

'kaltmachen F v/t (sep, -ge-, h) bump off

kam [ka:m] pret of **kommen**

Kamee [ka'me:ə] f (-; -n) cameo

Kamel [ka'me:l] n (-s; -e) zo camel

Ka'melhaar n (-[e]s) camelhair

Kamera ['kaməra] f (-; -s) camera

Kamerad [kamə'ra:t] m (-en; -en [kamə'ra:dən]) companion, F mate, pal, buddy; **Kameradin** [kamə'ra:dɪn] f (-; -nen) companion

Kame'radschaft f (-; no pl) comrade-ship

Kameramann m cameraman

'Kamera,korder m (-s; -) camcorder

Kamille [ka'mɪlə] f (-; -n) BOT camomile

Kamin [ka'mi:n] m (-s; -e) fireplace; chimney (a. MOUNT); **am ~** by the fire (-side); **~kehrer** [ka'mi:nke:rɐ] m (-s; -) chimney sweep; **~sims** m, n mantel-piece

Kamm [kam] m (-[e]s; Kämme ['kɛmə]) comb, zo a. crest (a. fig)

kämmen ['kɛmən] v/t (ge-, h) comb; **sich (die Haare) ~** comb one's hair

Kammer ['kamɐ] f (-; -n) (small) room; storeroom, closet; garret; POL, ECON chamber; JUR division

'Kammermu,sik f chamber music

'Kammgarn n worsted (yarn)

Kampagne [kam'panjə] f (-; -n) campaign

Kampf [kampf] *m* (-[e]s; *Kämpfe* ['kɛmpfə]) fight (*a.* fig), struggle (*a.* fig), *esp* MIL combat, battle (*a.* fig); SPORT contest, match; *boxing*: fight, bout; *fig* conflict; '**kampfbereit** *adj* ready for battle (MIL combat); **kämpfen** ['kɛmpfən] *v/i* (ge-, h) fight (**gegen** against; **mit** with; **um** for) (*a.* fig); struggle (*a.* fig); *fig* contend, wrestle

Kampfer ['kampfɐ] *m* (-s; *no pl*) CHEM camphor

Kämpfer ['kɛmpfɐ] *m* (-s; -), '**Kämpferin** *f* (-; -nen) fighter (*a.* fig); **kämpferisch** ['kɛmpfərɪʃ] *adj* fighting, aggressive

'**Kampf flugzeug** *n* MIL combat aircraft; **~kraft** *f* (-; *no pl*) fighting strength; **~richter** *m* SPORT judge; **~sportarten** *pl* martial arts

Kanada ['kanada] Canada; **Kanadier** [ka'naːdjɐ] *m* (-s; -), **Ka'nadierin** [ka-'naːdjərɪn] *f* (-; -nen), **ka'nadisch** *adj* Canadian

Kanal [ka'naːl] *m* (-s; *Kanäle* [ka'nɛːlə]) canal; channel (*a.* TV, TECH, fig); sewer, drain; **der ~** the (English) Channel

Kanalisation [kanaliza'tsjoːn] *f* (-; -en) sewerage (system); canalization

kanalisieren [kanali'ziːrən] *v/t* (*no -ge-*, h) sewer; canalize; *fig* channel

Ka'naltunnel *m* Channel Tunnel, F Chunnel

Kanarienvogel [ka'naːrjənfoːgəl] *m* canary

Kandidat [kandi'daːt] *m* (-en; -en), **Kandi'datin** *f* (-; -nen) candidate; **Kandidatur** [kandida'tuːrɛ] *f* (-; -en) candidacy, *Br a.* candidature; **kandidieren** [kandi'diːrən] *v/i* (*no -ge-*, h) stand *or* run for election; **~ für ...** run for the office of ...

Känguru, **Känguruh** ['kɛŋguru] *n* (-s; -s) ZO kangaroo

Kaninchen [ka'niːnçən] *n* (-s; -) ZO rabbit

Kanister [ka'nɪstɐ] *m* (-s; -) (fuel) can

Kanne ['kanə] *f* (-; -n) pot; can

Kannibale [kani'baːlə] *m* (-n; -n) cannibal

kannte ['kantə] *pret of* **kennen**

Kanon ['kaːnɔn] *m* (-s; -s) MUS canon

Kanone [ka'noːnə] *f* (-; -n) MIL gun; cannon; F ace, *esp* SPORT *a.* crack

Kante ['kantə] *f* (-; -n) edge; '**kanten** *v/t* (ge-, h) set on edge; tilt; edge (*skis*)

'**Kanten** *m* (-s; -) crust

kantig ['kantɪç] *adj* angular, square(d)

Kantine [kan'tiːnə] *f* (-; -n) canteen

Kanton [kan'toːn] *m* (-s; -e) POL canton

Kanu ['kaːnu] *n* (-s; -s) canoe

Kanüle [ka'nyːlə] *f* (-; -n) MED cannula, (drain) tube

Kanzel ['kantsəl] *f* (-; -n) REL pulpit; AVIAT cockpit

Kanzlei [kants'lai] *f* (-; -en) office

Kanzler ['kantslɐ] *m* (-s; -) chancellor

Kanzlerin ['kantslərɪn] *f* (-; -nen) chancellor

Kap [kap] *n* (-s; -s) cape, headland

Kapazität [kapatsi'tɛːt] *f* (-; -en) capacity; *fig* authority

Kapelle [ka'pɛlə] *f* (-; -n) REL chapel; MUS band

Ka'pellmeister *m* MUS conductor

kapern ['kaːpɛn] *v/t* (ge-, h) MAR capture, seize

kapieren [ka'piːrən] F *v/t* (*no -ge-*, h) get; **kapiert?** got it?

Kapital [kapi'taːl] *n* (-s; -e; -ien) ECON capital, funds; **~anlage** *f* investment

Kapitalismus [kapita'lɪsmʊs] *m* (-; *no pl*) capitalism; **Kapita'list** *m* (-en; -en), **kapita'listisch** *adj* capitalist

Kapi'talverbrechen *n* capital crime, JUR felony

Kapitän [kapi'tɛːn] *m* (-s; -e) captain (*a.* SPORT)

Kapitel [ka'pɪtəl] *n* (-s; -) chapter (*a.* fig); F *fig* story

Kapitulation [kapitula'tsjoːn] *f* (-; -en) capitulation, surrender (*a.* fig)

kapitulieren [kapitu'liːrən] *v/i* (*no -ge-*, h) capitulate, surrender (*a.* fig)

Kaplan [ka'plaːn] *m* (-s; *Kapläne* [ka-'plɛːnə]) REL curate

Kappe ['kapə] *f* (-; -n) cap, TECH *a.* top, hood; '**kappen** *v/t* (ge-, h) cut (*rope*); lop, top (*tree*)

Kapsel ['kapsəl] *f* (-; -n) capsule

kaputt [ka'pʊt] F *adj* broken (*a.* fig) TECH out of order; *fig* dead beat; ruined; **~ machen** F *v/t* (sep, -ge-, h) break, wreck (*a.* fig), ruin; *fig* → **~ma chen**; **~gehen** F *v/i* (irr, **gehen**, sep -ge-, sein) break; MOT *etc* break down *fig* break up; **~machen** *v/t* (sep, -ge-, h) F *fig* wreck, ruin

Kapuze [ka'puːtsə] f (-; -n) hood; cowl

Karabiner [kara'biːnɐ] m (-s; -) carbine; **~haken** m karabiner, snaplink

Karaffe [ka'rafə] f (-; -n) decanter

Karambolage [karambo'laːʒə] f (-; -n) collision, crash

Karat [ka'raːt] n (-[e]s; -e) carat

Karate [ka'raːtə] n (-[s]; no pl) SPORT karate

Karawane [kara'vaːnə] f (-; -n) caravan

Kardinal [kardi'naːl] m (-s; Kardinäle [kardi'nɛːlə]) REL cardinal

Karfiol [kar'fjoːl] Austrian m (-s; no pl) BOT cauliflower

Kar'freitag [kaːɐ'fraitaːk] m REL Good Friday

karg [kark], **kärglich** ['kɛrklɪç] adj meager, Br -re, scanty; frugal; poor

kariert [ka'riːɐt] adj checked, checkered, Br chequered; squared

Karies ['kaːrjɛs] f (-; no pl) MED (dental) caries

Karikatur [karika'tuːɐ] f (-; -en) mst cartoon, esp fig caricature; **Karikaturist** [karikatu'rɪst] m (-en; -en) cartoonist

karikieren [kari'kiːrən] v/t (no -ge-, h) caricature

Karneval ['karnəval] m (-s; -e, -s) carnival

Karo ['kaːro] n (-s; -s) square, check; cards: diamonds

Karosserie [karɔsə'riː] f (-; -n) MOT body

Karotte [ka'rɔtə] f (-; -n) BOT carrot

Karpfen ['karpfən] m (-s; -) ZO carp

Karre ['karə] f (-; -n), **'Karren** m (-s; -) cart; wheelbarrow; F MOT jalopy

Karriere [ka'rjeːrə] f (-; -n) career; **~machen** work one's way up, get to the top

Karte ['kartə] f (-; -n) card; ticket; GEOGR map; chart; GASTR menu; **gute (schlechte) ~n** a good (bad) hand

Kartei [kar'tai] f (-; -en) card index; **~karte** f index or file card

'Karten|haus n house of cards (a. fig); MAR chartroom; **~spiel** n card game; deck (Br pack) of cards; **~tele,fon** n cardphone; **~vorverkauf** m advance booking; box office

Kartoffel [kar'tɔfəl] f (-; -n) BOT potato; **~brei** m mashed potatoes; **~chips** pl (potato) chips, Br crisps; **~kloß** m, **~knödel** m potato dumpling; **~puffer** m potato fritter; **~schalen** pl potato

peelings; **~schäler** m potato peeler

Karton [kar'tɔŋ] m (-s; -s) cardboard; pasteboard; cardboard box

Karussell [karʊ'sɛl] n (-s; -s) roundabout, car(r)ousel, merry-go-round

Karwoche ['kaːɐvɔxə] f REL Holy Week

Kaschmir ['kaʃmiːɐ] m (-s; -e) cashmere

Käse ['kɛːzə] m (-s; -) cheese

Kaserne [ka'zɛrnə] f (-; -n) barracks

Ka'sernenhof m barrack square

käsig ['kɛːzɪç] adj cheesy; pasty

Kasino [ka'ziːno] n (-s; -s) casino; MIL (officers') mess

Kasperle ['kaspɛlə] n, m (-s; -) Punch; **~the,ater** n Punch and Judy show

Kassa ['kasa] Austrian f (-; Kassen), **Kasse** ['kasə] f (-; -n) till; cash register; checkout (counter); cash desk; cashier's counter; THEA etc box office; F **gut (knapp) bei Kasse sein** be flush (be a bit hard up)

'Kassen|beleg m, **~bon** m sales slip, Br receipt; **~erfolg** m THEA etc box-office success; **~pati,ent** m MED health plan (Am medicaid, Br NHS) patient; **~schlager** F m blockbuster; **~wart** ['kasənvart] m (-[e]s; -e) treasurer

Kassette [ka'sɛtə] f (-; -n) box, case; MUS, TV, PHOT etc cassette; casket

Kas'setten... in cpds ...rekorder etc: cassette ...

kassieren [ka'siːrən] v/t and v/i (no -ge-, h) collect, take (the money)

Kassierer [ka'siːrɐ] m (-s; -), **Kas'siererin** f (-; -nen) cashier; teller; collector

Kastanie [kas'taːnjə] f (-; -n) BOT chestnut

Kasten ['kastən] m (-s; Kästen ['kɛstən]) box (a. F TV, SPORT etc); case; chest

kastrieren [kas'triːrən] v/t (no -ge-, h) MED, VET castrate

Kasus ['kaːzus] m (-; -) LING case

Katalog [kata'loːk] m (-[e]s; -e) catalog(ue Br)

Katalysator [kataly'zaːtoːɐ] m (-s; -en [katalyza'toːrən]) CHEM catalyst; MOT catalytic converter

katastrophal [katastro'faːl] adj disastrous (a. fig); **Katastrophe** [katas-

'tro:fə] f (-; -n) catastrophe, disaster (a. fig)

Kata'strophen|gebiet n disaster area; **~schutz** m disaster control

Katechismus [katɛ'çɪsmʊs] m (-; -men) REL catechism

Kategorie [katego'ri:] f (-; -n) category

Kater ['ka:tɐ] m (-s; -) ZO male cat, tom-cat; F hangover

kath. abbr of **katholisch** Cath., Catholic

Kathedrale [kate'dra:lə] f (-; -n) cathedral

Katholik [kato'li:k] m (-en; -en), **Katho'likin** f (-; -nen), **katholisch** [ka'to:lɪʃ] adj (Roman) Catholic

Kätzchen ['kɛtsçən] n (-s; -) ZO kitten, pussy (a. BOT)

Katze ['katsə] f (-; -n) ZO cat; kitten

Kauderwelsch ['kaudɐvɛlʃ] n (-[s]; no pl) gibberish

kauen ['kauən] v/t and v/i (ge-, h) chew

kauern ['kauɐn] v/i and v/refl (ge-, h) crouch, squat

Kauf [kauf] m (-[e]s; Käufe ['kɔyfə]) purchase (a. ECON), F buy; purchasing, buying; **ein guter~** a bargain, F a good buy; **zum ~ anbieten** offer for sale

'**kaufen** v/t (ge-, h) buy (a. fig), purchase

Käufer ['kɔyfɐ] m (-s; -), **Käuferin** f (-; -nen) buyer; customer

'**Kauffrau** f (-; -en) businesswoman

'**Kauf|haus** n department store; **~kraft** f (-; no pl) ECON purchasing power

käuflich ['kɔyflɪç] adj for sale; fig venal

'**Kaufmann** m (-[e]s; -leute) businessman; dealer, trader, merchant; storekeeper; Br mst shopkeeper; grocer

kaufmännisch ['kaufmɛnɪʃ] adj commercial, business; **~er Angestellter** clerk

'**Kaufvertrag** m contract of sale

'**Kaugummi** m (-s; -s) chewing gum

kaum [kaum] adv hardly; **~ zu glauben** hard to believe

Kaution [kau'tsjo:n] f (-; -en) security; JUR bail

Kautschuk ['kautʃʊk] m (-s; -e) (india) rubber

Kavalier [kava'li:ɐ] m (-s; -e) gentleman

Kaviar ['ka:vjar] m (-s; -e) caviar(e)

keck [kɛk] adj cheeky, saucy, pert

Kegel ['ke:gəl] m (-s; -) skittle, pin; MATH, TECH cone; **~bahn** f bowling (esp Br skittle) alley

'**kegelförmig** ['ke:gəlfœrmɪç] adj conical

'**Kegelkugel** f bowling (esp Br skittle) ball

'**kegeln** v/i (ge-, h) bowl, go bowling, esp Br play (at) skittles or ninepins

Kehle ['ke:lə] f (-; -n) ANAT throat

'**Kehlkopf** m ANAT larynx

Kehre ['ke:rə] f (-; -n) (sharp) bend

'**kehren** v/t (ge-, h) sweep; **j-m den Rücken ~** turn one's back on s.o.

Kehricht ['ke:rɪçt] m (-s; no pl) sweepings; **~schaufel** f dustpan

kehrtmachen ['ke:ɐtmaxən] v/i (sep, -ge-, h) turn back

keifen ['kaifən] v/i (ge-, h) nag, bitch

Keil [kail] m (-[e]s; -e) wedge; gusset

Keiler ['kailɐ] m (-s; -) ZO wild boar

'**Keilriemen** m MOT fan belt

Keim [kaim] m (-[e]s; -e) BIOL, MED germ; BOT bud, sprout; fig seed(s)

'**keimen** v/i (ge-, h) BOT germinate, sprout; fig form, grow; stir

'**keimfrei** adj MED sterile

'**keimtötend** adj MED germicidal

'**Keimzelle** f BIOL germ cell

kein [kain] indef pron **1.** adj: **~(e)** no, not any; **~ anderer** no one else; **~(e) ... mehr** not any more ...; **~ Geld (~e Zeit) mehr** no money (time) left; **~ Kind mehr** no longer a child **2.** su: **~er, ~e, ~(e)s** none, no one, nobody; **~er von beiden** neither (of the two); **~er von uns** none of us; '**keines'falls** adv by no means, under no circumstances; '**keineswegs** [kainəs've:ks] adv by no means, not in the least; '**keinmal** adv not once, not a single time

Keks [ke:ks] m, n (-es; -e) cookie, Br biscuit

Kelch [kɛlç] m (-[e]s; -e) cup (a. BOT); REL chalice

Kelle ['kɛlə] f (-; -n) GASTR ladle, scoop; TECH trowel; signaling disk

Keller ['kɛlɐ] m (-s; -) cellar; → **~geschoss** n, **~geschoß** Austrian n basement; **~wohnung** f basement (apartment, esp Br flat)

Kellner ['kɛlnɐ] m (-s; -) waiter

Kellnerin ['kɛlnərɪn] f (-; -nen) waitress

keltern ['kɛltɐn] v/t (ge-, h) press

kennen ['kɛnən] v/t (irr, ge-, h) know, be acquainted with; **~ lernen → kennenlernen**

'kennenlernen v/t (sep, -ge-, h) get to know, become acquainted with; meet s.o.; **als ich ihn kennenlernte** when I first met him

Kenner ['kɛnɐ] m (-s; -), **'Kennerin** f (-; -nen) expert; **kenntlich** ['kɛntlɪç] adj recognizable (**an** dat by); **Kenntnis** f (-; -se) knowledge; **gute ~se in** (dat) a good knowledge of

'Kennwort n password

'Kennzeichen n mark, sign; (distinguishing) feature, characteristic; MOT license (Br registration) number

'kennzeichnen v/t (ge-, h) mark; fig characterize

kentern ['kɛntɐn] v/i (ge-, sein) MAR capsize

Keramik [ke'raːmɪk] f (-; -en) ceramics

Kerbe ['kɛrbə] f (-; -n) notch

Kerker ['kɛrkɐ] m (-s; -) dungeon

Kerl [kɛrl] F m (-s; -e) fellow, guy; **armer ~** poor devil; **ein anständiger ~** a decent sort

Kern [kɛrn] m (-[e]s; -e) BOT pip, seed, stone, kernel; TECH core (a. fig); PHYS nucleus; **~...** in cpds **...energie, ...forschung, ...physik, ...reaktor, ...technik** etc: nuclear ...; **~fach** n PED basic subject; **~fa,milie** f nuclear family; **~gehäuse** n BOT core

'kernge'sund adj F (as) sound as a bell

kernig ['kɛrnɪç] adj full of seeds (Br pips); fig robust; pithy

'Kernkraft f PHYS nuclear power; **~gegner** m anti-nuclear activist; **~werk** n nuclear power station or plant

'kernlos adj BOT seedless

'Kernspaltung f PHYS nuclear fission

'Kernwaffen pl MIL nuclear weapons; **'kernwaffenfrei** adj: **~e Zone** MIL nuclear-free zone; **'Kernwaffenversuch** m MIL nuclear test

'Kernzeit f ECON core time

Kerze ['kɛrtsə] f (-; -n) candle; SPORT shoulder stand

kess [kɛs] F adj cheeky, saucy, pert

Kessel ['kɛsəl] m (-s; -) kettle; TECH boiler; tank

Kette ['kɛtə] f (-; -n) chain (a. fig); necklace; **e-e ~ bilden** form a line

'Ketten... in cpds **...antrieb, ...laden, ...rauchen, ...raucher, ...reaktion** etc: chain ...

'ketten v/t (ge-, h) chain (**an** acc to)

'Kettenfahrzeug n tracked vehicle

Ketzer ['kɛtsɐ] m (-s; -) heretic

Ketzerei [kɛtsə'raɪ] f (-; -en) heresy

keuchen ['kɔʏçən] v/i (ge-, h) pant, gasp

'Keuchhusten m MED whooping cough

Keule ['kɔʏlə] f (-; -n) club; GASTR leg

keusch [kɔʏʃ] adj chaste

'Keuschheit f (-; no pl) chastity

Kfz [kaː'ʔɛf'tsɛt] abbr of **Kraftfahrzeug** motor vehicle; **Kf'z-Brief** m, **Kf'z-Schein** m vehicle registration document; **Kf'z-Steuer** f road or automobile tax; **Kf'z-Werkstatt** f garage

KG [kaː'geː] abbr of **Kommanditgesellschaft** ECON limited partnership

kichern ['kɪçɐn] v/i (ge-, h) giggle

Kiebitz ['kiːbɪts] m (-es; -e) ZO peewit, lapwing; F kibitzer

Kiefer[1] ['kiːfɐ] m (-s; -) ANAT jaw(bone)

Kiefer[2] f (-; -n) BOT pine(tree)

Kiel [kiːl] m (-[e]s; -e) MAR keel; **~flosse** f AVIAT tail fin; **~raum** m MAR bilge; **~wasser** n (-s; -) MAR wake (a. fig)

Kieme ['kiːmə] f (-n; -n) ZO gill

Kies [kiːs] m (-es; -e) gravel (a. **mit ~ bestreuen**); F dough

Kiesel ['kiːzəl] m (-s; -) pebble

Kilo ['kiːlo] n (-s; -) → **Kilogramm**

Kilo|'gramm ['kiːlo'gram] n kilogram(me); **~hertz** [kiːlo'hɛrts] n (-; -) kilohertz; **~'meter** m kilometer, Br kilometre; **~'watt** n ELECTR kilowatt

Kind [kɪnt] n (-[e]s; -er ['kɪndɐ]) child; **ein ~ erwarten** be expecting a baby

'Kinder|arzt m, **~ärztin** f p(a)ediatrician; **~garten** m kindergarten, nursery school; **~gärtnerin** ['kɪndɐgɛrtnərɪn] f (-; -nen) nursery-school or kindergarten teacher; **~geld** n child benefit; **~hort** ['kɪndɐhɔrt] m (-[e]s; -e), **~krippe** f day nursery; **~lähmung** f MED polio(-myelitis)

'kinderlieb adj fond of children

'kinderlos adj childless

'Kinder|mädchen n nurse(maid), nanny; **~spiel** fig n: **ein ~ sein** be child's play; **~stube** fig f manners, upbringing; **~wagen** m baby carriage, buggy, Br pram; **~zimmer** n children's room

Kindes|alter ['kɪndəs'ʔaltɐ] n childhood; infancy; **~entführung** f kidnap-(p)ing; **~misshandlung** f child abuse

'Kindheit f (-; no pl) (**von ~ an** from) childhood

K

kindisch ['kɪndɪʃ] *adj* childish

'**kindlich** *adj* childlike

Kinn [kɪn] *n* (-[e]s; -e) ANAT chin;~**backe** *f*,~**backen** *m* (-s; -) ANAT jaw(-bone);~**haken** *m boxing:* hook (to the chin), uppercut

Kino ['kiːno] *n* (-s; -s) *(no pl)* motion pictures, *esp Br* cinema, F *the* movies; movie theater, *esp Br* cinema

'**Kinobesucher** *m*, '**Kinogänger** ['kiːnogɛŋɐ] *m* (-s; -) moviegoer, *Br* cinemagoer

Kippe ['kɪpə] *f*(-; -n) F butt, *esp Br* stub; SPORT upstart

'**kippen 1.** *v/i* (ge-, sein) tip *or* topple (over) **2.** *v/t* (ge-, h) tilt, tip over *or* up

Kirche ['kɪrçə] *f* (-; -n) church; **in die ~ gehen** go to church

'**Kirchen|buch** *n* parish register;~**diener** *m* sexton;~**gemeinde** *f* parish;~**jahr** *n* Church *or* ecclesiastical year;~**lied** *n* hymn;~**mu,sik** *f* sacred *or* church music;~**schiff** *n* ARCH nave;~**steuer** *f* church tax;~**stuhl** *m* pew;~**tag** *m* church congress

'**Kirchgang** *m* churchgoing; **Kirchgänger** ['kɪrçgɛŋɐ] *m* (-s; -) churchgoer

'**kirchlich** *adj* church, ecclesiastical

'**Kirchturm** *m* steeple; spire; church tower

Kirsche ['kɪrʃə] *f* (-; -n) BOT cherry

Kissen ['kɪsən] *n* (-s;-) pillow; cushion;~**bezug** *m*,~**hülle** *f* pillowcase, pillowslip

Kiste ['kɪstə] *f* (-; -n) box, chest; crate

Kitsch [kɪtʃ] *m* (-[e]s; *no pl*) kitsch; trash; F slush

'**kitschig** *adj* kitschy; trashy; slushy

Kitt [kɪt] *m* (-[e]s; -e) cement; putty

Kittel ['kɪtəl] *m* (-s; -) smock; overall; MED (white) coat

'**kitten** *v/t* (ge-, h) cement; putty

Kitzel ['kɪtsəl] *m* (-s; -) tickle, *fig a.* thrill, kick; **Kitzeln** *v/i and v/t* (ge-, h) tickle; **Kitzler** ['kɪtslɐ] *m* (-s; -) ANAT clitoris; **kitzlig** ['kɪtslɪç] *adj* ticklish (*a. fig*)

kläffen ['klɛfən] *v/i* (ge-, h) yap, yelp

klaffend ['klafənt] *adj* gaping; yawning

Klage ['klaːgə] *f* (-; -n) complaint; lament; JUR action, (law)suit

'**klagen** *v/i* (ge-, h) complain (*über acc* of, about; *bei* to); lament; JUR go to court; *gegen j-n ~* JUR sue s.o.

Kläger ['klɛːgɐ] *m* (-s; -), '**Klägerin** *f* (-; -nen) JUR plaintiff

kläglich ['klɛːklɪç] → **jämmerlich**

Klamauk [kla'mauk] *m* (-s; *no pl*) racket; THEA *etc* slapstick

klamm [klam] *adj* numb; clammy

Klammer ['klamɐ] *f* (-; -n) TECH cramp; clamp; clip; clothespin, *Br* (clothes) peg; MED brace; MATH, PRINT bracket(s); '**klammern** *v/t* (ge-, h) fasten *or* clip together; *sich ~ an* (*acc*) cling to

klang [klaŋ] *pret of* **klingen**

Klang *m* (-[e]s; *Klänge* ['klɛŋə]) sound; tone; clink; ringing

'**klangvoll** *adj* sonorous; *fig* illustrious

Klappe ['klapə] *f*(-; -n) flap; hinged lid; MOT tailgate, *Br* tailboard; TECH, BOT, ANAT valve; F trap; '**klappen** (ge-, h) **1.** *v/i:* **nach oben ~** lift up, raise; put *or* fold up; **nach unten ~** lower, put down; **es lässt sich (nach hinten) ~** it folds (backward) **2.** *v/i* clap, clack; F work, work out (well)

Klapper ['klapɐ] *f* (-; -n) rattle

'**klappern** *v/i* (ge-, h) clatter, rattle (*mit et.* s.th.)

'**Klapperschlange** *f* ZO rattlesnake

Klapp|fahrrad ['klapfaːraːt] *n* folding bicycle;~**fenster** *n* top-hung window;~**messer** *n* jack knife, clasp knife

klapprig ['klaprɪç] *adj* MOT rattly, ramshackle; F shaky

'**Klappsitz** *m* folding *or* tip-up seat

'**Klappstuhl** *m* folding chair

'**Klapptisch** *m* folding table

Klaps [klaps] *m* (-es; -e) slap, pat; smack

klar [klaːɐ] *adj* clear (*a. fig*); **ist dir ~, dass ...?** do you realize that ...?; **das ist mir (nicht ganz) ~** I (don't quite) understand; **(na) ~!** of course!; **alles ~?** everything okay?

Kläranlage ['klɛːɐʔanlaːgə] *f* sewage works

klären ['klɛːrən] *v/t* (ge-, h) TECH purify, treat; *fig* clear up; settle; SPORT clear

'**Klarheit** *f*(-; *no pl*) clearness, *fig a.* clarity

Klarinette [klari'netə] *f* (-; -n) MUS clarinet

'**Klarsicht...** *in cpds* transparent

Klasse ['klasə] *f*(-; -n) class (*a.* POL), PED *a.* grade, *Br* form; classroom; F **klasse sein** be super, be fantastic

'**Klassen|arbeit** *f* (classroom) test;

~buch n classbook, Br (class) register; **~kame,rad** m classmate; **~lehrer(in)** homeroom teacher, Br form teacher, a. form master (mistress); **~sprecher** m class representative; **~zimmer** n classroom

klassifizieren [klasifi'tsi:rən] v/t (no -ge-, h) classify; '**Klassifi'zierung** f (-; -en) classification

Klassiker ['klasikɐ] m (-s; -) classic

klassisch ['klasɪʃ] adj classic(al)

Klatsch [klatʃ] F m (-es; no pl) gossip

'**Klatschbase** f gossip

'**klatschen** v/i and v/t (ge-, h) clap, applaud; F slap, bang; splash; F gossip; **in die Hände ~** clap one's hands

'**klatschhaft** adj gossipy

'**Klatschmaul** F n (old) gossip

'**klatsch'nass** F adj soaking wet

klauben ['klaubən] Austrian v/t (ge-, h) pick; gather

Klaue ['klauə] f (-; -n) zo claw; pl fig clutches

klauen ['klauən] F v/t (ge-, h) pinch

Klausel ['klauzəl] f (-; -n) JUR clause; condition

Klausur [klau'zu:ɐ] f (-; -en) test (paper), exam(ination)

Klavier [kla'vi:ɐ] n (-s; -e) MUS piano; **~ spielen** play the piano; **~kon,zert** n MUS piano concerto; piano recital

Klebeband ['kle:bəbant] n (-[e]s; -bänder) adhesive tape; **kleben** ['kle:bən] (ge-, h) **1.** v/t glue, paste; stick **2.** v/i stick, cling (**an** dat to) (a. fig); **klebrig** ['kle:brɪç] adj sticky

Kleb|stoff ['kle:pʃtɔf] m adhesive; glue; **~streifen** m adhesive tape

kleckern ['klekɐn] F (ge-, h) **1.** v/i make a mess **2.** v/t spill

Klecks [kleks] F m (-es; -e) (ink)blot; blob; **klecksen** ['kleksən] F v/i (ge-, h) blot, make blots

Klee [kle:] m (-s; no pl) BOT clover

'**Kleeblatt** n cloverleaf

Kleid [klait] n (-[e]s; -er ['klaidɐ]) dress; pl clothes; **kleiden** ['klaidən] v/t (ge-, h) dress, clothe; **j-n gut ~** suit s.o.; **sich gut** etc **~** dress well etc

Kleider|bügel ['klaidɐby:gəl] m (coat) hanger; **~bürste** f clothes brush; **~haken** m coat hook; **~schrank** m wardrobe; **~ständer** m coat stand; **~stoff** m dress material

'**kleidsam** adj becoming

'**Kleidung** f (-; no pl) clothes, clothing

'**Kleidungsstück** n article of clothing

Kleie ['klaiə] f (-; -n) AGR bran

klein [klain] adj small, esp F little (a. fig: ger, brother); short; **von ~ auf** from an early age; **ein ~ wenig** a little bit; **Groß und Klein** young and old; **die Kleinen** the little ones; **~ schneiden** cut up (into small pieces)

'**Klein|anzeige** f want ad, Br small ad; **~bildkamera** f 35 mm camera; **~fa,milie** f nuclear family; **~geld** n (small) change; **~holz** n matchwood

Kleinigkeit ['klainɪçkait] f (-; -en) little thing, trifle; little something; **e-e ~ sein** be nothing, be child's play

'**Kleinkind** n baby, infant

'**Kleinkram** F m odds and ends

'**kleinlaut** adj subdued

'**kleinlich** adj small-minded; petty; mean; pedantic, fussy

'**kleinschneiden** v/t (irr, **schneiden**, sep, -ge-, h) → **klein**

'**Kleinstadt** f small town; '**kleinstädtisch** adj small-town, provincial

'**Kleintrans,porter** m MOT pick-up

'**Kleinwagen** m MOT small or compact car, F runabout

Kleister ['klaistɐ] m (-s; -) paste

Klemme ['klemə] f (-; -n) TECH clamp; (hair) clip; F **in der ~ sitzen** be in a fix or tight spot; '**klemmen** v/i and v/t (ge-, h) jam; stick; be stuck, be jammed; **sich ~** jam one's finger or hand

Klempner ['klempnɐ] m (-s; -) plumber

Klepper ['klepɐ] m (-s; -) zo nag

Klerus ['kle:rus] m (-; no pl) REL clergy

Klette ['kletə] f (-; -n) BOT bur(r); fig leech

klettern ['kletɐn] v/i (ge-, sein) climb; **auf e-n Baum ~** climb (up) a tree

'**Kletterpflanze** f BOT climber

Klient [kli'ɛnt] m (-en; -en), **Kli'entin** f (-; -nen) client

Klima ['kli:ma] n (-s; -s) climate, fig a. atmosphere

'**Klimaanlage** f air-conditioning

klimatisch [kli'ma:tɪʃ] adj climatic

klimpern ['klɪmpɐn] v/i (ge-, h) jingle, chink (**mit et.** s.th.); F MUS strum (away) (**auf** dat on)

K

Klinge ['klɪŋə] f (-; -n) blade

Klingel ['klɪŋəl] f (-; -n) bell

'**Klingelknopf** m bell (push)

'**klingeln** v/i (ge-, h) ring (the bell); **es klingelt** the (door)bell is ringing

'**klingen** v/i (irr, ge-, h) sound; bell, metal etc: ring; glasses etc: clink

Klinik ['kliːnɪk] f (-; -en) hospital; clinic

klinisch ['kliːnɪʃ] adj clinical

Klinke ['klɪŋkə] f (-; -n) (door) handle

Klippe ['klɪpə] f (-; -n) cliff, rock(s); fig obstacle

klirren ['klɪrən] v/i (ge-, h) window: rattle; glasses etc: clink; broken glass: tinkle; swords: clash; keys, coins: jingle

Klischee [kli'ʃeː] n (-s; -s) cliché

klobig ['kloːbɪç] adj bulky, clumsy

klopfen ['klɔpfən] (ge-, h) 1. v/i heart etc: beat, throb; knock (an acc at; on); tap; pat; **es klopft** there's a knock at the door 2. v/t beat; knock; drive (nail etc)

Klosett [klo'zɛt] n (-s; -s) lavatory, toilet

Kloß [kloːs] m (-es; Klöße ['kløːsə]) clod, lump (a. fig); GASTR dumpling

Kloster ['kloːstɐ] n (-s; Klöster ['kløːstɐ]) REL monastery; convent

Klotz [klɔts] m (-es; Klötze ['klœtsə]) block; log

Klub [klʊb] m (-s; -s) club

'**Klubsessel** m lounge chair

Kluft [klʊft] f (-; Klüfte ['klʏftə]) gap (a. fig); abyss

klug [kluːk] adj intelligent, clever, F bright, smart; wise; **daraus (aus ihm) werde ich nicht ~** I don't know what to make of it (him)

'**Klugheit** f (-; no pl) intelligence, cleverness, F brains; good sense; knowledge

Klumpen ['klʊmpən] m (-s; -) lump; clod; nugget; '**Klumpfuß** m MED club foot; '**klumpig** adj lumpy; cloddish

knabbern ['knabɐn] v/t and v/i (ge-, h) nibble, gnaw

Knabe ['knaːbə] m (-n; -n) boy

'**knabenhaft** adj boyish

Knäckebrot ['knɛkəbroːt] n crispbread

knacken ['knakən] v/t and v/i (ge-, h) crack; twig: snap; fire, radio: crackle

Knacks F m (-es; -e) crack; fig defect

Knall [knal] m (-[e]s; -e) bang; crack, report; pop; F **e-n ~ haben** be nuts

'**Knallbon‚bon** m, n cracker

'**knallen** v/i and v/t (ge-, h) bang; slam;

crack; pop; F crash (**gegen** into); F **j-m e-e ~** slap s.o.('s face)

'**knallig** F adj flashy, loud

'**Knallkörper** m firecracker

knapp [knap] adj scarce; scanty, meager, Br meagre (food, pay etc); bare (a. majority etc); limited (time etc); narrow (escape etc); tight (dress etc); brief; **~ an Geld** (**Zeit** etc) short of money (time etc); **mit ~er Not** only just, barely

Knappe ['knapə] m (-n; -n) miner

'**knapphalten** v/t (irr, halten, sep, -ge-, h): **j-n ~** keep s.o. short

'**Knappheit** f (-; no pl) shortage

Knarre ['knarə] f (-; -n) rattle; F gun

'**knarren** v/i (ge-, h) creak

Knast [knast] F m (-[e]s; Knäste ['knɛstə]) sl clink

knattern ['knatɐn] v/i (ge-, h) crackle; MOT roar

Knäuel ['knɔyəl] m, n (-s; -s) ball; tangle

Knauf [knauf] m (-[e]s; Knäufe ['knɔyfə]) knob; pommel

knaus(e)rig ['knauz(ə)rɪç] F adj stingy

knautschen ['knautʃən] v/t and v/i (ge-, h) crumple

'**Knautschzone** f MOT crumple zone

Knebel ['kneːbəl] m (-s; -), '**knebeln** v/t (ge-, h) gag (a. fig)

kneifen ['knaifən] v/t and v/i (irr, ge-, h) pinch (**j-m in den Arm** s.o.'s arm); F chicken out; '**Kneifzange** f pincers

Kneipe ['knaipə] F f (-; -n) saloon, bar, esp Br pub

kneten ['kneːtən] v/t (ge-, h) knead; mo(u)ld; '**Knetmasse** f Plasticine®, Play-Doh®

Knick [knɪk] m (-[e]s; -e, -s) fold, crease; bend; '**knicken** v/t (ge-, h) fold, crease; bend; break; **nicht ~!** do not bend!

Knicks [knɪks] m (-es; -e) curts(e)y; **e-n ~ machen** → '**knicksen** v/i (ge-, h) curts(e)y (**vor** dat to)

Knie [kniː] n (-s; - ['kniːə, kniː]) ANAT knee; '**~beuge** f SPORT knee bend; '**~kehle** f ANAT hollow of the knee

knien [kniːn] v/i (ge-, h) kneel, be on one's knees (**vor** dat before)

'**Kniescheibe** f ANAT kneecap

'**Kniestrumpf** m knee(-length) sock

kniff [knɪf] pret of **kneifen**

Kniff m (-[e]s; -e) crease, fold; pinch; trick, knack

kniff(e)lig ['knɪf(ə)lɪç] adj tricky

knipsen ['knɪpsən] *v/t and v/i* (ge-, h) F PHOT take a picture (of); punch, clip

Knirps [knɪrps] *m* (-es; -e) little guy

knirschen ['knɪrʃən] *v/i* (ge-, h) crunch; *mit den Zähnen* ~ grind *or* gnash one's teeth

knistern ['knɪstən] *v/i* (ge-, h) crackle; rustle

knittern ['knɪtən] *v/t and v/i* (ge-, h) crumple, crease, wrinkle

Knoblauch ['kno:plaux] *m* (-[e]s; *no pl*) BOT garlic

Knöchel ['knœçəl] *m* (-s; -) ANAT ankle; knuckle

Knochen ['knɔxən] *m* (-s; -) ANAT bone

'**Knochenbruch** *m* MED fracture

knochig ['knɔxɪç] *adj* bony

Knödel ['knø:dəl] *m* (-s; -) dumpling

Knolle ['knɔlə] *f* (-; -n) BOT tuber; bulb

Knopf [knɔpf] *m* (-es; *Knöpfe* ['knœpfə]), **knöpfen** ['knœpfən] *v/t* (ge-, h) button

'**Knopfloch** *n* buttonhole

Knorpel ['knɔrpəl] *m* (-s; -) GASTR gristle; ANAT cartilage

knorrig ['knɔrɪç] *adj* gnarled, knotted

Knospe ['knɔspə] *f* (-; -n), '**knospen** *v/i* (ge-, h) BOT bud

knoten [kno:tən] *v/t* (ge-, h) knot, make a knot in; '**Knoten** *m* (-s; -) knot (*a. fig*); '**Knotenpunkt** *m* center, *Br* centre; RAIL junction

knüllen ['knʏlən] *v/t and v/i* (ge-, h) crumple

Knüller ['knʏlɐ] F *m* (-s; -) smash (hit); scoop

knüpfen ['knʏpfən] *v/t* (ge-, h) tie; weave

Knüppel ['knʏpəl] *m* (-s; -) stick, cudgel; truncheon; ~**schaltung** *f* floor shift

knurren ['knurən] *v/i* (ge-, h) growl, snarl; *fig* grumble (*über acc* at); *stomach*: rumble

knusp(e)rig ['knʊsp(ə)rɪç] *adj* crisp, crunchy

knutschen ['knu:tʃən] F *v/i* (ge-, h) pet, neck, smooch

k.o. [ka:'ʔo:] *adj* knocked out; *fig* beat

Koalition [koali'tsjo:n] *f* (-; -en) *esp* POL coalition; *Große* ~ grand coalition

Kobold ['ko:bɔlt] *m* (-[e]s; -e) (hob)goblin, imp (*a. fig*)

Koch [kɔx] *m* (-s; *Köche* ['kœçə]) cook; chef; ~**buch** *n* cookbook, *Br*

cookery book

'**kochen** (ge-, h) **1.** *v/t* cook; boil (*eggs etc*); make (*coffee etc*) **2.** *v/i* cook, do the cooking; boil (*a. fig*); *gut* ~ be a good cook; F *vor Wut* ~ boil with rage; ~*d heiß* boiling hot

Kocher ['kɔxɐ] *m* (-s; -) ELECTR cooker

Köchin ['kœçɪn] *f* (-; -nen) cook; chef

'**Koch|löffel** *m* (wooden) spoon; ~**nische** *f* kitchenette; ~**platte** *f* hotplate; ~**salz** *n* common salt; ~**topf** *m* saucepan, pot

Köder ['kø:dɐ] *m* (-s; -) bait, decoy (*both a. fig*); lure; '**ködern** *v/t* (ge-, h) bait, decoy (*both a. fig*)

Kodex ['ko:dɛks] *m* (-es; -, -e) code

kodieren [ko'di:rən] *v/t* (no -ge-, h) (en)code; **Ko'dierung** *f* (-; -en) (en)coding

Koffein [kɔfe'i:n] *n* (-s; *no pl*) caffeine

Koffer ['kɔfɐ] *m* (-s; -) (suit)case; trunk; ~**radio** *n* portable (radio); ~**raum** *m* MOT trunk, *Br* booth

Kognak® ['kɔnjak] *m* (-s; -s) cognac® *brandy from the Cognac region in France*

Kohl [ko:l] *m* (-[e]s; -e) BOT cabbage

Kohle ['ko:lə] *f* (-; -n) coal; ELECTR carbon; F dough

'**Kohlehy|drat** *n* carbohydrate

'**Kohlen...** *in cpds* ...*dioxid etc*: CHEM carbon ...; ~**bergwerk** *n* coalmine, colliery; ~**ofen** *m* coal-burning stove

'**Kohlensäure** *f* CHEM carbonic acid; GASTR F fizz; '**kohlensäurehaltig** *adj* carbonated, F fizzy

'**Kohlen|stoff** *m* CHEM carbon; ~**wasserstoff** *m* CHEM hydrocarbon

'**Kohle|pa|pier** *n* carbon paper; ~**zeichnung** *f* charcoal drawing

Kohlrabi [ko:l'ra:bi] *m* (-s; -s) BOT kohlrabi

Koje ['ko:jə] *f* (-; -n) MAR berth, bunk

Kokain [koka'i:n] *n* (-s; *no pl*) cocaine

kokettieren [koke'ti:rən] *v/i* (no -ge-, h) flirt; *fig* ~ *mit* toy with

Kokosnuss ['ko:kɔsnʊs] *f* BOT coconut

Koks [ko:ks] *m* (-es; *no pl*) coke; F dough; *sl* coke, snow

Kolben ['kɔlbən] *m* (-s; -) butt; TECH piston; ~**stange** *f* TECH piston rod

Kolibri ['ko:libri] *m* (-s; -s) ZO humming bird

Kolleg [kɔ'le:k] *n* (-s; -s) UNIV course (of lectures)

Kollege [kɔ'leːgə] m (-n; -n), **Kol'legin** f (-; -nen) colleague

Kollegium [kɔ'leːgjʊm] n (-s; -ien) UNIV faculty, Br teaching staff

Kollekte [kɔ'lɛktə] f (-; -n) REL collection

Kollektion [kɔlɛk'tsjoːn] f (-; -en) ECON collection; range

kollektiv [kɔlɛk'tiːf] adj, **Kollek'tiv** n (-s; -e) collective (a. in cpds)

Koller ['kɔlɐ] F m (-s; -) fit; rage

kollidieren [kɔli'diːrən] v/i (no -ge-, sein) collide; **Kollision** [kɔli'zjoːn] f (-; -en) collision, fig a. clash, conflict

Kölnischwasser ['kœlnɪʃvasɐ] n (-s; -) (eau de) cologne

Kolonie [kolo'niː] f (-; -n) colony

kolonisieren [koloni'ziːrən] v/t (no -ge-, h) colonize; **Koloni'sierung** f (-; -en) colonization

Kolonne [ko'lɔnə] f (-; -n) column; MIL convoy; gang, crew

Koloss [ko'lɔs] m (-es; -e) colossus, fig a. giant (of a man)

kolossal [kolo'saːl] adj gigantic

Kombi ['kɔmbi] m (-[s]; -s) MOT station wagon, Br estate (car)

Kombination [kɔmbina'tsjoːn] f (-; -en) combination; set; coveralls, Br overalls; flying suit; soccer: combined move

kombinieren [kɔmbi'niːrən] (no -ge-, h) **1.** v/t combine **2.** v/i reason

Kombüse [kɔm'byːzə] f (-; -n) MAR galley

Komet [ko'meːt] m (-en; -en) ASTR comet

Komfort [kɔm'foːɐ] m (-s; no pl) (modern) conveniences; luxury

komfortabel [kɔmfɔr'taːbəl] adj comfortable; well-appointed; luxurious

Komik ['koːmɪk] f (-; no pl) humo(u)r; comic effect; **Komiker** ['koːmikɐ] m (-s; -) comedian; **komisch** ['koːmɪʃ] adj comic(al), funny; strange, odd

Komitee [komi'teː] n (-s; -s) committee

Komma ['kɔma] n (-s; -s, -ta) comma; **sechs ~ vier** six point four

Kommandant [kɔman'dant] m (-en; -en), **Kommandeur** [kɔman'døːɐ] m (-s; -e) MIL commander, commanding officer; **kommandieren** [kɔman'diːrən] v/i and v/t (no -ge-, h) command, be in command of; **Kommando** [kɔ'mando] n (-s; -s) command; order;

MIL commando; **Kom'mandobrücke** f MAR (navigating) bridge

kommen ['kɔmən] v/i (irr, ge-, sein) come; arrive; get; reach; **zu spät ~** be late; **weit ~** get far; **zur Schule ~** start school; **ins Gefängnis ~** go to jail; **~ lassen** send for s.o., call s.o.; order s.th.; **~ auf** (acc) think of, hit upon; remember; **hinter et. ~** find s.th. out; **um et. ~** lose s.th.; miss s.th.; **zu et. ~** come by s.th.; **wieder zu sich ~** come round or to; **wohin kommt ...?** where does ... go?; **daher kommt es, dass** that's why; **woher kommt es, dass ...?** why is it that ...?, F how come ...?

Kommentar [kɔmɛn'taːɐ] m (-s; -e) commentary; **kein ~!** no comment

Kommentator [kɔmɛn'taːtoːɐ] m (-s; -en [kɔmɛnta'toːrən]), **Kommentatorin** [kɔmɛnta'toːrɪn] f (-; -nen) commentator

kommentieren [kɔmɛn'tiːrən] v/t (no -ge-, h) comment (on)

kommerzialisieren [kɔmɛrtsjali'ziːrən] v/t (no -ge-, h) commercialize

Kommissar [kɔmɪ'saːɐ] m (-s; -e) commissioner; superintendent

Kommission [kɔmɪ'sjoːn] f (-; -en) commission; committee

Kommode [kɔ'moːdə] f (-; -n) bureau, Br chest (of drawers)

Kommunal... [kɔmu'naːl-] in cpds ...politik etc: local ...; **Kommune** [kɔ'muːnə] f (-; -n) commune

Kommunikation [kɔmunika'tsjoːn] f (-; no pl) communication

Kommunion [kɔmu'njoːn] f (-; -en) REL (Holy) Communion

Kommunismus [kɔmu'nɪsmʊs] m (-; no pl) POL communism; **Kommunist** [kɔmu'nɪst] m (-en; -en), **Kommu'nistin** f (-; -nen), **kommu'nistisch** adj POL communist

Komödie [ko'møːdjə] f (-; -n) comedy; **~ spielen** put on an act, play-act

kompakt [kɔm'pakt] adj compact

Kom'paktanlage f stereo system, music center (Br centre)

Kompanie [kɔmpa'niː] f (-; -n) MIL company

Kompass ['kɔmpas] m (-es; -e) compass

kompatibel [kɔmpa'tiːbəl] adj compatible (a. IT)

komplett [kɔm'plɛt] adj complete

Komplex [kɔm'plɛks] m (-es; -e) complex (a. PSYCH)

Kompliment [kɔmpli'mɛnt] n (-[e]s; -e) compliment; **j-m ein ~ machen** pay s.o. a compliment

Komplize [kɔm'pliːtsə] m (-n; -n) accomplice

komplizieren [kɔmpli'tsiːrən] v/t (no -ge-, h) complicate; **kompliziert** [kɔmpli'tsiːɐt] adj complicated, complex

Kom'plizin f (-; -nen) accomplice

Komplott [kɔm'plɔt] n (-[e]s; -e) plot, conspiracy

komponieren [kɔmpo'niːrən] v/t and v/i (no -ge-, h) MUS compose; write; **Komponist** [kɔmpo'nɪst] m (-en; -en) MUS composer; **Komposition** [kɔmpozi'tsjoːn] f (-; -en) MUS composition

Kompott [kɔm'pɔt] n (-[e]s; -e) GASTR compot(e), stewed fruit

Kompresse [kɔm'prɛsə] f (-; -n) MED compress

komprimieren [kɔmpri'miːrən] v/t (no -ge-, h) compress

Kompromiss [kɔmpro'mɪs] m (-es; -e) compromise; **kompro'misslos** adj uncompromising

kompromittieren [kɔmprɔmɪ'tiːrən] v/t (no -ge-, h) compromise (**sich** o.s.); **~d** adj compromising

Kondensator [kɔndɛn'zaːtoːɐ] m (-s; -en [kɔndɛnza'toːrən]) ELECTR capacitor; TECH condenser; **kondensieren** [kɔndɛn'ziːrən] v/t (no -ge-, h) condense

Kondensmilch [kɔn'dɛnsmɪlç] f condensed milk

Kondition [kɔndi'tsjoːn] f (-; -en) condition; (no pl) SPORT condition, shape, form; **gute ~** (great) stamina

konditional [kɔndɪtsjoˈnaːl] adj LING conditional

Konditi'onstraining n fitness training

Konditor [kɔn'diːtoːɐ] m (-s; -en [kɔndi-'toːrən]) confectioner, pastrycook

Konditorei [kɔndito'rai] f (-; -en) cake shop; café, tearoom; **~waren** pl confectionery

Kondom [kɔn'doːm] n, m (-s; -e) condom

Kondukteur [kɔndʊk'tøːɐ] Swiss m (-s; -e) → **Schaffner**

Konfekt [kɔn'fɛkt] n (-[e]s; -e) sweets, chocolates

Konfektion [kɔnfɛk'tsjoːn] f (-; no pl) ready-made clothing; **Konfekti'ons...** in cpds ready-made ..., off-the-peg ...

Konferenz [kɔnfe'rɛnts] f (-; -en) conference

Konfession [kɔnfɛ'sjoːn] f (-; -en) religion, denomination; **konfessionell** [kɔnfɛsjoˈnɛl] adj confessional, denominational; **Konfessi'onsschule** f denominational school

Konfirmand [kɔnfɪr'mant] m (-en; -en), **Konfir'mandin** f (-; -nen) REL confirmand; **Konfirmation** [kɔnfɪrma'tsjoːn] f (-; -en) REL confirmation; **konfirmieren** [kɔnfɪr'miːrən] v/t (no -ge-, h) confirm

konfiszieren [kɔnfɪs'tsiːrən] v/t (no -ge-, h) JUR confiscate

Konfitüre [kɔnfi'tyːrə] f (-; -n) jam

Konflikt [kɔn'flɪkt] m (-[e]s; -e) conflict

konfrontieren [kɔnfrɔn'tiːrən] v/t (no -ge-, h) confront

konfus [kɔn'fuːs] adj confused, mixed-up

Kongress [kɔn'grɛs] m (-es; -e) convention, Br congress

König ['køːnɪç] m (-s; -e) king

Königin ['køːnɪgɪn] f (-; -nen) queen

königlich ['køːnɪklɪç] adj royal

Königreich ['køːnɪkraiç] n kingdom

Konjugation [kɔnjuga'tsjoːn] f (-; -en) LING conjugation; **konjugieren** [kɔnju-'giːrən] v/t (no -ge-, h) LING conjugate

Konjunktiv ['kɔnjʊŋktiːf] m (-s; -e) LING subjunctive (mood)

Konjunktur [kɔnjʊŋk'tuːɐ] f (-; -en) economic situation

konkret [kɔn'kreːt] adj concrete

Konkurrent [kɔnku'rɛnt] m (-en; -en), **Konkur'rentin** f (-; -nen) competitor, rival; **Konkurrenz** [kɔnku'rɛnts] f (-; no pl) competition; **die~** one's competitors; **außer ~** not competing; → **konkurrenzlos**

konkur'renzfähig adj competitive

Konkur'renzkampf m competition

konkur'renzlos adj without competition, unrival(l)ed

konkurrieren [kɔnku'riːrən] v/i (no -ge-, h) compete

Konkurs [kɔn'kʊrs] m (-es; -e) ECON, JUR bankruptcy; **in ~ gehen** go bankrupt;

K

..masse f JUR bankrupt's estate

können ['kœnən] v/t and v/i (irr, ge-, h), v/aux (irr, no -ge-, h) can, be able to; may, be allowed to; **kann ich gehen** etc? can or may I go etc?; **du kannst nicht** you cannot or can't; **ich kann nicht mehr** I can't go on; I can't manage or eat any more; **es kann sein** it may be; **ich kann nichts dafür** it's not my fault; **e-e Sprache ~** know or speak a language

'Können n (-s; no pl) ability, skill

Könner ['kœnɐ] m (-s; -), **'Könnerin** f (-; -nen) master, expert; esp SPORT ace, crack

konnte ['kɔntə] pret of **können**

konsequent [kɔnzə'kvɛnt] adj consistent; **Konsequenz** [kɔnzə'kvɛnts] f (-; -en) (no pl) consistency; consequence

konservativ [kɔnzɛrva'tiːf] adj conservative

Konserven [kɔn'zɛrvən] pl canned (Br a. tinned) foods; **..büchse** f, **..dose** f can, Br a. tin; **..fa,brik** f cannery

konservieren [kɔnzɛr'viːrən] v/t (no -ge-, h) preserve; **Konser-'vierungsmittel** n preservative

Konsonant [kɔnzo'nant] m (-en; -en) LING consonant

konstruieren [kɔnstru'iːrən] v/t (no -ge-, h) construct; design

Konstrukteur [kɔnstruk'tøːɐ] m (-s; -e) TECH designer; **Konstruktion** [kɔnstruk'tsjoːn] f (-; -en) construction

Konsul ['kɔnzʊl] m (-s; -n) consul

Konsulat [kɔnzu'laːt] n (-[e]s; -e) consulate

konsultieren [kɔnzʊl'tiːrən] v/t (no -ge-, h) consult

Konsum¹ [kɔn'zuːm] m (-s; no pl) consumption

Konsum² ['kɔnzuːm] m (-s; -s) cooperative (society or store), F co-op

Konsument [kɔnzu'mɛnt] m (-en; -en), **Konsu'mentin** f (-; -nen) consumer; **Kon'sumgesellschaft** f consumer society; **konsumieren** [kɔnzu'miːrən] v/t (no -ge-, h) consume

Kontakt [kɔn'takt] m (-[e]s; -e) contact (a. ELECTR); **~ aufnehmen** get in touch; **~ haben** or **in ~ stehen mit** be in contact or touch with; **den ~ verlieren** lose

touch; **kon'taktfreudig** adj sociable

Kon'taktlinsen pl OPT contact lenses

Konter ['kɔntɐ] m (-s; -), **'kontern** v/i (ge-, h) counter (a. fig)

Kontinent [kɔnti'nɛnt] m (-[e]s; -e) continent

Konto ['kɔnto] n (-s; Konten) account

'Kontoauszug m (bank) statement

Kontrast [kɔn'trast] m (-[e]s; -e) contrast (a. PHOT, TV etc)

Kontrolle [kɔn'trɔlə] f (-; -n) control; supervision; check(up)

Kontrolleur [kɔntrɔ'løːɐ] m (-s; -e), **Kontrol'leurin** f (-; -nen) inspector, RAIL a. conductor

kontrollieren [kɔntrɔ'liːrən] v/t (no -ge-, h) check; check up on s.o.; control

Kon'trollpunkt m checkpoint

Kontroverse [kɔntro'vɛrzə] f (-; -n) controversy

konventionell [kɔnvɛntsjo'nɛl] adj conventional

Konversation [kɔnvɛrza'tsjoːn] f (-; -en) conversation; **Konversati-'onslexikon** n encyclop(a)edia

Konzentration [kɔntsɛntra'tsjoːn] f (-; -en) concentration

Konzentrati'onslager n concentration camp

konzentrieren [kɔntsɛn'triːrən] v/t and v/refl (no -ge-, h) concentrate; **sich auf et. ~** concentrate on s.th.

Konzept [kɔn'tsɛpt] n (-[e]s; -e) (rough) draft; conception; **j-n aus dem ~ bringen** put s.o. out

Konzern [kɔn'tsɛrn] m (-[e]s; -e) ECON combine, group

Konzert [kɔn'tsɛrt] n (-[e]s; -e) MUS concert; concerto; **..halle** f, **..saal** m concert hall, auditorium

Konzession [kɔntsɛ'sjoːn] f (-; -en) concession; license, Br licence

Kopf [kɔpf] m (-[e]s; Köpfe ['kœpfə]) head (a. fig); top; fig a. brains, mind; **~ hoch!** chin up!; **j-m über den ~ wachsen** outgrow s.o.; fig be too much for s.o.; **sich den ~ zerbrechen (über** acc) rack one's brains (over); **sich et. aus dem ~ schlagen** put s.th. out of one's mind; **~ an ~** neck and neck; **~ball** m SPORT header; headed goal; **..bede-ckung** f headgear; **ohne ~** bareheaded

köpfen ['kœpfən] v/t (ge-, h) behead, decapitate; SPORT head (**ins Tor** home)

'Kopf|ende n head; ~hörer pl head-phones; ~jäger m headhunter; ~kissen n pillow

'kopflos adj headless; fig panicky

'Kopf|rechnen n mental arithmetic; ~sa.lat m BOT lettuce; ~schmerzen pl headache; ~sprung m SPORT header; ~stand m SPORT headstand; ~tuch n scarf, (head)kerchief

kopf'über adv headfirst (a. fig)

'Kopfweh n → Kopfschmerzen

'Kopfzerbrechen n: j-m ~ machen give s.o. a headache

Kopie [ko'pi:] f (-; -n), ko'pieren v/t (no -ge-, h) copy; Kopiergerät [ko-'pi:ɐgəre:t] n copier

Koppel¹ ['kɔpəl] f (-; -n) paddock

Koppel² n (-s; -) MIL belt

'koppeln v/t (ge-, h) couple; link

Koralle [ko'ralə] f (-; -n) ZO coral

Korb [kɔrp] m (-[e]s; Körbe ['kœrbə]) basket

Kord [kɔrt] m (-[e]s; -e) corduroy

Kordel ['kɔrdəl] f (-; -n) cord

'Kordhose f corduroys

Korinthe [ko'rɪntə] f (-; -n) currant

Kork [kɔrk] m (-[e]s; -e) BOT cork

'Korkeiche f BOT cork oak

Korken ['kɔrkən] m (-s; -) cork; ~zieher ['kɔrkentsi:ɐ] m (-s; -) corkscrew

Korn¹ [kɔrn] n (-[e]s; Körner ['kœrnɐ]) BOT grain; seed; (no pl) grain, Br a. corn; (pl -e) TECH front sight

Korn² F m (-[e]s; -e) (grain) schnapps

körnig ['kœrnɪç] adj grainy

Körper ['kœrpɐ] m (-s; -) body (a. PHYS, CHEM), MATH a. solid; ~bau m (-[e]s; no pl) build, physique

'körperbehindert adj (physically) disabled or handicapped

'Körper|geruch m body odo(u)r, BO; ~größe f height; ~kraft f physical strength

'körperlich adj physical

'Körperpflege f personal hygiene

'Körperschaft f (-; -en) corporation, (corporate) body

'Körper|teil m part of the body; ~verletzung f JUR bodily injury

korrekt [kɔ'rɛkt] adj correct

Korrektur [kɔrɛk'tu:ɐ] f (-; -en) correction; PED etc grading, Br marking

Korrespondent [kɔrɛspɔn'dɛnt] m (-en; -en), Korrespon'dentin f (-; -nen) correspondent; Korrespondenz [kɔrɛspɔn'dɛnts] f (-; -en) correspondence; korrespondieren [kɔrɛspɔn-'di:rən] v/i (no -ge-, h) correspond (mit with)

Korridor ['kɔrido:ɐ] m (-s; -e) corridor; hall

korrigieren [kɔri'gi:rən] v/t (no -ge-, h) correct; PED etc grade, Br mark

korrupt [kɔ'rʊpt] adj corrupt(ed)

Korruption [kɔrʊp'tsjo:n] f (-; -en) corruption

Korsett [kɔr'zɛt] n (-s; -s) corset (a. fig)

Kosename ['ko:zəna:mə] m pet name

Kosmetik [kɔs'me:tɪk] f (-; no pl) beauty culture; cosmetics, toiletries

Kosmetikerin [kɔs'me:tikərɪn] f (-; -nen) beautician, cosmetician

Kost [kɔst] f (-; no pl) food, diet; board

'kostbar adj precious, valuable; costly

'Kostbarkeit f (-; -en) precious object, treasure (a. fig)

kosten¹ ['kɔstən] v/t (ge-, h) cost, be; fig take (time etc); was or wie viel kostet ...? how much it ...?

'kosten² v/t (ge-, h) taste, try

'Kosten pl cost(s); price; expenses; charges; auf j-s ~ at s.o.'s expense

'kostenlos 1. adj free 2. adv free of charge

köstlich ['kœstlɪç] adj delicious; fig priceless; sich ~ amüsieren have great fun, F have a ball

'Kostprobe f taste, sample (a. fig)

'kostspielig adj expensive, costly

Kostüm [kɔs'ty:m] n (-s; -e) costume, dress; suit; ~fest n fancy-dress ball

Kot [ko:t] m (-[e]s; no pl) excrement, zo a. droppings

Kotelett [kotə'lɛt] n (-s; -s) chop, cutlet

Koteletten [kotə'lɛtən] pl sideburns

'Kotflügel m MOT fender, Br wing

kotzen ['kɔtsən] V v/i (ge-, h) puke

Krabbe ['krabə] f (-; -n) ZO shrimp; prawn

krabbeln ['krabəln] v/i (ge-, sein) crawl

Krach [krax] m (-[e]s; Kräche ['krɛçə]) crash, bang; (no pl) noise; F quarrel, fight

'krachen v/i (ge-, h) crack, bang, crash

Kracher ['kraxɐ] m (-s; -) (fire)cracker

krächzen ['krɛçtsən] v/t and v/i (ge-, h) croak

Kraft [kraft] f (-; Kräfte ['krɛftə])

strength, force (*a.* POL), power (*a.* ELECTR, TECH, POL); **in ~ sein (setzen, treten)** JUR *etc* be in (put into, come into) force; **~brühe** *f* GASTR consommé, clear soup; **~fahrer(in)** driver, motorist; **~fahrzeug** *n* motor vehicle

kräftig ['krɛftɪç] *adj* strong (*a.* fig), powerful; substantial (*food*); good

'kraftlos *adj* weak, feeble

'Kraft|probe *f* test of strength; **~stoff** *m* MOT fuel; **~verschwendung** *f* waste of energy; **~werk** *n* power station

Kragen ['kraːɡən] *m* (-s; -) collar

Krähe ['krɛːə] *f* (-; -n) ZO crow

krähen ['krɛːən] *v/i* (ge-, h) crow

Krake ['kraːkə] *m* (-n; -n) ZO octopus

Kralle ['kralə] *f* (-; -n) ZO claw (*a.* fig)

'krallen *v/refl* (ge-, h) cling (**an** *acc* on), clutch (*at*)

Kram [kraːm] F *m* (-[e]s; *no pl*) stuff, (one's) things

Krampf [krampf] *m* (-[e]s; *Krämpfe* ['krɛmpfə]) MED cramp; spasm, convulsion; **~ader** *f* varicose vein

'krampfhaft fig *adj* forced (*smile etc*); desperate (*attempt etc*)

Kran [kraːn] *m* (-[e]s; *Kräne* ['krɛːnə]) TECH crane

Kranich ['kraːnɪç] *m* (-s; -e) ZO crane

krank [kraŋk] *adj* ill, sick; **~ werden** get sick, *Br* fall ill; **Kranke** *m, f* (-n; -n) sick person, patient; **die ~n** the sick

kränken ['krɛŋkən] *v/t* (ge-, h) hurt (*s.o.'s feelings*), offend

'Kranken|bett *n* sickbed; **~geld** *n* sickness benefit; **~gymnastik** *f* physiotherapy; **~haus** *n* hospital; **~kasse** *f* health insurance scheme; **in e-r ~ sein** be a member of a health insurance scheme *or* plan; **~pflege** *f* nursing; **~pfleger** *m* male nurse; **~schein** *m* health insurance certificate; **~schwester** *f* nurse; **~versicherung** *f* health insurance; **~wagen** *m* ambulance; **~zimmer** *n* sickroom

'krankhaft *adj* morbid (*a.* fig)

'Krankheit *f* (-; -en) illness, sickness, disease

'Krankheitserreger *m* germ

kränklich ['krɛŋklɪç] *adj* sickly, ailing

Kränkung ['krɛŋkʊŋ] *f* (-; -en) insult, offense, *Br* offence

Kranz [krants] *m* (-es; *Kränze* ['krɛntsə]) wreath; fig ring, circle

krass [kras] *adj* crass, gross; blunt

Krater ['kraːtɐ] *m* (-s; -) crater

kratzen ['kratsən] *v/t and v/refl* (ge-, h) scratch (o.s.); scrape (*von* off)

Kratzer ['kratsɐ] *m* (-s; -) scratch (*a.* MED)

kraulen ['kraulən] **1.** *v/t* (ge-, h) stroke; run one's fingers through **2.** *v/i* (ge-, sein) SPORT do the crawl

kraus [kraus] *adj* curly (*hair*); wrinkled

Krause ['krauzə] *f* (-; -n) ruff; friz(z)

kräuseln ['krɔʏzəln] *v/t and v/refl* (ge-, h) curl, friz(z); *water:* ripple

Kraut [kraut] *n* (-[e]s; *Kräuter* ['krɔʏtɐ]) BOT herb; tops, leaves; cabbage

Krawall [kra'val] *m* (-s; -e) riot; F row, racket

Krawatte [kra'vatə] *f* (-; -n) tie

kreativ [krea'tiːf] *adj* creative

Kreativität [kreativi'tɛːt] *f* (-; *no pl*) creativity

Kreatur [krea'tuːɐ] *f* (-; -en) creature

Krebs [kreːps] *m* (-es; -e) ZO crayfish; MED cancer; AST Cancer; **sie ist (ein)** ~ she's (a) Cancer; **~ erregend → krebserregend**

Krebs. MED cancerous; **krebserregend** *adj* MED carcinogenic; **~geschwulst** *f* MED carcinoma; **~kranke** *m, f* cancer patient

Kredit [kre'diːt] *m* (-[e]s; -e) ECON credit; loan; **~karte** *f* credit card, *pl coll* F plastic money

Kreide ['kraidə] *f* (-; -n) chalk; crayon

Kreis [krais] *m* (-es; -e) circle (*a.* fig); POL district, county; **~bahn** *f* AST orbit

kreischen ['kraiʃən] *v/i* (ge-, h) screech; squeal

Kreisel ['kraizəl] *m* (-s; -) (spinning) top; PHYS gyro(scope); **'kreiseln** *v/i* (ge-, h, sein) spin around

kreisen ['kraizən] *v/i* (ge-, h, sein) (move in a) circle, revolve, rotate; circulate

kreisförmig ['kraisfœrmɪç] *adj* circular

'Kreislauf *m* MED, ECON circulation; BIOL cycle (*a.* fig), TECH, ELECTR *a.* circuit; **~störungen** *pl* MED circulatory trouble

Kreis|säge *f* circular saw; **~verkehr** *m* traffic circle, *Br* roundabout

Krempe ['krɛmpə] *f* (-; -n) brim

Kren [kreːn] *Austrian m* (-[e]s; *no pl*) GASTR horseradish

Krepp [krɛp] *m* (-s; -s) crepe

Kreuz [krɔʏts] *n* (-es; -e) cross (*a.* fig) ANAT (small of the) back; *cards:* club(s)

MUS sharp; **über~** crosswise; F **j-n aufs ~ legen** take s.o. in; **kreuzen** ['krɔʏtsən] **1.** v/t and v/refl (ge-, h) cross; clash **2.** v/i (ge-, sein) MAR cruise

'Kreuzer ['krɔʏtsɐ] m (-s; -) MAR cruiser

'Kreuzfahrer m HIST crusader

'Kreuzfahrt f MAR cruise

kreuzigen ['krɔʏtsɪgən] v/t (ge-, h) crucify; '**Kreuzigung** f (-; -en) crucifixion

'Kreuzotter f ZO adder

'Kreuzschmerzen pl backache

'Kreuzung f (-; -en) RAIL, MOT crossing, junction; intersection, crossroads; BIOL cross(breed)ing; cross(breed); fig cross

'Kreuzverhör n JUR cross-examination; **ins ~ nehmen** cross-examine

'kreuzweise adv crosswise, crossways

'Kreuz|worträtsel n crossword (puzzle); **~zug** HIST m crusade

kriechen ['kriːçən] v/i (irr, ge-, sein) creep, crawl; fig **vor j-m ~** toady to s.o.

Kriecher ['kriːçɐ] contp m (-s; -) toady

'Kriechspur f MOT slow lane

Krieg [kriːk] m (-[e]s; -e ['kriːgə]) war; **~ führen gegen** be at war with

kriegen ['kriːgən] F v/t (ge-, h) get; catch

Krieger ['kriːgɐ] m (-s; -) warrior

'Kriegerdenkmal n war memorial

kriegerisch ['kriːgərɪʃ] adj warlike, martial

'Kriegführung f (-; no pl) warfare

'Kriegs|beil fig n: **das ~ begraben** bury the hatchet; **~dienstverweigerer** m (-s; -) conscientious objector; **~erklärung** f declaration of war; **~gefangene** m prisoner of war, P.O.W.; **~gefangenschaft** f captivity; **~recht** n JUR martial law; **~schauplatz** m theater (Br theatre) of war; **~schiff** n warship; **~teilnehmer** m (war) veteran, Br ex-serviceman; **~verbrechen** n war crime; **~verbrecher** m war criminal

Krimi ['kriːmi] F m (-[s]; -s) (crime) thriller, detective novel

Kriminal|beamte [krimi'naːlbəʔamtə] m detective, plain-clothesman; **~polizei** f criminal investigation department; **~roman** m → **Krimi**

kriminell [krimi'nɛl] adj, **Krimi'nelle** m, f (-n; -n) criminal

Krippe ['krɪpə] f (-; -n) crib, manger (a. REL); REL crèche, Br crib

Krise ['kriːzə] f (-; -n) crisis

'Krisenherd m esp POL trouble spot

Kristall[1] [krɪs'tal] m (-s; -e) crystal

Kris'tall[2] n (s; no pl), **~glas** n crystal

kristallisieren [krɪstali'ziːrən] v/i and v/refl (no -ge-, h) crystallize

Kriterium [kri'teːrjʊm] n (-s; -ien) criterion (**für** of)

Kritik [kri'tiːk] f (-; -en) criticism; THEA, MUS etc review, critique; **gute ~en** a good press; **~ üben an** (dat) criticize; **Kritiker(in)** ['kriːtikɐ, 'kriːtikərɪn] m(f) (-s; -/-; -nen) critic; **kri'tiklos** adj uncritical; **kritisch** ['kriːtɪʃ] adj critical (a. fig) (**gegenüber** of); **kritisieren** [kriti'ziːrən] v/t (no -ge-, h) criticize

kritzeln ['krɪtsəln] v/t and v/i (ge-, h) scrawl, scribble

kroch [krɔx] pret of **kriechen**

Krokodil [kroko'diːl] n (-s; -e) ZO crocodile

Krone ['kroːnə] f (-; -n) crown; coronet

krönen ['krøːnən] v/t (ge-, h) crown; **j-n zum König ~** crown s.o. king

'Kronleuchter m chandelier

'Kronprinz m crown prince

'Kronprin,zessin f crown princess

'Krönung f (-; -en) coronation; fig crowning event, climax, high point

Kropf [krɔpf] m (-[e]s; Kröpfe ['krœpfə]) MED goiter, Br goitre; ZO crop

Kröte ['krøːtə] f (-; -n) ZO toad

Krücke ['krʏkə] f (-; -n) crutch

Krug [kruːk] m (-[e]s; Krüge ['kryːgə]) jug, pitcher; mug, stein; tankard

Krümel ['kryːməl] m (-s; -) crumb

krümelig ['kryːməlɪç] adj crumbly

'krümeln v/t and v/i (ge-, h) crumble

krumm [krʊm] adj crooked (a. fig), bent

krummbeinig ['krʊmbaɪnɪç] adj bow-legged

krümmen ['krʏmən] v/t (ge-, h) bend (a. TECH), crook; **sich ~** bend; writhe (with pain); '**Krümmung** f (-; -en) bend, curve; GEOGR, MATH, MED curvature

Krüppel ['krʏpəl] m (-s; -) cripple

Kruste ['krʊstə] f (-; -n) crust

Kto. abbr of **Konto** a/c, account

Kübel ['kyːbəl] m (-s; -) bucket, pail; tub

Kubik|meter [ku'biːkmeːtɐ] n, m cubic meter (Br metre); **~wurzel** f MATH cube root

Küche ['kʏçə] f (-; -en) kitchen; GASTR cooking, cuisine; **kalte (warme) ~** cold (hot) meals

Kuchen ['ku:xən] m (-s; -) cake; tart, pie

'**Küchen|geräte** pl kitchen utensils (or appliances); **~geschirr** n kitchen crockery, kitchenware; **~herd** m cooker; **~schrank** m (kitchen) cupboard

Kuckuck ['kʊkʊk] m (-s; -s) ZO cuckoo

Kufe ['ku:fə] f (-; -n) runner; AVIAT skid

Kugel ['ku:gəl] f (-; -n) ball; bullet; MATH, GEOGR sphere; SPORT shot

kugelförmig ['ku:gəlfœrmɪç] adj ball-shaped, spherical; MATH spheric(al)

'**Kugelgelenk** n TECH, ANAT ball (and socket) joint

'**Kugellager** n TECH ball bearing

'**kugeln** v/i (ge-, sein) and v/t (h) roll

'**Kugelschreiber** ['ku:gəlʃraibɐ] m (-s; -) ballpoint (pen)

'**kugelsicher** adj bulletproof

'**Kugelstoßen** n (-s; no pl) SPORT shot put(ting); **Kugelstoßer** ['ku:gəlʃto:sɐ] m (-s; -), **Kugelstoßerin** ['ku:gəlʃto:sərɪn] f (-; -nen) SPORT shot-putter

Kuh [ku:] f (-; Kühe ['ky:ə]) ZO cow

kühl [ky:l] adj cool (a. fig); '**Kühle** f (-; no pl) cool(ness); '**kühlen** v/t (ge-, h) cool; chill; refrigerate; refresh

'**Kühler** ['ky:lɐ] m (-s; -) MOT radiator

'**Kühlerhaube** f MOT hood, Br bonnet

'**Kühlmittel** n coolant

'**Kühlraum** m cold-storage room

'**Kühlschrank** m fridge, refrigerator

'**Kühltruhe** f deep-freeze, freezer

'**Kühlwasser** n MOT cooling water

kühn [ky:n] adj bold

'**Kühnheit** f (-; no pl) boldness

'**Kuhstall** m cowshed

Küken ['ky:kən] n (-s; -) ZO chick (a. fig)

Kukuruz ['kʊkʊrʊts] Austrian m → **Mais**

Kuli ['ku:li] F m (-s; -s) ballpoint

Kulissen [ku'lɪsən] pl THEA wings; scenery; **hinter den ~** backstage, esp fig behind the scenes

Kult [kʊlt] m (-[e]s; -e) cult; rite, ritual (act)

kultivieren [kʊlti'vi:rən] v/t (no -ge-, h) cultivate

Kultur [kʊl'tu:ɐ] f (-; -en) culture (a. BIOL), civilization; AGR cultivation

Kul'turbeutel m toilet bag

kulturell [kʊltu'rɛl] adj cultural

Kul'turgeschichte f history of civilization; **~zentrum** n cultural center (Br centre)

Kultusmi,nister ['kʊltʊsminɪstɐ] m minister of education and cultural affairs

Kummer ['kʊmɐ] m (-s; no pl) grief, sorrow; trouble, worry; **~ haben mit** have trouble or problems with

kümmerlich ['kymɐlɪç] adj miserable; poor, scanty; **kümmern** ['kymɐn] v/refl and v/t (ge-, h) **sich ~ um** look after, take care of, mind; care or worry about, be interested in

Kumpel ['kʊmpəl] m (-s; -) miner; F mate, buddy, pal

Kunde ['kʊndə] m (-n; -n) customer, client; '**Kundendienst** m after-sales service; (customer) service; service department; TECH servicing

Kundgebung ['kʊntge:bʊŋ] f (-; -en) meeting, rally, demonstration

kündigen ['kyndɪgən] v/i and v/t (ge-, h) cancel; **j-m ~** give s.o. his / her / one's notice; dismiss s.o., F sack or fire s.o.

'**Kündigung** f (-; -en) cancellation; (period of) notice

Kundin ['kʊndɪn] f (-; -nen) customer, client

Kundschaft ['kʊntʃaft] f (-; -en) customers, clients

Kunst [kʊnst] f (-; Künste ['kʏnstə]) art; skill; **~...** in cpds ...herz, ...leder, ...licht etc: artificial ...; **~akade,mie** f academy of arts; **~ausstellung** f art exhibition; **~dünger** m AGR artificial fertilizer; **~erziehung** f PED art (education); **~faser** f man-made or synthetic fiber (Br fibre); **~fehler** m professional blunder; **~fliegen** n stunt flying, aerobatics; **~geschichte** f history of art; **~gewerbe** n, **~handwerk** n arts and crafts

Künstler ['kʏnstlɐ] m (-s; -), **Künstlerin** ['kʏnstlərɪn] f (-; -nen) artist, MUS, THEA a. performer

künstlerisch ['kʏnstlərɪʃ] adj artistic

künstlich ['kʏnstlɪç] adj artificial; false; synthetic; man-made

'**Kunst|schwimmen** n water ballet; **~seide** f rayon; **~springen** n springboard diving; **~stoff** m plastic; **~stück** n trick, stunt, esp fig feat; **~turnen** n gymnastics; **~turner** m gymnast

'**kunstvoll** adj artistic; elaborate

'**Kunstwerk** n work of art

Kupfer ['kʊpfɐ] n (-s; no pl) copper (**aus**

of); **~stich** m copperplate (engraving)

Kupon ['kuˈpoːɪ] m (-s; -s) coupon

Kuppe ['kupə] f (-; -n) (rounded) hilltop; ANAT head

Kuppel ['kupəl] f (-; -n) ARCH dome; cupola

Kuppelei [kupəˈlai] f (-; -en) JUR procuring

kuppeln v/i (ge-, h) MOT put the clutch in or out; **Kupplung** ['kupluŋ] f (-; -en) MOT clutch

Kur [kuːɐ] f (-; -en) course of treatment; cure

Kür [kyːɐ] f (-; -en) SPORT free skating; free exercises

Kurbel ['kurbəl] f (-; -n) crank, handle; **~kurbeln** v/t (ge-, h) crank; wind (up etc); **Kurbelwelle** f TECH crankshaft

Kürbis ['kyrbɪs] m (-ses; -se) BOT pumpkin, gourd, squash

Kurgast m visitor

kurieren [kuˈriːrən] v/t (no -ge-, h) cure (**von** of)

kurios [kuˈrjoːs] adj curious, odd, strange

Kürlauf m SPORT free skating

Kurort m health resort, spa

Kurpfuscher ['kuːɐpfuʃɐ] m (-s; -) quack (doctor)

Kurs [kurs] m (-es; -e) AVIAT, MAR course (a. fig); PED etc class(es); ECON (exchange) rate; (stock) price

Kürschner ['kyrʃnɐ] m (-s; -) furrier

kursieren [kurˈziːrən] v/i (no -ge-, h) circulate (a. fig)

Kurve ['kurvə] f (-; -n) curve (a. MATH and fig); bend, turn; **kurvenreich** adj winding, full of bends; F curvaceous

kurz [kurts] adj short; brief; **~e Hose** shorts; **(bis) vor ~em** (until) recently; **(erst) seit ~em** (only) for a short time; **~ vorher (darauf)** shortly before (after[wards]); **~ vor uns** just ahead of us; **~ nacheinander** in quick succession; **~ fortgehen** etc go away for a short time or a moment; **~ gesagt** in short; **zu ~ kommen** go short; **~ angebunden** curt

Kurzarbeit f ECON short time

kurzarbeiten v/i (sep, ge-, h) ECON work short time

kurzatmig ['kurtsʔaːtmɪç] adj short of breath

Kürze ['kyrtsə] f (-; no pl) shortness; brevity; **in ~** soon, shortly, before long

kürzen v/t (ge-, h) shorten (**um** by); abridge; cut, reduce (a. MATH)

kurzerhand ['kurtsɐ'hant] adv without hesitation, on the spot

kurzfassen v/refl (sep, -ge-, h): **sich ~** be brief, put it briefly

kurzfristig 1. adj short-term **2.** adv at short notice

Kurzgeschichte f short story

kurzlebig ['kurtsleːbɪç] adj short-lived

kürzlich ['kyrtslɪç] adv recently, not long ago

Kurz|nachrichten pl news summary; **~schluss** m ELECTR short circuit, F short; **~schrift** f shorthand

kurzsichtig adj nearsighted, Br shortsighted

Kurzstrecke f short distance

Kürzung f (-; -en) cut, reduction (a. MATH)

Kurzwaren pl notions, Br haberdashery

kurzweilig ['kurtsvailɪç] adj entertaining

Kurzwelle f PHYS, radio: short wave

kuschelig ['kuʃəlɪç] F adj cozy, Br cosy, snug; **kuscheln** ['kuʃəln] v/refl (ge-, h) snuggle, cuddle (**an** acc up to; **in** acc in)

Kusine f → **Cousine**

Kuss [kus] m (-es; Küsse ['kysə]) kiss

kussecht adj kiss-proof

küssen ['kysən] v/t (ge-, h) kiss

Küste ['kystə] f (-; -n) coast, shore; **an der ~** on the coast; **an die ~** ashore

Küsten|gewässer pl coastal waters; **~schifffahrt** f coastal shipping; **~schutz** m, **~wache** f coast guard

Küster ['kystɐ] m (-s; -) REL verger, sexton

Kutsche ['kutʃə] f (-; -n) carriage, coach; **Kutscher** ['kutʃɐ] m (-s; -) coachman

Kutte ['kutə] f (-; -n) (monk's) habit

Kutteln ['kutəln] pl GASTR tripe

Kutter ['kutɐ] m (-s; -) MAR cutter

Kuvert [kuˈveːɐ] n (-s; -s) envelope

Kybernetik [kybɐˈneːtɪk] f (-; no pl) cybernetics

L

labil [la'biːl] *adj* unstable

Labor [la'boːɐ] *n* (-s; -e) laboratory, F lab; **Laborant(in)** [labo'rant(ɪn)] (-en; -en/-; -nen) laboratory assistant

Labyrinth [laby'rɪnt] *n* (-[e]s; -e) labyrinth, maze (*both a. fig*)

Lache ['laxə] *f* (-; -n) pool, puddle

lächeln ['lɛçəln] *v/i* (*ge-, h*), **Lächeln** *n* (-s; *no pl*) smile

lachen ['laxən] *v/i* (*ge-, h*) laugh (*über acc* at); **Lachen** *n* (-s; *no pl*) laugh (-ter); **j-n zum ~ bringen** make s.o. laugh; **lächerlich** ['lɛçɐlɪç] *adj* ridiculous; **~ machen** ridicule, make fun of; **sich ~ machen** make a fool of o.s.

Lachs [laks] *m* (-es; -e) ZO salmon

Lack [lak] *m* (-[e]s; -e) varnish; lacquer; MOT paint(work)

lackieren [la'kiːrən] *v/t* (*no -ge-, h*) varnish; lacquer; paint (*a.* MOT)

Lackschuhe *pl* patent-leather shoes

Ladefläche ['laːdəflɛçə] *f* loading space

Ladegerät *n* ELECTR battery charger

Ladehemmung *f* MIL jam

laden ['laːdən] *v/t* (*irr, ge-, h*) load; ELECTR charge; IT boot (up); *fig et.* **auf sich ~** burden o.s. with s.th.

Laden *m* (-s; *Läden* ['lɛːdən]) store, *Br* shop; shutter; **~dieb** *m* shoplifter; **~diebstahl** *m* shoplifting; **~inhaber** *m* storekeeper, *Br* shopkeeper; **~kasse** *f* till; **~schluss** *m* closing time; **nach ~** after hours; **~tisch** *m* counter

Laderampe *f* loading platform *or* ramp

Laderaum *m* loading space; MAR hold

Ladung *f* (-; -en) load, freight; AVIAT, MAR cargo; ELECTR, MIL charge; **e-e ~ ...** a load of ...

lag [laːk] *pret of* **liegen**

Lage ['laːgə] *f* (-; -n) situation, position (*both a. fig*); location; layer; round (*of beer etc*); **in schöner (ruhiger) ~** beautifully (peacefully) situated; **in der ~ sein zu** *inf* be able to *inf*, be in a position to *inf*

Lager ['laːgɐ] *n* (-s; -) bed; camp (*a. fig*); ECON stock, store; GEOL deposit; TECH bearing; **et. auf ~ haben** have s.th. in store (*a. fig for s.o.*); **~feuer** *n* campfire; **~haus** *n* warehouse

lagern (*ge-, h*) **1.** *v/i* camp; ECON be stored **2.** *v/t* store, keep; MED lay, rest; **kühl ~** keep in a cool place

Lagerraum *m* storeroom

Lagerung ['laːgərʊŋ] *f* (-; *no pl*) storage

Lagune [la'guːnə] *f* (-; -n) lagoon

lahm [laːm] *adj* lame; **lahmen** ['laːmən] *v/i* (*ge-, h*) be lame (*auf dat* in)

lähmen ['lɛːmən] *v/t* (*ge-, h*) paralyze, *Br* paralyse; bring *traffic etc* to a standstill

lahmlegen *v/t* (*sep, -ge-, h*) → **lähmen**

Lähmung *f* (-; -en) MED paralysis

Laib [laip] *m* (-[e]s; -e ['laibə]) loaf

Laich [laiç] *m* (-[e]s; -e), **laichen** ['laiçən] *v/i* (*ge-, h*) spawn

Laie ['laiə] *m* (-n; -n) layman; amateur

laienhaft *adj* amateurish

Laienspiel *n* amateur play

Laken ['laːkən] *n* (-s; -) sheet; bath towel

Lakritze [la'krɪtsə] *f* (-; -n) liquorice

lallen ['lalən] *v/i and v/t* (*ge-, h*) speak drunkenly; *baby*: babble

Lamm [lam] *n* (-[e]s; *Lämmer* ['lɛmɐ]) ZO lamb; **~fell** *n* lambskin

Lampe ['lampə] *f* (-; -n) lamp, light; bulb

Lampenfieber *n* stage fright

Lampenschirm *m* lampshade

Lampion [lam'pjoː] *m* (-s; -s) Chinese lantern

Land [lant] *n* (-[e]s; *Länder* ['lɛndɐ]) land; country; AGR ground, soil; ECON land, property; **an ~ gehen** MAR go ashore; **auf dem ~e** in the country; **aufs ~ fahren** go into the country; **außer ~es gehen** go abroad; **~arbeiter** *m* farmhand; **~bevölkerung** *f* country *or* rural population

Landebahn ['landəbaːn] *f* AVIAT runway

landeinwärts *adv* up-country, inland

landen ['landən] *v/i* (*ge-, sein*) land; *fig* **~ in** (*dat*) end up in

Landenge *f* neck of land, isthmus

Landeplatz *m* AVIAT landing field

Länderspiel ['lɛndɐʃpiːl] *n* SPORT international match

Landesgrenze *f* national border; **~innere** *n* interior; **~regierung** *f* Land (*Austrian* Provincial) government;

~sprache f national language

'**landesüblich** adj customary

'**Landesverrat** m treason

'**Land|flucht** f rural exodus; **~friedensbruch** m JUR breach of the public peace; **~gericht** n JUR appr regional superior court; **~haus** n country house, cottage; **~karte** f map; **~kreis** m district

'**landläufig** adj customary, current, common

ländlich ['lɛntlɪç] adj rural; rustic

'**Land|rat** m, **~rätin** ['lantrɛːtɪn] f (-; -nen) appr District Administrator

'**Landschaft** f (-; -en) countryside; scenery; esp PAINT landscape

'**landschaftlich** adj scenic

'**Landsmann** m (-[e]s; -leute) (fellow) countryman; **Landsmännin** ['lantsmɛnɪn] f (-; -nen) fellow countrywoman

'**Land|straße** f country (or ordinary) road; **~streicher(in)** tramp; **~streitkräfte** pl MIL land forces; **~tag** m Land parliament

'**Landung** f (-; -en) landing, AVIAT a. touchdown

'**Landungssteg** m MAR gangway

'**Land|vermesser** ['lantfɛʁmɛsɐ] m (-s; -) land surveyor; **~vermessung** f (-; -en) land surveying; **~weg** m: **auf dem ~e** by land; **~wirt(in)** farmer

'**Landwirtschaft** f (-; no pl) agriculture, farming; '**landwirtschaftlich** adj agricultural

'**Landzunge** f GEOGR promontory, spit

lang [laŋ] adj and adv long; F tall; **drei Jahre (einige Zeit) ~** for three years (some time); **den ganzen Tag ~** all day long; **seit ~em** for a long time; **vor ~er Zeit** (a) long (time) ago; **über kurz oder ~** sooner or later; **~ ersehnt** long-hoped-for; **~ erwartet** long-awaited; **gleich ~** the same length

langatmig ['laŋʔaːtmɪç] adj long-winded

lange ['laŋə] adv (for a) long (time); **es ist schon ~ her(, seit)** it has been a long time (since); **(noch) nicht ~ her** not long ago; **noch ~ hin** still a long way off; **es dauert nicht ~** it won't take long; **ich bleibe nicht ~ fort** I won't be long; **wie ~ noch?** how much longer?

Länge ['lɛŋə] f (-; -n) length; GEOGR longitude; **der ~ nach** (at) full length;

(sich) in die ~ ziehen stretch (a. fig)

langen ['laŋən] F v/i/ (nach) reach (**nach** for); be enough; **mir langt es** I've had enough, fig a. I'm sick of it

'**Längen|grad** m GEOGR degree of longitude; **~maß** n linear measure

'**Langeweile** f (-; no pl) boredom; **~ haben** be bored; **aus ~** to pass the time

'**langfristig** adj long-term

'**langjährig** ['laŋjɛːrɪç] adj long-standing; **~e Erfahrung** many years of experience

'**Langlauf** m (-[e]s; no pl) SPORT cross-country (skiing)

'**langlebig** ['laŋleːbɪç] adj long-lived

'**länglich** ['lɛŋlɪç] adj longish, oblong

längs [lɛŋs] **1.** prp (gen) along(side) **2.** adv lengthwise

'**langsam** adj slow; **~er werden** or **fahren** slow down

'**Langschläfer** ['laŋʃlɛːfɐ] m (-s; -), **~schläferin** ['laŋʃlɛːfərɪn] f (-; -nen) late riser

längst [lɛŋst] adv long ago or before; **~ vorbei** long past; **ich weiß es ~** I have known it for a long time; **längstens** ['lɛŋstəns] adv at (the) most

'**Langstrecken...** in cpds long-distance ...; AVIAT, MIL long-range ...

'**langweilen** v/t (ge-, h) bore; **sich ~** be bored; **langweilig** ['laŋvailɪç] adj boring, dull

'**Langwelle** f PHYS, radio: long wave

langwierig ['laŋviːrɪç] adj lengthy, protracted (a. MED)

Lanze ['lantsə] f (-; -n) lance, spear

Lappalie [la'paːljə] f (-; -n) trifle

Lappen ['lapən] m (-s; -) (piece of) cloth; rag (a. fig)

läppisch ['lɛpɪʃ] adj silly; ridiculous

Lärche ['lɛrçə] f (-; -n) BOT larch

Lärm [lɛrm] m (-s; no pl) noise

lärmen ['lɛrmən] v/i (ge-, h) be noisy; **~d** adj noisy

Larve ['larfə] f (-; -n) mask; zo larva

las [laːs] pret of **lesen**

lasch [laʃ] F adj slack, lax

Lasche ['laʃə] f (-; -n) flap; tongue

Laser ['leːzɐ] m (-s; -) PHYS laser; **~drucker** m IT laser printer; **~strahl** m PHYS laser beam; **~technik** f laser technology

lassen ['lasən] v/t (irr, ge-, h) and v/aux

(*irr, no -ge-, h*) let, leave; *j-n et. tun* ~ let s.o. do s.th.; allow s.o. to do s.th.; make s.o. do s.th.; *j-n (et.) zu Hause* ~ leave s.o. (s.th.) at home; *j-n allein (in Ruhe)* ~ leave s.o. alone; *sich die Haare schneiden* ~ have *or* get one's hair cut; *sein Leben* ~ *(für)* lose (give) one's life (for); *rufen* ~ send for, call in; *es lässt sich machen* it can be done; *lass alles so, wie (wo) es ist* leave everything as (where) it is; *er kann das Rauchen etc nicht* ~ he can't stop smoking etc; *lass das!* stop it! → *grüßen*, *kommen*

lässig ['lɛsɪç] *adj* casual; careless

Last [last] *f* (-; -*en*) load, burden, weight (*all a. fig*); *j-m zur* ~ *fallen* be a burden to s.o.; *j-m et. zur* ~ *legen* charge s.o. with s.th.; **lasten** ['lastən] *v/i* (*ge-, h*) ~ *auf* (*dat*) *a. fig* weigh *or* rest (up)on

'**Lastenaufzug** *m* freight elevator, *Br* goods lift

Laster[1] ['lastɐ] *m* (-*s*; -) → *Lastwagen*

Laster[2] *n* (-*s*; -) vice

lästern ['lɛstɐn] *v/i* (*ge-, h*) ~ *über* (*acc*) run down

lästig ['lɛstɪç] *adj* troublesome, annoying; (*j-m*) ~ *sein* be a nuisance (to s.o.)

'**Last|kahn** *m* barge; ~*tier* *n* pack animal; ~*wagen* *m* MOT truck, *Br a.* lorry; ~*wagenfahrer* *m* MOT truck (*Br a.* lorry) driver, trucker

Latein [la'taın] *n* (-*s*; *no pl*) Latin

La'teina,merika Latin America; **La'teinameri,kaner(in)**, **la'teinameri,kanisch** *adj* Latin American

la'teinisch *adj* Latin

Laterne [la'tɛrnə] *f* (-; -*n*) lantern; streetlight

La'ternenpfahl *m* lamppost

Latte ['latə] *f* (-; -*n*) lath; pale; SPORT bar

'**Lattenzaun** *m* paling, picket fence

Lätzchen ['lɛtsçən] *n* (-*s*; -) bib

Laub [laup] *n* (-[*e*]*s*; *no pl*) foliage, leaves; '**Laubbaum** *m* deciduous tree

Laube ['laubə] *f* (-; -*n*) arbo(u)r

'**Laubfrosch** *m* ZO tree frog

'**Laubsäge** *f* fretsaw

Lauch [laux] *m* (-[*e*]*s*; -*e*) BOT leek

Lauer ['lauɐ] *f*: *auf der* ~ *liegen* *or* *sein* lie in wait; '**lauern** *v/i* (*ge-, h*) lurk; ~ *auf* (*acc*) lie in wait for

Lauf [lauf] *m* (-[*e*]*s*; *Läufe* ['lɔyfə]) run; course; *gun*: barrel; *im* ~*(e)* *der Zeit* in

the course of time; ~*bahn* *f* career; ~*diszi,plin* *f* SPORT track event

laufen ['laufən] *v/i and v/t* (*irr, -ge-, sein*) run (*a. TECH, MOT, ECON*); walk; *fig* work, run; *j-n* ~ *lassen* let s.o. go; let s.o. off; ~*d* **1.** *fig adj* present, current (*a. ECON*); continual; *auf dem Laufenden sein* be up to date **2.** *adv* continuously; regularly; always

'**laufenlassen** *v/t* (*irr, lassen, sep, no -ge-, h*) → *laufen*

Läufer ['lɔyfɐ] *m* (-*s*; -) runner (*a. carpet*); *chess:* bishop; '**Läuferin** *f* (-; -*nen*) runner

'**Lauf|gitter** *n* playpen; ~*masche* *f* run, *Br* ladder; ~*schuhe* *pl* walking shoes; SPORT trainers; ~*steg* *m* footbridge; TECH, *fashion:* catwalk; MAR gangway

Lauge ['laugə] *f* (-; -*n*) suds; CHEM lye

Laune ['launə] *f* (-; -*n*) mood, temper; *gute (schlechte)* ~ *haben* be in a good (bad) mood *or* temper; **launenhaft**, '**launisch** *adj* moody; bad-tempered

Laus [laus] *f* (-; *Läuse* ['lɔyzə]) ZO louse

'**Lauschangriff** ['lauʃˀaŋɡrɪf] *m* bugging operation; **lauschen** ['lauʃən] *v/i* (*ge-, h*) listen (*dat* to); eavesdrop

lauschig ['lauʃɪç] *adj* snug, cozy, *Br* cosy

laut[1] [laut] **1.** *adj* loud; noisy **2.** *adv* loud(ly); ~ *vorlesen* read (out) aloud; (*sprich*) ~*er, bitte!* speak up, please!

laut[2] *prp* (*gen or dat*) according to

Laut *m* (-[*e*]*s*; -*e*) sound, noise

lauten ['lautən] *v/i* (*ge-, h*) read; be

läuten ['lɔytən] *v/i and v/t* (*ge-, h*) ring; *es läutet (an der Tür)* the (door)bell is ringing

lauter ['lautɐ] *adv* sheer (*nonsense etc*); nothing but; (so) many

'**lautlos** *adj* silent, soundless; hushed

'**Lautschrift** *f* phonetic transcription

'**Lautsprecher** *m* TECH (loud)speaker

'**Lautstärke** *f* loudness, ELECTR *a.* (sound) volume; *mit voller* ~ (at) full blast; ~*regler* *m* volume control

lauwarm ['lauvarm] *adj* lukewarm (*a. fig*)

Lava ['laːva] *f* (-; *Laven*) GEOL lava

Lavabo [la'vaːbo] *Swiss n* → *Waschbecken*

Lavendel [la'vɛndəl] *m* (-*s*; -) BOT lavender

Lawine [la'viːnə] *f* (-; -*n*) avalanche

Lazarett [latsa'rɛt] n (-[e]s; -e) (military) hospital

leben ['le:bən] (ge-, h) **1.** v/i live; be alive; **von et. ~** live on s.th. **2.** v/t live; 'Leben n (-s; -) life; **am ~ bleiben** stay alive; survive; **am ~ sein** be alive; **sich das ~ nehmen** take one's (own) life, commit suicide; **ums ~ kommen** lose one's life, be killed; **um sein ~ laufen (kämpfen)** run (fight) for one's life; **das tägliche ~** everyday life; **mein ~ lang** all my life; 'lebend adj living; lebendig[le'bɛndɪç] adj living; alive; fig lively

'Lebens|abend m old age, the last years of one's life; **~bedingungen** pl living conditions; **~dauer** f life-span; TECH (service) life; **~erfahrung** f experience of life; **~erwartung** f life expectancy

'lebensfähig adj MED viable (a. fig)

'Lebensgefahr f mortal danger; **in (unter) ~** in danger (at the risk) of one's life; 'lebensgefährlich adj dangerous (to life), perilous

'lebensgroß adj life-size(d)

'Lebensgröße f: **e-e Statue in ~** a life-size(d) statue

'Lebenshaltungskosten pl cost of living

'lebenslänglich **1.** adj lifelong; **~e Freiheitsstrafe** JUR life sentence **2.** adv for life

'Lebenslauf m personal record, curriculum vitae

'lebenslustig adj fond of life

'Lebensmittel pl food(stuffs), groceries; **~geschäft** n grocery, supermarket

'lebensmüde adj tired of life

'Lebens|notwendigkeit f vital necessity; **~retter(in)** lifesaver, rescuer; **~standard** m standard of living; **~unterhalt** m livelihood; **s-n ~ verdienen** earn one's living (**als** as; **mit** out of, by); **~versicherung** f life insurance; **~weise** f way of life

'lebenswichtig adj vital, essential

'Lebenszeichen n sign of life

'Lebenszeit f lifetime; **auf ~** for life

Leber ['le:bɐ] f (-; -n) ANAT liver; **~fleck** m mole; **~tran** m cod-liver oil

'Lebewesen n living being, creature

lebhaft ['le:phaft] adj lively; heavy (traffic etc)

'Lebkuchen m gingerbread

'leblos adj lifeless (a. fig)

'Lebzeiten pl: **zu s-n ~** in his lifetime

lechzen ['lɛçtsən] v/i (ge-, h) **~ nach** thirst for

leck [lɛk] adj leaking, leaky

Leck n (-[e]s; -s) leak

lecken [¹ ['lɛkən] v/t and v/i (ge-, h) a. **~ an** (dat) lick

lecken [²] v/i (ge-, h) leak

lecker ['lɛkɐ] adj delicious, tasty, F yummy; 'Leckerbissen m delicacy, treat (a. fig)

Leder ['le:dɐ] n (-s; -) leather; 'ledern adj leather(n); 'Lederwaren pl leather goods

ledig ['le:dɪç] adj single, unmarried

lediglich ['le:dɪklɪç] adv only, merely

Lee [le:] f (-; no pl) MAR lee; **nach ~** leeward

leer [le:ɐ] **1.** adj empty (a. fig); vacant (house etc); blank (page etc); ELECTR dead, Br flat; **~ stehend** unoccupied, vacant **2.** adv: **~ laufen** TECH idle; Leere ['le:rə] f (-; no pl) emptiness (a. fig); 'leeren v/t and v/refl (ge-, h) empty; 'Leergut n empties; 'Leerlauf m TECH idling; neutral (gear); fig running on the spot; 'Leertaste f space bar; 'Leerung f (-; -en) post collection

legal [le'ga:l] adj legal, lawful

legalisieren [legali'zi:rən] v/t (no -ge-, h) legalize; Legali'sierung f (-; -en) legalization

Legasthenie [legaste'ni:] f (-; -n) PSYCH dyslexia, F word blindness

Legastheniker [legas'te:nikɐ] m (-s; -), Legas'thenikerin f (-; -nen) PSYCH dyslexic

legen ['le:gən] v/t and v/i (ge-, h) lay (a. eggs); place, put; set (hair); **sich ~** lie down; fig calm down; pain: wear off

Legende [le'gɛndə] f (-; -n) legend

leger [le'ʒe:ɐ] adj casual, informal

Legislative [legɪsla'ti:və] f (-; -n) legislative power

legitim [legi'ti:m] adj legitimate

Lehm [le:m] m (-[e]s; -e) loam; clay

lehmig ['le:mɪç] adj loamy, F muddy

Lehne ['le:nə] f (-; -n) back(rest); arm (-rest); 'lehnen v/t and v/i lean (a. **sich ~**) rest (**an** acc, **gegen** against; **auf** acc on); **sich aus dem Fenster ~** lean out of the window; 'Lehnsessel m, 'Lehnstuhl m armchair, easy chair

L

Lehrbuch ['leːᵊbuːx] *n* textbook

Lehre ['leːrə] *f* (-; -*n*) science; theory; REL, POL teachings, doctrine; moral; ECON apprenticeship; *in der ~ sein* be apprenticed (*bei* to); *das wird ihm e-e ~ sein* that will teach him a lesson

'**lehren** *v/t* (*ge-, h*) teach, instruct; show

Lehrer ['leːrə] *m* (-*s*; -) teacher, instructor, *Br a.* master; **~ausbildung** *f* teacher training

Lehrerin ['leːrərɪn] *f* (-; -*nen*) (lady) teacher, *Br a.* mistress

'**Lehrer|kol,legium** *n* (teaching) staff; **~zimmer** *n* staff *or* teachers' room

'**Lehr|gang** *m* course (of instruction *or* study); training course; **~jahr** *n* year (of apprenticeship)

Lehrling ['leːrlɪŋ] *m* (-*s*; -*e*) apprentice, trainee

'**Lehr|meister** *m*, **~meisterin** *f* master; *fig* teacher; **~mittel** *pl* teaching aids; **~plan** *m* curriculum, syllabus; **~probe** *f* demonstration lesson

'**lehrreich** *adj* informative, instructive

'**Lehr|stelle** *f* apprenticeship; vacancy for an apprentice; **~stuhl** *m* professorship; **~tochter** *Swiss* apprentice; **~vertrag** *m* indenture(s); **~zeit** *f* apprenticeship

Leib [laip] *m* (-[*e*]*s*; *Leiber* ['laibə]) body; belly, ANAT abdomen; stomach; *bei lebendigem ~e* alive; *mit ~ und Seele* (with) heart and soul

'**Leibgericht** *n* GASTR favo(u)rite dish

'**leibhaftig** [laip'haftɪç] *adj*: *der ~e Teufel* the devil incarnate; *~es Ebenbild* living image; *ich sehe ihn noch ~ vor mir* I can see him (before me) now

'**leiblich** *adj* physical

'**Leib|rente** *f* life annuity; **~wache** *f*, **~wächter** *m* bodyguard; **~wäsche** *f* underwear

Leiche ['laiçə] *f* (-; -*n*) (dead) body, corpse

'**leichen'blass** *adj* deadly pale

'**Leichen|halle** *f* mortuary; **~schauhaus** *n* morgue; **~verbrennung** *f* cremation; **~wagen** *m* hearse

leicht [laiçt] *adj* light (*a. fig*); easy, simple; slight, minor; TECH light(weight); **~ möglich** quite possible; **~ gekränkt** easily offended; *es fällt mir (nicht) ~ (zu inf*) I find it easy (difficult) (to *inf*); *das ist ~ gesagt* it's not as easy

as that; *es geht ~ kaputt* it breaks easily; **~ verständlich** easy to understand

'**Leicht|ath,let** *m* SPORT (track-and-field) athlete; **~ath,letik** *f* SPORT track and field (events), athletics; **~ath,letin** *f* SPORT (track-and-field) athlete; **~gewicht** *n* SPORT lightweight

'**leichtgläubig** *adj* credulous

Leichtigkeit ['laiçtɪçkait] *f*: *mit ~* easily, with ease

'**leichtlebig** ['laiçtleːbɪç] *adj* happy-go-lucky

'**Leichtme,tall** *n* light metal

'**leichtnehmen** *v/t* (*irr, nehmen, sep, -ge-, h*): *et. ~* not worry about *or* s.th.; make light of s.th.; *nimm's leicht!* never mind!, don't worry about it!

'**Leichtsinn** *m* (-[*e*]*s; no pl*) carelessness; recklessness; '**leichtsinnig** *adj* careless; reckless

'**leichtverständlich** *adj* → **leicht**

Leid [lait] *n* (-[*e*]*s; no pl*) sorrow, grief; pain; *es tut mir ~* I'm sorry (*um* for; *wegen* about; *dass ich zu spät komme* for being late)

leiden ['laidən] *v/t and v/i* (*irr, ge-, h*) suffer (*an dat, unter dat* from); *j-n gut ~ können* like s.o.; *ich kann ... nicht ~* I don't like ...; I can't stand ...;

'**Leiden** *n* (-*s*; -) suffering(s); MED disease

'**Leidenschaft** *f* (-; -*en*) passion

'**leidenschaftlich** *adj* passionate, vehement

'**Leidensgenosse** *m*,

'**Leidensgenossin** *f* fellow sufferer

leider ['laidə] *adv* unfortunately; *~ ja (nein)* I'm afraid so (not)

'**leidlich** *adj* passable, F so-so

'**Leidtragende** *m, f*(-*n*; -*n*) mourner; *er ist der ~ dabei* he is the one who suffers for it

'**Leidwesen** *n*: *zu m-m ~* to my regret

Leierkasten ['laiəkastən] *m* barrel organ; **~mann** *m* organ grinder

leiern ['laiən] *v/i and v/t* (*ge-, h*) crank (up); *fig* drone

Leihbücherei ['laibyːçərai] *f* public library

leihen ['laiən] *v/t* (*irr, ge-, h*) lend; rent (*Br* hire) out; borrow (*von* from); rent hire

'**Leih|gebühr** *f* rental, lending fee **~haus** *n* pawnshop, pawnbroker's (shop); **~mutter** F f surrogate mother; **~wagen** m MOT rented (Br hire) car

'**leihweise** adv on loan

Leim [laim] m (-[e]s; -e), **leimen** ['laimən] v/t (ge-, h) glue

Leine ['lainə] f (-; -n) line; lead, leash

Leinen ['lainən] n (-s; -) linen; canvas; **in ~ gebunden** clothbound

'**Leinenschuh** m canvas shoe

'**Lein|samen** m BOT linseed; **~tuch** n (linen) sheet; **~wand** f linen; PAINT canvas; screen

leise ['laizə] adj quiet, a. low, soft (voice, a. music etc); fig slight, faint; **~r stellen** turn (the volume) down

Leiste ['laistə] f (-; -n) ledge; ANAT groin

'**leisten** v/t (ge-, h) do, work; achieve, accomplish; render (service etc); take (oath); **gute Arbeit ~** do a good job; **sich et. ~** treat o.s. to s.th.; **ich kann es mir (nicht) ~** I can('t) afford it

'**Leistung** f (-; -en) performance; achievement, PED a. (piece of) work, result, TECH a. output; service; benefit

'**Leistungsdruck** m (-[e]s; no pl) pressure, stress

'**leistungsfähig** adj efficient; (physically) fit; '**Leistungsfähigkeit** f (-; no pl) efficiency (a. TECH, ECON); fitness

'**Leistungs|kon,trolle** f (achievement or proficiency) test; **~kurs** m PED appr special subject; **~sport** m competitive sport(s)

Leitar,tikel m ['lait?arti:kəl] m editorial, esp Br leader, leading article

leiten ['laitən] v/t (ge-, h) lead, guide (a. fig), conduct (a. PHYS, MUS); run (a. PED), be in charge of, manage; TV etc direct; host; **~d** adj leading; PHYS conductive; **~e Stellung** key position; **~er Angestellter** executive

Leiter¹ ['laitə] f (-; -n) ladder

'**Leiter²** m (-s; -) leader; conductor (a. PHYS, MUS); ECON etc head, manager; chairman; → **Schulleiter**

Leiterin ['laitərin] f (-; -nen) leader; head; chairwoman

'**Leit|faden** m manual, guide; **~planke** f MOT guardrail, Br crash barrier; **~spruch** m motto

'**Leitung** f (-; -en) ECON management; head office; administration; chairmanship; organization; THEA etc direction; TECH main, pipe(s); ELECTR, TEL line;

die ~ haben be in charge; **unter der ~ von** MUS conducted by

'**Leitungsrohr** n pipe

'**Leitungswasser** n tap water

Lektion [lɛk'tsjo:n] f (-; -en) lesson

Lektüre [lɛk'ty:rə] f (-; -n) reading (matter); PED reader

Lende ['lɛndə] f (-; -n) ANAT loin; GASTR sirloin

lenken ['lɛŋkən] v/t (ge-, h) steer, drive; fig guide s.o.; direct (traffic etc)

Lenker ['lɛŋkə] m (-s; -) handlebar

'**Lenkrad** n MOT steering wheel

'**Lenkung** f (-; -en) MOT steering (system)

Leopard [leo'part] m (-en; -en) ZO leopard

Lerche ['lɛrçə] f (-; -n) ZO lark

lernen ['lɛrnən] v/t and v/i (ge-, h) learn; study; **er lernt leicht** he is a quick learner; **lesen ~** learn (how) to read

'**Lernmittelfreiheit** f free books etc

lesbar ['le:sba:ɐ] adj readable

Lesbierin ['lɛsbjərin] f (-; -nen), **lesbisch** ['lɛsbɪʃ] adj lesbian

'**Lesebuch** ['le:zəbu:x] n reader

'**Leselampe** f reading lamp

lesen ['le:zən] v/i and v/t (irr, ge-, h) read; AGR harvest

'**lesenswert** adj worth reading

Leser ['le:zɐ] m (-s; -) reader

'**Leseratte** F f bookworm

'**Leserbrief** m letter to the editor

'**Leserin** f (-; -nen) reader

'**leserlich** adj legible

'**Lesestoff** m reading matter

'**Lesezeichen** n bookmark

Lesung f (-; -en) reading (a. PARL)

Letzt [lɛtst] f: **zu guter ~** in the end

letzte ['lɛtstə] adj last; latest; **zum ~n Mal(e)** for the last time; **in ~r Zeit** recently; **als Letzter ankommen** etc arrive etc last; **Letzter sein** be last (a. SPORT); **das ist das Letzte!** that's the limit!; '**letztens** adv finally; **erst ~** just recently; **letztere** ['lɛtstərə] adj latter; **der (die) das) Letztere** the latter

Leuchtanzeige ['lɔyçt?antsaigə] f luminous or LED display light; **leuchten** ['lɔyçtən] v/i (ge-, h) shine; glow; '**Leuchten** n (-s; no pl) shining; glow; '**leuchtend** adj shining (a. fig); bright; **Leuchter** ['lɔyçtɐ] m (-s; -) candlestick

'**Leucht|farbe** f luminous paint; **~re,klame** f neon sign(s); **~(stoff)röhre** f

ELECTR fluorescent lamp; ~turm m lighthouse; ~ziffer f luminous figure

leugnen ['lɔygnən] v/t and v/i (ge-, h) deny (et. getan zu haben having done s.th.)

Leute ['lɔytə] pl people, F folks

Leutnant ['lɔytnant] m (-s; -s) MIL second lieutenant

Lexikon ['lɛksikɔn] n (-s; -ka, -ken) encyclop(a)edia; dictionary

Libelle [li'bɛlə] f (-; -n) zo dragonfly

liberal [libe'ra:l] adj liberal

Libero ['li:bero] m (-s; -s) soccer: sweeper

licht ['lɪçt] adj bright; fig lucid

Licht n (-[e]s; -er ['lɪçtə]) light; (no pl) brightness; ~ machen switch or turn on the light(s)

'Licht|bild n photo(graph); slide; ~bildervortrag m slide lecture; ~blick m ray of hope; bright moment

lichtempfindlich adj sensitive to light; PHOT sensitive; 'Lichtempfindlichkeit f (light) sensitivity; PHOT speed

lichten ['lɪçtən] v/t (ge-, h) clear; den Anker ~ MAR weigh anchor; sich ~ get thin(ner); fig be thinning (out)

'Licht|geschwindigkeit f speed of light; ~hupe f MOT (headlight) flash(er); die ~ betätigen flash one's lights; ~jahr n light year; ~ma,schine f MOT generator; ~orgel f colo(u)r organ; ~pause f blueprint; ~schacht m well; ~schalter m (light) switch

'lichtscheu fig adj shady

'Licht|schutzfaktor m sun protection factor, SPF; ~strahl m ray or beam of light (a. fig)

'Lichtung f (-; -en) clearing

Lid [li:t] n (-[e]s; Lider ['li:dɐ]) ANAT (eye)lid; ~schatten m eye shadow

lieb [li:p] adj dear; sweet; nice, kind; good; ~ gewinnen get fond of; ~ haben love, be fond of; Liebe ['li:bə] f (-; no pl) love (zu of, for); aus ~ zu out of love for; ~ auf den ersten Blick love at first sight; 'lieben v/t (ge-, h) love, a. be in love with s.o.; make love to

'liebenswert adj lovable, charming, sweet

'liebenswürdig adj kind; 'Liebenswürdigkeit f (-; no pl) kindness

lieber ['li:bɐ] adv rather, sooner; ~ ha-

ben prefer, like better; ich möchte ~ (nicht) ... I'd rather (not) ...; du solltest ~ (nicht) ... you had better (not) ...

'Liebes|brief m love letter; ~erklärung f: j-m e-e ~ machen declare one's love to s.o.; ~kummer m: ~ haben be lovesick; ~paar n lovers

'liebevoll adj loving, affectionate

'liebgewinnen v/t (irr, gewinnen, sep, h) → lieb

'liebhaben v/t (irr, haben, sep, -ge-, h) → lieb; Liebhaber ['li:phabɐ] m (-s; -) lover (a. fig); ~... in cpds ...preis, ...stück etc: collector's ...; Liebhaberei [li:phabə'raɪ] f (-; -en) hobby

Liebkosung [li:p'ko:zʊŋ] f (-; -en) caress

'lieblich adj lovely, charming, sweet (a. wine)

'Liebling m (-s; -e) darling; favo(u)rite

'Lieblings... in cpds mst favo(u)rite

'lieblos adj unloving, cold; unkind (words etc); fig careless

Lied [li:t] n (-[e]s; -er ['li:dɐ]) song; tune

liederlich ['li:dɐlɪç] adj slovenly, sloppy

Liedermacher ['li:dɐmaxɐ] m (-s; -) singer-songwriter

lief [li:f] pret of laufen

Lieferant [lifə'rant] m (-en; -en) ECON supplier; lieferbar ['li:fɐba:ɐ] adj ECON available; 'Lieferfrist f ECON term of delivery; liefern ['li:fɐn] v/t (ge-, h) ECON deliver; j-m et. ~ supply s.o. with s.th.; Lieferung ['li:fərʊŋ] f (-; -en) ECON delivery; supply

'Lieferwagen m MOT (delivery) van

Liege ['li:gə] f (-; -n) couch

liegen ['li:gən] v/i (irr, ge-, h) lie, a. be (situated); (krank) im Bett ~ be (ill) in bed; nach Osten (der Straße) ~ face east (the street); daran liegt es(, dass) that's (the reason) why; es (er) liegt mir nicht F it (he) is not my cup of tea; mir liegt viel (wenig) daran it means a lot (doesn't mean much) to me; ~ bleiben stay in bed; be left behind; ~ lassen leave (behind); F j-n links ~ lassen ignore s.o., give s.o. the cold shoulder

'liegenbleiben v/i (irr, bleiben, sep, -ge-, sein) → liegen; ~lassen v/i (irr, lassen, sep, no -ge-, h) → liegen

'Liege|sitz m reclining seat; ~stuhl m deckchair; ~stütz m (-es; -e) SPORT push-up, *Br* press-up; **~wagen** *m* RAIL couchette

lieh [liː] *pret of* **leihen**

ließ [liːs] *pret of* **lassen**

Lift [lɪft] *m* (-[e]s; -e, -s) elevator, *Br* lift; ski lift

Liga ['liːɡa] *f* (-; *Ligen*) league, SPORT *a.* division

Likör [li'køːʀ] *m* (-s; -e) liqueur

lila ['liːla] *adj* purple, violet

Lilie ['liːljə] *f* (-; -n) BOT lily

Liliputaner [lilipu'taːnɐ] *m* (-s; -) dwarf, midget

Limonade [limo'naːdə] *f* (-; -n) pop; lemon soda, *Br* lemonade

Limousine [limu'ziːnə] *f* (-; -n) MOT sedan, *Br* saloon car; limousine

Linde ['lɪndə] *f* (-; -n) BOT lime (tree), linden

lindern ['lɪndɐn] *v/t* (ge-, h) relieve, ease, alleviate; **Linderung** ['lɪndərʊŋ] *f* (-; *no pl*) relief, alleviation

Lineal [line'aːl] *n* (-s; -e) ruler

Linie ['liːnjə] *f* (-; -n) line; **auf s-e ~ achten** watch one's weight

'**Linien|flug** *m* AVIAT scheduled flight; **~richter** *m* SPORT linesman

'**linientreu** *adj* POL: **~ sein** follow the party line

linieren [li'niːrən], **liniieren** [lini'iːrən] *v/t* (*no* -ge-, h) rule, line

linke ['lɪŋkə] *adj* left (*a.* POL); **auf der ~n Seite** on the left(-hand side); '**Linke** *m, f* (-n; -n) POL leftist, left-winger

linkisch ['lɪŋkɪʃ] *adj* awkward, clumsy

links [lɪŋks] *adv* on the left (*a.* POL); on the wrong side; **nach ~** (to the) left; **~ von** to the left of

Links... *in cpds* ...*verkehr etc:* left-hand

Links'außen *m* (-; -) SPORT outside left, left wing

Linkshänder ['lɪŋkshɛndɐ] *m* (-s; -), '**Linkshänderin** *f* (-; -nen) left-hander

'**Linksradi,kale** *m, f* (-n; -n) POL left--wing extremist

Linse ['lɪnzə] *f* (-; -n) BOT lentil; OPT lens

Lippe ['lɪpə] *f* (-; -n) ANAT lip

'**Lippenstift** *m* lipstick

liquidieren [likvi'diːrən] *v/t* (*no* -ge-, h) ECON liquidate (*a.* POL)

lispeln ['lɪspəln] *v/i* (ge-, h) (have a) lisp

List [lɪst] *f* (-; -en) trick; (*no pl*) cunning

Liste ['lɪstə] *f* (-; -n) list; roll

listig ['lɪstɪç] *adj* cunning, tricky, sly

Liter ['liːtɐ] *n, m* (-s; -) liter, *Br* litre

literarisch [litə'raːrɪʃ] *adj* literary

Literatur [litəra'tuːɐ] *f* (-; -en) literature; **~...** *in cpds* ...*kritik etc:* mst literary

Litfaßsäule ['lɪtfaszɔylə] *f* advertising pillar

litt [lɪt] *pret of* **leiden**

Lizenz [li'tsɛnts] *f* (-; -en) license, *Br* licence

Lkw, LKW ['ɛlkaveː] *m* (-[s]; -) *abbr of* **Lastkraftwagen** truck, *Br a.* lorry

Lob [loːp] *n* (-[e]s; *no pl*), **loben** ['loːbən] *v/t* (ge-, h) praise; '**lobenswert** *adj* praiseworthy, laudable

Loch [lɔx] *n* (-[e]s; *Löcher* ['lœçɐ]) hole (*a. fig*); puncture; **lochen** ['lɔxən] *v/t* (ge-, h) punch (*a.* TECH); **Locher** ['lɔxɐ] *m* (-s; -) punch

Locke ['lɔkə] *f* (-; -n) curl; lock

locken¹ ['lɔkən] *v/t and v/refl* (ge-, h) curl

locken² *v/t* (ge-, h) lure, entice, *fig a.* attract, tempt

'**Locken|kopf** *m* curly head; **~wickler** ['lɔkənvɪklɐ] *m* (-s; -) curler, roller

locker ['lɔkɐ] *adj* loose; slack; *fig* relaxed; '**lockern** *v/t* (ge-, h) loosen, slacken; relax (*a. fig*); **sich ~** loosen, (be)come loose; SPORT limber up; *fig* relax

lockig ['lɔkɪç] *adj* curly, curled

'**Lockvogel** *m* decoy (*a. fig*)

lodern ['loːdɐn] *v/i* (ge-, h) blaze, flare

Löffel ['lœfəl] *m* (-s; -) spoon; ladle

'**löffeln** *v/t* (ge-, h) spoon up

log [loːk] *pret of* **lügen**

Logbuch ['lɔkbuːx] *n* MAR log

Loge ['loːʒə] *f* (-; -n) THEA box; lodge

Logik ['loːɡɪk] *f* (-; *no pl*) logic

logisch ['loːɡɪʃ] *adj* logical

'**logischer'weise** *adv* obviously

Lohn [loːn] *m* (-[e]s; *Löhne* ['løːnə]) ECON wages, pay(ment); *fig* reward; **~empfänger** *m* wageworker, *Br* wage earner

lohnen ['loːnən] *v/refl* (ge-, h) be worth (-while), pay; **es (die Mühe) lohnt sich** it's worth it (the trouble); **das Buch (der Film) lohnt sich** the book (film) is worth reading (seeing); **~d** *adj* paying; *fig* rewarding

'**Lohn|erhöhung** *f* raise, *Br* increase in

wages, rise; **~steuer** f income tax; **~stopp** m wage freeze

Loipe ['lɔypə] f (-; -n) (cross-country) course

Lok [lɔk] f (-; -s) → **Lokomotive**

Lokal [lo'kaːl] n (-s; -e) restaurant; bar, saloon, esp Br pub

Lo'kal... in cpds mst local

Lokführer m RAIL engineer, Br train driver

Lokomotive [lokomo'tiːvə] f (-; -n) RAIL engine

Lorbeer ['lɔrbeːɐ] m (-s; -en) BOT laurel; GASTR bay leaf

Lore ['loːrə] f (-; -n) TECH tipcart

los [loːs] adj and adv off; dog etc: loose; **~ sein** be rid of; **was ist ~?** what's the matter?, F what's up?; what's going on (here)?; **hier ist nicht viel ~** there's nothing much going on here; F **da ist was ~!** that's where the action is!; F **also ~!** okay, let's go!

Los [loːs] n (-es; -e) ['loːzə] lot, a fig a. fate; (lottery) ticket, number

'losbinden v/t (irr, **binden**, sep, -ge-, h) untie

Löschblatt ['lœʃblat] n blotting paper

löschen ['lœʃən] v/t (ge-, h) extinguish, put out; quench (thirst); blot (ink); wipe off the blackboard; erase, IT a. delete; slake (lime), MAR unload

'Löschpa,pier n blotting paper

lose ['loːzə] adj loose

Lösegeld ['løːzəgɛlt] n ransom

losen ['loːzən] v/i (ge-, h) draw lots (**um** for)

lösen ['løːzən] v/t (ge-, h) undo (knot etc); loosen, relax; TECH release; take off; solve (problem etc); settle (conflict etc); buy, get (ticket etc); dissolve (a. CHEM); **sich ~** come loose or undone; fig free o.s. (**von** from)

'losfahren v/i (irr, **fahren**, sep, -ge-, sein) leave; drive off; **~gehen** v/i (irr, **gehen**, sep, -ge-, sein) leave; start, begin; shot etc: go off; F **da j-n ~** go for s.o.; **ich gehe jetzt los** I'm off now; **~ketten** v/t (sep, -ge-, h) unchain; **~kommen** v/i (irr, **kommen**, sep, -ge-, sein) get away (**von** from); **~lassen** v/t (irr, **lassen**, sep, -ge-, h) let go; **den Hund ~ auf** (acc) set the dog on; **~legen** F v/i (sep, -ge-, h) get cracking

löslich ['løːslɪç] adj CHEM soluble

'losmachen v/t (sep, -ge-, h) → **lösen**; **~reißen** v/t (irr, **reißen**, sep, -ge-, h) tear off; **sich ~** break away; esp fig tear o.s. away (both: **von** from); **~sagen** v/refl (sep, -ge-, h) **sich ~ von** break with; **~schlagen** v/i (irr, **schlagen**, sep, -ge-, h) strike (**auf j-n** out at s.o.); **~schnallen** v/t (sep, -ge-, h) unbuckle; **sich ~** MOT, AVIAT unfasten one's seat belt; **~stürzen** v/i (sep, -ge-, sein) **~ auf** (acc) rush at

Losung ['loːzʊŋ] f (-; -en) MIL password; fig slogan

Lösung ['løːzʊŋ] f (-; -en) solution (a. fig); settlement

Lösungsmittel n solvent

'loswerden v/t (irr, **werden**, sep, -ge-, sein) get rid of; spend (money); lose

'losziehen v/i (irr, **ziehen**, sep, -ge-, sein) set out, take off, march away

Lot [loːt] n (-[e]s; -e) plumbline

löten ['løːtən] v/t (ge-, h) TECH solder

Lotion ['loːtsjoːn] f (-; -en) lotion

Lotse ['loːtsə] m (-n; -n), **'lotsen** v/t (ge-, h) MAR pilot

Lotterie [lɔtə'riː] f (-; -n) lottery; **~gewinn** m prize; **~los** n lottery ticket

Lotto ['lɔto] n (-s; -s) lotto, bingo; Br national lottery; in Germany: Lotto; (im) **~ spielen** do Lotto; **~schein** m Lotto coupon; **~ziehung** f Lotto draw

Löwe ['løːvə] m (-n; -n) zo lion; AST Leo; **er ist (ein) ~** he's a(a) Leo

'Löwenzahn m BOT dandelion

Löwin ['løːvɪn] f (-; -nen) zo lioness

loyal [loa'jaːl] adj loyal, faithful

Luchs [lʊks] m (-es; -e) zo lynx

Lücke ['lʏkə] f (-; -n) gap (a. fig); **'Lückenbüßer** m stopgap; **'lückenhaft** adj full of gaps; fig incomplete; **'lückenlos** adj without a gap; fig complete; **'Lückentest** m PSYCH completion or fill-in test

lud [luːt] pret of **laden**

Luft [lʊft] f (-; no pl) air; **an der frischen ~** (out) in the fresh air; (**frische**) **~ schöpfen** get a breath of fresh air; **die ~ anhalten** catch (esp fig a. hold) one's breath; **tief ~ holen** take a deep breath; **in die ~ sprengen** (F **fliegen**) blow up

'Luftangriff m air raid; **~ballon** m balloon; **~bild** n aerial photograph or view; **~blase** f air bubble; **~brücke**

airlift

'luftdicht *adj* airtight

'Luftdruck *m* (-[e]s; *no pl*) PHYS, TECH air pressure

lüften ['lʏftən] *v/t and v/i* (ge-, h) air, ventilate; *fig* reveal

'Luft|fahrt *f* (-; *no pl*) aviation, aeronautics; **~feuchtigkeit** *f* (atmospheric) humidity; **~gewehr** *n* airgun

'luftig *adj* airy; breezy; light (*dress etc*)

'Luft|kissen *n* air cushion; **~kissenfahrzeug** *n* hovercraft; **~krankheit** *f* air-sickness; **~krieg** *m* air warfare; **~kurort** *m* (climatic) health resort

'luftleer *adj*: **~er Raum** vacuum

'Luft|linie *f*: **50 km ~** 50 km as the crow flies; **~post** *f* air mail; **~pumpe** *f* air pump; bicycle pump; **~röhre** *f* ANAT windpipe, trachea; **~schlange** *f* streamer; **~schloss** *n* castle in the air; **~sprünge** *pl*: **~ machen vor Freude** jump for joy

'Lüftung *f* (-; -en) airing; TECH ventilation

'Luft|veränderung *f* change of air; **~verkehr** *m* air traffic; **~verschmutzung** *f* air pollution; **~waffe** *f* MIL air force; **~weg** *m*: **auf dem ~** by air; **~zug** *m* draft, *Br* draught

Lüge ['ly:gə] *f* (-; -n) lie; **lügen** *v/i* (irr, ge-, h) lie, tell a lie *or* lies; **das ist gelogen** that's a lie; **Lügner(in)** ['ly:gnɐ, 'ly:gnərɪn] *m(f)* (-s; -/-; -nen) liar; **lügnerisch** ['ly:gnərɪʃ] *adj* false

Luke ['lu:kə] *f* (-; -n) hatch; skylight

Lümmel ['lʏməl] F *m* (-s; -) rascal

lumpen ['lʊmpən] F *v/t*: **sich nicht ~ lassen** be generous

'Lumpen *m* (-s; -) rag; **in ~** in rags

lumpig ['lʊmpɪç] F *adj*: **für ~e zwei Euro** for a paltry two euros

Lunge ['lʊŋə] *f* (-; -n) ANAT lungs; (**auf**) ~

'Lungen|entzündung *f* MED pneumonia; **~flügel** *m* ANAT lung; **~zug** *m*: **e-n ~ machen** inhale

Lupe ['lu:pə] *f* (-; -n) magnifying glass; **unter die ~ nehmen** scrutinize (closely)

Lust [lʊst] *f* (-; *Lüste* ['lʏstə]) (*no pl*) desire, interest; pleasure, delight; lust; **~ haben auf et.** (**et. zu tun**) feel like (doing) s.th.; **hättest du ~ auszugehen?** would you like to go out?, how about going out?; **ich habe keine ~** I don't feel like it, I'm not in the mood for it; **die ~ an et. verlieren** (**j-m die ~ an et. nehmen**) (make s.o.) lose all interest in s.th.

lüstern ['lʏstɐn] *adj* greedy (**nach** for)

lustig ['lʊstɪç] *adj* funny; cheerful; **er ist sehr ~** he is full of fun; **es war sehr ~** it was great fun; **sich ~ machen über** (*acc*) make fun of

'lustlos *adj* listless, indifferent

'Lustmord *m* sex murder

'Lustspiel *n* THEA comedy

lutschen ['lʊtʃən] *v/i and v/t* (ge-, h) suck

Luv [lu:f] *f* (-; *no pl*) MAR windward, weather side

luxuriös [lʊksu'rjøːs] *adj* luxurious

Luxus ['lʊksʊs] *m* (-; *no pl*) luxury; **~artikel** *m* luxury (article); **~ausführung** *f* deluxe version; **~hotel** *n* five-star (*or* luxury) hotel

Lymphdrüse ['lʏmfdry:zə] *f* ANAT lymph gland

lynchen ['lʏnçən] *v/t* (ge-, h) lynch

Lyrik ['ly:rɪk] *f* (-; *no pl*) poetry

Lyriker ['ly:rikɐ] *m* (-s; -), **Lyrikerin** *f* (-; -nen) (lyric) poet

lyrisch ['ly:rɪʃ] *adj* lyrical (*a. fig*)

M

machbar ['maxbaːə] *adj* feasible

machen ['maxən] *v/t* (ge-, h) do; make; GASTR make, prepare; fix (*a. fig*); be, come to, amount to; take, pass (*test etc*); make, go on (*a trip etc*); **Hausaufgaben ~** do one's homework; **da**

(**-gegen**) **kann man nichts ~** it can't be helped; **mach, was du willst!** do as you please!; (**nun**) **mach mal** *or* **schon!** hurry up!, come on *or* along now!; **mach's gut!** take care (of yourself)!, good luck!; (**das**) **macht nichts** it doesn't matter; **mach dir nichts d-(a)raus!** never mind!, don't worry!; **das macht mir nichts aus** I don't mind or care; **was** or **wie viel macht das?** how much is it?; **sich et. (nichts) ~ aus** (not) care about; (not) care for

'**Machenschaften** pl machinations; **un-saubere** (esp POL) sleaze (esp POL)

Macher ['maxɐ] m (-s; -) man of action, doer

Macho ['matʃo] m (-s; -s) macho

Macht [maxt] f (-; **Mächte** ['mɛçtə]) power (**über** acc of); **an der ~** in power; **mit aller ~** with all one's might

Machthaber ['maxthaːbɐ] m (-s; -) POL ruler

mächtig ['mɛçtɪç] adj powerful, mighty (a. F); enormous, huge

'**Machtkampf** m struggle for power

'**machtlos** adj powerless

'**Macht|missbrauch** m abuse of power; **~poli,tik** f power politics; **~übernahme** f takeover; **~wechsel** m transition of power

Mädchen ['mɛːtçən] n (-s; -) girl; maid

'**mädchenhaft** adj girlish

'**Mädchen|name** m girl's name; maiden name; **~schule** f girls' school

Made ['maːdə] f (-; -n) zo maggot; worm

Mädel ['mɛːdəl] n (-s; -s) girl

'**madig** adj maggoty, worm-eaten; F'**madigmachen** v/t (sep, ge-, h): F **j-m et. ~** spoil s.th. for s.o.

Magazin [maga'tsiːn] n (-s; -e) maga-zine (a. MIL, PHOT, TV); store(room), warehouse

Magd [maːkt] f (-; **Mägde** ['mɛːktə]) (fe-male) farmhand

Magen ['maːgən] m (-s; **Mägen** ['mɛː-gən]) ANAT stomach; **~beschwerden** pl MED stomach trouble; **~geschwür** n MED (stomach) ulcer; **~schmerzen** pl stomachache

mager ['maːgɐ] adj lean, thin, skinny; GASTR low-fat (cheese), lean (meat), skim (milk); fig meager, Br meagre

Magie [ma'giː] f (-; no pl) magic

magisch ['maːgɪʃ] adj magic(al)

Magister [ma'gɪstɐ] m (-s; -) UNIV Mas-ter of Arts or Science; Austrian → **Apo-theker**

Magistrat [magɪs'traːt] m (-[e]s; -e) mu-nicipal council

Magnet [ma'gneːt] m (-[e]s, -en; -e[n])

magnet (a. fig); **~ ... in cpds ...band, ...feld, ...nadel** etc: magnetic ...

mag'netisch adj magnetic (a. fig)

magnetisieren [magneti'ziːrən] v/t (no -ge-, h) magnetize

Mahagoni [maha'goːni] n (-s; no pl) mahogany

Mähdrescher ['mɛːdrɛʃɐ] m (-s; -) AGR combine (harvester); **mähen** ['mɛːən] v/t (ge-, h) mow; cut; AGR reap

mahlen ['maːlən] v/t (irr, ge-, h) grind; mill

'**Mahlzeit** f (-; -en) meal; feed(ing)

Mähne ['mɛːnə] f (-; -n) zo mane (a. F)

mahnen ['maːnən] v/t (ge-, h) remind; ECON send s.o. a reminder

'**Mahngebühr** f reminder fee

'**Mahnmal** n memorial

'**Mahnung** f (-; -en) reminder

Mai [mai] m (-[e]s; -e) May; **der Erste ~** May Day; **~baum** m maypole; **~glöck-chen** n BOT lily of the valley; **~käfer** m zo cockchafer

Mais [mais] m (-es; -e) BOT corn, Br maize

Majestät [majes'tɛːt] f: **Seine** (**Ihre, Eu-re**) **~** His (Her, Your) Majesty

majes'tätisch adj majestic

Majonäse f → **Mayonnaise**

Major [ma'joːɐ] m (-s; -e) MIL major

makaber [ma'kaːbɐ] adj macabre

Makel ['maːkəl] m (-s; -) blemish (a. fig)

mäkelig ['mɛːkəlɪç] F adj picky, esp Br choos(e)y

'**makellos** adj immaculate (a. fig)

mäkeln ['mɛːkəln] F v/i (ge-, h) carp, pick, nag (**an** dat at)

Makler ['maːklɐ] m (-s; -) ECON real es-tate agent; broker; **~gebühr** f fee, com-mission

'**Maklerin** f (-; -nen) ECON → **Makler**

mal [maːl] adv MATH times, multiplied by; by; F → **einmal**; **12 ~ 5 ist** (**gleich**) **60** 12 times or multiplied by 5 is or equals 60; **ein 7 ~ 4 Meter großes Zim-mer** a room 7 meters by 4

Mal¹ n (-[e]s; -e) time; **zum ersten** (**letz-ten**) **~e** for the first (last) time; **mit e-m ~e** all of a sudden; **ein für alle ~e** once and for all

Mal² n mark

malen ['maːlən] v/t (ge-, h) paint

Maler ['maːlɐ] m (-s; -) painter

Malerei [maːlə'rai] f (-; -en) painting

Malerin ['ma:lərɪn] *f* (-; -nen) (woman) painter

'**malerisch** *fig adj* picturesque

Malkasten *m* paintbox

'**malnehmen** → *multiplizieren*

Malz [malts] *n* (-es; *no pl*) malt

'**Malzbier** *n* malt beer

Mama ['mama] F *f* (-; -s) mom(my), *Br* mum(my)

Mammut ['mamʊt] *n* (-s; -e, -s) ZO mammoth

man [man] *indef pron* you, one; they, people; *wie schreibt ~ das?* how do you spell it?; *~ sagt, dass* they *or* people say (that); *~ hat mir gesagt* I was told

Manager ['mɛnɪdʒɐ] *m* (-s; -), '**Managerin** *f* (-; -nen) ECON executive; SPORT manager

manch [manç] m **['mançɐ]**, **~e** ['man-çə], **~es** ['mançəs] *indef pron* some; quite a few, many

'**manchmal** *adv* sometimes, occasionally

Mandant [man'dant] *m* (-en; -en), **Mandantin** *f* (-; -nen) JUR client

Mandarine [manda'ri:nə] *f* (-; -n) BOT tangerine

Mandat [man'da:t] *n* (-[e]s; -e) POL mandate; seat; **Mandatar** [manda'ta:ɐ] *Austrian m* → *Abgeordnete*

Mandel ['mandəl] *f* (-; -n) BOT almond; ANAT tonsil; **~entzündung** *f* MED tonsillitis

Manege [ma'ne:ʒə] *f* (-; -n) (circus) ring

Mangel[1] ['maŋəl] *m* (-s; **Mängel** ['mɛŋəl]) (*no pl*) lack (**an** *dat* of), shortage; TECH defect, fault; shortcoming; *aus ~ an* (*dat*) for lack of

'**Mangel**[2] *f* (-; -n) mangle

'**mangelhaft** *adj* poor (*quality etc*); defective (*goods etc*); PED poor, unsatisfactory, failing

mangeln *v/t* (*ge-, h*) mangle

mangels *prp* (*gen*) for lack *or* want of

Mangelware *f*: **~ sein** be scarce

Manie [ma'ni:] *f* (-; -n) mania (*a. fig*)

Manieren [ma'ni:rən] *pl* manners

manierlich [ma'ni:ɐlɪç] *adv*: *sich ~ betragen* behave (decently)

Manifest [mani'fɛst] *n* (-[e]s; -e) manifesto

manipulieren [manipu'li:rən] *v/t* (*no ge-, h*) manipulate

Mann [man] *m* (-[e]s; **Männer** ['mɛnɐ]) man; husband

Männchen ['mɛnçən] *n* (-s; -) ZO male

'**Manndeckung** *f* SPORT man-to-man marking

Mannequin ['manəkɛ̃:] *n* (-s; -s) model

mannigfach ['manɪçfax], '**mannigfaltig** *adj* many and various

männlich ['mɛnlɪç] *adj* BIOL male; masculine (*a.* LING)

'**Mannschaft** *f* (-; -en) SPORT team; MAR, AVIAT crew

Manöver [ma'nø:vɐ] *n* (-s; -), **manövrieren** [manø'vri:rən] *v/i* (*no -ge-, h*) maneuver, *Br* manoeuvre

Mansarde [man'zardə] *f* (-; -n) room *or* apartment in the attic

Manschette [man'ʃɛtə] *f* (-; -n) cuff; TECH gasket

Man'schettenknopf *m* cuff-link

Mantel ['mantəl] *m* (-s; **Mäntel** ['mɛn-təl]) coat; *tire*: casing, *bicycle*: tire (*Br* tyre) cover; TECH jacket, shell

Manuskript [manu'skrɪpt] *n* (-[e]s; -e) manuscript; copy

Mappe ['mapə] *f* (-; -n) briefcase; school bag, satchel; folder

Märchen ['mɛːɐçən] *n* (-s; -) fairytale (*a. fig*); **~land** *n* (-[e]s; *no pl*) fairyland

Marder ['mardɐ] *m* (-s; -) ZO marten

Margarine [marga'ri:nə] *f* (-; *no pl*) margarine

Margerite [margə'ri:tə] *f* (-; -n) BOT marguerite

Marienkäfer [ma'ri:ənkɛːfɐ] *m* ZO ladybug, *Br* ladybird

Marihuana [mari'hua:na] *n* (-s; *no pl*) marijuana, *sl* grass; **~ziga,rette** *f sl* joint

Marille [ma'rɪlə] *Austrian f* (-; -n) BOT apricot

Marine [ma'ri:nə] *f* (-; -n) MIL navy

ma'rineblau *adj* navy blue

Marionette [marjo'nɛtə] *f* (-; -n) puppet (*a. fig*); **Mario'nettenthe,ater** *n* puppet show

Mark[1] *n* (-[e]s; *no pl*) marrow; BOT pulp

Mark[2] [mark] *f* (-; -) *hist* (*former monetary unit of Germany*) mark

Marke ['markə] *f* (-; -n) ECON brand; TECH make; trademark; stamp; badge, tag; mark; **markieren** [mar'ki:rən] *v/t* (*no -ge-, h*) mark (*a.* SPORT); F *fig* act; **Mar'kierung** *f* (-; -en) mark

Markise [mar'ki:zə] *f* (-; -n) awning, sun

M

blind

Markt [markt] m (-[e]s; Märkte ['mɛrktə]) ECON market; **auf den ~ bringen** put on the market; **~platz** m market place; **~wirtschaft** f market economy

Marmelade [marmə'la:də] f (-; -n) jam

Marmor ['marmo:ɐ] m (-s; -e) marble

Marsch[1] [marʃ] m (-[e]s; Märsche ['mɛrʃə]) march (a. MUS)

Marsch[2] f (-; -en) GEOGR marsh, fen

Marschall ['marʃal] m (-s; Marschälle ['marʃɛlə]) MIL marshal

'Marschbefehl m MIL marching orders

marschieren [mar'ʃi:rən] v/i (no -ge-, sein) march

Marsmensch ['marsmɛnʃ] m Martian

Marter ['martɐ] f (-; -n) torture

'martern v/t (ge-, h) torture

'Marterpfahl m stake

Martinshorn ['marti:nshɔrn] n (police etc) siren

Märtyrer ['mɛrtyrɐ] m (-s; -), **'Märtyrerin** ['mɛrtyrərɪn] f (-; -nen) martyr (a. fig)

Marxismus [mar'ksɪsmʊs] m (-; no pl) POL Marxism; **Marxist** [mar'ksɪst] m (-en; -en), mar'xistisch adj POL Marxist

März [mɛrts] m (-[es]; -e) March

Marzipan [martsi'pa:n] n (-s; -e) marzipan

Masche ['maʃə] f (-; -n) stitch; mesh; F trick

'Maschendraht m wire netting

Maschine [ma'ʃi:nə] f (-; -n) machine; MOT engine; AVIAT plane; motorcycle

Ma'schinen|bau m (-[e]s; no pl) mechanical engineering; **~gewehr** n MIL machinegun

ma'schinenlesbar adj machine-readable

Ma'schinen|öl n engine oil; **~pis,tole** f MIL submachine gun, machine pistol; **~schaden** m engine trouble or failure; **~schlosser** m (engine) fitter

Masern ['ma:zɐn] pl MED measles

Maserung ['ma:zərʊŋ] f (-; -en) grain

Maske ['maskə] f (-; -n) mask (a. IT)

'Maskenball m fancy-dress ball

Maskenbildner ['maskənbɪldnɐ] m (-s; -), **'Maskenbildnerin** f (-; -nen) THEA etc make-up artist

maskieren [mas'ki:rən] v/t (no -ge-, h) mask; **sich ~** put on a mask

maskulin [masku'li:n] adj masculine (a. LING)

maß [ma:s] pret of **messen**

Maß[1] n (-es; -e) measure (für of); dimension, measurements, size; fig extent, degree; **~e und Gewichte** weights and measures; **nach ~ (gemacht)** made to measure; **in gewissem (hohem) ~e** to a certain (high) degree; **in zunehmendem ~e** increasingly; **~ halten → maßhalten**

Maß[2] f (-; -[e]) liter (Br litre) of beer

Massage [ma'sa:ʒə] f (-; -n) massage

Massaker [ma'sa:kɐ] n (-s; -) massacre

Masse ['masə] f (-; -n) mass; substance; bulk; F **e-e~ Geld** etc loads or heaps of; **die (breite) ~,** POL **die ~n** pl the masses

'Maßeinheit f unit of measure(ment)

'Massen... in cpds ...medien, ...mörder etc: mass ...; **~andrang** m crush

'massenhaft F adv masses or loads of

'Massen|karambo,lage f MOT pileup; **~produkti,on** f ECON mass production

Masseur [ma'sø:ɐ] m (-s; -e) masseur

Masseurin [ma'sø:rɪn] f (-; -nen), **Masseuse** [ma'sø:zə] f (-; -n) masseuse

'maßgebend, 'maßgeblich ['ma:sge:p-lɪç] adj authoritative

'maßhalten v/i (irr, halten, sep, -ge-, h) be moderate (in dat in)

massieren [ma'si:rən] v/t (no -ge-, h) massage

massig ['masɪç] adj massive, bulky

mäßig ['mɛ:sɪç] adj moderate; poor

mäßigen ['mɛ:sɪgən] v/t and v/refl (ge-, h) moderate; **'Mäßigung** f (-; no pl) moderation; restraint

massiv [ma'si:f] adj solid

Mas'siv n (-s; -e) GEOL massif

'Maßkrug m beer mug, stein

'maßlos adj immoderate; gross (exaggeration)

'Maßnahme ['ma:sna:mə] f (-; -n) measure, step

'Maßregel f rule; **'maßregeln** v/t (ge-, h) reprimand; discipline

'Maßstab m scale; fig standard; **im ~ 1:10** on the scale of 1:10

maßstabgetreu adj true to scale

'maßvoll adj moderate

Mast[1] [mast] m (-[e]s; -en) MAR, TECH mast

Mast[2] f (-; -en) AGR fattening

'Mastdarm m ANAT rectum

mästen ['mɛstən] *v/t* (*ge-*, *h*) AGR fatten; F stuff *s.o.*

masturbieren [mastʊr'biːrən] *v/i* (*no -ge-*, *h*) masturbate

Match [mɛtʃ] *n* (*-[e]s*; *-s*, *-e*) game, *Br* match; ~**ball** *m* tennis: match point

Material [mate'rjaːl] *n* (*-s*; *-ien*) material (*a. fig*); TECH materials

Materialismus [materja'lɪsmʊs] *m* (*-*; *no pl*) PHILOS materialism; **Materialist** [materja'lɪst] *m* (*-en*; *-en*) materialist; **materia'listisch** *adj* materialistic

Materie [ma'teːrjə] *f* (*-*; *-n*) matter (*a. fig*); *fig* subject (matter); **materiell** [mate'rjɛl] *adj* material

Mathematik [matema'tiːk] *f* (*-*; *no pl*) mathematics; **Mathematiker** [mate'maːtikɐ] *m* (*-s*; *-*) mathematician; **mathe'matisch** *adj* mathematical

Matinee [mati'neː] *f* (*-*; *-n*) THEA *etc* morning performance

Matratze [ma'tratsə] *f* (*-*; *-n*) mattress

Matrize [ma'triːtsə] *f* (*-*; *-n*) stencil

Matrose [ma'troːzə] *m* (*-n*; *-n*) MAR sailor, seaman

Matsch [matʃ] F *m* (*-[e]s*; *no pl*) mud, slush; **'matschig** *adj* muddy, slushy

matt [mat] *adj* weak; exhausted, worn out; dull, pale (*color*); PHOT mat(t); frosted (*glass*); chess: checkmate

Matte ['matə] *f* (*-*; *-n*) mat

Mattigkeit ['matɪçkait] *f* (*-*; *no pl*) exhaustion, weakness

'Mattscheibe *f* screen; PHOT focus(s)ing screen; F (boob) tube, *Br* telly, box

Matura [ma'tuːra] *Austrian, Swiss f* → **Abitur**

Mauer ['mauɐ] *f* (*-*; *-n*) wall; ~**blümchen** *fig n* wallflower

'mauern *v/i* (*ge-*, *h*) lay bricks

Mauerwerk *n* (*-[e]s*; *no pl*) masonry, brickwork

Maul [maul] *n* (*-[e]s*; *Mäuler* ['mɔylɐ]) ZO mouth; *sl* **halt's ~!** shut up!

maulen ['maulən] F *v/i* (*ge-*, *h*) grumble, sulk, pout

'Maul|korb *m* muzzle (*a. fig*); ~**tier** *n* mule; ~**wurf** *m* ZO mole; ~**wurfshaufen** *m*, ~**wurfshügel** *m* molehill

Maurer ['maurɐ] *m* (*-s*; *-*) bricklayer; ~**kelle** *f* trowel; ~**meister** *m* master bricklayer

Maus [maus] *f* (*-*; *Mäuse* ['mɔyzə]) ZO mouse (*a. IT*)

'Mausefalle ['mauzəfalə] *f* mousetrap

Mauser ['mauzɐ] *f* (*-*; *no pl*) ZO mo(u)lt (*-ing*); **in der ~ sein** be mo(u)lting

Maut [maut] *Austrian f* (*-*; *-en*) toll; ~**straße** *f* turnpike, toll road

maximal [maksi'maːl] **1.** *adj* maximum **2.** *adv* at (the) most; **Maximum** ['maksimʊm] *n* (*-s*; *-ma*) maximum

Mayonnaise [majo'nɛːzə] *f* (*-*; *-n*) GASTR mayonnaise

Mäzen [mɛ'tseːn] *m* (*-s*; *-e*) patron; SPORT sponsor

Mechanik [me'çaːnɪk] *f* (*-*; *-en*) (*no pl*) PHYS mechanics; TECH mechanism; **Mechaniker** [me'çaːnikɐ] *m* (*-s*; *-*) mechanic; **mechanisch** [me'çaːnɪʃ] *adj* TECH mechanical; **mechanisieren** [meçani'ziːrən] *v/t* (*no -ge-*, *h*) mechanize; **Mechani'sierung** *f* (*-*; *-en*) mechanization; **Mechanismus** [meça'nɪsmʊs] *m* (*-*; *-men*) TECH mechanism; works

meckern ['mɛkɐn] *v/i* (*ge-*, *h*) ZO bleat; F grumble, bitch (**über** *acc* at, about)

Medaille [me'daljə] *f* (*-*; *-n*) medal

Me'daillengewinner *m* medal(l)ist

Medaillon [medal'joː] *n* (*-s*; *-s*) locket

Medien ['meːdjən] *pl* mass media; teaching aids; audio-visual aids

Medikament [medika'mɛnt] *n* (*-[e]s*; *-e*) drug; medicine

meditieren [medi'tiːrən] *v/i* (*no -ge-*, *h*) meditate (**über** *acc* on)

Medizin [medi'tsiːn] *f* (*-*; *-en*) (*no pl*) (science of) medicine; medicine, remedy (**gegen** for)

Mediziner [medi'tsiːnɐ] *m* (*-s*; *-*), **Medizinerin** *f* (*-*; *-nen*) (medical) doctor; UNIV medical student

medizinisch [medi'tsiːnɪʃ] *adj* medical

Meer [meːɐ] *n* (*-[e]s*; *-e* ['meːrə]) sea (*a. fig*), ocean; ~**enge** *f* GEOGR straits

Meeres|boden ['meːrəsboːdən] *m* seabed; ~**früchte** *pl* GASTR seafood; ~**spiegel** *m* sea level

'Meerjungfrau *f* MYTH mermaid

'Meerrettich *m* (*-s*; *-e*) horseradish

Meerschweinchen ['meːɐʃvaincən] *n* (*-s*; *-*) ZO guinea pig

Megabyte [mega'bait] *n* IT megabyte

Mehl [meːl] *n* (*-[e]s*; *-e*) flour; meal

mehlig ['meːlɪç] *adj* mealy

'Mehlspeise *Austrian f* sweet (dish)

mehr [meːɐ] *indef pron and adv* more;

M

immer ~ more and more; *nicht* ~ no longer, not any longer (*or* more); *noch* ~ even more; *es ist kein … ~ da* there isn't any … left

mehrdeutig ['meːɐdɔʏtɪç] *adj* ambiguous

mehrere ['meːrərə] *adj and indef pron* several

'**Mehrheit** *f* (-; -en) majority

'**Mehrkosten** *pl* extra costs

'**mehrmals** *adv* several times

Mehr|wegflasche *f* returnable (*or* deposit) bottle; ~**wertsteuer** *f* ECON value-added tax (*abbr* VAT); ~**zahl** *f* (-; *no pl*) majority; LING plural (form)

'**Mehrzweck…** *in cpds* …*fahrzeug etc*: multi-purpose …

meiden ['maɪdən] *v/t* (*irr*, ge-, h) avoid

Meile ['maɪlə] *f* (-; -n) mile

'**meilenweit** *adv* (for) miles

mein [maɪn] *poss pron and adj* my; *das ist ~er* (~*e*, ~[*e*]*s*) that's mine

'**Meineid** *m* JUR perjury

meinen ['maɪnən] *v/t* (ge-, h) think, believe; mean; say; ~ *Sie wirklich?* do you (really) think so?; *wie ~ Sie das?* what do you mean by that?; *wie ~ es gut* they mean well; *ich habe es nicht so gemeint* I didn't mean it; *wie ~ Sie?* (I beg your) pardon?

'**meinetwegen** ['maɪnətveːgən] *adv* for my sake; because of me; F I don't mind *or* care!

'**Meinung** *f* (-; -en) opinion (*über acc*, *von* about, of); *meiner ~ nach* in my opinion; *der ~ sein, dass* be of the opinion that, feel *or* believe that; *s-e ~ äußern* express one's opinion; *s-e ~ ändern* change one's mind; *ich bin Ihrer* (*anderer*) ~ I (don't) agree with you; *j-m die ~ sagen* give s.o. a piece of one's mind

'**Meinungs|austausch** *m* exchange of views (*über acc* on); ~**forscher** *m* pollster; ~**freiheit** *f* (-; *no pl*) freedom of speech *or* opinion; ~**umfrage** *f* opinion poll; ~**verschiedenheit** *f* disagreement (*über acc* about)

Meise ['maɪzə] *f* (-; -n) zo titmouse

Meißel ['maɪsəl] *m* (-s; -) chisel

'**meißeln** *v/t and v/i* (ge-, h) chisel, carve

meist [maɪst] **1.** *adj* most; *das ~e* (*davon*) most of it; *die ~en* (*von ihnen*) most of them; *die ~en Leute* most peo-

ple; *die ~e Zeit* most of the time **2.** *adv* → **meistens**; *am ~en* (the) most; most (of all); **meistens** ['maɪstəns] *adv* usually; most of the time

Meister ['maɪstə] *m* (-s; -) master (*a. fig*); SPORT champion, F champ

'**meisterhaft 1.** *adj* masterly **2.** *adv* in a masterly manner *or* way

'**Meisterin** *f* (-; -nen) master (*a. fig*); SPORT champion

meistern ['maɪstən] *v/t* (ge-, h) master

'**Meisterschaft** *f* (-; -en) (*no pl*) mastery; SPORT championship, cup; title

'**Meister|stück** *n*, ~**werk** *n* masterpiece

Melancholie [melaŋkoˈliː] *f* (-; -n) melancholy; **melancholisch** [melaŋˈkoːlɪʃ] *adj* melancholy; ~ *sein* feel depressed, F have the blues

Melange [meˈlãːʒə] *Austrian f* (-; -n) coffee with milk

melden ['mɛldən] (ge-, h) **1.** *v/t* report *s.th.* *or s.o.* (*bei* to); *radio etc*: announce, report; *j-m et.* ~ notify s.o. of s.th. **2.** *v/refl*: *sich* ~ report (*bei* to, *für*, *zu* for); register (*bei* with); PED *etc*: put up one's hand; TEL answer the phone; SPORT enter (*für*, *zu* for); volunteer (*für*, *zu* for)

'**Meldung** *f* (-; -en) report, news, announcement; information, notice; notification; registration (*bei* with); SPORT entry (*für*, *zu* for)

melken ['mɛlkən] *v/t* (*irr*, ge-, h) milk

Melodie [meloˈdiː] *f* (-; -n) MUS melody, tune; **melodisch** [meˈloːdɪʃ] *adj* MUS melodious, melodic

Melone [meˈloːnə] *f* (-; -n) BOT melon; F derby, Br bowler (hat)

Memoiren [meˈmoaːrən] *pl* memoirs

Menge ['mɛŋə] *f* (-; -n) amount, quantity; MATH set; F *e-e ~ Geld* plenty (*or* lots) of money; → **Menschenmenge**

'**Mengenlehre** *f* (-; *no pl*) MATH set theory; PED new math(ematics)

Mensa ['mɛnza] *f* (-; -s, *Mensen*) cafeteria, Br refectory, canteen

Mensch [mɛnʃ] *m* (-en; -en) human being; man; person, individual; *pl* people; mankind; *kein ~* nobody; ~*!* wow!

Menschen|affe *m* zo ape; ~**fresser** *m* cannibal; ~**freund** *m* philanthropist; ~**handel** *m* slave trade; ~**kenntnis** *f*: ~ *haben* know human nature; ~**leben** *n* human life '**menschenleer** adj deserted

'**Menschen|menge** f crowd; ~**rechte** pl human rights; ~**seele** f: **keine** ~ not a (living) soul

'**menschenunwürdig** adj degrading; *housing etc*: unfit for human beings

'**Menschen|verstand** m: **gesunder** ~ common sense; ~**würde** f human dignity

Menschheit: **die** ~ mankind, the human race

'**menschlich** adj human; humane

'**Menschlichkeit** f (-; *no pl*) humanity

Menstruation [mɛnstrua'tsjoːn] f (-; -en) MED menstruation

Mentalität [mɛntali'tɛːt] f (-; -en) mentality

Menü [me'nyː] n (-s; -s) set meal (*or* lunch); IT menu

Meridian [meri'djaːn] m (-s; -e) GEOGR, ASTR meridian

merkbar ['mɛrkbaːɐ] adj marked, distinct; noticeable; '**Merkblatt** n leaflet; **merken** ['mɛrkən] v/t (ge-, h) notice; feel; find (out), discover; **sich et.** ~ remember s.th., keep *or* bear s.th. in mind; '**merklich** adj → **merkbar**; '**Merkmal** n sign; feature, trait

'**merkwürdig** adj strange, odd, curious

'**merkwürdiger|weise** adv strangely enough

messbar ['mɛsbaːɐ] adj measurable

'**Messbecher** m measuring cup

Messe ['mɛsə] f (-; -n) ECON fair; REL mass; MIL, MAR mess

messen ['mɛsən] v/t (irr, ge-, h) measure; take (*temperature etc*); **sich nicht mit j-m** ~ **können** be no match for s.o.; **gemessen an** (*dat*) compared with

Messer ['mɛsɐ] n (-s; -) knife; **bis aufs** ~ to the knife; **auf des** ~**s Schneide stehen** be on a razor edge, be touch and go (**ob** whether)

Messerstecherei [mɛsəʃtɛçə'rai] f (-; -en) knife fight

'**Messerstich** m stab (with a knife)

Messing ['mɛsɪŋ] n (-s; -e) brass

'**Messinstru**,**ment** n measuring instrument

'**Messung** f (-; -en) measuring; reading

Metall [me'tal] n (-s; -e) metal

metallen [me'talən] n, **me'tallisch** adj metallic

Me'tallwaren pl hardware

Metamorphose [metamɔr'foːzə] f (-; -n) metamorphosis

Metastase [meta'staːzə] f (-; -n) MED metastasis

Meteor [mete'oːɐ] m (-s; -e) ASTR meteor

Meteorit [meteo'riːt] m (-en; -e[n]) ASTR meteorite

Meteorologe [meteoro'loːgə] m (-n; -n) meteorologist; **Meteorologie** [meteorolo'giː] f (-; *no pl*) meteorology; **Meteoro'login** f (-; -nen) meteorologist

Meter ['meːtɐ] n, m (-s; -) meter, *Br* metre; ~**maß** n tape measure

Methode [me'toːdə] f (-; -n) method, TECH *a.* technique; **methodisch** [me'toːdɪʃ] adj methodical

metrisch ['meːtrɪʃ] adj metric; ~**es Maßsystem** metric system

Metropole [metro'poːlə] f (-; -n) metropolis

Metzger ['mɛtsgɐ] m (-s; -) butcher

Metzgerei [mɛtsgə'rai] f (-; -en) butcher's (shop)

Meute ['mɔytə] f (-; -n) pack (of hounds); *fig* mob, pack

Meuterei [mɔytə'rai] f (-; -en) mutiny; **Meuterer** ['mɔytərɐ] m (-s; -) mutineer; **meutern** ['mɔytɐn] v/i (ge-, h) mutiny (**gegen** against)

MEZ abbr of **Mitteleuropäische Zeit** CET, Central European Time

miau [mi'au] int ZO meow, *Br* miaow

miauen [mi'auən] v/i (*no -ge-, h*) ZO meow, *Br* miaow

mich [mɪç] pers pron me; ~ (**selbst**) myself

mied [miːt] pret of **meiden**

Mieder ['miːdɐ] n (-s; -) corset(s); bodice; ~**höschen** n pantie girdle; ~**waren** pl foundation garments

Miene ['miːnə] f (-; -n) expression, look, air; **gute** ~ **zum bösen Spiel machen** grin and bear it

mies [miːs] F rotten, lousy

Miete ['miːtə] f (-; -n) rent; hire charge; **zur** ~ **wohnen** be a tenant; lodge (*bei* with); '**mieten** v/t (ge-, h) rent; (take on) lease; AVIAT, MAR charter; **ein Auto** *etc* ~ rent (*Br* hire) a car *etc*; **Mieter(in)** ['miːtɐ, 'miːtərɪn] m(f) (-s; -/-; -nen) tenant, lodger

'**Mietshaus** n apartment building *or* house, *Br* block of flats, tenement

M

'Mietvertrag m lease (contract)

'Mietwohnung f apartment, Br (rented) flat

Migräne [mi'grɛːnə] f (-; -n) MED migraine

Mikro ['miːkro] F n (-s; -s) mike

Mikro... ['miːkro-] in cpds ...chip, ...computer, ...elektronik, ...film, ...prozessor etc: micro...

Mikrofon [mikro'foːn] n (-s; -e) microphone

Mikroskop [mikro'skoːp] n (-s; -e) microscope; mikro'skopisch adj microscopic(al)

Mikrowelle ['miːkrovelə] F f, 'Mikrowellenherd m microwave oven

Milbe ['mɪlbə] f (-; -n) ZO mite

Milch [mɪlç] f (-; no pl) milk; ~geschäft n dairy, creamery; ~glas n frosted glass

milchig ['mɪlçɪç] adj milky

'Milch|kaffee m white coffee; ~ännchen n (milk) jug; ~kanne f milk can; ~mann F m milkman; ~mixgetränk n milk shake; ~pro,dukte pl dairy products; ~pulver n powdered milk; ~reis m rice pudding; ~straße f ASTR Milky Way, Galaxy; ~tüte f milk carton; ~wirtschaft f dairy farming; ~zahn m milk tooth

mild [mɪlt] adj mild, soft; gentle

milde ['mɪldə] adv mildly; ~ ausgedrückt to put it mildly

'Milde f (-; no pl) mildness, gentleness; leniency, mercy

mildern ['mɪldən] v/t (ge-, h) lessen, soften; ~d adj: ~e Umstände JUR mitigating circumstances

'mildtätig adj charitable

Milieu [mi'ljøː] n (-s; -s) environment; social background

Militär [mili'tɛːr] n (-s; no pl) the military, armed forces; army; ~dienst m (-[e]s; no pl) military service; ~dikta,tur f military dictatorship; ~gericht n court martial

militärisch [mili'tɛːrɪʃ] adj military

Militarismus [milita'rɪsmʊs] m (-; no pl) militarism; Militarist [milita'rɪst] m (-en; -en) militarist; milita'ristisch adj militaristic

'Mili'tärre'gierung f military government

Milliarde [mɪl'jardə] f (-; -n) billion, Br old use a. a thousand million(s)

Millimeter ['mɪlimeːtɐ] n, m (-s; -) millimet|er, Br -re;~pa,pier n graph paper

Million [mɪl'joːn] f (-; -en) million

Millionär [mɪljo'nɛːr] m (-s; -e), Millio'närin f (-; -nen) millionaire

Milz [mɪlts] f (-; no pl) ANAT spleen

Mimik ['miːmɪk] f (-; no pl) facial expression

minder ['mɪndɐ] 1. adj → geringer, weniger 2. adv less; nicht ~ no less

'Minderheit f (-; -en) minority

minderjährig ['mɪndɐjɛːrɪç] adj: ~ sein be under age, be a minor; Minderjährige ['mɪndɐjɛːrɪgə] m, f (-n; -n) minor

'Minderjährigkeit f (-; no pl) minority

'minderwertig adj inferior, of inferior quality; 'Minderwertigkeit f (-; no pl) inferiority; ECON inferior quality

'Minderwertigkeitskom,plex m PSYCH inferiority complex

mindest ['mɪndəst] adj least; das Mindeste the (very) least; nicht im Mindesten not in the least, not at all

'Mindest... in cpds ...alter, ...einkommen, ...lohn etc: minimum ...

mindestens ['mɪndəstəns] adv at least

'Mindest|haltbarkeitsdatum n pull date, Br best-before (or best-by, sell-by) date; ~maß n minimum; auf ein ~ herabsetzen reduce to a minimum

Mine ['miːnə] f (-; -n) mine (a. MAR, MIL); lead; cartridge; refill

Mineral [minə'raːl] n (-s; -e, -ien) mineral; Mineralogie [mineralo'giː] f (-; no pl) mineralogy

Mine'ralöl n mineral oil

Mine'ralwasser n mineral water

Miniatur [minja'tuːr] f (-; -en) miniature

Minigolf ['mɪnigɔlf] n miniature (Br crazy) golf

minimal [mini'maːl] adj, adv minimal; minimum; at least; Minimum ['miːnimʊm] n (-s; -ma) minimum

Minirock ['miːnirɔk] m miniskirt

Minister [mi'nɪstɐ] m (-s; -), Mi'nisterin f (-; -nen) minister, secretary, Br a. secretary of state

Ministerium [minɪs'teːrɪʊm] n (-s; -ien) ministry, department, Br a. office

Mi'nisterpräsi,dent m, Mi'nisterpräsi,dentin f prime minister

minus ['miːnʊs] adv MATH minus; bei 10 Grad ~ at 10 degrees below zero

Minute [mi'nuːtə] f (-; -n) minute

Mi'nutenzeiger *m* minute hand

Mio *abbr of* **Million(en)** m, million

mir [miːɐ] *pers pron* (to) me

Mischbatte,rie ['mɪʃbatəriː] *f* mixing faucet, *Br* mixer tap

'**Mischbrot** *n* wheat and rye bread

mischen ['mɪʃən] *v/t* (ge-, h) mix; blend (*tea etc*); shuffle (*cards*); **sich ~** mingle or mix (**unter** with)

'**Mischling** *m* (-s; -e) *esp contp* half-caste; BOT, ZO hybrid; mongrel

'**Mischmasch** F *m* (-[e]s; -e) hotch-potch, jumble

'**Misch|ma,schine** *f* TECH mixer; **~pult** *n* radio, TV: mixer, mixing console

'**Mischung** *f* (-; -en) mixture; blend; assortment

'**Mischwald** *m* mixed forest

miserabel [mizə'raːbəl] F *adj* lousy, rotten

miss'achten [mɪs'ʔaxtən] *v/t* (*no* -ge-, h) disregard, ignore; despise

Miss'achtung *f* disregard; contempt; neglect (*all: gen of*)

'**Missbildung** *f* (-; -en) deformity, malformation

miss'billigen *v/t* (*no* -ge-, h) disapprove of

'**Missbrauch** *m* abuse (*a.* JUR); misuse; **miss'brauchen** *v/t* (*no* -ge-, h) abuse; misuse

miss'deuten *v/t* (*no* -ge-, h) misinterpret

'**Misserfolg** *m* failure; F flop

'**Missernte** *f* bad harvest, crop failure

miss'fallen *v/i* (*irr*, **fallen**, *no* -ge-, h) *j-m* **~** displease s.o.; '**Missfallen** *n* (-s; *no pl*) displeasure, dislike

'**missgebildet** *adj* deformed, malformed; '**Missgeburt** *f* deformed child *or* animal; freak

'**Missgeschick** *n* (-[e]s; -e) mishap

miss'glücken *v/i* (*no* -ge-, sein) fail

miss'gönnen *v/t* (*no* -ge-, h) *j-m et.* **~** envy s.o. s.th.

'**Missgriff** *m* mistake

miss'handeln *v/t* (*no* -ge-, h) ill-treat, maltreat (*a. fig*); batter

Miss'handlung *f* ill-treatment, maltreatment, *esp* JUR assault and battery

Mission [mɪˈsjoːn] *f* (-; -en) mission (*a.* POL *and fig*); **Missionar(in)** [mɪsjo-ˈnaːɐ, mɪsjoˈnaːrɪn] *m(f)* (-s; -e/-; -nen) missionary

'**Missklang** *m* dissonance, discord (*both a. fig*)

'**Misskre,dit** *m* discredit

misslang [mɪsˈlaŋ] *pret of* **misslingen**; **misslingen** [mɪsˈlɪŋən] *v/i* (*irr*, *no* -ge-, sein) fail; **misslungen** [mɪsˈlʊŋən] *pp of* **misslingen**; **das ist mir ~** I've bungled it

'**missmutig** *adj* bad-tempered, grumpy, glum

miss'raten 1. *v/i* (*irr*, **raten**, *no* -ge-, sein) fail; turn out badly **2.** *adj* wayward

miss'trauen *v/i* (*no* -ge-, h) distrust; '**Misstrauen** *n* (-s; *no pl*) distrust, suspicion (*both:* **gegenüber** of)

'**Misstrauens|antrag** *m* PARL motion of no confidence; **~votum** *n* PARL vote of no confidence

misstrauisch ['mɪstrauɪʃ] *adj* distrustful, suspicious

'**Missverhältnis** *n* disproportion

'**Missverständnis** *n* (-ses; -se) misunderstanding; '**missverstehen** *v/t* (*irr*, **stehen**, *no* -ge-, h) misunderstand

'**Misswahl** *f* beauty contest *or* competition

Mist [mɪst] *m* (-[e]s; *no pl*) AGR dung, manure; F trash, rubbish

'**Mistbeet** *n* AGR hotbed

Mistel ['mɪstəl] *f* (-; -n) BOT mistletoe

'**Mistgabel** *f* AGR dung fork

'**Misthaufen** *m* AGR manure heap

mit [mɪt] *prp* (*dat*) *and adv* with; **~ Gewalt** by force; **~ Absicht** on purpose; **~ dem Auto** (**der Bahn** *etc*) by car (train *etc*); **~ 20 Jahren** at (the age of) 20; **~ 100 Stundenkilometern** at 100 kilometers per hour; **~ einem Mal(e)** all of a sudden; (all) at the same time; **~ lauter Stimme** in a loud voice; **~ anderen Worten** in other words; **ein Mann ~ dem Namen ...** a man by the name of ...; *j-n* **~ Namen kennen** know s.o. by name; **~ der Grund dafür, dass** one of the reasons why; **~ der Beste** one of the best

'**Mitarbeit** *f* cooperation; assistance; PED activity, class participation

'**Mitarbeiter** *m*, '**Mitarbeiterin** *f* colleague; employee; assistant; **freie(r) Mitarbeiter(in)** freelance

'**mit|bekommen** F *v/t* (*irr*, **kommen**, *sep*, *no* -ge-, h) get; catch; **~benutzen** *v/t* (*sep*, *no* -ge-, h) share

'**Mit**|**bestimmungsrecht** n (right of) codetermination, worker participation; ~**bewerber(in)** (rival) competitor; fellow applicant; ~**bewohner(in)** roommate, Br flatmate

'**mitbringen** v/t (irr, **bringen**, sep, -ge-, h) bring s.th. or s.o. with one; **j-m et.** ~ bring s.o. s.th.; **Mitbringsel** ['mɪt-brɪŋzəl] F n (-s; -) little present; souvenir

'**Mitbürger** m, '**Mitbürgerin** f fellow citizen

mitei'nander adv with each other, with one another; together, jointly

'**miterleben** v/t (sep, no -ge-, h) live to see

'**Mitesser** m MED blackhead

'**mitfahren** v/i (irr, **fahren**, sep, -ge-, sein) **mit j-m** ~ drive or go with s.o.; **j-n** ~ **lassen** give s.o. a lift

'**Mitfahr**|**gelegenheit** f lift; ~**zen**|**trale** f car pool(ing) service

'**mitfühlend** adj sympathetic

'**mitgeben** v/t (irr, **geben**, sep, -ge-, h) **j-m et.** ~ give s.o. s.th. (to take along)

'**Mitgefühl** n (-[e]s; no pl) sympathy

'**mitgehen** v/i (irr, **gehen**, sep, -ge-, sein) **mit j-m** ~ go or come along with s.o.; F **et.** ~ **lassen** walk off with s.th.

'**Mitgift** f (-; -en) dowry

'**Mitglied** n member (**bei** of)

'**Mitgliedsbeitrag** m subscription

'**Mitgliedschaft** f (-; -en) membership

'**mithaben** v/t (irr, **haben**, sep, -ge-, h) **ich habe kein Geld mit** I haven't got any money with me or on me

'**Mithilfe** f (-; no pl) assistance, help, cooperation (**bei** in; **von** of)

mit'hilfe prp: ~ **von** (or gen) with the help of, fig a. by means of

'**mithören** v/t (sep, -ge-, h) listen in to; overhear

'**Mitinhaber** m, '**Mitinhaberin** f joint owner

'**mitkommen** v/i (irr, **kommen**, sep, -ge-, sein) come along (**mit** with); fig keep pace (**mit** with), follow; PED get on, keep up (with the class)

'**Mitlaut** m LING consonant

'**Mitleid** n (-[e]s; no pl) pity (**mit** for); **aus** ~ out of pity; ~ **haben mit** feel sorry for

mitleidig ['mɪtlaidɪç] adj compassionate, sympathetic

'**mitleidslos** adj pitiless

'mitmachen (sep, -ge-, h) **1.** v/i join in **2.** v/t take part in; follow (a fashion etc); F go through

'**Mitmenschen**: **die** ~ one's fellow human beings; people

'**mitnehmen** v/t (irr, **nehmen**, sep, -ge-, h) take s.th. or s.o. with one; **j-n** (**im Auto**) ~ give s.o. a lift

'**mitreden** v/t (sep, -ge-, h) **et. mitzureden haben** (**bei**) have a say (in)

'**mitreißen** v/t (irr, **reißen**, sep, -ge-, h) drag along; fig carry away (mst passive); ~**d** fig adj electrifying (speech etc)

'**mitschneiden** v/t (irr, **schneiden**, sep, -ge-, h) radio, TV record, tape(-record)

'**mitschreiben** v/t (irr, **schreiben**, sep, -ge-, h) **1.** v/t take down; take, do (a test) **2.** v/i take notes

'**Mitschuld** f (-; no pl) partial responsibility; '**mitschuldig** adj: ~ **sein** be partly to blame (**an** dat for)

'**Mitschüler** m, '**Mitschülerin** f classmate; schoolmate, fellow student

'**mitspielen** v/i (sep, -ge-, h) SPORT, MUS play; join in a game etc; **in e-m Film** etc ~ be or appear in a film etc

'**Mitspieler** m, '**Mitspielerin** f partner, SPORT a. team-mate

Mittag ['mɪtaːk] m (-s; -e) noon, midday; **heute** ~ at noon today; **zu** ~ **essen** (have) lunch; ~**essen** n lunch; **was gibt es zum** ~? what's for lunch?

'mittags adv at noon; **12 Uhr** ~ 12 o'clock noon

'**Mittags**|**pause** f lunch break; ~**ruhe** f midday rest; ~**schlaf** m after-dinner nap; ~**zeit** f lunchtime

Mitte ['mɪtə] f (-; -n) middle; center, Br centre (a. POL); ~ **Juli** in the middle of July; ~ **dreißig** in one's mid thirties

'**mitteilen** v/t (sep, -ge-, h) **j-m et.** ~ inform s.o. of s.th.; '**mitteilsam** adj communicative; '**Mitteilung** f (-; -en) report, information, message

Mittel ['mɪtəl] n (-s; -) means, way; measure; PHARM remedy (**gegen** for) (a. fig); average; MATH mean; PHYS medium; pl means, money

'**Mittelalter** n (-s; no pl) Middle Ages

'**mittelalterlich** adj medi(a)eval

'**Mittel**|**ding** n cross (**zwischen** between); ~**feld** n SPORT midfield; ~**feldspieler(in)** midfield player, midfielder; ~**finger** m ANAT middle finger

'mittelfristig *adj* medium-term

'Mittelgewicht *n* (-[e]s; *no pl*) SPORT middleweight (class)

'mittelgroß *adj* of medium height; medium-sized

'Mittel|klasse *f* middle class (*a.* MOT); ~linie *f* SPORT halfway line

'mittellos *adj* without means

'mittelmäßig *adj* average

'Mittelpunkt *m* center, *Br* centre (*a. fig*)

mittels *prp* (*gen*) by (means of), through

'Mittelschule *f* → **Realschule**

'Mittel|strecke *f* SPORT middle distance; ~streckenra,kete *f* MIL medium-range missile; ~streifen *m* MOT median strip, *Br* central reservation; ~stufe *f* PED junior highschool, *Br* middle school; ~stürmer(in) SPORT center (*Br* centre) forward; ~weg *m* middle course; ~welle *f* radio: medium wave (*abbr* AM); ~wort *n* (-[e]s; -wörter) LING participle

mitten ['mɪtn] *adv*: ~ **in** (**auf, unter** *dat*) in the midst *or* middle of

mitten'drin F *adv* right in the middle

mitten'durch F *adv* right through (the middle); right in two

Mitternacht ['mɪtɐnaxt] *f* midnight

mittlere ['mɪtlərə] *adj* middle, central; average, medium

mittlerweile ['mɪtlɐ'vaɪlə] *adv* meanwhile, (in the) meantime

Mittwoch ['mɪtvɔx] *m* (-[s]; -e) Wednesday

mit'unter *adv* now and then

'Mitverantwortung *f* share of the responsibility

mitwirken *v/i* (*sep*, -ge-, *h*) take part (**bei** in); 'Mitwirkende *m, f* (-*n*; -*n*) THEA, MUS performer; *pl* THEA the cast; 'Mitwirkung *f* (-; *no pl*) participation

'Mixbecher *m* shaker

mixen ['mɪksən] *v/t* (*ge*-, *h*) mix

Mixer ['mɪksɐ] *m* (-*s*; -) mixer; 'Mixgetränk *n* mixed drink, cocktail, shake

Möbel ['mø:bəl] *pl* furniture; ~spediti,on *f* removal firm; ~stück *n* piece of furniture; ~wagen *m* moving (*Br* furniture) van

mobil [mo'bi:l] *adj* mobile; ~ **machen** MIL mobilize

Mobiliar [mobi'lja:ɐ] *n* (-*s*; *no pl*) furniture

Mo'biltele,fon *n* mobile phone

möblieren [mø'bli:rən] *v/t* (*no* -ge-, *h*) furnish

mochte ['mɔxtə] *pret of* **mögen**

Mode ['mo:də] *f* (-; -n) fashion; **in** ~ in fashion; ~ **sein** be in fashion, F be in; **die neueste** ~ the latest fashion; **mit der** ~ **gehen** follow the fashion; **in** (**aus der**) ~ **kommen** come into (go out of) fashion

Modell [mo'dɛl] *n* (-*s*; -*e*) model; **j-m** ~ **stehen** *or* **sitzen** pose *or* sit for s.o.; ~bau *m* model construction; ~baukasten *m* model construction kit; ~eisenbahn *f* model railway

modellieren [modɛ'li:rən] *v/t* (*no* -ge-, *h*) model

Modem ['mo:dɛm] *m, n* (-*s*; -*s*) IT modem

'Modenschau *f* fashion show

Moderator [mode'ra:to:ɐ] *m* (-*s*; -*en* [modera'to:rən]), Modera'torin *f* (-; -*nen*) TV presenter, host, anchorman (anchorwoman)

moderieren [mode'ri:rən] *v/t* (*no* -ge-, *h*) TV *etc* present, host

moderig ['mo:dəriç] *adj* musty, mo(u)ldy

modern¹ ['mo:dɛn] *v/i* (*ge*-, *h*, *sein*) mo(u)ld, rot, decay

modern² [mo'dɛrn] *adj* modern; fashionable

modernisieren [modɛrni'zi:rən] *v/t* (*no* -ge-, *h*) modernize, bring up to date

'Mode|schmuck *m* costume jewel(le)ry; ~schöpfer(in) fashion designer; ~waren *pl* fashionwear; ~wort *n* (-[e]s; -*wörter*) vogue word, F in word; ~zeichner(in) fashion designer; ~zeitschrift *f* fashion magazine

modisch ['mo:dɪʃ] *adj* fashionable, stylish

Modul¹ [mo'du:l] *n* (-*s*; -*e*) IT module

Modul² ['mo:dul] *m* (-*s*;-*n*) MATH, TECH module

Mofa ['mo:fa] *n* (-*s*; -*s*) (small) moped, motorized bicycle

mogeln ['mo:gəln] F *v/i* (*ge*-, *h*) cheat; crib

mögen ['mø:gən] *v/t* (*irr*, *ge*-, *h*) *and v/aux* (*irr*, *no* -ge-, *h*) like; **er mag sie** (**nicht**) he likes (doesn't like) her; **lieber** ~ like better, prefer; **nicht** ~ dislike; **was möchten Sie?** what would you

M

like?; **ich möchte, dass du es weißt** I'd like you to know (it); **ich möchte lieber bleiben** I'd rather stay; **es mag sein (, dass)** it may be (that)

möglich ['mø:klɪç] **1.** adj possible; **alle ~en** all sorts of; **sein Möglichstes tun** do what one can; do one's utmost; **nicht ~!** you don't say (so)!; **so bald (schnell, oft) wie ~** as soon (quickly, often) as possible **2.** adv: **~st bald** etc as soon etc as possible; '**möglicher'weise** adv possibly; '**Möglichkeit** f (-; -en) possibility; opportunity; chance; **nach ~** if possible

Mohammedaner [moham e'da:nɐ] m (-s; -), **mohamme'danisch** adj Muslim

Mohn [mo:n] m (-[e]s; -e) BOT poppy

Möhre ['mø:rə] f (-; -n), **Mohrrübe** ['mo:rry:bə] f BOT carrot

Molch [mɔlç] m (-[e]s; -e) ZO salamander

Mole ['mo:lə] f (-; -n) MAR mole, jetty

Molekül [mole'ky:l] n (-s; -e) CHEM molecule

molk [mɔlk] pret of **melken**

Molkerei [mɔlkə'rai] f (-; -en) dairy

Moll [mɔl] n (-; no pl) MUS minor (key); **a-Moll** A minor

mollig ['mɔlɪç] F adj snug, cozy, Br cosy; plump, chubby

Moment [mo'mɛnt] m (-[e]s; -e) moment; **(e-n) ~ bitte!** just a moment please!; **im ~** at the moment

Monarch [mo'narç] m (-en; -en) monarch; **Monarchie** [monar'çi:] f (-; -en) monarchy; **Monarchin** [mo'narçɪn] f (-; -nen) monarch; **Monarchist** [monar'çɪst] m (-en; -en) monarchist

Monat ['mo:nat] m (-[e]s; -e) month; **zweimal im** or **pro ~** twice a month

'**monatelang** adv for months

'**monatlich** adj and adv monthly

'**Monats|binde** f sanitary napkin (Br towel); **~karte** f commuter ticket, Br (monthly) season ticket

Mönch [mœnç] m (-[e]s; -e) monk; friar

Mond [mo:nt] m (-[e]s; -e ['mo:ndə]) moon; **~finsternis** f lunar eclipse

'**mondhell** adj moonlit

'**Mond|landefähre** f lunar module; **~landung** f moon landing; **~oberfläche** f moon surface, lunar soil; **~schein** m (-[e]s; no pl) moonlight; **~sichel** f crescent; **~umkreisung** f

~umlaufbahn f lunar orbit

Monitor ['mo:nito:ɐ] m (-s; -en [moni'to:rən]) TV etc monitor

Monolog [mono'lo:k] m (-[e]s; -e) monolog(ue Br)

Monopol [mono'po:l] n (-s; -e) ECON monopoly

monoton [mono'to:n] adj monotonous

Monotonie [monoto'ni:] f (-; -n) monotony

Monoxid ['mo:nɔksi:t] n CHEM monoxide

Monster ['mɔnstɐ] n (-s; -) monster

Montag ['mo:nta:k] m (-[e]s; -e) Monday

Montage [mɔn'ta:ʒə] f (-; -n) TECH assembly; installation; **auf ~ sein** be away on a field job; **~band** n (-[e]s; -bänder) TECH assembly line; **~halle** f TECH assembly shop

Monteur [mɔn'tø:ɐ] m (-s; -e) TECH fitter; esp MOT, AVIAT mechanic

montieren [mɔn'ti:rən] v/t (no -ge-, h) TECH assemble; fit, attach; instal(l)

Moor [mo:ɐ] n (-[e]s; -e) bog, moor (-land); **moorig** ['mo:rɪç] adj boggy

Moos [mo:s] n (-es; -e) BOT moss

moosig ['mo:zɪç] adj mossy

Moped ['mo:pɛt] n (-s; -s) moped

Mops [mɔps] m (-es; Möpse ['mœpsə]) ZO pug(dog)

Moral [mo'ra:l] f (-; no pl) morals, moral standards; MIL etc morale; **mo'ralisch** adj moral; **moralisieren** [morali'zi:rən] v/i (no -ge-, h) moralize

Morast [mo'rast] m (-[e]s; -e) morass; mire, mud

Mord [mɔrt] m (-[e]s; -e ['mɔrdə]) murder (**an** dat of); **e-n ~ begehen** commit murder; **~anschlag** m esp POL assassination attempt

Mörder ['mœrdɐ] m (-s; -), '**Mörderin** f (-; -nen) murderer; (hired) killer; esp POL assassin

'**Mord|kommissi,on** f homicide division, Br murder squad; **~pro,zess** m JUR murder trial

'**Mords|angst** F f: **e-e ~ haben** be scared stiff; **~glück** F n stupendous luck; **~kerl** F m devil of a fellow; **~wut** F f: **e-e ~ haben** be in a hell of a rage

'**Mord|verdacht** m suspicion of murder; **~versuch** m attempted murder

morgen ['mɔrgən] adv tomorrow; **~**

Abend (*früh*) tomorrow night (morning); **~** *Mittag* at noon tomorrow; **~** *in e-r Woche* a week from tomorrow; **~** *um diese Zeit* this time tomorrow; *...* *von* **~** tomorrow's ..., ... of tomorrow

'Morgen *m* (-*s*; -) morning; AGR acre; *heute* **~** this morning; *am* (*frühen*) **~** (early) in the morning; *am nächsten* **~** the next morning; **~***essen Swiss n* breakfast; **~***grauen n* dawn; *im* or *bei* **~***at dawn;***~***land n* (-[*e*]*s*; *no pl*) Orient; **~***mantel m,***~***rock m* dressing gown

'morgens *adv* in the morning; *von* **~** *bis abends* from morning till night

morgig ['mɔrgɪç] *adj* tomorrow's ...

Morphium ['mɔrfjʊm] *n* (-*s*; *no pl*) PHARM morphine

morsch [mɔrʃ] *adj* rotten; **~** *werden* rot

Morsealpha,bet [mɔrzəalfabeːt] *n* Morse code

Mörser ['mœrzɐ] *m* (-*s*; -) mortar (*a.* MIL)

'Morsezeichen *n* Morse signal

Mörtel ['mœrtəl] *m* (-*s*; -) mortar

Mosaik [moza'iːk] *n* (-*s*; -*en*) mosaic

Mosa'ikstein *m* piece

Moschee [mɔ'ʃeː] *f* (-; -*n*) mosque

Moskito [mɔs'kiːto] *m* (-*s*; -*s*) ZO mosquito

Moslem ['mɔslɛm] *m* (-*s*; -*s*), moslemisch [mɔs'leːmɪʃ] *adj*, Moslime [mɔs'liːmə] *f* (-; -*n*) Muslim

Most [mɔst] *m* (-[*e*]*s*; -*e*) grape juice; cider

Motiv [mo'tiːf] *n* (-*s*; -*e*) motive; PAINT, MUS motif;Motivation [motiva'tsjoːn] *f* (-; -*en*) motivation; motivieren [moti-'viːrən] *v/t* (*no* -*ge*-, *h*) motivate

Motor ['moːtoːɐ, mo'toːɐ] *m* (-*s*; -*en* [mo'toːrən]) motor, engine; **~***boot n* motor boat;**~***haube f* hood, *Br* bonnet

motorisieren [motori'ziːrən] *v/t* (*no* -*ge*-, *h*) motorize

'Motor|leistung *f* (engine) performance;**~***rad n* motorcycle, F motorbike; **~** *fahren* ride a motorcycle; **~***radfahrer(in)* motorcyclist, biker; **~***roller m* (motor) scooter; **~***säge f* power saw;**~***schaden m* engine trouble (*or* failure)

Motte ['mɔtə] *f* (-; -*n*) ZO moth

'Mottenkugel *f* mothball

'mottenzerfressen *adj* moth-eaten

Motto ['mɔto] *n* (-*s*; -*s*) motto

Möwe ['møːvə] *f* (-; -*n*) ZO (sea)gull

Mücke ['mʏkə] *f* (-; -*n*) ZO gnat, midge, mosquito; *aus e-r* **~** *e-n Elefanten machen* make a mountain out of a molehill; 'Mückenstich *m* gnat bite

müde ['myːdə] *adj* tired; weary; sleepy; **~** *sein* (*werden*) be (get) tired (*fig e-r Sache* of s.th.)

'Müdigkeit *f* (-; *no pl*) tiredness

Muff [mʊf] *m* (-[*e*]*s*; -*e*) muff

Muffe ['mʊfə] *f* (-; -*n*) TECH sleeve, socket

Muffel ['mʊfəl] F *m* (-*s*; -) sourpuss

muff(e)lig ['mʊf(ə)lɪç], muffig ['mʊfɪç] F *adj* musty; *contp* sulky, sullen

Mühe ['myːə] *f* (-; -*n*) trouble; effort; difficulty (*mit* with s.th.); (*nicht*) *der* **~** *wert* (not) worth the trouble; *j-m* **~** *machen* give s.o. trouble; *sich* **~** *geben* try hard; *sich die* **~** *sparen* save o.s. the trouble; *mit* **~** *und Not* (just) barely

'mühelos *adv* without difficulty

mühen ['myːən] *v/refl* (*ge*-, *h*) struggle, work hard

'mühevoll *adj* laborious

Mühle ['myːlə] *f* (-; -*n*) mill; morris

Mühsal ['myːzaːl] *f* (-; -*e*) toil

mühsam ['myːzaːm], 'mühselig 1. *adj* laborious 2. *adv* with difficulty

Mulatte [mu'latə] *m* (-*n*; -*n*), Mu'lattin *f* (-; -*nen*) mulatto

Mulde ['mʊldə] *f* (-; -*n*) hollow

Mull [mʊl] *m* (-[*e*]*s*; -*e*) muslin; *esp* MED gauze

Müll [mʏl] *m* (-*s*; *no pl*) garbage, trash, *Br* refuse, rubbish; **~***abfuhr f* garbage (*Br* refuse) collection; **~***beseitigung f* waste disposal; **~***beutel m* garbage bag, *Br* dustbin liner

'Mullbinde *f* MED gauze bandage

'Müll|con,tainer *m* garbage (*Br* rubbish) skip; **~***depo,nie f* dump; **~***eimer m* garbage can, *Br* dustbin; **~***fahrer m* garbage man, *Br* dustman; **~***halde f* dump; **~***haufen m* garbage (*Br* rubbish) heap; **~***kippe f* dump; **~***schlucker m* garbage (*Br* refuse) chute; **~***tonne f* garbage can, *Br* dustbin; **~***verbrennungsanlage f* (waste) incineration plant; **~***wagen m* garbage truck, *Br* dustcart

Multiplikation [mʊltiplika'tsjoːn] *f* (-; -*en*) MATH multiplication; multiplizieren [mʊltipli'tsiːrən] *v/t* (*no* -*ge*-, *h*)

M

MATH multiply (*mit* by)

Mumie ['mu:mjə] f (-; -n) mummy

Mumps [mʊmps] m, f (-; no pl) MED mumps

Mund [mʊnt] m (-[e]s; Münder ['mʏndɐ]) mouth; F **den ~ vollnehmen** talk big; **halt den ~!** shut up!; ~art f dialect

münden ['mʏndən] v/i (ge-, h, sein) ~ **in** (acc) river etc: flow into; road etc: lead into

'Mundgeruch m bad breath

'Mundhar,monika f MUS mouth organ, harmonica

mündig ['mʏndɪç] adj emancipated; ~ (**werden**) JUR (come) of age

mündlich ['mʏntlɪç] adj oral; verbal

'Mundstück n mouthpiece; tip

'Mündung f (-; -en) river: mouth; gun: muzzle

'Mund|wasser n mouthwash; ~werk F n: **ein loses ~** a loose tongue; ~winkel m corner of the mouth

'Mund-zu-'Mund-Beatmung f (-; -en) MED mouth-to-mouth resuscitation, F kiss of life

Munition [muni'tsjo:n] f (-; -en) ammunition

munkeln ['mʊŋkəln] F v/t (ge-, h) **man munkelt, dass** rumo(u)r has it that

Münster ['mʏnstɐ] n (-s; -) cathedral, minster

munter ['mʊntɐ] adj awake; lively; merry

Münze ['mʏntsə] f (-; -n) coin; medal

'Münz|einwurf m (coin) slot; ~fernsprecher m pay phone; ~tank(auto,mat) m coin-operated (gas, Br petrol) pump; ~wechsler m (-s; -) change machine

mürbe ['mʏrbə] adj tender; brittle; GASTR crisp; 'Mürbeteig m short pastry; shortcake

Murmel ['mʊrməl] f (-; -n) marble

'murmeln v/t and v/i (ge-, h) murmur

'Murmeltier n zo marmot

murren ['mʊrən] v/i (ge-, h) complain (**über** acc about)

mürrisch ['mʏrɪʃ] adj sullen; grumpy

Mus [mu:s] n (-es; -e) mush; stewed fruit

Muschel ['mʊʃəl] f (-; -n) zo mussel; shell

Museum [mu'ze:ʊm] n (-s; Museen) museum

Musik [mu'zi:k] f (-; no pl) music

musikalisch [muzi'ka:lɪʃ] adj musical

Mu'sik|anlage f hi-fi or stereo set; ~auto,mat m, ~box f juke box

Musiker ['mu:zikɐ] m (-s; -), 'Musikerin f (-; -nen) musician

Mu'sik|instru,ment n musical instrument; ~ka,pelle f band; ~kas,sette f music cassette; ~lehrer(in) music teacher; ~stunde f music lesson

musisch ['mu:zɪʃ] adv: ~ **interessiert** (**begabt**) fond of (gifted for) fine arts and music

musizieren [muzi'tsi:rən] v/i (no -ge-, h) make music

Muskat [mʊs'ka:t] m (-[e]s; -e), ~nuss f BOT nutmeg

Muskel ['mʊskəl] m (-s; -n) ANAT muscle; ~kater F m aching muscles; ~zerrung f MED pulled muscle

muskulös [mʊsku'lø:s] adj muscular, brawny

Müsli ['my:sli] n (-s; -) GASTR granola, Br muesli

Muss n (-; no pl) necessity; **es ist ein ~** it is a must

Muße ['mu:sə] f (-; no pl) leisure; spare time

müssen ['mʏsən] v/i (irr, ge-, h) and v/aux (irr, no -ge-, h) must, have (got) to; **du musst den Film sehen!** you must see the film!; **ich muss jetzt (m-e) Hausaufgaben machen** I have (got) to do my homework now; **sie muss krank sein** she must be ill; **du musst es nicht tun** you need not do it; **das müsstest du (doch) wissen** you ought to know (that); **sie müsste zu Hause sein** she should (ought to be) (at) home; **das müsste schön sein!** that would be nice!; **du hättest ihm helfen ~** you ought to have helped him

müßig ['my:sɪç] adj idle; useless

musste ['mʊstə] pret of **müssen**

Muster ['mʊstɐ] n (-s; -) pattern; sample; model

'muster|gültig, ~haft adj exemplary; **sich ~ benehmen** behave perfectly

'Musterhaus n showhouse

'mustern v/t (ge-, h) eye s.o.; size s.o. up; MIL **gemustert werden** F have one's medical; Musterung f ['mʊstərʊŋ] f (-; -en) MIL medical (examination for military service)

Mut [mu:t] m (-[e]s; no pl) courage; j-m

~ **machen** encourage s.o.; **den ~ verlieren** lose courage; → **zumute**
mutig ['muːtɪç] *adj* courageous, brave
'**mutlos** *adj* discouraged
'**mutmaßen** *v/t* (*ge-, h*) speculate
'**mutmaßlich** *adj* probable; presumed
'**Mutprobe** *f* test of courage
Mutter ['mʊtɐ] *f* (-; *Mütter* ['mʏtɐ]) mother; TECH nut; **~boden** *m*, **~erde** *f* AGR topsoil
mütterlich ['mʏtəlɪç] *adj* motherly
'**mütterlicherseits** *adv*: **Onkel** *etc* ~ maternal uncle *etc*
'**Mutterliebe** *f* motherly love
'**mutterlos** *adj* motherless
'**Mutter|mal** *n* birthmark, mole; **~milch** *f* mother's milk; **~schaftsurlaub** *m* maternity leave; **~schutz** *m* JUR legal protection of expectant and nursing mothers; **~söhnchen** *contp n* sissy; **~sprache** *f* mother tongue; **~sprachler** ['mʊtɐʃpraːxlɐ] *m* (-s; -) native speaker; **~tag** *m* Mother's Day
Mutti ['mʊti] F *f* (-; -s) mom(my), *esp Br* mum(my)
'**mutwillig** *adj* wanton
Mütze ['mʏtsə] *f* (-; -n) cap
MwSt *abbr of* **Mehrwertsteuer** VAT, value-added tax
mysteriös [mʏsteˈrjøːs] *adj* mysterious
mystisch ['mʏstɪʃ] *adj* mystic(al)
mythisch ['myːtɪʃ] *adj* mythical
Mythologie [mytoloˈgiː] *f* (-; -n) mythology
Mythos ['myːtɔs] *m* (-; *Mythen*) myth

N

N *abbr of* **Nord(en)** N, north
na [na] *int* well; ~ **und?** so what?; ~ **gut!** all right then; ~ **ja** (oh) well; ~(, ~)**!** come on!, come now!; ~ **so (et)was!** what do you know!; *Br* I say!; ~, **dann nicht!** oh, forget it!; ~ **also!** there you are!; ~, **warte!** just you wait!
Nabe ['naːbə] *f* (-; -n) TECH hub
Nabel ['naːbəl] *m* (-s; -) ANAT navel
'**Nabelschnur** *f* ANAT umbilical chord
nach [naːx] *prp* (*dat*) *and adv* to, toward(s), for; after; *time*: after, past; according to, by; ~ **Hause** home; **abfahren** ~ leave for; ~ **rechts** (**Süden**) to the right (south); ~ **oben** up(stairs); ~ **unten** down(stairs); ~ **vorn** (**hinten**) to the front (back); **der Reihe** ~ one after the other; *s-e Uhr* ~ **dem Radio stellen** set one's watch by the radio; ~ **m-r Uhr** by my watch; **suchen** (**fragen**) ~ look (ask) for; ~ **Gewicht** (**Zeit**) by weight (the hour); **riechen** (**schmecken**) ~ smell (taste) of; ~ **und** ~ gradually; ~ **wie vor** as before, still
nachahmen ['naːxaːmən] *v/t* (*sep, -ge-, h*) imitate, copy; take off
'**Nachahmung** *f* (-; -en) imitation
Nachbar ['naxbaːɐ] *m* (-n; -n), '**Nachbarin** *f* (-; -nen) neighbo(u)r; '**Nachbarschaft** *f* (-; *no pl*) neighbo(u)rhood, vicinity
'**Nachbau** *m* (-[e]s; -ten) TECH reproduction; '**nachbauen** *v/t* (*sep, -ge-, h*) copy, reproduce
'**Nachbildung** *f* (-; -en) copy, imitation; replica; dummy
'**nachblicken** *v/i* (*sep, -ge-, h*) look after
nach'dem *cj* after, when; **je ~ wie** depending on how
'**nachdenken** *v/i* (*irr, denken, sep, -ge-, h*) think; ~ **über** (*acc*) think about, think *s.th.* over
'**nachdenklich** *adj* thoughtful; **es macht e-n ~** it makes you think
'**Nachdruck**[1] *m* (-[e]s; *no pl*) emphasis, stress
'**Nachdruck**[2] (-[e]s; -e) reprint
'**nachdrucken** *v/t* (*sep, -ge-, h*) reprint
nachdrücklich ['naːxdrʏklɪç] *adj* emphatic; forceful; ~ **raten** (**empfehlen**) advise (recommend) strongly
'**nacheifern** *v/i* (*sep, -ge-, h*) *j-m* ~ emulate s.o.
nachei'nander *adv* one after the other, in (*or* by) turns
'**nacherzählen** *v/t* (*sep, no -ge-, h*) retell; '**Nacherzählung** *f* (-; -en) PED reproduction
'**Nachfolge** *f* (-; *no pl*) succession; *j-s* ~ **antreten** succeed s.o.; '**nachfolgen** *v/i*

(*sep*, *-ge-*, *sein*) (*dat*) succeed *s.o.*;
'**Nachfolger**(in) ['na:xfɔlgɐ,
'na:xfɔlgərɪn] (*-s*; *-/-*; *-nen*) successor
'**nachforschen** *v/i* (*sep*, *-ge-*, *h*) investigate; '**Nachforschung** *f* (*-*; *-en*) investigation, inquiry
'**Nachfrage** *f* (*-*; *-n*) inquiry; ECON demand; '**nachfragen** *v/i* (*sep*, *-ge-*, *h*) inquire, ask
'**nach|fühlen** *v/t* (*sep*, *-ge-*, *h*) *j-m et.* ~
understand how s.o. feels; ~**füllen** *v/t*
(*sep*, *-ge-*, *h*) refill; ~**geben** *v/i* (*irr*, **geben**, *sep*, *-ge-*, *h*) give (way); *fig* give in
'**Nachgebühr** *f* (*-*; *-en*) *post* surcharge
'**nachgehen** *v/i* (*irr*, **gehen**, *sep*, *-ge-*,
sein) follow (*a. fig*); *watch*: be slow;
e-r Sache ~ investigate s.th.; *s-r Arbeit*
~ go about one's work
'**Nachgeschmack** *m* (*-[e]s*; *no pl*) after-
taste (*a. fig*)
nachgiebig ['na:xgi:bɪç] *adj* yielding,
soft (*both a. fig*); '**Nachgiebigkeit** *f*
(*-*; *no pl*) yieldingness, softness (*both
a. fig*)
nachhaltig ['na:xhaltɪç] *adj* lasting, en-
during
nach'hause → **Haus**
nach'her *adv* afterwards; *bis ~!* see you
later!, so long!
'**Nachhilfe** *f* help, assistance; PED →
~**stunden** *pl*, ~**unterricht** *m* PED private lesson(s), coaching
'**nachholen** *v/t* (*sep*, *-ge-*, *h*) make up for,
catch up on
'**Nachkomme** *m* (*-n*; *-n*) descendant, *pl
esp* JUR issue; '**nachkommen** *v/i* (*irr*,
kommen, *sep*, *-ge-*, *sein*) follow, come
later; (*dat*) comply with
'**Nachkriegs-**... *in cpds* postwar ...
Nachlass ['na:xlas] *m* (*-es*; *-lässe*
['na:xlɛsə]) ECON reduction, discount;
JUR estate
'**nachlassen** *v/i* (*irr*, **lassen**, *sep*, *-ge-*, *h*)
decrease, diminish; *good*: come down;
effect etc: wear off; *student etc*: slacken one's effort; *interest etc*: flag; *health etc*: fail, deteriorate
nachlässig *adj* careless, negligent
'**nach|laufen** *v/i* (*irr*, **laufen**, *sep*, *-ge-*,
sein) run after; ~**lesen** *v/t* (*irr*, **lesen**,
sep, *-ge-*, *h*) look up; ~**machen** *v/t*
(*sep*, *-ge-*, *h*) imitate, copy; counterfeit,
forge
'**Nachmittag** *m* afternoon; *heute* ~ this

afternoon
'**nachmittags** *adv* in the afternoon
Nachnahme ['na:xna:mə] *f* (*-*; *-n*) ECON
cash on delivery; *per* ~ *schicken* send
C.O.D.
'**Nach|name** *m* surname, last (*or* family)
name; ~**porto** *n* surcharge
'**nachprüfen** *v/t* (*sep*, *-ge-*, *h*) check (up),
make sure (of)
'**nachrechnen** *v/t* (*sep*, *-ge-*, *h*) check
'**Nachrede** *f*: *üble* ~ malicious gossip;
JUR defamation (of character), slander
Nachricht ['na:xrɪçt] *f* (*-*; *-en*) news;
message; report; information, notice;
pl news (report), newscast; *e-e gute*
(*schlechte*) ~ good (bad) news; *Sie hören ~en* here is the news
'**Nachrichten|dienst** *m* news service;
MIL intelligence service; ~**satel,lit** *m*
communications satellite; ~**spre-
cher(in)** newscaster, *esp Br* newsread-
er; ~**technik** *f* telecommunications
'**Nachruf** *m* obituary
'**nach|rüsten** *v/i* (*sep*, *-ge-*, *h*) POL, MIL
close the armament gap; ~**sagen** *v/t*
(*sep*, *-ge-*, *h*) *j-m Schlechtes* ~ speak
badly of s.o.; *man sagt ihm nach, dass
er ...* he is said to *inf*
'**Nachsai,son** *f* off-peak season; *in der*
~ out of season
'**nachschlagen** (*irr*, **schlagen**, *sep*, *-ge-*,
h) 1. *v/t* look up 2. *v/i*: ~ *in* (*dat*) consult;
'**Nachschlagewerk** *n* reference book
'**Nach|schlüssel** *m* duplicate (*or* skele-
ton) key; ~**schrift** *f* postscript; dictation;
~**schub** *m esp* MIL supplies
'**nach|sehen** (*irr*, **sehen**, *sep*, *-ge-*, *h*) 1.
v/i follow with one's eyes; (have a)
look; ~ *ob* (go and) see whether 2. *v/t*
look *or* go over *or* through; correct,
mark; *check* (*a.* TECH); ~**senden** *v/t*
([*irr*, **senden**,] *sep*, *-ge-*, *h*) send on, forward; *bitte ~!* *post* please forward!
'**Nachsilbe** *f* LING suffix
'**nachsitzen** *v/i* (*irr*, **sitzen**, *sep*, *-ge-*, *h*)
stay in (after school), be kept in; ~ *las-
sen* keep in, detain
'**Nachspann** *m* (*-[e]s*; *-e*) *film*: credits *pl*
'**Nachspiel** *n* sequel, consequences
'**nachspielen** *v/i* (*sep*, *-ge-*, *h*) SPORT *5
Minuten* ~ *lassen* allow 5 minutes
for injury time; '**Nachspielzeit** *f esp*
soccer: injury time
'**nach|spio,nieren** *v/i* (*no -ge-*, *h*) spy

(up)on; **~sprechen** *v/t (irr,* **sprechen**, *sep, -ge-, h)* **j-m et. ~** say or repeat s.th. after to s.o.

nächst'beste [nɛːçst'bɛstə] *adj* first, F any old; next-best, second-best

nächste ['nɛːçstə] *adj* next; nearest *(a. relative);* **in den ~n Tagen (Jahren)** in the next few days (years); **in ~r Zeit** in the near future; **was kommt als Nächstes?** what comes next?; **der Nächste, bitte!** next please!

nachstehen *v/i (irr,* **stehen**, *sep, -ge-, h)* **j-m in nichts ~** be in no way inferior to s.o.

nachstellen *(sep, -ge-, h)* **1.** *v/t* put back *(watch);* TECH (re)adjust **2.** *v/i:* **j-m ~** be after s.o.; **'Nachstellung** *f (-; -en)* persecution

'Nächstenliebe *f* charity

Nacht [naxt] *f (-; Nächte* ['nɛçtə]*)* night; **Tag und ~** night and day; **die ganze ~** all night (long); **heute Nacht** tonight; last night

'Nachtdienst *m* night duty; **~ haben** PHARM be open all night

'Nachteil *m* disadvantage, drawback; **im ~ sein** be at a disadvantage *(gegenüber* compared with); **nachteilig** ['naxtaɪlɪç] *adj* disadvantageous

'Nacht|essen *Swiss* → **Abendbrot;** **~falter** *m* ZO moth; **~hemd** *n* nightgown, nightdress, F nightie; nightshirt

Nachtigall ['naxtɪgal] *f (-; -en)* ZO nightingale

'Nachtisch *m (-[e]s; no pl)* dessert; sweet

nächtlich ['nɛçtlɪç] *adj* nightly; at or by night

'Nachtlo̱kal *n* nightclub

Nachtrag ['naːxtraːk] *m (-[e]s; -träge* ['naːxtrɛːgə]*)* supplement; **'nachtragen** *fig v/t (irr,* **tragen**, *sep, -ge-, h)* **j-m et. ~** bear s.o. a grudge; **'nachtragend** *adj* unforgiving; **nachträglich** ['naːxtrɛːklɪç] *adj* additional; later; belated

nachts *adv* at night, in the night(time)

'Nachtschicht *f* night shift; **~ haben** be on night shift

'nachtschlafend *adj:* **zu ~er Zeit** in the middle of the night

'Nachttisch *m* bedside table

'Nachttopf *m* chamber pot

'Nachtwächter *m* night watchman

'nachwachsen *v/i (irr,* **wachsen**, *sep, -ge-, sein)* grow again

'Nachwahl *f* PARL special election, *Br* by-election

Nachweis ['naːxvaɪs] *m (-es; -e)* proof, evidence; **'nachweisbar** *adj* demonstrable; *esp* CHEM *etc* detectable

'nachweisen *v/t (irr,* **weisen**, *sep, -ge-, h)* prove; *esp* CHEM *etc* detect

'nachweislich *adv* as can be proved

'Nach|welt *f (-; no pl)* posterity; **~wirkung** *f* aftereffect(s), *pl a.* aftermath; **~wort** *n (-[e]s; -worte)* epilog(ue)

'Nachwuchs *m (-es; no pl)* young talent, F new blood; *in cpds* **~autor,** **...schauspieler** *etc:* talented *or* promising young ..., up-and-coming ...

'nach|zahlen *v/t (sep, -ge-, h)* pay extra; **~zählen** *v/t (sep, -ge-, h)* count over (again), check

'Nachzahlung *f* additional *or* extra payment

Nachzügler ['naːxtsyːklɐ] *m (-s; -)* straggler, latecomer

Nacken ['nakən] *m (-s; -)* ANAT (back *or* nape of the) neck; **~stütze** *f* headrest

nackt [nakt] *adj* naked; *esp* PAINT, PHOT nude; bare *(a. fig); fig* plain; **völlig ~** stark naked; **sich ~ ausziehen** strip; **~ baden** swim in the nude; **j-n ~ malen** paint s.o. in the nude

Nadel ['naːdəl] *f (-; -n)* needle; pin; brooch; **~baum** *m* BOT conifer(ous tree); **~öhr** *n* eye of a needle; **~stich** *m* pinprick *(a. fig)*

Nagel ['naːgəl] *m (-s; Nägel* ['nɛːgəl]*)* nail; **an den Nägeln kauen** bite one's nails; **~lack** *m* nail varnish *or* polish

nageln *v/t (ge-, h)* nail **(an** *acc,* **auf** *acc* to)

'nagel'neu *F adj* brand-new

'Nagelpflege *f* manicure

nagen ['naːgən] *(ge-, h)* **1.** *v/i* gnaw **(an** *dat* at); **an e-m Knochen ~** pick a bone **2.** *v/t* gnaw; **Nagetier** *n* ZO rodent

'Nahaufnahme *f* PHOT *etc* close-up

nahe ['naːə] *adj* near, close **(bei** to); nearby; **~ kommen** *(dat)* come close to; *fig* →**nahekommen;** →**nahelegen;** →**naheliegen;** →**naheliegend;** **Nähe** ['nɛːə] *f (-; no pl)* nearness; neighbo(u)rhood, vicinity; **in der ~ des Bahnhofs** near the station; **ganz in der ~** quite near, close by; **in deiner**

N

~ near you

nahegehen v/i (irr, **gehen**, sep, -ge-, sein): **j-m** ~ affect s.o. deeply

'**nahekommen** v/i (irr, **kommen**, sep, -ge-, sein) fig come close to

'**nahelegen** v/t (sep, -ge-, h) suggest

'**naheliegen** v/i (irr, **liegen**, sep, -ge-, h) seem likely; '**naheliegend** adj likely, obvious

nahen ['na:ən] v/i (ge-, sein) approach

nähen ['nɛ:ən] v/t and v/i (ge-, h) sew; make

Nähere ['nɛ:ərə] n (-n; no pl) details, particulars

nähern ['nɛ:rən] v/refl (ge-, h) approach, get near(er) or close(r) (dat to)

'**nahezu** adv nearly, almost

'**Nähgarn** n (sewing) cotton

'**Nahkampf** m MIL close combat

nahm [na:m] pret of **nehmen**

'**Nähma¦schine** f sewing machine

'**Nähnadel** f (sewing) needle

nähren ['nɛ:rən] v/t (ge-, h) feed; fig nurture

nahrhaft ['na:ɐhaft] adj nutritious, nourishing

Nährstoff ['nɛ:ɐʃtɔf] m nutrient

Nahrung ['na:rʊŋ] f (-; no pl) food, nourishment; AGR feed; diet

'**Nahrungsmittel** pl food(stuffs)

Nährwert ['nɛ:ɐveːɐt] m nutritional value

Naht [na:t] f (-; **Nähte** ['nɛ:tə]) seam; MED suture

'**Nahverkehr** m local traffic; '**Nahverkehrszug** m local or commuter train

'**Nähzeug** n sewing kit

naiv [na'i:f] adj naive; **Naivität** [naivi'tɛːt] f (-; no pl) naivety

Name ['na:mə] m (-ns; -n) name; **im ~ von** on behalf of; **nur dem ~n nach** in name only; '**namenlos** adj nameless, fig a. unspeakable; '**namens** adv by (the) name of, named, called

'**Namens¦tag** m name day; ~**vetter** m namesake; ~**zug** m signature

namentlich ['na:məntlɪç] adj and adv by name

nämlich ['nɛ:mlɪç] adv that is (to say), namely; you see or know

nannte ['nantə] pret of **nennen**

Napf [napf] m (-[e]s; **Näpfe** ['nɛpfə]) bowl, basin

Narbe ['narbə] f (-; -n) scar

narbig ['narbɪç] adj scarred

Narkose [nar'ko:zə] f (-; -n) MED an(a)esthesia; **in** ~ under an an(a)esthetic

Narr [nar] m (-en; -en) fool; **j-n zum ~en halten** fool s.o.; '**narrensicher** adj foolproof; **närrisch** ['nɛrɪʃ] adj foolish; ~ **vor** (dat) mad with

Narzisse [nar'tsɪsə] f (-; -n) BOT daffodil

nasal [na'za:l] adj nasal

naschen ['naʃən] v/i and v/t (ge-, h) nibble (**an** dat at); **gern** ~ have a sweet tooth; **Nascherei** [naʃə'raiən] pl dainties, goodies, sweets; '**naschhaft** adj sweet-toothed

Nase ['na:zə] f (-; -n) ANAT nose (a. fig); **sich die ~ putzen** blow one's nose; **in der ~ bohren** pick one's nose; F **die ~ voll haben (von)** be fed up (with)

'**Nasen¦bluten** n MED nosebleed; ~**loch** n nostril; ~**spitze** f tip of the nose

Nashorn n ZO rhinoceros, F rhino

nass [nas] adj wet; **triefend** ~ soaking (wet); **Nässe** ['nɛsə] f (-; no pl) wet (-ness); '**nässen** (ge-, h) **1.** v/t wet **2.** v/i MED weep

'**nasskalt** adj damp and cold, raw

Nation [na'tsjoːn] f (-; -en) nation

national [natsjo'na:l] adj national

Natio'nalhymne f national anthem

Nationalismus [natsjona'lɪsmʊs] m (-; no pl) nationalism; **Nationalität** [natsjonali'tɛːt] f (-; -en) nationality

Natio'nal¦mannschaft f SPORT national team; ~**park** m national park

Natio'nalsozia¦lismus m HIST National Socialism, contp Nazism; **Natio'nalsozia¦list** m, **natio'nalsozia¦listisch** adj HIST National Socialist, contp Nazi

Natter ['natə] f (-; -n) ZO adder, viper (a. fig)

Natur [na'tu:ɐ] f (-; -en) nature; **von** ~ **(aus)** by nature

Naturalismus [natura'lɪsmʊs] m (-; no pl) naturalism

Na'tur¦ereignis n, ~**erscheinung** f natural phenomenon; ~**forscher** m naturalist; ~**geschichte** f natural history; ~**gesetz** n law of nature

na'turgetreu adj true to life; lifelike

Na'turkata¦strophe f (natural) catastrophe or disaster, act of God

natürlich [na'tyːɐlɪç] **1.** adj natural **2.**

adv naturally, of course

Na'tur|schätze *pl* natural resources; ~schutz *m* nature conservation; unter ~ protected; ~schützer [ˈnaˈtuːɐʃytsɐ] *m* (-s; -) conservationist; ~schutzgebiet *n* nature reserve; national park; ~wissenschaft *f* (natural) science

n. Chr. *abbr of* nach Christus AD, Anno Domini

Nebel [ˈneːbəl] *m* (-s; -) fog; mist; haze; smoke; ~horn *n* foghorn; ~leuchte *f* мот fog light

neben [ˈneːbən] *prp* (*dat and acc*) beside, next to; besides, apart from; compared with; ~ anderem among other things; setz dich ~ mich sit by me *or* by my side

neben'an *adv* next door

neben'bei *adv* in addition, at the same time; ~ (gesagt) by the way

'Nebenberuf *m* second job, sideline; 'nebenberuflich *adv* as a sideline

Nebenbuhler [ˈneːbənbuːlɐ] *m* (-s; -), 'Nebenbuhlerin *f* (-; -nen) rival

'nebenei'nander *adv* side by side; next (door) to each other; ~ bestehen coexist

'Neben|einkünfte *pl*, ~einnahmen *pl* extra money; ~fach *n* PED *etc* minor (subject), *Br* subsidiary subject; ~fluss *m* tributary; ~gebäude *n* next-door *or* adjoining building; annex(e); ~haus *n* house next door; ~kosten *pl* extras; ~mann *m*: dein ~ the person next to you; ~pro,dukt *n* by-product; ~rolle *f* THEA supporting role, minor part (*a. fig*); cameo (role); ~sache *f* minor matter; das ist ~ that's of little *or* no importance

'nebensächlich *adj* unimportant

'Neben|satz *m* LING subordinate clause; ~stelle *f* TEL extension; ~straße *f* side street; minor road; ~strecke *f* RAIL branch line; ~tisch *m* next table; ~verdienst *m* extra earnings; ~wirkung *f* side effect; ~zimmer *n* adjoining room

neblig [ˈneːblɪç] *adj* foggy; misty; hazy

necken [ˈnɛkən] *v/t* (ge-, h) tease

Neckerei [nɛkəˈrai] *f* (-; -en) teasing

'neckisch *adj* playful, teasing

Neffe [ˈnɛfə] *m* (-n; -n) nephew

negativ [ˈneːgatiːf] *adj* negative

'Negativ *n* (-s; -e) PHOT negative

nehmen [ˈneːmən] *v/t* (*irr*, ge-, h) take (*a.*

sich ~); j-m et. ~ take s.th. (away) from s.o. (*a. fig*); sich e-n Tag frei ~ take a day off; j-n an die Hand ~ take s.o. by the hand

Neid [nait] *m* (-es; *no pl*) envy; reiner ~ sheer envy; neidisch [ˈnaidɪʃ] *adj* envious (auf *acc* of)

Neige [ˈnaigə] *f*: zur ~ gehen draw to its close; run out

'neigen (ge-, h) 1. *v/t and refl* bend, incline 2. *v/i*: zu et. ~ tend to (do) s.th.

'Neigung *f* (-; -en) inclination (*a. fig*), slope, incline; *fig* tendency

nein [nain] *adv* no

Nektar [ˈnɛktaːɐ] *m* (-s; -e) BOT nectar

Nelke [ˈnɛlkə] *f* (-; -n) BOT carnation; GASTR clove

nennen [ˈnɛnən] *v/t* (*irr*, ge-, h) name, call; mention; sich ~ call o.s., be called; man nennt ihn ... he is called ...; das nenne ich ...! that's what I call ...!

'nennenswert *adj* worth mentioning

Nenner [ˈnɛnɐ] *m* (-s; -) MATH denominator

'Nennwert *m* ECON nominal *or* face value; zum ~ at par

Neo..., neo... [neo-] *in cpds* ...faschist *etc*: neo-...

Neon [ˈneːɔn] *n* (-s; *no pl*) CHEM neon

'Neonröhre *f* neon tube

Nepp [nɛp] F *m* (-s; *no pl*) rip-off

neppen [ˈnɛpən] F *v/t* (ge-, h) fleece, rip s.o. off

Nerv [nɛrf] *m* (-s; -en) ANAT nerve; j-m auf die ~en fallen *or* gehen get on s.o.'s nerves; die ~en behalten (verlieren) keep (lose) one's head

nerven [ˈnɛrfən] F *v/t and v/i* (ge-, h) be a pain in the neck (j-n to s.o.)

'Nervenarzt *m*, 'Nervenärztin *f* neurologist

'nervenaufreibend *adj* nerve-racking

'Nerven|belastung *f* nervous strain; ~kitzel *m* thrill, F kick(s)

'nervenkrank *adj* mentally ill

'Nerven|säge F *f* pain in the neck; ~system *n* nervous system; ~zusammenbruch *m* nervous breakdown

nervös [nɛrˈvøːs] *adj* nervous

Nervosität [nɛrvoziˈtɛːt] *f* (-; *no pl*) nervousness

Nerz [nɛrts] *m* (-es; -e) ZO mink

Nessel [ˈnɛsəl] *f* (-; -n) BOT nettle

Nest [nɛst] *n* (-[e]s; -er [ˈnɛstɐ]) ZO nest;

F *contp* one-horse town

nett [nɛt] *adj* nice; kind; **so ~ sein und et.** (*or et. zu*) **tun** be so kind as to do s.th.

netto ['nɛto] *adv* ECON net

Netz [nɛts] *n* (*-es*; *-e*) net; RAIL, TEL, IT network; ELECTR mains; **~haut** *f* ANAT retina; **~karte** *f* RAIL area season ticket

neu [nɔy] *adj* new; fresh; *fig* modern; **neuere Sprachen** modern languages; **neueste Nachrichten** (**Mode**) latest news (fashion); **von neuem** anew, afresh; **seit neu(st)em** since (very) recently; **viel Neues** a lot of new things; **was gibt es Neues?** what's the news?, what's new?; '**neuartig** *adj* novel

'**Neubau** *m* (*-[e]s*; *-ten*) new building; **~gebiet** *n* new housing estate

neuerdings ['nɔyɐdɪŋs] *adv* lately, recently

Neuerer ['nɔyɐrɐ] *m* (*-s*; *-*) innovator; '**Neuerung** *f* (*-*; *-en*) innovation

'**Neugestaltung** *f* reorganization, reformation

'**Neugier** *f*, **Neugierde** ['nɔygi:rdə] *f* (*-*; *no pl*) curiosity; '**neugierig** *adj* curious (**auf** *acc* about); F *contp* nos(e)y; **ich bin ~, ob** I wonder if; **Neugierige** ['nɔygi:rɪgə] *contp pl* rubbernecks

'**Neuheit** *f* (*-*; *-en*) novelty

'**Neuigkeit** ['nɔyɪçkaɪt] *f* (*-*; *-en*) (piece of) news

'**Neujahr** *n* New Year('s Day); **Prost ~!** Happy New Year!

'**neulich** *adv* the other day

'**Neuling** ['nɔylɪŋ] *m* (*-s*; *-e*) newcomer, F greenhorn

'**neumodisch** *contp adj* newfangled

'**Neumond** *m* new moon

neun [nɔyn] *adj* nine; '**neunte** *adj* ninth; '**Neuntel** *n* (*-s*; *-*) ninth (part); '**neuntens** *adv* ninthly; '**neunzehn** *adj* nineteen; '**neunzehnte** *adj* nineteenth; '**neunzig** *adj* ninety; '**neunzigste** *adj* ninetieth

Neurose [nɔy'ro:zə] *f* (*-*; *-n*) MED neurosis; **neurotisch** [nɔy'ro:tɪʃ] *adj* MED neurotic

'**neusprachlich** *adj* modern-language

neutral [nɔy'tra:l] *adj* neutral; **Neutralität** [nɔytrali'tɛ:t] *f* (*-*; *no pl*) neutrality

Neutronen... [nɔy'tro:nən-] PHYS *in cpds* ...*bombe etc*: neutron ...

Neutrum ['nɔytrʊm] *n* (*-s*; *-tra*) LING neuter

'**Neuverfilmung** *f* remake

'**neuwertig** *adj* as good as new

'**Neuzeit** *f* (*-; no pl*) modern times

nicht [nɪçt] *adv* not; **überhaupt ~** not at all; **~ (ein)mal, gar ~ erst** not even; **~ mehr** not any more *or* longer; **sie ist nett** *indef hier*), **~ (wahr)?** she's nice (lives here), isn't (doesn't) she?; **~ so ... wie** not as ... as; **noch ~** not yet; **~ besser** (*als*) no (*or* not any) better (than); **ich** (*auch*) **~** I don't *or* I'm not (either); (*bitte*) **~!** (please) don't!

'**Nicht...** *in cpds* ...*mitglied, ...schwimmer etc*: *mst* non-...; **~beachtung** *f* disregard; non-observance

Nichte ['nɪçtə] *f* (*-*; *-n*) niece

nichtig ['nɪçtɪç] *adj* trivial; JUR void, invalid

'**Nichtraucher** *m*, '**Nichtraucherin** *f* non-smoker

nichts *indef pron* nothing, not anything; **~ anderes** als nothing but; **gar ~** nothing at all; F **das ist ~** that's no good; **~ sagend** meaningless; **Nichts** *n* (*-s*; *no pl*) nothing(ness); **aus dem ~ appear** *etc* from nowhere; **build** *etc* from nothing

nichtsdesto'weniger *adv* nevertheless

nichtsnutzig ['nɪçtsnʊtsɪç] *adj* good-for-nothing, worthless

'**nichtssagend** *adj* meaningless

Nichtstuer ['nɪçtstu:ɐ] *m* (*-s*; *-*) do-nothing, F bum

nicken ['nɪkən] *v/i* (*ge-*, *h*) nod (one's head)

nie [ni:] *adv* never, at no time; **fast ~** hardly ever; **~ und nimmer** never ever

nieder ['ni:dɐ] **1.** *adj* low **2.** *adv* down; '**Niedergang** *m* (*-[e]s*; *no pl*) decline

'**niedergeschlagen** *adj* depressed, (feeling) down

'**Niederlage** *f* defeat, F beating

'**niederlassen** *v/refl* (*irr*, *lassen*, *sep*, *-ge-*, *h*) settle (down); ECON set up (*als* as); '**Niederlassung** *f* (*-*; *-en*) ECON establishment; branch

'**nieder|legen** *v/t* (*sep*, *-ge-*, *h*) lay down (*a. office etc*); **die Arbeit ~** (go on) strike, down tools, F walk out; **sich ~** lie down; go to bed; **~metzeln** *v/t* (*sep*, *-ge-*, *h*) massacre

'**Niederschlag** *m* METEOR rain(fall);

PHYS fallout; CHEM precipitate; *boxing*: knock-down; 'niederschlagen *v/t* (*irr*, **schlagen**, *sep*, *-ge-*, *h*) knock down; cast down (*eyes*); fig put down (*revolt etc*); JUR quash; **sich ~** CHEM precipitate

'niederschmettern fig *v/t* (*sep*, *-ge-*, *h*) shatter, crush

'niederträchtig *adj* base, mean

Niederung ['niːdərʊŋ] *f* (*-*; *-en*) lowland(s)

niedlich ['niːtlɪç] *adj* pretty, sweet, cute

niedrig ['niːdrɪç] *adj* low (*a. fig*); *fig* light (*sentence etc*); **~ fliegen** fly low

niemals ['niːmaːls] → **nie**

niemand ['niːmant] *indef pron* nobody, no one, not anybody; **~ von ihnen** none of them; 'Niemandsland *n* (*-[e]s*; *no pl*) no-man's-land

Niere ['niːrə] *f* (*-*; *-n*) ANAT kidney

nieseln ['niːzəln] *v/i* (*ge-*, *h*) drizzle

'Nieselregen *m* drizzle

niesen ['niːzən] *v/i* (*ge-*, *h*) sneeze

Niete¹ ['niːtə] *f* (*-*; *-n*) TECH rivet

Niete² *f* (*-*; *-n*) blank; F failure

Nikolaustag ['nɪkolaustaːk] *m* St. Nicholas' Day

Nikotin [niko'tiːn] *n* (*-s*; *no pl*) CHEM nicotine

Nilpferd ['niːlpfeːrt] *n* ZO hippopotamus, F hippo

Nippel ['nɪpəl] *m* (*-s*; *-*) TECH nipple

nippen ['nɪpən] *v/i* (*ge-*, *h*) sip (**an** *dat* at)

nirgends ['nɪrgənts] *adv* nowhere

Nische ['niːʃə] *f* (*-*; *-n*) niche, recess

nisten ['nɪstən] *v/i* (*ge-*, *h*) ZO nest

'Nistplatz *m* ZO nesting place

Niveau [ni'voː] *n* (*-s*; *-s*) level, *fig a.* standard

Nixe ['nɪksə] *f* (*-*; *-n*) water nymph, mermaid

noch [nɔx] *adv* still; **~ nicht** not yet; **~ nie** never before; **er hat nur ~ 5 Euro (Minuten)** he has only 5 euros (minutes) left; (**sonst**) **~ et. ?** anything else?; **ich möchte ~ et.** (**Tee**) I'd like some more (tea); **~ ein(e, -n)..., bitte** another ..., please; **~ einmal** once more *or* again; **~ zwei Stunden** another two hours, two hours to go; **~ besser** (**schlimmer**) even better (worse); **~ gestern** only yesterday; (*und*) **wenn es ~ so ... ist** however (*or* no matter how) ... it may be

nochmalig ['nɔxmaːlɪç] *adj* new, renewed

'nochmals *adv* once more *or* again

Nockerl ['nɔkɐl] *Austrian n* (*-s*; *-n*) GASTR small dumpling

Nomade [no'maːdə] *m* (*-n*; *-n*), No-'madin *f* (*-*; *-nen*) nomad

Nominativ ['noːminatiːf] *m* (*-s*; *-e*) LING nominative (case)

nominieren [nomi'niːrən] *v/t* (*no -ge-*, *h*) nominate

Nonne ['nɔnə] *f* (*-*; *-n*) REL nun

'Nonnenkloster *n* REL convent

Norden ['nɔrdən] *m* (*-s*; *no pl*) north; **nach ~** north(wards); nordisch ['nɔrdɪʃ] *adj* northern; SPORT **~e Kombination** Nordic Combined

nördlich ['nœrtlɪç] **1.** *adj* north(ern); northerly **2.** *adv*: **~ von** north of

Nordlicht ['nɔrtlɪçt] *n* (*-[e]s*; *-er*) ASTR northern lights

Nord'osten *m* northeast; nord'östlich *adj* northeast(ern); northeasterly

'Nordpol *m* North Pole

Nord'westen *m* northwest

nord'westlich *adj* northwest(ern); northwesterly

'Nordwind *m* north wind

nörgeln ['nœrgəln] *v/i* (*ge-*, *h*) nag (**an** *dat* at)

Nörgler ['nœrglɐ] *m* (*-s*; *-*), 'Nörglerin *f* (*-*; *-nen*) nagger

Norm [nɔrm] *f* (*-*; *-en*) standard, norm

normal [nɔr'maːl] *adj* normal; F **nicht ganz ~** not quite right in the head

Nor'mal... *esp* TECH *in cpds* ...**maß**, ...**zeit** *etc*: standard ...; **~ben,zin** *n* regular (gas, *Br* petrol)

normalerweise [nɔr'maːlɐ'vaizə] *adv* normally, usually

normalisieren [nɔrmali'ziːrən] *v/refl* (*no -ge-*, *h*) return to normal

normen ['nɔrmən] *v/t* (*ge-*, *h*) standardize

Norwegen ['nɔrveːgən] Norway

Norweger ['nɔrveːgɐ] *m* (*-s*; *-*), 'Norwegerin ['nɔrveːgərɪn] *f* (*-*; *-nen*), 'norwegisch *adj* Norwegian

Not [noːt] *f* (*-*; *Nöte* ['nøːtə]) need; want; poverty; hardship; misery; difficulty; emergency; distress; **~ leidend** needy; **in ~ sein** be in trouble; **zur ~** if need be, if necessary

Notar [no'taːr] *m* (*-s*; *-e*), No'tarin *f* (*-*; *-nen*) JUR notary (public)

'Not|aufnahme f MED emergency room, Br casualty; ~ausgang m emergency exit; ~behelf m (-[e]s; -e) makeshift, expedient; ~bremse f emergency brake; ~dienst m emergency duty

'notdürftig adj scanty; temporary

Note ['noːtə] f (-; -n) note (a. MUS and POL); ECON bill, esp Br (bank)note; PED grade, Br mark; pl MUS (sheet) music; ~n lesen read music

Notebook ['noutbuk] n (-s; -s) IT notebook

'Notendurchschnitt m PED etc average

'Notenständer m music stand

'Notfall m emergency

'notfalls adv if necessary

'notgedrungen adv: et. ~ tun be forced to do s.th.

notieren [no'tiːrən] v/t (no -ge-, h) make a note of, note (down); ECON quote

nötig ['nøːtɪç] adj necessary; ~ haben need; ~ brauchen need badly; das Nötigste the (bare) necessities or essentials; nötigen ['nøːtɪgən] v/t (ge-, h) force, compel; press, urge; 'Nötigung f (-; -en) coercion; JUR intimidation

Notiz [no'tiːts] f (-; -en) note; keine ~ nehmen von take no notice of, ignore; sich ~en machen take notes; ~block m memo pad, Br notepad; ~buch n notebook

'Notlage f awkward (or difficult) situation; difficulties; emergency

'notlanden v/i (-ge-, sein) AVIAT make an emergency landing; 'Notlandung f AVIAT emergency landing

'Notlösung f expedient

'Notlüge f white lie

notorisch [no'toːrɪʃ] adj notorious

'Not|ruf m TEL emergency call; ~rufsäule f TEL emergency phone; ~sig,nal n emergency or distress signal; ~stand m state of (national) emergency; ~standsgebiet n disaster area; ECON depressed area; ~standsgesetze pl POL emergency laws; ~verband m MED emergency dressing

'Notwehr f (-; no pl) JUR self-defense, Br self-defence

'notwendig adj necessary

'Notwendigkeit f (-; -en) necessity

'Notzucht f (-; no pl) JUR rape

Novelle [no'vɛlə] f (-; -n) novella; PARL amendment

November [no'vɛmbɐ] m (-[s]; -) November

Nr. abbr of Nummer No., no., number

Nu [nuː] m: im ~ in no time

Nuance ['nyãːsə] f shade

nüchtern ['nʏçtɐn] adj sober (a. fig); matter-of-fact; auf ~en Magen on an empty stomach; ~ werden (machen) sober up

'Nüchternheit f (-; no pl) sobriety

Nudel ['nuːdəl] f (-; -n) noodle

nuklear [nukle'aːɐ] adj nuclear

null [nʊl] adj zero, Br nought; TEL 0; SPORT nil, nothing; tennis: love; ~ Grad zero degrees; ~ Fehler no mistakes; gleich Null sein be nil

'Null|di,ät f low-calorie (or F starvation) diet; ~punkt m zero (point or fig level); ~ta,rif m free fare(s); zum ~ free (of charge)

Numerus clausus ['nuːmerus 'klauzus] m (-; no pl) UNIV restricted admission(s)

Nummer ['nʊmɐ] f (-; -n) number; issue; size; nummerieren [nʊmə'riːrən] v/t (no -ge-, h) number

'Nummernschild n MOT license plate, Br numberplate

nun [nuːn] adv now; well

nur [nuːɐ] adv only, just; merely; nothing but; er tut ~ so he's just pretending; ~ so (zum Spaß) just for fun; warte ~! just you wait!; mach ~!, ~ zu! go ahead!; → Erwachsene

Nuss [nʊs] f (-; Nüsse ['nʏsə]) BOT nut; ~baum m walnut (tree); ~knacker m nutcracker; ~schale f nutshell

Nüstern ['nʏstɐn] pl ZO nostrils

Nutte ['nʊtə] F f (-; -n) hooker, sl tart

Nutzanwendung ['nʊts'anvɛndʊŋ] f practical application; 'nutzbar adj usable; ~ machen utilize; exploit; harness; 'nutzbringend adj profitable, useful

nütze ['nʏtsə] adj useful; zu nichts ~ sein be (of) no use; be good for nothing

Nutzen ['nʊtsən] m (-s; -) use; profit, gain; advantage; ~ ziehen aus (dat) benefit or profit from or by; zum ~ von (or gen) for the benefit of

'nutzen, 'nützen (ge-, h) 1. v/i: j-m ~ be of use to s.o.; es nützt nichts (es zu tun) it's no use (doing it) 2. v/t use, make use of; take advantage of

nützlich ['nʏtslɪç] *adj* useful, helpful; advantageous; **sich ~ machen** make o.s. useful

'**nutzlos** *adj* useless, (of) no use

'**Nutzung** *f* (-; -en) use, utilization

Nylon® ['nailɔn] *n* (-s; *no pl*) nylon®; **~strümpfe** *pl* nylon® stockings

Nymphe ['nʏmfə] *f* (-; -n) nymph

O

O *abbr of* **Osten** E, east

o *int* oh!; **o weh!** oh dear!

o. Ä. *abbr of* **oder Ähnliche(s)** or the like

Oase [o'a:zə] *f* (-; -n) oasis (*a. fig*)

ob [ɔp] *cj* whether, if; **als ~** as if, as though; **und ~!** and how!, you bet!

Obacht ['o:baxt] *f*: **~ geben auf** (*acc*) pay attention to; (**gib**) **~!** watch out!

Obdach ['ɔpdax] *n* (-[e]s; *no pl*) shelter

'**obdachlos** *adj* homeless, without shelter; '**Obdachlose** *m*, *f* (-n; -n) homeless person; '**Obdachlosena,syl** *n* shelter for the homeless

Obduktion [ɔpdʊk'tsjo:n] *f* (-; -en) MED autopsy

obduzieren [ɔpdu'tsi:rən] *v/t* (*no -ge-*, *h*) MED perform an autopsy on

oben ['o:bən] *adv* above; up; on (the) top; at the top (*a. fig*); on the surface; upstairs; **da ~** up there; **von ~ bis unten** from top to bottom (*or* toe); **links ~** at (the) top left; **siehe ~** see above; F **~ ohne** topless; **von ~ herab** *fig* patronizing(ly), condescending(ly); **~ erwähnt** *or* **genannt** above-mentioned; **~'an** *adv* at the top; **~'auf** *adv* on the top; on the surface; F feeling great; **~'drein** *adv* besides, into the bargain, at that; **~'hin** *adv* superficially

Ober ['o:bɐ] *m* (-s; -) waiter

'**Ober|arm** *m* ANAT upper arm; **~arzt** *m*, **~ärztin** *f* assistant medical director; **~befehl** *m* MIL supreme command; **~begriff** *n* generic term; **~bürgermeister** *m* mayor, *Br* Lord Mayor

obere ['o:bərə] *adj* upper, top, *fig a.* superior

'**Oberfläche** *f* surface (*a. fig*) (**an** *dat* on); '**oberflächlich** *adj* superficial

'**oberhalb** *prp* (*gen*) above

'**Ober|hand** *f*: **die ~ gewinnen** (**über** *acc*) get the upper hand (of); **~haupt** *n* head, chief; **~haus** *n* (-es; *no pl*) *Br*

PARL House of Lords; **~hemd** *n* shirt; **~herrschaft** *f* (-; *no pl*) supremacy

Oberin ['o:bərɪn] *f* (-; -nen) REL Mother Superior

'**oberirdisch** *adj* above ground; ELECTR overhead

'**Ober|kellner** *m* head waiter; **~kiefer** *m* ANAT upper jaw; **~körper** *m* upper part of the body; **den ~ frei machen** strip to the waist; **~leder** *n* uppers; **~leitung** *f* chief management; ELECTR overhead contact line; **~lippe** *f* ANAT upper lip

Obers ['o:bɐs] *Austrian n* (-; *no pl*) GASTR cream

'**Oberschenkel** *m* ANAT thigh

'**Oberschule** *f* *appr* highschool, *Br* grammar school

Oberst ['o:bɐst] *m* (-en; -en) MIL colonel

oberste ['o:bɐstə] *adj* up(per)most, top (-most); highest; *fig* chief, first

'**Ober|stufe** *f* *appr* senior highschool, *Br appr* senior classes; **~teil** *n* top

ob'gleich *cj* (al)though

Obhut ['ɔphu:t] *f* (-; *no pl*) care, charge; **in s-e ~ nehmen** take care of *or* charge of

obig ['o:bɪç] *adj* above(-mentioned)

Objekt [ɔp'jɛkt] *n* (-[e]s; -e) object (*a.* LING); ECON property

objektiv [ɔpjɛk'ti:f] *adj* objective; impartial, unbias(s)ed

Objek'tiv *n* (-s; -e) PHOT (object) lens

Objektivität [ɔpjɛktivi'tɛ:t] *f* (-; *no pl*) objectivity; impartiality

Oblate [o'bla:tə] *f* (-; -n) wafer; REL host

obligatorisch [ɔbliga'to:rɪʃ] *adj* compulsory

Oboe [o'bo:ə] *f* (-; -n) MUS oboe

Oboist [obo'ɪst] *m* (-en; -en) MUS oboist

Observatorium [ɔpzɛrva'to:rjʊm] *n* (-s; -rien) ASTR observatory

Obst [o:pst] *n* (-[e]s; *no pl*) fruit; **~garten** *m* orchard; **~kon,serven** *pl* canned fruit; **~laden** *m* fruit store, *esp Br* fruiterer's (shop); **~torte** *f*

fruit pie (*Br* flan)

obszön [ɔps'tsøːn] *adj* obscene, filthy

ob'wohl *cj* (al)though

Occasion [ɔka'zjoːn] *Swiss f* (-; -en) bargain, good buy

Ochse ['ɔksə] *m* (-n; -n) zo ox, bullock; F blockhead

od. *abbr of* **oder** or

öde ['øːdə] *adj* deserted, desolate; waste; *fig* dull, dreary, tedious

oder ['oːdɐ] *cj* or; ~ **aber** or else, otherwise; ~ **vielmehr** or rather; ~ **so** or so; **er kommt doch, ~?** he's coming, isn't he?; **du kennst ihn ja nicht, ~ doch?** you don't know him, or do you?

Ofen ['oːfən] *m* (-s; *Öfen* ['øːfən]) stove; oven; TECH furnace; **~rohr** *n* stovepipe

offen ['ɔfən] **1.** *adj* open (*a. fig*); vacant (*post*); *fig* frank **2.** *adv*: ~ **gesagt** frankly (speaking); ~ **s-e Meinung sagen** speak one's mind (freely); ~ **stehen** be open; ECON be outstanding

'offenbar *adj* obvious, evident; apparent; **offenbaren** [ɔfən'baːrən] *v/t* (ge-, h) reveal, disclose, show; **Offen-'barung** *f* (-; -en) revelation

'Offenheit *f* (-; *no pl*) openness, frankness

'offenherzig *adj* open-hearted, frank, candid; *fig* revealing (*dress*)

'offensichtlich *adj* → **offenbar**

offensiv [ɔfɛn'ziːf] *adj*, **Offensive** [ɔfɛn'ziːvə] *f* (-; -n) offensive

'offenstehen *v/i* (*irr, stehen, sep, -ge-, h*): **j-m** ~ *fig* be open to s.o.

öffentlich ['œfəntlɪç] *adj* public; **~e Verkehrsmittel** *pl* public transport; **~e Schulen** *pl* public (*Br* state) schools; **~ auftreten** appear in public

'Öffentlichkeit *f* (-; *no pl*) the public; **in aller ~** in public, openly; **an die ~ bringen** make public

offiziell [ɔfi'tsjɛl] *adj* official

Offizier [ɔfi'tsiːɐ] *m* (-s; -e) MIL (commissioned) officer

öffnen ['œfnən] *v/t and v/refl* (ge-, h) open; **Öffner** ['œfnɐ] *m* (-s; -) opener; **'Öffnung** *f* (-; -en) opening

'Öffnungszeiten *pl* business *or* office hours

oft [ɔft] *adv* often, frequently

oh [oː] *int* o(h)!

ohne ['oːnə] *prp* (*acc*) and *cj* without; ~

mich! count me out!; ~ **ein Wort** (**zu sagen**) without (saying) a word

ohne|'gleichen *adv* unequal(l)ed, unparalleled; ~**'hin** *adv* anyhow, anyway

Ohnmacht ['oːnmaxt] *f* (-; -en) MED unconsciousness; *fig* helplessness; **in ~ fallen** faint, pass out; **'ohnmächtig** *adj* MED unconscious; *fig* helpless; ~ **werden** faint, pass out

Ohr [oːɐ] *n* (-[e]s; -en ['oːrən]) ANAT ear; F **j-n übers ~ hauen** cheat s.o.; **bis über die ~en verliebt** (**verschuldet**) head over heels in love (over your head in debt)

Öhr [øːɐ] *n* (-[e]s; -e ['øːrə]) eye

Ohrenarzt ['oːrən?aːɐtst] *m* ear specialist

'ohrenbetäubend *adj* deafening

'Ohren|schmerzen *pl* earache; **~schützer** *pl* earmuffs; **~zeuge** *m* earwitness

'Ohrfeige *f* slap in the face (*a. fig*); **ohrfeigen** ['oːɐfaigən] *v/t* (ge-, h) **j-n** ~ slap s.o.'s face

'Ohr|läppchen ['oːɐlɛpçən] *n* (-s; -) ANAT earlobe; **~ring** *m* earring

oje [o'jeː] *int* oh dear!, dear me!

Ökologe [øko'loːgə] *m* (-n; -n) ecologist; **Ökologie** [økolo'giː] *f* (-; *no pl*) ecology; **ökologisch** [øko'loːgɪʃ] *adj* ecological

Ökonomie [økono'miː] *f* (-; *no pl*) economy; ECON economics; **ökonomisch** [øko'noːmɪʃ] *adj* economical; ECON economic

Ökosys,tem ['øːkozysteːm] *n* ecosystem

Oktave [ɔk'taːvə] *f* (-; -n) MUS octave

Oktober [ɔk'toːbɐ] *m* (-[s]; -) October

ökumenisch [øku'meːnɪʃ] *adj* REL ecumenical

Öl [øːl] *n* (-[e]s; *Öle*) oil; petroleum; **nach ~ bohren** drill for oil; **auf ~ stoßen** strike oil; **'Ölbaum** *m* BOT olive (tree)

Oldtimer ['oʊldtaimɐ] *m* (-s; -) MOT veteran car

ölen ['øːlən] *v/t* (ge-, h) oil, TECH *a.* lubricate

'Öl|farbe *f* oil (paint); **~feld** *n* oilfield; **~förderland** *n* oil-producing country; **~förderung** *f* oil production; **~gemälde** *n* oil painting; **~heizung** *f* oil heating

ölig ['øːlɪç] *adj* oily, greasy (*both a. fig*)

oliv [o'li:f] *adj* olive

Olive [o'li:və] *f* (-; -*n*) BOT olive

'Öl|leitung *f*(oil) pipeline; ~messtab *m* MOT dipstick; ~pest *f* oil pollution; ~quelle *f* oil well; ~sar,dine *f* canned (*Br a.* tinned) sardine; ~stand *m* oil level; ~tanker *m* MAR oil tanker; ~teppich *m* oil slick

'Ölung *f* (-; *no pl*) oiling, TECH *a.* lubrication; *Letzte* ~ REL extreme unction

'Öl|wanne *f* MOT oil pan, *Br* sump; ~wechsel *m* MOT oil change

Olympia... [o'lympia-]*in cpds* ...mannschaft, ...medaille *etc*: Olympic ...

Olympiade [olym'bja:də] *f*(-; -*n*) SPORT Olympic Games, Olympics

'Ölzeug *n* oilskins

Oma ['o:ma] F *f* (-; -*s*) grandma

Omi ['o:mi] F *f* (-; -*s*) granny

Omnibus ['ɔmnibus] *m* → *Bus*

onanieren [ona'ni:rən] *v/i* (*no -ge-, h*) masturbate

Onkel ['ɔŋkəl] *m* (-*s*; -) uncle

Online... ['ɔnlain-] IT online ...

Opa ['o:pa] F *m* (-*s*; -*s*) grandpa

Oper ['o:pɐ] *f* (-; -*n*) MUS opera; opera (house)

Operation [opəra'tsjo:n] *f* (-; -*en*) MED operation; *e-e* ~ *vornehmen* perform an operation; Operati'onssaal *m* MED operating room (*Br* theatre)

Operette [opə'rɛtə] *f*(-;-*n*) MUS operetta

operieren [opə'ri:rən] (*no -ge-, h*) **1.** *v/t* MED *j-n* ~ operate on s.o. (*wegen* for); *operiert werden* be operated on, have an operation; *sich* ~ *lassen* undergo an operation **2.** *v/i* MED, MIL operate; proceed

'Opernsänger(in) opera singer

Opfer ['ɔpfɐ] *n* (-*s*; -) sacrifice; offering; victim; *ein* ~ *bringen* make a sacrifice; (*dat*) *zum* ~ *fallen* fall victim to

'opfern *v/t and v/i* (*ge-, h*) sacrifice

Opium ['o:pjum] *n* (-*s*; *no pl*) opium

Opposition [ɔpozi'tsjo:n] *f* (-; -*en*) opposition (*a.* PARL)

Optik ['ɔptik]*f*(-;*no pl*) optics; PHOT optical system

Optiker ['ɔptikɐ] *m* (-*s*; -), 'Optikerin *f* (-; -*nen*) optician

optimal [ɔpti'ma:l] *adj* optimum, best

Optimismus [ɔpti'mismus] *m* (-; *no pl*) optimism; Optimist(in) [ɔpti'mist(in)] (-*en*; -*en*/-; -*nen*) optimist; opti-

'mistisch *adj* optimistic

Option [ɔp'tsjo:n] *f* (-; -*en*) option

optisch ['ɔpti∫] *adj* optical

Orange [o'ra:ʒə] *f* (-; -*n*) BOT orange

Orchester [ɔr'kɛstɐ] *n* (-*s*; -) MUS orchestra

Orchidee [ɔrçi'de:] *f* (-; -*n*) BOT orchid

Orden ['ɔrdən] *m* (-*s*; -) medal, decoration; *esp* REL order

'Ordensschwester *f* REL sister, nun

ordentlich ['ɔrdəntliç] **1.** *adj* tidy, neat, orderly; proper; thorough; decent (*a.* F); respectable; full (*member etc*); JUR ordinary; reasonable (*performance etc*); F good, sound **2.** *adv*: *s-e Sache* ~ *machen* do a good job; *sich* ~ *benehmen* (*anziehen*) behave (dress) properly *or* decently

ordinär [ɔrdi'nɛ:ɐ] *adj* vulgar; common

ordnen ['ɔrdnən] *v/t* (*ge-, h*) put in order; arrange, sort (out); file; settle

Ordner ['ɔrdnɐ] *m* (-*s*; -) file; folder; attendant, guard

'Ordnung *f* (-; *no pl*) order; orderliness, tidiness; arrangement; system, set-up; class; *in* ~ all right; TECH *etc* in (good) order; *in* ~ *bringen* put right (*a. fig*); tidy up; repair, fix (*a. fig*); (*in*) ~ *halten* keep (in) order; *et. ist nicht in* ~ (*mit*) there is s.th. wrong (with)

'ordnungsgemäß **1.** *adj* correct, regular **2.** *adv* duly, properly

'Ordnungs|strafe *f* JUR fine, penalty; ~zahl *f* MATH ordinal number

Organ [ɔr'ga:n] *n* (-*s*; -*e*) organ; ~empfänger *m* MED organ recipient; ~handel *m* sale of (transplant) organs

Organisation [ɔrganiza'tsjo:n]*f*(-;-*en*) organization; Organisator [ɔrgani-'za:tor] *m* (-*s*; -*en* [ɔrganiza'to:rən]) organizer; Organisa'torin *f* (-; -*nen*) organizer; organisatorisch [ɔrganiza-'to:riʃ] *adj* organizational

organisch [ɔr'ga:niʃ] *adj* organic

organisieren [ɔrgani'zi:rən] *v/t* organize; F get (hold of); *sich* ~ organize; ECON unionize; organisiert [ɔrgani-'zi:ɐt] *adj* organized; ECON unionized

Organismus [ɔrga'nismus] *m* (-; -*men*) BIOL organism

Organist [ɔrga'nist] *m* (-*en*; -*en*), Orga-'nistin *f* (-; -*nen*) MUS organist

Or'ganspender *m* MED (organ) donor

Orgasmus [ɔr'gasmus] *m* (-; -*men*) orgasm

Orgel ['ɔrgəl] f (-; -n) MUS organ

'**Orgelpfeife** f MUS organ pipe

Orgie ['ɔrgjə] f (-; -n) orgy

Orientale [orjɛn'ta:lə] m (-n; -n), **Orien'talin** f (-; -nen), **orien'talisch** adj oriental

orientieren [orjɛn'ti:rən] v/t (no -ge-, h) inform (**über** acc about), brief (on); **sich ~** orient(ate) o.s. (a. fig) (**nach** by); inform o.s.; **Orien'tierung** f (-; no pl) orientation, fig a. information; **die ~ verlieren** lose one's bearings

Orien'tierungssinn m (-[e]s; no pl) sense of direction

original [origi'na:l] adj original; real, genuine; TV live; **Origi'nal** n (-s; -e) original; fig real (or quite a) character

Origi'nal... in cpds ...aufnahme, ...ausgabe etc: original ...; **~übertragung** f live broadcast or program(me)

originell [origi'nɛl] adj original; ingenious; witty

Orkan [ɔr'ka:n] m (-[e]s; -e) hurricane

or'kanartig adj violent; fig thunderous

Ort [ɔrt] m (-[e]s; -e) place; village, (small) town; spot, point; scene; **vor ~ mining**: at the (pit) face; fig in the field, on the spot

orten ['ɔrtən] v/t (ge-, h) locate, spot

orthodox [ɔrto'dɔks] adj orthodox

Orthographie [ɔrtogra'fi:] f (-; -n) orthography

Orthopäde [ɔrto'pɛ:də] m (-n; -n), **Ortho'pädin** f (-; -nen) MED orthop(a)edic specialist

örtlich ['œrtlıç] adj local

'**Ortsbestimmung** f AVIAT, MAR location; LING adverb of place

'**Ortschaft** f → **Ort**

'**Ortsgespräch** n TEL local call

'**Ortskenntnis** f: **~ besitzen** know a place

'**Ortsnetz** n TEL local exchange

'**Ortszeit** f local time

Öse ['øːzə] f (-; -n) eye; eyelet

Ostblock ['ɔstblɔk] m (-[e]s; no pl) HIST POL East(ern) Bloc

Osten ['ɔstən] m (-s; no pl) east; POL the East; **nach ~** east(wards)

Oster|ei ['oːstɐ'ʔai] n Easter egg; **~hase** m Easter bunny or rabbit

Ostern ['oːstɐn] n (-; -) Easter (**zu, an** at); **frohe ~!** Happy Easter!

Österreicher ['øːstəraiçɐ] m (-s; -), '**Österreicherin** ['øːstəraiçərɪn] f (-; -nen), '**österreichisch** adj Austrian

östlich ['œstlıç] **1.** adj east(ern); easterly **2.** adv: **~ von** to the east of

ostwärts ['ɔstvɛrts] adv east(wards)

'**Ostwind** m east wind

Otter ['ɔtɐ] zo **1.** m (-s; -) otter **2.** f (-; -n) adder, viper

outen ['autən] v/t (ge-, h) out

Ouvertüre [uver'ty:rə] f (-; -n) MUS overture

oval [o'va:l] adj, **O'val** n (-s; -e) oval

Oxid [ɔ'ksi:t] n (-[e]s; -e [ɔ'ksi:də]) CHEM oxide; **oxidieren** [ɔksi'di:rən] v/t (no -ge-, h) and v/i (h, sein) CHEM oxidize; **Oxyd** n → **Oxid**

Ozean ['oːtsea:n] m (-s; -e) ocean, sea

Ozon [o'tso:n] n (-s; no pl) CHEM ozone

o'zonfreundlich adj ozone-friendly

O'zon|loch n ozone hole; **~schicht** f ozone layer; **~schild** m ozone shield; **~werte** pl ozone levels

P

paar [pa:ɐ] indef pron: **ein~** a few, some, F a couple of; **ein ~ Mal** a few times

Paar n (-[e]s; -e) pair; couple; **ein ~ (neue) Schuhe** a (new) pair of shoes

paaren [pa:rən] v/t and v/refl (ge-, h) zo mate; fig combine

'**Paarlauf** m SPORT pair skating

'**Paarung** f (-; -en) zo mating, copulation; SPORT matching

'**paarweise** adv in pairs, in twos

Pacht [paxt] f (-; -en) lease; rent

'**pachten** v/t (ge-, h) (take on) lease

Pächter ['pɛçtɐ] m (-s; -), '**Pächterin** f (-; -nen) leaseholder; AGR tenant

'**Pacht|vertrag** m lease; **~zins** m rent

Pack[1] [pak] m → **Packen**

Pack[2] contp n (-[e]s; no pl) rabble

Päckchen ['pɛkçən] n (-s; -) pack, Br

packet; small parcel; **packen** ['pakən] v/t and v/i (ge-, h) pack; make up (parcel etc); grab, seize (**an** dat by); fig grip; '**Packen** m (-s; -) pack, pile (a. fig); **Pa**-**cker** ['pakɐ] m (-s; -) packer; removal man; '**Packpa,pier** n packing or brown paper; '**Packung** f (-; -en) package, box; pack, Br packet

Pädagoge [peda'go:gə] m (-n; -n), **Päda'gogin** f (-; -nen) teacher; education(al)ist

päda'gogisch adj pedagogic, educational; **~e Hochschule** college of education

Paddel ['padəl] n (-s; -) paddle

'**Paddelboot** n canoe

'**paddeln** v/i (ge-, h, sein) paddle, canoe

Page ['pa:ʒə] m (-n; -n) page(boy)

Paket [pa'ke:t] n (-[e]s; -e) package; parcel; **~karte** f parcel post slip, Br parcel mailing form; **~post** f parcel post; **~schalter** m parcel counter; **~zustellung** f parcel delivery

Pakt [pakt] m (-[e]s; -e) POL pact

Palast [pa'last] m (-[e]s; Paläste [pa-'lɛstə]) palace

Palme ['palmə] f (-; -n) BOT palm (tree)

Palm'sonntag m REL Palm Sunday

Pampelmuse ['pampəlmu:zə] f (-; -n) BOT grapefruit

paniert [pa'ni:ɐt] adj GASTR breaded

Panik ['pa:nik] f (-; -en) panic; **in ~ geraten** (**versetzen**) panic; **in ~** panic-stricken, F panicky; **panisch** ['pa:nɪʃ] adj: **~e Angst** mortal terror

Panne ['panə] f (-; -n) breakdown, MOT a. engine trouble; fig mishap

'**Pannenhilfe** f MOT breakdown service

Panter, Panther ['pantɐ] m (-s; -) ZO panther

Pantoffel [pan'tɔfəl] m (-s; -n) slipper; **~held** F m henpecked husband

Pantomime [panto'mi:mə] THEA **1.** f (-; -n) mime, dumb show **2.** m (-n; -n) mime (artist); **panto'mimisch** adv: **~ darstellen** mime

Panzer ['pantsɐ] m (-s; -) armo(u)r (a. fig); MIL tank; ZO shell; **~glas** n bulletproof glass

'**panzern** v/t (ge-, h) armo(u)r; → **gepanzert**

'**Panzerschrank** m safe

Panzerung ['pantsərʊŋ] f (-; -en) armo(u)r plating

Papa [pa'pa:] F m (-s; -s) dad(dy), pa

Papagei [papa'gai] m (-en; -en) ZO parrot

Papeterie [papetə'ri:] Swiss f (-; -n) stationer('s shop)

Papier [pa'pi:ɐ] n (-s; -e) paper; pl papers, documents; identification (paper)

Pa'pier... in cpds ...geld, ...handtuch, ...serviette, ...tüte etc: mst paper ...; **~geschäft** n stationer('s store, Br shop); **~korb** m wastepaper basket; **~krieg** F m red tape; **~schnitzel** pl scraps of paper; **~waren** pl stationery

Pappe ['papə] f (-; -n) cardboard, pasteboard

Pappel ['papəl] f (-; -n) BOT poplar

'**Papp|kar,ton** m cardboard box, carton; **~teller** m paper plate

Paprika ['paprika] m (-s; -[s]) BOT sweet pepper; (no pl) GASTR paprika

Papst [pa:pst] m (-[e]s; Päpste ['pɛ:ps-tə]) pope; '**päpstlich** adj papal

Parade [pa'ra:də] f (-; -n) parade; soccer etc: save; boxing, fencing: parry

Paradeiser [para'daizɐ] Austrian m (-s; -) BOT tomato

Paradies [para'di:s] n (-es; -e) paradise

paradiesisch [para'di:zɪʃ] fig adj heavenly, delightful

paradox [para'dɔks] adj paradoxical

Paragraph [para'gra:f] m (-en; -en) JUR article, section; paragraph

parallel [para'le:l] adj, **Paral'lele** f (-; -n) parallel

Parasit [para'zi:t] m (-en; -en) parasite

Parfüm [par'fy:m] n (-s; -s) perfume, Br a. scent; **Parfümerie** [parfymə'ri:] f (-; -n) perfumery; **parfümieren** [parfy-'mi:rən] v/t (no -ge-, h) perfume, scent; **sich ~** put on perfume

parieren [pa'ri:rən] v/t and v/i (no -ge-, h) SPORT parry, fig a. counter (**mit** with); pull up (horse); obey

Park [park] m (-s; -s) park

parken ['parkən] v/i and v/t (ge-, h) MOT park; **Parken verboten!** no parking!

Parkett [par'kɛt] n (-[e]s; -e, -s) parquet (floor); THEA orchestra, Br stalls; dance floor

'**Park|gebühr** f parking fee; **~(hoch)haus** n parking garage, Br multi-storey car park

parkieren [par'ki:rən] Swiss v/t and v/i

→ **parken**

'Park|kralle f wheel clamp; ~lücke f parking space; ~platz m parking lot, Br car park; → **Parklücke; e-n ~ suchen (finden)** look for (find) somewhere to park the car; ~scheibe f parking disk (Br disc); ~sünder m parking offender; ~uhr f MOT parking meter; ~wächter m park keeper; MOT parking lot (Br car park) attendant

Parlament [parla'mɛnt] n (-[e]s; -e) parliament; parlamentarisch [parlamɛn-'taːrɪʃ] adj parliamentary

Parodie [paro'diː] f (-; -n), paro'dieren v/t (no -ge-, h) parody

Parole [pa'roːlə] f (-n; -n) MIL password; fig watchword, POL a. slogan

Partei [par'tai] f (-; -en) party (a. POL); **j-s ~ ergreifen** take sides with s.o., side with s.o.; par'teiisch adj partial (**für** to); prejudiced (**gegen** against)

par'teilos adj POL independent

Par'tei|mitglied n POL party member; ~pro,gramm n POL platform; ~tag m POL convention; ~zugehörigkeit f POL party membership

Parterre [par'tɛrə] n (-s; -s) first (Br ground) floor

Partie [par'tiː] f (-; -n) game, SPORT a. match; part, passage (a. MUS); **e-e gute etc ~ sein** be a good etc match

Partisan [parti'zaːn] m (-s; -en; -en), Parti'sanin f (-; -nen) MIL partisan, guerilla

Partitur [parti'tuːr] f (-; -en) MUS score

Partizip [parti'tsiːp] n (-s; -ien) LING participle

Partner ['partnɐ] m (-s; -), 'Partnerin f (-; -nen) partner

'Partnerschaft f (-; -en) partnership

'Partnerstadt f twin town

paschen ['paʃən] Austrian v/t and v/i (ge-, h) smuggle; Pascher ['paʃɐ] Austrian m (-s; -) smuggler

Pass [pas] m (-es; Pässe ['pɛsə]) passport; SPORT, GEOGR pass; **langer ~** SPORT long ball

Passage [pa'saːʒə] f (-; -n) passage

Passagier [pasa'ʒiːr] m (-s; -e) passenger; ~flugzeug n passenger plane; airliner

Passa'gierin f (-; -nen) passenger

Passah ['pasa] n (-s; no pl), 'Passahfest n REL Passover

Passant [pa'sant] m (-en; -en), Pas-'santin f (-; -nen) passerby

'Passbild n passport photo(graph)

passen ['pasən] v/i (ge-, h) fit (**j-m** s.o.; **auf** or **für** or **zu et.** s.th.); suit (**j-m** s.o.), be convenient; cards, SPORT pass; **~ zu** go with, match; **sie ~ gut zueinander** they are well suited to each other; **passt es Ihnen morgen?** would tomorrow suit you or be all right (with you)?; **das (es) passt mir gar nicht** I don't like that (him) at all; **das passt (nicht) zu ihm** that's just like him (not like him, not his style); ~d adj fitting; matching; suitable, right

passierbar [pa'siːrbaːr] adj passable

passieren [pa'siːrən] (no -ge-) **1.** v/i (sein) happen **2.** v/t (h) pass (through)

Pas'sierschein m pass, permit

Passion [pa'sjoːn] f (-; -en) passion; REL Passion

passiv ['pasiːf] adj passive

'Passiv n (-s; no pl) LING passive (voice)

Paste ['pastə] f (-; -n) paste

Pastell [pas'tɛl] n (-[e]s; -e) PAINT pastel

Pastete [pas'teːtə] f (-; -n) GASTR pie

Pate ['paːtə] m (-s; -n) godfather; 'Patenkind n godchild

'Patenschaft f (-; -en) sponsorship

Patent [pa'tɛnt] n (-[e]s; -e) patent; MIL commission; ~amt n patent office; ~anwalt m JUR patent agent

patentieren [patɛn'tiːrən] v/t (no -ge-, h) patent; **(sich) et. ~ lassen** take out a patent for s.th.

Pa'tentinhaber m patentee

pathetisch [pa'teːtɪʃ] adj pompous

Patient [pa'tsjɛnt] m (-en; -en), Pa-'tientin f (-; -nen) MED patient

Patin ['paːtɪn] f (-; -nen) godmother

Patriot [patri'oːt] m (-en; -en) patriot

patri'otisch adj patriotic

Patrone [pa'troːnə] f (-; -n) cartridge

Patrouille [pa'truljə] f (-; -n) MIL patrol; patrouillieren [patrul'jiːrən] v/i (no -ge-, h) MIL patrol

Patsche ['patʃə] F f: **in der ~ sitzen** be in a fix or jam

'patschen F v/i (ge-, h) (s)plash

'patsch'nass adj soaking wet

patzen ['patsən] F v/i (ge-, h), Patzer ['patsɐ] F m (-s; -) blunder

Pauke ['paukə] f (-; -n) MUS bass drum; kettledrum

'**pauken** F v/i and v/t (ge-, h) cram

Pauschale [pau'ʃa:lə] f (-; -n) lump sum

Pau'schal|gebühr f flat rate; **~reise** f package tour; **~urteil** n sweeping judg(e)ment

Pause¹ ['pauzə] f (-; -n) recess, Br break, esp THEA, SPORT intermission, Br interval; pause; rest (a. MUS)

'**Pause²** f (-; -n) TECH tracing

'**pausen** v/t (ge-, -n) TECH trace

'**pausenlos** adj uninterrupted, nonstop

'**Pausenzeichen** n radio: interval signal; PED bell

pausieren [pau'zi:rən] v/i (no -ge-, h) pause, rest

Pavian ['pa:vja:n] m (-s; -e) ZO baboon

Pavillon ['paviljoɲ] m (-s; -s) pavilion

Pazifist [patsi'fist] m (-en; -en), Pazi'fistin f (-; -nen), pazi'fistisch adj pacifist

PC [pe:'tse:] m (-[s]; -[s]) abbr of **personal computer** PC

Pech [pɛç] n (-s; no pl) pitch; F bad luck; **~strähne** F f run of bad luck; **~vogel** F m unlucky fellow

pedantisch [pe'dantɪʃ] adj pedantic, fussy

Pegel ['pe:gəl] m (-s; -) level (a. fig)

peilen ['pailən] v/t (ge-, h) sound

peinigen ['painɪgən] v/t (ge-, h) torment

Peiniger ['painɪgɐ] m (-s; -) tormentor

peinlich ['painlɪç] adj embarrassing; **~ genau** meticulous (**bei, in** dat in); **es war mir ~** I was or felt embarrassed

Peitsche ['paitʃə] f (-; -n), '**peitschen** v/t (ge-, h) whip

'**Peitschenhieb** m lash

Pelle ['pɛlə] f (-; -n) skin; peel; '**pellen** v/t (ge-, h) peel; '**Pellkar,toffeln** pl potatoes (boiled) in their jackets

Pelz [pɛlts] m (-es; -e) fur; skin

'**pelzgefüttert** adj fur-lined

'**Pelzgeschäft** n fur(rier's) store (Br shop)

pelzig ['pɛltsɪç] adj furry; MED furred

'**Pelzmantel** m fur coat

'**Pelztiere** pl furred animals, furs

Pendel ['pɛndəl] n (-s; -) pendulum

'**pendeln** v/i (ge-, h) swing; RAIL etc shuttle; commute

'**Pendeltür** f swing door

'**Pendelverkehr** m RAIL etc shuttle service; commuter traffic; **Pendler(in)** ['pɛndlɐ, 'pɛndlərɪn] m(f) (-s; -/-;

-nen) RAIL etc commuter

Penis ['pe:nɪs] m (-s; -se) ANAT penis

Penner ['pɛnɐ] F m (-s; -) tramp, bum

Pension [pa..'sjo:n] f (-; -en) (old age) pension; boarding-house, private hotel; **in ~ sein** be retired; **Pensionär(in)** [pa..sjo'nɛ:ɐ, pa..sjo'nɛ:rɪn] m(f) (-s; -e/-;-nen) (old age) pensioner; boarder; **Pensionat** [pa..sjo'na:t] n (-[e]s; -e) boarding school

pensionieren [pa..sjo'ni:rən] v/t (no -ge-, h) pension (off); **sich ~ lassen** retire; **Pensio'nierung** f (-; -en) retirement

Pensionist [pa..sjo'nist] Austrian, Swiss m (-en; -en) (old age) pensioner

Pensi'onsgast m boarder

Pensum ['pɛnzum] n (-s; Pensen, Pensa) (work) quota, stint

per [pɛr] prp (acc) per; by

perfekt [pɛr'fɛkt] adj perfect; **~ machen** settle

'**Perfekt** n (-s; -e) LING present perfect

Pergament [perga'mɛnt] n (-[e]s; -e) parchment

Periode [pe'rjo:də] f (-; -n) period, MED a. menstruation

periodisch [pe'rjo:dɪʃ] adj periodic(al)

Peripherie [perife'ri:] f (-; -n) periphery, outskirts; **~geräte** pl IT peripheral equipment

Perle ['pɛrlə] f (-; -n) pearl; bead

'**perlen** v/i (ge-, h) sparkle, bubble

'**Perlenkette** f pearl necklace

'**Perlmuschel** f ZO pearl oyster

Perlmutt ['pɛrlmut] n (-s; no pl) mother-of-pearl

Perron [pe'ro..:] m (-s; -s) Swiss platform

Perser ['pɛrzɐ] m (-s; -) Persian; Persian carpet; **Perserin** ['pɛrzərɪn] f (-; -nen) Persian (woman); **Persien** ['pɛrzjən] Persia; **persisch** ['pɛrzɪʃ] adj Persian

Person [pɛr'zo:n] f (-; -en) person, THEA etc a. character; **ein Tisch für drei ~en** a table for three

Personal [pɛrzo'na:l] n (-s; no pl) staff, personnel; **zu wenig ~ haben** be understaffed; **~abbau** m staff reduction; **~abteilung** f personnel department; **~ausweis** m identity card; **~chef** m staff manager

Personalien [pɛrzo'na:ljən] pl particulars, personal data

P

Perso'nalpro,nomen *n* LING personal pronoun

Per'sonen|(kraft)wagen *m* (*Br a.* motor)car, auto(mobile); **~zug** *m* passenger train; local *or* commuter train

personifizieren [pɛrzonifiˈtsiːrən] *v/t* (*no -ge-, h*) personify

persönlich [pɛrˈzøːnlɪç] *adj* personal

Per'sönlichkeit *f* (-; *-en*) personality

Perücke [peˈrʏkə] *f* (-; *-n*) wig

pervers [pɛrˈvɛrs] *adj* perverted; **~er Mensch** pervert

Pessimismus [pɛsiˈmɪsmʊs] *m* (-; *no pl*) pessimism; **Pessimist(in)** [pɛsiˈmɪst(ɪn)] (*-en; -en/-; -nen*) pessimist; **pessi'mistisch** *adj* pessimistic

Pest [pɛst] *f* (-; *no pl*) MED plague

Pestizid [pɛstiˈtsiːt] *n* (*-s; -e*) pesticide

Petersilie [peːtɐˈziːljə] *f* (-; *-n*) BOT parsley

Petroleum [peˈtroːleʊm] *n* (*-s; no pl*) kerosene, *Br* paraffin; **~lampe** *f* kerosene (*Br* paraffin) lamp

petzen [ˈpɛtsən] F *v/i* (*ge-, h*) tell tales, *Br a.* sneak

Pfad [pfaːt] *m* (*-[e]s; -e* [ˈpfaːdə]) path, track; **~finder** *m* boy scout; **~finderin** [ˈpfaːtfɪndərɪn] *f* (-; *-nen*) girl scout, *Br* girl guide

Pfahl [pfaːl] *m* (*-[e]s; Pfähle* [ˈpfɛːlə]) stake; post; pole

Pfand [pfant] *n* (*-[e]s; Pfänder* [ˈpfɛndɐ]) security; pawn, pledge; deposit; forfeit

'Pfandbrief *m* ECON mortgage bond

pfänden [ˈpfɛndən] *v/t* (*ge-, h*) seize

'Pfandhaus *n* → **Leihhaus**

Pfandleiher [ˈpfantlaiɐ] *m* (*-s; -*) pawnbroker

'Pfandschein *m* pawn ticket

'Pfändung *f* (-; *-en*) JUR seizure

Pfanne [ˈpfanə] *f* (-; *-n*) pan, skillet

'Pfannkuchen *m* pancake

Pfarrbezirk [ˈpfarbətsɪrk] *m* parish

Pfarrer [ˈpfarɐ] *m* (*-s; -*) vicar; pastor; (parish) priest

'Pfarr|gemeinde *f* parish; **~haus** *n* parsonage; rectory, vicarage; **~kirche** *f* parish church

Pfau [pfau] *m* (*-[e]s; -en*) ZO peacock

Pfeffer [ˈpfɛfɐ] *m* (*-s; -*) pepper; **~kuchen** *m* gingerbread; **~minze** [ˈpfɛfɐmɪntsə] *f* (-; *no pl*) BOT peppermint

'pfeffern *v/t* (*ge-, h*) pepper

'Pfefferstreuer *m* (*-s; -*) pepper caster

pfeffrig [ˈpfɛfrɪç] *adj* peppery

Pfeife [ˈpfaifə] *f* (-; *-n*) whistle; pipe (*a.* MUS); **'pfeifen** *v/i* and *v/t* (*irr, ge-, h*) whistle (*j-m* to s.o.); F ~ **auf** (*acc*) not give a damn about

Pfeil [pfail] *m* (*-[e]s; -e*) arrow

Pfeiler [ˈpfailɐ] *m* (*-s; -*) pillar; pier

Pfennig [ˈpfɛnɪç] *m* (*-s; -e*) hist (*former monetary unit of Germany*) pfennig; *fig* penny

Pferch [pfɛrç] *m* (*-[e]s; -e*) fold, pen

'pferchen *v/t* (*ge-, h*) cram (*in acc* into)

Pferd [pfeːrt] *n* (*-[e]s; -e*) ZO horse (*a.* SPORT); **zu ~e** on horseback

Pferde|geschirr [ˈpfeːrdəgəʃɪr] *n* harness; **~koppel** *f* paddock; **~rennen** *n* horserace; **~stall** *m* stable; **~stärke** *f* TECH horsepower; **~wagen** *m* (horse-drawn) carriage

pfiff [pfɪf] *pret of* **pfeifen**

Pfiff *m* (*-[e]s; -e*) whistle

pfiffig [ˈpfɪfɪç] *adj* smart

Pfingsten [ˈpfɪŋstən] *n* (-; *-*) REL Pentecost, *Br* Whitsun (**zu, an** *at*)

'Pfingst'montag *m* REL Whit Monday

'Pfingstrose *f* BOT peony

Pfingst'sonntag *m* REL Pentecost, *Br* Whit Sunday

Pfirsich [ˈpfɪrzɪç] *m* (*-s; -e*) BOT peach

Pflanze [ˈpflantsə] *f* (-; *-n*) plant; **~n fressend** ZO herbivorous

'pflanzen *v/t* (*ge-, h*) plant

'Pflanzenfett *n* vegetable fat

'pflanzlich *adj* vegetable

'Pflanzung *f* (-; *-en*) plantation

Pflaster [ˈpflastɐ] *n* (*-s; -*) pavement; MED Band-Aid®, *Br* plaster

'pflastern *v/t* (*ge-, h*) pave

'Pflasterstein *m* paving stone

Pflaume [ˈpflaumə] *f* (-; *-n*) BOT plum

Pflege [ˈpfleːgə] *f* (-; *no pl*) care; MED nursing; fig cultivation; TECH maintenance; *j-n in ~ nehmen* take s.o. into one's care; **~...** *in cpds* ...eltern, ...kind, ...sohn *etc*: foster ...; ...heim, ...kosten, ...personal *etc*: nursing ...

'pflegebedürftig *adj* needing care

'Pflegefall *m* constant-care patient

'pflegeleicht *adj* wash-and-wear, easy--care

'pflegen *v/t* (*ge-, h*) care for, look after, *esp* MED *a.* nurse; TECH maintain; fig cultivate; keep up (*custom etc*); **sie pflegte zu sagen** she used to or would say; **Pfleger** ['pfle:gɐ] m (-s; -) male nurse; **Pflegerin** ['pfle:gərɪn] f (-; -nen) nurse; **'Pflegestelle** f nursing place

Pflicht [pflɪçt] f (-; -en) duty (**gegen** to); SPORT compulsory events

'pflichtbewusst adj conscientious

'Pflicht|bewusstsein n sense of duty; **~erfüllung** f performance of one's duty; **~fach** n PED compulsory subject

'pflichtgemäß, **~getreu** adj dutiful; **~vergessen** adv: **~ handeln** neglect one's duty

'Pflichtversicherung f compulsory insurance

Pflock ['pflɔk] m (-[e]s; Pflöcke ['pflœkə]) peg, pin; plug

pflücken ['pflʏkən] v/t (ge-, h) pick, gather

Pflug [pflu:k] m (-[e]s; Pflüge ['pfly:gə]), **pflügen** ['pfly:gən] v/t and v/i (ge-, h) plow, Br plough

Pforte ['pfɔrtə] f (-; -n) gate, door, entrance; **Pförtner** ['pfœrtnɐ] m (-s; -) doorman, doorkeeper, porter

Pfosten ['pfɔstən] m (-s; -) post

Pfote ['pfo:tə] f (-; -n) zo paw (a. F)

pfropfen ['pfrɔpfən] v/t (ge-, h) stopper; cork; plug; AGR graft; F cram, stuff

'Pfropfen m (-s; -) stopper; cork; plug; MED clot

pfui [pfui] int ugh!; *audience*: boo!

Pfund [pfʊnt] n (-[e]s; -e ['pfʊndə]) pound (453,59 g); pound (sterling); **10 ~** ten pounds

'pfundweise adv by the pound

pfuschen ['pfʊʃən] F v/i (ge-, h), **Pfuscherei** [pfʊʃəˈrai] F f (-; -en) bungle, botch

Pfütze ['pfʏtsə] f (-; -n) puddle, pool

Phänomen [feno'me:n] n (-s; -e) phenomenon; **phänomenal** [fenomeˈnaːl] adj phenomenal

Phantasie etc → **Fantasie** etc

pharmazeutisch [farma'tsɔʏtɪʃ] adj pharmaceutic(al)

Phase ['fa:zə] f (-; -n) phase (a. ELECTR), stage

Philosoph [filo'zo:f] m (-en; -en) philosopher; **Philosophie** [filozo'fi:] f (-; -n) philosophy; **philosophieren** [filozo'fi:rən] v/i (no -ge-, h) philoso-

phize (**über** acc on); **Philo'sophin** f (-; -nen) (woman) philosopher; **philosophisch** [filo'zo:fɪʃ] adj philosophical

phlegmatisch [fle'gma:tɪʃ] adj phlegmatic

Phonetik [fo'ne:tɪk] f (-; no pl) phonetics; **pho'netisch** adj phonetic

Phosphor ['fɔsfo:ɐ] m (-s; -e) CHEM phosphorus

Photo... → **Foto...**

Phrase ['fra:zə] contp f (-; -n) cliché (phrase)

Physik [fy'zi:k] f (-; no pl) physics

physikalisch [fyziˈkaːlɪʃ] adj physical

Physiker ['fy:zikɐ] m (-s; -), **'Physikerin** f (-; -nen) physicist

physisch ['fy:zɪʃ] adj physical

Pianist [pja'nɪst] m (-en; -en), **Pia-'nistin** f (-; -nen) MUS pianist

Piano ['pja:no] n (-s; -s) MUS piano

Picke ['pɪkə] f (-; -n) TECH pick(axe)

Pickel[1] ['pɪkəl] m (-s; -) TECH pick(axe)

Pickel[2] m (-s; -) MED pimple; **pickelig** ['pɪkəlɪç] adj MED pimpled, pimply

picken ['pɪkən] v/i and v/t (ge-, h) zo peck, pick

Picknick ['pɪknɪk] n (-s; -e, -s) picnic

'picknicken v/i (ge-, h) (have a) picnic

piekfein ['pi:kfain] F adj posh

piep(s)en ['pi:p(s)ən] v/i (ge-, h) chirp, cheep; ELECTR bleep

Pietät [pjeˈtɛːt] f (-; no pl) reverence; piety; **pie'tätlos** adj irreverent; **pie-'tätvoll** adj reverent

Pik [pi:k] n (-s; -[s], -[s]) *cards*: spade(s)

pikant [pi'kant] adj piquant, spicy (*both a. fig*)

Pilger ['pɪlgɐ] m (-s; -) pilgrim; **'Pilgerfahrt** f pilgrimage; **'Pilgerin** f (-; -nen) pilgrim; **'pilgern** v/i (ge-, sein) (go on a) pilgrimage

Pille ['pɪlə] f (-; -n) pill; F **die ~ nehmen** be on the pill

Pilot [pi'lo:t] m (-en; -en), **Pi'lotin** f (-; -nen) pilot

Pilz [pɪlts] m (-es; -e) BOT mushroom (a. fig); toadstool; MED fungus; **~e suchen (gehen)** go mushrooming

Pinguin ['pɪŋgui:n] m (-s; -e) zo penguin

pinkeln ['pɪŋkəln] F v/i (ge-, h) (have a) pee, piddle

Pinsel ['pɪnzəl] m (-s; -) (paint)brush

P

'Pinselstrich *m* brushstroke

Pinzette [pɪn'tsɛtə] *f* (-; -n) tweezers

Pionier [pjo'niːɐ] *m* (-s; -e) pioneer, MIL *a.* engineer

Pirat [pi'raːt] *m* (-en; -en) pirate

Pisse ['pɪsə] V *f* (-; *no pl*), 'pissen V *v/i* (*ge-*, *h*) piss

Piste ['pɪstə] *f* (-; -n) course; AVIAT runway

Pistole [pɪs'toːlə] *f* (-; -n) pistol, gun

Pkw, PKW ['peːkaːveː] *abbr of* Personenkraftwagen (*Br a.* motor)car, automobile

Plache ['plaxə] *Austrian f* (-; -n) awning, tarpaulin

placieren *etc* → platzieren *etc*

plädieren [plɛ'diːrən] *v/i* (*no -ge-*, *h*) JUR plead (für for); Plädoyer [plɛdoa'jeː] *n* (-s; -s) JUR final speech, pleading

Plage ['plaːgə] *f* (-; -n) trouble, misery; plague; nuisance, F pest; 'plagen *v/t* (*ge-*, *h*) trouble; bother; pester; sich ~ toil, drudge

Plakat [pla'kaːt] *n* (-[e]s; -e) poster, placard, bill

Plakette [pla'kɛtə] *f* (-; -n) plaque, badge

Plan [plaːn] *m* (-[e]s; Pläne ['plɛːnə]) plan; intention

Plane ['plaːnə] *f* (-; -n) awning, tarpaulin

'planen *v/t* (*ge-*, *h*) plan, make plans for

Planet [pla'neːt] *m* (-en; -en) ASTR planet

planieren [pla'niːrən] *v/t* (*no -ge-*, *h*) TECH level, plane, grade

Planke ['plaŋkə] *f* (-; -n) plank, (thick) board

plänkeln ['plɛŋkəln] *v/i* (*ge-*, *h*) skirmish

'planlos *adj* without plan; aimless

'planmäßig 1. *adj* scheduled (*arrival etc*) 2. *adv* according to plan

Plan(t)schbecken ['planʃbɛkən] *n* paddling pool

plan(t)schen ['planʃən] *v/i* (*ge-*, *h*) splash

Plantage [plan'taːʒə] *f* (-; -n) plantation

Plappermaul ['plapɐmaul] F *n* chatterbox

plappern ['plapɐn] F *v/i* (*ge-*, *h*) chatter, prattle, babble, jabber

plärren ['plɛrən] F *v/i and v/t* (*ge-*, *h*) blubber; bawl; *radio:* blare

Plastik¹ ['plastɪk] *f* (-; -en) sculpture

'Plastik² *n* (-s; *no pl*) plastic; ~... *in cpds* ...besteck *etc*: plastic ...

plastisch ['plastɪʃ] *adj* plastic; three-dimensional; *fig* graphic

Platin ['plaːtiːn] *n* (-s; *no pl*) platinum

plätschern ['plɛtʃɐn] *v/i* (*ge-*, *h*) ripple (*a. fig*), splash

platt [plat] *adj* flat, level, even; *fig* trite; F flabbergasted

Platte ['platə] *f* (-; -n) sheet, plate; slab; board; panel; MUS record, disk, *Br* disc; IT disk; GASTR dish; F bald pate; kalte ~ GASTR plate of cold cuts (*Br* meats)

plätten ['plɛtən] *v/t* (*ge-*, *h*) iron, press

'Platten|spieler *m* record player; ~teller *m* turntable

'Plattform *f* platform

'Plattfuß *m* MED flat foot

'Plattheit *fig f* (-; -en) triviality; platitude

Plättli ['plɛtli] *Swiss n* (-s; -s) tile

Platz [plats] *m* (-es; Plätze ['plɛtsə]) place, spot; site; room, space; square; circus; seat; es ist (nicht) genug ~ there's (there isn't) enough room; ~ machen für make room for; make way for; ~ nehmen take a seat, sit down; ist dieser ~ noch frei? is this seat taken?; j-n vom ~ stellen SPORT send s.o. off; auf eigenem ~ SPORT at home; auf die Plätze, fertig, los! SPORT on your marks, get set, go!

'Platz|anweiser *m* (-s; -) usher; ~anweiserin *f* (-; -nen) usherette

Plätzchen ['plɛtsçən] *n* (-s; -) (little) place, spot; GASTR cookie, *Br* biscuit

platzen ['platsən] *v/i* (*ge-*, *sein*) burst (*a. fig*); crack, split; explode (*a. fig* vor *dat* with), blow up; F come to grief or nothing, fall through, blow up, *sl* go phut; break up

platzieren [pla'tsiːrən] *v/t* (*no -ge-*, *h*) place; sich ~ SPORT be placed

Plat'zierung *f* (-; -en) place, placing

'Platzkarte *f* reservation (ticket)

Plätzli ['plɛtsli] *Swiss n* (-s; -) cutlet

'Platz|pa,trone *f* blank (cartridge); ~regen *m* cloudburst, downpour; ~reservierung *f* seat reservation; ~verweis *m*: e-n ~ erhalten SPORT be sent off; ~wart *m* (-s; -e) SPORT groundkeeper, *Br* groundsman; ~wunde *f* MED cut, laceration

Plauderei [plaudə'rai] *f* (-; -en) chat

plaudern ['plaudɐn] *v/i* (*ge-*, *h*) (have a) chat

plauschen ['plauʃən] *Austrian v/i* (have a) chat

pleite ['plaitə] F *adj* broke

'**Pleite** F *f* (-; -*n*) bankruptcy; *fig* flop; **pleitegehen** go broke

Plombe ['plɔmbə] *f* (-; -*n*) TECH seal; MED filling; **plombieren** [plɔm'biːrən] *v/t* (*no* -*ge*-, *h*) TECH seal; MED fill

plötzlich ['plœtslɪç] **1.** *adj* sudden **2.** *adv* suddenly, all of a sudden

plump [plump] *adj* clumsy; **plumps** *int* thud, plop; **plumpsen** ['plumpsən] *v/i* (*ge*-, *sein*) thud, plop, flop

Plunder ['plundə] F *m* (-*s*; *no pl*) trash, junk

Plünderer ['plyndərə] *m* (-*s*; -) looter, plunderer; **plündern** ['plyndən] *v/i and v/t* (*ge*-, *h*) plunder, loot

Plural ['pluːraːl] *m* (-*s*; -*e*) LING plural

plus [plus] *adv* plus

Plusquamperfekt ['pluskvamperfɛkt] *n* (-*s*; -*e*) LING past perfect

Pneu [pnɔy] *Swiss m* (-*s*; -*s*) tire, *Br* tyre

Po [poː] F *m* (-*s*; -*s*) bottom, behind

Pöbel ['pøːbəl] *m* (-*s*; *no pl*) mob, rabble

pochen ['pɔxən] *v/i* (*ge*-, *h*) knock, rap (*both*: **an** *acc* at)

Pocke ['pɔkə] *f* (-; -*n*) MED pock

'**Pocken** *pl* MED smallpox; ~**impfung** *f* MED smallpox vaccination

Podest [po'dɛst] *n, m* (-[*e*]*s*; -*e*) platform; *fig* pedestal

Podium ['poːdjum] *n* (-*s*; -*ien*) podium, platform; '**Podiumsdiskussi,on** *f* panel discussion

Poesie [poe'ziː] *f* (-; -*n*) poetry

Poet [po'eːt] *m* (-*en*; -*en*), **Po'etin** *f* (-; -*nen*) poet

poetisch [po'eːtɪʃ] *adj* poetic(al)

Pointe ['poɛ̃ːtə] *f* (-; -*n*) point, punch line

Pokal [po'kaːl] *m* (-*s*; -*e*) goblet; SPORT cup; ~**endspiel** *n* SPORT cup final; ~**sieger** *m* SPORT cup winner; ~**spiel** *n* SPORT cup tie

pökeln ['pøːkəln] *v/t* (*ge*-, *h*) salt

Pol [poːl] *m* (-*s*; -*e*) GEOGR pole

polar [po'laːɐ] *adj* polar

Pole ['poːlə] *m* (-*n*; -*n*) Pole

Polemik [po'leːmɪk] *f* (-; -*en*) polemic(s); **po'lemisch** *adj* polemic(al)

polemisieren [polemi'ziːrən] *v/i* (*no* -*ge*-, *h*) polemize

'**Polen** Poland

Police [po'liːsə] *f* (-; -*n*) policy

Polier [po'liːɐ] *m* (-*s*; -*e*) TECH foreman

polieren [po'liːrən] *v/t* (*no* -*ge*-, *h*) polish

Polin ['poːlɪn] *f* (-; -*nen*) Pole, Polish woman

Politik [poli'tiːk] *f* (-; *no pl*) politics; policy (*a. fig*); **Politiker(in)** [po'liːtikɐ, po-'liːtikərɪn] *m(f)* (-*s*; -/-; -*nen*) politician; **politisch** [po'liːtɪʃ] *adj* political; **politisieren** [politi'ziːrən] *v/i* (*no* -*ge*-, *h*) talk politics

Polizei [poli'tsai] *f* (-; *no pl*) police; ~**auto** *n* police car; ~**beamt|e** *m*, -**in** *f* police officer

poli'zeilich *adj* (of or by the) police

Poli'zei|prä,sidium *n* police headquarters; ~**re,vier** *n* police station; precinct, *Br* district; ~**schutz** *m*: **unter ~** under police guard; ~**streife** *f* police patrol; ~**stunde** *f* closing time; ~**wache** *f* police station

Polizist [poli'tsɪst] *m* (-*en*; -*en*) policeman; **Poli'zistin** *f* (-; -*nen*) policewoman

polnisch ['pɔlnɪʃ] *adj* Polish

Polster ['pɔlstə] *n* (-*s*; -) upholstery; cushion; pad(ding); *fig* bolster; ~**garni,tur** *f* three-piece suite; ~**möbel** *pl* upholstered furniture

'**polstern** *v/t* (*ge*-, *h*) upholster; pad

'**Polster|sessel** *m* easy chair, armchair; ~**stuhl** *m* upholstered chair

Polsterung ['pɔlstəruŋ] *f* (-; -*en*) upholstery; padding

poltern ['pɔltən] *v/i* (*ge*-, *h*) rumble; *fig* bluster

Pommes frites [pɔm'frɪt] *pl* French fries, French fried potatoes, *Br* chips

Pomp [pɔmp] *m* (-[*e*]*s*; *no pl*) pomp

pompös [pɔm'pøːs] *adj* showy

Pony[1] ['pɔni] *n* (-*s*; -*s*) ZO pony

'**Pony**[2] *m* (-*s*; -*s*) fringe, bangs

Popgruppe ['pɔpgrupə] *f* MUS pop group

'**Popmu,sik** *f* pop music

populär [popu'lɛːɐ] *adj* popular

Popularität [populari'tɛːt] *f* (-; *no pl*) popularity

Pore ['poːrə] *f* (-; -*n*) pore

Porno ['pɔrno] F *m* (-*s*; -*s*), ~**film** *m* porn (film), blue movie; ~**heft** *n* porn magazine

porös [po'røːs] *adj* porous

Portemonnaie [pɔrtmɔ'neː] *n* (-*s*; -*s*)

P

purse
Portier [por'tje:] *m* (-s; -s) doorman, porter
Portion [por'tsjo:n] *f* (-; -en) portion, share; helping, serving
Portmonee *n* → *Portemonnaie*
Porto ['porto] *n* (-s; -s, -ti) postage
Porträt [por'tre:] *n* (-s; -s) portrait
porträtieren [portre'ti:rən] *v/t* (*no -ge-, h*) portray
Portugal ['portugal] Portugal
Portugiese [portu'gi:zə] *m* (-n; -n), **Portu'giesin** *f* (-; -nen), **portu'giesisch** *adj* Portuguese
Porzellan [portse'la:n] *n* (-s; -e) china, porcelain
Posaune [po'zaunə] *f* (-; -n) MUS trombone; *fig* trumpet
Pose ['po:zə] *f* (-; -n) pose, attitude
Position [pozi'tsjo:n] *f* (-; -en) position (*a. fig*)
positiv ['po:ziti:f] *adj* positive
possessiv [pose'si:f] *adj* LING possessive; **Posses'sivpro,nomen** *n* LING possessive pronoun
Post® [post] *f* (-; *no pl*) mail, *esp Br* post; letters; **mit der Post®** by post *or* mail; **Postamt** *n* post office; **Postanweisung** *f* money order; **Postbote** *m* mailman, *Br* postman
Posten ['postən] *m* (-s; -) post; job, position; MIL sentry; ECON item; lot, parcel
'Postfach *n* (PO) box
postieren [pos'ti:rən] *v/t* (*no -ge-, h*) post, station, place; **sich ~** station o.s.
'Postkarte *f* postcard
'Postkutsche *f* stagecoach
'postlagernd *adj* (in care of) general delivery, *Br* poste restante
'Postleitzahl *f* zip code, *Br* post(al) code; **~sparbuch** *n* post-office savings book; **~stempel** *m* postmark
'postwendend *adv* by return mail, *Br* by return (of post)
'Postwertzeichen *n* (postage) stamp; **~zustellung** *f* postal *or* mail delivery
Potenz [po'tents] *f* (-; -en) (*no pl*) MED potency; MATH power
Pracht [praxt] *f* (-; *no pl*) splendo(u)r, magnificence
prächtig ['preçtiç] *adj* splendid, magnificent, *fig a.* great, super
Prädikat [predi'ka:t] *n* (-[e]s; -e) LING

predicate
prägen ['pre:gən] *v/t* (*ge-, h*) stamp, coin (*a. fig*)
prahlen ['pra:lən] *v/i* (*ge-, h*) brag, boast (*both:* **mit** of), talk big, show off; **Prahler** ['pra:lə] *m* (-s; -) boaster, braggart; **Prahlerei** [pra:lə'rai] *f* (-; -en) boasting, bragging; **'prahlerisch** *adj* boastful; showy
Praktikant [prakti'kant] *m* (-en; -en), **Prakti'kantin** *f* (-; -nen) trainee; **Praktiken** ['praktikən] *pl* practices; **'Praktikum** *n* (-s; -ka) practical training; **'praktisch 1.** *adj* practical; useful, handy; **~er Arzt** general practitioner **2.** *adv* practically; virtually; **praktizieren** [prakti'tsi:rən] *v/t* (*no -ge-, h*) practice (*Br* practise) medicine *or* law
Prälat [pre'la:t] *m* (-en; -en) REL prelate
Praline [pra'li:nə] *f* (-; -n) chocolate
prall [pral] *adj* tight; well-rounded; bulging; blazing (*sun*)
prallen ['pralən] *v/i* (*ge-, sein*) **~ gegen** (*or* **auf** acc) crash *or* bump into
Prämie ['pre:mjə] *f* (-; -n) premium; prize; bonus; **prämieren** [pre'mi:rən], **prämiieren** [premi'i:rən] *v/t* (*no -ge-, h*) award a prize to
Pranke ['praŋkə] *f* (-; -n) zo paw (*a. F*)
Präparat [prepa'ra:t] *n* (-[e]s; -e) preparation
präparieren [prepa'ri:rən] *v/t* (*no -ge-, h*) prepare; MED, BOT, ZO dissect
Präposition [prepozi'tsjo:n] *f* (-; -en) LING preposition
Prärie [pre'ri:] *f* (-; -n) prairie
Präsens ['pre:zens] *n* (-; -sentia [pre-'zentsja]) LING present (tense)
präsentieren [prezen'ti:rən] *v/t* (*no -ge-, h*) present; offer
Präservativ [prezerva'ti:f] *n* (-s; -e) condom
Präsident [prezi'dent] *m* (-en; -en), **Präsi'dentin** *f* (-; -nen) president; chairman (chairwoman); **präsidieren** [prezi'di:rən] *v/i* preside (**in** dat over)
Präsidium [pre'zi:djum] *n* (-s; -ien) presidency
prasseln ['prasəln] *v/i* (*ge-, h*) rain etc: patter; *fire:* crackle
Präteritum [pre'te:ritum] *n* (-s; -ta) LING past (tense)
Praxis ['praksis] *f* (-; *Praxen*) (*no pl*) practice (*a.* MED, JUR); MED doctor's of-

fice, *Br* surgery

Präzedenzfall [prɛtse'dɛntsfal] *m* precedent

präzis [prɛ'tsiːs], **präzise** [prɛ'tsiːzə] *adj* precise; **Präzision** [prɛtsi'zjoːn] *f* (-; *no pl*) precision

predigen ['preːdɪgən] *v/i and v/t* (*ge-, h*) preach

Prediger ['preːdɪgɐ] *m* (-s; -), 'Predigerin *f* (-; -nen) preacher

Predigt ['preːdɪçt] *f* (-; -en) sermon

Preis [prais] *m* (-es; -e) price (*a. fig*); prize; *film etc*: award; reward; **um je-den ~** at all costs

'**Preisausschreiben** *n* competition

Preiselbeere ['praizəlbeːrə] *f* BOT cranberry

preisen ['praizən] *v/t* (*irr, ge-, h*) praise

'**Preiserhöhung** *f* rise *or* increase in price(s)

'**preisgeben** *v/t* (*irr, geben, sep, -ge-, h*) abandon; reveal, give away

'**preisgekrönt** *adj* prize-winning; *film etc*: award-winning

'**Preis|gericht** *n* jury; ~lage *f* price range; ~liste *f* price list; ~nachlass *m* discount; ~rätsel *n* competition; ~richter(in) judge; ~schild *n* price tag; ~stopp *m* price freeze; ~träger(in) prizewinner

'**preiswert** *adj* cheap

prellen ['prɛlən] *v/t* (*ge-, h*) *fig* cheat (**um** out of); **sich et. ~** MED bruise s.th.; 'Prellung *f* (-; -en) MED contusion, bruise

Premiere [prə'mjeːrə] *f* (-; -n) THEA *etc* first night, première

Premierminister [prə'mjeːminɪstɐ] *m*, Pre'miermi,nisterin [prə-'mjeːminɪstərɪn] *f* prime minister

Presse ['prɛsə] *f* (-; -n) (*no pl*) press; squeezer; ~... *in cpds* ...agentur, ...konferenz, ...fotograf *etc*: press ...; ~freiheit *f* freedom of the press; ~meldung *f* news item

'**pressen** *v/t* (*ge-, h*) press; squeeze

'**Presse|tri,büne** *f* press box; ~vertreter *m* reporter

'**Pressluft** *f* compressed air; ~... *in cpds* ...bohrer, ...hammer *etc*: pneumatic ...

Prestige [prɛs'tiːʒə] *n* (-s; *no pl*) prestige; ~verlust *m* loss of prestige *or* face

Preuße ['prɔʏsə] *m* (-n; -n), 'Preußin *f* (-; -nen), 'preußisch *adj* Prussian

prickeln ['prɪkəln] *v/i* (*ge-, h*) prickle; tingle

pries [priːs] *pret of* **preisen**

Priester ['priːstɐ] *m* (-s; -) priest; Priesterin ['priːstərɪn] *f* (-; -nen) priestess; 'priesterlich *adj* priestly

prima ['priːma] F *adj* great, super

primär [pri'mɛːɐ] *adj* primary

Primar|arzt [pri'maːɐʔaːɐtst] *Austrian m → Oberarzt*; ~schule *Swiss f → Grundschule*

Primel ['priːməl] *f* (-; -n) BOT primrose

primitiv [primi'tiːf] *adj* primitive

Prinz [prɪnts] *m* (-en; -en) prince

Prinzessin [prɪn'tsɛsɪn] *f* (-; -nen) princess

'**Prinzgemahl** *m* prince consort

Prinzip [prɪn'tsiːp] *n* (-s; -ien) principle (**aus** on; **im** in); prinzipiell [prɪntsi-'pjel] *adv* as a matter of principle

Prise ['priːzə] *f* (-; -n) **e-e ~ Salz** *etc* a pinch of salt *etc*

Prisma ['prɪsma] *n* (-s; -men) prism

Pritsche ['prɪtʃə] *f* (-; -n) plank bed; MOT platform

privat [pri'vaːt] *adj* private; personal

Pri'vat... *in cpds* ...leben, ...schule, ...detektiv *etc*: private ...; ~angelegenheit *f* personal *or* private matter *or* affair; **das ist m-e ~** that's my own business

Privileg [privi'leːk] *n* (-[e]s; -gien [privi-'leːgjən]) privilege

pro [proː] *prp* (*acc*) per; **2 Euro ~ Stück** two euros each

Pro *n*: **das ~ und Kontra** the pros and cons

Probe ['proːbə] *f* (-; -n) trial, test; sample; THEA rehearsal; MATH proof; **auf ~** on probation; **auf die ~ stellen** put to the test; ~alarm *m* test alarm, fire drill; ~aufnahmen *pl film*: screen test; ~fahrt *f* test drive; ~flug *m* test flight

'**proben** *v/i and v/t* (*ge-, h*) THEA *etc* rehearse

'**probeweise** *adv* on trial; on probation

'**Probezeit** *f* (time of) probation

probieren [pro'biːrən] *v/t* (*no -ge-, h*) try; taste

Problem [pro'bleːm] *n* (-s; -e) problem

problematisch [proble'maːtɪʃ] *adj* problematic(al)

Produkt [pro'dʊkt] *n* (-[e]s; -e) product (*a.* MATH); result

Produktion [produk'tsjo:n] *f* (-; *-en*)
production; output

produktiv [produk'ti:f] *adj* productive

Produktivität [produktivi'tɛ:t] *f* (-; *no pl*) productivity

Produzent [produ'tsɛnt] *m* (*-en*; *-en*), **Produ'zentin** *f* (-; *-nen*) producer;**produzieren** [produ'tsi:rən] *v/t* (*no -ge-*, *h*) produce

professionell [profɛsjo'nɛl] *adj* professional

Professor [pro'fɛso:ɐ] *m* (*-s*; *-en* [profɛ'so:rən]), **Profes'sorin** *f* (-; *-nen*) professor

Professur [profɛ'su:ɐ] *f* (-; *-en*) professorship, chair (*für* of)

Profi ['pro:fi] *m* (*-s*; *-s*) pro;**...** *in cpds* **...boxer, ...fußballer** *etc*: professional

Profil [pro'fi:l] *n* (*-s*; *-e*) profile; MOT tread; **profilieren** [profi'li:rən] *v/refl* (*no -ge-*, *h*) distinguish o.s.

Profit [pro'fi:t] *m* (*-[e]s*; *-e*) profit

profitieren [profi'ti:rən] *v/i* (*no -ge-*, *h*) profit (*von* or *bei et.* from or by s.th.)

Prognose [pro'gno:zə] *f* (-; *-n*) prediction; METEOR forecast; MED prognosis

Programm [pro'gram] *n* (*-s*; *-e*) program(me *Br*), TV *a.* channel; IT program;**~fehler** *m* IT program error, bug

programmieren [progra'mi:rən] *v/t* (*no -ge-*, *h*) program (*a.* IT)

Programmierer [progra'mi:rɐ] *m* (*-s*; *-*),**Program'miererin** *f* (-; *-nen*) IT programmer

Projekt [pro'jɛkt] *n* (*-[e]s*; *-e*) project

Projektion [projɛk'tsjo:n] *f* (-; *-en*) projection;**Projektor** [pro'jɛkto:ɐ] *m* (*-s*; *-en* [projɛk'to:rən]) projector

proklamieren [prokla'mi:rən] *v/t* (*no -ge-*, *h*) proclaim

Prokurist [proku'rɪst] *m* (*-en*; *-en*), **Proku'ristin** *f* (-; *-nen*) authorized signatory

Proletarier [prole'ta:rjɐ] *m* (*-s*; *-*),**proletarisch** [prole'ta:rɪʃ] *adj* proletarian

Prolog [pro'lo:k] *m* (*-[e]s*; *-e*) prologue

Promillegrenze [pro'mɪləgrɛntsə] *f* (blood) alcohol limit

prominent [promi'nɛnt] *adj* prominent

Prominenz [promi'nɛnts] *f* (-; *no pl*) notables; high society

Promotion [promo'tsjo:n] *f* (-; *-en*) UNIV doctorate;**promovieren** [promo'vi:rən] *v/i* (*no -ge-*, *h*) do one's doctorate

prompt [prɔmpt] *adj* prompt; quick

Pronomen [pro'no:mən] *n* (*-s*; *-mina*) LING pronoun

Propeller [pro'pɛlɐ] *m* (*-s*; *-*) propeller

Prophet [pro'fe:t] *m* (*-en*; *-en*) prophet; **pro'phetisch** *adj* prophetic

prophezeien [profe'tsaiən] *v/t* (*no -ge-*, *h*) prophesy, predict; **Prophe'zeiung** *f* (-; *-en*) prophecy, prediction

Proportion [propor'tsjo:n] *f* (-; *-en*) proportion

Proporz [pro'pɔrts] *m* (*-es*; *-e*) POL proportional representation

Prosa ['pro:za] *f* (-; *no pl*) prose

Prospekt [pro'spɛkt] *m* (*-[e]s*; *-e*) prospectus; brochure, pamphlet

prost [pro:st] *int* cheers!

Prostituierte [prostitu'i:rtə] *f* (*-n*; *-n*) prostitute

Protest [pro'tɛst] *m* (*-[e]s*; *-e*) protest; **aus ~** in (or as a) protest

Protestant [protɛs'tant] *m* (*-en*; *-en*), **Protes'tantin** *f* (-; *-nen*), **protes'tantisch** *adj* REL Protestant

protestieren [protɛs'ti:rən] *v/i* (*no -ge-*, *h*) protest

Prothese [pro'te:zə] *f* (-; *-n*) MED artificial limb; denture

Protokoll [proto'kɔl] *n* (*-s*; *-e*) record, minutes; protocol; (*das*) **~ führen** take *or* keep the minutes; **zu ~ nehmen** JUR record;**~führer** *m* keeper of the minutes

protokollieren [protoko'li:rən] *v/t and v/i* (*no -ge-*, *h*) take the minutes (of); JUR record

protzen ['prɔtsən] F *v/i* (*ge-*, *h*) show off (*mit et.* s.th.)

protzig ['prɔtsɪç] *adj* showy, flashy

Proviant [pro'vjant] *m* (*-s*; *no pl*) provisions, food

Provinz [pro'vɪnts] *f* (-; *-en*) province; *fig* country; **provinziell** [provɪn'tsjɛl] *adj* provincial (*a. contp*)

Provision [provi'zjo:n] *f* (-; *-en*) ECON commission

provisorisch [provi'zo:rɪʃ] *adj* provisional, temporary

provozieren [provo'tsi:rən] *v/t* (*no -ge-*, *h*) provoke

Prozent [pro'tsɛnt] *n* (*-[e]s*; *-e*) per cent; F *pl* discount;**~satz** *m* percentage

prozentual [protsɛn'tua:l] *adj* proportional; **~er Anteil** percentage

Prozess [pro'tsɛs] *m* (*-es*; *-e*) process (*a.* TECH, CHEM *etc*); JUR action; case; trial; *j-m den ~ machen* take s.o. to court; *e-n ~ gewinnen (verlieren)* win (lose) a case; **prozessieren** [protse'si:rən] *v/i* (*no -ge-*, *h*) JUR go to court; *gegen j-n ~* bring an action against s.o., take s.o. to court

Prozession [protse'sjo:n] *f* (*-; -en*) procession

Prozessor [pro'tsɛso:ɐ] *m* (*-s*; *-en* [protse'so:rən]) IT processor

prüde ['pry:də] *adj* prudish; *~ sein* be a prude

prüfen ['pry:fən] *v/t* (*ge-*, *h*) PED *etc* examine, test (*a.* TECH); check; inspect (*a.* TECH); *fig* consider; **~d** *adj* searching

Prüfer ['pry:fɐ] *m* (*-s*; *-*), **'Prüferin** *f* (*-; -nen*) PED *etc* examiner; *esp* TECH tester

Prüfling ['pry:flɪŋ] *m* (*-s*; *-e*) candidate

'Prüfstein *m* touchstone (*für* of)

'Prüfung *f* (*-; -en*) examination, F exam; test; check(ing), inspection; *e-e machen (bestehen, nicht bestehen)* take (pass, fail) an exam(ination)

'Prüfungsarbeit *f* examination *or* test paper

Prügel ['pry:gəl] F *pl* (*e-e Tracht*) *~ bekommen* get a (good) beating *or* hiding *or* thrashing; **Prüge'lei** F *f* (*-; -en*) fight; **'prügeln** F *v/t* (*ge-*, *h*) beat, flog; *sich ~* (have a) fight; **'Prügelstrafe** *f* corporal punishment

Prunk [prʊŋk] *m* (*-[e]s*; *no pl*) splendo(u)r, pomp; **'prunkvoll** *adj* splendid, magnificent

PS [pe:'ʔɛs] *abbr of* **Pferdestärke** horsepower, HP

Psalm [psalm] *m* (*-s*; *-en*) REL psalm

Pseudonym [psɔydo'ny:m] *n* (*-s*; *-e*) pseudonym

pst [pst] *int* sh!, ssh!; psst!

Psyche ['psy:çə] *f* (*-; -n*) mind, psyche

Psychiater [psy'çja:tɐ] *m* (*-s*; *-*), **Psy'chiaterin** *f* (*-; -nen*) psychiatrist; **psy'chiatrisch** [psy'çja:trɪʃ] *adj* psychiatric

psychisch ['psy:çɪʃ] *adj* mental, MED *a.* psychic

Psychoana'lyse ['psyçoanaly:zə] *f* psychoanalysis

Psychologe [psyço'lo:gə] *m* (*-n*; *-n*) psychologist (*a.* fig); **Psychologie**

[psyçolo'gi:] *f* (*-; no pl*) psychology; **Psycho'login** *f* (*-; -nen*) psychologist; **psycho'logisch** *adj* psychological

Psychose [psy'ço:zə] *f* (*-; -n*) MED psychosis

psychosomatisch [psyçozo'ma:tɪʃ] *adj* MED psychosomatic

Pubertät [pubɛr'tɛ:t] *f* (*-; no pl*) puberty

Publikum ['pu:blikʊm] *n* (*-s*; *no pl*) audience, TV *a.* viewers, *radio:* *a.* listeners; SPORT crowd, spectators; ECON customers; public

publizieren [publi'tsi:rən] *v/t* (*no -ge-*, *h*) publish

Pudding ['pʊdɪŋ] *m* (*-s*; *-e*, *-s*) pudding, *esp Br* blancmange

Pudel ['pu:dəl] *m* (*-s*; *-*) ZO poodle

Puder ['pu:dɐ] *m* (*-s*; *-*) powder

'Puderdose *f* powder compact

'pudern *v/t* (*ge-*, *h*) powder; *sich ~* powder one's face

'Puderzucker *m* confectioner's (*Br* icing) sugar

Puff[1] [pʊf] F *m* (*-s*; *-s*) brothel

Puff[2] *m* (*-[e]s*; *Püffe* ['pyfə]) hump; poke

Puffer ['pʊfɐ] *m* (*-s*; *-*) RAIL buffer (*a.* fig)

'Puffmais *m* popcorn

Pulli ['pʊli] F *m* (*-s*; *-s*) (light) sweater

Pullover [pʊ'lo:vɐ] *m* (*-s*; *-*) sweater, pullover

Puls [pʊls] *m* (*-es*; *-e*) MED pulse; pulse rate; **~ader** *f* ANAT artery

pulsieren [pʊl'zi:rən] *v/i* (*no -ge-*, *h*) MED pulsate (*a.* fig)

Pult [pʊlt] *n* (*-[e]s*; *-e*) desk

Pulver ['pʊlvɐ] *n* (*-s*; *-*) powder; F cash, *sl* dough; **pulv(e)rig** ['pʊlv(ə)rɪç] *adj* powdery; **pulverisieren** [pʊlveri-'zi:rən] *v/t* (*no -ge-*, *h*) pulverize

'Pulverkaffee *m* instant coffee

'Pulverschnee *m* powder snow

pumm(e)lig ['pʊm(ə)lɪç] F *adj* chubby, plump, tubby

Pumpe ['pʊmpə] *f* (*-; -n*) TECH pump

'pumpen *v/i and v/t* TECH pump; F lend; borrow

Punker ['paŋkɐ] F *m* (*-s*; *-*), **'Punkerin** *f* (*-; -nen*) punk

Punkt [pʊŋkt] *m* (*-[e]s*; *-e*) point (*a.* fig); dot; full stop, period; *fig* spot, place; *um ~ zehn (Uhr)* at ten (o'clock) sharp; *nach ~en gewinnen etc* SPORT win *etc* on points

P

punktieren [puŋk'tiːrən] *v/t (no -ge-, h)* dot; MED puncture

pünktlich ['pyŋktlɪç] *adj* punctual; ~ **sein** be on time; '**Pünktlichkeit** *f (-; no pl)* punctuality

'**Punkt|sieger** *m* SPORT winner on points; ~**spiel** *n* SPORT league game

Pupille [pu'pɪlə] *f (-; -n)* ANAT pupil

Puppe ['pupə] *f (-; -n)* doll, F *a.* chick; THEA puppet (*a. fig*); MOT dummy; zo chrysalis, pupa

'**Puppen|spiel** *n* puppet show; ~**stube** *f* doll's house; ~**wagen** *m* doll carriage, Br doll's pram

pur [puːɐ] *adj* pure (*a. fig*); *whisky etc*: straight, Br neat

Purpur ['purpur] *m (-s; no pl)* crimson

'**purpurrot** *adj* crimson

Purzelbaum ['purtsəlbaum] *m* somersault; *e-n* ~ *schlagen* turn a somersault

purzeln ['purtsəln] *v/i (ge-, sein)* tumble

Pute ['puːtə] *f (-; -n)* zo turkey (hen)

Puter ['puːtɐ] *m (-s; -)* zo turkey (cock)

Putsch [putʃ] *m (-[e]s; -e)* putsch, coup (d'état); '**putschen** *v/i (ge-, h)* revolt, make a putsch

Putz [puts] *m (-es; no pl)* ARCH plaster (-ing); **unter** ~ ELECTR concealed

putzen ['putsən] *(ge-, h)* **1.** *v/t* clean; polish; wipe; *sich die Nase* ~ blow one's nose; *sich die Zähne* ~ brush one's teeth **2.** *v/i* do the cleaning; ~ *(gehen)* work as a cleaner

'**Putzfrau** *f* cleaner, cleaning woman *or* lady

putzig ['putsɪç] *adj* funny, cute

'**Putzlappen** *m* cleaning rag

'**Putzmittel** *n* clean(s)er; polish

Puzzle ['pazəl] *n (-s; -s)* jigsaw (puzzle)

Pyjama [py'dʒaːma] *m (-s; -s)* pajamas, Br pyjamas

Pyramíde [pyra'miːdə] *f (-; -n)* pyramid

Q

Quacksalber ['kvakzalbɐ] *m (-s; -)* quack (doctor)

Quadrat [kva'draːt] *n (-[e]s; -e)* square; *ins* ~ *erheben* MATH square; ~**...** *in cpds* ...meile, ...meter, ...wurzel, ...zahl *etc*: square ...; **qua'dratisch** *adj* square; MATH quadratic

quaken ['kvaːkən] *v/i (ge-, h)* duck: quack; *frog*: croak

quäken ['kvɛːkən] *v/i (ge-, h)* squeak

Qual [kvaːl] *f (-; -en)* pain, torment, agony; anguish

quälen ['kvɛːlən] *v/t (ge-, h)* torment (*a. fig*); torture; *fig* pester, plague

Qualifikation [kvalifika'tsjoːn] *f (-; -en)* qualification; **Qualifikati'ons...** *in cpds* ...spiel *etc*: qualifying ...

qualifizieren [kvalifi'tsiːrən] *v/t and v/refl (no -ge-, h)* qualify

Qualität [kvali'tɛːt] *f (-; -en)* quality

qualitativ [kvalita'tiːf] *adj and adv* in quality

Quali'täts... *in cpds* ...arbeit, ...waren *etc*: high-quality ...

Qualm [kvalm] *m (-[e]s; no pl)* (thick) smoke; **qualmen** ['kvalmən] *v/i (ge-,*

h) smoke; F be a heavy smoker

'**qualvoll** *adj* very painful; agonizing

Quantität [kvanti'tɛːt] *f (-; -en)* quantity; **quantitativ** [kvantita'tiːf] *adj and adv* in quantity

Quantum ['kvantum] *n (-s; Quanten)* amount, *fig a.* share

Quarantäne [karan'tɛːnə] *f (-; -n)* (**unter** ~ **stellen** put in) quarantine

Quark [kvark] *m (-s; no pl)* curd, cottage cheese

Quartal [kvar'taːl] *n (-s; -e)* quarter (of a year)

Quartett [kvar'tɛt] *n (-[e]s; -e)* MUS quartet(te)

Quartier [kvar'tiːɐ] *n (-s; -e)* accommodation; *Swiss*: quarter

Quarz [kvaːɐts] *m (-es; -e)* MIN quartz

Quatsch [kvatʃ] F *m (-[e]s; no pl)* nonsense, rubbish, *sl* rot, crap, bullshit; ~ *machen* fool around; poke, F kid

quatschen ['kvatʃən] F *v/i (ge-, h)* talk rubbish; chat

Quecksilber ['kvɛkzɪlbɐ] *n (-s; no pl)* mercury, quicksilver

Quelle ['kvɛlə] *f (-; -n)* spring, source (*a.*

fig), well, *fig a.* origin; **'Quellen** *v/i* (*irr*, *ge-*, *sein*) pour (**aus** from)

'Quellenangabe *f* reference

quengeln ['kvɛŋəln] F *v/i* (*ge-*, *h*) whine

quer [kveːɐ] *adv* across; crosswise; **kreuz und ~** all over the place; **kreuz und ~ durch Deutschland fahren** travel all over Germany; **Quere** ['kveːrə] *f*: F **j-m in die ~ kommen** get in s.o.'s way

Querfeld'einlauf *m* SPORT cross-country race

'Querlatte *f* SPORT crossbar

'Querschläger *m* MIL ricochet

'Querschnitt *m* cross-section (*a. fig*)

'querschnitt(s)gelähmt *adj* MED paraplegic

'Querstraße *f* intersecting road; **zweite ~ rechts** second turning on the right

Querulant [kveru'lant] *m* (*-en*; *-en*), **Queru'lantin** *f* (*-; -nen*) querulous person

quetschen ['kvɛtʃən] *v/t and v/refl* (*ge-*, *h*) squeeze; MED bruise (o.s.)

'Quetschung *f* (*-; -en*) MED bruise

quiek(s)en ['kviːk(s)ən] *v/i* (*ge-*, *h*) squeak, squeal

quietschen ['kviːtʃən] *v/i* (*ge-*, *h*) squeal; screech; squeak, creak

quitt [kvɪt] *adj*: **mit j-m ~ sein** be quits *or* even with s.o. (*a. fig*)

quittieren [kvɪ'tiːrən] *v/t* (*no -ge-*, *h*) ECON give a receipt for

'Quittung *f* (*-; -en*) receipt; *fig* answer

quoll [kvɔl] *pret of* **quellen**

Quote ['kvoːtə] *f* (*-; -n*) quota; share; rate

'Quotenregelung *f* quota system

Quotient [kvo'tsjɛnt] *m* (*-en*; *-en*) MATH quotient

R

Rabatt [ra'bat] *m* (*-[e]s*; *-e*) ECON discount, rebate

Rabe ['raːbə] *m* (*-n*; *-n*) ZO raven

rabiat [ra'bjaːt] *adj* rough, tough

Rache ['raxə] *f* (*-; no pl*) revenge; **aus ~ für** in revenge for

Rachen ['raxən] *m* (*-s*; *-*) ANAT throat

rächen ['rɛçən] *v/t* (*ge-*, *h*) avenge *s.th.*; revenge *s.o.*; **sich an j-m für et. ~** revenge o.s. *or* take revenge on s.o. for s.th.; **Rächer** ['rɛçɐ] *m* (*-s*; *-*) avenger

rachsüchtig ['raxzʏçtɪç] *adj* revengeful, vindictive

Rad [raːt] *n* (*-[e]s*; *Räder* ['rɛːdɐ]) wheel; bicycle, F bike; **Rad fahren** ride a bicycle, F bike; **ein ~ schlagen** *peacock*: spread its tail; SPORT turn a (cart)wheel

Radar [ra'daːr] *m*, *n*, (*-s*; *-e*) radar; **~falle** *f* MOT speed trap; **~kon,trolle** *f* MOT radar speed check; **~schirm** *m* radar screen; **~stati,on** *f* radar station

radeln ['raːdəln] F *v/i* (*ge-*, *sein*) bike

Rädelsführer ['rɛːdəlsfyːrɐ] *m* ringleader

Räderwerk ['rɛːdɐvɛrk] *n* TECH gearing

'Radfahrer *m* (*-s*; *-*), **'Radfahrerin** *f* (*-; -nen*) cyclist

radieren [ra'diːrən] *v/t* (*no -ge-*, *h*) erase, rub out; *art*: etch

Radiergummi [ra'diːrɡumi] *m* eraser, *Br a.* rubber

Ra'dierung *f* (*-; -en*) *art*: etching

Radieschen [ra'diːsçən] *n* (*-s*; *-*) BOT (red) radish

radikal [radi'kaːl] *adj*, **Radi'kale** *m*, *f* (*-n*; *-n*) radical; **Radikalismus** [radika-'lɪsmʊs] *m* (*-; no pl*) radicalism

Radio ['raːdjo] *n* (*-s*; *-s*) radio; **im ~** on the radio; **~ hören** listen to the radio

radioak'tiv [radjoak'tiːf] *adj* PHYS radioactive; **~er Niederschlag** fall-out

Radioaktivi'tät *f* (*-; no pl*) radioactivity

'Radiowecker *m* clock radio

Radius ['raːdjʊs] *m* (*-s*; *Radien*) radius

'Rad|kappe *f* hubcap; **~rennbahn** *f* cycling track; **~rennen** *n* cycle race; **~sport** *m* cycling; **~sportler** *m* cyclist; **~weg** *m* cycle track *or* path, bikeway

raffen ['rafən] *v/t* (*ge-*, *h*) gather up; **an sich ~** grab

Raffinerie [rafinə'riː] *f* (*-; -n*) CHEM refinery

Raffinesse [rafi'nɛsə] *f* (*-; -n*) (*no pl*) shrewdness; refinement

raffiniert [rafi'niːɐt] *adj* refined (*a. fig*);

fig shrewd, clever

ragen ['ra:gən] *v/i* (*ge-*, *h*) tower (up), rise (high)

Rahe ['ra:ə] *f* (*-*; *-n*) MAR yard

Rahm [ra:m] *m* (*-[e]s*; *no pl*) cream

rahmen ['ra:mən] *v/t* (*ge-*, *h*) frame; PHOT mount; **Rahmen** (*-s*; *-*) frame; *fig* framework; setting; scope; **aus dem ~ fallen** be out of the ordinary

Rakete [ra'ke:tə] *f* (*-*; *-n*) rocket, MIL *a.* missile; **ferngelenkte ~** guided missile; **e-e ~ abfeuern (starten)** launch a rocket *or* missile

Ra'keten|antrieb *m* rocket propulsion; **mit ~** rocket-propelled; **~basis** *f* MIL rocket *or* missile base *or* site

rammen ['ramən] *v/t* (*ge-*, *h*) ram; MOT *etc* hit, collide with

Rampe ['rampə] *f* (*-*; *-n*) (loading) ramp

Rampenlicht *n* (*-[e]s*; *no pl*) THEA footlights; *fig* limelight

Ramsch [ramʃ] F *m* (*-es*; *no pl*) junk

Rand [rant] *m* (*-[e]s*; *Ränder* ['rɛndɐ]) edge, border; brink (*a. fig*); rim; brim; margin; **am ~(e) des Ruins** *etc* on the brink of ruin *etc*

randalieren [randa'li:rən] *v/i* (*no -ge-*, *h*) kick up a racket; **Randalierer** [randa'li:rɐ] *m* (*-s*; *-*) rowdy, hooligan

'Rand|bemerkung *f* marginal note; *fig* comment; **~gruppe** *f* fringe group

'randlos *adj* rimless

'Randstreifen *m* MOT shoulder

rang [raŋ] *pret of* **ringen**

Rang [raŋ] *m* (*-[e]s*; *Ränge* ['rɛŋə]) position, rank (*a.* MIL); THEA balcony, *Br* circle; *pl* SPORT terraces

rangieren [raŋ'ʒi:rən] (*no -ge-*, *h*) **1.** *v/t* RAIL switch, *Br* shunt **2.** *fig v/i* rank (**vor j-m** before s.o.)

'Rangordnung *f* hierarchy

Ranke ['raŋkə] *f* (*-*; *-n*) BOT tendril

'ranken *v/refl* (*ge-*, *h*) BOT creep, climb

rann [ran] *pret of* **rinnen**

rannte ['rantə] *pret of* **rennen**

Ranzen ['rantsən] *m* (*-s*; *-*) knapsack; satchel

ranzig ['rantsɪç] *adj* rancid, rank

Rappe ['rapə] *m* (*-n*; *-n*) ZO black horse

rar [ra:r] *adj* rare, scarce

Rarität [rari'tɛ:t] *f* (*-*; *-en*) curiosity; (*no pl*) rarity

rasch [raʃ] *adj* quick, swift; prompt

rascheln ['raʃəln] *v/i* (*ge-*, *h*) rustle

rasen ['ra:zən] *v/i* (*ge-*, *sein*) F MOT race, tear, speed; (*ge-*, *h*) rage; **~ vor Begeisterung** roar with enthusiasm

'Rasen *m* (*-s*; *-*) lawn, grass

'rasend *adj* breakneck; raging; agonizing; splitting; thunderous

'Rasen|mäher *m* lawn mower; **~platz** *m* lawn; *tennis*: grass court

Raserei [ra:zə'rai] *f* (*-*; *-en*) (*no pl*) frenzied rage; frenzy; madness; F MOT reckless driving

Rasier|appa,rat [ra'zi:ʀapara:t] *m* (safety) razor; *esp* **elektrischer ~** shaver; **~creme** *f* shaving cream

rasieren [ra'zi:rən] *v/t and v/refl* (*no -ge-*, *h*) shave

Ra'sier|klinge *f* razor blade; **~messer** *n* (straight) razor; **~pinsel** *m* shaving brush; **~seife** *f* shaving soap; **~wasser** *n* aftershave (lotion)

Rasse ['rasə] *f* (*-*; *-n*) race; ZO breed

'Rassehund *m* ZO pedigree dog

Rassel ['rasəl] *f* (*-*; *-n*), **'rasseln** *v/i* (*ge-*, *h*) rattle

'Rassen... *in cpds* **...diskriminierung**, **...konflikt**, **...probleme** *etc*: *mst* racial **...**; **~trennung** *f* POL (racial) segregation; HIST apartheid; **~unruhen** *pl* race riots

rassig ['rasɪç] *adj* classy

rassisch ['rasɪʃ] *adj* racial

Rassismus [ra'sɪsmʊs] *m* (*-*; *no pl*) POL racism; **Ras'sist(in)** (*-en*; *-en/-*; *-nen*), **ras'sistisch** *adj* POL racist

Rast [rast] *f* (*-*; *-en*) rest, stop; break; **rasten** ['rastən] *v/i* (*ge-*, *h*) rest, stop, take a break; **'rastlos** *adj* restless

'Rastplatz *m* resting place; MOT rest area, *Br* lay-by

'Raststätte *f* MOT service area

Rasur [ra'zu:ʀ] *f* (*-*; *-en*) shave

Rat [ra:t] *m* (*-[e]s*; *Räte* ['rɛ:tə]) (*no pl*) (piece of) advice; council; **j-n um ~ fragen** ask s.o.'s advice; **j-s ~ befolgen** take s.o.'s advice

Rate ['ra:tə] *f* (*-*; *-n*) rate; ECON instal(l)ment; **auf ~n** by instal(l)ments

raten ['ra:tən] *v/t and v/i* (*irr*, *ge-*, *h*) advise; guess; solve; **j-m zu et. ~** advise s.o. to do s.th.; **rate mal!** (have a) guess!

'Ratenzahlung *f* → **Abzahlung**

'Rateteam *n* TV *etc* panel

Ratgeber ['ra:tge:bɐ] *m* (*-s*; *-*),

'Ratgeberin f (-; -nen) adviser, counsel(l)or; m guide (**über** acc to)

'Rathaus n city (Br town) hall

ratifizieren [ratifi'tsiːrən] v/t (no -ge-, h) ratify

Ration [ra'tsjoːn] f (-; -en) ration

rational [ratsjo'naːl] adj rational

rationell [ratsjo'nɛl] adj efficient; economical

rationieren [ratsjo'niːrən] v/t (no -ge-, h) ration

'ratlos adj at a loss

'ratsam adj advisable, wise

'Ratschlag m piece of advice; **ein paar gute Ratschläge** some good advice

Rätsel ['rɛːtsəl] n (-s; -) puzzle; riddle (both a. fig); mystery

'rätselhaft adj puzzling; mysterious

Ratte ['ratə] f (-; -n) zo rat (a. contp)

rattern ['ratən] v/i (ge-, h, sein) rattle, clatter

rau [rau] adj rough, rugged (both a. fig); harsh; chapped; sore

Raub [raup] m (-[e]s; no pl) robbery; loot, booty; prey; ~bau m (-[e]s; no pl) overexploitation (**an** dat of); ~ **mit s-r Gesundheit treiben** ruin one's health

rauben ['raubən] v/t (ge-, h) rob, steal; kidnap; **j-m et.** ~ rob s.o. of s.th. (a. fig)

Räuber ['rɔybɐ] m (-s; -) robber

'Raub|fisch m predatory fish; ~mord m murder with robbery; ~mörder m murderer and robber; ~tier n beast of prey; ~überfall m holdup, (armed) robbery; mugging; ~vogel m bird of prey; ~zug m raid

Rauch [raux] m (-[e]s; no pl) smoke; CHEM etc fume; rauchen ['rauxən] v/i and v/t (ge-, h) smoke; CHEM etc fume; **Rauchen verboten!** no smoking; **Pfeife** ~ smoke a pipe; Raucher(in) ['rau-xɐ, 'rauxərin] m(f) (-s; -/-; -nen) smoker (m a. RAIL)

Räucher... ['rɔyçɐ-] in cpds ...aal, ...speck etc: smoked ...

'räuchern v/t (ge-, h) smoke

'Räucherstäbchen n joss stick

'Rauchfahne f trail of smoke

'rauchig ['rauxɪç] adj smoky

'Rauch|waren pl tobacco products; furs; ~zeichen n smoke signal

Räude ['rɔydə] f (-; -n) VET mange

'räudig adj VET mange

raufen ['raufən] (ge-, h) 1. v/t: **sich die Haare** ~ tear one's hair 2. v/i fight, scuffle; Rauferei [raufə'rai] f (-; -en) fight, scuffle

Raum [raum] m (-[e]s; Räume ['rɔymə]) room; space; area; (outer) space; ~anzug m spacesuit; ~deckung f SPORT zone marking

räumen ['rɔymən] v/t (ge-, h) leave, move out of; check out of; clear (**von** of); evacuate (a. MIL); **s-e Sachen in ...** (acc) ~ put one's things (away) in ...

'Raum|fähre f space shuttle; ~fahrer F m spaceman; ~fahrt f (-; no pl) space travel or flight; astronautics; ~fahrt... in cpds ...technik, ...zentrum etc: space ...; ~flug m space flight; ~inhalt m volume; ~kapsel f space capsule; ~la,bor n space lab

räumlich ['rɔymlɪç] adj three-dimensional

'Raum|schiff n spacecraft; spaceship; ~sonde f space probe; ~stati,on f space station

'Räumung f (-; -en) clearance; evacuation (a. MIL); JUR eviction

'Räumungsverkauf m ECON clearance sale

raunen ['raunən] v/i (ge-, h) whisper, murmur

Raupe ['raupə] f (-; -n) zo caterpillar, TECH a. track; 'Raupenschlepper m MOT caterpillar® tractor

'Raureif m hoarfrost

raus [raus] F int get out (of here)!

Rausch [rauʃ] m (-es; Räusche ['rɔyʃə]) drunkenness, intoxication; F high; fig ecstasy; **e-n** ~ **haben** be drunk; **s-n** ~ **ausschlafen** sleep it off

rauschen ['rauʃən] v/i (ge-, h) water etc: rush; brook: murmur; storm: roar; (ge-, sein) sweep; ~d adj thunderous (applause); ~es Fest lavish celebration

'Rauschgift n drug(s), narcotic(s); ~dezer,nat n narcotics or drugs squad; ~handel m drug traffic(king); ~händler m drug trafficker, F pusher

räuspern ['rɔyspən] v/refl (ge-, h) clear one's throat

Razzia ['ratsja] f (-; -ien) raid, roundup

Reagenzglas [rea'gɛntsglaːs] n CHEM test tube

reagieren [rea'giːrən] v/i (no -ge-, h) CHEM, MED react (**auf** acc to), fig a. respond (to); **Reaktion** [reak'tsjo:n] *f* (-; *-en*) CHEM, MED, PHYS, POL reaction (**auf** *acc* to), *fig a.* response (to)

Reaktor [re'akto:ɐ] *m* (-s; *-en* [reak-'to:rən]) PHYS (nuclear *or* atomic) reactor

real [re'a:l] *adj* real; concrete

realisieren [reali'zi:rən] *v/t* (*no -ge-, h*) realize

Realismus [rea'lɪsmus] *m* (-; *no pl*) realism; **rea'listisch** *adj* realistic

Realität [reali'tɛːt] *f* (-; *no pl*) reality

Re'alschule *f appr* (junior) highschool, *Br* secondary (modern) school

Rebe ['re:bə] *f* (-; *-n*) BOT vine

Rebell [re'bɛl] *m* (*-en*; *-en*) rebel

rebellieren [rebɛ'li:rən] *v/i* (*no -ge-, h*) rebel, revolt, rise (*all:* **gegen** against)

Re'bellin *f* (-; *-nen*) rebel

re'bellisch *adj* rebellious

Rebhuhn ['re:phu:n] *n* ZO partridge

'Rebstock *m* BOT vine

Rechen ['rɛçən] *m* (-s; -), **'rechen** *v/t* (*ge-, h*) rake

'Rechen|aufgabe *f* MATH (arithmetical) problem; **~fehler** *m* MATH arithmetical error, miscalculation; **~ma,schine** *f* calculator; computer

'Rechenschaft *f:* **~ ablegen über** (*acc*) account for; **zur ~ ziehen** call to account (**wegen** for)

'Rechen|schieber *m* MATH slide rule; **~werk** *n* IT arithmetic unit; **~zentrum** *n* computer center (*Br* centre)

rechnen ['rɛçnən] *v/i and v/t* (*ge-, h*) calculate, reckon; work out, do sums; count; **~ mit** *fig* expect; count on; **mit mir kannst du nicht ~!** count me out!

'Rechnen *n* (-s; *no pl*) arithmetic

Rechner ['rɛçnɐ] *m* (-s; -) calculator; computer

rechnerisch ['rɛçnərɪʃ] *adj* arithmetical

'Rechnung *f* (-; *-en*) MATH calculation; problem, sum; ECON invoice, bill, check; **die ~, bitte!** can I have the check, please?; **das geht auf m-e ~** that's on me

recht [rɛçt] **1.** *adj* right; correct; POL right-wing; **auf der ~en Seite** on the right(-hand side); **mir ist es ~** I don't mind **2.** *adv* right(ly), correctly; rather, quite; **ich weiß nicht ~** I don't really know; **es geschieht ihm ~** it serves

him right; **erst ~** all the more; **erst ~ nicht** even less; **du kommst gerade ~ (zu)** you're just in time (for); **j-m ~ geben** agree with s.o.; **~ haben** be right

Recht *n* (-[e]s; *-e*) right, claim (*both:* **auf** *acc* to); (*no pl*) JUR law; justice; **gleiches ~** equal rights; **~ haben → recht**; **j-m ~ geben → recht**; **im ~ sein** be in the right; **er hat es mit (vollem) ~ getan** he was (perfectly) right to do so; **ein ~ auf et. haben** be entitled to s.th.

'Rechteck *n* (-[e]s; *-e*) rectangle

'rechteckig *adj* rectangular

'rechtfertigen *v/t* (*ge-, h*) justify

'Rechtfertigung *f* (-; *-en*) justification

'rechtlich *adj* JUR legal

'rechtlos *adj* without rights; outcast

'rechtmäßig *adj* JUR lawful; legitimate; legal; **'Rechtmäßigkeit** *f* (-; *no pl*) JUR lawfulness, legitimacy

rechts [rɛçts] *adv* on the right(-hand side); **nach ~** to the right

Rechts... *in cpds* POL right-wing ...; **~anspruch** *m* legal claim (**auf** *acc* to); **~anwalt** *m*, **~anwältin** ['rɛçtsanvɛltɪn] *f* (-; *-nen*) lawyer

Rechts'außen *m* (-; -) *soccer:* outside right

'rechtschaffen *adj* honest

'Recht|schreibfehler *m* spelling mistake; **~schreibung** *f* (-; *no pl*) spelling, orthography

'rechtsextre,mistisch *adj* POL extreme right

'Rechtsfall *m* JUR (law) case

Rechtshänder ['rɛçtshɛndɐ] *m* (-s; -), **'Rechtshänderin** *f* (-; *-nen*) right-handed person; **sie ist Rechtshänderin** she is right-handed

'Rechtsprechung *f* (-; *no pl*) jurisdiction

'rechtsradi,kal *adj* POL extreme right-wing

'Rechtsschutz *m* legal protection; legal costs insurance

'rechtswidrig *adj* JUR illegal, unlawful

'rechtwink(e)lig *adj* rectangular

'rechtzeitig 1. *adj* punctual **2.** *adv* in time (**zu** for)

Reck [rɛk] *n* (-[e]s; *-e*) horizontal bar

recken ['rɛkən] *v/t* (*ge-, h*) stretch; **sich ~** stretch o.s.

recyceln [ri'saikəln] *v/t* (*no -ge-, h*) recycle; **Recyclingpa,pier** [ri-

'saiklɪŋpapiːɐ] *n* recycled paper

Redakteur [redak'tøːɐ] *m* (-s; -e), **Redak'teurin** *f* (-; -nen) editor

Redaktion [redak'tsjoːn] *f* (-; -en) (*no pl*) editing; editorial staff, editors; editorial office *or* department

redaktionell [redaktsjo'nɛl] *adj* editorial

Rede ['reːdə] *f* (-; -n) speech, address; talk (*von* of); *e-e ~ halten* make a speech; *direkte (indirekte) ~* LING direct (reported *or* indirect) speech; *j-n zur ~ stellen* take s.o. to task; *nicht der ~ wert* not worth mentioning

'**redegewandt** *adj* eloquent

reden ['reːdən] *v/i and v/t* (ge-, h) talk, speak (*both: mit* to; *über acc* about, of); *ich möchte mit dir ~* I'd like to talk to you; *die Leute ~* people talk; *j-n zum Reden bringen* make s.o. talk

'**Redensart** *f* saying, phrase

redlich ['reːtlɪç] *adj* upright, honest; *sich ~(e) Mühe geben* do one's best

Redner ['reːdnɐ] *m* (-s; -), '**Rednerin** *f* (-; -nen) speaker

'**Rednerpult** *n* speaker's desk

redselig ['reːtzeːlɪç] *adj* talkative

reduzieren [redu'tsiːrən] *v/t* (*no* -ge-, h) reduce (*auf acc* to)

Reeder ['reːdɐ] *m* (-s; -) shipowner

Reederei [reːdə'rai] *f* (-; -en) shipping company

reell [re'ɛl] *adj* reasonable, fair (*price*); real (*chance*); solid (*firm*)

Referat [refe'raːt] *n* (-[e]s; -e) paper; report; lecture; *ein ~ halten* read a paper

Referendar [referen'daːɐ] *m* (-s; -e), **Referen'darin** *f* (-; -nen) *appr* trainee teacher

Referent [refe'rɛnt] *m* (-en; -en), **Refe'rentin** *f* (-; -nen) speaker; **Referenz** [refe'rɛnts] *f* (-; -en) reference; **referieren** [refe'riːrən] *v/i* (*no* -ge-, h) (give a) report *or* lecture (*über acc* on)

reflektieren [reflɛk'tiːrən] *v/t and v/i* (*no* -ge-, h) reflect (*fig über acc* [up]on)

Reflex [re'flɛks] *m* (-es; -e) reflex

reflexiv [reflɛ'ksiːf] *adj* LING reflexive

Reform [re'fɔrm] *f* (-; -en) reform

Reformator [refɔr'maːtoːɐ] *m* (-s; -en [reforma'toːrən]), **Reformer(in)** [re-'fɔrmɐ, re'fɔrmərɪn] *m(f)* (-s; -/-; -nen) reformer

Re'formhaus *n* health food store (*Br*

shop)

reformieren [refɔr'miːrən] *v/t* (*no* -ge-, h) reform

Refrain [rə'frɛː] *m* (-s; -s) refrain, chorus

Regal [re'gaːl] *n* (-s; -e) shelf (unit), shelves

rege ['reːgə] *adj* lively; busy; active

Regel ['reːgəl] *f* (-; -n) rule; MED period, menstruation; *in der ~* as a rule

'**regelmäßig** *adj* regular

'**regeln** ['reːgəln] *v/t* (ge-, h) regulate, TECH *a.* adjust; ECON settle

'**regelrecht** *adj* regular (*a.* F)

'**Regeltechnik** *f* control engineering

'**Regelung** *f* (-; -en) regulation; adjustment; ECON settlement; TECH control

'**regelwidrig** *adj* against the rule(s); SPORT unfair; *~es Spiel* foul play

regen ['reːgən] *v/t and v/refl* (ge-, h) move, stir

'**Regen** *m* (-s; -) rain; *starker ~* heavy rain(fall); *~bogen* *m* rainbow; *~bogenhaut* *f* ANAT iris; *~guss* *m* (heavy) shower, downpour; *~mantel* *m* raincoat; *~schauer* *m* shower; *~schirm* *m* umbrella; *~tag* *m* rainy day; *~tropfen* *m* raindrop; *~wald* *m* rain forest; *~wasser* *n* rainwater; *~wetter* *n* rainy weather; *~wurm* *m* ZO earthworm; *~zeit* *f* rainy season, the rains

Regie [re'ʒiː] *f* (-; *no pl*) THEA, film *etc*: direction; *unter der ~ von* directed by

Re'gieanweisung *f* stage direction

regieren [re'giːrən] (*no* -ge-, h) **1.** *v/i* reign **2.** *v/t* govern (*a.* LING), rule

Re'gierung *f* (-; -en) government, administration; reign

Re'gierungs|bezirk *m* administrative district; *~chef* *m* head of government; *~wechsel* *m* change of government

Regime [re'ʒiːm] *n* (-s; -) POL regime

Re'gimekritiker *m* POL dissident

Regiment [regi'mɛnt] *n* (-[e]s; -er) (*no pl*) rule (*a.* fig); MIL regiment

Regisseur [reʒi'søːɐ] *m* (-s; -e), **Regis-'seurin** *f* (-; -nen) THEA, film *etc*: director, THEA *Br a.* producer

Register [re'gɪstɐ] *n* (-s; -) register (*a.* MUS), record; index; **registrieren** [regɪs'triːrən] *v/t* (*no* -ge-, h) register, record; fig note; **Registrierkasse** [regɪs'triːkasə] *f* cash register

Reglement [reglə'maː] *n* (-s; -s) regu-

R

lation, order, rule

Regler ['re:glɐ] *m* (-*s*; -) TECH control

regnen ['re:gnən] *v/i* (*ge-, h*) rain (*a. fig*); **es regnet in Strömen** it's pouring with rain; **'regnerisch** *adj* rainy

regulär [regu'lɛ:ɐ] *adj* regular; normal

regulierbar [regu'li:ɐba:ɐ] *adj* adjustable; controllable

regulieren [regu'li:rən] *v/t* (*no -ge-, h*) regulate, adjust; control

'Regung *f* (-; -*en*) movement; motion; emotion; impulse

'regungslos *adj* motionless

Reh [re:] *n* (-[*e*]*s*; -*e*) ZO deer, roe; doe; GASTR venison

rehabilitieren [rehabili'ti:rən] *v/t* (*no -ge-, h*) rehabilitate

'Reh|bock *m* ZO (roe)buck; **~keule** *f* GASTR leg of venison; **~kitz** *n* ZO fawn

Reibe ['raibə] *f* (-; -*n*), **Reibeisen** ['raip'ʔaizən] *n* (-*s*; -) grater, rasp

reiben ['raibən] *v/i and v/t* (*irr, ge-, h*) rub; grate, grind; **sich die Augen (Hände) ~** rub one's eyes (hands)

'Reibung *f* (-; -*en*) TECH *etc* friction

'reibungslos *adj* TECH *etc* frictionless; *fig* smooth

reich [raiç] *adj* rich (**an** *dat* in), wealthy; abundant

Reich *n* (-[*e*]*s*; -*e*) empire, kingdom (*a.* REL, BOT, ZO); *fig* world

reichen ['raiçən] (*ge-, h*) **1.** *v/t* reach; hand, pass; give, hold out (*one's hand*); **2.** *v/i* last, do; **~ bis** reach *or* come up to; **das reicht** that will do; F **mir reicht's!** I've had enough

'reichhaltig *adj* rich

'reichlich 1. *adj* rich, plentiful; plenty of **2.** *adv* rather; generously

'Reichtum *m* (-*s*; *no pl*) wealth (**an** *dat* of) (*a. fig*)

'Reichweite *f* reach; AVIAT, MIL *etc* range; **in (außer) (j-s) ~** within (out of) (s.o.'s) reach

reif [raif] *adj* ripe, *esp fig* mature

Reif *m* (-[*e*]*s*; *no pl*) white frost, hoarfrost

Reife ['raifə] *f* (-; *no pl*) ripeness, *esp fig* maturity; **'reifen** *v/i* (*ge-, sein*) ripen, mature (*both a. fig*)

Reifen ['raifən] *m* (-*s*; -) hoop; MOT *etc* tire, *Br* tyre; **~panne** *f* MOT flat tire (*Br* tyre), puncture, F flat

'Reifeprüfung *f* → **Abitur**

'reiflich *adj* careful

Reihe ['raiə] *f* (-; -*n*) line, row; number; series; **der ~ nach** in turn; **ich bin an der ~** it's my turn

'Reihenfolge *f* order

'Reihenhaus *n* row (*Br* terraced) house

'reihenweise *adv* in rows; F *fig* by the dozen

Reiher ['raiɐ] *m* (-*s*; -) ZO heron

Reim [raim] *m* (-[*e*]*s*; -*e*) rhyme

reimen ['raimən] *v/t and v/refl* (*ge-, h*) rhyme (**auf** *acc* with)

rein [rain] *adj* pure (*a. fig*); clean; *fig* clear (*conscience*); plain (*truth*); mere, sheer, nothing but

'Reinfall F *m* flop; let-down

'Reingewinn *m* ECON net profit

'reinhauen F *v/i* (*sep, -ge-, h*) tuck in

'Reinheit *f* (-; *no pl*) purity (*a. fig*); cleanness

reinigen ['rainıgən] *v/t* (*ge-, h*) clean; cleanse (*a.* MED); dry-clean; *fig* purify

'Reinigung *f* (-; -*en*) clean(s)ing; *fig* purification; (dry) cleaners; **chemische ~** dry cleaning; dry cleaner's

'Reinigungsmittel *n* cleaning agent, cleaner, detergent

'reinlich *adj* clean; cleanly

'reinrassig *adj* ZO purebred, pedigree; thoroughbred

'Reinschrift *f* fair copy

Reis [rais] *m* (-*es*; -*e*) BOT rice

Reise ['raizə] *f* (-; -*n*) trip; journey; tour; MAR voyage; **auf ~n sein** be travel(l)ing; **e-e ~ machen** take a trip; **gute ~!** have a nice trip!; **~andenken** *n* souvenir; **~bü,ro** *n* travel agency *or* bureau; **~führer** *m* guide(book); **~gesellschaft** *f* tourist party; tour operator; **~kosten** *pl* travel(l)ing expenses; **~krankheit** *f* travel sickness; **~leiter(in)** tour guide *or* manager, *Br* courier

'reisen *v/i* (*ge-, sein*) travel; **durch Frankreich ~** tour France; **ins Ausland ~** go abroad; **'Reisende** *m, f* (-*n*; -*n*) travel(l)er; tourist; passenger

'Reise|pass *m* passport; **~scheck** *m* travel(l)er's check (*Br* cheque); **~tasche** *f* travel(l)ing bag, holdall

Reisig ['raiziç] *n* (-*s*; *no pl*) brushwood

Reißbrett ['raisbrɛt] *n* drawing board

reißen ['raisən] (*irr, ge-*) **1.** *v/t* (*h*) tear (**in Stücke** to pieces), rip; pull, drag; ZO kill; F crack (*jokes*); SPORT knock down;

an sich ~ seize, snatch, grab **2.** v/i (sein) break, burst; **sich um et. ~** scramble for (or to get) s.th.; **~d** adj torrential

Reißer ['raisɐ] m (-s; -) thriller; hit

reißerisch ['raisərɪʃ] adj sensational, loud

'**Reiß|verschluss** m zipper; **den ~ an et. öffnen (schließen)** unzip (zip up) s.th.; **~zwecke** f thumbtack, Br drawing pin

reiten ['raitən] (irr, ge-) **1.** v/i (sein) ride, go on horseback **2.** v/t (h) ride

'**Reiten** n (-s; no pl) horseback riding

Reiter ['raitɐ] m (-s; -) rider, horseman

Reiterin ['raitərɪn] f (-; -nen) rider, horsewoman

'**Reitpferd** n saddle or riding horse

Reiz [raits] m (-es; -e) charm, attraction, appeal; thrill; MED, PSYCH stimulus; (für j-n) den ~ verlieren lose one's appeal (for s.o.); '**reizbar** adj irritable, excitable; **reizen** ['raitsən] (ge-, h) **1.** v/t irritate (a. MED), annoy; zo bait; provoke; appeal to, attract; tempt; challenge **2.** v/i cards: bid; '**reizend** adj charming, delightful; lovely, sweet, cute; '**reizlos** adj unattractive

'**Reizung** f (-; -en) irritation (a. MED)

'**reizvoll** adj attractive; challenging

'**Reizwort** n (-[e]s; -wörter) emotive word

rekeln ['rɛːkəln] F v/refl (ge-, h) loll

Reklamation [reklama'tsjoːn] f (-; -en) complaint

Reklame [re'klaːmə] f (-; -n) advertising, publicity; advertisement, F ad; ~ **machen für** advertise, promote

reklamieren [rekla'miːrən] v/i (no ge-, h) complain (**wegen** about), protest (against)

Rekord [re'kɔrt] m (-[e]s; -e) record; **e-n ~ aufstellen** set or establish a record

Rekrut [re'kruːt] m (-en; -en) MIL recruit

rekrutieren [rekru'tiːrən] v/t (no ge-, h) recruit

Rektor ['rɛktoːɐ] m (-s; -en [rɛk'toːrən]) principal, Br headmaster; UNIV president, Br rector; **Rektorin** [rɛk'toːrɪn] f (-; -nen) principal, Br headmistress; UNIV president, Br rector

relativ [rela'tiːf] adj relative

Relief [re'ljɛf] n (-s; -s) relief

Religion [reli'gjoːn] f (-; -en) religion

religiös [reli'gjøːs] adj religious

Reling ['reːlɪŋ] f (-; -s) MAR rail

Reliquie [re'liːkvjə] f (-; -n) relic

Rempelei [rɛmpə'lai] F f (-; -en), **rempeln** ['rɛmpəln] F v/t (ge-, h) jostle

Rennbahn ['rɛnbaːn] f racecourse, racetrack; cycling track

'**Rennboot** n racing boat; speedboat

rennen ['rɛnən] v/i and v/t (irr, ge-, sein) run; '**Rennen** n (-s; -) race (a. fig); heat

'**Renn|fahrer** m, **~fahrerin** f racing driver; racing cyclist; **~läufer** m ski racer; **~pferd** n racehorse, racer; **~rad** n racing bicycle, racer; **~sport** m racing; **~stall** m racing stable; **~wagen** m race (Br racing) car, racer

renommiert [reno'miːɐt] adj renowned

renovieren [reno'viːrən] v/t (no ge-, h) renovate, Br do up; redecorate

rentabel [rɛn'taːbəl] adj ECON profitable, paying

Rente ['rɛntə] f (-; -n) (old age) pension; **in ~ gehen** retire

'**Renten|alter** n retirement age; **~versicherung** f pension scheme

Rentier ['rɛntiːɐ] n (-s; -e) zo reindeer

rentieren [rɛn'tiːrən] v/refl (no ge-, h) ECON pay; fig be worth it

Rentner ['rɛntnɐ] m (-s; -), '**Rentnerin** ['rɛntnərɪn] f (-; -nen) (old age) pensioner

Reparatur [repara'tuːɐ] f (-; -en) repair; **~werkstatt** f repair shop; MOT garage

reparieren [repa'riːrən] v/t (no ge-, h) repair, mend, F fix

Reportage [repɔr'taːʒə] f (-; -n) report

Reporter [re'pɔrtɐ] m (-s; -), **Reporterin** f (-; -nen) reporter

Repräsentant [reprɛzɛn'tant] m (-en; -en) representative; **Repräsentantenhaus** n PARL House of Representatives; **Repräsentantin** f (-; -nen) representative; **repräsentieren** [reprɛzɛn'tiːrən] v/t (no ge-, h) represent

Repressalie [reprɛ'saːljə] f (-; -n) reprisal

Reproduktion [reprodukˈtsjoːn] f (-; -en) reproduction, print

reproduzieren [reprodu'tsiːrən] v/t (no ge-, h) reproduce

Reptil [rɛp'tiːl] n (-s; -ien) zo reptile

Republik [repu'bliːk] f (-; -en) republic

Republikaner [republi'kaːnɐ] m (-s; -), **Republikanerin** f (-; -nen), **republikanisch** adj POL republican

Reservat [rezɛr'vaːt] n (-[e]s; -e) (p)reserve; reservation

Reserve [re'zɛrvə] f (-; -n) reserve (a. MIL); ~... in cpds ...kanister, ...rad etc: spare ...

reservieren [rezɛr'viːrən] v/t (no -ge-, h) reserve (a. ~ lassen); j-m e-n Platz ~ keep or save a seat for s.o.; **reserviert** [rezɛr'viːrt] adj reserved (a. fig); aloof; **Reser'viertheit** f (-; no pl) aloofness

Residenz [rezi'dɛnts] f (-; -en) residence

Resignation [rezɪgnaˈtsjoːn] f (-; no pl) resignation; **resignieren** [rezɪˈgniːrən] v/i (no -ge-, h) give up; **resigniert** [rezɪˈgniːrt] adj resigned

Resoziali'sierung f (-; -en) rehabilitation

Respekt [re'spɛkt] m (-[e]s; no pl) respect (vor dat for); **respektieren** [respɛkˈtiːrən] v/t (no -ge-, h) respect; **re'spektlos** adj irreverent, disrespectful; **re'spektvoll** adj respectful

Ressort [rɛ'soːɐ] n (-s; -s) department, province

Rest [rɛst] m (-[e]s; -e) rest; pl remains, remnants; GASTR leftovers; F **das gab ihm den ~** that finished him (off)

Restaurant [rɛstoˈraː] n (-s; -s) restaurant

restaurieren [rɛstoˈriːrən] v/t (no -ge-, h) restore

'Restbetrag m remainder

'restlich adj remaining

'restlos adv completely

Resultat [rezʊl'taːt] n (-[e]s; -e) result (a. SPORT), outcome

Retorte [re'tɔrtə] f (-; -n) CHEM retort

Re'tortenbaby F n test-tube baby

retten ['rɛtən] v/t (ge-, h) save, rescue (both: aus dat, vor dat from)

Retter ['rɛtɐ] m (-s; -), **'Retterin** f (-; -nen) rescuer

Rettich ['rɛtɪç] m (-s; -e) BOT radish

'Rettung f (-; -en) rescue (aus dat, vor dat from); **das war s-e ~** that saved him

'Rettungs|boot n lifeboat; ~mannschaft f rescue party; ~ring m life belt, life buoy; ~schwimmer m lifeguard

Reue ['rɔYə] f (-; no pl) remorse, repentance (both: über acc for)

reumütig ['rɔYmyːtɪç] adj repentant

Revanche [re'vãːʃ(ə)] f (-; -n) revenge

revanchieren [revãˈʃiːrən] v/refl (no -ge-, h) have one's revenge (bei, an

dat on); make it up (bei j-m to s.o.)

Revers [re'veːɐ] n, m (-; -) lapel

revidieren [revi'diːrən] v/t (no -ge-, h) revise; ECON audit

Revier [re'viːɐ] n (-s; -e) district; zo territory (a. fig); → **Polizeirevier**

Revision [revi'zjoːn] f (-; -en) revision; ECON audit; JUR appeal

Revolte [re'vɔltə] f (-; -n), **revoltieren** [revɔl'tiːrən] v/i (no -ge-, h) revolt

Revolution [revolu'tsjoːn] f (-; -en) revolution; **revolutionär** [revolutsjo-'nɛːɐ] adj, **Revolutio'när(in)** (-s; -e/-; -nen) revolutionary

Revolver [re'vɔlvɐ] m (-s; -) revolver, F gun

Revue [re'vyː] f (-; -n) THEA (musical) show

Rezept [re'tsɛpt] n (-[e]s; -e) MED prescription; GASTR recipe (a. fig)

Rezession [retse'sjoːn] f (-; -en) ECON recession

Rhabarber [ra'barbɐ] m (-s; no pl) BOT rhubarb

rhetorisch [re'toːrɪʃ] adj rhetorical

Rheuma ['rɔYma] n (-s; no pl) MED rheumatism

rhythmisch ['rʏtmɪʃ] adj rhythmic(al)

Rhythmus ['rʏtmʊs] m (-; -men) rhythm

Ribisel ['riːbiːzəl] Austrian G f (-; -[n]) → **Johannisbeere**

richten ['rɪçtən] v/t (ge-, h) fix; get s.th. ready, prepare; do (room, one's hair); (sich) ~ an (acc) address (o.s.) to; put a question to; ~ auf (acc) direct or turn to; point or aim camera, gun etc at; ~ gegen direct against; sich ~ nach go by, act according to; follow (fashion etc); depend on; **ich richte mich ganz nach dir** I leave it to you

Richter(in) ['rɪçtɐ, 'rɪçtərɪn] m(f) (-s; -/-; -nen) judge

'richterlich adj judicial

'Richtgeschwindigkeit f MOT recommended speed

richtig ['rɪçtɪç] 1. adj right; correct, proper; true; real 2. adv: ~ nett (böse) really nice (angry); et. ~ machen do s.th. right; **m-e Uhr geht ~** my watch is right

'Richtigkeit f (-; no pl) correctness

richtigstellen v/t (sep, -ge-, h) fig put or set right

'Richt|linien pl guidelines; ~preis m

ECON recommended price

'**Richtung** f (-; -en) direction; POL leaning; PAINT etc style; '**richtungslos** adj aimless, disorient(at)ed

'**richtungweisend** adj pioneering

rieb [ri:p] pret of **reiben**

riechen ['ri:çən] v/i and v/t (irr, ge-, h) smell (**nach** of; **an** dat at)

rief [ri:f] pret of **rufen**

Riegel ['ri:gəl] m (-s; -) bolt, bar

Riemen ['ri:mən] m (-s; -) strap; TECH belt; MAR oar

Riese ['ri:zə] m (-n; -n) giant (a. fig)

rieseln ['ri:zəln] v/i (ge-, sein) trickle; rain: drizzle; snow: fall gently

'**Riesen...** in cpds mst giant ..., gigantic ..., enormous ...; **~erfolg** m huge success, film etc: a. smash hit

'**riesengroß**, '**riesenhaft** → **riesig**

'**Riesenrad** n Ferris wheel

riesig ['ri:zıç] adj enormous, gigantic, giant

Riesin f (-; -nen) giantess (a. fig)

riet [ri:t] pret of **raten**

Riff [rɪf] n (-[e]s; -e) GEOGR reef

Rille ['rɪlə] f (-; -n) groove

Rind [rɪnt] n (-[e]s; -er ['rɪndɐ]) ZO cow, pl cattle; GASTR beef

Rinde ['rɪndə] f (-; -n) BOT bark; GASTR rind; crust

Rinder|braten ['rɪndɐbra:tən] m roast beef; **~herde** f herd of cattle

'**Rind|fleisch** n GASTR beef; **~(s)leder** n cowhide; **~vieh** n ZO cattle

Ring [rɪŋ] m (-[e]s; -e) ring (a. fig); MOT ring road; subway etc: circle (line)

'**Ringbuch** n loose-leaf or ring binder

ringeln ['rɪŋəln] v/refl (ge-, h) curl, coil (a. ZO)

'**Ringelnatter** f ZO grass snake

'**Ringelspiel** Austrian n → **Karussell**

ringen ['rɪŋən] (irr, ge-, h) **1.** v/i SPORT wrestle (**mit** with), fig a. struggle (against, with; **um** for); **nach Atem ~** gasp (for breath) **2.** v/t wring

'**Ringen** n (-s; no pl) SPORT wrestling

'**Ringer** [-ŋɐ] m (-s; -) SPORT wrestler

ringförmig ['rɪŋfœrmıç] adj circular

'**Ringkampf** m SPORT wrestling match

'**Ringrichter** m SPORT referee

rings adv: **~ um** around

'**ringshe'rum**, '**rings'um**, '**ringsum'her** adv all around; everywhere

Rinne ['rɪnə] f (-; -n) groove, channel;

gutter; '**rinnen** v/i (irr, ge-, sein) run; flow, stream; **Rinnsal** ['rɪnza:l] n (-s; -e) trickle

'**Rinnstein** m gutter

Rippe ['rɪpə] f (-; -n) ANAT rib

'**Rippenfell** n ANAT pleura; **~entzündung** f MED pleurisy

'**Rippenstoß** m nudge in the ribs

Risiko ['ri:ziko] n (-s; -s, -ken) risk; **ein (kein) ~ eingehen** take a risk (no risks); **auf eigenes ~** at one's own risk

riskant [rɪs'kant] adj risky

riskieren [rɪs'ki:rən] v/t (no -ge-, h) risk

riss [rɪs] pret of **reißen**

Riss m (-es; -e) tear, rip, split (a. fig); crack; MED chap, laceration; **rissig** ['rɪsıç] adj chapped; cracky, cracked

Rist [rɪst] m (-es; -e) ANAT instep

ritt [rɪt] pret of **reiten**

Ritt m (-[e]s; -e) ride (on horseback)

Ritter ['rɪtɐ] m (-s; -) knight; **j-n zum ~ schlagen** knight s.o.

'**ritterlich** fig adj chivalrous

Ritz [rɪts] m (-es; -e), **Ritze** ['rɪtsə] f (-; -n) crack, chink; gap

Rivale [ri'va:lə] m (-n; -n), **Ri'valin** f (-; -nen) rival; **rivalisieren** [rivali'zi:rən] v/i (no -ge-, h) compete; **Rivalität** [rivali'tɛ:t] f (-; -en) rivalry

rk., **r.-k.** abbr of **römisch-katholisch** RC, Roman Catholic

Robbe ['rɔbə] f (-; -n) ZO seal

Robe ['ro:bə] f (-; -n) robe, gown

Roboter ['rɔbɔtɐ] m (-s; -) robot

robust [ro'bust] adj robust, strong, tough

roch [rɔx] pret of **riechen**

röcheln ['rœçəln] (ge-, h) **1.** v/i moan **2.** v/t gasp

Rock [rɔk] m (-[e]s; Röcke ['rœkə]) skirt

Rodelbahn ['ro:dəlba:n] f toboggan run

rodeln ['ro:dəln] v/i (ge-, sein) sled(ge), coast; SPORT toboggan

'**Rodelschlitten** m sled(ge); toboggan

roden ['ro:dən] v/t (ge-, h) clear; stub

Rogen ['ro:gən] m (-s; -) (hard) roe

Roggen ['rɔgən] m (-s; -) BOT rye

roh [ro:] adj raw; rough; fig brutal; **mit ~er Gewalt** with brute force

'**Rohbau** m (-[e]s; -ten) carcass

'**Rohkost** f raw vegetables and fruit

'**Rohling** m (-s; -e) TECH blank; fig brute

'**Rohmateri,al** n raw material

'**Rohöl** n crude (oil)

Rohr [roːɐ] n (-[e]s; -e ['roːrə]) TECH pipe, tube; duct; BOT reed; cane

Röhre ['røːrə] f (-; -n) pipe, tube (a. TV), TV etc valve

'**Rohr|leitung** f duct, pipe(s); plumbing; pipeline; **~stock** m cane; **~zucker** m cane sugar

'**Rohstoff** m raw material

Rollbahn ['rɔlbaːn] f AVIAT runway

Rolle ['rɔlə] f (-; -n) roll (a. SPORT), TECH a. roller; coil; caster, castor; THEA part, role (both a. fig); **e-e ~ Garn** a spool of thread, Br a reel of cotton; **das spielt keine~** that doesn't matter, that makes no difference; **Geld spielt k-e~** money is no object

'**rollen** v/i (ge-, sein) and v/t (ge-, h) roll

Roller ['rɔlə] m (-s; -) (motor) scooter

'**Roll|film** m PHOT roll film; **~kragen** m turtleneck, esp Br polo neck; **~laden** m rolling shutter

Rollo ['rɔlo] n (-s; -s) shades, Br (roller) blind

'**Rollschuh** m roller skate; **~ laufen** roller-skate; **~bahn** f roller-skating rink; **~läufer** m roller skater

'**Rollstuhl** m wheelchair

'**Rolltreppe** f escalator

Roman [ro'maːn] m (-s; -e) novel

Romanik [ro'maːnɪk] f (-; no pl) ARCH Romanesque (style or period)

romanisch [ro'maːnɪʃ] adj LING Romance; ARCH Romanesque

Romanist [roma'nɪst] m (-en; -en), **Roma'nistin** f (-; -nen) student of Romance languages

Ro'manschriftsteller m, **Ro'manschriftstellerin** f novelist

Romantik [ro'mantɪk] f (-; no pl) romance; HIST Romanticism

romantisch [ro'mantɪʃ] adj romantic

Römer ['røːmɐ] m (-s; -), **'Römerin** f (-; -nen), **römisch** ['røːmɪʃ] adj Roman

Rommee ['rɔmeː] n (-s; -s) rummy

röntgen ['rœntɡən] v/t (ge-, h) MED X-ray

'**Röntgen|appa‚rat** m MED X-ray apparatus;**~aufnahme** f,**~bild** n MED X-ray; **~strahlen** pl PHYS X-rays; **~untersuchung** f MED X-ray

rosa ['roːza] adj pink; fig rose-col-o(u)red;**Rose** ['roːzə] f (-; -n) BOT rose

'**Rosenkohl** m BOT Brussels sprouts

'**Rosenkranz** m REL rosary

rosig ['roːzɪç] adj rosy (a. fig)

Rosine [ro'ziːnə] f (-; -n) raisin

'**Rosshaar** n (-[e]s; no pl) horsehair

Rost [rɔst] m (-[e]s; -e) (no pl) CHEM rust; TECH grate; GASTR grid(iron), grill; **rosten** ['rɔstən] v/i (ge-, sein) rust

rösten ['rœstən] v/t (ge-, h) roast (a. F); toast; fry

'**Rostfleck** m rust stain; '**rostfrei** adj rustproof, stainless; '**rostig** adj rusty

rot [roːt] adj red (a. POL); **~ glühend** red--hot; **~ werden** blush; **in den ~en Zahlen** ECON in the red

Rot n (-s; -) red; **die Ampel steht auf ~** the lights are red; **bei ~** at red

'**rotblond** adj sandy(-haired)

Röte ['røːtə] f (-; no pl) redness, red (colo[u]r); fig blush

Röteln ['røːtəln] pl MED German measles

röten ['røːtən] v/refl (ge-, h) redden; flush

'**rothaarig** adj red-haired

'**Rothaarige** m, f (-n; -n) redhead

rotieren [ro'tiːrən] v/i (no ge-, h) rotate

'**Rotkehlchen** n (-s; -) ZO robin

'**Rotkohl** m BOT red cabbage

rötlich ['røːtlɪç] adj reddish

'**Rot|stift** m red crayon or pencil; **~wein** m red wine;**~wild** n ZO (red) deer

Rotznase ['rɔtsnaːzə] F f snotty nose

Route ['ruːtə] f (-; -n) route

Routine [ru'tiːnə] f (-;no pl) routine; experience;**~sache** f routine (matter)

routiniert [ruti'niːrt] adj experienced

Rübe ['ryːbə] f (-; -n) BOT turnip; (sugar) beet

Rubin [ru'biːn] m (-s; -e) MIN ruby

Rübli ['ryːpli] Swiss n (-s; -) BOT carrot

Rubrik [ru'briːk] f (-; -en) heading; column

Ruck [rʊk] m (-[e]s; -e) jerk, jolt, start; fig POL swing

Rückantwortschein ['rʏkantvɔrtʃaɪn] m reply coupon

'**ruckartig** adj jerky, abrupt

'**rückbezüglich** adj LING reflexive

'**Rückblende** f flashback (**auf** acc to)

'**Rückblick** m review (**auf** acc of); **im ~** in retrospect

rücken ['rʏkən] **1.** v/t (ge-, h) move, shift, push **2.** v/i (ge-, sein) move; move over; **näher ~** approach

'**Rücken** *m* (-*s*; -) ANAT back (*a.* *fig*);~deckung *fig* *f* backing, support;~lehne *f* back(rest);~mark *n* ANAT spinal cord; ~schmerzen *pl* backache; ~schwimmen *n* backstroke;~wind *m* following wind, tailwind;~wirbel *m* ANAT dorsal vertebra

'**Rück|erstattung** *f* (-; -*en*) refund; ~fahrkarte *f* round-trip ticket, *Br* a. return (ticket); ~fahrt *f* return trip; *auf der ~* on the way back;~fall *m* relapse

'**rückfällig** *adj*: ~ *werden* relapse

'**Rückflug** *m* return flight

'**Rückgabe** *f* (-; *no pl*) return

'**Rückgang** *m* drop, fall; ECON recession

'**rückgängig** *adj*: ~ *machen* cancel

'**Rück|gewinnung** *f* (-; *no pl*) recovery; ~grat *n* ANAT spine, backbone (*both a.* *fig*); ~halt *m* (-[*e*]*s*; *no pl*) support; ~hand *f*,~handschlag *m* tennis: backhand;~kauf *m* ECON repurchase

'**Rückkehr** *f* [ˈrʏkkeːɐ] *f* (-; *no pl*) return; *nach s-r~ aus ...* on his return from ...

'**Rück|kopplung** *f* ELECTR feedback (*a.* *fig*);~lage *f* (-; -*n*) reserve(s); savings; ~lauf *m* TECH rewind

'**rückläufig** *adj* falling, downward

'**Rücklicht** *n* (-[*e*]*s*; -*er*) MOT rear light, taillight

'**rücklings** [ˈrʏklɪŋs] *adv* backward(s); from behind

'**Rückporto** *n* return postage

'**Rückreise** *f* → *Rückfahrt*

'**Rucksack** [ˈrʊkzak] *m* rucksack, backpack; ~tou,rismus *m* backpacking; ~tou,rist *m* backpacker

'**Rück|schlag** *m* SPORT return; *fig* setback;~schluss *m* conclusion;~schritt *m* *fig* step back(ward); ~seite *f* back; reverse; flip side;~sendung *f* return

'**Rücksicht** *f* (-; -*en*) consideration, regard; *aus (ohne) ~ auf (acc)* out of (without any) consideration *or* regard for; *~ nehmen auf (acc)* show consideration for; '**rücksichtslos** *adj* inconsiderate (*gegen* of), thoughtless (of); ruthless; reckless; '**rücksichtsvoll** *adj* considerate (*gegen* of), thoughtful

'**Rück|sitz** *m* MOT back seat;~spiegel *m* MOT rear-view mirror; ~spiel *n* SPORT return match;~stand *m* CHEM residue; *mit der Arbeit (e-m Tor) im ~ sein* be behind with one's work (down by one goal)

'**rückständig** *adj* backward; underdeveloped; ~*e Miete* arrears of rent

'**Rück|stau** *m* MOT tailback;~stelltaste *f* backspace key; ~tritt *m* resignation; withdrawal; TECH → ~trittbremse *f* coaster (*Br* back-pedal) brake

rückwärts [ˈrʏkvɛrts] *adv* backward(s); *~ aus* (*dat*) *... fahren* back out of ...; *~ in* (*acc*) *... fahren* back into ...

'**Rückwärtsgang** *m* MOT reverse (gear)

'**Rückweg** *m* way back

'**ruckweise** *adv* jerkily, in jerks

'**rückwirkend** *adj* retroactive

'**Rück|wirkung** *f* reaction (*auf acc* upon); ~zahlung *f* repayment; ~zieher *m* (-*s*; -) soccer: overhead kick; F *e-n ~ machen* back (*or* chicken) out (*von* of);~zug *m* retreat

Rüde [ˈryːdə] *m* (-*n*; -*n*) ZO male (dog *ect*)

Rudel [ˈruːdəl] *n* (-*s*; -) ZO pack; herd

Ruder [ˈruːdɐ] *n* (-*s*; -) AVIAT, MAR rudder; SPORT oar; *am ~* at the helm (*a.* *fig*); ~boot *n* rowing boat, rowboat

Ruderer [ˈruːdərɐ] *m* (-*s*; -) rower, oarsman; '**Ruderin** *f* (-; -*nen*) rower, oarswoman; '**rudern** *v/i and v/t* (*ge-, h*) row

'**Ruder|re,gatta** *f* (rowing) regatta, boat race;~sport *m* rowing

Ruf [ruːf] *m* (-[*e*]*s*; -*e*) call (*a.* *fig*); cry, shout; *fig* reputation; '**rufen** *v/i and v/t* (*irr, ge-, h*) call (*nach* for) cry, shout; ~ *nach* call for (*a.* *fig*); ~ *lassen* send for; *um Hilfe ~* call *or* cry for help

'**Rufnummer** *f* telephone number

'**Rufweite** *f*: *in* (*außer*) ~ within (out of) call(ing distance)

Rüge [ˈryːgə] *f* (-; -*n*) reproof, reproach (*both: wegen* for); '**rügen** *v/t* (*ge-, h*) reprove, reproach

Ruhe [ˈruːə] *f* (-; *no pl*) quiet, calm; silence; rest; peace; calm(ness); *zur ~ kommen* come to rest; *j-n in ~ lassen* leave s.o. in peace; *lass mich in ~!* leave me alone!; *et. in ~ tun* take one's time (doing s.th.); *die ~ behalten* F keep (one's) cool, play it cool; *sich zur ~ setzen* retire; *~, bitte!* (be) quiet, please!; '**ruhelos** *adj* restless

ruhen *v/i* (*ge-, h*) rest (*auf dat* on)

'**Ruhe|pause** *f* break;~stand *m* (-[*e*]*s*; *no pl*) retirement; ~tag *m* a day's rest; *Montag ~* closed on Mondays

ruhig [ˈruːɪç] *adj* quiet; silent; calm;

R

cool; TECH smooth; **~ bleiben** F keep (one's) cool, play it cool

Ruhm [ruːm] *m* (-[e]s; *no pl*) fame, *esp* POL, MIL *etc* glory; **rühmen** ['ryːmən] *v/t* (ge-, h) praise (**wegen** for); **sich e-r Sache ~** boast of s.th.; **rühmlich** ['ryːmlɪç] *adj* laudable, praiseworthy

'ruhmlos *adj* inglorious

'ruhmreich *adj* glorious

Ruhr [ruːɐ] *f* (-; *no pl*) MED dysentery

Rührei er ['ryːɐʔaiɐ] *pl* scrambled eggs

rühren ['ryːrən] *v/t* (ge-, h) stir; move (*a. fig.*); *fig* touch, affect; *das rührt mich gar nicht* that leaves me cold; *rührt euch!* MIL (stand) at ease!; **~d** *fig adj* touching, moving; very kind

rührig ['ryːrɪç] *adj* active, busy

rührselig ['ryːɐzeːlɪç] *adj* sentimental

'Rührung *f* (-; *no pl*) emotion

Ruin [ruˈiːn] *m* (-s; *no pl*) ruin

Ruine [ruˈiːnə] *f* (-; *-n*) ruin

ruinieren [ruiˈniːrən] *v/t* (*no -ge-*, h) ruin

rülpsen ['rʏlpsən] *v/i* (ge-, h), **Rülpser** ['rʏlpsɐ] *m* (-s; -) belch

Rumäne [ruˈmɛːnə] *m* (-n; -n) Romanian; **Rumänien** Romania; **Ru'mänin** *f* (-; *-nen*), **ru'mänisch** *adj* Romanian

Rummel ['rʊməl] F *m* (-s; *no pl*) (hustle and) bustle; F ballyhoo; **~platz** F *m* amusement park, fairground

rumoren [ruˈmoːrən] *v/i* (*no -ge-*, h) rumble

Rumpelkammer ['rʊmpəlkamɐ] F *f* lumber room

rumpeln ['rʊmpəln] F *v/i* (ge-, h, *sein*) rumble

Rumpf [rʊmpf] *m* (-es; *Rümpfe* ['rʏmpfə]) ANAT trunk; MAR hull; AVIAT fuselage

rümpfen ['rʏmpfən] *v/t* (ge-, h) *die Nase ~* turn up one's nose (**über** *acc* at), sneer (at)

rund [rʊnt] 1. *adj* round (*a. fig*) 2. *adv* about; *~ um* (a)round; **'Rundblick** *m* panorama; **Runde** ['rʊndə] *f* (-; *-n*) round (*a. fig and* SPORT); *racing*: lap; *s-e ~ machen in* (*dat*) patrol; *die ~ machen* go the round(s)

'Rundfahrt *f* tour (**durch** round)

'Rundfunk *m* (-s; *no pl*) radio; broad-

casting corporation; *im ~* on the radio; *im ~ übertragen or senden* broadcast; *~hörer(in)* listener, *pl a.* (radio) audience; *~sender m* broadcasting *or* radio station

'Rundgang *m* tour (**durch** of)

'rundhe'raus *adv* frankly, plainly

'rundhe'rum *adv* all around

'rundlich *adj* plump, chubby

'Rundreise *f* tour (**durch** of); **~schau** *f* review; **~schreiben** *n* circular (letter); **~spruch** *Swiss m* → **Rundfunk**

'Rundung *f* (-; *-en*) curve

rundweg [rʊntˈvɛk] *adv* flatly, plainly

runter ['rʊntɐ] F *adv* → **herunter**

Runzel ['rʊntsəl] *f* (-; *-n*) wrinkle

runz(e)lig ['rʊnts(ə)lɪç] *adj* wrinkled

'runzeln *v/t* (ge-, h) *die Stirn ~* frown (**über** *acc* at)

Rüpel ['ryːpəl] *m* (-s; -) lout

rupfen ['rʊpfən] *v/t* (ge-, h) pluck

Rüsche ['ryːʃə] *f* (-; *-n*) frill, ruffle

Ruß [ruːs] *m* (-es; *no pl*) soot

Russe ['rʊsə] *m* (-n; -n) Russian

Rüssel ['rʏsəl] *m* (-s; -) ZO trunk; snout

rußen ['ruːsən] *v/i* (ge-, h) smoke

rußig ['ruːsɪç] *adj* sooty

Russin ['rʊsɪn] *f* (-; *-nen*), **russisch** ['rʊsɪʃ] *adj* Russian

'Russland Russia

rüsten ['rʏstən] (ge-, h) 1. *v/i* MIL arm 2. *v/refl* get ready, prepare (**zu, für** for); arm o.s. (**gegen** for)

rüstig ['rʏstɪç] *adj* vigorous, sprightly

rustikal [rʊstiˈkaːl] *adj* rustic

'Rüstung *f* (-; *-en*) MIL armament; armo(u)r

'Rüstungs|indus,trie *f* armament industry; **~wettlauf** *m* arms race

'Rüstzeug *n* equipment

Rute ['ruːtə] *f* (-; *-n*) rod (*a. fig*), switch

Rutschbahn ['rʊtʃbaːn] *f*, **Rutsche** ['rʊtʃə] *f* (-; *-n*) slide, chute; **'rutschen** *v/i* (ge-, h, *sein*) slide, slip; glide; MOT *etc* skid; **rutschig** ['rʊtʃɪç] *adj* slippery

'rutschsicher *adj* MOT *etc* non-skid

rütteln ['rʏtəln] (ge-, h) 1. *v/t* shake 2. *v/i* jolt; *an der Tür ~* rattle at the door

S

S *abbr of* **Süd(en)** S, south

S. *abbr of* **Seite** p., page

s. *abbr of* **siehe** see

Saal [zaːl] *m* (-[e]s; **Säle** ['zɛːlə]) hall

Saat [zaːt] *f* (-; -en) (*no pl*) sowing; seed(s) (*a. fig*); crop(s)

Sabbat ['zabat] *m* (-s; -e) sabbath (day)

sabbern ['zabɐn] F *v/i* (*ge-*, *h*) slobber, slaver

Säbel ['zɛːbəl] *m* (-s; -) saber, *Br* sabre (*a.* SPORT), sword; '**säbeln** F *v/t* (*ge-*, *h*) cut, hack

Sabotage [zabo'taːʒə] *f* (-; -n) sabotage; **Saboteur** [zabo'tøːɐ] *m* (-s; -e) saboteur; **sabotieren** [zabo'tiːrən] *v/t* (*no -ge-*, *h*) sabotage

Sach|bearbeiter ['zaxbəʔarbaitɐ] *m*, ~**bearbeiterin** ['zaxbəʔarbaitərɪn] *f* official in charge; ~**beschädigung** *f* damage to property; ~**buch** *n* specialized book, *pl coll* nonfiction

'**sachdienlich** *adj*: ~**e Hinweise** relevant information

Sache ['zaxə] *f* (-; -n) thing; matter, business; issue, problem, question; cause; JUR matter, case; *pl* things, clothes; **zur ~ kommen** (**bei der ~ bleiben**) come (keep) to the point; **nicht zur ~ gehören** be irrelevant

'**sachgerecht** *adj* proper

'**Sachkenntnis** *f* expert knowledge

'**sachkundig** *adj* expert

'**sachlich** *adj* matter-of-fact, business-like; unbias(s)ed, objective; practical, technical; ~ **richtig** factually correct

sächlich ['zɛçlɪç] *adj* LING neuter

'**Sachre,gister** *n* (subject) index

'**Sachschaden** *m* damage to property

sacht [zaxt] *adj* soft, gentle; slow

'**Sach|verhalt** *m* (-[e]s; -e) facts (of the case); ~**verstand** *m* know-how; ~**verständige** *m*, *f* (-n; -n) expert; JUR expert witness; ~**wert** *m* (-[e]s; *no pl*) real value; ~**zwänge** *pl* inherent necessities

Sack [zak] *m* (-[e]s; **Säcke** ['zɛkə]) sack, bag; V balls; **sacken** ['zakən] F *v/i* (*ge-*, *sein*) sink; '**Sackgasse** *f* blind alley (*a. fig*), dead end (*a. fig*), *fig* impasse

Sadismus [za'dɪsmus] *m* (-; *no pl*) sadism; **Sadist** [za'dɪst] *m* (-en; -en) sad-

ist; **sa'distisch** *adj* sadistic

säen ['zɛːən] *v/t and v/i* (*ge-*, *h*) sow (*a. fig*)

Safari [za'faːri] *f* (-; -s) safari; ~**park** *m* wildlife reserve, safari park

Saft [zaft] *m* (-[e]s; **Säfte** ['zɛftə]) juice; BOT sap (*both a. fig*); **saftig** ['zaftɪç] *adj* juicy (*a. fig*), lush; F fancy (*prices etc*)

Sage ['zaːgə] *f* (-; -n) legend, myth

Säge ['zɛːgə] *f* (-; -n) saw

'**Sägemehl** *n* sawdust

sagen ['zaːgən] *v/i and v/t* (*ge-*, *h*) say; **j-m et.** ~ tell s.o. s.th.; **die Wahrheit** ~ tell the truth; **er lässt dir** ~ he asked me to tell you; ~ **wir ...** (let's) say ...; **man sagt, er sei reich** he is said to be rich; **er lässt sich nichts** ~ he will not listen to reason; **das hat nichts zu** ~ it doesn't matter; **et. (nichts) zu** ~ **haben** (**bei**) have a say (no say) (in); **das sagt mir nichts** it doesn't mean anything to me; **unter uns gesagt** between you and me

sägen ['zɛːgən] *v/t and v/i* (*ge-*, *h*) saw

'**sagenhaft** *adj* legendary; F fabulous, incredible, fantastic

'**Sägespäne** *pl* sawdust

'**Sägewerk** *n* sawmill

sah [zaː] *pret of* **sehen**

Sahne ['zaːnə] *f* (-; *no pl*) cream

Saison [zɛ'zõ:] *f* (-; -s) season; **in der** ~ in season

sai'sonbedingt *adj* seasonal

Saite ['zaitə] *f* (-; -n) MUS string, chord (*a. fig*); '**Saiteninstru,ment** *n* MUS string(ed) instrument

Sakko ['zako] *m*, *n* (-s; -s) (sports) jacket, sport(s) coat

Sakristei [zakrıs'tai] *f* (-; -en) REL vestry, sacristy

Salat [za'laːt] *m* (-[e]s; -e) BOT lettuce; GASTR salad; ~**sauce** *f* salad dressing

Salbe ['zalbə] *f* (-; -n) ointment

'**Salbung** *f* (-; -en) unction

'**salbungsvoll** *adj* unctuous

Saldo ['zaldo] *m* (-s; -s, -di) ECON balance

Salon [za'lõ:] *m* (-s; -s) salon; MAR saloon; drawing room

salopp [za'lɔp] *adj* casual; *contp* sloppy

Salpeter [zal'peːtɐ] *m* (-s; *no pl*) CHEM salt|peter (*Br* -petre), niter, *Br* nitre

Salto ['zalto] *m* (-s; -s, -ti) somersault

Salut [za'luːt] *m* (-[e]s; -e) MIL salute; **~ schießen** fire a salute

salutieren [zalu'tiːrən] *v/i* (*no -ge-, h*) MIL (give a) salute

Salve ['zalvə] *f* (-; -n) MIL volley (*a. fig*); salute

Salz [zalts] *n* (-es; -e) salt

'Salzbergwerk *n* salt mine

salzen ['zaltsən] *v/t* ([*irr,*] *ge-, h*) salt

salzfrei ['zaltsfrai] *adj* salt-free, no-salt *diet*

salzig ['zaltsɪç] *adj* salty

'Salz|kar,toffeln *pl* boiled potatoes; **~säure** *f* (-; *no pl*) CHEM hydrochloric acid; **~stange** *f* pretzel (*Br* salt) stick; **~streuer** *m* (-s; -) salt shaker, *Br* salt cellar; **~wasser** *n* salt water

Same [za:mə] *m* (-n; -n), **'Samen** *m* (-s; -) BOT seed (*a. fig*); BIOL sperm, semen

'Samen|bank *f* (-; -en) MED, VET sperm bank; **~erguss** *m* ejaculation; **~korn** *n* BOT seedcorn

Sammel... ['zaməl-] *in cpds* ...**begriff**, ...**bestellung**, ...**konto** *etc*: collective ...; **~büchse** *f* collecting box

'sammeln *v/t* (*ge-, h*) collect; gather, pick; accumulate; **sich ~** assemble; *fig* compose o.s.

Sammler ['zamlɐ] *m* (-s; -), **'Sammlerin** *f* (-; -nen) collector

'Sammlung *f* (-; -en) collection

Samstag ['zamsta:k] *m* (-[e]s; -e) Saturday

samt [zamt] *prp* (*dat*) together *or* along with

Samt *m* (-[e]s; -e) velvet

sämtlich ['zɛmtlɪç] *adj:* **~e** *pl* all the; the complete *works etc*

Sanatorium [zana'toːrjɔm] *n* (-s; -ien) sanatorium, sanitarium

Sand [zant] *m* (-[e]s; -e) sand

Sandale [zan'daːlə] *f* (-; -n) sandal

Sandalette [zanda'lɛtə] *f* (-; -n) high-heeled sandal

'Sand|bahn *f* SPORT dirt track; **~bank** *f* (-; -bänke) sandbank; **~boden** *m* sandy soil; **~burg** *f* sandcastle

sandig ['zandɪç] *adj* sandy

'Sand|mann *m*, **~männchen** *n* sandman; **~pa,pier** *n* sandpaper; **~sack** *m* sand bag; **~stein** *m* sandstone; **~strand**

m sandy beach

sandte ['zantə] *pret of* **senden**

'Sanduhr *f* hourglass

sanft [zanft] *adj* gentle, soft; mild; easy (*death*)

sanftmütig ['zanftmyːtɪç] *adj* gentle, mild

sang [zaŋ] *pret of* **singen**

Sänger ['zɛŋɐ] *m* (-s; -), **Sängerin** ['zɛŋərɪn] *f* (-; -nen) singer

sanieren [za'niːrən] *v/t* (*no -ge-, h*) redevelop (*a.* ECON), rehabilitate (*a.* ARCH)

Sa'nierung *f* (-; -en) redevelopment, rehabilitation; **Sa'nierungsgebiet** *n* redevelopment area

sanitär [zani'tɛːɐ] *adj* sanitary

Sanitäter [zani'tɛːtɐ] *m* (-s; -) paramedic; MIL medic, *Br* medical orderly

sank [zaŋk] *pret of* **sinken**

Sankt [zaŋkt] Saint, ABBR St

Sardelle [zar'dɛlə] *f* (-; -n) ZO anchovy

Sardine [zar'diːnə] *f* (-; -n) ZO sardine

Sarg [zark] *m* (-[e]s; *Särge* ['zɛrgə]) casket, *esp Br* coffin

Sarkasmus [zar'kasmʊs] *m* (-; *no pl*) sarcasm; **sar'kastisch** *adj* sarcastic

saß [zaːs] *pret of* **sitzen**

Satan ['zaːtan] *m* (-s; -e) Satan; *fig* devil

Satellit [zatɛ'liːt] *m* (-en; -en) satellite (*a. fig*); **über ~** by *or* via satellite

Satel'liten... *in cpds* ...**bild**, ...**staat**, ...**stadt**, ...**-TV**: satellite ...

Satin [za'tɛ̃ː] *m* (-s; -s) satin; sateen

Satire [za'tiːrə] *f* (-; -n) satire (**auf** *acc* upon); **Satiriker** [za'tiːrikɐ] *m* (-s; -) satirist; **sa'tirisch** *adj* satiric(al)

satt [zat] *adj* F full (up); **ich bin ~** I've had enough, F I'm full (up); **sich ~ essen** eat one's fill (**an** *dat* of)

Sattel ['zatəl] *m* (-s; *Sättel* ['zɛtəl]) saddle; **'satteln** *v/t* (*ge-, h*) saddle; **'Sattelschlepper** *m* MOT semi-trailer truck, *Br* articulated lorry

'satthaben *v/t* (*irr, haben, sep, -ge-, h*) F be tired *or* F sick of, be fed up with

sättigen ['zɛtɪgən] (*ge-, h*) **1.** *v/t* satisfy; feed; CHEM, PHYS saturate **2.** *v/i* be substantial, be filling; **'Sättigung** *f* (-; -en) satiety; CHEM, ECON saturation (*a. fig*)

Sattler ['zatlɐ] *m* (-s; -) saddler

Sattlerei [zatlə'rai] *f* (-; -en) saddlery

Satz [zats] *m* (-es; *Sätze* ['zɛtsə]) leap; LING sentence; *tennis etc:* set; ECON rate; MUS movement; **~aussage** *f* LING predicate; **~bau** m (-[e]s; no pl) LING syntax; construction; **~gegenstand** m LING subject

Satzung ['zatsʊŋ] f (-; -en) statute

'Satzzeichen n LING punctuation mark

Sau [zau] f (-; Säue ['zɔʏə]) ZO sow; HUNT wild sow; F swine, pig

sauber ['zaubɐ] adj clean (a. F fig); pure; neat (a. fig), tidy; decent; iro fine, nice; **~ halten** keep clean (**sich** o.s.); **~ machen** clean (up); **'Sauberkeit** f (-; no pl) clean(li)ness; tidiness, neatness; purity; decency; **'saubermachen** v/t and v/i (sep, -ge-, h) → **sauber**, **säubern** ['zɔʏbɐn] v/t (ge-, h) clean (up); cleanse (a. MED)

sauer ['zauɐ] adj sour (a. fig), acid (a. CHEM); GASTR pickled; F mad (**auf** acc at), cross (with); **~ werden** turn sour; F get mad; **saurer Regen** acid rain

säuerlich ['zɔʏɐlɪç] adj sharp; F wry

'Sauerstoff m (-[e]s; no pl) CHEM oxygen; **~gerät** n MED oxygen apparatus; **~zelt** n MED oxygen tent

'Sauerteig m leaven

saufen ['zaufən] v/t and v/i (irr, ge-, h) ZO drink; F booze; **Säufer(in)** ['zɔʏfɐ, 'zɔʏfərɪn] m(f) f (-s; -/-; -nen) drunkard, F boozer

saugen ['zaugən] v/i and v/t (a/t) ([irr,] ge-, h) suck (**an et.** [at] s.th.)

säugen ['zɔʏgən] v/t (ge-, h) suckle (a. ZO), nurse, breastfeed

'Säugetier n mammal

saugfähig ['zaukfɛːɪç] adj absorbent

Säugling ['zɔʏklɪŋ] m (-s; -e) baby, infant

'Säuglings|heim n (baby) nursery; **~pflege** f infant care; **~schwester** f baby nurse; **~stati,on** f neonatal care unit; **~sterblichkeit** f infant mortality

Säule ['zɔʏlə] f (-; -n) column; pillar (a. fig); **'Säulengang** m colonnade

Saum [zaum] m (-[e]s; Säume ['zɔʏmə]) hem(line); seam; **säumen** ['zɔʏmən] v/t (ge-, h) hem; border, edge; line

Sauna ['zauna] f (-; -s, Saunen) sauna

Säure ['zɔʏrə] f (-; -n) CHEM acid

säurehaltig ['zɔʏrəhaltɪç] adj acid

sausen ['zauzən] v/i (ge-, sein) F rush, dash; (ge-, h) ears: buzz; wind: howl

'Saustall m pigsty (a. F contp)

Saxophon [zakso'foːn] n (-s; -e) MUS saxophone, F sax

S-Bahn ['ɛsbaːn] f rapid transit, Br suburban train

Schabe ['ʃaːbə] f (-; -n) ZO cockroach

'schaben v/t (ge-, h) scrape (**von** from)

schäbig ['ʃɛːbɪç] adj shabby, fig a. mean

Schablone [ʃa'bloːnə] f (-; -n) stencil; fig stereotype

Schach [ʃax] n (-s; no pl) chess; **~!** check!; **~ und matt!** checkmate!; **j-n in ~ halten** keep s.o. in check; **~brett** n chessboard; **~feld** n square; **~fi,gur** f chessman, piece

schach'matt adj: **j-n ~ setzen** checkmate s.o.

'Schachspiel n (game of) chess; chessboard and men

Schacht [ʃaxt] m (-[e]s; Schächte ['ʃɛçtə]) shaft, mining: a. pit

Schachtel ['ʃaxtəl] f (-; -n) box; carton; **e-e ~ Zigaretten** a pack (esp Br packet) of cigarettes

Schachzug m move (a. fig)

schade ['ʃaːdə] pred adj: **es ist ~** it's a pity; **wie ~!** what a pity or shame!; **zu ~ sein für** be too good for

Schädel ['ʃɛːdəl] m (-s; -) ANAT skull; **~bruch** m MED fracture of the skull

schaden ['ʃaːdən] v/i (ge-, h) damage, do damage to, harm, hurt; **der Gesundheit ~** be bad for one's health; **das schadet nichts** it doesn't matter; **es könnte ihm nicht ~** it wouldn't hurt him

Schaden m (-s; Schäden ['ʃɛːdən]) damage (**an** dat to); esp TECH trouble, defect (a. MED); fig disadvantage; ECON loss; **j-m ~ zufügen** do s.o. harm; **~ersatz** m damages; **~ leisten** pay damages; **~freude** f: **~ empfinden über** (acc) gloat over

schadenfroh adv gloatingly

schadhaft ['ʃaːthaft] adj damaged; defective, faulty; leaking (pipes)

schädigen ['ʃɛːdɪgən] v/t (ge-, h) damage, harm

schädlich ['ʃɛːtlɪç] adj harmful, injurious; bad (for your health)

Schädling ['ʃɛːtlɪŋ] m (-s; -e) BIOL pest

'Schädlings|bekämpfung f pest control; **~bekämpfungsmittel** n pesticide

Schadstoff ['ʃaːtʃtɔf] m harmful substance; pollutant

'schadstoffarm adj MOT low-emission

Schaf [ʃaːf] n (-[e]s; -e) zo sheep
'Schafbock m zo ram
Schäfer ['ʃɛːfɐ] m (-s; -) shepherd; ~hund m sheepdog; **Deutscher~** German shepherd, esp Br Alsatian
'Schaffell n sheepskin; zo fleece
schaffen¹ ['ʃafən] v/t (irr, ge-, h) create
'schaffen² (ge-, h) **1.** v/t cause, bring about; manage, get s.th. done; take; **es ~** make it, a. succeed **2.** v/i work; **j-m zu ~ machen** cause s.o. trouble; **sich zu ~ machen an** (dat) tamper with
Schaffner ['ʃafnɐ] m (-s; -),
'Schaffnerin f (-; -nen) conductor; Br RAIL guard
Schafott [ʃaˈfɔt] n (-[e]s; -e) scaffold
Schaft [ʃaft] m (-[e]s; Schäfte ['ʃɛftə]) shaft; stock; shank; leg
'Schafwolle f sheep's wool
'Schafzucht f sheep breeding
schäkern ['ʃɛːkɐn] v/i (ge-, h) joke; flirt
schal [ʃaːl] adj stale, flat, fig a. empty
Schal m (-s; -s) scarf
Schale [ˈʃaːlə] f (-; -n) bowl, dish; GASTR shell; peel, skin; schälen ['ʃɛːlən] v/t (ge-, h) peel, pare; **sich ~** skin: peel (off)
Schall [ʃal] m (-[e]s; -e) sound; ~dämpfer m silencer (a. Br MOT), MOT muffler
'schalldicht adj soundproof
schallen ['ʃalən] v/i (irr, ge-, h) sound; ring (out); **~des Gelächter** roars of laughter
'Schall|geschwindigkeit f speed of sound; ~mauer f sound barrier; ~platte f record, disk, Br disc; ~welle f PHYS sound wave
schalten ['ʃaltən] v/i and v/t (ge-, h) switch, turn; MOT shift (esp Br change) gear; F get it; react; Schalter ['ʃaltɐ] m (-s; -) counter; RAIL ticket window; AVIAT desk; ELECTR switch
'Schalt|hebel m MOT gear lever; TECH, AVIAT control lever; ELECTR switch lever; ~jahr n leap year; ~tafel f ELECTR switchboard, control panel; ~uhr f time switch
'Schaltung f (-; -en) MOT gearshift; ELECTR circuit
Scham [ʃaːm] f (-; no pl) shame; **vor ~** with shame; schämen ['ʃɛːmən] v/refl (ge-, h) be or feel ashamed (gen, **wegen** of); **du solltest dich (was) ~!** you ought to be ashamed of yourself!

'Scham|gefühl n (-[e]s; no pl) sense of shame; ~haare pl pubic hair
'schamhaft adj bashful
'schamlos adj shameless; indecent
Schande ['ʃandə] f (-; no pl) shame, disgrace; schänden ['ʃɛndən] v/t (ge-, h) disgrace; desecrate; rape
'Schandfleck ['ʃantflɛk] m eyesore
schändlich ['ʃɛndlɪç] adj disgraceful
'Schandtat f atrocity
Schanze ['ʃantsə] f (-; -n) SPORT ski jump
Schar [ʃaːɐ] f (-; -en ['ʃaːrən]) troop, band; F horde; crowd; zo flock
'scharen v/refl (ge-, h) **sich ~ um** gather round
scharf [ʃarf] adj sharp (a. fig), PHOT a. in focus; clear; savage, fierce (dog); live (ammunition), armed (bomb etc); GASTR hot; F hot, sexy; F **~ sein auf** (acc) be keen on; **~ (ein)stellen** PHOT focus; F **~e Sachen** hard liquor
Schärfe ['ʃɛrfə] f (-; -n) sharpness (a. PHOT); fig severity, fierceness
'scharfsichtig adj sharp-sighted; fig clear-sighted
'Scharfsinn m (-[e]s; no pl) acumen
'scharfsinnig adj sharp-witted, shrewd
'scharfstellen v/t (sep, -ge-, h) → **scharf**
Scharlach m (-[e]s; no pl) scarlet; MED scarlet fever
'scharlachrot adj scarlet
Scharlatan ['ʃarlatan] m (-s; -e) charlatan, fraud
Scharnier [ʃarˈniːɐ] n (-s; -e) TECH hinge
Schärpe ['ʃɛrpə] f (-; -n) sash
scharren ['ʃarən] v/i (ge-, h) scrape, scratch
schartig ['ʃartɪç] adj jagged, notchy
Schaschlik ['ʃaʃlɪk] m, n (-s; -s) GASTR shish kebab
Schatten ['ʃatən] m (-s; -) shadow (a. fig); shade; **im ~** in the shade
'schattenhaft adj shadowy
Schattierung [ʃaˈtiːrʊŋ] f (-; -en) shade; fig colo(u)r
schattig ['ʃatɪç] adj shady
Schatz [ʃats] m (-es; Schätze ['ʃɛtsə]) treasure; fig darling; ~amt n POL Treasury Department, Br Treasury
schätzen ['ʃɛtsən] v/t (ge-, h) estimate,

value (*both*: **auf** *acc* at); appreciate; think highly of; F reckon, guess

'Schatz|kammer f treasury (*a. fig*); ~kanzler m Chancellor of the Exchequer; ~meister(in) treasurer

'Schätzung f (-; -en) estimate; valuation

Schau [ʃaʊ] f (-; -en) show, exhibition; **zur ~ stellen** exhibit, display

Schauder ['ʃaʊdɐ] m (-s; -) shudder

'schauderhaft adj horrible, dreadful

'schaudern v/i (ge-, h) shudder, shiver (*both*: **vor** *dat* with)

schauen ['ʃaʊən] v/i (ge-, h) look (**auf** *acc* at)

Schauer ['ʃaʊɐ] m (-s; -) METEOR shower; shudder, shiver; ~geschichte f horror story (*a. fig*)

'schauerlich adj dreadful, horrible

Schaufel ['ʃaʊfəl] f (-; -n) shovel; dustpan; 'schaufeln v/t (ge-, h) shovel; dig

'Schaufenster n shop window; ~auslage f window display; ~bummel m: **e-n ~ machen** go window-shopping; ~dekorati,on f window dressing

Schaukel ['ʃaʊkəl] f (-; -n) swing

'schaukeln (ge-, h) 1. v/i swing; *boat etc*: rock 2. v/t rock

'Schaukel|pferd n rocking horse; ~stuhl m rocking chair, rocker

Schaulustige ['ʃaʊlʊstɪɡə] pl (curious) onlookers, F rubbernecks

Schaum [ʃaʊm] m (-[e]s; Schäume ['ʃɔʏmə]) foam; GASTR froth, head; lather; spray; **schäumen** ['ʃɔʏmən] v/i (ge-, h) foam (*a. fig*), froth; lather; spray

'Schaumgummi m foam rubber

schaumig ['ʃaʊmɪç] adj foamy, frothy

'Schaumlöscher m foam extinguisher

'Schauplatz m scene

'Schaupro,zess m JUR show trial

schaurig ['ʃaʊrɪç] adj creepy; horrible

'Schauspiel n THEA play; *fig* spectacle

'Schauspieler(in) actor (actress)

'Schauspielschule f drama school

Schausteller ['ʃaʊʃtɛlɐ] m (-s; -) showman

Scheck [ʃɛk] m (-s; -s) ECON check, Br cheque; ~heft n checkbook, Br chequebook

'scheckig ['ʃɛkɪç] adj spotty

'Scheckkarte f check cashing (Br cheque) card

scheffeln ['ʃɛfəln] F v/t (ge-, h) rake in

Scheibe ['ʃaɪbə] f (-; -n) disk, Br disc; slice; pane; target

'Scheiben|bremse f MOT disk (Br disc) brake; ~wischer m MOT windshield (Br windscreen) wiper

Scheide ['ʃaɪdə] f (-; -n) sheath; scabbard; ANAT vagina; 'scheiden (*irr, ge-*) 1. v/t (h) separate, part (*both*: **von** from); divorce; **sich ~ lassen** get a divorce, **von j-m**: divorce s.o. 2. v/i (sein) part; **~ aus** (*dat*) retire from

'Scheideweg m crossroads

'Scheidung f (-; -en) divorce

'Scheidungsklage f JUR divorce suit

Schein¹ [ʃaɪn] m (-[e]s; -e) certificate; blank, Br form; bill, Br note

Schein² m (-[e]s; *no pl*) light; *fig* appearance; **et. (nur) zum ~ tun** pretend to do s.th.

'scheinbar adj seeming, apparent

scheinen ['ʃaɪnən] v/i (irr, ge-, h) shine; *fig* seem, appear, look

'scheinheilig adj hypocritical

'Scheinwerfer m searchlight; MOT headlight; THEA spotlight

Scheiß... ['ʃaɪs-] V damn ..., fucking ..., *esp Br* bloody ...

Scheiße ['ʃaɪsə] V f (-; *no pl*), 'scheißen V v/i (*irr, ge-, h*) shit, crap

Scheit [ʃaɪt] n (-[e]s; -e) piece of wood

Scheitel ['ʃaɪtəl] m (-s; -) parting

'scheiteln v/t (ge-, h) part

'Scheiterhaufen ['ʃaɪtɐhaʊfən] m pyre; HIST stake

scheitern ['ʃaɪtɐn] v/i (ge-, sein) fail, go wrong

Schelle ['ʃɛlə] f (-; -n) (little) bell; TECH clamp, clip

'Schellfisch ['ʃɛlfɪʃ] m ZO haddock

Schelm [ʃɛlm] m (-[e]s; -e) rascal

schelmisch ['ʃɛlmɪʃ] adj impish

Schema ['ʃeːma] n (-s; -s, -ta) pattern, system; schematisch [ʃeˈmaːtɪʃ] adj schematic; mechanical

Schemel ['ʃeːməl] m (-s; -) stool

schemenhaft ['ʃeːmənhaft] adj shadowy

Schenkel ['ʃɛŋkəl] m (-s; -) ANAT thigh; shank; MATH leg

schenken ['ʃɛŋkən] v/t (ge-, h) give (as a present) (**zu** for)

'Schenkung f (-; -en) JUR donation

Scherbe ['ʃɛrbə] f (-; -n), 'Scherben m (-s; -) (broken) piece, fragment

S

Schere ['ʃeːrə] f (-; -n) scissors; zo claw

scheren¹ ['ʃeːrən] v/t (irr, ge-, h) zo shear; BOT clip; cut

'scheren² v/refl (ge-, h) **sich ~ um** bother about

Scherereien [ʃeːrə'raiən] pl trouble, bother

Schermaus ['ʃeːrmaus] Austrian f zo mole

Scherz [ʃɛrts] m (-es; -e) joke; **im (zum) ~** for fun; scherzen ['ʃɛrtsən] v/i (ge-, h) joke (**über** acc at); 'scherzhaft adj joking; **~ gemeint** meant as a joke

scheu [ʃɔy] adj shy (a. zo); bashful; **~ machen** frighten; Scheu f (-; no pl) shyness; awe; scheuen ['ʃɔyən] (ge-, h) **1.** v/i shy (**vor** dat at), take fright (at); v/t shun, avoid; fear; **sich ~, et. zu tun** be afraid of doing s.th.

scheuern ['ʃɔyən] v/t and v/i (ge-, h) scrub, scour; chafe

'Scheuertuch n floor cloth

'Scheuklappen pl blinders, Br blinkers (both a. fig)

'scheumachen v/t (sep, -ge-, h) → scheu

Scheune ['ʃɔynə] f (-; -n) barn

Scheusal ['ʃɔyzaːl] n (-s; -e) monster (a. fig); fig beast

scheußlich ['ʃɔyslɪç] adj horrible (a. F), atrocious

Schicht [ʃɪçt] f (-; -en) layer; coat; film; ECON shift; class; schichten ['ʃɪçtən] v/t (ge-, h) arrange in layers, pile up
'schichtweise adv in layers

schick [ʃɪk] adj smart, chic, stylish

schicken ['ʃɪkən] v/t (ge-, h) send (**nach, zu** to); **das schickt sich nicht** that isn't done

Schickeria [ʃɪkə'riːa] F f (-; no pl) smart set, beautiful people, trendies

Schickimicki [ʃɪki'mɪki] F contp m (-s; -s) trendy

Schicksal ['ʃɪkzaːl] n (-s; -e) fate, destiny; lot

Schiebe|dach ['ʃiːbədax] n MOT sliding roof, sunroof; ~fenster n sliding window; sash window

schieben ['ʃiːbən] v/t (irr, ge-, h) push

Schieber ['ʃiːbɐ] m (-s; -) TECH slide; bolt; F profiteer

'Schiebetür f sliding door

'Schiebung F f (-; -en) swindle, fix (a. SPORT)

schied [ʃiːt] pret of **scheiden**

'Schiedsrichter ['ʃiːtsrɪçtɐ] m, 'Schiedsrichterin f soccer: referee; tennis: umpire; judge, esp pl a. jury

schief [ʃiːf] adj crooked, not straight; sloping, oblique (a. MATH); leaning; fig false

Schiefer ['ʃiːfɐ] m (-s; -) GEOL slate

'Schiefertafel f slate

'schiefgehen v/i (irr, gehen, sep, -ge-, sein) F go wrong

schielen ['ʃiːlən] v/i (ge-, h) squint, be cross-eyed

schien [ʃiːn] pret of **scheinen**

Schienbein ['ʃiːnbain] n ANAT shin (-bone)

Schiene ['ʃiːnə] f (-; -n) TECH etc rail; MED splint

'schienen v/t (ge-, h) MED splint

Schießbude ['ʃiːsbuːdə] f shooting gallery

schießen ['ʃiːsən] v/i and v/t (irr, ge-, h) shoot, fire (both: **auf** acc at); SPORT score; Schießerei [ʃiːsə'rai] f (-; -en) shooting; gunfight

'Schieß|pulver n gunpowder; ~scharte f MIL loophole, embrasure; ~scheibe f target; ~stand m shooting range

Schiff [ʃɪf] n (-[e]s; -e) MAR ship, boat; ARCH nave; **mit dem ~** by boat

Schiffahrt f → **Schifffahrt**

'schiffbar adj navigable

'Schiffbau m (-[e]s; no pl) shipbuilding

'Schiffbruch m shipwreck (a. fig); **~ erleiden** be shipwrecked

Schiffer ['ʃɪfɐ] m (-s; -) sailor; skipper

'Schifffahrt f (-; no pl) shipping, navigation

'Schiffs|junge m ship's boy; ~ladung f shipload; cargo; ~schraube f (ship's) propeller; ~werft f shipyard

Schikane [ʃi'kaːnə] f (-; -n) a. pl harassment; **aus reiner ~** out of sheer spite; F **mit allen ~n** with all the trimmings

schikanieren [ʃika'niːrən] v/t (no -ge-, h) harass; bully

Schild¹ [ʃɪlt] n (-[e]s; -er ['ʃɪldɐ]) sign, plate

Schild² m (-[e]s; -e) shield

'Schilddrüse f ANAT thyroid (gland)

schildern ['ʃɪldɐn] v/t (ge-, h) describe; depict, portray

Schilderung ['ʃɪldərʊŋ] f (-; -en) description, portrayal; account

'**Schildkröte** f zo tortoise; turtle

Schilf [ʃɪlf] n (-[e]s; no pl) BOT reed(s)

schillern ['ʃɪlən] v/i (ge-, h) be iridescent; **~d** adj iridescent; fig dubious

Schimmel ['ʃɪməl] m zo white horse; BOT mo(u)ld; **schimm(e)lig** ['ʃɪm(ə)lɪç] adj mo(u)ldy, musty; '**schimmeln** v/i (ge-, h, sein) go mo(u)ldy

Schimmer ['ʃɪmɐ] m (-s; -) glimmer (a. fig), gleam, fig a. trace, touch

'**schimmern** v/i (ge-, h) shimmer, glimmer, gleam

Schimpanse [ʃɪm'panzə] m (-n; -n) zo chimpanzee

schimpfen ['ʃɪmpfən] v/i and v/t (ge-, h) scold (**mit j-m** s.o.); F tell s.o. off, bawl s.o. out; **~ über** (acc) complain about

'**Schimpfwort** n swearword

Schindel ['ʃɪndəl] f (-; -n) shingle

schinden ['ʃɪndən] v/t (irr, ge-, h) maltreat; slave-drive; **sich ~** drudge, slave away; **Schinder** ['ʃɪndɐ] m (-s; -) slave driver; **Schinderei** [ʃɪndə'raɪ] f (-; -en) slavery, drudgery

Schinken ['ʃɪŋkən] m (-s; -) ham

Schippe ['ʃɪpə] f (-; -n), '**schippen** v/t (ge-, h) shovel

Schirm [ʃɪrm] m (-[e]s; -e) umbrella; sunshade; TV, IT etc: screen; shade; peak, visor; **~herr(in)** patron, sponsor; **~herrschaft** f patronage, sponsorship; **unter der ~ von** under the auspices of; **~mütze** f peaked cap; **~ständer** m umbrella stand

schiss [ʃɪs] pret of scheißen

Schlacht [ʃlaxt] f (-; -en) battle (**bei** of)

'**schlachten** v/t (ge-, h) slaughter, kill, butcher

Schlachter ['ʃlaxtɐ] m (-s; -) butcher

'**Schlacht|feld** n MIL battlefield, battleground; **~haus** n, **~hof** m slaughterhouse; **~plan** m MIL plan of action (a. fig); **~schiff** n MIL battleship

Schlacke ['ʃlakə] f (-; -n) cinders; GEOL, METALL slag

Schlaf [ʃlaːf] m (-[e]s; no pl) sleep; **e-n leichten (festen) ~ haben** be a light (sound) sleeper; F fig **im ~** blindfold

'**Schlafanzug** m pajamas, Br pyjamas

Schläfe ['ʃlɛːfə] f (-; -n) ANAT temple

schlafen ['ʃlaːfən] v/i (irr, ge-, h) sleep (a. fig); **~ gehen, sich ~ legen** go to bed; **fest ~** be fast asleep; **j-n ~ legen** put s.o. to bed or to sleep

schlaff [ʃlaf] adj slack (a. fig); flabby; limp

'**Schlaf|gelegenheit** f sleeping accommodation; **~krankheit** f MED sleeping sickness; **~lied** n lullaby

'**schlaflos** adj sleepless

'**Schlaflosigkeit** f (-; no pl) sleeplessness, MED insomnia

'**Schlafmittel** n MED sleeping pill(s)

'**Schlafmütze** fig f sleepyhead; slowpoke, Br slowcoach

schläfrig ['ʃlɛːfrɪç] adj sleepy, drowsy

'**Schlaf|saal** m dormitory; **~sack** m sleeping bag; **~ta,blette** f sleeping pill

'**schlaftrunken** adj (very) drowsy

'**Schlaf|wagen** m RAIL sleeping car, sleeper; **~wandler(in)** [ʃlaːfvandlɐ, ʃlaːfvandlərɪn] (-s; -/-; -nen) sleepwalker, somnambulist; **~zimmer** n bedroom

Schlag [ʃlaːk] m (-[e]s; Schläge ['ʃlɛːgə]) blow (a. fig); slap; punch; pat, tap; a. tennis: stroke; ELECTR shock (a. fig); MED beat; pl beating; → **Schlaganfall**; **~ader** f ANAT artery; **~anfall** m MED (apoplectic) stroke

'**schlagartig 1.** adj sudden, abrupt **2.** adv all of a sudden, abruptly

'**Schlagbaum** m barrier

'**Schlagbohrer** m TECH percussion drill

schlagen ['ʃlaːgən] (irr, ge-, h) **1.** v/t hit, beat (a. GASTR and fig), strike, knock, fell, cut (down); **sich ~** fight (**um** over); **sich geschlagen geben** admit defeat **2.** v/i hit, beat (a. heart etc), strike (a. clock), knock; **an** or **gegen et. ~** hit s.th., bump or crash into s.th.

Schlager ['ʃlaːgɐ] m (-s; -) MUS hit (a. fig), (pop) song

Schläger ['ʃlɛːgɐ] m (-s; -) tennis etc: racket; table tennis, cricket, baseball: bat; golf: club; hockey: stick; contp thug; **Schlägerei** [ʃlɛːgə'raɪ] f (-; -en) fight, brawl

'**schlagfertig** adj quick-witted; **~e Antwort** (witty) repartee

'**Schlag|instru,ment** n MUS percussion instrument; **~kraft** f (-; no pl) striking power (a. MIL.); **~loch** n pot-hole; **~obers** Austrian n, **~sahne** f whipped cream; **~seite** f MAR list; **~ haben** be listing; **~stock** m baton, truncheon; **~wort** n catchword, slogan; **~zeile** f headline

'**Schlagzeug** n MUS drums

Schlagzeuger ['ʃlaːktsɔʏgɐ] m (-s; -)

S

MUS drummer

schlaksig ['ʃlaːksɪç] adj lanky, gangling

Schlamm [ʃlam] m (-[e]s; -e) mud

schlammig ['ʃlamɪç] adj muddy

Schlampe ['ʃlampə] F f (-; -n) slut

schlampig ['ʃlampɪç] F adj sloppy

schlang [ʃlaŋ] pret of **schlingen**

Schlange ['ʃlaŋə] f (-; -n) zo snake, serpent (a. fig); fig line, esp Br queue; ~ **stehen** line up, stand in line, esp Br queue (up) (**nach** for); **schlängeln** ['ʃlɛŋəln] v/refl (ge-, h) wind or weave (one's way); person: worm one's way

'**Schlangenlinie** f serpentine line; **in ~n fahren** weave

schlank [ʃlaŋk] adj slim, slender; **j-n ~ machen** make s.o. look slim; **~e Unternehmensstruktur** ECON lean management; '**Schlankheitskur** f: **e-e ~ machen** be slimming; '**schlankmachen** v/t (sep, -ge-, h): **j-n ~** → **schlank**

schlapp [ʃlap] F adj worn out; weak; **Schlappe** ['ʃlapə] F f (-; -n) setback, beating; '**schlappmachen** F v/i (sep, -ge-, h) flake out; '**Schlappschwanz** F m weakling, wimp

schlau [ʃlaʊ] adj clever, smart, bright; sly, cunning, crafty

Schlauch [ʃlaʊx] m (-[e]s; Schläuche ['ʃlɔʏçə]) tube; hose; ~**boot** n (inflatable or rubber) dinghy

Schlaufe ['ʃlaʊfə] f (-; -n) loop

schlecht [ʃlɛçt] adj bad; poor; **mir ist (wird) ~** I feel (I'm getting) sick to my stomach; **~ aussehen** look ill; **sich ~ fühlen** feel bad; **~ werden** GASTR go bad; **es geht ihm sehr ~** he is in a bad way; **~ gelaunt** in a bad temper or mood, bad-tempered; F **j-n ~ machen** run s.o. down, backbite s.o.

'**schlechtmachen** v/t (sep, -ge-, h): F **j-n ~ machen** run s.o. down, backbite s.o.

schleichen ['ʃlaɪçən] v/i (irr, ge-, sein) creep (a. fig), sneak; '**Schleichweg** m secret path; '**Schleichwerbung** f plugging; **für et. ~ machen** plug s.th.

Schleier ['ʃlaɪɐ] m (-s; -) veil (a. fig); haze; '**schleierhaft** adj: F **es ist mir ~** it's a mystery to me

Schleife ['ʃlaɪfə] f (-; -n) bow; ribbon; AVIAT, IT, ELECTR, GEOGR loop

schleifen[1] ['ʃlaɪfən] v/t and v/i (ge-, h) drag (along); rub

'**schleifen**[2] v/t (irr, ge-, h) grind (a.

TECH), sharpen; sand(paper); cut; F drill s.o. hard

Schleifer ['ʃlaɪfə] m (-s; -), '**Schleifma,schine** f TECH grinder

'**Schleifpa,pier** n sandpaper

'**Schleifstein** m grindstone; whetstone

Schleim [ʃlaɪm] m (-[e]s; -e) slime; MED mucus; '**Schleimhaut** f ANAT mucous membrane; **schleimig** ['ʃlaɪmɪç] adj slimy (a. fig); MED mucous

schlemmen ['ʃlɛmən] v/i (ge-, h) feast

schlendern ['ʃlɛndən] v/i (ge-, sein) stroll, saunter, amble

schlenkern ['ʃlɛŋkən] v/i and v/t (ge-, h) dangle, swing (**mit den Armen** one's arms)

schleppen ['ʃlɛpən] v/t (ge-, h) drag (a. fig); MOT, MAR tow; **sich ~** drag (on); ~**d** adj dragging; fig drawling

Schlepper ['ʃlɛpə] m (-s; -) MAR tug; MOT tractor

'**Schlepp|lift** m T-bar (lift), drag lift, ski tow; ~**tau** n tow-rope; **im (ins) ~ in tow** (a. fig)

Schleuder ['ʃlɔʏdə] f (-; -n) catapult, slingshot; TECH spin drier

'**schleudern** (ge-, h) **1.** v/t fling, hurl (both a. fig); spin-dry **2.** v/i MOT skid

'**Schleudersitz** m AVIAT ejection (esp Br ejector) seat

schleunigst ['ʃlɔʏnɪçst] adv immediately

Schleuse ['ʃlɔʏzə] f (-; -n) sluice; lock

schlich [ʃlɪç] pret of **schleichen**

schlicht [ʃlɪçt] adj plain, simple

schlichten ['ʃlɪçtən] v/t (ge-, h) settle

'**Schlichtung** f (-; -en) settlement

schlief [ʃliːf] pret of **schlafen**

schließen ['ʃliːsən] v/t and v/i (irr, ge-, h) shut, close (down); fig close, finish; **~ aus** (dat) conclude from; **nach ... zu ~** judging by ...

'**Schließfach** ['ʃliːsfax] n safe-deposit box; RAIL etc; (left luggage) locker

schließlich ['ʃliːslɪç] adv finally; eventually, in the end; after all

schliff [ʃlɪf] pret of **schleifen**[2]

Schliff m (-[e]s; -e) cut; polish (a. fig)

schlimm [ʃlɪm] adj bad; awful; **das ist nicht** or **halb so ~** it's not as bad as that; **das Schlimme daran** the bad thing about it

'**schlimmsten**|**falls** adv at (the) worst

Schlinge ['ʃlɪŋə] f (-; -n) loop; noose;

HUNT snare (*a. fig*); MED sling

Schlingel ['ʃlɪŋəl] *m* (*-s*; -) rascal

schlingen ['ʃlɪŋən] *v/t* (*irr, ge-, h*) wind, twist; tie; wrap (*um* [a]round); gobble; **sich um et.** ~ wind (a)round s.th.

schlingern ['ʃlɪŋɐn] *v/i* (*ge-, h*) MAR roll

'**Schlingpflanze** *f* BOT creeper, climber

Schlips [ʃlɪps] *m* (*-es*; -*e*) necktie, *esp Br* tie

schlitteln ['ʃlɪtəln] *Swiss v/i* (*ge-, sein*) go sledging, go tobogganing

Schlitten ['ʃlɪtən] *m* (*-s*; -) sled, *Br* sledge; sleigh; SPORT toboggan; ~ **fahren** go sledging, go tobogganing

Schlittschuh ['ʃlɪtʃuː] *m* ice-skate (*a.* ~ **laufen**); ~**läufer(in)** ice-skater

Schlitz [ʃlɪts] *m* (*-es*; -*e*) slit; slot

schlitzen ['ʃlɪtsən] (*v/t ge-, h*) slit, slash

schloss [ʃlɔs] *pret of* **schließen**

Schloss *n* (*-es*; *Schlösser* ['ʃlœsɐ]) TECH lock; ARCH castle, palace; **ins** ~ **fallen** *door*: slam shut; **hinter** ~ **und Riegel** locked up, under lock and key

Schlosser ['ʃlɔsɐ] *m* (*-s*; -) metal-worker; locksmith; **Schlosserei** [ʃlɔsə'raɪ] *f* (-; -*en*) metalwork shop

schlottern ['ʃlɔtɐn] *v/i* (*ge-, h*) shake, tremble (*both*: **vor** *dat* with); bag

Schlucht [ʃlʊxt] *f* (-; -*en*) canyon, gorge, ravine

schluchzen ['ʃlʊxtsən] *v/i* (*ge-, h*), **Schluchzer** ['ʃlʊxtsɐ] *m* (*-s*; -) sob

Schluck [ʃlʊk] *m* (*-[e]s*; -*e*) draught, swallow; sip; gulp; '**Schluckauf** *m* (*-s*; *no pl*) hiccups; (*e-n*) ~ **haben** have (the) hiccups; **schlucken** ['ʃlʊkən] *v/t and v/i* (*ge-, h*) swallow (*a. fig*)

'**Schluckimpfung** *f* MED oral vaccination

schlug [ʃluːk] *pret of* **schlagen**

Schlummer ['ʃlʊmɐ] *m* (*-s*; *no pl*) slumber; '**schlummern** *v/i* (*ge-, h*) lie asleep; *fig* slumber

schlüpfen ['ʃlʏpfən] *v/i* (*ge-, sein*) slip, slide; ZO hatch (out); **Schlüpfer** ['ʃlʏpfɐ] *m* (*-s*; -) briefs, panties

schlüpfrig ['ʃlʏpfrɪç] *adj* slippery; *contp* risqué, off-colo(u)r

'**Schlupfwinkel** ['ʃlʊpfvɪŋkəl] *m* hiding place

schlurfen ['ʃlʊrfən] *v/i* (*ge-, sein*) shuffle (along)

schlürfen ['ʃlʏrfən] *v/t and v/i* (*ge-, h*) slurp

Schluss [ʃlʊs] *m* (*-es*; *no pl*) end; conclusion; ending; ~ **machen** finish; break up; ~ **machen mit** stop *s.th.*, put an end to *s.th.*; **zum** ~ finally; (*ganz*) *bis zum* ~ to the (very) end; ~ **für heute!** that's all for today!

Schlüssel ['ʃlʏsəl] *m* (*-s*; -) key (**für, zu** to); ~**bein** *n* ANAT collarbone; ~**blume** *f* BOT cowslip, primrose; ~**bund** *m* a bunch of keys; ~**kind** F *n* latchkey child; ~**loch** *n* keyhole; ~**wort** *n* keyword, IT a. password

'**Schlussfolgerung** *f* conclusion

schlüssig ['ʃlʏsɪç] *adj* conclusive; **sich** ~ **werden** make up one's mind (**über** *acc* about)

'**Schluss**|**licht** *n* MOT *etc*: tail-light; ~**pfiff** *m* SPORT final whistle; ~**phase** *f* final stage(s); ~**verkauf** *m* ECON (end-of-season) sale

schmächtig ['ʃmɛçtɪç] *adj* slight, thin, frail

schmackhaft ['ʃmakhaft] *adj* tasty

schmal [ʃmaːl] *adj* narrow; thin, slender (*a. fig*); **schmälern** ['ʃmɛːlɐn] *v/t* (*ge-, h*) detract from

'**Schmalfilm** *m* cinefilm

'**Schmalspur** *f* RAIL narrow ga(u)ge

'**Schmalspur...** *fig in cpds* small-time ...

Schmalz [ʃmalts] *n* (*-es*; -*e*) grease; lard

schmalzig ['ʃmaltsɪç] F *adj* schmaltzy, mushy, *Br* soapy

schmarotzen [ʃma'rɔtsən] F *v/i* (*no -ge-, h*) sponge (*bei* on)

Schmarotzer [ʃma'rɔtsɐ] *m* (*-s*; -) BOT, ZO parasite, *fig a.* sponger

schmatzen ['ʃmatsən] *v/i* smack (one's lips), eat noisily

schmecken ['ʃmɛkən] *v/i and v/t* (*ge-, h*) taste (**nach** of); **gut** (**schlecht**) ~ taste good (bad); (*wie*) **schmeckt dir ...?** (how) do you like ...? (*a. fig*); **es schmeckt süß** (**nach nichts**) it has a sweet (no) taste

Schmeichelei [ʃmaɪçə'laɪ] *f* (-; -*en*) flattery; '**schmeichelhaft** *adj* flattering; '**schmeicheln** *v/i* (*ge-, h*) flatter (*j-m* s.o.); **Schmeichler(in)** ['ʃmaɪçlɐ, 'ʃmaɪçlərɪn] *m*(*f*) (*-s*; -/-; -*nen*) flatterer; **schmeichlerisch** ['ʃmaɪçlərɪʃ] *adj* flattering

schmeißen ['ʃmaɪsən] F *v/t and v/i* (*irr, ge-, h*) throw, chuck; slam; **mit Geld um**

S

sich ~ throw one's money about

'**Schmeißfliege** f zo blowfly, bluebottle

schmelzen ['ʃmɛltsən] v/i (irr, ge-, sein) and v/t (h) melt; thaw; TECH smelt

'**Schmelz|ofen** m (s)melting furnace; **~tiegel** m melting pot (a. fig)

Schmerz [ʃmɛrts] m (-es; -en) pain (a. fig), ache; fig grief, sorrow

schmerzen ['ʃmɛrtsən] v/i and v/t (ge-, h) hurt (a. fig), ache; esp fig pain

'**schmerzfrei** adj without pain

'**schmerzhaft** adj painful

'**schmerzlich** adj painful, sad

'**schmerzlos** adj painless

'**Schmerzmittel** n PHARM painkiller

'**schmerzstillend** adj painkilling

Schmetterling ['ʃmɛtɐlɪŋ] m (-s; -e) zo butterfly

schmettern ['ʃmɛtɐn] (ge-, h) **1.** v/t smash (a. tennis); F MUS belt out **2.** v/i (sein) crash, slam; MUS blare

Schmied [ʃmiːt] m (-[e]s; -e) (black)-smith; **Schmiede** ['ʃmiːdə] f (-; -n) forge, smithy; '**Schmiedeeisen** n wrought iron; '**schmieden** v/t and v/i (ge-, h) forge; fig make (plans etc)

schmiegen ['ʃmiːgən] v/refl (ge-, h) **sich ~ an** (acc) snuggle up to; dress etc: cling to

Schmiere ['ʃmiːrə] f (-; -n) grease

'**schmieren** v/t (ge-, h) TECH grease, oil, lubricate; spread (butter etc); contp scribble, scrawl; **Schmiererei** [ʃmiːrə-'rai] f (-; -en) scrawl; graffiti

schmierig ['ʃmiːrɪç] adj greasy; dirty; filthy; contp slimy

Schmiermittel ['ʃmiːɐmɪtəl] n TECH lubricant

Schminke ['ʃmɪŋkə] f (-; -n) make-up (a. THEA); '**schminken** v/t (ge-, h) make s.o. up; **sich ~** make o.s. or one's face up

Schmirgelpa,pier ['ʃmɪrgəlpapiːɐ] n emery paper

schmiss [ʃmɪs] pret of **schmeißen**

schmollen ['ʃmɔlən] v/i (ge-, h) sulk, be sulky, pout

schmolz [ʃmɔlts] pret of **schmelzen**

schmoren ['ʃmoːrən] v/t and v/i (ge-, h) GASTR braise, stew (a. fig)

Schmuck [ʃmʊk] m (-[e]s; no pl) jewel-(le)ry, jewels; decoration(s), orna-ment(s); **schmücken** ['ʃmʏkən] v/t (ge-, h) decorate; '**schmucklos** adj un-

adorned; plain; '**Schmuckstück** n piece of jewel(le)ry; fig gem

Schmuggel ['ʃmʊgəl] m (-; no pl), **Schmuggelei** [ʃmʊgə'lai] f (-; -en) smuggling; '**schmuggeln** v/t and v/i (ge-, h) smuggle; '**Schmuggelware** f smuggled goods; **Schmuggler** ['ʃmʊg-lɐ] m (-s; -) smuggler

schmunzeln ['ʃmʊntsəln] v/i (ge-, h) smile to o.s.

schmusen ['ʃmuːzən] F v/i (ge-, h) (kiss and) cuddle, smooch

Schmutz [ʃmʊts] m (-es; no pl) dirt, filth, fig a. smut; **~fleck** m smudge

schmutzig ['ʃmʊtsɪç] adj dirty, filthy (both a. fig); **~ werden, sich ~ machen** get dirty

Schnabel ['ʃnaːbəl] m (-s; Schnäbel ['ʃnɛːbəl]) zo bill, beak

Schnalle ['ʃnalə] f (-; -n) buckle

'**schnallen** v/t (ge-, h) buckle; **et. ~ an** (acc) strap s.th. to

schnalzen ['ʃnaltsən] v/i (ge-, h) snap one's fingers; click one's tongue

schnappen ['ʃnapən] (ge-, h) **1.** v/i snap, snatch (both: nach at); F **nach Luft ~** gasp for breath **2.** F v/t catch

'**Schnappschuss** m PHOT snapshot

Schnaps [ʃnaps] m (-es; Schnäpse ['ʃnɛpsə]) spirits, schnapps, F booze

schnarchen ['ʃnarçən] v/i (ge-, h) snore

schnarren ['ʃnarən] v/i (ge-, h) rattle; voice: rasp

schnattern ['ʃnatɐn] v/i (ge-, h) zo cack-le; chatter (a. F)

schnauben ['ʃnaubən] v/i and v/t (ge-, h) snort; **sich die Nase ~** blow one's nose

schnaufen ['ʃnaufən] v/i (ge-, h) breathe hard, pant, puff

Schnauze ['ʃnautsə] f (-; -n) zo snout, mouth, muzzle; F AVIAT, MOT nose; TECH spout; V trap, kisser; V **die ~ halten** keep one's trap shut

Schnecke ['ʃnɛkə] f (-; -n) zo snail; slug; '**Schnecken|haus** n zo snail shell; **~tempo n: im ~** at a snail's pace

Schnee [ʃneː] m (-s; no pl) snow (a. sl); **~ räumen** remove snow; **~ball** m snow-ball; **~ballschlacht** f snowball fight

'**schneebedeckt** adj snow-capped

'**Schnee|fall** m snowfall; **~flocke** f snowflake; **~gestöber** ['ʃneːgəʃtøːbə] n (-s; -) snow flurry; **~glöckchen** n

BOT snowdrop; **~grenze** f snow line; **~mann** m snowman; **~matsch** m slush; **~mo,bil** n snowmobile; **~pflug** m snowplow, Br snowplough; **~regen** m sleet; **~sturm** m snowstorm, blizzard; **~verwehung** f snowdrift

'schnee'weiß adj snow-white

Schneewittchen [ʃneːˈvɪtçən] n (-s; no pl) Snow White

Schneid [ʃnait] F m (-[e]s; no pl) grit, guts; **~brenner** m TECH cutting torch

Schneide ['ʃnaidə] f (-; -n) edge

'**schneiden** v/t and v/i (irr, ge-, h) cut (a. fig), film etc: a. edit; GASTR carve

Schneider ['ʃnaidɐ] m (-s; -) tailor; **Schneiderei** [ʃnaidəˈrai] f (-; -en) (no pl) tailoring, dressmaking; tailor's or dressmaker's shop; '**Schneiderin** f (-; -nen) dressmaker; seamstress; '**schneidern** v/i and v/t (ge-, h) do dressmaking; make, sew

'**Schneidezahn** m incisor

schneidig ['ʃnaidɪç] adj dashing; smart

schneien ['ʃnaiən] v/i (ge-, h) snow

schnell [ʃnɛl] adj fast, quick; prompt; rapid; **es geht ~** it won't take long; (**mach[f]**) **~!** hurry up!

'**Schnell...** in cpds **...dienst, ...paket, ...zug** etc: mst express ...

schnellen ['ʃnɛlən] v/t (ge-, h) and v/i (ge-, sein) shoot, spring

'**Schnellhefter** m folder

Schnelligkeit ['ʃnɛlɪçkait] f (-; no pl) speed; quickness, rapidity

'**Schnell|imbiss** m snack bar; **~straße** f expressway, thruway, Br motorway

schnetzeln ['ʃnɛtsəln] esp Swiss v/t (ge-, h) GASTR chop up

schnippisch ['ʃnɪpɪʃ] adj sassy, pert

schnipsen ['ʃnɪpsən] v/i (ge-, h) snap one's fingers

schnitt [ʃnɪt] pret of **schneiden**

Schnitt m (-[e]s; -e) cut (a. fig); average

'**Schnittblumen** pl cut flowers

Schnitte ['ʃnɪtə] f (-; -n) slice; open sandwich

schnittig ['ʃnɪtɪç] adj stylish; MOT sleek

Schnitt|lauch m BOT chives; **~muster** n pattern; **~punkt** m (point of) intersection; **~stelle** f film etc: cut; IT interface; **~wunde** f MED cut

Schnitzel[1] ['ʃnɪtsəl] n (-s; -) GASTR cutlet; **Wiener ~** schnitzel

'**Schnitzel**[2] n, m (-s; -) chip; scrap

schnitzen ['ʃnɪtsən] v/t (ge-, h) carve, cut (in wood); **Schnitzer** ['ʃnɪtsɐ] m (-s; -) (wood) carver; **Schnitzerei** [ʃnɪtsəˈrai] f (-; -en) (wood) carving

Schnorchel ['ʃnɔrçəl] m (-s; -), '**schnorcheln** v/i (ge-, h) snorkel

Schnörkel ['ʃnœrkəl] m (-s; -) flourish; ARCH scroll

schnorren ['ʃnɔrən] F v/t (ge-, h) mooch, Br cadge

schnüffeln ['ʃnʏfəln] v/i (ge-, h) sniff (**an** dat at); F snoop (about or around)

Schnuller ['ʃnʊlɐ] m (-s; -) pacifier, Br dummy

Schnulze ['ʃnʊltsə] F f (-; -n) tearjerker; schmal(t)zy song

'**Schnulzensänger** F m, '**Schnulzensängerin** f crooner

schnulzig ['ʃnʊltsɪç] F adj schmal(t)zy

Schnupfen ['ʃnʊpfən] m (-s; -) MED cold; **e-n ~ haben** (**bekommen**) have a (catch [a]) cold

'**Schnupftabak** m snuff

schnuppern ['ʃnʊpɐn] v/i (ge-, h) sniff (**an et.** [at] s.th.)

Schnur [ʃnuːɐ] f (-; **Schnüre** ['ʃnyːrə]) string, cord; ELECTR flex

Schnürchen ['ʃnyːɐçən] n: **wie am ~** like clockwork

schnüren ['ʃnyːrən] v/t (ge-, h) lace (up); tie up

schnurgerade adv dead straight

'**schnurlos** adj: **~es Telefon** cordless phone

Schnürlsamt ['ʃnyːɐlzamt] Austrian m corduroy

Schnurrbart ['ʃnʊrbaːɐt] m m(o)ustache

schnurren ['ʃnʊrən] v/i (ge-, h) purr

Schnür|schuh ['ʃnyːɐʃuː] m laced shoe; **~senkel** ['ʃnyːɐzɛŋkəl] m (-s; -) shoestring, Br shoelace

schnurstracks ['ʃnuːɐˈʃtraks] adv direct(ly), straight; straight away

schob [ʃoːp] pret of **schieben**

Schober ['ʃoːbɐ] m (-s; -) haystack, hayrick; barn

Schock [ʃɔk] m (-[e]s; -s) MED shock; **unter ~ stehen** be in (a state of) shock

schocken ['ʃɔkən] F v/t (ge-, h) shock

schockieren [ʃɔˈkiːrən] v/t (no -ge-, h) shock

Schokolade [ʃokoˈlaːdə] f (-; -n) chocolate; **e-e Tafel ~** a bar of chocolate

S

scholl [ʃɔl] pret of **schallen**

Scholle ['ʃɔlə] f (-; -n) clod; (ice)floe; ZO flounder, Br plaice

schon [ʃoːn] adv already; ever; even; ~ **damals** even then; ~ **1968** as early as 1968; ~ **der Gedanke** the very idea; **ist sie ~ da (zurück)?** has she come (is she back) yet?; **habt ihr ~ gegessen?** have you eaten yet?; **bist du ~ einmal dort gewesen?** have you ever been there?; **ich wohne hier ~ seit zwei Jahren** I've been living here for two years now; **ich kenne ihn ~, aber** I do know him, but; **er macht das ~** he'll do it all right; ~ **gut!** never mind!, all right!

schön [ʃøːn] 1. adj beautiful, lovely; METEOR a. fine, fair; nice (a. F iro); (na,) ~ all right 2. adv: ~ **warm (kühl)** nice and warm (cool); **ganz ~ teuer (schnell)** pretty expensive (fast); **j-n ganz ~ erschrecken (überraschen)** give s.o. quite a start (surprise)

schonen ['ʃoːnən] v/t (ge-, h) take care of, go easy on (a. TECH); spare; **sich ~** take it easy; save o.s. or one's strength; ~d 1. adj gentle; mild 2. adv: ~ **umgehen mit** take (good) care of; handle with care; go easy on

'Schönheit f (-; -en) beauty

'Schönheitspflege f beauty care

Schonung f (-; -en) (no pl) (good) care; rest; preservation; tree nursery

'schonungslos adj relentless; brutal

schöpfen ['ʃœpfən] v/t (ge-, h) scoop, ladle; draw (water); → **Luft, Verdacht**

Schöpfer ['ʃœpfɐ] m (-s; -), 'Schöpferin f (-; -nen) creator

schöpferisch ['ʃœpfərɪʃ] adj creative

'Schöpfung f (-; -en) creation

schor [ʃoːɐ] pret of **scheren**

Schorf [ʃɔrf] m (-[e]s; -e) MED scab

Schornstein ['ʃɔrnʃtaɪn] m chimney; MAR, RAIL funnel; ~feger m chimney sweep

schoss [ʃɔs] pret of **schießen**

Schoß [ʃoːs] m (-es; Schöße ['ʃøːsə]) lap; womb

Schote ['ʃoːtə] f (-; -n) BOT pod, husk

Schotte ['ʃɔtə] m (-n; -n) Scot(sman); pl the Scots, the Scottish (people)

Schotter ['ʃɔtɐ] m (-s; -) gravel, road metal

Schottin ['ʃɔtɪn] f (-; -nen) Scotswoman

'schottisch adj Scots, Scottish; Scotch

'Schottland Scotland

schräg [ʃrɛːk] 1. adj slanting, sloping, oblique; diagonal 2. adv: ~ **gegenüber** diagonally opposite

Schramme ['ʃramə] f (-; -n), 'schrammen v/t and v/i (ge-, h) scratch (a. MED)

Schrank [ʃraŋk] m (-[e]s; Schränke ['ʃrɛŋkə]) cupboard; closet; wardrobe

Schranke ['ʃraŋkə] f (-; -n) barrier (a. fig), RAIL a. gate; JUR bar; pl limits, bounds

'schrankenlos fig adj boundless

'Schrankenwärter m RAIL gatekeeper

'Schrankwand f wall units

Schraube ['ʃraʊbə] f (-;-n), 'schrauben v/t (ge-, h) screw

'Schrauben|schlüssel m TECH spanner, wrench; ~zieher m TECH screwdriver

Schraubstock ['ʃraʊpʃtɔk] m vise, Br vice

Schreck [ʃrɛk] m (-[e]s; -e) fright, shock; **j-m e-n ~ einjagen** give s.o. a fright, scare s.o.

Schrecken ['ʃrɛkən] m (-s; -) terror, fright; horror(s);

'Schreckensnachricht f dreadful news

'schreckhaft adj jumpy; skittish

'schrecklich adj awful, terrible; horrible, dreadful, atrocious

Schrei [ʃraɪ] m (-[e]s; -e) cry, shout, yell, scream (all: **um, nach** for)

schreiben ['ʃraɪbən] v/t and v/i (irr, ge-, h) write (**j-m** to s.o.); **über** acc about); type; spell; **falsch ~** misspell; **wie schreibt man ...?** how do you spell ...?

'Schreiben n (-s; -) letter

'Schreib|fehler m spelling mistake; ~heft n exercise book; ~kraft f typist; ~ma|schine f typewriter; ~materi|al n writing materials, stationery; ~schutz m IT write or file protection; ~tisch m desk

'Schreibung f (-; -en) spelling

'Schreibwaren pl stationery; ~geschäft n stationer's, stationery shop

'Schreibzen|trale f typing pool

schreien ['ʃraɪən] v/i and v/t (irr, ge-, h) cry, shout, yell, scream (all: **um, nach** [out] for); ~ **vor Schmerz (Angst)** cry out with pain (in terror); **es war**

zum Schreien it was a scream; **~d** *fig adj* loud (*colors*); flagrant (*abuse etc*), glaring (*injustices etc*)

Schreiner [ˈʃraɪnɐ] *m* (*-s*; *-*) → **Tischler**

schreiten [ˈʃraɪtən] *v/i* (*irr, ge-, sein*) stride

schrie [ʃriː] *pret of* **schreien**

schrieb [ʃriːp] *pret of* **schreiben**

Schrift [ʃrɪft] *f* (*-; -en*) (hand)writing, hand; PRINT type; character, letter; *pl* works, writings; **die Heilige ~** REL the Scriptures; **~art** *f* script; PRINT typeface; **~deutsch** *n* standard German

'schriftlich *adj* written; **~ übersetzen** translate in writing

Schriftsteller [ˈʃrɪftʃtɛlɐ] *m* (*-s*; *-*), **'Schriftstellerin** *f* (*-; -nen*) author, writer

'Schrift|verkehr *m*, **~wechsel** *m* correspondence; **~zeichen** *n* character, letter

schrill [ʃrɪl] *adj* shrill (*a. fig*), piercing

schritt [ʃrɪt] *pret of* **schreiten**

Schritt *m* (*-[e]s; -e*) step (*a. fig*); pace; *fig* **~e unternehmen** take steps; **~ fahren!** MOT caution; **~macher** *m* SPORT pacemaker (*a.* MED), pacesetter

'schrittweise *adv* step by step, gradually

schroff [ʃrɔf] *adj* steep; jagged; *fig* gruff

Schrot [ʃroːt] *m, n* (*-[e]s; -e*) (*no pl*) coarse meal; HUNT (small) shot; pellet; **~flinte** *f* shotgun

Schrott [ʃrɔt] *m* (*-[e]s; -e*) scrap (metal)

'Schrotthaufen *m* scrap heap

'Schrottplatz *m* scrapyard

schrubben [ˈʃrʊbən] *v/t* (*ge-, h*) scrub, scour

schrumpfen [ˈʃrʊmpfən] *v/i* (*ge-, sein*) shrink

Schub [ʃuːp] *m* (*-[e]s; Schübe* [ˈʃyːbə]) → **Schubkraft**; **~fach** *n* drawer; **~karren** *m* wheelbarrow; **~kasten** *m* drawer; **~kraft** *f* PHYS, TECH thrust; **~lade** *f* drawer

Schubs [ʃʊps] F *m* (*-es; -e*), **schubsen** [ˈʃʊpsən] F *v/t* (*ge-, h*) push

schüchtern [ˈʃʏçtɐn] *adj* shy, bashful

'Schüchternheit *f* (*-; no pl*) shyness, bashfulness

schuf [ʃuːf] *pret of* **schaffen**[1]

Schuft [ʃʊft] *m* (*-[e]s; -e*) *contp* bastard

schuften [ˈʃʊftən] F *v/i* (*ge-, h*) slave away, drudge

Schuh [ʃuː] *m* (*-[e]s; -e*) shoe; **j-m et. in die ~e schieben** put the blame for s.th. on s.o.; **~anzieher** *m* shoehorn; **~creme** *f* shoe polish; **~geschäft** *n* shoe store (*Br* shop); **~löffel** *m* shoehorn; **~macher** *m* shoemaker; **~putzer** [ˈʃuːpʊtsɐ] *m* (*-s*; *-*) shoeshine boy

'Schul|abbrecher *m* (*-s*; *-*) dropout; **~abgänger** [ˈʃuːlapɡɛŋɐ] *m* (*-s*; *-*) school leaver; **~amt** *n* school board, *Br* education authority; **~arbeit** *f* schoolwork; *pl* homework; **~besuch** *m* (school) attendance; **~bildung** *f* education; **~buch** *n* textbook

Schuld [ʃʊlt] *f* (*-; -en* [ˈʃʊldən]) (*no pl*) JUR guilt, *esp* REL sin; *mst pl* debt; **j-m die ~ (an et.) geben** blame s.o. (for s.th.); **es ist (nicht) deine ~** it is(n't) your fault; **~en haben (machen)** be in (run into) debt; → **zuschulden**

'schuldbewusst *adj*: **~e Miene** guilty look; **schulden** [ˈʃʊldən] *v/t* (*ge-, h*) **j-m et.** owe s.o. s.th.; **schuldig** [ˈʃʊldɪç] *adj esp* JUR guilty (**an** *dat* of); responsible or to blame (for); **j-m et. ~ sein** owe s.o. s.th.; **Schuldige** [ˈʃʊldɪɡə] *m, f* (*-n*; *-n*) culprit, JUR guilty person, offender

'schuldlos *adj* innocent

Schuldner [ˈʃʊldnɐ] *m* (*-s*; *-*); **'Schuldnerin** *f* (*-; -nen*) debtor

'Schuldschein *m* ECON promissory note, IOU (= I owe you)

Schule [ˈʃuːlə] *f* (*-; -n*) school (*a. fig*); **höhere ~** *appr* (senior) high school, *Br* secondary school; **auf** or **in der ~** at school; **in die** or **zur ~ gehen** (*kommen*) go to (start) school

'schulen *v/t* (*ge-, h*) train, school

Schüler [ˈʃyːlɐ] *m* (*-s*; *-*) student, schoolboy, *esp* Br *a*. pupil; **~austausch** *m* student exchange (program[me])

Schülerin [ˈʃyːlərɪn] *f* (*-; -nen*) student, schoolgirl, *esp* Br *a*. pupil

'Schülervertretung *f appr* student government (*Br* council)

'Schul|ferien *pl* vacation, *Br* holidays; **~fernsehen** *n* educational TV; **~funk** *m* schools programmes; **~gebäude** *n* school (building); **~geld** *n* school fee(s), tuition; **~heft** *n* exercise book; **~hof** *m* school yard, playground; **~kame,rad** *m* schoolfellow; **~leiter** *m* principal, *Br* headmaster, head teacher; ~leiterin f principal, Br headmistress; ~mappe f schoolbag; satchel; ~ordnung f school regulations

'schulpflichtig adj: **~es Kind** school-age child

'Schul‖schiff n training ship; ~schluss m end of school (or term); **nach~** after school; ~schwänzer ['ʃuːlʃvɛntsɐ] m (-s; -) truant; ~stunde f lesson, class, period; ~tasche f schoolbag

Schulter ['ʃʊltɐ] f (-; -n) ANAT shoulder

'Schulterblatt n ANAT shoulder-blade

'schulterfrei adj strapless

'schultern v/t (ge-, h) shoulder

'Schultertasche f shoulder bag

'Schulwesen n (-s; no pl) education(al system)

schummeln ['ʃʊməln] F v/i (ge-, h) cheat

Schund [ʃʊnt] m (-[e]s; no pl) trash, rubbish, junk

schund [ʃʊnt] pret of **schinden**

Schuppe ['ʃʊpə] f (-; -n) ZO scale; pl MED dandruff

'Schuppen m (-s; -) shed, esp F contp shack

schuppig ['ʃʊpɪç] adj ZO scaly

schüren ['ʃyːrən] v/t (ge-, h) stir up (a. fig)

schürfen ['ʃʏrfən] v/i (ge-, h) prospect (**nach** for)

'Schürfwunde f MED graze, abrasion

Schurke ['ʃʊrkə] m (-n; -n) esp THEA etc villain

Schurwolle ['ʃuːɐvɔlə] f virgin wool

Schürze ['ʃʏrtsə] f (-; -n) apron

Schuss [ʃʊs] m (-es; Schüsse ['ʃʏsə]) shot; GASTR dash; SPORT shot, soccer: a. strike; skiing: schuss (a. **~ fahren**); sl shot, fix; F **gut in ~ sein** be in good shape

Schüssel ['ʃʏsəl] f (-; -n) bowl, dish; basin

'Schuss‖waffe f firearm; ~wunde f MED gunshot or bullet wound

Schuster ['ʃuːstɐ] m (-s; -) shoemaker

Schutt [ʃʊt] m (-[e]s; no pl) rubble, debris

'Schüttelfrost m MED shivering fit, the shivers

schütteln ['ʃʏtəln] v/t (ge-, h) shake

schütten ['ʃʏtən] v/t (ge-, h) pour; throw

Schutz [ʃʊts] m (-es; no pl) protection (**gegen, vor** dat against), defense, Br

defence (against, from); shelter (from); safeguard (against); cover; ~blech n fender, Br mudguard; ~brille f goggles

Schütze ['ʃʏtsə] m (-n; -n) MIL rifleman; hunter; SPORT scorer; ASTR Sagittarius; **er ist (ein)** ~ he's (a) Sagittarius; **ein guter** ~ a good shot

schützen ['ʃʏtsən] v/t (ge-, h) protect (**gegen, vor** dat against, from), defend (against, from), guard (against, from); shelter (from); safeguard

'Schutzengel m guardian angel

'Schützengraben m MIL trench

'Schutzgeld n protection money; ~erpressung f protection racket

'Schutz‖haft f JUR protective custody; ~heilige m, f patron (saint); ~impfung f MED protective inoculation; vaccination; ~kleidung f protective clothing

Schützling ['ʃʏtslɪŋ] m (-s; -e) protégé(e)

'schutzlos adj unprotected; defenseless, Br defenceless

'Schutz‖maßnahme f safety measure; ~pa.tron m REL patron (saint); ~umschlag m dust cover; ~zoll m ECON protective duty (or tariff)

schwach [ʃvax] adj weak (a. fig); poor; faint; delicate, frail; **schwächer werden** grow weak; decline; fail; fade

Schwäche ['ʃvɛçə] f weakness (a. fig); MED infirmity; fig drawback, shortcoming; **e-e ~ haben für** be partial to; 'schwächen v/t (ge-, h) weaken (a. fig); lessen; 'schwächlich adj weakly, feeble; delicate, frail; 'Schwächling m (-s; -e) weakling (a. fig), softy, sissy

'schwachsinnig adj feeble-minded; F stupid, idiotic

'Schwachstrom m ELECTR low-voltage current

Schwager ['ʃvaːgɐ] m (-s; Schwäger ['ʃvɛːgɐ]) brother-in-law; Schwägerin ['ʃvɛːgərɪn] f (-; -nen) sister-in-law

Schwalbe ['ʃvalbə] f (-; -n) ZO swallow; soccer: dive

Schwall [ʃval] m (-[e]s; -e) gush, esp fig a. torrent

schwamm [ʃvam] pret of **schwimmen**

Schwamm m (-[e]s; Schwämme ['ʃvɛmə]) sponge; BOT fungus; F dry rot

Schwammerl ['ʃvaməl] Austrian m (-s; -[n]) → **Pilz**

schwammig ['ʃvamıç] *adj* spongy; puffy; *fig* woolly

Schwan [ʃvaːn] *m* (-[e]s; *Schwäne* ['ʃvɛːnə]) zo swan

schwand [ʃvant] *pret of* **schwinden**

schwang [ʃvaŋ] *pret of* **schwingen**

schwanger ['ʃvaŋɐ] *adj* pregnant; '**Schwangerschaft** *f* (-; -en) pregnancy; '**Schwangerschaftsabbruch** *m* abortion

schwanken ['ʃvaŋkən] *v/i* (ge-, h) sway, roll (*a.* MAR); stagger; *fig* ~ *zwischen ... und ...* waver between ... and ...; *prices*: range from ... to ...; '**Schwankung** *f* (-; -en) change, variation (*a.* ECON)

Schwanz [ʃvants] *m* (-es; *Schwänze* ['ʃvɛntsə]) zo tail (*a.* AVIAT, ASTR); V cock

schwänzen ['ʃvɛntsən] *v/i and v/t* (ge-, h) (*die Schule*) ~ play truant (F hooky)

Schwarm [ʃvarm] *m* (-[e]s; *Schwärme* ['ʃvɛrmə]) swarm; crowd, F bunch; zo shoal, school; F dream; idol

schwärmen ['ʃvɛrmən] *v/i* (ge-, *sein*) zo swarm; (ge-, h) ~ *für* be mad about; dream of; have a crush on *s.o.*; ~ *von* rave about

Schwarte ['ʃvartə] *f* (-; -n) rind; F *contp* (old) tome

schwarz [ʃvarts] *adj* black (*a. fig*); *Schwarzes Brett* bulletin board, *Br* notice board; ~ *auf weiß* in black and white

'**Schwarzarbeit** *f* (-; *no pl*) illicit work

'**Schwarzbrot** *n* rye bread

'**Schwarze** ['ʃvartsə] *m, f* (-n; -n) black (man *or* woman); *pl* the Blacks

schwärzen ['ʃvɛrtsən] *v/t* (ge-, h) blacken

'**Schwarz|fahrer** *m* fare dodger; ~händler *m* black marketeer; ~markt *m* black market; ~seher *m* pessimist; (TV) license (*Br* licence) dodger

Schwarz'weiß... *in cpds* ...film, ...fernseher etc: black-and-white ...

schwatzen ['ʃvatsən], **schwätzen** ['ʃvɛtsən] *v/i* (ge-, h) chat(ter); PED talk

Schwätzer ['ʃvɛtsɐ] *contp m* (-s; -), '**Schwätzerin** *f* (-; -nen) loudmouth

schwatzhaft ['ʃvatshaft] *adj* chatty

Schwebe|bahn ['ʃveːbəbaːn] *f* cableway, ropeway; ~balken *m* SPORT beam

schweben ['ʃveːbən] *v/i* (ge-, h) be suspended; zo, AVIAT hover (*a. fig*); glide;

esp JUR be pending; *in Gefahr* ~ be in danger

Schwede ['ʃveːdə] *m* (-n; -n) Swede

Schweden ['ʃveːdən] Sweden

Schwedin ['ʃveːdın] *f* (-; -nen) Swede

'**schwedisch** *adj* Swedish

Schwefel ['ʃveːfəl] *m* (-s; *no pl*) CHEM sulfur, *Br* sulphur; ~säure *f* CHEM sulfuric (*Br* sulphuric) acid

Schweif [ʃvaif] *m* (-[e]s; -e) zo tail (*a.* ASTR); **schweifen** ['ʃvaifən] *v/i* (ge-, *sein*) wander (*a. fig*), roam

schweigen ['ʃvaigən] *v/i* (*irr*, ge-, h) be silent; '**Schweigen** *n* (-s; *no pl*) silence; 'schweigend *adj* silent

schweigsam ['ʃvaikzaːm] *adj* quiet, taciturn, reticent

Schwein [ʃvain] *n* (-[e]s; -e) zo pig, hog; F *contp* (filthy) pig; swine, bastard; F ~ *haben* be lucky; '**Schweinebraten** *m* roast pork; '**Schweinefleisch** *n* pork; **Schweinerei** [ʃvainə'rai] F *f* (-; -en) mess; *fig* dirty trick; dirty *or* crying shame; filth(y story *or* joke)

'**Schweinestall** *m* pigsty (*a. fig*)

'**schweinisch** F *adj* filthy, obscene

'**Schweinsleder** *n* pigskin

Schweiß [ʃvais] *m* (-es; *no pl*) sweat, perspiration

schweißen *v/t* (ge-, h) TECH weld

Schweißer *m* (-s; -) TECH welder

'**schweißgebadet** *adj* soaked in sweat

'**Schweißgeruch** *m* body odo(u)r, BO

Schweiz [ʃvaits] Switzerland

Schweizer ['ʃvaitsɐ] *m* (-s; -), *adj* Swiss

Schweizerin ['ʃvaitsərın] *f* (-; -nen) Swiss woman *or* girl

schweizerisch ['ʃvaitsərıʃ] *adj* Swiss

schwelen ['ʃveːlən] *v/i* (ge-, h) smo(u)lder (*a. fig*)

schwelgen ['ʃvɛlgən] *v/i* (ge-, h) ~ *in* (*dat*) revel in

Schwelle ['ʃvɛlə] *f* (-; -n) threshold (*a. fig*); RAIL tie, *Br* sleeper

'**schwellen 1.** *v/i* (*irr*, ge-, *sein*) swell **2.** *v/t* (ge-, h) swell

'**Schwellung** *f* (-; -en) MED swelling

Schwemme ['ʃvɛmə] *f* (-; -n) ECON glut, oversupply; '**schwemmen** *v/t* (ge-, h) *an Land* ~ wash ashore

Schwengel ['ʃvɛŋəl] *m* (-s; -) clapper; handle

schwenken ['ʃvɛŋkən] *v/t* (ge-, h) *and* *v/i* (ge-, *sein*) swing, wave

S

schwer [ʃveːɐ] **1.** *adj* heavy; *fig* difficult, hard; GASTR strong, rich; MED *etc* serious, severe; heavy; violent (*storm etc*); **~e Zeiten** hard times; **es ~ haben** have a bad time; **100 Pfund ~ sein** weigh a hundred pounds **2.** *adv:* **~ arbeiten** work hard; → **schwerfallen**; → **hören**; **~ beschädigt** → **schwerbeschädigt**; **~ verdaulich** indigestible, heavy (*both a. fig*); **~ verständlich** difficult *or* hard to understand; **~ verwundet** seriously wounded

'schwerbeschädigt *adj* seriously disabled

Schwere ['ʃveːrə] *f* (-; *no pl*) weight (*a. fig*); *fig* seriousness

'schwerfallen *v/i* (*irr, fallen, sep, -ge-, sein*): **j-m ~** be difficult for s.o.; **es fällt ihm schwer zu …** he finds it difficult to …

'schwerfällig *adj* awkward, clumsy

'Schwergewicht *n* (-[e]s; *no pl*) heavyweight; *fig* (main) emphasis

'schwerhörig *adj* hard of hearing

'Schwer|indus,trie *f* heavy industry; **~kraft** *f* (-; *no pl*) PHYS gravity; **~me,tall** *n* heavy metal

schwermütig ['ʃveːrmyːtɪç] *adj* melancholy; **~ sein** have the blues

'Schwerpunkt *m* center (*Br* centre) of gravity; *fig* (main) emphasis

Schwert [ʃveːɐt] *n* (-[e]s; *-er*) sword

'Schwerverbrecher *m* dangerous criminal, JUR felon

'schwer|verdaulich *adj* → **schwer**; **~verständlich** *adj* → **schwer**; **~verwundet** *adj* → **schwer**

'schwerwiegend *fig adj* weighty, serious

Schwester ['ʃvestɐ] *f* (-; *-n*) sister, REL *a.* nun; MED nurse

schwieg [ʃviːk] *pret of* **schweigen**

Schwieger... ['ʃviːgɐ] *in cpds* ...**eltern**, ...**mutter**, ...**sohn** *etc:* ...-in-law

Schwiele ['ʃviːlə] *f* (-; *-n*) MED callus

schwielig ['ʃviːlɪç] *adj* horny

schwierig ['ʃviːrɪç] *adj* difficult, hard

'Schwierigkeit *f* (-; *-en*) difficulty, trouble; **in ~en geraten** get *or* run into trouble; **~en haben, et. zu tun** have difficulty in doing s.th.

Schwimmbad ['ʃvɪmbaːt] *n* (indoor) swimming pool; schwimmen ['ʃvɪmən] *v/i* (*irr, ge-, sein*) swim; float; **~**

gehen go swimming

'Schwimm|flosse *f* swimfin, *Br* flipper; **~gürtel** *m* swimming belt; **~haut** *f* ZO web; **~lehrer** *m* swimming instructor; **~weste** *f* life jacket

Schwindel ['ʃvɪndəl] *m* (-s; *no pl*) MED giddiness, dizziness; F swindle, fraud; **~ erregend** dizzy; 'schwindeler,regend *adj* dizzy

'schwindeln F *v/i* (*ge-, h*) fib, tell fibs

schwinden ['ʃvɪndən] *v/i* (*irr, ge-, sein*) dwindle, decline

Schwindler ['ʃvɪndlɐ] F *m* (-s; *-*), 'Schwindlerin *f* (-; *-nen*) swindler, crook; liar

schwindlig ['ʃvɪndlɪç] *adj* MED dizzy, giddy; **mir ist ~** I feel dizzy

Schwinge ['ʃvɪŋə] *f* (-; *-n*) ZO wing

'schwingen *v/i and v/t* (*irr, ge-, h*) swing; wave; PHYS oscillate; vibrate

'Schwingung *f* (-; *-en*) PHYS oscillation; vibration

Schwips [ʃvɪps] F *m:* **e-n ~ haben** be tipsy

schwirren ['ʃvɪrən] *v/i* (*ge-, sein*) whirr, whizz, *esp* ZO buzz (*a. fig*); (*ge-, h*) **mir schwirrt der Kopf** my head is buzzing

schwitzen ['ʃvɪtsən] *v/i* (*ge-, h*) sweat, perspire

schwoll [ʃvɔl] *pret of* **schwellen 1**

schwor [ʃvoːɐ] *pret of* **schwören**

schwören ['ʃvøːrən] *v/t and v/i* (*irr, ge-, h*) swear; JUR take an *or* the oath; *fig* **~ auf** (*acc*) swear by

schwul [ʃvuːl] F *adj* gay; *contp* queer

schwül [ʃvyːl] *adj* sultry (*a. fig*), close

schwülstig ['ʃvʏlstɪç] *adj* bombastic, pompous

Schwung [ʃvʊŋ] *m* (-[e]s; *Schwünge* ['ʃvʏŋə]) swing; *fig* verve, pep; drive; **in ~ kommen** get going; *et.* **in ~ bringen** get s.th. going; 'schwungvoll *adj* full of energy *or* verve; MUS swinging

Schwur [ʃvuːɐ] *m* (-[e]s; *Schwüre* ['ʃvyːrə]) oath; **~gericht** *n* JUR jury court

sechs [zɛks] *adj* six; *grade:* F, *Br a.* poor; 'Sechseck *n* (-[e]s; *-e*) hexagon; 'sechseckig *adj* hexagonal; 'sechsfach *adj* sixfold; 'sechsmal *adv* six times; Sechs'tagerennen *n* SPORT six-day race; sechstägig ['zɛkstɛːɡɪç] *adj* lasting *or* of six days; '**sechste** *adj* sixth; **Sechstel** ['zɛkstəl] *n* (-s; -) sixth (part); '**sechstens** *adv* sixthly, in the sixth place; **sechzehn(te)** ['zɛçtseːn(tə)] *adj* sixteen(th); **sechzig** ['zɛçtsɪç] *adj* sixty; '**sechzigste** *adj* sixtieth

See[1] [zeː] *m* (-s; -n) lake

See[2] *f* (-; *no pl*) sea, ocean; **auf** ~ at sea; **auf hoher** ~ on the high seas; **an der** ~ at the seaside; **zur** ~ **gehen (fahren)** go to sea (be a sailor); **in** ~ **stechen** put to sea; ~**bad** *n* seaside resort; ~**fahrt** *f* navigation; ~**gang** *m* (-[e]s; *no pl*) heavy sea; ~**hafen** *m* seaport; ~**hund** *m* ZO seal; ~**karte** *f* nautical chart

'**seekrank** *adj* seasick

'**Seekrankheit** *f* seasickness

Seele ['zeːlə] *f* (-; -n) soul (*a. fig*)

'**seelenlos** *adj* soulless

'**Seelenruhe** *f* peace of mind; **in aller** ~ as cool as you please

'**seelisch** *adj* mental

'**Seelsorge** *f* (-; *no pl*) pastoral care

Seelsorger ['zeːlzɔrɡɐ] *m* (-s; -), '**Seelsorgerin** *f* (-; -nen) pastor

'**See|macht** *f* sea power; ~**mann** *m* (-[e]s; -leute) seaman, sailor; ~**meile** *f* nautical mile; ~**not** *f* (-; *no pl*) distress (at sea); ~**notkreuzer** *m* MAR rescue cruiser; ~**räuber** *m* pirate; ~**reise** *f* voyage, cruise; ~**rose** *f* BOT water lily; ~**sack** *m* kit bag; ~**schlacht** *f* MIL naval battle; ~**streitkräfte** *pl* MIL naval forces, navy

'**seetüchtig** *adj* seaworthy

'**See|warte** *f* naval observatory; ~**weg** *m* sea route; **auf dem** ~ by sea; ~**zeichen** *n* seamark; ~**zunge** *f* ZO sole

Segel ['zeːɡəl] *n* (-s; -) sail; ~**boot** *n* sailboat, *Br* sailing boat; ~**fliegen** *n* gliding; ~**flugzeug** *n* glider

'**segeln** *v/i* (ge-, sein) sail, SPORT *a.* yacht

'**Segel|schiff** *n* sailing ship; sailing vessel; ~**sport** *m* sailing, yachting; ~**tuch** *n* canvas, sailcloth

Segen ['zeːɡən] *m* (-s; -) blessing (*a. fig*)

Segler ['zeːɡlɐ] *m* (-s; -) yachtsman

Seglerin ['zeːɡlərɪn] *f* (-; -nen) yachtswoman

segnen ['zeːɡnən] *v/t* (ge-, h) bless

Segnung *f* (-; -nen) blessing

Sehbeteiligung ['zeːbətailɪɡʊŋ] *f* (TV) ratings

sehen ['zeːən] *v/i and v/t* (*irr*, ge-, h) see; watch; notice; ~ **nach** look after; look for; **sich** ~ **lassen** show up; **das sieht man (kaum)** it (hardly) shows; **siehst du** (you) see; I told you; **siehe oben (unten, Seite ...)** see above (below, page ...); '**sehenlassen** *v/refl* (*irr*, **lassen**, *sep*, *no* -ge-, h) → **sehen**; '**sehenswert** *adj* worth seeing; '**Sehenswürdigkeit** *f* (-; -en) place *etc* worth seeing, sight, *pl* sights

'**Sehkraft** *f* (-; *no pl*) eyesight, vision

Sehne ['zeːnə] *f* (-; -n) ANAT sinew; string

sehnen ['zeːnən] *v/refl* (ge-, h) long (**nach** for), yearn (for); **sich danach** ~ **zu** *inf* be longing to *inf*

'**Sehnerv** *m* ANAT optic nerve

sehnig ['zeːnɪç] *adj* sinewy, GASTR *a.* stringy

sehnlichst ['zeːnlɪçst] *adj* dearest

'**Sehnsucht** *f*, '**sehnsüchtig** *adj* longing, yearning

sehr [zeːɐ] *adv* before adj and adv: very; with verbs: very much, greatly

'**Sehtest** *m* sight test

seicht [zaɪçt] *adj* shallow (*a. fig*)

Seide ['zaɪdə] *f* (-; -n), '**seiden** *adj* silk

Seidenpa,pier *n* tissue paper

'**Seidenraupe** *f* ZO silkworm

seidig ['zaɪdɪç] *adj* silky

Seife ['zaɪfə] *f* (-; -n) soap

'**Seifen|blase** *f* soap bubble; ~**lauge** *f* (soap)suds; ~**oper** *f* TV soap opera; ~**schale** *f* soap dish; ~**schaum** *m* lather

seifig ['zaɪfɪç] *adj* soapy

Seil [zaɪl] *n* (-[e]s; -e) rope

'**Seilbahn** *f* cable railway

'**seilspringen** *v/i* (*only inf*) skip

sein[1] [zaɪn] *v/i* (*irr*, ge-, sein) be; exist; **et.** ~ **lassen** stop *or* quit (doing) s.th.

sein[2] *poss pron* his, her, its; ~**er**, ~**e**, ~**(e)s** his, hers

Sein *n* (-s; *no pl*) being; existence

seiner|seits ['zaɪnɐzaɪts] *adv* for his part; ~**zeit** *adv* then, in those days

seines'gleichen ['zaɪnəsɡlaɪçən] *pron* his equals

seinet'wegen ['zaɪnətveːɡən] → **meinetwegen**

'**seinlassen** *v/t* (*irr*, *sep*, -ge-, h): **et.** ~ → **sein**

seit [zaɪt] *prp and cj* since; ~ **2002** since 2002; ~ **drei Jahren** for three years (now); ~ **langem (kurzem)** for a long (short) time; ~'dem **1.** adv since then, since that time, ever since **2.** cj since

Seite ['zaitə] f (-; -n) side (a. fig); page; **auf der linken** ~ on the left(-hand side); fig **auf der e-n** (**anderen**) ~ on the one (other) hand

'**Seiten|ansicht** f side view, profile; ~**blick** m sidelong glance; ~**hieb** m sideswipe; ~**linie** f esp soccer: touchline

seitens ['zaitəns] prp (gen) on the part of, by

'**Seitensprung** F m: **e-n** ~ **machen** cheat (on one's wife or husband)

'**Seitenstechen** n (-s; no pl) MED a stitch (in the side)

'**seitlich** adj side ..., at the side(s)

seitwärts ['zaitvɛrts] adv sideways, to the side

Sekretär [zekre'tɛːɐ] m (-s; -e) secretary; bureau; **Sekretariat** [zekreta-'rjaːt] n (-[e]s; -e) (secretary's) office; **Sekretärin** [zekre'tɛːrɪn] f (-; -nen) secretary

Sekt [zɛkt] m (-[e]s; -e) sparkling wine

Sekte ['zɛktə] f (-; -n) sect

Sektion [zɛk'tsjoːn] f (-; -en) section; MED autopsy

Sektor ['zɛktoːɐ] m (-s; -en [zɛk-'toːrən]) sector; fig field

Sekunde [ze'kundə] f (-; -n) second; **auf die** ~ to the second

Se'kundenzeiger m second(s) hand

selbe ['zɛlbə] adj same

selber ['zɛlbɐ] pron → **selbst** 1

selbst [zɛlbst] **1.** pron: **ich** (**du** etc) ~ I (you etc) myself (yourself etc); **mach es** ~ do it yourself; **et.** ~ **tun** do s.th. by oneself; **von** ~ by itself; ~ **gemacht** homemade **2.** adv even

'**Selbstachtung** f self-respect

'**selbständig** etc → **selbstständig** etc

'**Selbstbedienung** f self-service; ~**laden** m self-service store (Br shop)

'**Selbst|befriedigung** f masturbation; ~**beherrschung** f self-control; ~**bestimmung** f self-determination

'**selbstbewusst** adj self-confident, self-assured; '**Selbstbewusstsein** n self-confidence

'**Selbst|bildnis** n self-portrait; ~**erhaltungstrieb** m survival instinct; ~**erkenntnis** f (-; no pl) self-knowledge

'**selbstgerecht** adj self-righteous

'**Selbst|hilfe** f self-help; ~**hilfegruppe** f self-help group; ~**kostenpreis** m: **zum** ~ ECON at cost (price)

'**selbstkritisch** adj self-critical

'**Selbstlaut** m LING vowel

'**selbstlos** adj unselfish

'**Selbst|mord** m, ~**mörder(in)** suicide

'**selbstmörderisch** adj suicidal

'**selbstsicher** adj self-confident, self-assured

'**selbstständig** adj independent, self-reliant; self-employed; '**Selbstständigkeit** f (-; no pl) independence

'**Selbststudium** n (-s; no pl) self-study

'**selbst|süchtig** adj selfish, ego(-t)istic(al); ~**tätig** adj automatic

'**Selbsttäuschung** f self-deception

'**selbstverständlich 1.** adj natural; **das ist** ~ that's a matter of course **2.** adv of course, naturally; ~**!** a. by all means!; '**Selbstverständlichkeit** f (-; -en) matter of course

'**Selbst|verteidigung** f self-defense, Br self-defence; ~**vertrauen** n self-confidence, self-reliance; ~**verwaltung** f self-government, autonomy

'**selbstzufrieden** adj self-satisfied

selchen ['zɛlçən] Austrian → **räuchern**

selig ['zeːlɪç] adj REL blessed; late; fig overjoyed

Sellerie ['zɛləri] m (-s; -[s]), f (-; -) BOT celeriac; celery

selten ['zɛltən] **1.** adj rare; ~ **sein** be rare, be scarce **2.** adv rarely, seldom

'**Seltenheit** f (-; no pl) rarity

seltsam ['zɛltzaːm] adj strange, odd

Semester [ze'mɛstɐ] n (-s; -) UNIV semester, esp Br term

Semikolon [zemi'koːlɔn] n (-s; -s) LING semicolon

Seminar [zemi'naːɐ] n (-s; -e) UNIV department; seminar; REL seminary; teacher training college

sen. abbr of **senior** sen., Sen., Sr, Snr, senior

Senat [ze'naːt] m (-[e]s; -e) senate

Senator [ze'naːtoːɐ] m (-s; -en [zena-'toːrən]), **Sena'torin** f (-; -nen) senator

Sendemast m ELECTR mast

senden ['zɛndən] v/t (irr, [irr,] ge-, h) send (**mit der Post**® by mail, Br by post); ELECTR broadcast, transmit, a. televise

Sender ['zɛndɐ] m (-s; -) radio or television station; ELECTR transmitter

'Sende|reihe f TV or radio series; ~schluss m close-down, F sign-off; ~zeichen n call letters (Br sign); ~zeit f air time

'Sendung f (-; -en) broadcast, program (-me), a. telecast; ECON consignment, shipment; **auf ~ sein** be on the air

Senf [zɛnf] m (-[e]s; -e) mustard (a. BOT)

senil [ze'niːl] adj senile; Senilität [zenili'tɛːt] f (-; no pl) senility

Senior ['zeːnjoːɐ] **1.** m (-s; -en [ze-'njoːrən]) senior (a. SPORT); senior citizen **2.** adj senior

Seni'orenheim n old people's home

Seni'orin f (-; -nen) senior citizen

Senke ['zɛŋkə] f (-; -n) GEOGR depression, hollow; 'senken v/t (ge-, h) lower (a. one's voice), a. bow (one's head); ECON a. reduce, cut; **sich ~** drop, go or come down

'senkrecht adj vertical

Sensation [zɛnza'tsjoːn] f (-; -en) sensation; sensationell [zɛnzatsjo'nɛl] adj, Sensati'ons... in cpds ...blatt etc: sensational (...)

Sense ['zɛnzə] f (-; -n) AGR scythe

sensibel [zɛn'ziːbəl] adj sensitive

sensibilisieren [zɛnzibili'ziːrən] v/t (no -ge-, h) sensitize (**für** to)

sentimental [zɛntimɛn'taːl] adj sentimental; Sentimentalität [zɛntimɛntali'tɛːt] f (-; -en) sentimentality

September [zɛp'tɛmbɐ] m (-[s]; -) September

Serenade [zere'naːdə] f (-; -n) MUS serenade

Serie ['zeːrjə] f (-; -n) series, TV etc a. serial; set; **in ~** produce sell in series

'serienmäßig adj series(-produced); standard

'Serien|nummer f serial number; ~wagen m MOT standard-type car

seriös [ze'rjøːs] adj respectable; honest; serious

Serum ['zeːrʊm] n (-s; -ren, -ra) serum

Service[1] [zɛr'viːs] n (-[s]; -) set; service

Service[2] ['zøːvɪs] m, n (-; -s) service

servieren [zɛr'viːrən] v/t (no -ge-, h) serve; Serviererin [zɛr'viːrərɪn] f (-; -nen) waitress; Serviertochter [zɛr-'viːɐtɔxtə] Swiss f waitress

Serviette [zɛr'vjɛtə] f (-; -n) napkin, esp Br serviette

Servo|bremse ['zɛrvobrɛmzə] f MOT servo or power brake; ~lenkung f MOT servo(-assisted) or power steering

Sessel ['zɛsəl] m (-s; -) armchair, easy chair; ~lift m chair lift

sesshaft ['zɛshaft] adj: ~ werden settle (down)

Set [zɛt] n, m (-s; -s) place mat

setzen ['zɛtsən] v/t and v/i (ge-, h) put, set (a. PRINT, AGR, MAR), AGR a. plant; place; seat s.o.; ~ über (acc) jump over; cross (river); ~ auf (acc) bet on, back; **sich ~** sit down; CHEM etc settle; **sich ~ auf** (acc) get on, mount; **sich ~ in** (acc) get into; **sich zu j-m ~** sit beside or with s.o.; ~ **Sie sich bitte!** take or have a seat!

Setzer ['zɛtsɐ] m (-s; -) PRINT compositor, typesetter; Setzerei [zɛtsə'rai] f (-; -en) PRINT composing room

Seuche ['zɔʏçə] f (-; -n) epidemic (disease)

seufzen ['zɔʏftsən] v/i (ge-, h), Seufzer ['zɔʏftsɐ] m (-s; -) sigh

Sexismus [zɛ'ksɪsmʊs] m (-; no pl) sexism; Sexist [zɛ'ksɪst] m (-en; -en), se-'xistisch adj sexist

Sexual... [zɛ'ksuaːl-] in cpds ...erziehung, ...leben, ...trieb etc: sex(ual) ...; ~verbrechen n sex crime

sexuell [zɛ'ksuɛl] adj sexual; ~e Belästigung (sexual) harassment

sexy ['zɛksi] adj sexy

sezieren [ze'tsiːrən] v/t (no -ge-, h) MED dissect (a. fig); perform an autopsy on

Showgeschäft ['ʃougəʃɛft] n (-[e]s; no pl) show business

sich [zɪç] refl pron oneself; himself, herself, itself; pl themselves; yourself, pl yourselves; ~ ansehen look at oneself; look at each other

Sichel ['zɪçəl] f (-; -n) AGR sickle; ASTR crescent

sicher ['zɪçɐ] **1.** adj safe (**vor** dat from), secure (from); esp TECH proof (**gegen** against); fig certain, sure; reliable; (**sich**) ~ **sein** be sure (**e-r Sache** of s.th.; **dass** that); of course, sure(ly); **du hast** (**bist**) ~ ... you must have (be) ... **2.** adv safely; ~**/** of course, sure(ly); certainly; probably;

'Sicherheit f (-; -en) (no pl) security (a. MIL, POL, ECON); safety (a. TECH); fig certainty; skill; (**sich**) **in ~ bringen** get to safety; ECON cover

'Sicherheits... *esp* TECH *in cpds* ...glas, ...nadel, ...schloss *etc*: ~; ~gurt *m* seat belt, safety belt; ~maßnahme *f* safety (POL security) measure

'sicherlich *adv* → *sicher* 2

'sichern *v/t* (*ge-*, *h*) protect, safeguard; secure (*a.* MIL, TECH); IT save; *sich* ~ secure o.s. (*gegen, vor dat* against, from); 'sicherstellen *v/t* (*sep*, *-ge-*, *h*) secure; guarantee; Sicherung ['zɪçərʊŋ] *f* (-; *-en*) securing; safeguard(-ing); TECH safety device; ELECTR fuse

'Sicherungs|kasten *m* ELECTR fuse box; ~ko̱pie *f* IT backup; *e-e* ~ *machen* (*von*) back up

Sicht [zɪçt] *f* (-; *no pl*) visibility; view; *in* ~ *kommen* come into sight or view; *auf lange* ~ in the long run; 'sichtbar *adj* visible; sichten ['zɪçtən] *v/t* (*ge-*, *h*) sight; *fig* sort (through or out)

'Sichtkarte *f* season ticket

'sichtlich *adv* visibly

'Sichtweite *f* visibility; *in* (*außer*) ~ within (out of) sight

sickern ['zɪkɐn] *v/i* (*ge-*, *sein*) trickle, ooze, seep

sie [ziː] *pers pron* she; it; *pl* they; *Sie* you

Sieb [ziːp] *n* (*-[e]s*; *-e*) sieve; strainer

sieben¹ ['ziːbən] *v/t* (*ge-*, *h*) sieve, sift

'sieben² *adj* seven

Sieben'meter *m* SPORT penalty shot or throw

siebte ['ziːptə] *adj*, 'Siebtel *n* (*-s*; -) seventh; siebzehn(te) ['ziːptseːn(tə)] *adj* seventeen(th); siebzig ['ziːptsɪç] *adj* seventy; 'siebzigste *adj* seventieth

siedeln ['ziːdəln] *v/i* (*ge-*, *h*) settle

sieden ['ziːdən] *v/t and v/i* (*[irr,] ge-*, *h*) boil, simmer

'Siedepunkt *m* boiling point (*a. fig*)

Siedler ['ziːdlɐ] *m* (*-s*; -) settler

Siedlung ['ziːdlʊŋ] *f* (-; *-en*) settlement; housing development

Sieg [ziːk] *m* (*-[e]s*; *-e*) victory, SPORT *a.* win

Siegel ['ziːgəl] *n* (*-s*; -) seal, signet

'Siegellack *m* sealing wax

'siegeln *v/t* (*ge-*, *h*) seal

siegen ['ziːgən] *v/i* (*ge-*, *h*) win

Sieger ['ziːgɐ] *m* (*-s*; -), Siegerin ['ziːgərɪn] *f* (-; *-nen*) winner

'siegreich *adj* winning; victorious

Signal [zɪ'gnaːl] *n* (*-s*; *-e*), signalisieren [zɪgnali'ziːrən] *v/t* (*no -ge-*, *h*) signal

signieren [zɪ'gniːrən] *v/t* (*no -ge-*, *h*) sign

Silbe ['zɪlbə] *f* (-; *-n*) syllable

'Silbentrennung *f* LING syllabification

Silber ['zɪlbɐ] *n* (*-s*; *no pl*) silver; silverware; 'silbergrau *adj* silver-gray (*Br* -grey); 'Silberhochzeit *f* silver wedding; 'silbern *adj* silver

Silhouette [zi'luɛtə] *f* (-; *-n*) silhouette; skyline

Silikon [zili'koːn] *n* (*-s*; *-e*) CHEM silicone

Silizium [zi'liːtsjʊm] *n* (*-s*; *no pl*) CHEM silicon

Silvester [zɪl'vɛstɐ] *n* (*-s*; -) New Year's Eve

Sims [zɪms] *m*, *n* (*-es*; *-e*) ledge; windowsill

simulieren [zimu'liːrən] *v/t and v/i* TECH *etc* simulate; sham

simultan [zimul'taːn] *adj* simultaneous

Sinfonie [zɪnfo'niː] *f* (-; *-n*) MUS symphony

singen ['zɪŋən] *v/t and v/i* (*irr, ge-*, *h*) sing (*richtig* [*falsch*] in [out of] tune)

Singular ['zɪŋgulaːɐ] *m* (*-s*; *-e*) LING singular

'Singvogel ['zɪŋfoːgəl] *m* ZO songbird

sinken ['zɪŋkən] *v/i* (*irr, ge-*, *sein*) sink (*a. fig*), go down (*a.* ECON), ASTR *a.* set; *prices etc*: fall, drop

Sinn [zɪn] *m* (*-[e]s*; *-e*) sense (*für* of); mind; meaning; point, idea; *im* ~ *haben* have in mind; *es hat keinen* ~ (*zu warten etc*) it's no use or good (waiting *etc*); 'Sinnbild *n* symbol

'sinnentstellend *adj* distorting

Sinnes|organ ['zɪnəs'ʔorgaːn] *n* sense organ; ~tä̱uschung *f* hallucination; ~wandel *m* change of mind

'sinnlich *adj* sensuous; sensory; sensual; 'Sinnlichkeit *f* (-; *no pl*) sensuality

'sinnlos *adj* senseless; useless

'sinnverwandt *adj* synonymous

'sinnvoll *adj* meaningful; useful; wise, sensible

Sintflut ['zɪntfluːt] *f the* Flood

Sippe ['zɪpə] *f* (-; *-n*) (extended) family, clan

Sirene [zi'reːnə] *f* (-; *-n*) siren

Sirup ['ziːrʊp] *m* (*-s*; *-e*) sirup, *Br* syrup; treacle, molasses

Sitte ['zɪtə] *f* (-; *-n*) custom, tradition; *pl* morals; manners

'Sittenlosigkeit f (-; no pl) immorality

'Sittenpoli,zei f vice squad

'sittenwidrig adj immoral

'Sittlichkeitsverbrechen n sex crime

Situation [zitua'tsjo:n] f (-; -en) situation; position

Sitz [zɪts] m (-es; -e) seat; fit; ~blo,ckade f sit-down demonstration

sitzen ['zɪtsən] v/i (irr, ge-, h) sit (an dat at; auf dat on); be; fit; F do time; ~ bleiben keep one's seat; PED have to repeat a year; F ~ bleiben auf (dat) be left with; F j-n ~ lassen leave s.o. in the lurch, let s.o. down

'sitzen|bleiben v/i (irr, bleiben, sep, -ge-, sein) → sitzen; ~lassen v/t (irr, lassen, sep, no -ge-, sein) a. fig → sitzen

'Sitzplatz m seat

'Sitzstreik m sit-down strike

'Sitzung f (-; -en) session (a. PARL), meeting, conference

Skala ['ska:la] f (-; -en) scale, fig a. range

Skalp [skalp] m (-s; -e), skalpieren [skal'pi:rən] v/t (no -ge-, h) scalp

Skandal [skan'da:l] m (-s; -e) scandal; ein ~ sein be scandalous; skandalös [skanda'lø:s] adj scandalous, shocking

Skelett [ske'lɛt] n (-[e]s; -e) skeleton

Skepsis ['skɛpsɪs] f (-; no pl) skepticism, Br scepticism; Skeptiker ['skɛptikɐ] m (-s; -) skeptic, Br sceptic; skeptisch ['skɛptɪʃ] adj skeptical, Br sceptical

Ski [ʃiː] m (-s; -er ['ʃiːɐ]) ski; ~ laufen or fahren ski; ~brille f ski goggles; ~fahren n skiing; ~fahrer(in) skier; ~fliegen n ski flying; ~gebiet n skiing area; ~kurs m skiing course; ~läufer(in) skier; ~lehrer(in) ski instructor; ~lift m ski lift; ~schuh m ski boot; ~sport m skiing; ~springen n ski jumping; ~stock m ski pole

Skizze ['skɪtsə] f (-; -n), skizzieren [skɪ'tsi:rən] v/t (no -ge-, h) sketch

Sklave ['skla:və] m (-n; -n) slave (a. fig); Sklaverei [skla:və'raɪ] f (-; no pl) slavery; 'Sklavin f (-; -nen) slave (a. fig); 'sklavisch adj slavish (a. fig)

Skonto ['skɔnto] m, n (-s; -s) ECON (cash) discount

Skorpion [skɔr'pjo:n] m (-s; -e) ZO scorpion; ASTR Scorpio; er ist (ein) ~ he's a Scorpio

Skrupel ['skru:pəl] m (-s; -) scruple, qualm; 'skrupellos adj unscrupulous

Skulptur [skʊlp'tu:ɐ] f (-; -en) sculpture

Slalom ['sla:lɔm] m (-s; -s) slalom

Slawe ['sla:və] m (-n; -n), 'Slawin f (-; -nen) Slav; 'slawisch adj Slav(ic)

Slip [slɪp] m (-s; -s) briefs, panties

'Slipeinlage f panty liner

Slipper ['slɪpɐ] m (-s; -) loafer, esp Br slip-on (shoe)

Slowake [slo'va:kə] m (-n; -n) Slovak

Slowakei [slova'kaɪ] f Slovakia

Slo'wakin f (-; -nen), slo'wakisch adj Slovak

Smaragd [sma'rakt] m (-[e]s; -e) MIN, sma'ragdgrün adj emerald

Smiley ['smaɪli] n (-s; -s) smiley

Smog [smɔk] m (-[s]; -s) smog; Smog-alarm m smog alert

Smoking ['smo:kɪŋ] m (-s; -s) tuxedo, Br dinner jacket

SMS [esem'es] f (-; -) text (message); ich schicke dir eine ~ I'll text you, I'll send you a text (message)

Snob [snɔp] m (-s; -s) snob; Snobismus [sno'bɪsmʊs] m (-; no pl) snobbery; sno'bistisch adj snobbish

Snowboard ['sno:bɔ:et] n (-s; -s) snowboard; Snowboardfahren n snowboarding

so [zo:] 1. adv so; like this or that, this or that way; thus; such; (nicht) ~ groß wie (not) as big as; ~ ein(e) such a; ~ sehr so (F that) much; und ~ weiter and so on; oder ~ et. or s.th. like that; oder ~ or so; ~, fangen wir an! well or all right, let's begin!; F ~ weit sein be ready; es ist ~ weit it's time; ~ genannt so-called; doppelt ~ viel twice as much; ~ viel wie möglich as much as possible 2. cj so, therefore; ~ dass so that 3. int: ~! all right!, o.k.!; that's it!; ach ~! I see

s.o. abbr of siehe oben see above

so'bald [zo'balt] cj as soon as

Socke ['zɔkə] f (-; -n) sock

Sockel ['zɔkəl] m (-s; -) base; pedestal

Sodbrennen ['zo:tbrɛnən] n (-s; no pl) MED heartburn

soeben [zo'e:bən] adv just (now)

Sofa ['zo:fa] n (-s; -s) sofa, settee, davenport

sofern [zo'fɛrn] cj if, provided that; ~ nicht unless

soff [zɔf] pret of saufen

sofort [zo'fɔrt] *adv* at once, immediately, right away

So'fortbildkamera *f* PHOT instant camera

Software ['zɔftwɛːɐ] *f* IT software; **~paket** *n* software package

sog [zoːk] *pret of* **saugen**

Sog *m* (-[e]s; -e) suction, MAR *a.* wake

sogar [zo'gaːɐ] *adv* even

sogenannt ['zoːgənant] *adj* so-called

Sohle ['zoːlə] *f* (-; -n) sole; *mining:* floor

Sohn [zoːn] *m* (-[e]s; *Söhne* ['zøːnə]) son

Sojabohne ['zoːjaboːnə] *f* BOT soybean

so'lange [zo'laŋə] *cj* as long as

Solar... [zo'laːɐ-] *in cpds* ...*energie etc:* solar ...

solch [zɔlç] *dem pron* such, like this *or* that

Sold [zɔlt] *m* (-[e]s; -e) MIL pay

Soldat [zɔl'daːt] *m* (-en; -en), **Sol'datin** *f* (-; -nen) soldier

Söldner ['zœldnɐ] *m* (-s; -) MIL mercenary

Sole ['zoːlə] *f* (-; -n) brine, salt water

solidarisch [zoli'daːrɪʃ] *adj:* **sich ~ erklären mit** declare one's solidarity with

solide [zo'liːdə] *adj* solid, *fig a.* sound; reasonable (*prices*); steady (*person*)

Solist [zo'lɪst] *m* (-en; -en), **So'listin** *f* (-; -nen) soloist

Soll [zɔl] *n* (-[s]; -[s]) ECON debit; target, quota; **~ und Haben** debit and credit

sollen ['zɔlən] *v/i* (*ge-, h*) *and v/aux* (*irr, no -ge-, h*) be to; be supposed to; (*was*) **soll ich ...?** (what) shall I ...?; *du sollst est* **(nicht)** ... you should(n't) ...; you ought(n't) to; **was soll das?** what's the idea?

Solo ['zoːlo] *n* (-s, -s, *Soli*) *esp* MUS solo; SPORT solo attempt *etc*

so'mit [zo'mɪt] *cj* thus, so, consequently

Sommer ['zɔmɐ] *m* (-s; -) summer (time); *im* **~** in (the) summer; **~ferien** *pl* summer vacation (*Br* holidays); **~frische** *f* summer resort

'sommerlich *adj* summery

'Sommersprosse *f* freckle

'sommersprossig *adj* freckled

'Sommerzeit *f* summertime; daylight saving (*Br* summer) time

Sonate [zo'naːtə] *f* (-; -n) MUS sonata

Sonde ['zɔndə] *f* (-; -n) probe (*a.* MED)

Sonder... ['zɔndɐ-] *in cpds* ...*angebot,* ...*ausgabe,* ...*flug,* ...*preis,* ...*wunsch,* ...*zug etc:* special ...

'sonderbar *adj* strange, F funny

'Sonderling *m* (-s; -e) eccentric

'Sondermüll *m* hazardous (*or* special toxic) waste; **~depo,nie** *f* special waste dump

sondern ['zɔndɐn] *cj* but; *nicht nur ...,* **~ auch ...** not only ... but also ...

'Sonderschule *f* special school (for the handicapped *etc*)

Sonnabend ['zɔn?aːbənt] *m* Saturday

Sonne ['zɔnə] *f* (-; -n) sun

sonnen ['zɔnən] *v/refl* (*ge-, h*) sunbathe

'Sonnenaufgang *m* (*bei* **~** at) sunrise

'Sonnen|bad *n:* **ein ~ nehmen** sunbathe; **~bank** *f* (-; -*bänke*) sunbed; **~blume** *f* BOT sunflower; **~brand** *m* sunburn; **~bräune** *f* suntan; **~brille** *f* sunglasses; **~creme** *f* suntan lotion, *Br* sun cream; **~ener,gie** *f* solar energy; **~finsternis** *f* solar eclipse

'sonnen'klar F *adj* (as) clear as daylight

'Sonnen|kol,lektor *m* solar panel; **~licht** *n* (-[e]s, *no pl*) sunlight; **~öl** *n* suntan oil; **~schein** *m* sunshine; **~schirm** *m* sunshade; **~schutz** *m* suntan lotion; **~seite** *f* sunny side (*a.* fig); **~stich** *m* sunstroke; **~strahl** *m* sunbeam; **~sys,tem** *n* solar system; **~uhr** *f* sundial; **~untergang** *m* sunset

sonnig ['zɔnɪç] *adj* sunny (*a.* fig)

Sonntag ['zɔntaːk] *m* Sunday; (*am*) **~** on Sunday; **'sonntags** *adv* on Sundays

'Sonntagsfahrer *contp m* MOT Sunday driver

sonst [zɔnst] *adv* else; otherwise, or (else); normally, usually; **~ noch et.** (*jemand*)? anything (anyone) else?; **~ noch Fragen?** any other questions?; **~ nichts** nothing else; **alles wie ~** everything as usual; **nichts ist wie ~** nothing is as it used to be; **'sonstig** *adj* other

Sopran [zo'praːn] *m* (-s; -e) MUS, **Sopra-nistin** [zopra'nɪstɪn] *f* (-; -nen) MUS soprano

Sorge ['zɔrgə] *f* (-; -n) worry; sorrow; trouble; care; **sich ~n machen** (*um*) worry *or* be worried (about); **keine ~!** don't worry!; **sorgen** ['zɔrgən] (*ge-, h*) **1.** *v/i:* **~ für** care for, take care of; **dafür ~, dass** see (to it) that **2.** *v/refl:* **sich ~ um** worry *or* be worried about

'Sorgenkind *n* problem child

Sorgfalt ['zɔrkfalt] f (-; no pl) care

sorgfältig ['zɔrkfɛltɪç] adj careful

sorglos ['zɔrkloːs] adj carefree; careless

Sorte ['zɔrtə] f (-; -n) sort, kind, type; **sortieren** [zɔr'tiːrən] v/t (no -ge-, h) sort; arrange; **Sortiment** [zɔrti'mɛnt] n (-[e]s; -e) ECON assortment

Soße ['zoːsə] f (-; -n) sauce; gravy

sott [zɔt] pret of **sieden**

Souffleur [zu'fløːɐ] m (-s; -e), **Souffleuse** [zu'fløːzə] f (-; -n) THEA prompter; **soufflieren** [zu'fliːrən] v/i (no -ge-, h) THEA prompt (j-m s.o.)

souverän [zuvə'rɛːn] adj POL sovereign

Souveränität [zuvərɛni'tɛːt] f (-; no pl) POL sovereignty

so'viel [zo'fiːl] cj as far as; → **so**; **so'weit** cj as far as; → **so**; **so'wie** cj as well as, and … as well; as soon as; **sowie'so** adv anyway, anyhow, in any case

so'wohl [zo'voːl] cj: ~ *Lehrer als (auch) Schüler* both teachers and students

sozial [zo'tsjaːl] adj social

Sozi'al... in cpds ...arbeiter, ...demokrat, ...versicherung etc: social ...; ~**hilfe** f welfare, Br social security; ~ **beziehen** be on welfare (Br social security)

Sozialismus [zotsja'lɪsmʊs] m (-; no pl) socialism; **Sozialist(in)** (-en/-; -en / -nen), **sozia'listisch** adj socialist

Sozi'alkunde f PED social studies

Sozi'alstaat m welfare state

Soziologe [zotsjo'loːgə] m (-n; -n) sociologist; **Soziologie** [zotsjolo'giː] f (-; no pl) sociology; **Sozio'login** f (-; -nen) sociologist; **soziologisch** [zotsjo'loːgɪʃ] adj sociological

sozu'sagen adv so to speak

Spagat [ʃpa'gaːt] m: ~ *machen* do the splits

Spalier [ʃpa'liːɐ] n (-s; -e) BOT espalier; MIL etc lane

Spalt [ʃpalt] m (-[e]s; -e) crack, gap; **Spalte** ['ʃpaltə] f (-; -n) → **Spalt**; PRINT column; '**spalten** v/t ([irr], ge-, h) split (a. fig); POL divide; **sich** ~ split (up); '**Spaltung** f (-; -en) split(ting); PHYS fission; fig split; POL division

Span [ʃpaːn] m (-[e]s; Späne ['ʃpɛːnə]) chip; pl TECH shavings

Spange ['ʃpaŋə] f (-; -n) clasp

Spaniel ['ʃpaːnjəl] m (-s; -s) ZO spaniel

Spanien ['ʃpaːnjən] Spain

Spanier ['ʃpaːnjɐ] m (-s; -), **Spanierin** ['ʃpaːnjərɪn] f (-; -nen) Spaniard

spanisch ['ʃpaːnɪʃ] adj Spanish

spann [ʃpan] pret of **spinnen**

Spann m (-[e]s; -e) ANAT instep

Spanne ['ʃpanə] f (-; -n) span

'**spannen** (ge-, h) **1.** v/t stretch, tighten; put up (line); cock (gun); draw, bend (bow) **2.** v/i be (too) tight; ~**d** adj exciting, thrilling, gripping

'**Spannung** f (-; -en) tension (a. TECH, POL, PSYCH); ELECTR voltage; fig suspense, excitement

'**Spannweite** f span, fig a. range

Spar|buch ['ʃpaːrbuːx] n savings book; ~**büchse** f esp Br money box

sparen ['ʃpaːrən] v/i and v/t (ge-, h) save; economize; ~ *für or auf* (acc) save up for; **Sparer(in)** ['ʃpaːrɐ, 'ʃpaːrərɪn] m(f) (-s; -/-; -nen) saver

Spargel ['ʃpargəl] m (-s; -) BOT asparagus

'**Sparkasse** f savings bank

'**Sparkonto** n savings account

spärlich ['ʃpɛːrlɪç] adj sparse, scant; scanty; poor (attendance)

sparsam ['ʃpaːrzaːm] adj economical (mit of); ~ *leben* lead a frugal life; ~ *umgehen mit* use sparingly; go easy on

'**Sparsamkeit** f (-; no pl) economy

'**Sparschwein(chen)** n piggy bank

Spaß [ʃpaːs] m (-es; Späße ['ʃpɛːsə]), Austrian a. **Spass** fun; joke; make **aus (nur zum)** ~ (just) for fun; **es macht viel (keinen)** ~ it's great (no) fun; **j-m den** ~ **verderben** spoil s.o.'s fun; **er macht nur** ~ he is only joking (F kidding); **keinen** ~ **verstehen** have no sense of humo(u)r

spaßen ['ʃpaːsən] v/i (ge-, h) joke

spaßig ['ʃpaːsɪç] adj funny

'**Spaßvogel** m joker

spät [ʃpɛːt] adj and adv late; **am** ~**en Nachmittag** late in the afternoon; **wie** ~ **ist es?** what time is it?; **von früh bis** ~ from morning till night; **(fünf Minuten) zu** ~ **kommen** be (five minutes) late; **bis** ~**er!** see you (later)!; → **früher**

Spaten ['ʃpaːtən] m (-s; -) spade

'**spätestens** adv at the latest

Spatz [ʃpats] m (-en; -en) ZO sparrow

spazieren [ʃpa'tsiːrən]: ~ *fahren* go (take s.o.) for a drive; take s.o. out; ~ *gehen* go for a walk

Spazierfahrt [ʃpaˈtsiːɐfaːɐt] f drive, ride

Spa|ziergang m walk; **e-n ~ machen** go for a walk; **Spa'ziergänger(in)** [ʃpaˈtsiːɐɡɛŋɐ, ʃpaˈtsiːɐɡɛŋɐrɪn] (-s; -/-; -nen) walker

Specht [ʃpɛçt] m (-[e]s; -e) zo woodpecker

Speck [ʃpɛk] m (-[e]s; -e) bacon

speckig [ˈʃpɛkɪç] fig adj greasy

Spediteur [ʃpediˈtøːɐ] m (-s; -e) shipping agent; remover

Spedition [ʃpediˈtsjoːn] f (-; -en) shipping agency; moving (Br removal) firm

Speer [ʃpeːɐ] m (-[e]s; -e) spear; SPORT javelin

Speiche [ˈʃpaɪçə] f (-; -n) spoke

Speichel [ˈʃpaɪçəl] m (-s; no pl) saliva, spit

Speicher [ˈʃpaɪçɐ] m (-s; -) storehouse; tank, reservoir; ARCH attic; IT memory, store; **~dichte** f IT bit density; **~kapazität** f IT memory capacity

'speichern v/t (ge-, h) store (up)

Speicherung [ˈʃpaɪçɐrʊŋ] f (-; -en) storage

speien [ˈʃpaɪən] v/t (irr, ge-, h) spit; spout; volcano etc: belch

Speise [ˈʃpaɪzə] f (-; -n) food; dish; **~eis** n ice cream; **~kammer** f larder, pantry; **~karte** f menu

'speisen (ge-, h) **1.** v/i dine **2.** v/t feed (a. ELECTR etc)

'Speise|röhre f ANAT gullet; **~saal** m dining hall; **~wagen** m RAIL diner, esp Br dining car

Spekulant [ʃpekuˈlant] m (-en; -en) ECON speculator

Spekulation [ʃpekulaˈtsjoːn] f (-; -en) speculation, ECON a. venture

spekulieren [ʃpekuˈliːrən] v/i (no -ge-, h) ECON speculate (**auf** acc on; **mit** in)

Spende [ˈʃpɛndə] f (-; -n) gift; contribution; donation; **'spenden** v/t (ge-, h) give (a. fig); donate (a. MED); **Spender** [ˈʃpɛndɐ] m (-s; -) giver; donor (a. MED), **Spenderin** f (-; -nen) donor (a. MED)

spendieren [ʃpɛnˈdiːrən] v/t (no -ge-, h) **j-m et. ~** treat s.o. to s.th.

Spengler [ˈʃpɛŋlɐ] Austrian m → **Klempner**

Sperling [ˈʃpɛrlɪŋ] m (-s; -e) zo sparrow

Sperre [ˈʃpɛrə] f (-; -n) barrier, RAIL a. gate; fig stop; TECH lock(ing device); barricade; SPORT suspension; PSYCH mental block; ECON embargo

'sperren v/t (ge-, h) close; ECON embargo; cut off; stop (check); SPORT suspend; obstruct; **~ in** (acc) lock (up) in

'Sperr|holz n plywood; **~müllabfuhr** f removal of bulky refuse

'Sperrung f (-; -en) closing

Spesen [ˈʃpeːzən] pl expenses

Spezi [ˈʃpeːtsi] F m (-s; -[s]) buddy, pal

Spezial|ausbildung [ʃpeˈtsjaːlʔausbɪlduŋ] f special training; **~gebiet** n special field, special(i)ty; **~geschäft** n specialized shop or store

spezialisieren [ʃpetsjaliˈziːrən] v/refl (no -ge-, h) specialize (**auf** acc in); **Spezialist(in)** [ʃpetsjaˈlɪst(ɪn)] (-en; -en/-; -nen) specialist; **Spezialität** [ʃpetsjaliˈtɛːt] f (-; -en) special(i)ty; **speziell** [ʃpeˈtsjɛl] adj specific, particular

spezifisch [ʃpeˈtsiːfɪʃ] adj specific; **~es Gewicht** specific gravity

Sphäre [ˈsfɛːrə] f (-; -n) sphere (a. fig)

spicken [ˈʃpɪkən] (ge-, h) **1.** v/t GASTR lard (a. fig) **2.** F v/i PED crib

spie [ʃpiː] pret of **speien**

Spiegel [ˈʃpiːɡəl] m (-s; -) mirror (a. fig)

'Spiegelbild n reflection (a. fig)

Spiegelei n GASTR fried egg

'spiegel|glatt adj glassy; icy

'spiegeln v/i and v/t (ge-, h) reflect (a. fig); shine; **sich ~** be reflected (a. fig)

'Spiegelung f (-; -en) reflection

Spiel [ʃpiːl] n (-[e]s; -e) game (a. fig); match; play (a. THEA etc); gambling; fig gamble; **auf dem ~ stehen** be at stake; **aufs ~ setzen** risk; **'Spielca,sino** n casino; **spielen** [ˈʃpiːlən] v/i and v/t (ge-, h) play (a. fig) (**um** for); THEA act; perform; gamble; do (the pools etc); **Klavier** etc **~** play the piano etc; **'spielend** fig adv easily; **'Spieler** [ˈʃpiːlɐ] m (-s; -), **Spielerin** [ˈʃpiːlərɪn] f (-; -nen) player; gambler

'Spiel|feld n (playing) field, pitch; **~film** m feature film; **~halle** f amusement arcade, game room; **~kame,rad(in)** playmate; **~karte** f playing card; **~ka,sino** n casino; **~marke** f counter, chip; **~plan** m THEA etc program(me); **~platz** m playground; **~raum** fig m play, scope; **~regel** f rule (of the game); **~sachen**

pl toys; ~stand *m* score; ~uhr *f* music (*Br* musical) box; ~verderber(in) (*-s; -/-; -nen*) spoilsport; ~waren *pl* toys; ~zeit *f* THEA, SPORT season; playing (*film*: running) time

'Spielzeug *n* toy(s); ~... *in cpds* ...pistole *etc*: toy ...

Spieß [ʃpiːs] *m* (*-es; -e*) MIL spear; GASTR spit; skewer

spießen ['ʃpiːsən] *v/t* (*ge-, h*) skewer

Spießer ['ʃpiːsɐ] F *contp m* (*-s; -*), 'spießig F *contp adj* philistine

Spinat [ʃpiˈnaːt] *m* (*-[e]s; -e*) BOT spinach

Spind [ʃpɪnt] *n, m* (*-[e]s; -e*) locker

Spindel ['ʃpɪndəl] *f* (*-; -n*) spindle

Spinne ['ʃpɪnə] *f* (*-; -n*) ZO spider

'spinnen (*irr, ge-, h*) **1.** *v/t* spin (*a. fig*) **2.** F *contp v/i* be nuts; talk nonsense

Spinner ['ʃpɪnɐ] *m* (*-s; -*), 'Spinnerin *f* (*-; -nen*) spinner; F *contp* nut, crackpot

'Spinnrad *n* spinning wheel

'Spinnwebe *f* (*-; -n*) cobweb

Spion [ʃpjoːn] *m* (*-s; -e*) spy

Spionage [ʃpjoˈnaːʒə] *f* (*-; no pl*) espionage; spionieren [ʃpjoˈniːrən] *v/i* (*no -ge-, h*) spy; F snoop

Spi'onin *f* (*-; -nen*) spy

Spirale [ʃpiˈraːlə] *f* (*-; -n*), spiralförmig [ʃpiˈraːlfœrmɪç] *adj* spiral

Spirituosen [ʃpiriˈtuoːzən] *pl* spirits

Spiritus ['ʃpiːritus] *m* spirit

Spital [ʃpiˈtaːl] *Austrian, Swiss n* (*-s; Spitäler* [ʃpiˈtɛːlɐ]) hospital

spitz [ʃpɪts] *adj* pointed (*a. fig*); MATH acute; ~e *Zunge* sharp tongue

'Spitzbogen *m* ARCH pointed arch

Spitze ['ʃpɪtsə] *f* (*-; -n*) point; tip; ARCH spire; BOT, GEOGR top; head (*a. fig*); lace; F MOT top speed; *spitze sein* F be super, be (the) tops; *an der ~* at the top (*a. fig*)

Spitzel ['ʃpɪtsəl] *m* (*-s; -*) informer, F stoolpigeon

spitzen ['ʃpɪtsən] *v/t* (*ge-, h*) point, sharpen; purse; ZO prick up (*its ears*)

'Spitzen... *in cpds* top ...; hi-tech ...; ~technolo‚gie *f* high technology, hi tech

'spitzfindig *adj* quibbling

'Spitzfindigkeit *f* (*-; -en*) subtlety

'Spitzhacke *f* pickax(e), pick

'Spitzname *m* nickname

Splitter ['ʃplɪtɐ] *m* (*-s; -*), 'splittern *v/i*

(*ge-, h, sein*) splinter

'splitter'nackt F *adj* stark naked

sponsern ['ʃpɔnzɐn] *v/t* (*ge-, h*) sponsor

Sponsor ['ʃpɔnzɐ] *m* (*-s; -en* [ʃpɔn-ˈzoːrən]) sponsor

spontan [ʃpɔnˈtaːn] *adj* spontaneous

Sporen ['ʃpoːrən] *pl* spurs (*a.* ZO); BIOL spores

Sport [ʃpɔrt] *m* (*-[e]s; no pl*) sport(s); PED physical education; ~ *treiben* do sports

'Sport... *in cpds* ...ereignis, ...geschäft, ...hemd, ...verein, ...zentrum *etc*: mst sports ...; ~kleidung *f* sportswear

'Sportler ['ʃpɔrtlɐ] *m* (*-s; -*), Sportlerin ['ʃpɔrtlərɪn] *f* (*-; -nen*) athlete

'sportlich *adj* athletic; casual, sporty

'Sport|nachrichten *pl* sports news; ~platz *m* sports grounds; ~tauchen *n* scuba diving; ~wagen *m* stroller, Br pushchair; MOT sports car

Spott [ʃpɔt] *m* (*-[e]s; no pl*) mockery; derision

'spott'billig F *adj* dirt cheap

spotten ['ʃpɔtən] *v/i* (*ge-, h*) mock (*über acc* at; scoff (at); make fun (of)

Spötter ['ʃpœtɐ] *m* (*-s; -*) mocker, scoffer; 'spöttisch *adj* mocking, derisive

'Spottpreis *m*: *für e-n* ~ dirt cheap

sprach [ʃpraːx] *pret of* **sprechen**

Sprache ['ʃpraːxə] *f* (*-; -n*) language (*a. fig*); speech; *zur* ~ *kommen* (*bringen*) come up (bring *s.th.* up)

'Sprach|fehler *m* speech defect; ~gebrauch *m* usage; ~lehrer(in) language teacher

'sprachlich **1.** *adj* language ... **2.** *adv:* ~ *richtig* grammatically correct

'sprachlos *adj* speechless

'Sprach|rohr *fig n* mouthpiece; ~unterricht *m* language teaching; ~wissenschaft *f* linguistics

sprang [ʃpraŋ] *pret of* **springen**

Spraydose ['ʃpreːdoːzə] *f* spray can, aerosol (can)

Sprechanlage ['ʃprɛçanlaːgə] *f* intercom

sprechen ['ʃprɛçən] *v/t and v/i* (*irr, ge-, h*) speak (*j-n, mit j-m* to s.o.); talk (to) (*both:* *über acc, von* about, of); *nicht zu ~ sein* be busy; Sprecher(in) ['ʃprɛ-çɐ, 'ʃprɛçərɪn] *m(f)* (*-s; -/-; -nen*) speaker; announcer; spokesman (spokeswoman); 'Sprechstunde *f* of-

fice hours; MED office (*Br* consulting)
hours, *Br* surgery; '**Sprechzimmer** *n*
office, *Br a.* consulting room

spreizen ['∫praitsən] *v/t* (*ge*-, *h*) spread

sprengen ['∫prɛŋən] *v/t* (*ge*-, *h*) blow
up; blast; sprinkle; water; *fig* break up

'**Sprengkopf** *m* MIL warhead

'**Sprengstoff** *m* MIL explosive

'**Sprengung** *f* (-; -*en*) blasting; blowing
up

sprenkeln ['∫prɛŋkəln] *v/t* (*ge*-, *h*)
speck(le), spot, dot

Spreu [∫prɔy] *f* (-; *no pl*) chaff (*a. fig*)

Sprichwort ['∫priçvɔrt] *n* proverb, saying

'**sprichwörtlich** *adj* proverbial (*a. fig*)

sprießen ['∫priːsən] *v/i* (*irr*, *ge*-, *sein*)
BOT sprout

'**Springbrunnen** *m* fountain

springen ['∫priŋən] *v/i* (*irr*, *ge*-, *sein*)
jump, leap; *ball etc*: bounce; SPORT
dive; *glass etc*: crack; break; burst; *in
die Höhe* (*zur Seite*) ~ jump up (aside)

Springer ['∫priŋɐ] *m* (-*s*; -) jumper; diver; *chess*: knight

'**Springflut** *f* spring tide

'**Springreiten** *n* show jumping

Spritze ['∫pritsə] *f* (-; -*n*) MED injection,
F shot; syringe; '**spritzen 1.** *v/t and v/t*
(*ge*-, *h*) splash; spray (*a.* TECH, AGR);
MED inject; give *s.o.* an injection of **2.**
v/i (*ge*-, *sein*) spatter; gush (*aus* from);
Spritzer ['∫pritsɐ] *m* (-*s*; -) splash; dash

'**Spritzpistole** *f* TECH spray gun

'**Spritztour** F *f* MOT spin

spröde ['∫prøːdə] *adj* brittle (*a. fig*);
rough

spross [∫prɔs] *pret of* **sprießen**

Sprosse ['∫prɔsə] *f* (-; -*n*) rung

Spruch [∫prʊx] *m* (-[*e*]*s*; *Sprüche* ['∫pry-
çə]) saying; decision; *~band n* banner

Sprudel ['∫pruːdəl] *m* (-*s*; -) mineral water; '**sprudeln** *v/i* (*ge*-, *sein*) bubble

Sprühdose ['∫pryːdoːzə] *f* spray can,
aerosol (can); **sprühen** ['∫pryːən] *v/t
and v/i* (*ge*-, *h*) spray; throw out (*sparks*)

'**Sprühregen** *m* drizzle

Sprung [∫prʊŋ] *m* (-[*e*]*s*; *Sprünge*
['∫pryŋə]) jump, leap; SPORT dive;
crack, fissure; *~brett n* SPORT diving
board; springboard; *fig* stepping stone;
~schanze f ski jump

Spucke ['∫pʊkə] F *f* (-; *no pl*) spit

'**spucken** *v/i and v/t* (*ge*-, *h*) spit; F throw

up

Spuk [∫puːk] *m* (-[*e*]*s*; -*e*) apparition,
ghost; **spuken** ['∫puːkən] *v/i* (*ge*-, *h*)
~ in (*dat*) haunt; **hier spukt es** this
place is haunted

Spule ['∫puːlə] *f* (-; -*n*) spool, reel; bob-
bin; ELECTR coil; '**spulen** *v/t* (*ge*-, *h*)
spool, wind, reel

spülen ['∫pyːlən] *v/t and v/i* (*ge*-, *h*) wash
up, do the dishes; rinse; flush the toilet

'**Spülma,schine** *f* dishwasher

Spur [∫puːɐ] *f* (-; -*en*) track(s); trail;
print; lane; trace (*a. fig*); *j-m auf der
~ sein* be on *s.o.*'s trail; **spüren** ['∫pyː-
rən] *v/t* (*ge*-, *h*) feel, sense; notice

'**spurlos** *adv* without leaving a trace

'**Spurweite** *f* RAIL ga(u)ge; MOT track

St. *abbr of Sankt* St, Saint

Staat [∫taːt] *m* (-[*e*]*s*; -*en*) state; POL government; '**Staatenbund** *m* confedera-
cy, confederation; '**staatenlos** *adj*
stateless; '**staatlich 1.** *adj* state …; public, national **2.** *adv*: *~ geprüft* qualified,
registered

'**Staats|angehörige** *m, f* national, citi-
zen, subject; *~angehörigkeit f* (-; *no
pl*) nationality; *~anwalt m* JUR district
attorney, *Br* (public) prosecutor; *~be-
such m* official or state visit; *~bür-
ger(in)* citizen; *~chef m* head of state;
~dienst m civil (*or* public) service

'**staatseigen** *adj* state-owned

'**Staatsfeind** *m* public enemy

'**Staats|haushalt** *m* budget; *~kasse f*
treasury; *~mann m* statesman; *~ober-
haupt n* head of (the) state; *~sekre-
,tär(in)* undersecretary of state;
~streich m coup d'état; *~vertrag m*
treaty; *~wissenschaft f* political science

Stab [∫taːp] *m* (-[*e*]*s*; *Stäbe* ['∫tɛːbə])
staff (*a. fig*); bar; SPORT, MUS baton;
SPORT pole

Stäbchen ['∫tɛːpçən] *pl* chopstick

'**Stabhochsprung** *m* SPORT pole vault

stabil [∫taˈbiːl] *adj* stable (*a.* ECON, POL);
solid, strong; sound; **stabilisieren**
[∫tabiliˈziːrən] *v/t* (*no -ge-*, *h*) stabilize;
Stabilität [∫tabiliˈtɛːt] *f* (-; *no pl*) stability

stach [∫taːx] *pret of* **stechen**

Stachel ['∫taxəl] *m* (-*s*; -*n*) BOT, ZO spine,
prick; ZO sting; *~beere f* BOT gooseber-
ry; *~draht m* barbed wire

stachelig ['ʃtaxəlɪç] *adj* prickly

'**Stachelschwein** *n* zo porcupine

Stadel ['ʃtaːdəl] *Austrian m* (-s; -[n]) barn

Stadion ['ʃtaːdjɔn] *n* (-s; -ien) stadium

Stadium ['ʃtaːdjʊm] *n* (-s; -ien) stage, phase

Stadt [ʃtat] *f* (-; Städte ['ʃtɛːtə]) town; city; **die ~ Berlin** the city of Berlin; **in die ~ fahren** go downtown, *esp Br* go (in)to town; **~bahn** *f* urban railway

Städter ['ʃtɛːtɐ] *m* (-s; -), '**Städterin** *f* (-; -nen) city dweller, *F* townie, *often contp* city slicker

'**Stadt|gebiet** *n* urban area; **~gespräch** *fig n* talk of the town

städtisch ['ʃɛːtɪʃ] *adj* urban; POL municipal

'**Stadt|plan** *m* city map; **~rand** *m* outskirts; **~rat** *m* town council; city councilman, *Br* town council(l)or; **~rundfahrt** *f* sightseeing tour; **~streicher(in)** city vagrant; **~teil** *m*, **~viertel** *n* quarter

Staffel ['ʃtafəl] *f* (-; -n) SPORT relay race *or* team; MIL, AVIAT squadron

Staffelei [ʃtafə'laɪ] *f* (-; -en) PAINT easel

'**staffeln** *v/t* (ge-, h) grade, scale

stahl [ʃtaːl] *pret of* **stehlen**

Stahl [ʃtaːl] *m* (-[e]s; Stähle ['ʃtɛːlə]) steel

'**Stahlwerk** *n* steelworks

stak [ʃtaːk] *pret of* **stecken** 2

Stall [ʃtal] *m* (-[e]s; Ställe ['ʃtɛlə]) stable

'**Stallknecht** *m* stableman

Stamm [ʃtam] *m* (-[e]s; Stämme ['ʃtɛmə]) BOT stem (*a.* LING), trunk; tribe, stock; *fig* regulars; **~...** *in cpds* ...**gast**, ...**kunde**, ...**spieler** *etc*: regular ...; **~baum** *m* family tree; zo pedigree

stammeln ['ʃtaməln] *v/t* (ge-, h) stammer

stammen ['ʃtamən] *v/i* (ge-, h) **~ aus** (**von**) come from; be from; **~ von** *work of art etc*: be by

'**Stammformen** *pl* LING principal parts, *mst* tenses

stämmig ['ʃtɛmɪç] *adj* sturdy; stout

'**Stammkneipe** *f Br* local

stampfen ['ʃtampfən] (ge-, h) **1.** *v/t* mash **2.** *v/i* stamp (**mit dem Fuß** one's foot)

stand [ʃtant] *pret of* **stehen**

Stand *m* (-[e]s; Stände ['ʃtɛndə]) (*no pl*) stand(ing), standing *or* upright position; footing, foothold; ASTR position;

TECH *etc*: height, level (*a. fig*); reading; SPORT score; *racing*: standings; *fig* state; social standing, status; stand, stall; class; profession; **auf den neuesten ~ bringen** bring up to date; **e-n schweren ~ haben** have a hard time (of it); → **außerstande**; → **imstande**; → **instand**; → **zustande**

Standard ['ʃtandart] *m* (-s; -s) standard

'**Standbild** *n* statue

Ständchen ['ʃtɛntçən] *n* (-s; -) MUS serenade

Ständer ['ʃtɛndɐ] *m* (-s; -) stand; rack

'**Standesamt** ['ʃtandəsamt] *n* marriage license bureau, *Br* registry office; '**standesamtlich** *adj*: **~e Trauung** civil marriage; '**Standesbeamt|e** *m*, **-in** *f* civil magistrate, *Br* registrar

'**Standfoto** *n* still

'**standhaft** *adj* steadfast, firm; **~ bleiben** resist temptation

'**standhalten** *v/i* (*irr,* **halten**, *sep,* -ge-, h) withstand, resist

ständig ['ʃtɛndɪç] *adj* constant; permanent (*address*)

'**Stand|licht** *n* (-[e]s; *no pl*) MOT parking light; **~ort** *m* position; location; MIL post, garrison; **~pauke** F *f:* **j-m e-e ~ halten** give s.o. a talking-to; **~platz** *m* stand; **~punkt** *m* (point of view), standpoint; **~spur** *f* MOT (*Br* hard) shoulder; **~uhr** *f* grandfather clock

Stange ['ʃtaŋə] *f* (-; -n) pole; staff; rod, bar; carton (*of cigarettes*)

Stängel ['ʃtɛŋəl] *m* (-s; -) BOT stalk, stem

stank [ʃtaŋk] *pret of* **stinken**

Stanniol [ʃta'njoːl] *n* (-s; -e) tin foil

Stanze ['ʃtantsə] *f* (-; -n), '**stanzen** *v/t* (ge-, h) TECH punch

Stapel ['ʃtaːpəl] *m* (-s; -) pile, stack; heap; **vom ~ lassen** MAR launch (*a. fig*); **vom ~ laufen** MAR be launched

'**Stapellauf** *m* MAR launch

'**stapeln** *v/t* (ge-, h) pile (up), stack

stapfen ['ʃtapfən] *v/i* (ge-, sein) trudge

Star[1] [ʃtaːʁ] *m* (-[e]s; -e) zo starling; MED cataract

Star[2] *m* (-s; -s) THEA *etc*: star

starb [ʃtarp] *pret of* **sterben**

stark [ʃtark] **1.** *adj* strong (*a.* GASTR); powerful; *fig* heavy; F super, great **2.** *adv*: **~ beeindruckt** greatly impressed; **~ beschädigt** badly damaged; **Stärke** ['ʃtɛrkə] *f* (-; -n) (*no pl*) strength, power; intensity; degree; CHEM starch; 'stärken v/t (ge-, h) strengthen (a. fig); starch; sich ~ take some refreshment; 'Starkstrom m ELECTR high--voltage (or heavy) current; Stärkung f (-; -en) strengthening; refreshment; 'Stärkungsmittel n MED tonic

starr [ʃtar] adj stiff; rigid (a. TECH); frozen (face); ~er Blick (fixed) stare; ~ vor Kälte (Entsetzen) frozen (scared) stiff; 'starren v/i (ge-, h) stare (auf acc at); starrköpfig ['ʃtarkœpfɪç] adj stubborn, obstinate; 'Starrsinn m (-[e]s; no pl) stubbornness, obstinacy

Start [ʃtart] m (-[e]s; -s) start (a. fig); AVIAT take-off; rocket: lift-off
'Startbahn f AVIAT runway
'startbereit adj ready to start; AVIAT ready for take-off
starten ['ʃtartən] v/i (ge-, sein) and v/t (ge-, h) start (a. F); AVIAT take off; lift off; launch (a. fig)
Station [ʃtaˈtsjoːn] f (-; -en) station; MED ward; stationär [ʃtatsjoˈnɛːɐ] adj: ~er Patient MED in-patient; stationieren [ʃtatsjoˈniːrən] v/t (no -ge-, h) MIL station; deploy; Stationsvorsteher m RAIL stationmaster
Statist [ʃtaˈtɪst] m (-en; -en) THEA extra
Statistik [ʃtaˈtɪstɪk] f (-; -en) statistics; Sta'tistiker [ʃtaˈtɪstɪkɐ] m (-s; -) statistician; sta'tistisch adj statistical
Stativ [ʃtaˈtiːf] n (-s; -e) PHOT tripod
statt [ʃtat] prp instead of; ~ et. zu tun instead of doing s.th.; ~'dessen instead
Stätte ['ʃtɛtə] f (-; -n) place; scene
'stattfinden v/i (irr, finden, sep, -ge-, h) take place; happen
'stattlich adj imposing; handsome
Statue ['ʃtaːtuə] f (-; -n) statue
Statur [ʃtaˈtuːɐ] f (-; -en) build
Status ['ʃtaːtʊs] m (-; -) state; status; ~sym‚bol n status symbol; ~zeile f IT status line
Stau [ʃtau] m (-[e]s; -s, -e) MOT traffic jam or congestion
Staub [ʃtaup] m (-[e]s; TECH -e, Stäube ['ʃtɔybə]) dust (a. ~ wischen)
'Staubecken n reservoir
stauben ['ʃtaubən] v/i (ge-, h) give off or make dust; staubig ['ʃtaubɪç] adj dusty; 'staubsaugen v/i and v/t (ge-, h) vacuum, F Br hoover;

'Staubsauger m vacuum cleaner, F Br hoover; 'Staubtuch n duster
'Staudamm m dam
Staude ['ʃtaudə] f (-; -n) BOT herbacious plant
stauen ['ʃtauən] v/t (ge-, h) dam up; sich ~ MOT etc be stacked up
staunen ['ʃtaunən] v/i (ge-, h) be astonished or surprised (über acc at)
'Staunen n (-s; no pl) astonishment, amazement
Staupe ['ʃtaupə] f (-; -n) VET distemper
'Stausee m reservoir
stechen ['ʃtɛçən] v/i and v/t (irr, ge-, h) prick; zo sting, bite; stab; pierce; mit et. ~ in (acc) stick s.th. in(to); sich ~ prick o.s.; ~d fig adj piercing (look); stabbing (pain)
'Stechuhr f time clock
Steckbrief ['ʃtɛkbriːf] m JUR „wanted" poster
'steckbrieflich adv: er wird ~ gesucht JUR a warrant is out against him
'Steckdose f ELECTR (wall) socket
stecken ['ʃtɛkən] (ge-, h) 1. v/t stick; put; esp TECH insert (in acc into); pin (an acc to, on); AGR set, plant 2. v/i ([irr]) be; stick, be stuck; ~ bleiben get stuck; 'steckenbleiben v/i (irr, bleiben, sep, -ge-, sein) fig get stuck
'Steckenpferd n hobby horse; fig hobby
Stecker ['ʃtɛkɐ] m (-s; -) ELECTR plug
'Steck|kon‚takt m ELECTR plug (connection); ~nadel f pin; ~platz m IT slot
Steg [ʃteːk] m (-[e]s; -e) footbridge
Stegreif ['ʃteːkraif] m: aus dem ~ extempore, ad-lib; aus dem ~ sprechen or spielen etc extemporize, ad-lib
stehen ['ʃteːən] v/i (irr, ge-, h) stand; be; stand up; es steht ihr it suits (or looks well on) her; wie steht es (or das Spiel)? what's the score?; hier steht, dass it says here that; wo steht das? where does it say so or that?; wie steht es mit ...? what about ...?; F darauf stehe ich it turns me on; ~ bleiben stop; esp TECH come to a standstill (a. fig); leave behind; alles~ und liegen lassen drop everything; sich e-n Bart ~ lassen grow a beard
'stehen|bleiben v/i (irr, bleiben, sep, -ge-, sein) → stehen; ~lassen v/t (irr,

lassen, *sep*, *no -ge-*, *h*) → *stehen*

'**Steh|kragen** *m* stand-up collar; *~lampe* *f* floor (*Br* standard) lamp; *~leiter* *f* step ladder

stehlen ['ʃteːlən] *v/t and v/i* (*irr*, *ge-*, *h*) steal (*a. fig* **sich** *~*)

'**Stehplatz** *m* standing ticket; *pl* standing room

steif [ʃtaif] *adj* stiff (*vor dat* with)

Steigbügel ['ʃtaikbyːgə] *m* stirrup

steigen ['ʃtaigən] *v/i* (*irr*, *ge-*, *sein*) go, step; climb (*a.* AVIAT); *fig* rise, go up; *~ in* (*auf*) (*acc*) get on (*bus*, *bike etc*); *~ aus* (*von*) get off (*bus*, *horse etc*); *~ aus dem Bett ~* get out of bed

steigern ['ʃtaigən] *v/t* (*ge-*, *h*) raise, increase; heighten; improve; LING compare; *sich ~* improve, get better

Steigerung ['ʃtaigərʊŋ] *f* (*-*; *-en*) rise, increase; heightening; improvement; LING comparison

'**Steigung** *f* (*-*; *-en*) gradient; slope

steil [ʃtail] *adj* steep (*a. fig*)

Stein [ʃtain] *m* (*-[e]s*; *-e*) stone (*a.* BOT, MED), rock; *~bock* *m* ZO rock goat; ASTR Capricorn; *er ist (ein) ~* he's (a) Capricorn; *~bruch* *m* quarry

steinern ['ʃtainɐn] *adj* (of) stone; *fig* stony

'**Steingut** *n* (*-[e]s*; *-e*) earthenware

steinig ['ʃtainɪç] *adj* stony

steinigen ['ʃtainɪgən] *v/t* (*ge-*, *h*) stone

'**Steinkohle** *f* (hard) coal

Steinmetz ['ʃtainmɛts] *m* (*-en*; *-en*) stonemason

'**Steinzeit** *f* (*-*; *no pl*) Stone Age

Stellage [ʃtɛˈlaːʒə] *Austrian f* (*-*; *-n*) stand, rack, shelf

Stelle ['ʃtɛlə] *f* (*-*; *-n*) place; spot; point; job; authority; MATH figure; *freie ~* vacancy, opening; *auf der (zur) ~* on the spot; *an erster ~ stehen (kommen)* be (come) first; *an j-s ~* in s.o.'s place; *ich an deiner ~* if I were you

'**stellen** *v/t* (*ge-*, *h*) put; set (*trap*, *clock*, *task etc*); turn (*up*, *down etc*); ask (*question*); provide; corner, hunt down (*criminal etc*); *sich ~* give o.s. up, turn o.s. in; *sich gegen (hinter) j-n ~* *fig* oppose (back) s.o.; *sich schlafend etc ~* pretend to be asleep *etc*; *stell dich dorthin!* (go and) stand over there!

'**Stellen|angebot** *n* vacancy; *ich habe ein ~* I was offered a job; *~anzeige* *f*

job ad(vertisement), employment ad; *~gesuch* *n* application for a job

'**stellenweise** *adv* partly, in places

'**Stellung** *f* (*-*; *-en*) position; post, job; *~ nehmen zu* comment on, give one's opinion of; *~nahme* ['ʃtɛlʊŋnaːmə] *f* (*-*; *-n*) comment, opinion (*both*: *zu* on)

'**stellungslos** *adj* unemployed, jobless

'**stellvertretend** *adj* acting, deputy, vice-...; '**Stellvertreter(in)** (*-s*; *-/-*; *-nen*) representative; deputy

Stelze ['ʃtɛltsə] *f* (*-*; *-n*) stilt

'**stelzen** *v/i* (*ge-*, *sein*) stalk

stemmen ['ʃtɛmən] *v/t* (*ge-*, *h*) lift (*weight*); *sich ~ gegen* press o.s. against; *fig* resist *or* oppose s.th.

Stempel ['ʃtɛmpəl] *m* (*-s*; *-*) stamp; postmark; hallmark; BOT pistil

'**Stempelkissen** *n* ink pad

'**stempeln** (*ge-*, *h*) **1.** *v/t* stamp; cancel; hallmark **2.** F *v/i*: *~ gehen* be on the dole

Stengel → *Stängel*

Stenografie [ʃtenograˈfiː] *f* (*-*; *-n*) shorthand; **stenogra'fieren** *v/t* (*no -ge-*, *h*) take down in shorthand

Stenogramm [ʃtenoˈgram] *n* (*-[e]s*; *-e*) shorthand notes; **Stenotypistin** [ʃtenotyˈpɪstɪn] *f* (*-*; *-nen*) shorthand typist

Steppdecke ['ʃtɛpdɛkə] *f* quilt; **steppen** ['ʃtɛpən] (*ge-*, *h*) **1.** *v/t* quilt; stitch **2.** *v/i* tap dance; '**Stepptanz** *m* tap dancing

Sterbebett ['ʃtɛrbəbɛt] *n* deathbed

'**Sterbeklinik** *f* MED hospice

sterben ['ʃtɛrbən] *v/i* (*irr*, *ge-*, *sein*) die (*an dat* of) (*a. fig*); *im Sterben liegen* be dying

sterblich ['ʃtɛrplɪç] *adj* mortal

'**Sterblichkeit** *f* (*-*; *no pl*) mortality

Stereo ['ʃteːreo] *n* (*-s*; *-s*) stereo

steril [ʃteˈriːl] *adj* sterile; **Sterilisation** [ʃterilizaˈtsjoːn] *f* (*-*; *-en*) sterilization; **sterilisieren** [ʃteriliˈziːrən] *v/t* (*no -ge-*, *h*) sterilize

Stern [ʃtɛrn] *m* (*-[e]s*; *-e*) star (*a. fig*)

'**Sternbild** *n* ASTR constellation; sign of the zodiac

Sternchen *n* (*-s*; *-*) PRINT asterisk

'**Sternenbanner** *n* Star-Spangled Banner, Stars and Stripes

'**Sternenhimmel** *m* starry sky

'**sternklar** *adj* starry

S

'Stern|kunde f (-; no pl) astronomy; ~schnuppe f (-; -n) shooting or falling star; ~warte f (-; -n) observatory

stetig ['ʃteːtɪç] adj continual, constant; steady; stets [ʃteːts] adv always

Steuer[1] ['ʃtɔʏɐ] n (-s; -) MOT (steering) wheel; MAR helm, rudder

'Steuer[2] f (-; -n) tax (auf acc on)

'Steuer|beamte m revenue officer; ~berater m tax adviser

'Steuerbord n MAR starboard

'Steuer|erklärung f tax return; ~ermäßigung f tax allowance

'steuerfrei adj tax-free

'Steuerhinterziehung f tax evasion

'Steuer|knüppel m AVIAT control column or stick; ~mann m MAR helmsman; rowing: cox, coxswain

'steuern v/t and v/i (ge-, h) steer, AVIAT, MAR a. navigate, pilot, MOT a. drive; TECH control (a. fig); fig direct

'steuerpflichtig adj taxable

'Steuerrad n MOT steering wheel

'Steuerruder n MAR helm, rudder

'Steuersenkung f tax reduction

Steuerung ['ʃtɔʏərʊŋ] f (-; -en) steering (system); ELECTR, TECH control (a. fig)

'Steuerzahler m, 'Steuerzahlerin f tax-payer

Stich [ʃtɪç] m (-[e]s; -e) prick; ZO sting, bite, stab; stitch; cards: trick; engraving; im ~ lassen desert or abandon s.o., s.th., leave s.o. in the lurch, let s.o. down

Stichelei [ʃtɪçə'laɪ] f f (-; -en) dig, gibe

sticheln ['ʃɪçəln] F v/i (ge-, h) make digs, gibe (gegen at)

'Stichflamme f jet of flame

'stichhaltig adj valid, sound; watertight; nicht ~ sein F not hold water

'Stich|probe f spot check; ~tag m cutoff date; deadline; ~wahl f POL run-off; ~wort n (-[e]s; -e) THEA cue; (-[e]s; -wörter) headword; ~e pl notes; das Wichtigste in ~en an outline of the main points; ~wortverzeichnis n index; ~wunde f MED stab

sticken ['ʃtɪkən] v/t and v/i (ge-, h) embroider; Stickerei [ʃtɪkə'raɪ] f (-; -en) embroidery

stickig ['ʃtɪkɪç] adj stuffy

'Stickstoff m (-[e]s; no pl) CHEM nitrogen

Stief... [ʃtiːf-] in cpds ...mutter etc:

step...

Stiefel ['ʃtiːfəl] m (-s; -) boot

Stiefmütterchen ['ʃtiːfmʏtɐçən] n (-s; -) BOT pansy

stieg [ʃtiːk] pret of steigen

Stiege ['ʃtiːgə] Austrian f (-; -n) → Treppe

Stiel [ʃtiːl] m (-[e]s; -e) handle; stick; stem; BOT stalk

Stier [ʃtiːɐ] m (-[e]s; -e) ZO bull; ASTR Taurus; er ist (ein) ~ he's (a) Taurus

'Stierkampf m bullfight

stieß [ʃtiːs] pret of stoßen

Stift [ʃtɪft] m (-[e]s; -e) pen; pencil; crayon; TECH pin; peg

stiften ['ʃtɪftən] v/t (ge-, h) donate; fig cause; 'Stiftung f (-; -en) donation

Stil [ʃtiːl] m (-[e]s; -e) style (a. fig); in großem ~ in (grand) style; fig on a large scale; stilistisch [ʃti'lɪstɪʃ] adj stylistic

still [ʃtɪl] adj quiet, silent; still; sei(d) ~! be quiet!; halt ~! keep still!; sich ~ verhalten keep quiet (or still)

Stille ['ʃtɪlə] f (-; no pl) silence, quiet (-ness); in aller ~ quietly; secretly

Stilleben n → Stillleben

stillen ['ʃtɪlən] v/t (ge-, h) nurse, breastfeed; fig relieve (pain); satisfy (curiosity etc); quench (one's thirst)

'stillhalten v/i (irr, halten, sep, -ge-, h) keep still

'Stillleben n PAINT still life

'stilllegen v/t (sep, -ge-, h) close down

'stillos adj lacking style, tasteless

'stillschweigend adj tacit

'Stillstand m (-[e]s; no pl) standstill, stop, fig a. stagnation (a. ECON); deadlock; 'stillstehen v/i (irr, stehen, sep, -ge-, h) (have) stop(ped), (have) come to a standstill

'Stilmöbel pl period furniture

'stilvoll adj stylish; ~ sein have style

'Stimmband n ANAT vocal cord

'stimmberechtigt adj entitled to vote

Stimme ['ʃtɪmə] f (-; -n) voice; POL vote; sich der ~ enthalten abstain

'stimmen (ge-, h) 1. v/i be right, be true, be correct; POL vote (für for; gegen against); es stimmt et. nicht (damit or mit ihm) there's s.th. wrong (with it or him); 2. v/t MUS tune; j-n traurig etc ~ make s.o. sad etc

'Stimmenthaltung f abstention

'**Stimmrecht** *n* right to vote

'**Stimmung** *f* (-; -*en*) mood; atmosphere; feeling

'**stimmungsvoll** *adj* atmospheric

'**Stimmzettel** *m* ballot (paper)

stinken ['ʃtɪŋkən] *v/i* (*irr*, *ge-*, *h*) stink (*a. fig*) (*nach* of)

Stipendium [ʃti'pɛndjʊm] *n* (-*s*; -*ien*) UNIV scholarship, grant

stippen ['ʃtɪpən] *v/t* (*ge-*, *h*) dip

'**Stippvi,site** F *f* flying visit

Stirn [ʃtɪrn] *f* (-; -*en*) ANAT forehead; *die ~ runzeln* frown

stöbern ['ʃtøːbən] F *v/i* (*ge-*, *h*) rummage (about)

stochern ['ʃtɔxən] *v/i* (*ge-*, *h*) *im Feuer ~* poke the fire; *im Essen ~* pick at one's food; *in den Zähnen ~* pick one's teeth

Stock [ʃtɔk] *m* (-[*e*]*s*; *Stöcke* ['ʃtœkə]) stick; cane; ARCH stor(e)y, floor; *im ers-ten ~* on the second (*Br* first) floor

'**stock'dunkel** F *adj* pitch-dark

stocken ['ʃtɔkən] *v/i* (*ge-*, *h*) stop (short); falter; *traffic*: be jammed; **~d 1.** *adj* halting **2.** *adv*: *~ lesen* stumble through a text; *~ sprechen* speak halt-ingly

'**Stockfleck** *m* mo(u)ld stain

'**Stockung** *f* (-; -*en*) holdup, delay

'**Stockwerk** *n* stor(e)y, floor

Stoff [ʃtɔf] *m* (-[*e*]*s*; -*e*) material, stuff (*a.* F); fabric, textile; cloth; CHEM, PHYS *etc* substance; *fig* subject (matter)

'**stofflich** *adj* material

'**Stofftier** *n* soft toy animal

'**Stoffwechsel** *m* BIOL metabolism

stöhnen ['ʃtøːnən] *v/i* (*ge-*, *h*) groan, moan (*a. fig*)

Stollen ['ʃtɔlən] *m* (-*s*; -) tunnel, gallery

stolpern ['ʃtɔlpən] *v/i* (*ge-*, *sein*) stumble (*über acc* over), trip (over) (*both a. fig*)

stolz [ʃtɔlts] *adj* proud (*auf acc* of)

Stolz *m* (-*es*; *no pl*) pride (*auf acc* in)

stolzieren [ʃtɔl'tsiːrən] *v/i* (*no -ge-*, *sein*) strut, stalk

stopfen ['ʃtɔpfən] *v/t* (*ge-*, *h*) darn, mend; stuff, fill (*a. pipe*)

Stoppel ['ʃtɔpəl] *f* (-; -*n*) stubble

'**Stoppelbart** F *m* stubbly beard

'**stoppelig** *adj* stubbly, bristly

'**Stoppelzieher** *Austrian m* corkscrew

stoppen ['ʃtɔpən] *v/i* and *v/t* (*ge-*, *h*)

stop (*a. fig*); *esp* SPORT time

'**Stopp**|**licht** *n* (-[*e*]*s*; -*er*) MOT stop light; *~schild* *n* stop sign; *~uhr* *f* stopwatch

Stöpsel ['ʃtœpsəl] *m* (-*s*; -) stopper; plug

Storch [ʃtɔrç] *m* (-[*e*]*s*; *Störche* ['ʃtœr-çəl]) ZO stork

stören ['ʃtøːrən] *v/t* and *v/i* (*ge-*, *h*) disturb; trouble; bother, annoy; be in the way; *lassen Sie sich nicht ~!* don't let me disturb you!; *darf ich Sie kurz ~?* may I trouble you for a minute?; *es (er) stört mich nicht* it (he) doesn't bother me, I don't mind (him); *stört es Sie(, wenn ich rauche)?* do you mind (my smoking *or* if I smoke)?

'**Störenfried** ['ʃtøːrənfriːt] *m* (-[*e*]*s*; -*e*) troublemaker; intruder

'**Störfall** ['ʃtøːrfal] *m* TECH accident

störrisch ['ʃtœrɪʃ] *adj* stubborn, obsti-nate

'**Störung** *f* (-; -*en*) disturbance; trouble (*a.* TECH); TECH breakdown; TV, *radio*: interference

Stoß [ʃtoːs] *m* (-*es*; *Stöße* ['ʃtøːsə]) push, shove; thrust; kick; butt; *esp* blow, knock; shock; MOT jolt; bump, *esp* TECH, PHYS impact; pile, stack; '**Stoßdämpfer** *m* MOT shock absorber; **stoßen** ['ʃtoː-sən] *v/t* and *v/i* (*ge-*, *h*) and *v/i* (*sein*) push, shove; thrust; kick; butt; knock, strike; pound; *~ gegen* or *an* (*acc*) bump or run into or against; *sich an den Kopf ~* (*an dat*) knock one's head (against); *~ auf* (*acc*) strike (*oil etc*); *fig* come across; meet with; '**stoßgesichert** *adj* shockproof, shock-resistant; '**Stoßstange** *f* MOT bumper; '**Stoßzahn** *m* ZO tusk; '**Stoßzeit** *f* rush hour, peak hours

stottern ['ʃtɔtən] *v/i* and *v/t* (*ge-*, *h*) stut-ter

Str. *abbr of* **Straße** St, Street; Rd, Road

'**Strafanstalt** *f* prison, penitentiary; '**strafbar** *adj* punishable, penal; *sich ~ machen* commit an offense (*Br* of-fence); **Strafe** ['ʃtraːfə] *f* (-; -*n*) punish-ment; JUR, ECON, SPORT penalty (*a. fig*); fine; *30 Euro ~ zahlen müssen* be fined 30 euros; *zur ~* as a punishment; '**strafen** *v/t* (*ge-*, *h*) punish

straff [ʃtraf] *adj* tight; *fig* strict

'**straffrei** *adj*: *~ ausgehen* go unpun-ished

'Straf|gefangene *m*, *f* prisoner, convict; ~gesetz *n* criminal law

sträflich ['ʃtrɛːflɪç] **1.** *adj* inexcusable **2.** *adv*: ~ **vernachlässigen** neglect badly

'Straf|mi,nute *f* SPORT penalty minute; ~pro,zess *m* JUR criminal action, trial; ~raum *m* SPORT penalty area (F box); ~stoß *m* SPORT penalty kick; ~tat *f* JUR criminal offense (Br offence); crime; ~zettel *m* ticket

Strahl [ʃtraːl] *m* (-[e]s, -en) ray (*a. fig*); beam; flash; jet; strahlen ['ʃtraːlən] *v/i* (*ge-, h*) radiate; shine (brightly); *fig* beam (**vor** with); 'Strahlen... in *cpds* PHYS ...*schutz etc*: radiation ...

'Strahlung *f* (-; -en) PHYS radiation

Strähne ['ʃtrɛːnə] *f* (-; -n) strand; streak

stramm [ʃtram] *adj* tight; ~stehen MIL stand to attention

strampeln ['ʃtrampəln] *v/i* (*ge-, h*) kick

Strand [ʃtrant] *m* (-[e]s; Strände ['ʃtrɛndə]) beach; **am** ~ on the beach

stranden ['ʃtrandən] *v/i* (*ge-, sein*) MAR strand; *fig* fail

'Strand|gut *n* flotsam and jetsam (*a. fig*); ~korb *m* roofed wicker beach chair

Strang [ʃtraŋ] *m* (-[e]s; Stränge ['ʃtrɛŋə]) rope; *esp* HALTER

Strapaze [ʃtra'paːtsə] *f* (-; -n) strain, exertion, hardship; strapazieren [ʃtrapa-'tsiːrən] *v/t* (*no -ge-, h*) wear *s.o. or s.th.* out, be hard on; strapazierfähig *adj* longwearing, Br hardwearing

strapaziös [ʃtrapa'tsjøːs] *adj* strenuous

Straße ['ʃtraːsə] *f* (-; -n) road; street; GEOGR strait; **auf der** ~ on the road; on (*Br a.* in) the street

'Straßen|arbeiten *pl* roadworks; ~bahn *f* streetcar, Br tram; ~ca,fé *n* sidewalk (Br pavement) café; ~karte *f* road map; ~kehrer ['ʃtraːsənkeːrə] *m* (-s; -) street sweeper; ~kreuzung *f* crossroads; intersection; ~lage *f* MOT roadholding; ~rand *m* roadside; **am** ~ at *or* by the roadside; ~sperre *f* road block

strategisch [ʃtra'teːgɪʃ] *adj* strategic

sträuben ['ʃtrɔʏbən] *v/t and v/refl* (*ge-, h*) ruffle (up); bristle (up); **sich** ~ **gegen** struggle against

Strauch [ʃtraʊx] *m* (-[e]s; Sträucher ['ʃtrɔʏçɐ]) BOT shrub, bush

straucheln ['ʃtraʊxəln] *v/i* (*ge-, sein*) stumble

Strauß¹ [ʃtraʊs] *m* (-es; -e) ZO ostrich

Strauß² *m* (-es; Sträuße ['ʃtrɔʏsə]) bunch, bouquet

Strebe ['ʃtreːbə] *f* (-; -n) prop, stay (*a.* AVIAT, MAR); 'streben *v/i* (*ge-, h*) strive (**nach** for, after); Streber ['ʃtreːbɐ] *m* (-s; -) pusher; PED *etc* grind, Br swot; strebsam ['ʃtreːpzaːm] *adj* ambitious

Strecke ['ʃtrɛkə] *f* (-; -n) distance (*a.* SPORT, MATH), way; route; RAIL line; SPORT course; stretch; **zur** ~ **bringen** kill; *esp fig* hunt down; 'strecken *v/t* (*ge-, h*) stretch (out), extend

Streich [ʃtraɪç] *m* (-[e]s; -e) trick, prank, practical joke; **j-m e-n** ~ **spielen** play a trick *or* joke on *s.o.*

streicheln ['ʃtraɪçəln] *v/t* (*ge-, h*) stroke, caress

streichen ['ʃtraɪçən] *v/t and v/i* (*irr, ge-, h*) paint; spread; cross out; cancel; MAR strike; MUS bow; **mit der Hand** ~ **über** (*acc*) run one's hand over; ~ **durch** roam (*acc*); Streicher(in) ['ʃtraɪçɐ, 'ʃtraɪçərɪn] *m(f)* (-s; -/-; -nen) MUS string player, *pl* the strings

'Streich|holz *n* match; ~instru,ment *n* MUS string instrument; ~or,chester *n* MUS string orchestra

'Streichung *f* (-; -en) cancellation; cut

Streife ['ʃtraɪfə] *f* (-; -n) patrol; **auf~ ge-hen** go on patrol; **auf~ sein in** (*dat*) patrol

'streifen *v/t and v/i* (*ge-, h*) touch, brush (against); MOT scrape against; graze; slip (**von** off); *fig* touch on; ~ **durch** roam (*acc*), wander through

'Streifen *m* (-s; -) stripe; strip

'Streifenwagen *m* squad (Br patrol) car

'Streifschuss *m* MED graze

'Streifzug *m* tour (**durch** of)

Streik [ʃtraɪk] *m* (-[e]s; -s) strike, walkout

'Streikbrecher *m* strikebreaker, Br blackleg, *contp* scab

streiken ['ʃtraɪkən] *v/i* (*ge-, h*) (go *or* be on) strike; F *fig* refuse (to work *etc*)

'Streikende *m*, *f* (-n; -n) striker

'Streikposten *m* picket

Streit [ʃtraɪt] *m* (-[e]s; -e) quarrel, argument; fight; POL *etc* dispute; ~ **anfan-gen** pick a fight *or* quarrel; ~ **suchen** be looking for trouble; streiten ['ʃtraɪ-tən] *v/i and v/refl* (*irr, ge-, h*) quarrel,

argue, fight (*all*: **wegen, über** *acc* about, over); **sich ~ um** fight for
'**Streitfrage** *f* (point at) issue
streitig ['ʃtraɪtɪç] *adj*: **j-m et. ~ machen** dispute s.o.'s right to s.th.
'**Streitkräfte** *pl* MIL (armed) forces
'**streitsüchtig** *adj* quarrelsome
streng [ʃtrɛŋ] *adj* strict; severe; harsh; rigid; **~ genommen** strictly speaking
Strenge ['ʃtrɛŋə] *f* (-; *no pl*) strictness; severity; harshness; rigidity
'**strenggläubig** *adj* REL orthodox
Stress [ʃtrɛs] *m* (-*es*; *no pl*) stress; **im ~** under stress
Streu [ʃtrɔy] *f* (-; -*en*) AGR litter
'**streuen** *v/t and v/i* (*ge-, h*) scatter (*a.* PHYS); spread; sprinkle; grit
streunen ['ʃtrɔynən] *v/i* (*ge-, sein*), **~d** *adj* stray
strich [ʃtrɪç] *pret of* **streichen**
Strich [ʃtrɪç] *m* (-*[e]s*; -*e*) line; stroke; F red-light district; F **auf den ~ gehen** walk the streets; **~junge** F *m* male prostitute; **~kode** *m* bar code
'**strichweise** *adv* in parts; **~ Regen** scattered showers
Strick [ʃtrɪk] *m* (-*[e]s*; -*e*) cord; rope
stricken ['ʃtrɪkən] *v/t and v/i* (*ge-, h*) knit
'**Strick|jacke** *f* cardigan; **~leiter** *f* rope ladder; **~nadel** *f* knitting needle; **~waren** *pl* knitwear; **~zeug** *n* knitting (things)
Striemen ['ʃtriːmən] *m* (-*s*; -) welt, weal
stritt [ʃtrɪt] *pret of* **streiten**
strittig ['ʃtrɪtɪç] *adj* controversial; **~er Punkt** point at issue
Stroh [ʃtroː] *n* (-*[e]s*; *no pl*) straw; thatch; **~dach** *n* thatch(ed) roof; **~halm** *m* straw; **~hut** *m* straw hat; **~witwe** F *f* grass widow; **~witwer** F *m* grass widower
Strom [ʃtroːm] *m* (-*[e]s*; *Ströme* ['ʃtrøːmə]) (large) river; current (*a.* ELECTR); **ein ~ von** a stream of (*a. fig*); **es gießt in Strömen** it's pouring (with rain)
strom'ab(wärts) *adv* downstream
strom'auf(wärts) *adv* upstream
'**Stromausfall** *m* ELECTR power failure, blackout
strömen ['ʃtrøːmən] *v/i* (*ge-, sein*) stream (*a. fig*), flow, run; pour (*a. fig*)
'**Stromkreis** *m* ELECTR circuit
'**stromlinienförmig** *adj* streamlined

'**Stromschnelle** *f* (-; -*n*) GEOGR rapid
'**Stromstärke** *f* ELECTR amperage
Strömung *f* (-; -*en*) current, *fig a.* trend
Strophe ['ʃtroːfə] *f* (-; -*n*) stanza, verse
strotzen ['ʃtrɔtsən] *v/i* (*ge-, h*) **~ von** be full of, abound with; **~ vor** (*dat*) be bursting with
Strudel ['ʃtruːdəl] *m* (-*s*; -) whirlpool (*a. fig*), eddy
Struktur [ʃtrʊk'tuːɐ] *f* (-; -*en*) structure, pattern
Strumpf [ʃtrʊmpf] *m* (-*[e]s*; *Strümpfe* ['ʃtrʏmpfə]) stocking
'**Strumpfhose** *f* pantyhose, *Br* tights
struppig ['ʃtrʊpɪç] *adj* shaggy
Stück [ʃtʏk] *n* (-*[e]s*; -*e*) piece; part; lump; AGR head (*a. pl*); THEA play; **2 Euro das ~** 2 euros each; **im** or **am ~** in one piece; **in ~e schlagen** (**reißen**) smash (tear) to pieces; ECON by the piece; '**stückweise** *adv* bit by bit (*a. fig*); ECON by the piece
Student [ʃtu'dɛnt] *m* (-*en*; -*en*), **Studentin** *f* (-; -*nen*) student; **Studie** ['ʃtuːdjə] *f* (-; -*n*) study (**über** *acc* of); '**Studienplatz** *m* university *or* college place; **studieren** [ʃtu'diːrən] *v/t and v/i* (*no -ge-, h*) study, be a student (of) (**an** *dat* at); **Studium** ['ʃtuːdjʊm] *n* (-*s*; -*ien*) studies
Stufe ['ʃtuːfə] *f* (-; -*n*) step; level; stage
'**Stufenbarren** *m* SPORT uneven parallel bars
Stuhl [ʃtuːl] *m* (-*[e]s*; *Stühle* ['ʃtyːlə]) chair; MED stool; **~gang** *m* (-*[e]s*; *no pl*) MED (bowel) movement; **~lehne** *f* back of a chair
stülpen ['ʃtʏlpən] *v/t* (*ge-, h*) put (**auf** *acc*, **über** *acc* over, on)
stumm [ʃtʊm] *adj* dumb, mute; *fig* silent
Stummel ['ʃtʊməl] *m* (-*s*; -) stub, stump, butt
'**Stummfilm** *m* silent film
Stümper ['ʃtʏmpɐ] F *m* (-*s*; -) bungler
stumpf [ʃtʊmpf] *adj* blunt, dull (*a. fig*)
Stumpf *m* (-*[e]s*; *Stümpfe* ['ʃtʏmpfə]) stump, stub
'**stumpfsinnig** *adj* dull; monotonous
Stunde ['ʃtʊndə] *f* (-; -*n*) hour; PED class, lesson; period
'**Stundenkilo,meter** *m* kilometer (*Br* kilometre) per hour
'**stundenlang 1.** *adj*: **nach ~em Warten** after hours of waiting **2.** *adv* for hours

S

(and hours)

'**Stunden|lohn** *m* hourly wage; **~plan** *m* schedule, *Br* timetable

'**stundenweise** *adv* by the hour

'**Stundenzeiger** *m* hour hand

stündlich ['ʃtʏntlɪç] **1.** *adj* hourly **2.** *adv* hourly, every hour

Stupsnase ['ʃtʊpsnaːzə] *F f* snub nose

stur [ʃtuːɐ] *F adj* pigheaded

Sturm [ʃtʊrm] *m* (-[e]s; *Stürme* ['ʃtʏrmə]) storm (*a. fig*); **stürmen** ['ʃtʏrmən] *v/t* (*ge-, h*) *and v/i* (*ge-, sein*) storm; SPORT attack; rush; **Stürmer(in)** ['ʃtʏrmɐ, 'ʃtʏrmərɪn] *m(f)* (*-s; -/-; -nen*) SPORT forward; *esp soccer*: striker; **stürmisch** ['ʃtʏrmɪʃ] *adj* stormy; *fig* wild, vehement

Sturz [ʃtʊrts] *m* (-es; *Stürze* ['ʃtʏrtsə]) fall (*a. fig*); POL etc: overthrow

stürzen ['ʃtʏrtsən] **1.** *v/i* (*ge-, sein*) fall; crash; rush, dash; **schwer ~** have a bad fall **2.** *v/t* (*ge-, h*) throw; POL etc: overthrow; **j-n ins Unglück ~** ruin s.o.; **sich stürzen aus** throw o.s. out of; **sich ~ auf** (*acc*) throw o.s. at

'**Sturzflug** *m* AVIAT nosedive

'**Sturzhelm** *m* crash helmet

Stute ['ʃtuːtə] *f* (-; -n) ZO mare

Stütze ['ʃtʏtsə] *f* (-; -n) support, prop; *fig a.* aid

stutzen ['ʃtʊtsən] (*ge-, h*) **1.** *v/t* trim, clip **2.** *v/i* stop short; (*begin to*) wonder

stützen ['ʃtʏtsən] *v/t* (*ge-, h*) support (*a. fig*); **sich ~ auf** (*acc*) lean on; *fig* be based on

'**Stütz|pfeiler** *m* ARCH supporting column; **~punkt** *m* MIL base (*a. fig*)

Styropor® ['ʃtyroˈpoːɐ] *n* (-s; *no pl*) Styrofoam®, *Br* polystyrene®

s. u. *abbr of siehe unten* see below

Subjekt [zʊpˈjɛkt] *n* (-[e]s; -e) LING subject; *contp* character

subjektiv [zʊpjɛkˈtiːf] *adj* subjective

Substantiv ['zʊpstantiːf] *n* (-s; -e) LING noun

Substanz [zʊpˈstants] *f* (-; -en) substance (*a. fig*)

subtrahieren [zʊptraˈhiːrən] *v/t* (*no -ge-, h*) MATH subtract; **Subtraktion** [zʊptrakˈtsjoːn] *f* (-; -en) MATH subtraction

subventionieren [zʊpvɛntsjoˈniːrən] *v/t* (*no -ge-, h*) subsidize

Suche ['zuːxə] *f* (-; *no pl*) search (**nach** for); **auf der ~ nach** in search of; '**suchen** *v/t and v/i* (*ge-, h*) look for; search for; **gesucht: ...** wanted: ...; **was hat er hier zu ~?** what's he doing here?; **er hat hier nichts zu ~** he has no business to be here; **Sucher** ['zuːxɐ] *m* (*-s; -*) PHOT viewfinder

Sucht [zʊxt] *f* (-; *Süchte* ['zʏçtə]) addiction (**nach** to); mania (for); **süchtig** ['zʏçtɪç] *adj:* **~ sein** be addicted to *drugs etc*, be a *drug etc* addict; **Süchtige** ['zʏçtɪgə] *m, f* (*-n; -n*) addict

Süden ['zyːdən] *m* (-s; *no pl*) south; **nach ~** south(wards)

Südfrüchte ['zyːtfrʏçtə] *pl* tropical *or* southern fruits

'**südlich 1.** *adj* south(ern); southerly **2.** *adv:* **~ von** (to the) south of

Süd'osten *m* southeast; **süd'östlich** *adj* southeast(ern); southeasterly

'**Südpol** *m* South Pole

'**südwärts** ['zyːdvɛrts] *adv* southward(s)

Süd'westen *m* southwest; **süd-** '**westlich** *adj* southwest(ern); southwesterly

'**Südwind** *m* south wind

Sülze ['zʏltsə] *f* (-; -n) GASTR jellied meat

Summe ['zʊmə] *f* (-; -n) sum (*a. fig*); amount; (*sum*) total

summen ['zʊmən] *v/i and v/t* (*ge-, h*) buzz, hum

summieren [zʊˈmiːrən] *v/refl* (*no -ge-, h*) add up (**auf** *acc* to)

Sumpf [zʊmpf] *m* (-es; *Sümpfe* ['zʏmpfə]) swamp, bog

'**sumpfig** *adj* swampy, marshy

Sünde ['zʏndə] *f* (-; -n) sin (*a. fig*)

'**Sündenbock** *m* scapegoat

Sünder ['zʏndɐ] *m* (*-s; -*), **'Sünderin** *f* (*-; -nen*) sinner

sündig ['zʏndɪç] *adj* sinful; **sündigen** ['zʏndɪgən] *v/i* (*ge-, h*) (commit a) sin

Super... ['zuːpɐ-] *in cpds ...macht etc: mst* super ...

'**Super** *n* (-s; *no pl*), **~ben,zin** *n* super *or* premium (gasoline), *Br* four-star (petrol)

Superlativ ['zuːpɐlatiːf] *m* (-s; -e) LING superlative (*a. fig*)

'**Supermarkt** *m* supermarket

Suppe ['zʊpə] *f* (-; -n) soup

'**Suppen...** *in cpds ...löffel, ...teller, ...küche etc*: soup ...

Surfbrett ['zøːɐfbrɛt] n sail board; surfboard; 'surfen v/i (ge-, h) surf

surren ['zʊrən] v/i (ge-, h) whirr; buzz

süß [zyːs] adj sweet, sugary (both a. fig)

Süße ['zyːsə] f (-; no pl) sweetness

'süßen v/t (ge-, h) sweeten

Süßigkeiten ['zyːsɪçkaitən] pl sweets,
candy

'süßlich adj sweetish; contp mawkish,
sugary

'süß'sauer adj GASTR sweet-and-sour

'Süßstoff m sweetener

'Süßwasser n fresh water

Symbol [zym'boːl] n (-s; -e) symbol;
Symbolik [zym'boːlɪk] f (-; no pl) sym-
bolism; sym'bolisch adj symbolic(al)

Symmetrie [zyme'triː] f (-; -n) symmetry; symmetrisch [zy'meːtrɪʃ] adj
symmetric(al)

Sympathie [zympa'tiː] f (-; -n) liking
(für for); sympathy; Sympathisant(in)
[zympati'zant(ɪn)] (-en; -en/-; -nen)
sympathizer; sympathisch [zym-

'paːtɪʃ] adj nice, likable; er ist mir ~
I like him

Symphonie [zymfo'niː] f (-; -n) etc →
Sinfonie

Symptom [zymp'toːm] n (-s; -e) symptom

Synagoge [zyna'goːgə] f (-; -n) syna-
gogue

synchron [zyn'kroːn] adj TECH synchro-
nous; synchronisieren [zynkroni-
'ziːrən] v/t (no -ge-, h) synchronize;
film etc: dub

synonym [zyno'nyːm] adj synonymous

Syno'nym n (-s; -e) synonym

Synthese [zyn'teːzə] f (-; -n) synthesis

synthetisch [zyn'teːtɪʃ] adj synthetic

System [zys'teːm] n (-s; -e) system

systematisch [zyste'maːtɪʃ] adj sys-
tematic, methodical

Sys'temfehler m IT system error

Szene ['stseːnə] f (-; -n) scene (a. fig)

Szenerie [stsenə'riː] f (-; -n) scenery;
setting

T

Tabak ['taːbak] m (-s; -e) tobacco; ~ge-
schäft n tobacconist's; ~waren pl tobacco products

Tabelle [ta'bɛlə] f (-; -n) table (a. MATH,
SPORT)

Ta'bellen|kalkulati,on f IT spreadsheet;
~platz m SPORT position

Tablett [ta'blɛt] n (-[e]s; -s) tray

Tablette [ta'blɛtə] f (-; -n) tablet

tabu [ta'buː] adj, Ta'bu n (-s; -s) taboo

Tabulator [tabu'laːtoːɐ] m (-s; -en
[tabula'toːrən]) tabulator

Tachometer [taxo'meːtɐ] m, n (-s; -)
MOT speedometer

Tadel ['taːdəl] m (-s; -) blame; censure,
reproof, rebuke; 'tadellos adj faultless; blameless; excellent; perfect

'tadeln v/t (ge-, h) criticize, blame; censure, reprove, rebuke (all: wegen for)

Tafel ['taːfəl] f PED etc: blackboard; (bulletin, esp Br notice) board; sign; tablet,
plaque; GASTR bar (of chocolate)

täfeln ['tɛːfəln] v/t (ge-, h) panel

'Täfelung f (-; -en) panel(l)ing

Taft [taft] m (-[e]s; -e) taffeta

Tag [taːk] m (-[e]s; -e ['taːgə]) day; daylight; welchen ~ haben wir heute?
what day is it today?; heute (morgen)
in 14 ~en two weeks from today (tomorrow); e-s ~es one day; den ganzen ~ all day; am ~e during the day;
~ und Nacht night and day; am helllichten ~ in broad daylight; ein freier
~ a day off; guten ~! hello!, hi!; how
do you do?; (j-m) guten ~ sagen say
hello (to s.o.); F sie hat ihre ~e she
has her period; unter ~e underground;
→ zutage

Tage|bau ['taːgəbau] m (-[e]s; -e) open-
cast mining; ~buch n diary; ~ führen
keep a diary

'tagelang adv for days

'tagen v/i (ge-, h) meet, hold a meeting;
JUR be in session

'Tages|anbruch m: bei ~ at daybreak, at
dawn; ~gespräch n talk of the day;
~karte f day ticket; GASTR menu for
the day; ~licht n (-[e]s; no pl) daylight;
~mutter f childminder; ~ordnung f
agenda; ~stätte f day care center (Br

centre); ~**tour** f day trip; ~**zeit** f time of day; **zu jeder** ~ at any hour; ~**zeitung** f daily (paper)

'**tageweise** adv by the day

täglich ['tɛːklɪç] adj and adv daily

'**Tagschicht** f ECON day shift

'**tagsüber** adv during the day

'**Tagung** f (-; -en) conference

Taille ['taljə] f (-; -n) waist; waistline

tailliert [ta'jiːɐt] adj waisted, tapered

Takelage [takəˈlaːʒə] f (-; -n) MAR rigging

Takt [takt] m (-[e]s; -e) (no pl) MUS time, measure, beat; MUS bar; MOT stroke; (no pl) tact; **den** ~ **halten** MUS keep time

Taktik ['taktɪk] f (-; -en) MIL tactics (a. fig); '**taktisch** adj tactical

'**taktlos** adj tactless

'**Taktstock** m MUS baton

'**Taktstrich** m MUS bar

'**taktvoll** adj tactful

Tal [taːl] n (-[e]s; Täler ['tɛːlɐ]) valley

Talar [ta'laːɐ] m (-s; -e) robe, gown

Talent [ta'lɛnt] n (-[e]s; -e) talent (a. person), gift; **talentiert** [talɛnˈtiːɐt] adj talented, gifted

Talg [talk] m (-[e]s; -e) tallow; GASTR suet

Talisman ['taːlɪsman] m (-s; -e) talisman, charm

Talk|master ['tɔːkmaːstɐ] m (-s; -) TV talk (Br chat) show host; ~**show** ['tɔːkʃou] f (-; -s) TV talk (Br chat) show

'**Talsperre** f dam, barrage

Tampon ['tampɔn] m (-s; -s) tampon

Tandler ['tandlɐ] Austrian m (-s; -) second-hand dealer

Tang [taŋ] m (-[e]s; -e) BOT seaweed

Tank [taŋk] m (-s; -s) tank; **tanken** ['taŋkən] v/t (ge-; h) get some gasoline (Br petrol), fill up; **Tanker** ['taŋkɐ] m (-s; -) MAR tanker; '**Tankstelle** f filling (or gas, Br petrol) station; '**Tankwart** m (-[e]s; -e) gas station (Br petrol pump) attendant

Tanne ['tanə] f (-; -n) BOT fir (tree)

'**Tannenbaum** m Christmas tree

'**Tannenzapfen** m BOT fir cone

Tante ['tantə] f (-; -n) aunt; ~ **Lindy** Aunt Lindy; ~**Emma-Laden** F m mom-and-pop store, Br corner shop

Tantiemen [ta_'tjeːmən] pl royalties

Tanz [tants] m (-es; Tänze ['tɛntsə]), **tanzen** ['tantsən] v/i (ge-; h, sein) and v/t (ge-; h) dance; **Tänzer** ['tɛntsɐ]

m (-s; -), **Tänzerin** ['tɛntsərɪn] f (-; -nen) dancer

'**Tanz|fläche** f dance floor; ~**kurs** m dancing lessons; ~**mu,sik** f dance music; ~**schule** f dancing school

Tapete [ta'peːtə] f (-; -n), **tapezieren** [tape'tsiːrən] v/t (no -ge-; h) wallpaper

tapfer ['tapfɐ] adj brave; courageous

'**Tapferkeit** f (-; no pl) bravery; courage

Tarif [ta'riːf] m (-[e]s; -e) rate(s), tariff; (wage) scale; ~**lohn** m standard wage(s); ~**verhandlungen** pl wage negotiations, collective bargaining

tarnen ['tarnən] v/t (ge-; h) camouflage; fig disguise

'**Tarnung** f (-; -en) camouflage

Tasche ['taʃə] f (-; -n) bag; pocket

'**Taschen|buch** n paperback; ~**dieb** m pickpocket; ~**geld** n allowance, Br pocket money; ~**lampe** f flashlight, Br torch; ~**messer** n penknife, pocket-knife; ~**rechner** m pocket calculator; ~**schirm** m telescopic umbrella; ~**tuch** n handkerchief, F hankie; ~**uhr** f pocket watch

Tasse ['tasə] f (-; -n) cup; **e-e** ~ **Tee** etc a cup of tea etc

Tastatur [tasta'tuːɐ] f (-; -en) keyboard, keys; **Taste** ['tastə] f (-; -n) key

tasten ['tastən] (ge-; h) **1.** v/i grope (**nach** for), feel (for); fumble (for) **2.** v/t touch, feel; **sich** ~ feel or grope (a. fig) one's way

'**Tastente,fon** n push-button phone

'**Tastsinn** m (-[e]s; no pl) sense of touch

tat [taːt] pret of **tun**

Tat f (-; -en) act, deed; action; JUR offense, Br offence; **j-n auf frischer** ~ **ertappen** catch s.o. in the act

'**tatenlos** adj inactive, passive

'**Täter** ['tɛːtɐ] m (-s; -), '**Täterin** f (-; -nen) culprit; JUR offender

tätig ['tɛːtɪç] adj active; busy; ~ **sein bei** be employed with; ~ **werden** act, take action; '**Tätigkeit** f (-; -en) activity; work; occupation, job

'**Tatkraft** f (-; no pl) energy

'**tatkräftig** adj energetic, active

tätlich ['tɛːtlɪç] adj violent; ~ **werden gegen** assault; '**Tätlichkeiten** pl (acts of) violence; JUR assault (and battery)

'**Tatort** m JUR scene of the crime

tätowieren [tɛto'viːrən] v/t (no -ge-; h), **Täto,wierung** f (-; -en) tattoo

'Tatsache f fact
'tatsächlich 1. adj actual, real **2.** adv actually, in fact; really
tätscheln ['tɛːtʃəln] v/t (ge-, h) pat, pet
Tatze ['tatsə] f (-; -n) zo paw (a. fig)
Tau[1] [tau] n (-[e]s; -e) rope
Tau[2] m (-[e]s; no pl) dew
taub [taup] adj deaf (fig **gegen** to); numb, benumbed
Taube ['taubə] f (-; -n) zo pigeon; esp fig dove; **'Taubenschlag** m pigeonhouse
'Taubheit f (-; no pl) deafness; numbness
'taubstumm adj deaf-and-dumb
'Taubstumme m, f (-n; -n) deaf mute
tauchen ['tauxən] **1.** v/i (ge-, h, sein) dive (**nach** for); sport skin-dive; submarine: a. submerge; stay underwater **2.** v/t (h) dip (**in** acc into); duck; **Taucher** ['tauxɐ] m (-s; -) (sport skin) diver; **'Tauchsport** m skin diving
tauen ['tauən] v/i (ge-, sein) and v/t (ge-, h) thaw, melt
Taufe ['taufə] f (-; -n) baptism, christening; **'taufen** v/t (ge-, h) baptize, christen; **'Taufpate** m godfather; **'Taufpatin** f godmother; **'Taufschein** m certificate of baptism
taugen ['taugən] v/i (ge-, h) be good or fit or of use or suited (**all: zu, für** for); **nichts ~** be no good; F **taugt es was?** is it any good?; **'tauglich** ['tauklɪç] adj esp MIL fit (for service)
Taumel ['tauməl] m (-s; no pl) dizziness; rapture, ecstasy; **'taumelig** adj dizzy; **'taumeln** v/i (ge-, sein) stagger, reel
Tausch [tauʃ] m (-[e]s; -e) exchange, F swap; **tauschen** ['tauʃən] v/t (ge-, h) exchange, F swap (both: **gegen** for); switch; change; **ich möchte nicht mit ihm ~** I wouldn't like to be in his shoes
täuschen ['tɔyʃən] v/t (ge-, h) deceive, fool; delude; cheat; a. sport feint; **sich ~** deceive o.s.; be mistaken; **sich ~ lassen von** be taken in by; **~de Ähnlichkeit** striking similarity; **'Täuschung** f (-; -en) deception; delusion; JUR deceit; a. PED cheating
tausend ['tauzənt] adj a thousand
'tausendst adj thousandth
'Tausendstel n (-s; -) thousandth (part)
'Tautropfen m dewdrop
'Tauwetter n thaw
'Tauziehen n (-s; no pl) sport tug-of-

-war (a. fig)
Taxi ['taksi] n (-s; -s) taxi(cab), cab
taxieren [ta'ksiːrən] v/t (no -ge-, h) rate, estimate (**auf** acc at)
'Taxistand m cabstand, esp Br taxi rank
Technik ['tɛçnɪk] f (-; -en) (no pl) technology, engineering; technique (a. sport etc), mus execution
Techniker ['tɛçnikɐ] m (-s; -), **'Technikerin** f (-; -nen) engineer; technician (a. sport etc)
technisch ['tɛçnɪʃ] adj technical; technological; **~e Hochschule** school etc of technology
Technologie [tɛçnolo'giː] f (-; -n) technology; **technologisch** [tɛçno'loːgɪʃ] adj technological
Tee [teː] m (-s; -s) tea; (**e-n**) **~ trinken** have some tea; (**e-n**) **~ machen** or **kochen** make some tea; **~beutel** m teabag; **~kanne** f teapot; **~löffel** m teaspoon
Teer [teːɐ] m (-[e]s; -e), **teeren** ['teːrən] v/t (ge-, h) tar
'Teesieb n tea strainer
'Teetasse f teacup
Teich [taiç] m (-[e]s; -e) pool, pond
Teig [taik] m (-[e]s; -e) dough, paste
teigig ['taigɪç] adj doughy, pasty
'Teigwaren pl pasta
Teil [tail] m, n (-[e]s; -e) part; portion, share; component; **zum ~** partly, in part; **~...** in cpds ...erfolg etc: partial ...
'teilbar adj divisible
'Teilchen n (-s; -) particle
teilen ['tailən] v/t (ge-, h) divide; share
'teilhaben v/i (irr, **haben**, sep, -ge-, h) **~ an** (dat) (have a) share in; **Teilhaber(in)** ['tailhaːbɐ (-bərɪn)] (-s; -/-; -nen) econ partner
Teilnahme ['tailnaːmə] f (-; no pl) participation (**an** dat in); fig interest in); sympathy (for)
'teilnahmslos adj indifferent; esp MED apathetic; **'Teilnahmslosigkeit** f (-; no pl) indifference; apathy
'teilnehmen v/i (irr, **nehmen**, sep, -ge-, h) **~ an** (dat) take part or participate in; share (in); **'Teilnehmer(in)** ['tailneːmɐ (-mərɪn)] (-s; -/-; -nen) participant; UNIV student; sport competitor
teils adv partly
'Teilstrecke f stage, leg
'Teilung f (-; -en) division

T

'teilweise *adv* partly, in part
'Teilzahlung *f* → *Abzahlung, Rate*
Teint [tɛ:] *m* (-s; -s) complexion
Tel. *abbr of Telefon* tel., telephone
Telefon [tele'fo:n] *n* (-s; -e) telephone, phone; **am ~** on the (tele)phone; **~ haben** have a (Br be on the) (tele)phone; **ans ~ gehen** answer the (tele)phone; **~anruf** *m* (tele)phone call; **~anschluss** *m* telephone connection; **~appa,rat** *m* telephone, phone
Telefonat [telefo'na:t] *n* (-[e]s; -e) → *Te-lefongespräch*
Tele'fon|buch *n* telephone directory, phone book; **~gebühr** *f* telephone charge; **~gespräch** *n* (tele)phone call
telefonieren [telefo'ni:rən] *v/i* (no -ge-, h) (tele)phone; be on the phone; **mit j-m ~** talk to s.o. on the phone
telefonisch [tele'fo:nɪʃ] **1.** *adj* telephonic, telephone … **2.** *adv* by (tele)phone, over the (tele)phone
Tele'fon|karte *f* phonecard; **~leitung** *f* telephone line; **~netz** *n* telephone network; **~nummer** *f* (tele)phone number; **~zelle** *f* (tele)phone booth, *esp Br* (tele)phone box, *Br* call box; **~zen,trale** *f* switchboard
Telegramm [tele'gram] *n* (-s; -e) telegram, wire, cable(gram)
Teleobjektiv ['te:leɔpjɛkti:f] *n* telephoto lens
Telephon *n* → *Telefon*
Teletext ['te:lətɛkst] *m* teletext
Teller ['tɛlɐ] *m* (-s; -) plate; **~wäscher** ['tɛlɐvɛʃɐ] *m* (-s; -) dishwasher
Tempel ['tɛmpəl] *m* (-s; -) temple
Temperament [tɛmpəra'mɛnt] *n* (-[e]s; -e) temper(ament); life, F pep
tempera'mentlos *adj* lifeless, dull; **~voll** *adj* full of life *or* F pep
Temperatur [tɛmpəra'tu:ɐ] *f* (-; -en) temperature; **j-s ~ messen** take s.o.'s temperature
Tempo ['tɛmpo] *n* (-s; -s, -pi) speed; *MUS* time; **mit ~** … at a speed of … an hour
Tendenz [tɛn'dɛnts] *f* (-; -en) tendency, trend; leaning; tendenziös [tɛndɛn-'tsjø:s] *adj* tendentious; tendieren [tɛn'di:rən] *v/i* (no -ge-, h) tend (**zu** towards; *dazu, et. zu tun* to do s.th.)
Tennis ['tɛnɪs] *n* (-; *no pl*) tennis; **~platz** *m* tennis court; **~schläger** *m* tennis racket; **~spieler(in)** tennis player

Tenor [te'no:ɐ] *m* (-s; *Tenöre* [te'nø:rə]) *MUS* tenor
Teppich ['tɛpɪç] *m* (-s; -e) carpet
'Teppichboden *m* fitted carpet, wall-to--wall carpeting
Termin [tɛr'mi:n] *m* (-s; -e) date; deadline; engagement; **e-n ~ vereinbaren (einhalten, absagen)** make (keep, cancel) an appointment
Terminal ['tœ:rmɪnəl] *m, n* (-s; -s) *AVIAT* terminal; *n* (-s; -s) *IT* terminal
Terrasse [tɛ'rasə] *f* (-; -n) terrace
ter'rassenförmig [tɛ'rasənfœrmɪç] *adj* terraced, in terraces
Terrine [tɛ'ri:nə] *f* (-; -n) tureen
Territorium [teri'to:rjʊm] *n* (-s; -ien) territory
Terror ['tɛro:ɐ] *m* (-s; *no pl*) terror
terrorisieren [tɛrori'zi:rən] *v/t* (no -ge-, h) terrorize
Terrorismus [tɛro'rɪsmʊs] *m* (-; *no pl*) terrorism; Terrorist(in) [tɛro'rɪst(ɪn)] (-en; -en/-; -nen), terro'ristisch *adj* terrorist
Testament [tɛsta'mɛnt] *n* (-[e]s; -e) (last) will; *JUR* last will and testament
testamentarisch [tɛstamɛn'ta:rɪʃ] *adv* by will
Testa'mentsvollstrecker *m* executor
Testbild ['tɛstbɪlt] *n* *TV* test card
testen ['tɛstən] *v/t* (no -ge-, h) test
'Testpi,lot *m* test pilot
Tetanus ['te:tanus] *m* (-; *no pl*) *MED* tetanus
Teufel ['tɔʏfəl] *m* (-s; -) devil (*a. fig*); **wer (wo, was) zum ~ …?** who (where, what) the hell …? 'Teufelskerl F *m* devil of a fellow; 'Teufelskreis *m* vicious circle; teuflisch ['tɔʏflɪʃ] *adj* devilish, diabolic(al)
Text [tɛkst] *m* (-[e]s; -e) text; *MUS* words, lyrics
Texter ['tɛkstɐ] *m* (-s; -), 'Texterin *f* (-; -nen) *MUS* songwriter
Textil… [tɛks'ti:l-] *in cpds* textile …
Textilien [tɛks'ti:ljən] *pl* textiles
'Textverarbeitung *f* word processing
Theater [te'a:tɐ] *n* (-s; -) theater, *Br* theatre; F **~ machen (um)** make a fuss (about); **~besucher** *m* theatergoer, *Br* theatregoer; **~karte** *f* theater (*Br* theatre) ticket; **~kasse** *f* box office;

teuer ['tɔʏɐ] *adj* expensive; **wie~ ist es?** how much is it?

~stück *n* play

Thema ['te:ma] *n* (*-s; Themen*) subject, topic; MUS theme; **das ~ wechseln** change the subject

Theologe [teo'lo:gə] *m* (*-n; -n*) theologian; **Theologie** [teolo'gi:] *f* (*-; -n*) theology; **Theo'login** *f* (*-; -nen*) theologian; **theo'logisch** *adj* theological

Theoretiker [teo're:tikɐ] *m* (*-s; -*) theorist; **theo'retisch** *adj* theoretical

Theorie [teo'ri:] *f* (*-; -n*) theory

Therapeut [tera'pɔyt] *m* (*-en; -en*), **Thera'peutin** *f* (*-; -nen*) therapist; **Therapie** [tera'pi:] *f* (*-; -n*) therapy

Thermometer [tɛrmo'me:tɐ] *n* (*-s; -*) thermometer

Thermosflasche® ['tɛrmɔsflaʃə] *f* thermos®

These ['te:zə] *f* (*-; -n*) thesis

Thon [to:n] *Swiss m* (*-s; -s*) tuna (fish)

Thrombose [trɔm'bo:zə] *f* (*-; -n*) MED thrombosis

Thron [tro:n] *m* (*-[e]s; -e*) throne

Thronfolger ['tro:nfɔlgɐ] *m* (*-s; -*), **Thronfolgerin** ['tro:nfɔlgərin] *f* (*-; -nen*) successor to the throne

Thunfisch ['tu:nfɪʃ] *m* tuna (fish)

Tick [tɪk] F *m* (*-[e]s; -s*) quirk

ticken ['tɪkən] *v/i* (*ge-, h*) tick

Tiebreak, Tie-Break ['taɪbreɪk] *m, n tennis:* tiebreak(er)

tief [ti:f] *adj* deep (*a. fig*); low

Tief *n* (*-s; -s*) METEOR depression (*a.* PSYCH, ECON), low (*a. fig*)

Tiefe ['ti:fə] *f* (*-; -n*) depth (*a. fig*)

Tief|ebene *f* lowland(s); **~flieger** *m* low-flying air plane; **~gang** *m* MAR draft, *Br* draught; *fig* depth; **~ga,rage** *f* parking *or* underground garage, *Br* underground car park

'tiefgekühlt *adj* deep-frozen

Tiefkühl|fach *n* freezing compartment; **~kost** *f* frozen foods; **~schrank** *m*, **~truhe** *f* freezer, deep-freeze

Tier [ti:ɐ] *n* (*-[e]s; -e*) animal; F **hohes ~** bigwig, big shot; **~arzt** *m*, **~ärztin** *f* veterinarian, *Br* veterinary surgeon, F vet; **~freund** *m* animal lover; **~garten** *m* → **Zoo**; **~heim** *n* animal shelter

tierisch ['ti:rɪʃ] *adj* animal; *fig* bestial, brutish

Tierkreis *m* ASTR zodiac; **~zeichen** *n* sign of the zodiac

'Tiermedi,zin *f* veterinary medicine

Tierquäle'rei *f* cruelty to animals

'Tier|reich *n* animal kingdom; **~schutz** *m* protection of animals; **~schutzverein** *m* society for the prevention of cruelty to animals; **~versuch** *m* MED experiment with animals

Tiger ['ti:gɐ] *m* (*-s; -*) ZO tiger

Tigerin ['ti:gərin] *f* (*-; -nen*) ZO tigress

tilgen ['tɪlgən] *v/t* (*ge-, h*) ECON pay off

Tinte ['tɪntə] *f* (*-; -n*) ink

'Tintenfisch *m* ZO squid

Tipp [tɪp] *m* (*-s; -s*) hint, tip; tip-off; **j-m e-n ~ geben** tip s.o. off

tippen ['tɪpən] *v/i and v/t* (*ge-, h*) tap; type; F guess; do *lotto etc*

Tisch [tɪʃ] *m* (*-[e]s; -e*) table; **am ~ sitzen** sit at the table; **bei ~** at table; **den ~ decken (abräumen)** lay (clear) the table; **~decke** *f* tablecloth; **~gebet** *n* REL grace: **das ~ sprechen** say grace

Tischler ['tɪʃlɐ] *m* (*-s; -*) joiner; cabinet-maker

'Tisch|platte *f* tabletop; **~tennis** *n* table tennis; **~tuch** *n* tablecloth

Titel ['ti:tl] *m* (*-s; -*) title; **~bild** *n* cover picture; **~blatt** *n*, **~seite** *f* title page; cover, front page

Toast [to:st] *m* (*-[e]s; -s*), **toasten** ['to:stən] *v/t* (*ge-, h*) toast

toben ['to:bən] *v/i* (*ge-, h*) rage (*a. fig*); romp; **tobsüchtig** ['to:pzʏçtɪç] *adj* raving mad; **'Tobsuchtsanfall** *m* tantrum

Tochter ['tɔxtɐ] *f* (*-; Töchter* ['tœçtɐ]) daughter; **~gesellschaft** *f* ECON subsidiary (company)

Tod [to:t] *m* (*-[e]s; no pl*) death (*a. fig*) **(durch** from); **tod...** *in cpds* **...ernst, ...müde, ...sicher:** dead ...

Todes|ängste ['to:dəsɛŋstə] *pl:* **~ ausstehen** be scared to death; **~anzeige** *f* obituary (notice); **~fall** *m* (case of) death; **~kampf** *m* agony; **~opfer** *n* casualty; **~strafe** *f* JUR capital punishment; death penalty; **~ursache** *f* cause of death; **~urteil** *n* JUR death sentence

Todfeind *m* deadly enemy

'tod'krank *adj* mortally ill

tödlich ['tø:tlɪç] *adj* fatal; deadly; *esp fig* mortal

'Todsünde *f* mortal *or* deadly sin

Toilette [toa'lɛtə] *f* (*-; -n*) bathroom, *Br* toilet, lavatory; *pl* rest rooms, *Br* ladies' *or* men's rooms

T

Toi'letten... *in cpds* ...papier, ...seife *etc*: toilet ...; ~tisch *m* dressing table

tolerant [tole'rant] *adj* tolerant (**gegen** of, towards); Toleranz [tole'rants] *f* (-; -en) tolerance (*a.* TECH); tolerieren [tole'ri:rən] *v/t* (*no* -ge-, *h*) tolerate

toll [tɔl] *adj* wild; F great, fantastic

'tollkühn *adj* daredevil

'Tollwut *f* VET rabies; 'tollwütig ['tɔlvy:tıç] *adj* VET rabid

Tomate [to'ma:tə] *f* (-; -n) BOT tomato

Ton[1] [to:n] *m* (-[e]s; -e) clay

Ton[2] *m* (-[e]s; *Töne* ['tø:nə]) tone (*a.* MUS, PAINT), PAINT *a.* shade; sound (*a.* TV, *film*); note; stress; **kein** ~ not a word; ~art *f* MUS key; ~band *n* (-[e]s; -bänder) (recording) tape; ~bandgerät *n* tape recorder

tönen ['tø:nən] (ge-, *h*) **1.** *v/i* sound, ring **2.** *v/t* tinge, tint, shade

'Ton|fall *m* tone (of voice); accent; ~film *m* sound film; ~kopf *m* ELECTR (magnetic) head; ~lage *f* MUS pitch; ~leiter *f* MUS scale

Tonne ['tɔnə] *f* (-; -n) barrel; (metric) ton

'Tontechniker *m* sound engineer

'Tönung *f* (-; -en) tint, tinge, shade

Topf [tɔpf] *m* (-[e]s; *Töpfe* ['tœpfə]) pot; saucepan

Topfen ['tɔpfən] *Austrian m* (-s; *no pl*) GASTR curd(s)

'Töpfer ['tœpfɐ] *m* (-s; -) potter

Töpferei [tœpfə'rai] *f* (-; -en) pottery

'Töpferin *f* (-; -nen) potter

'Töpferscheibe *f* potter's wheel

'Töpferware *f* pottery, earthenware

Tor [to:ɐ] *n* (-[e]s; -e) gate; *soccer etc*: goal; **ein** ~ **schießen** score (a goal); **im** ~ **stehen** keep goal

Torf [tɔrf] *m* (-[e]s; -e) peat

'Torfmull *m* peat dust

'Torhüter ['to:ɐhy:tɐ] *m* → **Torwart**

torkeln ['tɔrkəln] F *v/i* (ge-, *h*, sein) reel, stagger

'Torlatte *f* SPORT crossbar

'Torlinie *f* SPORT goal line

torpedieren [tɔrpe'di:rən] *v/t* (*no* -ge-, *h*) MIL torpedo (*a. fig*)

'Tor|pfosten *m* SPORT goalpost; ~raum *m* SPORT goalmouth; ~schuss *m* SPORT shot at goal; ~schütze *m* SPORT scorer

Torte ['tɔrtə] *f* (-; -n) pie, *esp Br* flan; cream cake, gateau

'Torwart ['to:ɐvart] *m* (-[e]s; -e) SPORT

goalkeeper, F goalie

tosen ['to:zən] *v/i* (ge-, *h*) roar; thunder; ~d *adj* thunderous (*applause*)

tot [to:t] *adj* dead (*a. fig*); late; ~ **geboren** MED stillborn; ~ **umfallen** drop dead

total [to'ta:l] *adj* total, complete

totalitär [totali'tɛ:ɐ] *adj* POL totalitarian

'Tote *m, f* (-*n*; -*n*) dead man *or* woman; (dead) body, corpse; *mst pl* casualty; *pl the* dead; töten ['tø:tən] *v/t* (ge-, *h*) kill

'Totenbett *n* deathbed

'toten'blass *adj* deadly pale

'Toten|gräber ['to:tngrɛ:bɐ] *m* (-s; -) gravedigger; ~kopf *m* skull; skull and crossbones; ~maske *f* death mask; ~messe *f* REL mass for the dead, requiem (*a.* MUS); ~schädel *m* skull; ~schein *m* death certificate

'toten'still *adj* deathly still

'totlachen F *v/refl* (sep, -ge-, *h*) kill o.s. laughing

Toto ['to:to] *m, f n* (-s; -s) football pools

'Totschlag *m* (-[e]s; *no pl*) JUR manslaughter; 'totschlagen *v/t* (*irr*, **schlagen**, *sep*, -ge-, *h*) kill; *j-n* ~ beat s.o. to death; **die Zeit** ~ kill time

'totschweigen *v/t* (*irr*, **schweigen**, *sep*, -ge-, *h*) hush up

Toupet [tu'pe:] *n* (-s; -s) toupee

toupieren [tu'pi:rən] *v/t* (*no* -ge-, *h*) Br backcomb

Tour [tu:ɐ] *f* (-; -en) tour (**durch** of), trip; excursion; TECH turn, revolution; **auf** ~en **kommen** MOT pick up speed; F *krumme* ~en underhand methods

Touren... ['tu:rən-] *in cpds* ...rad *etc*: touring ...

Tourismus [tu'rɪsmʊs] *m* (-; *no pl*) tourism; ~geschäft *n* tourist industry

Tourist [tu'rɪst] *m* (-*en*; -*en*), Tou'ristin *f* (-; -nen) tourist; tou'ristisch *adj* touristic

Tournee [tʊr'ne:] *f* (-; -s, -n) tour; **auf** ~ **gehen** go on tour

Trab [tra:p] *m* (-[e]s; *no pl*) trot

Trabant [tra'bant] *m* (-*en*; -*en*) ASTR satellite; Tra'bantenstadt *f* satellite town

traben ['tra:bən] *v/i* (ge-, sein) trot

Traber ['tra:bɐ] *m* (-s; -) zo trotter

'Trabrennen *n* trotting race

Tracht [traxt] *f* (-; -en) costume; uniform; dress; F *e-e* ~ *Prügel* a thrashing

trächtig ['trɛçtıç] *adj* zo with young,

pregnant

Tradition [tradi'tsjoːn] *f* (-; -en) tradition; **traditionell** [traditsjo'nɛl] *adj* traditional

traf [traːf] *pret of* **treffen**

Trafik [tra'fɪk] *Austrian f* (-; -en) → **Tabakgeschäft**; **Trafikant** [trafi'kant] *Austrian m* (-en; -en) tobacconist

Tragbahre ['traːkbaːrə] *f* stretcher

'**tragbar** *adj* portable; wearable; *fig* bearable; *person:* acceptable

Trage ['traːgə] *f* (-; -n) stretcher

träge ['trɛːgə] *adj* lazy, indolent; PHYS inert (*a. fig*)

tragen ['traːgən] (*irr, ge-, h*) **1.** *v/t* carry; wear; *fig* bear; **sich gut ~** wear well **2.** *v/i* BOT bear fruit; *fig* hold; **~d** *adj* ARCH supporting; *fig* leading

Träger ['trɛːgɐ] *m* (-s; -) carrier; porter; (shoulder) strap; TECH support; ARCH girder; *fig* bearer

'**trägerlos** *adj* strapless

'**Tragetasche** *f* carrier bag; carrycot

'**tragfähig** *adj* load-bearing; *fig* sound

'**Tragfläche** *f* AVIAT wing

Trägheit ['trɛːkhait] *f* (-; *no pl*) laziness, indolence; PHYS inertia (*a. fig*)

Tragik ['traːgɪk] *f* (-; *no pl*) tragedy

tragisch ['traːgɪʃ] *adj* tragic

Tragödie [tra'gøːdjə] *f* (-; -n) tragedy

'**Tragriemen** *m* strap; sling

'**Tragweite** *f* range; *fig* significance

Trainer ['trɛːnɐ] *m* (-s; -), '**Trainerin** *f* (-; -nen) SPORT trainer, coach; **trainieren** [trɛ'niːrən] *v/i and v/t* (*no -ge-, h*) SPORT train, coach

'**Training** *n* (-s; -s) training

'**Trainingsanzug** *m* track suit

Traktor ['traktoːɐ] *m* (-s; -en [trak'toːrən]) MOT tractor

trällern ['trɛlɐn] *v/t and v/i* (*ge-, h*) warble, trill

Tram [tram] *Austrian f* (-; -s), *Swiss n* (-s; -s) streetcar, *Br* tram

trampeln ['trampəln] *v/i* (*ge-, sein*) trample, stamp

'**Trampelpfad** *m* beaten track

trampen ['trɛmpən] *v/i* (*ge-, sein*) hitchhike; **Tramper(in)** ['trɛmpɐ, 'trɛmpərɪn] (-s; -/-; -nen) hitchhiker

Träne ['trɛːnə] *f* (-; -n) tear; **in ~n ausbrechen** burst into tears; '**tränen** *v/i* (*ge-, h*) water; '**Tränengas** *n* tear gas

trank [traŋk] *pret of* **trinken**

Tränke ['trɛŋkə] *f* (-; -n) watering place

'**tränken** *v/t* (*ge-, h*) ZO water; soak, drench

Transfer [trans'feːɐ] *m* (-s; -s) transfer (*a.* SPORT)

Transformator [transfɔr'maːtoːɐ] *m* (-s; -en [transfɔrma'toːrən]) ELECTR transformer

Transfusion [transfu'zjoːn] *f* (-; -en) MED transfusion

Transistor [tran'zɪstoːɐ] *m* (-s; -en [tranzɪs'toːrən]) ELECTR transistor

Transit [tran'ziːt] *m* (-s; -e) transit

transitiv ['tranzitiːf] *adj* LING transitive

transparent [transpa'rɛnt] *adj* transparent

Transpa'rent *n* (-[e]s; -e) banner

Transplantation [transplanta'tsjoːn] *f* (-; -en), **transplantieren** [transplan'tiːrən] *v/t* (*no -ge-, h*) MED transplant

Transport [trans'pɔrt] *m* (-[e]s; -e) transport; shipment; **transportabel** [transpɔr'taːbəl], **trans'portfähig** *adj* transportable; **transportieren** [transpɔr'tiːrən] *v/t* (*no -ge-, h*) transport, ship, carry, MOT *a.* haul

Trans'portmittel *n* (means of) transport(ation); **~unternehmen** *n* hauler, *Br* haulier

Trapez [tra'peːts] *n* (-es; -e) MATH trapezoid, *Br* trapezium; SPORT trapeze

trappeln ['trapəln] *v/i* (*ge-, sein*) clatter; patter

trat [traːt] *pret of* **treten**

Traube ['traubə] *f* (-; -n) BOT bunch of grapes; grape; *pl* grapes; *fig* cluster

'**Traubensaft** *m* grape juice

'**Traubenzucker** *m* glucose

trauen ['trauən] (*ge-, h*) **1.** *v/t* marry **2.** *v/i* trust (*j-m s.o.*); **sich ~, et. zu tun** dare (to) do s.th.; **ich traute meinen Augen nicht** I couldn't believe my eyes

Trauer ['trauɐ] *f* (-; *no pl*) grief, sorrow; mourning; **in ~ sein** in mourning; **~fall** *m* death; **~feier** *f* funeral service; **~marsch** *m* MUS funeral march

'**trauern** *v/i* (*ge-, h*) mourn (**um** for)

'**Trauerrede** *f* funeral oration

'**Trauerzug** *m* funeral procession

träufeln ['trɔyfəln] *v/t* (*ge-, h*) drip, trickle

Traum [traum] *m* (-[e]s; *Träume* ['trɔymə]) dream (*a. fig*); **~... in** *cpds* ...**beruf**, ...**mann** *etc:* dream ..., ... of

T

one's dreams; **träumen** ['trɔʏmən] v/i and v/t (ge-, h) dream (a. fig) (**von** about, of); **schlecht ~** have bad dreams; **Träumer** ['trɔʏmɐ] m (-s; -) dreamer (a. fig); **Träumerei** [trɔʏmə-'raɪ] fig f (day)dream(s), reverie (a. MUS)

träumerisch ['trɔʏmərɪʃ] adj dreamy

traurig ['traʊrɪç] adj sad (**über** acc, **wegen** about)

'Traurigkeit f (-; no pl) sadness

'Trauring m wedding ring

'Trauschein m marriage certificate

'Trauung f (-; -en) marriage, wedding

'Trauzeuge m, **'Trauzeugin** f witness to a marriage

Trecker ['trɛkɐ] m (-s; -) MOT tractor

Treff [trɛf] F m (-s; -s) meeting place

treffen ['trɛfən] v/t and v/i (irr, ge-, h) hit (a. fig) hurt; meet s.o.; take (measures etc); **nicht ~** miss; **sich ~ (mit** j-m) meet (s.o.); **gut ~** PHOT etc: capture well; **'Treffen** n (-s; -) meeting; **'treffend 1.** adj apt (remark etc) **2.** adv: **~ gesagt** well put; **Treffer** ['trɛfɐ] m (-s; -) hit (a. fig), SPORT goal; win; **'Treffpunkt** m meeting place

Treibeis ['traɪpʔaɪs] n drift ice

treiben ['traɪbən] (irr, ge-, h) **1.** v/t (h) drive (a. TECH and fig); SPORT etc: do; push, press s.o.; BOT put forth; F do, be up to **2.** v/i (sein) drift (a. fig), float; BOT shoot (up); **sich ~ lassen** drift along (a. fig), **~de Kraft** driving force; **'Treiben** n (-s; no pl) doings, goingson; **geschäftiges ~** bustle

'treibenlassen v/refl (irr, **lassen**, sep, no -ge-, h) → **treiben**

'Treib|haus n hothouse; **~hausef,fekt** m greenhouse effect; **~holz** n driftwood; **~riemen** m TECH driving belt; **~sand** m quicksand; **~stoff** m fuel

trennen ['trɛnən] v/t (ge-, h) separate; sever; part; divide (a. LING, POL); segregate; TEL disconnect; **sich ~** separate (**von** from), part (a. fig); **sich ~ von** part with s.th.; leave s.o.; **'Trennung** f (-; -en) separation; division; segregation

'Trennwand f partition

Treppe ['trɛpə] f (-; -n) staircase, stairs

'Treppen|absatz m landing; **~geländer** n banisters; **~haus** n staircase; hall

Tresor [tre'zoːɐ] m (-s; -e) safe; strongroom, vault

treten ['treːtən] v/i and v/t (irr, ge-, h) kick; step (**aus** out of; **in** acc into; **auf** acc on[to]); pedal (away)

treu [trɔʏ] adj faithful (a. fig); loyal; devoted; **Treue** ['trɔʏə] f (-; no pl) fidelity, faithfulness, loyalty

'Treuhänder(in) ['trɔʏhɛndɐ, 'trɔʏhɛndərɪn] m(f) (-s; -/-; -nen) JUR trustee

'treulos adj faithless, disloyal, unfaithful (all: **gegen** to)

Tribüne [tri'byːnə] f (-; -n) platform; stand

Trichter ['trɪçtɐ] m (-s; -) funnel; crater

Trick [trɪk] m (-s; -s) trick; **~aufnahme** f trick shot; **~betrüger(in)** confidence trickster

trieb [triːp] pret of **treiben**

Trieb m (-[e]s; -e ['triːbə]) BOT (young) shoot, sprout; fig impulse, drive; sex drive; **~feder** f mainspring (a. fig)

triefen ['triːfən] v/i (ge-, h) drip, be dripping (**von** with)

triftig ['trɪftɪç] adj weighty; good

Trikot [tri'koː] n (-s; -s) SPORT shirt, jersey; leotard

Triller ['trɪlɐ] m (-s; -) MUS trill; **'trillern** v/i and v/t (ge-, h) trill; zo warble

trimmen ['trɪmən] v/refl (ge-, h) keep fit

'Trimmpfad m fitness trail

trinkbar ['trɪŋkbaːɐ] adj drinkable

trinken ['trɪŋkən] v/t and v/i (irr, ge-, h) drink (**auf** acc to); have; **et. zu ~** a drink; **Trinker(in)** ['trɪŋkɐ (-kərɪn)] (-s; -/-; -nen) drinker, alcoholic

'Trink|geld n tip; **j-m (zwei Euro) ~ geben** tip s.o. (two euros); **~spruch** m toast; **~wasser** n drinking water

Trio ['triːo] n (-s; -s) MUS trio (a. fig)

trippeln ['trɪpəln] v/i (ge-, sein) mince

Tripper ['trɪpɐ] m (-s; -) MED gonorrh(o)ea

Tritt [trɪt] m (-[e]s; -e) kick; step

'Trittbrett n step; MOT running board

'Trittleiter f stepladder

Triumph [tri'ʊmf] m (-[e]s; -e) triumph

triumphal [triʊm'faːl] adj triumphant

triumphieren [triʊm'fiːrən] v/i (no -ge-, h) triumph (**über** acc over)

trocken ['trɔkən] adj dry (a. fig)

'Trocken-... in cpds dried ...; drying ...

'Trockenhaube f hairdryer

'Trockenheit f (-; no pl) dryness; AGR drought

'**trockenlegen** *v/t* (*sep*, *-ge-*, *h*) drain; change (*a baby*)

trocknen ['trɔknən] *v/t* (*ge-*, *h*) *and v/i* (*sein*) dry

Trockner ['trɔknɐ] *m* (*-s*; *-*) dryer

Troddel ['trɔdəl] *f* (*-*; *-n*) tassel

Trödel ['trøːdəl] *m* (*-s*; *no pl*) junk

trödeln ['trøːdəln] *v/i* (*ge-*, *h*) dawdle

Trödler ['trøːdlɐ] *m* (*-s*; *-*) junk dealer; dawdler

trog [troːk] *pret of* **trügen**

Trog *m* (*-[e]s*; *Tröge* ['trøːgə]) trough

Trommel ['trɔməl] *f* (*-*; *-n*) MUS drum (*a. TECH*); **~fell** *n* ANAT eardrum

'**trommeln** *v/i and v/t* (*ge-*, *h*) drum

Trommler ['trɔmlɐ] *m* (*-s*; *-*) drummer

Trompete [trɔm'peːtə] *f* (*-*; *-n*) MUS trumpet; **trom'peten** *v/i and v/t* (*no -ge-*, *h*) trumpet (*a. ZO*); **Trompeter** [trɔm'peːtɐ] *m* (*-s*; *-*) trumpeter

Tropen ['troːpən]: **die ~ pl** the tropics

'**Tropen…** *in cpds* tropical …

Tropf [trɔpf] *m* (*-[e]s*; *Tröpfe* ['trœpfə]) MED drip

Tröpfchen ['trœpfçən] *n* (*-s*; *-*) droplet

tröpfeln ['trœpfəln] *v/i and v/t* (*ge-*, *h*) drip; **es tröpfelt** it's spitting

tropfen ['trɔpfən] *v/i and v/t* (*ge-*, *h*) drip, drop; 'Tropfen *m* (*-s*; *-*) drop (*a. fig*); **ein ~ auf den heißen Stein** a drop in the bucket; '**tropfenweise** *adv* in drops, drop by drop

Trophäe [tro'fɛːə] *f* (*-*; *-n*) trophy (*a. fig*)

tropisch ['troːpɪʃ] *adj* tropical

Trosse ['trɔsə] *f* (*-*; *-n*) cable

Trost [troːst] *m* (*-[e]s*; *no pl*) comfort, consolation; **ein schwacher ~** cold comfort

trösten ['trøːstən] *v/t* (*ge-*, *h*) comfort, console; **sich ~** console o.s. (**mit** with)

tröstlich ['trøːstlɪç] *adj* comforting

'**trostlos** *adj* miserable; desolate

Trott [trɔt] *m* (*-[e]s*; *-e*) trot; F **der alte ~** the old routine

Trottel ['trɔtəl] F *m* (*-s*; *-*) dope

trottelig ['trɔtəlɪç] F *adj* dopey

trotten ['trɔtən] *v/i* (*ge-*, *sein*) trot

Trottinett ['trɔtinet] *Swiss n* (*-s*; *-e*) scooter

Trottoir [trɔ'toaːr] *Swiss n* (*-s*, *-e*, *-s*) sidewalk, *Br* pavement

trotz [trɔts] *prp* (*gen*) in spite of, despite

Trotz *m* (*-es*; *no pl*) defiance; **j-m zum ~** to spite s.o.

'**trotzdem** *adv* in spite of it, nevertheless, F anyhow, anyway

trotzen ['trɔtsən] *v/i* (*ge-*, *h*) defy (*dat s.o. or s.th.*); sulk

trotzig ['trɔtsɪç] *adj* defiant; sulky

trüb [tryːp], **trübe** ['tryːbə] *adj* cloudy; muddy; dim; dull, *fig a.* gloomy

Trubel ['truːbəl] *m* (*-s*; *no pl*) (hustle and) bustle

trüben ['tryːbən] *v/t* (*ge-*, *h*) cloud; *fig* spoil, mar

Trübsal ['tryːpzaːl] *f*: **~ blasen** mope

'**trübselig** *adj* sad, gloomy; dreary

'**Trübsinn** *m* (*-[e]s*; *no pl*) melancholy, gloom, low spirits; '**trübsinnig** *adj* melancholy, gloomy

trug [truːk] *pret of* **tragen**

trügen ['tryːgən] (*irr*, *ge-*, *h*) **1.** *v/t* deceive **2.** *v/i* be deceptive

trügerisch ['tryːgərɪʃ] *adj* deceptive

'**Trugschluss** *m* fallacy

Truhe ['truːə] *f* (*-*; *-n*) chest

Trümmer ['trymɐ] *pl* ruins; debris; pieces, bits

Trumpf [trʊmpf] *m* (*-[e]s*; *Trümpfe* ['trʏmpfə]) trump (card) (*a. fig*); **~ sein** be trumps; *fig* **s-n ~ ausspielen** play one's trump card

Trunkenheit ['trʊŋkənhaɪt] *f* (*-*; *no pl*) esp JUR; **~ am Steuer** drunk (*Br* drink) driving

'**Trunksucht** *f* (*-*; *no pl*) alcoholism

Trupp [trʊp] *m* (*-s*; *-s*) band, party; group; **Truppe** ['trʊpə] *f* (*-*; *-n*) MIL troop, *pl* troops, forces; THEA company, troupe

'**Truppen|gattung** *f* MIL branch (of service); **~übungsplatz** *m* training area

Truthahn ['truːthaːn] *m* ZO turkey

Tscheche ['tʃɛçə] *m* (*-n*; *-n*) Czech; **Tschechien** ['tʃɛçjən] Czech Republic; '**Tschechin** *f* (*-*; *-nen*) Czech; '**tschechisch** *adj* Czech; **Tschechische Republik** Czech Republic

Tube ['tuːbə] *f* (*-*; *-n*) tube

Tuberkulose [tuberku'loːzə] *f* (*-*; *-n*) MED tuberculosis

Tuch [tuːx] *n* (*-[e]s*) (*pl -e*) cloth; (*pl Tücher* ['tyːçɐ]) scarf

'**Tuchfühlung** *f*: **auf ~** in close contact

tüchtig ['tʏçtɪç] *adj* (cap)able, competent; skil(l)ful; efficient; F *fig* good

'**Tüchtigkeit** *f* (*-*; *no pl*) (cap)ability, qualities; skill; efficiency

tückisch ['tʏkɪʃ] *adj* malicious; MED insidious; treacherous

tüfteln ['tʏftəln] F *v/i* (ge-, h) puzzle (**an** *dat* over)

Tugend ['tuːɡənt] *f* (-; -en) virtue (*a. fig*)

Tulpe ['tʊlpə] *f* (-; -n) BOT tulip

Tumor ['tuːmoːɐ] *m* (-s; -en [tuˈmoːrən]) MED tumo(u)r

Tümpel ['tʏmpəl] *m* (-s; -) pool

Tumult [tuˈmʊlt] *m* (-[e]s; -e) tumult, uproar

tun [tuːn] *v/t and v/i* (*irr*, ge-, h) do; take (*a step etc*); F put; **zu~haben** have work to do; be busy; **ich weiß (nicht)**, **was ich~ soll or muss** I (don't) know what to do; **so ~**, **als ob** pretend to *inf*

Tünche ['tʏnçə] *f* (-; -n), **'tünchen** *v/t* (ge-, h) whitewash

Tunfisch *m* → **Thunfisch**

Tunke ['tʊŋkə] *f* (-; -n) sauce

Tunnel ['tʊnəl] *m* (-s; -) tunnel

Tüpfelchen ['tʏpfəlçən] *n*: **das ~ auf dem i** the icing on the cake

tupfen ['tʊpfən] *v/t* (ge-, h) dab

'Tupfen *m* (-s; -) dot, spot

Tupfer ['tʊpfɐ] *m* (-s; -) MED swab

Tür [tyːɐ] *f* (-; -en ['tyːrən]) door (*a. fig*); **die ~(en) knallen** slam the door(s); F **j-n vor die ~ setzen** throw s.o. out; **Tag der offenen ~** open house (*Br* day)

Turban ['tʊrbaːn] *m* (-s; -e) turban

Turbine [tʊrˈbiːnə] *f* (-; -n) TECH turbine

Turbolader ['tʊrbolaːdɐ] *m* (-s; -) MOT turbo(charger)

Türke ['tʏrkə] *m* (-n; -n) Turk; **Türkei** [tʏrˈkai] *f* Turkey; **Türkin** ['tʏrkɪn] *f* (-; -nen) Turk(ish woman); **'türkisch** *adj* Turkish

'Tür|klingel *f* doorbell; **~klinke** *f* door handle; **~knauf** *m* doorknob

Turm [tʊrm] *m* (-[e]s; **Türme** ['tʏrmə])
tower; steeple; *chess*: castle, rook

türmen ['tʏrmən] *v/t* (ge-, h) pile up (*a. sich ~*)

'Turmspitze *f* spire

'Turmspringen *n* SPORT platform diving

turnen ['tʊrnən] *v/i* (ge-, h) SPORT do gymnastics; **Turnen** *n* (-s; *no pl*) SPORT gymnastics; PED physical education (*abbr* PE); **Turner** ['tʊrnɐ] *m* (-s; -), **Turnerin** ['tʊrnərɪn] *f* (-; -nen) SPORT gymnast

'Turnhalle *f* gymnasium, F gym

'Turnhemd *n* gym shirt

'Turnhose *f* gym shorts

Turnier [tʊrˈniːɐ] *n* (-s; -e) tournament

Tur'niertanz *m* ballroom dancing

'Turn|lehrer(in) gym(nastics) *or* PE teacher; **~schuh** *m* sneaker, *Br* trainer; **~verein** *m* gymnastics club

'Tür|pfosten *m* doorpost; **~rahmen** *m* doorframe; **~schild** *n* doorplate; **~sprechanlage** *f* entryphone

Tusche ['tʊʃə] *f* (-; -n) Indian ink; watercolo(u)r

'Tuschkasten *m* paintbox

Tüte ['tyːtə] *f* (-; -n) (paper *or* plastic) bag; **e-e ~ ...** a bag of ...

TÜV [tyf] *abbr of* **Technischer Überwachungs-Verein** *Br appr* MOT (test), compulsory car inspection; (*nicht*) **durch den ~ kommen** pass (fail) its *or* one's MOT

Typ [tyːp] *m* (-s; -en) type; model; F fellow, guy; **Type** ['tyːpə] *f* (-; -n) TECH type; F character

Typhus ['tyːfus] *m* (-; *no pl*) MED typhoid (fever)

typisch ['tyːpɪʃ] *adj* typical (**für** of)

Tyrann [tyˈran] *m* (-en; -en) tyrant

Tyrannei [tyraˈnai] *f* (-; -en) tyranny

tyrannisch [tyˈranɪʃ] *adj* tyrannical

tyrannisieren [tyraniˈziːrən] *v/t* (*no -ge-*, h) tyrannize, bully

U

u. a. *abbr of* **unter anderem** among other things; **und andere** and others

U-Bahn ['uːbaːn] *f* underground, subway, *in London*: tube

übel ['yːbəl] *adj* bad; **mir ist~** I feel sick; **et. ~ nehmen** be offended by s.th.; **~**

~riechend foul-smelling, foul

'Übel *n* (-s; -) evil

'Übelkeit *f* (-; -en) nausea

'übelnehmen *v/t* (*irr*, **nehmen**, *sep*, -ge-, h) → **übel**

'Übeltäter *m*, **'Übeltäterin** *f esp iro* culprit

üben ['y:bən] *v/t and v/i* (*ge-, h*) practice, Br practise; **Klavier** *etc* ~ practice the piano *etc*

über ['y:bɐ] *prp* (*dat or acc*) over; above (*a. fig*); more than; across; *fig* about, of, *lecture etc a.* on; **sprechen (nachdenken** *etc*) ~ (*acc*) talk (think *etc*) about; ~ **Nacht bleiben** stay overnight; ~ **München nach Rom** to Rome via Munich

über'all *adv* everywhere; ~ **in ...** (*dat*) *a.* throughout ..., all over ...

über'anstrengen *v/t and v/refl* (*no -ge-, h*) overstrain (*o.s.*)

über'arbeiten *v/t* (*no -ge-, h*) revise; **sich ~** overwork *o.s.*

überaus *adv* most, extremely

überbelichten *v/t* (*no -ge-, h*) PHOT overexpose

über'bieten *v/t* (*irr*, **bieten**, *no -ge-, h*) *at auction*: outbid (**um** by); *fig* beat, *a.* outdo *s.o.*

'Überblick *m* view; *fig* overview (**über** *acc* of); general idea, outline

über'blicken *v/t* (*no -ge-, h*) overlook; *fig* be able to calculate

über'bringen *v/t* (*irr*, **bringen**, *no -ge-, h*) deliver; **Über'bringer(in)** (*-s; -/-; -nen*) ECON bearer

über'brücken *v/t* (*no -ge-, h*) bridge (*a. fig*); **~dacht** [y:bɐ'daxt] *adj* roofed, covered; **~'dauern** *v/t* (*no -ge-, h*) outlast, survive; **~'denken** *v/t* (*irr*, **denken**, *no -ge-, h*) think *s.th.* over

'überdimensio,nal *adj* oversized

'Überdosis *f* MED overdose

über'drüssig ['y:bɐdrʏsɪç] *adj*: ~ **sein** be weary or sick (*gen* of)

'über|durchschnittlich *adj* above--average; **~eifrig** *adj* overzealous

über'eilen *v/t* (*no -ge-, h*) rush; **nichts~!** don't rush things!; **über'eilt** *adj* rash, hasty

überei'nander *adv* on top of each other; *talk etc* about one another; **~schlagen** *v/t* (*irr*, **schlagen**, *sep, -ge-, h*): **die Beine ~** cross one's legs

über'einkommen *v/i* (*irr*, **kommen**, *sep, -ge-, sein*) agree; **Über'einkommen** *n* (*-s; -*), **Über'einkunft** *f* (*-; -künfte*) agreement

über'einstimmen *v/i* (*sep, -ge-, h*) tally, correspond (with); **mit j-m ~** agree with

s.o. (**in** *dat* on); **Über'einstimmung** *f* (*-; -en*) agreement; correspondence; **in ~ mit** in accordance with

über'fahren *v/t* (*irr*, **fahren**, *no -ge-, h*) run *s.o.* over, knock *s.o.* down

'Überfahrt *f* MAR crossing

'Überfall *m* assault (**auf** *acc* on); hold-up (on, of); mugging (of); MIL raid (on); invasion (of); **über'fallen** *v/t* (*irr*, **fallen**, *no -ge-, h*) attack, assault; hold up; mug; MIL raid; invade

'überfällig *adj* overdue

über'fliegen *v/t* (*irr*, **fliegen**, *no -ge-, h*) fly over or across; *fig* glance over, skim (through)

über'fließen *v/i* (*irr*, **fließen**, *sep, -ge-, sein*) overflow

'Überfluss *m* (*-es; no pl*) abundance (**an** *dat* of); affluence; **im ~ haben** abound in; **'überflüssig** *adj* superfluous

über'|fluten *v/t* (*no -ge-, h*) flood (*a. fig*); **~'fordern** *v/t* (*no -ge-, h*) overtax

überfragt [y:bɐ'fra:kt] *adj*: F **da bin ich ~** you've got me there

über'führen *v/t* (*no -ge-, h*) transport; JUR convict (**e-r Tat** of a crime)

Über'führung *f* (*-; -en*) transfer; JUR conviction; MOT overpass, Br flyover; footbridge

über'füllt *adj* overcrowded, packed

über'füttern *v/t* (*no -ge-, h*) overfeed

'Übergang *m* crossing; *fig* transition

über'geben *v/t* (*irr*, **geben**, *no -ge-, h*) hand over; MIL surrender; **sich ~** vomit

über'gehen¹ *v/t* (*irr*, **gehen**, *no -ge-, h*) pass over, ignore

'übergehen² *v/i* (*irr*, **gehen**, *sep, -ge-, sein*) pass (**zu** on to); ~ **in** (*acc*) change or turn (in)to

'übergeschnappt F *adj* cracked

'Übergewicht *n* (**~ haben** be) overweight; *fig* predominance

'übergewichtig *adj* overweight

'überglücklich *adj* overjoyed

über'greifen *v/i* (*irr*, **greifen**, *sep, -ge-, h*) ~ **auf** (*acc*) spread to

'Übergriff *m* infringement (**auf** *acc* of); (act of) violence

'Übergröße *f* outsize; **in ~n** outsized, oversize(d)

überhandnehmen *v/i* (*irr*, **nehmen**, *sep, -ge-, h*) become rampant

über'häufen *v/t* (*no -ge-, h*) swamp; shower

über'haupt *adv* ... at all; anyway; ~ **nicht** (**nichts**) not (nothing) at all

überheblich [y:bə'he:plıç] *adj* arrogant

Über'heblichkeit *f* (-; *no pl*) arrogance

über'hitzen *v/t* (*no* -ge-, *h*) overheat (*a. fig*); ~höht [y:bə'hø:t] *adj* excessive; ~

'holen *v/t* (*no* -ge-, *h*) pass, overtake (*a.* SPORT); TECH overhaul, service; ~holt *adj* outdated, antiquated; ~'hören *v/t* (*no* -ge-, *h*) miss, not catch *or* get; ignore

überirdisch *adj* supernatural

über'kleben *v/t* (*no* -ge-, *h*) paste up, cover

'überkochen *v/i* (*sep*, -ge-, *sein*) boil over

über'kommen *v/t* (*irr*, **kommen**, *no* -ge-, *h*) ... **überkam ihn** he was seized with *or* overcome by ...; ~'laden *v/t* (*irr*, **laden**, *no* -ge-, *h*) overload (*a.* ELECTR); *fig* clutter; ~'lassen *v/t* (*irr*, **lassen**, *no* -ge-, *h*) *j-n et.* ~ let s.o. have s.th., leave s.th. to s.o. (*a. fig*); *j-n sich selbst* ~ leave s.o. to himself; *j-n s-m Schicksal* ~ leave s.o. to his fate; ~'lasten *v/t* (*no* -ge-, *h*) overload (*a.* ELECTR); *fig* overburden

'überlaufen[1] *v/i* (*irr*, **laufen**, *sep*, -ge-, *sein*) run *or* flow over; MIL desert

über'laufen[2] *v/t* (*irr*, **laufen**, *no* -ge-, *h*) *es überlief mich heiß und kalt* I went hot and cold

über'laufen[3] *adj* overcrowded

'Überläufer *m* MIL deserter; POL defector

über'leben *v/t and v/i* (*no* -ge-, *h*) survive (*a. fig*); live through *s.th.*

Über'lebende *m, f* (-*n*; -*n*) survivor

'überlebensgroß *adj* larger than life

über'legen[1] *v/t and v/i* (*no* -ge-, *h*) think about *s.th.*, think *s.th.* over; consider; *lassen Sie mich* ~ let me think; *ich habe es mir* (*anders*) *überlegt* I've made up (changed) my mind

über'legen[2] *adj* superior (*j-m* to s.o.)

Über'legenheit *f* (-; *no pl*) superiority

über'legt *adj* deliberate; prudent

Über'legung *f* (-; -*en*) consideration, reflection

'überleiten *v/i* (*sep*, -ge-, *h*) ~ *zu* lead up *or* over to

über'liefern *v/t* (*no* -ge-, *h*) hand down, pass on; Über'lieferung *f* (-; -*en*) tradition

über'listen *v/t* (*no* -ge-, *h*) outwit

'Übermacht *f* (-; *no pl*) superiority; *esp* MIL superior forces; *in der* ~ *sein* be superior in numbers; 'übermächtig *adj* superior; *fig* overpowering

'Übermaß *n* (-*es*; *no pl*) excess (*an dat* of); 'übermäßig *adj* excessive

übermenschlich *adj* superhuman

über'mitteln *v/t* (*no* -ge-, *h*) convey

'übermorgen *adv* the day after tomorrow

über'müdet *adj* overtired

'übermütig ['y:bəmy:tıç] *adj* high-spirited

über'nächst *adj the* next but one; ~*e Woche* the week after next

übernachten [y:bə'naxtən] *v/i* (*no* -ge-, *h*) stay overnight (*bei j-m* at s.o.'s [house], with s.o.), spend the night (at, with)

Über'nachtung *f* (-; -*en*) night; ~ *und Frühstück* bed and breakfast

Übernahme ['y:bəna:mə] *f* (-; -*n*) taking (over); adoption

'überna,türlich *adj* supernatural

über'nehmen *v/t* (*irr*, **nehmen**, *no* -ge-, *h*) take over; adopt; take (*responsibility etc*); undertake *to do*

über'prüfen *v/t* (*no* -ge-, *h*) check, examine; verify; *esp* POL screen

Über'prüfung *f* check, examination; verification; screening

über'queren *v/t* (*no* -ge-, *h*) cross; ~'ragen *v/t* (*no* -ge-, *h*) tower above (*a. fig*); ~'ragend *adj* outstanding

überraschen [y:bə'raʃən] *v/t* (*no* -ge-, *h*) surprise; *j-n bei et.* ~ *a.* catch s.o. doing *s.th.*; Über'raschung *f* (-; -*en*) surprise

über'reden *v/t* (*no* -ge-, *h*) persuade (*et. zu tun* to do s.th.); *j-n zu et.* ~ talk s.o. into (doing) s.th.; Über'redung *f* (-; *no pl*) persuasion

'überregio,nal *adj* national

über'reichen *v/t* (*no* -ge-, *h*) present, hand *s.th.* over (*dat* to); ~'reizen *v/t* (*no* -ge-, *h*) overexcite; ~'reizt *adj* overwrought, F on edge

'Überrest *m* remains; *pl* relics; GASTR leftovers

über'rumpeln *v/t* (*no* -ge-, *h*) (take *s.o.* by) surprise; ~'runden *v/t* (*no* -ge-, *h*) SPORT lap

übersät [y:bə'zɛ:t] *adj*: ~ *mit* strewn

with *garbage*; studded with *stars*

übersättigt [y:bɐ'zɛtɪçt] *adj* sated, surfeited

Überschall… *in cpds* supersonic …

über|'schatten *v/t (no -ge-,h)* overshadow *(a. fig)*; **~'schätzen** *v/t (no -ge-,h)* overrate, overestimate

Überschlag *m* AVIAT loop; SPORT somersault; ECON rough estimate

überschlagen¹ *(irr, schlagen, sep, -ge-)* **1.** *v/t (h)* cross *(one's legs)*; **2.** *v/i (sein) fig ~ in (acc)* turn into

über|'schlagen² *(no -ge-, h)* **1.** *v/t* skip; ECON make a rough estimate of **2.** *v/refl* turn (right) over; go head over heels; *voice:* break

'überschnappen F *v/i (no -ge-, sein)* crack up

über|'schneiden *v/refl (irr, schneiden, no -ge-, h)* overlap *(a. fig)*; intersect; **~'schreiben** *v/t (irr, schreiben, no -ge-, h)* make *s.th.* over *(dat* to); **~'schreiten** *v/t (irr, schreiten, no -ge-, h)* cross; *fig* go beyond; pass; break *(the speed limit etc)*

Überschrift *f* heading, title; headline; caption

Überschuss *m*, **überschüssig** ['y:bɐʃʏsɪç] *adj* surplus

über|'schütten *v/t (no -ge-, h) ~ mit* cover with; shower with; heap *s.th.* on

'überschwänglich ['y:bɐʃvɛŋlɪç] *adj* effusive

über|'schwemmen *v/t (no -ge-, h)*, **Über'schwemmung** *f (-; -en)* flood

'überschwenglich → überschwänglich

'Übersee: in (nach) ~ oversea

über|'sehen *v/t (irr, sehen, no -ge-, h)* overlook; ignore

über|'setzen¹ *v/t (no -ge-, h)* translate *(in acc* into)

'übersetzen² *(sep, -ge-)* **1.** *v/i (h, sein)* cross *(über e-n Fluss* a river); **2.** *v/t (h)* take over

Übersetzer [y:bɐ'zɛtsɐ] *m (-s; -)*, **Über'setzerin** *f (-; -nen)* translator

Über'setzung *f (-; -en)* translation *(aus dat* from; *in acc* into)

'Übersicht *f (-; -en)* overview *(über acc* of); outline, summary

'übersichtlich *adj* clear(ly arranged)

'übersiedeln *v/i (sep, -ge-, sein)* move *(nach* to); **'Übersied(e)lung** *f* move

über'spannen *v/t (no -ge-, h)* span

über'spannt *fig adj* eccentric; extravagant

über|'spielen *v/t (no -ge-, h)* record; tape; *fig* cover up

über'spitzt *adj* exaggerated

über|'springen *v/t (irr, springen, no -ge-, h)* jump (over), *esp* SPORT *a.* clear; *fig* skip

über|'stehen¹ *v/t (irr, stehen, no -ge-, h)* get over; survive *(a. fig)*, live through

'überstehen² *v/i (irr, stehen, sep, -ge-, h)* jut out

über|'steigen *fig v/t (irr, steigen, no -ge-, h)* exceed; **~'stimmen** *v/t (no -ge-, h)* outvote

'überstreifen *v/t (sep, -ge-, h)* slip *s.th.* on; **~'strömen** *v/i (sep, -ge-, sein)* overflow *(vor dat* with)

'Überstunden *pl* overtime; **~ machen** work overtime

über|'stürzen *v/t (no -ge-, h) et. ~* rush things; **sich ~** *events:* follow in rapid succession; **~'stürzt** *adj* (over)hasty; rash; **~'teuert** *adj* overpriced; **~'tönen** *v/t (no -ge-, h)* drown (out)

über'tragbar *adj* transferable; MED contagious

über'tragen¹ *adj* figurative

über'tragen² *v/t (irr, tragen, no -ge-, h)* broadcast, *a.* televise; translate; MED, TECH transmit; MED transfuse *(blood)*; JUR, ECON transfer

Über'tragung *f (-; -en)* radio, TV broadcast; transmission; translation; MED transfusion; JUR, ECON transfer

über'treffen *v/t (irr, treffen, no -ge-, h)* outstrip, outdo, surpass, beat

über'treiben *v/i and v/t (irr, treiben, no -ge-, h)* exaggerate; overdo

Über'treibung *f (-; -en)* exaggeration

'übertreten¹ *v/i (irr, treten, sep, -ge-, sein) ~ zu* go over to, REL convert to

über'treten² *v/t (irr, treten, no -ge-, h)* **1.** *v/t* break, violate **2.** *v/i* SPORT foul (a jump *or* throw); **Über'tretung** *f (-; -en)* violation, JUR *a.* offen|se, *Br* -ce

'Übertritt *m* change *(zu* to); REL, POL conversion (to)

übervölkert [y:bɐ'fœlkɐt] *adj* overpopulated

über'wachen *v/t (no -ge-, h)* supervise, oversee; control; observe

Über'wachung *f (-; -en)* supervision,

control; observance; surveillance

überwältigen [y:bɐ'vɛltɪgən] *v/t* (*no -ge-, h*) overwhelm, overpower, *fig a* overcome; **~d** *adj* overwhelming, overpowering

über'weisen *v/t* (*irr, weisen, no -ge-, h*) ECON transfer (**an j-n** to s.o.'s account); remit; MED refer (**an** *acc* to)

Über'weisung *f* (-; *-en*) ECON transfer; remittance; MED referral

'überwerfen[1] *v/t* (*irr, werfen, sep, -ge-, h*) slip *s.th.* on

über'werfen[2] *v/refl* (*irr, werfen, no -ge-, h*) **sich ~ (mit j-m)** fall out with each other (with s.o.)

über'wiegen *v/i* (*irr, wiegen, no -ge-, h*) predominate; **~d** *adj* predominant; vast (*majority*)

über'winden *v/t* (*irr, winden, no -ge-, h*) overcome (*a. fig*); defeat; **sich ~ zu** *inf* bring o.s. to *inf*; **~wintern** [y:bɐ-'vɪntən] *v/i* (*no -ge-, h*) spend the winter (*in dat* in); **~wuchern** *v/t* (*no -ge-, h*) overgrow

'Überzahl *f* (-; *no pl*) majority; **in der ~ sein** outnumber *s.o.*

über'zeugen *v/t* (*no -ge-, h*) convince (**von** of), persuade; **sich ~, dass** make sure that; **von sich selbst ~** be or feel (quite) sure of o.s.; **überzeugt** [y:bɐ'tsɔʏkt] *adj* convinced; **~ sein** *a.* be or feel (quite) sure; **Über'zeugung** *f* (-; *-en*) conviction

'überziehen[1] *v/t* (*irr, ziehen, sep, -ge-, h*) put *s.th.* on

über'ziehen[2] *v/t* (*irr, ziehen, no -ge-, h*) TECH *etc* cover; ECON overdraw

Über'ziehungskre,dit *m* ECON overdraft (facility)

'Überzug *m* cover; coat(ing)

üblich ['y:plɪç] *adj* usual, normal; **es ist ~** it's the custom; **wie ~** as usual

'U-Boot *n* submarine

übrig ['y:brɪç] *adj* remaining; **die Übrigen** *pl* the others, the rest; **~ sein** (**haben**) be (have) left; **~ bleiben** be left, remain; **es bleibt mir nichts anderes ~** (**als zu** *inf*) there is nothing else I can do (but *inf*); **~ lassen** leave

übrigens ['y:brɪgəns] *adv* by the way

'übriglassen *v/t* (*irr, lassen, sep, -ge-, sein*) (*a. fig*) → **übrig**

Übung ['y:bʊŋ] *f* (-; *-en*) exercise; practice; **in** (**aus der**) **~** in (out of) practice

Ufer ['u:fɐ] *n* (-*s*; -) shore; bank; **ans ~**

ashore

Uhr [u:ɐ] *f* (-; *-en* ['u:rən]) clock; watch; **um vier ~** at four o'clock

'Uhr|armband *n* watchstrap; **~macher** *m* (-*s*; -) watchmaker; **~werk** *n* clockwork; **~zeiger** *m* hand; **~zeigersinn** *m*: **im ~** clockwise; **entgegen dem ~** counterclockwise, *Br* anticlockwise

Uhu ['u:hu] *m* (-*s*; -*s*) ZO eagle owl

UKW [u:ka:'ve:] *abbr of* **Ultrakurzwelle** VHF, very high frequency

Ulk [ʊlk] *m* (-*s*; -*e*) joke; hoax

ulkig ['ʊlkɪç] *adj* funny

Ulme ['ʊlmə] *f* (-; -*n*) BOT elm

Ultimatum [ʊlti'ma:tʊm] *n* (-*s*; -*ten*) ultimatum; **j-m ein ~ stellen** deliver an ultimatum to s.o.

um [ʊm] *prp* (*acc*) *and cj* (a)round; at; about, around; **~ Geld** for money; **~ e-e Stunde (10 cm)** by an hour (10 cm); **~ ... willen** for the sake of ...; **~ zu** *inf* (in order) to *inf*; **~ sein** F be over; **die Zeit ist ~** time's up; → **umso**

umarmen [ʊm'ʔarmən] *v/t* (*no -ge-, h*) (*a. sich ~*) embrace, hug

Um'armung *f* (-; -*en*) embrace, hug

'Umbau *m* (-[*e*]*s*; -*e*, -*ten*) rebuilding, reconstruction; **'umbauen** *v/t* (*sep, -ge-, h*) rebuild, reconstruct

'um|binden *v/t* (*irr, binden, sep, -ge-, h*) put *s.th.* on; **~blättern** *v/i* (*sep, -ge-, h*) turn (over) the page; **~bringen** *v/t* (*irr, bringen, sep, -ge-, h*) kill; **sich ~** kill o.s.; **~buchen** *v/t* (*sep, -ge-, h*) change; ECON transfer (**auf** *acc* to); **~denken** *v/i* (*irr, denken, sep, -ge-, h*) change one's way of thinking; **~dispo,nieren** *v/i* (*sep, no -ge-, h*) change one's plans; **~drehen** *v/t* (*sep, -ge-, h*) turn (round); **sich ~** turn round

Um'drehung *f* (-; -*en*) turn; PHYS, TECH rotation, revolution

umei'nander *adv* care *etc* about *or* for each other

'umfahren[1] *v/t* (*irr, fahren, sep, -ge-, h*) run down

um'fahren[2] *v/t* (*irr, fahren, no -ge-, h*) drive (MAR sail) round

'umfallen *v/i* (*irr, fallen, sep, -ge-, sein*) fall down *or* over; collapse; **tot ~** drop dead

'Umfang *m* circumference; size; extent; **in großem ~** on a large scale

'umfangreich *adj* extensive; voluminous

um'fassen fig v/t (no -ge-, h) cover; include; **~d** adj comprehensive; complete

'**Umformen** v/t (sep, -ge-, h) turn, change; ELECTR, LING, MATH a. transform, convert (all: **in** acc [in]to)

'**Umformer** m (-s; -) ELECTR converter

'**Umfrage** f opinion poll

'**Umgang** m (-[e]s; no pl) company; **~ haben mit** associate with; **beim ~ mit** when dealing with

um'gänglich ['ʊmɡɛŋlɪç] adj sociable

'**Umgangs|formen** pl manners; **~sprache** f colloquial speech; **die englische ~** colloquial English

um'geben v/t (irr, **geben**, no -ge-, h) surround (**mit** with); **Um'gebung** f (-; -en) surroundings; environment

'**umgehen**[1] v/i (irr, **gehen**, sep, -ge-, sein) **~ mit** deal with, handle; **~ können mit** have a way with, be good with

um'gehen[2] v/t (irr, **gehen**, no -ge-, h) avoid; bypass

'**umgehend** adv immediately

Um'gehungsstraße f bypass; beltway, Br ring road

umgekehrt ['ʊmɡəkeːɐt] **1.** adj reverse; opposite; (**genau**) **~** (just) the other way round **2.** adv the other way round; **und ~** and vice versa

'**umgraben** v/t (irr, **graben**, sep, -ge-, h) dig (up), break up

'**Umhang** m cape; '**umhängen** v/t (sep, -ge-, h) put around or over s.o.'s shoulders etc; rehang

'**umhauen** v/t (irr, **hauen**, sep, -ge-, h) fell, cut down; F knock s.o. out

um'her adv (a)round, about

um'herstreifen v/i (sep, -ge-, sein) roam or wander around

'**umkehren** (sep, -ge-) **1.** v/i (sein) turn back **2.** v/t (h) reverse

'**Umkehrung** f (-; -en) reversal (a. fig)

'**umkippen** (sep, -ge-) **1.** v/t (h) tip over, upset **2.** v/i (sein) fall down or over, overturn

'**Umkleide|ka|bine** f changing cubicle; **~raum** m esp SPORT changing or locker room; THEA dressing room

'**umkommen** v/i (irr, **kommen**, sep, -ge-,

sein) be killed (**bei** in), die (in); F **~ vor** (dat) be dying with

'**Umkreis** m: **im ~ von** within a radius of; **um'kreisen** v/t (no -ge-, h) circle; ASTR revolve around; satellite etc: orbit

'**umkrempeln** v/t (sep, -ge-, h) roll up

'**Umlauf** m circulation; PHYS, TECH rotation; ECON circular; **im** (**in**) **~ sein** (**bringen**) be in (put into) circulation, circulate; **~bahn** f ASTR orbit

'**um|laufen** v/i (irr, **laufen**, sep, -ge-, sein) circulate; **~legen** v/t (sep, -ge-, h) put on; move; share (expenses etc); TECH pull; F do s.o. in, bump s.o. off

um'leiten v/t (sep, -ge-, h) divert; '**Umleitung** f (-; -en) detour, Br diversion

'**umliegend** adj surrounding

'**umpacken** v/t (sep, -ge-, h) repack

'**umpflanzen** v/t (sep, -ge-, h) repot

umranden ['ʊm'randən] v/t (no -ge-, h), **Um'randung** f (-; -en) edge, border

'**umräumen** v/t (sep, -ge-, h) rearrange

um'rechnen v/t (sep, -ge-, h) convert (**in** acc into); '**Umrechnung** f (-; -en) conversion; '**Umrechnungskurs** m exchange rate

'**umreißen** v/t (irr, **reißen**, sep, -ge-, h) knock s.o. down

um'ringen v/t (no -ge-, h) surround

'**Umriss** m outline (a. fig), contour

'**um|rühren** v/t (sep, -ge-, h) stir; **~rüsten** v/t (sep, -ge-, h) TECH convert (**auf** acc to); **~satteln** F v/i (sep, -ge-, h) **~ von … auf** (acc) … switch from … to …

'**Umsatz** m ECON sales

'**umschalten** v/t and v/i (sep, -ge-, h) switch (over) (**auf** acc to) (a. fig)

'**Umschlag** m envelope; cover, wrapper; jacket; cuff, Br turn-up; MED compress; ECON handling; '**umschlagen** (irr, **schlagen**, sep, -ge-, h) **1.** v/t (h) cut down, fell; turn up; turn down; ECON handle **2.** v/i (sein) turn over; fig change (suddenly)

'**Umschlagplatz** m trading center (Br centre)

'**umschnallen** v/t (sep, -ge-, h) buckle on

'**umschreiben**[1] v/t (irr, **schreiben**, sep, -ge-, h) rewrite

um'schreiben[2] v/t (irr, **schreiben**, no -ge-, h) paraphrase

Um'schreibung f (-; -en) paraphrase

'**Umschrift** f transcription

'**umschulen** v/t (sep, -ge-, h) retrain; transfer to another school

umschwärmt [ʊmˈʃvɛrmt] adj idolized

'**Umschwung** m (drastic) change, esp POL a. swing

um|segeln v/t (no -ge-, h) sail round; circumnavigate

'**um|sehen** v/refl (irr, **sehen**, sep, -ge-, h) look around (**in e-m Laden** a shop; **nach** for); look back (**nach** at); **sich ~ nach** be looking for; **~setzen** v/t (sep, -ge-, h) move (a. PED); ECON sell; **~ in** (acc) convert (in)to; **in die Tat ~** put into action; **sich ~** change places

'**umsiedeln** v/i (sep, -ge-, sein) and v/t (h) resettle; → **umziehen**

'**Umsied(e)lung** f (-; -en) resettlement

'**Umsiedler** m (-s; -) resettler

'**umso 1. je später** etc, **~ schlechter** etc the later etc the worse etc **2. ~ besser** so much the better

um'**sonst** adv free (of charge), for nothing; F for free; fig in vain

um'**spannen** v/t (no -ge-, h) span (a. fig)

'**umspringen** v/i (irr, **springen**, sep, -ge-, sein) shift, change (suddenly) (a. fig); **~ mit** treat (badly)

'**Umstand** m circumstance; fact; detail; **unter diesen** (**keinen**) **Umständen** under the (no) circumstances; **unter Umständen** possibly; **keine Umstände machen** not cause s.o. any trouble; not go to any trouble; no put o.s. out; **in anderen Umständen sein** be expecting

umständlich ['ʊmʃtɛntlɪç] adj awkward; complicated; long-winded; **das ist** (**mir**) **viel zu ~** that's far too much trouble (for me)

'**Umstands|kleid** n maternity dress; **~wort** n (-[e]s; -wörter) LING adverb

'**Umstehende: die ~n** pl the bystanders

'**umsteigen** v/i (irr, **steigen**, sep, -ge-, sein) change (**nach** for), RAIL a. change trains (for)

'**umstellen** v/t (sep, -ge-, h) change (**auf** acc to), make a change or changes in, esp TECH a. switch (over) (to), convert (to); adjust (to); rearrange (a. furniture), reorganize; reset (watch); **sich ~ auf** (acc) change or switch (over) to; adjust (o.s.) to, get used to

'**Umstellung** f (-; -en) change; switch, conversion; adjustment; rearrange-

ment, reorganization

'**umstimmen** v/t (sep, -ge-, h) **j-n ~** change s.o.'s mind

'**umstoßen** v/t (irr, **stoßen**, sep, -ge-, h) knock over, upset (a. fig)

umstritten [ʊmˈʃtrɪtən] adj controversial

'**Umsturz** m overthrow; '**umstürzen** v/i (sep, -ge-, sein) overturn, fall over

'**Umtausch** m, '**umtauschen** v/t (sep, -ge-, h) exchange (**gegen** for)

'**umwälzend** adj revolutionary

'**Umwälzung** f (-; -en) radical change

'**umwandeln** v/t (sep, -ge-, h) turn (**in** acc into), transform (into), esp CHEM, ELECTR, PHYS a. convert ([in]to)

'**Umwandlung** f (-; -en) transformation, conversion

'**Umweg** m roundabout route or way (a. fig), esp MOT a. detour; **ein ~ von 10 Minuten** ten minutes out of the way; fig **auf ~en** in a roundabout way

'**Umwelt** f (-; no pl) environment

'**Umwelt...** in cpds mst environmental ...; **~forschung** f ecology

'**umwelt|freundlich** adj environment friendly, non-polluting; **~schädlich** adj harmful, noxious, polluting

'**Umwelt|schutz** m conservation, environmental protection, pollution control; **~schützer** m environmentalist, conservationist; **~schutzpa,pier** n recycled paper; **~sünder** m (environmental) polluter; **~verschmutzer** m (-s; -) polluter; **~verschmutzung** f (environmental) pollution; **~zerstörung** f ecocide

'**umziehen** (irr, **ziehen**, sep -ge-) **1.** v/i (sein) move (**nach** to); **2.** v/refl (h) change (one's clothes)

umzingeln [ʊmˈtsɪŋəln] v/t (no -ge-, h) surround, encircle

'**Umzug** m move (**nach** to), removal (to); parade

unabhängig ['ʊnaphɛŋɪç] adj independent (**von** of); **~ davon, ob** (**was**) regardless of whether (what); '**Unabhängigkeit** f (-; no pl) independence (**von** from)

'**unabsichtlich** adj unintentional; **et. ~ tun** do s.th. by mistake

unab'**wendbar** adj inevitable

'**unachtsam** adj careless, negligent

'**Unachtsamkeit** f (-; no pl) carelessness, negligence

unan'fechtbar *adj* incontestable

'un|angebracht *adj* inappropriate; **~ sein** be out of place; **~angemessen** *adj* unreasonable; inadequate; **~angenehm** *adj* unpleasant; embarrassing

unan'nehmbar *adj* unacceptable

Unannehmlichkeiten ['ʊnʔanːə·mlɪkkaitən] *pl* trouble, difficulties

'unansehnlich *adj* unsightly

'unanständig *adj* indecent, obscene

unan'tastbar *adj* inviolable

'unappetitlich *adj* unappetizing

Unart ['ʊnʔaːrt] *f* (-; *-en*) bad habit

'unartig *adj* naughty, bad

'unaufdringlich *adj* unobtrusive

'unauffällig *adj* inconspicuous, unobtrusive

unauf'findbar *adj* not to be found, untraceable

'unaufgefordert *adv* without being asked, of one's own accord

unaufhörlich [ʊnʔʔaufˈhøːrlɪç] *adj* continuous

'unaufmerksam *adj* inattentive

'Unaufmerksamkeit *f* (-; *no pl*) inattention, inattentiveness

'unaufrichtig *adj* insincere

unaus'löschlich [ʊnʔausˈlœʃlɪç] *adj* indelible; **~stehlich** [ʊnʔausˈʃteːlɪç] *adj* unbearable

'unbarmherzig *adj* merciless

'un|beabsichtigt *adj* unintentional; **~beachtet** *adj* unnoticed; **~beaufsichtigt** *adj* unattended; **~bebaut** *adj* undeveloped; **~bedacht** ['ʊnbədaxt] *adj* thoughtless; **~bedenklich 1.** *adj* safe **2.** *adv* without hesitation; **~bedeutend** *adj* insignificant; minor; **~bedingt 1.** *adj* unconditional, absolute **2.** *adv* by all means, absolutely; *need etc* badly; **~befahrbar** *adj* impassable; **~befangen** *adj* unprejudiced, unbias(s)ed; unembarrassed; **~befriedigend** *adj* unsatisfactory; **~befriedigt** *adj* dissatisfied; **~begabt** *adj* untalented; **~begreiflich** *adj* inconceivable, incomprehensible; **~begrenzt** *adj* unlimited, boundless; **~begründet** *adj* unfounded

'Unbehagen *n* (-s; *no pl*) uneasiness, discomfort; **'unbehaglich** *adj* uneasy, uncomfortable

unbehelligt [ʊnbəˈhɛlɪçt] *adj* unmolested

'un|beherrscht *adj* uncontrolled, lacking self-control; **~beholfen** ['ʊnbəhɔlfən] *adj* clumsy, awkward; **~beirrt** *adj* unwavering; **~bekannt** *adj* unknown

'Unbekannte *f* (-; *-n*) MATH unknown quantity

'un|bekümmert *adj* light-hearted, cheerful; **~belehrbar** *adj*: **er ist ~** he'll never learn; **~beliebt** *adj* unpopular; **er ist überall ~** nobody likes him; **~bemannt** *adj* unmanned; **~bemerkt** *adj* unnoticed; **~benutzt** *adj* unused; **~bequem** *adj* uncomfortable; inconvenient; **~berechenbar** *adj* unpredictable; **~berechtigt** *adj* unauthorized; unjustified; **~beschädigt** *adj* undamaged; **~bescheiden** *adj* immodest

un|be'schränkt *adj* unlimited; absolute (*power*); **~beschreiblich** ['ʊnbə·ˈʃraiplɪç] *adj* indescribable; **~besehen** *adv* unseen; **~besiegbar** ['ʊnbə·ˈziːkbaːɐ] *adj* invincible

'un|besonnen *adj* thoughtless, imprudent; rash; **~bespielbar** *adj* SPORT unplayable; **~beständig** *adj* unstable; METEOR changeable, unsettled; **~bestätigt** *adj* unconfirmed

unbe'stechlich *adj* incorruptible

'unbestimmt *adj* indefinite (*a.* LING); uncertain; vague

un|be'streitbar *adj* indisputable; **~bestritten** [ʊnbəˈʃtrɪtən] *adj* undisputed

'un|beteiligt *adj* not involved; indifferent; **~betont** *adj* unstressed

unbeugsam [ʊnˈbɔykzaːm] *adj* inflexible

'un|bewacht *adj* unwatched, unguarded (*a. fig*); **~bewaffnet** *adj* unarmed; **~beweglich** *adj* immovable; motionless

unbe'wohnbar *adj* uninhabitable

'unbewohnt *adj* uninhabited; unoccupied, vacant

'unbewusst *adj* unconscious

unbe'zahlbar *fig adj* invaluable, priceless; **'unbezahlt** *adj* unpaid

'unblutig 1. *adj* bloodless **2.** *adv* without bloodshed

'unbrauchbar *adj* useless

und [ʊnt] *cj* and; F **na ~?** so what?

'undankbar *adj* ungrateful (**gegen** to); thankless; **'Undankbarkeit** *f* (-; *no pl*) ingratitude, ungratefulness

undefi'nierbar *adj* undefinable

un'denkbar *adj* unthinkable

'undeutlich *adj* indistinct; inarticulate; *fig* vague

'undicht *adj* leaky

'unduldsam *adj* intolerant; 'Unduldsamkeit *f* (-; *no pl*) intolerance

undurch|'dringlich *adj* impenetrable; ~'führbar *adj* impracticable

'undurch|lässig *adj* impervious, impermeable; ~sichtig *adj* opaque; *fig* mysterious

'uneben *adj* uneven; 'Unebenheit *f* (-; *no pl*) unevenness; (-; -en) bump

'unecht *adj* false; artificial; imitation ...; *F contr* fake, phon(e)y

'unehelich *adj* illegitimate

'unehrenhaft *adj* dishono(u)rable

'unehrlich *adj* dishonest

'uneigennützig *adj* unselfish

'uneinig *adj*: (sich) ~ sein disagree (**über** *acc* on); 'Uneinigkeit *f* (-; *no pl*) disagreement; dissension

unein'nehmbar *adj* impregnable

'un|empfänglich *adj* insusceptible (**für** to); ~empfindlich *adj* insensitive (**gegen** to)

un'endlich *adj* infinite; endless, never-ending; Un'endlichkeit *f* (-; *no pl*) infinity (*a. fig*)

unent|behrlich [ʊnʔɛnt'beːɐlɪç] *adj* indispensable; ~geltlich [ʊnʔɛnt'gɛltlɪç] *adj and adv* free (of charge)

'unentschieden *adj* undecided; ~ **enden** SPORT end in a draw *or* tie; **es steht** ~ the score is even; 'Unentschieden *n* (-s; -) SPORT draw, tie

'unentschlossen *adj* irresolute

unent'schuldbar *adj* inexcusable

unentwegt [ʊnʔɛnt'veːkt] *adv* untiringly; continuously

'un|erfahren *adj* inexperienced; ~erfreulich *adj* unpleasant; ~erfüllt *adj* unfulfilled; ~ergiebig *adj* unproductive; ~erheblich *adj* irrelevant (**für** to); insignificant

unerhört [ʊnʔɛːɐ'høːɐt] *adj* outrageous

'un|erkannt *adj* unrecognized; ~erklärlich *adj* inexplicable; ~erlässlich *adj* essential, indispensable; ~erlaubt *adj* unallowed; unauthorized; ~erledigt *adj* unsettled (*a.* ECON)

uner'messlich *adj* immeasurable

unermüdlich [ʊnʔɛɐ'myːtlɪç] *adj* inde-

fatigable; untiring

uner'reichbar *adj* inaccessible; *esp fig* unattainable; uner'reicht *adj* unequal(l)ed

unersättlich [ʊnʔɛɐ'zɛtlɪç] *adj* insatiable

'unerschlossen *adj* undeveloped

uner|schöpflich [ʊnʔɛɐ'ʃœpflɪç] *adj* inexhaustible; ~schütterlich [ʊnʔɛɐ'ʃytɛlɪç] *adj* imperturbable; ~schwinglich [ʊnʔɛɐ'ʃvɪŋlɪç] *adj* exorbitant; **für j-n** ~ **sein** be beyond s.o.'s means; ~setzlich [ʊnʔɛɐ'zɛtslɪç] *adj* irreplaceable; ~träglich [ʊnʔɛɐ'trɛːklɪç] *adj* unbearable

'unerwartet *adj* unexpected

'unerwünscht *adj* unwanted

'unfähig *adj* incompetent; incapable (**zu tun** of doing), unable (to *inf*)

'Unfähigkeit *f* (-; *no pl*) incompetence; incapacity, inability

'Unfall *m* accident; crash

'Unfallstelle *f* scene of the accident

un'fehlbar *adj* infallible (*a.* REL); unfailing

unförmig ['ʊnfœrmɪç] *adj* shapeless; misshapen; monstrous

'unfrankiert *adj* unstamped

'unfrei *adj* not free; *post* unpaid

'unfreiwillig *adj* involuntary; unconscious (*humor*)

'unfreundlich *adj* unfriendly (**zu** to), unkind (to); *fig* cheerless

'Unfrieden *m* (-s; *no pl*) discord; ~ **stiften** make mischief

'unfruchtbar *adj* infertile; 'Unfruchtbarkeit *f* (-; *no pl*) infertility

Unfug ['ʊnfuːk] *m* (-[e]s; *no pl*) nonsense; ~ **treiben** be up to mischief, fool around

Ungar ['ʊŋɡar] *m* (-n; -n), 'Ungarin *f* (-; -nen), 'ungarisch *adj* Hungarian; 'Ungarn Hungary

'ungastlich *adj* inhospitable

'un|geachtet *prp* (*gen*) regardless of; despite; ~geahnt *adj* unthought-of; ~gebeten *adj* uninvited, unasked; ~gebildet *adj* uneducated; ~geboren *adj* unborn; ~gebräuchlich *adj* uncommon, unusual; ~gebührlich ['ʊnɡəbyːɐlɪç] *adj* unseemly; ~gebunden *fig adj* free, independent; **frei und** ~ footloose and fancy-free; ~gedeckt *adj* ECON uncovered; SPORT unmarked

'**Ungeduld** f (-; no pl) impatience

'**ungeduldig** adj impatient

'**ungeeignet** adj unfit; unqualified; inappropriate

ungefähr ['ʊngəfɛːɐ̯] **1.** adj approximate; rough **2.** adv approximately, roughly, about, around, ... or so; **so ~** something like that

'**ungefährlich** adj harmless; safe

'**ungeheuer** adj enormous (a. fig), huge, vast

'**Ungeheuer** n (-s; -) monster (a. fig)

unge'heuerlich adj monstrous

'**ungehindert** adj and adv unhindered

'**ungehobelt** fig adj uncouth, rough

'**ungehörig** adj improper, unseemly

'**ungehorsam** adj disobedient

Ungehorsam m (-s; no pl) disobedience

'**un|gekocht** adj uncooked; **~gekünstelt** adj unaffected; **~gekürzt** adj unabridged; **~gelegen** adj inconvenient; **j-m ~ kommen** be inconvenient for s.o.

ungelenk ['ʊngəlɛŋk] adj awkward, clumsy

'**ungelernt** adj unskilled

'**ungemütlich** adj uncomfortable; F **~ werden** get nasty

'**ungenau** adj inaccurate; fig vague; '**Ungenauigkeit** f (-; -en) inaccuracy

ungeniert ['ʊnʒeniːɐ̯t] adj uninhibited

'**un|genießbar** adj uneatable; undrinkable; F unbearable; **~genügend** adj insufficient; PED poor, unsatisfactory; grade: a. F; **~gepflegt** adj neglected; untidy, unkempt; **~gerade** adj uneven; odd; **~gerecht** adj unfair, unjust; '**Ungerechtigkeit** f (-; no pl) injustice, unfairness

'**ungern** adv unwillingly; **et. ~ tun** hate or not like to do s.th.

'**un|geschehen** adj: **~ machen** undo; **~geschickt** adj awkward, clumsy; **~geschliffen** adj uncut (diamond etc); unpolished (a. fig); **~geschminkt** adj without make-up; fig unvarnished, plain (truth); **~gesetzlich** adj illegal, unlawful; **~gestört** adj undisturbed; **~gestraft** adj: **~ davonkommen** get off unpunished (F scot-free); **~gesund** adj unhealthy; **~geteilt** adj undivided (a. fig)

Ungetüm ['ʊngətyːm] n (-s; -e) monster, fig a. monstrosity

'**ungewiss** adj uncertain; **j-n im Ungewissen lassen** keep s.o. in the dark (**über** acc about); '**Ungewissheit** f (-; no pl) uncertainty

'**ungewöhnlich** adj unusual

'**ungewohnt** adj strange, unfamiliar;

Ungeziefer ['ʊngətsiːfɐ] n (-s; no pl) vermin

'**ungezogen** adj naughty, bad; spoilt

'**ungezwungen** adj relaxed, informal; easygoing

'**ungläubig** adj incredulous, unbelieving (a. REL)

unglaublich [ʊn'glauplɪç] adj incredible, unbelievable

'**unglaubwürdig** adj implausible; unreliable (witness etc)

'**ungleich** adj unequal, different; unlike; **~mäßig** adj uneven; irregular

'**Unglück** n (-[e]s; -e) (no pl) bad luck, misfortune; misery; accident; disaster; '**unglücklich** adj unhappy, miserable; unfortunate; '**unglücklicher'weise** adv unfortunately

'**ungültig** adj invalid; **für ~ erklären** JUR invalidate

'**Ungunst** f: **zu ~en → zuungunsten**; '**ungünstig** adj unfavo(u)rable; disadvantageous

'**ungut** adj: **~es Gefühl** misgivings (**bei et.** about s.th.); **nichts für ~!** no offense (Br offence) meant!

'**unhaltbar** adj untenable; intolerable; SPORT unstoppable

'**unhandlich** adj unwieldy

'**unhar'monisch** adj MUS discordant

'**Unheil** n (-s; no pl) mischief; evil; disaster; '**unheilbar** adj MED incurable

'**unheilvoll** adj disastrous; sinister

'**unheimlich** adj creepy, spooky, eerie; F tremendous; F **~ gut** terrific, fantastic

'**unhöflich** adj impolite; rude

'**Unhöflichkeit** f (-; no pl) impoliteness; rudeness

'**unhörbar** adj inaudible

'**unhygienisch** adj insanitary

Uniform [uni'fɔrm] f (-; -en) uniform

'**uninteressant** adj uninteresting

uninteressiert ['ʊn'ʔɪntəresiːɐ̯t] adj uninterested (**an** dat in)

Union [u'njoːn] f (-; -en) union

Universität [univerzi'tɛːt] f (-; -en) university

Universum [uni'vɛrzʊm] *n* (*-s; no pl*) universe

Unke ['ʊŋkə] *f* (*-; -n*) zo toad

'unkenntlich *adj* unrecognizable

'Unkenntnis *f* (*-; no pl*) ignorance

'unklar *adj* unclear; uncertain; confused, muddled; *im Unklaren sein* (*lassen*) be (leave *s.o.*) in the dark

'unklug *adj* imprudent, unwise

'Unkosten *pl* expenses, costs

'Unkraut *n* (*-[e]s; no pl*) weed(s); ~ *jäten* weed (the garden)

unkündbar ['ʊnkʏntbaːɐ] *adj* permanent (*post*)

'unlängst *adv* lately, recently

'unleserlich *adj* illegible

'unlogisch *adj* illogical

un'lösbar *adj* insoluble

'unmännlich *adj* unmanly, effeminate

'unmäßig *adj* excessive

'Unmenge *f* vast quantity *or* number(s) (*von* of), F loads (of), tons (of)

'Unmensch *m* monster, brute

'unmenschlich *adj* inhuman, cruel

'Unmenschlichkeit *f* (*-; -en*) (*no pl*) inhumanity; cruelty

un'merklich *adj* imperceptible

'unmissverständlich *adj* unmistakable

'unmittelbar 1. *adj* immediate, direct **2.** *adv*: ~ *nach* (*hinter*) right after (behind)

'unmöbliert *adj* unfurnished

'unmodern *adj* out of fashion *or* style

'unmöglich 1. *adj* impossible **2.** *adv*: *ich kann es ~ tun* I can't possibly do it

'unmoralisch *adj* immoral

'unmündig *adj* JUR under age

'unmusikalisch *adj* unmusical

'unnachahmlich *adj* inimitable

'unnachgiebig *adj* unyielding

'unnachsichtig *adj* strict, severe

unnahbar [ʊn'naːbaːɐ] *adj* standoffish, cold

'unnatürlich *adj* unnatural (*a. fig*); affected

'unnötig *adj* unnecessary, needless

'unnütz ['ʊnnʏts] *adj* useless

'unordentlich *adj* untidy; ~ *sein* room *etc*: be (in) a mess; **'Unordnung** *f* (*-; no pl*) disorder, mess

'unparteiisch *adj* impartial, unbias(s)ed; **'Unparteiische** *m, f* (*-n; -n*) SPORT referee

'unpassend *adj* unsuitable; improper; inappropriate

'unpassierbar *adj* impassable

unpässlich ['ʊnpɛslɪç] *adj* indisposed

'unpersönlich *adj* impersonal (*a.* LING)

'unpolitisch *adj* unpolitical

'unpraktisch *adj* impractical

'unpünktlich *adj* unpunctual

'unrecht *adj* wrong; ~ *haben* be wrong; *j-m ~ tun* do s.o. wrong; **'Unrecht** *n* (*-[e]s; no pl*) injustice; wrong; *zu* ~ wrong(ful)ly; ~ *haben* → *unrecht*; ~ *tun* → *unrecht*

'unrechtmäßig *adj* unlawful

'unregelmäßig *adj* irregular (*a.* LING)

'Unregelmäßigkeit *f* (*-; -en*) irregularity

'unreif *adj* unripe; *fig* immature

'Unreife *fig f* immaturity

'unrein *adj* unclean; impure (*a.* REL)

'Unreinheit *f* (*-; -en*) impurity

'unrichtig *adj* incorrect, wrong

'Unruhe *f* (*-; -n*) (*no pl*) restlessness, unrest (*a.* POL); anxiety, alarm; *pl* disturbances, riots

'unruhig *adj* restless; uneasy; worried, alarmed; MAR rough

uns [ʊns] *pers pron* (to) us; each other; ~ (*selbst*) (to) ourselves; *ein Freund von* ~ a friend of ours

'un|sachgemäß *adj* improper; ~**sachlich** *adj* unobjective; ~**sanft** *adj* rude, rough; ~**sauber** *adj* unclean, *esp fig a.* impure; SPORT unfair; *fig* underhand; ~**schädlich** *adj* harmless; ~**scharf** *adj* PHOT blurred, out of focus

un'schätzbar *adj* inestimable, invaluable

'un|scheinbar *adj* inconspicuous; plain; ~**schlüssig** *adj* irresolute; undecided; ~**schön** *adj* unsightly; *fig* unpleasant

'Unschuld *f* (*-; no pl*) innocence; *fig* virginity

'unschuldig *adj* innocent (*an dat* of)

'unselbstständig *adj* dependent on others; **'Unselbstständigkeit** *f* lack of independence, dependence on others

unser ['ʊnzɐ] *poss pron* our; ~*er*, ~*e*, ~*es* ours

'unsicher *adj* unsafe, insecure; self-conscious; uncertain; **'Unsicherheit** *f* (*-; -en*) (*no pl*) insecurity, unsafeness;

self-consciousness; uncertainty
'**unsichtbar** adj invisible
'**Unsinn** m (-[e]s; no pl) nonsense
'**unsinnig** adj nonsensical, stupid; absurd
'**Unsitte** f bad habit; abuse
'**unsittlich** adj immoral, indecent
'**unsozial** adj unsocial
'**unsportlich** adj unathletic; fig unfair
'**unsterblich 1.** adj immortal (a. fig) **2.** adv: ~ **verliebt** madly in love (**in** acc with); '**Unsterblichkeit** f immortality
'**Unstimmigkeit** f (-; -en) discrepancy; pl disagreements
'**unsympathisch** adj disagreeable; **er (es) ist mir** ~ I don't like him (it)
'**untätig** adj inactive; idle; '**Untätigkeit** f (-; no pl) inactivity
'**untauglich** adj unfit (a. MIL); incompetent
un'**teilbar** adj indivisible
unten ['ʊntən] adv (down) below, down (a. **nach** ~); downstairs; ~ **an** (dat) at the bottom of the page etc; **siehe** ~ see below; **von oben bis** ~ from top to bottom
unter ['ʊntɐ] prp under; below (a. fig); among; fig less than; ~ **anderem** among other things; ~ **uns (gesagt)** between you and me; ~ **Wasser** underwater
'**Unterarm** m ANAT forearm
'**unter|belichtet** adj PHOT underexposed; ~**besetzt** adj understaffed
'**Unterbewusstsein** n subconscious; **im** ~ subconsciously
unter|'bieten v/t (irr, **bieten**, no -ge-, h) underbid; undercut; beat (record); ~'**binden** fig v/t (irr, **binden**, no -ge-, h) put a stop to; prevent
unter'brechen v/t (irr, **brechen**, no -ge-, h) interrupt; **Unter'brechung** f (-; -en) interruption
'**unterbringen** v/t (irr, **bringen**, sep, -ge-, h) accommodate, put s.o. up; find a place for, put (**in** acc into); '**Unterbringung** f (-; -en) accommodation
unter'dessen adv in the meantime, meanwhile
unter'drücken v/t (no -ge-, h) oppress; suppress; **Unter'drücker** m (-s; -) oppressor; **Unter'drückung** f (-; -en) oppression

untere ['ʊntərə] adj lower (a. fig)
'**unterentwickelt** adj underdeveloped
'**unterernährt** adj undernourished, underfed; '**Unterernährung** f (-; no pl) undernourishment, malnutrition
Unter'führung f (-; -en) underpass, Br a. subway
'**Untergang** m ASTR setting; MAR sinking; fig downfall; decline; fall; '**untergehen** v/i (irr, **gehen**, sep, -ge-, sein) go down (a. fig), ASTR a. set, MAR a. sink
'**untergeordnet** adj subordinate, inferior; secondary
'**Untergewicht** n (-[e]s; no pl), '**untergewichtig** adj underweight
unter'graben fig v/t (irr, **graben**, no -ge-, h) undermine
'**Untergrund** m subsoil; POL underground; **in den** ~ **gehen** go underground; ~**bahn** f → **U-Bahn**
unterhalb prp (gen) below, under
'**Unterhalt** m (-[e]s; no pl) support, maintenance (a. JUR); **unter'halten** v/t (irr, **halten**, no -ge-, h) entertain; support; **sich** ~ (**mit**) talk (to, with); **sich (gut)** ~ enjoy o.s., have a good time; **unter'haltsam** adj entertaining; **Unter'haltung** f (-; -en) talk, conversation; entertainment; **Unter'haltungsindus,trie** f show business
Unter|'händler m negotiator; ~**haus** n (-es; no pl) Br PARL House of Commons; ~**hemd** n undershirt, Br vest; ~**holz** n (-es; no pl) undergrowth; ~**hose** f shorts, esp Br underpants, panties, Br pants; **e-e lange** ~, **lange** ~**n** (a pair of) long johns
'**unterirdisch** adj underground
'**Unterkiefer** m ANAT lower jaw
'**Unterkleid** n slip
'**unterkommen** v/i (irr, **kommen**, sep, -ge-, sein) find accommodation; find work or a job (**bei** with)
Unterkunft ['ʊntɐkʊnft] f (-; -künfte ['ʊntɐkʏnftə]) accommodation, lodging(s); MIL quarters; ~ **und Verpflegung** board and lodging
'**Unterlage** f TECH base; pl documents; data
unter'lassen v/t (irr, **lassen**, no -ge-, h) omit, fail to do s.th.; stop or quit doing s.th.; **Unter'lassung** f (-; -en) omission (a. JUR)

U

'unter|legen¹ v/t (sep, -ge-, h) underlay

unter'legen² adj inferior (dat to)

Unter'legenheit f (-; no pl) inferiority

'Unterleib m ANAT abdomen, belly

'Untermieter m, 'Untermieterin f roomer, Br lodger

unter'nehmen v/t (irr, nehmen, no -ge-, h) make, take, go on a trip etc; et. ~ do s.th. (gegen about s.th.), take action (against s.o.); Unter'nehmen n (-s; -) firm, business; venture; undertaking, enterprise; MIL operation; Unter'nehmensberater(in) management consultant; Unter'nehmer m (-s; -) businessman, entrepreneur; employer; Unter'nehmerin f (-; -nen) businesswoman; unter'nehmungslustig adj active, dynamic; adventurous

'Unteroffizier m MIL non-commissioned officer

'unterordnen v/t and v/refl (sep, -ge-, h) subordinate (o.s.)

Unter'redung f (-; -en) talk(s)

Unterricht ['untərɪçt] m (-[e]s; no pl) instruction, teaching; PED school, classes, lessons; unter'richten v/i and v/t (no -ge-, h) teach; give lessons; inform (über acc of); 'Unterrichtsstunde f lesson, PED a. class, period

'Unterrock m slip

unter'sagen v/t (no -ge-, h) prohibit

unter'schätzen v/t (no -ge-, h) underestimate; underrate

unter'scheiden v/t and v/i (irr, scheiden, no -ge-, h) distinguish (zwischen between; von from); tell apart; sich ~ differ (von from; in dat in; durch by); Unter'scheidung f (-; -en) distinction; Unterschied ['untərʃiːt] m (-[e]s; -e) difference; im ~ zu unlike, as opposed to; 'unterschiedlich adj different; varying

unter'schlagen v/t (irr, schlagen, no -ge-, h) embezzle; Unter'schlagung f (-; -en) embezzlement

Unterschlupf ['untərʃlupf] m (-[e]s; no pl) hiding place

unter'schreiben v/t and v/i (irr, schreiben, no -ge-, h) sign

'Unterschrift f signature; caption

'Unterseeboot n → U-Boot

Untersetzer ['untɛzɛtsɐ] m (-s; -) coaster; saucer

unter'setzt adj thickset, stocky

'Unterstand m shelter, MIL a. dugout

unter'stehen (irr, stehen, no -ge-, h) 1. v/i (dat) be under (the control of) 2. v/refl dare; ~ Sie sich (et. zu tun)! don't you dare ([to] do s.th.)!

'unterstellen¹ v/t (sep, -ge-, h) put s.th. in; store; sich ~ take shelter

unter'stellen² v/t (no -ge-, h) assume; j-m ~, dass er ... insinuate that s.o. ...; Unter'stellung f (-; -en) insinuation

unter'streichen v/t (irr, streichen, no -ge-, h) underline (a. fig)

unter'stützen v/t (no -ge-, h) support; back (up); Unter'stützung f (-; -en) support; aid; welfare (payments)

unter'suchen v/t (no -ge-, h) examine (a. MED), investigate (a. JUR); search; CHEM analyze; Unter'suchung f (-; -en) examination (a. MED), investigation (a. JUR), a. (medical) checkup; CHEM analysis

Unter'suchungs|gefangene m, f JUR prisoner on remand; ~gefängnis n JUR remand prison; ~haft f: in ~ sein JUR be on remand; ~richter m JUR examining magistrate

Untertan ['untətaːn] m (-s; -en) subject

'Untertasse f saucer

'untertauchen (sep, -ge-) 1. v/i (sein) dive, submerge; fig disappear; esp POL go underground 2. v/t duck

'Unterteil n, m lower part, bottom

unter'teilen v/t (no -ge-, h) subdivide; Unter'teilung f (-; -en) subdivision

'Untertitel m subtitle; film: a. caption

'Unterton m undertone

Unter'treibung f (-; -en) understatement

'untervermieten v/t (no -ge-, h) sublet

unter'wandern v/t (no -ge-, h) infiltrate

'Unterwäsche f underwear

'Unterwasser... in cpds underwater ...

unterwegs [untə'veːks] adv on the or one's way (nach to)

unter'weisen v/t (irr, weisen, no -ge-, h) instruct; Unter'weisung f (-; -en) instruction

'Unterwelt f (-; no pl) underworld

unter'werfen v/t (irr, werfen, no -ge-, h) subject (dat to); subjugate; sich ~ submit (to); Unter'werfung f (-; -en) subjection; submission (**unter** acc to)

unter'würfig [ʊntɐˈvʏrfɪç] adj servile

unter'zeichnen v/t (no -ge-, h) sign; Unter'zeichnete m, f (-n; -n) the undersigned; Unter'zeichnung f (-; -en) signing

'unter'ziehen[1] v/t (irr, ziehen, sep, -ge-, h) put s.th. on underneath

unter'ziehen[2] v/t (irr, ziehen, no -ge-, h) sich e-r Behandlung, Prüfung etc ~ undergo (treatment etc), take (an examination etc)

'Untiefe f shallow, shoal

un|'tragbar adj unbearable, intolerable; ~trennbar adj inseparable

'untreu adj unfaithful (dat to)

un|'tröstlich adj inconsolable; ~trüglich [ʊnˈtryːklɪç] adj unmistakable

'Untugend f vice, bad habit

'unüber'legt adj thoughtless; ~sichtlich adj blind (bend etc)

unüber'trefflich [ʊnʔyːbɐˈtrɛflɪç] adj unsurpassable, matchless; ~troffen [ʊnʔyːbɐˈtrɔfən] adj unequal(l)ed; ~windlich [ʊnʔyːbɐˈvɪntlɪç] adj insuperable, invincible

unum|gänglich [ʊnʔʊmˈɡɛŋlɪç] adj inevitable; ~schränkt [ʊnʔʊmˈʃrɛŋkt] adj unlimited; POL absolute; ~stritten [ʊnʔʊmˈʃtrɪtən] adj undisputed; ~wunden [ʊnʔʊmˈvʊndən] adv straight out, frankly

ununterbrochen ['ʊnʔʊntɐbrɔxən] adj uninterrupted; continuous

un|ver'änderlich adj unchanging; ~ver'antwortlich adj irresponsible; ~ver'besserlich adj incorrigible; ~ver'bindlich adj noncommittal, ECON not binding; ~ver'daulich adj indigestible (a. fig)

'unverdient adj undeserved

'unverdünnt adj undiluted; straight

unver'einbar adj incompatible

'unverfälscht adj unadulterated

'unverfänglich adj harmless

'unverfroren adj brazen, impertinent

'unvergänglich adj immortal, eternal

unver'gesslich adj unforgettable

'unver'gleichlich adj incomparable

'unverhältnismäßig adv disproportionately; ~ hoch excessive

'unverheiratet adj unmarried, single

unverhofft ['ʊnfɛɐhɔft] adj unhoped-

for; unexpected

unverhohlen ['ʊnfɛɐhoːlən] adj undisguised, open

'unverkäuflich adj not for sale; unsal(e)able

unver'kennbar adj unmistakable

'unverletzt adj unhurt

unvermeidlich [ʊnfɛɐˈmaɪtlɪç] adj inevitable

'unvermindert adj undiminished

'unvermittelt adj abrupt, sudden

'Unvermögen n (-s; no pl) inability, incapacity

'unvermutet adj unexpected

'unvernünftig adj unreasonable; foolish

'unverschämt adj rude, impertinent; outrageous (price etc); 'Unverschämtheit f (-; -en) impertinence; die ~ haben zu inf have the nerve to inf

'unverschuldet adj through no fault of one's own

unversehens ['ʊnfɛɐzeːəns] adv unexpectedly, all of a sudden

un|'versehrt adj unhurt; undamaged; ~versöhnlich adj irreconcilable (a. fig), implacable; ~versorgt adj unprovided for; ~verständlich adj unintelligible; es ist mir ~ I can't see how or why, F it beats me; ~versucht adj: nichts ~ lassen leave nothing undone

unver'wundbar adj invulnerable

unver|wüstlich [ʊnfɛɐˈvyːstlɪç] adj indestructible; ~zeihlich [ʊnfɛɐˈtsaɪlɪç] adj inexcusable; ~züglich [ʊnfɛɐˈtsyːklɪç] 1. adj immediate, prompt 2. adv immediately, without delay

'unvollendet adj unfinished

'unvollkommen adj imperfect

'unvollständig adj incomplete

'unvorbereitet adj unprepared

'unvoreingenommen adj unprejudiced, unbias(s)ed

'unvorhergesehen adj unforeseen

'unvorhersehbar adj unforeseeable

'unvorsichtig adj careless; 'Unvorsichtigkeit f (-; no pl) carelessness

unvor'stellbar adj unthinkable

'unvorteilhaft adj unbecoming

'unwahr adj untrue; 'Unwahrheit f untruth; 'unwahrscheinlich adj improbable, unlikely; F fantastic

U

unwegsam [ˈʊnvɛːkzaːm] *adj* difficult, rough (*terrain*)

unweigerlich [ʊnˈvaɪɡɐlɪç] *adv* inevitably

'unweit *prp* (*gen*) not far from

'Unwetter *n* (-s; -) disastrous (thunder)-storm

'unwichtig *adj* unimportant

unwider|legbar [ʊnviːdɐˈleːkbaːɐ] *adj* irrefutable; **~ruflich** [ʊnviːdɐˈruːflɪç] *adj* irrevocable; **~stehlich** [ʊnviːdɐˈʃteːlɪç] *adj* irresistible

'Unwille(n) *m* indignation (**über** *acc* at); **'unwillig** *adj* indignant (**über** *acc* at); unwilling, reluctant

'unwillkürlich *adj* involuntary

'unwirklich *adj* unreal

'unwirksam *adj* ineffective

unwirsch [ˈʊnvɪrʃ] *adj* surly, gruff

unwirtlich [ˈʊnvɪrtlɪç] *adj* inhospitable

'unwirtschaftlich *adj* uneconomic(al)

'unwissend *adj* ignorant

'Unwissenheit *f* (-; *no pl*) ignorance

'unwohl *adj* unwell; uneasy

'unwürdig *adj* unworthy (*gen* of)

unzählig [ʊnˈtsɛːlɪç] *adj* innumerable, countless

unzer'brechlich *adj* unbreakable

unzer'reißbar *adj* untearable

unzer'störbar *adj* indestructible

unzer'trennlich *adj* inseparable

'Unzucht *f* (-; *no pl*) sexual offense (*Br* offence); **'unzüchtig** *adj* indecent; obscene

'unzufrieden *adj* discontent(ed) (**mit** with), dissatisfied (with); **'Unzufriedenheit** *f* discontent, dissatisfaction

'unzugänglich *adj* inaccessible

'unzulänglich *adj* inadequate

'unzulässig *adj* inadmissible

unzu'mutbar *adj* unacceptable; unreasonable

'unzurechnungsfähig *adj* JUR irresponsible; **'Unzurechnungsfähigkeit** *f* (-; *no pl*) JUR irresponsibility

'unzureichend *adj* insufficient

'unzusammenhängend *adj* incoherent

'unzuverlässig *adj* unreliable, untrustworthy; uncertain

üppig [ˈʏpɪç] *adj* luxuriant, lush (*both a.*

fig); voluptuous, luscious; opulent; rich

uralt [ˈuːɐʔalt] *adj* ancient (*a. iro*)

Uran [uˈraːn] *n* (-s; *no pl*) uranium

'Uraufführung *f* première, first performance (*film:* showing)

urbar [ˈuːɐbaːɐ] *adj* arable; **~ machen** cultivate; reclaim

'Urbevölkerung *f*, **'Ureinwohner** *pl* aboriginal inhabitants; *in Australia:* Aborigines

'Urenkel *m* great-grandson

'Urenkelin *f* great-granddaughter

'Urgroß... *in cpds* ...eltern, ...mutter, ...vater: great-grand...

Urheberrecht [ˈuːɐheːbɐɾeçt] *n* copyright (**an** *dat* on, for)

Urin [uˈriːn] *m* (-s; -e) urine; **urinieren** [uriˈniːrən] *v/i* (*no -ge-,* h) urinate

Urkunde [ˈuːɐkʊndə] *f* (-; *-n*) document; diploma; **'Urkundenfälschung** *f* forgery of documents

Urlaub [ˈuːɐlaʊp] *m* (-[e]s; *-e*) vacation, *Br* holiday(s); MIL leave; **in** *or* **im ~ sein** (**auf ~ gehen**) be (go) on vacation (*Br* holiday); **e-n Tag** (**ein paar Tage**) **~ nehmen** take a day (a few days) off; **Urlauber(in)** [ˈuːɐlaʊbɐ, ˈuːɐlaʊbərɪn] *m(f)* (-s; -/-; *-nen*) vacationist, vacationer, *Br* holidaymaker

Urne [ˈʊrnə] *f* (-; *-n*) urn; ballot box

Ursache *f* (-; *-n*) cause; reason; **keine ~!** not at all, you're welcome

'Ursprung *m* origin

ursprünglich [ˈuːɐʃprʏŋlɪç] *adj* original; natural, unspoilt

Urteil [ˈʊrtaɪl] *n* (-[e]s; *-e*) judg(e)ment; JUR sentence; **sich ein ~ bilden** form a judg(e)ment (**über** *acc* about)

'urteilen *v/i* (*ge-*, h) judge (**über** *j-n, et.* s.o., s.th.; **nach** by)

'Urwald *m* primeval forest; jungle

urwüchsig [ˈuːɐvʏksɪç] *adj* coarse, earthy

'Urzeit *f* prehistoric times

usw. *abbr of* **und so weiter** etc, and so on

Utensilien [utɛnˈziːljən] *pl* utensils

Utopie [utoˈpiː] *f* (-; *-n*) illusion

utopisch [uˈtoːpɪʃ] *adj* utopian; fantastic

V

Vagabund [vaga'bʊnt] *m* (-en; -en) vagabond, tramp, F bum

vage ['va:gə] *adj* vague

Vakuum ['va:kuʊm] *n* (-s; -kua, -kuen) vacuum

Vampir ['vampi:ɐ] *m* (-s; -e) ZO vampire (*a. fig*)

Vanille [va'nɪljə] *f* (-; *no pl*) vanilla

variabel [va'rja:bəl] *adj* variable

Variante [va'rjantə] *f* (-; -n) variant

Variation [varja'tsio:n] *f* (-; -en) variation

Varietee, *a.* **Varieté** [varje'te:] *n* (-s; -s) vaudeville, *Br* variety theatre, music hall

variieren [vari'i:rən] *v/i and v/t* (*no* -*ge*-, *h*) vary

Vase ['va:zə] *f* (-; -n) vase

Vater ['fa:tɐ] *m* (-s; *Väter* ['fɛ:tɐ]) father

'Vaterland *n* native country

'Vaterlandsliebe *f* patriotism

väterlich ['fɛ:tɐlɪç] *adj* fatherly, paternal

'Vaterschaft *f* (-; -en) JUR paternity

'Vater'unser *n* (-s; -) REL Lord's Prayer

V-Ausschnitt ['fau'aʊsʃnɪt] *m* V-neck

v. Chr. *abbr of* **vor Christus** BC, before Christ

Vegetarier [vege'ta:rjɐ] *m* (-s; -), **Vege'tarierin** *f* (-; -nen), **vegetarisch** [vege'ta:rɪʃ] *adj* vegetarian

Vegetation [vegeta'tsio:n] *f* (-; -en) vegetation; **vegetieren** [vege'ti:rən] *v/i* (*no* -*ge*-, *h*) vegetate

Veilchen ['faɪlçən] *n* (-s; -) BOT violet

Velo ['ve:lo] *Swiss n* (-s; -s) bicycle, F bike

Ventil [vɛn'ti:l] *n* (-s; -e) TECH valve; *fig* vent, outlet

Ventilation [vɛntila'tsio:n] *f* (-; -en) ventilation; **Ventilator** [vɛntila'to:ɐ] *m* (-s; -en [vɛntila'to:rən]) fan

verabreden [fɛɐ'ʔapre:dən] *v/t* (*no* -*ge*-, *h*) agree (up)on, arrange; appoint, fix; **sich ~** make a date (*or* an appointment) (**mit** with); **Ver'abredung** *f* (-; -en) appointment; date

ver'abreichen *v/t* (*no* -*ge*-, *h*) give; MED administer; **ver'abscheuen** *v/t* (*no* -*ge*-, *h*) loathe, detest

verabschieden [fɛɐ'ʔapʃi:dən] *v/t* (*no* -*ge*-, *h*) say goodbye to (*a.* **sich ~ von**); dismiss; JUR pass; **Ver'abschiedung** *f* (-; -en) dismissal; JUR passing

ver'achten *v/t* (*no* -*ge*-, *h*) despise; **verächtlich** [fɛɐ'ʔɛçtlɪç] *adj* contemptuous; **Ver'achtung** *f* (-; *no pl*) contempt

verallgemeinern [fɛɐ'ʔalgə'maɪnɐn] *v/t* (*no* -*ge*-, *h*) generalize

ver'altet *adj* antiquated, out of date

Veranda [ve'randa] *f* (-; -den) porch, *Br* veranda(h)

veränderlich [fɛɐ'ʔɛndɐlɪç] *adj* changeable (*a.* METEOR), variable (*a.* MATH, LING); **ver'ändern** *v/t and v/refl* (*no* -*ge*-, *h*), **Ver'änderung** *f* change

verängstigt [fɛɐ'ʔɛŋstɪçt] *adj* frightened, scared

ver'anlagen *v/t* (*no* -*ge*-, *h*) ECON assess; **veranlagt** [fɛɐ'ʔanla:kt] *adj* inclined (**zu, für** to); **künstlerisch** (**musikalisch**) **~ sein** have a gift *or* bent for art (music); **Ver'anlagung** *f* (-; -en) (pre)disposition (*a.* MED); talent; gift; ECON assessment

ver'anlassen *v/t* (*no* -*ge*-, *h*) make arrangements (*or* arrange) for *s.th.*; **j-n zu et. ~** make s.o. do s.th.

Ver'anlassung *f* (-; -en) cause (**zu** for)

ver'anschaulichen *v/t* (*no* -*ge*-, *h*) illustrate; **~anschlagen** *v/t* (*no* -*ge*-, *h*) estimate (**auf** *acc* at)

ver'anstalten *v/t* (*no* -*ge*-, *h*) arrange, organize; hold, give (*concert, party etc*); **Ver'anstaltung** *f* (-; -en) event, SPORT *a.* meet, *Br* meeting

ver'antworten *v/t* (*no* -*ge*-, *h*) take the responsibility for; **ver'antwortlich** *adj* responsible; **j-n ~ machen für** hold s.o. responsible for; **Ver'antwortung** *f* (-; *no pl*) responsibility; **auf eigene ~** at one's own risk; **j-n zur ~ ziehen** call s.o. to account; **Ver'antwortungsgefühl** *n* (-[e]s; *no pl*) sense of responsibility; **ver'antwortungslos** *adj* irresponsible

ver'arbeiten *v/t* (*no* -*ge*-, *h*) process; *fig* digest; **et. ~ zu** manufacture (*or* make) s.th. into; **~ärgern** *v/t* (*no* -*ge*-, *h*) make

s.o. angry, annoy

ver'armt *adj* impoverished

ver'arschen *v/t (no -ge-, h) j-n ~* take the piss out of s.o.

Verb [vɛrp] *n (-s; -en* ['vɛrbən]) LING verb

Verband [fɛr'bant] *m (-es; Verbände* [fɛr'bɛndə]) MED dressing, bandage; ECON association; MIL formation, unit; ~(s)kasten *m* MED first-aid kit *or* box; ~(s)zeug *m* MED dressing material

ver'bannen *v/t (no -ge-, h)* banish (*a. fig*), exile; Ver'bannung *f (-; -en)* banishment, exile

verbarrika'dieren *v/t (no -ge-, h)* barricade; block

ver'bergen *v/t (irr, bergen, no -ge-, h)* hide (*a. sich ~*), conceal

ver'bessern *v/t (no -ge-, h)* improve; correct; Ver'besserung *f (-; -en)* improvement; correction

ver'beugen *v/refl (no -ge-, h),* Ver'beugung *f (-; -en)* bow (*vor* to)

ver'biegen *v/t (irr, biegen, no -ge-, h)* twist; ~'bieten *v/t (irr, bieten, no -ge-, h)* forbid; prohibit; → *verboten*

ver'billigen *v/t (no -ge-, h)* reduce in price; verbilligt [fɛr'bɪlɪçt] *adj* reduced, at reduced prices

verbinden *v/t (irr, binden, no -ge-, h)* MED dress, bandage; bandage *s.o.* up; *a.* TECH connect, join, link (up); TEL put *s.o.* through (*mit* to); combine (*a.* CHEM *sich ~*); *fig* unite; associate; *j-m die Augen ~* blindfold s.o.; *damit sind beträchtliche Kosten verbunden* that involves considerable cost(s *pl*); *falsch verbunden!* wrong number!

verbindlich [fɛr'bɪntlɪç] *adj* obligatory, compulsory (*a.* PED); obliging

Ver'bindlichkeit *f (-; -en) (no pl)* obligingness; *pl* ECON liabilities

Ver'bindung *f (-; -en)* connection; combination; CHEM compound; UNIV fraternity, *Br* society; *sich in ~ setzen mit* get in touch with; *in~ stehen (bleiben)* be (keep) in touch

verbissen [fɛr'bɪsən] *adj* dogged

ver'bittert *adj* bitter, embittered

ver'blassen [fɛr'blasən] *v/i (no -ge-, sein)* fade (*a. fig*)

Verbleib [fɛr'blaɪp] *m (-[e]s; no pl)* whereabouts; ver'bleiben *v/i (irr, blei-*

ben, *no -ge-, sein)* remain

verbleit [fɛr'blaɪt] *adj* leaded

ver'blendet *fig adj* blind

Ver'blendung *fig f (-; -en)* blindness

verblichen [fɛr'blɪçən] *adj* faded

verblüffen [fɛr'blʏfən] *v/t (no -ge-, h)* amaze, F flabbergast

Ver'blüffung *f (-; -en)* amazement

ver'blühen *v/i (no -ge-, sein)* fade, wither (*both a. fig*)

ver'bluten *v/i (no -ge-, sein)* MED bleed to death

verborgen [fɛr'bɔrgən] *adj* hidden, concealed; *im Verborgenen* in secret

Verbot [fɛr'boːt] *n (-[e]s; -e)* prohibition, ban (on *s.th.*); ver'boten *adj: Rauchen ~* no smoking

Ver'brauch *m (-[e]s; no pl)* consumption (*an dat* of); ver'brauchen *v/t (no -ge-, h)* consume, use up

Verbraucher [fɛr'brauxɐ] *m (-s; -),* Ver'braucherin *f (-; -nen)* consumer; ~schutz *m* consumer protection

ver'brechen *v/t (no -ge-, h)* crime; *ein ~ begehen* commit a crime; Ver'brecher(in) *(-s; -/-; -nen),* ver'brecherisch *adj* criminal

ver'breiten *v/t and v/refl (no -ge-, h)* spread (*in dat, über acc* over, through); circulate

verbreitern [fɛr'braɪtɐn] *v/t and v/refl (no -ge-, h)* widen, broaden

Ver'breitung *f (-; no pl)* spread(ing); circulation

ver'brennen *v/i (irr, brennen, no -ge-, sein) and v/t (h)* burn (up); cremate

Ver'brennung *f (-; -en)* burning; cremation; TECH combustion; MED burn

ver'bringen *v/t (irr, bringen, no -ge-, h)* spend, pass

verbrüdern [fɛr'bryːdɐn] *v/refl (no -ge-, h)* fraternize; Verbrüderung [fɛr'bryːdərʊŋ] *f (-; -en)* fraternization

ver'brühen *v/t (no -ge-, h)* scald

ver'buchen *v/t (no -ge-, h)* book

verbünden [fɛr'bʏndən] *v/refl (no -ge-, h)* ally o.s. (*mit* to, with)

Ver'bündete *m, f (-n; -n)* ally (*a. fig*)

ver'bürgen *v/refl (no -ge-, h) sich ~ für* vouch for, guarantee

ver'büßen *v/t (no -ge-, h) e-e Strafe ~* serve a sentence, serve time

verchromt [fɛr'kroːmt] *adj* chromium-plated

Verdacht [fɛɐˈdaxt] m (-[e]s; -e) suspicion; ~ **schöpfen** become suspicious

verdächtig [fɛɐˈdɛçtɪç] adj suspicious, suspect; **Verdächtige** [fɛɐˈdɛçtɪɡə] m, f (-n; -n) suspect; **ver'dächtigen** v/t (no -ge-, h) suspect (**j-n e-r Tat** s.o. of [doing] s.th.); **Ver'dächtigung** f (-; -en) suspicion

verdammen [fɛɐˈdamən] v/t (no -ge-, h) condemn (**zu** to), damn (a. REL); **Ver'dammnis** f (-; no pl) REL damnation; **ver'dammt 1.** adj damned, F a. damn, darn(ed), Br sl a. bloody; F ~ (**noch mal)!** damn (it)! **2.** adv: ~ **gut etc** damn (Br sl a. bloody) good etc; **Ver-'dammung** f (-; -en) condemnation; REL damnation

ver'dampfen v/t (no -ge-, h) and v/i (sein) evaporate

ver'danken v/t (no -ge-, h) **j-m (e-m Umstand) et. ~** owe s.th. to s.o. (s.th.)

verdarb [fɛɐˈdarp] pret of **verderben**

ver'dauen [fɛɐˈdaʊən] v/t (no -ge-, h) digest (a. fig)

ver'daulich adj digestible; **leicht (schwer) ~** easy (hard) to digest

Ver'dauung f (-; no pl) digestion

ver'deck n (-[e]s; -e) top; **ver'decken** v/t (no -ge-, h) cover (up) (a. fig)

ver'denken v/t (irr, **denken**, no -ge-, h) **ich kann es ihm nicht ~(, dass er …)** I can't blame him (for doing)

verderben [fɛɐˈdɛrbən] (irr, no -ge-) **1.** v/i (sein) spoil (a. fig); GASTR go bad **2.** v/t (h) spoil (a. fig), ruin; **sich den Magen ~** upset one's stomach

Ver'derben n (-s; no pl) ruin

verderblich [fɛɐˈdɛrplɪç] adj perishable; **leicht ~e Lebensmittel** perishables

ver'dichten v/t (no -ge-, h) compress, condense

ver'dienen v/t (no -ge-, h) earn, make; fig deserve

Ver'dienst[1] m (-[e]s; -e) earnings; salary; wages; gain, profit

Ver'dienst[2] n (-[e]s; -e) merit; **es ist sein ~, dass** it is thanks to him that

ver'dient adj (well-)deserved

ver'doppeln v/t and v/refl (no -ge-, h) double

verdorben [fɛɐˈdɔrbən] **1.** pp of **verderben 2.** adj GASTR spoilt, bad (both a. fig); MED upset

ver'dorren [fɛɐˈdɔrən] v/i (no -ge-, sein) wither, dry up; ~'**drängen** v/t (no -ge-, h) supplant, supersede; replace; PHYS displace; PSYCH repress, suppress; ~'**drehen** v/t (no -ge-, h) twist, fig a. distort; **die Augen ~** roll one's eyes; **j-m den Kopf ~** turn s.o.'s head; ~'**dreht** F fig adj mixed up; ~'**dreifachen** v/t and v/refl (no -ge-, h) treble, triple

verdrießen [fɛɐˈdriːsən] v/t (irr, no -ge-, h) annoy; **verdrießlich** [fɛɐˈdriːslɪç] adj glum, morose, sullen; **verdross** [fɛɐˈdrɔs] pret of **verdrießen**; **verdrossen** [fɛɐˈdrɔsən] **1.** pp of **verdrießen 2.** adj grumpy, sullen; **Verdruss** [fɛɐ-'drʊs] m (-es; -e) annoyance

ver'dummen (no -ge-) **1.** v/t (h) make stupid, stultify **2.** v/i (sein) become stultified

ver'dunkeln v/t and v/refl (no -ge-, h) darken; black out; fig obscure

Ver'dunk(e)lung f (-; -en) darkening; blackout; JUR collusion

ver'dünnen v/t (no -ge-, h) dilute

ver'dunsten v/i (no -ge-, sein) evaporate

ver'dursten v/i (no -ge-, sein) die of thirst

verdutzt [fɛɐˈdʊtst] adj puzzled

ver'edeln v/t (no -ge-, h) BOT graft; TECH process, refine; **Ver'ed(e)lung** f (-; -en) BOT grafting; TECH processing, refinement

ver'ehren v/t (no -ge-, h) admire; adore, worship (both a. fig), esp REL a. revere, venerate; **Ver'ehrer(in)** (-s; -/-; -nen) admirer, esp film etc: a. fan; **Ver-'ehrung** f (-; no pl) admiration; adoration, worship; esp REL reverence, veneration

vereidigen [fɛɐˈʔaidɪɡən] v/t (no -ge-, h) swear s.o. in; JUR put s.o. under an oath

Verein [fɛɐˈʔain] m (-[e]s; -e) club (a. SPORT); society, association

vereinbar [fɛɐˈʔainbaːɐ] adj compatible (**mit** with); **vereinbaren** [fɛɐ-'ʔainbaːrən] v/t (no -ge-, h) agree (up)on, arrange; **Ver'einbarung** f (-; -en) agreement, arrangement

ver'einen → vereinigen

ver'einfachen v/t (no -ge-, h) simplify

Ver'einfachung f (-; -en) simplification

ver'einheitlichen v/t (no -ge-, h) standardize

ver'einigen v/t and v/refl (no -ge-, h) unite (**zu** into); combine, join

Ver'einigung f (-; -en) union; combination; alliance

ver'einsamen v/i (no -ge-, sein) become lonely or isolated

vereinzelt [fɛɐˈʔaintsəlt] adj occasional, odd; ~ **Regen** scattered showers

ver'eiteln v/t (no -ge-, h) prevent; frustrate; ~'enden v/i (no -ge-, sein) esp zo die, perish; ~'engen v/t and v/refl (no -ge-, h) narrow

ver'erben v/t (no -ge-, h) **j-m et.** ~ leave (BIOL transmit) s.th. to s.o.; **sich ~ (auf** acc) be passed on or down (to) (a. BIOL and fig); Ver'erbung f (-; no pl) BIOL heredity; Ver'erbungslehre f BIOL genetics

verewigen [fɛɐˈʔeːvɪɡən] v/t (no -ge-, h) immortalize

ver'fahren (irr, fahren, no -ge-) 1. v/i (sein) proceed; ~ **mit** deal with 2. v/refl (h) MOT get lost

Ver'fahren n (-s; -) procedure, method, esp TECH a. technique, way; JUR (legal) proceedings (**gegen** against)

Ver'fall m (-[e]s; no pl) decay (a. fig); dilapidation; fig decline; ECON et expiry; ver'fallen (irr, fallen, no -ge-, sein) 1. v/i decay (a. fig), dilapidate; esp fig decline; ECON expire; MED waste away; become addicted to; (**wieder**) ~ **in** (acc) fall (back) into; ~ **auf** (acc) hit (up)on 2. adj decayed; dilapidated; Ver'fallsdatum n expiry date; GASTR pull date, Br best-before (or best-by) date; PHARM sell-by date

ver'fälschen v/t (no -ge-, h) falsify; distort; GASTR adulterate

verfänglich [fɛɐˈfɛŋlɪç] adj delicate, tricky; embarrassing, compromising

ver'färben v/refl (no -ge-, h) discolo(u)r

ver'fassen v/t (no -ge-, h) write

Verfasser [fɛɐˈfasɐ] m (-s; -), Ver'fasserin f (-; -nen) author

Ver'fassung f (-; -en) state (of health or of mind), condition; POL constitution

ver'fassungs|mäßig adj POL constitutional; ~widrig adj unconstitutional

ver'faulen v/i (no -ge-, sein) rot, decay

ver'fechten v/t (irr, fechten, no -ge-, h), Ver'fechter(in) (-s; -/-; -nen) advocate

ver'fehlen v/t (no -ge-, h) miss (**sich** each other); Ver'fehlung f (-; -en) offense, Br offence

verfeinden [fɛɐˈfaindən] v/refl (no -ge-, h) become enemies; ver'feindet adj hostile; ~ **sein** be enemies

verfeinern [fɛɐˈfainən] v/t and v/refl (no -ge-, h) refine

ver'filmen v/t (no -ge-, h) film; Ver'filmung f (-; -en) filming; film version

ver'flechten v/t (irr, flechten, no -ge-, h) intertwine (a. **sich ~**)

ver'fluchen v/t (no -ge-, h) curse

ver'flucht → **verdammt**

ver'folgen v/t (no -ge-, h) pursue (a. fig); chase, hunt (both a. fig); POL, REL persecute; follow (track etc); fear etc: haunt s.o.; **j-n gerichtlich ~** prosecute s.o.; Verfolger [fɛɐˈfɔlɡɐ] m (-s; -) pursuer; persecutor; Ver'folgung f (-; -en) pursuit (a. cycling); chase; hunt; persecution; **gerichtliche ~** prosecution

ver'frachten v/t (no -ge-, h) freight; ship; F bundle s.o., s.th. (**in** acc) into

verfremden [fɛɐˈfrɛmdən] v/t (no -ge-, h) esp art: alienate

ver'früht adj premature

verfügbar [fɛɐˈfyːkbaːɐ] adj available; ver'fügen (no -ge-, h) 1. v/t decree, order 2. v/i: ~ **über** (acc) have at one's disposal; Ver'fügung f (-; -en) decree, order; (no pl) disposal; **j-m zur ~ stehen (stellen)** be (place) at s.o.'s disposal

ver'führen v/t (no -ge-, h) seduce (**et. zu tun** into doing s.th.); Ver'führer m (-s; -) seducer; Ver'führerin f (-; -nen) seductress; ver'führerisch adj seductive; tempting; Ver'führung f (-; -en) seduction

vergangen [fɛɐˈɡaŋən] adj gone, past; **im ~en Jahr** last year; Ver'gangenheit f (-; no pl) past; LING past tense

vergänglich [fɛɐˈɡɛŋlɪç] adj transitory, transient

vergasen [fɛɐˈɡaːzən] v/t (no -ge-, h) gas; CHEM gasify; Vergaser [fɛɐˈɡaːzɐ] m (-s; -) MOT carburet(t)or

vergaß [fɛɐˈɡaːs] pret of **vergessen**

ver'geben v/t (irr, geben, no -ge-, h) give away (a. fig); award (prize etc); forgive; ver'gebens adv in vain; vergeblich [fɛɐˈɡeːplɪç] 1. adj futile 2. adv in vain; Ver'gebung f (-; -en) forgiveness, pardon

ver'gehen (*irr*, **gehen**, *no* -ge-, *sein*) **1.** *v/i time etc*: go by, pass; *pain, effect etc*: wear off; **~ vor** (*dat*) be dying with; **wie die Zeit vergeht!** how time flies! **2.** *v/refl* **sich ~ an** (*dat*) violate; rape

Vergehen *n* (-*s*; -) JUR offen|se, *Br* -ce

ver'gelten *v/t* (*irr*, **gelten**, *no* -ge-, *h*) repay; reward; **Ver'geltung** *f* (-; -*en*) retaliation (*a.* MIL)

vergessen [fɛɐˈɡɛsən] **1.** *v/t* (*irr*, *no* -ge-, *h*) forget; leave **2.** *pp of* **vergessen** 1; **Ver'gessenheit** *f*: **in ~ geraten** fall into oblivion; **vergesslich** [fɛɐˈɡɛslɪç] *adj* forgetful

vergeuden [fɛɐˈɡɔʏdən] *v/t* (*no* -ge-, *h*), **Ver'geudung** *f* (-; -*en*) waste

vergewaltigen [fɛɐɡəˈvaltɪɡən] *v/t* (*no* -ge-, *h*) rape, violate (*a.* fig)

Verge'waltigung *f* (-; -*en*) rape, violation (*a.* fig)

vergewissern [fɛɐɡəˈvɪsɐn] *v/refl* (*no* -ge-, *h*) make sure (**e-r Sache** of s.th.; **ob** whether; **dass** that)

ver'gießen *v/t* (*irr*, **gießen**, *no* -ge-, *h*) shed (*blood, tears*); spill

ver'giften *v/t* (*no* -ge-, *h*) poison (*a.* fig); contaminate; **Ver'giftung** *f* (-; -*en*) poisoning (*a.* fig); contamination

ver'gittert *adj* barred (*window etc*)

Ver'gleich *m* (-*[e]s*; -*e*) comparison; JUR compromise; **ver'gleichbar** *adj* comparable (**mit** to, with); **ver'gleichen** *v/t* (*irr*, **gleichen**, *no* -ge-, *h*) compare (**mit** with *or* to); **... ist nicht zu ~ mit** ... cannot be compared to; ... cannot compare with; **vergleichen mit** compared to *or* with; **ver'gleichsweise** *adv* comparatively, relatively

ver'glühen *v/i* (*no* -ge-, *sein*) burn out (*or* up)

vergnügen [fɛɐˈɡnyːɡən] *v/refl* (*no* -ge-, *h*) enjoy o.s. (**mit et.** doing s.th.)

Ver'gnügen *n* (-*s*; -) pleasure, enjoyment, fun; **mit ~** with pleasure; **viel ~!** have fun!, have a good time!

vergnügt [fɛɐˈɡnyːkt] *adj* cheerful

Ver'gnügung *f* (-; -*en*) pleasure, amusement, entertainment

Ver'gnügungspark *m* amusement park

ver'gnügungssüchtig *adj* pleasure-seeking

Ver'gnügungsviertel *n* nightlife district

ver|'golden *v/t* (*no* -ge-, *h*) gild; **~göt-**

tern [fɛɐˈɡœtən] *v/t* (*no* -ge-, *h*) idolize, adore; **~'graben** *v/t* (*irr*, **graben**, *no* -ge-, *h*) bury (*a.* fig)

ver'greifen *v/refl* (*irr*, **greifen**, *no* -ge-, *h*) **sich ~ an** (*dat*) lay hands on

vergriffen [fɛɐˈɡrɪfən] *adj* out of print

vergrößern [fɛɐˈɡrøːsɐn] *v/t* (*no* -ge-, *h*) enlarge (*a.* PHOT); increase; OPT magnify; **sich ~** increase, grow, expand; **Ver'größerung** *f* (-; -*en*) increase; PHOT enlargement; OPT magnification; **Ver'größerungsglas** *n* OPT magnifying glass

Vergünstigung [fɛɐˈɡʏnstɪɡʊn] *f* (-; -*en*) privilege

vergüten [fɛɐˈɡyːtən] *v/t* (*no* -ge-, *h*) reimburse, pay (for); **Ver'gütung** *f* (-; -*en*) reimbursement

ver'haften *v/t* (*no* -ge-, *h*), **Ver'haftung** *f* (-; -*en*) arrest

ver'halten[1] *v/refl* (*irr*, **halten**, *no* -ge-, *h*) behave, conduct o.s., act; **sich ruhig ~** keep quiet

ver'halten[2] *adj* restrained; subdued

Ver'halten *n* (-*s*; *no pl*) behavio(u)r, conduct; **Ver'haltensforschung** *f* behavio(u)ral science; **ver'haltensgestört** *adj* disturbed, maladjusted

Verhältnis [fɛɐˈhɛltnɪs] *n* (-*ses*; -*se*) relationship, relations; attitude; proportion, relation, *esp* MATH ratio; F affair; *pl* circumstances, conditions; **über j-s ~se** beyond s.o.'s means; **ver'hältnismäßig** *adv* comparatively, relatively

Ver'hältniswort *n* (-*[e]s*; -*wörter*) LING preposition

ver'handeln *no* (-ge-, *h*) **1.** *v/i* negotiate **2.** *v/t* JUR hear; **Ver'handlung** *f* (-; -*en*) negotiation, talk; JUR hearing; trial; **Ver'handlungsbasis** *f* ECON asking price

ver'hängen *v/t* (*no* -ge-, *h*) cover (**mit** with); impose (**über** *acc* on)

Verhängnis [fɛɐˈhɛnnɪs] *n* (-*ses*; -*se*) fate; disaster; **ver'hängnisvoll** *adj* fatal, disastrous

verharmlosen [fɛɐˈharmloːzən] *v/t* (*no* -ge-, *h*) play s.th. down

verhärmt [fɛɐˈhɛrmt] *adj* careworn

ver'hasst *adj* hated; hateful

ver'hätscheln *v/t* (*no* -ge-, *h*) coddle, pamper, spoil

V

ver'hauen F *v/t* (*no -ge-, h*) spank

verheerend [fɛɐˈheːrənt] *adj* disastrous

ver'heilen *v/i* (*no -ge-, sein*) heal (up)

verheimlichen [fɛɐˈhaimlɪçən] *v/t* (*no -ge-, h*) hide, conceal

ver'heiraten *v/t* (*no -ge-, h*) marry (*s.o. off*) (*mit* to); **sich** ~ get married

ver'heiratet *adj* married (*mit* to)

ver'heißungsvoll *adj* promising

ver'helfen *v/i* (*irr, helfen, no -ge-, h*) **j-m zu et.** ~ help s.o. to get s.th.

ver'herrlichen *v/t* (*no -ge-, h*) glorify, *contp a.* idolize; Ver'herrlichung *f* (*-; -en*) glorification

ver'hexen *v/t* (*no -ge-, h*) bewitch

ver'hindern *v/t* (*no -ge-, h*) prevent (*dass j. et. tut* s.o. from doing s.th.); ver'hindert *adj* unable to come; F ein ~**er** ... a would-be ...; Ver-'hinderung *f* (*-; -en*) prevention

ver'höhnen *v/t* (*no -ge-, h*) deride, mock (at), jeer (at)

Verhör [fɛɐˈhøːɐ] *n* (*-[e]s; -e*) JUR interrogation; ver'hören (*no -ge-, h*) **1.** *v/t* interrogate, question **2.** *v/refl* get it wrong

ver'hüllen *v/t* (*no -ge-, h*) cover, veil

ver'hungern *v/i* (*no -ge-, sein*) die of hunger, starve (to death)

Ver'hungern *n* (*-s; no pl*) starvation

ver'hüten *v/t* (*no -ge-, h*) prevent

Ver'hütung *f* (*-; -en*) prevention

Ver'hütungsmittel *n* MED contraceptive

ver'irren *v/refl* (*no -ge-, h*) get lost, lose one's way, go astray (*a. fig*)

Ver'irrung *f* (*-; -en*) aberration

ver'jagen *v/t* (*no -ge-, h*) chase *or* drive away

verjähren [fɛɐˈjɛːrən] *v/i* (*no -ge-, sein*) JUR come under the statute of limitations; ver'jährt *adj* JUR statute-barred

verjüngen [fɛɐˈjʏŋən] *v/t* (*no -ge-, h*) make s.o. (look) younger, rejuvenate; **sich** ~ ARCH, TECH taper (off)

ver'kabeln *v/t* (*no -ge-, h*) ELECTR cable

Ver'kauf *m* sale; ver'kaufen *v/t* (*no -ge-, h*) sell; **zu** ~ for sale; **sich gut** ~ sell well; Ver'käufer *m* (*-s; -*) (sales)clerk, salesman, *Br* shop assistant; ECON seller; Ver'käuferin *f* (*-; -nen*) (sales)clerk, saleslady, *Br* shop assistant; ver-'käuflich *adj* for sale; **schwer** ~ hard to sell

Verkehr [fɛɐˈkeːɐ] *m* (*-s; no pl*) traffic;

transportation, *Br* transport; *fig* contact, dealings; intercourse; circulation; **starker** (**schwacher**) ~ heavy (light) traffic; ver'kehren (*no -ge-, h*) **1.** *v/i* bus *etc*: run; ~ **in** (*dat*) frequent; ~ **mit** associate *or* mix with; have intercourse with **2.** *v/t* turn (*in acc* into); **ins Gegenteil** ~ reverse

Ver'kehrs|ader *f* arterial road; ~ampel *f* traffic light(s); ~behinderung *f* hold-up, delay; *zur* ~ Obstruction of traffic; ~delikt *n* traffic offense (*Br* offence); ~flugzeug *n* airliner; ~funk *m* traffic bulletin; ~insel *f* traffic island; ~meldung *f* traffic announcement, flash; ~mi,nister *m* minister of transportation; ~minis,terium *n* ministry of transportation; ~mittel *n* means of transportation; **öffentliche** ~ public transportation; ~opfer *n* road casualty; ~poli,zei *f* traffic police; ~rowdy *m* F road hog

ver'kehrssicher *adj* MOT roadworthy

Ver'kehrs|sicherheit *f* MOT road safety; roadworthiness; ~stau *m* traffic jam; ~sünder(in) F traffic offender; ~teilnehmer(in) road user; ~unfall *m* traffic accident; (car) crash; ~unterricht *m* traffic instruction; ~zeichen *n* traffic sign

ver'kehrt *adj and adv* wrong; upside down; inside out

ver'kennen *v/t* (*irr, kennen, no -ge-, h*) mistake, misjudge; ~'klagen *v/t* (*no -ge-, h*) JUR sue (*auf acc, wegen* for); ~'klappen *v/t* (*no -ge-, h*) dump (into the sea); ~'kleben *v/t* (*no -ge-, h*) glue (together)

ver'kleiden *v/t* (*no -ge-, h*) disguise (*als* as), dress *s.o.* up (as); TECH cover, (en)-case; panel; **sich** ~ disguise o.s., dress (o.s.) up; Ver'kleidung *f* (*-; -en*) disguise; TECH cover, encasement; panel-(l)ing; MOT fairing

verkleinern [fɛɐˈklainɐn] *v/t* (*no -ge-, h*) make smaller, reduce, diminish; Ver-'kleinerung [fɛɐˈklainəruŋ] *f* (*-; -en*) reduction

ver'klingen *v/i* (*irr, klingen, no -ge-, sein*) die away

ver'knallt F *adj*: ~ **sein in** (*acc*) be madly in love with, have a crush on

ver'knoten *v/t* (*no -ge-, h*) knot; ~-'knüpfen *v/t* (*no -ge-, h*) knot together;

fig connect, combine; ~'**kohlen** *v/i* (*no -ge-, sein*) char; ~'**kommen 1.** *v/i* (*irr, kommen, no -ge-, sein*) become run-down *or* dilapidated; go to seed; GASTR go bad **2.** *adj* run-down, dilapidated; neglected; depraved, rotten (to the core); ~'**korken** *v/t* (*no -ge-, h*) cork (up); ~'**körpern** *v/t* (*no -ge-, h*) personify; embody; *esp* THEA impersonate; ~'**kriechen** *v/refl* (*irr, kriechen, no -ge-, h*) hide; ~'**krümmt** *adj* crooked, curved (*a.* MED); ~'**krüppelt** *adj* crippled; ~'**kümmern** *v/i* (*no -ge-, sein*) BIOL become stunted; ~'**kümmert** *adj* BIOL stunted

ver'künden [fɛɐ'kʏndən] *v/t* (*no -ge-, h*) announce; proclaim; JUR pronounce; REL preach; **Ver'kündung** *f* (*-; -en*) announcement; proclamation; JUR pronouncement; REL preaching

ver'kürzen *v/t* (*no -ge-, h*) shorten; reduce; ~'**laden** *v/t* (*irr, laden, no -ge-, h*) load (*auf acc* onto; *in acc* into)

Verlag [fɛɐ'la:k] *m* (*-[e]s; -e* [fɛɐ'la:gə]) publishing house *or* company, publisher(s)

ver'lagern *v/t and v/refl* (*no -ge-, h*) shift (*auf acc* to)

ver'langen *v/t* (*no -ge-, h*) ask for; demand; claim; charge; take, call for; **Ver'langen** *n* (*-s; -*) desire (*nach* for); longing (for), yearning (for); *auf ~* by request; ECON on demand

ver'längern [fɛɐ'lɛŋən] *v/t* (*no -ge-, h*) lengthen; make longer; prolong, extend (*a.* ECON); **Verlängerung** [fɛɐ'lɛŋərʊŋ] *f* (*-; -en*) lengthening; prolongation, extension; SPORT overtime, *Br* extra time

ver'langsamen *v/t and v/refl* (*no -ge-, h*) slacken; slow down (*both a. fig*)

ver'lassen (*irr, lassen, no -ge-, h*) **1.** *v/t* leave; abandon, desert **2.** *v/refl: sich ~ auf* (*acc*) rely *or* depend on

ver'lässlich [fɛɐ'lɛslɪç] *adj* reliable, dependable

Ver'lauf *m* course; **ver'laufen** (*irr, laufen, no -ge-*) **1.** *v/i* (*sein*) run; go; end (up) **2.** *v/refl* (*h*) get lost, lose one's way

ver'leben *v/t* (*no -ge-, h*) spend; have

ver'legen¹ *v/t* (*no -ge-, h*) move; mislay; TECH lay; put off, postpone; publish

ver'legen² *adj* embarrassed

Ver'legenheit *f* (*-; -en*) (*no pl*) embar-

rassment; embarrassing situation

Verleger [fɛɐ'le:gɐ] *m* (*-s; -*), **Ver'legerin** *f* (*-; -nen*) publisher

Verleih [fɛɐ'lai] *m* (*-[e]s; -e*) (*no pl*) hire, rental; *film*: distributor(s)

ver'leihen *v/t* (*irr, leihen, no -ge-, h*) lend, loan; MOT *etc* rent (*Br* hire) out; award (*prize etc*); grant (*privilege etc*); **Ver'leihung** *f* (*-; -en*) award(ing), presentation; grant(ing)

ver'leiten *v/t* (*no -ge-, h*) *j-n zu et. ~* make s.o. do s.th., lead s.o. to do s.th.

ver'lernen *v/t* (*no -ge-, h*) forget

ver'lesen (*irr, lesen, no -ge-, h*) **1.** *v/t* read (*or* call) out **2.** *v/refl* make a slip (in reading); misread *s.th.*

ver'letzen [fɛɐ'lɛtsən] *v/t* (*no -ge-, h*) hurt, injure, *fig a.* offend; *sich ~* hurt o.s., get hurt; ~**d** *adj* offensive

Ver'letzte *m, f* (*-n; -n*) injured person; *pl the* injured; **Ver'letzung** *f* (*-; -en*) injury, *esp pl a.* hurt; JUR violation

ver'leugnen *v/t* (*no -ge-, h*) deny; renounce

ver'leumden [fɛɐ'lɔʏmdən] *v/t* (*no -ge-, h*) defame; JUR slander, libel; **ver'leumderisch** *adj* JUR slanderous, libel(l)ous; **Ver'leumdung** *f* (*-; -en*) JUR slander; libel

ver'lieben *v/refl* (*no -ge-, h*) fall in love (*in acc* with); **verliebt** [fɛɐ'li:pt] *adj* in love (*in acc* with); amorous (*look etc*); **Ver'liebte** *m, f* (*-n; -n*) lover

ver'lieren [fɛɐ'li:rən] *v/t and v/i* (*irr, no -ge-, h*) lose; **Ver'lierer(in)** (*-s; -/-; -nen*) loser

ver'loben *v/refl* (*no -ge-, h*) get engaged (*mit* to); **Ver'lobte** [fɛɐ'lo:ptə] **1.** *m* (*-n; -n*) fiancé **2.** *f* (*-n; -n*) fiancée; **Ver'lobung** *f* (*-; -en*) engagement

ver'locken *v/t* (*no -ge-, h*) tempt; ~**d** *adj* tempting

Ver'lockung *f* (*-; -en*) temptation

ver'logen [fɛɐ'lo:gən] *adj* untruthful, lying

verlor [fɛɐ'lo:ɐ] *pret of* **verlieren**

verloren [fɛɐ'lo:rən] **1.** *pp of* **verlieren 2.** *adj* lost; wasted; *~ gehen* be *or* get lost; **ver'lorengehen** *v/i* (*irr, gehen, sep, -ge-, sein*) → **verloren**

ver'losen *v/t* (*no -ge-, h*) raffle (off); **Ver'losung** *f* (*-; -en*) raffle

Verlust [fɛɐ'lʊst] *m* (*-[e]s; -e*) loss (*a. fig*); *pl esp* MIL casualties

V

ver'machen v/t (no -ge-, h) leave, will

Vermächtnis [fɛɐ'mɛçtnɪs] n (-ses; -se) legacy (a. fig)

ver'markten v/t (no -ge-, h) market, merchandize; **Ver'marktung** f (-; -en) marketing, merchandizing

ver'mehren v/t and v/refl increase (**um** by), multiply (by) (a. BIOL); BIOL reproduce, esp ZO a. breed; **Ver'mehrung** f (-; -en) increase; BIOL reproduction

vermeidbar [fɛɐ'maitbaːɐ] adj avoidable; **ver'meiden** v/t (irr, **meiden**, no -ge-, h) avoid

vermeintlich [fɛɐ'maintlɪç] adj supposed, alleged

ver'mengen v/t (no -ge-, h) mix, mingle, blend

Vermerk [fɛɐ'mɛrk] m (-[e]s; -e) note

ver'merken v/t (no -ge-, h) make a note of

ver'messen[1] v/t (irr, **messen**, no -ge-, h) measure; survey

ver'messen[2] adj presumptuous

Ver'messung f (-; -en) measuring; survey(ing)

ver'mieten v/t (no -ge-, h) let, rent, lease (out); rent (Br hire) out (cars etc); **zu ~** for rent, Br to let, for hire

Ver'mieter n (-s; -) landlord

Ver'mieterin f (-; -nen) landlady

Ver'mietung f (-; -en) letting, renting

ver'mischen v/t and v/refl (no -ge-, h) mix, mingle, blend (**mit** with); **ver'mischt** adj mixed; miscellaneous

vermissen [fɛɐ'mɪsən] v/t (no -ge-, h) miss; **ver'misst** adj missing; **die Vermissten** pl the missing

ver'mitteln (no -ge-, h) **1.** v/t arrange; give, convey (impression etc); **j-m et. ~** get or find s.o. s.th. **2.** v/i mediate (**zwischen** between); **Ver'mittler** m (-s; -) mediator, go-between; ECON agent, broker; **Ver'mittlung** f (-; -en) mediation; arrangement; agency, office; (telephone) exchange; operator

ver'modern v/i (no -ge-, sein) rot, mo(u)lder

Ver'mögen n (-s; -) fortune, property, possessions; ECON assets

ver'mögend adj well-to-do, well-off

vermummen [fɛɐ'mʊmən] v/refl (no -ge-, h) mask o.s., disguise o.s.

vermuten [fɛɐ'muːtən] v/t (no -ge-, h) suppose, expect, think, guess; ver-

'**mutlich** adv probably; **Ver'mutung** f (-; -en) supposition; speculation

vernachlässigen [fɛɐ'naːxlɛsɪɡən] v/t (no -ge-, h), **Ver'nachlässigung** f (-; -en) neglect

ver'narben v/i (no -ge-, sein) scar over; fig heal

ver'narrt adj: **~ in** (acc) mad or crazy about

ver'nehmen v/t (irr, **nehmen**, no -ge-, h) JUR question, interrogate

ver'nehmlich adj clear, distinct

Ver'nehmung f (-; -en) JUR interrogation, examination

ver'neigen v/refl (no -ge-, h), **Ver'neigung** f (-; -en) bow (**vor** dat to) (a. fig)

ver'neinen (no -ge-, h) **1.** v/t deny **2.** v/i say no, answer in the negative; **~d** adj negative

Ver'neinung f (-; -en) denial, negative (a. LING)

ver'nichten v/t (no -ge-, h) destroy; **~d** adj devastating (a. fig); crushing

Ver'nichtung f (-; -en) destruction; extermination

Vernunft [fɛɐ'nʊnft] f (-; no pl) reason; **~ annehmen** listen to reason; **j-n zur ~ bringen** bring s.o. to reason

vernünftig [fɛɐ'nʏnftɪç] adj sensible, reasonable (a. ECON); F decent

ver'öden v/i (no -ge-, sein) become deserted

ver'öffentlichen v/t (no -ge-, h) publish; **Ver'öffentlichung** f (-; -en) publication

ver'ordnen v/t (no -ge-, h) order, MED a. prescribe (**gegen** for); **Ver'ordnung** f (-; -en) order; MED prescription

ver'pachten v/t (no -ge-, h) lease

Ver'pächter m lessor

ver'packen v/t (no -ge-, h) pack (up); TECH package; wrap up

Ver'packung f (-; -en) pack(ag)ing; wrapping; **Ver'packungsmüll** m superfluous packaging

ver'passen v/t (no -ge-, h) miss; **~'patzen** F v/t (no -ge-, h) mess up, spoil; **~pesten** [fɛɐ'pɛstən] v/t (no -ge-, h) pollute, foul, contaminate; stink up (Br out); **~'petzen** F v/t (no -ge-, h) **j-n ~** tell on s.o. (**bei** to); **~'pfänden** v/t (no -ge-, h) pawn; fig pledge

ver'pflanzen v/t (no -ge-, h), **Ver'pflanzung** f (-; -en) transplant (a. MED)

ver'pflegen v/t (no -ge-, h) feed

Ver'pflegung f (-; -en) food

ver'pflichten v/t (no -ge-, h) oblige; engage; **sich ~, et. zu tun** undertake (ECON agree) to do s.th.; ver'pflichtet adj: **~ sein (sich ~ fühlen) et. zu tun** be (feel) obliged to do s.th.; Ver'pflichtung f (-; -en) obligation; duty; ECON, JUR liability; engagement, commitment

ver'pfuschen F v/t (no -ge-, h) bungle, botch

ver'plappern v/refl (no -ge-, h) blab

verpönt [fɛɛ'pøːnt] adj taboo

ver'prügeln F v/t (no -ge-, h) beat s.o. up

Ver'putz m (-es; no pl), ver'putzen v/t (no -ge-, h) ARCH plaster

verquollen [fɛɛ'kvɔlən] adj face etc: puffy, swollen; wood: warped

Verrat [fɛɛ'raːt] m (-[e]s; no pl) betrayal (**an** dat of); treachery (to); JUR treason (to); ver'raten v/t (irr, **raten**, no -ge-, h) betray, give away (both a. fig); **sich ~** betray o.s., give o.s. away

Verräter [fɛɛ'rɛːtɐ] m (-s; -), Ver'räterin f (-; -nen) traitor

verräterisch [fɛɛ'rɛːtərɪʃ] adj treacherous; fig telltale

ver'rechnen (no -ge-, h) **1.** v/t offset (**mit** against); **2.** v/refl miscalculate, make a mistake (a. fig); **sich um zwei Euro ~** be two euros out

Ver'rechnungsscheck m ECON voucher check, Br crossed cheque

ver'regnet adj rainy

ver'reisen v/i (no -ge-, sein) go away (**geschäftlich** on business); ver'reist adj away (**geschäftlich** on business)

verrenken [fɛɛ'rɛŋkən] v/t (no -ge-, h) MED dislocate, luxate; **sich et. ~** MED dislocate s.th.; **sich den Hals ~** crane one's neck; Ver'renkung f (-; -en) MED dislocation, luxation

ver'richten v/t (no -ge-, h) do, perform, carry out

ver'riegeln v/t (no -ge-, h) bolt, bar

verringern [fɛɛ'rɪŋɐn] v/t (no -ge-, h) decrease, lessen (both a. **sich ~**), reduce, cut down; Ver'ringerung f (-; -en) reduction, decrease

ver'rosten v/i (no -ge-, sein) rust, get rusty (a. fig)

verrotten [fɛɛ'rɔtən] v/i (no -ge-, sein) rot; ver'rottet adj rotten

ver'rücken v/t (no -ge-, h) move, shift

ver'rückt adj mad, crazy (both a. fig **nach** about); **wie ~** like mad; **~ werden** go mad, go crazy; **j-n ~ machen** drive s.o. mad; Ver'rückte m, f (-n; -n) madman (madwoman), lunatic, maniac (all a. F); Ver'rücktheit f (-; -en) (no pl) madness, craziness; crazy thing

Ver'ruf m: **in ~ bringen** bring discredit (up)on; **in ~ kommen** get into discredit

ver'rufen adj disreputable, notorious

ver'rutschen v/i (no -ge-, sein) slip, get out of place

Vers [fɛrs] m (-es; -e ['fɛrzə]) verse; line

ver'sagen (no -ge-, h) **1.** v/i fail (a. MED), MOT etc a. break down; gun etc: misfire **2.** v/t deny, refuse; Ver'sagen n (-s; no pl) failure; Ver'sager m (-s; -) failure

ver'salzen v/t (no -ge-, h) oversalt

ver'sammeln v/t (no -ge-, h) gather, assemble; **sich ~** a. meet; Ver'sammlung f (-; -en) assembly, meeting

Versand [fɛɛ'zant] m (-[e]s; no pl) dispatch, shipment; **~... in** cpds ...haus, ...katalog etc: mail-order ...

ver'säumen v/t (no -ge-, h) miss; **~ et. zu tun** fail to do s.th.; Ver'säumnis [fɛɛ'zɔʏmnɪs] n (-ses; -se) omission

ver'schaffen v/t (no -ge-, h) get, find; **sich ~** a. obtain; ver'schämt adj bashful; ver'schanzen v/refl (no -ge-, h) entrench o.s. (fig **hinter** behind); ver'schärfen v/t (no -ge-, h) aggravate; tighten up; increase; **sich ~** get worse; ver'schenken v/t (no -ge-, h) give away (a. fig); ver'scherzen v/t (no -ge-, h) forfeit; ver'scheuchen v/t (no -ge-, h) chase away (a. fig); ver'schicken v/t (no -ge-, h) send off, esp ECON a. dispatch

ver'schieben v/t (irr, **schieben**, no -ge-, h) move, shift (a. **sich ~**); postpone, put off; Ver'schiebung f (-; -en) shift(ing); postponement

verschieden [fɛɛ'fiːdən] adj different (**von** from); **~e ... pl** various ..., several...; **~artig** adj different; various

ver'schiedentlich adv repeatedly

Ver'schiedenheit f (-; -en) difference

ver'schiffen v/t (no -ge-, h) ship

Ver'schiffung f (-; -en) shipment

ver'schimmeln v/i (no -ge-, sein) get mo(u)ldy; ver'schlafen (irr, **schlafen**, no -ge-, h) **1.** v/i oversleep **2.** v/t sleep through **3.** adj sleepy (a. fig)

Ver'schlag *m* shed

ver'schlagen¹ *v/t (irr, schlagen, no -ge-, h)* take s.o.'s breath away; *j-m die Sprache ~* leave s.o. speechless; *es hat ihn nach X ~* he ended up in X

ver'schlagen² *adj* sly, cunning

verschlechtern [fɛɐˈʃlɛçtɐn] *v/t and v/refl (no -ge-, h)* make (*refl* get) worse, worsen, deteriorate

Ver'schlechterung *f (-; -en)* deterioration; change for the worse

ver'schleiern *v/t (no -ge-, h)* veil (*a. fig*)

Verschleiß [fɛɐˈʃlais] *m (-es; no pl)* wear (and tear); ver'schleißen *v/t (irr, no -ge-, h)* wear out

ver'schleppen *v/t (no -ge-, h)* carry off; POL displace; draw out, delay; MED neglect; ~'schleudern *v/t (no -ge-, h)* waste; ECON sell dirt cheap; ~'schließen *v/t (irr, schließen, no -ge-, h)* close (*a. fig* one's eyes); lock (up)

ver'schlingen *v/t (irr, schlingen, no -ge-, h)* devour (*a. fig*); gulp (down)

verschliss [fɛɐˈʃlis] *pret of* verschleißen; verschlissen [fɛɐˈʃlisən] *pp of* verschleißen

verschlossen [fɛɐˈʃlɔsən] *adj* closed; *fig* aloof, reserved; Ver'schlossenheit *f (-; no pl)* aloofness

ver'schlucken *v/t (no -ge-, h)* 1. *v/t* swallow (*fig* up); 2. *v/refl* choke; *ich habe mich verschluckt* it went down the wrong way

Ver'schluss *m* fastener; clasp; catch; lock; cover, lid; cap, top; PHOT shutter; *unter ~* under lock and key

ver'schlüsseln *v/t (no -ge-, h)* (en)code, (en)cipher

verschmähen [fɛɐˈʃmɛːən] *v/t (no -ge-, h)* disdain, scorn

ver'schmelzen *v/i (irr, schmelzen, no -ge-, sein) and v/t (h)* merge, fuse (*both a.* ECON, POL *etc*); melt; Ver'schmelzung *f (-; -en)* fusion (*a. fig*)

ver'schmerzen *v/t (no -ge-, h)* get over s.th.; ~'schmieren *v/t (no -ge-, h)* smear, smudge

verschmitzt [fɛɐˈʃmɪtst] *adj* mischievous

ver'schmutzen *(no -ge-)* 1. *v/t (h)* soil, dirty; pollute 2. *v/i (sein)* get dirty; get polluted; ~'schnaufen F *v/i and v/refl*

(*no -ge-, h*) stop for breath

ver'schneit *adj* snow-covered, snowy

Ver'schnitt *m* blend; waste

verschnupft [fɛɐˈʃnʊpft] *adj*: *~ sein* MED have a cold; F be in a huff

ver'schnüren *v/t (no -ge-, h)* tie up

verschollen [fɛɐˈʃɔlən] *adj* missing; JUR presumed dead

ver'schonen *v/t (no -ge-, h)* spare; *j-n mit et. ~* spare s.o. s.th.

verschönern [fɛɐˈʃøːnɐn] *v/t (no -ge-, h)* embellish; Verschönerung [fɛɐˈʃøːnərʊŋ] *f (-; -en)* embellishment

verschossen [fɛɐˈʃɔsən] *adj* faded; F *~ sein in (acc)* have a crush on

ver'schränken [fɛɐˈʃrɛŋkən] *v/t (no -ge-, h)* fold; cross (one's legs)

ver'schreiben *(irr, schreiben, no -ge-, h)* 1. *v/t* MED prescribe (*gegen* for); 2. *v/refl* make a slip of the pen

ver'schreibungspflichtig *adj* PHARM available on prescription only

verschroben [fɛɐˈʃroːbən] *adj* eccentric, odd

ver'schrotten *v/t (no -ge-, h)* scrap

ver'schüchtert *adj* intimidated

ver'schulden *v/t (no -ge-, h)* be responsible for, cause, be the cause of; *sich ~* get into debt; ver'schuldet *adj* in debt

ver'schütten *v/t (no -ge-, h)* spill; bury s.o. (alive)

verschwägert [fɛɐˈʃvɛːgɐt] *adj* related by marriage

ver'schweigen *v/t (irr, schweigen, no -ge-, h)* keep s.th. a secret, hide

verschwenden [fɛɐˈʃvɛndən] *v/t (no -ge-, h)* waste; Verschwender [fɛɐˈʃvɛndɐ] *m (-s; -)* spendthrift; ver'schwenderisch [fɛɐˈʃvɛndərɪʃ] *adj* wasteful, extravagant; lavish; Ver'schwendung *f (-; -en)* waste

verschwiegen [fɛɐˈʃviːgən] *adj* discreet; hidden; secret; Ver'schwiegenheit *f (-; no pl)* secrecy, discretion

ver'schwimmen *v/i (irr, schwimmen, no -ge-, sein)* become blurred

ver'schwinden *v/i (irr, schwinden, no -ge-, sein)* disappear, vanish; F *verschwinde!* beat it!; Ver'schwinden *n (-s; no pl)* disappearance

verschwommen [fɛɐˈʃvɔmən] *adj* blurred (*a.* PHOT), *fig a.* vague, hazy

ver'schwören *v/refl (irr, schwören, no*

-ge-, *h*) conspire, plot; **Verschwörer** [fɛɐˈʃvøːrə] *m* (*-s*; *-*) conspirator; **Verˈschwörung** *f* (*-*; *-en*) conspiracy, plot

verschwunden [fɛɐˈʃvʊndən] *adj* missing

verˈsehen (*irr*, **sehen**, *no -ge-*, *h*) **1.** *v/t* hold (*an office etc*); **~ mit** provide with **2.** *v/refl* make a mistake; **Verˈsehen** *n* (*-s*; *-*) mistake, error; **aus ~** → **versehentlich** [fɛɐˈzeːəntlɪç] *adv* by mistake, unintentionally

Versehrte [fɛɐˈzeːɐtə] *m*, *f* (*-n*; *-n*) disabled person

verˈsengen *v/t* (*no -ge-*, *h*) singe, scorch; **~ˈsenken** *v/t* (*no -ge-*, *h*) sink; **sich ~ in** (*acc*) become absorbed in

verˈsessen [fɛɐˈzɛsən] *adj*: **~ auf** (*acc*) keen on, mad *or* crazy about

verˈsetzen *v/t* (*no -ge-*, *h*) move, shift; transfer; PED promote, *Br* move s.o. up; give (*s.o. a kick etc*); pawn; AGR transplant; F *j-n* **~** stand s.o. up; *j-n* **in die Lage ~ zu** *inf* put s.o. in a position to *inf*, enable s.o. to *inf*; **sich in j-s Lage ~** put o.s. in s.o.'s place; **Verˈsetzung** *f* (*-*; *-en*) transfer; PED promotion

verˈseuchen *v/t* (*no -ge-*, *h*) contaminate; **Verˈseuchung** *f* (*-*; *-en*) contamination

verˈsichern *v/t* (*no -ge-*, *h*) ECON insure (**bei** with); assure (*j-m et.* s.o. of s.th.), assert; **sich ~** insure o.s.; make sure (**dass** that); **Verˈsicherte** *m*, *f* (*-n*; *-n*) *the* insured; **Verˈsicherung** *f* (*-*; *-en*) insurance; assurance, assertion

Verˈsicherungs|gesellschaft *f* insurance company; **~po‚lice** *f*, **~schein** *m* insurance policy

ver|ˈsickern *v/i* (*no -ge-*, *sein*) trickle away; **~ˈsiegeln** *v/t* (*no -ge-*, *h*) seal; **~ˈsiegen** *v/i* (*no -ge-*, *sein*) dry up, run dry; **~ˈsilbern** *v/t* (*no -ge-*, *h*) silver-plate; F turn *s.th.* into cash; **~ˈsinken** *v/i* (*irr*, **sinken**, *no -ge-*, *sein*) sink; → **versunken**

Version [vɛrˈzjoːn] *f* (*-*; *-en*) version

ˈVersmaß *n* meter, *Br* metre

verˈsöhnen [fɛɐˈzøːnən] *v/t* (*no -ge-*, *h*) reconcile; **sich (wieder) ~** make it up (*mit* with); **verˈsöhnlich** *adj* conciliatory; **Verˈsöhnung** *f* (*-*; *-en*) reconciliation; *esp* POL appeasement

verˈsorgen *v/t* (*no -ge-*, *h*) provide (**mit** with), supply (with); support; take care of, look after; **Verˈsorgung** *f* (*-*; *no pl*) supply (**mit** with); support; care

verˈspäten *v/refl* (*no -ge-*, *h*) be late; **verˈspätet** *adj* belated, late, RAIL *etc* a. delayed; **Verˈspätung** *f* (*-*; *-en*) being *or* coming late, RAIL *etc* delay; **20 Minuten ~ haben** be 20 minutes late

verˈspeisen *v/t* (*no -ge-*, *h*) eat (up)

verˈsperren *v/t* (*no -ge-*, *h*) bar, block (up), obstruct (*a. view*); lock

verˈspielen *v/t* (*no -ge-*, *h*) lose; **verˈspielt** *adj* playful

verˈspotten *v/t* (*no -ge-*, *h*) make fun of, ridicule

verˈsprechen (*irr*, **sprechen**, *no -ge-*, *h*) **1.** *v/t* promise (*a. fig*); **sich zu viel ~** (**von**) expect too much (of) **2.** *v/refl* make a mistake *or* slip; **Verˈsprechen** *n* (*-s*; *-*) promise; **ein ~ geben** (**halten**, **brechen**) make (keep, break) a promise; **Verˈsprecher** F *m* (*-s*; *-*) slip (of the tongue)

verˈstaatlichen *v/t* (*no -ge-*, *h*) ECON nationalize; **Verˈstaatlichung** *f* (*-*; *-en*) ECON nationalization

Verstädterung [fɛɐˈʃtɛːtərʊŋ] *f* (*-*; *-en*) urbanization

Verstand [fɛɐˈʃtant] *m* (*-[e]s*; *no pl*) mind, intellect; reason, (common) sense; intelligence, brains; **nicht bei ~** out of one's mind, not in one's right mind; **den ~ verlieren** go out of one's mind; **verstandesmäßig** [fɛɐˈʃtandəsmɛːsɪç] *adj* rational

verˈständig *adj* reasonable, sensible

verständigen [fɛɐˈʃtɛndɪgən] *v/t* (*no -ge-*, *h*) inform (**von** of), notify (of); call (*doctor, police etc*); **sich ~** communicate; come to an agreement (**über** *acc* on); **Verˈständigung** *f* (*-*; *no pl*) communication (*a.* TEL); agreement

verständlich [fɛɐˈʃtɛntlɪç] *adj* audible; intelligible; comprehensible; understandable; **schwer** (**leicht**) **~** difficult (easy) to understand; *j-m et.* **~ machen** make s.th. clear to s.o.; **sich ~ machen** make o.s. understood

Verständnis [fɛɐˈʃtɛntnɪs] *n* (*-ses*; *no pl*) comprehension, understanding; sympathy; (**viel**) **~ haben** be (very) understanding; **~ haben für** understand; appreciate

verˈständnislos *adj* uncomprehending; blank (*look etc*)

ver'ständnisvoll *adj* understanding, sympathetic; knowing (*look etc*)

ver'stärken *v/t* (*no -ge-, h*) reinforce (*a. TECH, MIL*); strengthen (*a. TECH*); *radio, PHYS* intensify; **Ver'stärker** *m* (*-s; -*) amplifier; **Ver'stärkung** *f* (*-; -en*) strengthening; reinforcement(s *MIL*); amplification; intensification

ver'stauben *v/i* (*no -ge-, sein*) get dusty

verstauchen [fɛɐˈʃtaʊxən] *v/t* (*no -ge-, h*), **Ver'stauchung** *f* (*-; -en*) sprain

ver'stauen *v/t* (*no -ge-, h*) stow away

Versteck [fɛɐˈʃtɛk] *n* (*-[e]s; -e*) hiding place, hideout, hideaway

ver'stecken *v/t and v/refl* (*no -ge-, h*) hide (*a. fig*); **Verstecken spielen** play (at) hide-and-seek

ver'stehen *v/t* (*irr, stehen, no -ge-, h*) understand, F get; catch; see; realize; know; **es ~ zu inf** know how to *inf*; **zu ~ geben** give *s.o.* to understand, suggest; **ich verstehe!** I see!; **falsch ~** misunderstand; **was ~ Sie unter ...?** what do you mean *or* understand by ...?; **sich (gut) ~** get along (well) (*mit* with); **es versteht sich von selbst** it goes without saying

ver'steifen (*no -ge-, h*) **1.** *v/t* stiffen (*a. sich ~*); *TECH* strut, brace **2.** *v/refl*: **sich auf et. ~** insist on (doing) s.th.

ver'steigern *v/t* (*no -ge-, h*) auction off; **Ver'steigerung** *f* (*-; -en*) auction (sale)

ver'steinern *v/i* (*no -ge-, sein*) petrify (*a. fig*)

ver'stellbar *adj* adjustable

ver'stellen *v/t* (*no -ge-, h*) block; move; set *s.th.* wrong *or* the wrong way; *TECH* adjust, regulate; disguise (*one's voice etc*); **sich ~** pretend

Ver'stellung *f* (*-; no pl*) disguise, make-believe, (false) show

ver'steuern *v/t* (*no -ge-, h*) pay duty *or* tax on

verstiegen [fɛɐˈʃtiːɡən] *adj* high-flown

ver'stimmen *v/t* (*no -ge-, h*) *MUS* put out of tune; *fig* annoy; **ver'stimmt** *adj* annoyed; *MUS* out of tune; *MED* upset; **Ver'stimmung** *f* (*-; -en*) annoyance

ver'stockt [fɛɐˈʃtɔkt] *adj* stubborn, obstinate; **~stohlen** [fɛɐˈʃtoːlən] *adj* furtive, stealthy

ver'stopfen *v/t* (*no -ge-, h*) plug (up); block, jam; *MED* constipate; **ver'stopft**

adj MED constipated; **Ver'stopfung** *f* (*-; -en*) block(age); *MED* constipation

verstorben [fɛɐˈʃtɔrbən] *adj* late, deceased; **Ver'storbene** *m, f* (*-n; -n*) the deceased; **die ~n** the deceased

verstört [fɛɐˈʃtøːɐt] *adj* upset; distracted; wild (*look etc*)

Ver'stoß *m* offense, *Br* offence (*gegen* against), violation (*of*)

ver'stoßen (*irr, stoßen, no -ge-*) **1.** *v/t* expel (*aus* from); disown **2.** *v/i*: **~ gegen** offend against, violate

ver'strahlt *adj* (radioactively) contaminated

ver'streichen (*irr, streichen, no -ge-*) **1.** *v/i* (*sein*) *time*: pass, go by; *date*: expire **2.** *v/t* (*h*) spread

ver'streuen *v/t* (*no -ge-, h*) scatter

verstümmeln [fɛɐˈʃtʏməln] *v/t* (*no -ge-, h*) mutilate (*a. fig*); **Ver'stümmelung** *f* (*-; -en*) mutilation (*a. fig*)

ver'stummen *v/i* (*no -ge-, sein*) grow silent; stop; die down

Versuch [fɛɐˈzuːx] *m* (*-[e]s; -e*) attempt, try; trial, test; *PHYS* experiment; **mit et. (j-m) e-n ~ machen** give s.th. (s.o.) a try; **ver'suchen** *v/t* (*no -ge-, h*) try, attempt; taste; *REL* tempt; **es ~** have a try (at it)

Ver'suchs... *in cpds ...bohrung etc*: test ..., trial ...; **~ka,ninchen** *n* guinea pig; **~stadium** *n* experimental stage; **~tier** *n* laboratory *or* test animal

ver'suchsweise *adv* by way of trial

Ver'suchung *f* (*-; -en*) temptation; **j-n in ~ führen** tempt s.o.

versunken [fɛɐˈzʊŋkən] *fig adj*: **~ in** (*acc*) absorbed *or* lost in

ver'süßen *v/t* (*no -ge-, h*) sweeten

ver'tagen *v/t and v/refl* (*no -ge-, h*) adjourn; **Ver'tagung** *f* (*-; -en*) adjournment

ver'tauschen *v/t* (*no -ge-, h*) exchange (*mit* for)

verteidigen [fɛɐˈtaɪdɪɡən] *v/t* (*no -ge-, h*) defend (*sich* o.s.); **Verteidiger(in)** [fɛɐˈtaɪdɪɡə (-ɡərɪn)] (*-s; -/-; -nen*) defender, *SPORT a.* back; *fig* advocate; **Ver'teidigung** *f* (*-; -en*) defense, *Br* defence

Ver'teidigungs... *in cpds ...politik etc*: *mst* defense ..., *Br* defence ...; **~mi,nister** *m* Secretary of Defense, *Br* Minister of Defence; **~minis,terium**

n Department of Defense, *Br* Ministry of Defence

ver'teilen *v/t (no -ge-, h)* distribute; hand out; Ver'teiler *m (-s; -)* distributor; Ver'teilung *f (-; -en)* distribution

ver'tiefen *v/t and v/refl (no -ge-, h)* deepen *(a. fig);* **sich ~ in** *(acc)* become absorbed in; Ver'tiefung *f (-; -en)* hollow, depression, dent; *fig* deepening

vertikal [verti'ka:l] *adj*, Verti'kale *f (-; -n)* vertical

ver'tilgen *v/t (no -ge-, h)* exterminate; F consume; Ver'tilgung *f (-; no pl)* extermination

vertonen [fɛɐ'to:nən] *v/t (no -ge-, h)* set to music

Vertrag [fɛɐ'tra:k] *m (-[e]s; Verträge [fɛɐ'trɛ:gə])* contract; *POL* treaty

ver'tragen *v/t (irr, tragen, no -ge-, h)* endure, bear, stand; **ich kann ... nicht ~** ... doesn't agree with me; I can't stand ...; **er kann viel ~** he can take a lot; he can hold his drink; F **ich (es) könnte ... ~** I (it) could do with ...; **sich (gut) ~** get along (well) *(mit* with); **sich wieder ~** make it up

ver'traglich *adv* by contract

verträglich [fɛɐ'trɛ:klɪç] *adj* easy to get on with; *GASTR* (easily) digestible

ver'trauen *v/i (no -ge-, h)* trust **(auf** *acc* in); Ver'trauen *n (-s; no pl)* confidence, trust, faith; **im ~ (gesagt)** between you and me; **wenig ~ erweckend aussehen** inspire little confidence

Ver'trauens|frage *f:* **die ~ stellen** *PARL* ask for a vote of confidence; **~sache** *f:* **das ist ~** that is a matter of confidence; **~stellung** *f* position of trust

ver'trauensvoll *adj* trustful, trusting

Ver'trauensvotum *n PARL* vote of confidence

ver'trauenswürdig *adj* trustworthy

ver'traulich *adj* confidential; familiar

ver'traut *adj* familiar; close

Ver'traute *m, f (-n; -n)* confidant(e *f)*

Ver'trautheit *f (-; no pl)* familiarity

ver'treiben *v/t (irr, treiben, no -ge-, h)* drive *or* chase away *(a. fig);* pass *(the time);* *ECON* sell; **~ aus** drive out of; Ver'treibung *f (-; -en)* expulsion **(aus** from)

ver'treten *v/t (irr, treten, no -ge-, h)* substitute for, replace, stand in for; *POL, ECON* represent; *PARL a.* sit for; *JUR*

act for *s.o.;* **j-s Sache ~** *JUR* plead s.o.'s cause; **die Ansicht ~, dass** argue that; **sich den Fuß ~** sprain one's ankle; F **sich die Beine ~** stretch one's legs

Ver'treter *m (-s; -)*, Ver'treterin *f (-; -nen)* substitute, deputy; *POL, ECON* representative; *ECON a.* agent; *MED* locum

Ver'tretung *f (-; -en)* substitution, replacement; substitute, stand-in, *a.* supply teacher; *ECON, POL* representation

Vertrieb [fɛɐ'tri:p] *m (-[e]s; no pl)* *ECON* sale, distribution

Vertriebene [fɛɐ'tri:bənə] *m, f (-n; -n)* *POL* expellee, refugee

ver'trocknen *v/i (no -ge-, sein)* dry up; **~'trödeln** F *v/t (no -ge-, h)* dawdle away, waste; **~'trösten** *v/t (no -ge-, h)* put *s.o.* off; **~'tuschen** F *v/t (no -ge-, h)* cover up; **~'übeln** *v/t (no -ge-, h)* take amiss; **ich kann es ihr nicht ~** I can't blame her for it; **~'üben** *v/t (no -ge-, h)* commit

verunglücken [fɛɐ'ʔʊnglʏkən] *v/i (no -ge-, sein)* have an accident; *fig* go wrong; **tödlich ~** die in an accident

ver'ursachen *v/t (no -ge-, h)* cause

ver'urteilen *v/t (no -ge-, h)* condemn **(zu** to) *(a. fig)*, sentence (to), convict **(wegen** of); Ver'urteilung *f (-; -en)* condemnation *(a. fig)*

ver'vielfachen *v/t (no -ge-, h)* multiply

vervielfältigen [fɛɐ'fi:lfɛltɪgən] *v/t (no -ge-, h)* copy, duplicate; Ver'vielfältigung *f (-; -en)* duplication; copy

ver'vollkommnen *v/t (no -ge-, h)* perfect; improve

vervollständigen [fɛɐ'fɔlʃtɛndɪgən] *v/t (no -ge-, h)* complete

ver'wachsen *adj MED* deformed, crippled; *fig* **~ mit** deeply rooted in, bound up with; **~'wackelt** F *adj PHOT* blurred

ver'wahren *v/t (no -ge-, h)* keep (in a safe place); **sich ~ gegen** protest against

verwahrlost [fɛɐ'va:ɐlo:st] *adj* uncared-for, neglected

ver'walten *v/t (no -ge-, h)* manage, *esp POL a.* administer; Ver'walter *m (-s; -)* manager; administrator; Ver'waltung *f (-; -en)* administration, management; Ver'waltungs... *in cpds* ...gericht, ...kosten *etc:* administrative ...

V

ver'wandeln v/t (no -ge-, h) change, turn (both a. sich ~), esp PHYS, CHEM a. transform, convert (all: in acc into); Ver'wandlung f (-; -en) change, transformation; conversion

verwandt [fɛɐ'vant] adj related (mit to); Ver'wandte m, f (-n; -n) relative; (alle) m-e ~n (all) my relatives or relations; der nächste ~ the next of kin; Ver'wandtschaft f (-; -en) relationship; (no pl) relations

ver'warnen v/t (no -ge-, h) Br caution; SPORT book; Ver'warnung f (-; -en) Br caution; SPORT booking

ver'waschen adj washed-out

ver'wässern v/t (no -ge-, h) water down (a. fig)

ver'wechseln v/t (no -ge-, h) confuse (mit with), mix up (with), mistake (for) Ver'wechs(e)lung f (-; -en) mistake, F mix-up

ver'wegen adj daring, bold

Ver'wegenheit f (-; no pl) boldness, daring

ver'weichlicht adj soft

ver'weigern v/t (no -ge-, h) refuse; disobey; Ver'weigerung f (-; -en) denial, refusal

ver'weilen v/i (no -ge-, h) stay; fig rest

Verweis [fɛɐ'vais] m (-es; -e) reprimand, reproof; reference (auf acc to)

ver'weisen v/t (irr, weisen, no -ge-, h) refer (auf acc, an acc to); expel (gen from)

ver'welken v/i (no -ge-, sein) wither, fig a. fade

ver'wenden v/t (no -ge-, h) use; spend (time etc) (auf acc on); Ver'wendung f (-; -en) use; keine ~ haben für have no use for

ver'werfen v/t (irr, werfen, no -ge-, h) drop, give up; reject

ver'werten v/t (no -ge-, h) use, make use of

verwesen [fɛɐ've:zən] v/i (no -ge-, sein), Ver'wesung f (-; no pl) decay

ver'wickeln fig v/t (no -ge-, h) involve; sich ~ in (acc) get caught in; ver'wickelt fig adj complicated; ~ sein (werden) in (acc) be (get) involved in; Ver'wicklung fig f (-; -en) involvement; complication

ver'wildern v/i (no -ge-, sein) grow (or run) wild; ver'wildert adj wild (a.

fig), overgrown

ver'winden v/t (irr, winden, no -ge-, h) get over s.th.

ver'wirklichen v/t (no -ge-, h) realize; sich ~ come true; sich selbst ~ fulfil(l) o.s.; Ver'wirklichung f (-; -en) realization

ver'wirren v/t (no -ge-, h) tangle (up); fig confuse; ver'wirrt fig adj confused; Ver'wirrung fig f (-; -en) confusion

ver'wischen v/t (no -ge-, h) blur (a. fig); cover (track etc)

verwittern [fɛɐ'vɪtən] v/i (no -ge-, sein) GEOL weather

verwöhnen [fɛɐ'vø:nən] v/t (no -ge-, h) spoil; ver'wöhnt adj spoilt

verworren [fɛɐ'vɔrən] adj confused, muddled; complicated

verwundbar [fɛɐ'vʊntbaːɐ] adj vulnerable (a. fig); ver'wunden v/t (no -ge-, h) wound

ver'wunderlich adj surprising

Verwunderung [fɛɐ'vʊndərʊŋ] f (-; no pl) (zu m-r etc ~ to my etc) surprise

Ver'wundete m, f (-n; -n) wounded (person), casualty

Ver'wundung f (-; -en) wound, injury

ver'wünschen v/t (no -ge-, h), Ver'wünschung f (-; -en) curse

ver'wüsten v/t (no -ge-, h) lay waste, devastate, ravage; Ver'wüstung f (-; -en) devastation, ravage

ver'zählen v/refl (no -ge-, h) count wrong; ~'zaubern v/t (no -ge-, h) enchant, fig a. charm; ~ in (acc) turn into; ~'zehren v/t (no -ge-, h) consume (a. fig)

ver'zeichnen v/t (no -ge-, h) record, keep a record of, list; fig achieve; suffer; Ver'zeichnis n (-ses; -se) list, catalog(ue); record, register; index

verzeihen [fɛɐ'tsaiən] v/t and v/i (irr, no -ge-, h) forgive s.o.; pardon, excuse s.th.; ver'zeihlich adj pardonable; Ver'zeihung f (-; no pl) pardon; (j-n) um ~ bitten apologize (to s.o.); ~! (I'm) sorry!; excuse me!

ver'zerren v/t (no -ge-, h) distort (a. fig); sich ~ become distorted

Ver'zerrung f (-; -en) distortion

Verzicht [fɛɐ'tsɪçt] m (-[e]s; -e) renunciation (auf acc of); mst giving up, doing without etc

ver'zichten *v/i* (*no* -ge-, *h*) ~ **auf** (*acc*) do without; give up; renounce (*a.* JUR)

verzieh [fɛɐ'tsiː] *pret of* **verzeihen**

ver'ziehen (*irr, ziehen, no* -ge-) **1.** *v/i* (*sein*) move (**nach** to); **2.** *v/t* (*h*) spoil; **das Gesicht** ~ make a face; **sich** ~ *wood:* warp; *storm etc:* pass (over); F disappear **3.** *pp of* **verziehen**

ver'zieren *v/t* (*no* -ge-, *h*) decorate

Ver'zierung *f* (-; -en) decoration, ornament

ver'zinsen *v/t* (*no* -ge-, *h*) pay interest on; **sich** ~ yield interest

Ver'zinsung *f* (-; -en) interest

ver'zögern *v/t* (*no* -ge-, *h*) delay; **sich** ~ be delayed; Ver'zögerung *f* (-; -en) delay

ver'zollen *v/t* (*no* -ge-, *h*) pay duty on; **et. (nichts) zu ~ haben** have s.th. (nothing) to declare

verzückt [fɛɐ'tsʏkt] *adj* ecstatic; Ver-'zückung *f* (-; -en) ecstasy; **in ~ geraten** go into ecstasies *or* raptures (**wegen, über** *acc* over)

Verzug [fɛɐ'tsuːk] *m* (-[e]s; *no pl*) delay; ECON default

ver'zweifeln *v/i* (*no* -ge-, *h*) despair (**an** *dat* of); ver'zweifelt *adj* desperate, despairing

Ver'zweiflung *f* (-; *no pl*) despair; **j-n zur ~ bringen** drive s.o. to despair

verzweigen [fɛɐ'tsvaɪɡən] *v/refl* (*no* -ge-, *h*) branch

verzwickt [fɛɐ'tsvɪkt] F *adj* tricky

Veteran [vete'raːn] *m* (-en; -en) MIL veteran (*a. fig*)

Veterinär [veteri'nɛːɐ] *m* (-s; -e), Veteri-'närin *f* (-; -nen) veterinarian, *Br* veterinary surgeon, F vet

Veto ['veːto] *n* (-s; -s) veto; **(s)ein ~ einlegen gegen** veto

Vetter ['fɛtɐ] *m* (-s; -n) cousin

'Vetternwirtschaft *f* (-; *no pl*) nepotism

vgl. *abbr of* **vergleiche** cf., confer

VHS *abbr of* **Volkshochschule** adult education program(me); adult evening classes

Vibration [vibra'tsjoːn] *f* (-; -en) vibration; vibrieren [vi'briːrən] *v/i* (*no* -ge-, *h*) vibrate

Video ['viːdeo] *n* (-s; -s) video (*a. in cpds* ...aufnahme, ...clip, ...kamera, ...kassette, ...recorder etc*); **auf ~ aufnehmen** video(tape), tape; ~**band** *n* videotape;

~**text** *m* teletext

Videothek [video'teːk] *f* (-; -en) video (-tape) library; video store (*Br* shop)

Vieh [fiː] *n* (-[e]s; *no pl*) cattle; **20 Stück** ~ 20 head of cattle; ~**bestand** *m* livestock; ~**händler** *m* cattle dealer

'viehisch *contp adj* bestial, brutal

'Vieh|markt *m* cattle market; ~**zucht** *f* cattle breeding, stockbreeding; ~**züchter** *m* cattle breeder, stockbreeder

viel [fiːl] *adj und adv* a lot (of), plenty (of), F lots of; ~**e** many; **nicht** ~ not much; **nicht** ~**e** not many; **sehr** ~ a great deal (of); **sehr** ~**e** very many, a lot (of); **das** ~**e Geld** all that money; **ziemlich** ~ quite a lot (of); **ziemlich** ~**e** quite a few; ~ **besser** much better; ~ **teurer** much more expensive; **e-r zu** ~ one too many; ~ **zu** ~ far too much; ~ **zu wenig** not nearly enough; ~ **lieber** much rather; **wie** ~ how much (*pl* many); ~ **beschäftigt** very busy; ~ **sagend** meaningful; ~ **versprechend** promising; 'vieldeutig [-dɔʏtɪç] *adj* ambiguous; vielerlei [-'fiːlɐ'laɪ] *adj* all kinds *or* sorts of; 'vielfach **1.** *adj* multiple **2.** *adv* in many cases, (very) often; 'Vielfalt *f* (-; *no pl*) (great) variety (*gen* of); 'vielfarbig *adj* multicolo(u)red

vielleicht [fi'laɪçt] *adv* perhaps, maybe; ~ **ist er …** he may *or* might be …

'vielmals *adv:* **(ich) danke (Ihnen)** ~ thank you very much; **entschuldigen Sie** ~ I'm very sorry, I do apologize

viel'mehr *cj* rather

'viel|sagend *adj* meaningful; ~**seitig** ['fiːlzaɪtɪç] *adj* versatile

'Vielseitigkeit *f* (-; *no pl*) versatility

'vielversprechend *adj* promising

vier [fiːɐ] *adj* four; **zu viert sein** be four; **auf allen ~en** on all fours; **unter ~ Augen** in private, privately

'Vierbeiner [-baɪnɐ] *m* (-s; -) zo quadruped, four-legged animal

'vierbeinig *adj* four-legged

'Viereck *n* quadrangle, quadrilateral

'viereckig *adj* quadrangular, square

'Vierer ['fiːrɐ] *m* (-s; -) *rowing:* four

'vierfach *adj* fourfold; ~**e Ausfertigung** four copies

'vierfüßig ['fiːɐfyːsɪç] *adj* four-footed

'Vierfüßler ['fiːɐfyːslɐ] *m* (-s; -) zo quadruped

'vierhändig ['fiːɐhɛndɪç] *adj* MUS four-

V

handed

'vierjährig ['fiːɐjɛːrɪç] *adj* four-year-old, of four

Vierlinge ['fiːɐlɪŋə] *pl* quadruplets, quads

'viermal *adv* four times

'Vierradantrieb *m* MOT four-wheel drive

'vierseitig ['fiːɐzaɪtɪç] *adj* MATH quadrilateral

'vierspurig ['fiːɐʃpuːrɪç] *adj* MOT four-lane

'vierstöckig ['fiːɐʃtœkɪç] *adj* four-storied, *Br* four-storey …

'Viertaktmotor *m* four-stroke engine

vierte ['fiːɐtə] *adj* fourth

Viertel ['fɪrtəl] *n* (-s; -) fourth (part); quarter; (*ein*) **~** *vor* (*nach*) (a) quarter to (past); **~fi,nale** *n* SPORT quarter finals

Viertel'jahr *n* three months

'vierteljährlich 1. *adj* quarterly **2.** *adv* every three months, quarterly

vierteln ['fɪrtəln] *v/t* (ge-, h) quarter

'Viertel|note *f* MUS quarter note, *Br* crotchet; **~pfund** *n* quarter of a pound

Viertel'stunde *f* quarter of an hour

viertens ['fiːɐtəns] *adv* fourthly

vierzehn ['fɪrtseːn] *adj* fourteen; **~** *Tage* two weeks, *esp Br* a. a fortnight

'vierzehnte *adj* fourteenth

vierzig ['fɪrtsɪç] *adj* forty

'vierzigste *adj* fortieth

Villa ['vɪla] *f* (-; *Villen*) villa

violett [vio'lɛt] *adj* violet, purple

Violine [vio'liːnə] *f* (-; -n) MUS violin

virtuell [vɪr'tuɛl] *adj* virtual; **Virtuelle Realität** [vɪr'tuɛlə] *f* virtual reality, Cyberspace

virtuos [vɪr'tuoːs] *adj* virtuoso …, masterly; **Virtuose** [vɪr'tuoːzə] *m* (-n; -n) virtuoso; **Virtuosität** [vɪrtuoziˈtɛːt] *f* (-; *no pl*) virtuosity

Virus ['viːrus] *n, m* (-; *Viren*) MED virus

Visier [vi'ziːɐ] *n* (-s; -e) sights; visor

Vision [vi'zjoːn] *f* (-; -en) vision

Visite [vi'ziːtə] *f* (-; -n) MED round

Vi'sitenkarte *f* (visiting) card

Visum ['viːzum] *n* (-s; *Visa*) visa

vital [vi'taːl] *adj* vigorous; **Vitalität** [vitali'tɛːt] *f* (-; *no pl*) vigo(u)r

Vitamin [vita'miːn] *n* (-s; -e) vitamin

Vitrine [vi'triːnə] *f* (-; -n) (glass) cabinet; showcase

Vize… ['fiːtsə-] *in cpds* vice(-)…

Vogel ['foːgəl] *m* (-s; *Vögel* ['føːgəl]) ZO bird

'Vogelbauer *n* birdcage

'vogelfrei *adj* outlawed

'Vogel|futter *n* birdseed; **~grippe** *f* bird flu, avian flu; **~käfig** *m* birdcage; **~kunde** *f* ornithology

vögeln ['føːgəln] V *v/t and v/i* (ge-, h) screw

'Vogel|nest *n* bird's nest; **~perspektive** *f* bird's-eye view; **~scheuche** *f* scarecrow (*a. fig*); **~schutzgebiet** *n* bird sanctuary; **~warte** *f* ornithological station; **~zug** *m* bird migration

Vokabel [vo'kaːbəl] *f* (-; -n) word; *pl* → **Vokabular** [vokabu'laːɐ] *n* (-s; -e) vocabulary

Vokal [vo'kaːl] *m* (-s; -e) LING vowel

Volant [vo'laː…] Austrian *m* → **Lenkrad**

Volk [fɔlk] *n* (-[e]s; *Völker* ['fœlkɐ]) people, nation; *the* people; ZO swarm; *ein Mann aus dem* **~** a man of the people

Völker|kunde ['fœlkɐkʊndə] *f* ethnology; **~mord** *m* genocide; **~recht** *n* (-[e]s; *no pl*) international law; **~wanderung** *f* migration of peoples; F mass exodus

'Volks|abstimmung *f* POL referendum; **~fest** *n* funfair; **~hochschule** *f* adult evening classes; **~lied** *n* folk song; **~mund** *m*: *im* **~** in the vernacular; **~musik** *f* folk music; **~repu,blik** *f* people's republic; **~schule** HIST *f* → **Grundschule**; **~sport** *m* popular sport; **~sprache** *f* vernacular; **~stamm** *m* tribe, race; **~tanz** *m* folk dance; **~tracht** *f* national costume

'volkstümlich ['fɔlkstyːmlɪç] *adj* popular, folk …; traditional

'Volks|versammlung *f* public meeting; **~wirt** *m* economist; **~wirtschaft** *f* (national) economy; → **~wirtschaftslehre** *f* economics; **~zählung** *f* census

voll [fɔl] **1.** *adj* full (*a. fig*); full up (*a.* F); F plastered; thick, rich (*hair*); **~er** full of, filled with, *a.* covered with *dirt etc* **2.** *adv* fully; completely, totally, wholly; *pay etc* in full, the full price; *hit etc* full, straight, right; **~** *entwickelt* fully developed; (*nicht*) *für* **~** *nehmen* (not) take seriously

'vollauf *adv* perfectly, quite

'vollauto,matisch *adj* fully automatic

'Vollbart *m* (full) beard

'Vollbeschäftigung *f* full employment

'Vollblut… *in cpds* full-blooded (*a. fig*)

'Vollblüter ['fɔlblyːtɐ] *m* (-s; -) ZO thoroughbred

voll'**bringen** v/t (irr, **bringen**, no -ge-, h) accomplish, achieve; perform

'**Volldampf** m full steam; F **mit ~** (at) full blast

voll'**enden** v/t (no -ge-, h) finish, complete; voll'**endet** adj completed; fig perfect; voll'**ends** ['fɔlɛnts] adv completely; **Voll'endung** f (-; no pl) finishing, completion; fig perfection

voll'**führen** v/t (no -ge-, h) perform

'**vollfüllen** v/t (sep, -ge-, h) (**gießen**) fill (up)

'**Vollgas** n (-es; no pl) MOT full throttle; ~ **geben** F step on it

völlig ['fœlɪç] **1.** adj complete, absolute, total **2.** adv completely; ~ **unmöglich** absolutely impossible

'**volljährig** ['fɔljɛːrɪç] adj JUR ~ **sein** (**werden**) be (come) of age; **noch nicht** ~ under age; '**Volljährigkeit** f (-; no pl) JUR majority

voll'**kommen** adj perfect; → **völlig**

Voll'kommenheit f (-; no pl) perfection

'**Vollkornbrot** n wholemeal bread

'**vollmachen** v/t (sep, -ge-, h) fill (up); F soil, dirty; **um das Unglück voll zu machen** to crown it all

Voll|macht f (-; -en) full power(s), authority; JUR power of attorney; ~ **haben** be authorized; **~milch** f full-cream milk; **~mond** m full moon

'**vollpacken** v/t (sep, -ge-, h) load (**mit** with) (a. fig)

'**Vollpensi,on** f full board

'**vollschlank** adj plump

'**vollständig** adj complete; → **völlig**

'**vollstopfen** v/t (sep, -ge-, h) stuff, fig a. cram, pack (all: **mit** with)

voll'**strecken** v/t (no -ge-, h) JUR execute; **Voll'streckung** f (-; -en) JUR execution

'**volltanken** v/t (sep, -ge-, h): **bitte ~!** MOT fill her up, please!

'**Voll|treffer** m direct hit; bull's eye (a. fig); **~versammlung** f plenary session

'**vollwertig** adj full

'**Vollwertkost** f wholefoods

vollzählig ['fɔltsɛːlɪç] adj complete

voll'**ziehen** v/t (irr, **ziehen**, no -ge-, h) execute; perform; **sich ~** take place; **Voll'ziehung** f (-; no pl), **Voll'zug** m (-[e]s; no pl) execution

Volontär [volɔn'tɛːɐ] m (-s; -e), Volon-

'**tärin** f (-; -nen) unpaid trainee

Volt [vɔlt] n (-; -) ELECTR volt

Volumen [vo'luːmən] n (-s; -, -mina) volume; size

von [fɔn] prp from; instead of gen: of; passive: by; about s.o. or s.th.; **südlich** ~ south of; **weit ~** far from; ~ **Hamburg** from Hamburg; ~ **nun an** from now on; **ein Freund ~ mir** a friend of mine; **die Freunde ~ Alice** Alice's friends; **ein Brief** (**Geschenk**) ~ **Tom** a letter (gift) from Tom; **ein Buch** (**Bild**) ~ **Orwell** (**Picasso**) a book (painting) by Orwell (Picasso); **der König** (**Bürgermeister** etc) ~ ... the King (Mayor etc) of ...; **ein Kind ~ 10 Jahren** a child of ten; **müde ~ der Arbeit** tired from work; **es war nett** (**gemein**) ~ **dir** it was nice (mean) of you; **reden** (**hören**) ~ talk (hear) about or of; ~ **Beruf** (**Geburt**) by profession (birth); ~ **selbst** by itself; ~ **mir aus!** I don't mind or care

von'statten|gehen v/i (irr, **gehen**, sep, -ge-, sein) go, come off

vor [foːɐ] prp (dat and acc) in front of; outside; before; ... ago; with, for; ~ **der Klasse** in front of the class; ~ **der Schule** in front of or outside the school; before school; ~ **kurzem** (**e-r Stunde**) a short time (an hour) ago; **5 Minuten ~ 12** five (minutes) to twelve; ~ **j-m liegen** be or lie ahead of s.o. (a. fig and SPORT); ~ **sich hin** smile etc to o.s.; **sicher ~** safe from; ~ **Kälte** with cold; ~ **Angst** for fear; ~ **allem** above all; ~ **sich gehen** go on, happen

'**Vorabend** m eve (a. fig)

'**Vorahnung** f presentiment, foreboding

voran [fo'ran] adv at the head (dat of), in front (of); before; **Kopf ~** head first; **~gehen** v/i (irr, **gehen**, sep, -ge-, sein) go in front or first; esp fig lead the way; **~kommen** v/i (irr, **kommen**, sep, -ge-, sein) get on or along (a. fig), make headway

'**Voranzeige** f preannouncement; film: trailer

'**vorarbeiten** v/i (sep, -ge-, h) work in advance; fig pave the way

'**Vorarbeiter** m foreman

voraus [fo'raus] adv ahead (dat of); **im Voraus** in advance, beforehand

vo'**rausgehen** v/i (irr, **gehen**, sep, -ge-,

sein) precede; → *vorangehen*

vo'rausgesetzt *cj:* ~, *dass* provided that

Vo'raussage *f* (-; -n) prediction; METEOR forecast; vo'raussagen *v/t* (*sep*, *-ge-*, *h*) predict; forecast

vo'raus|schicken *v/t* (*sep*, *-ge-*, *h*) send on ahead; ~sehen *v/t* (*irr*, *sehen*, *sep*, *-ge-*, *h*) foresee, see s.th. coming

vo'raussetzen *v/t* (*sep*, *-ge-*, *h*) assume; take s.th. for granted

Vo'raussetzung *f* (-; -en) condition, prerequisite; assumption; *die* ~*en erfüllen* meet the requirements

Vo'raussicht *f* (-; *no pl*) foresight; *aller* ~ *nach* in all probability

vo'raussichtlich *adv* probably; *er kommt* ~ *morgen* he is expected to arrive tomorrow

Vo'rauszahlung *f* advance payment

'Vorbedeutung *f* omen

'Vorbedingung *f* prerequisite

Vorbehalt ['fo:ɐbəhalt] *m* (-[e]s; -e) reservation; 'vorbehalten **1.** *v/t* (*irr*, *halten*, *sep*, *no -ge-*, *h*) *sich* (*das Recht*) ~ *zu inf* reserve the right to *inf* **2.** *adj* reserved; 'vorbehaltlos **1.** *adj* unconditional **2.** *adv* without reservation

vor'bei *adv* time: over, past; finished; gone; *space*: past, by; *jetzt ist alles* ~ it's all over now; ~*!* missed!; ~fahren *v/i* (*irr*, *fahren*, *sep*, *-ge-*, *sein*) go (*or* drive) past (*an dat s.o. or s.th.*), pass (*s.o. or s.th.*); ~gehen *v/i* (*irr*, *gehen*, *sep*, *-ge-*, *sein*) walk past; *a.* fig go by, pass; *shot etc*: miss; ~ *kommen v/i* (*irr*, *kommen*, *sep*, *-ge-*, *sein*) pass (*an dat s.th.*); get past (*an obstacle etc*); F drop in (*bei j-m* on s.o.); fig avoid; ~*lassen v/t* (*irr*, *lassen*, *sep*, *-ge-*, *h*) let *s.o.* pass

'Vorbemerkung *f* preliminary remark

'vorbereiten *v/t and v/refl* (*sep*, *no -ge-*, *h*) prepare (*auf acc* for); 'Vorbereitung *f* (-; -en) preparation (*auf acc* for)

'vorbestellen *v/t* (*sep*, *no -ge-*, *h*) book (*or* order) in advance; reserve (*room*, *seat etc*); 'Vorbestellung *f* (-; -en) advance booking; reservation

'vorbestraft *adj:* ~ *sein* have a police record

'vorbeugen (*sep*, *-ge-*, *h*) **1.** *v/i* prevent (*e-r Sache* s.th.); **2.** *v/refl* bend forward; ~*d adj* preventive, MED *a.* pro-

phylactic

'Vorbeugung *f* (-; -en) prevention

'Vorbild *n* model, pattern; (*j-m*) *ein* ~ *sein* set an example (to s.o.); *sich j-n zum* ~ *nehmen* follow s.o.'s example

'vorbildlich *adj* exemplary

'Vorbildung *f* education(al background)

'vor|bringen *v/t* (*irr*, *bringen*, *sep*, *-ge-*, *h*) bring forward; say, state; ~*da,tieren v/t* (*sep*, *-ge-*, *h*) antedate; postdate

Vorder... ['fɔrdɐ-] *in cpds* ...achse, ...rad, ...sitz, ...tür, ...zahn *etc*: front ...

vordere ['fɔrdərə] *adj* front

'Vorder|grund *m* foreground (*a.* fig); ~*mann m: mein* ~ the man *or* boy in front of me; ~*seite f* front (side); head

'vor|dräge(l)n *v/refl* (*sep*, *-ge-*, *h*) cut into line, *Br* jump the queue; ~*dringen v/i* (*irr*, *dringen*, *sep*, *-ge-*, *sein*) advance; ~ (*bis*) *zu* work one's way through to (*a.* fig)

'Vordruck *m* (-[e]s; -e) form, blank

'voreilig *adj* hasty, rash, precipitate; ~*e Schlüsse ziehen* jump to conclusions

'voreingenommen *adj* prejudiced, bias(s)ed; 'Voreingenommenheit *f* (-; *no pl*) prejudice, bias

'vorenthalten *v/t* (*irr*, *halten*, *sep*, *no -ge-*, *h*) keep back, withhold (*both: j-m et.* s.th. from s.o.)

'Vorentscheidung *f* preliminary decision

'vorerst *adv* for the present, for the time being

Vorfahr ['fo:ɐfaːɐ] *m* (-en; -en) ancestor

'vorfahren *v/i* (*irr*, *fahren*, *sep*, *-ge-*, *sein*) drive up (*or* on); 'Vorfahrt *f* (-; *no pl*) right of way, priority

'Vorfall *m* incident, occurrence, event

'vor|fallen *v/i* (*irr*, *fallen*, *sep*, *-ge-*, *sein*) happen, occur; ~*finden v/t* (*irr*, *finden*, *sep*, *-ge-*, *h*) find

'Vorfreude *f* anticipation

'vorführen *v/t* (*sep*, *-ge-*, *h*) show, present; perform (*trick etc*); demonstrate; JUR bring (*j-m* before s.o.); 'Vorführer *m* demonstrator; 'Vorführung *f* presentation, show(ing); performance; demonstration; JUR production

'Vorführwagen *m* MOT demonstrator, *Br* demonstration car

'Vorgabe *f* handicap

'Vorgang *m* event, occurrence, happening; file, record(s); BIOL, TECH process; **e-n ~ schildern** give an account of what happened; **Vorgänger(in)** ['foːɐɡɛŋɐ, 'foːɐɡɛŋərin] *m(f)* (*-s; -/-; -nen*) predecessor

'**Vorgarten** *m* front yard (*Br* garden)

'**vorgeben** *v/t* (*irr,* **geben,** *sep, -ge-,* h SPORT give; *fig* use s.th. as a pretext

'**Vorgebirge** *n* foothills

'**vorgefasst** *adj* preconceived

'**vorgefertigt** *adj* prefabricated

'**Vorgefühl** *n* presentiment

'**vorgehen** *v/i* (*irr,* **gehen,** *sep, -ge-, sein*) go on; come first; act; JUR sue (**gegen j-n** s.o.); proceed; *watch:* be fast; '**Vorgehen** *n* (*-s; no pl*) procedure

'**vorgeschichtlich** *adj* prehistoric

'**Vor**|**geschmack** *m* foretaste (**auf** *acc* of); **~gesetzte** *m, f* (*-n; -n*) superior, F boss

'**vorgestern** *adv* the day before yesterday

'**vorgreifen** *v/i* (*irr,* **greifen,** *sep, -ge-,* h) anticipate *s.o.* or *s.th.*

'**vorhaben** *v/t* (*irr,* **haben,** *sep, -ge-,* h) plan, intend; **haben Sie heute Abend et. vor?** have you anything on tonight?; **was hat er jetzt wieder vor?** what is he up to now?; '**Vorhaben** *n* (*-s; -*) plan(s), intention; TECH, ECON *a.* project

'**Vorhalle** *f* (entrance) hall, lobby

'**vorhalten** *v/t* (*irr,* **halten,** *sep, -ge-,* h) **1.** *v/t:* **j-m et. ~** hold s.th. in front of s.o.; *fig* blame s.o. for (doing) s.th. **2.** *v/i* last; '**Vorhaltungen** *pl* reproaches; **j-m ~ machen (für et.)** reproach s.o. (with s.th., for being …)

'**Vorhand** *f* (*-; no pl*) tennis: forehand

vorhanden [foːɐ'handən] *adj* available; in existence; **~ sein** exist; **es ist nichts mehr ~** there's nothing left; **Vor**-'**handensein** *n* (*-s; no pl*) existence

'**Vorhang** *m* curtain

'**Vorhängeschloss** *n* padlock

vor'**her** *adv* before, earlier; in advance, beforehand

vor'**herbestimmen** *v/t* (*sep, no -ge-,* h) predetermine

vorherig [foːɐ'heːrɪç] *adj* previous

'**Vorherrschaft** *f* (*-; no pl*) predominance; '**vorherrschen** *v/i* (*sep, -ge-,* h) predominate, prevail; '**vorherrschend** *adj* predominant, prevailing

vor'**hersehbar** *adj* foreseeable

vor'**hersehen** *v/t* (*irr,* **sehen,** *sep, -ge-,* h) foresee

vor'**hin** *adv* a (little) while ago

'**Vorhut** *f* (*-; -en*) MIL vanguard

vorig ['foːrɪç] *adj* last; former, previous

vorjährig ['foːɐjɛːrɪç] *adj* of last year, last year' …

'**Vorkämpfer** *m,* '**Vorkämpferin** *f* champion, pioneer

Vorkehrungen ['foːɐkeːruŋən] *pl:* **~ treffen** take precautions

'**Vorkenntnisse** *pl* previous knowledge *or* experience (**in** *dat* of)

'**vorkommen** *v/i* (*irr,* **kommen,** *sep, -ge-, sein*) be found; happen; **es kommt mir … vor** it seems … to me

'**Vorkommen** *n* (*-s; -*) MIN deposit(s)

Vorkommnis ['foːɐkɔmnɪs] *n* (*-ses; -se*) occurrence, incident, event

'**Vorkriegs…** *in cpds* prewar …

'**vorladen** *v/t* (*irr,* **laden,** *sep, -ge-,* h) JUR summon; '**Vorladung** *f* (*-; -en*) JUR summons

'**Vorlage** *f* model; pattern; copy; presentation; PARL bill; *soccer etc:* pass

'**vorlassen** *v/t* (*irr,* **lassen,** *sep, -ge-,* h) let *s.o.* go first; let *s.o.* pass; **vorgelassen werden** be admitted (**bei** to)

'**Vorlauf** *m* recorder: fast-forward; SPORT (preliminary) heat; '**Vorläufer** *m* forerunner, precursor; '**vorläufig 1.** *adj* provisional, temporary **2.** *adv* for the present, for the time being

vorlaut *adj* pert, cheeky

'**Vorleben** *n* (*-s; no pl*) former life, past

'**vorlegen** *v/t* (*sep, -ge-,* h) present; produce; show

'**Vorleger** *m* (*-s; -*) rug; mat

'**vorlesen** *v/t* (*irr,* **lesen,** *sep, -ge-,* h) read out (aloud); **j-m et. ~** read s.th. to s.o.; '**Vorlesung** *f* (*-; -en*) lecture (**über** *acc* on; **vor** *dat* to); **e-e ~ halten** (give a) lecture

'**vorletzte** *adj* last but one; **~ Nacht (Woche)** the night (week) before last

'**Vorliebe** *f* (*-; -n*) preference, special liking

'**vorliebnehmen** *v/i* (*irr,* **nehmen,** *sep, -ge-,* h) **mit** make do with

'**vorliegen** *v/i* (*irr,* **liegen,** *sep, -ge-,* h) **es liegen (keine) … vor** there are (no) …; **was liegt gegen ihn vor?** what is he charged with?; **~d** *adj* present, in question

'**vor**|**lügen** v/t (irr, **lügen**, sep, -ge-, h) **j-m et.** ~ tell s.o. lies; **~machen** v/t (sep, -ge-, h) **j-m et.** ~ show s.th. to s.o., show s.o. how to do s.th.; *fig* fool s.o.

'**Vormachtstellung** f supremacy

'**Vormarsch** m MIL advance (a. fig)

'**vormerken** v/t (sep, -ge-, h) **j-n** ~ put s.o.'s name down

'**Vormittag** m morning; **heute** ~ this morning

'**vormittags** adv in the morning; **sonntags** ~ on Sunday mornings

'**Vormund** m (-[e]s; -e) JUR guardian; **~schaft** f (-; -en) JUR guardianship

vorn [fɔrn] adv in front; **nach** ~ forward; **von** ~ from the front; from the beginning; **j-n von** ~(e) **sehen** see s.o.'s face; **noch einmal von** ~(e) (**anfangen**) (start) all over again

'**Vorname** m first or Christian name, forename

vornehm ['foːɐneːm] adj distinguished; noble; fashionable, exclusive, F smart, posh; **die** ~**e Gesellschaft** (high) society; ~ **tun** put on airs

'**vornehmen** v/t (irr, **nehmen**, sep, -ge-, h) carry out, do; make (*changes etc*); **sich et.** ~ decide or resolve to do s.th.; make plans for s.th.; **sich fest vorgenommen haben zu** inf have the firm intention to inf, be determined to inf

'**vornherein** adv: **von** ~ from the start or beginning

'**Vorort** m suburb

'**Vorposten** m outpost (a. MIL)

'**vorprogram,mieren** v/t (sep, no -ge-, sein) (pre)program(me); fig **das war vorprogrammiert** that was bound to happen

'**Vorrang** m (-[e]s; no pl) precedence (**vor** dat over), priority (over)

'**Vorrat** m (-[e]s; -räte) store, stock, supply (all: **an** dat of); GASTR provisions, ECON resources, reserves; **e-n** ~ **anlegen an** (dat) stockpile; **vorrätig** ['foːɐrɛːtɪç] adj available; ECON in stock

'**Vorrecht** n privilege

'**Vorredner** m previous speaker

'**Vorrichtung** f TECH device

'**vorrücken** (sep, -ge-) **1.** v/t (h) move forward **2.** v/i (sein) advance

'**Vorrunde** f SPORT preliminary round

'**vorsagen** v/i (sep, -ge-, h) **j-m** ~ prompt s.o.

'**Vorsai,son** f off-peak season

'**Vorsatz** m resolution; intention; JUR intent; **vorsätzlich** ['foːɐzɛtslɪç] adj intentional; *esp* JUR wil(l)ful

'**Vorschau** f preview (**auf** acc of), film, TV a. trailer

'**Vorschein** m: **zum** ~ **bringen** produce; fig bring out; **zum** ~ **kommen** appear; fig come to light

'**vor**|**schieben** v/t (irr, **schieben**, sep, -ge-, h) push forward; slip (*bolt*); fig use as a pretext; **~schießen** F v/t (irr, **schießen**, sep, -ge-, h) advance (*money*)

'**Vorschlag** m suggestion, proposal (a. PARL etc); **den** ~ **machen** → '**vorschlagen** v/t (irr, **schlagen**, sep, -ge-, h) suggest, propose

'**Vorschlussrunde** f SPORT semifinal

'**vorschnell** adj hasty, rash

'**vorschreiben** fig v/t (irr, **schreiben**, sep, -ge-, h) prescribe; tell; **ich lasse mir nichts** ~ I won't be dictated to; '**Vorschrift** f rule, regulation; instruction, direction; **Dienst nach** ~ **machen** work to rule

'**vorschrifts**|**mäßig** adj correct, proper; **~widrig** adj and adv contrary to regulations

'**Vorschub** m: ~ **leisten** (dat) encourage; JUR aid and abet

'**Vorschul...** in cpds pre-school ...

'**Vorschule** f preschool

'**Vorschuss** m advance

'**vorschützen** v/t (sep, -ge-, h) use s.th. as a pretext

'**vorsehen** (irr, **sehen**, sep, -ge-, h) **1.** v/t plan; JUR provide; ~ **für** intend (or designate) for **2.** v/refl **sich et.** ~ be careful, take care, watch out (**vor** dat for)

'**Vorsehung** f (-; no pl) providence

'**vorsetzen** v/t (sep, -ge-, h) **j-m et.** ~ put s.th. before s.o.; offer s.o. s.th.

'**Vorsicht** f (-; no pl) caution, care; ~**!** look or watch out!, (be) careful!; ~ **Stufe!** mind the step!; '**vorsichtig** adj careful, cautious; '**vorsichtshalber** ['foːɐzɪçtshalbɐ] adv to be on the safe side; '**Vorsichtsmaßnahme** f precaution, precautionary measure; ~**n treffen** take precautions

'**Vorsilbe** f LING prefix

'vorsingen *v/t and v/i* (*irr*, **singen**, *sep*, *-ge-*, *h*) **j-m et. ~** sing s.th. to s.o.; (have an) audition

'Vorsitz *m* chair(manship), presidency; **den ~ haben** (**übernehmen**) be in (take) the chair, preside (**bei** over, at)

'Vorsitzende *m*, *f* (*-n*; *-n*) chairman (chairwoman), president

'Vorsorge *f* (*-*; *no pl*) precaution; **~ treffen** take precautions; **~untersuchung** *f* MED preventive checkup

'vorsorglich **1.** *adj* precautionary **2.** *adv* as a precaution

'Vorspann *m* (*-[e]s*; *-e*) *film etc*: credits

'Vorspeise *f* hors d'œuvre, *Br* starter

'Vorspiel *n* MUS prelude (*a. fig*); foreplay; 'vorspielen *v/t* (*sep*, *-ge-*, *h*) **j-m et. ~** play s.th. to s.o.

'vorsprechen (*irr*, **sprechen**, *sep*, *-ge-*, *h*) **1.** *v/t* pronounce (**j-m** for s.o.); **2.** *v/i* call (**bei** at); THEA (have an) audition

'vorspringen *fig v/i* (*irr*, **springen**, *sep*, *-ge-*, *sein*) project, protrude (*both a.* ARCH); 'Vorsprung *m* ARCH projection; SPORT lead; **e-n ~ haben** be leading (**von** by); *esp fig* **e-n ~ von zwei Jahren haben** be two years ahead

'Vorstadt *f* suburb

'Vorstand *m* ECON board (of directors); managing committee (*of a club etc*)

'vorstehen *v/i* (*irr*, **stehen**, *sep*, *-ge-*, *h*) project, protrude

'vorstellen *v/t* (*sep*, *-ge-*, *h*) introduce (**sich** o.s.; **j-n j-m** s.o. to s.o.); put *watch* forward (*vtw* mean); **sich et.** (**j-n als ...**) **~** imagine s.th. (s.o. as ...); **so stelle ich mir ... vor** that's my idea of ...; **sich ~ bei** have an interview with *a firm etc*; 'Vorstellung *f* (*-*; *-en*) introduction; interview; THEA performance, *film etc*: *a.* show; idea; expectation

'Vorstellungs|kraft *f* (*-*; *no pl*), **~vermögen** *n* (*-s*; *no pl*) imagination

Vorstopper ['foːɐʃtɔpɐ] *m* (*-s*; *-*) SPORT center (*Br* centre) back

'Vorstoß *m* MIL advance; *fig* attempt

'Vorstrafe *f* previous conviction

'vorstrecken *v/t* (*sep*, *-ge-*, *h*) advance (*money*)

'Vorstufe *f* preliminary stage

'vortäuschen *v/t* (*sep*, *-ge-*, *h*) feign, fake

'Vorteil *m* advantage (*a.* SPORT); benefit, profit; **die ~e und Nachteile** the pros

and cons; 'vorteilhaft *adj* advantageous, profitable; 'Vorteilsregel *f* SPORT advantage rule

Vortrag ['foːtraːk] *m* (*-[e]s*; *Vorträge* ['foːtrɛːɡə]) talk, *esp* UNIV lecture; MUS *etc* recital; **e-n ~ halten** give a talk or lecture (**vor** *dat* to; **über** *acc* on)

'vortragen *v/t* (*irr*, **tragen**, *sep*, *-ge-*, *h*) express, state; MUS *etc* perform, play; recite (*poem etc*)

'vortreten *v/i* (*irr*, **treten**, *sep*, *-ge-*, *sein*) step forward; *fig* protrude, stick out

'Vortritt *m* (*-[e]s*; *no pl*) precedence; **j-m den ~ lassen** let s.o. go first

vorüber [foˈryːbɐ] *adv*: **~ sein** be over; **~gehen** *v/i* (*irr*, **gehen**, *sep*, *-ge-*, *sein*) pass, go by; **~gehend** *adj* temporary

'Vorübung *f* preparatory exercise

'Voruntersuchung *f* JUR, MED preliminary examination

'Vorurteil *n* prejudice; 'vorurteilslos *adj* unprejudiced, unbias(s)ed

'Vorverkauf *m* THEA advance booking

'vorverlegen *v/t* (*sep*, *no -ge-*, *h*) advance

'Vorwahl *f* TEL area (*Br* STD *or* dialling) code; POL primary, *Br* preliminary election

'Vorwand *m* pretext, excuse

vorwärts ['foːɐvɛrts] *adv* forward, on (-ward), ahead; **~!** come on!, let's go!; 'vorwärtskommen *v/i* (*irr*, **kommen**, *sep*, *-ge-*, *sein*) make headway (*a. fig*)

vorweg [foˈɐˈvɛk] *adv* beforehand

vor'wegnehmen *v/t* (*irr*, **nehmen**, *sep*, *-ge-*, *h*) anticipate

'vor|weisen *v/t* (*irr*, **weisen**, *sep*, *-ge-*, *h*) produce, show; **et. ~ können** boast s.th.; **~werfen** *fig v/t* (*irr*, **werfen**, *sep*, *-ge-*, *h*) **j-m et. ~** reproach s.o. with s.th.

'vorwiegend *adv* predominantly, chiefly, mainly, mostly

'vorwitzig *adj* cheeky, pert

'Vorwort *n* (*-[e]s*; *-e*) foreword; preface

'Vorwurf *m* reproach; **j-m Vorwürfe machen** (**wegen**) reproach s.o. (for); 'vorwurfsvoll *adj* reproachful

'Vorzeichen *n* omen, sign (*a.* MATH)

'vorzeigen *v/t* (*sep*, *-ge-*, *h*) show; produce

'vorzeitig *adj* premature, early

'vorziehen *v/t* (*irr*, **ziehen**, *sep*, *-ge-*, *h*) draw; *fig* prefer

V

'Vorzimmer *n* anteroom; outer office; Austrian → **Hausflur**

'Vorzug *m* advantage; merit

vorzüglich [foːˈɛˈtsyːklɪç] *adj* excellent, exquisite

'vorzugsweise *adv* preferably

Votum ['voːtʊm] *n* (-s; -ta, -ten) vote

VP *abbr of* **Vollpension** full board; (full) board and lodging

vulgär [vʊlˈgɛːɐ] *adj* vulgar

Vulkan [vʊlˈkaːn] *m* (-s; -e) volcano; ~ausbruch *m* volcanic eruption

vul'kanisch *adj* volcanic

W

W *abbr of* **West(en)** W, west; **Watt** W, watt(s)

Waage ['vaːgə] *f* (-; -n) scale(s *Br*); balance; ASTR Libra; **sich die** ~ **halten** balance each other; **er ist (e-e)** ~ he's (a) Libra; 'waagerecht *adj* horizontal

Waagschale ['vaːkˌʃaːlə] *f* scale

Wabe ['vaːbə] *f* (-; -n) honeycomb

wach [vax] *adj* awake; ~ **rütteln** rouse; *fig* → **wachrütteln**; ~ **werden** wake (up), *esp fig* → **wachwerden**

Wache ['vaxə] *f* (-; -n) guard (*a.* MIL); sentry; MAR, MED *etc* watch; police station; ~ **haben** be on guard (MAR watch); ~ **halten** keep watch; 'wachen *v/i* (ge-, h) (keep) watch (**über** *acc* over)

'Wachhund *m* watchdog

'Wachmann *m* (-[e]s; -männer, -leute) watchman; Austrian → **Polizist**

Wacholder [va'xɔldɐ] *m* (-s; -) BOT juniper

'wach|rufen *v/t* (irr, rufen, sep, -ge-, h) call up, evoke; ~rütteln *v/t* (sep, -ge-, h) *fig* rouse (*a. fig*)

Wachs [vaks] *n* (-es; -e) wax

wachsam ['vaxzaːm] *adj* watchful, on one's guard, vigilant; 'Wachsamkeit *f* (-; *no pl*) watchfulness, vigilance

wachsen¹ ['vaksən] *v/i* (irr, ge-, sein) grow (*a.* **sich** ~ **lassen**), *fig a.* increase

'wachsen² *v/t* (ge-, h) wax

'Wachs|fi,gurenkabi,nett *n* waxworks; ~tuch *n* oilcloth

'Wachstum *n* (-s; *no pl*) growth, *fig a.* increase

Wachtel ['vaxtəl] *f* (-; -n) ZO quail

Wächter ['vɛçtɐ] *m* (-s; -) guard

'Wachtmeister *m* (-s; *no pl*) patrolman, *Br* (police) constable

'Wach(t)turm *m* watchtower

'wachwerden *v/i* (irr, **werden**, sep, -ge-,

sein) *fig* awake; → **wach**

wackelig ['vakəlɪç] *adj* shaky (*a. fig*), loose (*tooth*); 'wackeln *v/i* (ge-, h) shake; *table etc*: wobble; *tooth*: be loose; PHOT move; ~ **mit** waggle

Wade ['vaːdə] *f* (-; -n) ANAT calf

Waffe ['vafə] *f* (-; -n) weapon (*a. fig*), *pl a.* arms

Waffel ['vafəl] *f* (-; -n) waffle; wafer

'Waffen|gewalt *f*: **mit** ~ by force of arms; ~schein *m* gun license (*Br* licence); ~stillstand *m* armistice (*a. fig*); truce

wagen ['vaːgən] *v/t* (ge-, h) dare; risk; **sich** ~ venture

'Wagen *m* (-s; -) MOT car; RAIL car, *Br* carriage

wägen ['vɛːgən] *lit v/t* (irr, ge-, h) weigh (*one's words etc*)

'Wagen|heber *m* TECH jack; ~ladung *f* cartload

Waggon [va'goː] *m* (-s, -s) (railroad) car, *Br* (railway) carriage; freight car, *Br* goods waggon

Wagnis ['vaːknɪs] *n* (-ses; -se) venture, risk

Wa'gon *m* → **Waggon**

Wahl [vaːl] *f* (-; -en) choice; alternative; selection; POL election; voting, poll; vote; **die** ~ **haben** (**s-e** ~ **treffen**) have the (make one's) choice; **keine** (**ande-re**) ~ **haben** have no choice or alternative; 'wahlberechtigt *adj* POL entitled to vote; 'Wahlbeteiligung *f* POL poll, (voter) turnout; **hohe** (**niedrige**) ~ heavy (light) poll; 'Wahlbezirk *m* → **Wahlkreis**

wählen ['vɛːlən] *v/t and v/i* (ge-, h) choose, pick, select; POL vote (for); elect; TEL dial; 'Wähler *m* (-s; -) voter

'Wahlergebnis *n* election result

wählerisch ['vɛːlərɪʃ] *adj* F picky (**in** *dat*

about), *esp Br* choos(e)y

'Wählerschaft *f* (-; -en) electorate, voters

'Wahl|fach *n* PED *etc* elective, optional subject; ~ka,bine *f* voting (*esp Br* polling) booth; ~kampf *m* election campaign; ~kreis *m* electoral district, *Br* constituency; ~lo,kal *n* polling place (*Br* station)

'wahllos *adj* indiscriminate

'Wahl|pro,gramm *n* election platform; ~recht *n* (-[e]s; *no pl*) (right to) vote, suffrage, franchise; ~rede *f* election speech

'Wählscheibe *f* TEL dial

'Wahl|sieg *m* election victory; ~sieger *m* election winner; ~spruch *m* motto; ~urne *f* ballot box; ~versammlung *f* election rally

'Wahnsinn *m* (-[e]s; *no pl*) madness (*a.* F), insanity

'wahnsinnig **1.** *adj* mad (*a.* F), insane, F *a.* crazy; F awful, terrible **2.** F *adv* terribly, awfully; madly (*in love*)

'Wahnsinnige *m, f* (-n; -n) madman (madwoman), lunatic, maniac (*all a.* F)

'Wahnvorstellung *f* delusion, hallucination

wahr [va:ɐ] *adj* true; real; genuine

wahren ['va:rən] *v/t* (ge-, h) protect; **den Schein ~** keep up appearances

während ['vɛ:rənt] **1.** *prp* (*gen*) during **2.** *cj* while; whereas

'wahrhaft, wahr'haftig *adv* really, truly

'Wahrheit *f* (-; -en) truth

'wahrheits|gemäß, ~getreu *adj* true, truthful; ~liebend *adj* truthful

wahrnehmbar ['va:ɐne:mba:ɐ] *adj* noticeable, perceptible; 'wahrnehmen *v/t* (*irr*, **nehmen**, *sep*, -ge-, h) perceive, notice; seize, take (*chance etc*); look after (*s.o.'s interests etc*); 'Wahrnehmung *f* (-; -en) perception

'wahrsagen *v/i* (*sep*, -ge-, h) *j-m ~* tell s.o. his fortune; *sich ~ lassen* have one's fortune told; 'Wahrsager(in) ['va:ɐza:gɐ, 'va:ɐza:gərɪn] *m* (*f*) (-s; -/-; -nen) fortune-teller

wahr'scheinlich **1.** *adj* probable, likely **2.** *adv* probably, (very *or* most) likely; **~ gewinnt er** (**nicht**) he is (not) likely to win; Wahr'scheinlichkeit *f* (-; -en) probability, likelihood

Währung ['vɛ:rʊŋ] *f* (-; -en) currency

'Währungs... *in cpds* ...politik, ...reform *etc*: monetary ...

'Wahrzeichen *n* landmark

Waise ['vaizə] *f* (-; -n) orphan

'Waisenhaus *n* orphanage

Wal [va:l] *m* (-[e]s; -e) zo whale

Wald [valt] *m* (-[e]s; Wälder ['vɛldɐ]) wood(s), forest; ~brand *m* forest fire

'waldreich *adj* wooded

'Waldsterben *n* dying of forests

'Walfang *m* whaling

'Walfänger *m* whaler

Walkman® *m* (-s; -men) personal stereo, Walkman®

Wall [val] *m* (-[e]s; Wälle ['vɛlə]) mound; MIL rampart

Wallach ['valax] *m* (-[e]s; -e) zo gelding

wallen ['valən] *v/i* (ge-, sein) flow

'Wallfahrer *m*, 'Wallfahrerin *f* pilgrim

'Wallfahrt *f* pilgrimage

'Walnuss *f* BOT walnut

'Walross *n* zo walrus

Walze ['valtsə] *f* (-; -n) roller; cylinder; TECH, MUS barrel

'walzen *v/t* (ge-, h) roll (*a.* TECH)

wälzen ['vɛltsən] *v/t* (ge-, h) roll (*a.* **sich ~**); *fig* turn *s.th.* over in one's mind

Walzer ['valtsɐ] *m* (-s; -) MUS waltz (*a.* **~ tanzen**)

wand [vant] *pret of* **winden**

Wand *f* (-; Wände ['vɛndə]) wall, *fig a.* barrier

Wandale [van'da:lə] *m* (-n; -n) vandal; Wandalismus [vanda'lɪsmʊs] *m* (-; *no pl*) vandalism

Wandel ['vandəl] *m* (-s; *no pl*), 'wandeln *v/t* and *v/i*refl (ge-, h) change

Wanderer ['vandərɐ] *m* (-s; -), 'Wanderin *f* (-; -nen) hiker

wandern ['vandɐn] *v/i* (ge-, sein) hike; ramble (*about*); *eyes etc*: roam, wander

'Wander|po,kal *m* challenge cup; ~preis *m* challenge trophy; ~schuhe *pl* walking shoes; ~tag *m* (school) outing *or* excursion

'Wanderung *f* (-; -en) walking tour, hike; zo *etc* migration

'Wand|gemälde *n* mural; ~ka,lender *m* wall calendar; ~karte *f* wallchart

Wandlung ['vandlʊŋ] *f* (-; -en) change

'Wand|schrank *m* closet, *Br* built-in cupboard; ~tafel *f* blackboard

wandte ['vantə] *pret of* **wenden**

'Wandteppich *m* tapestry

W

Wange ['vaŋə] f (-; -n) ANAT cheek

Wankelmotor ['vaŋkəlmoːtoːɐ] m rotary piston or Wankel engine

wankelmütig ['vaŋkəlmyːtɪç] adj fickle

wanken ['vaŋkən] v/i (ge-, sein) stagger, reel; fig rock

wann [van] interr adv when, (at) what time; **seit ~?** (for) how long?, since when?

Wanne ['vanə] f (-; -n) tub (a. F); bath (-tub)

Wanze ['vantsə] f (-; -n) zo bug (a. F)

Wapitihirsch [va'piːtihɪrʃ] m zo elk

Wappen ['vapən] n (-s; -) (coat of) arms

'Wappenkunde f heraldry

wappnen ['vapnən] fig v/refl (ge-, h) arm o.s.

war [vaːɐ] pret of **sein**[1]

warb [varp] pret of **werben**

Ware ['vaːrə] f (-; -n) coll mst goods; article; product

'Waren|haus n department store; **~lager** n stock; **~probe** f sample; **~zeichen** n trademark

warf [varf] pret of **werfen**

warm [varm] adj warm (a. fig); GASTR hot; **schön ~** nice and warm; **~ halten** keep warm; **~ machen** warm (up)

Wärme ['vɛrmə] f (-; no pl) warmth; PHYS heat; **~iso,lierung** f heat insulation

'wärmen v/t (ge-, h) warm

'Wärmflasche f hot-water bottle

'warmherzig adj warm-hearted

'warmmachen v/t (sep, -ge-, h) → **warm**

Warm'wasser|bereiter m (-s; -) water heater; **~versorgung** f hot-water supply

'Warn|blinkanlage f MOT warning flasher; **~dreieck** n MOT warning triangle

warnen ['varnən] v/t (ge-, h) warn (**vor** dat of, against); **j-n davor ~, et. zu tun** warn s.o. not to do s.th.

'Warn|schild n danger sign; **~sig,nal** n warning signal; **~streik** m token strike

'Warnung f (-; -en) warning

'Warteliste f waiting list

warten[1] ['vartən] v/i (ge-, h) wait (**auf** acc for); **j-n ~ lassen** keep s.o. waiting

'warten[2] v/t (ge-, h) TECH service, maintain

Wärter ['vɛrtɐ] m (-s; -), **'Wärterin** f (-; -nen) attendant; zo keeper

'Warte|saal m, **~zimmer** n waiting room

'Wartung f (-; -en) TECH maintenance

warum [va'rʊm] interr adv why

Warze ['vartsə] f (-; -n) MED wart

was [vas] **1.** interr pron what; **~ gibt's?** what is it?, F what's up?; what's for lunch etc?; **~ soll's?** so what?; **~ machen Sie?** what are you doing?; what do you do?; **~ kostet ...?** how much is ...?; **~ für ...?** what kind or sort of ...?; **~ für e-e Farbe (Größe)?** what colo(u)r (size)?; **~ für ein Unsinn** what nonsense!; **~ für e-e gute Idee!** what a good idea! **2.** rel pron what; **~ (auch) immer** whatever; **alles, ~ ich habe (brauche)** all I have (need); **ich weiß nicht, ~ ich tun (sagen) soll** I don't know what to do (say); **..., ~ mich ärgerte...**, which made me angry **3.** F indef pron → **etwas**

waschbar ['vaʃbaːɐ] adj washable

'Waschbecken n washbowl, Br washbasin

Wäsche ['vɛʃə] f (-; -n) washing; (no pl) laundry; linen; underwear; **in der ~** in the wash; **schmutzige ~ waschen** wash one's dirty linen in public

'waschecht adj washable; fast (color); fig trueborn, genuine

'Wäsche|klammer f clothespin, Br clothes peg; **~leine** f clothesline

waschen ['vaʃən] v/t and v/refl (irr, ge-, h) wash; **sich die Haare (Hände) ~** wash one's hair (hands)

Wäscherei [vɛʃə'raɪ] f (-; -en) laundry

'Wasch|lappen m washcloth, Br flannel, facecloth; **~ma,schine** f washing machine, F washer

'waschma,schinenfest adj machine-washable

Wasch|mittel n, **~pulver** n washing powder; **~raum** m lavatory, washroom; **~sa,lon** m laundromat, Br launderette; **~straße** f MOT car wash

Wasser ['vasɐ] n (-s; -) water; **~ball** m beach ball; SPORT water polo; **~bett** n water bed; **~dampf** m steam

'wasserdicht adj waterproof; esp MAR watertight (a. fig)

'Wasser|fall m waterfall; falls; **~farbe** f water colo(u)r; **~flugzeug** n seaplane; **~graben** m SPORT water jump; **~hahn** m tap, faucet

wässerig ['vɛsərɪç] adj watery; **j-m den Mund ~ machen** make s.o.'s mouth water

'**Wasser|kessel** *m* kettle; **~klo,sett** *n* water closet, W.C.; **~kraft** *f* (-; *no pl*) water power; **~kraftwerk** *n* hydroelectric power station *or* plant; **~lauf** *m* watercourse; **~leitung** *f* waterpipe(s); **~mangel** *m* (-*s*; *no pl*) water shortage; **~mann** *m* (-[*e*]*s*; *no pl*) ASTR Aquarius; **er ist (ein) ~** he's (an) Aquarius

'**wassern** *v/i* (*ge-, h*) AVIAT touch down on water; *spacecraft*: splash down

'**wässern** ['vɛsən] *v/t* (*ge-, h*) water; AGR irrigate; GASTR soak; PHOT rinse

'**Wasserpflanze** *f* BOT aquatic plant

'**Wasserrohr** *n* TECH water pipe

'**Wasserscheide** *f* GEOGR watershed

'**wasserscheu** *adj* afraid of water

'**Wasser|ski 1.** *m* water ski **2.** *n* (-*s*; *no pl*) water skiing; **~ fahren** water-ski; **~spiegel** *m* water level; **~sport** *m* water *or* aquatic sports, aquatics; **~spülung** *f* TECH flushing cistern; **Toilette mit~** (flush) toilet, W.C.; **~stand** *m* water level; **~stoff** *m* (-[*e*]*s*; *no pl*) CHEM hydrogen; **~stoffbombe** *f* MIL hydrogen bomb, H-bomb; **~strahl** *m* jet of water; **~straße** *f* waterway; **~tier** *n* aquatic animal; **~verschmutzung** *f* water pollution; **~versorgung** *f* water supply; **~waage** *f* (*Br* spirit) level; **~welle** *f* water wave; **~werk(e)** *n*(*pl*) waterworks; **~zeichen** *n* watermark

waten ['vaːtən] *v/i* (*ge-, sein*) wade

watscheln ['vaːtʃəln] *v/i* (*ge-, sein*) waddle

Watt¹ [vat] *n* (-*s*; -) ELECTR watt

Watt² *n* (-[*e*]*s*; -*en*) GEOGR mud flats

Watte ['vatə] *f* (-; -*n*) cotton wool

wattiert [va'tiːrt] *adj* padded; quilted

weben ['veːbən] *v/t* and *v/i* ([*irr*,] *ge-, h*) weave; **Weber** ['veːbə] *m* (-*s*; -) weaver; **Weberei** [veːbə'rai] *f* (-; -*en*) weaving mill; '**Weberin** *f* (-; -*nen*) weaver; '**Webstuhl** ['veːpʃtuːl] *m* loom

Wechsel ['vɛksəl] *m* (-*s*; -) change; exchange; ECON bill of exchange; allowance; '**Wechselgeld** *n* (small) change

wechselhaft *adj* changeable

'**Wechseljahre** *pl* MED menopause

'**Wechselkurs** *m* ECON exchange rate

'**wechseln** *v/t* and *v/i* (*h*) change; exchange; vary; **~d** *adj* varying

'**wechselseitig** ['vɛksəlzaitiç] *adj* mutual, reciprocal

'**Wechsel|strom** *m* ELECTR alternating current; **~stube** *f* ECON exchange office; **~wirkung** *f* interaction

wecken ['vɛkən] *v/t* (*ge-, h*) wake (up), call; *fig* awaken (*memories etc*); rouse (*s.o.'s curiosity etc*)

Wecker ['vɛkə] *m* (-*s*; -) alarm (clock)

wedeln ['veːdəln] *v/i* (*ge-, h*) wave (**mit et.** s.th.); *skiing*: wedel; **mit dem Schwanz~** wag its tail

weder ['veːdə] *cj*: **~ ... noch ...** neither ... nor ...

Weg [veːk] *m* (- [*e*]*s; -e* ['veːgə]) way (*a. fig*); road (*a. fig*); path; route; walk; **auf friedlichem (legalem) ~e** by peaceful (legal) means; **j-m aus dem ~ gehen** get (*fig* keep) out of s.o.'s way; **j-n aus dem ~ räumen** put s.o. out of the way; **vom ~ abkommen** lose one's way; → **halb**

weg [vɛk] *adv* away; gone; off; F in raptures (*over* over, about); **Finger ~!** (keep your) hands off!; **nichts wie ~!** let's get out of here!; F **~ sein** be out; **~bleiben** *v/i* (*irr*, **bleiben**, *sep*, *-ge-, sein*) stay away; be left out; **~bringen** F *v/t* (*irr*, **bringen**, *sep*, *-ge-, h*) take away; **~ von** *... etc* so away from

wegen ['veːgən] *prp* (*gen*) because of; for the sake of; due *or* owing to; JUR for

wegfahren ['vɛkfaːrən] (*irr*, **fahren**, *sep*, *-ge-*) **1.** *v/i* (*sein*) leave **2.** *v/t* (*h*) take away, remove

'**wegfallen** *v/i* (*irr*, **fallen**, *sep*, *-ge-, sein*) be dropped; stop, be stopped

'**Weggang** ['vɛkgaŋ] *m* (-[*e*]*s*; *no pl*) leaving; '**weggehen** *v/i* (*irr*, **gehen**, *sep*, *-ge-, sein*) go away (*a. fig*), leave; *stain etc*: come off; ECON be sold

weg|jagen ['vɛkjaːgən] *v/t* (*sep*, *-ge-, h*) drive *or* chase away; **~kommen** F *v/i* (*irr*, **kommen**, *sep*, *-ge-, sein*) get away; get lost; **gut ~** come off well; **mach, dass du wegkommst!** get out of here!; *sl* get lost!; **~lassen** *v/t* (*irr*, **lassen**, *sep*, *-ge-, h*) let s.o. go; leave s.th. out; **~laufen** *v/i* (*irr*, **laufen**, *sep*, *-ge-, sein*) run away ([**vor**] *from* s.o.) (*a. fig*); **~legen** *v/t* (*sep*, *-ge-, h*) put away; **~nehmen** *v/t* (*irr*, **nehmen**, *sep*, *-ge-, h*) take away (**von** from); take up (*room, time*); steal (*s.o.'s girlfriend etc*); **j-m et.~** take s.th. (away) from s.o.; **~räumen**

W

v/t (*sep*, *-ge-*, *h*) clear away, remove; ~**schaffen** *v/t* (*sep*, *-ge-*, *h*) remove; ~**schicken** *v/t* (*sep*, *-ge-*, *h*) send away *or* off; ~**sehen** *v/i* (*irr*, **sehen**, *sep*, *-ge-*, *h*) look away; ~**setzen** *v/t* (*sep*, *-ge-*, *h*) move

Wegweiser ['veːkvaɪzɐ] *m* (*-s*; *-*) signpost; *fig* guide

Wegwerf... ['vɛkvɛrf-] *in cpds* ...**geschirr**, ...**besteck**, ...**rasierer** *etc*: throwaway ..., disposable ...; ...**flasche** *etc*: non-returnable ...; '**wegwerfen** *v/t* (*irr*, **werfen**, *sep*, *-ge-*, *h*) throw away

weg|wischen ['vɛkvɪʃən] *v/t* (*sep*, *-ge-*, *h*) wipe off; ~**ziehen** (*irr*, **ziehen**, *sep*, *-ge-*) **1.** *v/i* (*sein*) move away **2.** *v/t* (*h*) pull away

weh [veː] *adv*: ~ **tun** → **wehtun**

wehen ['veːən] *v/i* (*ge-*, *h*) blow; wave

'**Wehen** *pl* MED labo(u)r

wehmütig ['veːmyːtɪç] *adj* melancholy; wistful

Wehr[1] [veːɐ] *n* (*-[e]s*; *-e* ['veːrə]) weir

Wehr[2] *f*: **sich zur ~ setzen** → **wehren**

'**Wehrdienst** *m* (*-[e]s*; *no pl*) military service; ~**verweigerer** *m* (*-s*; *-*) conscientious objector

wehren ['veːrən] *v/refl* (*ge-*, *h*) defend o.s. (**gegen** against), fight (*a*. *fig* **gegen et.** s.th.); '**wehrlos** *adj* defenseless, *Br* defenceless; *fig* helpless

'**Wehrpflicht** *f* (*-*; *no pl*) compulsory military service; '**wehrpflichtig** *adj* liable to military service; '**Wehrpflichtige** *m* (*-n*; *-n*) draftee, *Br* conscript

'**wehtun** *v/t* (**j-m** s.o.; *fig* s.o.'s feelings); be aching; **sich** (**am Finger**) ~ hurt o.s. (hurt one's finger)

Weib [vaɪp] *n* (*-[e]s*; *-er* ['vaɪbɐ]) *contp* woman; bitch; '**Weibchen** *n* (*-s*; *-*) ZO female; '**weibisch** ['vaɪbɪʃ] *adj* effeminate, F sissy; '**weiblich** *adj* female; feminine (*a*. LING)

weich [vaɪç] *adj* soft (*a*. *fig*), tender; GASTR done; soft-boiled (*egg*); ~ **werden** soften; *fig* give in

Weiche ['vaɪçə] *f* (*-*; *-n*) RAIL switch, points

weichen ['vaɪçən] *v/i* (*irr*, *ge-*, *sein*) give way (*dat* to), yield (to); go (away)

'**weichlich** *adj* soft, effeminate, F sissy

'**Weichling** *m* (*-s*; *-e*) weakling, F softy, sissy

'**weichmachen** *v/t* (*sep*, *-ge-*, *h*): F **j-n** ~ soften s.o. up

'**Weichspüler** *m* (*-s*; *-*) fabric softener

'**Weichtier** *n* ZO mollusk, *Br* mollusc

Weide[1] ['vaɪdə] *f* (*-*; *-n*) BOT willow

'**Weide**[2] *f* (*-*; *-n*) AGR pasture; **auf die** (**der**) ~ to (at) pasture; '**Weideland** *n* pasture(land), range; '**weiden** *v/t* and *v/i* (*ge-*, *h*) graze, pasture; *fig* **sich an** (*dat*) feast on; *contp* gloat over

weigern ['vaɪɡɐn] *v/refl* (*ge-*, *h*) refuse

Weigerung ['vaɪɡərʊŋ] *f* (*-*; *-en*) refusal

Weihe ['vaɪə] *f* (*-*; *-n*) REL consecration; ordination; '**weihen** *v/t* (*ge-*, *h*) consecrate; **zum Priester** ~ ordain s.o. priest

Weiher ['vaɪɐ] *m* (*-s*; *-*) pond

Weihnachten ['vaɪnaxtən] *n* (*-*; *-*) Christmas, F Xmas

'**Weihnachts|abend** *m* Christmas Eve; ~**baum** *m* Christmas tree; ~**einkäufe** *pl* Christmas shopping; ~**geschenk** *n* Christmas present; ~**lied** *n* (Christmas) carol; ~**mann** *m* Father Christmas, Santa Claus; ~**markt** *m* Christmas fair; ~**tag** *m* Christmas Day; **zweiter** ~ day after Christmas, *esp Br* Boxing Day; ~**zeit** *f* Christmas season

'**Weih|rauch** *m* REL incense; ~**wasser** *n* (*-s*; *no pl*) REL holy water

weil [vaɪl] *cj* because; since, as

'**Weilchen** *n*: **ein** ~ a little while

Weile ['vaɪlə] *f*: **e-e** ~ a while

Wein [vaɪn] *m* (*-[e]s*; *-e*) wine; BOT vine; ~**(an)bau** *m* (*-[e]s*; *no pl*) wine growing; ~**beere** *f* grape; ~**berg** *m* vineyard; ~**brand** *m* brandy

weinen ['vaɪnən] *v/i* (*ge-*, *h*) cry (**vor** *dat* with; **nach** for; **wegen** about, over); weep (**um** for, over; **über** *acc* at; **vor** *dat* for, with); '**weinerlich** ['vaɪnɐlɪç] *adj* tearful; whining

'**Wein|fass** *n* wine cask *or* barrel; ~**flasche** *f* wine bottle; ~**händler** *m* wine merchant; ~**hauer** *Austrian m* → **Winzer**; ~**karte** *f* wine list; ~**keller** *m* wine cellar *or* vault, vaults; ~**kellerei** *f* winery; ~**kenner** *m* wine connoisseur; ~**lese** *f* vintage; ~**presse** *f* wine press; ~**probe** *f* wine tasting; ~**rebe** *f* BOT vine

'**weinrot** *adj* claret

'**Weinstock** *m* BOT vine

'**Weintraube** *f* → **Traube**

weise ['vaɪzə] *adj* wise

'**Weise** *f* (*-*; *-n*) way; MUS tune; **auf diese**

(*die gleiche*) **~** this (the same) way; *auf m-e* (*s-e*) **~** my (his) way

weisen ['vaizən] *v/t and v/i* (*irr, ge-, h*) show; *j-n von der Schule* **~** expel s.o. from school; **~** *auf* (*acc*) point to *or* at; *von sich* **~** reject; repudiate

Weisheit ['vaishait] *f* (*-; -en*) wisdom; *mit s-r* **~** *am Ende sein* be at one's wit's end

'**Weisheitszahn** *m* wisdom tooth

weismachen ['vaismaxən] F *v/t*: *j-m* **~**, *dass* make s.o. believe that; *du kannst mir nichts* **~** you can't fool me

weiß [vais] *adj* white; **~** *werden or* **machen** whiten; '**Weißbrot** *n* white bread; '**Weiße** *m, f* (*-n; -n*) white, white man (woman), *pl* the whites

'**weißen** *v/t* (*ge-, h*) whitewash

'**Weißkohl** *m*, '**Weißkraut** *n* BOT (green, *Br* white) cabbage

'**weißlich** *adj* whitish

'**weißmachen** *v/t* (*sep, -ge-, h*) → *weiß*

'**Weißwein** *m* white wine

Weisung ['vaizʊŋ] *f* (*-; -en*) instruction, directive

weit [vait] **1.** *adj* wide, *clothes*: *a.* big; long (*way, trip etc*) **2.** *adv* far, a long way (*a. time and fig*); **~** *weg* far away (*von* from); *von* **~** *em* from a distance; **~** *und breit* far and wide; *bei* **~** *em* by far; *bei* **~** *em nicht so ...* not nearly as ...; **~** *über* (*acc*) well over; **~** *besser* far *or* much better; *zu* **~** *gehen* go too far; *es* **~** *bringen* go far; *wir haben es* **~** *gebracht* we have come a long way; **~** *blickend* *fig* farsighted; **~** *reichend* far-reaching; **~** *verbreitet* widespread

'**weit** *ab adv* far away (*von* from)

'**weit** *aus adv* (by) far, much

Weite ['vaitə] *f* (*-; -n*) width; vastness; expanse; *esp* SPORT distance

'**weiten** *v/t and v/refl* (*ge-, h*) widen

weiter ['vaitɐ] *adv* on, further; (*mach*) **~** *!* go on!; (*geh*) **~** *!* move on!; *und so* **~** and so on *or* forth, et cetera; *nichts* **~** nothing else; **~** *arbeiten* *v/i* (*sep, -ge-, h*) go on working; **~** *bilden* *v/refl* (*sep, -ge-, h*) improve one's knowledge; continue one's education *or* training

'**Weiterbildung** *f* (*-; no pl*) further education *or* training

weitere ['vaitərə] *adj* further, additional; *alles Weitere* the rest; *bis auf* **~** *s* until further notice; *ohne* **~** *s* easily;

Weiteres more, (further) details

'**weiter** *geben v/t* (*irr, geben, sep, -ge-, h*) pass (*dat, an acc* to) (*a. fig*); **~** *gehen* *v/i* (*irr, gehen, sep, -ge-, sein*) move on; *fig* continue, go on

'**weiter** *hin adv* further(more); *et.* **~** *tun* go on doing s.th., continue to do s.th.

'**weiter** *kommen* *v/i* (*irr, kommen, sep, -ge-, sein*) get on (*fig* in life); **~** *leben* *v/i* (*sep, -ge-, h*) live on, *fig a.* survive; **~** *machen* *v/t and v/i* (*sep, -ge-, h*) go *or* carry on, continue

'**Weiterverkauf** *m* resale

'**weit** *gehend* **1.** *adj* considerable **2.** *adv* largely; **~** *läufig* *adj* spacious; distant (*relative*); **~** *sichtig* *adj* MED farsighted (*a. fig*), *Br* longsighted

'**Weitsprung** *m* broad (*Br* long) jump

'**Weitwinkelobjek,tiv** *n* PHOT wide-angle lens

Weizen ['vaitsən] *m* (*-s; -*) BOT wheat

welche ['velçə], **welcher** ['velçɐ], **welches** ['velçəs] **1.** *interr pron* what, which; *welcher?* which one?; *welcher von beiden?* which of the two? **2.** *rel pron* who, that; which, that **3.** F *welche indef pron* some, any

welk [velk] *adj* faded, withered; flabby

welken ['velkən] *v/i* (*ge-, sein*) fade, wither

'**Wellblech** *n* corrugated iron

Welle ['velə] *f* (*-; -n*) wave (*a.* PHYS *and fig*); TECH shaft; '**wellen** *v/t and v/refl* (*ge-, h*) wave

'**Wellenlänge** *f* ELECTR wavelength

'**Wellensittich** ['velənzitiç] *m* (*-s; -e*) ZO budgerigar, F budgie

'**wellig** ['veliç] *adj* wavy

Welt [velt] *f* (*-; -en*) world; *die ganze* **~** the whole world; *auf der ganzen* **~** all over *or* throughout the world; *das beste etc ... der* **~** the best *etc ...* in the world, the world's best *etc ...*; *zur* **~** *kommen* be born; *zur* **~** *bringen* give birth to

'**Weltall** *n* universe

'**weltberühmt** *adj* world-famous

Weltgewicht ['veltgəviçt] *n* (*-[e]s; no pl*), '**Weltgewichtler** *m* (*-s; -*) SPORT welterweight

'**weltfremd** *adj* naive, unrealistic

'**Weltfriede(n)** *m* world peace

'**Weltgeschichte** *f* world history

'**weltklug** *adj* worldlywise

'**Weltkrieg** *m* world war; *der Zweite ~* World War II

'**Weltkugel** *f* globe

'**weltlich** *adj* worldly

'**Welt|litera,tur** *f* world literature; *~macht* *f* POL world power; *~markt* *m* ECON world market; *~meer* *n* ocean; *~meister(in)* world champion; *~meisterschaft* *f* world championship; *esp* soccer: World Cup; *~raum* *m* (-[e]s; no pl) (outer) space; *~reich* *n* empire; *~reise* *f* world trip; *~re,kord* *m* world record; *~stadt* *f* metropolis; *~untergang* *m* end of the world

'**weltweit** *adj* worldwide

'**Weltwirtschaft** *f* world economy

'**Weltwirtschaftskrise** *f* worldwide economic crisis

'**Weltwunder** *n* wonder of the world

Wende ['vɛndə] *f* (-; -n) turn (a. swimming); change; *~kreis* *m* ASTR, GEOGR tropic; MOT turning circle

Wendeltreppe ['vɛndəltrɛpə] *f* spiral staircase

'**wenden** *v/t and v/i* (ge-, h) *and v/refl* ([irr.] ge-, h) turn (*nach* to; *gegen* against); MOT turn (round); GASTR turn over; *sich an j-n um Hilfe ~* turn to s.o. for help; *bitte ~* please turn over, pto

'**Wendepunkt** *m* turning point

wendig ['vɛndɪç] *adj* MOT, MAR maneuverable, *Br* manoeuvrable; *fig* nimble

'**Wendung** *f* (-; -en) turn, *fig a.* change; expression, phrase

wenig ['ve:nɪç] *indef pron and adv* little; *~(e)* *pl* few; *nur ~e* only few; only a few; *(in) ~er als* (in) less than; *am ~sten* least of all; *er spricht ~* he doesn't talk much; *(nur) ein (klein) ~* (just) a little (bit)

'**wenigstens** *adv* at least

wenn [vɛn] *cj* when; if; *~ ... nicht* if ... not, unless; *~ auch* (al)though, even though; *wie* *or als* as as though, as if; *~ ich nur ... wäre!* if only I were ...!; *~ auch noch so ...* no matter how ...; *und ~ nun ...?* what if ...?

wer [ve:ɐ] **1.** *interr pron* who, which; *~ von euch?* which of you? **2.** *rel pron* who; *~ auch (immer)* who(so)ever **3.** *F indef pron* somebody, anybody

Werbe|abteilung ['vɛrbəʔaptaɪluŋ] *f* publicity department; *~agen,tur* *f* advertising agency; *~feldzug* *m* advertis-

ing campaign; *~fernsehen* *n* commercial television; *~film* *m* promotion(al) film; *~funk* *m* radio commercials

werben ['vɛrbən] (*irr, ge-, h*) **1.** *v/i* advertise (*für et.* s.th.), promote (s.th.), give *s.th.* *or s.o.* publicity; *esp* POL make propaganda (*für* for), canvass (for); *~ um* court (*a. fig*) **2.** *v/t* recruit; canvass, solicit

'**Werbesendung** *f*, '**Werbespot** ['vɛrbəspɔt] *m* (-s; -s) (TV) commercial

'**Werbung** *f* (-; *no pl*) advertising, (sales) promotion; *a.* POL *etc* publicity, propaganda; recruitment; *~ machen für et.* advertise s.th.

Werdegang ['ve:ɐdəgaŋ] *m* career

werden ['ve:ɐdən] *v/i* (*irr, ge-, sein*) *and v/aux* become, get; turn, go; grow; turn out; *wir ~* we will (*or* shall), we are going to; *geliebt ~* be loved (*von* by); *was willst du ~?* what do you want to be?; *mir wird schlecht* I'm going to be sick; *F es wird schon wieder (~)* it'll be all right

werfen ['vɛrfən] *v/i and v/t* (*irr, ge-, h*) throw (*a. zo*) ([*mit*] *et. nach* s.th. at); drop (*bombs*); cast (*shadow*)

Werft [vɛrft] *f* (-; -en) MAR shipyard, dockyard

Werk [vɛrk] *n* (-[e]s; -e) work, deed; TECH mechanism; ECON works, factory; *ans ~ gehen* set *or* go to work; *~bank* *f* (-; -bänke) TECH workbench; *~meister* *m* TECH foreman

'**Werkstatt** *f* (-; -stätten) workshop; MOT garage

'**Werktag** *m* workday

'**werktags** *adv* on workdays

'**werktätig** *adj* working

'**Werkzeug** *n* tool (*a. fig*); *coll* tools; instrument; *~macher* *m* toolmaker

wert [ve:ɐt] *adj* worth; *die Mühe (e-n Versuch) ~* worth the trouble (a try); *fig nichts ~* no good; *Wert* *m* (-[e]s; -e) value, *esp fig a.* worth; use; *pl* data, figures; *... im ~(e) von 20 Dollar* 20 dollars' worth of ...; *großen ~ legen auf* (*acc*) set great store by

werten ['ve:ɐtən] *v/t* (ge-, h) value; *a.* SPORT rate, judge

'**Wertgegenstand** *m* article of value

'**wertlos** *adj* worthless

'**Wertpa,piere** *pl* securities

'**Wertsachen** *pl* valuables

'**Wertung** f (-; -en) valuation; a. SPORT rating, judging; score, points

'**wertvoll** adj valuable

Wesen ['ve:zən] n (-s; -) being, creature; fig essence; nature, character

'**wesentlich** adj essential; considerable; **im Wesentlichen** on the whole

weshalb [vɛs'halp] interr adv → **warum**

Wespe ['vɛspə] f (-; -n) zo wasp

Weste ['vɛstə] f (-; -n) vest, Br waistcoat

Westen ['vɛstən] m (-s; no pl) west; POL West

Western ['vɛstən] m (-s; -) western

'**westlich 1.** adj western; westerly; POL West(ern) **2.** adv: **~ von** (to the) west of

'**Westwind** m west(erly) wind

Wettbewerb ['vɛtbəvɛrp] m (-[e]s; -e) competition (a. ECON), contest

'**Wettbü**,**ro** n betting office

Wette ['vɛtə] f (-; -n) bet; **e-e ~ abschließen** make a bet; **um die ~ laufen** etc race (**mit j-m** s.o.)

'**wetteifern** v/i (ge-; h) compete (**mit** with; **um** for)

'**wetten** v/i and v/t (ge-; h) bet; **mit j-m um 10 Dollar ~** bet s.o. ten dollars; **~ auf** (acc) bet on, back

Wetter ['vɛtə] n (-s; -) weather

'**Wetterbericht** m weather report

'**Wetterfahne** f weather vane

'**wetterfest** adj weatherproof

'**Wetter**|**karte** f weather chart; **~lage** f weather situation; **~leuchten** n sheet lightning; **~vorhersage** f weather forecast; **~warte** f weather station

'**Wett**|**kampf** m competition, contest; **~kämpfer(in)** contestant, competitor; **~lauf** m race (a. fig **mit** against); **~läufer(in)** runner

'**wettmachen** v/t (sep, -ge-, h) make up for

'**Wettrennen** n race

'**Wettrüsten** n (-s; no pl) arms race

'**Wettstreit** m contest, competition

wetzen ['vɛtsən] v/t (ge-; h) whet, sharpen

wich [vɪç] pret of **weichen**

wichtig ['vɪçtɪç] adj important

'**Wichtigkeit** f (-; no pl) importance

'**wickeln** v/t (ge-; h) change (baby); **~ in** (acc) wrap in; **~ um** wrap (a)round

Widder ['vɪdə] m (-s; -) zo ram; ASTR Aries; **er ist (ein)** ~ he's (an) Aries

wider ['vi:də] prp (acc) **~ Willen** against

one's will; **~ Erwarten** contrary to expectations

'**Widerhaken** m barb

'**widerhallen** v/i (sep, -ge-, h) resound (**von** with)

wider'legen v/t (no -ge-, h) refute, disprove

'**widerlich** adj sickening, disgusting

'**widerrechtlich** adj illegal, unlawful

'**Widerruf** m JUR revocation; withdrawal; **wider'rufen** v/t (irr, **rufen**, no -ge-, h) revoke; withdraw

Widersacher ['vi:dəzaxə] m (-s; -) adversary, rival

'**Widerschein** m reflection

wider'setzen v/refl (no -ge-, h) (dat) oppose, resist

'**widersinnig** adj absurd

'**widerspenstig** ['vi:dəʃpɛnstɪç] adj unruly, stubborn

'**widerspiegeln** v/t (sep, -ge-, h) reflect (a. fig); **sich ~ in** (dat) be reflected in

wider'sprechen v/i (irr, **sprechen**, no -ge-, h) (dat) contradict

'**Widerspruch** m contradiction

widersprüchlich ['vi:dəʃprʏçlɪç] adj contradictory

'**widerspruchslos** adv without contradiction

'**Widerstand** m resistance (a. ELECTR), opposition; **~ leisten** offer resistance (dat to); '**widerstandsfähig** adj resistant (a. TECH); **wider'stehen** v/i (irr, **stehen**, no -ge-, h) (dat) resist

wider'streben v/i (no -ge-, h) **es widerstrebt mir, dies zu tun** I hate doing or to do that; **~d** adv reluctantly

widerwärtig ['vi:dəvɛrtɪç] adj disgusting

'**Widerwille** m aversion (**gegen** to), dislike (of, for); disgust (at)

'**widerwillig** adj reluctant, unwilling

widmen ['vɪtmən] v/t (ge-; h) dedicate; '**Widmung** f (-; -en) dedication

wie [vi:] **1.** interr adv how; **~ geht es Gordon?** how is Gordon?; **~ ist er?** what's he like?; **~ ist das Wetter?** what's the weather like?; **~ heißen Sie?** what's your name?; **~ nennt man ...?** what do you call ...?; **~ wäre (ist, steht) es mit ...?** what or how about ...?; **~ viele ...?** how many ...?; **2.** cj like; as; **~ neu (verrückt)** like new (mad); **doppelt so ... ~** twice as ... as; **~ (zum Beispiel)**

such as, like; **~ üblich** as usual; **~ er sagte** as he said; **ich zeige (sage) dir, ~ (...)** I'll show (tell) you how (...)

wieder ['viːdɐ] *adv* again; *in cpds often* re...; **immer ~** again and again; **~ aufbauen** reconstruct; **~ aufnehmen** resume; **~ beleben** MED resuscitate, revive (*a. fig*); **~ erkennen** recognize (**an** *dat* by); **~ finden** find (what one has lost); *fig* regain; **~ gutmachen** make up for; **~ herstellen** restore; **~ sehen** see or meet again; **~ verwendbar** reusable; **~ verwerten** TECH recycle

Wieder|aufbau *m* (-[*e*]*s*; *no pl*) reconstruction, rebuilding; **~'aufbereitung** *f* TECH recycling, reprocessing (*a.* NUCL); **~'aufbereitungsanlage** *f* TECH reprocessing plant; **~'aufleben** *n* (-*s*; *no pl*) revival; **~'aufnahme** *f* (-; *no pl*) resumption

'**wiederbekommen** *v/t* (*irr, kommen, sep, no -ge-, h*) get back

'**Wieder|belebung** *f* (-; *-en*) MED resuscitation; **~belebungsversuch** *m* MED attempt at resuscitation

'**wiederbringen** *v/t* (*irr, bringen, sep, -ge-, h*) bring back; return

Wieder'einführung *f* reintroduction

Wieder'entdeckung *f* rediscovery

'**Wiedergabe** *f* TECH reproduction, playback; '**wiedergeben** *v/t* (*irr, geben, sep, -ge-, h*) give back, return; *fig* describe; TECH play back, reproduce

Wieder'gutmachung *f* (-; *-en*) reparation

'**wiederholen**[1] *v/t* (*sep, -ge-, h*) (go and) get *s.o.* or *s.th.* back

wieder'holen[2] *v/t* (*no -ge-, h*) repeat; PED revise, review; THEA replay; *sich* **~** repeat o.s. (*a. fig*); **wieder'holt** *adv* repeatedly, several times

Wieder'holung *f* (-; *-en*) repetition; PED review; TV etc rerun; SPORT replay

Wiederkehr ['viːdɐkeːɐ] *f* (-; *no pl*) return; recurrence; '**wiederkehren** *v/i* (*sep, -ge-, sein*) return; recur

'**wiederkommen** *v/i* (*irr, kommen, sep, -ge-, sein*) come back, return

'**Wiedersehen** *n* (-*s*; -) seeing *s.o.* again; reunion; **auf ~!** goodbye!

wiederum ['viːdərʊm] *adv* again; on the other hand

'**Wieder|vereinigung** *f* reunion, *esp* POL *a.* reunification; **~verkauf** *m* resale;

~verwendung *f* reuse; **~verwertung** *f* (-; *-en*) TECH recycling; **~wahl** *f* POL re-election

Wiege ['viːgə] *f* (-; *-n*) cradle

wiegen[1] ['viːgən] *v/t and v/i* (*irr, ge-, h*) weigh

'**wiegen**[2] *v/t* (*ge-, h*) rock (**in den Schlaf** to sleep)

'**Wiegenlied** *n* lullaby

wiehern ['viːɐn] *v/i* (*ge-, h*) ZO neigh

wies [viːs] *pret of* **weisen**

Wiese ['viːzə] *f* (-; *-n*) meadow

Wiesel ['viːzəl] *n* (-*s*; -) ZO weasel

wieso [vi'zoː] *interr adv →* **warum**

wievielt [vi'fiːlt] *adj*: **zum ~en Male?** how many times?

wild [vɪlt] *adj* wild (*a. fig*) (F **auf** *acc* about); violent

Wild *n* (-[*e*]*s*; *no pl*) HUNT game; GASTR *mst* venison; **~bach** *m* torrent

Wilde ['vɪldə] *m*, *f* (-*n*; *-n*) savage; F **wie ein ~r** like mad

Wilderer ['vɪldərɐ] *m* (-*s*; -) poacher

wildern *v/i* (*ge-, h*) poach

'**Wildhüter** *m* gamekeeper

'**Wildkatze** *f* ZO wild cat

'**Wildleder** *n* suede

Wildnis *f* (-; *-se*) wilderness

'**Wild|park** *m*, **~reser,vat** *n* game park or reserve; **~schwein** *n* ZO wild boar

Wille ['vɪlə] *m* (-*ns*; *-n*) will; intention; **s-n ~n durchsetzen** have or get one's own way; **j-m s-n ~n lassen** let *s.o.* have his (own) way

'**willenlos** *adj* weak(-willed)

'**Willenskraft** *f* (-; *no pl*) willpower; **durch ~ erzwingen** will

'**willensstark** *adj* strong-willed

willig ['vɪlɪç] *adj* willing

will'kommen *adj* welcome (*a.* **~ heißen**) (**in** *dat* to)

willkürlich ['vɪlkyːɐlɪç] *adj* arbitrary; random

wimmeln ['vɪməln] *v/i* (*ge-, h*) **~ von** be teeming with

wimmern ['vɪmɐn] *v/i* (*ge-, h*) whimper

Wimpel ['vɪmpəl] *m* (-*s*; -) pennant

Wimper ['vɪmpɐ] *f* (-; *-n*) eyelash; **ohne mit der ~ zu zucken** without turning a hair; '**Wimperntusche** *f* mascara

Wind [vɪnt] *m* (-[*e*]*s*; *-e* ['vɪndə]) wind

Winde ['vɪndə] *f* (-; *-n*) winch, windlass, hoist

Windel ['vɪndəl] *f* (-; *-n*) diaper, *Br* nappy

winden ['vɪndən] v/t (*irr, ge-, h*) wind, TECH *a.* hoist; **sich ~** wind (one's way); writhe (*with pain etc*)

'**Windhund** *m* ZO greyhound

windig ['vɪndɪç] *adj* windy

'**Wind|mühle** f windmill; **~pocken** *pl* MED chickenpox; **~richtung** f direction of the wind; **~schutzscheibe** f MOT windshield, *Br* windscreen; **~stärke** f wind force

'**windstill** *adj*, '**Windstille** f calm

'**Windstoß** *m* gust

'**Windsurfen** *n* windsurfing

'**Windung** f (*-; -en*) bend, turn (*a.* TECH)

Wink [vɪŋk] *m* (*-[e]s; -e*) sign; *fig* hint

Winkel ['vɪŋkəl] *m* (*-s; -*) corner; MATH angle; '**winkelig** *adj* angular; crooked

winken ['vɪŋkən] v/i (*ge-, h*) wave (one's hand *etc*), signal; beckon

winseln ['vɪnzəln] v/i (*ge-, h*) whimper, whine

Winter ['vɪntɐ] *m* (*-s; -*) winter

'**winterlich** *adj* wintry

'**Winter|reifen** *m* MOT snow tire (*Br* tyre); **~schlaf** *m* ZO hibernation; **~spiele** *pl*: **Olympische~** SPORT Winter Olympics; **~sport** *m* winter sports

Winzer ['vɪntsɐ] *m* (*-s; -*) winegrower

winzig ['vɪntsɪç] *adj* tiny, diminutive

Wipfel ['vɪpfəl] *m* (*-s; -*) (tree)top

Wippe ['vɪpə] f (*-; -n*), '**wippen** v/i (*ge-, h*) seesaw

wir [viːɐ] *pers pron* we; **~ drei** the three of us; F **~ sind's!** it's us!

Wirbel ['vɪrbəl] *m* (*-s; -*) whirl (*a. fig*); ANAT vertebra

'**wirbeln** v/i (*ge-, sein*) whirl

'**Wirbel|säule** f ANAT spinal column, spine; **~sturm** *m* cyclone, tornado; **~tier** *n* vertebrate; **~wind** *m* whirlwind

wirken ['vɪrkən] (*ge-, h*) **1.** v/i work; be effective (**gegen** against); look; **anregend** *etc* **~** have a stimulating *etc* effect (**auf** *acc* [up]on); **~ als** act as **2.** v/t weave; *fig* work (*miracles etc*)

wirklich ['vɪrklɪç] *adj* real, actual; true, genuine; '**Wirklichkeit** f (*-; -en*) reality; **in~** in reality, actually

wirksam ['vɪrkzaːm] *adj* effective

'**Wirkung** f (*-; -en*) effect

'**wirkungslos** *adj* ineffective

'**wirkungsvoll** *adj* effective

wirr [vɪr] *adj* confused, mixed-up; hair:

tousled; **Wirren** ['vɪrən] *pl* disorder, confusion; **Wirrwarr** ['vɪrvar] *m* (*-s; no pl*) confusion, mess, welter

Wirt [vɪrt] *m* (*-[e]s; -e*) landlord; '**Wirtin** f (*-; -nen*) landlady; '**Wirtschaft** f (*-; -en*) ECON, POL economy; business; → **Gastwirtschaft**; '**wirtschaften** v/i (*ge-, h*) keep house; manage one's money *or* affairs *or* business; economize; **gut** (**schlecht**) **~** be a good (bad) manager; '**Wirtschafterin** f (*-; -nen*) housekeeper; '**wirtschaftlich** *adj* economic; economical; '**Wirtschafts...** ECON *in cpds* ...*gemeinschaft*, ...*gipfel*, ...*krise*, ...*system*, ...*wunder etc*: economic ...

'**Wirtshaus** *n* → **Gastwirtschaft**

wischen ['vɪʃən] v/t (*ge-, h*) wipe; **Staub ~** dust

wispern ['vɪspɐn] v/t *and* v/i (*ge-, h*) whisper

wissbegierig ['vɪsbəgiːrɪç] *adj* curious

wissen ['vɪsən] v/t *and* v/i (*irr, ge-, h*) know; **ich möchte ~** I'd like to know, I wonder; **soviel ich weiß** as far as I know; **weißt du** you know; **weißt du noch?** (do you) remember?; **woher weißt du das?** how do you know?; **man kann nie ~** you never know; **ich will davon (von ihm) nichts ~** I don't want anything to do with it (him)

'**Wissen** *n* (*-s; no pl*) knowledge; know-how; **m-s ~s** as far as I know

'**Wissenschaft** f (*-; -en*) science

'**Wissenschaftler** *m* (*-s; -*), '**Wissenschaftlerin** f (*-; -nen*) scientist

'**wissenschaftlich** *adj* scientific

'**wissenswert** *adj* worth knowing; **Wissenswertes** useful facts; **alles Wissenswerte** (**über** *acc*) all you need to know (about)

wittern ['vɪtɐn] v/t (*ge-, h*) scent, smell (*both a. fig*)

Witwe ['vɪtvə] f (*-; -n*) widow

Witwer ['vɪtvɐ] *m* (*-s; -*) widower

Witz [vɪts] *m* (*-es; -e*) joke; **~e reißen** crack jokes

witzig ['vɪtsɪç] *adj* funny; witty

wo [voː] *adv* where; **~ ... doch** when, although

wob [voːp] *pret of* **weben**

wobei [voˈbai] *adv*: **~ bist du?** what are you at?; **~ mir einfällt** which reminds me

Woche ['vɔxə] f (*-; -n*) week

W

'Wochen... in cpds ...lohn, ...markt, ...zeitung etc: weekly ...; ~ende n weekend; am~ on (Br at) the weekend

'wochenlang 1. adj: ~es Warten (many) weeks of waiting 2. adv for weeks

'Wochenschau f film: newsreel

'Wochentag m weekday

wöchentlich ['vœçəntlıç] 1. adj weekly 2. adv weekly, every week; einmal ~ once a week

wodurch [vo'dʊrç] adv how; through which

wofür [vo'fy:ɐ] adv for which; ~? what (...) for?

wog [vo:k] pret of wiegen¹ and wägen

Woge ['vo:gə] f (-; -n) wave, esp fig a. surge; breaker; 'wogen v/i (ge-, h) surge, heave (both a. fig)

woher [vo'he:ɐ] adv where ... from; ~ weißt du (das)? how do you know?

wohin [vo'hın] adv where (... to)

wohl [vo:l] adv and cj well; probably, I suppose; sich~ fühlen → wohlfühlen; ~ oder übel willy-nilly, whether you etc like it or not; ~ kaum hardly

Wohl n (-[e]s; no pl) well-being; auf j-s~ trinken drink to s.o.('s health); zum~! to your health!; F cheers!

'wohlbehalten adv safely

'Wohlfahrtsstaat m welfare state

'wohlfühlen v/refl (sep, -ge-, h): sich~ feel well, be well; feel good; feel at home (bei with); ich fühle mich nicht wohl I don't feel well

'wohl|gemerkt adv mind you; ~genährt adj well-fed; ~gesinnt adj: j-m~ sein be well-disposed towards s.o.; ~habend adj well-off, well-to-do

wohlig ['vo:lıç] adj snug, cozy, Br cosy

'Wohl|stand m (-[e]s; no pl) prosperity, affluence; ~standsgesellschaft f affluent society

'Wohltat f (-; no pl) pleasure; relief; blessing; 'Wohltäter(in) benefactor (benefactress); 'wohltätig adj charitable; für ~e Zwecke for charity

'Wohltätigkeits... in cpds ...ball, ...konzert etc: charity ...

'wohltun v/i (irr, tun, sep, -ge-, h): j-m~ do so. good

'wohlverdient adj well-deserved

'wohlwollend adj benevolent

wohnen ['vo:nən] v/i (ge-, h) live (in dat in; bei j-m with s.o.); stay (in dat at; bei with)

'Wohngebiet n residential area

'Wohngemeinschaft f: (mit j-m) in e-r ~ leben share an apartment (Br a flat) or a house (with s.o.)

wohnlich ['vo:nlıç] adj comfortable, snug, cozy, Br cosy

'Wohnmo,bil n (-s; -e) camper, motor home (Br caravan)

'Wohn|siedlung f housing development (Br estate); ~sitz m residence; ohne festen ~ of no fixed abode

'Wohnung f (-; -en) apartment, Br flat; m-e etc ~ my etc place

'Wohnungs|amt n housing office; ~bau m (-[e]s; no pl) house building; ~not f housing shortage

'Wohnwagen m trailer, Br caravan; mobile home

'Wohnzimmer n sitting or living room

wölben ['vœlbən] v/refl (ge-, h), 'Wölbung f (-; -en) vault, arch

Wolf [vɔlf] m (-[e]s; Wölfe ['vœlfə]) zo wolf

Wolke ['vɔlkə] f (-; -n) cloud

'Wolkenbruch m cloudburst

'Wolkenkratzer m (-s; -) skyscraper

'wolkenlos adj cloudless

wolkig ['vɔlkıç] adj cloudy, clouded

Woll... [vɔl-] in cpds ...schal, ...socken etc: wool(l)en ...; ~decke f blanket

Wolle ['vɔlə] f (-; -n) wool

wollen ['vɔlən] v/t and v/i (ge-, h) and v/aux (no -ge-, h) want (to); lieber~ prefer; ~ wir (gehen etc)? shall we (go etc)?; ~ Sie bitte ... will or would you please ...; wie (was, wann) du willst as (whatever, whenever) you like; sie will, dass ich komme she wants me to come; ich wollte, ich wäre (hätte) ... I wish I were (had) ...

womit [vo'mıt] adv with which; ~? what ... with?

Wonne ['vɔnə] f (-; -n) joy, delight

woran [vo'ran] adv: ~ denkst du? what are you thinking of?; ~ liegt es, dass ... ? how is it that ...?; ~ sieht man, welche (ob) ... ? how can you tell which (if) ...?

worauf [vo'rauf] adv after which; on which; ~? what ... on?; ~ wartest du? what are you waiting for?

woraus [vo'raus] adv from which; ~ ist es? what's it made of?

worin [voˈrɪn] *adv* in which; **~?** where?

Wort [vɔrt] *n* (-[e]s; -e, **Wörter** [ˈvœrtɐ]) word; **mit anderen ~en** in other words; **sein ~ geben** (**halten, brechen**) give (keep, break) one's word; **j-n beim ~ nehmen** take s.o. at his word; **ein gutes ~ einlegen für** put in a good word for; **j-m ins ~ fallen** cut s.o. short

'Wortart *f* LING part of speech

Wörter|buch [ˈvœrtɐbuːx] *n* dictionary; **~verzeichnis** *n* vocabulary, list of words

'Wortführer *m* spokesman; **'Wortführerin** *f* spokeswoman

'wortkarg *adj* taciturn

wörtlich [ˈvœrtlɪç] *adj* literal; **~e Rede** LING direct speech

'Wort|schatz *m* vocabulary; **~spiel** *n* pun; **~stellung** *f* LING word order

worüber [voˈryːbɐ] *adv* about which; **~ lachen Sie?** what are you laughing at *or* about?

worum [voˈrʊm] *adv* about which; **~ handelt es sich?** what is it about?

worunter [voˈrʊntɐ] *adv* among which; **~?** what ... under?

wovon [voˈfɔn] *adv* about which; **~ redest du?** what are you talking about?

wovor [voˈfoːɐ] *adv* of which; **~ hast du Angst?** what are you afraid of?

wozu [voˈtsuː] *adv*: **~ er mir rät** what he advised me to do; **~?** what (...) for?; why?

Wrack [vrak] *n* (-[e]s; -s) MAR wreck (*a. fig*)

wrang [vraŋ] *pret of* **wringen**

wringen [ˈvrɪŋən] *v/t* (*irr, ge-, h*) wring

Wucher [ˈvuːxɐ] *m* (-s; *no pl*) usury

Wucherer [ˈvuːxərɐ] *m* (-s; -) usurer

'wuchern *v/i* (*ge-, h*) grow (*fig* be) rampant; **Wucherung** [ˈvuːxərʊŋ] *f* (-; -en) MED growth

Wuchs [vuːks] *m* (-es; *no pl*) growth; build

wuchs [vuːks] *pret of* **wachsen**[1]

Wucht [vʊxt] *f* (-; *no pl*) force; impact

wuchtig [ˈvʊxtɪç] *adj* massive; powerful

wühlen [ˈvyːlən] *v/i* (*ge-, h*) dig; *zo* root; rummage (**in** *dat* in, through)

Wulst [vʊlst] *m* (-es; **Wülste** [ˈvʏlstə], *f*-; **Wülste**) bulge; roll (*of fat*)

wulstig [ˈvʊlstɪç] *adj* bulging; thick

wund [vʊnt] *adj* MED sore; **~e Stelle** MED sore; **~er Punkt** *fig* sore point

Wunde [ˈvʊndə] *f* (-; -n) MED wound

Wunder [ˈvʊndɐ] *n* (-s; -) miracle, *fig a.* wonder; **~ wirken** work wonders; (**es ist**) **kein ~, dass du müde bist** no wonder you are tired; **'wunderbar** *adj* wonderful, marvel(l)ous

'Wunderkind *n* infant prodigy

'wunderlich *adj* funny, odd; senile

'wundern *v/refl* (*ge-, h*) be surprised *or* astonished (**über** *acc* at)

'wundervoll *adj* wonderful

'Wundstarrkrampf *m* (-es; *no pl*) MED tetanus

Wunsch [vʊnʃ] *m* (-[e]s; **Wünsche** [ˈvʏnʃə]) wish; request; **auf j-s ~** at s.o.'s request; **auf eigenen ~** at one's own request; (**je**) **nach ~** as desired

wünschen [ˈvʏnʃən] *v/t* (*ge-, h*) wish; **sich et.** (**zu Weihnachten** *etc*) **~** want s.th. (for Christmas *etc*); **das habe ich mir** (**schon immer**) **gewünscht** that's what I (always) wanted; **alles, was man sich nur ~ kann** everything one could wish for; **ich wünschte, ich wäre** (**hätte**) **...** I wish I were (had) ...

'wünschenswert *adj* desirable

wurde [ˈvʊrdə] *pret of* **werden**

Würde [ˈvʏrdə] *f* (-; -n) dignity

'würdelos *adj* undignified

'Würdenträger *m* dignitary

'würdevoll *adj* dignified

würdig [ˈvʏrdɪç] *adj* worthy (*gen* of); dignified; **würdigen** [ˈvʏrdɪgən] *v/t* (*ge-, h*) appreciate; **j-n keines Blickes ~** ignore s.o. completely; **'Würdigung** *f* (-; -en) appreciation

Wurf [vʊrf] *m* (-[e]s; **Würfe** [ˈvʏrfə]) throw; *zo* litter

Würfel [ˈvʏrfəl] *m* (-s; -) cube (*a.* MATH); dice; **'würfeln** *v/i* (*ge-, h*) throw dice (**um** for); play dice; GASTR dice; **e-e Sechs ~** throw a six

'Würfelzucker *m* lump sugar

'Wurfgeschoss *n* missile

würgen [ˈvʏrgən] *v/i and v/t* (*ge-, h*) choke; throttle *s.o.*

Wurm [vʊrm] *m* (-[e]s; **Würmer** [ˈvʏrmɐ]) *zo* worm; **wurmen** [ˈvʊrmən] F *v/t* (*ge-, h*) gall *s.o.*; **'wurmstichig** [ˈvʊrmʃtɪçɪç] *adj* worm-eaten

Wurst [vʊrst] *f* (-; **Würste** [ˈvʏrstə]) sausage

Würstchen [ˈvʏrstçən] *n* (-s; -) small

sausage, frankfurter, wiener; hot dog

Würze ['vʏrtsə] f (-; -n) spice (a. fig)

Wurzel ['vʊrtsəl] f (-; -n) root (a. MATH); **~n schlagen** take root (a. fig)

'wurzeln v/i (ge-, h) **~ in** (dat) be rooted in (a. fig)

'würzen v/t (ge-, h) spice, season, flavo(u)r; **würzig** ['vʏrtsɪç] adj spicy, well-seasoned

wusch [vuːʃ] pret of **waschen**

wusste ['vʊstə] pret of **wissen**

Wust [vuːst] F m (-[e]s; no pl) tangled mass

wüst [vyːst] adj waste; confused; wild, dissolute

Wüste ['vyːstə] f (-; -n) desert

Wut [vuːt] f (-; no pl) rage, fury; **e-e ~ haben** be furious (**auf** acc with)

'Wutanfall m fit of rage

wüten ['vyːtən] v/i (ge-, h) rage (a. fig); **~d** adj furious (**auf** acc with; **über** acc at), F mad (at)

'wutschnaubend adj fuming

X, Y

X-Beine ['ɪksbainə] pl knock-knees; **sie hat ~** she's knock-kneed

x-beinig ['ɪksbainɪç] adj knock-kneed

x-be'liebig adj: **jede(r, -s) x-Beliebige** ... any ... you like, F any old ...

'x-mal F adv umpteen times

x-te ['ɪkstə] adj: **zum ~n Male** for the umpteenth time

Xylophon [ksylo'foːn] n (-s; -e) MUS xylophone

Yacht [jaxt] f (-; -en) MAR yacht

Yoga ['joːga] m, n (-[s]; no pl) yoga

Z

Zacke ['tsakə] f (-; -n), **'Zacken** m (-s; -) (sharp) point; tooth; **zackig** ['tsakɪç] adj serrated; jagged; fig smart

zaghaft ['tsaːkhaft] adj timid

zäh [tsɛː] adj tough (a. fig); **~flüssig** adj thick, viscous; fig slow-moving (traffic)

Zähigkeit ['tsɛːɪçkait] f (-; no pl) toughness, fig a. stamina

Zahl [tsaːl] f (-; -en) number; figure

'zahlbar adj payable (**an** acc to; **bei** at)

zählbar ['tsɛːlbaːɐ] adj countable

zahlen ['tsaːlən] v/i and v/t (ge-, h) pay; **~, bitte!** the check (Br bill), please!

zählen ['tsɛːlən] v/t and v/i (ge-, h) count (**bis** up to; fig **auf** acc on); **~ zu** rank with the best etc

'zahlenmäßig 1. adj numerical **2.** adv: **j-m ~ überlegen sein** outnumber s.o.

Zähler ['tsɛːlɐ] m (-s; -) counter (a. TECH); MATH numerator; ELECTR etc meter

'Zahlkarte f post deposit (Br paying-in) slip

'zahllos adj countless

'Zahlmeister m MIL paymaster; MAR purser

'zahlreich 1. adj numerous **2.** adv in great number

'Zahltag m payday

'Zahlung f (-; -en) payment

'Zählung f (-; -en) count; POL census

'Zahlungs|aufforderung f request for payment; **~bedingungen** pl terms of payment; **~befehl** m order to pay

'zahlungsfähig adj solvent

'Zahlungs|frist f term of payment; **~mittel** n currency; **gesetzliches ~** legal tender; **~schwierigkeiten** pl financial difficulties; **~ter,min** m date of payment

'zahlungsunfähig adj insolvent

'Zählwerk n TECH counter

'Zahlwort n LING numeral

zahm [tsaːm] adj tame (a. fig)

zähmen ['tsɛːmən] v/t (ge-, h) tame (a. fig); **'Zähmung** f (-; no pl) taming

Zahn [tsaːn] m (-[e]s; Zähne ['tsɛːnə]) tooth, TECH a. cog; **~arzt** m, **~ärztin** f dentist, dental surgeon; **~bürste** *f* toothbrush; **~creme** *f* toothpaste

zahnen ['tsa:nən] *v/i* (*ge-*, *h*) cut one's teeth, teethe

'**Zahnfleisch** *n* gums

'**zahnlos** *adj* toothless

'**Zahn|lücke** *f* gap between the teeth; **~medi,zin** *f* dentistry; **~pasta**, **~paste** *f* toothpaste; **~radbahn** *f* rack railroad; **~schmerzen** *pl* toothache; **~spange** *f* MED brace; **~stein** *m* tartar; **~stocher** *m* (*-s*; *-*) toothpick

Zange ['tsaŋə] *f* (*-*; *-n*) TECH pliers; pincers; tongs; MED forceps; ZO pincer

zanken ['tsaŋkən] *v/refl* (*ge-*, *h*) quarrel (**wegen** about; **um** over), fight, argue (about; over)

zänkisch ['tsɛŋkɪʃ] *adj* quarrelsome

Zäpfchen ['tsɛpfçən] *n* (*-s*; *-*) ANAT uvula; PHARM suppository

zapfen ['tsapfən] *v/t* (*ge-*, *h*) tap

'**Zapfen** *m* (*-s*; *-*) faucet, *Br* tap; TECH peg, pin; bung; tenon; pivot; BOT cone

'**Zapfenstreich** *m* MIL tattoo, taps

'**Zapf|hahn** *m* faucet, *Br* tap; MOT nozzle; **~säule** *f* MOT gasoline (*Br* petrol) pump

zappelig ['tsapəlɪç] *adj* fidgety

zappeln ['tsapəln] *v/i* (*ge-*, *h*) fidget, wriggle

zappen ['zɛpən] F *v/i* (*ge-*, *h*) TV zap

zart [tsa:ɐt] *adj* tender; gentle; **~ fühlend** sensitive

'**Zartgefühl** *n* (*-[e]s*; *no pl*) delicacy (of feeling), sensitivity, tact

zärtlich ['tsɛːɐtlɪç] *adj* tender, affectionate (**zu** with); '**Zärtlichkeit** *f* (*-*; *-en*) (*no pl*) tenderness, affection; caress

Zauber ['tsaubɐ] *m* (*-s*; *-*) magic, spell, charm (*all a. fig*), fig enchantment; **Zauberei** [tsaubə'rai] *f* (*-*; *-en*) magic, witchcraft; **Zauberer** ['tsaubərɐ] *m* (*-s*; *-*) magician, sorcerer, wizard (*a. fig*); '**zauberhaft** *fig adj* enchanting, charming; **Zauberin** ['tsaubərɪn] *f* (*-*; *-nen*) sorceress

'**Zauber|kraft** *f* magic power; **~künstler** *m* magician, conjurer; **~kunststück** *n* conjuring trick

'**zaubern** (*ge-*, *h*) **1.** *v/i* practise magic; do conjuring tricks **2.** *v/t* conjure (up)

'**Zauberspruch** *m* spell

zaudern ['tsaudɐn] *v/i* (*ge-*, *h*) hesitate

Zaum [tsaum] *m* (*-[e]s*; *Zäume* ['tsɔymə]) bridle; **im ~ halten** control (**sich** o.s.), keep in check

zäumen ['tsɔymən] *v/t* (*ge-*, *h*) bridle

'**Zaumzeug** *n* (*-[e]s*; *-e*) bridle

Zaun [tsaun] *m* (*-[e]s*; *Zäune* ['tsɔynə]) fence; **~gast** *m* onlooker; **~pfahl** *m* pale

z. B. *abbr of* **zum Beispiel** e.g., for example, for instance

Zebra ['tse:bra] *n* (*-s*; *-s*) ZO zebra

'**Zebrastreifen** *m* MOT zebra crossing

Zeche ['tsɛçə] *f* (*-*; *-n*) check, *Br* bill; (coal) mine, pit; **die ~ bezahlen müssen** F have to foot the bill

Zeh [tse:] *m* (*-s*; *-en*), **Zehe** ['tse:ə] *f* (*-*; *-n*) ANAT toe; **große** (**kleine**) **~** big (little) toe; '**Zehennagel** *m* ANAT toenail

'**Zehenspitze** *f* tip of the toe; **auf ~n gehen** (walk on) tiptoe

zehn [tse:n] *adj* ten; '**zehnfach** *adj* tenfold; '**zehnjährig** ['tse:nje:rɪç] *adj* ten-year-old (*boy etc*); ten-year *anniversary etc*; *absence etc* of ten years

Zehnkampf *m* SPORT decathlon

'**zehnmal** *adv* ten times; '**zehnte** *adj* tenth; '**Zehntel** *n* (*-s*; *-*) tenth; '**zehntens** *adv* tenthly

Zeichen ['tsaiçən] *n* (*-s*; *-*) sign; mark; signal; **zum ~** gen as a token of; **~block** *m* sketch pad; **~brett** *n* drawing board; **~dreieck** *n* MATH set square; **~folge** *f* IT string; **~lehrer(in)** art teacher; **~setzung** *f* (*-*; *no pl*) LING punctuation; **~sprache** *f* sign language; **~trickfilm** *m* (animated) cartoon

zeichnen ['tsaiçnən] *v/i and v/t* (*ge-*, *h*) draw; mark (*a. fig*); sign; fig leave its mark on *s.o.*; '**Zeichnen** *n* (*-s*; *no pl*) drawing; PED art; '**Zeichner** ['tsaiçnɐ] *m* (*-s*; *-*) *mst* graphic artist; draftsman, *Br* draughtsman; '**Zeichnung** *f* (*-*; *-en*) drawing; diagram; ZO marking

Zeigefinger ['tsaigəfɪŋɐ] *m* ANAT forefinger, index finger; **zeigen** ['tsaigən] (*ge-*, *h*) **1.** *v/t* show (*a.* **sich ~**); **2.** *v/i*: **~ nach** point to; (**mit dem Finger**) **~ auf** (*acc*) point (one's finger) at; **Zeiger** ['tsaigɐ] *m* (*-s*; *-*) hand; TECH pointer, needle; '**Zeigestock** *m* pointer

Zeile ['tsailə] *f* (*-*; *-n*) line (*a.* TV); **j-m ein paar ~n schreiben** drop s.o. a line

Zeit [tsait] *f* (*-*; *-en*) time; age, era; LING tense; **vor einiger ~** some time ago, a

Z

while ago; *in letzter* ~ lately, recently; *in der* (*or* **zur**) ~ *gen* in the days of; *... aller* ~*en* ... of all time; *die* ~ *ist um* time's up; *e-e* ~ *lang* for some time, for a while; *sich* ~ *lassen* take one's time; *es wird* ~*, dass* ... it's time to *inf*; *das waren noch* ~*en* those were the days; ~ *raubend* → *zeitraubend*; → *zurzeit*

'**Zeit|abschnitt** *m* period (of time); ~**alter** *n* age; ~**bombe** *f* time bomb (*a. fig*); ~**druck** *m*: *unter* ~ *stehen* be pressed for time; ~**fahren** *n* (*-s*; *no pl*) *cycling*: time trials

'**zeitgemäß** *adj* modern, up-to-date

'**Zeitgenosse** *m*, '**Zeitgenossin** *f*, '**zeitgenössisch** ['tsaitgənœsɪʃ] *adj* contemporary

'**Zeit|geschichte** *f* (*-*; *no pl*) contemporary history; ~**gewinn** *m* (*-[e]s*; *no pl*) gain of time; ~**karte** *f* season ticket

'**Zeitlang** *f* → **Zeit**

zeit'lebens *adv* all one's life

'**zeitlich 1.** *adj* time ... **2.** *adv*: *et.* ~ *planen or* **abstimmen** time s.th.

'**zeitlos** *adj* timeless; classic

'**Zeit|lupe** *f*: *in* ~ in slow motion; ~*not f*: *in* ~ *sein* be pressed for time; ~**punkt** *m* moment; ~**raffer** *m*: *im* ~ in quick motion

'**zeitraubend** *adj* time-consuming

'**Zeitraum** *m* period (of time)

'**Zeitschrift** *f* magazine

Zeitung ['tsaitʊŋ] *f* (*-*; *-en*) (news)paper

'**Zeitungs|abonne,ment** *n* subscription to a paper; ~**ar,tikel** *m* newspaper article; ~**ausschnitt** *m* (newspaper) clipping (*Br* cutting); ~**junge** *m* paper boy; ~**kiosk** *m* newspaper kiosk; ~**no,tiz** *f* press item; ~**pa,pier** *n* newspaper; ~**stand** *m* newsstand; ~**verkäufer(in)** newsdealer, *Br* news vendor

'**Zeitverlust** *m* (*-[e]s*; *no pl*) loss of time

'**Zeitverschiebung** *f* AVIAT time lag

'**Zeitverschwendung** *f* waste of time

'**Zeitvertreib** ['tsaitfɐtraip] *m* (*-[e]s*; *-e*) pastime; *zum* ~ to pass the time

zeitweilig ['tsaitvailɪç] *adj* temporary

'**zeitweise** *adv* at times, occasionally

'**Zeitwort** *n* (*-[e]s*; *-wörter*) LING verb

'**Zeitzeichen** *n radio*: time signal

'**Zeitzünder** *m* MIL time fuse

Zelle ['tsɛlə] *f* (*-*; *-n*) cell

Zellstoff ['tsɛlʃtɔf] *m*, **Zellulose** [tsɛlu-

'**lo:zə**] *f* (*-*; *-n*) TECH cellulose

Zelt [tsɛlt] *n* (*-[e]s*; *-e*) tent; **zelten** ['tsɛl-tən] *v/i* (*ge-*, *h*) camp; '**Zeltlager** *n* camp; '**Zeltplatz** *m* campsite

Zement [tse'mɛnt] *m* (*-[e]s*; *-e*), **zemen-tieren** [tsemen'tiːrən] *v/t* (*no -ge-*, *h*) cement

Zenit [tse'niːt] *m* (*-[e]s*; *no pl*) zenith

zensieren [tsɛn'ziːrən] *v/t* (*no -ge-*, *h*) censor; PED mark, grade; **Zensor** ['tsɛnzoːɐ] *m* (*-s*; *-en* [tsɛn'zoːrən]) censor; **Zensur** [tsɛn'zuːɐ] *f* (*-*; *-en* [tsɛn'zuːrən]) (*no pl*) censorship; PED mark, grade

Zentimeter [tsɛnti'meːtɐ] *n*, *m* (*-s*; *-*) centimeter, *Br* centimetre

Zentner ['tsɛntnɐ] *m* (*-s*; *-*) 50 kilograms, metric hundredweight

zentral [tsɛn'traːl] *adj* central

Zentrale [tsɛn'traːlə] *f* (*-*; *-n*) head office; headquarters; TEL switchboard; TECH control room

Zen'tral|heizung *f* central heating; ~**verriegelung** *f* MOT central locking

Zentrum ['tsɛntrʊm] *n* (*-s*; *Zentren*) center, *Br* centre

Zepter ['tsɛptɐ] *n* (*-s*; *-*) scepter, *Br* sceptre

zer'brechen *v/i* (*irr*, *brechen*, *no -ge-*, *sein*) *and v/t* (*h*) break; → **Kopf**

zer'brechlich *adj* fragile

zer'bröckeln *v/t* (*no -ge-*, *h*) *and v/i* (*sein*) crumble

zer'drücken *v/t* (*no -ge-*, *h*) crush

Zeremonie [tseremo'niː] *f* (*-*; *-n*) ceremony

zeremoniell [tseremo'njɛl] *adj*, **Zeremoni'ell** *n* (*-s*; *-e*) ceremonial

Zer'fall *m* (*-[e]s*; *no pl*) disintegration, decay; **zer'fallen** *v/i* (*irr*, *fallen*, *no -ge-*, *sein*) disintegrate, decay; ~ *in* (*acc*) break up into

zer'|fetzen *v/t* (*no -ge-*, *h*) tear to pieces; ~**fressen** *v/t* (*irr*, *fressen*, *no -ge-*, *h*) eat (holes in); CHEM corrode; ~'**gehen** *v/i* (*irr*, *gehen*, *no -ge-*, *sein*) melt, dissolve; ~'**hacken** *v/t* (*no -ge-*, *h*) chop (*a.* ELECTR)

zerknirscht [tsɐ'knɪrʃt] *adj* remorseful

zer'|knittern *v/t* (*no -ge-*, *h*) (c)rumple, crease; ~'**knüllen** *v/t* (*no -ge-*, *h*) crumple up; ~'**kratzen** *v/t* (*no -ge-*, *h*) scratch; ~'**krümeln** *v/t* (*no -ge-*, crumble; **~'lassen** v/t (irr, **lassen**, no -ge-, h) melt; **~'legen** v/t (no -ge-, h) take apart or to pieces; TECH dismantle; GASTR carve; CHEM, LING, fig analyze, Br analyse

zer'lumpt adj ragged, tattered

zer'mahlen v/t (no -ge-, h) grind

zer'mürben v/t (no -ge-, h) wear down

zer'quetschen v/t (no -ge-, h) crush

Zerrbild ['tsɛɐbɪlt] n caricature

zer'reiben v/t (irr, **reiben**, no -ge-, h) rub to powder, pulverize

zer'reißen (irr, **reißen**, no -ge-) **1.** v/t (h) tear up or to pieces; **sich die Hose ~** tear one's trousers **2.** v/i (sein) tear; break

zerren ['tsɛrən] (ge-, h) **1.** v/t tug, drag, pull (a. MED); **2.** v/i: **~ an** (dat) tug (or strain) at

'Zerrung f (-; -en) MED pulled muscle

zerrütten [tsɛɐ'rʏtən] v/t (no -ge-, h) ruin; **zer'rüttet** adj: **~e Ehe** (**Verhältnisse**) broken marriage (home)

zer|'sägen v/t (no -ge-, h) saw up; **~schellen** [tsɛɐ'ʃɛlən] v/i (no -ge-, sein) be smashed, AVIAT a. crash; **~'schlagen 1.** v/t (irr, **schlagen**, no -ge-, h) smash (to pieces); fig smash; **sich ~** come to nothing **2.** adj: **sich ~ fühlen** be (all) worn out, F be dead beat; **~'schmettern** v/t (no -ge-, h) smash (to pieces), shatter (a. fig); **~'schneiden** v/t (irr, **schneiden**, no -ge-, h) cut (up); **~'setzen** v/t (no -ge-, h) CHEM decompose (a. sich ~); fig corrupt, undermine; **~'splittern** v/t (no -ge-, h) and v/i (sein) split (up), splinter; shatter; **~'springen** v/i (irr, **springen**, no -ge-, sein) crack; shatter; **~'stampfen** v/t (no -ge-, h) pound; GASTR mash

zer'stäuben v/t (no -ge-, h) spray; **Zerstäuber** [tsɛɐ'ʃtɔʏbɐ] m (-s; -) atomizer, sprayer

zer'stören v/t (no -ge-, h) destroy, ruin (both a. fig); **Zer'störer** m (-s; -) destroyer (a. MAR); **zer'störerisch** adj destructive; **Zer'störung** f (-; -en) destruction

zer'streuen v/t and v/refl (no -ge-, h) scatter, disperse; break up (crowd etc); fig take s.o.'s (refl one's) mind off things; **zer'streut** fig adj absent-minded; **Zer'streutheit** f (-; no pl) ab-

sent-mindedness; **Zer'streuung** fig f (-; -en) diversion, distraction

zer'stückeln v/t (no -ge-, h) cut up or (in)to pieces; dismember (body)

Zertifikat [tsɛrtifi'kaːt] n (-[e]s; -e) certificate

zer'treten v/t (irr, **treten**, no -ge-, h) crush (a. fig)

zer'trümmern v/t (no -ge-, h) smash

zerzaust [tsɛɐ'tsaust] adj tousled, dishevel(l)ed

Zettel ['tsɛtəl] m (-s; -) slip (of paper); note; label, sticker

Zeug [tsɔʏk] n (-[e]s; -e) stuff (a. F); things; **er hat das ~ dazu** he's got what it takes; **dummes ~** nonsense

Zeuge ['tsɔʏgə] m (-n; -n) witness

zeugen[^1] v/i (ge-, h) give evidence (**für** for); fig **~ von** testify to

zeugen[^2] v/t (ge-, h) BIOL procreate; father

'Zeugen|aussage f JUR testimony, evidence; **~bank** f (-; -bänke) JUR witness stand (Br box)

'Zeugin f (-; -nen) JUR (female) witness

Zeugnis ['tsɔʏknɪs] n (-ses; -se) report card, Br (school) report; certificate, diploma; reference; pl credentials

'Zeugung f (-; -en) BIOL procreation

z. H(d). abbr of **zu Händen** attn, attention

Zickzack ['tsɪktsak] m (-[e]s; -e) (a. **im ~ fahren**) zigzag

Ziege ['tsiːgə] f (-; -n) ZO (nanny) goat; F contp (**blöde**) **~** (silly old) cow

Ziegel ['tsiːgəl] m (-s; -) brick; tile

'Ziegeldach n tiled roof

Ziegelei [tsiːgə'lai] f (-; -en) brickyard

'Ziegelstein m brick

'Ziegen|bock m ZO billy goat; **~leder** n kid (leather); **~peter** ['tsiːgənpeːtɐ] m (-s; -) MED mumps

ziehen ['tsiːən] (irr, -ge-) **1.** v/t (h) pull, draw; take off one's hat (**vor** dat to) (a. fig); AGR grow; pull or take out (**aus** of); **j-n ~ an** (dat) pull s.o. by; **auf sich ~** attract (attention etc); **sich ~** run; stretch; **→ Länge, Erwägung 2.** v/i (h) pull (**an** dat at); (sein) move; ZO etc migrate; go; travel; wander, roam; **es zieht** there's a draft (Br draught)

Ziehharmonika ['tsiːharmoːnika] f (-; -s) MUS accordion

[^1]: zeugen¹
[^2]: zeugen²

'Ziehung f (-; -en) draw

Ziel [tsiːl] n (-[e]s; -e) aim, target, mark (all a. fig), fig a. goal, objective; destination; SPORT finish; **sich ein ~ setzen** set o.s. a goal; **sein ~ erreichen** reach one's goal; **sich zum ~ gesetzt haben, et. zu tun** aim to do or at doing s.th.

'Zielband n (-[e]s; -bänder) SPORT tape

zielen ['tsiːlən] v/i (ge-, h) (take) aim (**auf** acc at)

'Ziellinie f SPORT finishing line

'ziellos adj aimless

'Zielscheibe f target, fig a. object

zielstrebig ['tsiːlʃtreːbɪç] adj purposeful, determined

ziemlich ['tsiːmlɪç] **1.** adj quite a **2.** adv rather, fairly, quite, F pretty; **~ viele** quite a few

Zierde ['tsiːɐdə] f (-; -n) (**zur** as a) decoration; **zieren** ['tsiːrən] v/t (ge-, h) decorate; **sich ~** be coy; make a fuss

zierlich ['tsiːɐlɪç] adj dainty; petite

Zierpflanze ['tsiːɐpflantsə] f ornamental plant

Ziffer ['tsɪfɐ] f (-; -n) figure

'Zifferblatt n dial, face

Zigarette [tsiga'rɛtə] f (-; -n) cigarette

Ziga'retten|auto,mat m cigarette machine; **~stummel** m cigarette end, stub, butt

Zigarre [tsi'garə] f (-; -n) cigar

Zimmer ['tsɪmɐ] n (-s; -) room; apartment; **~einrichtung** f furniture; **~mädchen** n (chamber)maid; **~mann** m carpenter

'zimmern v/t (ge-, h) build, make

'Zimmer|pflanze f indoor plant; **~service** m room service; **~suche** f: **auf ~ sein** be looking (or hunting) for a room; **~vermittlung** f accommodation office

zimperlich ['tsɪmpɐlɪç] adj prudish; soft, F sissy

Zimt [tsɪmt] m (-[e]s; -e) cinnamon

Zink [tsɪŋk] n (-[e]s; no pl) CHEM zinc

Zinke ['tsɪŋkə] f (-; -n) tooth; prong

Zinn [tsɪn] n (-[e]s; no pl) CHEM tin; pewter

Zins [tsɪns] m (-es; -en) ECON interest (a. pl); **3% ~en bringen** bear interest at 3%; **'zinslos** adj ECON interest-free; **'Zinssatz** m ECON interest rate

Zipfel ['tsɪpfəl] m (-s; -) corner; point; tail; GASTR end; **~mütze** f pointed cap

zirka ['tsɪrka] adv about, approximately

Zirkel ['tsɪrkəl] m (-s; -) circle (a. fig); MATH compasses, dividers

zirkulieren [tsɪrku'liːrən] v/i (no ge-, h) circulate

Zirkus ['tsɪrkus] m (-; -se) circus

zirpen ['tsɪrpən] v/i (ge-, h) chirp

zischen ['tsɪʃən] v/i and v/t (ge-, h) hiss; fat etc: sizzle; fig whiz(z)

ziselieren [tsizə'liːrən] v/t (no -ge-, h) TECH chase

Zitat [tsi'taːt] n (-[e]s; -e) quotation, F quote; **zitieren** [tsi'tiːrən] v/t (no -ge-,h) quote, cite (a. JUR); JUR summon

Zitrone [tsi'troːnə] f (-; -n) BOT lemon

Zi'tronen|limo,nade f lemon soda or pop, Br (fizzy) lemonade; **~saft** m lemon juice; **~schale** f lemon peel

zitterig ['tsɪtərɪç] adj shaky; **zittern** ['tsɪtɐn] v/i (ge-, h) tremble, shake (both: **vor** dat with)

zivil [tsi'viːl] adj civil, civilian

Zi'vil n (-s; no pl) civilian clothes; **Polizist in ~** plainclothes policeman

Zi'vildienst m MIL alternative service (in lieu of military service)

Zivilisation [tsiviliza'tsjoːn] f (-; -en) civilization; **zivilisieren** [tsivili'ziːrən] v/t (no -ge-, h) civilize

Zivilist [tsivi'lɪst] m (-en; -en) civilian

Zi'vilrecht n (-[e]s; no pl) JUR civil law

Zi'vilschutz m civil defen|se, Br -ce

Znüni ['tsnyːni] n (-s; -) Swiss m, n (-s; -) mid-morning snack, tea (or coffee) break

zog [tsoːk] pret of **ziehen**

zögern ['tsøːɡɐn] v/i (ge-, h) hesitate; **'Zögern** n (-s; no pl) hesitation

Zoll[1] [tsɔl] m (-[e]s; -) inch

Zoll[2] n (-[e]s; Zölle ['tsœlə]) (no pl) customs; duty

'Zollabfertigung f customs clearance

'Zollbeamte m customs officer

'Zollerklärung f customs declaration

'zollfrei adj duty-free

'Zollkon,trolle f customs examination

'zollpflichtig adj liable to duty

'Zollstock m (folding) rule

Zone ['tsoːnə] f (-; -n) zone

Zoo [tsoː] m (-s; -s) zoo

'Zoohandlung f pet shop

Zoologe [tsoo'loːɡə] m (-n; -n) zoologist; **Zoologie** [tsoolo'giː] f (-; no pl) zoology; **Zoo'login** f (-; -nen) zoologist; **zoo'logisch** adj zoological

Zopf [tsɔpf] *m* (-[e]s; *Zöpfe* ['tsœpfə]) plait; pigtail

Zorn [tsɔrn] *m* (-[e]s; *no pl*) anger

zornig ['tsɔrnɪç] *adj* angry

Zote ['tsoːtə] *f* (-; -n) filthy joke, obscenity

zottelig ['tsɔtəlɪç] *adj* shaggy

z. T. *abbr of* **zum Teil** partly

zu [tsuː] **1.** *prp* (*dat*) to, toward(s); at; *purpose:* for; **~ Fuß** (*Pferd*) on foot (horseback); **~ Hause** (*Ostern etc*) at home (Easter *etc*); **~ Weihnachten** give *etc* for Christmas; **Tür** (*Schlüssel*) **~** ... door (key) to ...; **~ m-r Überraschung** to my surprise; **wir sind ~ dritt** there are three of us; **~ zweien** two by two; **~ zwei Euro** at *or* for two euros; *sport* **1 ~ 1** one all; **2 ~ 1 gewinnen** win two one, win by two goals *etc* to one; → **zum, zur 2.** *adv* too; F closed, shut; **ein ~ großes Risiko** too much of a risk; **~ viel** too much, too many; **~ wenig** too little, too few **3.** *cj* to; **es ist ~ erwarten** it is to be expected

Zubehör ['tsuːbəhøːɐ] *n* (-[e]s; -e) accessories

zubereiten *v/t* (*sep, no* -ge-, *h*) prepare; **Zubereitung** *f* (-; -en) preparation

zu|binden *v/t* (*irr, binden, sep,* -ge-, *h*) tie (up); **~bleiben** *v/i* (*irr, bleiben, sep,* -ge-, *sein*) stay shut; **~blinzeln** *v/i* (*sep,* -ge-, *h*) wink at

Zubringer *m* (-s; -), **~straße** *f* MOT feeder (road), access road

Zucht [tsʊxt] *f* (-; -en) breed; zo breeding; BOT cultivation; **züchten** ['tsʏçtən] *v/t* (*ge-*, *h*) zo breed; BOT grow, cultivate; **Züchter(in)** ['tsʏçtɐ, 'tsʏçtərɪn] *m(f)* (-s; -/-; -nen) zo breeder; BOT grower

Zuchtperle *f* culture(d) pearl

zucken ['tsʊkən] *v/i* (*ge-*, *h*) jerk; twitch (**mit et.** s.th.); wince; *lightning:* flash

zücken ['tsʏkən] *v/t* (*ge-*, *h*) draw (*weapon*); F pull out (*one's wallet etc*)

Zucker ['tsʊkɐ] *m* (-s; -) sugar; **~dose** *f* sugar bowl; **~guss** *m* icing, frosting

zuckerkrank *adj*, **Zuckerkranke** *m, f* (-n; -n) MED diabetic

Zuckerkrankheit *f* MED diabetes

Zuckermais *m* sweet corn

zuckern *v/t* (*ge-*, *h*) sugar

Zuckerrohr *n* BOT sugarcane

Zuckerrübe *f* BOT sugar beet

Zuckerwatte *f* candy floss

Zuckerzange *f* sugar tongs

Zuckung *f* (-; -en) twitch(ing); tic; convulsion, spasm

zudecken *v/t* (*sep,* -ge-, *h*) cover (up)

zudem [tsuˈdeːm] *adv* besides, moreover

zudrehen *v/t* (*sep,* -ge-, *h*) turn off; **j-m den Rücken ~** turn one's back on s.o.

zudringlich *adj:* **~ werden** F get fresh (**j-m gegenüber** with s.o.)

zudrücken *v/t* (*sep,* -ge-, *h*) close, push *s.th.* shut; → **Auge**

zuerst [tsuˈʔeːɐst] *adv* first; at first; first (of all), to begin with

Zufahrt *f* approach; drive(way)

Zufahrtsstraße *f* access road

Zufall *m* chance; **durch ~** by chance, by accident; **zufallen** *v/i* (*irr, fallen, sep,* -ge-, *sein*) *door etc:* slam (shut); *fig* fall to *s.o.*; **mir fallen die Augen zu** I can't keep my eyes open; **zufällig 1.** *adj* accidental, chance ... **2.** *adv* by accident, by chance; **~ tun** happen to do

Zuflucht *f:* **~ suchen** (**finden**) look for (find) refuge *or* shelter (**vor** *dat* from; **bei** with); (**s-e**) **~ nehmen zu** resort to

zufrieden [tsuˈfriːdən] *adj* content(ed), satisfied; **~ stellen** satisfy; **~ stellend** satisfactory

zuˈfrieden|geben *v/refl* (*irr, geben, sep,* -ge-, *h*): **sich ~ mit** content o.s. with

Zuˈfriedenheit *f* (-; *no pl*) contentment, satisfaction

zuˈfrieden|lassen *v/t* (*irr, lassen, sep,* -ge-, *h*) leave s.o. alone; **~stellen** *v/t* (*sep,*-ge-, *h*) satisfy; **~stellend** *adj* satisfactory

zufrieren *v/i* (*irr, frieren, sep,* -ge-, *sein*) freeze up *or* over

zufügen *v/t* (*sep,* -ge-, *h*) do, cause; **j-m Schaden ~** *a.* harm s.o.

Zufuhr ['tsuːfuːɐ] *f* (-; -en) supply

Zug [tsuːk] *m* (-[e]s; *Züge* ['tsyːgə]) RAIL train; procession, line; parade; *fig* feature; trait; tendency; *chess etc:* move (*a. fig*); *swimming:* stroke; pull (*a.* TECH), PHYS *a.* tension; *smoking:* puff; draft, *Br* draught; PED stream; **im ~e gen** in the course of; **in e-m ~** at one go; **~ um ~** step by step; **in großen Zügen** in broad outlines

Zugabe *f* addition; THEA encore

Zugang *m* access (*a. fig*); **zugänglich**

['tsu:gɛnlɪç] adj accessible (**für** to) (a. fig)

'Zugbrücke f drawbridge

'zugeben v/t (irr, **geben**, sep, -ge-, h) add; fig admit

'zugehen v/i (irr, **gehen**, sep, -ge-, sein) F door etc: close, shut; **~ auf** (acc) walk up to, approach (a. fig); **es geht auf 8 Uhr zu** it's getting on for 8; **es ging lustig zu** we had a lot of fun

'Zugehörigkeit f (-; no pl) membership

'Zügel ['tsy:gəl] m (-s; -) rein (a. fig)

'zügeln 1. v/t (ge-, h) curb, control, bridle 2. Swiss v/i (ge-, sein) move

'Zugeständnis n concession

'zugestehen v/t (irr, **stehen**, sep, no -ge-, h) concede, grant

'zugetan adj attached (dat to)

'Zugführer m RAIL conductor, Br guard

zugig ['tsu:gɪç] adj drafty, Br draughty

'Zugkraft f TECH traction; (no pl) attraction, draw, appeal

'zugkräftig adj: **~ sein** be a draw

zu'gleich [tsu'glaɪç] adv at the same time

'Zugluft f (-; no pl) draft, Br draught

'Zugma,schine f MOT tractor

'zugreifen v/i (irr, **greifen**, sep, -ge-, h) grab (at) it; fig grab the opportunity; **greifen Sie zu!** help yourself!; **mit ~** lend a hand

'Zugriffscode m IT access code

'Zugriffszeit f IT access time

zugrunde [tsu'grʊndə] adv: **~ gehen** (**an** dat) perish (of); **e-r Sache et. ~ legen** base s.th. on s.th.; **~ richten** ruin

zugunsten [tsu'gʊnstən] prp (gen) in favo(u)r of

zu'gute [tsu'gu:tə] adv: **~ halten → zugutehalten**; **~ kommen → zugutekommen**; zu'gutehalten v/t (irr, **halten**, sep, -ge-, h): **j-m et. ~** give s.o. credit for s.th.; make allwances for s.o.'s ...; ~kommen v/t (irr, **kommen**, sep, -ge-, sein): **j-m ~** be for the benefit of s.o.

'Zugvogel m ZO bird of passage

'zuhalten v/t (irr, **halten**, sep, -ge-, h) keep shut; **sich die Ohren** (**Augen**) **~** cover one's ears (eyes) with one's hands; **sich die Nase ~** hold one's nose

Zuhälter ['tsu:hɛltɐ] m (-s; -) pimp

Zuhause [tsu'hauzə] n (-s; no pl) home

zu'hause adv → **Haus**

'zuhören v/i (sep, -ge-, h) listen (dat to)

Zuhörer m, 'Zuhörerin f listener, pl a. the audience

'zujubeln v/i (sep, -ge-, h) cheer

'zukleben v/t (sep, -ge-, h) seal

'zuknöpfen v/t (sep, -ge-, h) button (up)

'zukommen v/i (irr, **kommen**, sep, -ge-, sein) **~ auf** (acc) come up to; fig be ahead of; **die Dinge auf sich ~ lassen** wait and see

Zukunft ['tsu:kʊnft] f (-; no pl) future (a. LING)

'zukünftig 1. adj future 2. adv in future

'zulächeln v/i (sep, -ge-, h) smile at

'Zulage f bonus

'zulangen F v/i (sep, -ge-, h) tuck in

'zulassen v/t (irr, **lassen**, sep, -ge-, h) F keep s.th. closed; fig allow; MOT etc license, register; **j-n zu et. ~** admit s.o. to s.th.; 'zulässig adj admissible (a. JUR); **~ sein** be allowed; 'Zulassung f (-; -en) admission; MOT etc license, Br licence

'zulegen v/t (sep, -ge-, h) add; F **sich ... ~** get s.o. s.th.; adopt (name)

zu'letzt [tsu'lɛtst] adv in the end; come etc last; finally; **wann hast du ihn ~ gesehen?** when did you last see him?

zu'liebe [tsu'li:bə] adv: **j-m ~** for s.o.'s sake

zum [tsʊm] prp zu dem → zu; **~ ersten Mal** for the first time; et. **~ Kaffee** s.th. with one's coffee; **~ Schwimmen** etc **gehen** go swimming etc

'zumachen F (sep, -ge-, h) 1. v/t close, shut; button (up) 2. v/i close (down)

'zumauern v/t (sep, -ge-, h) brick or wall up

zumutbar ['tsu:mu:tba:ɐ] adj reasonable; zu'mute [tsu'mu:tə] adv: **mir ist ... ~** I feel ...; 'zumuten v/t (sep, -ge-, h) **j-m et. ~** expect s.th. of s.o.; **sich zu viel ~** overtax o.s.; 'Zumutung f: **das ist e-e ~** that's asking or expecting a bit much

zu'nächst [tsu'nɛ:çst] adv → **zuerst**

'zunageln v/t (sep, -ge-, h) nail up

'zunähen v/t (sep, -ge-, h) sew up

Zunahme ['tsu:na:mə] f (-; -n) increase

'Zuname m surname

'zünden ['tsyndən] v/i (sep, -ge-, h) kindle; ELECTR, MOT ignite; fire; **~d** fig adj stirring

Zünder ['tsyndɐ] m (-s; -) MIL fuse; pl Austrian matches

Zünd|holz ['tsʏntholts] *n* match; **~kerze** *f* MOT spark plug; **~schlüssel** *m* MOT ignition key; **~schnur** *f* fuse

'**Zündung** *f* (-; -en) MOT ignition

zunehmen *v/i* (*irr*, **nehmen**, *sep*, -ge-, h) increase (**an** *dat* in); put on weight; *moon:* wax; *days:* grow longer

Zuneigung *f* (-; -en) affection

Zunft [tsʊnft] HIST *f* (-; *Zünfte* ['tsʏnftə]) guild

Zunge [tsʊŋə] *f* (-; -n) ANAT tongue; *es* *liegt mir auf der ~* it's on the tip of my tongue

züngeln ['tsʏŋəln] *v/i* (ge-, h) *flames:* lick, flicker

'**Zungenspitze** *f* tip of the tongue

'**zunicken** *v/i* (*sep*, -ge-, h) (*dat*) nod at

zunutze [tsu'nʊtsə] *adv:* **sich et.** ~ **machen** make (good) use of s.th.; take advantage of s.th.

zupfen [tsʊpfən] *v/t and v/i* (ge-, h) pull (**an** *dat* at), pick, pluck (at) (*a.* MUS)

zur [tsuːɐ] *prp* **zu der → zu**; ~ **Schule** (**Kirche**) **gehen** go to school (church); ~ **Hälfte** half (of it *or* them); ~ **Belohnung** *etc* as a reward *etc*

'**zurechnungsfähig** *adj* JUR responsible; 'Zurechnungsfähigkeit *f* (-; *no* *pl*) JUR responsibility

zu'recht|finden *v/refl* (*irr*, **finden**, *sep*, -ge-, h) find one's way; *fig* cope, manage; **~kommen** *v/i* (*irr*, **kommen**, *sep*, -ge-, sein) get along (**mit** with); cope (with); **~legen** *v/t* (*sep*, -ge-, h) arrange; *fig* **sich et.** ~ think s.th. out; **~machen** F *v/t* (*sep*, -ge-, h) get ready, prepare, fix; **sich** ~ do o.s. up; **~rücken** *v/t* (*sep*, -ge-, h) put s.th. straight (*a. fig*)

zu'rechtweisen *v/t* (*irr*, **weisen**, *sep*, -ge-, h), Zu'rechtweisung *f* reprimand

'**zu|reden** *v/i* (*sep*, -ge-, h) *j-m* ~ encourage s.o.; **~reiten** *v/t* (*irr*, **reiten**, *sep*, -ge-, h) break in; **~richten** F *fig v/t* (*sep*, -ge-, h) **übel** ~ batter, *a.* beat s.o. up badly, *a.* make a mess of s.th., ruin

zurück [tsu'rʏk] *adv* back; behind (*a. fig*); **~behalten** *v/t* (*irr*, **halten**, *sep*, no -ge-, h) keep back, retain; **~bekommen** *v/t* (*irr*, **kommen**, *sep*, no -ge-, h) get back; **~bleiben** *v/i* (*irr*, **bleiben**, *sep*, -ge-, sein) stay behind, be left behind; fall behind (*a.* PED *etc*); **~blicken** *v/i* (*sep*, -ge-, h) look back (**auf** *acc* at, *fig* on); **~bringen** *v/t* (*irr*, **bringen**, *sep*,

-ge-, h) bring *or* take back, return; **~datieren** *v/t* (*sep*, no -ge-, h) backdate (**auf** *acc* to); **~fallen** *fig v/i* (*irr*, **fallen**, *sep*, -ge-, sein) fall behind, SPORT *a.* drop back; **~finden** *v/i* (*irr*, **finden**, *sep*, -ge-, h) find one's way back (**nach, zu** to); *fig* return (to); **~fordern** *v/t* (*sep*, -ge-, h) reclaim; **~führen** *v/t* (*sep*, -ge-, h) lead back; ~ **auf** (*acc*) attribute to; **~geben** *v/t* (*irr*, **geben**, *sep*, -ge-, h) give back, return; **~geblieben** *fig adj* backward; retarded; **~gehen** *v/i* (*irr*, **gehen**, *sep*, -ge-, sein) go back, return; *fig* decrease; go down, drop; **~gezogen** *fig adj* secluded; **~greifen** *v/i* (*irr*, **greifen**, *sep*, -ge-, h) ~ **auf** (*acc*) fall back (up)on

zu'rück|halten (*irr*, **halten**, *sep*, -ge-, h) **1.** *v/t* hold back **2.** *v/refl* control o.s.; be careful; **~d** *adj* reserved

Zu'rückhaltung *f* (-; *no pl*) reserve

zu'rück|kehren *v/i* (*sep*, -ge-, sein) return; **~kommen** *v/i* (*irr*, **kommen**, *sep*, -ge-, sein) come back, return (*both* *fig* **auf** *acc* to); **~lassen** *v/t* (*irr*, **lassen**, *sep*, -ge-, h) leave (behind); **~legen** *v/t* (*sep*, -ge-, h) put back; put aside, save (*money*); cover, do (*miles*); **~nehmen** *v/t* (*irr*, **nehmen**, *sep*, -ge-, h) take back (*a. fig*); **~rufen** (*irr*, **rufen**, *sep*, -ge-, h) **1.** *v/t* call back (*a.* TEL); ECON recall; **ins** **Gedächtnis** ~ recall **2.** *v/i* TEL call back; **~schlagen** (*irr*, **schlagen**, *sep*, -ge-, h) **1.** *v/t* beat off; *tennis:* return; fold back **2.** *v/i* hit back; MIL retaliate (*a. fig*); **~schrecken** *v/i* (*sep*, -ge-, sein) ~ **vor** (*dat*) shrink from; **vor nichts** ~ stop at nothing; **~setzen** *v/t* (*sep*, -ge-, h) MOT back (up); *fig* neglect s.o.; **~stehen** *v/i* (*irr*, **stehen**, *sep*, -ge-, h) stand aside; **~stellen** *v/t* (*sep*, -ge-, h) put back (*a.* watch); put aside; MIL defer; **~strahlen** *v/t* (*sep*, -ge-, h) reflect; **~treten** *v/i* (*irr*, **treten**, *sep*, -ge-, sein) step *or* stand back; resign (**von e-m Amt** [**Posten**] one's office [post]); ECON, JUR withdraw (**von** from); **~weichen** *v/i* (*irr*, **weichen**, *sep*, -ge-, sein) fall back (*a.* MIL); **~weisen** *v/t* (*irr*, **weisen**, *sep*, -ge-, h) turn down; *fig* dismiss; **~zahlen** *v/t* (*sep*, -ge-, h) pay back (*a. fig*); **~ziehen** *v/t* (*irr*, **ziehen**, *sep*, -ge-, h) draw back; *fig* withdraw; **sich** ~ retire, withdraw, MIL *a.* retreat

'**Zuruf** *m* shout; '**zurufen** *v/t* (*irr*, **rufen**,

Z

sep, *-ge-, h) j-m et. ~* shout s.th. to s.o.

zur'zeit *adv* at the moment, at present

'**Zusage** *f* promise; assent

'**zusagen** *v/i and v/t (sep, -ge-, h)* accept (an invitation); *(dat)* suit, appeal to; *s-e* **Hilfe ~** promise to help

zusammen [tsu'zamən] *adv* together; *alles ~* (all) in all; *das macht ~ …* that makes … altogether

Zu'sammenarbeit *f (-; no pl)* cooperation; *in ~ mit* in collaboration with; **zu'sammenarbeiten** *v/i (sep, -ge-, h)* cooperate, collaborate

zu'sammenbeißen *v/t (irr, beißen, sep, -ge-, h) die Zähne ~* clench one's teeth

zu'sammenbrechen *v/i (irr, brechen, sep, -ge-, sein)* break down, collapse (*both a. fig*); **Zu'sammenbruch** *m* breakdown, collapse

zu'sammen|fallen *v/i (irr, fallen, sep, -ge-, sein)* coincide; **~falten** *v/t (sep, -ge-, h)* fold up

zu'sammenfassen *v/t (sep, -ge-, h)* summarize, sum up; **Zu'sammenfassung** *f (-; -en)* summary

zu'sammen|fügen *v/t (sep, -ge-, h)* join (together); **~gesetzt** *adj* compound; **~halten** *v/i and v/t (irr, halten, sep, -ge-, h)* hold together (*a. fig*); F stick together

Zu'sammenhang *m (-[e]s; -hänge)* connection; context; *im ~ stehen (mit)* be connected (with)

zu'sammenhängen *v/i (irr, hängen, sep, -ge-, h)* be connected; **~d** *adj* coherent

zu'sammenhang(s)los *adj* incoherent, disconnected

zu'sammen|klappen *v/i (sep, -ge-, sein) and v/t (h)* TECH fold up; F break down; **~kommen** *v/i (irr, kommen, sep, -ge-, sein)* meet

Zu'sammenkunft [tsu'zamənkʊnft] *f (-; -künfte* [tsu'zamənkʏnftə]*)* meeting

zu'sammen|legen *(sep, -ge-, h)* **1.** *v/t* combine; fold up **2.** *v/i* club together; **~nehmen** *v/t (irr, nehmen, sep, -ge-, h)* muster (up); *sich ~* pull o.s. together; **~packen** *v/t (sep, -ge-, h)* pack up; **~passen** *v/i (sep, -ge-, h)* harmonize; match; **~rechnen** *v/t (sep, -ge-, h)* add up; **~reißen** F *v/refl (irr, reißen, sep, -ge-, h)* pull o.s. together; **~rollen** *v/t (sep, -ge-, h)* roll up; *sich ~* coil up; **~rot-**

~ten [tsu'zamənrɔtən] *v/refl (sep, -ge-, h)* band together; **~rücken** *(sep, -ge-, sein)* move up; **~schlagen** *v/t (irr, schlagen, sep, -ge-, h)* clap (hands); click (*one's heels*); beat s.o. up; smash (up)

zu'sammenschließen *v/refl (irr, schließen, sep, -ge-, h)* join, unite; **Zu-'sammenschluss** *m* union

zu'sammen|schreiben *v/t (irr, schreiben, sep, -ge-, h)* write in one word; **~schrumpfen** *v/i (sep, -ge-, sein)* shrink

zu'sammensetzen *v/t (sep, -ge-, h)* put together; TECH assemble; *sich ~ aus (dat)* consist of, be composed of; **Zu-'sammensetzung** *f (-; -en)* composition; CHEM, LING compound; TECH assembly

zu'sammenstellen *v/t (sep, -ge-, h)* put together; arrange

Zu'sammenstoß *m* collision (*a. fig*), crash; impact; *fig* clash; **zu-'sammenstoßen** *v/i (irr, stoßen, sep, -ge-, sein)* collide (*a. fig*); *fig* clash; **~ mit** run or bump into; *fig* have a clash with

zu'sammentreffen *v/i (irr, treffen, sep, -ge-, h)* meet, encounter; coincide (*mit* with); **Zu'sammentreffen** *n (-s; -)* meeting; coincidence; encounter

zu'sammen|treten *v/i (irr, treten, sep, -ge-, sein)* meet; **~tun** *v/refl (irr, tun, sep, -ge-, h)* join (forces); F team up; **~wirken** *v/i (sep, -ge-, h)* combine; **~zählen** *v/t (sep, -ge-, h)* add up; **~ziehen** *(irr, ziehen, sep, -ge-)* **1.** *v/t and v/refl (h)* contract **2.** *v/i (sein)* move in (*mit* with); **~zucken** *v/i (sep, -ge-, sein)* wince, flinch

'**Zusatz** *m* addition; *chemical etc* additive; **~… in** *cpds mst* additional …, supplementary …; auxiliary …; **zusätzlich** ['tsu:zɛtslɪç] *adj* additional, extra

'**zuschauen** *v/i (sep, -ge-, h)* look on (*bei et.* at s.th.); *j-m ~* watch s.o. (*bei et.* doing s.th.)

Zuschauer ['tsu:fauɐ] *m (-s; -)*, '**Zuschauerin** *f (-; -nen)* spectator; TV viewer, *pl a. the* audience

'**Zuschauerraum** *m* auditorium

'**Zuschlag** *m* extra charge; RAIL *etc* excess fare; bonus; *auction:* knocking down; '**zuschlagen** *v/i (irr, schlagen,* *sep*, *-ge-*, *sein*) *and v/t* (*h*) *door etc*: slam *or* bang shut; *boxing etc*: hit, strike (a blow); *fig* act; **j-m et. ~** *auction*: knock s.th. down to s.o.

'zu|schließen *v/t* (*irr*, **schließen**, *sep*, *-ge-*, *h*) lock (up); **~schnallen** *v/t* (*sep*, *-ge-*, *h*) buckle (up); **~schnappen** *v/i* (*sep*, *-ge-*) (*h*) *dog*: snap; (*sein*) *door etc*: snap shut; **~schneiden** *v/t* (*irr*, **schneiden**, *sep*, *-ge-*, *h*) cut out; cut (to size); **~schnüren** *v/t* (*sep*, *-ge-*, *h*) tie (*or* lace) up; **~schrauben** *v/t* (*sep*, *-ge-*, *h*) screw shut; **~schreiben** *v/t* (*irr*, **schreiben**, *sep*, *-ge-*, *h*) ascribe *or* attribute (*dat* to)

'Zuschrift *f* letter

zuschulden [tsu'ʃʊldən] *adv*: **sich et.** (**nichts**) **~ kommen lassen** do s.th. (nothing) wrong

'Zuschuss *m* allowance; subsidy

'zuschütten *v/t* (*sep*, *-ge-*, *h*) fill up

'zusehen → **zuschauen**

zusehends ['tsu:se:ənts] *adv* noticeably; rapidly

'zusetzen (*sep*, *-ge-*, *h*) **1.** *v/t* add; lose (money) **2.** *v/i* lose money; **j-m ~** press s.o. (hard)

'zuspielen *v/t* (*sep*, *-ge-*, *h*) SPORT pass

'zuspitzen *v/t* (*sep*, *-ge-*, *h*) point; **sich ~** become critical

'Zuspruch *m* (-[*e*]*s*; *no pl*) encouragement; words of comfort

'Zustand *m* condition, state, F shape

zustande [tsu'ʃtandə] *adv*: **~ bringen** bring about, manage (to do); **~ kommen** come about; **es kam nicht ~** it didn't come off

'zuständig *adj* responsible (**für** for), in charge (of)

'zustehen *v/i* (*irr*, **stehen**, *sep*, *-ge-*, *h*) **j-m steht et.** (**zu tun**) **zu** s.o. is entitled to (do) s.th.

'zustellen *v/t* (*sep*, *-ge-*, *h*) *post*: deliver; 'Zustellung *f post*: delivery

'zustimmen *v/i* (*sep*, *-ge-*, *h*) agree (*dat to s.th.*; *with s.o.*); 'Zustimmung *f* approval, consent; (**j-s**) **~ finden** meet with (s.o.'s) approval

'zustoßen *v/i* (*irr*, **stoßen**, *sep*, *-ge-*, *sein*) **j-m ~** happen to s.o.

zutage [tsu'ta:gə] *adv*: **~ bringen** (**kommen**) bring (come) to light

'Zutaten *pl* ingredients

'zuteilen *v/t* (*sep*, *-ge-*, *h*) assign, allot;

'Zuteilung *f* (-; *-en*) allotment; ration

'zutragen *v/refl* (*irr*, **tragen**, *sep*, *-ge-*, *h*) happen

'zutrauen *v/t* (*sep*, *-ge-*, *h*) **j-m et. ~** credit s.o. with s.th.; **sich zu viel ~** overrate o.s.

zutraulich ['tsu:traʊlɪç] *adj* trusting; zo friendly

'zutreffen *v/i* (*irr*, **treffen**, *sep*, *-ge-*, *h*) be true; **~ auf** (*acc*) apply to, go for; **~d** *adj* true, correct

'zutrinken *v/i* (*irr*, **trinken**, *sep*, *-ge-*, *h*) **j-m ~** drink to s.o.

'Zutritt *m* (-[*e*]*s*; *no pl*) admission; access; **~ verboten!** no admittance!

zu'ungunsten *adv* to s.o.'s disadvantage

zuverlässig ['tsu:fɛɐlɛsɪç] *adj* reliable, dependable; safe; 'Zuverlässigkeit *f* (-; *no pl*) reliability, dependability

Zuversicht ['tsu:fɛɐzɪçt] *f* (-; *no pl*) confidence; 'zuversichtlich *adj* confident, optimistic

zuviel → **zu**

zu'vor [tsu'fo:ɐ] *adv* before, previously; first

zu'vorkommen *v/i* (*irr*, **kommen**, *sep*, *-ge-*, *sein*) anticipate; prevent; **j-m ~** a. F beat s.o. to it; **~d** *adj* obliging; polite

Zuwachs ['tsu:vaks] *m* (-*es*; *no pl*) increase, growth; 'zuwachsen *v/i* (*irr*, **wachsen**, *sep*, *-ge-*, *sein*) become overgrown; MED close

zu'weilen [tsu'vaɪlən] *adv* occasionally, now and then

'zuweisen *v/t* (*irr*, **weisen**, *sep*, *-ge-*, *h*) assign

'zuwenden *v/t and v/refl* ([*irr*, **wenden**,] *sep*, *-ge-*, *h*) turn to (*a. fig*)

'Zuwendung *f* (-; *-en*) payment; (*no pl*) attention; (loving) care, love, affection

zuwenig → **zu**

'zuwerfen *v/t* (*irr*, **werfen**, *sep*, *-ge-*, *h*) slam (shut); **j-m et. ~** throw s.o. s.th.; **j-m e-n Blick ~** cast a glance at s.o.

zu'wider [tsu'vi:dɐ] *adj*: **... ist mir ~** I hate *or* detest ...; **~handeln** *v/i* (*sep*, *-ge-*, *h*) (*dat*) act contrary to; violate

'zu|winken *v/i* (*sep*, *-ge-*, *h*) wave to; signal to; **~zahlen** *v/t* (*sep*, *-ge-*, *h*) pay extra; **~ziehen** (*irr*, **ziehen**, *sep*, *-ge-*) **1.** *v/t* (*h*) draw (*curtains etc*); pull tight; *fig* consult; **sich ~** MED catch **2.** v/i (sein) move in

zuzüglich ['tsu:tsy:kliç] prp (gen) plus

Zvieri ['tsfi:ri] Swiss m, n (-s; -s) afternoon snack, tea or coffee break

zwang [tsvaŋ] pret of **zwingen**

Zwang m (-[e]s; Zwänge ['tsvɛŋə]) compulsion, constraint; restraint; coercion; force; **~ sein** be compulsory; **zwängen** ['tsvɛŋən] v/t (ge-, h) press, squeeze, force; 'zwanglos adj informal; casual; 'Zwanglosigkeit f (-; no pl) informality

'Zwangs|arbeit f JUR hard labo(u)r; ~herrschaft f (-; no pl) despotism, tyranny; ~lage f predicament

'zwangsläufig adv inevitably

'Zwangs|maßnahme f sanction; ~vollstreckung f JUR compulsory execution; ~vorstellung f PSYCH obsession

'zwangsweise adv by force

'zwanzig ['tsvantsiç] adj twenty

'zwanzigste adj twentieth

zwar [tsva:ɐ] adv: **ich kenne ihn ~, aber** ... I do know him, but ..., I know him all right, but ...; **und ~** that is (to say), namely

Zweck m (-[e]s; -e) purpose, aim; **s-n ~ erfüllen** serve its purpose; **es hat keinen ~ (zu warten** etc) it's no use (waiting etc); 'zwecklos adj useless

'zweckmäßig adj practical; wise; TECH, ARCH functional; 'Zweckmäßigkeit f (-; no pl) practicality, functionality

zwecks prp (gen) for the purpose of

zwei [tsvai] adj two

zweibeinig ['tsvaibainiç] adj two-legged

'Zweibettzimmer n twin-bedded room

zweideutig ['tsvaidɔytiç] adj ambiguous; off-colo(u)r

Zweier ['tsvaiɐ] m (-s; -) rowing: pair

zweierlei ['tsvaiɐ'lai] adj two kinds of

'zweifach adj double, twofold

'Zweifa'milienhaus n duplex, Br two-family house

'Zweifel ['tsvaifəl] m (-s; -) doubt

'zweifelhaft adj doubtful, dubious

'zweifellos adv undoubtedly, no or without doubt

'zweifeln v/i (ge-, h) **~ an** (dat) doubt s.th., have one's doubts about

Zweig [tsvaik] m (-[e]s; -e) BOT branch

(a. fig); twig; ~geschäft n, ~niederlassung f, ~stelle f branch

'zweijährig ['tsvaijɛːriç] adj two-year-old, of two (years)

'Zweikampf m duel

'zweimal adv twice

'zweimalig adj (twice) repeated

'zwei|motorig ['tsvaimoto:riç] adj twin-engined; ~reihig ['tsvairaiiç] adj double-breasted (suit); ~schneidig adj double-edged, two-edged (both a. fig); ~seitig ['tsvaizaitiç] adj two-sided; reversible; POL bilateral; IT double-sided

'Zweisitzer ['tsvaizitsɐ] m (-s; -) esp MOT two-seater

'zwei|sprachig ['tsvaiʃpra:xiç] adj bilingual; ~stimmig ['tsvaiʃtimiç] adj MUS ... for two voices; ~stöckig ['tsvaiʃtœkiç] adj two-storied, Br two-storey ...

zweit [tsvait] adj second; **ein ~er** ... another ...; **jede(r, -s) ~e** ... every other ...; **aus ~er Hand** second-hand; **wir sind zu ~** there are two of us

'zweitbeste adj second-best

'zweiteilig adj two-piece (suit etc)

'zweitens ['tsvaitəns] adv secondly

'zwei|klassig ['tsvaitklasiç] adj, 'zweitrangig ['tsvaitraŋiç] adj second-class or -rate

Zwerchfell ['tsvɛrçfɛl] n ANAT diaphragm

Zwerg [tsvɛrk] m (-[e]s; -e ['tsvɛrgə]) dwarf; gnome; fig midget; **~... in** cpds BOT dwarf ...; ZO pygmy ...

Zwetsch(g)e ['tsvɛtʃ(g)ə] f (-; -n) BOT plum

zwicken ['tsvikən] v/t and v/i (ge-, h) pinch, nip

Zwieback ['tsvi:bak] m (-[e]s; -e, -bäcke ['tsvi:bɛkə]) rusk, zwieback

Zwiebel ['tsvi:bəl] f (-; -n) GASTR onion; BOT bulb

Zwiegespräch ['tsvi:gəʃprɛːç] n dialog(ue)

'Zwielicht n (-[e]s; no pl) twilight

'Zwiespalt m (-[e]s; -e) conflict

'zwiespältig ['tsvi:ʃpɛltiç] adj conflicting

'Zwietracht f (-; no pl) discord

Zwilling ['tsviliŋ] m (-s; -e) twin; pl ASTR Gemini; **er ist (ein) ~** he's a (a) Gemini

'Zwillings|bruder m twin brother;

~schwester *f* twin sister

Zwinge ['tsvɪŋə] *f* (-; *-n*) TECH clamp

zwingen ['tsvɪŋən] *v/t* (*irr, ge-, h*) force, compel; **~d** *adj* compelling; cogent

Zwinger ['tsvɪŋɐ] *m* (*-s*; -) kennels

zwinkern ['tsvɪŋkɐn] *v/i* (*ge-, h*) wink, blink

Zwirn [tsvɪrn] *m* (-[*e*]*s*; *-e*) thread, yarn, twist

zwischen ['tsvɪʃən] *prp* (*dat and acc*) between; among

'zwischen'durch F *adv* in between

'Zwischen|ergebnis *n* intermediate result; **~fall** *m* incident; **~händler** *m* ECON middleman; **~landung** *f* AVIAT stopover; **ohne ~** nonstop

'Zwischen|raum *m* space, interval; **~ruf** *m* (loud) interruption; *pl* heckling; **~rufer** *m* (*-s*; -) heckler; **~spiel** *n* interlude; **~stati|on** *f* stop(over); **~ machen** (*in dat*) stop over (in); **~wand** *f* partition (wall); **~zeit** *f*: **in der ~** in the meantime, meanwhile

Zwist [tsvɪst] *m* (-[*e*]*s*; *-e*) discord

zwitschern ['tsvɪtʃɐn] *v/i* (*ge-, h*) twitter, chirp

Zwitter ['tsvɪtɐ] *m* (*-s*; -) BIOL hermaphrodite

zwölf [tsvœlf] *adj* twelve; **um ~ (Uhr)** at twelve (o'clock); at noon; at midnight

'zwölfte *adj* twelfth

Zyankali [tsya:n'ka:li] *n* (*-s*; *no pl*) CHEM potassium cyanide

Zyklus ['tsy:klus] *m* (-; *-klen*) cycle; series, course

Zylinder [tsi'lɪndɐ] *m* (*-s*; -) top hat; MATH, TECH cylinder; **zylindrisch** [tsi-'lɪndrɪʃ] *adj* cylindrical

Zyniker ['tsy:nikɐ] *m* (*-s*; -) cynic

zynisch ['tsy:nɪʃ] *adj* cynical

Zynismus [tsy'nɪsmus] *m* (-; *-men*) cynicism

Zypresse [tsy'prɛsə] *f* (-; *-n*) BOT cypress

Zyste ['tsʏstə] *f* (-; *-n*) MED cyst

z.Z(t). *abbr of* **zur Zeit** at the moment, at present

ENGLISH – GERMAN

A

A, a A, a *n*; *from A to Z* von A bis Z

A grade Eins

a, *before vowel:* **an** *indef art* ein(e); per, pro, je; *not a(n)* kein(e); *all of a size* alle gleich groß; *100 dollars a year* 100 Dollar im Jahr; *twice a week* zweimal die *or* in der Woche

a·back: *taken ~* überrascht, verblüfft; bestürzt

a·ban·don aufgeben, preisgeben; verlassen; überlassen

a·base erniedrigen, demütigen

a·base·ment Erniedrigung *f*, Demütigung *f*

a·bashed verlegen

ab·at·toir *Br* Schlachthof *m*

ab·bess REL Äbtissin *f*

ab·bey REL Kloster *n*; Abtei *f*

ab·bot REL Abt *m*

ab·bre·vi·ate (ab)kürzen

ab·bre·vi·a·tion Abkürzung *f*, Kurzform *f*

ABC Abc *n*, Alphabet *n*

ab·di·cate *Amt, Recht etc* aufgeben, verzichten auf (*acc*); *~ (from) the throne* abdanken

ab·di·ca·tion Verzicht *m*; Abdankung *f*

ab·do·men ANAT Unterleib *m*

ab·dom·i·nal ANAT Unterleibs...

ab·duct JUR *j-n* entführen

ab·er·ra·tion Verirrung *f*

a·bet → *aid 1*

ab·hor verabscheuen

ab·hor·rence Abscheu *m* (*of* vor *dat*)

ab·hor·rent zuwider (*to* dat); abstoßend

a·bide *v/i: ~ by the law etc* sich an das Gesetz *etc* halten; *v/t: he can't ~ him* er kann ihn nicht ausstehen

a·bil·i·ty Fähigkeit *f*

ab·ject abschwören; entsagen (*dat*)

a·blaze in Flammen; *fig* glänzend, funkelnd (*with* vor *dat*)

a·ble fähig; geschickt; *be ~ to inf* in der Lage sein zu *inf*, können

a·ble-bod·ied kräftig

ab·nor·mal abnorm, ungewöhnlich; anomal

a·board an Bord; *all ~!* MAR alle Mann *or* Reisenden an Bord!; RAIL alles einsteigen!; *~ a bus* in e-m Bus; *go ~ a train* in

e-n Zug einsteigen

a·bode *a. place of ~* Aufenthaltsort *m*, Wohnsitz *m*; *of or with no fixed ~* ohne festen Wohnsitz

a·bol·ish abschaffen, aufheben

ab·o·li·tion Abschaffung *f*, Aufhebung *f*

A-bomb → *atom(ic) bomb*

a·bom·i·na·ble abscheulich, scheußlich; **a·bom·i·nate** verabscheuen; **a·bom·i·na·tion** Abscheu *m*

ab·o·rig·i·nal 1. eingeboren, Ur...; **2.** Ureinwohner *m*

ab·o·rig·i·ne Ureinwohner *m*

a·bort *v/t* abbrechen (*a.* MED *Schwangerschaft*); MED *Kind* abtreiben; *v/i* fehlschlagen, scheitern; MED e-e Fehlgeburt haben; **a·bor·tion** MED Fehlgeburt *f*; Schwangerschaftsabbruch *m*, Abtreibung *f*; *have an ~* abtreiben (lassen)

a·bor·tive misslungen, erfolglos

a·bound reichlich vorhanden sein; Überfluss haben, reich sein (*in* an *dat*); voll sein (*with* von)

a·bout 1. *prp* um (... herum); bei (*dat*); (irgendwo) herum in (*dat*); um, gegen, etwa; im Begriff, dabei; über (*acc*) **2.** *adv* herum, umher; in der Nähe; etwa, ungefähr

a·bove 1. *prp* über (*dat or acc*), oberhalb (*gen*); *fig* über, erhaben über (*acc*); *~ all* vor allem **2.** *adv* oben; darüber **3.** *adj* obig, oben erwähnt

a·breast nebeneinander; *keep ~ of, be ~ of fig* Schritt halten mit

a·bridge (ab-, ver)kürzen

a·bridg(e)·ment Kürzung *f*; Kurzfassung *f*

a·broad im *or* ins Ausland; überall(hin)

a·brupt abrupt; jäh; schroff

ab·scess MED Abszess *m*

ab·sence Abwesenheit *f*; Mangel *m*

ab·sent 1. abwesend; fehlend; nicht vorhanden; *be ~* fehlen (*from school* in der Schule; *from work* am Arbeitsplatz); **2.** *~ o.s. from* fernbleiben (*dat*) *or* von; **ab·sent-mind·ed** zerstreut, geistesabwesend

ab·so·lute absolut; unumschränkt; vollkommen; unbedingt; CHEM rein, unvermischt

ab·so·lu·tion REL Absolution f

ab·solve freisprechen, lossprechen

ab·sorb absorbieren, aufsaugen, einsaugen; *fig* ganz in Anspruch nehmen

ab·sorb·ing *fig* fesselnd, packend

ab·stain sich enthalten (*from gen*)

ab·ste·mi·ous enthaltsam; mäßig

ab·sten·tion Enthaltung f; POL Stimmenthaltung f

ab·sti·nence Abstinenz f, Enthaltsamkeit f

ab·sti·nent abstinent, enthaltsam

ab·stract 1. abstrakt **2.** *das* Abstrakte; Auszug m **3.** abstrahieren; entwenden

ab·stract·ed *fig* zerstreut

ab·strac·tion Abstraktion f; abstrakter Begriff

ab·surd absurd; lächerlich

a·bun·dance Überfluss m; Fülle f; Überschwang m

a·bun·dant reich, reichlich

a·buse 1. Missbrauch m; Beschimpfung(en pl) f; **~ of drugs** Drogenmissbrauch m; **~ of power** Machtmissbrauch m **2.** missbrauchen; beschimpfen; **a·bu·sive** beleidigend, Schimpf...

a·but (an)grenzen (*on* an *acc*)

a·byss Abgrund m (*a. fig*)

ac·a·dem·ic 1. Hochschullehrer m **2.** akademisch; **a·cad·e·mi·cian** Akademiemitglied n; **a·cad·e·my** Akademie f; **~ of music** Musikhochschule f

ac·cede: ~ to zustimmen (*dat*); Amt antreten; *Thron* besteigen

ac·cel·e·rate *v/t* beschleunigen; *v/i* schneller werden, MOT *a.* beschleunigen, Gas geben

ac·cel·e·ra·tion Beschleunigung f

ac·cel·e·ra·tor MOT Gaspedal n

ac·cent 1. Akzent m (*a.* LING); **2.** → **ac·cen·tu·ate** akzentuieren, betonen

ac·cept annehmen; akzeptieren; hinnehmen; **ac·cept·a·ble** annehmbar; *person:* tragbar; **ac·cept·ance** Annahme f; Aufnahme f

ac·cess Zugang m (*to* zu); *fig* Zutritt m (*to* bei, zu); IT Zugriff m (*to* auf *acc*)

ac·ces·sa·ry → **accessory**

ac·cess code IT Zugriffskode m

ac·ces·si·ble (leicht) zugänglich

ac·ces·sion (Neu)Anschaffung f (*to* für); Zustimmung f (*to* zu); Antritt m (*e·s Amtes*); **~ to power** Machtübernahme f; **~ to the throne** Thronbesteigung f

ac·ces·so·ry JUR Komplize m, Komplizin f, Mitschuldige m, f; *mst pl* Zubehör n, *fashion:* a. Accessoires pl, TECH *a.* Zubehörteile pl

ac·cess road Zufahrts- or Zubringerstraße f; **~ time** IT Zugriffszeit f

ac·ci·dent Unfall m, Unglück n, Unglücksfall m; NUCL Störfall m; **by~** zufällig

ac·ci·den·tal zufällig; versehentlich

ac·claim feiern (*as* als)

ac·cla·ma·tion lauter Beifall; Lob n

ac·cli·ma·tize (sich) akklimatisieren or eingewöhnen

ac·com·mo·date unterbringen; Platz haben für, fassen; anpassen (*to dat* or an *acc*)

ac·com·mo·da·tion Unterkunft f, Unterbringung f; **~ of·fice** Zimmervermittlung f

ac·com·pa·ni·ment MUS Begleitung f

ac·com·pa·ny begleiten (*a.* MUS)

ac·com·plice JUR Komplize m, Komplizin f, Helfershelfer(in)

ac·com·plish erreichen; leisten

ac·com·plished fähig, tüchtig

ac·com·plish·ment Fähigkeit f, Talent n

ac·cord 1. Übereinstimmung f; *of one's own* ~ von selbst; *with one* ~ einstimmig **2.** übereinstimmen (*with* mit)

ac·cord·ance: in ~ with entsprechend (*dat*)

ac·cord·ing: ~ to laut; nach

ac·cord·ing·ly folglich, also; (dem)entsprechend

ac·cost *j-n* ansprechen

ac·count 1. ECON Rechnung f, Berechnung f; Konto n; Rechenschaft f; Bericht m; **by all ~s** nach allem, was man so hört; *of no ~* ohne Bedeutung; *on no ~* auf keinen Fall; *on ~ of* wegen; *take into~, take~ of* in Betracht or Erwägung ziehen, berücksichtigen; *turn s.th. to (good)* ~ et. (gut) ausnutzen; *keep ~s* die Bücher führen; *call to ~* zur Rechenschaft ziehen; *give (an)* ~ *of* Rechenschaft ablegen über (*acc*); *give an ~ of* Bericht erstatten über (*acc*) **2.** *v/i:* ~ *for* Rechenschaft über *et.* ablegen; (sich) erklären

ac·count·a·ble verantwortlich; erklärlich

ac·coun·tant ECON Buchhalter(in)
ac·count·ing ECON Buchführung *f*
acct *abbr of **account*** Konto *n*
ac·cu·mu·late (sich) (an)häufen *or* ansammeln
ac·cu·mu·la·tion Ansammlung *f*
ac·cu·mu·la·tor ELECTR Akkumulator *m*
ac·cu·ra·cy Genauigkeit *f*
ac·cu·rate genau
ac·cu·sa·tion Anklage *f*; Anschuldigung *f*, Beschuldigung *f*
ac·cu·sa·tive *a.* **~ case** LING Akkusativ *m*
ac·cuse JUR anklagen; beschuldigen (*of* gen); ***the ~d*** der *or* die Angeklagte, die Angeklagten *pl*
ac·cus·er JUR Ankläger(in)
ac·cus·ing anklagend, vorwurfsvoll
ac·cus·tom gewöhnen (**to** an *acc*)
ac·cus·tomed gewohnt, üblich; gewöhnt (**to** an *acc*, zu *inf*)
ace Ass *n* (*a. fig*); ***have an ~ in the hole*** (*Br* **up one's sleeve**) *fig* (noch) e-n Trumpf in der Hand haben; ***within an ~*** um ein Haar
ache 1. schmerzen, wehtun **2.** *anhaltender* Schmerz
a·chieve zustande bringen; *Ziel* erreichen; **a·chieve·ment** Zustandebringen *n*, Leistung *f*, Ausführung *f*
ac·id 1. sauer; *fig* beißend, bissig **2.** CHEM Säure *f*; **a·cid·i·ty** Säure *f*
ac·id rain saurer Regen
ac·knowl·edge anerkennen; zugeben; *Empfang* bestätigen
ac·knowl·edg(e)·ment Anerkennung *f*; (Empfangs)Bestätigung *f*; Eingeständnis *n*
a·corn BOT Eichel *f*
a·cous·tics Akustik *f*
ac·quaint bekannt machen; **~ s.o. with s.th.** j-m et. mitteilen; **be ~ed with** kennen; **ac·quaint·ance** Bekanntschaft *f*; Bekannte *m, f*
ac·quire erwerben; sich aneignen
ac·qui·si·tion Erwerb *m*; Anschaffung *f*, Errungenschaft *f*
ac·quit JUR freisprechen (*of* von); **~ o.s. well** s-e Sache gut machen
ac·quit·tal JUR Freispruch *m*
a·cre Acre *m* (*4047 qm*)
ac·rid scharf, beißend
ac·ro·bat Akrobat(in)
ac·ro·bat·ic akrobatisch

a·cross 1. *adv* hinüber, herüber; (quer) durch; drüben, auf der anderen Seite; über Kreuz **2.** *prp* (quer) über (*acc*); (quer) durch; auf der anderen Seite von (*or gen*), jenseits (*gen*); über (*dat*); **come ~, run ~** *fig* stoßen auf (*acc*)
act 1. *v/i* handeln; sich verhalten *or* benehmen; (ein)wirken; funktionieren; (Theater) spielen; *v/t* THEA spielen (*a. fig*), *Stück* aufführen; **~ as** fungieren als **2.** Handlung *f*, Tat *f*; JUR Gesetz *n*; THEA Akt *m*; **act·ing** THEA Spiel(en) *n*
ac·tion Handlung *f* (*a.* THEA), Tat *f*; *film etc*: Action *f*; Funktionieren *n*; (Ein-)Wirkung *f*; JUR Klage *f*, Prozess *m*; MIL Gefecht *n*, Einsatz *m*; **take ~** handeln
ac·ti·vate *v/t* aktivieren; **ac·tive** aktiv; tätig, rührig; lebhaft (*a.* ECON), rege; wirksam
ac·tiv·ist *esp* POL Aktivist(in)
ac·tiv·i·ty Tätigkeit *f*; Aktivität *f*; Betriebsamkeit *f*; *esp* ECON Lebhaftigkeit *f*; **~ va·ca·tion** Aktivurlaub *m*
ac·tor Schauspieler *m*
ac·tress Schauspielerin *f*
ac·tu·al wirklich, tatsächlich, eigentlich
ac·u·men Scharfsinn *m*
ac·u·punc·ture MED Akupunktur *f*
a·cute akut (*shortage, pain etc*); brennend (*problem etc*); scharf (*hearing etc*); scharfsinnig; MATH spitz (*angle*)
ad F → ***advertisement***
ad·a·mant unerbittlich
a·dapt anpassen (**to** *dat or* an *acc*); *Text* bearbeiten (**from** nach); TECH umstellen (**to** auf *acc*); umbauen (**to** für)
a·dapt·a·ble anpassungsfähig
ad·ap·ta·tion Anpassung *f*; Bearbeitung *f*
a·dapt·er, a·dapt·or ELECTR Adapter *m*
add *v/t* hinzufügen; **~ up** zusammenzählen, addieren; *v/i:* **~** *to* vermehren, beitragen zu, hinzukommen zu; **~ up** MATH ergeben; F sich summieren; *fig* e-n Sinn ergeben; **~ up to** *fig* hinauslaufen auf (*acc*)
ad·der ZO Natter *f*
ad·dict Süchtige *m, f*; **alcohol (drug) ~** Alkoholsüchtige (Drogen- *or* Rauschgiftsüchtige); (*Fußball- etc*) Fanatiker(in), (*Film- etc*)Narr *m*
ad·dict·ed süchtig, abhängig (**to** von); **be**

~ **to alcohol** (**drugs**) alkoholsüchtig (drogenabhängig *or* -süchtig) sein

ad·dic·tion Sucht *f*, Süchtigkeit *f*

ad·di·tion Hinzufügen *n*; Zusatz *m*; Zuwachs *m*; ARCH Anbau *m*; MATH Addition *f*; **in ~** außerdem; **in ~ to** außer (*dat*)

ad·di·tion·al zusätzlich

ad·dress 1. *Worte* richten (**to** an *acc*), *j-n* anreden *or* ansprechen **2.** Adresse *f*, Anschrift *f*; Rede *f*, Ansprache *f*

ad·dress·ee Empfänger(in)

ad·ept erfahren, geschickt (**at, in** in *dat*)

ad·e·qua·cy Angemessenheit *f*

ad·e·quate angemessen

ad·here (**to**) kleben, haften (an *dat*); *fig* festhalten (an *dat*); **ad·her·ence** Anhaften *n*; *fig* Festhalten *n*; **ad·her·ent** Anhänger(in)

ad·he·sive 1. klebend **2.** Klebstoff *m*; ~ **plas·ter** MED Heftpflaster *n*; ~ **tape** Klebeband *n*, Klebstreifen *m*; MED Heftpflaster *n*

ad·ja·cent angrenzend, anstoßend (**to** an *acc*); benachbart

ad·jec·tive LING Adjektiv *n*, Eigenschaftswort *n*

ad·join (an)grenzen an (*acc*)

ad·journ *v/t* verschieben, (*v/i* sich) vertagen; **ad·journ·ment** Vertagung *f*, Verschiebung *f*

ad·just anpassen; TECH einstellen, regulieren; **ad·just·a·ble** TECH verstellbar, regulierbar; **ad·just·ment** Anpassung *f*; TECH Einstellung *f*

ad·lib aus dem Stegreif (sprechen *or* spielen)

ad·min·is·ter verwalten; PHARM geben, verabreichen; ~ **justice** Recht sprechen

ad·min·is·tra·tion Verwaltung *f*; POL Regierung *f*; Amtsperiode *f*

ad·min·is·tra·tive Verwaltungs...

ad·min·is·tra·tor Verwaltungsbeamte *m*

ad·mi·ra·ble bewundernswert; großartig

ad·mi·ral MAR Admiral *m*

ad·mi·ra·tion Bewunderung *f*

ad·mire bewundern; verehren

ad·mir·er Verehrer *m*

ad·mis·si·ble zulässig

ad·mis·sion Eintritt *m*, Zutritt *m*; Aufnahme *f*; Eintrittsgeld *n*; Eingeständnis *n*; ~ **free** Eintritt frei

ad·mit *v/t* zugeben; (her)einlassen (**to,**

into in *acc*), eintreten lassen; zulassen (**to** zu); **ad·mit·tance** Einlass *m*, Eintritt *m*, Zutritt *m*; **no~** Zutritt verboten

ad·mon·ish ermahnen; warnen (**of, against** vor *dat*)

a·do Getue *n*, Lärm *m*; **without more** *or* **further** ~ ohne weitere Umstände

ad·o·les·cence Jugend *f*, Adoleszenz *f*

ad·o·les·cent 1. jugendlich, heranwachsend **2.** Jugendliche *m, f*

a·dopt adoptieren; übernehmen; **~ed child** Adoptivkind *n*

a·dop·tion Adoption *f*

a·dop·tive par·ents Adoptiveltern *pl*

a·dor·a·ble F bezaubernd, entzückend

a·do·ra·tion Anbetung *f*, Verehrung *f*

a·dore anbeten, verehren

a·dorn schmücken, zieren

a·dorn·ment Schmuck *m*, Verzierung *f*

a·droit geschickt

ad·ult 1. erwachsen **2.** Erwachsene *m, f*; **~s only** nur für Erwachsene!; ~ **edu·ca·tion** Erwachsenenbildung *f*

a·dul·ter·ate verfälschen, *Wein* panschen

a·dul·ter·er Ehebrecher *m*

a·dul·ter·ess Ehebrecherin *f*

a·dul·ter·ous ehebrecherisch

a·dul·ter·y Ehebruch *m*

ad·vance 1. *v/i* vordringen, vorrücken (*a. time*); Fortschritte machen; *v/t* vorrücken; *Termin etc* vorverlegen; *Argument etc* vorbringen; *Geld* vorstrecken, F vorschießen; (be)fördern; *Preis* erhöhen; *Wachstum etc* beschleunigen **2.** Vorrücken *n*, Vorstoß *m* (*a. fig*); Fortschritt *m*; ECON Vorschuss *m*; Erhöhung *f*; **in ~** im Voraus

ad·vanced fortgeschritten; ~ **for one's years** weit *or* reif für sein Alter

ad·vance·ment Fortschritt *m*, Verbesserung *f*

ad·van·tage Vorteil *m* (*a.* SPORT); ~ **rule** SPORT Vorteilsregel *f*; **take ~ of** ausnutzen

ad·van·ta·geous vorteilhaft

ad·ven·ture Abenteuer *n*, Wagnis *n*

ad·ven·tur·er Abenteurer *m*

ad·ven·tur·ess Abenteu(r)erin *f*

ad·ven·tur·ous abenteuerlich; verwegen, kühn

ad·verb LING Adverb *n*, Umstandswort *n*

ad·ver·sa·ry Gegner(in)

ad·ver·tise ankündigen, bekannt machen; inserieren; Reklame machen (für)

ad·ver·tise·ment Anzeige f, Inserat n

ad·ver·tis·ing 1. Reklame f, Werbung f **2.** Reklame..., Werbe...; ~ **a·gen·cy** Werbeagentur f; ~ **cam·paign** Werbefeldzug m

ad·vice Rat(schlag) m; ECON Benachrichtigung f; *take medical* ~ e-n Arzt zu Rate ziehen; *take my* ~ hör auf mich

ad·vice| cen·ter, Br ~ **cen·tre** Beratungsstelle f

ad·vis·ab·le ratsam

ad·vise v/t j-n beraten; j-m raten; esp ECON benachrichtigen, avisieren; v/i sich beraten

ad·vis·er esp Br, **ad·vis·or** Berater m

ad·vi·so·ry beratend

ad·vo·cate 1. befürworten, verfechten **2.** Befürworter(in), Verfechter(in)

aer·i·al 1. luftig; Luft... **2.** Antenne f

aer·i·al| pho·to·graph, ~ **view** Luftaufnahme f, Luftbild n

aer·o... Aero..., Luft...

aer·o·bics SPORT Aerobic n

aer·o·drome esp Br Flugplatz m

aer·o·dy·nam·ic aerodynamisch

aer·o·dy·nam·ics Aerodynamik f

aer·o·nau·tics Luftfahrt f

aer·o·plane Br Flugzeug n

aer·o·sol Spraydose f, Sprühdose f

aes·thet·ic etc → **esthetic** etc

a·far: *from* ~ von weit her

af·fair Angelegenheit f, Sache f; F Ding n, Sache f; Affäre f

af·fect beeinflussen; MED angreifen, befallen; bewegen, rühren; e-e Vorliebe haben für; vortäuschen

af·fec·tion Liebe f, Zuneigung f

af·fec·tion·ate liebevoll, herzlich

af·fil·i·ate als Mitglied aufnehmen; angliedern

af·fin·i·ty Affinität f; (geistige) Verwandtschaft; Neigung f (**for**, **to** zu)

af·firm versichern; beteuern; bestätigen; **af·fir·ma·tion** Versicherung f, Beteuerung f; Bestätigung f

af·fir·ma·tive 1. bejahend **2.** *answer in the* ~ bejahen

af·fix (**to**) anheften, ankleben (an acc), befestigen (an dat); beifügen, hinzufügen (dat)

af·flict heimsuchen, plagen; ~ed with geplagt von, leidend an (dat)

af·flic·tion Gebrechen n; Elend n, Not f

af·flu·ence Überfluss m; Wohlstand m

af·flu·ent reich, reichlich; ~ **so·ci·e·ty** Wohlstandsgesellschaft f

af·ford sich leisten; gewähren, bieten; *I can* ~ *it* ich kann es mir leisten

af·front 1. beleidigen **2.** Beleidigung f

a·float MAR flott, schwimmend; *set* ~ MAR flottmachen; *fig Gerücht etc* in Umlauf setzen

a·fraid: *be* ~ **of** sich fürchten or Angst haben vor (dat); *I'm* ~ **she won't come** ich fürchte, sie wird nicht kommen; *I'm* ~ *I must go now* leider muss ich jetzt gehen

a·fresh von neuem

Af·ri·ca Afrika n; **Af·ri·can 1.** afrikanisch **2.** Afrikaner(in)

af·ter 1. adv hinterher, nachher, danach **2.** prp nach; hinter (dat) (... her); ~ **all** schließlich (doch) **3.** cj nachdem **4.** adj später; Nach...; ~ **ef·fect** MED Nachwirkung f (a. fig)

af·ter·glow Abendrot n

af·ter·math Nachwirkungen pl, Folgen pl

af·ter·noon Nachmittag m; *this* ~ heute Nachmittag; *good* ~! guten Tag!

af·ter·taste Nachgeschmack m

af·ter·thought nachträglicher Einfall

af·ter·ward, Br **af·ter·wards** nachher, später

a·gain wieder; wiederum; ferner; ~ **and** ~, *time and* ~ immer wieder; *as much* ~ noch einmal so viel

a·gainst gegen; an (dat or acc); *as* ~ verglichen mit; *he was* ~ *it* er war dagegen

age 1. (Lebens)Alter n; Zeit(alter n) f; Menschenalter n; (*old*) ~ (hohes) Alter; *at the* ~ *of* im Alter von; *s.o.* **your** ~ in deinem or Ihrem Alter; (*come*) *of* ~ mündig or volljährig (werden); *be* **over** ~ die Altersgrenze überschritten haben; *under* ~ minderjährig; unmündig; *wait for* ~s F e-e Ewigkeit warten **2.** alt werden or machen

a·ged[1] alt, betagt

aged[2]: ~ *twenty* 20 Jahre alt

age·less zeitlos; ewig jung

a·gen·cy Agentur f; Geschäftsstelle f, Büro n

a·gen·da Tagesordnung f

a·gent Agent m (a. POL), Vertreter m; (*Grundstücks- etc*)Makler m; CHEM

Wirkstoff *m*, Mittel *n*

ag·glom·er·ate (sich) zusammenballen; (sich) (an)häufen

ag·gra·vate erschweren, verschlimmern; F ärgern

ag·gre·gate 1. sich belaufen auf (*acc*) **2.** gesamt **3.** Gesamtmenge *f*, Summe *f*; TECH Aggregat *n*

ag·gres·sion Angriff *m*

ag·gres·sive aggressiv, Angriffs...; *fig* energisch

ag·gres·sor Angreifer *m*

ag·grieved verletzt, gekränkt

a·ghast entsetzt, entsetzt

ag·ile flink, behend

a·gil·i·ty Flinkheit *f*, Behendigkeit *f*

ag·i·tate *v/t fig* aufregen, aufwühlen; *Flüssigkeit* schütteln; *v/i* POL agitieren, hetzen (**against** gegen)

ag·i·ta·tion Aufregung *f*; POL Agitation *f*

ag·i·ta·tor POL Agitator *m*

a·go: a year ~ vor e-m Jahr

ag·o·ny Qual *f*; Todeskampf *m*

a·gree *v/i* übereinstimmen; sich vertragen; einig werden, sich einigen (**on** über *acc*); übereinkommen; ~ **to** zustimmen (*dat*), einverstanden sein mit

a·gree·a·ble (**to**) angenehm (für); übereinstimmend (mit)

a·gree·ment Übereinstimmung *f*; Vereinbarung *f*; Abkommen *n*

ag·ri·cul·tur·al landwirtschaftlich

ag·ri·cul·ture Landwirtschaft *f*

a·ground MAR gestrandet; *run* ~ stranden, auf Grund laufen

a·head vorwärts, voraus; vorn; *go* ~*!* nur zu!, mach nur!; *straight* ~ geradeaus

aid 1. unterstützen, *j-m* helfen (**in** bei); fördern; *he was accused of* ~*ing and abetting* JUR er wurde wegen Beihilfe angeklagt **2.** Hilfe *f*, Unterstützung *f*

AIDS, **Aids** MED Aids *n*

ail kränklich sein; **ail·ment** Leiden *n*

aim 1. *v/i* zielen (**at** auf *acc*, nach); ~ **at** beabsichtigen; *be* ~*ing to do s.th.* vorhaben, et. zu tun; *v/t:* ~ **at** *Waffe etc* richten auf *or* gegen (*acc*) **2.** Ziel *n* (*a. fig*); Absicht *f*; *take* ~ **at** zielen auf (*acc*) *or* nach; **aim·less** ziellos

air¹ 1. Luft *f*; Luftzug *m*; Miene *f*, Aussehen *n*; *by* ~ auf dem Luftwege; *in the open* ~ im Freien; *on the* ~ im Rundfunk *or* Fernsehen; *be on the* ~ senden;

in Betrieb sein; *go off the* ~ die Sendung beenden (*person*); sein Programm beenden (*station*); *give o.s.* ~*s, put on* ~*s* vornehm tun **2.** (aus)lüften; *fig* an die Öffentlichkeit bringen; erörtern

air² MUS Arie *f*, Weise *f*, Melodie *f*

air·bag MOT Airbag *m*

air·base MIL Luftstützpunkt *m*

air·bed Luftmatratze *f*

air·borne AVIAT in der Luft; MIL Luftlande...

air·brake TECH Druckluftbremse *f*

air·bus AVIAT Airbus *m*, Großraumflugzeug *n*

air-con·di·tioned mit Klimaanlage

air-con·di·tion·ing Klimaanlage *f*

air·craft car·ri·er MAR, MIL Flugzeugträger *m*

air·field Flugplatz *m*

air force MIL Luftwaffe *f*

air host·ess AVIAT Stewardess *f*

air jack·et Schwimmweste *f*

air·lift AVIAT Luftbrücke *f*

air·line AVIAT Fluggesellschaft *f*

air·lin·er AVIAT Verkehrsflugzeug *n*

air·mail Luftpost *f*; *by* ~ mit Luftpost

air·man MIL Flieger *m*

air·plane Flugzeug *n*

air pock·et AVIAT Luftloch *n*

air pol·lu·tion Luftverschmutzung *f*

air·port Flughafen *m*

air raid MIL Luftangriff *m*

air-raid| pre·cau·tions MIL Luftschutz *m*; ~ **shel·ter** MIL Luftschutzraum *m*

air route AVIAT Flugroute *f*

air·sick luftkrank

air·space Luftraum *m*

air·strip (behelfsmäßige) Start- und Landebahn

air ter·mi·nal Flughafenabfertigungsgebäude *n*

air·tight luftdicht

air time Sendezeit *f*

air traf·fic AVIAT Flugverkehr *m*

air-traf·fic| con·trol AVIAT Flugsicherung *f*; ~ **con·trol·ler** AVIAT Fluglotse *m*

air·way AVIAT Fluggesellschaft *f*

air·wor·thy AVIAT flugtüchtig

air·y luftig

aisle ARCH Seitenschiff *n*; Gang *m*

a·jar halb offen, angelehnt

a·kin verwandt (**to** mit)

a·lac·ri·ty Bereitwilligkeit *f*

a·larm 1. Alarm(zeichen *n*) *m*; Wecker *m*; Angst *f* **2.** alarmieren; beunruhigen; **~ clock** Wecker *m*

al·bum Album *n* (*a. record*)

al·bu·mi·nous BIOL eiweißhaltig

al·co·hol Alkohol *m*; **al·co·hol·ic 1.** alkoholisch **2.** Alkoholiker(in)

al·co·hol·ism Alkoholismus *m*, Trunksucht *f*

a·lert 1. wachsam; munter **2.** Alarm *m*; Alarmbereitschaft *f*; **on the ~** auf der Hut; **in** Alarmbereitschaft **3.** warnen (**to** vor *dat*), alarmieren

al·ga BOT Alge *f*

al·ge·bra MATH Algebra *f*

al·i·bi JUR Alibi *n*

a·li·en 1. ausländisch; fremd **2.** Ausländer(in); Außerirdische *m*, *f*

a·li·en·ate veräußern; entfremden; *esp art:* verfremden; **a·li·en·a·tion** Entfremdung *f*; *esp art:* Verfremdung *f*

a·light 1. in Flammen **2.** aussteigen; absteigen, absitzen; ZO sich niederlassen; AVIAT landen

a·lign (sich) ausrichten (**with** nach)

a·like 1. *adj* gleich **2.** *adv* gleich, ebenso

al·i·mo·ny JUR Unterhalt *m*

a·live lebendig; (noch) am Leben; lebhaft; **~ and kicking** gesund und munter; **be ~ with** wimmeln von

all 1. *adj* all; ganz; jede(r, -s) **2.** *pron* alles; alle *pl* **3.** *adv* ganz, völlig; **~ at once** auf einmal; **~ the better** desto besser; **~ but** beinahe, fast; **~ in** F fertig, ganz erledigt; **~ right** in Ordnung; **for ~ that** dessen ungeachtet, trotzdem; **for ~ I know** soviel ich weiß; **at ~** überhaupt; **not at ~** überhaupt nicht; **the score was two ~** das Spiel stand zwei zu zwei

all-A·mer·i·can typisch amerikanisch; die ganzen USA vertretend

al·lay beruhigen; lindern

al·le·ga·tion *unerwiesene* Behauptung

al·lege behaupten

al·leged angeblich, vermeintlich

al·le·giance Treue *f*

al·ler·gic MED allergisch (**to** gegen)

al·ler·gy MED Allergie *f*

al·le·vi·ate mildern, lindern

al·ley (enge *or* schmale) Gasse; Garten-, Parkweg *m*; *bowling:* Bahn *f*

al·li·ance Bündnis *n*

al·li·ga·tor ZO Alligator *m*

al·lo·cate zuteilen, anweisen

al·lo·ca·tion Zuteilung *f*

al·lot zuteilen, an-, zuweisen

al·lot·ment Zuteilung *f*; Parzelle *f*

al·low erlauben, bewilligen, gewähren; zugeben; ab-, anrechnen, vergüten; **~ for** einplanen, berücksichtigen (*acc*)

al·low·a·ble erlaubt, zulässig

al·low·ance Erlaubnis *f*; Bewilligung *f*; Taschengeld *n*; Vergütung *f*; *fig* Nachsicht *f*; **make~(s) for s.th.** et. berücksichtigen

al·loy TECH **1.** Legierung *f* **2.** legieren

all-round vielseitig

all·round·er Alleskönner *m*; Allroundsportler *m*, -spieler *m*

al·lude anspielen (**to** auf *acc*)

al·lure locken, an-, verlocken

al·lure·ment Verlockung *f*

al·lu·sion Anspielung *f*

all-wheel drive MOT Allradantrieb *m*

al·ly 1. (sich) vereinigen, verbünden (**to**, **with** mit); **2.** Verbündete *m*, *f*, Bundesgenosse *m*, Bundesgenossin *f*; **the Allies** MIL die Alliierten *pl*

al·might·y allmächtig; **the Almighty** REL der Allmächtige

al·mond BOT Mandel *f*

al·most fast, beinah(e)

alms Almosen *n*

a·loft (hoch) (dr)oben

a·lone allein; **let ~**, **leave ~** in Ruhe lassen, bleiben lassen; **let ~ ...** geschweige denn ...

a·long 1. *adv* weiter, vorwärts; da; dahin; **all ~** die ganze Zeit; **~ with** (zusammen) mit; **come ~** mitkommen, mitgehen; **get ~** vorwärtskommen, weiterkommen; auskommen, sich vertragen (**with s.o.** mit j-m); **take ~** mitnehmen **2.** *prp* entlang (*dat*), längs (*gen*)

a·long·side Seite an Seite; neben

a·loof abseits; reserviert, zurückhaltend, verschlossen; **a·loof·ness** Reserviertheit *f*; Verschlossenheit *f*

a·loud laut

al·pha·bet Alphabet *n*

al·pine (Hoch)Gebirgs...; alpin

al·read·y bereits, schon

al·right → **all right**

Al·sa·tian *esp Br* ZO Deutscher Schäferhund

al·so auch, ferner

al·tar REL Altar *m*

al·ter ändern, sich (ver)ändern; ab-, um-

ändern; **al·ter·a·tion** Änderung *f* (*to* an
dat), Veränderung *f*

al·ter·nate 1. abwechseln (lassen) **2.** abwechselnd; **al·ter·nat·ing cur·rent**
ELECTR Wechselstrom *m*

al·ter·na·tion Abwechslung *f*; Wechsel
m

al·ter·na·tive 1. alternativ, wahlweise **2.**
Alternative *f*, Wahl *f*, Möglichkeit *f*

al·though obwohl, obgleich

al·ti·tude Höhe *f*; *at an* ~ *of* in e-r Höhe
von

al·to·geth·er im Ganzen, insgesamt;
ganz (und gar), völlig

al·u·min·i·um *Br*, **a·lu·mi·num** Aluminium *n*

al·ways immer, stets

am, AM *abbr of* **before noon** (*Latin* **ante
meridiem**) morgens, vorm., vormittags

a·mal·gam·ate (sich) zusammenschließen, ECON *a.* fusionieren

a·mass anhäufen, aufhäufen

am·a·teur Amateur(in); Dilettant(in);
Hobby…

a·maze in Erstaunen setzen, verblüffen;
a·maze·ment Staunen *n*, Verblüffung
f; **a·maz·ing** erstaunlich

am·bas·sa·dor POL Botschafter *m* (*to* in
e-m Land); **am·bas·sa·dress** POL Botschafterin *f* (*to* in *e-m Land*)

am·ber Bernstein *m*

am·bi·gu·i·ty Zwei-, Mehrdeutigkeit *f*

am·big·u·ous zwei-, mehr-, vieldeutig

am·bi·tion Ehrgeiz *m*

am·bi·tious ehrgeizig, strebsam

am·ble 1. Passgang *m* **2.** im Passgang gehen *or* reiten; schlendern

am·bu·lance Krankenwagen *m*

a·men *int* REL amen

a·mend verbessern, berichtigen; PARL
abändern, ergänzen; **a·mend·ment**
Bess(e)rung *f*; Verbesserung *f*; PARL
Abänderungsantrag *m*, Ergänzungs-
antrag *m*; Zusatzartikel *m* zur Verfassung; **a·mends** (Schaden)Ersatz *m*;
make ~ Schadenersatz leisten, es wieder gutmachen; *make* ~ *to s.o. for s.th.*
j-n für et. entschädigen

a·men·i·ty *often pl* Annehmlichkeiten *pl*

A·mer·i·ca Amerika *n*; **A·mer·i·can 1.** a-
merikanisch **2.** Amerikaner(in)

A·mer·i·can·is·m LING Amerikanismus
m

A·mer·i·can·ize (sich) amerikanisieren

A·mer·i·can plan Vollpension *f*

a·mi·a·ble liebenswürdig, freundlich

am·i·ca·ble freundschaftlich, *a.* JUR gütlich

a·mid(st) inmitten (*gen*), (mitten) in *or*
unter

a·miss verkehrt, falsch, übel; *take s.th.*
~ et. übel nehmen, et. verübeln

am·mo·ni·a CHEM Ammoniak *n*

am·mu·ni·tion Munition *f*

am·nes·ty JUR **1.** Amnestie *f* **2.** begnadigen

a·mok: run ~ Amok laufen

a·mong(st) (mitten) unter, zwischen

am·o·rous verliebt

a·mount 1. (*to*) sich belaufen (auf *acc*);
hinauslaufen (auf *acc*); **2.** Betrag *m*,
(Gesamt)Summe *f*; Menge *f*

am·per·age ELECTR Stromstärke *f*

am·ple weit, groß, geräumig; reich,
reichlich, beträchtlich

am·pli·fi·ca·tion Erweiterung *f*; PHYS
Verstärkung *f*

am·pli·fi·er ELECTR Verstärker *m*

am·pli·fy erweitern; ELECTR verstärken

am·pli·tude Umfang *m*, Weite *f*, Fülle *f*;
ELECTR, PHYS Amplitude *f*

am·pu·tate MED amputieren

a·muck → *amok*

a·muse (*o.s.* sich) amüsieren, unterhalten, belustigen

a·muse·ment Unterhaltung *f*, Vergnügen *n*, Zeitvertreib *m*; ~ *park* Vergnü-
gungspark *m*, Freizeitpark *m*

a·mus·ing amüsant, unterhaltend

an → *a*

an·a·bol·ic ster·oid PHARM Anabolikum
n

a·nae·mi·a *Br* → **anemia**

an·aes·thet·ic *Br* → **anesthetic**

a·nal ANAT anal, Anal…

a·nal·o·gous analog, entsprechend

a·nal·o·gy Analogie *f*, Entsprechung *f*

an·a·lyse *esp Br*, **an·a·lyze** analysieren;
zerlegen

a·nal·y·sis Analyse *f*

an·arch·y Anarchie *f*, Gesetzlosigkeit *f*;
Chaos *n*

a·nat·o·mize MED zerlegen; zergliedern;
a·nat·o·my MED Anatomie *f*; Zerglie-
derung *f*, Analyse *f*

an·ces·tor Vorfahr *m*, Ahn *m*

an·ces·tress Vorfahrin *f*, Ahnfrau *f*

an·chor MAR **1.** Anker *m*; *at* ~ vor Anker

2. verankern

an·chor·man TV Moderator *m*

an·chor·wom·an TV Moderatorin *f*

an·cho·vy ZO Anschovis *f*, Sardelle *f*

an·cient 1. alt, antik; uralt **2.** *the ~s* HIST die Alten, die antiken Klassiker

and und

an·ec·dote Anekdote *f*

a·ne·mi·a MED Blutarmut *f*, Anämie *f*

an·es·thet·ic MED **1.** betäubend, Narkose... **2.** Betäubungsmittel *n*

an·gel Engel *m*

an·ger 1. Zorn *m*, Ärger *m* (*at* über *acc*); **2.** erzürnen, (ver)ärgern

an·gle[1] Winkel *m* (*a.* MATH)

an·gle[2] angeln (*for* nach)

an·gler Angler(in)

An·gli·can REL **1.** anglikanisch **2.** Anglikaner(in)

An·glo-Sax·on 1. angelsächsisch **2.** Angelsachse *m*

an·gry zornig, verärgert, böse (*at, with* über *acc*, mit *dat*)

an·guish Qual *f*, Schmerz *m*

an·gu·lar winkelig; knochig

an·i·mal 1. Tier *n* **2.** tierisch; **~ lov·er** Tierfreund *m*; **~ shel·ter** Tierheim *n*

an·i·mate beleben; aufmuntern, anregen

an·i·mat·ed lebendig; lebhaft, angeregt; **~ car·toon** Zeichentrickfilm *m*

an·i·ma·tion Lebhaftigkeit *f*; Animation *f*; Herstellung *f* von Zeichentrickfilmen; IT bewegtes Bild

an·i·mos·i·ty Animosität *f*, Feindseligkeit *f*

an·kle ANAT (Fuß)Knöchel *m*

an·nals Jahrbücher *pl*

an·nex 1. anhängen; annektieren **2.** Anhang *m*; ARCH Anbau *m*

an·ni·ver·sa·ry Jahrestag *m*; Jahresfeier *f*

an·no·tate mit Anmerkungen versehen; kommentieren

an·nounce ankündigen; bekannt geben; *radio*, TV ansagen; durchsagen; **an·nounce·ment** Ankündigung *f*; Bekanntgabe *f*; *radio*, TV Ansage *f*; Durchsage *f*; **an·nounc·er** *radio*, TV Ansager(in), Sprecher(in)

an·noy ärgern; belästigen

an·noy·ance Störung *f*, Belästigung *f*; Ärgernis *n*

an·noy·ing ärgerlich, lästig

an·nu·al 1. jährlich, Jahres... **2.** einjährige Pflanze; Jahrbuch *n*

an·nu·i·ty (Jahres)Rente *f*

an·nul für ungültig erklären, annullieren; **an·nul·ment** Annullierung *f*, Aufhebung *f*

an·o·dyne MED **1.** schmerzstillend **2.** schmerzstillendes Mittel

a·noint REL salben

a·nom·a·lous anomal

a·non·y·mous anonym

an·o·rak Anorak *m*

an·oth·er ein anderer; ein Zweiter; noch eine(r, -s)

an·swer 1. *v/t et.* beantworten; *j-m* antworten; entsprechen (*dat*); Zweck erfüllen; TECH *dem* Steuer gehorchen; JUR *e-r* Vorladung Folge leisten; *e-r* Beschreibung entsprechen; **~ the bell** or **door** (die Tür) aufmachen; **~ the telephone** ans Telefon gehen; *v/i* antworten (*to* auf *acc*); entsprechen (*to dat*); **~ for** einstehen für **2.** Antwort *f* (*to* auf *acc*)

an·swer·a·ble verantwortlich

an·swer·ing ma·chine TEL Anrufbeantworter *m*

ant ZO Ameise *f*

an·tag·o·nism Feindschaft *f*

an·tag·o·nist Gegner(in)

an·tag·o·nize bekämpfen; sich *j-n* zum Feind machen

Ant·arc·tic antarktisch

an·te·ced·ent vorhergehend, früher (*to* als)

an·te·lope ZO Antilope *f*

an·ten·na[1] ZO Fühler *m*

an·ten·na[2] ELECTR Antenne *f*

an·te·ri·or vorhergehend, früher (*to* als); vorder

an·them MUS Hymne *f*

an·ti... Gegen..., gegen ... eingestellt, Anti..., anti...

an·ti·air·craft MIL Fliegerabwehr..., Flugabwehr...

an·ti·bi·ot·ic MED Antibiotikum *n*

an·ti·bod·y BIOL Antikörper *m*, Abwehrstoff *m*

an·tic·i·pate voraussehen, ahnen; erwarten; zuvorkommen; vorwegnehmen; **an·tic·i·pa·tion** (Vor)Ahnung *f*; Erwartung *f*; Vorwegnahme *f*; Vorfreude *f*; *in ~* im Voraus

an·ti·clock·wise Br entgegen dem Uhrzeigersinn

an·tics Mätzchen pl

an·ti·dote Gegengift n, Gegenmittel n

an·ti·for·eign·er vi·o·lence Gewalt f gegen Ausländer

an·ti·freeze Frostschutzmittel n

an·ti·lock brak·ing sys·tem MOT Antiblockiersystem n (abbr **ABS**)

an·ti·mis·sile MIL Raketenabwehr...

an·ti·nu·cle·ar ac·tiv·ist Kernkraftgegner(in)

an·tip·a·thy Abneigung f

an·ti·quat·ed veraltet

an·tique 1. antik, alt 2. Antiquität f

an·tique| deal·er Antiquitätenhändler(in); ~ shop esp Br, ~ store Antiquitätenladen m

an·tiq·ui·ty Altertum n, Vorzeit f

an·ti·sep·tic MED 1. antiseptisch 2. antiseptisches Mittel

ant·lers ZO Geweih n

a·nus ANAT After m

an·vil Amboss m

anx·i·e·ty Angst f, Sorge f

anx·ious besorgt, beunruhigt (**about** wegen); begierig, gespannt (**for** auf acc); bestrebt (**to do** zu tun)

an·y 1. adj and pron (irgend)eine(r, -s), (irgend)welche(r, -s); (irgend)etwas; jede(r, -s) (beliebige); einige pl, welche pl; **not ~** keiner 2. adv irgend(wie), ein wenig, (noch) etwas

an·y·bod·y (irgend)jemand; jeder

an·y·how irgendwie; trotzdem, jedenfalls; wie dem auch sei

an·y·one → **anybody**

an·y·thing (irgend)etwas; alles; **~ but** alles andere als; **~ else?** sonst noch etwas?; **not ~** nichts

an·y·way → **anyhow**

an·y·where irgendwo(hin); überall

a·part einzeln, für sich; beiseite; **~ from** abgesehen von

a·part·heid POL Apartheid f, Politik f der Rassentrennung

a·part·ment Wohnung f; **~ build·ing, ~ house** Mietshaus n

ap·a·thet·ic apathisch, teilnahmslos, gleichgültig; **ap·a·thy** Apathie f, Teilnahmslosigkeit f

ape ZO (Menschen)Affe m

ap·er·ture Öffnung f

a·pi·a·ry Bienenhaus n

a·piece für jedes Stück, pro Stück, je

a·pol·o·gize sich entschuldigen (**for** für; **to** bei); a·pol·o·gy Entschuldigung f; Rechtfertigung f; **make an ~** (**for s.th.**) sich (für et.) entschuldigen

ap·o·plex·y MED Schlaganfall m, F Schlag m

a·pos·tle REL Apostel m

a·pos·tro·phe LING Apostroph m

ap·pal(l) erschrecken, entsetzen

ap·pal·ling erschreckend, entsetzlich

ap·pa·ra·tus Apparat m, Vorrichtung f, Gerät n

ap·par·ent offenbar; anscheinend; scheinbar

ap·pa·ri·tion Erscheinung f, Gespenst n

ap·peal 1. JUR Berufung or Revision einlegen, Einspruch erheben, Beschwerde einlegen; appellieren, sich wenden (**to** an acc); **~ to** gefallen (dat), zusagen (dat), wirken auf (acc); j-n dringend bitten (**for** um); 2. JUR Revision f, Berufung f; Beschwerde f; Einspruch m; Appell m (**to** an acc), Aufruf m; Wirkung f, Reiz m; Bitte f (**to** an acc; **for** um); **~ for mercy** JUR Gnadengesuch n

ap·peal·ing flehend; ansprechend

ap·pear (er)scheinen; sich zeigen; öffentlich auftreten; sich ergeben or herausstellen; ap·pear·ance Erscheinen n; Auftreten n; Äußere n, Erscheinung f, Aussehen n; Anschein m, äußerer Schein; **keep up ~s** den Schein wahren; **to** or **by all ~s** allem Anschein nach

ap·pease besänftigen, beschwichtigen; Durst etc stillen; Neugier befriedigen

ap·pend an-, hinzu-, beifügen

ap·pend·age Anhang m; Anhängsel n

ap·pen·di·ci·tis MED Blinddarmentzündung f

ap·pen·dix Anhang m; a. **vermiform ~** ANAT Wurmfortsatz m, Blinddarm m

ap·pe·tite (**for**) Appetit m (auf acc); fig Verlangen n (nach)

ap·pe·tiz·er Appetithappen m, appetitanregendes Gericht or Getränk

ap·pe·tiz·ing appetitanregend

ap·plaud applaudieren, Beifall spenden; loben

ap·plause Applaus m, Beifall m

ap·ple BOT Apfel m

ap·ple pie (warmer) gedeckter Apfelkuchen

ap·ple sauce Apfelmus n; sl Schmus m,

Quatsch *m*

ap·pli·ance Vorrichtung *f*; Gerät *n*; Mittel *n*

ap·plic·a·ble anwendbar (*to* auf *acc*)

ap·pli·cant Antragsteller(in), Bewerber(in) (*for* um)

ap·pli·ca·tion Anwendung *f* (*to* auf *acc*); Bedeutung *f* (*to* für); Gesuch *n* (*for* um); Bewerbung *f* (*for* um)

ap·ply v/t (*to*) (auf)legen, auftragen (auf *acc*); anwenden (auf *acc*); verwenden (für); ~ *o.s. to* sich widmen (*dat*); v/i (*to*) passen, zutreffen, sich anwenden lassen (auf *acc*); gelten (für); sich wenden (an *acc*); ~ *for* sich bewerben um, *et.* beantragen

ap·point bestimmen, festsetzen; verabreden; ernennen (*s.o. governor* j-n zum …); berufen (*to* auf e-*n* Posten)

ap·point·ment Bestimmung *f*; Verabredung *f*; Termin *m*; Ernennung *f*, Berufung *f*; Stelle *f*; ~ *book* Terminkalender *m*

ap·por·tion verteilen, zuteilen

ap·prais·al (Ab)Schätzung *f*

ap·praise (ab)schätzen, taxieren

ap·pre·cia·ble nennenswert, spürbar

ap·pre·ci·ate v/t schätzen, würdigen; dankbar sein für; v/i im Wert steigen

ap·pre·ci·a·tion Würdigung *f*; Dankbarkeit *f*; (richtige) Beurteilung *f*; ECON Wertsteigerung *f*

ap·pre·hend ergreifen, fassen; begreifen; befürchten; **ap·pre·hen·sion** Ergreifung *f*, Festnahme *f*; Besorgnis *f*; **ap·pre·hen·sive** ängstlich, besorgt (*for* um; *that* dass)

ap·pren·tice 1. Auszubildende *m*, *f*, Lehrling *m*, *Swiss* Lehrtochter *f* **2.** in die Lehre geben; **ap·pren·tice·ship** Lehrzeit *f*, Lehre *f*, Ausbildung *f*

ap·proach 1. v/i näher kommen, sich nähern; v/t sich nähern (*dat*); herangehen *or* herantreten an (*acc*) **2.** (Heran)Nahen *n*; Einfahrt *f*, Zufahrt *f*, Auffahrt *f*; Annäherung *f*; Methode *f*

ap·pro·ba·tion Billigung *f*, Beifall *m*

ap·pro·pri·ate 1. sich aneignen; verwenden; PARL bewilligen **2.** (*for, to*) angemessen (*dat*), passend (für, zu)

ap·prov·al Billigung *f*; Anerkennung *f*, Beifall *m*; **ap·prove** billigen, anerkennen; **ap·proved** bewährt

ap·prox·i·mate annähernd, ungefähr

a·pri·cot BOT Aprikose *f*

A·pril (*abbr* **Apr**) April *m*

a·pron Schürze *f*

apt geeignet, passend; treffend; begabt; ~ *to* geneigt zu

ap·ti·tude (*for*) Begabung *f* (für), Befähigung *f* (für), Talent *n* (zu)

ap·ti·tude test Eignungsprüfung *f*

aq·ua| jog·ging SPORT Aquajogging *n*; ~ **plan·ing** *Br* MOT Aquaplaning *n*

a·quar·i·um Aquarium *n*

A·quar·i·us ASTR Wassermann *m*; **he (she) is (an)** ~ er (sie) ist (ein) Wassermann

a·quat·ic Wasser…; ~ **plant** Wasserpflanze *f*; ~**s**, ~ **sports** Wassersport *m*

aq·ue·duct Aquädukt *m*

Ar·ab Araber(in); **A·ra·bi·a** Arabien *n*

Ar·a·bic 1. arabisch **2.** LING Arabisch *n*

ar·a·ble AGR anbaufähig; Acker…

ar·bi·tra·ry willkürlich, eigenmächtig

ar·bi·trate entscheiden, schlichten

ar·bi·tra·tion Schlichtung *f*

ar·bi·tra·tor Schiedsrichter *m*; Schlichter *m*

ar·bo(u)r Laube *f*

arc Bogen *m*; ELECTR Lichtbogen *m*

ar·cade Arkade *f*; Lauben-, Bogengang *m*; Durchgang *m*, Passage *f*

arch¹ 1. Bogen *m*; Gewölbe *n* **2.** (sich) wölben; krümmen

arch² erste(r, -s), oberste(r, -s), Haupt…, Erz…

arch³ schelmisch

ar·cha·ic veraltet

arch·an·gel Erzengel *m*

arch·bish·op REL Erzbischof *m*

ar·cher Bogenschütze *m*

ar·cher·y Bogenschießen *n*

ar·chi·tect Architekt(in)

ar·chi·tec·ture Architektur *f*

ar·chives Archiv *n*

arch·way (Bogen)Gang *m*

arc·tic arktisch, nördlich, Polar…

ar·dent feurig, glühend; *fig* leidenschaftlich, heftig; eifrig

ar·do(u)r Leidenschaft *f*, Glut *f*, Feuer *n*; Eifer *m*

are *du* bist, *wir or sie or Sie* sind, *ihr* seid

ar·e·a (Boden)Fläche *f*; Gegend *f*, Gebiet *n*; Bereich *m*

ar·e·a code TEL Vorwahl(nummer) *f*

a·re·na Arena *f*

Ar·gen·ti·na Argentinien *n*

Ar·gen·tine 1. argentinisch **2.** Argentinier(in)

ar·gue argumentieren; streiten; diskutieren; **ar·gu·ment** Argument *n*; Wortwechsel *m*, Auseinandersetzung *f*

ar·id dürr, trocken (*a. fig*)

Ar·ies ASTR Widder *m*; *he (she) is (an)* ~ er (sie) ist (ein) Widder

a·rise entstehen; auftauchen, auftreten

ar·is·toc·ra·cy Aristokratie *f*, Adel *m*

a·ris·to·crat Aristokrat(in), Adlige, *m, f*

a·ris·to·crat·ic aristokratisch, adlig

a·rith·me·tic[1] Rechnen *n*

a·rith·me·tic[2] arithmetisch, Rechen...

a·rith·met·ic u·nit IT Rechenwerk *n*

ark Arche *f*; *Noah's* ~ die Arche Noah

arm[1] ANAT Arm *m*; Armlehne *f*; *keep s.o. at* ~*'s length* sich j-n vom Leibe halten

arm[2] MIL (sich) bewaffnen; (auf)rüsten

ar·ma·ment MIL Bewaffnung *f*; Aufrüstung *f*

arm-chair Lehnstuhl *m*, Sessel *m*

ar·mi·stice MIL Waffenstillstand *m*

ar·mo(u)r 1. MIL Rüstung *f*, Panzer *m* (*a. fig*, ZO); **2.** panzern

ar·mo(u)red car gepanzertes Fahrzeug

arm·pit ANAT Achselhöhle *f*

arms Waffen *pl*; Waffengattung *f*; ~ **con·trol** Rüstungskontrolle *f*

ar·my MIL Armee *f*, Heer *n*

a·ro·ma Aroma *n*, Duft *m*

ar·o·mat·ic aromatisch, würzig

a·round 1. *adv* (rings)herum, (rund-) herum, ringsumher, überall; umher, herum; in der Nähe; da **2.** *prp* um, um... herum, rund um; in (*dat*) ... herum; ungefähr, etwa

a·rouse (auf)wecken; *fig* aufrütteln, erregen

ar·range (an)ordnen; festlegen, festsetzen; arrangieren (*a.* MUS); vereinbaren; MUS, THEA bearbeiten

ar·range·ment Anordnung *f*; Vereinbarung *f*; Vorkehrung *f*; MUS Arrangement *n*, Bearbeitung *f* (*a.* THEA)

ar·rears Rückstand *m*, Rückstände *pl*

ar·rest JUR **1.** Verhaftung *f*, Festnahme *f* **2.** verhaften, festnehmen

ar·riv·al Ankunft *f*; Erscheinen *n*; Ankömmling *m*; ~*s* AVIAT, RAIL *etc* 'Ankunft' (*timetable*); *day of* ~ Anreisetag; **ar·rive** (an)kommen, eintreffen, erscheinen; ~ *at fig* erreichen (*acc*), kom-

men zu

ar·ro·gance Arroganz *f*, Überheblichkeit *f*

ar·ro·gant arrogant, überheblich

ar·row Pfeil *m*

ar·row·head Pfeilspitze *f*

ar·se·nic CHEM Arsen *n*

ar·son JUR Brandstiftung *f*

art 1. Kunst *f* **2.** Kunst...; ~ *exhibition* Kunstausstellung *f*; → *arts*

ar·te·ri·al ANAT Schlagader...

ar·te·ri·al road Hauptverkehrsstraße *f*, Verkehrsader *f*

ar·te·ri·o·scle·ro·sis MED Arteriosklerose *f*, Arterienverkalkung *f*

ar·te·ry ANAT Arterie *f*, Schlagader *f*; (Haupt)Verkehrsader *f*

art·ful schlau, verschmitzt

art gal·le·ry Gemäldegalerie *f*

ar·thri·tis MED Arthritis *f*, Gelenkentzündung *f*

ar·ti·choke BOT Artischocke *f*

ar·ti·cle Artikel *m* (*a.* LING)

ar·tic·u·late 1. deutlich (aus)sprechen **2.** deutlich ausgesprochen; gegliedert

ar·tic·u·lat·ed Gelenk...; ~ *lorry* Br MOT Sattelschlepper *m*

ar·tic·u·la·tion (deutliche) Aussprache; TECH Gelenk *n*

ar·ti·fi·cial künstlich, Kunst...; ~ *person* juristische Person

ar·til·le·ry MIL Artillerie *f*

ar·ti·san Handwerker *m*

art·ist Künstler(in)

ar·tis·tic künstlerisch, Kunst...

art·less schlicht; naiv

arts Geisteswissenschaften *pl*; **Arts De·partment**, Br **Faculty of Arts** philosophische Fakultät

as 1. *adv* so, ebenso; wie; als **2.** *cj* (gerade) wie, so wie; ebenso wie; als, während; obwohl, obgleich; da, weil; ~ ... ~ (eben)so ... wie; ~ *for*, ~ *to* was ... (an-)betrifft; ~ *from* von *e-m* Zeitpunkt an, ab; ~ *it were* sozusagen; ~ *Hamlet* THEA als Hamlet

as·bes·tos Asbest *m*

as·cend (auf)steigen; ansteigen; besteigen; **as·cen·dan·cy, as·cen·den·cy** Überlegenheit *f*; Einfluss *m*

as·cen·sion Aufsteigen *n* (*esp* ASTR); Aufstieg *m*; **As·cen·sion (Day)** REL Himmelfahrt(stag *m*) *f*

as·cent Aufstieg *m*; Besteigung *f*; Steigung *f*

as·cet·ic asketisch

a·sep·tic MED **1.** aseptisch, keimfrei **2.** aseptisches Mittel

ash[1] BOT Esche *f*; Eschenholz *n*

ash[2] *a.* **ashes** Asche *f*

a·shamed beschämt; *be ~ of* sich schämen für (*o. gen*)

ash·en Aschen…; aschfahl, aschgrau

a·shore am *or* ans Ufer *or* Land

ash·tray Asch(en)becher *m*

Ash Wednes·day Aschermittwoch *m*

A·sia Asien *n*; **A·sian, A·si·at·ic 1.** asiatisch **2.** Asiat(in)

a·side beiseite (*a.* THEA), seitwärts; *~ from* abgesehen von

ask *v/t* fragen (*s.th.* nach et.); verlangen (*of, from s.o.* von j-m); bitten (*s.o.* [*for*] *s.th.* j-n um et.; *that* darum, dass); erbitten; *~* (*s.o.*) *a question* (j-m) e-e Frage stellen; *v/i ~ for* bitten um; fragen nach; *he ~ed for it or for trouble* er wollte es ja so haben; *to be had for the ~ing* umsonst zu haben sein

a·skew schief

a·sleep schlafend; *be* (*fast, sound*) *~* (fest) schlafen; *fall ~* einschlafen

as·par·a·gus BOT Spargel *m*

as·pect Lage *f*, Aspekt *m*, Seite *f*, Gesichtspunkt *m*

as·phalt 1. Asphalt *m* **2.** asphaltieren

as·pic GASTR Aspik *m*, Gelee *n*

as·pi·rant Bewerber(in)

as·pi·ra·tion Ambition *f*, Bestrebung *f*

as·pire streben (*to, after* nach)

ass ZO Esel *m*

as·sail angreifen; *be ~ed with doubts* von Zweifeln befallen werden

as·sail·ant Angreifer(in)

as·sas·sin (*esp* politischer) Mörder, Attentäter *m*; **as·sas·sin·ate** *esp* POL ermorden; *be ~d* e-m Attentat *or* Mordanschlag zum Opfer fallen; **as·sas·sin·a·tion** (*of*) (*esp* politischer) Mord (an *dat*), Ermordung *f* (*gen*), Attentat *n* (auf *acc*)

as·sault 1. Angriff *m*, Überfall *m* **2.** angreifen, überfallen

as·sem·blage Ansammlung *f*; TECH Montage *f*; **as·sem·ble** (sich) versammeln; TECH montieren

as·sem·bly Versammlung *f*, Gesellschaft *f*; TECH Montage *f*; *~ line* TECH Fließband *n*

as·sent 1. Zustimmung *f* **2.** (*to*) zustimmen (*dat*); billigen (*acc*)

as·sert behaupten; geltend machen; *~ o.s.* sich behaupten, sich durchsetzen

as·ser·tion Behauptung *f*; Erklärung *f*; Geltendmachung *f*

as·sess Kosten etc festsetzen; Einkommen etc (zur Steuer) veranlagen (*at* mit); *fig* abschätzen, beurteilen

as·sess·ment Festsetzung *f*; (Steuer)Veranlagung *f*; *fig* Einschätzung *f*

as·set ECON Aktivposten *m*; *fig* Plus *n*, Gewinn *m*; *pl* ECON Aktiva *pl*; JUR Vermögen(smasse *f*) *n*; Konkursmasse *f*

as·sign an-, zuweisen; bestimmen; zuschreiben; **as·sign·ment** An-, Zuweisung *f*; Aufgabe *f*; Auftrag *m*; JUR Abtretung *f*; Übertragung *f*

as·sim·i·late (sich) angleichen *or* anpassen (*to, with* dat)

as·sim·i·la·tion Assimilation *f*, Angleichung *f*, Anpassung *f* (*all*: *to* an *acc*)

as·sist *j-m* beistehen, helfen; *j-n* unterstützen; **as·sist·ance** Beistand *m*, Hilfe *f*; **as·sist·ant 1.** stellvertretend, Hilfs… **2.** Assistent(in), Mitarbeiter(in); (*shop*) *~* Br Verkäufer(in); *~ant referee* SPORT Schiedsrichterassistent(in)

as·so·ci·ate 1. vereinigen, verbinden, zusammenschließen; assoziieren; *~ with* verkehren mit **2.** Teilhaber(in)

as·so·ci·a·tion Vereinigung *f*, Verbindung *f*; Verein *m*

as·sort sortieren, aussuchen, zusammenstellen; **as·sort·ment** ECON (*of*) Sortiment *n* (von), Auswahl *f* (an *dat*)

as·sume annehmen, voraussetzen; übernehmen

as·sump·tion Annahme *f*, Voraussetzung *f*; Übernahme *f*; *the Assumption* REL Mariä Himmelfahrt *f*

as·sur·ance Zusicherung *f*, Versicherung *f*; *esp* Br (Lebens)Versicherung *f*; Sicherheit *f*, Gewissheit *f*; Selbstsicherheit *f*; **as·sure** *j-m* versichern; *esp* Br *j-s* Leben versichern; **as·sured 1.** sicher *m*, *f*; *esp* Br Versicherte *m*, *f*; **as·sur·ed·ly** ganz gewiss

as·te·risk PRINT Sternchen *n*

asth·ma MED Asthma *n*

as·ton·ish in Erstaunen setzen; *be ~ed* erstaunt sein (*at* über *acc*)

as·ton·ish·ing erstaunlich

as·ton·ish·ment (Er)Staunen n, Verwunderung f

as·tound verblüffen

a·stray: go ~ vom Weg abkommen; fig auf Abwege geraten; irregehen; **lead ~** fig irreführen; verleiten

a·stride rittlings (of auf dat)

as·trin·gent MED 1. adstringierend 2. Adstringens n

as·trol·o·gy Astrologie f

as·tro·naut Astronaut m, (Welt)Raumfahrer m

as·tron·o·my Astronomie f

as·tute scharfsinnig; schlau

a·sun·der auseinander, entzwei

a·sy·lum Asyl n; **right of ~** Asylrecht n

a·sy·lum seek·er Asylant(in), Asylbewerber(in)

at prp place: in, an, bei, auf; direction: auf, nach, gegen, zu; occupation: bei, beschäftigt mit, in; manner, state: in, bei, zu, unter; price etc: für, um; time, age: um, bei; **~ the baker's** beim Bäcker; **~ the door** an der Tür; **~ school** in der Schule; **~ 10 dollars** für 10 Dollar; **~ 18** mit 18 (Jahren); **~ the age of** im Alter von; **~ 8 o'clock** um 8 Uhr

a·the·ism Atheismus m

ath·lete SPORT (Leicht)Athlet(in)

ath·let·ic SPORT athletisch

ath·let·ics SPORT (Leicht)Athletik f

At·lan·tic 1. a. **~ Ocean** der Atlantik **2.** atlantisch

at·mo·sphere Atmosphäre f (a. fig)

at·mo·spher·ic atmosphärisch

at·oll Atoll n

at·om Atom n; **~ bomb** Atombombe f

a·tom·ic atomar, Atom...; **~ age** Atomzeitalter n; **~ bomb** Atombombe f; **~ en·er·gy** Atomenergie f; **~ pile** Atomreaktor m; **~ pow·er** Atomkraft f; **~-pow·ered** atomgetrieben; **~ waste** Atommüll m; **~ weight** CHEM Atomgewicht n

at·om·ize atomisieren; Flüssigkeit zerstäuben; **at·om·iz·er** Zerstäuber m

a·tro·cious grässlich; grausam

a·troc·i·ty Scheußlichkeit f; Greueltat f

at sign IT at-Zeichen n

at·tach v/t (to) anheften, ankleben (an acc), befestigen, anbringen (an dat), Wert, Wichtigkeit etc beimessen (dat); **be ~ed to** fig hängen an; **at·tach·ment**

Befestigung f; Bindung f (**to** an acc); Anhänglichkeit f (**to** an acc)

at·tack 1. angreifen **2.** Angriff m; MED Anfall m

at·tempt 1. versuchen **2.** Versuch m; **an ~ on s.o.'s life** ein Mordanschlag or Attentat auf j-n

at·tend v/t (ärztlich) behandeln; Kranke pflegen; teilnehmen an (dat), Schule, Vorlesung etc besuchen; fig begleiten; v/i anwesend sein; erscheinen; **~** j-n (im Laden) bedienen; **are you being ~ed to?** werden Sie schon bedient?; **~ to s.th.** etwas erledigen; **at·tend·ance** Dienst m, Bereitschaft f; Pflege f; Anwesenheit f, Erscheinen n; Besucher pl, Teilnehmer pl; Besuch(erzahl f) m, Beteiligung f; **at·tend·ant** Begleiter(in); Aufseher(in); (Tank-)Wart m

at·ten·tion Aufmerksamkeit f (a. fig); **pay ~** aufpassen

at·ten·tive aufmerksam

at·tic Dachboden m; Dachkammer f

at·ti·tude (Ein)Stellung f; Haltung f

at·tor·ney Bevollmächtigte m, f; JUR (Rechts)Anwalt m, (Rechts)Anwältin f; **power of ~** Vollmacht f

At·tor·ney Gen·er·al JUR Justizminister; Br erster Kronanwalt

at·tract anziehen; Aufmerksamkeit erregen; fig reizen; **at·trac·tion** Anziehung f, Anziehungskraft f, Reiz m; Attraktion f, THEA etc Zugnummer f, Zugstück n; **at·trac·tive** anziehend; attraktiv; reizvoll

at·trib·ute¹ zuschreiben (**to** dat); zurückführen (**to** auf acc)

at·tri·bute² Attribut n (a. LING), Eigenschaft f, Merkmal n

at·tune: ~ to fig einstellen auf (acc)

au·ber·gine BOT Aubergine f

au·burn kastanienbraun

auc·tion 1. Auktion f, Versteigerung f **2.** mst **~ off** versteigern

auc·tion·eer Auktionator m

au·da·cious unverfroren, dreist

au·dac·i·ty Unverfrorenheit f, Dreistigkeit f

au·di·ble hörbar

au·di·ence Publikum n, Zuhörer pl, Zuschauer pl, Besucher pl, Leser(kreis m) pl; Audienz f

au·di·o·vis·u·al aids audiovisuelle Unterrichtsmittel *pl*

au·dit ECON **1.** Buchprüfung *f* **2.** prüfen

au·di·tion MUS Vorsingen *n*; THEA Vorsprechen *n*; *have an* ~ vorsingen, THEA vorsprechen

au·di·tor ECON Buchprüfer *m*; UNIV Gasthörer(in)

au·di·to·ri·um Zuhörer-, Zuschauerraum *m*; Vortrags-, Konzertsaal *m*

Aug *abbr of* **August** Aug., August *m*

au·ger TECH großer Bohrer

Au·gust (*abbr* **Aug**) August *m*

aunt Tante *f*

au pair (**girl**) Au-pair-Mädchen *n*

aus·pic·es: *under the* ~ *of* unter der Schirmherrschaft (*gen*)

aus·tere streng; enthaltsam; dürftig; einfach, schmucklos

Aus·tra·li·a Australien; **Aus·tra·li·an 1.** australisch **2.** Australier(in)

Aus·tri·a Österreich *n*

Aus·tri·an 1. österreichisch **2.** Österreicher(in)

au·then·tic authentisch; zuverlässig; echt

au·thor Urheber(in); Autor(in), Verfasser(in), Schriftsteller(in)

au·thor·ess Autorin *f*, Verfasserin *f*, Schriftstellerin *f*

au·thor·i·ta·tive gebieterisch, herrisch; maßgebend

au·thor·i·ty Autorität *f*; Nachdruck *m*, Gewicht *n*; Vollmacht *f*; Einfluss *m* (**o·ver** auf *acc*); Ansehen *n*; Quelle *f*; Autorität *f*, Kapazität *f*; *mst pl* Behörde *f*

au·thor·ize *j-n* autorisieren, ermächtigen, bevollmächtigen

au·thor·ship Urheberschaft *f*

au·to Auto *n*

au·to... auto..., selbst..., Auto..., Selbst...

au·to·bi·og·ra·phy Autobiografie *f*

au·to·graph Autogramm *n*

au·to·mat® Automatenrestaurant *n*

au·to·mate automatisieren

au·to·mat·ic 1. automatisch **2.** Selbstladepistole *f*, -gewehr *n*; Auto *n* mit Automatik; ~**tel·ler ma·chine** (*abbr* **ATM**) Geld-, Bankautomat *m*

au·to·ma·tion TECH Automation *f*

au·tom·a·ton Roboter *m*

au·to·mo·bile Auto *n*, Automobil *n*

au·ton·o·my POL Autonomie *f*

au·top·sy MED Autopsie *f*

au·to·tel·ler Geld-, Bankautomat *m*

au·tumn Herbst *m*

au·tum·nal herbstlich, Herbst...

aux·il·i·a·ry helfend, Hilfs...

a·vail *to no* ~ vergeblich

a·vail·a·ble verfügbar, vorhanden; erreichbar; ECON lieferbar, vorrätig, erhältlich

av·a·lanche Lawine *f*

av·a·rice Habsucht *f*

av·a·ri·cious habgierig

a·venge rächen; **a·veng·er** Rächer(in)

a·ve·nue Allee *f*; Boulevard *m*, Prachtstraße *f*

av·e·rage 1. Durchschnitt *m* **2.** durchschnittlich, Durchschnitts...

a·verse abgeneigt (**to** *dat*)

a·ver·sion Widerwille *m*, Abneigung *f*

a·vert abwenden (*a. fig*)

avian flu Vogelgrippe *f*

a·vi·a·ry Vogelhaus *n*, Voliere *f*

a·vi·a·tion Luftfahrt *f*

a·vi·a·tor Flieger *m*

av·id gierig (**for** nach); begeistert

av·o·ca·do BOT Avocado *f*

a·void (ver)meiden; ausweichen

a·void·ance Vermeidung *f*

a·vow·al Bekenntnis *n*, (Ein)Geständnis *n*

a·wait erwarten, warten auf (*acc*)

a·wake 1. wach, munter **2.** *a.* **a·waken** *v/t* (auf)wecken; *v/i* aufwachen, erwachen;

a·wak·en·ing Erwachen *n*

a·ward 1. Belohnung *f*; Preis *m*, Auszeichnung *f* **2.** zuerkennen, *Preis etc* verleihen

a·ware: *be* ~ *of s.th.* von etwas wissen, sich e-r Sache bewusst sein; *become* ~ *of s.th.* etwas merken

a·way weg, fort; (weit) entfernt; immer weiter, d(a)rauflos; SPORT Auswärts...; ~ *match* SPORT Auswärtsspiel *n*

awe 1. Furcht *f*, Scheu *f* **2.** *j-m* (Ehr-)Furcht *or* großen Respekt einflößen

aw·ful furchtbar, schrecklich

awk·ward ungeschickt, linkisch; unangenehm; unhandlich, sperrig; ungünstig, ungelegen

awl Ahle *f*, Pfriem *m*

aw·ning Plane *f*; Markise *f*

a·wry schief

ax(e) Axt *f*, Beil *n*

ax·is MATH *etc* Achse *f*

B

ax·le TECH (Rad)Achse f, Welle f
ay(e) PARL Jastimme f

A-Z Br appr Stadtplan m
az·ure azurblau, himmelblau

B

B, b B, b n
b abbr of **born** geb., geboren
bab·ble **1.** stammeln; plappern, schwatzen; plätschern **2.** Geplapper n, Geschwätz n
babe kleines Kind, Baby n; F Puppe f
ba·boon ZO Pavian m
ba·by **1.** Baby n, Säugling m, kleines Kind; F Puppe f **2.** Baby…, Kinder…; klein; ~ bug·gy, ~ car·riage Kinderwagen m; ~-changing room Babywickelraum m; ~ food Babynahrung f
ba·by·hood Säuglingsalter n
ba·by·ish contp kindisch
ba·by·mind·er Br Tagesmutter f
ba·by·sit babysitten
ba·by·sit·ter Babysitter(in)
bach·e·lor Junggeselle m
back **1.** Rücken m; Rückseite f; (Rück)Lehne f; hinterer or rückwärtiger Teil; SPORT Verteidiger m **2.** adj Hinter…, Rück…, hintere(r, -s), rückwärtig; ECON rückständig; alt, zurückliegend **3.** adv zurück, rückwärts **4.** v/t mit e-m Rücken versehen; wetten or setzen auf (acc); a. ~ **up** unterstützen; zurückbewegen; MOT zurückstoßen mit; ~ **up** IT e-e Sicherungskopie machen von; v/i often ~ **up** sich rückwärts bewegen, zurückgehen or -fahren, MOT a. zurückstoßen; ~ **in(to a parking space)** MOT rückwärts einparken; ~ **up** IT e-e Sicherungskopie machen
back·ache Rückenschmerzen pl
back·bite verleumden, schlechtmachen
back·bone ANAT Rückgrat n (a. fig)
back·break·ing erschöpfend, mörderisch
back·chat Br freche Antwort(en pl)
back·comb Br toupieren
back door Hintertür f; fig Hintertürchen n
back·er Unterstützer m, Geldgeber m
back·fire MOT Früh- or Fehlzündung haben; fig fehlschlagen
back·ground Hintergrund m

back·hand SPORT Rückhand f, Rückhandschlag m
back·heel·er soccer: Hackentrick m
back·ing Unterstützung f
back num·ber alte Nummer
back·pack großer Rucksack
back·pack·er Rucksacktourist(in)
back·pack·ing Rucksacktourismus m
back·ped·al brake Br Rücktritt m, Rücktrittbremse f
back seat MOT Rücksitz m
back·side Gesäß n, F Hintern m, Po m
back·space (key) IT Rücktaste f
back stairs Hintertreppe f
back street Seitenstraße f
back·stroke Rückenschwimmen n
back talk freche Antwort(en pl)
back·track fig e-n Rückzieher machen
back·up Unterstützung f; TECH Ersatzgerät n; IT Backup n, Sicherungskopie f; MOT Rückstau m
back·ward **1.** adj Rück…, Rückwärts…; zurückgeblieben; rückständig; **a ~ glance** ein Blick zurück **2.** adv a. **backwards** rückwärts, zurück
back·yard Garten m hinter dem Haus; Br Hinterhof m
ba·con Speck m
bac·te·ri·a BIOL Bakterien pl
bad schlecht, böse, schlimm; **go ~** schlecht werden, verderben; **he is in a ~ way** es geht ihm schlecht; **he is ~ly off** es geht ihm finanziell schlecht; **~ly wounded** schwer verwundet; **want ~ly** dringend brauchen
badge Abzeichen n; Dienstmarke f
bad·ger **1.** ZO Dachs m **2.** j-n plagen, j-m zusetzen
bad·min·ton Federball(spiel n) m, SPORT Badminton n
bad-tempered schlecht gelaunt
bag **1.** Beutel m, Sack m; Tüte f; Tasche f **2.** in e-n Beutel etc tun; in Beutel verpacken or abfüllen; HUNT zur Strecke bringen; schlottern
bag·gage (Reise)Gepäck n; ~ car RAIL

Gepäckwagen *m*; ~ check Gepäckschein *m*; ~ claim AVIAT Gepäckausgabe *f*; ~ room RAIL Gepäckaufbewahrung *f*

bag·gy bauschig; ausgebeult

bag·pipes MUS Dudelsack *m*

bail 1. Bürge *m*; JUR Kaution *f*; *be out on* ~ gegen Kaution auf freiem Fuß sein; *go* or *stand* ~ *for s.o.* für j-n Kaution stellen 2. ~ *out* JUR j-n gegen Kaution freibekommen; AVIAT (mit dem Fallschirm) abspringen

bai·liff (Guts)Verwalter *m*; Br JUR Gerichtsvollzieher *m*

bait 1. Köder *m* (*a. fig*) 2. mit e-m Köder versehen; *fig* ködern

bake backen, im (Back)Ofen braten; TECH brennen; dörren

bak·er Bäcker *m*

bak·er·y Bäckerei *f*

bak·ing pow·der Backpulver *n*

bal·ance 1. Waage *f*; Gleichgewicht *n* (*a. fig*); ECON Bilanz *f*; Saldo *m*, Kontostand *m*, Guthaben *n*; Restbetrag *m*; *keep one's* ~ das Gleichgewicht halten; *lose one's* ~ das Gleichgewicht verlieren; *fig* die Fassung verlieren; ~ *of payments* ECON Zahlungsbilanz *f*; ~ *of power* POL Kräftegleichgewicht *n*; ~ *of trade* ECON Handelsbilanz *f* 2. *v/t* abwägen; im Gleichgewicht halten, balancieren; ECON ausgleichen; *v/i* balancieren; ECON sich ausgleichen; ~ *each other* sich die Waage halten

bal·ance sheet ECON Bilanz *f*

bal·co·ny Balkon *m* (*a.* THEA)

bald kahl

bale¹ Ballen *m*

bale²: ~ *out* Br AVIAT (mit dem Fallschirm) abspringen

bale·ful hasserfüllt

balk 1. Balken *m* 2. stutzen; scheuen

ball¹ 1. Ball *m*; Kugel *f*; ANAT (Hand-, Fuß)Ballen *m*; Knäuel *m, n*; Kloß *m*; *long* ~ SPORT langer Pass 2. ballen; sich zusammenballen

ball² 1. Ball *m*, Tanzveranstaltung *f*

bal·lad Ballade *f*

bal·last 1. Ballast *m* 2. mit Ballast beladen

ball bear·ing TECH Kugellager *n*

bal·let Ballett *n*

bal·lis·tics MIL Ballistik *f*

bal·loon Ballon *m*; Sprech-, Denk-

blase *f* 2. sich (auf)blähen

bal·lot 1. Stimmzettel *m*; (geheime) Wahl *f* 2. *(for)* stimmen (für), (in geheimer Wahl) wählen (*acc*); ~ box Wahlurne *f*; ~ pa·per Stimmzettel *m*

ball·point (pen) Kugelschreiber *m*, F Kuli *m*

ball·room Ballsaal *m*, Tanzsaal *m*

balls V Eier *pl*

balm Balsam *m* (*a. fig*)

balm·y lind, mild

ba·lo·ney F Quatsch *m*

Balt·ics: *the* ~ das Baltikum

bal·us·trade Balustrade *f*, Brüstung *f*, Geländer *n*

bam·boo BOT Bambus(rohr *n*) *m*

bam·boo·zle F betrügen, j-n übers Ohr hauen

ban 1. (amtliches) Verbot, Sperre *f*; REL Bann *m* 2. verbieten

ba·nal banal, abgedroschen

ba·na·na BOT Banane *f*

band 1. Band *n*; Streifen *m*; Schar *f*, Gruppe *f*; *contp* Bande *f*; (Musik)Kapelle *f*, (Tanz-, Unterhaltungs)Orchester *n*, (*Jazz-, Rock*)Band *f* 2. ~ *together* sich zusammentun or -rotten

ban·dage MED 1. Bandage *f*; Binde *f*; Verband *m*; (Heft)Pflaster *n* 2. bandagieren; verbinden

'Band-Aid® MED (Heft)Pflaster *n*

B & B *abbr of bed and breakfast* Übernachtung *f* mit Frühstück

ban·dit Bandit *m*

band·lead·er MUS Bandleader *m*

band·mas·ter MUS Kapellmeister *m*

ban·dy krumm

ban·dy-legged säbelbeinig, o-beinig

bang 1. heftiger Schlag; Knall *m*; *mst pl* Pony *m* 2. dröhnend (zu)schlagen

ban·gle Armreif *m*, Fußreif *m*

ban·ish verbannen

ban·ish·ment Verbannung *f*

ban·is·ter *a. pl* Treppengeländer *n*

ban·jo MUS Banjo *n*

bank¹ ECON 1. Bank *f* (*a.* MED); 2. *v/t* bei e-r Bank einzahlen; *v/i* ein Bankkonto haben (*with* bei)

bank² (Erd)Wall *m*; Böschung *f*; (*Fluss-etc*)Ufer *n*; (*Sand-, Wolken*)Bank *f*

bank ac·count Bankkonto *n*

bank bill Banknote *f*, Geldschein *m*

bank·book Sparbuch *n*

bank code ECON Bankleitzahl *f*

B

bank·er Bankier *m*, Banker *m*; **~'s card**
Scheckkarte *f*

bank hol·i·day *Br* gesetzlicher Feiertag
m

bank·ing ECON **1.** Bankgeschäft *n*, Bank-
wesen *n* **2.** Bank...

bank note *Br* → **bank bill**

bank rate ECON Diskontsatz *m*

bank·rupt JUR **1.** Konkursschuldner *m* **2.**
bankrott; **go~** in Konkurs gehen, Bankrott machen **3.** *j-n*, *Unternehmen* Bankrott machen; **bank·rupt·cy** JUR Bankrott *m*, Konkurs *m*

bank sort·ing code → **bank code**

ban·ner Transparent *n*

banns Aufgebot *n*

ban·quet Bankett *n*

ban·ter necken

bap·tism REL Taufe *f*

bap·tize REL taufen

bar **1.** Stange *f*, Stab *m*; SPORT (Tor-,
Quer-, Sprung)Latte *f*; Riegel *m*;
Schranke *f*, Sperre *f*; *fig* Hindernis *n*;
(*Gold- etc*)Barren *m*; MUS Taktstrich
m; *ein* Takt *m*; dicker Strich; JUR (Ge-
richts)Schranke *f*; JUR Anwaltschaft *f*;
Bar *f*; Lokal *n*, Imbissstube *f*; *pl* Gitter
n; **a ~ of chocolate** ein Riegel *or* e-e
Tafel Schokolade; **a ~ of soap** ein
Stück Seife **2.** zuriegeln, verriegeln;
versperren; einsperren; (ver)hindern;
ausschließen

barb Widerhaken *m*

bar·bar·i·an **1.** barbarisch **2.** Barbar(in)

bar·be·cue **1.** Bratrost *m*, Grill *m*; Barbecue *n* **2.** auf dem Rost *or* am Spieß
braten, grillen

barbed wire Stacheldraht *m*

bar·ber (Herren)Friseur *m*, (-)Frisör *m*

bar code Strichkode *m*

bare **1.** nackt, bloß; kahl; leer **2.** entblößen

bare·faced unverschämt, schamlos

bare·foot, bare·foot·ed barfuß

bare·head·ed barhäuptig

bare·ly kaum

bar·gain **1.** Geschäft *n*, Handel *m*; vor-
teilhaftes Geschäft, Gelegenheitskauf
m; **a (dead) ~** spottbillig; **it's a ~!** abgemacht! **2.** (ver)handeln; **~ sale** Verkauf
m zu herabgesetzten Preisen; Ausverkauf *m*

barge **1.** Lastkahn *m* **2. ~ in** F hereinplatzen (**on** bei)

bark[1] BOT Borke *f*, Rinde *f*

bark[2] **1.** bellen; **~ up the wrong tree** F
auf dem Holzweg sein; an der falschen
Adresse sein **2.** Bellen *n*

bar·ley BOT Gerste *f*; Graupe *f*

barn Scheune *f*; (Vieh)Stall *m*

ba·rom·e·ter Barometer *n*

bar·on Baron *m*; Freiherr *m*

bar·on·ess Baronin *f*; Freifrau *f*

bar·racks MIL Kaserne *f*; *contp* Mietskaserne *f*

bar·rage Staudamm *m*; MIL Sperrfeuer
n; *fig* (Wort- *etc*)Schwall *m*

bar·rel Fass *n*, Tonne *f*; (*Gewehr*)Lauf
m; TECH Trommel *f*, Walze *f*

bar·rel or·gan MUS Drehorgel *f*

bar·ren unfruchtbar; trocken

bar·rette Haarspange *f*

bar·ri·cade **1.** Barrikade *f* **2.** verbarrika-
dieren; sperren

bar·ri·er Schranke *f* (*a. fig*), Barriere *f*,
Sperre *f*; Hindernis *n*

bar·ris·ter *Br* JUR Barrister *m*

bar·row Karre *f*

bar·ter **1.** Tausch(handel) *m* **2.** tauschen
(**for** gegen)

base[1] gemein

base[2] **1.** Basis *f*; Grundlage *f*; Fundament *n*; Fuß *m*; MIL Standort *m*; MIL
Stützpunkt *m* **2.** gründen, stützen (**on**
auf *acc*)

base[3] CHEM Base *f*

base·ball SPORT Baseball(spiel *n*) *m*

base·board Scheuerleiste *f*

base·less grundlos

base·line *tennis etc*: Grundlinie *f*

base·ment ARCH Fundament *n*; Keller-
geschoss *n*

bash·ful scheu, schüchtern

ba·sic[1] **1.** Grund..., grundlegend **2.** *pl*
Grundlagen *pl*

ba·sic[2] CHEM basisch

ba·sic·al·ly im Grunde

ba·sin Becken *n*, Schale *f*, Schüssel *f*;
Tal-, Wasser-, Hafenbecken *n*

ba·sis Basis *f*; Grundlage *f*

bask sich sonnen (*a. fig*)

bas·ket Korb *m*

bas·ket·ball SPORT Basketball(spiel *n*) *m*

bass[1] MUS Bass *m*

bass[2] ZO (Fluss-, See)Barsch *m*

bas·tard Bastard *m*

baste[1] GASTR mit Fett begießen

baste[2] (an)heften

bat¹ ZO Fledermaus f; *as blind as a ~* stockblind

bat² *baseball, cricket* **1.** Schlagholz n, Schläger m; F *right off the ~* sofort **2.** am Schlagen sein

batch Stapel m, Stoß m

bate: *with ~d breath* mit angehaltenem Atem

bath 1. (Wannen)Bad n; pl Bad n, Badeanstalt f; Badeort m; *have a ~* Br, *take a ~* baden, ein Bad nehmen **2.** Br *v/t* j-n baden, ein Bad nehmen; *v/i* baden, ein Bad nehmen

bathe *v/t* baden (a. MED); *v/i* baden, ein Bad nehmen; schwimmen

bath foam Badeschaum m

bath-ing 1. Baden n **2.** Bade...

bath-ing suit → *swimsuit*

bath-robe Bademantel m; Morgenrock m, Schlafrock m

bath-room Badezimmer n; Toilette f

bath-tub Badewanne f

bat-on Stab m; MUS Taktstock m; Schlagstock m, Gummiknüppel m

bat-tal-i-on MIL Bataillon n

bat-ten Latte f

bat-ter¹ heftig schlagen; misshandeln; verbeulen; *~ down, ~ in* einschlagen

bat-ter² GASTR Rührteig m

bat-ter³ *baseball, cricket:* Schläger m, Schlagmann m

bat-ter-y ELECTR Batterie f; JUR Tätlichkeit f, Körperverletzung f; *assault and ~* JUR tätliche Beleidigung

bat-ter-y charg-er ELECTR Ladegerät n

bat-ter-y-op-e-rat-ed ELECTR batteriebetrieben

bat-tle 1. MIL Schlacht f (*of* bei); fig Kampf m (*for* um) **2.** kämpfen

bat-tle-field, bat-tle-ground MIL Schlachtfeld n

bat-tle-ments ARCH Zinnen pl

bat-tle-ship MIL Schlachtschiff n

baulk → *balk*

Ba-va-ri-a Bayern n

Ba-var-i-an 1. bay(e)risch **2.** Bayer(in)

bawd-y obszön

bawl brüllen, schreien; *~ s.o. out* mit j-m schimpfen

bay¹ GEOGR Bai f, Bucht f; ARCH Erker m

bay² *~ tree* BOT Lorbeer(baum) m

bay³ 1. ZO bellen, Laut geben **2.** *hold or keep at ~* j-n in Schach halten; *et.* von sich fernhalten

bay⁴ 1. rotbraun **2.** ZO Braune m

bay-o-net MIL Bajonett n

bay-ou GEOGR sumpfiger Flussarm

bay win-dow ARCH Erkerfenster n

ba-zaar Basar m

BC *abbr of before Christ* v. Chr., vor Christus

be sein; *to form the passive:* werden; stattfinden; *he wants to ~ a doctor etc* er möchte Arzt etc werden; *how much are the shoes?* was kosten die Schuhe?; *that's five dollars* das macht or kostet fünf Dollar; *she is reading* sie liest gerade; *there is, there are* es gibt

beach Strand m; *~ ball* Wasserball m; *~ bug-gy* MOT Strandbuggy m

beach-wear Strandkleidung f

bea-con Leucht-, Signalfeuer n

bead (*Glas-, Schweiß- etc*)Perle f; pl REL Rosenkranz m

bead-y klein, rund und glänzend

beak ZO Schnabel m; TECH Tülle f

beam 1. Balken m; (Licht)Strahl m; AVIAT etc Peil-, Leit-, Richtstrahl m **2.** ausstrahlen; strahlen (a. fig *with* vor dat)

bean BOT Bohne f; *be full of ~s* F aufgekrazt sein; → *spill 1*

bear¹ ZO Bär m

bear² tragen; zur Welt bringen, gebären; ertragen, aushalten; *I can't ~ him (it)* ich kann ihn (es) nicht ausstehen or leiden; *~ out* bestätigen

bear-a-ble erträglich

beard Bart m; BOT Grannen pl

beard-ed bärtig

bear-er Träger(in), ECON Überbringer(in), Inhaber(in)

bear-ing Ertragen n; Betragen n; (Körper)Haltung f; fig Beziehung f; Lage f, Richtung f, Orientierung f; *take one's ~s* sich orientieren; *lose one's ~s* die Orientierung verlieren

beast (a. *wildes*) Tier; Bestie f

beast-ly scheußlich

beast of prey ZO Raubtier n

beat 1. schlagen; (ver)prügeln; besiegen; übertreffen; F *~ s.o. to it* j-m zuvorkommen; *~ it!* F hau ab!; *that's all!* das ist doch der Gipfel or die Höhe!; *that ~s me* F das ist mir zu hoch; *~ about the bush* wie die Katze um den heißen Brei herumschleichen; *~ down* ECON drücken, herunterhan-

B

deln; **~ s.o. up** j-n zusammenschlagen **2.** Schlag *m*; MUS Takt(schlag) *m*; *jazz:* Beat *m*; Pulsschlag *m*; Runde *f*, Revier *n* **3.** (**dead**) **~** F wie erschlagen, fix und fertig

beat·en track Trampelpfad *m*; **off the ~** ungewohnt, ungewöhnlich

beat·ing (Tracht *f*) Prügel *pl*

beau·ti·cian Kosmetikerin *f*

beau·ti·ful schön

beau·ty Schönheit *f*; *Sleeping Beauty* Dornröschen *n*; **~care** Schönheitspflege *f*; **~par·lo(u)r**, **~ sal·on** Schönheitssalon *m*

bea·ver ZO Biber *m*; Biberpelz *m*

be·cause weil; **~ of** wegen (*gen*)

beck·on (zu)winken (*dat*)

be·come *v/i* werden (**of** aus); *v/t* sich schicken für; *j-m* stehen, *j-n* kleiden

be·com·ing passend; schicklich; kleidsam

bed **1.** Bett *n*; ZO Lager *n*; AGR Beet *n*; Unterlage *f*; **~ and breakfast** Zimmer *n* mit Frühstück **2. ~ down** sein Nachtlager aufschlagen

bed·clothes Bettwäsche *f*

bed·ding Bettzeug *n*; AGR Streu *f*

bed·lam Tollhaus *n*

bed·rid·den bettlägerig

bed·room Schlafzimmer *n*

bed·side: at the ~ am (*a. Kranken*)Bett

bed·side lamp Nachttischlampe *f*

bed·sit F, **bed·sit·ter**, **bed·sit·ting room** *Br* möbliertes Zimmer; Einzimmerappartement *n*

bed·spread Tagesdecke *f*

bed·stead Bettgestell *n*

bed·time Schlafenszeit *f*

bee ZO Biene *f*

beech BOT Buche *f*

beech·nut BOT Buchecker *f*

beef GASTR Rindfleisch *n*

beef·bur·ger GASTR *Br* Hamburger *m*

beef tea GASTR (Rind)Fleischbrühe *f*

beef·y F bullig

bee·hive Bienenkorb *m*, Bienenstock *m*

bee·keep·er Imker *m*

bee·line: make a ~ for F schnurstracks losgehen auf (*acc*)

beep·er TECH Piepser *m*

beer Bier *n*

beet BOT Runkelrübe *f*, Rote Bete, Rote Rübe

bee·tle ZO Käfer *m*

beet·root BOT *Br* Rote Bete, Rote Rübe

be·fore 1. *adv space:* vorn, voran; *time:* vorher, früher, schon (früher) **2.** *cj* bevor, ehe, bis **3.** *prp* vor; **be·fore·hand** zuvor, im Voraus, vorweg

be·friend sich *j-s* annehmen

beg *v/t et.* erbitten (**of s.o.** von j-m); betteln um; *j-n* bitten; *v/i* betteln; (dringend) bitten

be·get (er)zeugen

beg·gar 1. Bettler(in); F Kerl *m* **2.** *it* **~s all description** es spottet jeder Beschreibung

be·gin beginnen, anfangen

be·gin·ner Anfänger(in)

be·gin·ning Beginn *m*, Anfang *m*

be·grudge missgönnen

be·guile täuschen; betrügen (**of, out of** um); sich *die Zeit* vertreiben

be·half: in (*Br* **on**) **~ of** im Namen von (*or gen*)

be·have sich (gut) benehmen

be·hav·io(u)r Benehmen *n*, Betragen *n*, Verhalten *n*

be·hav·io(u)r·al sci·ence PSYCH Verhaltensforschung *f*

be·head enthaupten

be·hind 1. *adv* hinten, dahinter; zurück **2.** *prp* hinter (*dat or acc*) **3.** F Hinterteil *n*, Hintern *m*

beige beige

be·ing Sein *n*, Dasein *n*, Existenz *f*; (Lebe)Wesen *n*, Geschöpf *n*; *j-s* Wesen *n*, Natur *f*

be·lat·ed verspätet

belch 1. aufstoßen, rülpsen; *a.* **~ out** speien, ausstoßen **2.** Rülpser *m*

bel·fry Glockenturm *m*, -stuhl *m*

Bel·gian 1. belgisch **2.** Belgier(in)

Bel·gium Belgien *n*

be·lief Glaube *m* (**in** an *acc*)

be·liev·a·ble glaubhaft

be·lieve glauben (**in** an *acc*); *I couldn't* **~** *my ears* (**eyes**) ich traute m-n Ohren (Augen) nicht

be·liev·er REL Gläubige *m, f*

be·lit·tle *fig* herabsetzen

bell Glocke *f*; Klingel *f*

bell·boy *Br*, **bell·hop** (Hotel)Page *m*

bel·lig·er·ent kriegerisch; streitlustig; aggressiv; Krieg führend

bel·low 1. brüllen **2.** Gebrüll *n*

bel·lows Blasebalg *m*

bel·ly 1. Bauch *m*; Magen *m* **2. ~ out** (an)-

schwellen lassen; bauschen

bel·ly·ache F Bauchweh *n*

be·long gehören; **~ to** gehören *dat or* zu

be·long·ings Habseligkeiten *pl*, Habe *f*

be·loved 1. (innig) geliebt **2.** Geliebte *m*, *f*

be·low 1. *adv* unten **2.** *prp* unter (*dat or acc*)

belt 1. Gürtel *m*; Gurt *m*; GEOGR Zone *f*, Gebiet *n*; TECH (Treib)Riemen *m* **2.** **~ out** MUS schmettern; *a.* **~ up** den Gürtel (*gen*) zumachen; **~ up** MOT sich anschnallen; **belt·ed** mit e-m Gürtel

belt·way Umgehungsstraße *f*; Ringstraße *f*

be·moan betrauern, beklagen

bench Sitzbank *f*, Bank *f*; (a. SPORT); TECH Werkbank *f*; JUR Richterbank *f*; Richter *m or pl*

bend 1. Biegung *f*, Kurve *f*; **drive s.o. round the~** F j-n noch wahnsinnig machen **2.** (sich) biegen *or* krümmen; neigen; beugen; *fig* richten (**to, on** auf *acc*)

be·neath → **below**

ben·e·dic·tion REL Segen *m*

ben·e·fac·tor Wohltäter *m*

ben·ef·i·cent wohltätig

ben·e·fi·cial wohltuend, zuträglich, nützlich

ben·e·fit 1. Nutzen *m*, Vorteil *m*; Wohltätigkeitsveranstaltung *f*; (*Sozial-, Versicherungs- etc*)Leistung *f*; (*Arbeitslosen- etc*)Unterstützung *f*; (*Kranken- etc*)Geld *n* **2.** nützen; **~ by, ~ from** Vorteil haben von *or* durch, Nutzen ziehen aus

be·nev·o·lence Wohlwollen *n*

be·nev·o·lent wohltätig; wohlwollend

be·nign MED gutartig

bent 1. **~ on doing** entschlossen zu tun **2.** Hang *m*, Neigung *f*; Veranlagung *f*

ben·zene CHEM Benzol *n*

ben·zine CHEM Leichtbenzin *n*

be·queath JUR vermachen

be·quest JUR Vermächtnis *n*

be·reave berauben

be·ret Baskenmütze *f*

ber·ry BOT Beere *f*

berth 1. MAR Liege-, Ankerplatz *m*; Koje *f*; RAIL (Schlafwagen)Bett *n* **2.** MAR festmachen, anlegen

be·seech (inständig) bitten (um); anflehen

be·side *prp* neben (*dat or acc*); **~ o.s.** au-

ßer sich (**with** vor); **~ the point**, **~ the question** nicht zur Sache gehörig

be·sides 1. *adv* außerdem **2.** *prp* abgesehen von, außer (*dat*)

be·siege belagern

best 1. *adj* beste(r, -s) höchste(r, -s), größte(r, -s), meiste; **~ before** GASTR haltbar bis **2.** *adv* am besten **3.** *der, die, das* Beste; **all the ~!** alles Gute!, viel Glück!; **to the ~ of …** nach bestem …; **make the ~ of** das Beste machen aus (*dat*); **at ~** bestenfalls; **be at one's ~** in Hoch- *or* Höchstform sein

best-be·fore date, best-by date Mindesthaltbarkeitsdatum *n*

bes·ti·al *fig* tierisch, bestialisch

be·stow geben, verleihen (**on** *dat*)

best-sell·er Bestseller *m*

bet 1. Wette *f*; **make a ~** e-e Wette abschließen **2.** wetten; **~ s.o. ten dollars** mit j-m um zehn Dollar wetten; **you~** F und ob!

be·tray verraten (*a. fig*); verleiten

be·tray·al Verrat *m*

be·tray·er Verräter(in)

bet·ter 1. *adj* besser; **he is ~** es geht ihm besser; **~ and ~** immer besser **2.** *das* Bessere; **get the ~ of** die Oberhand gewinnen über (*acc*); *et.* überwinden **3.** *adv* besser; mehr; **do ~ than** es besser machen als; **know ~** es besser wissen; **so much the ~** desto besser; **you had ~ go** Br, F **you ~ go** es wäre besser, wenn du gingest; **~ off** (finanziell) besser gestellt; **he is ~ off than I am** es geht ihm besser als mir **4.** *v/t* verbessern; *v/i* sich bessern

be·tween 1. *adv* dazwischen; **in ~** zwischendurch; F **few and far ~** (ganz) vereinzelt **2.** *prp* zwischen (*dat or acc*); unter (*dat*); **~ you and me** unter uns *or* im Vertrauen (gesagt)

bev·el TECH abkanten, abschrägen

bev·er·age Getränk *n*

bev·y ZO Schwarm *m*, Schar *f*

be·ware (**of**) sich in Acht nehmen (vor *dat*), sich hüten (vor *dat*); **~ of the dog!** Vorsicht, bissiger Hund!

be·wil·der verwirren

be·wil·der·ment Verwirrung *f*

be·witch bezaubern, verhexen

be·yond 1. *adv* darüber hinaus **2.** *prp* jenseits (*gen*); über … (*acc*) hinaus

bi… zwei, zweifach, zweimal

B

bi·as Neigung *f*; Vorurteil *n*

bi·as(s)ed voreingenommen; JUR befangen

bi·ath·lete SPORT Biathlet *m*

bi·ath·lon SPORT Biathlon *n*

bib (Sabber)Lätzchen *n*

Bi·ble Bibel *f*

bib·li·cal biblisch, Bibel...

bib·li·og·ra·phy Bibliografie *f*

bi·car·bon·ate *a.* ~ **of soda** CHEM doppeltkohlensaures Natron

bi·cen·te·na·ry *Br,* bi·cen·ten·ni·al Zweihundertjahrfeier *f*

bi·ceps ANAT Bizeps *m*

bick·er sich zanken *or* streiten

bi·cy·cle Fahrrad *n*

bid **1.** *auction:* bieten **2.** ECON Gebot *n,* Angebot *n*

bi·en·ni·al zweijährlich; BOT zweijährig; bi·en·ni·al·ly alle zwei Jahre

bier (Toten)Bahre *f*

big groß; dick, stark; **talk** ~ F den Mund voll nehmen

big·a·my Bigamie *f*

big busi·ness Großunternehmertum *n*

big·head F Angeber *m*

big shot, big·wig F hohes Tier

bike F **1.** (Fahr)Rad *n* **2.** Rad fahren

bik·er Motorradfahrer(in); Radfahrer(in), Radler(in)

bi·lat·er·al bilateral

bile Galle *f* (*a. fig*)

bi·lin·gual zweisprachig

bill[1] ZO Schnabel *m*

bill[2] ECON Rechnung *f*; POL (Gesetzes)Vorlage *f*; JUR (An)Klageschrift *f*; Plakat *n*; Banknote *f*, (Geld)Schein *m*

bill·board Reklametafel *f*

bill·fold Brieftasche *f*

bil·li·ards Billard(spiel) *n*

bil·li·on Milliarde *f*

bill|| of de·liv·er·y ECON Lieferschein *m*; ~ **of ex·change** ECON Wechsel *m*; ~ **of sale** JUR Verkaufsurkunde *f*

bil·low **1.** Woge *f*; (*Rauch- etc*) Schwaden *m* **2.** *a.* ~ **out** sich bauschen *or* blähen

bil·ly goat ZO Ziegenbock *m*

bin (großer) Behälter

bi·na·ry MATH, PHYS *etc* binär, Binär...

bi·na·ry code IT Binärcode *m*

bi·na·ry num·ber MATH Binärzahl *f*

bind *v/t* (an-, ein-, um-, auf-, fest-, ver-) binden; *a.* vertraglich binden, verpflichten; einfassen; *v/i* binden

bind·er (*esp Buch*)Binder(in); Einband *m*; Aktendeckel *m*

bind·ing **1.** bindend, verbindlich **2.** Einband *m*; Einfassung *f*, Borte *f*

bin·go Bingo *n*

bi·noc·u·lars Fern-, Opernglas *n*

bi·o·chem·is·try Biochemie *f*

bi·o·de·gra·da·ble biologisch abbaubar, umweltfreundlich

bi·og·ra·pher Biograf *m*

bi·og·ra·phy Biografie *f*

bi·o·log·i·cal biologisch

bi·ol·o·gist Biologe *m,* Biologin *f*

bi·ol·o·gy Biologie *f*

bi·o·rhythms Biorhythmus *m*

bi·o·tope Biotop *n*

bi·ped ZO Zweifüßer *m*

birch BOT Birke *f*

bird ZO Vogel *m*

bird·cage Vogelkäfig *m*

bird flu Vogelgrippe *f*

bird of pas·sage ZO Zugvogel *m*

bird of prey ZO Raubvogel *m*

bird sanc·tu·a·ry Vogelschutzgebiet *n*

bird·seed Vogelfutter *n*

bird's-eye view Vogelperspektive *f*

bi·ro® Kugelschreiber *m*

birth Geburt *f*; Herkunft *f*; **give** ~ **to** gebären, zur Welt bringen

birth cer·tif·i·cate Geburtsurkunde *f*

birth con·trol Geburtenregelung *f*

birth·day Geburtstag *m*; **happy** ~**!** alles Gute *or* herzlichen Glückwunsch zum Geburtstag!

birth·mark Muttermal *n*

birth·place Geburtsort *m*

birth·rate Geburtenziffer *f*

bis·cuit *Br* Keks *m, n,* Plätzchen *n*

bi·sex·u·al bisexuell

bish·op REL Bischof *m*; *chess:* Läufer *m*

bish·op·ric REL Bistum *n*

bi·son ZO Bison *m*; Wisent *m*

bit Bisschen *n,* Stück(chen) *n*; Gebiss *n* (*am Zaum*); IT Bit *n*; **a (little)** ~ ein (kleines) bisschen

bitch ZO Hündin *f*; F *contp* Miststück *n,* Schlampe *f*

bit den·si·ty IT Speicherdichte *f*

bite **1.** Beißen *n*; Biss *m*; Bissen *m,* Happen *m*; TECH Fassen *n,* Greifen *n* **2.** (an-)beißen; ZO stechen; GASTR brennen; *fig* schneiden (*cold etc*); beißen (*smoke etc*); TECH fassen, greifen

bit·ter bitter; *fig* verbittert

bit·ters GASTR Magenbitter *m*

biz F ~ *business*

black 1. schwarz; dunkel; finster; *have* **s.th. in ~ and white** et. schwarz auf weiß haben *or* besitzen; *be ~ and blue* blaue Flecken haben; *beat s.o. ~ and blue* j-n grün und blau schlagen **2.** schwärzen; **~ out** verdunkeln **3.** Schwarz *n*; Schwärze *f*; Schwarze *m*, *f*

black·ber·ry BOT Brombeere *f*

black·bird ZO Amsel *f*

black·board (Schul-, Wand)Tafel *f*

black box AVIAT Flugschreiber *m*

black cur·rant BOT schwarze Johannisbeere

black·en *v/t* schwärzen; *fig* anschwärzen; *v/i* schwarz werden

black eye blaues Auge, Veilchen *n*

black·head MED Mitesser *m*

black ice Glatteis *n*

black·ing schwarze Schuhwichse

black·leg *Br* Streikbrecher *m*

black·mail 1. Erpressung *f* **2.** j-n erpressen; **black·mail·er** Erpresser(in)

black mar·ket Schwarzmarkt *m*

black·ness Schwärze *f*

black·out Verdunkelung *f*; Black-out *n*, *m*; ELECTR Stromausfall *m*; Ohnmacht *f*

black pud·ding GASTR Blutwurst *f*

black sheep *fig* schwarzes Schaf

black·smith Schmied *m*

blad·der ANAT Blase *f*

blade TECH Blatt *n*, Schaufel *f*; Klinge *f*; Schneide *f*; BOT Halm *m*

blame 1. Tadel *m*; Schuld *f* **2.** tadeln; *be to ~ for* schuld sein an (*dat*)

blame·less untadelig

blanch *v/t* bleichen; GASTR blanchieren; *v/i* erbleichen, bleich werden

blank 1. leer; unausgefüllt, unbeschrieben; ECON Blanko...; verdutzt **2.** Leere *f*; leerer Raum, Lücke *f*; unbeschriebenes Blatt, Formular *n*; *lottery*: Niete *f*; ~ **car·tridge** Platzpatrone *f*; ~ **check** (*Br* cheque) ECON Blankoscheck *m*

blan·ket 1. (Woll)Decke *f* **2.** zudecken

blare brüllen, plärren (*radio etc*), schmettern (*trumpet*)

blas·pheme lästern

blas·phe·my Gotteslästerung *f*

blast 1. Windstoß *m*; MUS Ton *m*; TECH Explosion *f*; Druckwelle *f*; Sprengung *f* **2.** sprengen; *fig* zunichtemachen; ~

off (*into space*) in den Weltraum schießen; **~ off** abheben, starten (*rocket*); **~!** verdammt!; **~ you!** der Teufel soll dich holen!; **~ed** verdammt, verflucht

blast fur·nace TECH Hochofen *m*

blast-off Start *m* (*of a rocket*)

bla·tant offenkundig, eklatant

blaze 1. Flamme(n *pl*) *f*, Feuer *n*; heller Schein; *fig* Ausbruch *m* **2.** brennen, lodern; leuchten

blaz·er Blazer *m*

bla·zon Wappen *n*

bleach bleichen

bleak öde, kahl; rau; *fig* trüb, freudlos, finster

blear·y trübe, verschwommen

bleat ZO **1.** Blöken *n* **2.** blöken

bleed *v/i* bluten; *v/t* MED zur Ader lassen; F schröpfen

bleed·ing MED Blutung *f*; Aderlass *m*

bleep 1. Piepton *m* **2.** j-n anpiepsen

bleep·er *Br* F Piepser *m*

blem·ish 1. (*a.* Schönheits)Fehler *m*; Makel *m* **2.** entstellen

blend 1. (sich) (ver)mischen; GASTR verschneiden **2.** Mischung *f*; GASTR Verschnitt *m*

blend·er Mixer *m*, Mixgerät *n*

bless segnen; preisen; *be* **~ed with** gesegnet sein mit; (*God*) **~ you!** alles Gute!; Gesundheit!; **~ me!**, **~ my heart!**, **~ my soul!** F du meine Güte!

bless·ed selig, gesegnet; F verflixt

bless·ing Segen *m*

blight BOT Mehltau *m*

blind 1. blind (*fig* **to** gegen[über]); unübersichtlich **2.** Rouleau *n*, Rollo *n*; **the ~** die Blinden (*pl*) **3.** blenden; *fig* blind machen (**to** für, gegen)

blind al·ley Sackgasse *f*

blind·ers Scheuklappen *pl*

blind·fold 1. blindlings **2.** j-m die Augen verbinden **3.** Augenbinde *f*

blind·ly *fig* blindlings

blind·ness Blindheit *f*; Verblendung *f*

blind·worm ZO Blindschleiche *f*

blink 1. Blinzeln *n* **2.** blinzeln, zwinkern; blinken

blink·ers *Br* Scheuklappen *pl*

bliss Seligkeit *f*, Wonne *f*

blis·ter MED, TECH **1.** Blase *f* **2.** Blasen hervorrufen auf (*dat*); Blasen ziehen *or* TECH werfen

blitz MIL **1.** heftiger Luftangriff **2.** schwer

B

bombardieren

bliz·zard Blizzard *m*, Schneesturm *m*

bloat·ed (an)geschwollen, (auf)gedunsen; *fig* aufgeblasen

bloat·er GASTR Bückling *m*

blob Klecks *m*

block 1. Block *m*, Klotz *m*; Baustein *m*, (Bau)Klötzchen *n*; (*Schreib-, Notiz-*) Block *m*; (Häuser)Block *m*; TECH Verstopfung *f*; *fig geistige etc* Sperre; ~ (*of flats*) Wohn-, Mietshaus *n* **2.** *a.* ~ *up* (ab-, ver)sperren, blockieren, verstopfen

block·ade 1. Blockade *f* **2.** blockieren

block·bust·er F Kassenmagnet *m*, Kassenschlager *m*

block·head F Dummkopf *m*

block let·ters Blockschrift *f*

blog IT Blog *m*, *n*

blond 1. Blonde *m* **2.** blond; hell (*skin*)

blonde 1. blond **2.** Blondine *f*

blood Blut *n*; *in cold* ~ kaltblütig; ~ **bank** MED Blutbank *f*; ~ **clot** MED Blutgerinnsel *n*; ~ **cor·pus·cle** MED Blutkörperchen *n*

blood·cur·dling grauenhaft

blood do·nor MED Blutspender(in)

blood group MED Blutgruppe *f*

blood·hound ZO Bluthund *m*

blood pres·sure MED Blutdruck *m*

blood·shed Blutvergießen *n*

blood·shot blutunterlaufen

blood test MED Blutprobe *f*

blood·thirst·y blutdürstig

blood ves·sel ANAT Blutgefäß *n*

blood·y blutig; *Br* F verdammt, verflucht

bloom 1. Blume *f*, Blüte *f*; *fig* Blüte(zeit) *f* **2.** blühen; *fig* (er)strahlen

blos·som 1. Blüte *f* **2.** blühen; *fig* ~ *into* erblühen zu

blot 1. Klecks *m*; *fig* Makel *m* **2.** beklecksen

blotch Klecks *m*; Hautfleck *m*

blotch·y fleckig

blot·ter (Tinten)Löscher *m*

blot·ting pa·per Löschpapier *n*

blouse Bluse *f*

blow¹ Schlag *m* (*a. fig*), Stoß *m*

blow² *v/i* blasen, wehen, keuchen, schnaufen; explodieren; platzen (*tire*), ELECTR durchbrennen; ~ *up* in die Luft fliegen; explodieren; *v/t:* ~ *one's nose* sich die Nase putzen; ~ *out* ausblasen;

~ *up* sprengen; PHOT vergrößern

blow-dry föhnen

blow·fly ZO Schmeißfliege *f*

blow·pipe Blasrohr *n*

blow-up PHOT Vergrößerung *f*

blud·geon Knüppel *m*

blue 1. blau; F melancholisch, traurig, schwermütig **2.** Blau *n*; *out of the* ~ *fig* aus heiterem Himmel

blue·ber·ry BOT Blau-, Heidelbeere *f*

blue·bot·tle ZO Schmeißfliege *f*

blue-col·lar work·er Arbeiter(in)

blues MUS Blues *m*; F Melancholie *f*; *have the* ~ F den Moralischen haben

bluff¹ Steilufer *n*

bluff² 1. Bluff *m* **2.** bluffen

blu·ish bläulich

blun·der 1. Fehler *m*, F Schnitzer *m* **2.** e-n (groben) Fehler machen; verpfuschen, F verpatzen

blunt stumpf; *fig* offen

blunt·ly freiheraus

blur [blɜː] **1.** *v/t* verwischen; verschmieren; PHOT, TV verwackeln, verzerren; *fig* trüben **2.** *v/i* verschwimmen (*a. fig*)

blurt: ~ *out* herausplatzen mit

blush 1. Erröten *n*, Schamröte *f* **2.** erröten, rot werden

blus·ter brausen (*wind*); *fig* poltern, toben

BO ABBR → *body odo(u)r*

boar ZO Eber *m*; Keiler *m*

board 1. Brett *n*; (Anschlag)Brett *n*; Konferenztisch *m*; Ausschuss *m*, Kommission *f*; Behörde *f*; Verpflegung *f*; Pappe *f*, Karton *m*; SPORT (Surf)Board *n*; *on* ~ *a train* in e-m Zug **2.** *v/t* dielen, verschalen; beköstigen; an Bord gehen; MAR entern; RAIL *etc* einsteigen in; *v/i* in Kost sein, wohnen

board·er Kostgänger(in); Pensionsgast *m*; Internatsschüler(in)

board game Brettspiel *n*

board·ing| card AVIAT Bordkarte *f*; ~ **house** Pension *f*, Fremdenheim *n*; ~ **school** Internat *n*

board of di·rec·tors ECON Aufsichtsrat *m*

Board of Trade Handelskammer *f*; *Br* Handelsministerium *n*

board·walk Strandpromenade *f*

boast 1. Prahlerei *f* **2.** (*of, about*) sich rühmen (*gen*), prahlen (mit)

boat Boot *n*; Schiff *n*

bob 1. Knicks *m*; kurzer Haarschnitt; *Br* HIST F Schilling *m* **2.** *v/t Haar* kurz schneiden; *v/i* sich auf und ab bewegen; knicksen
bob·bin Spule *f* (*a.* ELECTR)
bob·sleigh SPORT Bob *m*
bod·ice Mieder *n*; Oberteil *n*
bod·i·ly körperlich
bod·y Körper *m*, Leib *m*; Leiche *f*; JUR Körperschaft *f*; Hauptteil *m*; MOT Karosserie *f*; MIL Truppenkörper *m*
bod·y·guard Leibwache *f*; Leibwächter *m*
bod·y| o·do(u)r (*abbr* **BO**) Körpergeruch *m*; ~ **stock·ing** Body *m*
bod·y·work MOT Karosserie *f*
Boer 1. Bure *m* **2.** Buren...
bog Sumpf *m*, Morast *m*
bo·gus falsch; Schwindel...
boil[1] MED Geschwür *n*, Furunkel *m*, *n*
boil[2] **1.** kochen, sieden **2.** Kochen *n*, Sieden *n*
boil·er (Dampf)Kessel *m*; Boiler *m*
boil·er suit Overall *m*
boil·ing point Siedepunkt *m* (*a. fig*)
bois·ter·ous ungestüm; heftig, laut; lärmend
bold kühn, verwegen; keck, dreist, unverschämt; steil; PRINT fett; *words in* ~ *print* fett gedruckt; **bold·ness** Kühnheit *f*, Verwegenheit *f*; Dreistigkeit *f*
bol·ster 1. Keilkissen *n* **2.** ~ *up* (unter)stützen; *j-m* Mut machen
bolt 1. Bolzen *m*; Riegel *m*; Blitz(strahl) *m*; plötzlicher Satz, Fluchtversuch *m* **2.** *adv:* ~ *upright* kerzengerade **3.** *v/t* verriegeln; F hinunterschlingen; *v/i* davonlaufen, ausreißen; ZO scheuen, durchgehen
bomb 1. Bombe *f*; *the* ~ die Atombombe **2.** bombardieren; **bom·bard** bombardieren; **bomb·er** AVIAT Bomber *m*; Bombenleger *m*
bomb·proof bombensicher
bomb·shell Bombe *f* (*a. fig*)
bo·nan·za *fig* Goldgrube *f*
bond Bund *m*, Verbindung *f*; ECON Schuldverschreibung *f*, Obligation *f*; *in* ~ ECON unter Zollverschluss
bond·age Hörigkeit *f*
bonds *fig* Bande *pl*
bone 1. ANAT Knochen *m*, *pl a.* Gebeine *pl*; ZO Gräte *f* **2.** die Knochen auslösen (aus); entgräten

bon·fire Feuer *n* im Freien; Freudenfeuer *n*
bon·net Haube *f*; *Br* Motorhaube *f*
bo·nus ECON Bonus *m*, Prämie *f*; Gratifikation *f*
bon·y knöchern; knochig
boo *int* buh!; THEA ~ *off the stage*, *soccer:* ~ *off the park* auspfeifen
boobs *sl* Titten *pl*
boo·by F Trottel *m*
book 1. Buch *n*; Heft *n*; Liste *f*; Block *m* **2.** buchen; eintragen; SPORT verwarnen; *Fahrkarte etc* lösen; *Platz etc* (vor)bestellen, reservieren lassen; *Gepäck* aufgeben; ~ *in esp Br* sich (*im Hotel*) eintragen; ~ *in at* absteigen in (*dat*); ~*ed up* ausgebucht, ausverkauft, belegt
book·case Bücherschrank *m*
book·ing Buchen *n*, (Vor)Bestellung *f*; SPORT Verwarnung *f*; ~ *clerk* Schalterbeamte *m*, -beamtin *f*; ~ *of·fice* Fahrkartenausgabe *f*, -schalter *m*; THEA Kasse *f*
book·keep·er ECON Buchhalter(in)
book·keep·ing ECON Buchhaltung *f*, Buchführung *f*
book·let Büchlein *n*, Broschüre *f*
book·mak·er Buchmacher *m*
book·mark(·er) Lesezeichen *n*
book·sell·er Buchhändler(in)
book·shelf Bücherregal *n*
book·shop *esp Br*, **book·store** Buchhandlung *f*
book·worm *fig* Bücherwurm *m*
boom[1] ECON **1.** Boom *m*, Aufschwung *m*, Hochkonjunktur *f*, Hausse *f* **2.** e-n Boom erleben
boom[2] MAR Baum *m*, Spiere *f*; TECH (Kran)Ausleger *m*; *film*, TV (Mikrofon)Galgen *m*
boom[3] dröhnen, donnern
boor·ish ungehobelt
boost 1. hochschieben; ECON in die Höhe treiben; ankurbeln; ELECTR verstärken; TECH erhöhen; *fig* stärken, Auftrieb geben (*dat*) **2.** Erhöhung *f*; Auftrieb *m*; ELECTR Verstärkung *f*
boot[1] Stiefel *m*; *Br* MOT Kofferraum *m*
boot[2]: ~ (*up*) IT laden
boot[3]: *to* ~ obendrein
boot·ee (*Damen*)Halbstiefel *m*
booth (Markt- *etc*)Bude *f*; (Messe-) Stand *m*; (Wahl- *etc*)Kabine *f*; (Tele-

B

fon)Zelle *f*

boot·lace Schnürsenkel *m*

boot·y Beute *f*

booze F **1.** saufen **2.** Zeug *n;* Sauferei *f*

bor·der 1. Rand *m,* Saum *m,* Einfassung *f;* Rabatte *f;* Grenze *f* **2.** einfassen; (um)säumen; grenzen (**on** an *acc*)

bore[1] **1.** Bohrloch *n;* TECH Kaliber *n* **2.** bohren

bore[2] **1.** Langweiler *m;* langweilige *or* lästige Sache **2.** *j-n* langweilen; **be ~d** sich langweilen

bore·dom Lang(e)weile *f*

bor·ing langweilig

bor·ough Stadtteil *m;* Stadtgemeinde *f;* Stadtbezirk *m*

bor·row (sich) *et.* borgen *or* (aus)leihen

bos·om Busen *m;* *fig* Schoß *m*

boss F **1.** Boss *m,* Chef *m* **2.** *a.* **~ about, ~ around** herumkommandieren

boss·y F herrisch

bo·tan·i·cal botanisch

bot·a·ny Botanik *f*

botch 1. Pfusch *m* **2.** verpfuschen

both beide(s); **~ ... and ...** sowohl ... als (auch) ...

both·er 1. Belästigung *f,* Störung *f,* Plage *f,* Mühe *f* **2.** belästigen, stören, plagen; **don't ~!** bemühen Sie sich nicht!

bot·tle 1. Flasche *f* **2.** in Flaschen abfüllen; **~ bank** *Br* Altglascontainer *m*

bot·tle·neck *fig* Engpass *m*

bot·tle o·pen·er Flaschenöffner *m*

bot·tom unterster Teil, Boden *m,* Fuß *m,* Unterseite *f;* Grund *m;* F Hintern *m,* Popo *m;* **be at the ~ of s.th.** hinter e-r Sache stecken; **get to the ~ of s.th.** e-r Sache auf den Grund gehen

bough Ast *m,* Zweig *m*

boul·der Geröllblock *m,* Findling *m*

bounce 1. aufprallen *or* aufspringen (lassen); springen, hüpfen, stürmen; ECON F platzen (*check*) **2.** Sprung *m,* Satz *m;* F Schwung *m*

bounc·ing kräftig, stramm

bound[1] unterwegs (**for** nach)

bound[2] *mst pl* Grenze *f, fig a.* Schranke *f*

bound[3] **1.** Sprung *m,* Satz *m* **2.** springen, hüpfen; auf-, abprallen

bound·a·ry Grenze *f*

bound·less grenzenlos

boun·te·ous, boun·ti·ful freigebig, reichlich

boun·ty Freigebigkeit *f;* großzügige Spende *f;* Prämie *f*

bou·quet Bukett *n* (*a.* GASTR), Strauß *m;* GASTR Blume *f*

bout SPORT (*Box-, Ring*)Kampf *m;* MED Anfall *m*

bou·tique Boutique *f*

bow[1] **1.** Verbeugung *f* **2.** *v/i* sich verbeugen *or* verneigen (**to** vor *dat*); *fig* sich beugen *or* unterwerfen (**to** *dat*); *v/t* biegen; beugen, neigen

bow[2] MAR Bug *m*

bow[3] Bogen *m;* Schleife *f*

bow·els ANAT Darm *m;* Eingeweide *pl*

bowl[1] Schale *f,* Schüssel *f,* Napf *m;* (*Zucker*)Dose *f;* Becken *n;* (*Pfeifen-*) Kopf *m*

bowl[2] **1.** (*Bowling-, Kegel- etc*)Kugel *f* **2.** kegeln; rollen (*bowling ball*); *cricket:* werfen

bow·leg·ged o-beinig

bowl·er[1] Bowlingspieler(in); Kegler(in)

bowl·er[2], *a.* **~ hat** *esp Br* Bowler *m,* F Melone *f*

bowl·ing Bowling *n;* Kegeln *n;* **go ~** kegeln; **~ al·ley** Kegelbahn *f;* **~ ball** Kegelkugel *f*

box[1] Kasten *m,* Kiste *f;* Büchse *f,* Dose *f,* Kästchen *n;* Schachtel *f;* Behälter *m;* TECH Gehäuse *n;* Postfach *n;* *Br* (*Tele-*fon)Zelle *f;* JUR Zeugenstand *m;* THEA Loge *f;* MOT, ZO Box *f*

box[2] **1.** SPORT boxen; F **s.o.'s ears** *j-n* ohrfeigen **2.** F **a ~ on the ear** e-e Ohrfeige

box[3] [bɒks] BOT Buchsbaum *m*

box·er Boxer *m*

box·ing Boxen *n,* Boxsport *m*

Box·ing Day *Br* der zweite Weihnachtsfeiertag

box num·ber Chiffre(nummer) *f*

box of·fice Theaterkasse *f*

boy Junge *m,* Knabe *m,* Bursche *m*

boy·cott 1. boykottieren **2.** Boykott *m*

boy·friend Freund *m*

boy·hood Knabenjahre *pl,* Jugend (-zeit) *f*

boy·ish jungenhaft

boy scout Pfadfinder *m*

bra BH *m* (*Büstenhalter*)

brace 1. TECH Strebe *f,* Stützbalken *m;* (*Zahn*)Klammer *f,* (-)Spange *f* **2.** TECH verstreben, versteifen, stützen

brace·let Armband *n*

brac·es Br Hosenträger pl

brack·et TECH Träger m, Halter m, Stütze f; PRINT Klammer f; (esp Alters-, Steuer)Klasse f; **lower income ~** niedrige Einkommensgruppe

brack·ish brackig, salzig

brag prahlen (**about** mit)

brag·gart Prahler m, F Angeber m

braid 1. Zopf m; Borte f, Tresse f **2.** flechten; mit Borte besetzen

brain ANAT Gehirn n, often pl fig a. Verstand m, Intelligenz f, Kopf m

brain·storm Geistesblitz m

brain·wash j-n e-r Gehirnwäsche unterziehen

brain·wash·ing Gehirnwäsche f

brain·wave Br Geistesblitz m

brain·y F gescheit

braise GASTR schmoren

brake TECH **1.** Bremse f **2.** bremsen

brake·light MOT Bremslicht n

bram·ble BOT Brombeerstrauch m

bran AGR Kleie f

branch 1. Ast m, Zweig m; fig Fach n; Linie f (des Stammbaumes); ECON Zweigstelle f, Filiale f **2.** sich verzweigen; abzweigen

brand 1. ECON (Schutz-, Handels)Marke f, Warenzeichen n; Markenname m; Sorte f, Klasse f; Brandmal n **2.** einbrennen; brandmarken

bran·dish schwingen

brand name ECON Markenname m

brand-new nagelneu

bran·dy Kognak m, Weinbrand m

brass Messing n; F Unverschämtheit f

brass band MUS Blaskapelle f

bras·sière Büstenhalter m

brat contp Balg m, n, Gör n

brave 1. tapfer, mutig, unerschrocken **2.** trotzen; mutig begegnen (dat)

brav·er·y Tapferkeit f

brawl 1. Krawall m; Rauferei f **2.** Krawall machen; raufen

brawn·y muskulös

bray 1. ZO Eselsschrei m **2.** ZO schreien; fig wiehern

bra·zen unverschämt, unverfroren, frech

Bra·zil Brasilien n; **Bra·zil·ian 1.** brasilianisch **2.** Brasilianer(in)

breach 1. Bruch m; fig Verletzung f; MIL Bresche f **2.** e-e Bresche schlagen in (acc)

bread Brot n; **brown ~** Schwarzbrot n; **know which side one's ~ is buttered** F s-n Vorteil (er)kennen

breadth Breite f

break 1. Bruch m; Lücke f; Pause f (Br a. PED), Unterbrechung f; (plötzlicher) Wechsel, Umschwung m; (Tages)Anbruch m; **give s.o. a ~** F j-m e-e Chance geben; **take a ~** e-e Pause machen; **without a ~** ununterbrochen **2.** v/t (ab-, auf-, durch-, zer)brechen; zerschlagen, kaputt machen; ZO a. **~ in** zähmen, abrichten, zureiten; Gesetz, Vertrag etc brechen; Kode etc knacken; schlechte Nachricht (schonend) beibringen; v/i brechen (a. fig) (zer)brechen, (zer)reißen, kaputtgehen; anbrechen (Tag); METEOR umschlagen; fig ausbrechen (**into** in Tränen etc); **~ away** ab-, losbrechen; sich losmachen or losreißen; **~ down** ein-, niederreißen, Haus abbrechen; zusammenbrechen (a. fig); versagen; MOT e-e Panne haben; fig scheitern; **~ in** einbrechen, eindringen; **~ into** einbrechen in (ein Haus etc); **~ off** abbrechen, fig a. Schluss machen mit; **~ out** ausbrechen; **~ through** durchbrechen; fig den Durchbruch schaffen; **~ up** abbrechen, beenden, schließen; (sich) auflösen; fig zerbrechen, auseinanderbrechen

break·a·ble zerbrechlich

break·age Bruch m

break·a·way 1. Trennung f **2.** Splitter...

break·down Zusammenbruch m (a. fig); TECH Maschinenschaden m; MOT Panne f; **nervous ~** MED Nervenzusammenbruch m; **~ lor·ry** Br MOT Abschleppwagen m; **~ ser·vice** Br MOT Pannendienst m, Pannenhilfe f; **~ truck** Br MOT Abschleppwagen m

break·fast 1. Frühstück n; **have ~ → 2.** frühstücken

break·through fig Durchbruch m

break·up Aufhebung f; Auflösung f

breast ANAT Brust f; Busen m; fig Herz n

breast·stroke Brustschwimmen n

breath Atem(zug) m; Hauch m; **be out of ~** außer Atem sein; **waste one's ~** in den Wind reden

breath·a·lyse Br, **breath·a·lyze** F (ins Röhrchen) blasen or pusten lassen

breath·a·lys·er® Br, **breath·alyz·er®** Alkoholtestgerät n, F Röhrchen n

B

breathe atmen
breath·less atemlos
breath·tak·ing atemberaubend
breech·es Kniebund-, Reithosen *pl*
breed 1. ZO Rasse *f*, Zucht *f* **2.** *v/t* BOT, ZO züchten; *v/i* BIOL sich fortpflanzen
breed·er Züchter(in); Zuchttier *n*; PHYS Brüter *m*
breed·ing BIOL Fortpflanzung *f*; (Tier-)Zucht *f*; *fig* Erziehung *f*; (gutes) Benehmen
breeze Brise *f*
breth·ren *esp* REL Brüder *pl*
brew brauen; *Tee* zubereiten, aufbrühen
brew·er (Bier)Brauer *m*
brew·er·y Brauerei *f*
bri·ar → **brier**
bribe 1. Bestechungsgeld *n*, -geschenk *n*; Bestechung *f* **2.** bestechen
brib·er·y Bestechung *f*
brick Ziegel(stein) *m*, Backstein *m*; *Br* Baustein *m*, (Bau)Klötzchen *n*
brick·lay·er Maurer *m*
brick·yard Ziegelei *f*
brid·al Braut…; **bride** Braut *f*
bride·groom Bräutigam *m*
brides·maid Brautjungfer *f*
bridge 1. Brücke *f* **2.** e-e Brücke schlagen über (*acc*); *fig* überbrücken
bri·dle 1. Zaum *m*; Zügel *m* **2.** (auf)zäumen; zügeln; **~ path** Reitweg *m*
brief 1. kurz, bündig **2.** instruieren, genaue Anweisungen geben (*dat*)
brief·case Aktenmappe *f*
briefs Slip *m*
bri·er BOT Dornstrauch *m*; Wilde Rose
bri·gade MIL Brigade *f*
bright hell, glänzend; klar; heiter; lebhaft; gescheit
bright·en *v/t a.* **~ up** heller machen, aufhellen, erhellen; aufheitern; *v/i a.* **~ up** sich aufhellen
bright·ness Helligkeit *f*; Glanz *m*; Heiterkeit *f*; Gescheitheit *f*
brill *Br* F super, toll
bril·liance, **bril·lian·cy** Glanz *m*; *fig* Brillanz *f*
bril·liant 1. glänzend; hervorragend, brillant **2.** Brillant *m*
brim 1. Rand *m*; Krempe *f* **2.** bis zum Rande füllen *or* voll sein
brim·ful(l) randvoll
brine Sole *f*; Lake *f*
bring bringen, mitbringen, herbringen;

j-n dazu bringen (**to do** zu tun); **~ about** zustande bringen; bewirken; **~ forth** hervorbringen; **~ off** *et.* fertigbringen, schaffen; **~ on** verursachen; **~ out** herausbringen; **~ round** *Ohnmächtigen* wieder zu sich bringen; *Kranken* wieder auf die Beine bringen; **~ up** auf-, großziehen; erziehen; zur Sprache bringen
brink Rand *m* (*a. fig*)
brisk flott; lebhaft; frisch
bris·tle 1. Borste *f*; (Bart)Stoppel *f* **2.** *a.* **~ up** sich sträuben; zornig werden; strotzen, wimmeln (**with** von)
bris·tly stoppelig, Stoppel…
Brit F Brite *m*, Britin *f*
Brit·ain Britannien *n*
Brit·ish britisch; **the ~** die Briten *pl*
Brit·on Brite *m*, Britin *f*
brit·tle spröde, zerbrechlich
broach *Thema* anschneiden
broad breit; weit; hell; deutlich (*hint etc*); derb (*humor etc*); stark (*accent*); allgemein; weitherzig; liberal
broad·cast 1. im Rundfunk *or* Fernsehen bringen, ausstrahlen, übertragen; senden **2.** *radio*, TV Sendung *f*
broad·cast·er Rundfunk-, Fernsehsprecher(in)
broad·en verbreitern, erweitern
broad jump SPORT Weitsprung *m*
broad·mind·ed liberal
bro·cade Brokat *m*
bro·chure Broschüre *f*, Prospekt *m*
brogue fester Straßenschuh
broil grillen
broke F pleite, abgebrannt
bro·ken zerbrochen, kaputt; gebrochen (*a. fig*); zerrüttet
brok·en-heart·ed verzweifelt, untröstlich
bro·ker ECON Makler *m*
bron·chi·tis MED Bronchitis *f*
bronze 1. Bronze *f* **2.** bronzefarben; Bronze…
brooch Brosche *f*
brood ZO **1.** Brut *f* **2.** Brut… **3.** brüten (*a. fig*)
brook Bach *m*
broom Besen *m*
broth GASTR Fleischbrühe *f*
broth·el Bordell *n*
broth·er Bruder *m*; **~(s) and sister(s)** Geschwister *pl*

broth·er·hood REL Bruderschaft *f*
broth·er-in-law Schwager *m*
broth·er·ly brüderlich
brow ANAT (Augen)Braue *f*; Stirn *f*; GEOGR Rand *m*
brow·beat einschüchtern
brown 1. braun **2.** Braun *n* **3.** bräunen; braun werden
browse grasen, weiden; *fig* schmökern
bruise 1. MED Quetschung *f*, blauer Fleck **2.** quetschen; anstoßen; MED e-e Quetschung *or* e-n blauen Fleck bekommen
brunch Brunch *m*
brush 1. Bürste *f*; Pinsel *m*; ZO (*Fuchs-*) Rute *f*; Scharmützel *n*; Unterholz *n* **2.** bürsten; fegen; streifen; *~ away*, *~ off* j-n streifen; *~ away*, *~ off* wegbürsten, abwischen; *~ aside*, *~ away et.* abtun; *~ up (on) fig* aufpolieren, auffrischen
brush·wood Gestrüpp *n*, Unterholz *n*
brusque brüsk, barsch
Brus·sels sprouts BOT Rosenkohl *m*
bru·tal brutal, roh
bru·tal·i·ty Brutalität *f*
brute 1. brutal; *with ~ force* mit roher Gewalt **2.** Vieh *n*; F Untier *n*, Scheusal *n*; Rohling *m*; *brut·ish fig* tierisch
bub·ble 1. Blase *f* **2.** sprudeln; *~ bath* Badeschaum *m*
buck[1] **1.** ZO Bock *m* **2.** bocken
buck[2] F Dollar *m*
buck·et Eimer *m*, Kübel *m*
buck·le Schnalle *f*, Spange *f* **2.** *a. ~ up* zu-, festschnallen; *~ on* anschnallen
buck·skin Wildleder *n*
bud 1. BOT Knospe *f*; *fig* Keim *m* **2.** knospen, keimen
bud·dy F Kamerad *m*; Kumpel *m*, Spezi *m*
budge *v/i* sich (von der Stelle) rühren; *v/t* (vom Fleck) bewegen
bud·ger·i·gar ZO Wellensittich *m*
bud·get 1. Budget *n*, Etat *m*; PARL Haushaltsplan *m* **2.** preisgünstig; *~ airline* Billigflieger *m*
bud·gie F → **budgerigar**
buf·fa·lo ZO Büffel *m*
buff·er TECH Puffer *m*
buf·fet[1] schlagen; *~ about* durchrütteln, durchschütteln
buf·fet[2] Büfett *n*, Anrichte *f*
buf·fet[3] (*Frühstücks- etc*)Büfett *n*; Theke *f*

bug 1. ZO Wanze *f* (*a.* F *fig*); Insekt *n*; IT Programmfehler *m* **2.** F Wanzen anbringen in (*dat*); F ärgern
bug·ging| de·vice Abhörgerät *n*; *~ op·e·ra·tion* Lauschangriff *m*
bug·gy Kinderwagen *m*; MOT Buggy *m*
bu·gle MUS Wald-, Signalhorn *n*
build 1. (er)bauen, errichten **2.** Körperbau *m*, Figur *f*, Statur *f*; **build·er** Erbauer *m*; Bauunternehmer *m*
build·ing 1. (Er)Bauen *n*; Bau *m*, Gebäude *n* **2.** Bau…; *~ site* Baustelle *f*
built-in eingebaut, Einbau…
built-up: *~ area* bebautes Gelände *or* Gebiet; geschlossene Ortschaft
bulb BOT Zwiebel *f*, Knolle *f*; ELECTR (Glüh)Birne *f*
bulge 1. (Aus)Bauchung *f*, Ausbuchtung *f* **2.** sich (aus)bauchen; hervorquellen
bulk Umfang *m*, Größe *f*, Masse *f*; Großteil *m*; *in ~* ECON lose, unverpackt; en gros; bulk·y sperrig
bull ZO Bulle *m*, Stier *m*
bull·dog ZO Bulldogge *f*
bull·doze planieren; F einschüchtern
bull·doz·er TECH Bulldozer *m*, Planierraupe *f*
bul·let Kugel *f*
bul·le·tin Bulletin *n*, Tagesbericht *m*
bul·le·tin board Schwarzes Brett
bul·let-proof kugelsicher
bull·fight Stierkampf *m*
bul·lion Gold-, Silberbarren *m*
bul·lock ZO Ochse *m*
bull's-eye: *hit the ~* ins Schwarze treffen (*a. fig*)
bul·ly 1. tyrannische Person, Tyrann *m* **2.** einschüchtern, tyrannisieren
bul·wark Bollwerk *n* (*a. fig*)
bum F **1.** Gammler *m*; Tippelbruder *m*, Vagabund *m*; Nichtstuer *m* **2.** *v/t* schnorren; *~ around* herumgammeln
bum·ble·bee ZO Hummel *f*
bump 1. heftiger Schlag *or* Stoß; Beule *f*; Unebenheit *f* **2.** stoßen; rammen, auf *ein Auto* auffahren; zusammenstoßen; holpern; *~ into fig* j-n zufällig treffen; F *~ so. off* j-n umlegen
bump·er MOT Stoßstange *f*
bump·y holp(e)rig
bun süßes Brötchen; (Haar)Knoten *m*
bunch Bund *n*, Bündel *n*; F Verein *m*, Haufen *m*; *~ of flowers* Blumenstrauß

B

m; **~ of grapes** Weintraube *f*; **~ of keys** Schlüsselbund *m*, *n*

bun·dle 1. Bündel *n* (*a. fig*), Bund *n* **2.** *v/t a.* **~ up** bündeln

bun·ga·low Bungalow *m*

bun·gee elastisches Seil

bun·gee jump·ing Bungeespringen *n*

bun·gle 1. Pfusch *m* **2.** (ver)pfuschen

bunk Koje *f*; → **~ bed** Etagenbett *n*

bun·ny Häschen *n*

buoy 1. MAR Boje *f* **2.** **~ up** *fig* Auftrieb geben (*dat*)

bur·den 1. Last *f*; Bürde *f* **2.** belasten

bu·reau *Br* Schreibtisch *m*; (Spiegel-) Kommode *f*; Büro *n*

bu·reauc·ra·cy Bürokratie *f*

burg·er GASTR Hamburger *m*

bur·glar Einbrecher *m*

bur·glar·ize einbrechen in (*acc*)

bur·gla·ry Einbruch *m*

bur·gle *Br* → **burglarize**

bur·i·al Begräbnis *n*

bur·ly stämmig, kräftig

burn 1. MED Verbrennung *f*, Brandwunde *f*; verbrannte Stelle **2.** (ver-, an-) brennen; **~ down** ab-, niederbrennen; **~ out** ausbrennen; **~ up** auflodern; verbrennen; verglühen (*rocket etc*)

burn·ing brennend (*a. fig*)

burp F rülpsen, aufstoßen; ein Bäuerchen machen (lassen)

bur·row 1. zo Bau *m* **2.** graben; sich eingraben *or* vergraben

burst 1. Bersten *n*; Riss *m*; *fig* Ausbruch *m* **2.** *v/i* bersten, (zer)platzen; entspringen; explodieren; **~ from** sich losreißen von; **~ in on** *or* **upon s.o.** bei j-m hereinplatzen; **~ into tears** in Tränen ausbrechen; **~ out** *fig* herausplatzen; *v/t* (auf)sprengen

bur·y begraben, vergraben; beerdigen

bus Omnibus *m*, Bus *m*

bus driv·er Busfahrer *m*

bush Busch *m*; Gebüsch *n*

bush·el Bushel *m*, Scheffel *m* (*Am* 35,24 l, *Br* 36,37 l)

bush·y buschig

busi·ness Geschäft *n*; Arbeit *f*, Beschäftigung *f*, Beruf *m*, Tätigkeit *f*; Angelegenheit *f*; Sache *f*, Aufgabe *f*; **~ of the day** Tagesordnung *f*; **on ~** geschäftlich, beruflich; **you have no ~ doing** (*or* **to do**) *that* Sie haben kein recht, das zu tun; **that's none of your ~** das

geht Sie nichts an; → **mind** 2

busi·ness hours Geschäftszeit *f*

busi·ness·like geschäftsmäßig, sachlich

busi·ness·man Geschäftsmann *m*

busi·ness trip Geschäftsreise *f*

busi·ness·wom·an Geschäftsfrau *f*

bus stop Bushaltestelle *f*

bust¹ Büste *f*

bust²: **go ~** F pleitegehen

bus·tle 1. geschäftiges Treiben **2.** **~ about** geschäftig hin und her eilen

bus·y 1. beschäftigt; geschäftig; fleißig (*at* bei, *an dat*); belebt (*street*); arbeitsreich (*dat*); TEL besetzt **3.** (*mst ~ o.s.* sich) beschäftigen (*with* mit)

bus·y·bod·y aufdringlicher Mensch, Gschaftlhuber *m*

bus·y sig·nal TEL Besetztzeichen *n*

but 1. *cj* aber, jedoch; sondern; außer, als; ohne dass; dennoch; **~ then** and(e)-rerseits; *he could not ~ laugh* er musste einfach lachen **2.** *prp* außer (*dat*); *all ~ him* alle außer ihm; *the last ~ one* der Vorletzte; *the next ~ one* der Übernächste; *nothing ~* nichts als; *~ for* wenn nicht … gewesen wäre, ohne **3.** *adv* nur; erst; gerade; *all ~* fast, beinahe

butch·er 1. Fleischer *m*, Metzger *m* **2.** (*fig* ab)schlachten

but·ler Butler *m*

butt¹ 1. (*of rifle*) (Gewehr-)Kolben *m*; (*of cigar etc*) (Zigarren-)Stummel *m* (*of cigarette*) (Zigaretten-)Kippe *f*; (*with head etc*) (Kopf-)Stoß *m* **2.** (mit dem Kopf) stoßen; **~ in** F sich einmischen (*on* in *acc*)

butt² (*of wine, beer*) Wein-, Bierfass *n*; (*rainwater tank*) Regentonne *f*

butt³ (*backside*) F Hintern *m*

but·ter 1. Butter *f* **2.** mit Butter bestreichen

but·ter·cup BOT Butterblume *f*

but·ter·fly ZO Schmetterling *m*, Falter *m*

but·tocks ANAT Gesäß *n*, F *or* ZO Hinterteil *n*

but·ton 1. Knopf *m*; Button *m*, (Ansteck)Plakette *f*, Abzeichen *n* **2.** *mst* **~ up** zuknöpfen

but·ton·hole Knopfloch *n*

but·tress Strebepfeiler *m*

buy 1. Kauf *m* **2.** (an-, ein)kaufen (*of, from* von; *at* bei); *Fahrkarte* lösen; **~ out** *j-n* abfinden, auszahlen; *Firma* aufkaufen; **~ up** aufkaufen

buy·er Käufer(in); ECON Einkäufer(in)

buzz 1. Summen *n*, Surren *n*; Stimmengewirr *n* **2.** *v/i* summen, surren; **~ off!** F schwirr ab!, hau ab!

buz·zard ZO Bussard *m*

buzz·er ELECTR Summer *m*

by 1. *prp* (nahe *or* dicht) bei *or* an, neben (**side ~ side** Seite an Seite); vorbei *or* vorüber an; *time*: bis um, bis spätestens (**be back ~ 9.30** sei um 9 Uhr 30 zurück); während, bei (**~ day** bei Tage); per, mit (**~ bus** mit dem Bus; **~ rail** per Bahn); nach, …weise (**~ the dozen** dutzendweise); nach, gemäß (**~ my watch** nach *or* auf m-r Uhr); von (**~ nature** von Natur aus); von, durch (**a play ~** … ein Stück von …; **~ o.s.** allein); um (**~ an inch** um e-n Zoll); MATH mal (**2 ~ 4**); *geteilt*: durch (**6 ~ 3**) **2.** *adv* vorbei,

vorüber (**go ~** vorbeigehen, -fahren; *time*: vergehen); beiseite (**put ~** beiseitelegen, zurücklegen); **~ and large** im Großen und Ganzen

by… Neben…; Seiten…

bye, bye-bye *int* F Wiedersehen!, tschüs(s)!

by-e·lec·tion PARL Nachwahl *f*

by·gone 1. vergangen **2.** *let* **~s** *be* **~s** lass(t) das Vergangene ruhen

by·pass 1. Umgehungsstraße *f*; MED Bypass *m* **2.** umgehen; vermeiden

by-prod·uct Nebenprodukt *n*

by·road Nebenstraße *f*

by·stand·er Zuschauer(in), *pl die* Umstehenden *pl*

byte IT Byte *n*

by·way Nebenstraße *f*

by·word Inbegriff *m*; **be a ~ for** stehen für

C

C, c C, c *n*

C *abbr of* **Celsius** C, Celsius; **centigrade** hundertgradig

c *abbr of* **cent(s)** Cent *m or pl*; **century** Jh., Jahrhundert *n*; **circa** ca., zirca, ungefähr; **cubic** Kubik…

cab Droschke *f*, Taxi *n*; RAIL Führerstand *m*; MOT Fahrerhaus *n, a.* TECH Führerhaus *n*

cab·a·ret Varieteedarbietung(en *pl) f*

cab·bage BOT Kohl *m*

cab·in Hütte *f*; MAR Kabine *f*, Kajüte *f*; AVIAT Kanzel *f*

cab·i·net Schrank *m*, Vitrine *f*; POL Kabinett *n*

cab·i·net-mak·er Kunsttischler *m*

cab·i·net meet·ing POL Kabinettssitzung *f*

ca·ble 1. Kabel *n*; (Draht)Seil *n* **2.** telegrafieren; *j-m Geld* telegrafisch anweisen; TV verkabeln

ca·ble car Kabine *f*; Wagen *m*

ca·ble·gram (Übersee)Telegramm *n*

ca·ble| **rail·way** Drahtseil-, Kabinenbahn *f*; **~ tel·e·vi·sion, ~ TV** Kabelfernsehen *n*

cab rank, cab·stand Taxistand *m*

cack·la ZO **1.** Gegacker *n*, Geschnatter *n*

2. gackern, schnattern

cac·tus BOT Kaktus *m*

ca·dence MUS Kadenz *f*; (Sprech-)Rhythmus *m*

ca·det MIL Kadett *m*

cadge *Br* F schnorren

caf·é, caf·e Café *n*

caf·e·te·ri·a Cafeteria *f*, Selbstbedienungsrestaurant *n, a.* Kantine *f*, UNIV Mensa *f*

cage 1. Käfig *m*; *mining*: Förderkorb *m* **2.** einsperren

cake 1. Kuchen *m*, Torte *f*; Tafel *f Schokolade*, Stück *n Seife* **2. ~d with mud** schmutzverkrustet

ca·lam·i·ty großes Unglück, Katastrophe *f*

cal·cu·late *v/t* kalkulieren; be-, aus-, errechnen; F vermuten; *v/i*: **~ on** rechnen mit *or* auf (*acc*), zählen auf (*acc*)

cal·cu·la·tion Berechnung *f (a. fig)*; ECON Kalkulation *f*; *fig* Überlegung *f*

cal·cu·la·tor TECH (Taschen)Rechner *m*

cal·en·dar Kalender *m*

calf¹ ANAT Wade *f*

calf² ZO Kalb *n*

calf·skin Kalb(s)fell *n*

cal·i·ber, *esp Br* **cal·i·bre** Kaliber *n*

call 1. Ruf *m*; TEL Anruf *m*, Gespräch *n*; Ruf *m*, Berufung *f* (**to** in *ein Amt*; auf *e-n Lehrstuhl*); Aufruf *m*, Aufforderung *f*; Signal *n*; (kurzer) Besuch; **on ~** auf Abruf; TEL **be on ~** MED Bereitschaftsdienst haben; **make a ~** telefonieren **2.** *v/t* (herbei)rufen; (ein)berufen; TEL *j-n* anrufen; *j-n* berufen, ernennen (**to** zu); nennen; *Aufmerksamkeit* lenken (**to** auf *acc*); **be ~ed** heißen; **~ s.o. names** *j-n* beschimpfen, *j-n* beleidigen; *v/i* rufen; TEL anrufen; e-n (kurzen) Besuch machen (**on s.o., at s.o.'s** [*house*] bei *j-m*); **~ at a port** MAR e-n Hafen anlaufen; **~ for** rufen nach; *et.* anfordern; *et.* abholen; **to be ~ed for** postlagernd; **~ on** sich an *j-n* wenden (**for** wegen); appellieren an (*acc*) (**to do** zu tun); **~ on s.o.** *j-n* besuchen

call box *Br* Telefonzelle *f*
call·er Besucher(in); TEL Anrufer(in)
call-in → **phone-in**
call·ing Berufung *f*; Beruf *m*
cal·lous schwielig; *fig* gefühllos
cal·lus Schwiele *f*
calm 1. still, ruhig **2.** (Wind)Stille *f*, Ruhe *f* **3.** *often* **~ down** besänftigen, (sich) beruhigen
cal·o·rie Kalorie *f*; **high** *or* **rich in ~s** kalorienreich; **low in ~s** kalorienarm, kalorienreduziert
cal·o·rie-con·scious kalorienbewusst
calve ZO kalben
cam·cor·der Camcorder *m*, Kamerarekorder *m*
cam·el ZO Kamel *n*
cam·e·o Kamee *f*; THEA, *film*: kleine Nebenrolle, kurze Szene
cam·e·ra Kamera *f*, Fotoapparat *m*; **~ phone** Fotohandy *n*
cam·o·mile BOT Kamille *f*
cam·ou·flage 1. Tarnung *f* **2.** tarnen
camp 1. (*Zelt- etc*)Lager *n* **2.** lagern; **~ out** zelten, campen
cam·paign 1. MIL Feldzug *m* (*a. fig*); *fig* Kampagne *f*, Aktion *f*; POL Wahlkampf *m* **2.** *fig* kämpfen (**for** für; **against** gegen)
camp bed *Br*, **camp cot** Feldbett *n*
camp·er (van) Campingbus *m*, Wohnmobil *n*
camp·ground, camp·site Lagerplatz *m*; Zeltplatz *m*, Campingplatz *m*

cam·pus Campus *m*, Universitätsgelände *n*
can¹ *v/aux ich* kann, *du* kannst *etc*; dürfen, können
can² 1. Kanne *f*; (Blech-, Konserven-) Dose *f*, (-)Büchse *f* **2.** einmachen, eindosen
Can·a·da Kanada *n*; **Ca·na·di·an 1.** kanadisch **2.** Kanadier(in)
ca·nal Kanal *m* (*a.* ANAT)
ca·nar·y ZO Kanarienvogel *m*
can·cel (durch-, aus)streichen; entwerten; rückgängig machen; absagen; **be ~(l)ed** ausfallen
Can·cer ASTR Krebs *m*; **he** (**she**) **is** (**a**) **~** er (sie) ist (ein) Krebs
can·cer MED Krebs *m*
can·cer·ous MED Krebs…, krebsbefallen
can·cer pa·tient MED Krebskranke *m*, *f*
can·did aufrichtig, offen
can·di·date Kandidat(in) (**for** für), Bewerber(in) (**for** um)
can·died kandiert
can·dle Kerze *f*; Licht *n*; **burn the ~ at both ends** mit s-r Gesundheit Raubbau treiben
can·dle·stick Kerzenleuchter *m*, Kerzenständer *m*
can·do(u)r Aufrichtigkeit *f*, Offenheit *f*
can·dy 1. Kandis(zucker) *m*; Süßigkeiten *pl* **2.** kandieren; **~ floss** Zuckerwatte *f*; **~ store** Süßwarengeschäft *n*
cane BOT Rohr *n*; (Rohr)Stock *m*
ca·nine Hunde…
canned Dosen…, Büchsen…; **~ fruit** Obstkonserven *pl*
can·ne·ry Konservenfabrik *f*
can·ni·bal Kannibale *m*
can·non MIL Kanone *f*
can·ny schlau
ca·noe 1. Kanu *n*, Paddelboot *n* **2.** Kanu fahren, paddeln
can·on Kanon *m*; Regel *f*
can o·pen·er Dosen-, Büchsenöffner *m*
can·o·py Baldachin *m*
cant Jargon *m*; Phrase(n *pl*) *f*
can·tan·ker·ous F zänkisch, mürrisch
can·teen *esp Br* Kantine *f*; MIL Feldflasche *f*; Besteck(kasten *m*) *n*
can·ter 1. Kanter *m* **2.** kantern
can·vas Segeltuch *n*; Zelt-, Packleinwand *f*; Segel *pl*; PAINT Leinwand *f*; Gemälde *n*

can·vass 1. POL Wahlfeldzug *m*; ECON Werbefeldzug *m* **2.** *v/t* eingehend untersuchen *or* erörtern *or* prüfen; POL werben um (Stimmen); *v/i* POL e-n Wahlfeldzug veranstalten

can·yon GEOGR Cañon *m*, Schlucht *f*

cap 1. Kappe *f*; Mütze *f*; Haube *f*; Zündkapsel *f* **2.** (mit e-r Kappe *etc*) bedecken; *fig* krönen; übertreffen

ca·pa·bil·i·ty Fähigkeit *f*

cap·a·ble Fähig (**of** zu)

ca·pac·i·ty (Raum)Inhalt *m*; Fassungsvermögen *n*; Kapazität *f*; Aufnahmefähigkeit *f*; (TECH Leistungs)Fähigkeit *f* (**for** *ger* zu *inf*); **in my ~ as** in meiner Eigenschaft als

cape¹ GEOGR Kap *n*, Vorgebirge *n*

cape² Cape *n*, Umhang *m*

ca·per 1. Kapriole *f*, Luftsprung *m*; **cut ~s → 2.** Freuden- *or* Luftsprünge machen

ca·pil·la·ry ANAT Haar-, Kapillargefäß *n*

cap·i·tal 1. ECON Kapital *n*; Hauptstadt *f*; Großbuchstabe *m* **2.** Kapital...; Tod(es)...; Haupt...; großartig, prima; **~ crime** JUR Kapitalverbrechen *n*

cap·i·tal·ism ECON Kapitalismus *m*

cap·i·tal·ist ECON Kapitalist *m*

cap·i·tal·ize großschreiben; ECON kapitalisieren

cap·i·tal let·ter Großbuchstabe *m*; **~ pun·ish·ment** JUR Todesstrafe *f*

ca·pit·u·late kapitulieren (**to** vor *dat*)

cap·pu·cci·no Cappucino *m*

ca·pri·cious launisch

Cap·ri·corn ASTR Steinbock *m*; **he (she) is (a) ~** er (sie) ist (ein) Steinbock

cap·size MAR *v/i* kentern; *v/t* zum Kentern bringen

cap·sule Kapsel *f*

cap·tain 1. (An)Führer *m*; MAR, ECON Kapitän *m*; AVIAT Flugkapitän *m*; MIL Hauptmann *m*; SPORT (Mannschafts-) Kapitän *m*, Spielführer *m*

cap·tion Überschrift *f*, Titel *m*; Bildunterschrift *f*; *film*: Untertitel *m*

cap·ti·vate *fig* gefangen nehmen, fesseln; **cap·tive 1.** gefangen; gefesselt; **hold ~** gefangen halten **2.** Gefangene *m*, *f*; **cap·tiv·i·ty** Gefangenschaft *f*

cap·ture 1. Eroberung *f*; Gefangennahme *f* **2.** fangen, gefangen nehmen; erobern; erbeuten; MAR kapern

car Auto *n*, Wagen *m*; (Eisenbahn-,

Straßenbahn)Wagen *m*; Gondel *f* (*of a balloon etc*); Kabine *f*; **by ~** mit dem Auto, im Auto

car·a·mel Karamell *m*; Karamelle *f*

car·a·van Karawane *f*; Br Wohnwagen *m*; **~ site** Campingplatz *m* für Wohnwagen

car·a·way BOT Kümmel *m*

car·bine MIL Karabiner *m*

car·bo·hy·drate CHEM Kohle(n)hydrat *n*

car bomb Autobombe *f*

car·bon CHEM Kohlenstoff *m*; **→ carbon copy, carbon paper**

car·bon cop·y Durchschlag *m*

car·bon pa·per Kohlepapier *n*

car·bu·ret·(t)or MOT Vergaser *m*

car·case Br, **car·cass** Kadaver *m*, Aas *n*; GASTR Rumpf *m*

car·cin·o·gen·ic MED karzinogen, krebserregend

car·ci·no·ma MED Krebsgeschwulst *f*

card Karte *f*; **play ~s** Karten spielen; **have a ~ up one's sleeve** *fig* (noch) e-n Trumpf in der Hand haben

card·board Pappe *f*; **~ box** Pappschachtel *f*, Pappkarton *m*

car·di·ac MED Herz...; **~ pace·mak·er** MED Herzschrittmacher *m*

car·di·gan Strickjacke *f*

car·di·nal 1. Grund..., Haupt..., Kardinal...; scharlachrot **2.** REL Kardinal *m*

car·di·nal num·ber MATH Kardinalzahl *f*, Grundzahl *f*

card in·dex Kartei *f*

card phone Kartentelefon *n*

card·sharp·er Falschspieler *m*

car dump Autofriedhof *m*

care 1. Sorge *f*; Sorgfalt *f*; Vorsicht *f*; Obhut *f*, Pflege *f*; **needing ~** MED pflegebedürftig; **medical ~** ärztliche Behandlung; **take ~ of** aufpassen auf (*acc*); versorgen; **with ~!** Vorsicht! **2.** Lust haben (**to** *inf* zu *inf*); **~ about** sich kümmern um; **~ for** sorgen für, sich kümmern um; sich etwas machen aus; **I don't ~!** F meinetwegen!; **I couldn't ~ less** F es ist mir völlig egal

ca·reer 1. Karriere *f*, Laufbahn *f* **2.** Berufs...; Karriere... **3.** rasen

ca·reers ad·vice Berufsberatung *f*; **~ ad·vi·sor** Berufsberater *m*; **~ guid·ance** Berufsberatung *f*; **~ of·fice** Berufsberatungsstelle *f*; **~ of·fi·cer** Berufsberater *m*

care·free sorgenfrei, sorglos

care·ful vorsichtig; sorgsam bedacht (*of* auf *acc*); sorgfältig; *be ~!* pass auf!

care·less nachlässig, unachtsam; leichtsinnig, unvorsichtig; sorglos

care·less·ness Nachlässigkeit *f*, Unachtsamkeit *f*; Leichtsinn *m*; Sorglosigkeit *f*

ca·ress 1. Liebkosung *f*; Zärtlichkeit *f* **2.** liebkosen, streicheln

care·tak·er Hausmeister *m*; (Haus- *etc*) Verwalter *m*

care·worn abgehärmt, verhärmt

car fer·ry Autofähre *f*

car·go Ladung *f*

car hire *Br* Autovermietung *f*

car·i·ca·ture 1. Karikatur *f*, Zerrbild *n* **2.** karikieren

car·i·ca·tur·ist Karikaturist *m*

car·ies, *a.* **dental ~** MED Karies *f*

car·mine Karmin(rot) *n*

car·nap·per F Autoentführer *m*

car·na·tion BOT Nelke *f*

car·ni·val Karneval *m*

car·niv·o·rous ZO fleischfressend

car·ol Weihnachtslied *n*

carp[1] ZO Karpfen *m*

carp[2] nörgeln

car park *esp Br* Parkplatz *m*; Parkhaus *n*

car·pen·ter Zimmermann *m*

car·pet 1. Teppich *m*; **fitted ~** Teppichboden *m*; **sweep s.th. under the ~** *fig* et. unter den Teppich kehren **2.** mit Teppich(boden) auslegen

car phone Autotelefon *n*

car pool Fahrgemeinschaft *f*

car pool(·ing) ser·vice Mitfahrzentrale *f*

car·port MOT überdachter Abstellplatz

car rent·al Autovermietung *f*

car re·pair shop Autoreparaturwerkstatt *f*

car·riage Beförderung *f*, Transport *m*; Transportkosten *pl*; Kutsche *f*; *Br* RAIL (Personen)Wagen *m*

car·riage·way Fahrbahn *f*

car·ri·er Spediteur *m*; Gepäckträger *m* (*on a bicycle*); MIL Flugzeugträger *m*

car·ri·er bag *Br* Trag(e)tasche *f*, -tüte *f*

car·ri·on 1. Aas *n* **2.** Aas...

car·rot BOT Karotte *f*, Mohrrübe *f*

car·ry *v/t* bringen, führen, tragen (*a. v/i*)

fahren, befördern; (bei sich) haben *or* tragen; *Ansicht* durchsetzen; *Gewinn, Preis* davontragen; *Ernte, Zinsen* tragen; (weiter)führen, *Mauer* ziehen; *Antrag* durchbringen; **be carried** PARL *etc* angenommen werden; **~ s.th. too far** et. übertreiben, et. zu weit treiben; **get carried away** *fig* die Kontrolle über sich verlieren; sich hinreißen lassen; **~ forward, ~ over** ECON übertragen; **~ on** fortsetzen, weiterführen; ECON betreiben; **~ out, ~ through** aus-, durchführen

car·ry·cot *Br* (Baby)Trag(e)tasche *f*

cart 1. Karren *m*; Wagen *m*; Einkaufswagen *m*; **put the ~ before the horse** *fig* das Pferd beim Schwanz aufzäumen **2.** karren

car·ti·lage ANAT Knorpel *m*

cart·load Wagenladung *f*

car·ton Karton *m*; **a ~ of cigarettes** e-e Stange Zigaretten

car·toon Cartoon *m*, *n*; Karikatur *f*; Zeichentrickfilm *m*

car·toon·ist Karikaturist *m*

car·tridge Patrone *f* (*a.* MIL); (Film-) Patrone *f*, (Film)Kassette *f*; Tonabnehmer *m*

cart·wheel: turn ~s Rad schlagen

carve GASTR vorschneiden, zerlegen; TECH schnitzen; meißeln

carv·er (Holz)Schnitzer *m*; Bildhauer *m*; GASTR Tranchierer *m*; Tranchiermesser *n*; **carv·ing** Schnitzerei *f*

car wash Autowäsche *f*; (Auto)Waschanlage *f*, Waschstraße *f*

cas·cade Wasserfall *m*

case[1] 1. Behälter *m*; Kiste *f*, Kasten *m*; Etui *n*; Gehäuse *n*; Schachtel *f*; (Glas-) Schrank *m*; (Kissen)Bezug *m*; TECH Verkleidung *f* **2.** in ein Gehäuse *or* Etui stecken; TECH verkleiden

case[2] Fall *m* (*a.* JUR); LING *a.* Kasus *m*; MED (Krankheits)Fall *m*, Patient(in); Sache *f*, Angelegenheit *f*

case·ment Fensterflügel *m*; → **~ window** Flügelfenster *n*

cash 1. Bargeld *n*; Barzahlung *f*; **~ down** gegen bar; **~ on delivery** Lieferung *f* gegen bar; (per) Nachnahme *f* **2.** einlösen

cash·book ECON Kassenbuch *n*

cash desk Kasse *f*

cash dis·pens·er *esp Br* Geld-, Bankautomat *m*

cash·ier Kassierer(in)

cash·less bargeldlos

cash ma·chine Geld-, Bankautomat *m*

cash·mere Kaschmir *m*

cash·point *Br* → **cash machine**

cash reg·is·ter Registrierkasse *f*

cas·ing (Schutz)Hülle *f*; Verschalung *f*, Verkleidung *f*, Gehäuse *n*

cask Fass *n*

cas·ket Kästchen *n*; Sarg *m*

cas·sette (*Film-*, *Band-*, *Musik*)Kassette *f*; ~ deck Kassettendeck *n*; ~ player Kassettenrekorder *m*; ~ ra·di·o Radiorekorder *m*; ~ re·cord·er Kassettenrekorder *m*

cas·sock REL Soutane *f*

cast 1. Wurf *m*; TECH Guss(form *f*) *m*; Abguss *m*, Abdruck *m*; Schattierung *f*, Anflug *m*; Form *f*, Art *f*; Auswerfen *n* (*of a fishing line etc*); THEA Besetzung *f* 2. (ab-, aus-, hin-, um-, weg)werfen; ZO abwerfen (*skin*); verlieren (*teeth*); verwerfen; gestalten; TECH gießen; ~ up ausrechnen, zusammenzählen; THEA *Stück* besetzen; *Rollen* verteilen (*to* an *acc*); ~ lots losen (*for* um); ~ away wegwerfen; be ~ down niedergeschlagen sein; ~ off *Kleidung* ausrangieren; MAR losmachen; *Freund etc* fallen lassen; *knitting*: abketten; *v/i:* ~ about for, ~ around for suchen (nach), *fig a.* sich umsehen nach

cas·ta·net Kastagnette *f*

cast·a·way Schiffbrüchige *m*, *f*

caste Kaste *f* (*a. fig*)

cast·er Laufrolle *f*; *Br* (*Salz-*, *Zucker- etc*)Streuer *m*

cast i·ron Gusseisen *n*

cast-i·ron gusseisern

cas·tle Burg *f*, Schloss *n*; *chess*: Turm *m*

cast·or → **caster**

cast·or oil PHARM Rizinusöl *n*

cas·trate kastrieren

cas·u·al zufällig; gelegentlich; flüchtig; lässig

cas·u·al·ty Unfall *m*; Verunglückte *m*, *f*, Opfer *n*; MIL Verwundete *m*; Gefallene *m*; **casualties** Opfer *pl*, MIL *mst* Verluste *pl*; ~ (de·part·ment) MED Notaufnahme *f*; ~ ward MED Unfallstation *f*

cas·u·al wear Freizeitkleidung *f*

cat ZO Katze *f*

cat·a·log, *esp Br* cat·a·logue 1. Katalog

m; Verzeichnis *n*, Liste *f* 2. katalogisieren

cat·a·lyt·ic con·vert·er MOT Katalysator *m*

cat·a·pult *Br* Schleuder *f*; Katapult *n*, *m*

cat·a·ract Wasserfall *m*; Stromschnelle *f*; MED grauer Star

ca·tarrh MED Katarr(h) *m*

ca·tas·tro·phe Katastrophe *f*

catch 1. Fangen *n*; Fang *m*, Beute *f*; Halt *m*, Griff *m*; TECH Haken *m* (*a. fig*); (Tür)Klinke *f*; Verschluss *m* 2. *v/t* (auf-, ein)fangen; packen, fassen, ergreifen; überraschen, ertappen; *Blick etc* auffangen; F *Zug etc* (noch) kriegen, erwischen; *et.* erfassen, verstehen; *Atmosphäre etc* einfangen; sich *e-e Krankheit* holen; ~ (a) cold sich erkälten; ~ the eye ins Auge fallen; ~ s.o.'s eye j-s Aufmerksamkeit auf sich lenken; ~ s.o. up j-n einholen; be caught up in verwickelt sein in (*acc*); *v/i* sich verfangen, hängen bleiben; fassen, greifen; TECH ineinandergreifen; klemmen; einschnappen; ~ up with einholen

catch·er Fänger *m*

catch·ing packend; MED ansteckend (*a. fig*)

catch·word Schlagwort *n*; Stichwort *n*

catch·y MUS eingängig

cat·e·chis·m REL Katechismus *m*

cat·e·go·ry Kategorie *f*

ca·ter: ~ for Speisen und Getränke liefern für; *fig* sorgen für

cat·er·pil·lar ZO Raupe *f*

Cat·er·pil·lar® MOT Raupenfahrzeug *n*; ~ trac·tor® MOT Raupenschlepper *m*

cat·gut MUS Darmsaite *f*

ca·the·dral Dom *m*, Kathedrale *f*

Cath·o·lic REL 1. katholisch 2. Katholik(in)

cat·kin BOT Kätzchen *n*

cat·tle Vieh *n*; ~ breed·er Viehzüchter *m*; ~ breed·ing Viehzucht *f*; ~ dealer Viehhändler *m*; ~ mar·ket Viehmarkt *m*

ca(u)l·dron großer Kessel

cau·li·flow·er BOT Blumenkohl *m*

cause 1. Ursache *f*; Grund *m*; Sache *f* 2. verursachen; veranlassen

cause·less grundlos

cau·tion 1. Vorsicht *f*; Warnung *f*; Verwarnung *f* 2. warnen; verwarnen; JUR belehren

cau·tious behutsam, vorsichtig

cav·al·ry HIST MIL Kavallerie *f*

cave 1. Höhle *f* 2. *v/i:* ~ *in* einstürzen

cav·ern (große) Höhle

cav·i·ty Höhle *f*; MED Loch *n*

caw ZO 1. krächzen 2. Krächzen *n*

CD *abbr of compact disk* CD *f*; ~ bur·ner CD-Brenner *m*; ~ play·er CD-Spieler *m*; ~-ROM *abbr of compact disk read-only memory* CD-ROM; ~-ROM drive CD-ROM-Laufwerk *n*; ~ vid·e·o CD-Video *n*; ~ wri·ter CD-Brenner *m*

cease aufhören; beenden

cease-fire MIL Feuereinstellung *f*; Waffenruhe *f*

cease·less unaufhörlich

cei·ling (Zimmer)Decke *f*; ECON Höchstgrenze *f*, oberste Preisgrenze

cel·e·brate feiern; cel·e·brat·ed gefeiert, berühmt (*for* für, wegen)

cel·e·bra·tion Feier *f*

ce·leb·ri·ty Berühmtheit *f*

cel·e·ry BOT Sellerie *m*, *f*

ce·les·ti·al himmlisch

cel·i·ba·cy Ehelosigkeit *f*

cell BIOL Zelle *f*, ELECTR *a.* Element *n*

cel·lar Keller *m*

cel·list MUS Cellist(in)

cel·lo MUS (Violon)Cello *n*

cel·lo·phane® Cellophan® *n*

cel·lu·lar BIOL Zell(en)...

cel·lu·lar phone Handy *n*

Cel·tic keltisch

ce·ment 1. Zement *m*; Kitt *m* 2. zementieren; (ver)kitten

cem·e·tery Friedhof *m*

cen·sor 1. Zensor *m* 2. zensieren

cen·sor·ship Zensur *f*

cen·sure 1. Tadel *m*, Verweis *m* 2. tadeln

cen·sus Volkszählung *f*

cent Hundert *n*; Cent *m* (*1/100 Dollar*); *per* ~ Prozent *n*

cen·te·na·ry Hundertjahrfeier *f*, hundertjähriges Jubiläum

cen·ten·ni·al 1. hundertjährig 2. → *cen·tenary*

cen·ter 1. Zentrum *n*, Mittelpunkt *m*; *soccer:* Flanke *f* 2. (sich) konzentrieren; zentrieren; ~ *back soccer:* Vorstopper *m*; ~ *for·ward* SPORT Mittelstürmer(in); ~ *of grav·i·ty* PHYS Schwerpunkt *m*

cen·ti·grade: *10 degrees* ~ 10 Grad Celsius

cen·ti·me·ter, *Br* cen·ti·me·tre Zentimeter *m*, *n*

cen·ti·pede ZO Tausendfüß(l)er *m*

cen·tral zentral; Haupt..., Zentral...; Mittel...; ~ heat·ing Zentralheizung *f*

cen·tral·ize zentralisieren

cen·tral|| lock·ing MOT Zentralverriegelung *f*; ~ res·er·va·tion *Br* MOT Mittelstreifen *m*

cen·tre *Br* → *center*

cen·tu·ry Jahrhundert *n*

ce·ram·ics Keramik *f*, keramische Erzeugnisse *pl*

ce·re·al 1. Getreide... 2. BOT Getreide *n*; Getreidepflanze *f*; GASTR Getreideflocken *pl*, Frühstückskost *f*

ce·re·bral ANAT Gehirn...

cer·e·mo·ni·al 1. zeremoniell 2. Zeremoniell *n*

cer·e·mo·ni·ous zeremoniell; förmlich

cer·e·mo·ny Zeremonie *f*; Feier *f*, Feierlichkeit *f*; Förmlichkeit(en *pl*) *f*

cer·tain sicher, gewiss; zuverlässig; bestimmt; gewisse(r, -s); cer·tain·ly sicher, gewiss; *int* sicherlich, bestimmt, natürlich; cer·tain·ty Sicherheit *f*, Bestimmtheit *f*, Gewissheit *f*

cer·tif·i·cate Zeugnis *n*; Bescheinigung *f*; ~ *of* (*good*) *conduct* Führungszeugnis *n*; *General Certificate of Education advanced level* (*A level*) *Br* PED *appr* Abitur(zeugnis) *n*; *General Certificate of Education ordinary level* (*O level*) *Br* PED *appr* mittlere Reife; *medical* ~ ärztliches Attest

cer·ti·fy *et.* bescheinigen; beglaubigen

cer·ti·tude Sicherheit *f*, Bestimmtheit *f*, Gewissheit *f*

CET *abbr of Central European Time* MEZ, mitteleuropäische Zeit

cf (*Latin confer*) *abbr of compare* vgl., vergleiche

CFC *abbr of chlorofluorocarbon* FCKW, Fluorchlorkohlenwasserstoff *m*

chafe *v/t* warm reiben; aufreiben, wund reiben; *v/i* (sich durch)reiben, scheuern

chaff AGR Spreu *f*; Häcksel *n*

chaf·finch ZO Buchfink *m*

cha·grin 1. Ärger *m* 2. ärgern

chain 1. Kette *f*; *fig* Fessel *f* 2. (an)ket-

ten; fesseln
chain re·ac·tion Kettenreaktion *f*
chain-smoke F Kette rauchen
chain-smok·er Kettenraucher(in)
chain-smok·ing Kettenrauchen *n*
chain store Kettenladen *m*
chair Stuhl *m*; UNIV Lehrstuhl *m*; ECON
etc Vorsitz *m*; **be in the ~** den Vorsitz
führen; ~ **lift** Sessellift *m*
chair·man Vorsitzende *m*, Präsident *m*;
Diskussionsleiter *m*; ECON *Br* Generaldirektor *m*
chair·man·ship Vorsitz *m*
chair·wom·an Vorsitzende *f*, Präsiden-
tin *f*; Diskussionsleiterin *f*
chal·ice REL Kelch *m*
chalk 1. Kreide *f* **2.** mit Kreide schreiben
or zeichnen
chal·lenge 1. Herausforderung *f* **2.** herausfordern
chal·len·ger Herausforderer *m*
cham·ber TECH, PARL *etc* Kammer *f*
cham·ber·maid Zimmermädchen *n*
cham·ber of com·merce ECON Handelskammer *f*
cham·ois ZO Gämse *f*
cham·ois (leath·er) Fensterleder *n*
champ F SPORT → **champion**
cham·pagne Champagner *m*
cham·pi·on 1. Verfechter(in), Fürspre-
cher(in); SPORT Meister(in) **2.** verfechten, eintreten für; **cham·pi·on·ship**
SPORT Meisterschaft *f*
chance 1. Zufall *m*; Chance *f*, (günstige)
Gelegenheit *f*; Aussicht *f* (**of** auf *acc*);
Möglichkeit *f*; Risiko *n*; **by ~** zufällig;
take a ~ es darauf ankommen lassen;
take no ~s nichts riskieren (wollen)
2. zufällig **3.** F riskieren
chan·cel·lor Kanzler(in)
chan·de·lier Kronleuchter *m*
change 1. Veränderung *f*, Wechsel *m*;
Abwechslung *f*; Wechselgeld *n*; Kleingeld *n*; **for a ~** zur Abwechslung; ~ **for
the better** (**worse**) Bess(e)rung *f* (Ver-
schlechterung *f*); **2.** *v/t* (ver)ändern,
umändern; (aus)wechseln (aus-, ver-)
tauschen (**for** gegen); umbuchen;
MOT, TECH schalten; ~ **over** umschalten;
umstellen; ~ **trains** umsteigen; *v/i* sich
(ver)ändern, wechseln; sich umziehen
change·a·ble veränderlich
change ma·chine Münzwechsler *m*
change·o·ver Umstellung *f* (**to** auf *acc*)

chang·ing room *esp* SPORT Umkleidekabine *f*, Umkleideraum *m*
chan·nel 1. Kanal *m* (*a. fig*); (*Fernseh-
etc*)Kanal *m*, (*Fernseh- etc*)Programm
n; *fig* Weg *m* **2.** *fig* lenken
Chan·nel Tun·nel Kanaltunnel *m*, Euro-
tunnel *m*
chant 1. (Kirchen)Gesang *m*; Singsang
m **2.** in Sprechchören rufen
cha·os Chaos *n*
chap¹ 1. Riss *m* **2.** rissig machen *or* werden; aufspringen
chap² *Br* F Bursche *m*, Kerl *m*
chap·el ARCH Kapelle *f*; REL Gottesdienst *m*
chap·lain REL Kaplan *m*
chap·ter Kapitel *n*
char verkohlen
char·ac·ter Charakter *m*; Ruf *m*, Leu-
mund *m*; Schriftzeichen *n*, Buchstabe
m; *novel etc*: Figur *f*, Gestalt *f*; THEA
Rolle *f*; **char·ac·ter·is·tic 1.** charakteristisch (**of** für); **2.** Kennzeichen *n*;
char·ac·ter·ize charakterisieren
char·coal Holzkohle *f*
charge 1. *v/t* ELECTR (auf)laden; *Gewehr
etc* laden; *j-n* beauftragen (**with** mit);
j-n beschuldigen *or* anklagen (**with**
e-r Sache) (*a*. JUR); ECON berechnen,
verlangen, fordern (**for** für); MIL angreifen; stürmen; ~ **s.o. with s.th.** ECON
j-m et. in Rechnung stellen; *v/i*: ~ **at
s.o.** auf *j-n* losgehen **2.** Ladung *f* (*a.*
ELECTR *etc*); (Spreng)Ladung *f*; Beschuldigung *f*, *a*. JUR Anklage(-punkt
m) *f*; ECON Preis *m*; Forderung *f*; Gebühr *f*; *a*. *pl* Unkosten *pl*, Spesen *pl*;
Verantwortung *f*; Schützling *m*, Mündel *n*, *m*; **free of ~** kostenlos; **be in ~
of** verantwortlich sein für; **take ~ of**
die Leitung *etc* übernehmen, die Sache
in die Hand nehmen
char·ger Aufladegerät *n*
char·i·ot HIST Streit-, Triumphwagen *m*
cha·ris·ma Charisma *n*, Ausstrahlung *f*,
Ausstrahlungskraft *f*
char·i·ta·ble wohltätig
char·i·ty Nächstenliebe *f*; Wohltätigkeit
f; Güte *f*, Nachsicht *f*; milde Gabe
char·la·tan Scharlatan *m*; Quacksalber
m, Kurpfuscher *m*
charm 1. Zauber *m*; Charme *m*, Reiz *m*;
Talisman *m*, Amulett *n* **2.** bezaubern,
entzücken

charm·ing charmant, bezaubernd

chart (*See-, Himmels-, Wetter*)Karte *f*; Diagramm *n*, Schaubild *n*; *pl* MUS Charts *pl*, Hitliste(n *pl*) *f*

char·ter 1. Urkunde *f*; Charta *f*; Chartern *n* **2.** chartern, mieten

char·ter flight Charterflug *m*

char·wom·an Putzfrau *f*, Raumpflegerin *f*

chase 1. Jagd *f*; Verfolgung *f* **2.** *v/t* jagen, hetzen; Jagd machen auf (*acc*); TECH ziselieren; *v/i* rasen, rennen

chasm Kluft *f*, Abgrund *m*

chaste keusch; schlicht

chas·tise züchtigen

chas·ti·ty Keuschheit *f*

chat 1. Geplauder *n*, Schwätzchen *f*, Plauderei *f*; IT Chat *m* **2.** plaudern; IT chatten

chat show *Br* TV Talkshow *f*

chat show host *Br* TV Talkmaster *m*

chat·ter 1. plappern; schnattern; klappern **2.** Geplapper *n*; Klappern *n*

chat·ter·box F Plappermaul *n*

chat·ty gesprächig

chauf·feur Chauffeur *m*

chau·vi F Chauvi *m*

chau·vin·ist Chauvinist *m*; F *male ~ pig* Chauvi *m*; *contp* Chauvischwein *n*

cheap billig; *fig* schäbig, gemein

cheap·en (sich) verbilligen; *fig* herabsetzen

cheat 1. Betrug *m*, Schwindel *m*; Betrüger(in) **2.** betrügen; F schummeln

check 1. Schach(stellung *f*) *n*; Hemmnis *n*, Hindernis *n* (**on** für); Einhalt *m*; Kontrolle *f* (**on** gen); Kontrollabschnitt *m*, -schein *m*; Gepäckschein *m*; Garderobenmarke *f*; ECON Scheck *m* (**for** über); Häkchen *n* (**on** a list etc); ECON Kassenzettel *m*, Rechnung *f*; karierter Stoff **2.** *v/i* (plötzlich) innehalten; ~ **in** sich (*in e-m Hotel*) anmelden; einstempeln; AVIAT einchecken; ~ **out** (*aus e-m Hotel*) abreisen; ausstempeln; ~ **up** (**on**) F (*e-e Sache*) nachprüfen, (*e-e Sache, j-n*) überprüfen; *v/t* hemmen, hindern, aufhalten; zurückhalten; checken, kontrollieren, überprüfen; *auf e-r Liste* abhaken; *Mantel etc* in der Garderobe abgeben; *Gepäck* aufgeben

check card ECON Scheckkarte *f*

checked kariert

check·ers Damespiel *n*

check-in Anmeldung *f*; Einstempeln *n*; AVIAT Einchecken *n*

check-in| coun·ter, ~ desk AVIAT Abfertigungsschalter *m*

check·ing ac·count ECON Girokonto *n*

check·list Check-, Kontrollliste *f*

check·mate 1. (*Schach*)Matt *n* **2.** (schach)matt setzen

check-out Abreise *f*; Ausstempeln *n*

check-out coun·ter Kasse *f*

check·point Kontrollpunkt *m*

check·room Garderobe *f*; Gepäckaufbewahrung *f*

check-up Überprüfung *f*; MED Check-up *m*, Vorsorgeuntersuchung *f*

cheek ANAT Backe *f*, Wange *f*; *Br* Unverschämtheit *f*; **cheek·y** *Br* frech

cheer 1. Stimmung *f*, Fröhlichkeit *f*; Hoch *n*, Hochruf *m*, Beifall *m*, Beifallsruf *m*; *pl* SPORT Anfeuerungsrufe *pl*; *three ~s!* dreimal hoch!; *~s!* prost! **2.** *v/t* mit Beifall begrüßen; *a. ~ on* anspornen; *a. ~ up* aufheitern; *v/i* hoch rufen, jubeln; *a. ~ up* Mut fassen; *~ up!* Kopf hoch!; **cheer·ful** vergnügt

cheer·i·o *int Br* F tschüs(s)!

cheer·lead·er SPORT Einpeitscher *m*, Cheerleader *m*

cheer·less freudlos; unfreundlich

cheer·y vergnügt

cheese Käse *m*

chee·tah ZO Gepard *m*

chef Küchenchef *m*; Koch *m*

chem·i·cal 1. chemisch **2.** Chemikalie *f*

chem·ist Chemiker(in); Apotheker(in); Drogist(in)

chem·is·try Chemie *f*

chem·ist's shop Apotheke *f*; Drogerie *f*

chem·o·ther·a·py MED Chemotherapie *f*

cheque *Br* ECON Scheck *m*; *crossed ~* Verrechnungsscheck *m*; *~ ac·count* *Br* Girokonto *n*; *~ card* *Br* Scheckkarte *f*

cher·ry BOT Kirsche *f*

chess Schach(spiel) *n*; *a game of ~* e-e Partie Schach

chess·board Schachbrett *n*

chess·man, chess·piece Schachfigur *f*

chest Kiste *f*; Truhe *f*; ANAT Brust *f*, Brustkasten *m*; *get s.th. off one's ~* F sich et. von der Seele reden

chest·nut 1. BOT Kastanie *f* **2.** kastanienbraun

chest of drawers Kommode *f*

chew (zer)kauen

chew·ing gum Kaugummi *m*

chic schick, *Austrian* fesch

chick zo Küken *n*; junger Vogel; F Biene *f*, Puppe *f* (*girl*)

chick·en zo Huhn *n*; Küken *n*; GASTR (*Brat*)Hähnchen *n*, (*Brat*)Hühnchen *n*

chick·en-heart·ed furchtsam, feige

chick·en pox MED Windpocken *pl*

chic·o·ry BOT Chicorée *m*, *f*

chief 1. oberste(r, -s), Ober…, Haupt…, Chef…; wichtigste(r, -s) 2. Chef *m*; Häuptling *m*

chief·ly hauptsächlich

chil·blain MED Frostbeule *f*

child Kind *n*; ～a·buse JUR Kindesmisshandlung *f*; ～ben·e·fit *Br* Kindergeld *n*; ～birth Geburt *f*, Niederkunft *f*; ～hood Kindheit *f*; *from*～ von Kindheit an; ～ish kindlich; kindisch; ～like kindlich; ～mind·er Tagesmutter *f*; ～seat Kindersitz *m*, Babysitz *m*

chill 1. kalt, frostig, kühl (*a. fig*) 2. Frösteln *n*; Kälte *f*, Kühle *f* (*a. fig*); MED Erkältung *f* 3. abkühlen; *j-n* frösteln lassen; kühlen

chill·y kalt, frostig, kühl (*a. fig*)

chime 1. Glockenspiel *n*; Geläut *n* 2. läuten; schlagen (*clock*)

chim·ney Schornstein *m*

chim·ney sweep Schornsteinfeger *m*

chimp F, chim·pan·zee zo Schimpanse *m*

chin ANAT Kinn *n*; ～up! Kopf hoch!, halt die Ohren steif!

chi·na Porzellan *n*

Chi·na China *n*

Chi·nese 1. chinesisch 2. Chinese *m*, Chinesin *f*; LING Chinesisch *n*; *the* ～ die Chinesen *pl*

chink Ritz *m*, Spalt *m*

chip 1. Splitter *m*, Span *m*, Schnitzel *n*, *m*; dünne Scheibe; Spielmarke *f*; IT Chip *m* 2. *v/t* schnitzeln; anschlagen, abschlagen; *v/i* abbröckeln

chips (Kartoffel)Chips *pl*; *Br* Pommes frites *pl*, F Fritten *pl*

chi·rop·o·dist Fußpfleger(in), Pediküre *f*

chirp zo zirpen, zwitschern, piepsen

chis·el 1. Meißel *m* 2. meißeln

chit-chat Plauderei *f*

chiv·al·rous ritterlich

chive(s) BOT Schnittlauch *m*

chlo·ri·nate *Wasser etc* chloren

chlo·rine CHEM Chlor *n*

chlo·ro·fluo·ro·car·bon (*abbr* **CFC**) CHEM Fluorchlorkohlenwasserstoff *m* (*abbr* **FCKW**)

chlor·o·form MED 1. Chloroform *n* 2. chloroformieren

choc·o·late Schokolade *f*; Praline *f*; *pl* Pralinen *pl*, Konfekt *n*

choice 1. Wahl *f*; Auswahl *f* 2. auserlesen, ausgesucht, vorzüglich

choir ARCH, MUS Chor *m*

choke 1. *v/t* (er)würgen, (*a. v/i*) ersticken; ～ *back* Ärger *etc* unterdrücken, *Tränen* zurückhalten; ～ *down* hinunterwürgen; *a.* ～ *up* verstopfen 2. MOT Choke *m*, Luftklappe *f*

cho·les·te·rol MED Cholesterin *n*

choose (aus)wählen, aussuchen

choos·(e)y *esp Br* wählerisch

chop 1. Hieb *m*, (Handkanten)Schlag *m*; GASTR Kotelett *n* 2. *v/t* (zer)hacken, hauen; ～ *down* fällen; *v/i* hacken

chop·per Hackmesser *n*, Hackbeil *n*; F Hubschrauber *m*

chop·py unruhig (*sea*)

chop·stick Essstäbchen *n*

cho·ral MUS Chor…

cho·rale MUS Choral *m*

chord MUS Saite *f*; Akkord *m*

chore schwierige *or* unangenehme Aufgabe; *pl* Hausarbeit *f*

cho·rus MUS Chor *m*; Kehrreim *m*, Refrain *m*; Tanzgruppe *f*

Christ REL Christus *m*

chris·ten REL taufen

chris·ten·ing REL 1. Taufe *f* 2. Tauf…

Chris·tian REL 1. christlich 2. Christ(in)

Chris·ti·an·i·ty REL Christentum *n*

Chris·tian name Vorname *m*

Christ·mas Weihnachten *n and pl*; *at* ～ zu Weihnachten; ～ Day erster Weihnachtsfeiertag; ～ Eve Heiliger Abend

chrome Chrom *n*

chro·mi·um CHEM Chrom *n*

chron·ic chronisch; ständig, (an)dauernd

chron·i·cle Chronik *f*

chron·o·log·i·cal chronologisch

chro·nol·o·gy Zeitrechnung *f*; Zeitfolge *f*

chub·by F rundlich, pumm(e)lig; pausbäckig

chuck F werfen, schmeißen; ～ *out* *j-n*

rausschmeißen; *et.* wegschmeißen; ~ *up Job etc* hinschmeißen

chuck·le 1. ~ (*to o.s.*) (stillvergnügt) in sich hineinlachen **2.** leises Lachen

chum F Kamerad *m*, Kumpel *m*

chum·my F dick befreundet

chump Holzklotz *m*; F Trottel *m*

chunk Klotz *m*, Klumpen *m*

Chun·nel F → *Channel Tunnel*

church 1. Kirche *f* **2.** Kirch..., Kirchen...

church ser·vice REL Gottesdienst *m*

church·yard Kirchhof *m*

churl·ish grob, flegelhaft

churn 1. Butterfass *n* **2.** buttern; *Wellen* aufwühlen, peitschen

chute Stromschnelle *f*; Rutsche *f*, Rutschbahn *f*; F Fallschirm *m*

ci·der *a.* **hard** ~ Apfelwein *m*; (*sweet*) ~ Apfelmost *m*, Apfelsaft *m*

ci·gar Zigarre *f*

cig·a·rette Zigarette *f*

cinch F todsichere Sache

cin·der Schlacke *f*; *pl* Asche *f*

Cin·de·rel·la Aschenbrödel *n*, Aschenputtel *n*

cin·der track SPORT Aschenbahn *f*

cin·e·cam·e·ra (Schmal)Filmkamera *f*

cin·e·film Schmalfilm *m*

cin·e·ma *Br* Kino *n*; Film *m*

cin·na·mon Zimt *m*

ci·pher Geheimschrift *f*, Chiffre *f*; Null *f* (*a. fig*)

cir·cle 1. Kreis *m*; THEA Rang *m*; *fig* Kreislauf *m* **2.** (um)kreisen

cir·cuit Kreislauf *m*; ELECTR Stromkreis *m*; Rundreise *f*; SPORT Zirkus *m*; *short* ~ ELECTR Kurzschluss *m*

cir·cu·i·tous gewunden; weitschweifig; ~ *route* Umweg *m*

cir·cu·lar 1. kreisförmig; Kreis... **2.** Rundschreiben *n*; Umlauf *m*; (Post-) Wurfsendung *f*

cir·cu·late *v/i* zirkulieren, im Umlauf sein; *v/t* in Umlauf setzen

cir·cu·lat·ing li·bra·ry Leihbücherei *f*

cir·cu·la·tion (*a.* Blut)Kreislauf *m*, Zirkulation *f*; ECON Umlauf *m*; *newspaper etc*: Auflage *f*

cir·cum·fer·ence (Kreis)Umfang *m*

cir·cum·nav·i·gate umschiffen, umsegeln

cir·cum·scribe MATH umschreiben; *fig* begrenzen

cir·cum·spect umsichtig, vorsichtig

cir·cum·stance Umstand *m*; *pl* (Sach-) Lage *f*, Umstände *pl*; Verhältnisse *pl*; *in or under no* ~*s* unter keinen Umständen, auf keinen Fall; *in or under the* ~*s* unter diesen Umständen

cir·cum·stan·tial ausführlich; umständlich; ~ *ev·i·dence* JUR Indizien *pl*, Indizienbeweis *m*

cir·cus Zirkus *m*

CIS *abbr* of *Commonwealth of Independent States die* GUS, *die* Gemeinschaft unabhängiger Staaten

cis·tern Wasserbehälter *m*; Spülkasten *m*

ci·ta·tion Zitat *n*; JUR Vorladung *f*

cite zitieren; JUR vorladen

cit·i·zen Bürger(in); Städter(in); Staatsangehörige *m*, *f*

cit·i·zen·ship Staatsangehörigkeit *f*

cit·y 1. (Groß)Stadt *f*; *the City* die (Londoner) City **2.** städtisch, Stadt...; ~ *cen·tre Br* Innenstadt *f*, City *f*; ~ *coun·cil·*(l)*or* Stadtrat *m*, Stadträtin *f*; ~ *hall* Rathaus *n*; Stadtverwaltung *f*

civ·ic städtisch, Stadt...

civ·ics PED Staatsbürgerkunde *f*

civ·il staatlich, Staats...; (staats)bürgerlich, Bürger...; zivil, Zivil...; JUR zivilrechtlich; höflich

ci·vil·ian Zivilist *m*

ci·vil·i·ty Höflichkeit *f*

civ·i·li·za·tion Zivilisation *f*, Kultur *f*

civ·i·lize zivilisieren

civ·il rights (Staats)Bürgerrechte *pl*; ~ *ac·tiv·ist* Bürgerrechtler(in); ~ *move·ment* Bürgerrechtsbewegung *f*

civ·il| ser·vant Staatsbeamte *m*, -beamtin *f*; ~ *ser·vice* Staatsdienst *m*; ~ *war* Bürgerkrieg *m*

clad gekleidet

claim 1. Anspruch *m*; Anrecht *n* (*to* auf *acc*); Forderung *f*; Behauptung *f*; Claim *m* **2.** beanspruchen; fordern; behaupten

clair·voy·ant 1. hellseherisch **2.** Hellseher(in)

clam·ber (mühsam) klettern

clam·my feuchtkalt, klamm

clam·o·(u)r 1. Geschrei *n*, Lärm *m* **2.** lautstark verlangen (*for* nach)

clamp TECH Zwinge *f*

clan Clan *m*, Sippe *f*

clan·des·tine heimlich

clang klingen, klirren; erklingen lassen

clank 1. Gerassel *n*, Geklirr *n* **2.** rasseln *or* klirren (mit)

clap 1. Klatschen *n*; Schlag *m*, Klaps *m* **2.** schlagen *or* klatschen (mit)

clar·et roter Bordeaux(wein); Rotwein *m*

clar·i·fy *v/t* (auf)klären, klarstellen; *v/i* sich (auf)klären, klar werden

clar·i·net MUS Klarinette *f*

clar·i·ty Klarheit *f*

clash 1. Zusammenstoß *m*; Konflikt *m* **2.** zusammenstoßen; *fig* nicht zusammenpassen *or* harmonieren

clasp 1. Haken *m*, Schnalle *f*; Schloss *n*, (Schnapp)Verschluss *m*; Umklammerung *f* **2.** einhaken, zuhaken; ergreifen, umklammern

clasp knife Taschenmesser *n*

class 1. Klasse *f*; (Bevölkerungs-) Schicht *f*; (Schul)Klasse *f*; (Unterrichts)Stunde *f*; Kurs *m*; Jahrgang *m* **2.** (in Klassen) einteilen, einordnen, einstufen

clas·sic 1. Klassiker *m* **2.** klassisch

clas·si·cal klassisch

clas·sic car Klassiker *m*

clas·si·fi·ca·tion Klassifizierung *f*, Einteilung *f*

clas·si·fied klassifiziert; MIL, POL geheim; **~ ad** Kleinanzeige *f*

clas·si·fy klassifizieren, einstufen

class·mate Mitschüler(in)

class·room Klassenzimmer *n*

clat·ter 1. Geklapper *n* **2.** klappern (mit)

clause JUR Klausel *f*, Bestimmung *f*; LING Satz(teil *n*) *m*

claw 1. ZO Klaue *f*, Kralle *f*; (Krebs-) Schere *f* **2.** (zer)kratzen; umkrallen, packen

clay Ton *m*, Lehm *m*

clean 1. *adj* rein; sauber, glatt, eben; *sl* clean **2.** *adv* völlig, ganz und gar **3.** reinigen, säubern, putzen; **~ out** reinigen; **~ up** gründlich reinigen; aufräumen

clean·er Rein(e)machefrau *f*, (*Fenster- etc*)Putzer *m*; Reinigungsmittel *n*, Reiniger *m*; **take to the ~s** *et*. zur Reinigung bringen; F *j-n* ausnehmen

clean·ing: do the ~ sauber machen, putzen; **~ la·dy, ~ wom·an** Putzfrau *f*

clean·li·ness Reinlichkeit *f*

clean·ly 1. *adv* sauber **2.** *adj* reinlich

cleanse reinigen, säubern

cleans·er Putzmittel *n*, Reinigungsmittel *n*, Reiniger *m*

clear 1. klar; hell; rein; deutlich; frei (**of** von); ECON Netto…, Rein… **2.** *v/t* reinigen, säubern; Wald lichten, roden; wegräumen (*a.* **~ away**); *Tisch* abräumen; räumen, leeren; *Hindernis* nehmen; *Schuld* klären; ECON verzollen; JUR freisprechen; IT löschen; *v/i* klar *or* hell werden; METEOR aufklaren; sich verziehen (*fog*); **~ out** aufräumen; ausräumen, entfernen; F abhauen; **~ up** aufräumen; *Verbrechen etc* aufklären; METEOR aufklaren

clear·ance Räumung *f*; TECH lichter Abstand; Freigabe *f*; **~ sale** ECON Räumungsverkauf *m*, Ausverkauf *m*

clear·ing Lichtung *f*

cleave spalten

cleav·er Hackmesser *n*

clef MUS Schlüssel *m*

cleft Spalt *m*, Spalte *f*

clem·en·cy Milde *f*, Nachsicht *f*

clem·ent mild (*a.* METEOR)

clench *Lippen etc* (fest) zusammenpressen; *Zähne* zusammenbeißen; *Faust* ballen

cler·gy REL Klerus *m*, *die* Geistlichen *pl*

cler·gy·man REL Geistliche *m*

clerk Verkäufer(in); (Büro- *etc*)Angestellte *m, f*, (Bank-, Post)Beamte *m*, (-)Beamtin *f*

clev·er klug, gescheit; geschickt

click 1. Klicken *n* **2.** *v/i* klicken; zu-, einschnappen; *mit der Zunge* schnalzen; *v/t* klicken *or* einschnappen lassen; *mit der Zunge* schnalzen; **~ on** IT anklicken

cli·ent JUR Klient(in), Mandant(in); Kunde *m*, Kundin *f*, Auftraggeber(in)

cliff Klippe *f*, Felsen *m*

cli·mate Klima *n*

cli·max Höhepunkt *m*; Orgasmus *m*

climb klettern; (er-, be)steigen; **~ (up) a tree** auf e-n Baum klettern

climb·er Kletterer *m*, Bergsteiger(in); BOT Kletterpflanze *f*

clinch 1. TECH sicher befestigen; (ver)nieten; *boxing*: umklammern (*v/i* clinchen); *fig* entscheiden; **that ~ed it** damit war die Sache entschieden **2.** *boxing*: Clinch *m*

cling (**to**) festhalten (an *dat*), sich klammern (an *acc*); sich (an)schmiegen (an *acc*)

cling·film® *esp Br* Frischhaltefolie *f*

clin·ic Klinik *f*

clin·i·cal klinisch

clink 1. Klirren *n*, Klingen *n*; *sl* Knast *m* **2.** klingen *or* klirren (lassen); klimpern mit

clip[1] **1.** ausschneiden; *Schafe etc* scheren **2.** Schnitt *m*; Schur *f*; (*Film- etc*) Ausschnitt *m*; (*Video*)Clip *m*

clip[2] **1.** (*Heft-, Büro- etc*)Klammer *f*; (*Ohr*)Klipp *m* **2.** *a.* **~ on** anklammern

clip·per: (*a pair of*) **~s** (e-e) (*Nagel- etc*)-Schere *f*, Haarschneidemaschine *f*

clip·pings Abfälle *pl*, Schnitzel *pl*; (*Zeitungs- etc*)Ausschnitte *pl*

clit·o·ris ANAT Klitoris *f*

cloak 1. Umhang *m* **2.** *fig* verhüllen

cloak·room *Br* Garderobe *f*; Toilette *f*

clock 1. (*Wand-, Stand-, Turm*)Uhr *f*; **9 o'clock** 9 Uhr **2.** SPORT Zeit stoppen; **~ in, ~ on** einstempeln; **~ out, ~ off** ausstempeln; **~ ra·di·o** Radiowecker *m*

clock·wise im Uhrzeigersinn

clock·work Uhrwerk *n*; **like ~** wie am Schnürchen

clod (*Erd*)Klumpen *m*

clog 1. (*Holz*)Klotz *m*; Holzschuh *m* **2.** *a.* **~ up** verstopfen

clois·ter ARCH Kreuzgang *m*; REL Kloster *n*

close 1. *adj* geschlossen; knapp (*result etc*); genau, gründlich (*inspection etc*); eng (*anliegend*); stickig, schwül; eng (*friend*), nah (*relative*); **keep a ~ watch on** scharf im Auge behalten (*acc*) **2.** *adv* eng, nahe, dicht; **~ by** ganz in der Nähe, nahe *or* dicht bei **3.** Ende *n*, (Ab)Schluss *m*; **come** *or* **draw to a ~** sich dem Ende nähern; Einfriedung *f* **4.** *v/t* (ab-, ver-, zu)schließen, zumachen; ECON schließen; *Straße* (ab)sperren; *v/i* sich schließen; schließen, zumachen; enden, zu Ende gehen; **~ down** *Geschäft etc* schließen, *Betrieb* stilllegen; *radio*, TV das Programm beenden, Sendeschluss haben; **~ in** bedrohlich nahe kommen; hereinbrechen (*night*); **~ up** (ab-, ver-, zu)schließen; aufschließen, aufrücken

closed geschlossen, F *pred* zu

clos·et (*Wand*)Schrank *m*

close-up PHOT, *film*: Großaufnahme *f*

clos·ing date Einsendeschluss *m*

clos·ing time Laden-, Geschäftsschluss *m*; Polizeistunde *f* (*of a pub*)

clo·sure Abschluss *m*; **look for ~** mit et. abschließen wollen

clot 1. Klumpen *m*, Klümpchen *n*; **~ of blood** MED Blutgerinnsel *n* **2.** gerinnen; Klumpen bilden

cloth Stoff *m*, Tuch *n*; Lappen *m*

cloth-bound in Leinen gebunden

clothe (an-, be)kleiden; einkleiden

clothes Kleider *pl*, Kleidung *f*; Wäsche *f*

clothes bas·ket Wäschekorb *m*

clothes-horse Wäscheständer *m*

clothes-line Wäscheleine *f*

clothes peg *Br*, **clothes-pin** Wäscheklammer *f*

cloth·ing (Be)Kleidung *f*

cloud 1. Wolke *f*; *fig* Schatten *m* **2.** (sich) bewölken; (sich) trüben

cloud-burst Wolkenbruch *m*

cloud-less wolkenlos

cloud·y bewölkt; trüb; *fig* unklar

clout F Schlag *m*; POL Einfluss *m*

clove[1] GASTR (Gewürz)Nelke *f*; **~ of garlic** Knoblauchzehe *f*

clo·ven hoof ZO Huf *m* der Paarzeher

clo·ver BOT Klee *m*

clown Clown *m*, Hanswurst *m*

club 1. Keule *f*; Knüppel *m*; SPORT Schlagholz *n*; (*Golf*)Schläger *m*; Klub *m*; *pl card game:* Kreuz *n* **2.** einknüppeln auf (*acc*), niederknüppeln

club-foot MED Klumpfuß *m*

cluck ZO **1.** gackern; glucken **2.** Gackern *n*; Glucken *n*

clue Anhaltspunkt *m*, Fingerzeig *m*, Spur *f*

clump 1. Klumpen *m*; (*Baum- etc -*) Gruppe *f* **2.** trampeln

clum·sy unbeholfen, ungeschickt, plump

clus·ter 1. BOT Traube *f*, Büschel *n*; Haufen *m* **2.** sich drängen

clutch 1. Griff *m*; TECH Kupplung *f*; *fig* Klaue *f* **2.** (er)greifen; umklammern

clut·ter *fig* überladen

c/o *abbr of* **care of** c/o, (wohnhaft) bei

Co *abbr of* **company** ECON Gesellschaft *f*

coach 1. Reisebus *m*; *Br* RAIL (Personen)Wagen *m*; (*class*) Economyclass *f*; **~ party** (*Bus*) Reisegruppe *f*; SPORT Trainer(in); PED Nachhilfelehrer(in) **2.** SPORT trainieren; PED *j-m* Nachhilfeunterricht geben

coach·man Kutscher *m*

co·ag·u·late gerinnen (lassen)

coal (Stein)Kohle *f*; *carry ~s to New·castle* F *Br* Eulen nach Athen tragen

co·a·li·tion POL Koalition *f*; Bündnis *n*, Zusammenschluss *m*

coal·mine, coal·pit Kohlengrube *f*

coarse grob; rau; derb; ungeschliffen; gemein

coast 1. Küste *f* **2.** MAR die Küste entlangfahren; im Leerlauf (*car*) or im Freilauf (*bicycle*) fahren; rodeln

coast·er brake Rücktritt(bremse *f*) *m*

coast·guard (Angehörige *m* der) Küstenwache *f*

coast·line Küstenlinie *f*, -strich *m*

coat 1. Mantel *m*; ZO Pelz *m*, Fell *n*; (*Farb- etc*)Überzug *m*, Anstrich *m*, Schicht *f* **2.** (an)streichen, überziehen, beschichten

coat hang·er Kleiderbügel *m*

coat·ing (*Farb- etc*)Überzug *m*, Anstrich *m*; Schicht *f*; Mantelstoff *m*

coat of arms Wappen(schild *m*, *n*) *n*

coax überreden, beschwatzen

cob Maiskolben *m*

cob·bled: *~ street* Straße *f* mit Kopfsteinpflaster

cob·bler (Flick)Schuster *m*

cob·web Spinn(en)gewebe *n*

co·caine Kokain *m*

cock 1. ZO Hahn *m*; V Schwanz *m* **2.** aufrichten

cock·a·too ZO Kakadu *m*

cock·chaf·er ZO Maikäfer *m*

cock·eyed F schielend; (krumm und) schief

Cock·ney Cockney *m*, waschechter Londoner

cock·pit AVIAT Cockpit *n*

cock·roach ZO Schabe *f*

cock·sure F übertrieben selbstsicher

cock·tail Cocktail *m*

cock·y großspurig, anmaßend

co·co BOT Kokospalme *f*

co·coa Kakao *m*

co·co·nut BOT Kokosnuss *f*

co·coon (*Seiden*)Kokon *m*

cod ZO Kabeljau *m*, Dorsch *m*

COD *abbr of* **collect** (*Br* **cash**) **on delivery** per Nachnahme

cod·dle verhätscheln, verzärteln

code 1. Kode *m* **2.** verschlüsseln, chiffrieren; kodieren

cod·fish → *cod*

cod·ing Kodierung *f*

cod-liv·er oil Lebertran *m*

co·ed·u·ca·tion PED Gemeinschaftserziehung *f*

co·ex·ist gleichzeitig *or* nebeneinander bestehen *or* leben

co·ex·ist·ence Koexistenz *f*

cof·fee Kaffee *m*; **black**(**white**) *~* Kaffee ohne (mit) Milch; *~* **bar** *Br* Café *n*; Imbissstube *f*; *~* **bean** Kaffeebohne *f*; *~* **grind·er** Kaffeemühle *f*; *~* **machine** Kaffeeautomat *m*

cof·fee·mak·er Kaffeemaschine *f*

cof·fee| pot Kaffeekanne *f*; *~* **shop** Café *n*; Imbissstube *f*; *~* **ta·ble** Couchtisch *m*

cof·fin Sarg *m*

cog TECH (Rad)Zahn *m*; → **cog·wheel** TECH Zahnrad *n*

co·her·ence, co·her·en·cy Zusammenhang *m*

co·her·ent zusammenhängend

co·he·sion Zusammenhalt *m*

co·he·sive (fest) zusammenhaltend

coif·fure Frisur *f*

coil 1. *a. ~ up* aufrollen, (auf)wickeln; sich zusammenrollen **2.** Spirale *f* (*a.* TECH, MED); Rolle *f*, Spule *f*

coin 1. Münze *f* **2.** prägen

co·in·cide zusammentreffen; übereinstimmen; **co·in·ci·dence** (zufälliges) Zusammentreffen; Zufall *m*

coin-op·e·rat·ed: *~* (**gas**, *Br* **petrol**) **pump** Münztank(automat) *m*

coke Koks *m* (*a.* F *cocaine*)

Coke® F Coke *n*, Cola *n*, Coca *n*, *f*

cold 1. kalt **2.** Kälte *f*; MED Erkältung *f*; *catch* (*a*) *~* sich erkälten; *have a ~* erkältet sein

cold-blood·ed kaltblütig

cold cuts GASTR Aufschnitt *m*

cold-heart·ed kaltherzig

cold·ness Kälte *f*

cold sweat Angstschweiß *m*; *he broke out in a ~* ihm brach der Angstschweiß aus

cold war POL kalter Krieg

cold wave METEOR Kältewelle *f*

cole·slaw Krautsalat *m*

col·ic MED Kolik *f*

col·lab·o·rate zusammenarbeiten

col·lab·o·ra·tion Zusammenarbeit *f*; *in*

~ with gemeinsam mit

col·lapse 1. zusammenbrechen (*a. fig*), einstürzen; umfallen; *fig* scheitern **2.** Einsturz *m*; *fig* Zusammenbruch *m*

col·lap·si·ble Klapp..., zusammenklappbar

col·lar 1. Kragen *m*; (*Hunde- etc*)Halsband *n* **2.** beim Kragen packen; *j-n* festnehmen, F schnappen

col·lar·bone ANAT Schlüsselbein *n*

col·league Kollege *m*, Kollegin *f*, Mitarbeiter(in)

col·lect *v/t* (ein)sammeln; *Daten* erfassen; *Geld* kassieren; *j-n or et.* abholen; *Gedanken etc* sammeln; *v/i* sich (ver)sammeln; **col·lect·ed** *fig* gefasst

col·lect·ing box Sammelbüchse *f*

col·lec·tion Sammlung *f*; ECON Eintreibung *f*; REL Kollekte *f*; Abholung *f*

col·lec·tive gesammelt; Sammel...; **~ bargaining** ECON Tarifverhandlungen

col·lec·tive·ly insgesamt; zusammen

col·lec·tor Sammler(in); Steuereinnehmer *m*; ELECTR Stromabnehmer *m*

col·lege College *n*; Hochschule *f*; höhere Lehranstalt

col·lide zusammenstoßen, kollidieren (*a. fig*)

col·lie·ry Kohlengrube *f*

col·li·sion Zusammenstoß *m*, Kollision *f* (*a. fig*)

col·lo·qui·al umgangssprachlich

co·lon LING Doppelpunkt *m*

colo·nel MIL Oberst *m*

co·lo·ni·al·is·m POL Kolonialismus *m*

col·o·nize kolonisieren, besiedeln

col·o·ny Kolonie *f*

col·o(u)r 1. Farbe *f*; *pl* MIL Fahne *f*; MAR Flagge *f*; **what ~ is ...?** welche Farbe hat ...? **2.** *v/t* färben; anmalen, bemalen, anstreichen; *fig* beschönigen; *v/i* sich (ver)färben; erröten

col·o(u)r-blind farbenblind

col·o(u)red bunt; farbig

col·o(u)r·fast farbecht

col·o(u)r film PHOT Farbfilm *m*

col·o(u)r·ful farbenprächtig; *fig* farbig, bunt

col·o(u)r·ing Färbung *f*; Farbstoff *m*; Gesichtsfarbe *f*

col·o(u)r·less farblos

colt ZO (Hengst)Fohlen *n*

col·umn Säule *f*; PRINT Spalte *f*; MIL Kolonne *f*

col·umn·ist Kolumnist(in)

comb 1. Kamm *m* **2.** kämmen; striegeln

com·bat 1. Kampf *m*; **single ~** Zweikampf *m* **2.** kämpfen gegen, bekämpfen; **com·ba·tant** MIL Kämpfer *m*

com·bi·na·tion Verbindung *f*, Kombination *f*; **com·bine 1.** (sich) verbinden **2.** ECON Konzern *m*; AGR *a.* **~ harvester** Mähdrescher *m*

com·bus·ti·ble 1. brennbar **2.** Brennstoff *m*, Brennmaterial *n*

com·bus·tion Verbrennung *f*

come kommen; **to ~** künftig, kommend; **~ and go** kommen und gehen; **~ to see** besuchen; **~ about** geschehen, passieren; **~ across** auf *j-n or et.* stoßen; **~ along** mitkommen, mitgehen; **~ apart** auseinanderfallen; **~ away** sich lösen, ab-, losgehen (*button etc*); **~ back** zurückkommen; **~ by** zu et. kommen; **~ down** herunterkommen (*a. fig*); einstürzen; sinken (*prices*); überliefert werden; **~ down with** F erkranken an (*dat*); **~ for** abholen kommen, kommen wegen; **~ forward** sich melden; **~ from** kommen aus; kommen von; **~ home** nach Hause (*Austrian, Swiss a.* nachhause) kommen; **~ in** hereinkommen; eintreffen (*news*); einlaufen (*train*); **~ in!** herein!; **~ loose** sich ablösen, abgehen; **~ off** ab-, losgehen (*button etc*); **~ on!** los!, vorwärts!, komm!; **~ out** herauskommen; **~ over** vorbeikommen (*visitor*); **~ round** vorbeikommen (*visitor*); wieder zu sich kommen; **~ through** durchkommen; *Krankheit etc* überstehen, überleben; **~ to** sich belaufen auf (*acc*); wieder zu sich kommen; **~ up to** entsprechen (*dat*), heranreichen an (*acc*)

come·back Come-back *n*

co·me·di·an Komiker *m*

come·ly attraktiv, gut aussehend

com·fort 1. Komfort *m*, Bequemlichkeit *f*; Trost *m*; **cold ~** schwacher Trost **2.** trösten

com·for·ta·ble komfortabel, behaglich, bequem; tröstlich

com·fort·er Tröster *m*; *esp Br* Schnuller *m*; Steppdecke *f*

com·fort·less unbequem; trostlos

com·fort sta·tion Bedürfnisanstalt *f*

com·ic komisch; Komödien..., Lust-

company

spiel...; **com·i·cal** komisch, spaßig
com·ics Comics *pl*, Comic-Hefte *pl*
com·ma LING Komma *n*
com·mand 1. Befehl *m*; Beherrschung *f*; MIL Kommando *n* **2.** befehlen; MIL kommandieren; verfügen über (*acc*); beherrschen
com·mand·er MIL Kommandeur *m*, Befehlshaber *m*; ~ **in chief** MIL Oberbefehlshaber *m*
com·mand·ment REL Gebot *n*
com·mand mod·ule Kommandokapsel *f*
com·man·do MIL Kommando *n*
com·mem·o·rate gedenken (*gen*)
com·mem·o·ra·tion: in ~ of zum Gedenken *or* Gedächtnis an (*acc*)
com·mem·o·ra·tive Gedenk..., Erinnerungs...
com·ment 1. (*on*) Kommentar *m* (zu); Bemerkung *f* (zu); Anmerkung *f* (zu); **no ~!** kein Kommentar! **2.** *v/i* ~ **on** e-n Kommentar abgeben zu, sich äußern über (*acc*); *v/t* bemerken (**that** dass)
com·men·ta·ry Kommentar *m* (**on** zu)
com·men·ta·tor Kommentator *m*, *radio*, TV *a*. Reporter *m*
com·merce ECON Handel *m*
com·mer·cial 1. ECON Handels..., Geschäfts...; kommerziell, finanziell **2.** *radio*, TV Werbespot *m*, Werbesendung *f*; ~ **art** Gebrauchsgrafik *f*; ~ **art·ist** Gebrauchsgrafiker(in)
com·mer·cial·ize kommerzialisieren
com·mer·cial tel·e·vi·sion Werbefernsehen *n*; kommerzielles Fernsehen
com·mis·e·rate: ~ with Mitleid empfinden mit
com·mis·e·ra·tion Mitleid *n* (**for** mit)
com·mis·sion 1. Auftrag *m*; Kommission *f*, Ausschuss *m*; ECON Kommission *f*, Provision *f*; Begehung *f* (*of a crime*) **2.** beauftragen; *et.* in Auftrag geben
com·mis·sion·er Beauftragte *m*, *f*; Kommissar(in)
com·mit anvertrauen, übergeben (**to** *dat*); JUR *j-n* einweisen (**to** in *acc*); *Verbrechen* begehen; *j-n* verpflichten (**to** zu), *j-n* festlegen (**to** auf *acc*)
com·mit·ment Verpflichtung *f*; Engagement *n*
com·mit·tal JUR Einweisung *f*
com·mit·tee Komitee *n*, Ausschuss *m*

com·mod·i·ty ECON Ware *f*, Artikel *m*
com·mon 1. gemeinsam, gemeinschaftlich; allgemein; alltäglich; gewöhnlich, einfach **2.** Gemeindeland *n*; **in ~** gemeinsam (**with** mit)
com·mon·er Bürgerliche *m*, *f*
com·mon law (ungeschriebenes englisches) Gewohnheitsrecht
com·mon·place 1. Gemeinplatz *m* **2.** alltäglich; abgedroschen
Com·mons: the ~, the House of ~ *Br* PARL das Unterhaus
com·mon sense gesunder Menschenverstand
Com·mon·wealth: the ~ (of Nations) das Commonwealth
com·mo·tion Aufregung *f*; Aufruhr *m*, Tumult *m*
com·mu·nal Gemeinde...; Gemeinschafts...; *com·mune* Kommune *f*
com·mu·ni·cate *v/t* mitteilen; *v/i* sich besprechen; sich in Verbindung setzen (**with s.o.** mit *j-m*); (durch e-e Tür) verbunden sein
com·mu·ni·ca·tion Mitteilung *f*; Verständigung *f*, Kommunikation *f*; Verbindung *f*; *pl* Kommunikationsmittel *pl*; Verkehrswege *pl*
com·mu·ni·ca·tions sat·el·lite Nachrichtensatellit *m*
com·mu·ni·ca·tive mitteilsam, gesprächig
Com·mu·nion *a. Holy ~* REL (heilige) Kommunion, Abendmahl *n*
com·mu·nis·m POL Kommunismus *m*
com·mu·nist POL **1.** Kommunist(in) *2.* kommunistisch
com·mu·ni·ty Gemeinschaft *f*; Gemeinde *f*
com·mute JUR Strafe *mildernd* umwandeln; RAIL *etc* pendeln
com·mut·er Pendler(in); ~ **train** Pendlerzug *m*, Nahverkehrszug *m*
com·pact 1. Puderdose *f*; MOT Kleinwagen *m* **2.** *adj* kompakt; eng, klein; knapp (*style*); ~ **car** MOT Kleinwagen *m*; ~ **disk** (*abbr CD*) Compact Disc *f*, CD *f*; ~ **disk play·er** CD-Player *m*, CD-Spieler *m*
com·pan·ion Begleiter(in); Gefährte *m*, Gefährtin *f*; Gesellschafter(in); Handbuch *n*, Leitfaden *m*
com·pan·ion·ship Gesellschaft *f*
com·pa·ny Gesellschaft *f*, ECON *a*. Firma

f; MIL Kompanie f; THEA Truppe f; **keep s.o.** ~ j-m Gesellschaft leisten

com·pa·ra·ble vergleichbar

com·par·a·tive 1. vergleichend; verhältnismäßig **2.** a. ~ **degree** LING Komparativ m; **com·par·a·tive·ly** vergleichsweise; verhältnismäßig

com·pare 1. v/t vergleichen; **~d with** im Vergleich zu; v/i sich vergleichen lassen **2. beyond ~, without ~** unvergleichlich

com·pa·ri·son Vergleich m

com·part·ment Fach n; RAIL Abteil n

com·pass Kompass m; **pair of ~es** Zirkel m

com·pas·sion Mitleid n

com·pas·sion·ate mitleidig

com·pat·i·ble vereinbar; **be ~ (with)** passen (zu), zusammenpassen; IT etc kompatibel sein (mit)

com·pat·ri·ot Landsmann m, Landsmännin f

com·pel (er)zwingen

com·pel·ling bezwingend

com·pen·sate j-n entschädigen; et. ersetzen; ausgleichen

com·pen·sa·tion Ersatz m; Ausgleich m; Schadenersatz m, Entschädigung f; Bezahlung f, Gehalt n

com·pere Br Conférencier m

com·pete sich (mit)bewerben (**for** um); konkurrieren; SPORT (am Wettkampf) teilnehmen

com·pe·tence Können n, Fähigkeit f

com·pe·tent fähig, tüchtig; fachkundig, sachkundig

com·pe·ti·tion Wettbewerb m; Konkurrenz f

com·pet·i·tive konkurrierend

com·pet·i·tor Mitbewerber(in); Konkurrent(in); SPORT (Wettbewerbs-)Teilnehmer(in)

com·pile kompilieren, zusammentragen, zusammenstellen

com·pla·cence, com·pla·cen·cy Selbstzufriedenheit f, Selbstgefälligkeit f; **com·pla·cent** selbstzufrieden, selbstgefällig

com·plain sich beklagen or beschweren (**about** über acc; **to** bei); klagen (**of** über acc)

com·plaint Klage f, Beschwerde f; MED Leiden n, pl MED a. Beschwerden pl

com·ple·ment 1. Ergänzung f **2.** ergänzen

com·ple·men·ta·ry (sich) ergänzend

com·plete 1. vollständig; vollzählig **2.** vervollständigen; beenden, abschließen

com·ple·tion Vervollständigung f; Abschluss m; ~ **test** PSYCH Lückentext m

com·plex 1. zusammengesetzt; komplex, vielschichtig **2.** Komplex m (a. PSYCH)

com·plex·ion Gesichtsfarbe f, Teint m

com·plex·i·ty Komplexität f, Vielschichtigkeit f

com·pli·ance Einwilligung f; Befolgung f; **in ~ with** gemäß (dat)

com·pli·ant willfährig

com·pli·cate komplizieren

com·pli·cat·ed kompliziert

com·pli·ca·tion Komplikation f (a. MED)

com·plic·i·ty JUR Mitschuld f, Mittäterschaft f (**in** an dat)

com·pli·ment 1. Kompliment n; Empfehlung f; Gruß m **2.** v/t j-m ein Kompliment or Komplimente machen (**on** über acc)

com·ply (with) einwilligen (in acc); (e-e Abmachung etc) befolgen

com·po·nent Bestandteil m; TECH, ELECTR Bauelement n

com·pose zusammensetzen, -stellen; MUS komponieren; verfassen; **be ~d of** bestehen or sich zusammensetzen aus; **~ o.s.** sich beruhigen

com·posed ruhig, gelassen

com·pos·er MUS Komponist(in)

com·po·si·tion Zusammensetzung f; MUS Komposition f; PED Aufsatz m

com·po·sure Fassung f, (Gemüts)Ruhe f

com·pound[1] Lager n; Gefängnishof m; (Tier)Gehege n

com·pound[2] 1. Zusammensetzung f; Verbindung f; LING zusammengesetztes Wort **2.** zusammengesetzt; ~ **inter·est** ECON Zinseszinsen pl **3.** v/t zusammensetzen; steigern, esp verschlimmern

com·pre·hend begreifen, verstehen

com·pre·hen·si·ble verständlich

com·pre·hen·sion Verständnis n; Begriffsvermögen n, Verstand m; **past ~** unfassbar, unfasslich

com·pre·hen·sive 1. umfassend **2.** a. ~ **school** Br Gesamtschule f

com·press zusammendrücken, -pressen; **~ed air** Druckluft f

com·pres·sion PHYS Verdichtung f; TECH Druck m

com·prise einschließen, umfassen; bestehen aus

com·pro·mise 1. Kompromiss m **2.** v/t bloßstellen, kompromittieren; v/i e-n Kompromiss schließen

com·pro·mis·ing kompromittierend; verfänglich

com·pul·sion Zwang m

com·pul·sive zwingend, Zwangs...; PSYCH zwanghaft

com·pul·so·ry obligatorisch; Pflicht..., Zwangs...

com·punc·tion Gewissensbisse pl; Reue f; Bedenken pl

com·pute berechnen; schätzen

com·put·er Computer m, Rechner m

com·put·er|-aid·ed computergestützt; **~-con**trolled computergesteuert

com·put·er| game Computerspiel n; **~ graph·ics** Computergrafik f

com·put·er·ize(sich) auf Computer umstellen; computerisieren; mit Hilfe e-s Computers errechnen or zusammenstellen

com·put·er| pre·dic·tion Hochrechnung f; **~ sci·ence** Informatik f; **~ sci·en·tist** Informatiker m; **~ vi·rus** IT Computervirus m

com·rade Kamerad m; (Partei)Genosse m

con[1] → **contra**

con[2] F reinlegen, betrügen

con·ceal verbergen; verheimlichen

con·cede zugestehen, einräumen

con·ceit Einbildung f, Dünkel m

con·ceit·ed eingebildet (**of** auf acc)

con·cei·va·ble denkbar, begreiflich

con·ceive v/i schwanger werden; v/t Kind empfangen; sich et. vorstellen or denken

con·cen·trate (sich) konzentrieren

con·cept Begriff m; Gedanke m

con·cep·tion Vorstellung f, Begriff m; BIOL Empfängnis f

con·cern 1. Angelegenheit f; Sorge f; ECON Geschäft n, Unternehmen n **2.** betreffen, angehen; beunruhigen

con·cerned besorgt; beteiligt (**in** an dat)

con·cern·ing prp betreffend, hinsichtlich (gen), was ... (acc) (an)betrifft

con·cert MUS Konzert n

con·cert hall Konzerthalle f, -saal m

con·ces·sion Zugeständnis n; Konzession f

con·cil·i·a·to·ry versöhnlich, vermittelnd

con·cise kurz, knapp

con·cise·ness Kürze f

con·clude schließen, beenden; Vertrag etc abschließen; et. folgern, schließen (**from** aus); **to be ~d** Schluss folgt

con·clu·sion (Ab)Schluss m, Ende n; Abschluss m (**of** a contract etc); (Schluss)Folgerung f; → **jump**

con·clu·sive schlüssig

con·coct (zusammen)brauen; fig aushecken, ausbrüten

con·coc·tion Gebräu n; fig Erfindung f

con·crete[1] konkret

con·crete[2] **1.** Beton m **2.** Beton... **3.** betonieren

con·cur übereinstimmen

con·cur·rence Zusammentreffen n; Übereinstimmung f

con·cus·sion MED Gehirnerschütterung f

con·demn verurteilen (a. JUR); verdammen; für unbrauchbar or unbewohnbar etc erklären; **~ to death** JUR zum Tode verurteilen; **con·dem·na·tion** Verurteilung f (a. JUR); Verdammung f

con·den·sa·tion Kondensation f; Zusammenfassung f

con·dense kondensieren; zusammenfassen

con·densed milk Kondensmilch f

con·dens·er TECH Kondensator m

con·de·scend sich herablassen

con·de·scend·ing herablassend, gönnerhaft

con·di·ment Gewürz n, Würze f

con·di·tion 1. Zustand m; (körperlicher or Gesundheits)Zustand m; SPORT Kondition f, Form f; Bedingung f; pl Verhältnisse pl, Umstände pl; **out of ~** in schlechter Verfassung, in schlechtem Zustand **2.** bedingen; in Form bringen

con·di·tion·al 1. (**on**) bedingt (durch), abhängig (von) **2.** a. **~ clause** LING Bedingungs-, Konditionalsatz m; a. **~ mood** LING Konditional m

con·do → **condominium**

con·dole kondolieren (**with** dat)

con·do·lence Beileid n

con·dom Kondom *n*, *m*

con·do·min·i·um Eigentumswohnanlage *f*; Eigentumswohnung *f*

con·done verzeihen, vergeben

con·du·cive dienlich, förderlich (**to** *dat*)

con·duct 1. Führung *f*; Verhalten *n*, Betragen *n* 2. führen; PHYS leiten; MUS dirigieren; **~ed tour** Führung *f* (**of** durch); **con·duc·tor** Führer *m*, Leiter *m*; (*Bus-*, *Straßenbahn*)Schaffner *m*; RAIL Zugbegleiter *m*; MUS Dirigent *m*; PHYS Leiter *m*; ELECTR Blitzableiter *m*

cone Kegel *m*; GASTR Eistüte *f*; BOT Zapfen *m*

con·fec·tion Konfekt *n*

con·fec·tion·er Konditor *m*

con·fec·tion·e·ry Süßigkeiten *pl*, Süß-, Konditoreiwaren *pl*; Konfekt *n*; Konditorei *f*; Süßwarengeschäft *n*

con·fed·e·ra·cy (Staaten)Bund *m*; **the Confederacy** HIST die Konföderation

con·fed·er·ate 1. verbündet 2. Verbündete *m*, Bundesgenosse *m* 3. (sich) verbünden

con·fed·er·a·tion Bund *m*, Bündnis *n*; (Staaten)Bund *m*

con·fer *v/t* Titel *etc* verleihen (**on** *dat*); *v/i* sich beraten

con·fe·rence Konferenz *f*

con·fess gestehen; beichten

con·fes·sion Geständnis *n*; REL Beichte *f*

con·fes·sion·al REL Beichtstuhl *m*

con·fes·sor REL Beichtvater *m*

con·fi·dant(e) Vertraute *m* (*f*)

con·fide: **~ s.th. to s.o.** j-m et. anvertrauen; **~ in s.o.** sich j-m anvertrauen

con·fi·dence Vertrauen *n*; Selbstvertrauen *n*; **~ man → conman**; **~ trickster** Trickbetrüger *m*

con·fi·dent überzeugt, zuversichtlich

con·fi·den·tial vertraulich

con·fine begrenzen, beschränken; einsperren; **be ~d of** entbunden werden von; **con·fine·ment** Haft *f*; Beschränkung *f*; MED Entbindung *f*

con·firm bestätigen; bekräftigen; REL konfirmieren, firmen

con·fir·ma·tion Bestätigung *f*; REL Konfirmation *f*, Firmung *f*

con·fis·cate beschlagnahmen

con·fis·ca·tion Beschlagnahme *f*

con·flict 1. Konflikt *m*, Zwiespalt *m* 2.

im Widerspruch stehen (**with** zu)

con·flict·ing widersprüchlich, zwiespältig

con·form (sich) anpassen (**to** *dat*, an *acc*)

con·found verwirren, durcheinanderbringen

con·front gegenübertreten, -stehen (*dat*); sich stellen (*dat*); konfrontieren

con·fron·ta·tion Konfrontation *f*

con·fuse verwechseln; verwirren; **con·fused** verwirrt; verlegen; verworren; **con·fu·sion** Verwirrung *f*; Verlegenheit *f*; Verwechslung *f*

con·geal erstarren (lassen); gerinnen (lassen)

con·gest·ed überfüllt; verstopft

con·ges·tion MED Blutandrang *m*; *a.* **traffic ~** Verkehrsstockung *f*, Verkehrsstörung *f*, Verkehrsstau *m*

con·grat·u·late beglückwünschen, *j-m* gratulieren

con·grat·u·la·tion Glückwunsch *m*; **~s!** ich gratuliere!, herzlichen Glückwunsch!

con·gre·gate (sich) versammeln

con·gre·ga·tion REL Gemeinde *f*

con·gress Kongress *m*; **Congress** PARL der Kongress

Con·gress·man PARL Kongressabgeordnete *m*; **Con·gress·wom·an** PARL Kongressabgeordnete *f*

con·ic, **con·i·cal** *esp* TECH konisch, kegelförmig

co·ni·fer BOT Nadelbaum *m*

con·jec·ture 1. Vermutung *f* 2. vermuten

con·ju·gal ehelich

con·ju·gate LING konjugieren, beugen

con·ju·ga·tion LING Konjugation *f*, Beugung *f*

con·junc·tion Verbindung *f*; LING Konjunktion *f*, Bindewort *n*

con·junc·ti·vi·tis MED Bindehautentzündung *f*

con·jure zaubern; *Teufel etc* beschwören; **~ up** heraufbeschwören (*a. fig*)

con·jur·er *esp Br* → **conjuror**

con·jur·ing trick Zauberkunststück *n*

con·jur·or Zauberer *m*, Zauberin *f*, Zauberkünstler(in)

con·man Betrüger *m*; Hochstapler *m*

con·nect verbinden; ELECTR anschließen, zuschalten; RAIL, AVIAT *etc* Anschluss haben (**with** an *acc*)

con·nect·ed verbunden; (logisch) zusammenhängend (*speech etc*); **be well** ~ gute Beziehungen haben

con·nec·tion, *Br* **con·nex·ion** Verbindung *f*, Anschluss *m* (*a.* ELECTR, RAIL, AVIAT, TEL); Zusammenhang *m*; *mst pl* Beziehungen *pl*, Verbindungen *pl*; Verwandte *pl*

con·quer erobern; (be)siegen

con·quer·or Eroberer *m*

con·quest Eroberung *f* (*a. fig*); erobertes Gebiet

con·science Gewissen *n*

con·sci·en·tious gewissenhaft; Gewissens…; **con·sci·en·tious·ness** Gewissenhaftigkeit *f*

con·sci·en·tious ob·jec·tor MIL Wehrdienstverweigerer *m*

con·scious MED bei Bewusstsein; bewusst; **be ~ of** sich bewusst sein (*gen*) **con·scious·ness** Bewusstsein *n* (*a.* MED)

con·script MIL **1.** einberufen **2.** Wehrpflichtige *m*; **con·scrip·tion** MIL Einberufung *f*; Wehrpflicht *f*

con·se·crate REL weihen; widmen

con·se·cra·tion REL Weihe *f*

con·sec·u·tive aufeinanderfolgend; fortlaufend

con·sent 1. Zustimmung *f* **2.** einwilligen, zustimmen

con·se·quence Folge *f*, Konsequenz *f*; Bedeutung *f*

con·se·quent·ly folglich, daher

con·ser·va·tion Erhaltung *f*; Naturschutz *m*; Umweltschutz *m*; ~ **area** (Natur)Schutzgebiet *n*

con·ser·va·tion·ist Naturschützer(in); Umweltschützer(in)

con·ser·va·tive 1. erhaltend; konservativ; vorsichtig **2. Conservative** POL Konservative *m*, *f*

con·ser·va·to·ry Treibhaus *n*, Gewächshaus *n*; Wintergarten *m*

con·serve erhalten

con·sid·er *v/t* nachdenken über (*acc*); betrachten als, halten für; sich überlegen, erwägen; in Betracht ziehen; berücksichtigen; *v/i* nachdenken, überlegen

con·sid·e·ra·ble ansehnlich, beträchtlich; **con·sid·e·ra·bly** bedeutend, ziemlich, (sehr) viel

con·sid·er·ate rücksichtsvoll

con·sid·e·ra·tion Erwägung *f*, Überle-

gung *f*; Berücksichtigung *f*; Rücksicht (-nahme) *f*; **take into** ~ in Erwägung *or* in Betracht ziehen

con·sid·er·ing in Anbetracht (der Tatsache, dass)

con·sign ECON *Waren* zusenden

con·sign·ment ECON (Waren)Sendung *f*; Zusendung *f*

con·sist: ~ **in** bestehen in (*dat*); ~ **of** bestehen aus

con·sis·tence, **con·sis·ten·cy** Konsistenz *f*, Beschaffenheit *f*; Übereinstimmung *f*; Konsequenz *f*

con·sis·tent übereinstimmend, vereinbar (**with** mit); konsequent; SPORT *etc*: beständig

con·so·la·tion Trost *m*

con·sole trösten

con·sol·i·date festigen; *fig* zusammenschließen, -legen

con·so·nant LING Konsonant *m*, Mitlaut *m*

con·spic·u·ous deutlich sichtbar; auffallend

con·spi·ra·cy Verschwörung *f*

con·spi·ra·tor Verschwörer *m*

con·spire sich verschwören

con·sta·ble *Br* Polizist *m*

con·stant konstant, gleichbleibend; (be)ständig, (an)dauernd

con·stant-care pa·tient MED Pflegefall *m*

con·ster·na·tion Bestürzung *f*

con·sti·pat·ed MED verstopft

con·sti·pa·tion MED Verstopfung *f*

con·sti·tu·en·cy POL *Br* Wählerschaft *f*; Wahlkreis *m*

con·sti·tu·ent (wesentlicher) Bestandteil; POL Wähler(in)

con·sti·tute ernennen, einsetzen; bilden, ausmachen

con·sti·tu·tion POL Verfassung *f*; Konstitution *f*, körperliche Verfassung

con·sti·tu·tion·al konstitutionell; POL verfassungsmäßig

con·strained gezwungen, unnatürlich

con·strict zusammenziehen

con·stric·tion Zusammenziehung *f*

con·struct bauen, errichten, konstruieren

con·struc·tion Konstruktion *f*; Bau *m*, Bauwerk *n*; **under** ~ im Bau (befindlich); ~ **site** Baustelle *f*

con·struc·tive konstruktiv

con·struc·tor Erbauer *m*, Konstrukteur *m*

con·sul Konsul *m*

con·su·late Konsulat *n*; ~ gen·e·ral Generalkonsulat *n*

con·sul gen·e·ral Generalkonsul *m*

con·sult *v/t* konsultieren, um Rat fragen; in *e-m Buch* nachschlagen; *v/i* (sich) beraten

con·sul·tant (fachmännischer) Berater; *Br* Facharzt *m*

con·sul·ta·tion Konsultation *f*, Beratung *f*, Rücksprache *f*

con·sult·ing beratend; ~ hours *Br* MED Sprechstunde *f*; ~ room *Br* MED Sprechzimmer *n*

con·sume *v/t Essen etc* zu sich nehmen, verzehren (*a. fig*); verbrauchen, konsumieren; zerstören, vernichten

con·sum·er ECON Verbraucher(in); ~ so·ci·e·ty Konsumgesellschaft *f*

con·sum·mate 1. vollendet 2. vollenden; *Ehe* vollziehen

con·sump·tion Verbrauch *m*

cont *abbr of* continued Forts., Fortsetzung *f*; fortgesetzt

con·tact 1. Berührung *f*; Kontakt *m*; Ansprechpartner(in), Kontaktperson *f* (*a.* MED); *make* ~s Verbindungen anknüpfen *or* herstellen 2. sich in Verbindung setzen mit, Kontakt aufnehmen mit; ~ lens Kontaktlinse *f*, -schale *f*, Haftschale *f*

con·ta·gious MED ansteckend (*a. fig*)

con·tain enthalten; *fig* zügeln, zurückhalten; con·tain·er Behälter *m*; ECON Container *m*; con·tain·er·ize ECON auf Containerbetrieb umstellen; in Containern transportieren

con·tam·i·nate verunreinigen; infizieren, vergiften; (*a.* radioaktiv) verseuchen; *radioactively* ~d verstrahlt; ~d soil Altlasten *pl*; con·tam·i·na·tion Verunreinigung *f*; Vergiftung *f*; (*a.* radioaktive) Verseuchung

contd *abbr of* continued (→ cont)

con·tem·plate (nachdenklich) betrachten; nachdenken über (*acc*); erwägen, beabsichtigen

con·tem·pla·tion (nachdenkliche) Betrachtung; Nachdenken *n*

con·tem·pla·tive nachdenklich

con·tem·po·ra·ry 1. zeitgenössisch 2. Zeitgenosse *m*, Zeitgenossin *f*

con·tempt Verachtung *f*

con·temp·ti·ble verachtenswert

con·temp·tu·ous geringschätzig, verächtlich

con·tend kämpfen, ringen (*for* um; *with* mit); con·tend·er *esp* SPORT Wettkämpfer(in)

con·tent[1] Gehalt *m*, Aussage *f*, *pl* Inhalt *m*; (*table of*) ~s Inhaltsverzeichnis *n*

con·tent[2] 1. zufrieden 2. befriedigen; ~ o.s. sich begnügen

con·tent·ed zufrieden

con·tent·ment Zufriedenheit *f*

con·test 1. (Wett)Kampf *m*; Wettbewerb *m* 2. sich bewerben um; bestreiten, *a.* JUR anfechten

con·tes·tant Wettkämpfer(in), (Wettkampf)Teilnehmer(in)

con·text Zusammenhang *m*

con·ti·nent Kontinent *m*, Erdteil *m*; *the Continent Br* das (europäische) Festland; con·ti·nen·tal kontinental, Kontinental…

con·tin·gen·cy Möglichkeit *f*, Eventualität *f*; ~ plan Notplan *m*

con·tin·gent 1. *be* ~ *on* abhängen von 2. Kontingent *n* (*a.* MIL)

con·tin·u·al fortwährend, unaufhörlich

con·tin·u·a·tion Fortsetzung *f*; Fortbestand *m*, Fortdauer *f*

con·tin·ue *v/t* fortsetzen, fortfahren mit; beibehalten; *to be* ~d Fortsetzung folgt; *v/i* fortdauern; andauern, anhalten; fortfahren, weitermachen

con·ti·nu·i·ty Kontinuität *f*

con·tin·u·ous ununterbrochen; ~ form LING Verlaufsform *f*

con·tort verdrehen; verzerren

con·tor·tion Verdrehung *f*; Verzerrung *f*

con·tour Umriss *m*

con·tra wider, gegen

con·tra·band ECON Schmuggelware *f*

con·tra·cep·tion MED Empfängnisverhütung *f*

con·tra·cep·tive MED 1. empfängnisverhütend 2. Verhütungsmittel *n*

con·tract 1. Vertrag *m* 2. (sich) zusammenziehen; sich *e-e Krankheit* zuziehen; *e-n* Vertrag abschließen; sich vertraglich verpflichten

con·trac·tion Zusammenziehung *f*

con·trac·tor *a.* building ~ Bauunternehmer *m*

con·tra·dict widersprechen (*dat*)

con·tra·dic·tion Widerspruch *m*

con·tra·dic·to·ry (sich) widersprechend

con·tra·ry 1. entgegengesetzt (*to dat*); gegensätzlich; **~ to expectations** wider Erwarten **2.** Gegenteil *n*; **on the ~** im Gegenteil

con·trast 1. Gegensatz *m*; Kontrast *m* **2.** *v/t* gegenüberstellen, vergleichen; *v/i* sich abheben (**with** von, gegen); im Gegensatz stehen (**with** zu)

con·trib·ute beitragen, beisteuern; spenden (**to** für)

con·tri·bu·tion Beitrag *m*; Spende *f*

con·trib·u·tor Beitragende *m*, *f*; Mitarbeiter(in)

con·trib·u·to·ry beitragend

con·trite zerknirscht

con·trive zustande bringen; es fertig bringen

con·trol 1. Kontrolle *f*, Herrschaft *f*, Macht *f*, Gewalt *f*, Beherrschung *f*; Aufsicht *f*; TECH Steuerung *f*; *mst pl* TECH Steuervorrichtung *f*; **get** (**have, keep**) **under ~** unter Kontrolle bringen (haben, halten); **get out of ~** außer Kontrolle geraten; **lose ~ of** die Herrschaft *or* Gewalt *or* Kontrolle verlieren über **2.** beherrschen, die Kontrolle haben über (*acc*); *e-r Sache* Herr werden, (erfolgreich) bekämpfen; kontrollieren, überwachen; ECON (staatlich) lenken, *Preise* binden; ELECTR, TECH steuern, regeln, regulieren; **~ desk** ELECTR Schalt-, Steuerpult *n*; **~ pan·el** ELECTR Schalttafel *f*; **~ tow·er** AVIAT Kontrollturm *m*, Tower *m*

con·tro·ver·sial umstritten

con·tro·ver·sy Kontroverse *f*, Streit *m*

con·tuse MED sich *et.* prellen *or* quetschen; **con·tu·sion** MED Prellung *f*, Quetschung *f*

con·va·lesce gesund werden, genesen

con·va·les·cence Rekonvaleszenz *f*, Genesung *f*

con·va·les·cent 1. genesend **2.** Rekonvaleszent(in), Genesende *m*, *f*

con·vene (sich) versammeln; zusammenkommen; *Versammlung* einberufen

con·ve·ni·ence Annehmlichkeit *f*, Bequemlichkeit *f*; *Br* Toilette *f*; **all** (**modern**) **~s** aller Komfort; **at your earliest ~** möglichst bald; **con·ve·ni·ent** bequem; günstig, passend

con·vent REL (Nonnen)Kloster *n*

con·ven·tion Zusammenkunft *f*, Tagung *f*, Versammlung *f*; Abkommen *n*; Konvention *f*, Sitte *f*; **con·ven·tion·al** herkömmlich, konventionell

con·verge konvergieren; zusammenlaufen, -strömen

con·ver·sa·tion Gespräch *n*, Unterhaltung *f*

con·ver·sa·tion·al Unterhaltungs...; **~ English** Umgangsenglisch *n*

con·verse sich unterhalten

con·ver·sion Umwandlung *f*, Verwandlung *f*; Umbau *m*; Umstellung *f* (**to** auf *acc*); REL Bekehrung *f*, Übertritt *m*; MATH Umrechnung *f*; **~ ta·ble** Umrechnungstabelle *f*

con·vert (sich) umwandeln *or* verwandeln; umbauen (**into** zu); umstellen (**to** auf *acc*); REL *etc* (sich) bekehren; MATH umrechnen

con·vert·er ELECTR Umformer *m*

con·vert·i·ble 1. umwandelbar, verwandelbar; ECON konvertierbar **2.** MOT Kabrio(lett) *n*

con·vey befördern, transportieren, bringen; überbringen, übermitteln; *Ideen etc* mitteilen, vermitteln

con·vey·ance Beförderung *f*, Transport *m*; Übermittlung *f*; Verkehrsmittel *n*

con·vey·or belt TECH Förderband *n*

con·vict 1. Verurteilte *m*, *f*; Strafgefangene *m*, *f* **2.** JUR (**of**) überführen (*gen*); verurteilen (wegen)

con·vic·tion Überzeugung *f*; JUR Verurteilung *f*

con·vince überzeugen

con·voy 1. MAR Geleitzug *m*, Konvoi *m*; MOT (Wagen)Kolonne *f*; (Geleit-)Schutz *m* **2.** Geleitschutz geben (*dat*), eskortieren

con·vul·sion MED Zuckung *f*, Krampf *m*; **con·vul·sive** MED krampfhaft, krampfartig, konvulsiv

coo ZO gurren (*a. fig*)

cook 1. Koch *m*; Köchin *f* **2.** kochen

cook·book Kochbuch *n*

cook·er *Br* Ofen *m*, Herd *m*

cook·e·ry Kochen *n*; Kochkunst *f*

cook·e·ry book *Br* Kochbuch *n*

cook·ie (süßer) Keks, Plätzchen *n*

cook·ing GASTR Küche *f*

cook·y → cookie

cool 1. kühl; *fig* kalt(blütig), gelassen;

abweisend; gleichgültig; F **klasse**, prima, cool **2.** Kühle f; F (Selbst)Beherrschung f **3.** (sich) abkühlen; **~ down, ~ off** sich beruhigen

coon F zo Waschbär m

coop 1. Hühnerstall m **2. ~ up, ~ in** einsperren, einpferchen

co-op F Co-op m

co·op·e·rate zusammenarbeiten; mitwirken, helfen

co·op·e·ra·tion Zusammenarbeit f; Mitwirkung f, Hilfe f

co·op·e·ra·tive 1. zusammenarbeitend; kooperativ, hilfsbereit; ECON Gemeinschafts…, Genossenschafts… **2.** a. **~ society** Genossenschaft f; Co-op m, Konsumverein m; a. **~ store** Co-op m, Konsumladen m

co·or·di·nate 1. koordinieren, aufeinander abstimmen **2.** koordiniert, gleichgeordnet; **co·or·di·na·tion** Koordinierung f, Koordination f; harmonisches Zusammenspiel

cop F Bulle m

cope: ~ with gewachsen sein (dat), fertigwerden mit

cop·i·er Kopiergerät n, Kopierer m

co·pi·ous reich(lich); weitschweifig

cop·per 1. MIN Kupfer n; Kupfermünze f **2.** kupfern, Kupfer…

cop·pice, copse Gehölz n

cop·y Kopie f; Abschrift f; Nachbildung f; Durchschlag m; Exemplar n; (Zeitungs)Nummer f; PRINT Satzvorlage f; **fair ~** Reinschrift f **2.** kopieren; abschreiben, e-e Kopie anfertigen von; IT Daten übertragen; nachbilden; nachahmen

cop·y·book Schreibheft n

cop·y·ing Kopier…

cop·y·right Urheberrecht n, Copyright n

cor·al zo Koralle f

cord 1. Schnur f (a. ELECTR), Strick m; Kordsamt m **2.** ver-, zuschnüren

cor·di·al[1] Fruchtsaftkonzentrat n; MED Stärkungsmittel n

cor·di·al[2] herzlich

cor·di·al·i·ty Herzlichkeit f

cord·less schnurlos

cord·less phone schnurloses Telefon

cor·don 1. Kordon m, Postenkette f **2. ~ off** abriegeln, absperren

cor·du·roy Kord m; (**a pair of**) **~s** (e-e) Kordhose

core 1. Kerngehäuse n; Kern m, fig a. das Innerste **2.** entkernen

core time ECON Kernzeit f

cork 1. Kork(en m **2.** a. **~ up** zu-, verkorken; **cork·screw** Korkenzieher m

corn[1] 1. Korn n, Getreide n; a. **Indian ~** Mais m **2.** pökeln

corn[2] MED Hühnerauge n

cor·ner 1. Ecke f; Winkel m; esp MOT Kurve f; soccer: Eckball m, Ecke f; fig schwierige Lage, Klemme f **2.** Eck… **3.** in die Ecke (fig Enge) treiben; **~ kick** soccer: Eckball m, Eckstoß m; **~ shop** Br Tante-Emma-Laden m

cor·net MUS Kornett n; Br GASTR Eistüte f

corn·flakes Cornflakes pl

cor·nice ARCH Gesims n, Sims m

cor·o·na·ry 1. ANAT Koronar… **2.** F MED Herzinfarkt m

cor·o·na·tion Krönung f

cor·o·net Adelskrone f

cor·po·ral MIL Unteroffizier m

cor·po·ral pun·ish·ment körperliche Züchtigung

cor·po·rate gemeinsam; Firmen…

cor·po·ra·tion JUR Körperschaft f; Stadtverwaltung f; ECON (Aktien)Gesellschaft f

corpse Leichnam m, Leiche f

cor·pu·lent beleibt

cor·ral 1. Korral m, Hürde f, Pferch m **2.** Vieh in e-n Pferch treiben

cor·rect 1. korrekt, richtig, a. genau (time) **2.** korrigieren, verbessern, berichtigen

cor·rec·tion Korrektur f, Verbess(e)-rung f; Bestrafung f

cor·rect·ness Richtigkeit f

cor·re·spond (with, to) entsprechen (dat), übereinstimmen (mit); korrespondieren (**with** mit)

cor·re·spon·dence Übereinstimmung f; Korrespondenz f, Briefwechsel m; **~ course** Fernkurs m

cor·re·spon·dent 1. entsprechend **2.** Briefpartner(in); Korrespondent(in)

cor·re·spon·ding entsprechend

cor·ri·dor Korridor m, Gang m

cor·rob·o·rate bekräftigen, bestätigen

cor·rode zerfressen; CHEM korrodieren; rosten; **cor·ro·sion** CHEM Korrosion f; Rost m; **cor·ro·sive** CHEM ätzend; fig

coup

nagend, zersetzend

cor·ru·gat·ed i·ron Wellblech *n*

cor·rupt 1. korrupt, bestechlich, käuflich; *moralisch* verdorben **2.** bestechen; *moralisch* verderben

cor·rupt·i·ble korrupt, bestechlich, käuflich

cor·rup·tion Verdorbenheit *f*; Unredlichkeit *f*; Korruption *f*; Bestechlichkeit *f*; Bestechung *f*

cor·set Korsett *n*

cos·met·ic 1. kosmetisch, Schönheits… **2.** kosmetisches Mittel, Schönheitsmittel *n*

cos·me·ti·cian Kosmetiker(in)

cos·mo·naut Kosmonaut *m*, (Welt-)Raumfahrer *m*

cos·mo·pol·i·tan 1. kosmopolitisch **2.** Weltbürger(in)

cost 1. Preis *m*; Kosten *pl*; Schaden *m* **2.** kosten

cost·ly kostspielig; teuer erkauft

cost of liv·ing Lebenshaltungskosten *pl*

cos·tume Kostüm *n*, Kleidung *f*, Tracht *f*

co·sy *Br* → **cozy**

cot Feldbett *n*; *Br* Kinderbett *n*

cot·tage Cottage *n*, (kleines) Landhaus; Ferienhaus *n*, Ferienhäuschen *n*

cot·ton 1. Baumwolle *f*; Baumwollstoff *m*; (Baumwoll)Garn *n*, (Baumwoll-)Zwirn *m*; (Verband)Watte *f* **2.** baumwollen, Baumwoll…

cot·ton·wood BOT *e-e* amer. Pappel

cot·ton wool *Br* (Verband)Watte *f*

couch Couch *f*, Sofa *n*; Liege *f*

cou·chette RAIL Liegewagenplatz *m*; *a.* ~ **coach** Liegewagen *m*

cou·gar ZO Puma *m*

cough 1. Husten *m* **2.** husten

coun·cil Rat *m*, Ratsversammlung *f*; ~ **house** *Br* gemeindeeigenes Wohnhaus

coun·cil·(l)or Ratsmitglied *n*, Stadtrat *m*, Stadträtin *f*

coun·sel 1. Beratung *f*; Rat(schlag) *m*; *Br* JUR (Rechts)Anwalt *m*; ~ **for the defense** (*Br* **defence**) Verteidiger *m*; ~ **for the prosecution** Anklagevertreter *m* **2.** *j-m* raten; zu *et.* raten; ~**ing center** (*Br* ~**ling centre**) Beratungsstelle *f*

coun·sel·(l)or (Berufs- *etc*)Berater(in); JUR (Rechts)Anwalt *m*

count¹ Graf *m*

count² 1. Zählung *f*; JUR Anklagepunkt

m **2.** *v/t* (ab-, auf-, aus-, nach-, zusammen)zählen; aus-, berechnen; *fig* halten für, betrachten als; *v/i* zählen; gelten; ~ **down** Geld hinzählen; den Count-down durchführen für, letzte (Start)Vorbereitungen treffen für; ~ **on** zählen auf (*acc*), sich verlassen auf (*acc*), sicher rechnen mit

count·down Count-down *m*, *n*, letzte (Start)Vorbereitungen *pl*

coun·te·nance Gesichtsausdruck *m*; Fassung *f*, Haltung *f*

coun·ter¹ TECH Zähler *m*; *Br* Spielmarke *f*

coun·ter² Ladentisch *m*; Theke *f*; (Bank-, Post®)Schalter *m*

coun·ter³ 1. (ent)gegen, Gegen… **2.** entgegentreten (*dat*), entgegnen (*dat*), bekämpfen; abwehren

coun·ter·act entgegenwirken (*dat*); neutralisieren

coun·ter·bal·ance 1. Gegengewicht *n* **2.** ein Gegengewicht bilden zu, ausgleichen

coun·ter·clock·wise entgegen dem Uhrzeigersinn

coun·ter·es·pi·o·nage Spionageabwehr *f*

coun·ter·feit 1. falsch, gefälscht **2.** Fälschung *f* **3.** Geld, Unterschrift *etc* fälschen; ~ **mon·ey** Falschgeld *n*

coun·ter·foil Kontrollabschnitt *m*

coun·ter·mand Befehl *etc* widerrufen; Ware abbestellen

coun·ter·pane Tagesdecke *f*

coun·ter·part Gegenstück *n*; genaue Entsprechung

coun·ter·sign gegenzeichnen

count·ess Gräfin *f*

count·less zahllos

coun·try 1. Land *n*, Staat *m*; Gegend *f*, Landschaft *f*; **in the** ~ auf dem Lande **2.** Land…, ländlich

coun·try·man Landbewohner *m*; Bauer *m*; *a.* **fellow** ~ Landsmann *m*

coun·try road Landstraße *f*

coun·try·side (ländliche) Gegend; Landschaft *f*

coun·try·wom·an Landbewohnerin *f*; Bäuerin *f*; *a.* **fellow** ~ Landsmännin *f*

coun·ty (Land)Kreis *m*; *Br* Grafschaft *f*; ~ **seat** Kreis(haupt)stadt *f*; ~ **town** *Br* Grafschaftshauptstadt *f*

coup Coup *m*; Putsch *m*

cou·ple 1. Paar *n*; *a~ of* F ein paar **2.** (zusammen)koppeln; TECH kuppeln; ZO (sich) paaren

cou·pon Gutschein *m*; Kupon *m*, Bestellzettel *m*

cour·age Mut *m*

cou·ra·geous mutig, beherzt

cou·ri·er Kurier *m*, Eilbote *m*; Reiseleiter *m*

course AVIAT, MAR Kurs *m (a. fig)*; SPORT (Renn)Bahn *f*, (Renn)Strecke *f*, (Golf-)Platz *m*; Verlauf *m*; GASTR Gang *m*; Reihe *f*, Zyklus *m*; Kurs *m*, Lehrgang *m*; *of ~* natürlich, selbstverständlich; *the ~ of events* der Gang der Ereignisse, der Lauf der Dinge

court 1. Hof *m*; kleiner Platz; SPORT Platz *m*, (Spiel)Feld *n*; JUR Gericht *n*, Gerichtshof *m*; *go to ~* JUR prozessieren; *take s.o. to ~* JUR gegen j-n prozessieren; j-m den Prozess machen **2.** *j-m* den Hof machen; werben um

cour·te·ous höflich; **cour·te·sy** Höflichkeit *f*; *by ~ of* mit freundlicher Genehmigung von (*or gen*)

court·house Gerichtsgebäude *n*

court·ier Höfling *m*

court·ly höflich; höflich

court mar·tial MIL Kriegsgericht *n*

court-mar·tial MIL vor ein Kriegsgericht stellen

court·room Gerichtssaal *m*

court·ship Werben *n*

court·yard Hof *m*

cous·in Cousin *m*, Vetter *m*; Cousine *f*, Kusine *f*

cove kleine Bucht

cov·er 1. Decke *f*; Deckel *m*; Buchdeckel *m*, Einband *m*; Umschlag *m*; Titelseite *f*; Hülle *f*; Überzug *m*, Bezug *m*; Schutzhaube *f*, Schutzplatte *f*; Abdeckhaube *f*; Briefumschlag *m*; GASTR Gedeck *n*; Deckung *f*; Schutz *m*; *fig* Tarnung *f*; *take ~* in Deckung gehen; *under plain ~* in neutralem Umschlag; *under separate ~* mit getrennter Post **2.** (be-, zu)decken; einschlagen, einwickeln; verbergen; decken, schützen; ECON (ab)decken; versichern; *Thema* erschöpfend behandeln; *radio*, TV berichten über (*acc*); sich über *e-e* Fläche *etc* erstrecken; *Strecke* zurücklegen; SPORT *Gegenspieler* decken; j-n beschatten; *~ up* ab-, zudecken; *fig* ver-

heimlichen, vertuschen; *~ up for s.o.* j-n decken

cov·er·age Berichterstattung *f (of* über *acc)*

cov·er girl Covergirl *n*, Titelblattmädchen *n*

cov·er·ing Decke *f*; Überzug *m*; Hülle *f*; (Fußboden)Belag *m*

cov·er sto·ry Titelgeschichte *f*

cow¹ ZO Kuh *f*

cow² einschüchtern

cow·ard 1. feig(e) **2.** Feigling *m*

cow·ard·ice Feigheit *f*

cow·ard·ly feig(e)

cow·boy Cowboy *m*

cow·er kauern; sich ducken

cow·herd Kuhhirt *m*

cow·hide Rind(s)leder *n*

cow·house Kuhstall *m*

cowl Mönchskutte *f*; Kapuze *f*; TECH Schornsteinkappe *f*

cow·shed Kuhstall *m*

cow·slip BOT Schlüsselblume *f*; Sumpfdotterblume *f*

cox, **cox·swain** Bootsführer *m*; *rowing*: Steuermann *m*

coy schüchtern, scheu

coy·ote ZO Kojote *m*, Präriewolf *m*

co·zy 1. behaglich, gemütlich **2.** → *egg* **cosy, tea cosy**

CPU *abbr of* **central processing unit** IT Zentraleinheit *f*

crab ZO Krabbe *f*, Taschenkrebs *m*

crack 1. Knall *m*; Sprung *m*, Riss *m*; Spalt(e *f*) *m*, Ritze *f*; (heftiger) Schlag **2.** erstklassig **3.** *v/i* krachen, knallen, knacken; (zer)springen; überschnappen (*voice*); *a. ~ up* zusammenbrechen; F *~ up* überschnappen; *get ~ing* F loslegen; *v/t* knallen mit (*Peitsche*), knacken mit (*Fingern*); zerbrechen; *Nuss*, F *Kode, Safe etc* knacken; *~ a joke* e-n Witz reißen; **crack·er** GASTR Cracker *m*, Kräcker *m*; Schwär·mer *m*, Knallfrosch *m*, Knallbonbon *m*, *n*

crack·le knattern, knistern, prasseln

cra·dle 1. Wiege *f* **2.** wiegen; betten

craft¹ Boot(e *pl*) *n*, Schiff(e *pl*) *n*; Flugzeug(e *pl*) *n*; (Welt)Raumfahrzeug(e *pl*) *n*

craft² Handwerk *n*, Gewerbe *n*; Schlauheit *f*, List *f*

crafts·man (Kunst)Handwerker *m*

craft·y gerissen, listig, schlau

crag Klippe *f*, Felsenspitze *f*

cram *v/t* (voll)stopfen; nudeln, mästen; mit *j-m* pauken; *v/i* pauken, büffeln (**for** für)

cramp 1. MED Krampf *m*; TECH Klammer *f*; *fig* Fessel *f* **2.** einengen, hemmen

cran·ber·ry BOT Preiselbeere *f*

crane[1] TECH Kran *m*

crane[2] **1.** ZO Kranich *m* **2.** den Hals recken; **~ one's neck** sich den Hals verrenken (**for** nach)

crank 1. TECH Kurbel *f*; TECH Schwengel *m*; F Spinner *m*, komischer Kauz **2.** (an)kurbeln

crank·shaft TECH Kurbelwelle *f*

crank·y wack(e)lig; verschroben; schlecht gelaunt

cran·ny Riss *m*, Ritze *f*

crape Krepp *m*, Flor *m*

crash 1. Krach *m*, Krachen *n*; MOT Unfall *m*, Zusammenstoß *m*; AVIAT Absturz *m*; ECON Zusammenbruch *m*, (Börsen)Krach *m* **2.** *v/t* zertrümmern; e-n Unfall haben mit; AVIAT abstürzen mit; *v/i* krachend einstürzen, zusammenkrachen; *esp* ECON zusammenbrechen; krachen (**against, into** gegen); MOT zusammenstoßen, verunglücken; AVIAT abstürzen **3.** Schnell…, Sofort…; **~ bar·ri·er** MOT Leitplanke *f*; **~ course** Schnell-, Intensivkurs *m*; **~ di·et** radikale Schlankheitskur; **~ hel·met** Sturzhelm *m*

crash-land AVIAT e-e Bruchlandung machen (mit); **crash land·ing** AVIAT Bruchlandung *f*

crate (Latten)Kiste *f*

cra·ter Krater *m*; Trichter *m*

crave sich sehnen (**for, after** nach)

crav·ing heftiges Verlangen

craw·fish → **crayfish**

crawl 1. Kriechen *n* **2.** kriechen; krabbeln; kribbeln; wimmeln (**with** von); *swimming:* kraulen; **it makes my skin ~** F mir läuft e-e Gänsehaut über den Rücken

cray·fish ZO Flusskrebs *m*

cray·on Zeichen-, Buntstift *m*

craze Verrücktheit *f*, F Fimmel *m*; **be the ~** Mode sein

cra·zy verrückt (**about** nach)

creak knarren, quietschen

cream 1. GASTR Rahm *m*, Sahne *f*; Creme *f*; *fig* Auslese *f*, Elite *f* **2.** creme-

(-farben); **cream·y** sahnig; weich

crease 1. (Bügel)Falte *f* **2.** (zer)knittern

cre·ate (er)schaffen; hervorrufen; verursachen

cre·a·tion Schöpfung *f*

cre·a·tive schöpferisch

cre·a·tor Schöpfer *m*

crea·ture Geschöpf *n*; Kreatur *f*

crèche (Kinder)Krippe *f*; (Weihnachts)Krippe *f*

cre·den·tials Beglaubigungsschreiben *n*; Referenzen *pl*; Zeugnis *n*; Ausweis *m*, Ausweispapiere *pl*

cred·i·ble glaubwürdig

cred·it 1. Glaube(n) *m*; Ruf *m*, Ansehen *n*; Verdienst *n*; ECON Kredit *m*; Guthaben *n*; **~ (side)** Kredit(seite *f*) *n*, Haben *n*; **on ~** auf Kredit **2.** *j-m* glauben; *j-m* trauen; ECON gutschreiben; **~ s.o. with s.th.** *j-m* et. zutrauen; *j-m* et. zuschreiben

cred·i·ta·ble achtbar, ehrenvoll (**to** für)

cred·it card ECON Kreditkarte *f*

cred·i·tor ECON Gläubiger *m*

cred·its *film*: Vorspann *m*, Nachspann *m*

cred·it·wor·thy ECON kreditwürdig

cred·u·lous leichtgläubig

creed REL Glaubensbekenntnis *n*

creek Bach *m*; *Br* kleine Bucht

creep kriechen; schleichen (*a. fig*); **~ in** (sich) hinein- *or* hereinschleichen; sich einschleichen (*mistake etc*); **it makes my flesh ~** mir läuft e-e Gänsehaut über den Rücken

creep·er BOT Kriech-, Kletterpflanze *f*

creep·y unheimlich

cre·mate verbrennen, einäschern

cres·cent Halbmond *m*

cress BOT Kresse *f*

crest ZO Haube *f*, Büschel *n*; (*Hahnen*)Kamm *m*; Bergrücken *m*, Kamm *m*; (*Wellen*)Kamm *m*; Federbusch *m*; **fam·ily ~** Familienwappen *n*

crest·fal·len niedergeschlagen

cre·vasse GEOL (Gletscher)Spalte *f*

crev·ice GEOL Riss *m*, Spalte *f*

crew AVIAT, MAR Besatzung *f*, Crew *f*, MAR Mannschaft *f*

crib 1. (Futter)Krippe *f*; Kinderbettchen *n*; *esp Br* (Weihnachts)Krippe *f*; F PED Spickzettel *m* **2.** F abschreiben, spicken

crick **a ~ in one's back** (**neck**) ein steifer Rücken (Hals)

crick·et[1] zo Grille *f*

crick·et[2] SPORT Kricket *n*

crime JUR Verbrechen *n*; *coll* Verbrechen *pl*; ~ **nov·el** Kriminalroman *m*

crim·i·nal 1. kriminell; Kriminal..., Straf... **2.** Verbrecher(in), Kriminelle *m, f*

crimp kräuseln

crim·son karmesinrot; puterrot

cringe sich ducken

crin·kle 1. Falte *f*, Fältchen *n* **2.** (sich) kräuseln; knittern

crip·ple 1. Krüppel *m* **2.** zum Krüppel machen; *fig* lähmen

cri·sis Krise *f*

crisp knusp(e)rig, mürbe; frisch, knackig (*vegetable*); scharf, frisch (*air*); kraus (*hair*)

crisp·bread Knäckebrot *n*

crisps *a.* **potato** ~ *Br* (Kartoffel)Chips *pl*

criss-cross 1. Netz *n* sich schneidender Linien **2.** kreuz und quer ziehen durch; kreuz und quer (ver)laufen

cri·te·ri·on Kriterium *n*

crit·ic Kritiker(in)

crit·i·cal kritisch; bedenklich

crit·i·cis·m Kritik *f* (**of** an *dat*)

crit·i·cize kritisieren; kritisch beurteilen; tadeln

cri·tique Kritik *f*, Besprechung *f*, Rezension *f*

croak zo krächzen; quaken (*both a. fig*)

cro·chet 1. Häkelei *f*; Häkelarbeit *f* **2.** häkeln

crock·e·ry Geschirr *n*

croc·o·dile zo Krokodil *n*

cro·ny F alter Freund

crook 1. Krümmung *f*; Hirtenstab *m*; F Gauner *m* **2.** (sich) krümmen *or* biegen; **crook·ed** gekrümmt krumm; F unehrlich, betrügerisch

croon schmachtend singen; summen

croon·er Schnulzensänger(in)

crop 1. AGR (Feld)Frucht *f*; Ernte *f*; zo Kropf *m*; kurzer Haarschnitt; kurz geschnittenes Haar **2.** zo abfressen, abweiden; *Haar* kurz schneiden; ~ **up** *fig* plötzlich auftauchen

cross 1. Kreuz *n* (*a. fig*); BIOL Kreuzung *f*; *soccer:* Flanke *f* **2.** böse, ärgerlich **3.** (sich) kreuzen; *Straße* überqueren; *Plan etc* durchkreuzen; BIOL kreuzen;

~ **off**, ~ **out** ausstreichen, durchstreichen; ~ **o.s.** sich bekreuzigen; ~ **one's arms** die Arme verschränken; ~ **one's legs** die Beine übereinanderschlagen; **keep one's fingers** ~**ed** den Daumen drücken

cross·bar SPORT Tor-, Querlatte *f*

cross·breed Mischling *m*, Kreuzung *f*

cross-coun·try Querfeldein..., Gelände...; ~ **skiing** Skilanglauf *m*

cross-ex·am·i·na·tion JUR Kreuzverhör *n*; **cross-ex·am·ine** JUR ins Kreuzverhör nehmen

cross-eyed: be ~ schielen

cross·ing (*Straßen- etc*)Kreuzung *f*; Straßenübergang *m*; *Br* Fußgängerüberweg *m*; MAR Überfahrt *f*

cross·road Querstraße *f*

cross·roads (Straßen)Kreuzung *f*; *fig* Scheideweg *m*

cross-sec·tion Querschnitt *m*

cross·walk Fußgängerüberweg *m*

cross·wise kreuzweise

cross·word (puz·zle) Kreuzworträtsel *n*

crotch ANAT Schritt *m*

crotch·et MUS *Br* Viertelnote *f*

crouch 1. sich ducken **2.** Hockstellung *f*

crow 1. zo Krähe *f*; Krähen *n* **2.** krähen

crow·bar TECH Brecheisen *n*

crowd 1. (Menschen)Menge *f*; Masse *f*; Haufen *m* **2.** sich drängen; *Straßen etc* bevölkern; vollstopfen

crowd·ed überfüllt, voll

crown 1. Krone *f* **2.** krönen; *Zahn* überkronen; **to** ~ **it all** zu allem Überfluss

cru·cial entscheidend, kritisch

cru·ci·fix REL Kruzifix *n*

cru·ci·fix·ion REL Kreuzigung *f*

cru·ci·fy REL kreuzigen

crude roh, unbearbeitet; *fig* roh, grob

crude (oil) Rohöl *n*

cru·el grausam; roh, gefühllos

cru·el·ty Grausamkeit *f*; ~ **to animals** Tierquälerei *f*; **society for the prevention of** ~ **to animals** Tierschutzverein *m*; ~ **to children** Kindesmisshandlung *f*

cru·et Essig-, Ölfläschchen *n*

cruise 1. Kreuzfahrt *f*, Seereise *f* **2.** kreuzen, e-e Kreuzfahrt *or* Seereise machen; AVIAT, MOT mit Reisegeschwindigkeit fliegen *or* fahren; ~ **mis·sile** MIL Marschflugkörper *m*

cruis·er Kreuzfahrtschiff *n*; MIL MAR

Kreuzer *m*; (Funk)Streifenwagen *m*

crumb Krume *f*, Krümel *m*

crum·ble zerkrümeln, zerbröckeln

crum·ple *v/t* zerknittern; *v/i* knittern; zusammengedrückt werden; ~ **zone** MOT Knautschzone *f*

crunch geräuschvoll (zer)kauen; knirschen

cru·sade HIST Kreuzzug *m* (*a. fig*)

crush 1. Gedränge *n*; *have a ~ on s.o.* für j-n schwärmen, F in j-n verknallt sein **2.** *v/t* zerquetschen, zermalmen, zerdrücken; TECH zerkleinern, zermahlen; auspressen; *fig* nieder-, zerschmettern, vernichten; *v/i* sich drängen; ~ **bar·ri·er** Barriere *f*, Absperrung *f*

crust (Brot)Kruste *f*, (Brot)Rinde *f*

crus·ta·cean ZO Krebs-, Krusten-, Schalentier *n*

crust·y krustig

crutch Krücke *f*

cry 1. Schrei *m*, Ruf *m*; Geschrei *n*; Weinen *n* **2.** schreien, rufen (*for* nach); weinen; heulen, jammern

crypt Gruft *f*, Krypta *f*

crys·tal Kristall *m*; Uhrglas *n*

crys·tal·line kristallen

crys·tal·lize kristallisieren

cub ZO Junge *n*

cube Würfel *m* (*a.* MATH); PHOT Blitzwürfel *m*; MATH Kubikzahl *f*

cube root MATH Kubikwurzel *f*

cu·bic, cu·bi·cal würfelförmig; kubisch; Kubik...

cu·bi·cle Kabine *f*

cuck·oo ZO Kuckuck *m*

cu·cum·ber BOT Gurke *f*; (*as*) *cool as a* ~ F eiskalt, kühl und gelassen

cud AGR wiedergekäutes Futter; *chew the* ~ wiederkäuen; *fig* überlegen

cud·dle *v/t* an sich drücken; schmusen mit; *v/i:* ~ *up* sich kuscheln *or* schmiegen (*to* an *acc*)

cud·gel 1. Knüppel *m* **2.** prügeln

cue[1] THEA *etc* Stichwort *n* (*a. fig*); *fig* Wink *m*

cue[2] *billiards:* Queue *n*

cuff[1] Manschette *f*; (Hosen-, *Br* Ärmel-) Aufschlag *m*

cuff[2] **1.** Klaps *m* **2.** *j-m* e-n Klaps geben

cuff link Manschettenknopf *m*

cui·sine GASTR Küche *f*

cul·mi·nate gipfeln (*in* in *dat*)

cu·lottes (*a pair of* ein) Hosenrock *m*

cul·prit Schuldige *m, f*, Täter(in)

cul·ti·vate AGR anbauen, bebauen; kultivieren; *Freundschaft etc* pflegen

cul·ti·vat·ed AGR bebaut; *fig* gebildet, kultiviert

cul·ti·va·tion AGR Kultivierung *f*, Anbau *m*; *fig* Pflege *f*

cul·tu·ral kulturell; Kultur...

cul·ture Kultur *f* (*a.* BIOL); ZO Zucht *f*

cul·tured kultiviert; gezüchtet, Zucht...

cum·ber·some lästig, hinderlich; klobig

cu·mu·la·tive sich (an)häufend, anwachsend; Zusatz...

cun·ning 1. schlau, listig **2.** List *f*, Schlauheit *f*

cup 1. Tasse *f*; Becher *m*; Schale *f*; Kelch *m*; SPORT Cup *m*, Pokal *m* **2.** *die Hand* hohl machen; *she~ped her chin in her hand* sie stützte das Kinn in die Hand

cup·board (Geschirr-, Speise-, *Br a.* Wäsche-, Kleider)Schrank *m*

cup·board bed Schrankbett *n*

cup fi·nal SPORT Pokalendspiel *n*

cu·po·la ARCH Kuppel *f*

cup tie SPORT Pokalspiel *n*

cup win·ner SPORT Pokalsieger *m*

cur Köter *m*; Schurke *m*

cu·ra·ble MED heilbar

cu·rate REL Hilfsgeistliche *m*

cu·ra·tive heilkräftig; ~ *power* Heilkraft *f*

curb 1. Kandare *f* (*a. fig*); Bordstein *m* **2.** an die Kandare legen (*a. fig*); *fig* zügeln

curd *a. pl* Dickmilch *f*, Quark *m*

cur·dle *v/t Milch* gerinnen lassen; *v/i* gerinnen, dick werden; *the sight made my blood* ~ bei dem Anblick erstarrte mir das Blut in den Adern

cure 1. MED Kur *f*; (Heil)Mittel *n*; Heilung *f* **2.** MED heilen; GASTR pökeln; räuchern; trocknen

cur·few MIL Ausgangsverbot *n*, -sperre *f*

cu·ri·o Rarität *f*

cu·ri·os·i·ty Neugier *f*; Rarität *f*

cu·ri·ous neugierig; wissbegierig; seltsam, merkwürdig

curl 1. Locke *f* **2.** (sich) kräuseln *or* locken; **curl·er** Lockenwickler *m*; **curl·y** gekräuselt; gelockt, lockig

cur·rant BOT Johannisbeere *f*; GASTR Korinthe *f*

cur·ren·cy ECON Währung *f*; *foreign* ~ Devisen *pl*

cur·rent 1. laufend; gegenwärtig, aktuell; üblich, gebräuchlich; **~ events** Tagesereignisse *pl* **2.** Strömung *f*, Strom *m* (*both a. fig*); ELECTR Strom *m*; **~ account** *Br* ECON Girokonto *n*

cur·ric·u·lum Lehr-, Stundenplan *m*; **~ vi·tae** Lebenslauf *m*

cur·ry[1] GASTR Curry *m*, *n*

cur·ry[2] *Pferd* striegeln

curse 1. Fluch *m*, Verwünschung *f* **2.** (ver)fluchen, verwünschen

curs·ed verflucht

cur·sor IT Cursor *m*

cur·so·ry flüchtig, oberflächlich

curt knapp; barsch, schroff

cur·tail *Ausgaben etc* kürzen; *Rechte* beschneiden

cur·tain 1. Vorhang *m*, Gardine *f*; **draw the ~s** die Vorhänge auf- *or* zuziehen **2.** **~ off** von Vorhängen abteilen

curt·s(e)y 1. Knicks *m* **2.** knicksen (**to** vor *dat*)

cur·va·ture Krümmung *f*

curve 1. Kurve *f*; Krümmung *f*, Biegung *f* **2.** (sich) krümmen *or* biegen

cush·ion 1. Kissen *n*, Polster *n* **2.** polstern; *Stoß etc* dämpfen

cuss 1. Fluch *m* **2.** (ver)fluchen

cus·tard Eiercreme *f*, Vanillesoße *f*

cus·to·dy JUR Haft *f*; Sorgerecht *n*

cus·tom Brauch *m*, Gewohnheit *f*; ECON Kundschaft *f*

cus·tom·a·ry üblich

cus·tom-built nach Kundenangaben gefertigt

cus·tom·er Kunde *m*, Kundin *f*, Auftraggeber(in)

cus·tom house Zollamt *n*

cus·tom-made maßgefertigt, Maß...

cus·toms Zoll *m*; **~ clear·ance** Zollabfertigung *f*; **~ of·fi·cer**, **~ of·fi·cial** Zollbeamte *m*

cut 1. Schnitt *m*; MED Schnittwunde *f*; GASTR Schnitte *f*, Stück *n*; (Zu)Schnitt *m* (*clothes*); TECH Schnitt *m*, Schliff *m*; Haarschnitt *m*; *fig* Kürzung *f*, Senkung *f*; *cards*: Abheben *n* **2.** schneiden; ab-, an-, auf-, aus-, be-, durch-, zer-, zuschneiden; *Edelstein etc* schleifen; *Gras* mähen, *Bäume* fällen, *Holz* hacken; MOT *Kurve* schneiden; *Löhne etc* kürzen; *Preise* herabsetzen, senken; *Karten* abheben; **~ one's teeth** Zähne bekommen, zahnen; **~ s.o.** (**dead**) *fig* F

j-n schneiden; **~ s.o.** *or* **s.th. short** j-n *or* et. unterbrechen, j-m ins Wort fallen; **~ across** quer durch ... gehen; **~ back** *Pflanze* beschneiden, stutzen; einschränken; **~ down** *Bäume* fällen; verringern, einschränken, reduzieren; **~ in** F sich einmischen, unterbrechen; **~ in on s.o.** MOT j-n schneiden; **~ off** abschneiden; unterbrechen, trennen; *Strom etc* sperren; **~ out** (her)ausschneiden; *Kleid etc* zuschneiden; **be ~ out for** wie geschaffen sein für; **~ up** zerschneiden

cut·back Kürzung *f*

cute F schlau; niedlich, süß

cu·ti·cle Nagelhaut *f*

cut·le·ry (Ess)Besteck *n*

cut·let GASTR Kotelett *n*; (*Kalbs-, Schweine*)Schnitzel *n*; Hacksteak *n*

cut-off date Stichtag *m*

cut-price, **cut-rate** ECON herabgesetzt, ermäßigt; Billig...

cut·ter Zuschneider *m*; (*Glas-, Diamant*)Schleifer *m*; Schneidemaschine *f*, -werkzeug *n*; *film*: Cutter(in); MAR Kutter *m*

cut·throat 1. Mörder *m*; Killer *m* **2.** mörderisch

cut·ting 1. schneidend; scharf; TECH Schneid(e)..., Fräs... **2.** Schneiden *n*; BOT Steckling *m*; *esp Br* Ausschnitt *m*

cut·tings Schnipsel *pl*; Späne *pl*

cut·ting torch TECH Schneidbrenner *m*

Cy·ber·space → virtual reality

cy·cle[1] Zyklus *m*; Kreis(lauf) *m*

cy·cle[2] **1.** Fahrrad *n* **2.** Rad fahren

cy·cle| path, **~ track** (Fahr)Radweg *m*

cy·cling Radfahren *n*

cy·clist Radfahrer(in); Motorradfahrer(in)

cy·clone Wirbelsturm *m*

cyl·in·der Zylinder *m*, TECH *a*. Walze *f*, Trommel *f*

cyn·ic Zyniker(in); **cyn·i·cal** zynisch; **cyn·i·cism** Zynismus *m*

cy·press BOT Zypresse *f*

cyst MED Zyste *f*

czar → tsar

Czech 1. tschechisch; **~ Republic** Tschechien *n*, Tschechische Republik **2.** Tscheche *m*, Tschechin *f*; LING Tschechisch *n*

D

D, d D, d n

d *abbr of* **died** gest., gestorben

dab 1. Klecks m, Spritzer m **2.** betupfen, abtupfen

dab·ble bespritzen; **~ at, ~ in** sich oberflächlich *or contp* in dilettantischer Weise beschäftigen mit

dachs·hund zo Dackel m

dad F, **dad·dy** F Papa m, Vati m

dad·dy long·legs zo Schnake f; Weberknecht m

daf·fo·dil bot gelbe Narzisse

dag·ger Dolch m; **be at ~s drawn** fig auf Kriegsfuß stehen (**with** mit)

dai·ly 1. täglich; **the ~ grind** *or* **rut** das tägliche Einerlei **2.** Tageszeitung f; Putzfrau f

dain·ty 1. zierlich, reizend; wählerisch **2.** Leckerbissen m

dair·y Molkerei f; Milchwirtschaft f; Milchgeschäft n

dai·sy bot Gänseblümchen n

dal·ly: ~ about herumtrödeln

dam 1. (Stau)Damm m **2.** *a.* **~ up** stauen, eindämmen

dam·age 1. Schaden m, (Be)Schädigung f; *pl* jur Schadenersatz **2.** (be)schädigen

dam·ask Damast m

damn 1. verdammen; verurteilen; **~** (**it**)**!** F verflucht!, verdammt! **2.** *adj and adv* F → **damned 3.** **I don't give a ~** F das ist mir völlig gleich(gültig) *or* egal

dam·na·tion Verdammung f; rel Verdammnis f

damned F verdammt

damn·ing vernichtend, belastend

damp 1. feucht, klamm **2.** Feuchtigkeit f **3.** *a.* **damp·en** an-, befeuchten; dämpfen; **damp·ness** Feuchtigkeit f

dance 1. Tanz m; Tanzveranstaltung f **2.** tanzen

danc·er Tänzer(in)

danc·ing 1. Tanzen n **2.** Tanz...

dan·de·li·on bot Löwenzahn m

dan·druff (Kopf)Schuppen pl

Dane Däne m, Dänin f

dan·ger Gefahr f; **be out of ~** außer Lebensgefahr sein; **~ ar·e·a** Gefahrenzone f, Gefahrenbereich m

dan·ger·ous gefährlich

dan·ger zone → danger area

dan·gle baumeln (lassen)

Da·nish 1. dänisch **2.** ling Dänisch n

dank feucht, nass(kalt)

dare *v/i* es wagen, sich (ge)trauen; **I ~ say** ich glaube wohl; allerdings; **how ~ you!** was fällt dir ein!; untersteh dich!; *v/t et.* wagen

dare·dev·il Draufgänger m

dar·ing 1. kühn, verwegen, waghalsig **2.** Mut m, Kühnheit f, Verwegenheit f

dark 1. dunkel; finster; *fig* düster, trüb(e); geheim(nisvoll) **2.** Dunkel n, Dunkelheit f; **before** (**at, after**) **~** vor (bei, nach) Einbruch der Dunkelheit; **keep s.o. in the ~ about s.th.** j-n über et. im Ungewissen lassen

Dark Ag·es das frühe Mittelalter

dark·en (sich) verdunkeln *or* verfinstern

dark·ness Dunkelheit f, Finsternis f

dark·room phot Dunkelkammer f

dar·ling 1. Liebling m **2.** lieb; F goldig

darn stopfen, ausbessern

dart 1. Wurfpfeil m; Sprung m, Satz m; **~s** Darts n **2.** *v/t* werfen, schleudern; *v/i* schießen, stürzen

dart·board Dartsscheibe f

dash 1. Schlag m; Klatschen n; gastr Prise f (*of* salt), Schuss m (*of* rum *etc*), Spritzer m (*of lemon etc*); Gedankenstrich m; sport Sprint m; *fig* Anflug m; **a ~ of blue** ein Stich ins Blaue; **make a ~ for** losstürzen auf (*acc*) **2.** *v/t* schleudern, schmettern; *Hoffnung etc* zerstören, zunichtemachen; *v/i* stürmen; **~ off** davonstürzen

dash·board mot Armaturenbrett n

dash·ing schneidig, forsch

da·ta Daten *pl* (*a.* it), Angaben *pl*; **~ base** it Datenbank f; **~ car·ri·er** Datenträger m; **~ in·put** Dateneingabe f; **~ me·di·um** Datenträger m; **~ mem·o·ry** Datenspeicher m; **~ out·put** Datenausgabe f; **~ pro·cess·ing** Datenverarbeitung f; **~ pro·tec·tion** jur Datenschutz m; **~ stor·age** Datenspeicher m; **~ trans·fer** Datenübertragung f

date¹ bot Dattel f

date² 1. Datum n; Zeit f, Zeitpunkt m;

Termin *m*; Verabredung *f*; F (Verabredungs)Partner(in); *out of* ~ veraltet, unmodern; *up to* ~ zeitgemäß, modern, auf dem Laufenden **2.** datieren; F sich verabreden mit, (aus)gehen mit

dat·ed veraltet, überholt

da·tive *a.* ~ *case* LING Dativ *m*, dritter Fall

daub (be)schmieren

daugh·ter Tochter *f*

daugh·ter-in-law Schwiegertochter *f*

daunt entmutigen

dav·en·port Sofa *n*

daw zo Dohle *f*

daw·dle F (herum)trödeln

dawn 1. (Morgen)Dämmerung *f*; *at* ~ bei Tagesanbruch **2.** dämmern; ~ *on* fig *j*-m dämmern

day Tag *m*; *often pl* (Lebens)Zeit *f*; *any* ~ jederzeit; *these* ~*s* heutzutage; *the other* ~ neulich; *the* ~ *after tomorrow* übermorgen; *the* ~ *before yesterday* vorgestern; *open all* ~ durchgehend geöffnet; *let's call it a* ~*!* machen wir Schluss für heute!, Feierabend!

day·break Tagesanbruch *m*

day care cen·ter (*Br* cen·tre) → *day nursery*

day·dream 1. Tag-, Wachtraum *m* **2.** (mit offenen Augen) träumen

day·dream·er Träumer(in)

day·light Tageslicht *n*; *in broad* ~ am helllichten Tag

day nur·se·ry (Kinder)Tagesstätte *f*

day off freier Tag

day re·turn *Br* Tagesrückfahrkarte *f*

day·time: *in the* ~ am Tag, bei Tage

daze 1. blenden; betäuben **2.** *in a* ~ benommen, betäubt

dead 1. tot; unempfindlich (*to* für); matt; blind (*window etc*); erloschen; ECON flau; tot (*capital etc*); völlig, total; *drop* ~ tot umfallen **2.** *adv* völlig, total; plötzlich, abrupt; genau, direkt; ~ *slow* MOT Schritt fahren!; ~ *tired* todmüde **3.** *the* ~ die Toten *pl*

dead·en abstumpfen; (ab)schwächen; dämpfen

dead end Sackgasse *f* (*a. fig*)

dead heat SPORT totes Rennen

dead·line letzter (Ablieferungs)Termin; Stichtag *m*

dead·lock fig toter Punkt

dead·locked fig festgefahren

dead·ly tödlich

deaf 1. taub **2.** *the* ~ die Tauben *pl*

deaf-and-dumb taubstumm

deaf·en taub machen; betäuben

deaf-mute Taubstumme *m*, *f*

deal 1. F Geschäft *n*, Handel *m*; Menge *f*; *it's a* ~*!* abgemacht!; *a good* ~ ziemlich viel; *a great* ~ sehr viel **2.** *v/t* (aus-, ver-, zu)teilen; *j*-m Karten geben; *j*-m *e*-*n Schlag* versetzen; *v/i* handeln (*in* mit *e*-*r Ware*); *sl* dealen; *cards*: geben; ~ *with* sich befassen mit, behandeln; ECON Handel treiben mit, Geschäfte machen mit; *deal·er* ECON Händler(in); *cards*: Geber(in); *sl* Dealer *m*; *deal·ing mst pl* Umgang *m*, Beziehungen *pl*

dean REL, UNIV Dekan *m*

dear 1. teuer; lieb; *Dear Sir* Sehr geehrter Herr … **2.** Liebste *m*, *f*, Schatz *m*; *my* ~ *e*-e Liebe, mein Lieber **3.** *int* (oh) ~*!*, ~ *me!* F du liebe Zeit!, ach herrje!; *dear·est* sehnlichst; *dear·ly* innig, von ganzem Herzen; ECON teuer

death Tod *m*; Todesfall *m*

death·bed Sterbebett *n*

death cer·tif·i·cate Totenschein *m*

death·ly tödlich; ~ *still* totenstill

death war·rant JUR Hinrichtungsbefehl *m*; fig Todesurteil *n*

de·bar: ~ *s.o. from* *j*-n ausschließen aus

de·base erniedrigen; mindern

de·ba·ta·ble umstritten

de·bate 1. Debatte *f*, Diskussion *f* **2.** debattieren, diskutieren

deb·it ECON **1.** Soll *n*; (Konto)Belastung *f*; ~ *and credit* Soll und Haben *n* **2.** *j*-*n*, *ein Konto* belasten

deb·ris Trümmer *pl*, Schutt *m*

debt Schuld *f*; *be in* ~ Schulden haben, verschuldet sein; *be out of* ~ schuldenfrei sein; *get into* ~ sich verschulden, Schulden machen

debt·or Schuldner(in)

de·bug TECH, IT Fehler beseitigen

de·but Debüt *n*

Dec *abbr of* **December** Dez., Dezember *m*

dec·ade Jahrzehnt *n*

dec·a·dent dekadent

de·caf·fein·at·ed koffeinfrei

de·camp F verschwinden

de·cant abgießen; umfüllen

de·cant·er Karaffe *f*

de·cath·lete SPORT Zehnkämpfer *m*

de·cath·lon SPORT Zehnkampf *m*
de·cay 1. zerfallen; verfaulen; kariös *or* schlecht werden (*tooth*) 2. Zerfall *m*; Verfaulen *n*
de·cease *esp* JUR Tod *m*, Ableben *n*
de·ceased *esp* JUR 1. *the~* der *or* die Verstorbene; die Verstorbenen *pl* 2. verstorben
de·ceit Betrug *m*; Täuschung *f*
de·ceit·ful betrügerisch
de·ceive betrügen; täuschen
de·ceiv·er Betrüger(in)
De·cem·ber (*abbr* *Dec*) Dezember *m*
de·cen·cy Anstand *m*
de·cent anständig; F annehmbar, (ganz) anständig; F nett
de·cep·tion Täuschung *f*
de·cep·tive trügerisch; *be* ~ täuschen, trügen
de·cide (sich) entscheiden; bestimmen; beschließen, sich entschließen
de·cid·ed entschieden; bestimmt; entschlossen
dec·i·mal MATH 1. *a.* ~ *fraction* Dezimalbruch *m* 2. Dezimal...
de·ci·pher entziffern
de·ci·sion Entscheidung *f*; Entschluss *m*; Entschlossenheit *f*; *make a* ~ e-e Entscheidung treffen; *reach* or *come to a* ~ zu e-m Entschluss kommen
de·ci·sive entscheidend; ausschlaggebend; entschieden
deck 1. MAR Deck *n*; Spiel *n*, Pack *m* (Spiel)Karten 2. ~ *out* schmücken
deck·chair Liegestuhl *m*
dec·la·ra·tion Erklärung *f*; Zollerklärung *f*; **de·clare** erklären; deklarieren, verzollen
de·clen·sion LING Deklination *f*
de·cline 1. abnehmen, zurückgehen; fallen; verfallen; (höflich) ablehnen; LING deklinieren 2. Abnahme *f*, Rückgang *m*, Verfall *m*
de·cliv·i·ty (Ab)Hang *m*
de·clutch MOT auskuppeln
de·code entschlüsseln
de·com·pose zerlegen; (sich) zersetzen; verwesen
de·con·tam·i·nate entgasen, entgiften, entseuchen, entstrahlen
de·con·tam·i·na·tion Entseuchung *f*
dec·o·rate verzieren, schmücken; tapezieren; (an)streichen; dekorieren
dec·o·ra·tion Verzierung *f*, Schmuck *m*,

Dekoration *f*; Orden *m*
dec·o·ra·tive dekorativ; Zier...
dec·o·ra·tor Dekorateur *m*; Maler *m* und Tapezierer *m*
de·co·rous anständig
de·co·rum Anstand *m*
de·coy 1. Lockvogel *m* (*a*, *fig*); Köder *m* (*a. fig*) 2. ködern; locken (*into* in *acc*); verleiten (*into* zu)
de·crease 1. Abnahme *f* 2. abnehmen; (sich) vermindern
de·cree 1. Dekret *n*, Erlass *m*, Verfügung *f*; *esp* JUR Entscheid *m*, Urteil *n* 2. verfügen
ded·i·cate widmen
ded·i·cat·ed engagiert
ded·i·ca·tion Widmung *f*; Hingabe *f*
de·duce ableiten; folgern
de·duct *Betrag* abziehen (*from* von); **de·duct·i·ble**: *tax-~* steuerlich absetzbar; **de·duc·tion** Abzug *m*; (Schluss)Folgerung *f*, Schluss *m*
deed Tat *f*; Heldentat *f*; JUR (Übertragungs)Urkunde *f*
deep 1. tief (*a. fig*) 2. Tiefe *f*
deep·en (sich) vertiefen, *fig a.* (sich) verstärken
deep freeze 1. tiefkühlen, einfrieren 2. Tiefkühl-, Gefriertruhe *f*
deep-fro·zen tiefgefroren
deep fry frittieren
deep·ness Tiefe *f*
deer zo Hirsch *m*; Reh *n*
de·face entstellen; unleserlich machen; ausstreichen
def·a·ma·tion Verleumdung *f*
de·fault 1. JUR Nichterscheinen *n* vor Gericht; SPORT Nichtantreten *n*; ECON Verzug *m* 2. s-n Verpflichtungen nicht nachkommen, ECON *a.* im Verzug sein; JUR nicht vor Gericht erscheinen; SPORT nicht antreten
de·feat 1. Niederlage *f* 2. besiegen, schlagen; vereiteln, zunichtemachen
de·fect Defekt *m*, Fehler *m*; Mangel *m*
de·fec·tive mangelhaft; schadhaft, defekt
de·fence *Br* → **defense**
de·fence·less *Br* → **defenseless**
de·fend (*from*, *against*) verteidigen (gegen), schützen (vor *dat*, gegen)
de·fen·dant Angeklagte *m*, *f*; Beklagte *m*, *f*
de·fend·er Verteidiger(in); SPORT Ab-

wehrspieler(in)

de·fense Verteidigung *f* (*a.* MIL, JUR, SPORT), Schutz *m*; SPORT Abwehr *f*; ***wit·ness for the* ~** Entlastungszeuge *m*

de·fense·less schutzlos, wehrlos

de·fen·sive 1. Defensive *f*, Verteidigung *f*, Abwehr *f* **2.** defensiv; Verteidigungs…, Abwehr…

de·fer aufschieben, verschieben

de·fi·ance Herausforderung *f*; Trotz *m*

de·fi·ant herausfordernd; trotzig

de·fi·cien·cy Unzulänglichkeit *f*; Mangel *m*

de·fi·cient mangelhaft, unzureichend

def·i·cit ECON Defizit *n*, Fehlbetrag *m*

de·file beschmutzen

de·fine definieren; erklären, bestimmen

def·i·nite bestimmt; endgültig, definitiv

def·i·ni·tion Definition *f*, Bestimmung *f*, Erklärung *f*

de·fin·i·tive endgültig, definitiv

de·flect *v/t* ablenken; *Ball* abfälschen; *v/i* abweichen

de·form entstellen, verunstalten

de·formed deformiert, verunstaltet; verwachsen

de·for·mi·ty Missbildung *f*

de·fraud betrügen (*of* um)

de·frost *v/t* Windschutzscheibe *etc* entfrosten; *Kühlschrank etc* abtauen, *Tiefkühlkost etc* auftauen; *v/i* ab-, auftauen

deft geschickt, gewandt

de·fy herausfordern; trotzen (*dat*)

de·gen·er·ate 1. entarten **2.** entartet

deg·ra·da·tion Erniedrigung *f*

de·grade erniedrigen, demütigen

de·gree Grad *m*; Stufe *f*; (akademischer) Grad; ***by* ~s** allmählich; ***take one's* ~** e-n akademischen Grad erwerben, promovieren

de·hy·drate austrocknen; TECH das Wasser entziehen (*dat*)

de·i·fy vergöttern; vergöttlichen

deign sich herablassen

de·i·ty Gottheit *f*

de·ject·ed niedergeschlagen, mutlos, deprimiert

de·jec·tion Niedergeschlagenheit *f*

de·lay 1. Aufschub *m*; Verzögerung *f*; RAIL *etc* Verspätung *f* **2.** ver-, aufschieben; verzögern; aufhalten; *be·~ed* sich verzögern; RAIL *etc* Verspätung haben

del·e·gate 1. abordnen, delegieren; *Voll-*

machten etc übertragen **2.** Delegierte *m*, *f*, bevollmächtigter Vertreter

del·e·ga·tion Übertragung *f*; Abordnung *f*, Delegation *f*

de·lete (aus)streichen; IT löschen

de·lib·e·rate absichtlich, vorsätzlich; bedächtig, besonnen

de·lib·e·ra·tion Überlegung *f*; Beratung *f*; Bedächtigkeit *f*

del·i·ca·cy Delikatesse *f*, Leckerbissen *m*; Zartheit *f*; Feingefühl *n*, Takt *m*

del·i·cate delikat (*a. fig*), schmackhaft; zart; fein; zierlich; zerbrechlich; heikel; empfindlich

del·i·ca·tes·sen Delikatessen *pl*, Feinkost *f*; Feinkostgeschäft *n*

de·li·cious köstlich

de·light 1. Vergnügen *n*, Entzücken *n* **2.** entzücken, erfreuen; ~ *in* (große) Freude haben an (*dat*)

de·light·ful entzückend

de·lin·quen·cy Kriminalität *f*

de·lin·quent 1. straffällig **2.** Straffällige *m*, *f*; → *juvenile 1*

de·lir·i·ous MED im Delirium, fantasierend; **de·lir·i·um** MED Delirium *n*

de·liv·er ausliefern, (ab)liefern; *Briefe* zustellen; *Rede etc* halten; befreien, erlösen; *be ~ed of* MED entbunden werden von

de·liv·er·ance Befreiung *f*

de·liv·er·er Befreier(in)

de·liv·er·y (Ab-, Aus)Lieferung *f*; *post* Zustellung *f*; Halten *n* (e-r Rede); Vortrag(sweise *f*) *m*; MED Entbindung *f*

de·liv·er·y van *Br* MOT Lieferwagen *m*

dell kleines Tal

de·lude täuschen

del·uge Überschwemmung *f*; *fig* Flut *f*

de·lu·sion Täuschung *f*; Wahn(vorstellung *f*) *m*

de·mand 1. Forderung *f* (*for* nach); Anforderung *f* (*on* an *acc*); Nachfrage *f* (*for* nach), Bedarf *m* (*for* an *dat*); *on* ~ auf Verlangen **2.** verlangen, fordern; (*fordernd*) fragen nach; erfordern

de·mand·ing anspruchsvoll

de·ment·ed wahnsinnig

dem·i·… Halb…, halb…

de·mil·i·ta·rize entmilitarisieren

dem·o F Demo *f*

de·mo·bi·lize demobilisieren

de·moc·ra·cy Demokratie *f*

dem·o·crat Demokrat(in)

dem·o·crat·ic demokratisch

de·mol·ish demolieren; ab-, ein-, niederreißen; zerstören

dem·o·li·tion Demolierung *f*; Niederreißen *n*, Abbruch *m*

de·mon Dämon *m*; Teufel *m*

dem·on·strate demonstrieren; beweisen; zeigen; vorführen

dem·on·stra·tion Demonstration *f*, *a.* Kundgebung *f*, *a.* Vorführung *f*; ~ **car** *Br* Vorführwagen *m*

dem·on·stra·tor Demonstrant(in); Vorführer(in); MOT Vorführwagen *m*

de·mor·al·ize demoralisieren

de·mote degradieren

de·mure ernst, zurückhaltend

den ZO Höhle *f* (*a. fig*); F Bude *f*

de·ni·al Ablehnung *f*; Leugnen *n*; Verweigerung *f*; *official* ~ Dementi *n*

den·ims Jeans *pl*

Den·mark Dänemark *n*

de·nom·i·na·tion REL Konfession *f*; ECON Nennwert *m*

de·note bezeichnen; bedeuten

de·nounce (öffentlich) anprangern

dense dicht; *fig* beschränkt, begriffsstutzig; **den·si·ty** Dichte *f*

dent 1. Beule *f*, Delle *f* **2.** ver-, einbeulen

den·tal Zahn…; ~ **plaque** Zahnbelag *m*; ~ **plate** (Zahn)Prothese *f*; ~ **surgeon** Zahnarzt *m*, Zahnärztin *f*

den·tist Zahnarzt *m*, Zahnärztin *f*

den·tures (Zahn)Prothese *f*, (künstliches) Gebiss

de·nun·ci·a·tion Denunziation *f*

de·nun·ci·a·tor Denunziant(in)

de·ny abstreiten, bestreiten, dementieren, (ab)leugnen; *j-m et.* verweigern, abschlagen

de·o·do·rant De(s)odorant *n*, Deo *n*

de·part abreisen; abfahren, abfliegen; abweichen (*from* von)

de·part·ment Abteilung *f*, UNIV *a.* Fachbereich *m*; POL Ministerium *n*

De·part·ment| of De·fense Verteidigungsministerium *n*; ~ **of State** *a.* **State Department** Außenministerium *n*; ~ **of the En·vi·ron·ment** *Br* Umweltministerium *n*; ~ **of the In·te·ri·or** Innenministerium *n*

de·part·ment store Kaufhaus *n*, Warenhaus *n*

de·par·ture Abreise *f*; RAIL *etc* Abfahrt *f*; AVIAT Abflug *m*; *fig* Abweichung *f*; ~**s**

AVIAT, RAIL *etc* 'Abfahrt' (*timetable*); **day of** ~ Abreisetag *m*; ~ **gate** AVIAT Flugsteig *m*; ~ **lounge** AVIAT Abflughalle *f*

de·pend: ~ **on** sich verlassen auf (*acc*); abhängen von; angewiesen sein auf (*acc*); *that* ~*s* das kommt darauf an

de·pend·a·bil·i·ty Zuverlässigkeit *f*

de·pend·a·ble zuverlässig

de·pen·dant Angehörige *m*, *f*

de·pen·dence Abhängigkeit *f*; Vertrauen *n*

de·pen·dent 1. (**on**) abhängig (von); angewiesen (auf *acc*); **2.** → **dependant**

de·plor·a·ble bedauerlich, beklagenswert; **de·plore** beklagen, bedauern

de·pop·u·late entvölkern

de·port ausweisen, *Ausländer a.* abschieben; deportieren

de·pose *j-n* absetzen; JUR unter Eid erklären

de·pos·it 1. absetzen, abstellen; CHEM, GEOL (sich) ablagern *or* absetzen; deponieren, hinterlegen; ECON *Betrag* anzahlen **2.** CHEM Ablagerung *f*, GEOL *a.* (*Erz- etc*)Lager *n*; Deponierung *f*, Hinterlegung *f*; ECON Anzahlung *f*; *make a* ~ e-e Anzahlung leisten (**on** für)

dep·ot Depot *n*; Bahnhof *m*

de·prave *moralisch* verderben

de·pre·ci·ate an Wert verlieren

de·press (nieder)drücken; deprimieren, bedrücken

de·pressed deprimiert, niedergeschlagen; ECON flau (*market*); Not leidend (*industry*); ~ **ar·e·a** ECON Notstandsgebiet *n*

de·press·ing deprimierend, bedrückend

de·pres·sion Depression *f*, Niedergeschlagenheit *f*; ECON Depression *f*, Flaute *f*; Senke *f*, Vertiefung *f*; METEOR Tief(druckgebiet) *n*

de·prive: ~ **s.o. of s.th.** j-m et. entziehen *or* nehmen; **de·prived** benachteiligt

dept, Dept *abbr of* **department** Abt., Abteilung *f*

depth 1. Tiefe *f* **2.** Tiefen…

dep·u·ta·tion Abordnung *f*

dep·u·tize: ~ **for s.o.** j-n vertreten

dep·u·ty (Stell)Vertreter(in); PARL Abgeordnete *m*, *f*; *a.* ~ **sheriff** Hilfssheriff *m*

de·rail: be ~**ed** entgleisen

de·ranged geistesgestört

der·by F Melone f

der·e·lict heruntergekommen, baufällig

de·ride verhöhnen, verspotten

de·ri·sion Hohn m, Spott m

de·ri·sive höhnisch, spöttisch

de·rive herleiten (*from* von); (sich) ableiten (*from* von); abstammen (*from* von); ~ *pleasure from* Freude finden or haben an (*dat*)

der·ma·tol·o·gist Dermatologe m, Hautarzt m

de·rog·a·to·ry abfällig, geringschätzig

der·rick TECH Derrickkran m; MAR Ladebaum m; TECH Bohrturm m

de·scend herab-, hinabsteigen, herunter-, hinuntersteigen, -gehen, -kommen; AVIAT niedergehen; abstammen, herkommen (*from* von); ~ *on* herfallen über (*acc*); überfallen (*acc*) (*visitor etc*)

de·scen·dant Nachkomme m

de·scent Herab-, Hinuntersteigen n, -gehen n; AVIAT Niedergehen n; Gefälle n; Abstammung f, Herkunft f

de·scribe beschreiben

de·scrip·tion Beschreibung f, Schilderung f; Art f, Sorte f; **de·scrip·tive** beschreibend; anschaulich

des·e·crate entweihen

de·seg·re·gate die Rassentrennung aufheben in (*dat*); **de·seg·re·ga·tion** Aufhebung f der Rassentrennung

des·ert¹ 1. Wüste f 2. Wüsten…

de·sert² v/t verlassen, im Stich lassen; v/i MIL desertieren

de·sert·er MIL Deserteur m

de·ser·tion (JUR a. böswilliges) Verlassen; MIL Fahnenflucht f

de·serve verdienen

de·serv·ed·ly verdientermaßen

de·serv·ing verdienstvoll

de·sign 1. Design n, Entwurf m, (TECH Konstruktions)Zeichnung f; Design n, Muster n; (a. böse)Absicht 2. entwerfen, TECH konstruieren; gestalten; ausdenken; bestimmen, vorsehen (*for* für)

des·ig·nate et. or j-n bestimmen

de·sign·er Designer(in); TECH Konstrukteur m; (*Mode*)Schöpfer(in)

de·sir·a·ble erwünscht, wünschenswert; begehrenswert

de·sire 1. Wunsch m, Verlangen n, Begierde f (*for* nach); 2. wünschen; begehren

de·sist Abstand nehmen (*from* von)

desk Schreibtisch m; Pult n; Empfang m, Rezeption f; Schalter m

desk·top com·put·er Desktop-Computer m; ~ **pub·lish·ing** (*abbr* **DTP**) IT Desktop-Publishing n

des·o·late einsam, verlassen; trostlos

de·spair 1. Verzweiflung f; **drive s.o. to** ~ j-n zur Verzweiflung bringen 2. verzweifeln (*of* an *dat*)

de·spair·ing verzweifelt

de·spatch → **dispatch**

des·per·ate verzweifelt; F hoffnungslos, schrecklich

des·per·a·tion Verzweiflung f

des·pic·a·ble verachtenswert, verabscheuungswürdig

de·spise verachten

de·spite trotz (*gen*)

de·spon·dent mutlos, verzagt

des·pot Despot m, Tyrann m

des·sert Nachtisch m, Dessert n

des·ti·na·tion Bestimmung f; Bestimmungsort m

des·tined bestimmt; MAR etc unterwegs (*for* nach)

des·ti·ny Schicksal n

des·ti·tute mittellos

de·stroy zerstören, vernichten; *Tier* töten, einschläfern; **de·stroy·er** Zerstörer(in); MAR MIL Zerstörer m

de·struc·tion Zerstörung f, Vernichtung f; **de·struc·tive** zerstörend, vernichtend; zerstörerisch

de·tach (ab-, los)trennen, (los)lösen

de·tached einzeln, frei or allein stehend; unvoreingenommen; distanziert; ~ **house** Einzelhaus n

de·tach·ment (Los)Lösung f, (Ab-)Trennung f; MIL (Sonder)Kommando n

de·tail 1. Detail n, Einzelheit f; MIL (Sonder)Kommando n; **in** ~ ausführlich 2. genau schildern; MIL abkommandieren

de·tailed detailliert, ausführlich

de·tain aufhalten; JUR in (Untersuchungs)Haft behalten

de·tect entdecken, (heraus)finden

de·tec·tion Entdeckung f

de·tec·tive Kriminalbeamte m, Detektiv m; ~ **nov·el**, ~ **sto·ry** Kriminalroman m

de·ten·tion JUR Haft f; PED Nachsitzen n

de·ter abschrecken (*from* von)

de·ter·gent Reinigungs-, Wasch-, Geschirrspülmittel *n*

de·te·ri·o·rate (sich) verschlechtern, nachlassen; verderben

de·ter·mi·na·tion Entschlossenheit *f*, Bestimmtheit *f*; Entschluss *m*; Feststellung *f*, Ermittlung *f*; de·ter·mine *et.* beschließen, bestimmen; feststellen, ermitteln; (sich) entscheiden; sich entschließen; de·ter·mined entschlossen

de·ter·rence Abschreckung *f*

de·ter·rent 1. abschreckend 2. Abschreckungsmittel *n*

de·test verabscheuen

de·throne entthronen

de·to·nate *v/t* zünden; *v/i* detonieren, explodieren

de·tour Umweg *m*; Umleitung *f*

de·tract: ~ *from* ablenken von; schmälern (*acc*)

de·tri·ment Nachteil *m*, Schaden *m*

deuce *cards etc:* Zwei *f*; *tennis:* Einstand *m*

de·val·u·a·tion Abwertung *f*

de·val·ue abwerten

dev·a·state verwüsten

dev·a·stat·ing verheerend, vernichtend; F umwerfend, toll

de·vel·op (sich) entwickeln; *Naturschätze, Bauland* erschließen, *Altstadt etc* sanieren; de·vel·op·er PHOT Entwickler *m*; (Stadt)Planer *m*

de·vel·op·ing Entwicklungs...; ~ country, ~ nation Entwicklungsland *n*

de·vel·op·ment Entwicklung *f*; Erschließung *f*, Sanierung *f*

de·vi·ate abweichen (*from* von)

de·vi·a·tion Abweichung *f*

de·vice Vorrichtung *f*, Gerät *n*; Plan *m*, Trick *m*; *leave s.o. to his own ~s* j-n sich selbst überlassen

dev·il Teufel *m* (*a. fig*)

dev·il·ish teuflisch

de·vi·ous abwegig; gewunden; unaufrichtig; ~ *route* Umweg *m*

de·vise (sich) ausdenken

de·void: ~ *of* ohne (*acc*)

de·vote widmen (*to dat*); de·vot·ed ergeben; hingebungsvoll; eifrig, begeistert; dev·o·tee begeisterter Anhänger; de·vo·tion Ergebenheit *f*; Hingabe *f*; Frömmigkeit *f*, Andacht *f*

de·vour verschlingen

de·vout fromm; sehnlichst, innig

dew Tau *m*; dew·y taufeucht, taufrisch

dex·ter·i·ty Gewandtheit *f*

dex·ter·ous, dex·trous gewandt

di·a·bol·i·cal teuflisch

di·ag·nose diagnostizieren

di·ag·no·sis Diagnose *f*

di·ag·o·nal 1. diagonal 2. Diagonale *f*

di·a·gram Diagramm *n*, grafische Darstellung

di·al 1. Zifferblatt *n*; TEL Wählscheibe *f*; Skala *f* 2. TEL wählen; ~ *direct* durchwählen (*to* nach); *direct ~(l)ing* Durchwahl *f*

di·a·lect Dialekt *m*, Mundart *f*

di·al·ling code *Br* TEL Vorwahl (-nummer) *f*

di·a·log, *Br* di·a·logue Dialog *m*, (Zwie)Gespräch *n*

di·am·e·ter Durchmesser *m*; *in ~* im Durchmesser

di·a·mond Diamant *m*; Raute *f*, Rhombus *m*; *cards:* Karo *n*

di·a·per Windel *f*

di·a·phragm ANAT Zwerchfell *n*; OPT Blende *f*; TEL Membran(e) *f*

di·ar·rh(o)e·a MED Durchfall *m*

di·a·ry Tagebuch *n*

dice 1. Würfel *m* 2. GASTR in Würfel schneiden; würfeln

dic·tate diktieren; *fig* vorschreiben

dic·ta·tion Diktat *n*

dic·ta·tor Diktator *m*

dic·ta·tor·ship Diktatur *f*

dic·tion Ausdrucksweise *f*, Stil *m*

dic·tion·a·ry Wörterbuch *n*

die[1] sterben; ZO eingehen, verenden; ~ *of hunger* verhungern; ~ *of thirst* verdursten; ~ *away* sich legen (*wind*); verklingen (*sound*); ~ *down* nachlassen; herunterbrennen; schwächer werden; ~ *out* aussterben (*a. fig*)

die[2] Würfel *m*

di·et 1. Diät *f*; Nahrung *f*, Kost *f*; *be on a ~* Diät leben; *put s.o. on a ~* j-m e-e Diät verordnen 2. Diät leben

di·e·ti·cian Diätassistent(in)

dif·fer sich unterscheiden; anderer Meinung sein (*with, from* als); abweichen

dif·fe·rence Unterschied *m*; Differenz *f*; Meinungsverschiedenheit *f*

dif·fe·rent verschieden; andere(r, -s); anders (*from* als)

dif·fe·ren·ti·ate (sich) unterscheiden

dif·fi·cult schwierig

dif·fi·cul·ty Schwierigkeit *f*, *pl* Unannehmlichkeiten *pl*

dif·fi·dence Schüchternheit *f*

dif·fi·dent schüchtern

dif·fuse 1. *fig* verbreiten 2. diffus; *esp* PHYS zerstreut; weitschweifig

dif·fu·sion CHEM, PHYS (Zer)Streuung *f*

dig 1. graben; ~ *(up)* umgraben; ~ *(up or out)* ausgraben *(a. fig)*; ~ *s.o. in the ribs* j-m e-n Rippenstoß geben 2. F Puff *m*, Stoß *m*; Seitenhieb *m* *(at* auf *acc)*

di·gest 1. verdauen; ~ *well* leicht verdaulich sein 2. Abriss *m*; Auswahl *f*; **di·gest·i·ble** verdaulich; **di·ges·tion** Verdauung *f*; **di·ges·tive** verdauungsfördernd; Verdauungs…

dig·ger *(esp* Gold)Gräber *m*

di·git Ziffer *f*; *three-~ number* dreistellige Zahl

di·gi·tal digital, Digital…; ~ *camera* Digitalkamera *f*; ~ *clock* Digitaluhr *f*; ~ *television*, ~ TV Digitalfernsehen *n* ~ *watch* Digitaluhr *f*

dig·ni·fied würdevoll, würdig

dig·ni·ta·ry Würdenträger(in)

dig·ni·ty Würde *f*

di·gress abschweifen

dike 1. Deich *m*, Damm *m*; Graben *m* 2. eindeichen, eindämmen

di·lap·i·dat·ed verfallen, baufällig, klapp(e)rig

di·late (sich) ausdehnen *or* (aus)weiten; *Augen* weit öffnen

dil·a·to·ry verzögernd, hinhaltend; langsam

dil·i·gence Fleiß *m*

dil·i·gent fleißig, emsig

di·lute 1. verdünnen; *fig* verwässern 2. verdünnt; *fig* verwässert

dim 1. (halb)dunkel, düster; undeutlich, verschwommen; schwach, trüb(e) *(light)* 2. (sich) verdunkeln *or* verdüstern; (sich) trüben; undeutlich werden; ~ *one's headlights* MOT abblenden

dime Zehncentstück *n*

di·men·sion Dimension *f*, Maß *n*, Abmessung *f*; *pl a.* Ausmaß *n*

di·min·ish (sich) vermindern *or* verringern

di·min·u·tive klein, winzig

dim·ple Grübchen *n*

din Getöse *n*, Lärm *m*

dine essen, speisen; ~ *in* zu Hause essen;

~ *out* auswärts essen, essen gehen

din·er Speisende *m*, *f*; Gast *m*; Speiselokal *n*; RAIL Speisewagen *m*

din·ghy MAR Jolle *f*; Dingi *n*; Beiboot *n*; Schlauchboot *n*

din·gy schmutzig, schmudd(e)lig

din·ing car RAIL Speisewagen *m*

din·ing room Ess-, Speisezimmer *n*

din·ner (Mittag-, Abend)Essen *n*; Diner *n*, Festessen *n*; ~ *jack·et* Smoking *m*; ~ *par·ty* Dinnerparty *f*, Abendgesellschaft *f*; ~ *ser·vice*, ~ *set* Speiseservice *n*, Tafelgeschirr *n*

din·ner·time Essens-, Tischzeit *f*

di·no F → *dinosaur*

di·no·saur ZO Dinosaurier *m*

dip 1. *v/t* (ein)tauchen; senken; schöpfen; ~ *one's headlights* Br MOT abblenden; *v/i* (unter)tauchen; sinken; sich neigen, sich senken 2. (Ein-, Unter-)Tauchen *n*; F kurzes Bad; Senkung *f*, Neigung *f*, Gefälle *n*; GASTR Dip *m*

diph·ther·i·a MED Diphtherie *f*

di·plo·ma Diplom *n*

di·plo·ma·cy Diplomatie *f*

di·plo·mat Diplomat *m*

dip·lo·mat·ic diplomatisch

dip·per Schöpfkelle *f*

dire schrecklich; höchste(r, -s), äußerste(r, -s)

di·rect 1. *adj* direkt; gerade; unmittelbar; offen, aufrichtig 2. *adv* direkt, unmittelbar 3. richten; lenken, steuern; leiten; anordnen; *j-n* anweisen; *j-m* den Weg zeigen; *Brief* adressieren; Regie führen bei; ~ *cur·rent* ELECTR Gleichstrom *m*; ~ *train* durchgehender Zug

di·rec·tion Richtung *f*; Leitung *f*, Führung *f*; *film etc:* Regie *f*; *mst pl* Anweisung *f*, Anleitung *f*; ~*s for use* Gebrauchsanweisung *f*; *sense of* ~ Ortssinn *m*; ~ *in·di·ca·tor* MOT Fahrtrichtungsanzeiger *m*, Blinker *m*

di·rec·tive Anweisung *f*

di·rect·ly 1. *adv* sofort 2. *cj* F sobald, sowie

di·rec·tor Direktor *m*; *film etc:* Regisseur(in)

di·rec·to·ry Adressbuch *n*

di·rect speech LING wörtliche Rede

di·rect train durchgehender Zug

dirt Schmutz *m*; (lockere) Erde

dirt cheap F spottbillig

dirt·y 1. schmutzig (*a. fig*) **2.** *v/t* beschmutzen; *v/i* schmutzig werden, schmutzen

dis·a·bil·i·ty Unfähigkeit *f*

dis·a·bled 1. arbeitsunfähig, erwerbsunfähig, invalid(e); MIL kriegsversehrt; *körperlich or geistig* behindert **2. the** ~ die Behinderten *pl*

dis·ad·van·tage Nachteil *m*; Schaden *m*; **dis·ad·van·ta·geous** nachteilig, ungünstig

dis·a·gree nicht übereinstimmen; uneinig sein; nicht bekommen (**with s.o.** j-m); **dis·a·gree·a·ble** unangenehm; **dis·a·gree·ment** Verschiedenheit *f*, Unstimmigkeit *f*, Uneinigkeit *f*; Meinungsverschiedenheit *f*

dis·ap·pear verschwinden

dis·ap·pear·ance Verschwinden *n*

dis·ap·point *j-n* enttäuschen; *Hoffnungen etc* zunichtemachen

dis·ap·point·ing enttäuschend

dis·ap·point·ment Enttäuschung *f*

dis·ap·prov·al Missbilligung *f*

dis·ap·prove missbilligen; dagegen sein

dis·arm *v/t* entwaffnen (*a. fig*); *v/i* MIL, POL abrüsten; **dis·ar·ma·ment** Entwaffnung *f*; MIL, POL Abrüstung *f*

dis·ar·range in Unordnung bringen

dis·ar·ray Unordnung *f*

di·sas·ter Unglück *n*, Unglücksfall *m*, Katastrophe *f*; ~ **ar·e·a** Katastrophen-, Notstandsgebiet *n*; ~ **con·trol** Katastrophenschutz *m*

di·sas·trous katastrophal, verheerend

dis·be·lief Unglaube *m*; Zweifel *m* (**in** an *dat*); **dis·be·lieve** *et.* bezweifeln, nicht glauben

disc *Br* → **disk**

dis·card *Karten* ablegen, *Kleidung etc a.* ausrangieren; *Freund etc* fallen lassen

di·scern wahrnehmen, erkennen

di·scern·ing kritisch, scharfsichtig

di·scern·ment Scharfblick *m*

dis·charge 1. *v/t* entladen, ausladen; *j-n* befreien, entbinden; *j-n* entlassen; *Gewehr etc* abfeuern; von sich geben, ausströmen, -senden, -stoßen; MED absondern; *Pflicht etc* erfüllen; *Zorn etc* auslassen (**on** an *dat*); *v/i* ELECTR sich entladen; sich ergießen, münden (*river*); MED eitern **2.** MAR Entladung *f*; MIL Abfeuern *n*; Ausströmen *n*; MED Absonde-

derung *f*, Ausfluss *m*; Ausstoßen *n*; ELECTR Entladung *f*; Entlassung *f*; Erfüllung *f* (*e-r Pflicht*)

di·sci·ple Schüler *m*; Jünger *m*

dis·ci·pline 1. Disziplin *f* **2.** disziplinieren; **well ~d** diszipliniert; **badly ~d** disziplinlos, undiszipliniert

dis·claim abstreiten, bestreiten; *Verantwortung* ablehnen; JUR verzichten auf (*acc*)

dis·close bekannt geben *or* machen; enthüllen, aufdecken

dis·clo·sure Enthüllung *f*

dis·co Disko *f*

dis·col·o(u)r (sich) verfärben

dis·com·fort 1. Unbehagen *n*; Unannehmlichkeit *f* **2.** *j-m* Unbehagen verursachen

dis·con·cert aus der Fassung bringen

dis·con·nect trennen (*a.* ELECTR); TECH auskuppeln; ELECTR *Gerät* abschalten; *Gas, Strom, Telefon* abstellen; TEL *Gespräch* unterbrechen

dis·con·nect·ed zusammenhang(s)los

dis·con·so·late untröstlich

dis·con·tent Unzufriedenheit *f*

dis·con·tent·ed unzufrieden

dis·con·tin·ue aufgeben, aufhören mit; unterbrechen

dis·cord Uneinigkeit *f*, Zwietracht *f*; Zwist *m*; MUS Missklang *m*

dis·cord·ant nicht übereinstimmend; MUS unharmonisch, misstönend

dis·co·theque Diskothek *f*

dis·count ECON Diskont *m*; Preisnachlass *m*, Rabatt *m*, Skonto *m*, *n*

dis·cour·age entmutigen; abschrecken, abhalten; *j-m* abraten (**from** von)

dis·cour·age·ment Entmutigung *f*; Abschreckung *f*

dis·course 1. Unterhaltung *f*, Gespräch *n*; Vortrag *m* **2.** e-n Vortrag halten (**on** über *acc*)

dis·cour·te·ous unhöflich

dis·cour·te·sy Unhöflichkeit *f*

dis·cov·er entdecken; ausfindig machen, (heraus)finden

dis·cov·er·y Entdeckung *f*

dis·cred·it 1. Zweifel *m*; Misskredit *m*, schlechter Ruf; **bring ~ (up)on** in Verruf bringen **2.** nicht glauben; in Misskredit bringen

di·screet besonnen, vorsichtig; diskret, verschwiegen

di·screp·an·cy Diskrepanz *f*, Widerspruch *m*

di·scre·tion Ermessen *n*, Gutdünken *n*; Diskretion *f*, Verschwiegenheit *f*

di·scrim·i·nate unterscheiden; **~ against** benachteiligen, diskriminieren; **di·scrim·i·nat·ing** kritisch, urteilsfähig; **di·scrim·i·na·tion** unterschiedliche (*esp* nachteilige) Behandlung; Diskriminierung *f*, Benachteiligung *f*; Urteilsfähigkeit *f*

dis·cus SPORT Diskus *m*

dis·cuss diskutieren, erörtern, besprechen; **dis·cus·sion** Diskussion *f*, Besprechung *f*

dis·cus| throw SPORT Diskuswerfen *n*; **~ throw·er** SPORT Diskuswerfer(in)

dis·ease Krankheit *f*

dis·eased krank

dis·em·bark von Bord gehen (lassen); MAR *Waren* ausladen

dis·en·chant·ed: be~ with sich keine Illusionen mehr machen über (*acc*)

dis·en·gage (sich) frei machen; losmachen; TECH auskuppeln, loskuppeln

dis·en·tan·gle entwirren; (sich) befreien

dis·fa·vo(u)r Missfallen *n*; Ungnade *f*

dis·fig·ure entstellen

dis·grace 1. Schande *f*; Ungnade *f* **2.** Schande bringen über (*acc*), *j-m* Schande bereiten

dis·grace·ful schändlich; skandalös

dis·guise 1. verkleiden (**as** als); *Stimme etc* verstellen; *et.* verbergen, verschleiern **2.** Verkleidung *f*; Verstellung *f*; Verschleierung *f*; *in~* maskiert, verkleidet; *fig* verkappt; **in the ~ of** verkleidet als

dis·gust 1. Ekel *m*, Abscheu *m* **2.** (an)ekeln; empören, entrüsten

dis·gust·ing ekelhaft

dish 1. flache Schüssel; (Servier)Platte *f*; GASTR Gericht *n*, Speise *f*; **the ~es** das Geschirr; **wash** *or* **do the ~es** abspülen, abwaschen **2. ~ out** F austeilen; *often* **~ up** *Speisen* anrichten, auftragen; F *Geschichte etc* auftischen

dish·cloth Geschirrtuch *n*

dish·heart·en entmutigen

di·shev·el(l)ed zerzaust

dis·hon·est unehrlich, unredlich

dis·hon·est·y Unehrlichkeit *f*; Unredlichkeit *f*

dis·hon·o(u)r 1. Schande *f* **2.** Schande

bringen über (*acc*); ECON *Wechsel* nicht honorieren *or* einlösen

dis·hon·o(u)·ra·ble schändlich, unehrenhaft

dish·wash·er Tellerwäscher *m*, Spüler(in); TECH Geschirrspülmaschine *f*, Geschirrspüler *m*

dish·wa·ter Spülwasser *n*

dis·il·lu·sion 1. Ernüchterung *f*, Desillusion *f* **2.** ernüchtern, desillusionieren; **be~ed with** sich keine Illusionen mehr machen über (*acc*)

dis·in·clined abgeneigt

dis·in·fect MED desinfizieren

dis·in·fec·tant Desinfektionsmittel *n*

dis·in·her·it JUR enterben

dis·in·te·grate (sich) auflösen; verfallen, zerfallen

dis·in·ter·est·ed uneigennützig, selbstlos; objektiv, unvoreingenommen

disk Scheibe *f*; (Schall)Platte *f*; Parkscheibe *f*; IT Diskette *f*; ANAT Bandscheibe *f*; **slipped ~** MED Bandscheibenvorfall *m*

disk drive IT Diskettenlaufwerk *n*

disk·ette IT Floppy *f*, Diskette *f*

disk jock·ey Diskjockey *m*

disk park·ing MOT Parken *n* mit Parkscheibe

dis·like 1. Abneigung *f*, Widerwille *m* (**of, for** gegen); **take a ~ to s.o.** gegen j-n e-e Abneigung fassen **2.** nicht leiden können, nicht mögen

dis·lo·cate MED sich den Arm etc verrenken *or* ausrenken

dis·loy·al treulos, untreu

dis·mal trüb(e), trostlos, elend

dis·man·tle TECH demontieren

dis·may 1. Schreck(en) *m*, Bestürzung *f*; **in~, with~** bestürzt; **to my~** zu m-r Bestürzung **2.** *v/t* erschrecken, bestürzen

dis·miss *v/t* entlassen; wegschicken; ablehnen; *Thema etc* fallen lassen; JUR abweisen; **dis·miss·al** Entlassung *f*; Aufgabe *f*; JUR Abweisung *f*

dis·mount *v/i* absteigen, absitzen (**from** von); *v/t* demontieren; TECH auseinandernehmen

dis·o·be·di·ence Ungehorsam *m*

dis·o·be·di·ent ungehorsam

dis·o·bey nicht gehorchen, ungehorsam sein (gegen)

dis·or·der Unordnung *f*; Aufruhr *m*; MED Störung *f*

dis·or·der·ly unordentlich; ordnungswidrig; unruhig; aufrührerisch

dis·or·gan·ize durcheinanderbringen; desorganisieren

dis·own nicht anerkennen; *Kind* verstoßen; ablehnen

di·spar·age verächtlich machen, herabsetzen; gering schätzen

di·spar·i·ty Ungleichheit *f*; ~ *of* or *in age* Altersunterschied *m*

dis·pas·sion·ate leidenschaftslos; objektiv

di·spatch 1. schnelle Erledigung; Sendung *f*; Abfertigung *f*; Eile *f*; Botschaft *f*; Bericht *m* **2.** schnell erledigen; absenden, abschicken, *Telegramm etc* aufgeben, abfertigen

di·spel *Menge etc* zerstreuen (*a. fig*), *Nebel* zerteilen

di·spen·sa·ble entbehrlich

di·spen·sa·ry Werks-, Krankenhaus-, Schul-, MIL Lazarettapotheke *f*

di·spen·sa·tion Austeilung *f*; Befreiung *f*; Dispens *m*; *göttliche* Fügung

di·spense austeilen; *Recht* sprechen; *Arzneien* zubereiten und abgeben; ~ *with* auskommen ohne; überflüssig machen; **di·spens·er** Spender *m*, *a.* Abroller *m* (*for adhesive tape etc*), (*Briefmarken- etc*) Automat *m*

di·sperse verstreuen; (sich) zerstreuen

di·spir·it·ed entmutigt

dis·place verschieben; ablösen, entlassen; *j-n* verschleppen; ersetzen; verdrängen

dis·play 1. Entfaltung *f*; (Her)Zeigen *n*; (protzige) Zurschaustellung; IT Display *n*, Bildschirm *m*, Datenanzeige *f*; ECON Display *n*, Auslage *f*; *be on ~* ausgestellt sein **2.** entfalten; zur Schau stellen; zeigen

dis·please *j-m* missfallen

dis·pleased ungehalten

dis·plea·sure Missfallen *n*

dis·pos·a·ble Einweg...; Wegwerf...

dis·pos·al Beseitigung *f*, Entsorgung *f*; Endlagerung *f*; Verfügung(srecht *n*) *f*; *be* (*put*) *at s.o.'s ~* j-m zur Verfügung stehen (stellen)

dis·pose *v/t* (an)ordnen, einrichten; geneigt machen, bewegen; *v/i*: ~ *of* verfügen über (*acc*); erledigen; loswerden; wegschaffen, beseitigen; *Abfall, a. Atommüll etc* entsorgen

dis·posed geneigt; ...gesinnt

dis·po·si·tion Veranlagung *f*

dis·pos·sess enteignen, vertreiben; berauben (*of gen*)

dis·pro·por·tion·ate(·ly) unverhältnismäßig

dis·prove widerlegen

di·spute 1. Disput *m*, Kontroverse *f*; Streit *m*; Auseinandersetzung *f* **2.** streiten (über *acc*); bezweifeln

dis·qual·i·fy unfähig or untauglich machen; für untauglich erklären; SPORT disqualifizieren

dis·re·gard 1. Nichtbeachtung *f*; Missachtung *f* **2.** nicht beachten

dis·rep·u·ta·ble übel; verrufen

dis·re·pute schlechter Ruf

dis·re·spect Respektlosigkeit *f*; Unhöflichkeit *f*

dis·re·spect·ful respektlos; unhöflich

dis·rupt unterbrechen

dis·sat·is·fac·tion Unzufriedenheit *f*

dis·sat·is·fied unzufrieden (*with* mit)

dis·sect MED sezieren, zerlegen, zergliedern (*a. fig*)

dis·sen·sion Meinungsverschiedenheit(en *pl*) *f*, Differenz(en *pl*) *f*; Uneinigkeit *f*

dis·sent 1. abweichende Meinung **2.** anderer Meinung sein (*from* als)

dis·sent·er Andersdenkende *m, f*

dis·si·dent Andersdenkende *m, f*; POL Dissident(in), Regime-, Systemkritiker(in)

dis·sim·i·lar (*to*) unähnlich (*dat*); verschieden (von)

dis·sim·u·la·tion Verstellung *f*

dis·si·pate (sich) zerstreuen; verschwenden

dis·si·pat·ed ausschweifend, zügellos

dis·so·ci·ate trennen; ~ *o.s.* sich distanzieren (*from* von)

dis·so·lute → *dissipated*

dis·so·lu·tion Auflösung *f*

dis·solve (sich) auflösen

dis·suade *j-m* abraten (*from* von)

dis·tance 1. Abstand *m*; Entfernung *f*; Ferne *f*; Strecke *f*; *fig* Distanz *f*, Zurückhaltung *f*; *at a ~* von weitem; in einiger Entfernung; *keep s.o. at a ~* j-m gegenüber reserviert sein **2.** hinter sich lassen; ~ *race* SPORT Langstreckenlauf *m*; ~ *run·ner* SPORT Langstreckenläufer(in), Langstreckler(in)

dis·tant entfernt; fern, Fern…; distanziert

dis·taste Widerwille *m*, Abneigung *f*

dis·taste·ful ekelerregend; unangenehm; **be ~ to s.o.** j-m zuwider sein

dis·tem·per VET Staupe *f*

dis·tend (sich) (aus)dehnen; (auf)blähen; sich weiten

dis·til(l) destillieren

dis·tinct verschieden; deutlich, klar

dis·tinc·tion Unterscheidung *f*; Unterschied *m*; Auszeichnung *f*; Rang *m*

dis·tinc·tive unterscheidend; kennzeichnend, bezeichnend

dis·tin·guish unterscheiden; auszeichnen; **~ o.s.** sich auszeichnen

dis·tin·guished berühmt; ausgezeichnet; vornehm

dis·tort verdrehen; verzerren

dis·tract ablenken; **dis·tract·ed** beunruhigt, besorgt; (**by, with** vor *dat*) außer sich, wahnsinnig; **dis·trac·tion** Ablenkung *f*; Zerstreuung *f*; Wahnsinn *m*; **drive s.o. to ~** j-n wahnsinnig machen

dis·traught → **distracted**

dis·tress 1. Leid *n*, Kummer *m*, Sorge *f*; Not(lage) *f* **2.** beunruhigen, mit Sorge erfüllen

dis·tressed Not leidend; **~ ar·e·a** Notstandsgebiet *n*

dis·tress·ing besorgniserregend

dis·trib·ute ver-, aus-, zuteilen; ECON *Waren* vertreiben, absetzen; *Filme* verleihen; **dis·tri·bu·tion** Ver-, Aus-, Zuteilung *f*; ECON Vertrieb *m*, Absatz *m*; *film:* Verleih *m*

dis·trict Bezirk *m*; Gegend *f*

dis·trust 1. Misstrauen *n* **2.** misstrauen (*dat*); **dis·trust·ful** misstrauisch

dis·turb stören; beunruhigen

dis·turb·ance Störung *f*; Unruhe *f*; **~ of the peace** JUR Störung *f* der öffentlichen Sicherheit und Ordnung; **cause a ~** für Unruhe sorgen; ruhestörenden Lärm machen

dis·turbed geistig gestört; verhaltensgestört

dis·used nicht mehr benutzt (*machinery etc*), stillgelegt (*colliery etc*)

ditch Graben *m*

di·van Diwan *m*; **~ bed** Bettcouch *f*

dive 1. (unter)tauchen; *vom Sprungbrett* springen; e-n Hecht- *or* Kopfsprung machen (**for** nach); e-n Sturz-

flug machen **2.** *swimming:* Springen *n*; Kopfsprung *m*, Hechtsprung *m*; *soccer:* Schwalbe *f*; AVIAT Sturzflug *m*; F Spelunke *f*; **div·er** Taucher(in); SPORT Wasserspringer(in)

di·verge auseinanderlaufen; abweichen; **di·ver·gence** Abweichung *f*; **di·ver·gent** abweichend

di·verse verschieden; mannigfaltig

di·ver·si·fy verschieden(artig) *or* abwechslungsreich gestalten

di·ver·sion Ablenkung *f*; Zeitvertreib *m*; *Br* MOT Umleitung *f*

di·ver·si·ty Verschiedenheit *f*; Mannigfaltigkeit *f*

di·vert ablenken; *j-n* zerstreuen, unterhalten; *Br Verkehr* umleiten

di·vide 1. *v/t* teilen; ver-, aus-, aufteilen; trennen; MATH dividieren, teilen (**by** durch); *v/i* sich teilen; sich aufteilen; MATH sich dividieren *or* teilen lassen (**by** durch); **2.** GEOGR Wasserscheide *f*; **di·vid·ed** geteilt; **~ highway** Schnellstraße *f*

div·i·dend ECON Dividende *f*

di·vid·ers (**a pair of ~** ein) Stechzirkel *m*

di·vine göttlich

di·vine ser·vice REL Gottesdienst *m*

div·ing Tauchen *n*; SPORT Wasserspringen *n* **2.** Taucher…

div·ing·board Sprungbrett *n*

div·ing·suit Taucheranzug *m*

di·vin·i·ty Gottheit *f*; Göttlichkeit *f*; Theologie *f*

di·vis·i·ble teilbar

di·vi·sion Teilung *f*; Trennung *f*; Abteilung *f*; MIL, MATH Division *f*

di·vorce 1. (Ehe)Scheidung *f*; **get a ~** sich scheiden lassen (**from** von); **2.** JUR *j-n, Ehe* scheiden; **get ~d** sich scheiden lassen; **di·vor·cee** Geschiedene *m, f*

DIY ABBR → **do-it-yourself**

DIY store Baumarkt *m*

diz·zy schwind(e)lig

do *v/t* tun, machen; (zu)bereiten; *Zimmer* aufräumen; *Geschirr* abwaschen; *Wegstrecke* zurücklegen, schaffen; **~ you know him? no, I don't** kennst du ihn? nein; what can I **~ for you?** was kann ich für Sie tun?, womit kann ich (Ihnen) dienen?; **~ London** F London besichtigen; **have one's hair done** sich die Haare machen *or* frisieren las-

sen; ***have done reading**** fertig sein mit
Lesen; *v/i* tun, handeln; sich befinden;
genügen; ***that will ~** das genügt; ***how ~
you ~?*** guten Tag!; *~ **be quick*** beeil
dich doch; *~ **you like New York?** I ~* gefällt Ihnen New York? ja; *****she works
hard, doesn't she?*** sie arbeitet viel,
nicht wahr?; *~ **well** s-e Sache gut machen; gute Geschäfte machen; *~ **away
with** beseitigen, weg-, abschaffen; *****do
s.o.*** in F j-n umlegen; ***I'm done in** F
ich bin geschafft; *~ **up** Kleid etc zumachen; *Haus etc* instand setzen; *Päckchen* zurechtmachen; *~ **o.s.** up* sich zurechtmachen; ***I could ~ with ...*** ich
könnte ... brauchen *or* vertragen; *~
without auskommen *or* sich behelfen
ohne

doc F → *doctor*
do·cile gelehrig; fügsam
dock¹ stutzen, kupieren
dock² **1.** MAR Dock *n*; Kai *m*, Pier *m*; JUR
Anklagebank *f* **2.** *v/t* MAR (ein)docken;
Raumschiff koppeln; *v/i* MAR anlegen;
andocken, ankoppeln (*Raumschiff*)
dock·er Dock-, Hafenarbeiter *m*
dock·ing Docking *n*, Ankopp(e)lung *f*
dock·yard MAR Werft *f*
doc·tor Doktor *m* (*a*. UNIV), Arzt *m*,
Ärztin *f*
doc·tor·al: *~ **thesis** UNIV Doktorarbeit *f*
doc·trine Doktrin *f*, Lehre *f*
doc·u·ment **1.** Urkunde *f* **2.** (urkundlich)
belegen; **doc·u·men·ta·ry** **1.** urkundlich; *film etc:* Dokumentar... **2.** Doku-
mentarfilm *m*
dodge (rasch) zur Seite springen, ausweichen; F sich drücken (vor *dat*)
dodg·er Drückeberger *m*
doe zo (Reh)Geiß *f*, Ricke *f*
dog **1.** zo Hund *m* **2.** *j-n* beharrlich verfolgen
dog-eared mit Eselsohren (*book*)
dog·ged verbissen, hartnäckig
dog·ma Dogma *n*; Glaubenssatz *m*
dog·mat·ic dogmatisch
do-it-your·self **1.** Heimwerken *n* **2.**
Heimwerker...
do-it-your·self·er Heimwerker *m*
dole **1.** milde Gabe; *Br* F Stempelgeld *m*;
*****go** *or* **be on the ~** *Br* F stempeln gehen
2. *~ **out** sparsam ver- *or* austeilen
dole·ful traurig, trübselig
doll Puppe *f*

dol·lar Dollar *m*
dol·phin zo Delphin *m*
dome Kuppel *f*
do·mes·tic **1.** häuslich; inländisch, einheimisch; zahm **2.** Hausangestellte
m, *f*; *~ **an·i·mal** Haustier *n*
do·mes·ti·cate *Tier* zähmen
do·mes·tic/ **flight** AVIAT Inlandsflug *m*; *~
mar·ket ECON Binnenmarkt *m*; *~ **trade**
ECON Binnenhandel *m*; *~ **vi·olence**
häusliche Gewalt
dom·i·cile Wohnsitz *m*
dom·i·nant dominierend, (vor)herr-
schend
dom·i·nate beherrschen; dominieren
dom·i·na·tion (Vor)Herrschaft *f*
dom·i·neer·ing herrisch, tyrannisch
do·nate schenken; stiften; spenden (*a*.
MED); **do·na·tion** Schenkung *f*
done getan; erledigt; fertig; GASTR gar
don·key zo Esel *m*
do·nor Spender(in) (*a*. MED)
do-noth·ing F Nichtstuer *m*
doom **1.** Schicksal *n*, Verhängnis *n* **2.**
verurteilen, verdammen
Dooms·day der Jüngste Tag
door Tür *f*; Tor *n*; ***next ~** nebenan
door·bell Türklingel *f*
door han·dle Türklinke *f*
door·keep·er Pförtner *m*
door·knob Türknauf *m*
door·mat (Fuß)Abtreter *m*
door·step Türstufe *f*
door·way Türöffnung *f*
dope **1.** F Stoff *m* (*Rauschgift*); Betäubungsmittel *n*; SPORT Dopingmittel *n*;
sl Trottel *m* **2.** F *j-m* Stoff geben; SPORT
dopen; *~ **test** SPORT Dopingkontrolle *f*
dor·mant schlafend, ruhend; untätig
dor·mi·to·ry Schlafsaal *m*; Studenten-
wohnheim *n*
dor·mo·bile® Campingbus *m*, Wohnmobil *n*
dor·mouse zo Haselmaus *f*
dose **1.** Dosis *f* **2.** *j-m* e-e Medizin geben
dot **1.** Punkt *m*; Fleck *m*; ***on the ~** F auf
die Sekunde pünktlich **2.** punktieren;
tüpfeln; *fig* sprenkeln; *~**ted line** punk-
tierte Linie
dote: *~ **on** vernarrt sein in (*acc*)
dot·ing vernarrt
doub·le **1.** doppelt; Doppel...; zweifach
2. Doppelte *n*; Doppelgänger(in); *film*,
TV Double *n* **3.** (sich) verdoppeln; *film*,

TV *j-n* doubeln; *a.* ~ **up** falten; *Decke* zusammenlegen; ~ *back* kehrtmachen; ~ *up with* sich krümmen vor (*dat*)

dou·ble-breast·ed zweireihig

dou·ble-check genau nachprüfen

dou·ble chin Doppelkinn *n*

dou·ble-cross ein doppeltes *or* falsches Spiel treiben mit

dou·ble-deal·ing 1. betrügerisch **2.** Betrug *m*

dou·ble-deck·er Doppeldecker *m*

dou·ble-edged zweischneidig (*a. fig*); zweideutig

dou·ble fea·ture *film:* Doppelprogramm *n*

dou·ble-park MOT in zweiter Reihe parken

dou·bles *esp tennis:* Doppel *n*; **men's** ~ Herrendoppel *n*; **women's** ~ Damendoppel *n*

dou·ble-sid·ed IT zweiseitig

doubt 1. *v/i* zweifeln; *v/t* bezweifeln; misstrauen (*dat*) **2.** Zweifel *m*; **be in** ~ **about** Zweifel haben an (*dat*); **no** ~ ohne Zweifel

doubt·ful zweifelhaft

doubt·less ohne Zweifel

douche 1. Spülung *f* (*a.* MED); Spülapparat *m* **2.** spülen (*a.* MED)

dough Teig *m*

dough·nut *appr* Krapfen *m*, Berliner Pfannkuchen, Schmalzkringel *m*

dove ZO Taube *f*

dow·dy unelegant; unmodern

dow·el TECH Dübel *m*

down[1] Daunen *pl*; Flaum *m*

down[2] **1.** *adv* nach unten, herunter, hinunter, herab, hinab, abwärts; unten **2.** *prp* herab, hinab, herunter, hinunter; ~ *the river* flussabwärts **3.** *adj* nach unten gerichtet; deprimiert, niedergeschlagen; ~ *platform* Abfahrtsbahnsteig *m* (*in London*); ~ *train* Zug *m* (von London fort) **4.** *v/t* niederschlagen; *Flugzeug* abschießen; F *Getränk* runterkippen; ~ *tools* die Arbeit niederlegen, in den Streik treten

down·cast niedergeschlagen

down·fall Platzregen *m*; *fig* Sturz *m*

down·heart·ed niedergeschlagen

down·hill 1. *adv* bergab **2.** *adj* abschüssig; *skiing:* Abfahrts... **3.** Abhang *m*; *skiing:* Abfahrt *f*

down pay·ment ECON Anzahlung *f*

down·pour Regenguss *m*, Platzregen *m*

down·right 1. *adv* völlig, ganz und gar, ausgesprochen **2.** *adj* glatt (*lie etc*); ausgesprochen

downs Hügelland *n*

down·stairs die Treppe herunter *or* hinunter; (nach) unten

down·stream stromabwärts

down-to-earth realistisch

down·town 1. *adv* im *or* ins Geschäftsviertel **2.** *adj* im Geschäftsviertel (gelegen *or* tätig); **3.** Geschäftsviertel *n*, Innenstadt *f*, City *f*

down·ward(s) abwärts, nach unten

down·y flaumig

dow·ry Mitgift *f*

doze 1. dösen, ein Nickerchen machen **2.** Nickerchen *n*

doz·en Dutzend *n*

drab trist; düster; eintönig

draft 1. Entwurf *m*; (Luft)Zug *m*; Zugluft *f*; Zug *m*, Schluck *m*; MAR Tiefgang *m*; ECON Tratte *f*, Wechsel *m*; MIL Einberufung *f*; **beer on** ~, ~ **beer** Bier *n* vom Fass, Fassbier *n* **2.** entwerfen; *Brief etc* aufsetzen; MIL einberufen

draft·ee MIL Wehr(dienst)pflichtige *m*

drafts·man TECH Zeichner *m*

drafts·wom·an TECH Zeichnerin *f*

draft·y zugig

drag 1. Schleppen *n*, Zerren *n*; *fig* Hemmschuh *m*; F *et.* Langweiliges **2.** schleppen, zerren, ziehen, schleifen; *a.* ~ *behind* zurückbleiben, nachhinken; ~ *on* weiterschleppen; *fig* sich dahinschleppen; *fig* sich in die Länge ziehen

drag lift Schlepplift *m*

drag·on MYTH Drache *m*

drag·on·fly ZO Libelle *f*

drain 1. Abfluss(kanal) *m*, Abflussrohr *n*; Entwässerungsgraben *m* **2.** *v/t* abfließen lassen; entwässern; austrinken, leeren; *v/i:* ~ *off*, ~ *away* abfließen, ablaufen; **drain·age** Abfließen *n*, Ablaufen *n*, Entwässerung *f*; Entwässerungsanlage *f*, -system *n*

drain·pipe Abflussrohr *n*

drake ZO Enterich *m*, Erpel *m*

dram Schluck *m*

dra·ma Drama *n*; **dra·mat·ic** dramatisch; **dram·a·tist** Dramatiker *m*; **dram·a·tize** dramatisieren

drape 1. drapieren; in Falten legen **2.**

mst ~**s** Vorhänge *pl*

drap·er·y *Br* Textilien *pl*

dras·tic drastisch, durchgreifend

draught *Br* → **draft**

draughts *Br* Damespiel *n*

draughts·man *etc* → **draftsman** *etc*

draugh·ty *Br* → **drafty**

draw 1. *v/t* ziehen; *Vorhänge* auf-, zuziehen; *Atem* holen; *Tee* ziehen lassen; *fig Menge* anziehen; *Interesse* auf sich ziehen; zeichnen; *Geld* abheben; *Scheck* ausstellen; *v/i* ziehen; SPORT unentschieden spielen; ~ **back** zurückweichen; ~ **near** sich nähern; ~ **out** *Geld* abheben; *fig* in die Länge ziehen; ~ **up** *Schriftstück* aufsetzen; MOT (an)halten; vorfahren **2.** Ziehen *n*; *lottery*: Ziehung *f*; SPORT Unentschieden *n*; Attraktion *f*, Zugnummer *f*

draw·back Nachteil *m*, Hindernis *n*

draw·bridge Zugbrücke *f*

draw·er[1] Schublade *f*, Schubfach *n*

draw·er[2] Zeichner(in); ECON Aussteller(in)

draw·ing Zeichnen *n*; Zeichnung *f*; ~**board** Reißbrett *n*; ~ **pin** *Br* Reißzwecke *f*, Reißnagel *m*, Heftzwecke *f*; ~ **room** → **living room**; Salon *m*

drawl gedehnt sprechen

drawn abgespannt; SPORT unentschieden

dread 1. (große) Angst, Furcht *f* **2.** (sich) fürchten

dread·ful schrecklich, furchtbar

dream 1. Traum *m* **2.** träumen

dream·er Träumer(in)

dream·y träumerisch, verträumt

drear·y trübselig; trüb(e); langweilig

dredge 1. (Schwimm)Bagger *m* **2.** (aus)baggern

dredg·er (Schwimm)Bagger *m*

dregs Bodensatz *m*; *fig* Abschaum *m*

drench durchnässen

dress 1. Kleidung *f*; Kleid *n* **2.** (sich) ankleiden *or* anziehen; schmücken, dekorieren; zurechtmachen; GASTR zubereiten, *Salat* anmachen; MED *Wunde* verbinden; *Haare* frisieren; **get** ~**ed** sich anziehen; ~ **s.o. down** F j-m e-e Standpauke halten; ~ **up** (sich) fein machen; sich kostümieren *or* verkleiden

dress cir·cle THEA erster Rang

dress de·sign·er Modezeichner(in)

dress·er Anrichte *f*; Toilettentisch *m*

dress·ing An-, Zurichten *n*; Ankleiden *n*; MED Verband *m*; GASTR Dressing *n*, Füllung *f*

dressing-down F Standpauke *f*

dress·ing| **gown** *esp Br* Morgenrock *m*, -mantel *m*; SPORT Bademantel *m*; ~ **room** THEA *etc* (Künstler)Garderobe *f*; SPORT (Umkleide)Kabine *f*; ~ **ta·ble** Toilettentisch *m*

dress·mak·er (Damen)Schneider(in)

dress re·hears·al THEA *etc* Generalprobe *f*

drib·ble tröpfeln (lassen); sabbern, geifern; *soccer*: dribbeln

dried getrocknet, Dörr…

dri·er → **dryer**

drift 1. (Dahin)Treiben *n*; (Schnee)Verwehung *f*; Schnee-, Sandwehe *f*; *fig* Tendenz *f* **2.** (dahin)treiben; wehen; sich häufen

drill 1. TECH Bohrer *m*; MIL Drill *m* (*a. fig*), Exerzieren *n*; Säen *n*; MIL drillen (*a. fig*); **drill·ing site** TECH Bohrgelände *n*, Bohrstelle *f*

drink 1. Getränk *n* **2.** trinken; ~ **to s.o.** j-m zuprosten *or* zutrinken

drink-driv·ing *Br* Trunkenheit *f* am Steuer

drink·er Trinker(in)

drinks ma·chine Getränkeautomat *m*

drip 1. Tröpfeln *n*; MED Tropf *m* **2.** tropfen *or* tröpfeln (lassen); triefen

drip-dry bügelfrei

drip·ping Bratenfett *n*

drive 1. Fahrt *f*; Aus-, Spazierfahrt *f*; Zufahrt(sstraße) *f*; (private) Auffahrt; TECH Antrieb *m*; IT Laufwerk *n*; MOT (*Links- etc*)Steuerung *f*; PSYCH Trieb *m*; *fig* Kampagne *f*; *fig* Schwung *m*, Elan *m*, Dynamik *f* **2.** *v/t* treiben; *Auto etc* fahren, lenken, steuern; (im Auto *etc*) fahren; TECH (an)treiben; *a.* ~ **off** vertreiben; *v/i* treiben; (Auto) fahren; ~ **off** wegfahren; **what are you driving at?** F worauf wollen Sie hinaus?

drive-in 1. Auto…; ~ **cinema** *Br*, ~ **motion-picture theater** Autokino *n* **2.** Autokino *n*; Drive-in-Restaurant *n*; Autoschalter *m*, Drive-in-Schalter *m*

driv·el 1. faseln **2.** Geschwätz *n*, Gefasel *n*

driv·er MOT Fahrer(in); (*Lokomotiv-*) Führer *m*

driv·er's li·cense Führerschein *m*

driv·ing (an)treibend; TECH Antriebs…, Treib…; Trieb…; MOT Fahr…

driv·ing force *fig* Triebkraft *f*

driv·ing li·cence *Br* Führerschein *m*

driv·ing test Fahrprüfung *f*

driz·zle 1. Sprühregen *m* **2.** sprühen, nieseln

drone 1. ZO Drohne *f (a. fig)* **2.** summen; dröhnen

droop (schlaff) herabhängen

drop 1. Tropfen *m*; Fallen *n*, Fall *m*; *fig* Fall *m*, Sturz *m*; Bonbon *m*, *n*; *fruit* ~**s** Drops *pl* **2.** *v/t* tropfen (lassen); fallen lassen*(a. fig)*; *Brief* einwerfen; *Fahrgast* absetzen; senken; ~ **s.o. a few lines** j-m ein paar Zeilen schreiben; *v/i* tropfen; herab-, herunterfallen; umsinken, fallen; ~ **in** (kurz) hereinschauen; ~ **off** abfallen; zurückgehen, nachlassen; F einnicken; ~ **out** herausfallen; aussteigen (*of* aus); *a.* ~ **out of school** (*university*) die Schule (das Studium) abbrechen

drop·out Drop-out *m*, Aussteiger *m*; (Schul-, Studien)Abbrecher *m*

drought Trockenheit *f*, Dürre *f*

drown *v/t* ertränken; überschwemmen; *fig* übertönen; *v/i* ertrinken

drow·sy schläfrig; einschläfernd

drudge sich (ab)placken, schuften, sich schinden; **drudg·e·ry** (stumpfsinnige) Plackerei *f* od Schinderei od Schufterei

drug 1. Arzneimittel *n*, Medikament *n*; Droge *f*, Rauschgift *n*; **be on** ~**s** drogenabhängig *or* drogensüchtig sein; **be off** ~**s** clean sein **2.** j-m Medikamente geben; *j-n* unter Drogen setzen; ein Betäubungsmittel beimischen (*dat*); betäuben (*a. fig*); ~ **a·buse** Drogenmissbrauch *m*; Medikamentenmissbrauch *m*; ~ **ad·dict** Drogenabhängige *m*, *f*, Drogensüchtige *m*, *f*; **be a** ~ drogenabhängig *or* drogensüchtig sein

drug·gist Apotheker(in); Inhaber(in) e-s Drugstores

drug·store Apotheke *f*; Drugstore *m*

drug vic·tim Drogentote *m*, *f*

drum 1. MUS Trommel *f*; ANAT Trommelfell *n*; *pl* MUS Schlagzeug *n* **2.** trommeln; **drum·mer** MUS Trommler *m*; Schlagzeuger *m*

drunk 1. *adj* betrunken; **get** ~ sich betrinken **2.** Betrunkene *m*, *f*; → **drunk-**

ard

drunk·ard Trinker(in), Säufer(in)

drunk driv·ing Trunkenheit *f* am Steuer

drunk·en betrunken; ~ **driv·ing** *Br* Trunkenheit *f* am Steuer

dry 1. trocken, GASTR *a.* herb; F durstig **2.** trocknen; dörren; ~ **out** trocknen; e-e Entziehungskur machen, F trocken werden; ~ **up** austrocknen; versiegen

dry-clean chemisch reinigen

dry clean·er's chemische Reinigung

dry·er TECH Trockner *m*

dry goods Textilien *pl*

du·al doppelt, Doppel…; ~ **car·riageway** *Br* Schnellstraße *f*

dub *Film* synchronisieren

du·bi·ous zweifelhaft

duch·ess Herzogin *f*

duck 1. ZO Ente *f*; Ducken *n*; F Schatz *m* **2.** (unter)tauchen; (sich) ducken

duck·ling ZO Entchen *n*

due 1. zustehend; gebührend; angemessen; ECON fällig; ~ **to** wegen (*gen*); **be** ~ **to** zurückzuführen sein auf (*acc*) **2.** *adv* direkt, genau (*nach Osten etc*)

du·el Duell *n*

dues Gebühren *pl*; Beitrag *m*

du·et MUS Duett *n*

duke Herzog *m*

dull 1. dumm; träge, schwerfällig; stumpf; matt (*eyes etc*); schwach (*hearing*); langweilig; abgestumpft, teilnahmslos; dumpf; trüb(e); ECON flau **2.** stumpf machen *od* werden; (sich) trüben; mildern, dämpfen; *Schmerz* betäuben; *fig* abstumpfen

du·ly ordnungsgemäß; gebührend; rechtzeitig

dumb stumm; sprachlos; F doof, dumm, blöd

dum(b)·found·ed verblüfft, sprachlos

dum·my Attrappe *f*; Kleider-, Schaufensterpuppe *f*; MOT Dummy *m*, Puppe *f*; *Br* Schnuller *m*

dump 1. *v/t* (hin)plumpsen *or* (hin)fallen lassen; auskippen; *Schutt etc* abladen; *Schadstoffe in e-n Fluss etc* einleiten, *im Meer* verklappen (**into** in); ECON *Waren zu Dumpingpreisen verkaufen* **2.** Plumps *m*; Schuttabladeplatz *m*, Müllkippe *f*, Müllhalde *f*, (Müll)Deponie *f*; **dump·ing** ECON Dumping *n*, Ausfuhr *f* zu Schleuderpreisen

dune Düne *f*

dung AGR 1. Dung *m* 2. düngen
dun·geon (Burg)Verlies *n*
dupe betrügen, täuschen
du·plex 1. doppelt, Doppel... 2. *a*. ~ *apartment* Maisonette *f*, Maisonettewohnung *f*; *a*. ~ *house* Doppel-, Zweifamilienhaus *n*
du·pli·cate 1. doppelt; ~ *key* Zweit-, Nachschlüssel *m* 2. Duplikat *n*; Zweit-, Nachschlüssel *m* 3. doppelt ausfertigen; kopieren, vervielfältigen
du·plic·i·ty Doppelzüngigkeit *f*
dur·a·ble haltbar; dauerhaft
du·ra·tion Dauer *f*
du·ress Zwang *m*
dur·ing während
dusk (Abend)Dämmerung *f*
dusk·y dämmerig, düster (*a*. *fig*); schwärzlich
dust 1. Staub *m* 2. *v/t* abstauben; (be)streuen; *v/i* Staub wischen, abstauben
dust·bin *Br* Abfall-, Mülleimer *m*; Abfall-, Mülltonne *f*; ~ lin·er *Br* Müllbeutel *m*
dust·cart *Br* Müllwagen *m*
dust cov·er, dust jack·et Schutzumschlag *m*
dust·er Staubtuch *n*
dust·man *Br* Müllmann *m*
dust·pan Kehrichtschaufel *f*
dust·y staubig
Dutch 1. *adj* holländisch, niederländisch

2. *adv*: *go* ~ getrennte Kasse machen 3. LING Holländisch *n*, Niederländisch *n*; *the* ~ die Holländer *pl*, die Niederländer *pl*
Dutch·man Holländer *m*, Niederländer *m*; Dutch·wom·an Holländerin *f*, Niederländerin *f*
du·ti·a·ble ECON zollpflichtig
du·ty Pflicht *f*; Ehrerbietung *f*; ECON Abgabe *f*; Zoll *m*; Dienst *m*; *on* ~ diensthabend; *be on* ~ Dienst haben; *be off* ~ dienstfrei haben; du·ty-free zollfrei
DVD *abbr of* *Digital Versatile Disk* DVD; ~ *player* DVD-Player *m*; ~ re·corder DVD-Rekorder *m*
dwarf 1. Zwerg(in) 2. verkleinern, klein erscheinen lassen
dwell wohnen; *fig* verweilen (*on* bei)
dwell·ing Wohnung *f*
dwin·dle (dahin)schwinden, abnehmen
dye 1. Farbe *f*; *of the deepest* ~ *fig* von der übelsten Sorte 2. färben
dy·ing 1. sterbend; Sterbe... 2. Sterben *n*; ~ *of forests* Waldsterben *n*
dyke → *dike*[1, 2]
dy·nam·ic dynamisch, kraftgeladen
dy·nam·ics Dynamik *f*
dy·na·mite 1. Dynamit *n* 2. (mit Dynamit) sprengen
dys·en·te·ry MED Ruhr *f*
dys·pep·si·a MED Verdauungsstörung *f*

E, e E, e *n*
each jede(r, -s); ~ *other* einander, sich; je, pro Person, pro Stück
ea·ger begierig; eifrig
ea·ger·ness Begierde *f*; Eifer *m*
ea·gle ZO Adler *m*; HIST Zehndollarstück *n*; ea·gle-eyed scharfsichtig
ear BOT Ähre *f*; ANAT Ohr *n*; Öhr *n*; Henkel *m*
ear·ache Ohrenschmerzen *pl*
ear·drum ANAT Trommelfell *n*
earl *englischer* Graf
ear·lobe ANAT Ohrläppchen *n*
ear·ly früh; Früh...; Anfangs..., erste(r, -s); bald(ig); *as* ~ *as May* schon im Mai; *as* ~ *as possible* so bald wie möglich; ~

on schon früh, frühzeitig
ear·ly bird Frühaufsteher(in)
ear·ly warn·ing sys·tem MIL Frühwarnsystem *n*
ear·mark 1. Kennzeichen *n*; Merkmal *n* 2. kennzeichnen; zurücklegen (*for* für)
earn verdienen; einbringen
ear·nest 1. ernst, ernstlich, ernsthaft; ernst gemeint 2. Ernst *m*; *in* ~ im Ernst; ernsthaft
earn·ings Einkommen *n*
ear·phones Ohrhörer *pl*; Kopfhörer *pl*
ear·piece TEL Hörmuschel *f*
ear·ring Ohrring *m*
ear·shot *within* (*out of*) ~ in (außer) Hörweite

earth 1. Erde *f*; Land *n* 2. *v/t* ELECTR erden

earth·en irden

earth·en·ware Steingut(geschirr) *n*

earth·ly irdisch, weltlich; F denkbar

earth·quake Erdbeben *n*

earth·worm ZO Regenwurm *m*

ease 1. Bequemlichkeit *f*; (Gemüts)Ruhe *f*; Sorglosigkeit *f*; Leichtigkeit *f*; *at (one's)* ~ ruhig, entspannt; unbefangen; *be or feel ill at* ~ sich (in s-r Haut) nicht wohlfühlen 2. *v/t* erleichtern; beruhigen; *Schmerzen* lindern; *v/i mst* ~ *off*, ~ *up* nachlassen; sich entspannen (*situation etc*)

ea·sel Staffelei *f*

east 1. Ost, Osten *m* 2. *adj* östlich, Ost... 3. *adv* nach Osten, ostwärts

Eas·ter Ostern *n*; Oster...; ~ *bun·ny* Osterhase *m*; ~ *egg* Osterei *n*

eas·ter·ly östlich, Ost...

east·ern östlich, Ost...

east·ward(s) östlich, nach Osten

eas·y leicht; einfach; bequem; gemächlich, gemütlich; ungezwungen; *go* ~ *on* schonen, sparsam umgehen mit; *go* ~, *take it* ~ sich Zeit lassen; *take it* ~*!* immer mit der Ruhe!

eas·y chair Sessel *m*

eas·y·go·ing gelassen; ungezwungen

eat essen; (zer)fressen; ~ *out* essen gehen; ~ *up* aufessen

eat·a·ble essbar, genießbar

eat·er Esser(in)

eaves Dachrinne *f*, Traufe *f*

eaves·drop (heimlich) lauschen *or* horchen; ~ *on* belauschen

ebb 1. Ebbe *f* 2. zurückgehen; ~ *away* abnehmen; ~ *tide* Ebbe *f*

eb·o·ny Ebenholz *n*

ec·cen·tric 1. exzentrisch 2. Exzentriker *m*, Sonderling *m*

ec·cle·si·as·tic, ec·cle·si·as·ti·cal geistlich, kirchlich

ech·o 1. Echo *n* 2. widerhallen; *fig* echoen, nachsprechen

e·clipse ASTR (*Sonnen-, Mond*)Finsternis *f*; *fig* Niedergang *m*

e·co·cide Umweltzerstörung *f*

e·co·lo·gi·cal ökologisch, Umwelt...

e·col·o·gist Ökologe *m*

e·col·o·gy Ökologie *f*

ec·o·nom·ic Wirtschafts..., wirtschaftlich; ~ *growth* Wirtschaftswachstum *n*

e·co·nom·i·cal wirtschaftlich, sparsam

e·co·nom·ics Volkswirtschaft(slehre) *f*

e·con·o·mist Volkswirt *m*

e·con·o·mize sparsam wirtschaften (mit)

e·con·o·my 1. Wirtschaft *f*; Wirtschaftlichkeit *f*, Sparsamkeit *f*; Einsparung *f* 2. Spar...

e·co·sys·tem Ökosystem *n*

ec·sta·sy Ekstase *f*, Verzückung *f*

ec·stat·ic verzückt

ed·dy 1. Wirbel *m* 2. wirbeln

edge 1. Schneide *f*; Rand *m*; Kante *f*; Schärfe *f*; *be on* ~ nervös *or* gereizt sein 2. schärfen; (um)säumen; (sich) drängen

edge·ways, edge·wise seitlich, von der Seite

edg·ing Einfassung *f*, Rand *m*

edg·y scharf(kantig); F nervös; F gereizt

ed·i·ble essbar, genießbar

e·dict Edikt *n*

ed·i·fice Gebäude *n*

ed·it *Text* herausgeben, redigieren; IT editieren; *Zeitung* als Herausgeber leiten; e·di·tion (*Buch*)Ausgabe *f*; Auflage *f*; ed·i·tor Herausgeber(in); Redakteur(in); ed·i·to·ri·al 1. Leitartikel *m* 2. Redaktions...

EDP *abbr of* **electronic data processing** EDV, elektronische Datenverarbeitung

ed·u·cate erziehen; unterrichten

ed·u·cat·ed gebildet

ed·u·ca·tion Erziehung *f*; (Aus)Bildung *f*; Bildungs-, Schulwesen *n*; *Ministry of Education* *appr* Unterrichtsministerium

ed·u·ca·tion·al erzieherisch, pädagogisch, Erziehungs...; Bildungs...

ed·u·ca·tion·(al·)ist Pädagoge *m*

eel ZO Aal *m*

ef·fect (Aus)Wirkung *f*; Effekt *m*, Eindruck *m*; *pl* ECON Effekten *pl*; *be in* ~ in Kraft sein; *in* ~ in Wirklichkeit; *take* ~ in Kraft treten; ef·fec·tive wirksam; eindrucksvoll; tatsächlich

ef·fem·i·nate verweichlicht; weibisch

ef·fer·vesce brausen, sprudeln

ef·fer·ves·cent sprudelnd, schäumend

ef·fi·cien·cy Leistung *f*; Leistungsfähigkeit *f*; ~ *measure* ECON Rationalisierungsmaßnahme *f*; ef·fi·cient wirksam; leistungsfähig, tüchtig

ef·flu·ent Abwasser *n*, Abwässer *pl*

ef·fort Anstrengung *f*, Bemühung *f* (*at* um); Mühe *f*; *without ~* → **ef·fort·less** mühelos, ohne Anstrengung

ef·fron·te·ry Frechheit *f*

ef·fu·sive überschwänglich

egg[1] Ei *n*; *put all one's ~ s in one basket* alles auf eine Karte setzen

egg[2]: *~ on* anstacheln

egg co·sy *Br* Eierwärmer *m*

egg·cup Eierbecher *m*

egg·head F Eierkopf *m*

egg·shell Eierschale *f*

egg tim·er Eieruhr *f*

e·go·is·m Egoismus *m*, Selbstsucht *f*

e·go·ist Egoist(in)

E·gypt Ägypten *n*; **E·gyp·tian 1.** ägyptisch **2.** Ägypter(in)

ei·der·down Eiderdaunen *pl*; Daunendecke *f*

eight 1. acht **2.** Acht *f*

eigh·teen 1. achtzehn **2.** Achtzehn *f*

eigh·teenth achtzehnte(r, -s)

eight·fold achtfach

eighth 1. achte(r, -s) **2.** Achtel *n*

eighth·ly achtens

eigh·ti·eth achtzigste(r, -s)

eigh·ty 1. achtzig; *the eighties* die Achtzigerjahre **2.** Achtzig *f*

ei·ther jede(r, -s) (*von zweien*): eine(r, -s) (*von zweien*); beides; *~ ... or* entweder ... oder; *not ~* auch nicht

e·jac·u·late *v/t Samen* ausstoßen; *v/i* ejakulieren, e-n Samenerguss haben

e·jac·u·la·tion Samenerguss *m*

e·ject *j-n* hinauswerfen; TECH ausstoßen, auswerfen

eke: *~ out Vorräte etc* strecken; *Einkommen* aufbessern; *~ out a living* sich (mühsam) durchschlagen

e·lab·o·rate 1. sorgfältig (aus)gearbeitet; kompliziert **2.** sorgfältig ausarbeiten

e·lapse verfließen, verstreichen

e·las·tic 1. elastisch, dehnbar; *~ band Br* → **2.** Gummiring, Gummiband *n*

e·las·ti·ci·ty Elastizität *f*

e·lat·ed begeistert (*at, by* von)

el·bow 1. Ellbogen *m*; (scharfe) Biegung; TECH Knie *n*; *at one's ~* bei der Hand **2.** mit dem Ellbogen (weg)stoßen; *~ one's way through* sich (mit den Ellbogen) e-n Weg bahnen durch

el·der[1] **1.** ältere(r, -s) **2.** der, die Ältere;

(Kirchen)Älteste(r) *m*

el·der[2] BOT Holunder *m*

el·der·ly ältlich, ältere(r, -s)

el·dest älteste(r, -s)

e·lect 1. gewählt **2.** (aus-, er)wählen

e·lec·tion Wahl *f*; *~ vic·to·ry* POL Wahlsieg *m*; *~ win·ner* POL Wahlsieger *m*

e·lec·tor Wähler(in); POL Wahlmann *m*; HIST Kurfürst *m*; **e·lec·to·ral** Wähler..., Wahl...; *~ college* POL Wahlmänner *pl*; *~ district* POL Wahlkreis *m*; **elec·to·rate** POL Wähler(schaft *f*) *pl* (*f*)

e·lec·tric elektrisch, Elektro...

e·lec·tri·cal elektrisch; Elektro...; *~ en·gi·neer* Elektroingenieur *m*, Elektrotechniker *m*; *~ en·gi·neer·ing* Elektrotechnik *f*

e·lec·tric chair elektrischer Stuhl

e·lec·tri·cian Elektriker *m*

e·lec·tri·ci·ty Elektrizität *f*

e·lec·tric ra·zor Elektrorasierer *m*

e·lec·tri·fy elektrifizieren; elektrisieren (*a. fig*)

e·lec·tro·cute auf dem elektrischen Stuhl hinrichten; durch elektrischen Strom töten

e·lec·tron Elektron *n*

e·lec·tron·ic elektronisch, Elektronen...; *~ da·ta pro·cess·ing* elektronische Datenverarbeitung

el·e·gance Eleganz *f*; **el·e·gant** elegant; geschmackvoll; erstklassig

el·e·ment CHEM Element *n*; Urstoff *m*; (Grund)Bestandteil *m*; *pl* Anfangsgründe *pl*, Grundlage(n *pl*) *f*; Elemente *pl*, Naturkräfte *pl*

el·e·men·tal elementar; wesentlich

el·e·men·ta·ry elementar; Anfangs...; *~ school* Grundschule *f*

el·e·phant ZO Elefant *m*

el·e·vate erhöhen; *fig* erheben

el·e·vat·ed erhöht; *fig* gehoben, erhaben

el·e·va·tion Erhebung *f*; Erhöhung *f*; Höhe *f*; Erhabenheit *f*

el·e·va·tor TECH Lift *m*, Fahrstuhl *m*, Aufzug *m*

el·ev·en 1. elf **2.** Elf *f*

el·eventh 1. elfte(r, -s) **2.** Elftel *n*

elf Elf *m*, Elfe *f*; Kobold *m*

e·li·cit *et.* entlocken (*from dat*); ans (Tages)Licht bringen

el·i·gi·ble infrage kommend, geeignet, annehmbar, akzeptabel

E

e·lim·i·nate entfernen, beseitigen; ausscheiden; **e·lim·i·na·tion** Entfernung *f*, Beseitigung *f*; Ausscheidung *f*

é·lite Elite *f*; Auslese *f*

elk zo Elch *m*; Wapitihirsch *m*

el·lipse MATH Ellipse *f*

elm BOT Ulme *f*

e·lon·gate verlängern

e·lope (mit s-m *or* s-r Geliebten) ausreißen *or* durchbrennen

e·lo·quent redegewandt, beredt

else sonst, weiter; andere(r, -s)

else·where anderswo(hin)

e·lude beseitigen entgehen, ausweichen, sich entziehen (*all: dat*); *fig* nicht einfallen (*dat*)

e·lu·sive schwer fassbar

e·ma·ci·at·ed abgezehrt, ausgemergelt

em·a·nate ausströmen; ausgehen (**from** von); **em·a·na·tion** Ausströmen *n*; *fig* Ausstrahlung *f*

e·man·ci·pate emanzipieren

e·man·ci·pa·tion Emanzipation *f*

em·balm (ein)balsamieren

em·bank·ment (Bahn-, Straßen-) Damm *m*; (Erd)Damm *m*; Uferstraße *f*

em·bar·go ECON Embargo *n*, (Hafen-, Handels)Sperre *f*

em·bark AVIAT, MAR an Bord nehmen *or* gehen, MAR *a.* (sich) einschiffen; *Waren* verladen; **~ on** *et.* anfangen, *et.* beginnen

em·bar·rass in Verlegenheit bringen, verlegen machen, in e-e peinliche Lage bringen; **em·bar·rass·ing** unangenehm, peinlich; verfänglich

em·bar·rass·ment Verlegenheit *f*

em·bas·sy POL Botschaft *f*

em·bed (ein)betten, (ein)lagern

em·bel·lish verschönern; *fig* ausschmücken, beschönigen

em·bers Glut *f*

em·bez·zle unterschlagen

em·bez·zle·ment Unterschlagung *f*

em·bit·ter verbittern

em·blem Sinnbild *n*; Wahrzeichen *n*

em·bod·y verkörpern; enthalten

em·bo·lism MED Embolie *f*

em·brace 1. (sich) umarmen; einschließen **2.** Umarmung *f*

em·broi·der (be)sticken; *fig* ausschmücken; **em·broi·der·y** Stickerei *f*; *fig* Ausschmückung *f*

em·broil verwickeln (**in** in *acc*)

e·mend *Texte* verbessern, korrigieren

em·er·ald 1. Smaragd *m* **2.** smaragdgrün

e·merge auftauchen; sich herausstellen *or* ergeben

e·mer·gen·cy 1. Not *f*, Notlage *f*, Notfall *m*, Notstand *m*; **state of ~** POL Ausnahmezustand *m* **2.** Not…; ~ brake Notbremse *f*; ~ call Notruf *m*; ~ ex·it Notausgang *m*; ~ land·ing AVIAT Notlandung *f*; ~ num·ber Notruf(nummer *f*) *m*; ~ room MED Notaufnahme *f*

em·i·grant Auswanderer *m*, *esp* POL Emigrant(in)

em·i·grate auswandern, *esp* POL emigrieren

em·i·gra·tion Auswanderung *f*, *esp* POL Emigration *f*

em·i·nence Berühmtheit *f*, Bedeutung *f*; **Eminence** REL Eminenz *f*

em·i·nent hervorragend, berühmt; bedeutend; **~ly** ganz besonders, äußerst

e·mis·sion Ausstoß *m*, Ausstrahlung *f*, Ausströmen *n*; **~free** abgasfrei

e·mit aussenden, ausstoßen, ausstrahlen, ausströmen; von sich geben

e·mo·tion (Gemüts)Bewegung *f*, Gefühl *n*, Gefühlsregung *f*; Rührung *f*

e·mo·tion·al emotional; gefühlsmäßig; gefühlsbetont

e·mo·tion·al·ly emotional, gefühlsmäßig; **~ disturbed** seelisch gestört

e·mo·tion·less gefühllos

e·mo·tive word PSYCH Reizwort *n*

em·pe·ror Kaiser *m*

em·pha·sis Gewicht *n*; Nachdruck *m*

em·pha·size nachdrücklich betonen

em·phat·ic nachdrücklich; deutlich; bestimmt

em·pire Reich *n*, Imperium *n*; Kaiserreich *n*

em·pir·i·cal erfahrungsgemäß

em·ploy 1. beschäftigen, anstellen; an-, verwenden, gebrauchen **2.** Beschäftigung *f*

em·ploy·ee Angestellte *m*, *f*, Arbeitnehmer(in)

em·ploy·er Arbeitgeber(in)

em·ploy·ment Beschäftigung *f*, Arbeit *f*; ~ ad Stellenanzeige *f*; ~ a·gen·cy *Br* Arbeitsagentur *f*; ~ of·fice Arbeitsamt *n*

em·pow·er ermächtigen; befähigen

em·press Kaiserin *f*

emp·ti·ness Leere *f* (*a. fig*)

emp·ty 1. leer (*a. fig*) **2.** leeren, ausleeren, entleeren; sich leeren

em·u·late wetteifern mit; nacheifern (*dat*); es gleichtun (*dat*)

e·mul·sion Emulsion *f*

en·a·ble befähigen, es *j-m* ermöglichen; ermächtigen

en·act *Gesetz* erlassen; verfügen

en·am·el 1. Email *n*, Emaille *f*; ANAT (Zahn)Schmelz *m*; Glasur *f*, Lack *m*; Nagellack *m* **2.** emaillieren; glasieren; lackieren

en·cased: ~ *in* gehüllt in (*acc*)

en·chant bezaubern; **en·chant·ing** bezaubernd; **en·chant·ment** Bezauberung *f*; Zauber *m*

en·cir·cle einkreisen, umzingeln; umfassen, umschlingen

en·close einschließen, umgeben; beilegen, beifügen

en·clo·sure Einzäunung *f*; Anlage *f*

en·code verschlüsseln, chiffrieren; kodieren

en·com·pass umgeben

en·coun·ter 1. Begegnung *f*; Gefecht *n* **2.** begegnen (*dat*); auf *Schwierigkeiten etc* stoßen; mit *j-m feindlich* zusammenstoßen

en·cour·age ermutigen; fördern

en·cour·age·ment Ermutigung *f*; Anfeuerung *f*; Unterstützung *f*

en·cour·ag·ing ermutigend

en·croach (**on**) eingreifen (in *j-s Recht etc*), eindringen (in *acc*); über Gebühr in Anspruch nehmen (*acc*)

en·croach·ment Ein-, Übergriff *m*

en·cum·ber belasten; (be)hindern

en·cum·brance Belastung *f*

en·cy·clo·p(a)e·di·a Enzyklopädie *f*

end 1. Ende *n*; Ziel *n*, Zweck *m*; **no ~ of** unendlich viel(e), unzählige; **at the ~ of May** Ende Mai; **in the ~** am Ende, schließlich; **on ~** aufrecht; **stand on ~** zu Berge stehen (*hair*); **to no ~** vergebens; **go off the deep ~** F *fig* in die Luft gehen; **make** (**both**) **~s meet** durchkommen, finanziell über die Runden kommen **2.** enden; beend(-ig)en

en·dan·ger gefährden

en·dear beliebt machen (**to s.o.** bei *j-m*); **en·dear·ing** gewinnend; liebenswert; **en·dear·ment: words of ~, ~s** zärtliche Worte *pl*

en·deav·o(u)r 1. Bestreben *n*, Bemühung *f* **2.** sich bemühen

end·ing Ende *n*; Schluss *m*; LING Endung *f*

en·dive BOT Endivie *f*

end·less endlos, unendlich; TECH ohne Ende

en·dorse ECON *Scheck etc* indossieren; *et.* vermerken (**on** auf der Rückseite); billigen; **en·dorse·ment** Vermerk *m*; ECON Indossament *n*, Giro *n*

en·dow *fig* ausstatten; **~ s.o. with s.th.** *j-m et.* stiften; **en·dow·ment** Stiftung *f*; *mst pl* Begabung *f*, Talent *n*

en·dur·ance Ausdauer *f*; **beyond ~, past ~** unerträglich; **en·dure** ertragen

end us·er Endverbraucher *m*

en·e·my 1. Feind *m* **2.** feindlich

en·er·get·ic energisch; tatkräftig

en·er·gy Energie *f*

en·er·gy cri·sis Energiekrise *f*

en·er·gy-sav·ing energiesparend

en·er·gy sup·ply Energieversorgung *f*

en·fold einhüllen; umfassen

en·force (mit Nachdruck, *a.* gerichtlich) geltend machen; *Gesetz etc* durchführen; durchsetzen, erzwingen

en·force·ment ECON, JUR Geltendmachung *f*; Durchsetzung *f*, Erzwingung *f*

en·fran·chise *j-m* das Wahlrecht verleihen

en·gage *v/t j-s Aufmerksamkeit* auf sich ziehen; TECH einrasten lassen; MOT *e-n Gang* einlegen; *j-n* einstellen, anstellen, *Künstler* engagieren; *v/i* TECH einrasten, greifen; **~ in** sich einlassen auf (*acc*) or in (*acc*); sich beschäftigen mit

en·gaged verlobt (**to** mit); beschäftigt (**in, on** mit); besetzt (*a.* Br TEL); **~ tone** or **signal** Br TEL Besetztzeichen *n*

en·gage·ment Verlobung *f*; Verabredung *f*; MIL Gefecht *n*

en·gag·ing einnehmend; gewinnend

en·gine Maschine *f*; Motor *m*; RAIL Lokomotive *f*; **~ driv·er** Br RAIL Lokomotivführer *m*

en·gi·neer 1. Ingenieur *m*, Techniker *m*, Mechaniker *m*; RAIL Lokomotivführer *m*; MIL Pionier *m* **2.** bauen; *fig* (geschickt) in die Wege leiten

en·gi·neer·ing Technik *f*, Ingenieurwesen *n*, Maschinen- und Gerätebau *m*

En·gland England *n*

En·glish 1. englisch **2.** LING Englisch *n*;

the ~ die Engländer *pl*; **in plain** ~ *fig* unverblümt

Eng·lish·man Engländer *m*

Eng·lish·wom·an Engländerin *f*

en·grave (ein)gravieren, (ein)meißeln, (ein)schnitzen; *fig* einprägen

en·grav·er Graveur *m*

en·grav·ing (Kupfer-, Stahl)Stich *m*; Holzschnitt *m*

en·grossed: ~ **in** (voll) in Anspruch genommen von, vertieft *or* versunken in (*acc*)

en·hance erhöhen, verstärken, steigern

e·nig·ma Rätsel *n*

en·ig·mat·ic rätselhaft

en·joy sich erfreuen an (*dat*); genießen; **did you** ~ **it?** hat es Ihnen gefallen?; ~ **o.s.** sich amüsieren, sich gut unterhalten; ~ **yourself!** viel Spaß!; **I** ~ **my dinner** es schmeckt mir; **en·joy·a·ble** angenehm, erfreulich; **en·joy·ment** Vergnügen *n*, Freude *f*; Genuss *m*

en·large (sich) vergrößern *or* erweitern, ausdehnen; PHOT vergrößern; sich verbreiten *or* auslassen (**on** über *acc*)

en·large·ment Erweiterung *f*; Vergrößerung *f* (*a*. PHOT)

en·light·en aufklären, belehren

en·light·en·ment Aufklärung *f*

en·list MIL *v/t* anwerben; *v/i* sich freiwillig melden

en·liv·en beleben

en·mi·ty Feindschaft *f*

en·no·ble adeln; veredeln

e·nor·mi·ty Ungeheuerlichkeit *f*

e·nor·mous ungeheuer

e·nough genug

en·quire, **en·qui·ry** → **inquire, inquiry**

en·rage wütend machen

en·raged wütend (**at** über *acc*)

en·rap·ture entzücken, hinreißen

en·rap·tured entzückt, hingerissen

en·rich bereichern; anreichern

en·rol(l) (sich) einschreiben *or* eintragen; UNIV (sich) immatrikulieren

en·sign MAR *esp* (National)Flagge *f*; MIL Leutnant *m* zur See

en·sue (darauf-, nach)folgen

en·sure sichern

en·tail mit sich bringen, zur Folge haben

en·tan·gle verwickeln

en·ter *v/t* hinein-, hereingehen, -kommen, -treten in (*acc*), eintreten, einsteigen in (*acc*), betreten; einreisen in (*acc*); MAR, RAIL einlaufen, einfahren in (*acc*); eindringen in (*acc*); *Namen etc* eintragen, einschreiben; SPORT melden, nennen (**for** für); *fig* eintreten in (*acc*), beitreten (*dat*); IT eingeben; *v/i* eintreten, herein-, hineinkommen, herein-, hineingehen; THEA auftreten; sich eintragen *or* einschreiben *or* anmelden (**for** für); SPORT melden, nennen (**for** für)

en·ter key IT Eingabetaste *f*

en·ter·prise Unternehmen *n* (*a*. ECON); ECON Unternehmertum *n*; Unternehmungsgeist *m*; **en·ter·pris·ing** unternehmungslustig; wagemutig; kühn

en·ter·tain unterhalten; bewirten

en·ter·tain·er Entertainer(in), Unterhaltungskünstler(in)

en·ter·tain·ment Unterhaltung *f*; Entertainment *n*; Bewirtung *f*

en·thral(l) fesseln, bezaubern

en·throne inthronisieren

en·thu·si·asm Begeisterung *f*, Enthusiasmus *m*; **en·thu·si·ast** Enthusiast(in); **en·thu·si·as·tic** begeistert, enthusiastisch

en·tice (ver)locken

en·tice·ment Verlockung *f*, Reiz *m*

en·tire ganz, vollständig; ungeteilt

en·tire·ly völlig; ausschließlich

en·ti·tle betiteln; berechtigen (**to** zu)

en·ti·ty Einheit *f*

en·trails ANAT Eingeweide *pl*

en·trance Eintreten *n*, Eintritt *m*; Eingang *m*, Zugang *m*; Zufahrt *f*; Einlass *m*, Eintritt *m*, Zutritt *m*

en·trance | ex·am(·i·na·tion) Aufnahmeprüfung *f*; ~ **fee** Eintritt *m*, Eintrittsgeld *n*; Aufnahmegebühr *f*

en·treat inständig bitten, anflehen

en·trea·ty dringende *or* inständige Bitte

en·trench MIL verschanzen (*a*. *fig*)

en·tre·pre·neur ECON Unternehmer(in); **en·tre·pre·neu·ri·al** ECON unternehmerisch

en·trust anvertrauen (**s.th. to s.o.** j-m et.); *j-n* betrauen (**with** mit)

en·try Eintreten *n*, Eintritt *m*; Einreise *f*; Beitritt *m* (**into** zu); Einlass *m*, Zutritt *m*; Zugang *m*, Eingang *m*, Einfahrt *f*; Eintrag(ung *f*) *m*; Stichwort *n*; SPORT Nennung *f*, Meldung *f*; **no** ~**!** Zutritt verboten!, MOT keine Einfahrt!

en·try per·mit Einreiseerlaubnis *f*, -genehmigung *f*

en·try·phone Türsprechanlage *f*

en·try vi·sa Einreisevisum *n*

en·twine ineinander schlingen

e·nu·me·rate aufzählen

en·vel·op (ein)hüllen, einwickeln

en·ve·lope Briefumschlag *m*

en·vi·a·ble beneidenswert

en·vi·ous neidisch

en·vi·ron·ment Umgebung *f*, *a.* Milieu *n*; Umwelt *f*; en·vi·ron·men·tal Milieu...; Umwelt...; en·vi·ron·mental·ist Umweltschützer(in)

en·vi·ron·men·tal| law Umweltschutzgesetz *n*; ~ pol·lu·tion Umweltverschmutzung *f*

en·vi·ron·ment friend·ly umweltfreundlich

en·vi·rons Umgebung *f*

en·vis·age sich *et.* vorstellen

en·voy Gesandte *m*, Gesandtin *f*

en·vy **1.** Neid *m* **2.** beneiden

ep·ic **1.** episch **2.** Epos *n*

ep·i·dem·ic MED **1.** seuchenartig; ~ *disease* → **2.** Epidemie *f*, Seuche *f*

ep·i·der·mis ANAT Oberhaut *f*

ep·i·lep·sy MED Epilepsie *f*

ep·i·log, *Br* ep·i·logue Epilog *m*, Nachwort *n*

e·pis·co·pal REL bischöflich

ep·i·sode Episode *f*

ep·i·taph Grabinschrift *f*

e·poch Epoche *f*, Zeitalter *n*

eq·ua·ble ausgeglichen (*a.* METEOR)

e·qual **1.** gleich; gleichmäßig; ~ *to fig* gewachsen (*dat*); ~ *opportunities* Chancengleichheit *f*; ~ *rights for women* Gleichberechtigung *f* der Frau **2.** Gleiche *m*, *f* **3.** gleich (*dat*)

e·qual·i·ty Gleichheit *f*

e·qual·i·za·tion Gleichstellung *f*; Ausgleich *m*; e·qual·ize gleichmachen, gleichstellen, angleichen; SPORT ausgleichen; e·qual·iz·er SPORT Ausgleich *m*, Ausgleichstor *n*, -treffer *m*

eq·ua·nim·i·ty Gleichmut *m*

e·qua·tion MATH Gleichung *f*

e·qua·tor Äquator *m*

e·qui·lib·ri·um Gleichgewicht *n*

e·quip ausrüsten

e·quip·ment Ausrüstung *f*, Ausstattung *f*; TECH Einrichtung *f*; *fig* Rüstzeug *n*

e·quiv·a·lent **1.** gleichwertig, äquivalent;

---

gleichbedeutend (*to* mit); **2.** Äquivalent *n*, Gegenwert *m*

e·ra Zeitrechnung *f*; Zeitalter *n*

e·rad·i·cate ausrotten

e·rase ausradieren, ausstreichen, löschen (*a.* IT); *fig* auslöschen

e·ras·er Radiergummi *m*

e·rect **1.** aufrecht **2.** aufrichten; *Denkmal etc* errichten; aufstellen

e·rec·tion Errichtung *f*; MED Erektion *f*

er·mine ZO Hermelin *n*

e·rode GEOL erodieren

e·ro·sion GEOL Erosion *f*

e·rot·ic erotisch

err (sich) irren

er·rand Botengang *m*, Besorgung *f*; *go on an* ~, *run an* ~ e-e Besorgung machen

er·rat·ic sprunghaft, unstet, unberechenbar

er·ro·ne·ous irrig

er·ror Irrtum *m*, Fehler *m* (*a.* IT); *in* ~ irrtümlicherweise; ~ *of judg(e)ment* Fehleinschätzung *f*; ~*s excepted* ECON Irrtümer vorbehalten; ~ *mes·sage* IT Fehlermeldung *f*

e·rupt ausbrechen (*volcano etc*); durchbrechen (*teeth*); e·rup·tion (Vulkan-) Ausbruch *m*; MED Ausschlag *m*

ESA *abbr of* **European Space Agency** Europäische Weltraumbehörde

es·ca·late eskalieren; ECON steigen, in die Höhe gehen

es·ca·la·tion Eskalation *f*

es·ca·la·tor Rolltreppe *f*

es·ca·lope GASTR (*esp* Wiener) Schnitzel *n*

es·cape **1.** entgehen (*dat*); entkommen, entrinnen (*both dat*); entweichen; *j-m* entfallen **2.** Entrinnen *n*; Entweichen *n*, Flucht *f*; *have a narrow* ~ mit knapper Not davonkommen

es·cape chute AVIAT Notrutsche *f*

es·cape key IT Escape-Taste *f*

es·cort **1.** MIL Eskorte *f*; Geleit(schutz *m*) *n* **2.** MIL eskortieren; AVIAT, MAR Geleit(schutz) geben; geleiten

es·cutch·eon Wappenschild *m*, *n*

es·pe·cial besondere(r, -s)

es·pe·cial·ly besonders

es·pi·o·nage Spionage *f*

es·pla·nade (*esp* Strand)Promenade *f*

es·say Aufsatz *m*, kurze Abhandlung, Essay *m*, *n*

es·sence Wesen n; Essenz f; Extrakt m

es·sen·tial 1. wesentlich; unentbehrlich 2. mst pl das Wesentliche

es·sen·tial·ly im Wesentlichen, in der Hauptsache

es·tab·lish einrichten, errichten; ~ o.s. sich etablieren or niederlassen; beweisen, nachweisen; es·tab·lish·ment Einrichtung f, Errichtung f; ECON Unternehmen n, Firma f; the Establishment das Establishment, die etablierte Macht, die herrschende Schicht

es·tate (großes) Grundstück, Landsitz m, Gut n; JUR Besitz m, (Erb)Masse f, Nachlass m; housing ~ (Wohn)Siedlung f; industrial ~ Industriegebiet n; real ~ Liegenschaften pl; ~ a·gent Br Grundstücks-, Immobilienmakler m; ~ car Br MOT Kombiwagen m

es·teem Achtung f, Ansehen n (with bei); 2. achten, (hoch) schätzen

es·thet·ic ästhetisch

es·thet·ics Ästhetik f

es·ti·mate 1. (ab-, ein)schätzen; veranschlagen 2. Schätzung f; (Kosten)Voranschlag m; es·ti·ma·tion Meinung f; Achtung f, Wertschätzung f

es·tranged entfremdet

es·trange·ment Entfremdung f

es·tu·a·ry weite Flussmündung

etch ätzen; radieren

etch·ing Radierung f; Kupferstich m

e·ter·nal ewig

e·ter·ni·ty Ewigkeit f

e·ther Äther m

e·the·re·al ätherisch (a. fig)

eth·i·cal sittlich, ethisch

eth·ics Sittenlehre f, Ethik f

eu·ro Euro m

Eu·rope Europa n.

Eu·ro·pe·an 1. europäisch 2. Europäer(in); ~ Union (abbr EU) Europäische Union (abbr EU)

e·vac·u·ate entleeren; evakuieren; Haus etc räumen

e·vade (geschickt) ausweichen (dat); umgehen

e·val·u·ate schätzen; abschätzen, bewerten, beurteilen

e·vap·o·rate verdunsten, verdampfen (lassen); ~d milk Kondensmilch f

e·vap·o·ra·tion Verdunstung f, Verdampfung f

e·va·sion Umgehung f, Vermeidung f;

(Steuer)Hinterziehung f; Ausflucht f

e·va·sive ausweichend; be~ ausweichen

eve Vorabend m; Vortag m; on the ~ of unmittelbar vor (dat), am Vorabend (gen)

e·ven 1. adj eben, gleich; gleichmäßig; ausgeglichen; glatt; gerade (Zahl); get ~ with s.o. es j-m heimzahlen 2. adv selbst, sogar, auch; not~ nicht einmal; ~ though, ~ if wenn auch 3. ~ out sich einpendeln; sich ausgleichen

eve·ning Abend m; in the ~ am Abend, abends; ~ class·es Abendkurs m, Abendunterricht m; ~ dress Gesellschaftsanzug m; Frack m, Smoking m; Abendkleid n

e·ven·song REL Abendgottesdienst m

e·vent Ereignis n; Fall m; SPORT Disziplin f; SPORT Wettbewerb m; at all ~s auf alle Fälle; in the ~ of im Falle (gen)

e·vent·ful ereignisreich

e·ven·tu·al(·ly) schließlich

ev·er immer (wieder); je(mals); ~ after, ~ since seitdem; ~ so F sehr, noch so; for ~ für immer, auf ewig; Yours ~, ..., Ever yours, ... Viele Grüße, dein(e) or Ihr(e), ...; have you ~ been to Boston? bist du schon einmal in Boston gewesen?

ev·er·green 1. immergrün; unverwüstlich, esp immer wieder gern gehört 2. immergrüne Pflanze; MUS Evergreen m, n

ev·er·last·ing ewig

ev·er·more (for) ~ für immer

ev·ery jede(r, -s); alle(r, -s); ~ now and then von Zeit zu Zeit, dann und wann; ~ one of them jeder von ihnen; ~ other day jeden zweiten Tag, alle zwei Tage

ev·ery·bod·y jeder(mann)

ev·ery·day Alltags...

ev·ery·one jeder(mann)

ev·ery·thing alles

ev·ery·where überall(hin)

e·vict JUR zur Räumung zwingen; j-n gewaltsam vertreiben

ev·i·dence Beweis(material n) m, Beweise pl; (Zeugen)Aussage f; give ~ (als Zeuge) aussagen; ev·i·dent augenscheinlich, offensichtlich

e·vil 1. übel, schlimm, böse 2. Übel n; das Böse; e·vil-mind·ed bösartig

e·voke (herauf)beschwören; Erinnerungen wachrufen

ev·o·lu·tion Entwicklung f; BIOL Evolution f

e·volve (sich) entwickeln

ewe ZO Mutterschaf n

ex prp ECON ab; **~ works** ab Werk

ex… Ex…, ehemalig

ex·act 1. exakt, genau **2.** fordern, verlangen; **ex·act·ing** streng, genau; aufreibend, anstrengend; **ex·act·ly** exakt, genau; **~!** ganz recht!, genau!

ex·act·ness Genauigkeit f

ex·ag·ge·rate übertreiben

ex·ag·ge·ra·tion Übertreibung f

ex·am F Examen n

ex·am·i·na·tion Examen n, Prüfung f; Untersuchung f; JUR Vernehmung f, Verhör n; **ex·am·ine** untersuchen; JUR vernehmen, verhören; PED etc prüfen (**in** in dat; **on** über acc)

ex·am·ple Beispiel n; Vorbild n, Muster n; **for ~** zum Beispiel

ex·as·pe·rate wütend machen

ex·as·pe·rat·ing ärgerlich

ex·ca·vate ausgraben, ausheben, ausschachten

ex·ceed überschreiten; übertreffen

ex·ceed·ing übermäßig

ex·ceed·ing·ly außerordentlich, überaus

ex·cel v/t übertreffen; v/i sich auszeichnen

ex·cel·lence ausgezeichnete Qualität

Ex·cel·lency Exzellenz f

ex·cel·lent ausgezeichnet, hervorragend

ex·cept 1. ausnehmen, ausschließen **2.** prp ausgenommen, außer; **~ for** abgesehen von, bis auf (acc)

ex·cept·ing prp ausgenommen

ex·cep·tion Ausnahme f; Einwand m (**to** gegen); **make an ~** e-e Ausnahme machen; **take ~ to** Anstoß nehmen an (dat); **without ~** ohne Ausnahme, ausnahmslos; **ex·cep·tion·al** außergewöhnlich; **ex·cep·tion·al·ly** ungewöhnlich, außergewöhnlich

ex·cerpt Auszug m

ex·cess 1. Übermaß n; Überschuss m; Ausschweifung f **2.** Mehr…; **~ bag-gage** AVIAT Übergepäck n; **~ fare** (Fahrpreis)Zuschlag m

ex·ces·sive übermäßig, übertrieben

ex·cess| lug·gage → **excess baggage**; **~ post·age** Nachgebühr f

ex·change 1. (aus-, ein-, um)tauschen (**for** gegen); wechseln **2.** (Aus-, Um-)Tausch m; (esp Geld)Wechsel m; ECON a. **bill of ~** Wechsel m; Börse f; Wechselstube f; TEL Fernsprechamt n; ECON **foreign ~(s)** Devisen pl; **rate of ~** → **exchange rate**; **~ of·fice** Wechselstube f; **~ rate** Wechselkurs m; **~ student** Austauschschüler(in), Austauschstudent(in)

Ex·cheq·uer: Chancellor of the ~ Br Finanzminister m

ex·cise Verbrauchssteuer f

ex·ci·ta·ble reizbar, (leicht) erregbar

ex·cite erregen, anregen; reizen

ex·cit·ed erregt, aufgeregt

ex·cite·ment Aufregung f, Erregung f

ex·cit·ing erregend, aufregend, spannend

ex·claim (aus)rufen

ex·cla·ma·tion Ausruf m, (Auf)Schrei m; **~ mark** Br, **~ point** Ausrufe-, Ausrufungszeichen n

ex·clude ausschließen

ex·clu·sion Ausschließung f, Ausschluss m; **ex·clu·sive** ausschließlich; exklusiv; Exklusiv…; **~ of** abgesehen von, ohne

ex·com·mu·ni·cate REL exkommunizieren; **ex·com·mu·ni·ca·tion** REL Exkommunikation f

ex·cre·ment Kot m

ex·crete MED ausscheiden

ex·cur·sion Ausflug m

ex·cu·sa·ble entschuldbar

ex·cuse 1. entschuldigen; **~ me** entschuldige(n Sie) **2.** Entschuldigung f

ex·di·rec·to·ry num·ber Br TEL Geheimnummer f

ex·e·cute ausführen; vollziehen; MUS vortragen; hinrichten; JUR Testament vollstrecken; **ex·e·cu·tion** Ausführung f; Vollziehung f; JUR (Zwangs-) Vollstreckung f; Hinrichtung f; MUS Vortrag m; **put or carry a plan into ~** e-n Plan ausführen or verwirklichen

ex·e·cu·tion·er JUR Henker m, Scharfrichter m

ex·ec·u·tive 1. vollziehend, ausübend, POL Exekutiv…; ECON leitend **2.** POL Exekutive f, vollziehende Gewalt; ECON der, die leitende Angestellte; **~ board** Geschäftsleitung f;

ex·em·pla·ry vorbildlich

ex·em·pli·fy veranschaulichen

ex·empt 1. befreit, frei **2.** ausnehmen, befreien

ex·er·cise 1. Übung f; Ausübung f; PED Übung(sarbeit) f, Schulaufgabe f; MIL Manöver n; (körperliche) Bewegung; **do one's ~s** Gymnastik machen; **take** ~ sich Bewegung machen **2.** üben; ausüben; (sich) bewegen; sich Bewegung machen; MIL exerzieren

ex·er·cise book Schul-, Schreibheft n

ex·ert Einfluss etc ausüben; ~ **o.s.** sich anstrengen or bemühen; **ex·er·tion** Ausübung f; Anstrengung f, Strapaze f

ex·hale ausatmen; Gas, Geruch etc verströmen; Rauch ausstoßen

ex·haust 1. erschöpfen; Vorräte ver-, aufbrauchen **2.** TECH Auspuff m; a. ~ **fumes** TECH Auspuff-, Abgase pl

ex·haust·ed erschöpft, aufgebraucht (supplies), vergriffen (book)

ex·haus·tion Erschöpfung f

ex·haus·tive erschöpfend

ex·haust pipe TECH Auspuffrohr n

ex·hib·it 1. ausstellen; vorzeigen; fig zeigen, zur Schau stellen **2.** Ausstellungsstück n; JUR Beweisstück n

ex·hi·bi·tion Ausstellung f; Zurschaustellung f

ex·hil·a·rat·ing erregend, berauschend

ex·hort ermahnen

ex·ile 1. Exil n; im Exil Lebende m, f **2.** ins Exil schicken

ex·ist existieren; vorhanden sein; leben; bestehen; **ex·ist·ence** Existenz f; Vorhandensein n, Vorkommen n; Leben n, Dasein n; **ex·ist·ent** vorhanden

ex·it 1. Abgang m; Ausgang m; (Autobahn)Ausfahrt f; Ausreise f **2.** v/i verlassen; IT (das Programm) beenden; ~ **Macbeth** THEA Macbeth (geht) ab

ex·o·dus Auszug m; Abwanderung f; **general** ~ allgemeiner Aufbruch

ex·on·e·rate entlasten, entbinden, befreien

ex·or·bi·tant übertrieben, maßlos; unverschämt (price etc)

ex·or·cize böse Geister beschwören, austreiben (**from** aus); befreien (**of** von)

ex·ot·ic exotisch; fremd(artig)

ex·pand ausbreiten; (sich) ausdehnen or erweitern; ECON a. expandieren

ex·panse weite Fläche, Weite f

ex·pan·sion Ausbreitung f; Ausdehnung f, Erweiterung f

ex·pan·sive mitteilsam

ex·pat·ri·ate j-n ausbürgern, j-m die Staatsangehörigkeit aberkennen

ex·pect erwarten; F annehmen; **be ~ing** in anderen Umständen sein

ex·pec·tant erwartungsvoll; ~ **mother** werdende Mutter

ex·pec·ta·tion Erwartung f; Hoffnung f, Aussicht f

ex·pe·di·ent 1. zweckdienlich, zweckmäßig; ratsam **2.** (Hilfs)Mittel n, (Not)Behelf m

ex·pe·di·tion Expedition f, (Forschungs)Reise f

ex·pe·di·tious schnell

ex·pel (from) vertreiben (aus); ausweisen (aus); ausschließen (von, aus)

ex·pen·di·ture Ausgaben pl, (Kosten-) Aufwand m

ex·pense Ausgabe pl; pl ECON Unkosten pl, Spesen pl, Auslagen pl; **at the ~ of** auf Kosten (gen)

ex·pen·sive kostspielig, teuer

ex·pe·ri·ence 1. Erfahrung f; (Lebens) Praxis f; Erlebnis n **2.** erfahren, erleben; **ex·pe·ri·enced** erfahren

ex·per·i·ment 1. Versuch m **2.** experimentieren; **ex·per·i·men·tal** Versuchs…

ex·pert 1. erfahren, geschickt; fachmännisch **2.** Fachmann m; Sachverständige m, f

ex·pi·ra·tion Ablauf m, Ende n; Verfall m

ex·pire ablaufen, erlöschen; verfallen

ex·plain erklären

ex·pla·na·tion Erklärung f

ex·pli·cit ausdrücklich; ausführlich; offen, deutlich; (**sexually**) ~ freizügig (film etc)

ex·plode v/t zur Explosion bringen; v/i explodieren; fig ausbrechen (**with** in acc), platzen (**with** vor); fig sprunghaft ansteigen

ex·ploit 1. (Helden)Tat f **2.** ausbeuten; fig ausnutzen

ex·ploi·ta·tion Ausbeutung f, Auswertung f, Verwertung f, Abbau m

ex·plo·ra·tion Erforschung f

ex·plore erforschen

ex·plor·er Forscher(in); Forschungsreisende m, f

ex·plo·sion Explosion *f; fig* Ausbruch *m; fig* sprunghafter Anstieg

ex·plo·sive 1. explosiv; *fig* aufbrausend; *fig* sprunghaft ansteigend **2.** Sprengstoff *m*

ex·po·nent MATH Exponent *m*, Hochzahl *f*; Vertreter(in), Verfechter(in)

ex·port ECON **1.** exportieren, ausführen **2.** Export *m*, Ausfuhr *f; mst pl* Export-, Ausfuhrartikel *m*

ex·por·ta·tion ECON Ausfuhr *f*

ex·port·er ECON Exporteur *m*

ex·pose aussetzen; PHOT belichten; *Waren* ausstellen; *j-n* entlarven, bloßstellen, *et.* aufdecken

ex·po·si·tion Ausstellung *f*

ex·po·sure Aussetzen *n*, Ausgesetztsein *n* (**to** *dat*); *fig* Bloßstellung *f*, Aufdeckung *f*, Enthüllung *f*, Entlarvung *f*; PHOT Belichtung *f*, Aufnahme *f*; **die of ~** an Unterkühlung sterben; **~ me·ter** PHOT Belichtungsmesser *m*

ex·press 1. ausdrücklich, deutlich; Express…, Eil… **2.** Eilbote *m*; Schnellzug *m*; **by ~** → **3.** *adv* durch Eilboten; als Eilgut **4.** äußern, ausdrücken

ex·pres·sion Ausdruck *m*

ex·pres·sion·less ausdruckslos

ex·pres·sive ausdrucksvoll; **be ~ of** *et.* ausdrücken

ex·press let·ter *Br* Eilbrief *m*

ex·press·ly ausdrücklich, eigens

ex·press train Schnellzug *m*

ex·press·way Schnellstraße *f*

ex·pro·pri·ate JUR enteignen

ex·pul·sion (**from**) Vertreibung *f* (aus); Ausweisung *f* (aus)

ex·pur·gate reinigen

ex·qui·site erlesen; fein

ex·tant noch vorhanden

ex·tem·po·re aus dem Stegreif

ex·tem·po·rize aus dem Stegreif sprechen *or* spielen

ex·tend (aus)dehnen, (aus)weiten; *Hand etc* ausstrecken; *Betrieb etc* vergrößern, ausbauen; *Frist, Pass etc* verlängern; sich ausdehnen *or* erstrecken

ex·tend·ed fam·i·ly Großfamilie *f*

ex·ten·sion Ausdehnung *f*; Vergrößerung *f*, Erweiterung *f*; (Frist)Verlängerung *f*; ARCH Erweiterung *f*, Anbau *m*; TEL Nebenanschluss *m*, (-)Apparat *m*; *a.* **~ cord** (*Br* **lead**) ELECTR Verlängerungskabel *n*, -schnur *f*

ex·ten·sive ausgedehnt, umfassend

ex·tent Ausdehnung *f*; Umfang *m*, (Aus)Maß *n*, Grad *m*; **to some ~, to a certain ~** bis zu e-m gewissen Grade; **to such an ~ that** so sehr, dass

ex·ten·u·ate abschwächen, mildern; beschönigen; **extenuating circumstances** JUR mildernde Umstände *pl*

ex·te·ri·or 1. äußerlich, äußere(r, -s), Außen… **2.** *das* Äußere; Außenseite *f*; äußere Erscheinung

ex·ter·mi·nate ausrotten (*a. fig*), vernichten, *Ungeziefer, Unkraut a.* vertilgen

ex·ter·nal äußere(r, -s), äußerlich, Außen…

ex·tinct erloschen; ausgestorben

ex·tinc·tion Erlöschen *n*; Aussterben *n*, Untergang *m*; Vernichtung *f*, Zerstörung *f*

ex·tin·guish (aus)löschen; vernichten

ex·tin·guish·er (*Feuer*)Löscher *m*

ex·tort erpressen (**from** von)

ex·tra 1. *adj* zusätzlich, Extra…, Sonder…; **be ~** gesondert berechnet werden **2.** *adv* extra, besonders; **charge ~ for** *et.* gesondert berechnen **3.** Sonderleistung *f*; *esp* MOT Extra *n*; Zuschlag *m*; Extrablatt *n*; THEA, *film*: Statist(in)

ex·tract 1. Auszug *m* **2.** (heraus)ziehen; herauslocken; ableiten, herleiten

ex·trac·tion (Heraus)Ziehen *n*; Herkunft *f*

ex·tra·dite ausliefern; *j-s* Auslieferung erwirken

ex·tra·di·tion Auslieferung *f*

extra·or·di·na·ry außerordentlich; ungewöhnlich; Sonder…

ex·tra pay Zulage *f*

ex·tra·ter·res·tri·al außerirdisch

ex·tra time SPORT (Spiel)Verlängerung *f*

ex·trav·a·gance Übertriebenheit *f*; Verschwendung *f*; Extravaganz *f*

ex·trav·a·gant übertrieben, überspannt; verschwenderisch; extravagant

ex·treme 1. äußerste(r, -s), größte(r, -s), höchste(r, -s); außergewöhnlich; **~ right** POL rechtsextrem(istisch); **~ right wing** POL rechtsradikal **2.** *das* Äußerste; Extrem *n*; höchster Grad

ex·treme·ly äußerst, höchst

ex·trem·ism POL Extremismus *m*

ex·trem·ist POL Extremist(in)

E

ex·trem·i·ties Gliedmaßen *pl*, Extremitäten *pl*

ex·trem·i·ty *das* Äußerste; höchste Not; äußerste Maßnahme

ex·tri·cate herauswinden, herausziehen, befreien

ex·tro·vert Extrovertierte *m*, *f*

ex·u·be·rance Fülle *f*; Überschwang *m*; ex·u·be·rant reichlich, üppig; überschwänglich; ausgelassen

ex·ult frohlocken, jubeln

eye **1.** ANAT Auge *n*; Blick *m*; Öhr *n*; Öse *f*; **see ~ to ~ with s.o.** mit j-m völlig übereinstimmen; **be up to the ~s in work** bis über die Ohren in Arbeit stecken; **with an ~ to s.th.** im Hinblick auf et. **2.** ansehen; mustern

eye·ball ANAT Augapfel *m*

eye·brow ANAT Augenbraue *f*

eye-catch·ing ins Auge fallend, auffallend

eye doc·tor F Augenarzt *m*, -ärztin *f*

eye·glass·es *a.* **pair of** ~ Brille *f*

eye·lash ANAT Augenwimper *f*

eye·lid ANAT Augenlid *n*

eye·lin·er Eyeliner *m*

eye-o·pen·er: **that was an ~ to me** das hat mir die Augen geöffnet

eye shad·ow Lidschatten *m*

eye·sight Augen(licht *n*) *pl*, Sehkraft *f*

eye·sore F Schandfleck *m*

eye spe·cial·ist Augenarzt *m*, -ärztin *f*

eye·strain Ermüdung *f or* Überanstrengung *f* der Augen

eye·wit·ness Augenzeuge *m*, -zeugin *f*

F

F, f F, f *n*

fa·ble Fabel *f*; Sage *f*

fab·ric Gewebe *n*, Stoff *m*; Struktur *f*

fab·ri·cate fabrizieren (*mst fig*)

fab·u·lous sagenhaft, der Sage angehörend; fabelhaft

fa·cade, fa·çade ARCH Fassade *f*

face **1.** Gesicht *n*; Gesichtsausdruck *m*, Miene *f*; (Ober)Fläche *f*; Vorderseite *f*; Zifferblatt *n*; **~ to ~ with** Auge in Auge mit; **save (lose) one's ~** das Gesicht wahren (verlieren); **on the ~ of it** auf den ersten Blick; **pull a long ~** ein langes Gesicht machen; **have the ~ to do s.th.** die Stirn haben, et. zu tun **2.** *v/t* ansehen; gegenüberstehen (*dat*); (hinaus)gehen auf (*acc*); die Stirn bieten (*dat*); einfassen; ARCH bekleiden; *v/i*: **~ about** sich umdrehen

face·cloth, *Br* face flan·nel Waschlappen *m*

face-lift Facelifting *n*, Gesichtsstraffung *f*; *fig* Renovierung *f*, Verschönerung *f*

fa·ce·tious witzig

fa·cial **1.** Gesichts… **2.** Gesichtsbehandlung *f*

fa·cile leicht; oberflächlich

fa·cil·i·tate erleichtern

fa·cil·i·ty Leichtigkeit *f*; Oberflächlichkeit *f*; *mst pl* Erleichterung(en *pl*) *f*; Einrichtung(en *pl*) *f*, Anlage(n *pl*) *f*

fac·ing TECH Verkleidung *f*; *pl* Besatz *m*

fact Tatsache *f*, Wirklichkeit *f*, Wahrheit *f*; Tat *f*; *pl* Daten; **in ~** in der Tat, tatsächlich

fac·tion *esp* POL Splittergruppe *f*; Zwietracht *f*

fac·ti·tious künstlich

fac·tor Faktor *m*

fac·to·ry Fabrik *f*

fac·ul·ty Fähigkeit *f*; Kraft *f*; *fig* Gabe *f*; UNIV Fakultät *f*; Lehrkörper *m*

fad Mode *f*, Modeerscheinung *f*, -torheit *f*; (vorübergehende) Laune

fade (ver)welken (lassen); verschießen, verblassen (*color*); schwinden; immer schwächer werden (*person*); *film, radio, TV* **~ in** auf- *or* eingeblendet werden; auf- *or* einblenden; **~ out** aus- *or* abgeblendet werden; aus- *or* abblenden; **~d jeans** ausgewaschene Jeans *pl*

fail **1.** *v/i* versagen; misslingen, fehlschlagen; versiegen; nachlassen; durchfallen (*candidate*); *v/t* im Stich lassen; j-n in e-r Prüfung durchfallen lassen **2. without** ~ mit Sicherheit, ganz bestimmt; fail·ure Versagen *n*; Fehlschlag *m*, Misserfolg *m*; Versäumnis *n*; Versager *m*, F Niete *f*

faint **1.** schwach, matt **2.** ohnmächtig

werden, in Ohnmacht fallen (**with** vor);
3. Ohnmacht *f*

faint-heart·ed verzagt

fair[1] gerecht, ehrlich, anständig, fair;
recht gut, ansehnlich; schön (*weather*);
klar (*sky*); blond (*hair*); hell (*skin*); **play**
~ fair spielen; *fig* sich an die Spielregeln halten

fair[2] (Jahr)Markt *m*; Volksfest *n*; Ausstellung *f*, Messe *f*

fair game *fig* Freiwild *n*

fair·ground Rummelplatz *m*

fair·ly gerecht; ziemlich

fair·ness Gerechtigkeit *f*, Fairness *f*

fair play SPORT *and fig* Fair Play *n*, Fairness *f*

fai·ry Fee *f*; Zauberin *f*; Elf *m*, Elfe *f*

fai·ry·land Feen-, Märchenland *n*

fai·ry| sto·ry, ~ **tale** Märchen *n* (*a. fig*)

faith Glaube *m*; Vertrauen *n*; **faith·ful**
treu (**to** *dat*); **Yours ~ly** Hochachtungsvoll (*letter*); **faith·less** treulos

fake 1. Schwindel *m*; Fälschung *f*;
Schwindler *m* **2.** fälschen; imitieren,
nachmachen; vortäuschen, simulieren
3. gefälscht; fingiert

fal·con ZO Falke *m*

fall 1. Fallen *n*, Fall *m*; Sturz *m*; Verfall
m; Einsturz *m*; Herbst *m*; ECON Sinken
n (*of prices etc*); Gefälle *n*; *mst pl* Wasserfall *m* **2.** fallen, stürzen; ab-, einfallen; sinken; sich legen (*wind*); *in e-n
Zustand* verfallen; ~ **ill**, ~ **sick** krank
werden; ~ **in love with** sich verlieben
in (*acc*); ~ **short of** den Erwartungen
etc nicht entsprechen; ~ **back** zurückweichen; ~ **back on** *fig* zurückgreifen
auf (*acc*); ~ **for** hereinfallen auf (*acc*);
F sich in *j-n* verknallen; ~ **off** zurückgehen (*business, demand etc*), nachlassen; ~ **on** herfallen über (*acc*); ~ **out**
streiten (**with** mit); ~ **through** durchfallen (*a. fig*); ~ **to** reinhauen, tüchtig zugreifen

fal·la·cious trügerisch

fal·la·cy Trugschluss *m*

fall guy F *der* Lackierte, *der* Dumme

fal·li·ble fehlbar

fall·ing star Sternschnuppe *f*

fall·out Fall-out *m*, radioaktiver Niederschlag

fal·low ZO falb; AGR brach(liegend)

false falsch

false·hood, **false·ness** Falschheit *f*;

Unwahrheit *f*

false start Fehlstart *m*

fal·si·fi·ca·tion (Ver)Fälschung *f*

fal·si·fy (ver)fälschen

fal·si·ty Falschheit *f*, Unwahrheit *f*

fal·ter schwanken; stocken (*voice*);
stammeln; *fig* zaudern

fame Ruf *m*, Ruhm *m*

famed berühmt (**for** wegen)

fa·mil·i·ar 1. vertraut; gewohnt; familiär
2. Vertraute *m*, *f*

fa·mil·i·ar·i·ty Vertrautheit *f*; (plumpe)
Vertraulichkeit

fa·mil·i·ar·ize vertraut machen

fam·i·ly 1. Familie *f* **2.** Familien...,
Haus...; ~ **al·low·ance** → **child bene-
fit**; ~ **doc·tor** Hausarzt *m*; ~ **name**
Familien-, Nachname *m*; ~ **plan·ning** Familienplanung *f*; ~ **tree** Stammbaum *m*

fam·ine Hungersnot *f*; Knappheit *f* (**of**
an *dat*)

fam·ished verhungert; **be** ~ F am Verhungern sein

fa·mous berühmt

fan[1] **1.** Fächer *m*; Ventilator *m* **2.** (zu)fächeln; anfachen; *fig* entfachen

fan[2] (*Sport- etc*)Fan *m*

fa·nat·ic Fanatiker(in)

fa·nat·i·cal fanatisch

fan belt TECH Keilriemen *m*

fan·ci·er BOT, ZO Liebhaber(in), Züchter(in)

fan·ci·ful fantastisch

fan club Fanklub *m*

fan·cy 1. Fantasie *f*; Einbildung *f*; plötzlicher Einfall, Idee *f*; Laune *f*; Vorliebe
f, Neigung *f* **2.** ausgefallen; Fantasie...
3. sich vorstellen; sich einbilden; ~
that! stell dir vor!, denk nur!; sieh
mal einer an!

fan·cy| ball Kostümfest *n*, Maskenball
m; ~ **dress** (Masken)Kostüm *n*

fan·cy-free → **footloose**

fan·cy goods Modeartikel *pl*, -waren *pl*

fan·cy·work Stickerei *f*

fang ZO Reiß-, Fangzahn *m*; Hauer *m*;
Giftzahn *m*

fan mail Fanpost *f*, Verehrerpost *f*

fan·tas·tic fantastisch

fan·ta·sy Fantasie *f*

far 1. *adj* fern, entfernt, weit **2.** *adv* fern;
weit; (sehr) viel; **as ~ as** bis; **in so ~ as**
insofern als

far·a·way weit entfernt

F

fare 1. Fahrgeld *n*; Fahrgast *m*; Verpflegung *f*, Kost *f* **2.** *gut* leben; **he ~d well** es (er)ging ihm gut

fare dodg·er Schwarzfahrer(in)

fare·well 1. *int* lebe(n Sie) wohl! **2.** Abschied *m*, Lebewohl *n*

far·fetched *fig* weit hergeholt, gesucht

farm 1. Bauernhof *m*, Gut *n*, Gehöft *n*, Farm *f* **2.** *Land, Hof* bewirtschaften

farm·er Bauer *m*, Landwirt *m*, Farmer *m*

farm·hand Landarbeiter(in)

farm·house Bauernhaus *n*

farm·ing 1. Acker…, landwirtschaftlich **2.** Landwirtschaft *f*

farm·stead Bauernhof *m*, Gehöft *n*

farm·yard Wirtschaftshof *m*

far·off entfernt, fern

far right POL rechtsgerichtet

far·sight·ed weitsichtig, *fig a.* weitblickend

fas·ci·nate faszinieren

fas·ci·nat·ing faszinierend

fas·ci·na·tion Zauber *m*, Reiz *m*, Faszination *f*

fas·cism POL Faschismus *m*

fas·cist POL **1.** Faschist *m* **2.** faschistisch

fash·ion Mode *f*; Art *f* und Weise *f*; **be in ~** in Mode sein; **out of ~** unmodern; **fash·ion·a·ble** modisch, elegant; in Mode

fash·ion| pa·rade, ~ show Modenschau *f*

fast¹ 1. Fasten *n* **2.** fasten

fast² 1. schnell; fest; treu; echt, beständig (*color*); flott; **be ~** vorgehen (*watch*)

fast·back MOT (Wagen *m* mit) Fließheck *n*

fast breed·er (**re·ac·tor**) PHYS Schneller Brüter

fas·ten befestigen, festmachen, anheften, anschnallen, anbinden, zuknöpfen, zu-, verschnüren; *Blick etc* richten (**on** auf *acc*); sich festmachen *or* schließen lassen; **fas·ten·er** Verschluss *m*

fast food Schnellgericht(e *pl*) *n*

fast·food res·tau·rant Schnellimbiss *m*, Schnellgaststätte *f*

fas·tid·i·ous anspruchsvoll, heikel, wählerisch, verwöhnt

fast lane MOT Überholspur *f*

fat 1. fett; dick; fettig, fetthaltig **2.** Fett *n*; **be low in ~** fettarm sein

fa·tal tödlich; verhängnisvoll, fatal (**to** für); **fa·tal·i·ty** Verhängnis *n*; tödlicher

Unfall; (Todes)Opfer *n*

fate Schicksal *n*; Verhängnis *n*

fa·ther Vater *m*

Fa·ther Christ·mas *esp Br* der Weihnachtsmann, der Nikolaus

fa·ther·hood Vaterschaft *f*

fa·ther-in-law Schwiegervater *m*

fa·ther·less vaterlos

fa·ther·ly väterlich

fath·om 1. MAR Faden *m* **2.** MAR loten; *fig* ergründen

fath·om·less unergründlich

fa·tigue 1. Ermüdung *f*; Strapaze *f* **2.** ermüden

fat·ten dick *or contp* fett machen *or* werden; mästen; fat·ty fett; fettig

fau·cet TECH (Wasser)Hahn *m*

fault Fehler *m*; Defekt *m*; Schuld *f*; **find ~ with** et. auszusetzen haben an (*dat*); **be at ~** Schuld haben

fault·less fehlerfrei, fehlerlos

fault·y fehlerhaft, TECH *a.* defekt

fa·vo(u)r 1. Gunst *f*; Gefallen *m*; Begünstigung *f*; **in ~ of** zu Gunsten von (*or gen*); **do s.o. a ~** j-m ein Gefallen tun **2.** begünstigen; bevorzugen, vorziehen; wohlwollend gegenüberstehen; SPORT favorisieren; **fa·vo(u)r·a·ble** günstig; **fa·vo(u)r·ite 1.** Liebling *m*; SPORT Favorit *m* **2.** Lieblings…

fawn 1. ZO (Reh)Kitz *n*; Rehbraun *n* **2.** rehbraun

fax 1. Fax *n* **2.** faxen; **~ s.th. (through) to s.o.** j-m et. faxen

fax (ma·chine) Faxgerät *n*

fear 1. Furcht *f* (**of** vor *dat*); Befürchtung *f*; Angst *f* **2.** (be)fürchten; sich fürchten vor (*dat*)

fear·ful furchtsam; furchtbar

fear·less furchtlos

fea·si·ble durchführbar

feast 1. REL Fest *n*, Feiertag *m*; Festessen *n*; *fig* Fest *n*, (Hoch)Genuss *m* **2.** *v/t* festlich bewirten; *v/i* sich gütlich tun (**on** an *dat*), schlemmen

feat große Leistung; (Helden)Tat *f*

fea·ther 1. Feder *f*; *a. pl* Gefieder *n*; **birds of a ~** Leute vom gleichen Schlag; **birds of a ~ flock together** Gleich und Gleich gesellt sich gern; **that is a ~ in his cap** darauf kann er stolz sein **2.** mit Federn polstern *or* schmücken; *Pfeil* fiedern

feath·er·bed verhätscheln

feath·er·brained F hohlköpfig

feath·ered ZO gefiedert

feath·er·weight SPORT Federgewicht *n*, Federgewichtler *m*; Leichtgewicht *n* (*person*)

feath·er·y gefiedert; federleicht

fea·ture 1. (Gesichts)Zug *m*; (charakteristisches) Merkmal; *radio*, TV etc Feature *n*; Haupt-, Spielfilm *m* **2.** groß herausbringen; *film:* in der Hauptrolle zeigen; ~ film Haupt-, Spielfilm *m*

Feb *abbr of February* Febr., Februar *m*

Feb·ru·a·ry (*abbr* **Feb**) Februar *m*

fed·e·ral POL Bundes...

Fed·e·ral Re·pub·lic of Ger·man·y die Bundesrepublik Deutschland (*abbr* **BRD**)

fed·e·ra·tion POL Bundesstaat *m*; Föderation *f*, Staatenbund *m*; ECON, SPORT etc (Dach)Verband *m*

fee Gebühr *f*; Honorar *n*; (Mitglieds-) Beitrag *m*; Eintrittsgeld *n*

fee·ble schwach

feed 1. Futter *n*; Nahrung *f*; Fütterung *f*; TECH Zuführung *f*, Speisung *f* **2.** *v/t* füttern; ernähren; TECH *Maschine* speisen; IT eingeben; AGR weiden lassen; *be fed up with s.o.* (*s.th.*) j-n (et.) satthaben; *well fed* wohlgenährt; *v/i* (fr)essen; sich ernähren; weiden

feed·back ELECTR Feed-back *n*, Rückkoppelung *f*; *radio*, TV Reaktion *f*

feed·er Esser *m*

feed·er road Zubringer(straße *f*) *m*

feed·ing bot·tle (Saug)Flasche *f*

feel 1. (sich) fühlen; befühlen; empfinden; sich anfühlen; ~ *sorry for s.o.* j-n bedauern *or* bemitleiden **2.** Gefühl *n*; Empfindung *f*; **feel·er** ZO Fühler *m*; **feel·ing** Gefühl *n*

feign *Interesse etc* vortäuschen, *Krankheit a.* simulieren

feint Finte *f*

fell niederschlagen; fällen

fel·low 1. Gefährte *m*, Gefährtin *f*, Kamerad(in); Gegenstück *n*; F Kerl *m*; *old* ~ F alter Knabe; *the* ~ *of a glove* der andere Handschuh **2.** Mit...; ~ being Mitmensch *m*; ~ cit·i·zen Mitbürger *m*; ~ coun·try·man Landsmann *m*

fel·low·ship Gemeinschaft *f*; Kameradschaft *f*

fel·low trav·el·(l)er Mitreisende *m*, *f*, Reisegefährte *m*, -gefährtin *f*; POL Mit-

läufer(in)

fel·on JUR Schwerverbrecher *m*

fel·o·ny JUR (schweres) Verbrechen, Kapitalverbrechen *n*

felt Filz *m*; ~ **pen**, ~ **tip**, ~-**tip(ped) pen** Filzstift *m*, Filzschreiber *m*

fe·male 1. weiblich **2.** *contp* Weib *n*, Weibsbild *n*; ZO Weibchen *n*

fem·i·nine weiblich, Frauen...; feminin

fem·i·nism Feminismus *m*

fem·i·nist 1. Feminist(in) **2.** feministisch

fen Fenn *n*, Sumpf-, Marschland *n*

fence 1. Zaun *m*; *sl* Hehler *m* **2.** *v/t:* ~ *in* einzäunen, umzäunen; einsperren; ~ *off* abzäunen; *v/i* SPORT fechten; **fenc·er** SPORT Fechter *m*; **fenc·ing 1.** Einfriedung *f*; sport Fechten *n* **2.** Fecht...

fend: ~ *off* abwehren; ~ *for o.s.* für sich selbst sorgen

fend·er Schutzvorrichtung *f*; Schutzblech *n*; MOT Kotflügel *m*; Kamingitter *n*, Kaminvorsetzer *m*

fen·nel BOT Fenchel *m*

fer·ment 1. Ferment *n*; Gärung *f* **2.** gären (lassen)

fer·men·ta·tion Gärung *f*

fern BOT Farn(kraut *n*) *m*

fe·ro·cious wild; grausam

fe·ro·ci·ty Wildheit *f*

fer·ret 1. ZO Frettchen *n*; *fig* Spürhund *m* **2.** herumstöbern; ~ *out* aufspüren, aufstöbern

fer·ry 1. Fähre *f* **2.** übersetzen

fer·ry·boat Fährboot *n*, Fähre *f*

fer·ry·man Fährmann *m*

fer·tile fruchtbar; reich (*of*, *in* an *dat*)

fer·til·i·ty Fruchtbarkeit *f* (*a. fig*)

fer·ti·lize fruchtbar machen; befruchten; AGR düngen; **fer·ti·liz·er** AGR (*esp* Kunst)Dünger *m*, Düngemittel *n*

fer·vent glühend, leidenschaftlich

fer·vo(u)r Glut *f*; Inbrunst *f*

fes·ter MED eitern

fes·ti·val Fest *n*; Festival *n*, Festspiele *pl*

fes·tive festlich

fes·tiv·i·ty Festlichkeit *f*

fes·toon Girlande *f*

fetch holen; *Preis* erzielen; *Seufzer* ausstoßen; **fetch·ing** F reizend

fête, **fête 1.** Fest *n*; *village* ~ Dorffest *n* **2.** feiern

fet·id stinkend

fet·ter 1. Fessel *f* **2.** fesseln

feud Fehde *f*

F

feud·al Feudal…, Lehns…
feu·dal·ism Feudalismus *m*, Feudal-, Lehnssystem *n*
fe·ver MED Fieber *n*; **fe·ver·ish** MED fieb(e)rig, fieberhaft (*a. fig*)
few wenige; *a* ~ ein paar, einige; *no fewer than* nicht weniger als; *quite a* ~, *a good* ~ e-e ganze Menge
fi·an·cé Verlobte *m*
fi·an·cée Verlobte *f*
fi·as·co Fiasko *n*
fib F **1.** Flunkerei *f*, Schwindelei *f* **2.** schwindeln, flunkern
fi·ber, *Br* **fi·bre** Faser *f*
fi·ber·glass TECH Fiberglas *n*, Glasfaser *f*
fi·brous faserig
fick·le wankelmütig; unbeständig
fic·tion Erfindung *f*; Prosaliteratur *f*, Belletristik *f*; Romane *pl*
fic·tion·al erdichtet; Roman…
fic·ti·tious erfunden, fiktiv
fid·dle 1. Fiedel *f*, Geige *f*; *play first (second)* ~ *esp fig* die erste (zweite) Geige spielen; (*as*) *fit as a* ~ kerngesund **2.** MUS fiedeln; *a.* ~ *about or around (with)* herumfingern (an *dat*), spielen (mit)
fid·dler Geiger(in)
fi·del·i·ty Treue *f*; Genauigkeit *f*
fid·get F nervös machen; (herum)zappeln; **fid·get·y** zapp(e)lig, nervös
field Feld *n*; SPORT Spielfeld *n*; Arbeitsfeld *n*; Gebiet *n*; Bereich *m*; ~ *of vision* OPT Gesichtsfeld *n*; ~ *events* SPORT Sprung- und Wurfdisziplinen *pl*; ~ *glass·es a. pair of* ~ Feldstecher *m*, Fernglas *n*; ~ *mar·shal* MIL Feldmarschall *m*
field·work praktische (wissenschaftliche) Arbeit, *a.* Arbeit *f* im Gelände; ECON Feldarbeit *f*
fiend Satan *m*, Teufel *m*; F (*Frischluftetc*)Fanatiker(in)
fiend·ish teuflisch, boshaft
fierce wild; scharf; heftig; **fierce·ness** Wildheit *f*, Schärfe *f*; Heftigkeit *f*
fi·er·y feurig; hitzig
fif·teen 1. fünfzehn **2.** Fünfzehn *f*
fif·teenth fünfzehnte(r, -s)
fifth 1. fünfte(r, -s) **2.** Fünftel *n*
fifth·ly fünftens
fif·ti·eth fünfzigste(r, -s)
fif·ty 1. fünfzig **2.** Fünfzig *f*

fif·ty-fif·ty F halbe-halbe
fig BOT Feige *f*
fight 1. Kampf *m*; MIL Gefecht *n*; Schlägerei *f*; *boxing:* Kampf *m*, Fight *m* **2.** *v/t* bekämpfen; kämpfen gegen *or* mit, SPORT *a.* boxen gegen; *v/i* kämpfen, sich schlagen; SPORT boxen
fight·er Kämpfer *m*; SPORT Boxer *m*, Fighter *m*; *a.* ~ *plane* MIL Jagdflugzeug *n*
fight·ing Kampf *m*
fig·u·ra·tive bildlich
fig·ure 1. Figur *f*; Gestalt *f*; Zahl *f*, Ziffer *f*; Preis *m*; *be good at* ~*s* ein guter Rechner sein **2.** *v/t* abbilden, darstellen; F meinen, glauben; sich *et.* vorstellen; ~ *out* Problem lösen, F rauskriegen; verstehen; ~ *up* zusammenzählen; *v/i* erscheinen, vorkommen; ~ *on* rechnen mit; ~ *skat·er* Eiskunstläufer(in); ~ *skat·ing* Eiskunstlauf *m*
filch F klauen, stibitzen
file¹ 1. Ordner *m*; Karteikasten *m*; Akte *f*, Akten *pl*; Ablage *f*; IT Datei *f*; Reihe *f*; MIL Rotte *f*; *on* ~ bei den Akten **2.** *v/t* Briefe *etc* ablegen, zu den Akten nehmen, einordnen; *Antrag* einreichen, *Berufung* einlegen; *v/i* hintereinander marschieren
file² TECH **1.** Feile *f* **2.** feilen
file| man·age·ment IT Dateiverwaltung *f*; ~ *pro·tec·tion* IT Schreibschutz *m*
fil·et GASTR Filet *n*
fi·li·al kindlich, Kindes…
fil·ing Ablegen *n*
fil·ing cab·i·net Aktenschrank *m*
fill 1. (sich) füllen; an-, aus-, erfüllen, vollfüllen; *Pfeife* stopfen; *Zahn* füllen, plombieren; ~ *in* einsetzen; ~ *out* (*Br in*) *Formular* ausfüllen; ~ *up* vollfüllen; sich füllen **2.** Füllung *f*
fil·let → *filet*
fill·ing Füllung *f*; MED (*Zahn*)Füllung *f*, Plombe *f*; ~ *sta·tion* Tankstelle *f*
fil·ly ZO Stutenfohlen *n*
film 1. Häutchen *n*; Membran(e) *f*; Film *m* (*a.* PHOT); *take or shoot a* ~ e-n Film drehen **2.** (ver)filmen; sich verfilmen lassen; ~ *star esp Br* Filmstar *m*
fil·ter 1. Filter *m* **2.** filtern
fil·ter tip Filter *m*; Filterzigarette *f*
fil·ter-tipped: ~ *cigarette* Filterzigarette *f*

filth Schmutz m
filth·y schmutzig; fig unflätig
fin zo Flosse f; SPORT Schwimmflosse f
fi·nal **1.** letzte(r, -s); End..., Schluss...; endgültig **2.** SPORT Finale n; mst pl Schlussexamen n, -prüfung f
fi·nal dis·pos·al Endlagerung f
fi·nal·ist SPORT Finalist(in)
fi·nal·ly endlich, schließlich; endgültig
fi·nal whis·tle SPORT Schlusspfiff m, Abpfiff m
fi·nance **1.** Finanzwesen n; pl Finanzen pl **2.** finanzieren
fi·nan·cial finanziell
fi·nan·cier Finanzier m
finch zo Fink m
find **1.** finden; (an)treffen; herausfinden; JUR j-n für (nicht) schuldig erklären; beschaffen, besorgen; ~ out v/t et. herausfinden; v/i es herausfinden **2.** Fund m, Entdeckung f; find·ings Befund m; JUR Feststellung f, Spruch m
fine¹ **1.** adj fein; schön; ausgezeichnet, großartig; I'm ~ mir geht es gut **2.** adv F sehr gut, bestens
fine² **1.** Geldstrafe f, Bußgeld n **2.** zu e-r Geldstrafe verurteilen
fin·ger **1.** ANAT Finger m; → cross 3 **2.** betasten, (herum)fingern an (dat)
fin·ger·nail ANAT Fingernagel m
fin·ger·print Fingerabdruck m
fin·ger·tip Fingerspitze f
fin·i·cky pedantisch; wählerisch
fin·ish **1.** (be)enden, aufhören (mit); a. ~ off vollenden, zu Ende führen, erledigen, Buch etc auslesen; a. ~ off, ~ up aufessen, austrinken **2.** Ende n, Schluss m; SPORT Endspurt m, Finish n; Ziel n; Vollendung f, letzter Schliff
fin·ish·ing line SPORT Ziellinie f
Fin·land Finnland n
Finn Finne m, Finnin f
Finn·ish **1.** finnisch **2.** LING Finnisch n
fir a. ~ tree BOT Tanne f
fir cone BOT Tannenzapfen m
fire **1.** Feuer n; be on ~ in Flammen stehen, brennen; catch ~ Feuer fangen, in Brand geraten; set on ~, set ~ to anzünden **2.** v/t anzünden, entzünden; fig anfeuern; abfeuern; Ziegel etc brennen; F j-n rausschmeißen; heizen; v/i Feuer fangen (a. fig); feuern
fire a·larm Feueralarm m; Feuermelder m

fire·arms Schusswaffen pl
fire bri·gade Br Feuerwehr f
fire·bug F Feuerteufel m
fire·crack·er Knallfrosch m; Knallbonbon m, n
fire de·part·ment Feuerwehr f
fire en·gine Br Löschfahrzeug n
fire es·cape Feuerleiter f, -treppe f
fire ex·tin·guish·er Feuerlöscher m
fire fight·er Feuerwehrmann m
fire·guard Br Kamingitter n
fire hy·drant Br Hydrant m
fire·man Feuerwehrmann m; Heizer m
fire·place (offener) Kamin
fire·plug Hydrant m
fire·proof feuerfest
fire·rais·ing Br Brandstiftung f
fire·screen Kamingitter n
fire ser·vice Br Feuerwehr f
fire·side (offener) Kamin
fire sta·tion Feuerwache f
fire truck Löschfahrzeug n
fire·wood Brennholz n
fire·works Feuerwerk n
fir·ing squad MIL Exekutionskommando n
firm¹ fest; hart; standhaft
firm² Firma f
first **1.** adj erste(r, -s); beste(r, -s) **2.** adv erstens; zuerst; ~ of all an erster Stelle; zu allererst **3.** Erste(r, -s); at ~ zuerst, anfangs; from the ~ von Anfang an
first aid MED Erste Hilfe; ~ box, ~ kit Verband(s)kasten m
first·born erstgeborene(r, -s), älteste(r, -s)
first class RAIL etc 1. Klasse
first-class erstklassig
first floor Erdgeschoss n, Br erster Stock; → second floor
first·hand aus erster Hand
first leg SPORT Hinspiel n
first·ly erstens
first name Vorname m
first-rate erstklassig
firth Förde f, Meeresarm m
fish **1.** zo Fisch m **2.** fischen, angeln
fish·bone Gräte f
fish·er·man Fischer m
fish·er·y Fischerei f
fish fin·ger Br GASTR Fischstäbchen n
fish·hook Angelhaken m
fish·ing Fischen n, Angeln n; ~ line Angelschnur f; ~ rod Angelrute f; ~ tack-

le Angelgerät n

fish·mon·ger *esp Br* Fischhändler m

fish stick GASTR Fischstäbchen n

fish·y Fisch…; F verdächtig

fis·sion PHYS Spaltung f

fis·sure GEOL Spalt m, Riss m

fist Faust f

fit[1] **1.** geeignet, passend; tauglich; SPORT fit, (gut) in Form; **keep ~** sich fit halten **2.** v/t passend machen (**for** für), anpassen; TECH einpassen, einbauen; anbringen; **~ in** j-m e-n Termin geben, j-n, et. einschieben; a. **~ on** anprobieren; a. **~ out** ausrüsten, ausstatten, einrichten (**with** mit); a. **~ up** einrichten (**with** mit); montieren, installieren; v/i passen, sitzen (*dress etc*) **3.** Sitz m

fit[2] MED Anfall m; **give s.o. a ~** F j-n auf die Palme bringen; j-m e-n Schock versetzen

fit·ful unruhig (*sleep etc*)

fit·ness Tauglichkeit f; *esp* SPORT Fitness f, (gute) Form; **~ cen·ter** (*Br* **cen·tre**) Fitnesscenter n

fit·ted zugeschnitten; **~ carpet** Spannteppich m, Teppichboden m; **~ kitchen** Einbauküche f

fit·ter Monteur m; Installateur m

fit·ting 1. passend; schicklich **2.** Montage f, Installation f; *pl* Ausstattung f; Armaturen pl

five 1. fünf **2.** Fünf f

fix 1. befestigen, anbringen (**to** an *dat*); *Preis* festsetzen; fixieren; *Blick etc* richten (**on** auf *acc*); *Aufmerksamkeit etc* fesseln; reparieren, in Ordnung bringen (*a. fig*); *Essen* zubereiten **2.** Klemme f; *sl* Fix m

fixed fest; starr

fix·ings GASTR Beilagen pl

fix·ture Inventarstück n; **lighting ~** Beleuchtungskörper m

fizz zischen, sprudeln

flab·ber·gast F verblüffen; **be ~ed** F platt sein

flab·by schlaff

flac·cid schlaff, schlapp

flag[1] **1.** Fahne f, Flagge f **2.** beflaggen

flag[2] **1.** (Stein)Platte f, Fliese f **2.** mit (Stein)Platten *or* Fliesen belegen, fliesen

flag[3] nachlassen, erlahmen

flag·pole, flag·staff Fahnenstange f

flag·stone (Stein)Platte f, Fliese f

flake 1. Flocke f; Schuppe f **2.** *mst* **~ off** abblättern; F **~ out** schlappmachen

flak·y flockig; blätt(e)rig

flak·y pas·try GASTR Blätterteig m

flame 1. Flamme f (*a. fig*); **be in ~s** in Flammen stehen **2.** flammen, lodern

flam·ma·ble TECH brennbar, leicht entzündlich, feuergefährlich

flan GASTR Obst-, Käsekuchen m

flank 1. Flanke f **2.** flankieren

flan·nel Flanell m; *Br* Waschlappen m; *pl Br* Flanellhose f

flap 1. Flattern n, (Flügel)Schlag m; Klappe f **2.** mit *den Flügeln etc* schlagen; flattern

flare 1. flackern; sich weiten; **~ up** aufflammen; *fig* aufbrausen **2.** Lichtsignal n

flash 1. Aufblitzen n, Aufleuchten n, Blitz m; *radio etc*: Kurzmeldung f; PHOT F Blitz m; F Taschenlampe f; **like a ~** wie der Blitz; **in a ~** im Nu; **a ~ of lightning** ein Blitz **2.** (auf)blitzen *or* aufleuchten (lassen); zucken; rasen, flitzen

flash·back *film*: Rückblende f

flash freeze GASTR schnell einfrieren

flash·light PHOT Blitzlicht n; Taschenlampe f

flash·y protzig; auffallend

flask Taschenflasche f

flat[1] **1.** flach, eben, platt; schal; ECON flau; MOT platt (*tire*) **2.** *adv* **fall ~** danebengehen; **sing ~** zu tief singen **3.** Fläche f, Ebene f; flache Seite f; Flachland n, Niederung f; MOT Reifenpanne f

flat[2] *Br* Wohnung f

flat·foot·ed plattfüßig

flat·mate *Br* Mitbewohner(in)

flat·ten (ein)ebnen; abflachen; a. **~ out** flach(er) werden

flat·ter schmeicheln (*dat*)

flat·ter·er Schmeichler(in)

flat·ter·y Schmeichelei f

fla·vo(u)r 1. Geschmack m; Aroma n; Blume f; *fig* Beigeschmack m; Würze f **2.** würzen

fla·vo(u)r·ing Würze f, Aroma n

flaw Fehler m, TECH a. Defekt m

flaw·less einwandfrei, tadellos

flax BOT Flachs m

flea ZO Floh m

flea mar·ket Flohmarkt m

fleck Fleck(en) m; Tupfen m

fluff

fledged zo flügge

fledg(e)·ling zo Jungvogel m; fig Grünschnabel m

flee fliehen; meiden

fleece 1. Vlies n, esp Schafsfell n 2. F j-n neppen

fleet MAR Flotte f

flesh Fleisch n; flesh·y fleischig; dick

flex[1] esp ANAT biegen

flex[2] esp Br ELECTR (Anschluss-, Verlängerungs)Kabel n, (-)Schnur f

flex·i·ble flexibel, biegsam; fig anpassungsfähig; ~ working hours Gleitzeit f

flex·i·time Br, flex·time Gleitzeit f

flick schnippen; schnellen

flick·er 1. flackern; TV flimmern 2. Flackern n; TV Flimmern n

fli·er AVIAT Flieger m; Reklamezettel m

flight Flucht f; Flug m (a. fig); zo Schwarm m; a. ~ of stairs Treppe f; put to ~ in die Flucht schlagen; take (to) ~ die Flucht ergreifen; ~ at·tend·ant AVIAT Flugbegleiter(in); ~ con·nec·tion AVIAT Flugverbindung f

flight·less zo flugunfähig

flight| num·ber AVIAT Flugnummer f; ~ re·cord·er AVIAT Flugschreiber m

flight·y flatterhaft

flim·sy dünn; zart; fig fadenscheinig

flinch (zurück)zucken, zusammenfahren; zurückschrecken (from vor dat)

fling 1. werfen, schleudern; ~ o.s. sich stürzen; ~ open (to) Tür etc aufreißen (zuschlagen) 2. have a ~ sich austoben; have a ~ at es versuchen or probieren mit

flint Feuerstein m

flip schnippen, schnipsen; Münze hochwerfen

flip·pant respektlos, F schnodd(e)rig

flip·per zo Flosse f; Schwimmflosse f

flirt 1. flirten 2. be a ~ gern flirten

flir·ta·tion Flirt m

flit flitzen, huschen

float 1. v/i (auf dem Wasser) schwimmen, (im Wasser) treiben; schweben; a. ECON in Umlauf sein; v/t schwimmen or treiben lassen; MAR flottmachen; ECON Wertpapiere etc in Umlauf bringen; Währung floaten, den Wechselkurs (gen) freigeben 2. Festwagen m

float·ing 1. schwimmend, treibend; ECON umlaufend; frei (exchange rate);

frei konvertierbar (currency) 2. ECON Floating n

float·ing vot·er POL Wechselwähler(in)

flock 1. zo Herde f (a. REL); Menge f, Schar f 2. fig strömen

floe (treibende) Eisscholle

flog prügeln, schlagen

flog·ging Tracht f Prügel

flood 1. a. ~ tide Flut f; Überschwemmung f 2. überfluten, überschwemmen

flood·gate Schleusentor n

flood·lights ELECTR Flutlicht n

floor 1. (Fuß)Boden m; Stock m, Stockwerk n, Etage f; Tanzfläche f; → first floor, second floor; take the ~ das Wort ergreifen 2. e-n (Fuß)Boden legen in; zu Boden schlagen; fig F j-n umhauen

floor·board (Fußboden)Diele f

floor cloth Putzlappen m

floor·ing (Fuß)Bodenbelag m

floor lamp Stehlampe f

floor lead·er PARL Fraktionsführer m

floor-length bodenlang

floor show Nachtklubvorstellung f

floor-walk·er Aufsicht f

flop 1. sich (hin)plumpsen lassen; F durchfallen, danebengehen, ein Reinfall sein 2. Plumps m; F Flop m, Reinfall m, Pleite f; Versager m

flop·py (disk) IT Floppy Disk f, Diskette f

flor·id rot, gerötet

flor·ist Blumenhändler(in)

floun·der[1] zo Flunder f

floun·der[2] zappeln; strampeln; fig sich verhaspeln

flour (feines) Mehl

flour·ish 1. Schnörkel m; MUS Tusch m 2. v/i blühen, gedeihen; v/t schwenken

flow 1. fließen, strömen; wallen 2. Fluß m, Strom m (both a. fig)

flow·er 1. Blume f; Blüte f (a. fig) 2. blühen

flow·er·bed Blumenbeet n

flow·er·pot Blumentopf m

flu F MED Grippe f

fluc·tu·ate schwanken

fluc·tu·a·tion Schwankung f

flue Rauchfang m, Esse f

flu·en·cy Flüssigkeit f; (Rede)Gewandtheit f; flu·ent flüssig; gewandt; speak ~ French fließend Französisch sprechen

fluff 1. Flaum m; Staubflocke f 2. zo auf-

F

plustern; **fluff·y** flaumig

flu·id 1. flüssig **2.** Flüssigkeit *f*

flunk F durchfallen (lassen)

flu·o·res·cent fluoreszierend

flu·o·ride CHEM Fluor *n*

flu·o·rine CHEM Fluor *n*

flur·ry Windstoß *m*; (Regen-, Schnee-) Schauer *m*; *fig* Aufregung *f*, Unruhe *f*

flush 1. (Wasser)Spülung *f*; Erröten *n*; Röte *f* **2.** *v/t a.* ~ **out** (aus)spülen; ~ **down** hinunterspülen; ~ **the toilet** spülen; *v/i* erröten, rot werden; spülen **3.** **be** ~ F gut bei Kasse sein

flus·ter 1. nervös machen *or* werden **2.** Nervosität *f*

flute MUS **1.** Flöte *f* **2.** (auf der) Flöte spielen

flut·ter 1. flattern **2.** Flattern *n*; *fig* Erregung *f*

flux *fig* Fluss *m*

fly¹ ZO Fliege *f*

fly² Hosenschlitz *m*; Zeltklappe *f*

fly³ fliegen (lassen); stürmen, stürzen; flattern, wehen; (ver)fliegen (*time*); *Drachen* steigen lassen; ~ **at s.o.** auf j-n losgehen; ~ **into a passion or rage** in Wut geraten; **fly·er** → **flier**

fly·ing fliegend; Flug...; ~ **sau·cer** fliegende Untertasse; ~ **squad** Überfallkommando *n*; ~ **time** AVIAT Flugzeit *f*; ~ **vis·it** F Stippvisite *f*

fly·o·ver *Br* (Straßen-, Eisenbahn-) Überführung *f*

fly·screen Fliegenfenster *n*

fly·weight *boxing*: Fliegengewicht *n*, Fliegengewichtler *m*

fly·wheel TECH Schwungrad *n*

foal ZO Fohlen *n*

foam 1. Schaum *m* **2.** schäumen; ~ **ex·tin·guish·er** Schaumlöscher *m*, -löschgerät *n*; ~ **rub·ber** Schaumgummi *m*

foam·y schaumig

fo·cus 1. Brennpunkt *m*, *fig a.* Mittelpunkt *m*; OPT, PHOT Scharfeinstellung *f* **2.** OPT, PHOT scharf einstellen; *fig* konzentrieren (**on** auf *acc*)

fod·der AGR (Trocken)Futter *n*

foe POET Feind *m*, Gegner *m*

fog (dichter) Nebel

fog·gy neb(e)lig; *fig* nebelhaft

foi·ble (kleine) Schwäche

foil¹ Folie *f*; *fig* Hintergrund *m*

foil² vereiteln

foil³ *fencing*: Florett *n*

fold¹ 1. Falte *f*; Falz *m* **2.** ...fach, ...fältig **3.** (sich) falten; falzen; *Arme* verschränken; einwickeln; *often* ~ **up** zusammenfalten, -legen, -klappen

fold² AGR Schafhürde *f*, Pferch *m*; REL Herde *f*

fold·er Aktendeckel *m*; Schnellhefter *m*; Faltprospekt *m*, -blatt *n*, Broschüre *f*

fold·ing zusammenlegbar; Klapp...; ~ **bed** Klappbett *n*; ~ **bi·cy·cle** Klapprad *n*; ~ **boat** Faltboot *n*; ~ **chair** Klappstuhl *m*; ~ **door(s)** Falttür *f*

fo·li·age BOT Laub *n*, Laubwerk *n*

folk 1. Leute *pl*; *pl* F *m*-*e etc* Leute *pl* **2.** Volks...

folk·lore Volkskunde *f*; Volkssagen *pl*; Folklore *f*

folk mu·sic Volksmusik *f*

folk song Volkslied *n*; Folksong *m*

fol·low folgen (*dat*); folgen auf (*acc*); befolgen; verfolgen; *s-m Beruf etc* nachgehen; ~ **through** *Plan etc* bis zum Ende durchführen; ~ **up** *e-r Sache* nachgehen; *e-e Sache* weiterverfolgen; **as** ~**s** wie folgt; **fol·low·er** Nachfolger(in); Verfolger(in); Anhänger(in); **fol·low·ing 1.** Anhängerschaft *f*, Anhänger *pl*; Gefolge *n*; **the** ~ das Folgende; die Folgenden *pl* **2.** folgende(r, -s) **3.** im Anschluss an (*acc*)

fol·ly Torheit *f*

fond zärtlich; vernarrt (**of** in *acc*); **be** ~ **of** gernhaben, lieben

fon·dle liebkosen; streicheln; (ver)hätscheln

fond·ness Zärtlichkeit *f*; Vorliebe *f*

font REL Taufstein *m*, Taufbecken *n*

food Nahrung *f*, Essen *n*; Nahrungs-, Lebensmittel *pl*; AGR Futter *n*

fool 1. Narr *m*, Närrin *f*, Dummkopf *m*; **make a** ~ **of s.o.** j-n zum Narren halten; **make a** ~ **of o.s.** sich lächerlich machen **2.** zum Narren halten; betrügen (**out of** um); ~ **about,** ~ **around** herumtrödeln; Unsinn machen, herumalbern

fool·har·dy tollkühn

fool·ish dumm, töricht; unklug

fool·ish·ness Dummheit *f*

fool·proof kinderleicht; todsicher

foot 1. ANAT Fuß *m* (*a. linear measure* = *30,48 cm*); Fußende *n*; **on** ~ zu Fuß **2.** F *Rechnung* bezahlen; **have to** ~ **the bill** die Zeche bezahlen müssen; ~ **it** zu Fuß gehen

foot·ball Football(spiel *n*) *m*; *Br* Fußball(spiel *n*) *m*; Football-Ball *m*; *Br* Fußball *m*

foot·bal·ler *Br* Fußballer *m*

foot·ball | **hoo·li·gan** *Br* Fußballrowdy *m*; ~ **play·er** *Br* Fußballspieler *m*

foot·bridge Fußgängerbrücke *f*

foot·fall Tritt *m*, Schritt *m*

foot·hold fester Stand, Halt *m*

foot·ing Halt *m*, Stand *m*; *fig* Grundlage *f*, Basis *f*; **be on a friendly ~ with s.o.** ein gutes Verhältnis zu j-m haben; **lose one's ~** den Halt verlieren

foot·lights THEA Rampenlicht(er *pl*) *n*

foot·note Fußnote *f*

foot·path (Fuß)Pfad *m*, (Fuß)Weg *m*

foot·print Fußabdruck *m*, *pl a.* Fußspur(en *pl*) *f*

foot·sore *be* ~ wunde Füße haben

foot·step Tritt *m*, Schritt *m*; Fußstapfe *f*

foot·wear Schuhwerk *n*, Schuhe *pl*

fop Geck *m*, F Fatzke *m*

for 1. *prp* for; *purpose, direction:* zu; nach; *warten, hoffen etc* auf (*acc*); *sich sehnen etc* nach; *cause:* aus, vor (*dat*), wegen; *time:* ~ **three days** drei Tage (lang); seit drei Tagen; *distance:* **I walked ~ a mile** ich ging eine Meile (weit); *exchange:* (an)statt; als; **I ~ one** ich zum Beispiel; ~ **sure** sicher!, gewiss! **2.** *cj* denn, weil

for·age *a.* ~ **about** (herum)stöbern, (herum)wühlen (**in** *in dat;* **for** nach)

for·ay MIL Einfall *m*, Überfall *m*; *fig* Ausflug *m* (**into** *politics in die Politik*)

for·bid verbieten; hindern

for·bid·ding abstoßend

force 1. Stärke *f*, Kraft *f*, Gewalt *f*, Wucht *f*; **the** (**police**) ~ die Polizei; (**armed**) ~s MIL Streitkräfte *pl*; **by** ~ mit Gewalt; **come** *or* **put into** ~ in Kraft treten *or* setzen **2.** *j-n* zwingen; *et.* erzwingen; zwängen; drängen; *Tempo* beschleunigen; ~ **s.th. on s.o.** *j-m et.* aufzwingen *or* aufdrängen; ~ **o.s. on s.o.** sich *j-m* aufdrängen; ~ **open** aufbrechen

forced erzwungen; gezwungen, gequält; ~ **land·ing** AVIAT Notlandung *f*

force·ful energisch, kraftvoll; eindrucksvoll, überzeugend

for·ceps MED Zange *f*

for·ci·ble gewaltsam; eindringlich

ford 1. Furt *f* **2.** durchwaten

fore 1. vorder, Vorder...; vorn **2.** Vorderteil *m*, Vorderseite *f*, Front *f*

fore·arm ANAT Unterarm *m*

fore·bear *mst pl* Vorfahren *pl*, Ahnen *pl*

fore·bod·ing (böses) Vorzeichen; (*böse*) (Vor)Ahnung

fore·cast 1. voraussagen, vorhersehen; *Wetter* vorhersagen **2.** Voraussage *f*; METEOR Vorhersage *f*

fore·fa·ther Vorfahr *m*

fore·fin·ger Zeigefinger *m*

fore·foot ZO Vorderfuß *m*

fore·gone con·clu·sion ausgemachte Sache; **be a ~** *a.* von vornherein feststehen

fore·ground Vordergrund *m*

fore·hand SPORT Vorhand *f*, Vorhandschlag *m*; Vorhand...

fore·head ANAT Stirn *f*

for·eign fremd, ausländisch, Außen..., Auslands...; ~ **af·fairs** Außenpolitik *f*; ~ **aid** Auslandshilfe *f*

for·eign·er Ausländer(in)

for·eign | **lan·guage** Fremdsprache *f*; ~ **min·is·ter** POL Außenminister *m*

For·eign Of·fice *Br* POL Außenministerium *n*

for·eign pol·i·cy Außenpolitik *f*

For·eign Sec·re·ta·ry *Br* POL Außenminister *m*

for·eign trade ECON Außenhandel *m*

for·eign work·er Gastarbeiter(in)

fore·knowl·edge vorherige Kenntnis

fore·leg ZO Vorderbein *n*

fore·man TECH Vorarbeiter *m*, Polier *m*; Werkmeister *m*; JUR Sprecher *m*

fore·most vorderste(r, -s), erste(r, -s)

fore·name Vorname *m*

fo·ren·sic JUR Gerichts...; ~ **me·dicine** Gerichtsmedizin *f*

fore·run·ner Vorläufer(in)

fore·see vorhersehen, voraussehen

fore·see·a·ble vorhersehbar

fore·shad·ow ahnen lassen, andeuten

fore·sight Weitblick *m*; (weise) Voraussicht

for·est Wald *m* (*a. fig*); Forst *m*

fore·stall *et.* vereiteln; *j-m* zuvorkommen

for·est·er Förster *m*

for·est·ry Forstwirtschaft *f*

fore·taste Vorgeschmack *m*

fore·tell vorhersagen

for·ev·er, for ev·er für immer

fore·wom·an TECH Vorarbeiterin f

fore·word Vorwort n

for·feit verwirken; einbüßen

forge 1. Schmiede f 2. fälschen; schmieden

forg·er Fälscher m

for·ge·ry Fälschen n; Fälschung f

for·ge·ry-proof fälschungssicher

for·get vergessen

for·get·ful vergesslich

for·get-me-not BOT Vergissmeinnicht n

for·give vergeben, verzeihen

for·give·ness Verzeihung f; Vergebung f

for·giv·ing versöhnlich; nachsichtig

fork 1. Gabel f 2. (sich) gabeln

fork·lift truck MOT Gabelstapler m

form 1. Form f; Gestalt f; Formular n, Vordruck m; Br (Schul)Klasse f; Formalität f; Kondition f, Verfassung f; *in great*~ gut in Form 2. (sich) formen, (sich) bilden, gestalten

for·mal förmlich; formell

for·mal dress Gesellschaftskleidung f

for·mal·i·ty Förmlichkeit f; Formalität f

for·mat 1. Aufmachung f; Format n 2. IT formatieren

for·ma·tion Bildung f

form·a·tive bildend; gestaltend; ~ years Entwicklungsjahre pl

for·mat·ting IT Formatierung f

for·mer 1. früher; ehemalig 2. *the* ~ der or die or das Erstere

for·mer·ly früher

for·mi·da·ble furchterregend; gewaltig, riesig, gefährlich, schwierig

form teach·er Br Klassenlehrer(in), Klassenleiter(in)

for·mu·la Formel f; Rezept n

for·mu·late formulieren

for·sake aufgeben; verlassen

for·swear abschwören, entsagen (dat)

fort MIL Fort n, Festung f

forth weiter, fort; (her)vor; *and so* ~ und so weiter

forth·com·ing bevorstehend, kommend; in Kürze erscheinend (book) or anlaufend (film)

for·ti·eth vierzigste(r, -s)

for·ti·fi·ca·tion Befestigung f

for·ti·fy MIL befestigen; fig (ver)stärken

for·ti·tude (innere) Kraft or Stärke

fort·night esp Br vierzehn Tage

for·tress MIL Festung f

for·tu·i·tous zufällig

for·tu·nate glücklich; *be*~ Glück haben; for·tu·nate·ly glücklicherweise

for·tune Vermögen n; (glücklicher) Zufall, Glück n; Schicksal n

for·tune-tell·er Wahrsager(in)

for·ty 1. vierzig 2. Vierzig f

for·ward 1. adv nach vorn, vorwärts 2. adj Vorwärts...; fortschrittlich; vorlaut, dreist 3. soccer: Stürmer m 4. befördern, (ver)senden, schicken; *Brief etc* nachsenden

for·ward·ing a·gent Spediteur m

fos·sil GEOL Fossil n (a. F), Versteinerung f

fos·ter-child Pflegekind n

fos·ter-par·ents Pflegeeltern pl

foul 1. stinkend, widerlich; verpestet, schlecht (air, water); GASTR verdorben, faul; schmutzig, verschmutzt; METEOR stürmisch, schlecht; SPORT regelwidrig; esp Br F mies 2. SPORT Foul n, Regelverstoß m; *vicious*~ böses or übles Foul 3. beschmutzen, verschmutzen; SPORT foulen

found¹ gründen; stiften

found² TECH gießen

foun·da·tion ARCH Grundmauer f, Fundament n; fig Gründung f, Errichtung f; (gemeinnützige) Stiftung; fig Grundlage f, Basis f

found·er¹ Gründer(in); Stifter(in)

foun·der² MAR sinken; fig scheitern

found·ling JUR Findelkind n

foun·dry TECH Gießerei f

foun·tain Springbrunnen m; (Wasser-) Strahl m; ~ pen Füllfederhalter m

four 1. vier 2. Vier f; rowing: Vierer m; *on all*~*s* auf allen vieren

four star Br F Super n

four-star pet·rol Br Superbenzin n

four-stroke en·gine Viertaktmotor m

four·teen 1. vierzehn 2. Vierzehn f

four·teenth vierzehnte(r, -s)

fourth 1. vierte(r, -s) 2. Viertel n

fourth·ly viertens

four-wheel drive MOT Vierradantrieb m

fowl ZO Geflügel n

fox ZO Fuchs m

fox·glove BOT Fingerhut m

fox·y schlau, gerissen

frac·tion Bruchteil m; MATH Bruch m

frac·ture MED 1. (Knochen)Bruch m 2.

brechen
fra·gile zerbrechlich
frag·ment Bruchstück *n*
fra·grance Wohlgeruch *m*, Duft *m*
fra·grant wohlriechend, duftend
frail gebrechlich; zerbrechlich; zart, schwach; **frail·ty** Zartheit *f*; Gebrechlichkeit *f*; Schwäche *f*
frame 1. Rahmen *m*; (*Brillen- etc*)Gestell *n*; Körper(bau) *m*; **~ of mind** (Gemüts)Verfassung *f*, (-)Zustand *m* **2.** (ein)rahmen; bilden, formen, bauen; *a.* **~ up** F *j-m* etc. anhängen
frame-up F abgekartetes Spiel; Intrige *f*
frame·work TECH Gerüst *n*; *fig* Struktur *f*, System *n*
franc Franc *m*; Franken *m*
France Frankreich *n*
fran·chise POL Wahlrecht *n*; ECON Konzession *f*
frank 1. frei(mütig), offen; **~ly** (**speaking**) offen gesagt **2.** Brief freistempeln
frank·fur·ter GASTR Frankfurter (Würstchen *n*) *f*
frank·ness Offenheit *f*
fran·tic hektisch; **be ~** außer sich sein
fra·ter·nal brüderlich
fra·ter·ni·ty Brüderlichkeit *f*; Vereinigung *f*, Zunft *f*; UNIV Verbindung *f*
frat·er·ni·za·tion Verbrüderung *f*
frat·er·nize sich verbrüdern
fraud Betrug *m*; F Schwindel *m*
fraud·u·lent betrügerisch
fray ausfransen, (sich) durchscheuern
freak 1. Missgeburt *f*; Laune *f*; *in cpds* ...freak *m*, ...fanatiker *m*; Freak *m*, irrer Typ; **~ of nature** Laune *f* der Natur **2.** F *a.* **~ out** durchdrehen, die Nerven verlieren
freck·le Sommersprosse *f*
freck·led sommersprossig
free 1. frei; ungehindert; ungebunden; kostenlos, zum Nulltarif; freigebig; **~ and easy** zwanglos; sorglos; **set ~** freilassen **2.** befreien; freilassen
free climb·ing Freeclimbing *n*
free·dom Freiheit *f*
free fares Nulltarif *m*
free·lance frei, freiberuflich tätig, freischaffend
Free·ma·son Freimaurer *m*
free skat·ing Kür *f*
free·style SPORT Freistil *m*
free time Freizeit *f*

free trade ECON Freihandel *m*; **~ ar·e·a** ECON Freihandelszone *f*
free·way Schnellstraße *f*
free-wheel im Freilauf fahren
freeze 1. *v/i* (ge)frieren; erstarren; *v/t* gefrieren lassen; GASTR einfrieren (*a.* ECON), tiefkühlen **2.** Frost *m*, Kälte *f*; ECON, POL Einfrieren *n*; **wage ~, ~ on wages** ECON Lohnstopp *m*
freeze-dried gefriergetrocknet
freeze-dry gefriertrocknen
freez·er Gefriertruhe *f*, Tiefkühl-, Gefriergerät *n*; Gefrierfach *n*
freez·ing eisig; Gefrier...; **~ com·partment** Gefrierfach *n*; **~ point** Gefrierpunkt *m*
freight 1. Fracht *f*; Frachtgebühr *f* **2.** Güter... **3.** beladen; verfrachten
freight car RAIL Güterwagen *m*
freight·er MAR Frachter *m*, Frachtschiff *n*; AVIAT Transportflugzeug *n*
freight train Güterzug *m*
French 1. französisch **2.** LING Französisch *n*; **the ~** die Franzosen *pl*
French doors Terrassen-, Balkontür *f*
French fries GASTR Pommes frites *pl*
French·man Franzose *m*
French win·dows → **French doors**
French·wom·an Französin *f*
fren·zied wahnsinnig, rasend (**with** vor *dat*); hektisch; **fren·zy** Wahnsinn *m*; Ekstase *f*; Raserei *f*
fre·quen·cy Häufigkeit *f*; ELECTR Frequenz *f*
fre·quent 1. häufig **2.** (oft) besuchen
fresh frisch; neu; unerfahren; frech; **fresh·en** auffrischen (*wind*); **~ up** (**o.s.**) sich frisch machen
fresh·man UNIV Student(in) im ersten Jahr
fresh·ness Frische *f*; Frechheit *f*
fresh wa·ter Süßwasser *n*
fresh wa·ter Süßwasser...
fret sich Sorgen machen
fret·ful verärgert, gereizt; quengelig
FRG *abbr of* **Federal Republic of Germany** Bundesrepublik *f* Deutschland
Fri *abbr of* **Friday** Fr., Freitag *m*
fri·ar REL Mönch *m*
fric·tion TECH *etc* Reibung *f* (*a. fig*)
Fri·day (*abbr* **Fri**) Freitag *m*; **on ~** (*am*) Freitag; **on ~s** freitags
fridge F Kühlschrank *m*
friend Freund(in); Bekannte *m*, *f*; **make**

~s with sich anfreunden mit, Freundschaft schließen mit

friend·ly 1. freund(schaft)lich **2.** *esp Br* SPORT Freundschaftsspiel *n*

friend·ship Freundschaft *f*

fries F GASTR Fritten *pl*

frig·ate MAR Fregatte *f*

fright Schreck(en) *m*; **look a ~** F verboten aussehen; **fright·en** erschrecken; **be ~ed** erschrecken (**at, by, of** vor *dat*); Angst haben (**of** vor *dat*)

fright·ful schrecklich, fürchterlich

fri·gid PSYCH frigid(e); kalt, frostig

frill Krause *f*, Rüsche *f*

fringe 1. Franse *f*; Rand *m*; Pony *m* **2.** mit Fransen besetzen; **~ ben·e·fits** ECON Gehalts-, Lohnnebenleistungen *pl*; **~ e·vent** Randveranstaltung *f*; **~ group** *soziale* Randgruppe *f*

frisk herumtollen; F *j-n* filzen, durchsuchen; **frisk·y** lebhaft, munter

friz·zle F GASTR verbrutzeln

frizz·y gekräuselt, kraus

fro: **to and ~** hin und her

frock REL Kutte *f*

frog ZO Frosch *m*

frog·man Froschmann *m*, MIL *a.* Kampfschwimmer *m*

frol·ic herumtoben, herumtollen

from von; aus; von ... aus *or* her; von ... (an), seit; aus, vor (*dat*); **~ 9 to 5** (*o'clock*) von 9 bis 5 (Uhr)

front 1. Vorderseite *f*; Front *f* (*a.* MIL); **at the ~, in ~** vorn; **in ~ of** vor; **be in ~** in Führung sein **2.** Vorder... **3.** *a.* **~ on, to(wards)** gegenüberstehen, gegenüberliegen

front·age ARCH (Vorder)Front *f*

front cov·er Titelseite *f*

front door Haustür *f*, Vordertür *f*

front en·trance Vordereingang *m*

fron·tier 1. (Landes)Grenze *f*; HIST Grenzland *n*, Grenze *f* **2.** Grenz...

front-page F wichtig, aktuell

front-wheel drive MOT Vorderradantrieb *m*

frost 1. Frost *m*; *a.* **hoar ~, white ~** Reif *m* **2.** mit Reif überziehen; *Glas* mattieren; GASTR glasieren, mit Zuckerguss überziehen; mit (Puder)Zucker bestreuen

frost·bite MED Erfrierung *f*

frost·bit·ten MED erfroren

frost·ed glass Matt-, Milchglas *n*

frost·y eisig, frostig (*a. fig*)

froth 1. Schaum *m* **2.** schäumen; zu Schaum schlagen

froth·y schäumend; schaumig

frown 1. Stirnrunzeln *n*; **with a ~** stirnrunzelnd **2.** *v/i* die Stirn runzeln

fro·zen *adj* (eis)kalt; (ein-, zu)gefroren; Gefrier...

fro·zen foods Tiefkühlkost *f*

fru·gal sparsam; bescheiden; einfach

fruit Frucht *f*; Früchte *pl*; Obst *n*

fruit·er·er Obsthändler *m*

fruit·ful fruchtbar

fruit juice Fruchtsaft *m*

fruit·less unfruchtbar; erfolglos

fruit·y fruchtartig; fruchtig (*wine*)

frus·trate vereiteln; frustrieren

frus·tra·tion Vereitelung *f*; Frustration *f*

fry braten; **fried eggs** Spiegeleier *pl*; **fried potatoes** Bratkartoffeln *pl*

fry·ing pan Bratpfanne *f*

fuch·sia BOT Fuchsie *f*

fuck V ficken, vögeln; **~ off!** verpiss dich!; **get ~ed!** der Teufel soll ihn holen!; **fuck·ing** V Scheiß..., verflucht; **~ hell!** verdammte Scheiße!

fudge GASTR Fondant *m*

fu·el 1. Brennstoff *m*; MOT Treib-, Kraftstoff *m* **2.** MOT, AVIAT (auf)tanken

fu·el in·jec·tion en·gine MOT Einspritzmotor *m*

fu·gi·tive 1. flüchtig (*a. fig*) **2.** Flüchtling *m*

ful·fil *Br*, **ful·fill** erfüllen; vollziehen; **ful·fil·(l)ing** befriedigend; **ful·fil·(l)·ment** Erfüllung *f*, Ausführung *f*

full 1. voll; ganz; Voll...; **~ of** voll von, voller; **~ (up)** (voll) besetzt (*bus etc*); F voll, satt; **house ~!** THEA ausverkauft!; **~ of o.s.** (ganz) von sich eingenommen **2.** *adv* völlig, ganz **3.** **in ~** vollständig, ganz; **write out in ~** Wort *etc* ausschreiben

full board Vollpension *f*

full dress Gesellschaftskleidung *f*

full-fledged ZO flügge; *fig* richtig

full-grown ausgewachsen

full-length in voller Größe; bodenlang; abendfüllend (*film etc*)

full moon Vollmond *m*

full stop LING Punkt *m*

full time SPORT Spielende *n*

full-time ganztägig, Ganztags...; **~ job** Ganztagsbeschäftigung *f* ful·ly voll, völlig, ganz

ful·ly-fledged *Br* → **full-fledged**

ful·ly-'grown *Br* → **full-grown**

fum·ble tasten; fummeln

fume wütend sein

fumes Dämpfe *pl*, Rauch *m*; Abgase *pl*

fum·ing wutschnaubend

fun Scherz *m*, Spaß *m*; **for ∼** aus *or* zum Spaß; **make ∼ of** sich lustig machen über (*acc*), verspotten

func·tion 1. Funktion *f*; Aufgabe *f*; Veranstaltung *f* 2. funktionieren

func·tion·a·ry Funktionär *m*

func·tion key IT Funktionstaste *f*

fund ECON Fonds *m*; Geld(mittel *pl*) *n*

fun·da·men·tal 1. Grund..., grundlegend 2. **∼s** Grundlage *f*, Grundbegriffe *pl*

fun·da·men·tal·ist Fundamentalist *m*

fu·ne·ral Begräbnis *n*, Beerdigung *f*; ∼ march MUS Trauermarsch *m*; ∼ o·ra·tion Trauerrede *f*; ∼ pro·ces·sion Trauerzug *m*; ∼ ser·vice Trauerfeier *f*

fun·fair Rummelplatz *m*

fun·gus BOT Pilz *m*, Schwamm *m*

fu·nic·u·lar·a·∼ railway (Draht)Seilbahn *f*

funk·y F irre, schräg, schrill

fun·nel Trichter *m*; MAR, RAIL Schornstein *m*

fun·nies F Comics *pl*

fun·ny komisch, lustig, spaßig; sonderbar

fur Pelz *m*, Fell *n*; MED Belag *m*; TECH Kesselstein *m*

fu·ri·ous wütend

furl *Fahne, Segel* aufrollen, einrollen; *Schirm* zusammenrollen

fur·nace TECH Schmelzofen *m*, Hochofen *m*; (Heiz)Kessel *m*

fur·nish einrichten, möblieren; liefern; versorgen, ausrüsten, ausstatten (**with** mit)

fur·ni·ture Möbel *pl*; **sectional ∼** Anbaumöbel *pl*

furred MED belegt, pelzig

fur·ri·er Kürschner *m*

fur·row 1. Furche *f* 2. furchen

fur·ry pelzig; flauschig

fur·ther 1. weiter 2. fördern, unterstützen; ∼ ed·u·ca·tion *Br* Fortbildung *f*, Weiterbildung *f*

fur·ther·more *fig* weiter, überdies

fur·ther·most entfernteste(r, -s), äußerste(r, -s)

fur·tive heimlich, verstohlen

fu·ry Wut *f*, Zorn *m*

fuse 1. Zünder *m*; ELECTR Sicherung *f*; Zündschnur *f* 2. schmelzen; ELECTR durchbrennen

fuse box ELECTR Sicherungskasten *m*

fu·se·lage (Flugzeug)Rumpf *m*

fu·sion Verschmelzung *f*, Fusion *f*; PHYS **nuclear ∼** Kernfusion *f*

fuss 1. (unnötige) Aufregung; Wirbel *m*, F Theater *n* 2. sich (unnötig) aufregen; viel Aufhebens machen (**about** um, von); fuss·y aufgeregt, hektisch; kleinlich, pedantisch; heikel, wählerisch

fus·ty muffig; *fig* verstaubt

fu·tile nutzlos, zwecklos

fu·ture 1. (zu)künftig 2. Zukunft *f*; LING Futur *n*, Zukunft *f*; **in ∼** in Zukunft, künftig

fuzz feiner Flaum

fuzz·y kraus, wuschelig; unscharf, verschwommen; flaumig, flauschig

G

G, g G, g *n*

gab F Geschwätz *n*; **have the gift of the ∼** ein gutes Mundwerk haben

gab·ble 1. Geschnatter *n*, Geschwätz *n* 2. schnattern, schwatzen

ga·ble ARCH Giebel *m*

gad·fly ZO Bremse *f*

gad·get TECH Apparat *m*, Gerät *n*, Vorrichtung *f*; *often contp* technische Spielerei

gag 1. Knebel *m* (*a. fig*); F Gag *m* 2. knebeln; *fig* mundtot machen

gage 1. Eichmaß *n*; TECH Messgerät *n*, Lehre *f*; TECH Stärke *f*, Dicke *f*; RAIL Spur(weite) *f* 2. TECH eichen; (ab-, aus)messen

gai·e·ty Fröhlichkeit *f*

gain 1. gewinnen; erreichen, bekommen; zunehmen an (*dat*); vorgehen (um) (*watch*); ~ *speed* schneller werden; ~ *5 pounds* 5 Pfund zunehmen; ~ *in* zunehmen an (*dat*) **2.** Gewinn *m*; Zunahme *f*; ~ *of time* Zeitgewinn *m*

gait Gang *m*, Gangart *f*; Schritt *m*

gai·ter Gamasche *f*

gal F Mädchen *n*

ga·la **1.** Festlichkeit *f*; Gala (-veranstaltung) *f* **2.** Gala…

gal·ax·y ASTR Milchstraße *f*, Galaxis *f*

gale Sturm *m*

gall[1] Frechheit *f*

gall[2] **1.** wund geriebene Stelle **2.** wund reiben *or* scheuern; *fig* (ver)ärgern

gal·lant tapfer; galant; höflich

gal·lan·try Tapferkeit *f*; Galanterie *f*

gall blad·der ANAT Gallenblase *f*

gal·le·ry Galerie *f*; Empore *f*

gal·ley MAR Galeere *f*; Kombüse *f*; *a.* ~ *proof* PRINT Fahne *f*, Fahnenabzug *m*

gal·lon Gallone *f* (*3,79 l, Br 4,55 l*)

gal·lop 1. Galopp *m* **2.** galoppieren (lassen)

gal·lows Galgen *m*

gal·lows hu·mo(u)r Galgenhumor *m*

ga·lore in rauen Mengen

gam·ble 1. (um Geld) spielen **2.** Glücksspiel *n*

gam·bler (Glücks)Spieler(in)

gam·bol 1. Luftsprung *m* **2.** (herum-) tanzen, (herum)hüpfen

game (Karten-, Ball- *etc*)Spiel *n*; (einzelnes) Spiel (*a. fig*); HUNT Wild *n*; Wildbret *n*; *pl* Spiele *pl*; PED Sport *m*

game·keep·er Wildhüter *m*

game| park, ~ **re·serve** Wildpark *m*; Wildreservat *n*

gan·der ZO Gänserich *m*

gang 1. (Arbeiter)Trupp *m*; Gang *f*, Bande *f*, Clique *f*; Horde *f* **2.** ~ *up* sich zusammentun, *contp* sich zusammenrotten

gan·gling schlaksig

gang·ster Gangster *m*

gang| war, ~ **war·fare** Bandenkrieg *m*

gang·way Gang *m*; AVIAT, MAR Gangway *f*

gaol, gaol·bird, gaol·er *Br* → **jail** *etc*

gap Lücke *f*; Kluft *f*; Spalte *f*

gape gähnen; klaffen; gaffen

ga·rage 1. Garage *f* (Reparatur)Werkstatt *f* (und Tankstelle *f*); **2.** *Auto* in e-r Garage ab- *or* unterstellen; *Auto*

in die Garage fahren

gar·bage Abfall *m*, Müll *m*; ~ **bag** Müllbeutel *m*; ~ **can** Abfalleimer *m*, Mülleimer *m*; Abfalltonne *f*, Mülltonne *f*; ~ **truck** Müllwagen *m*

gar·den Garten *m*

gar·den·er Gärtner(in)

gar·den·ing Gartenarbeit *f*

gar·gle gurgeln

gar·ish grell, auffallend

gar·land Girlande *f*

gar·lic BOT Knoblauch *m*

gar·ment Kleidungsstück *n*; Gewand *n*

gar·nish GASTR garnieren

gar·ret Dachkammer *f*

gar·ri·son MIL Garnison *f*

gar·ter Strumpfband *n*; Sockenhalter *m*; Strumpfhalter *m*, Straps *m*

gas Gas *n*; F Benzin *n*, Sprit *m*

gas·e·ous gasförmig

gash klaffende Wunde

gas·ket TECH Dichtung(sring *m*) *f*

gas me·ter Gasuhr *f*, Gaszähler *m*

gas·o·lene, gas·o·line Benzin *n*; ~ **pump** Zapfsäule *f*

gasp 1. keuchen, röcheln; ~ *(for breath)* nach Atem ringen, F nach Luft schnappen **2.** Keuchen *n*, Röcheln *n*

gas sta·tion Tankstelle *f*

gas stove Gasofen *m*, Gasherd *m*

gas·works TECH Gaswerk *n*

gate Tor *n*; Pforte *f*; Schranke *f*, Sperre *f*; AVIAT Flugsteig *m*

gate·crash F uneingeladen kommen (zu); sich ohne zu bezahlen hineinschmuggeln (in *acc*)

gate·post Tor-, Türpfosten *m*

gate·way Tor(weg *m*) *n*, Einfahrt *f*

gate·way drug Einstiegsdroge *f*

gath·er *v/t* sammeln, *Informationen* einholen, einziehen; *Personen* versammeln; ernten, pflücken; zusammenziehen, kräuseln; *fig* folgern, schließen *(from* aus); ~ *speed* schneller werden; *v/i* sich (ver)sammeln; sich (an)sammeln; **gath·er·ing** Versammlung *f*; Zusammenkunft *f*

gau·dy auffällig, bunt, grell; protzig

gauge *Br* → **gage**

gaunt hager; ausgemergelt

gaunt·let Schutzhandschuh *m*

gauze Gaze *f*; MED Bandage *f*, Binde *f*

gav·el Hammer *m*

gaw·ky linkisch

gay 1. lustig, fröhlich; bunt, (farben-)prächtig; F schwul **2.** F Schwule *m*

gaze 1. (starrer) Blick **2.** starren; **~ at** starren auf (*acc*), anstarren

ga·zelle ZO Gazelle *f*

ga·zette Amtsblatt *n*

gear TECH Getriebe *n*; MOT Gang *m*; *mst in cpds* Vorrichtung *f*, Gerät *n*; F Kleidung *f*, Aufzug *m*; **shift** (*esp Br* **change**) **~(s)** MOT schalten; **shift** (*esp Br* **change**) **into second ~** MOT in den zweiten Gang schalten

gear·box MOT Getriebe *n*

gear le·ver *Br*, **gear shift**, **gear stick** *Br* MOT Schalthebel *m*

Gei·ger count·er PHYS Geigerzähler *m*

geld·ing ZO Wallach *m*

gem Edelstein *m*

Gem·i·ni ASTR Zwillinge *pl*; **he (she) is (a) ~** er (sie) ist (ein) Zwilling

gen·der LING Genus *n*, Geschlecht *n*

gene BIOL Gen *n*, Erbfaktor *m*

gen·e·ral 1. allgemein; Haupt..., General... **2.** MIL General *m*; **in ~** im Allgemeinen; **~ de·liv·er·y** (*in care of*) ~ postlagernd; **~ e·lec·tion** *Br* POL Parlamentswahlen *pl*

gen·e·ral·ize verallgemeinern

gen·e·ral·ly im Allgemeinen, allgemein

gen·e·ral prac·ti·tion·er (*abbr GP*) *appr* Arzt *m or* Ärztin *f* für Allgemeinmedizin

gen·e·rate erzeugen; **gen·e·ra·tion** Erzeugung *f*; Generation *f*

gen·e·ra·tor ELECTR Generator *m*; MOT Lichtmaschine *f*

gen·e·ros·i·ty Großzügigkeit *f*

gen·e·rous großzügig; reichlich

ge·net·ic genetisch; **~ code** BIOL Erbanlage *f*; **~ en·gin·eer·ing** Gentechnologie *f*; **~ fin·ger·print** genetischer Fingerabdruck

ge·net·ics BIOL Genetik *f*, Vererbungslehre *f*

ge·ni·al freundlich

gen·i·tive *a.* **~ case** LING Genitiv *m*, zweiter Fall

ge·ni·us Genie *n*

gen·o·cide Völkermord *m*

gent F *esp Br* Herr *m*; **gents** *Br* F Herrenklo *n*

gen·tle sanft, zart, sacht; mild

gen·tle·man Gentleman *m*; Herr *m*

gen·tle·man·ly gentlemanlike, vornehm

gen·tle·ness Sanftheit *f*, Zartheit *f*; Milde *f*

gen·try *Br* niederer Adel; Oberschicht *f*

gen·u·ine echt; aufrichtig

ge·og·ra·phy Geografie *f*

ge·ol·o·gy Geologie *f*

ge·om·e·try Geometrie *f*

germ BIOL, BOT Keim *m*; MED Bazillus *m*, Bakterie *f*, (Krankheits)Erreger *m*

Ger·man 1. deutsch **2.** Deutsche *m, f*; LING Deutsch *n*; **~ shep·herd** ZO Deutscher Schäferhund

Ger·man·y Deutschland *n*

ger·mi·nate BIOL, BOT keimen (lassen)

ger·und LING Gerundium *n*

ges·tic·u·late gestikulieren

ges·ture Geste *f*, Gebärde *f*

get *v/t* bekommen, erhalten; sich *et.* verschaffen *or* besorgen; erwerben, sich aneignen; holen; bringen; F erwischen; F kapieren, verstehen, checken; *j-n* dazu bringen (**to do** zu tun); *with pp*: lassen; **~ one's hair cut** sich die Haare schneiden lassen; **~ going** in Gang bringen; **~ s.th. ready** et. fertig machen; **have got** haben; **have got to** müssen; *v/i* kommen, gelangen; *with pp or adj*: werden; **~ tired** müde werden, ermüden; **~ going** in Gang kommen; *fig* in Schwung kommen; **~ home** nach Hause kommen; **~ ready** sich fertig machen; **~ about** herumkommen; sich herumsprechen *or* verbreiten (*rumor etc*); **~ ahead of** übertreffen (*acc*); **~ along** vorwärts-, vorankommen; auskommen (**with** mit *j-m*); zurechtkommen (**with** mit *et.*); **~ at** herankommen an (*acc*); **what is he getting at?** worauf will er hinaus?; **~ away** loskommen; entkommen; **~ away with** davonkommen mit; **~ back** zurückkommen; *et.* zurückbekommen; **~ in** hinein-, hereinkommen; einsteigen (**in** *acc*); **~ off** aussteigen (aus); davonkommen (**with** mit); **~ on** einsteigen (**in** *acc*); → **get along**; **~ out** herausgehen, hinausgehen; aussteigen (**of** aus); *et.* herausbekommen; **~ over s.th.** über et. hinwegkommen; **~ to** kommen nach; **~ together** zusammenkommen; **~ up** aufstehen

get·a·way Flucht *f*; **~ car** Fluchtauto *n*

get·up Aufmachung *f*

gey·ser GEOL Geysir *m*; *Br* TECH Durchlauferhitzer *m*

ghast·ly grässlich; schrecklich; (toten-) bleich

gher·kin Gewürzgurke f

ghet·to Getto n

ghost Geist m, Gespenst n; fig Spur f

ghost·ly geisterhaft

gi·ant 1. Riese m **2.** riesig

gib·ber·ish Kauderwelsch n

gib·bet Galgen m

gibe 1. spotten (**at** über acc); **2.** höhnische Bemerkung, Stichelei f

gib·lets GASTR Hühner-, Gänseklein n

gid·di·ness MED Schwindel(gefühl n) m; **gid·dy** schwindelerregend; **I feel ~** mir ist schwind(e)lig

gift Geschenk n; Talent n

gift·ed begabt

gift vouch·er Geschenkgutschein m; **~ wrap** Geschenkpapier n

gig F MUS Gig m, Auftritt m, Konzert n

gi·gan·tic gigantisch, riesenhaft, riesig, gewaltig

gig·gle 1. kichern **2.** Gekicher n

gild vergolden

gill zo Kieme f; BOT Lamelle f

gim·mick F Trick m; Spielerei f

gin Gin m

gin·ger 1. Ingwer m **2.** rötlich or gelblich braun;

gin·ger·bread Lebkuchen m, Pfefferkuchen m

gin·ger·ly behutsam, vorsichtig

gip·sy Br → **gypsy**

gi·raffe zo Giraffe f

gir·der TECH Tragbalken m

gir·dle Hüfthalter m, Hüftgürtel m

girl Mädchen n

girl·friend Freundin f

girl guide Br Pfadfinderin f

girl·hood Mädchenjahre pl, Jugend f, Jugendzeit f

girl·ish mädchenhaft; Mädchen...

girl scout Pfadfinderin f

girth (Sattel)Gurt m; (a. Körper)Umfang m

gist das Wesentliche, Kern m

give geben; schenken; spenden; Leben hingeben, opfern; Befehl etc geben, erteilen; Hilfe leisten; Schutz bieten; Grund etc angeben; THEA etc geben, aufführen; Vortrag halten; Schmerzen bereiten, verursachen; Grüße etc übermitteln; **~ her my love** bestelle ihr herzliche Grüße von mir; **~ birth to**

zur Welt bringen; **~ s.o. to understand that** j-m zu verstehen geben, dass; **~ way** nachgeben; Br MOT die Vorfahrt lassen (dat); **~ away** hergeben, weggeben, verschenken; j-n, et. verraten; **~ back** zurückgeben; **~ in** Gesuch etc einreichen; Prüfungsarbeit etc abgeben; nachgeben; aufgeben; **~ off** Geruch verbreiten; ausstoßen; ausströmen, verströmen; **~ on(to)** führen auf or nach, gehen nach; **~ out** aus-, verteilen; esp Br bekannt geben; zu Ende gehen (supplies, strength etc); F versagen (engine etc); **~ up** aufgeben; aufhören mit; j-n ausliefern; **~ o.s. up** sich (freiwillig) stellen (**to the police** der Polizei)

give-and-take beiderseitiges Entgegenkommen, Kompromiss(bereitschaft f) m

giv·en: be ~ to neigen zu (dat)

giv·en name Vorname m

gla·cial eisig; Eis...

gla·ci·er Gletscher m

glad froh, erfreut; **be ~ of** sich freuen über (acc); **glad·ly** gern(e)

glam·o(u)r Zauber m, Glanz m

glam·o(u)r·ous bezaubernd, reizvoll

glance 1. (schneller or flüchtiger) Blick (**at** auf acc); **at a ~** auf e-n Blick **2.** (schnell or flüchtig) blicken (**at** auf acc)

gland ANAT Drüse f

glare 1. grell scheinen or leuchten; wütend starren; **~ at s.o.** j-n wütend anstarren **2.** greller Schein, grelles Leuchten; wütender Blick

glar·ing fig schreiend

glass 1. Glas n; (Trink)Glas n; Glas (-gefäß) n; (Fern-, Opern)Glas n; Br F Spiegel m; Br Barometer n; (**a pair of**) **~es** (e-e) Brille f **2.** gläsern; Glas... **3. ~ in, ~ up** verglasen

glass case Vitrine f; Schaukasten m

glass·ful ein Glas (voll)

glass·house Gewächs-, Treibhaus n

glass·ware Glaswaren pl

glass·y gläsern; glasig

glaze 1. v/t verglasen; glasieren; v/i: a. **~ over** glasig werden (eyes) **2.** Glasur f

gla·zi·er Glaser m

gleam 1. schwacher Schein, Schimmer m **2.** leuchten, schimmern

glean v/t sammeln; v/i Ähren lesen

glee Fröhlichkeit f

glee club Gesangverein m

glee·ful ausgelassen, fröhlich

glen enges Bergtal *n*

glib gewandt; schlagfertig

glide 1. gleiten; segeln **2.** Gleiten *n*; AVIAT Gleitflug *m*; **glid·er** Segelflugzeug *n*; **glid·ing** Segelfliegen *n*

glim·mer 1. schimmern **2.** Schimmer *m*

glimpse 1. (nur) flüchtig zu sehen bekommen **2.** flüchtiger Blick

glint 1. glitzern, glänzen **2.** Glitzern *n*, Glanz *m*

glis·ten glitzern, glänzen

glit·ter 1. glitzern, funkeln, glänzen **2.** Glitzern *n*, Funkeln *n*, Glanz *m*

glo·bal Welt…, global, weltumspannend; umfassend; **~ warm·ing** Erwärmung *f* der Erdatmosphäre

globe (Erd)Kugel *f*; Globus *m*

gloom Düsterkeit *f*; Dunkelheit *f*; düstere *or* gedrückte Stimmung

gloom·y düster; hoffnungslos; niedergeschlagen; trübsinnig, trübselig

glo·ri·fi·ca·tion Verherrlichung *f*

glo·ri·fy verherrlichen

glo·ri·ous ruhmreich, glorreich; herrlich, prächtig

glo·ry Ruhm *m*; Herrlichkeit *f*, Pracht *f*

gloss 1. Glanz *m*; LING Glosse *f* **2. ~ over** beschönigen, vertuschen

glos·sa·ry Glossar *n*

gloss·y glänzend

glove Handschuh *m*; **~ com·part·ment** MOT Handschuhfach *n*

glow 1. glühen **2.** Glühen *n*; Glut *f*

glow·er finster blicken

glow-worm ZO Glühwürmchen *n*

glu·cose Traubenzucker *m*

glue 1. Leim *m* **2.** kleben

glum bedrückt

glut·ton *fig* Vielfraß *m*

glut·ton·ous gefräßig, unersättlich

gnarled knorrig; knotig (*hands etc*)

gnash knirschen (mit)

gnat ZO (Stech)Mücke *f*

gnaw (zer)nagen; (zer)fressen

gnome Gnom *m*; Gartenzwerg *m*

go 1. gehen, fahren, reisen (*to* nach); (fort)gehen; gehen, führen (*to* nach) (*road etc*); sich erstrecken, gehen (*to* bis zu); verkehren, fahren (*bus etc*); TECH gehen, laufen, funktionieren; vergehen (*time*); harmonieren (*with* mit), passen (*with* zu); ausgehen, ablaufen, ausfallen; werden (**~ mad**; **~**

blind); **be ~ing to** *inf* im Begriff sein zu *inf*, tun wollen, zun werden; **~ swimming** schwimmen gehen; **it is ~ing to rain** es gibt Regen; **I must be ~ing** ich muss gehen; **~ for a walk** e-n Spaziergang machen, spazieren gehen; **~ to bed** ins Bett gehen; **~ to school** zur Schule gehen; **~ to see** besuchen; **let ~** loslassen; **~ after** nachlaufen (*dat*); sich bemühen um; **~ ahead** vorangehen; vorausgehen, vorausfahren; **~ ahead with** beginnen mit; fortfahren mit; **~ at** losgehen auf (*acc*); **~ away** weggehen; **~ between** vermitteln zwischen (*dat*); **~ by** vorbeigehen, vorbeifahren; vergehen (*time*); *fig* sich halten an (*acc*), sich richten nach; **~ down** untergehen (*sun*); **~ for** holen; **~ in** hineingehen; **~ in for an examination** e-e Prüfung machen; **~ off** fortgehen, weggehen; losgehen (*gun etc*); **~ on** weitergehen, weiterfahren; *fig* fortfahren (**doing** zu tun); *fig* vor sich gehen, vorgehen; **~ out** hinausgehen; ausgehen (**with** mit); ausgehen (*light etc*); **~ through** durchgehen, durchnehmen; durchmachen; **~ up** steigen; hinaufgehen, -steigen; **~ without** sich behelfen ohne, auskommen ohne **2.** F Schwung *m*, Schmiss *m*; *esp Br* F Versuch *m*; **it's my ~** *esp Br* F ich bin dran *or* an der Reihe; **it's a ~!** F abgemacht!; **have a ~ at s.th.** *Br* F et. probieren

goad *fig* anstacheln

go-a·head[1]: **get the ~** grünes Licht bekommen; **give s.o. the ~** j-m grünes Licht geben

go-a·head[2] *Br* zielstrebig; unternehmungslustig

goal Ziel *n* (*a. fig*); SPORT Tor *n*; **keep ~** im Tor stehen; **score a ~** ein Tor schießen *or* erzielen; **consolation ~** Ehrentreffer *m*; **own ~** Eigentor *n*, Eigentreffer *m*; **shot at ~** Torschuss *m*

goal·ie F, **goal·keep·er** SPORT Torwart *m*, Torhüter *m*

goal kick *soccer*: Abstoß *m*

goal line SPORT Torlinie *f*

goal·mouth SPORT Torraum *m*

goal·post SPORT Torpfosten *m*

goat ZO Ziege *f*, Geiß *f*

gob·ble schlingen; *mst* **~ up** verschlingen (*a. fig*)

go-be·tween Vermittler(in), Mittels-

G

mann *m*

gob·lin Kobold *m*

god REL *God* Gott *m*; *fig* Abgott *m*

god·child Patenkind *n*

god·dess Göttin *f*

god·fa·ther Pate *m* (*a. fig*), Taufpate *m*

god·for·sak·en *contp* gottverlassen

god·head Gottheit *f*

god·less gottlos

god·like gottähnlich; göttlich

god·moth·er (Tauf)Patin *f*

god·pa·rent (Tauf)Pate, (Tauf)Patin *f*

god·send Geschenk *n* des Himmels

gog·gle glotzen

gog·gle box *Br* F TV Glotze *f*

gog·gles Schutzbrille *f*

go·ings-on F Treiben *n*, Vorgänge *pl*

gold 1. Gold *n* **2.** golden

gold·en *mst fig* golden, goldgelb

gold·finch ZO Stieglitz *m*

gold·fish ZO Goldfisch *m*

gold·smith Goldschmied *m*

golf 1. Golf(spiel) *n* **2.** Golf spielen

golf club Golfschläger *m*; Golfklub *m*

golf course, golf links Golfplatz *m*

gon·do·la Gondel *f*

gone *adj* fort; F futsch; vergangen; tot; F hoffnungslos

good 1. gut; artig; gütig; gründlich; *~ at* geschickt *or* gut in (*dat*); *real ~* F echt gut **2.** Nutzen *m*, Wert *m*; *das* Gute; *do* (*no*) *~* (nichts) nützen; *for ~* für immer; F *what ~ is ...?* was nützt ...?

good-by(e) 1. wish s.o. ~, say ~ to s.o. j-m Auf Wiedersehen sagen **2.** *int* (auf) Wiedersehen!

Good Fri·day REL Karfreitag *m*

good-hu·mo(u)red gut gelaunt; gutmütig

good-look·ing gut aussehend

good-na·tured gutmütig

good·ness Güte *f*; *thank ~!* Gott sei Dank!; (*my*) *~!, ~ gracious!* du meine Güte!, du lieber Himmel!; *for ~' sake* um Himmels willen!; *~ knows* weiß der Himmel

goods ECON Waren *pl*, Güter *pl*

good·will gute Absicht, guter Wille; ECON Firmenwert *m*

good·y F Bonbon *m*, *n*

goose ZO Gans *f*

goose·ber·ry BOT Stachelbeere *f*

goose·flesh, goose pim·ples *fig* Gänsehaut *f*

go·pher ZO Taschenratte *f*; Ziesel *m*

gore durchbohren, aufspießen

gorge 1. ANAT Kehle *f*, Schlund *m*; GEOGR enge (Fels)Schlucht **2.** verschlingen; schlingen, (sich) vollstopfen

gor·geous prächtig

go·ril·la ZO Gorilla *m*

gor·y F blutrünstig

gosh *int* F Mensch!, Mann!

gos·ling ZO junge Gans

go-slow *Br* ECON Bummelstreik *m*

Gos·pel REL Evangelium *n*

gos·sa·mer Altweibersommer *m*

gos·sip 1. Klatsch *m*, Tratsch *m*; Klatschbase *f* **2.** klatschen, tratschen

gos·sip·y geschwätzig; voller Klatsch und Tratsch (*letter etc*)

Goth·ic ARCH **1.** gotisch; *~ novel* Schauerroman *m* **2.** Gotik *f*

gourd BOT Kürbis *m*

gout MED Gicht *f*

gov·ern *v/t* regieren; lenken, leiten; *v/i* herrschen

gov·ern·ess Erzieherin *f*

gov·ern·ment Regierung *f*; Staat *m*

gov·er·nor Gouverneur *m*; Direktor *m*, Leiter *m*; F Alte *m*

gown Kleid *n*; Robe *f*, Talar *m*

grab 1. packen, (hastig *or* gierig) ergreifen, fassen **2.** (hastiger *or* gieriger) Griff; TECH Greifer *m*

grace 1. Anmut *f*, Grazie *f*; Anstand *m*; ECON Frist *f*, Aufschub *m*; Gnade *f*; REL Tischgebet *n* **2.** zieren, schmücken

grace·ful anmutig

grace·less ungraziös

gra·cious gnädig

gra·da·tion Abstufung *f*

grade 1. Grad *m*, Rang *m*; Stufe *f*; ECON Qualität *f*; RAIL *etc* Steigung *f*, Gefälle *n*; PED Klasse *f*; Note *f*, Zensur *f* **2.** sortieren, einteilen; abstufen

grade cross·ing RAIL schienengleicher Bahnübergang

grade school Grundschule *f*

gra·di·ent *Br* RAIL *etc* Steigung *f*, Gefälle *n*

grad·u·al stufenweise, allmählich

grad·u·al·ly nach und nach; allmählich

grad·u·ate 1. UNIV Hochschulabsolvent(in), Akademiker(in); Graduierte *m*, *f*; PED Schulabgänger(in) **2.** abstufen, staffeln; UNIV graduieren; PED die Abschlussprüfung bestehen

greedy

grad·u·a·tion Abstufung f, Staffelung f; UNIV Graduierung f; PED Absolvieren n (**from** gen)

graf·fi·ti Graffiti pl, Wandschmierereien pl

graft 1. MED Transplantat n; AGR Pfropfreis n **2.** MED Gewebe verpflanzen, transplantieren; AGR pfropfen

grain (Samen-, esp Getreide)Korn n; Getreide n; (Sand- etc)Körnchen n, (-)Korn n; Maserung f

gram Gramm n

gram·mar Grammatik f

gram·mar school Grundschule f; Br appr (humanistisches) Gymnasium

gram·mat·i·cal grammatisch, Grammatik...

gramme → **gram**

gra·na·ry Kornspeicher m

grand 1. fig großartig; erhaben; groß; Groß..., Haupt... **2.** F Riese m (1000 dollars or pounds)

grand·child Enkel m, Enkelin f

grand·daugh·ter Enkelin f

gran·deur Größe f, Erhabenheit f; Großartigkeit f

grand·fa·ther Großvater m

gran·di·ose großartig

grand·moth·er Großmutter f

grand·par·ents Großeltern pl

grand·son Enkel m

grand·stand SPORT Haupttribüne f

gran·ny F Oma f

grant 1. bewilligen, gewähren; Erlaubnis etc geben; Bitte etc erfüllen; et. zugeben; **take s.th. for ~ed** et. als selbstverständlich betrachten or hinnehmen **2.** Stipendium n; Bewilligung f, Unterstützung f

gran·u·lat·ed körnig, granuliert; **~ sugar** Kristallzucker m

gran·ule Körnchen n

grape BOT Weinbeere f, Weintraube f

grape·fruit BOT Grapefruit f, Pampelmuse f

grape·vine BOT Weinstock m

graph grafische Darstellung

graph·ic grafisch; anschaulich; **~ arts** Grafik f; **graph·ics** IT Grafik f

grap·ple: ~ with kämpfen mit, fig a. sich herumschlagen mit

grasp 1. (er)greifen, packen; fig verstehen, begreifen **2.** Griff m; Reichweite f (a. fig); fig Verständnis n

grass Gras n; Rasen m; Weide(land n) f; sl. Grass n (marijuana)

grass·hop·per ZO Heuschrecke f

grass roots POL Basis f

grass wid·ow Strohwitwe f

grass wid·ow·er Strohwitwer m

gras·sy grasbedeckt, Gras...

grate 1. (Kamin)Gitter n; (Feuer)Rost m **2.** reiben, raspeln; knirschen (mit); **~ on s.o.'s nerves** an j-s Nerven zerren

grate·ful dankbar

grat·er Reibe f

grat·i·fi·ca·tion Befriedigung f; Freude f; **grat·i·fy** erfreuen; befriedigen

grat·ing¹ kratzend, knirschend, quietschend; schrill; unangenehm

grat·ing² Gitter(werk) n

grat·i·tude Dankbarkeit f

gra·tu·i·tous unentgeltlich; freiwillig

gra·tu·i·ty Abfindung f; Gratifikation f; Trinkgeld n

grave¹ ernst; (ge)wichtig; gemessen

grave² Grab n

grave·dig·ger Totengräber m

grav·el 1. Kies m **2.** mit Kies bestreuen

grave·stone Grabstein m

grave·yard Friedhof m

grav·i·ta·tion PHYS Gravitation f, Schwerkraft f

grav·i·ty PHYS Schwerkraft f; Ernst m

gra·vy Bratensaft m; Bratensoße f

gray 1. grau **2.** Grau n **3.** grau machen or werden

gray·hound ZO Windhund m

graze¹ Vieh weiden (lassen); (ab)weiden; (ab)grasen

graze² 1. streifen; schrammen; Haut (ab-, auf)schürfen, (auf)schrammen **2.** Abschürfung f, Schramme f; Streifschuss m

grease 1. Fett n; TECH Schmierfett n, Schmiere f **2.** (ein)fetten; TECH schmieren; **greas·y** fett(ig), ölig; speckig; schmierig

great groß; Ur(groß)...; F großartig, super

Great Brit·ain Großbritannien n

great-grand·child Urenkel(in)

great-grand·par·ents Urgroßeltern pl

great·ly sehr

great·ness Größe f

Greece Griechenland n

greed Gier f; **greed·y** gierig (**for** auf acc, nach); habgierig; gefräßig

G

Greek 1. griechisch **2.** Grieche *m*, Griechin *f*; LING Griechisch *n*

green 1. grün; *fig* grün, unerfahren **2.** Grün *n*; Grünfläche *f*, Rasen *m*; *pl* grünes Gemüse, Blattgemüse *n*

green·back F Dollar *m*

green belt Grüngürtel *m*

green card Arbeitserlaubnis *f*

green·gro·cer *esp Br* Obst- und Gemüsehändler(in)

green·horn F Greenhorn *n*, Grünschnabel *m*

green·house Gewächs-, Treibhaus *n*; **~ ef·fect** Treibhauseffekt *m*

green·ish grünlich

greet grüßen; **greet·ing** Begrüßung *f*, Gruß *m*; *pl* Grüße *pl*

gre·nade MIL Granate *f*

grey *Br* → **gray**

grid Gitter *n*; ELECTR *etc* Versorgungsnetz *n*; Gitter(netz) *n* (*map etc*)

grid·i·ron Bratrost *m*

grief Kummer *m*

griev·ance (Grund *m* zur) Beschwerde *f*; Missstand *m*

grieve *v/t* betrüben, bekümmern; *v/i* bekümmert sein; **~ for** trauern um

griev·ous schwer, schlimm

grill 1. grillen **2.** Grill *m*; Bratrost *m*; GASTR *das* Gegrillte *n*

grim grimmig; schrecklich; erbittert; F schlimm

gri·mace 1. Fratze *f*, Grimasse *f* **2.** Grimassen schneiden

grime Schmutz *m*; Ruß *m*

grim·y schmutzig; rußig

grin 1. Grinsen *n* **2.** grinsen

grind 1. *v/t* (zer)mahlen, zerreiben, zerkleinern; *Messer etc* schleifen; *Fleisch* durchdrehen; **~ one's teeth** mit den Zähnen knirschen; *v/i* F schuften; pauken, büffeln **2.** Schinderei *f*, F Schufterei *f*; **the daily ~** das tägliche Einerlei

grind·er (*Messer- etc*)Schleifer *m*; TECH Schleifmaschine *f*; TECH Mühle *f*

grind·stone Schleifstein *m*

grip 1. packen (*a. fig*) **2.** Griff *m*; *fig* Gewalt *f*, Herrschaft *f*; Reisetasche *f*

grip·ping spannend

gris·ly grässlich, schrecklich

gris·tle GASTR Knorpel *m*

grit 1. Kies *m*, (grober) Sand; *fig* Mut *m* **2.** streuen; **~ one's teeth** die Zähne zusammenbeißen

griz·zly (bear) ZO Grislibär *m*, Graubär *m*

groan 1. stöhnen, ächzen **2.** Stöhnen *n*, Ächzen *n*

gro·cer Lebensmittelhändler *m*

gro·cer·ies Lebensmittel *pl*

gro·cer·y Lebensmittelgeschäft *n*

grog·gy F groggy, schwach *or* wackelig (auf den Beinen)

groin ANAT Leiste *f*, Leistengegend *f*

groom 1. Pferdepfleger *m*, Stallbursche *m*; Bräutigam *m* **2.** *Pferde* versorgen, striegeln; pflegen

groove Rinne *f*, Furche *f*; Rille *f*, Nut *f*

grope tasten; F *Mädchen* befummeln

gross 1. dick, feist; grob, derb; ECON Brutto... **2.** Gros *n*

gro·tesque grotesk

ground[1] gemahlen (*coffee etc*); **~ meat** Hackfleisch *n*

ground[2] **1.** (Erd)Boden *m*, Erde *f*; Boden *m*, Gebiet *n*; SPORT (*Spiel*)Platz *m*; ELECTR Erdung *f*; (Boden)Satz *m*; *fig* Beweggrund *m*; *pl* Grundstück *n*, Park *m*, Gartenanlage *f*; **on the ~(s) of** aufgrund (*gen*); **hold** *or* **stand one's ~** sich behaupten **2.** MAR auflaufen; ELECTR erden; *fig* gründen, stützen; **~ crew** AVIAT Bodenpersonal *n*; **~ floor** *esp Br* Erdgeschoss *n*; **~ forc·es** MIL Bodentruppen *pl*, Landstreitkräfte *pl*

ground·hog ZO Amer. Waldmurmeltier *n*

ground·ing ELECTR Erdung *f*; Grundlagen *pl*, Grundkenntnisse *pl*

ground·keep·er SPORT Platzwart *m*

ground·less grundlos

ground·nut *Br* BOT Erdnuss *f*

grounds·man *Br* SPORT Platzwart *m*

ground staff *Br* AVIAT Bodenpersonal *n*; **~ sta·tion** Bodenstation *f*

ground·work *fig* Grundlage *f*, Fundament *n*

group 1. Gruppe *f* **2.** (sich) gruppieren

group·ie F Groupie *n*

group·ing Gruppierung *f*

grove Wäldchen *n*, Gehölz *n*

grov·el (am Boden) kriechen

grow *v/i* wachsen; (allmählich) werden; **~ up** aufwachsen, heranwachsen; *v/t* BOT anpflanzen, anbauen, züchten; **~ a beard** sich e-n Bart wachsen lassen

grow·er Züchter *m*, Erzeuger *m*

growl knurren, brummen

grown-up 1. erwachsen **2.** Erwachsene *m*, *f*

growth Wachsen *n*, Wachstum *n*; Wuchs *m*, Größe *f*; *fig* Zunahme *f*, Anwachsen *n*; MED Gewächs *n*, Wucherung *f*

grub 1. ZO Larve *f*, Made *f*; F Futter *n* **2.** graben

grub·by schmudd(e)lig

grudge 1. missgönnen (*s.o. s.th.* j-m et.); **2.** Groll *m*

grudg·ing·ly widerwillig

gru·el Haferschleim *m*

gruff grob, schroff, barsch, unwirsch

grum·ble murren, F meckern (*über acc* about, at); ~ *at* schimpfen über (*acc*)

grump·y F schlecht gelaunt, mürrisch, missmutig, verdrießlich, verdrossen

grun·gy F schmudd(e)lig-schlampig; MUS schlecht und laut

grunt 1. grunzen; brummen; stöhnen **2.** Grunzen *n*; Stöhnen *n*

guar·an·tee 1. Garantie *f*; Kaution *f*, Sicherheit *f* **2.** (sich ver)bürgen für; garantieren

guar·an·tor JUR Bürge *m*, Bürgin *f*

guar·an·ty JUR Garantie *f*; Sicherheit *f*

guard 1. Wache *f*, (Wacht)Posten *m*, Wächter *m*; Wärter *m*, Aufseher *m*; Wache *f*, Bewachung *f*; *Br* Zugbegleiter *m*; Schutz(vorrichtung *f*) *m*; Garde *f*; *be on* ~ Wache stehen; *be on* (*off*) *one's* ~ (nicht) auf der Hut sein **2.** *v/t* bewachen, (be)schützen (*from* vor *dat*); *v/i* sich hüten *or* in Acht nehmen *or* schützen (*against* vor *dat*)

guard·ed vorsichtig, zurückhaltend

guard·i·an JUR Vormund *m* **2.** Schutz...

guard·i·an·ship JUR Vormundschaft *f*

gue(r)·ril·la MIL Guerilla *m*

gue(r)·ril·la war·fare Guerillakrieg *m*

guess 1. (er)raten; vermuten; schätzen; glauben, meinen **2.** Vermutung *f*

guess·work (reine) Vermutung(en *pl*)

guest Gast *m*

guest·house (Hotel)Pension *f*, Fremdenheim *n*

guest·room Gäste-, Fremdenzimmer *n*

guf·faw 1. schallendes Gelächter **2.** schallend lachen

guid·ance Führung *f*; (An)Leitung *f*

guide 1. (Reise-, Fremden)Führer(in); (Reise- *etc*)Führer *m* (*book*); Hand-

buch (*to gen*); *a* ~ *to London* ein London-Führer *m* **2.** leiten; führen; lenken

guide·book (Reise- *etc*)Führer *m*

guid·ed tour Führung *f*

guide·lines Richtlinien *pl* (*on gen*)

guild HIST Gilde *f*, Zunft *f*

guile·less arglos

guilt Schuld *f*

guilt·less schuldlos, unschuldig (*of an dat*)

guilt·y schuldig (*of gen*); schuldbewusst

guin·ea pig ZO Meerschweinchen *n*; *fig* Versuchsperson *f*, F Versuchskaninchen *n*

guise *fig* Gestalt *f*, Maske *f*

gui·tar MUS Gitarre *f*

gulch GEOGR tiefe Schlucht, Klamm *f*

gulf GEOGR Golf *m*; *fig* Kluft *f*

gull ZO Möwe *f*

gul·let ANAT Speiseröhre *f*; Gurgel *f*, Kehle *f*

gulp 1. (großer) Schluck **2.** *often* ~ *down Getränk* hinunterstürzen, *Speise* hinunterschlingen

gum¹ ANAT *mst pl* Zahnfleisch *n*

gum² **1.** Gummi *m*, *n*; Klebstoff *m*; Kaugummi *m*; (Frucht)Gummi *m* **2.** kleben

gump·tion F Grips *m*; Schneid *m*

gun 1. Gewehr *n*; Pistole *f*, Revolver *m*; Geschütz *n*, Kanone *f* **2.** ~ *down* niederschießen

gun·fight Feuergefecht *n*, Schießerei *f*

gun·fire Schüsse *pl*; MIL Geschützfeuer *n*

gun li·cence *Br*, **gun li·cense** Waffenschein *m*

gun·man Bewaffnete *m*

gun·point: *at* ~ mit vorgehaltener Waffe, mit Waffengewalt

gun·pow·der Schießpulver *n*

gun·run·ner Waffenschmuggler *m*

gun·run·ning Waffenschmuggel *m*

gun·shot Schuss *m*; *within* (*out of*) ~ in (außer) Schussweite

gur·gle 1. gurgeln, gluckern, glucksen **2.** Gurgeln *n*, Gluckern *n*, Glucksen *n*

gush 1. strömen, schießen (*from* aus); **2.** Schwall *m*, Strom *m* (*a. fig*)

gust Windstoß *m*, Bö *f*

gust F Eingeweide *pl*; Schneid *m*, Mumm *m*

gut·ter Gosse *f* (*a. fig*), Rinnstein *m*; Dachrinne *f*

G

guy F Kerl *m*, Typ *m*
guz·zle F saufen; fressen
gym F Fitnesscenter *n*; → *gymnasium*; → *gymnastics*
gym·na·si·um Turn-, Sporthalle *f*
gym·nast Turner(in)
gym·nas·tics Turnen *n*, Gymnastik *f*
gym shirt Turnhemd *n*

gym shorts Turnhose *f*
gy·n(a)e·col·o·gist Gynäkologe *m*, Gynäkologin *f*, Frauenarzt *m*, -ärztin *f*
gy·n(a)e·col·o·gy Gynäkologie *f*, Frauenheilkunde *f*
gyp·sy Zigeuner *m*, Zigeunerin *f*
gy·rate kreisen, sich (im Kreis) drehen, (herum)wirbeln

H

H, h H, h *n*
hab·it (An)Gewohnheit *f*; *esp* (Ordens-) Tracht *f*; **get into** (**out of**) **the ~ of smoking** sich das Rauchen angewöhnen (abgewöhnen); **ha·bit·u·al** gewohnheitsmäßig, Gewohnheits...
hack¹ hacken
hack² *contp* Schreiberling *m*
hack³ *contp* Klepper *m*
hack·er IT Hacker *m*
hack·neyed abgedroschen
had·dock ZO Schellfisch *m*
h(a)e·mor·rhage MED Blutung *f*
hag hässliches altes Weib, Hexe *f*
hag·gard abgespannt; verhärmt, abgehärmt; hager
hag·gle feilschen, handeln
hail 1. Hagel *m* **2.** hageln
hail·stone Hagelkorn *n*
hail·storm Hagelschauer *m*
hair *einzelnes* Haar; *coll* Haar *n*, Haare *pl*; **let one's ~ down** F aus sich herausgehen; **without turning a ~** ohne mit der Wimper zu zucken
hair·breadth → *hair's breadth*
hair·brush Haarbürste *f*
hair·cut Haarschnitt *m*
hair·do F Frisur *f*
hair·dress·er Friseur(in)
hair·dri·er, hair·dry·er Trockenhaube *f*; Haartrockner *m*, Föhn *m*
hair·grip *Br* Haarklammer *f*, Haarklemme *f*
hair·less ohne Haare, kahl
hair·pin Haarnadel *f*; **~ bend** MOT Haarnadelkurve *f*
hair·rais·ing haarsträubend
hair's breadth: by a ~ um Haaresbreite
hair slide *Br* Haarspange *f*
hair·split·ting Haarspalterei *f*

hair·spray Haarspray *m, n*
hair·style Frisur *f*
hair styl·ist Hair-Stylist *m*, Damenfriseur *m*
hair·y behaart, haarig
half 1. Hälfte *f*; **go halves** halbe-halbe machen, teilen **2.** halb; **~ an hour** e-e halbe Stunde; **~ a pound** ein halbes Pfund; **~ past ten** halb elf (Uhr); **~ way up** auf halber Höhe
half-breed Halbblut *n*
half-broth·er Halbbruder *m*
half-caste *esp contp* Mischling *m*
half-heart·ed halbherzig
half time SPORT Halbzeit *f*; **~ score** SPORT Halbzeitstand *m*
half-way halb; auf halbem Weg, in der Mitte; **~ line** *soccer*: Mittellinie *f*
half-wit·ted schwachsinnig
hal·i·but ZO Heilbutt *m*
hall Halle *f*, Saal *m*; Flur *m*, Diele *f*; *esp Br* Herrenhaus *n*; *Br* UNIV Speisesaal *m*; *Br* **~ of residence** Studentenheim *n*
hall·mark *fig* Kennzeichen *n*
Hal·low·e'en Abend *m* vor Allerheiligen
hal·lu·ci·na·tion Halluzination *f*
hall·way Halle *f*, Diele *f*; Korridor *m*
ha·lo ASTR Hof *m*; Heiligenschein *m*
halt 1. Halt *m* **2.** (an)halten
hal·ter Halfter *m, n*
halt·ing zögernd, stockend
halve halbieren
ham Schinken *m*; **~ and eggs** Schinken mit (Spiegel)Ei
ham·burg·er GASTR Hamburger *m*; Rinderhack *n*
ham·let Weiler *m*
ham·mer 1. Hammer *m* **2.** hämmern
ham·mock Hängematte *f*

ham·per[1] (Deckel)Korb *m*; Präsentkorb *m*; Wäschekorb *m*

ham·per[2] (be)hindern

ham·ster zo Hamster *m*

hand 1. Hand *f* (*a. fig*); Handschrift *f*; (Uhr)Zeiger *m*; *often in cpds* Arbeiter *m*; Fachmann *m*; *card game*: Blatt *n*, Karten *pl*; *change* ~*s* den Besitzer wechseln; *give or lend a* ~ mit zugreifen, *j-m* helfen (*with* bei); *shake* ~*s with j-m* die Hand schütteln *or* geben; *at* ~ in Reichweite; nahe; bei der *or* zur Hand; *at first* ~ aus erster Hand; *by* ~ mit der Hand; *on the one* ~ einerseits; *on the other* ~ andererseits; *on the right* ~ rechts; ~*s off!* Hände weg!; ~*s up!* Hände hoch! **2.** aushändigen, (über)geben, (über)reichen; ~ *around* herumreichen; ~ *down* weitergeben, überliefern; *in Prüfungsarbeit etc* abgeben; *Bericht, Gesuch etc* einreichen; ~ *on* weiterreichen, weitergeben; überliefern; ~ *out* austeilen, verteilen; ~ *over* übergeben, aushändigen (*to dat*); ~ *up* hinauf-, heraufreichen; ~*bag* Handtasche *f*; ~ *bag·gage* Handgepäck *n*; ~*ball* SPORT Handball *m*; *soccer*: Handspiel *n*; ~*bill* Handzettel *m*, Flugblatt *n*; ~*book* Handbuch *n*; ~*brake* TECH Handbremse *f*; ~*cart* Handwagen *m*; ~*cuffs* Handschellen *pl*; ~*ful* Handvoll *f*; F Plage *f*

hand·i·cap 1. Handikap *n*, MED *a.* Behinderung *f*, SPORT *a.* Vorgabe *f*; → *mental handicap, physical handicap* **2.** behindern, benachteiligen; **hand·i·capped** 1. gehandikapt, behindert, benachteiligt; → *mental, physical* **2.** *the* ~ MED die Behinderten *pl*

hand·ker·chief Taschentuch *n*

han·dle 1. Griff *m*; Stiel *m*; Henkel *m*; Klinke *f*; *fly off the* ~ F wütend werden **2.** anfassen, berühren; hantieren *or* umgehen mit; behandeln; ~*bar(s)* Lenkstange *f*

hand|**lug·gage** Handgepäck *n*; ~*made* handgearbeitet; ~*out* Handzettel *m*; Hand-out *n*, Informationsmaterial *n*; ~*rail* Geländer *n*; ~*s-free·kit* Freisprechanlage *f*; ~*shake* Händedruck *m*

hand·some gut aussehend; *fig* ansehnlich, beträchtlich (*sum etc*)

hands-on praktisch

hand|**spring** Handstandüberschlag *m*; ~*stand* Handstand *m*; ~*writ·ing* Handschrift *f*; ~*writ·ten* handgeschrieben

hand·y zur Hand; geschickt; handlich, praktisch; nützlich; *come in* ~ sich als nützlich erweisen; (sehr) gelegen kommen; ~*man* Handwerker *m*; *be a* ~ *a.* handwerklich geschickt sein

hang (auf-, be-, ein)hängen; *Tapete* ankleben; *j-n* (auf)hängen; ~ *o.s.* sich erhängen; ~ *about*, ~ *around* herumlungern; ~ *on* sich klammern (*to* an *acc*) (*a. fig*), festhalten (*to acc*); TEL am Apparat bleiben; ~ *up* TEL einhängen, auflegen; *she hung up on me* sie legte einfach auf

han·gar Hangar *m*, Flugzeughalle *f*

hang·er Kleiderbügel *m*

hang glid·er SPORT (Flug)Drachen *m*; Drachenflieger(in)

hang glid·ing SPORT Drachenfliegen *n*

hang·ing 1. Hänge… **2.** (Er)Hängen *n*

hang·ings Tapete *f*, Wandbehang *m*, Vorhang *m*

hang·man Henker *m*

hang·nail MED Niednagel *m*

hang·o·ver Katzenjammer *m*, Kater *m*

han·ker F sich sehnen (*after, for* nach)

han·kie, **han·ky** F Taschentuch *n*

hap·haz·ard willkürlich, planlos, wahllos

hap·pen (zufällig) geschehen; sich ereignen, passieren, vorkommen

hap·pen·ing Ereignis *n*, Vorkommnis *n*; Happening *n*

hap·pi·ly glücklich(erweise)

hap·pi·ness Glück *n*

hap·py glücklich; erfreut

hap·py-go-luck·y unbekümmert, sorglos

ha·rangue 1. (Straf)Predigt *f* **2.** *v/t j-m* e-e Strafpredigt halten

har·ass ständig belästigen; schikanieren; aufreiben, zermürben

har·ass·ment ständige Belästigung; Schikane(n *pl*) *f*; → *sexual harassment*

har·bo(u)r 1. Hafen *m*; Zufluchtsort *m* **2.** *j-m* Zuflucht *or* Unterschlupf gewähren; *Groll etc* hegen

hard hart (*a. fig*); fest; schwer, schwierig; heftig, stark; streng (*a. winter*); *fig* nüchtern (*facts etc*); *give s.o. a* ~ *time* j-m das Leben schwer machen; **~ of hearing** schwerhörig; **be ~ on s.th.** et. strapazieren; **~ up** F in (Geld)-Schwierigkeiten, knapp bei Kasse; F **the ~ stuff** die harten Sachen (*alcohol, drugs*)

hard·back gebundene Ausgabe

hard·boiled GASTR hart (gekocht); F *fig* hart, unsentimental, nüchtern

hard cash Bargeld *n*; klingende Münze

hard core harter Kern; **hard-core** zum harten Kern gehörend; hart

hard court *tennis*: Hartplatz *m*

hard·cov·er 1. gebunden **2.** Hard Cover *n*, gebundene Ausgabe

hard cur·ren·cy ECON harte Währung

hard disk IT Festplatte *f*

hard·en härten; hart machen *or* werden; (sich) abhärten

hard hat Schutzhelm *m*

hard-head·ed nüchtern, praktisch; starrköpfig, dickköpfig

hard-heart·ed hartherzig

hard la·bo(u)r JUR Zwangsarbeit *f*

hard line *esp* POL harter Kurs

hard-line *esp* POL hart, kompromisslos

hard·ly kaum

hard·ness Härte *f*; Schwierigkeit *f*

hard·ship Not *f*; Härte *f*; Strapaze *f*

hard shoul·der *Br* MOT Standspur *f*

hard·top MOT Hardtop *n*, *m*

hard·ware Eisenwaren *pl*; Haushaltswaren *pl*; IT Hardware *f*

hard-wear·ing strapazierfähig

har·dy zäh, robust, abgehärtet; BOT winterhart, winterfest

hare *zo* Hase *m*

hare·bell BOT Glockenblume *f*

hare·brained verrückt

hare·lip MED Hasenscharte *f*

harm 1. Schaden *m* **2.** verletzen; schaden (*dat*)

harm·ful schädlich

harm·less harmlos

har·mo·ni·ous harmonisch

har·mo·nize harmonieren; in Einklang sein *or* bringen

har·mo·ny Harmonie *f*

har·ness 1. (*Pferde- etc*)Geschirr *n* **2.** anschirren; anspannen (**to** an *acc*)

harp 1. MUS Harfe *f* **2.** MUS Harfe spielen

har·poon 1. Harpune *f* **2.** harpunieren

har·row AGR **1.** Egge *f* **2.** eggen

har·row·ing quälend, qualvoll, erschüt-

ternd

harsh rau; grell; streng; schroff, barsch

hart ZO Hirsch *m*

har·vest 1. Ernte(zeit) *f*; (Ernte)Ertrag *m* **2.** ernten

har·vest·er MOT Mähdrescher *m*

hash[1] GASTR Haschee *n*

hash[2] F Hasch *n*

hash browns GASTR Brat-, Röstkartoffeln *pl*

hash·ish Haschisch *n*

hasp TECH Haspe *f*

haste Eile *f*, Hast *f*

has·ten *j-n* antreiben; (sich be)einlen; *et.* beschleunigen

hast·y eilig, hastig, überstürzt; voreilig

hat Hut *m*

hatch[1]: *a.* **~ out** ZO ausbrüten; ausschlüpfen

hatch[2] Durchreiche *f*; AVIAT, MAR Luke *f*

hatch·back MOT (Wagen *m* mit) Hecktür *f*

hatch·et Beil *n*; **bury the ~** das Kriegsbeil begraben

hate 1. Hass *m* **2.** hassen

hate·ful verhasst; abscheulich

ha·tred Hass *m*

haugh·ty hochmütig, überheblich

haul 1. ziehen, zerren; schleppen; befördern, transportieren **2.** Ziehen *n*; Fischzug *m*, *fig* F *a.* Fang *m*; Beförderung *f*, Transport *m*; Transportweg *m*

haul·age Beförderung *f*, Transport *m*

haul·er, *Br* **haul·i·er** Transportunternehmer *m*

haunch ANAT Hüfte *f*, Hüftpartie *f*, Hinterbacke *f*; GASTR Keule *f*

haunt 1. spuken in (*dat*); häufig besuchen; *fig* verfolgen, quälen **2.** häufig besuchter Ort; Schlupfwinkel *m*

haunt·ing quälend; unvergesslich; eindringlich

have *v/t* haben; erhalten, bekommen; essen, trinken; **~ breakfast** frühstücken; **~ a cup of tea** e-n Tee trinken; *with inf*: müssen (**I ~ to go now** ich muss jetzt gehen); *with object and pp*: lassen (**I had my hair cut** ich ließ mir die Haare schneiden); **~ back** zurückbekommen; **~ on** *Kleidungsstück* anhaben, *Hut* aufhaben; *v/aux* haben; *v/i* often sein; **I ~ come** ich bin gekommen

ha·ven Hafen *m* (*mst fig*)

hav·oc Verwüstung *f*, Zerstörung *f*; **play**

~ with verwüsten, zerstören; *fig* verheerend wirken auf (*acc*)

hawk[1] ZO Habicht *m*, Falke *m*

hawk[2] hausieren mit; auf der Straße verkaufen; **hawk·er** Hausierer(in); Straßenhändler(in); Drücker(in)

haw·thorn BOT Weißdorn *m*

hay Heu *n*

hay fe·ver MED Heuschnupfen *m*

hay·loft Heuboden *m*

hay·stack Heuhaufen *m*

haz·ard Gefahr *f*, Risiko *n*

haz·ard·ous gewagt, gefährlich, riskant; **~ waste** Sonder-, Giftmüll *m*

haze Dunst(schleier) *m*

ha·zel 1. BOT Hasel(nuss)strauch *m* **2.** (hasel)nussbraun

ha·zel·nut BOT Haselnuss *f*

haz·y dunstig, diesig; *fig* unklar, verschwommen

H-bomb H-Bombe *f*, Wasserstoffbombe *f*

he 1. er **2.** Er *m*; ZO Männchen *n*; **~-goat** Ziegenbock *m*

head 1. Kopf *m*; (Ober)Haupt *n*; Chef *m*; (An)Führer(in), Leiter(in); Spitze *f*; Kopf(ende *n*) *n*; Kopf *m* (*of a page, nail etc*); Vorderseite *f*; Überschrift *f*; **20 dollars a ~** *or* **per ~** zwanzig Dollar pro Kopf *or* Person; **40 ~** (**of cattle**) 40 Stück (Vieh); **~s or tails?** Kopf oder Zahl?; **at the ~** *of* an der Spitze (*gen*); **~ over heels** kopfüber; bis über beide Ohren (*verliebt sein*); **bury one's ~ in the sand** den Kopf in den Sand stecken; **get it into one's ~ that …** es sich in den Kopf setzen, dass; **lose one's ~** den Kopf *or* die Nerven verlieren **2.** Ober…, Haupt…, Chef…, oberste(r, -s), erste(r, -s) **3.** *v/t* anführen, an der Spitze stehen von (*or gen*); voran-, vorausgehen (*dat*); (an)führen, leiten; *soccer:* köpfen; *v/i* (**for**) gehen, fahren (nach); lossteuern, losgehen (auf *acc*); MAR Kurs halten (auf *acc*)

head·ache Kopfweh *n*

head·band Stirnband *n*

head·dress Kopfschmuck *m*

head·er Kopfsprung *m*; *soccer:* Kopfball *m*

head·first kopfüber, mit dem Kopf voran; *fig* ungestüm, stürmisch

head·gear Kopfbedeckung *f*

head·ing Überschrift *f*, Titel(zeile *f*) *m*

head·land Landspitze *f*, Landzunge *f*

head·light MOT Scheinwerfer *m*

head·line Schlagzeile *f*; **news ~s** *radio*, *TV* das Wichtigste in Schlagzeilen

head·long kopfüber; *fig* ungestüm

head·mas·ter *Br* PED Direktor *m*, Rektor *m*

head·mis·tress *Br* PED Direktorin *f*, Rektorin *f*

head-on frontal, Frontal…; **~ collision** MOT Frontalzusammenstoß *m*

head·phones Kopfhörer *pl*

head·quar·ters (*abbr* **HQ**) MIL Hauptquartier *n*; Zentrale *f*

head·rest MOT Kopfstütze *f*

head·set Kopfhörer *pl*

head start SPORT Vorgabe *f*, Vorsprung *m* (*a. fig*)

head·strong halsstarrig

head teach·er → **headmaster, headmistress, principal**

head·wa·ters GEOGR Quellgebiet *n*

head·way Fortschritt(e *pl*) *m*; **make ~** (gut) vorankommen

head·word Stichwort *n*

head·y ZU Kopf steigend, berauschend

heal heilen; **~ over, ~ up** (zu)heilen

heal·ing Heilung *f*; **~ power** Heilkraft *f*

health Gesundheit *f*; **~ cer·tif·i·cate** Gesundheitszeugnis *n*; **~ club** Fitnessklub *m*, Fitnesscenter *n*; **~ food** Reform-, Biokost *f*; **~ food shop** *Br*, **~ food store** Reformhaus *n*, Bioladen *m*

health·ful gesund; heilsam

health| in·su·rance Krankenversicherung *f*; **~ re·sort** Kurort *m*; **~ service** Gesundheitsdienst *m*

health·y gesund

heap 1. Haufe(n) *m* **2.** *a.* **~ up** aufhäufen, *fig a.* anhäufen

hear hören; anhören; *j-m* zuhören; *Zeugen* vernehmen; *Lektion* abhören

hear·er (Zu)Hörer(in)

hear·ing Gehör *n*; Hören *n*; JUR Verhandlung *f*; JUR Vernehmung *f*; *esp* POL Hearing *n*, Anhörung *f*; **within** (**out of**) **~** in (außer) Hörweite

hear·ing aid Hörgerät *n*

hear·say Gerede *n*; **by ~** vom Hörensagen *n*

hearse Leichenwagen *m*

heart ANAT Herz *n* (*a. fig*); Kern *m*; *card games:* Herz(karte *f*) *n*, *pl* Herz *n*; **lose ~** den Mut verlieren; **take ~** sich ein

Herz fassen; **take s.th. to** ~ sich et. zu
Herzen nehmen; **with a heavy ~**
schweren Herzens

heart·ache Kummer *m*

heart at·tack MED Herzanfall *m*; Herzinfarkt *m*

heart·beat Herzschlag *m*

heart·break Leid *n*, großer Kummer

heart·break·ing herzzerreißend

heart·brok·en gebrochen, verzweifelt

heart·burn Sodbrennen *n*

heart·en ermutigen

heart fail·ure MED Herzversagen *n*

heart·felt innig, tief empfunden

hearth Kamin *m*

heart·less herzlos

heart·rend·ing herzzerreißend

heart trans·plant MED Herzverpflan-
zung *f*, Herztransplantation *f*

heart·y herzlich; gesund; herzhaft

heat 1. Hitze *f*; PHYS Wärme *f*; Eifer *m*;
ZO Läufigkeit *f*; SPORT (Einzel)Lauf *m*;
preliminary ~ Vorlauf *m* **2.** *v/t* heizen;
a. ~ **up** erhitzen, aufwärmen; *v/i* sich erhitzen (*a. fig*); **heat·ed** geheizt; heizbar; erhitzt, *fig a.* erregt

heat·er Heizgerät *n*, Heizkörper *m*

heath Heide *f*, Heideland *n*

hea·then REL **1.** Heide *m*, Heidin *f* **2.**
heidnisch

heath·er BOT Heidekraut *n*; Erika *f*

heat·ing Heizung *f* **2.** Heiz...

heat·proof hitzebeständig

heat shield Hitzeschild *n*

heat·stroke MED Hitzschlag *m*

heat wave Hitzewelle *f*

heave *v/t* (hoch)stemmen, (hoch)hie-
ven; *Anker* lichten; *Seufzer* ausstoßen;
v/i sich heben und senken, wogen

heav·en Himmel *m*

heav·en·ly himmlisch

heav·y schwer; stark (*rain, smoker,
drinker, traffic etc*); hoch (*fine, taxes
etc*); schwer (verdaulich); drückend,
lastend; Schwer...

heav·y cur·rent ELECTR Starkstrom *m*

heav·y-du·ty TECH Hochleistungs...;
strapazierfähig

heav·y-hand·ed ungeschickt

heav·y·weight *boxing*: Schwergewicht
n, Schwergewichtler *m*

He·brew 1. hebräisch **2.** Hebräer(in);
LING Hebräisch *n*

heck·le *Redner* durch Zwischenrufe or

Zwischenfragen stören; **heck·ler** Zwi-
schenrufer *m*; **heck·ling** Zwischenrufe

hec·tic hektisch

hedge 1. Hecke *f* **2.** *v/t*: *a.* ~ **in** mit e-r
Hecke einfassen; *v/i fig* ausweichen

hedge·hog ZO Stachelschwein *n*; *Br*
Igel *m*

hedge·row Hecke *f*

heed 1. beachten, Beachtung schenken
(*dat*) **2. give** *or* **pay to, take ~ of** → 1

heed·less: be ~ of nicht beachten, *Warnung etc* in den Wind schlagen

heel 1. ANAT Ferse *f*; Absatz *m*; **down at**
~ *fig* abgerissen; heruntergekommen
2. Absätze machen auf (*acc*)

hef·ty kräftig, stämmig; mächtig (*blow
etc*), gewaltig; F saftig (*prices, fine etc*)

heif·er ZO Färse *f*, junge Kuh

height Höhe *f*; (Körper)Größe *f*; Anhöhe *f*; *fig* Höhe(punkt *m*) *f*

height·en erhöhen; vergrößern

heir Erbe *m*; ~ **to the throne** Thronerbe
m, Thronfolger *m*

heir·ess Erbin *f*

heir·loom Erbstück *n*

hel·i·cop·ter AVIAT Hubschrauber *m*,
Helikopter *m*

hel·i·port AVIAT Hubschrauberlande-
platz *m*

hell 1. Hölle *f*; *a* ~ **of a noise** F ein Höllenlärm; **what the ~ ...?** F was zum Teufel ...? **2.** Höllen... **3.** *int* F verdammt!,
verflucht!; **hell·ish** F höllisch

hel·lo *int* hallo!

helm MAR Ruder *n*, Steuer *n*

hel·met Helm *m*

helms·man MAR Steuermann *m*

help 1. Hilfe *f*; Hausangestellte *f*; *a call*
or **cry for ~** ein Hilferuf, ein Hilfeschrei
2. helfen; ~ *o.s.* sich bedienen, zulangen; *I cannot ~ it* ich kann es nicht ändern; *I could not ~ laughing* ich musste einfach lachen

help·er Helfer(in)

help·ful hilfreich; nützlich

help·ing Portion *f*

help·less hilflos

help·less·ness Hilflosigkeit *f*

help men·u IT Hilfemenü *n*

hel·ter-skel·ter 1. *adv* holterdiepolter,
Hals über Kopf **2.** *adj* überstürzt

helve Stiel *m*, Griff *m*

Hel·ve·tian Schweizer ...

hem 1. Saum *m* **2.** säumen; ~ **in** einschließen

hem·i·sphere GEOGR Halbkugel *f*, Hemisphäre *f*

hem·line Saum *m*

hem·lock BOT Schierling *m*

hemp BOT Hanf *m*

hem·stitch Hohlsaum *m*

hen ZO Henne *f*, Huhn *n*; Weibchen *n*

hence daher; *a week ~* in e-r Woche

hence·forth von nun an

hen house Hühnerstall *m*

hen·pecked hus·band Pantoffelheld *m*

her sie; ihr; ihr(e); sich

her·ald 1. HIST Herold *m* 2. ankündigen

her·ald·ry Wappenkunde *f*, Heraldik *f*

herb BOT Kraut *n*; Heilkraut *n*

her·ba·ceous BOT krautartig; *~ plant* Staudengewächs *n*

herb·al BOT Kräuter…, Pflanzen…

her·bi·vore ZO Pflanzenfresser *m*

herd 1. Herde *f* (*a. fig*), Rudel *n* 2. *v/t* Vieh hüten; *v/i*: *a. ~ together* in e-r Herde leben; sich zusammendrängen

herds·man Hirt *m*

here hier; hierher; *~ you are* hier (bitte); *~'s to you!* auf dein Wohl!

here·a·bout(s) hier herum, in dieser Gegend

here·af·ter 1. künftig 2. *das* Jenseits

here·by hiermit

he·red·i·ta·ry BIOL erblich, Erb…

he·red·i·ty BIOL Erblichkeit *f*; ererbte Anlagen *pl*, Erbmasse *f*

here·in hierin

here·of hiervon

her·e·sy REL Ketzerei *f*

her·e·tic REL Ketzer(in)

here·up·on hierauf, darauf(hin)

here·with hiermit

her·i·tage Erbe *n*

her·maph·ro·dite BIOL Zwitter *m*

her·met·ic TECH hermetisch

her·mit Einsiedler *m*

he·ro Held *m*

he·ro·ic heroisch, heldenhaft, Helden…

her·o·in Heroin *n*

her·o·ine Heldin *f*

her·o·is·m Heldentum *n*

her·on ZO Reiher *m*

her·ring ZO Hering *m*

hers ihrs, ihre(r, -s)

her·self sie selbst; ihr selbst; sich (selbst); *by ~* von selbst, allein, ohne Hilfe

hes·i·tant zögernd, zaudernd, unschlüssig; hes·i·tate zögern, zaudern, unschlüssig sein, Bedenken haben; hes·i·ta·tion Zögern *n*, Zaudern *n*, Unschlüssigkeit *f*; *without ~* ohne zu zögern, bedenkenlos

heterosexual heterosexuell

hew hauen, hacken; *~ down* fällen, umhauen

hey *int* F he!, heda!

hey·day Höhepunkt *m*, Gipfel *m*; Blüte (-zeit) *f*

hi *inf* F hallo!

hi·ber·nate ZO Winterschlaf halten

hic·cough, hic·cup 1. Schluckauf *m* 2. den Schluckauf haben

hide[1] (sich) verbergen, verstecken; verheimlichen

hide[2] Haut *f*, Fell *n*

hide-and-seek Versteckspiel *n*

hide·a·way F Versteck *n*

hid·e·ous abscheulich, scheußlich

hide-out Versteck *n*

hid·ing[1] F Tracht *f* Prügel

hid·ing[2]: *be in ~* sich versteckt halten; *go into ~* untertauchen

hid·ing place Versteck *n*

hi-fi Hi-Fi *n*, Hi-Fi-Gerät *n*, -Anlage *f*

high 1. hoch; groß (*hopes etc*); GASTR angegangen; F blau; F high; *be in ~ spirits* in Hochstimmung sein; ausgelassen *or* übermütig sein 2. METEOR Hoch *n*; Höchststand *m*; High School *f*

high·brow F 1. Intellektuelle *m*, *f* 2. (betont) intellektuell

high-cal·o·rie kalorienreich

high-class erstklassig

high·er ed·u·ca·tion Hochschulausbildung *f*

high fi·del·i·ty High Fidelity *f*

high·grade hochwertig; erstklassig

high-hand·ed anmaßend, eigenmächtig

high-heeled hochhackig

high jump SPORT Hochsprung *m*

high jump·er SPORT Hochspringer(in)

high·land Hochland *n*

high·light 1. Höhe-, Glanzpunkt *m* 2. hervorheben

high·ly *fig* hoch; *think ~ of* viel halten von; high·ly-strung reizbar, nervös

high·ness *mst fig* Höhe *f*; *Highness* Hoheit *f* (*title*)

high-pitched schrill; steil (*roof*)

high-pow·ered TECH Hochleistungs…; *fig* dynamisch

high-pres·sure METEOR, TECH Hochdruck…

high-rank·ing hochrangig

high rise Hochhaus *n*

high road *esp Br* Hauptstraße *f*

high school High School *f*

high sea·son Hochsaison *f*

high so·ci·e·ty High Society *f*

high-spir·it·ed übermütig, ausgelassen

high street *Br* Hauptstraße *f*

high tea *Br* frühes Abendessen

high tech·nol·o·gy Hochtechnologie *f*

high ten·sion ELECTR Hochspannung *f*

high tide Flut *f*

high time: *it is* ~ es ist höchste Zeit

high wa·ter Hochwasser *n*

high·way Highway *m*, Haupt(verkehrs)-straße *f*; **High·way Code** *Br* Straßenverkehrsordnung *f*

hi·jack 1. *Flugzeug* entführen; *j-n, Geldtransport etc* überfallen **2.** (Flugzeug-) Entführung *f*; Überfall *m*

hi·jack·er Räuber *m*; (Flugzeug)Entführer(in)

hike 1. wandern **2.** Wanderung *f*

hik·er Wanderer *m*, Wanderin *f*

hik·ing Wandern *n*

hi·lar·i·ous ausgelassen

hi·lar·i·ty Ausgelassenheit *f*

hill Hügel *m*, Anhöhe *f*

hill·bil·ly *contp* Hinterwäldler *m*

hill·ock kleiner Hügel

hill·side (Ab)Hang *m*

hill·top Hügelspitze *f*

hill·y hügelig

hilt Heft *n*, Griff *m*

him ihn; ihm; F er; sich

him·self er *or* ihm *or* ihn selbst; sich; sich (selbst); *by* ~ von selbst, allein, ohne Hilfe

hind[1] ZO Hirschkuh *f*

hind[2] Hinter…

hin·der hindern (*from* an *dat*); hemmen

hind·most hinterste(r, -s), letzte(r, -s)

hin·drance Hindernis *n*

Hin·du Hindu *m*

Hin·du·ism Hinduismus *m*

hinge 1. TECH (Tür)Angel *f*, Scharnier *n* **2.** ~ *on fig* abhängen von

hint 1. Wink *m*, Andeutung *f*; Tipp *m*; Anspielung *f*; *take a* ~ e-n Wink verstehen **2.** andeuten; anspielen (*at* auf *acc*)

hip[1] ANAT Hüfte *f*

hip[2] BOT Hagebutte *f*

hip·po F → **hip·po·pot·a·mus** ZO Flusspferd *n*, Nilpferd *n*

hire 1. *Br Auto etc* mieten, *Flugzeug etc* chartern; *j-n* anstellen; *j-n* engagieren, anheuern; ~ *out Br* vermieten **2.** Miete *f*; Lohn *m*; *for* ~ zu vermieten; frei

hire car *Br* Leih-, Mietwagen *m*

hire pur·chase: *on* ~ *Br* ECON auf Abzahlung, auf Raten

his sein(e); seins, seine(r, -s)

hiss 1. zischen; fauchen (*cat*); auszischen **2.** Zischen *n*; Fauchen *n*

his·to·ri·an Historiker(in)

his·tor·ic historisch, geschichtlich (bedeutsam); **his·tor·i·cal** historisch, geschichtlich (belegt *or* überliefert); Geschichts…; ~ *novel* historischer Roman

his·to·ry Geschichte *f*; ~ *of civilization* Kulturgeschichte *f*; *contemporary* ~ Zeitgeschichte *f*

hit 1. schlagen; treffen (*a. fig*); MOT *etc j-n, et.* anfahren, *et.* rammen; F ~ *it off* (*with s.o.*) sich (mit j-m) gut vertragen; ~ *on* (zufällig) auf *et.* stoßen, *et.* finden **2.** Schlag *m*; *fig* (Seiten)Hieb *m*; (Glücks)Treffer *m*; Hit *m*

hit-and-run: ~ *driver* (unfall)flüchtiger Fahrer; ~ *offense* (*Br offence*) Fahrerflucht *f*

hitch 1. befestigen, festmachen, festhaken, anbinden, ankoppeln (*to* an *acc*); ~ *up* hochziehen; ~ *a ride or* lift im Auto mitgenommen werden **2.** Ruck *m*, Zug *m*; Schwierigkeit *f*, Haken *m*; *without a* ~ glatt, reibungslos

hitch·hike per Anhalter fahren, trampen; **hitch·hik·er** Anhalter(in), Tramper(in)

hi-tech → **high tech**

HIV: ~ *carrier* HIV-Positive *m, f*; ~ *negative* HIV-negativ; ~ *positive* HIV-positiv

hive Bienenstock *m*; Bienenschwarm *m*

hoard 1. Vorrat *m*, Schatz *m* **2.** *a.* ~ *up* horten, hamstern; **hoard·ing** Bauzaun *m*; *Br* Reklametafel *f*

hoar·frost (Rau)Reif *m*

hoarse heiser, rau

hoax 1. Falschmeldung *f*; (übler) Scherz **2.** *j-n* hereinlegen

hob·ble humpeln, hinken

hob·by Hobby *n*, Steckenpferd *n*
hob·by·horse Steckenpferd *n (a. fig)*
hob·gob·lin Kobold *m*
ho·bo F Landstreicher *m*
hock[1] weißer Rheinwein
hock[2] ZO Sprunggelenk *n*
hock·ey SPORT Eishockey *n*; *esp Br* Hockey *n*
hodge·podge Mischmasch *m*
hoe AGR **1.** Hacke *f* **2.** hacken
hog ZO (Haus-, Schlacht)Schwein *n*
hoist 1. hochziehen; hissen **2.** TECH Winde *f*, (Lasten)Aufzug *m*
hold 1. halten; festhalten; *Gewicht etc* tragen, aushalten; zurück-, abhalten (**from** von); *Wahlen, Versammlung etc* abhalten; *Stellung* halten; SPORT *Meisterschaft etc* austragen; *Aktien, Rechte etc* besitzen; *Amt* bekleiden; *Platz* einnehmen; *Rekord* halten; fassen, enthalten; Platz bieten für; der Ansicht sein (**that** dass); halten für; *fig* fesseln, in Spannung halten; (sich) festhalten; anhalten, andauern (*a. fig*); ~ **one's ground,** ~ **one's own** sich behaupten; ~ **the line** TEL am Apparat bleiben; ~ **responsible** verantwortlich machen; ~ **still** still halten; ~ **s.th. against s.o.** j-m et. vorhalten *or* vorwerfen; j-m et. übel nehmen *or* nachtragen; ~ **back** (sich) zurückhalten; *fig* zurückhalten mit; ~ **on** (sich) festhalten (**to** an *dat*); aus-, durchhalten; andauern; TEL am Apparat bleiben; ~ **out** aus-, durchhalten; reichen (*supplies etc*); ~ **up** hochheben; hochhalten; hinstellen (**as** als); aufhalten, verzögern; *j-n, Bank etc* überfallen **2.** Griff *m*, Halt *m*; Stütze *f*; Gewalt *f*, Macht *f*, Einfluss *m*; MAR Laderaum *m*, Frachtraum *m*; **catch** (**get, take**) ~ **of s.th.** et. ergreifen, et. zu fassen bekommen
hold·er TECH Halter *m*; *esp* ECON Inhaber(in)
hold·ing Besitz *m*; ~ **com·pa·ny** ECON Holding-, Dachgesellschaft *f*
hold·up (Verkehrs)Stockung *f*; (bewaffneter) (Raub)Überfall
hole **1.** Loch *n*; Höhle *f*, Bau *m*; *fig* F Klemme *f* **2.** durchlöchern
hol·i·day Feiertag *m*; freier Tag; *esp Br mst pl* Ferien *pl*, Urlaub *m*; **be on** ~ im Urlaub sein, Urlaub machen; ~ **home** Ferienhaus *n*, Ferienwohnung *f*

hol·i·day·mak·er Urlauber(in)
hol·i·ness Heiligkeit *f*; *His Holiness* Seine Heiligkeit
hol·ler F schreien
hol·low **1.** hohl **2.** Hohlraum *m*, (Aus)Höhlung *f*; Mulde *f*, Vertiefung *f* **3.** ~ **out** aushöhlen
hol·ly BOT Stechpalme *f*
hol·o·caust Massenvernichtung *f*, Massensterben *n*, (*esp* Brand)Katastrophe *f*; *the Holocaust* HIST der Holocaust
hol·ster (Pistolen)Halfter *m*, *n*
ho·ly heilig
ho·ly wa·ter REL Weihwasser *n*
Ho·ly Week REL Karwoche *f*
home 1. Heim *n*; Haus *n*; Wohnung *f*; Zuhause *n*; Heimat *f*; **at** ~ zu Hause; **make oneself at** ~ es sich bequem machen; **at** ~ **and abroad** im In- und Ausland **2.** *adj* häuslich, Heim... (*a.* SPORT); inländisch, Inlands...; Heimat... **3.** *adv* heim, nach Hause; zu Hause; daheim; *fig* ins Ziel, ins Schwarze; *return* ~ heimkehren; *strike* ~ sitzen, treffen
home ad·dress Privatanschrift *f*
home com·put·er Heimcomputer *m*
home·less heimatlos; obdachlos; ~ *per·son* Obdachlose *m*, *f*; *shelter for the* ~ Obdachlosenasyl *n*
home·ly einfach; unscheinbar, reizlos
home·made selbst gemacht, Hausmacher...
home mar·ket ECON Binnenmarkt *m*
Home| Of·fice *Br* POL Innenministerium *n*; ~ **Sec·re·ta·ry** *Br* POL Innenminister *m*
home·sick: be ~ Heimweh haben
home·sick·ness Heimweh *n*
home team SPORT Gastgeber *pl*
home·ward *adj* Heim..., Rück...
home·ward(s) *adv* nach Hause
home·work Hausaufgabe(n *pl*) *f*; *do one's* ~ s-e Hausaufgaben machen (*a. fig*)
hom·i·cide JUR Mord *m*; Totschlag *m*; Mörder(in)
hom·i·cide squad Mordkommission *f*
ho·mo·ge·ne·ous homogen, gleichartig
ho·mo·sex·u·al 1. homosexuell **2.** Homosexuelle *m*, *f*
hone TECH fein schleifen
hon·est ehrlich, rechtschaffen; aufrichtig; **hon·es·ty** Ehrlichkeit *f*, Rechtschaffenheit *f*; Aufrichtigkeit *f*

H

hon·ey Honig *m*; Liebling *m*, Schatz *m*

hon·ey·comb (Honig)Wabe *f*

hon·eyed *fig* honigsüß

hon·ey·moon **1.** Flitterwochen *pl*, Hochzeitsreise *f* **2. be ~ing** auf Hochzeitsreise sein

hon·ey·suck·le BOT Geißblatt *n*

honk MOT hupen

hon·or·ar·y Ehren...; ehrenamtlich

hon·o(u)r **1.** Ehre *f*; Ehrung *f*, Ehre(n *pl*) *f*; *pl* besondere Auszeichnung(en *pl*); *Your Hono(u)r* JUR Euer Ehren **2.** ehren; auszeichnen; ECON *Scheck etc* honorieren, einlösen

hon·o(u)r·a·ble ehrenvoll, ehrenhaft; ehrenwert

hood Kapuze *f*; MOT Verdeck *n*; (Motor)Haube *f*; TECH (Schutz)Haube *f*

hood·lum F Rowdy *m*; Ganove *m*

hood·wink *j-n* hinters Licht führen

hoof ZO Huf *m*

hook **1.** Haken *m*; Angelhaken *m* **2.** an-, ein-, fest-, zuhaken; angeln (*a. fig*)

hooked krumm, Haken...; F süchtig (**on** nach) (*a. fig*); **~ on heroin** (**television**) heroinsüchtig (fernsehsüchtig)

hook·er F Nutte *f*

hoo·li·gan Rowdy *m*

hoo·li·gan·ism Rowdytum *n*

hoop Reif(en) *m*

hoot **1.** ZO Schrei *m* (*a. fig*); MOT Hupen *n* **2.** *v/i* heulen; johlen; ZO schreien; MOT hupen; *v/t* auspfeifen, auszischen

Hoo·ver® Br **1.** Staubsauger *m* **2.** *mst* **hoover** (staub)saugen

hop[1] **1.** hüpfen, hopsen; hüpfen über (*acc*); **be ~ping mad** F e-e Stinkwut haben **2.** Sprung *m*

hop[2] BOT Hopfen *m*

hope **1.** Hoffnung *f* (*of* auf *acc*); **2.** hoffen (**for** auf *acc*); **~ for the best** das Beste hoffen; **I ~ so, let's ~ so** hoffentlich

hope·ful: **be ~ that** hoffen, dass

hope·ful·ly hoffnungsvoll; hoffentlich

hope·less hoffnungslos; verzweifelt

horde Horde *f* (*often contp*)

ho·ri·zon Horizont *m*

hor·i·zon·tal horizontal, waag(e)recht

hor·mone BIOL Hormon *n*

horn ZO Horn *n*, *pl* Geweih *n*; MOT Hupe *f*

hor·net ZO Hornisse *f*

horn·y schwielig; V geil

hor·o·scope Horoskop *n*

hor·ri·ble schrecklich, furchtbar, scheußlich

hor·rid *esp Br* grässlich, abscheulich; schrecklich

hor·rif·ic schrecklich, entsetzlich

hor·ri·fy entsetzen

hor·ror Entsetzen *n*; Abscheu *m*, Horror *m*; F Gräuel *m*

horse ZO Pferd *n*; Bock *m*, Gestell *n*; *wild ~s couldn't drag me there* keine zehn Pferde bringen mich dort hin

horse·back: **on ~** zu Pferde, beritten

horse chest·nut BOT Rosskastanie *f*

horse·hair Rosshaar *n*

horse·man (geübter) Reiter

horse·pow·er TECH Pferdestärke *f*

horse race Pferderennen *n*

horse rac·ing Pferderennen *n or pl*

horse·rad·ish BOT Meerrettich *m*

horse·shoe Hufeisen *n*

horse·wom·an (geübte) Reiterin

hor·ti·cul·ture Gartenbau *m*

hose[1] Schlauch *m*

hose[2] Strümpfe *pl*, Strumpfwaren *pl*

ho·sier·y Strumpfwaren *pl*

hos·pice Sterbeklinik *f*

hos·pi·ta·ble gastfreundlich

hos·pi·tal Krankenhaus *n*, Klinik *f*; *in the ~* im Krankenhaus

hos·pi·tal·i·ty Gastfreundschaft *f*

hos·pi·tal·ize ins Krankenhaus einliefern *or* einweisen

host[1] **1.** Gastgeber *m*; BIOL Wirt *m*; *radio*, TV Talkmaster *m*, Showmaster *m*, Moderator(in); *your ~ was ...* durch die Sendung führte Sie ... **2.** *radio*, TV F *Sendung* moderieren

host[2] Menge *f*, Masse *f*

host[3] REL *often* **Host** Hostie *f*

hos·tage Geisel *m*, *f*; *take s.o. ~* j-n als Geisel nehmen

hos·tel *esp Br* UNIV (Wohn)Heim *n*; *mst* **youth ~** Jugendherberge *f*

host·ess Gastgeberin *f*; Hostess *f* (*a.* AVIAT); AVIAT Stewardess *f*

hos·tile feindlich; feindselig (**to** gegen); **~ to foreigners** ausländerfeindlich

hos·til·i·ty Feindseligkeit *f* (**to** gegen); **~ to foreigners** Ausländerfeindlichkeit *f*

hot heiß (*a. fig and sl*); GASTR scharf; warm (*meal*); *fig* hitzig, heftig; ganz neu *or* frisch (*news etc*); *I am or feel ~* mir ist heiß

hot·bed Mistbeet *n*; *fig* Brutstätte *f*

hotch·potch *Br* → **hodgepodge**

hot dog GASTR Hot Dog *n*, *m*

ho·tel Hotel *n*

hot·head Hitzkopf *m*

hot·house Treib-, Gewächshaus *n*

hot line POL heißer Draht; TEL Hotline *f*

hot·plate Kochplatte *f*

hot spot *esp* POL Unruhe-, Krisenherd *m*

hot spring Thermalquelle *f*

hot-tem·pered jähzornig

hot-wa·ter bot·tle Wärmflasche *f*

hound ZO Jagdhund *m*

hour Stunde *f*; *pl* (*Arbeits*)Zeit *f*, (*Geschäfts*)Stunden *pl*; hour·ly stündlich

house **1.** Haus *n* **2.** unterbringen

house·bound aus Haus gefesselt

house·break·ing Einbruch *m*

house·hold **1.** Haushalt *m* **2.** Haushalts…

house hus·band Hausmann *m*

house·keep·er Haushälterin *f*

house·keep·ing Haushaltung *f*, Haushaltsführung *f*

house·maid Hausangestellte *f*, Hausmädchen *n*

house·man *Br* MED Assistenzarzt *m*, -ärztin *f*

House of Lords *Br* PARL Oberhaus *n*

house plant Zimmerpflanze *f*

house-warm·ing Hauseinweihung *f*, Einzugsparty *f*

house·wife Hausfrau *f*

house·work Hausarbeit *f*

hous·ing Wohnung *f*; ~ de·vel·opment, *Br* ~ es·tate Wohnsiedlung *f*

hov·er schweben; herumlungern; *fig* schwanken

hov·er·craft Hovercraft *n*, Luftkissenfahrzeug *n*

how wie; ~ *are you?* wie geht es dir?; ~ *about…?* wie steht's mit …?, wie wäre es mit …?; ~ *do you do?* guten Tag!; ~ *much?* wie viel?; ~ *many* wie viele?

how·ev·er **1.** *adv* wie auch (immer) **2.** *cj* jedoch

howl **1.** heulen; brüllen, schreien **2.** Heulen *n*; howl·er F grober Schnitzer

hub TECH (Rad)Nabe *f*; *fig* Mittelpunkt *m*, Angelpunkt *m*

hub·bub F Stimmengewirr *n*; Tumult *m*

hub·by F (Ehe)Mann *m*

huck·le·ber·ry BOT amerikanische Heidelbeere

hud·dle: ~ *together* (sich) zusammen-

drängen; ~*d up* zusammengekauert

hue[1] Farbe *f*; (Farb)Ton *m*

hue[2] ~ *and cry* *fig* großes Geschrei, heftiger Protest

huff: *in a* ~ verärgert, verstimmt

hug **1.** (sich) umarmen; an sich drücken **2.** Umarmung *f*

huge riesig, riesengroß

hulk F Koloss *m*; sperriges Ding

hull **1.** BOT Schale *f*, Hülse *f*; MAR Rumpf *m* **2.** enthülsen, schälen

hul·la·ba·loo Lärm *m*, Getöse *n*

hul·lo *int* hallo!

hum summen; brummen

hu·man **1.** menschlich, Menschen… **2.** *a.* ~ *being* Mensch *m*

hu·mane human, menschlich

hu·man·i·tar·i·an humanitär, menschenfreundlich

hu·man·i·ty die Menschheit, die Menschen *pl*; Humanität *f*, Menschlichkeit *f*; *pl* Geisteswissenschaften *pl*; Altphilologie *f*

hu·man·ly: ~ *possible* menschenmöglich

human rights Menschenrechte *pl*

hum·ble **1.** demütig; bescheiden **2.** demütigen; hum·ble·ness Demut *f*

hum·drum eintönig, langweilig

hu·mid feucht, nass

hu·mid·i·ty Feuchtigkeit *f*

hu·mil·i·ate demütigen, erniedrigen

hu·mil·i·a·tion Demütigung *f*, Erniedrigung *f*

hu·mil·i·ty Demut *f*

hum·ming·bird ZO Kolibri *m*

hu·mor·ous humorvoll, komisch

hu·mo(u)r **1.** Humor *m*; Komik *f* **2.** *j-m* s-n Willen lassen; eingehen auf (*acc*)

hump ZO Höcker *m*; MED Buckel *m*

hump·back(ed) → **hunchback(ed)**

hunch **1.** → **hump**; dickes Stück; (Vor)Ahnung *f* **2.** *a.* ~ *up* krümmen; ~ *one's shoulders* die Schultern hochziehen

hunch·back Buckel *m*; Bucklige *m*, *f*

hunch·backed buck(e)lig

hun·dred **1.** hundert **2.** Hundert *f*

hun·dredth **1.** hundertste(r, -s) **2.** Hundertstel *n*

hun·dred·weight *appr* Zentner *m* (= *50,8 kg*)

Hun·ga·ri·an **1.** ungarisch **2.** Ungar(in); LING Ungarisch *n*

H

Hun·ga·ry Ungarn *n*

hun·ger 1. Hunger *m (a. fig* **for** nach); **2.** *fig* hungern (*for, after* nach)

hun·ger strike Hungerstreik *m*

hun·gry hungrig

hunk dickes *or* großes Stück

hunt 1. jagen; Jagd machen auf (*acc*); verfolgen; suchen (*for, after* nach); *~ down* zur Strecke bringen; *~ for* Jagd machen auf (*acc*); *~ out, ~ up* aufspüren **2.** Jagd *f (a. fig)*, Jagen *n*; Verfolgung *f*; Suche *f* (*for, after* nach)

hunt·er Jäger *m*; Jagdpferd *n*

hunt·ing 1. Jagen *n* **2.** Jagd…

hunt·ing ground Jagdrevier *n*

hur·dle SPORT Hürde *f (a. fig)*

hur·dler SPORT Hürdenläufer(in)

hur·dle race SPORT Hürdenrennen *n*

hurl schleudern; *~ abuse at s.o.* j-m Beleidigungen ins Gesicht schleudern

hur·rah, hur·ray *int* hurra!

hur·ri·cane Hurrikan *m*, Wirbelsturm *m*; Orkan *m*

hur·ried eilig, hastig, übereilt

hur·ry 1. *v/t* schnell *or* eilig befördern *or* bringen; *often ~ up* j-n antreiben, hetzen; *et.* beschleunigen; *v/i* eilen, hasten; *~ (up)* sich beeilen; *~ up!* (mach) schnell! **2.** (große) Eile, Hast *f*; *be in a ~* es eilig haben

hurt verletzen; verwunden (*a. fig*); schmerzen, wehtun; schaden (*dat*)

hurt·ful verletzend

hus·band (Ehe)Mann *m*

hush 1. *int* still! **2.** Stille *f* **3.** zum Schweigen bringen; *~ up* vertuschen, totschweigen

hush mon·ey Schweigegeld *n*

husk BOT **1.** Hülse *f*, Schote *f*, Schale *f* **2.** enthülsen, schälen

hus·tle 1. (*in aller Eile*) *wohin* bringen *or* schicken; hasten, hetzen; sich beeilen **2.** *~ and bustle* Gedränge *n*; Gehetze *n*; Betrieb *m*, Wirbel *m*

hut Hütte *f*

hutch Stall *m*

hy·a·cinth BOT Hyazinthe *f*

hy·(a)e·na ZO Hyäne *f*

hy·brid BIOL Mischling *m*, Kreuzung *f*

hy·drant Hydrant *m*

hy·drau·lic hydraulisch

hy·drau·lics hydraulik *f*

hy·dro… Wasser…

hy·dro·car·bon CHEM Kohlenwasserstoff *m*

hy·dro·chlor·ic ac·id CHEM Salzsäure *f*

hy·dro·foil MAR Tragflächenboot *n*, Tragflügelboot *n*

hy·dro·gen CHEM Wasserstoff *m*; *~ bomb* Wasserstoffbombe

hy·dro·plane AVIAT Wasserflugzeug *n*; MAR Gleitboot *n*

hy·dro·plan·ing MOT Aquaplaning *n*

hy·e·na ZO Hyäne *f*

hy·giene Hygiene *f*

hy·gien·ic hygienisch

hymn Kirchenlied *n*, Choral *m*

hype F **1.** *a. ~ up* (übersteigerte) Publicity machen für **2.** (übersteigerte) Publicity; *media ~* Medienrummel *m*

hy·per… hyper…, übermäßig

hy·per·mar·ket *Br* Groß-, Verbrauchermarkt *m*

hy·per·sen·si·tive überempfindlich (*to* gegen)

hy·phen Bindestrich *m*

hy·phen·ate mit Bindestrich schreiben

hyp·no·tize hypnotisieren

hy·po·chon·dri·ac Hypochonder *m*

hy·poc·ri·sy Heuchelei *f*

hyp·o·crite Heuchler(in); **hyp·o·crit·i·cal** heuchlerisch, scheinheilig

hy·poth·e·sis Hypothese *f*

hys·te·ri·a MED Hysterie *f*

hys·ter·i·cal hysterisch

hys·ter·ics hysterischer Anfall; *go into ~* hysterisch werden

---

I

I, i I, i *n*

I ich; *it is ~* ich bin es

ice 1. Eis *n* **2.** *Getränke etc* mit *or* in Eis kühlen; GASTR glasieren, mit Zucker-

guss überziehen; *~d over* zugefroren (*lake etc*); *~d up* vereist (*road*)

ice age Eiszeit *f*

ice·berg Eisberg *m (a. fig)*

ice·bound eingefroren
ice cream (Speise)Eis n
ice-cream par·lo(u)r Eisdiele f
ice cube Eiswürfel m
iced eisgekühlt
ice floe Eisscholle f
ice hock·ey sport Eishockey n
ice lol·ly Br Eis n am Stiel
ice rink (Kunst)Eisbahn f
ice show Eisrevue f
ice skate Schlittschuh m
ice-skate Schlittschuh laufen
i·ci·cle Eiszapfen m
ic·ing gastr Glasur f, Zuckerguss m; **the ~ on the cake** das Tüpfelchen auf dem i
i·con rel Ikone f; it Icon n, (Bild)Symbol n
i·cy eisig; vereist
ID abbr of **identity** Identität f; **ID card** (Personal)Ausweis m
i·dea Idee f, Vorstellung f, Begriff m; Gedanke m, Idee f; **have no ~** keine Ahnung haben
i·deal 1. ideal 2. Ideal n
i·deal·ism Idealismus m
i·deal·ize idealisieren
i·den·ti·cal identisch (**to, with** mit); ~ twins eineiige Zwillinge pl
i·den·ti·fi·ca·tion Identifizierung f; ~ (pa·pers) Ausweis(papiere pl) m
i·den·ti·fy identifizieren; ~ **o.s.** sich ausweisen
i·den·ti·kit® pic·ture Br jur Phantombild n
i·den·ti·ty Identität f; ~ card (Personal)Ausweis m
i·de·o·log·i·cal ideologisch
i·de·ol·o·gy Ideologie f
id·i·om Idiom n, idiomatischer Ausdruck, Redewendung f
id·i·o·mat·ic idiomatisch
id·i·ot Idiot(in), contp a. Trottel m
id·i·ot·ic idiotisch, F a. blödsinnig, schwachsinnig
i·dle 1. untätig; faul, träge; nutzlos; leer, hohl (talk); tech stillstehend, außer Betrieb; mot leerlaufend, im Leerlauf 2. faulenzen; mot leerlaufen; mst ~ **away** Zeit vertrödeln
i·dol Idol n (a. fig) Götzenbild n
i·dol·ize abgöttisch verehren, vergöttern
i·dyl·lic idyllisch
if wenn, falls; ob; ~ **I were you** wenn ich du wäre

ig·loo Iglu m, n
ig·nite anzünden, (sich) entzünden; mot zünden; ig·ni·tion mot Zündung f
ig·ni·tion key mot Zündschlüssel m
ig·no·rance Unkenntnis f, Unwissenheit f; ig·no·rant: **be ~ of s.th.** et. nicht wissen or kennen, nichts wissen von et.
ig·nore ignorieren, nicht beachten
ill krank; schlimm, schlecht; **fall ~** krank werden, erkranken
ill-ad·vised schlecht beraten; unklug
ill-bred schlecht erzogen; ungezogen
il·le·gal illegal, ungesetzlich; ~ **parking** Falschparken n
il·le·gi·ble unleserlich
il·le·git·i·mate unehelich; unrechtmäßig
ill feel·ing Verstimmung f; **cause ~** böses Blut machen
ill-hu·mo(u)red schlecht gelaunt
il·li·cit unerlaubt, verboten
il·lit·e·rate ungebildet
ill-man·nered ungehobelt, ungezogen
ill-na·tured boshaft, bösartig
ill·ness Krankheit f
ill-tem·pered schlecht gelaunt
ill-timed ungelegen, unpassend
ill-treat misshandeln
il·lu·mi·nate beleuchten
il·lu·mi·nat·ing aufschlussreich
il·lu·mi·na·tion Beleuchtung f; pl Illumination f, Festbeleuchtung f
il·lu·sion Illusion f, Täuschung f
il·lu·sive, il·lu·so·ry illusorisch, trügerisch
il·lus·trate illustrieren; bebildern; erläutern, veranschaulichen
il·lus·tra·tion Erläuterung f; Illustration f; Bild n, Abbildung f
il·lus·tra·tive erläuternd
il·lus·tri·ous berühmt
ill will Feindschaft f
im·age Bild n; Ebenbild n; Image n; bildlicher Ausdruck, Metapher f
im·age·ry Bildersprache f, Metaphorik f
i·ma·gi·na·ble vorstellbar, denkbar
i·ma·gi·na·ry eingebildet, imaginär
i·ma·gi·na·tion Einbildung(skraft) f; Vorstellungskraft f, -vermögen n
i·ma·gi·na·tive ideenreich, einfallsreich; fantasievoll
i·ma·gine sich j-n or et. vorstellen; sich et. einbilden
im·bal·ance Unausgewogenheit f; pol etc Ungleichgewicht n

im·be·cile Idiot *m*, Trottel *m*

im·i·tate nachahmen, nachmachen, imitieren; im·i·ta·tion **1.** Nachahmung *f*, Imitation *f* **2.** nachgemacht, unecht, künstlich, Kunst…

im·mac·u·late unbefleckt, makellos; tadellos, fehlerlos

im·ma·te·ri·al unwesentlich, unerheblich (*to* für)

im·ma·ture unreif

im·mea·su·ra·ble unermesslich

im·me·di·ate unmittelbar; sofortig, umgehend; nächste(r, -s) (*family*)

im·me·di·ate·ly unmittelbar; sofort

im·mense riesig, *fig a.* enorm, immens

im·merse (ein)tauchen; **~ o.s. in** sich vertiefen in (*acc*)

im·mer·sion Eintauchen *n*

im·mer·sion heat·er Tauchsieder *m*

im·mi·grant Einwanderer *m*, Einwanderin *f*, Immigrant(in); im·mi·grate einwandern, immigrieren (*into* nach); im·mi·gra·tion Einwanderung *f*, Immigration *f*

im·mi·nent nahe bevorstehend; **~ danger** drohende Gefahr

im·mo·bile unbeweglich

im·mod·e·rate maßlos

im·mod·est unbescheiden; schamlos, unanständig

im·mor·al unmoralisch

im·mor·tal **1.** unsterblich **2.** Unsterbliche *m*, *f*

im·mor·tal·i·ty Unsterblichkeit *f*

im·mo·va·ble unbeweglich; *fig* unerschütterlich; hart, unnachgiebig

im·mune MED immun (*to* gegen); geschützt (*from* vor, gegen); **~ sys·tem** MED Immunsystem *n*

im·mu·ni·ty MED Immunität *f*

im·mu·nize MED immunisieren, immun machen (*against* gegen)

imp Kobold *m*; F Racker *m*

im·pact Zusammenprall *m*, Anprall *m*; Aufprall *m*; Wucht *f*; *fig* (Ein)Wirkung *f*, (starker) Einfluss (*on* auf *acc*)

im·pair beeinträchtigen

im·part (*to* dat) mitteilen; vermitteln

im·par·tial unparteiisch, unvoreingenommen; im·par·ti·al·i·ty Unparteilichkeit *f*, Objektivität *f*

im·pass·a·ble unpassierbar

im·passe *fig* Sackgasse *f*; **reach an ~** in e-e Sackgasse geraten

im·pas·sioned leidenschaftlich

im·pas·sive teilnahmslos; ungerührt; gelassen

im·pa·tience Ungeduld *f*

im·pa·tient ungeduldig

im·peach JUR anklagen (**for, of, with** gen); JUR anfechten; infrage stellen, in Zweifel ziehen

im·pec·ca·ble untadelig, einwandfrei

im·pede (be)hindern

im·ped·i·ment Hindernis *n* (**to** für); Behinderung *f*

im·pel antreiben; zwingen

im·pend·ing nahe bevorstehend, drohend

im·pen·e·tra·ble undurchdringlich; *fig* unergründlich

im·per·a·tive **1.** unumgänglich, unbedingt erforderlich; gebieterisch; LING Imperativ… **2.** *a.* **~ mood** LING Imperativ *m*, Befehlsform *f*

im·per·cep·ti·ble nicht wahrnehmbar, unmerklich

im·per·fect **1.** unvollkommen; mangelhaft **2.** *a.* **~ tense** LING Imperfekt *n*, 1. Vergangenheit

im·pe·ri·al·ism POL Imperialismus

im·pe·ri·al·ist POL Imperialist *m*

im·per·il gefährden

im·pe·ri·ous herrisch, gebieterisch

im·per·me·a·ble undurchlässig

im·per·son·al unpersönlich

im·per·so·nate *j-n* imitieren, nachahmen; verkörpern, THEA *etc* darstellen

im·per·ti·nence Unverschämtheit *f*, Frechheit *f*

im·per·ti·nent unverschämt, frech

im·per·tur·ba·ble unerschütterlich, gelassen

im·per·vi·ous undurchlässig; *fig* unzugänglich (**to** für)

im·pe·tu·ous ungestüm, heftig; impulsiv; vorschnell

im·pe·tus TECH Antrieb *m*, Impuls *m*

im·pi·e·ty Gottlosigkeit *f*; Pietätlosigkeit *f*, Respektlosigkeit *f* (**to** gegenüber)

im·pinge **~ on** sich auswirken auf (*acc*), beeinflussen (*acc*)

im·pi·ous gottlos; pietätlos, respektlos (**to** gegenüber)

im·plac·a·ble unversöhnlich

im·plant MED implantieren, einpflanzen; *fig* einprägen

im·plau·si·ble unglaubwürdig

im·ple·ment **1.** Werkzeug *n*, Gerät *n* **2.** ausführen

im·pli·cate *j-n* verwickeln, hineinziehen (*in* in *acc*); im·pli·ca·tion Verwicklung *f*; Folge *f*; Andeutung *f*

im·pli·cit vorbehaltlos, bedingungslos; impliziert, (stillschweigend *or* mit) inbegriffen

im·plore *j-n* anflehen; *et.* erflehen

im·ply implizieren, einbeziehen, mit enthalten; andeuten; bedeuten

im·po·lite unhöflich

im·pol·i·tic unklug

im·port ECON **1.** importieren, einführen **2.** Import *m*, Einfuhr *f*

im·por·tance Wichtigkeit *f*, Bedeutung *f*; im·por·tant wichtig, bedeutend

im·por·ta·tion → **import** 2

im·port du·ty ECON Einfuhrzoll *m*

im·port·er ECON Importeur *m*

im·pose auferlegen, aufbürden (**on** *dat*); *Strafe* verhängen (**on** gegen); *et.* aufdrängen, aufzwingen (**on** *dat*); ~ **o.s. on s.o.** sich j-m aufdrängen

im·pos·ing imponierend, eindrucksvoll, imposant

im·pos·si·bil·i·ty Unmöglichkeit *f*

im·pos·si·ble unmöglich

im·pos·ter, *Br* im·pos·tor Betrüger(in), *esp* Hochstapler(in)

im·po·tence Unvermögen *n*, Unfähigkeit *f*; Hilflosigkeit *f*; MED Impotenz *f*

im·po·tent unfähig; hilflos; MED impotent

im·pov·er·ish arm machen; **be ~ed** verarmen; verarmt sein

im·prac·ti·ca·ble undurchführbar; unpassierbar

im·prac·ti·cal unpraktisch; undurchführbar

im·preg·na·ble uneinnehmbar

im·preg·nate imprägnieren, tränken; BIOL schwängern

im·press aufdrücken, einprägen (*a. fig*); *j-n* beeindrucken; **be ~ed with** beeindruckt sein von

im·pres·sion Eindruck *m*; Abdruck *m*; **under the ~ that** in der Annahme, dass

im·pres·sive eindrucksvoll

im·print **1.** (auf)drücken (**on** auf *acc*); ~ **s.th. on s.o.'s memory** j-m et. ins Gedächtnis einprägen **2.** Abdruck *m*, Eindruck *m*; PRINT Impressum *n*

im·pris·on JUR inhaftieren

im·pris·on·ment Freiheitsstrafe *f*, Gefängnis(strafe *f*) *n*, Haft *f*

im·prob·a·ble unwahrscheinlich

im·prop·er ungeeignet, unpassend; unanständig, unschicklich; unrichtig

im·pro·pri·e·ty Unschicklichkeit *f*

im·prove *v/t* verbessern; *Wert etc* erhöhen, steigern; ~ **on** übertreffen; *v/i* sich (ver)bessern, besser werden, sich erholen; im·prove·ment (Ver)Besse)rung *f*; Steigerung *f*; Fortschritt *m* (**on** gegenüber *dat*)

im·pro·vise improvisieren

im·pru·dent unklug

im·pu·dence Unverschämtheit *f*

im·pu·dent unverschämt

im·pulse Impuls *m* (*a. fig*); Anstoß *m*, Anreiz *m*; im·pul·sive impulsiv

im·pu·ni·ty: **with** ~ straflos, ungestraft

im·pure unrein (*a.* REL), schmutzig; *fig* schlecht, unmoralisch

im·pu·ri·ty Unreinheit *f*

im·pute: ~ **s.th. to s.o.** j-n e-r Sache bezichtigen; j-m et. unterstellen

in **1.** *prp place:* in (*dat or acc*), an (*dat*), auf (*dat*): ~ **New York** in New York; ~ **the street** auf der Straße; **put it** ~ **your pocket** steck es in deine Tasche; *time:* in (*dat*), an (*dat*): ~ **1999** 1999; ~ **two hours** in zwei Stunden; ~ **the morning** am Morgen; *state, manner:* in (*dat*), auf (*acc*), mit; ~ **English** auf Englisch; *activity:* in (*dat*), bei, auf (*dat*): ~ **crossing the road** beim Überqueren der Straße; *author:* bei: ~ **Shakespeare** bei Shakespeare; *direction:* in (*acc, dat*), auf (*acc*), zu: **have confidence** ~ Vertrauen haben zu; *purpose:* in (*dat*), zu, als: ~ **defense of** zur Verteidigung *or* zum Schutz von; *material:* in (*dat*), aus, mit: **dressed** ~ **blue** in Blau (gekleidet); *amount etc:* in, von, aus, zu: **three** ~ **all** insgesamt *or* im Ganzen drei; **one** ~ **ten** eine(r, -s) von zehn; nach, gemäß: ~ **my opinion** m-r Meinung nach **2.** *adv* innen, drinnen; hinein, herein; da, (an)gekommen; da, zu Hause **3.** *adj* F in (Mode)

in·a·bil·i·ty Unfähigkeit *f*

in·ac·ces·si·ble unzugänglich, unerreichbar (**to** für *or dat*)

in·ac·cu·rate ungenau

in·ac·tive untätig

in·ac·tiv·i·ty Untätigkeit *f*

in·ad·e·quate unangemessen; unzulänglich, ungenügend

in·ad·mis·si·ble unzulässig, unstatthaft

in·ad·ver·tent unbeabsichtigt, versehentlich; **~ly** *a.* aus Versehen

in·an·i·mate leblos; langweilig

in·ap·pro·pri·ate unpassend, ungeeignet (**for, to** für)

in·apt ungeeignet, unpassend

in·ar·tic·u·late unartikuliert, undeutlich (ausgesprochen), unverständlich; unfähig(, deutlich) zu sprechen

in·at·ten·tive unaufmerksam

in·au·di·ble unhörbar

in·au·gu·ral **1.** Eröffnungs..., Antritts...; **~ speech → 2.** Antrittsrede *f*

in·au·gu·rate *j-n* (feierlich) (in sein Amt) einführen; einweihen, eröffnen; einleiten; in·au·gu·ra·tion Amtseinführung *f*; Einweihung *f*, Eröffnung *f*; Beginn *m*; **Inauguration Day** Tag *m* der Amtseinführung des neu gewählten Präsidenten der USA

in·born angeboren

in·cal·cu·la·ble unberechenbar; unermesslich

in·can·des·cent (weiß) glühend

in·ca·pa·ble unfähig (**of** zu *inf or gen*), nicht imstande (**of doing** zu tun)

in·ca·pac·i·tate unfähig *or* untauglich machen; in·ca·pac·i·ty Unfähigkeit *f*, Untauglichkeit *f*

in·car·nate leibhaftig; personifiziert

in·cau·tious unvorsichtig

in·cen·di·a·ry Brand...; *fig* aufwiegelnd, aufhetzend

in·cense¹ REL Weihrauch *m*

in·cense² in Wut bringen, erbosen

in·cen·tive Ansporn *m*, Anreiz *m*

in·ces·sant ständig, unaufhörlich

in·cest Inzest *m*, Blutschande *f*

inch **1.** Inch *m* (2,54 *cm*), Zoll *m* (*a. fig*); **by ~es, ~ by ~** allmählich; **every ~** durch und durch **2.** (sich) zentimeterweise *or* sehr langsam bewegen

in·ci·dence Vorkommen *n*

in·ci·dent Vorfall *m*, Ereignis *n*; POL Zwischenfall *m*

in·ci·den·tal nebensächlich, Neben...; beiläufig; in·ci·den·tal·ly nebenbei bemerkt, übrigens

in·cin·er·ate verbrennen

in·cin·er·a·tor TECH Verbrennungsofen *m*; Verbrennungsanlage *f*

in·cise einschneiden; aufschneiden; einritzen, einschnitzen

in·ci·sion (Ein)Schnitt *m*

in·ci·sive schneidend, scharf; *fig* treffend

in·ci·sor ANAT Schneidezahn *m*

in·cite anstiften; aufwiegeln, aufhetzen

in·cite·ment Anstiftung *f*; Aufhetzung *f*, Aufwieg(e)lung *f*

in·clem·ent rau

in·cli·na·tion Neigung *f* (*a. fig*)

in·cline **1.** *v/i* sich neigen (**to, towards** nach); *fig* neigen (**to, towards** zu); *v/t* neigen; *fig* veranlassen **2.** Gefälle *n*; (Ab)Hang *m*

in·close, in·clos·ure → **enclose, enclosure**

in·clude einschließen, enthalten; aufnehmen (**in** in *e-e* Liste etc); **the group ~d several ...** zu der Gruppe gehörten einige ...; **tax ~d** inklusive Steuer

in·clud·ing einschließlich

in·clu·sion Einschluss *m*, Einbeziehung *f*; in·clu·sive einschließlich, inklusive (**of** *gen*); **be ~ of** einschließen (*acc*)

in·co·her·ent unzusammenhängend, unklar, unverständlich

in·come ECON Einkommen *n*, Einkünfte *pl*; **~ tax** ECON Einkommensteuer *f*

in·com·ing hereinkommend; ankommend; nachfolgend, neu; **~ mail** Posteingang *m*

in·com·mu·ni·ca·tive verschlossen

in·com·pa·ra·ble unvergleichlich; unvergleichbar

in·com·pat·i·ble unvereinbar; unverträglich; inkompatibel

in·com·pe·tence Unfähigkeit *f*; Inkompetenz *f*; in·com·pe·tent unfähig; nicht fachkundig *or* sachkundig; unzuständig, inkompetent

in·com·plete unvollständig; unvollendet

in·com·pre·hen·si·ble unbegreiflich, unfassbar

in·com·pre·hen·sion Unverständnis *n*

in·con·cei·va·ble unbegreiflich, unfassbar; undenkbar

in·con·clu·sive nicht überzeugend; ergebnislos, erfolglos

in·con·gru·ous nicht übereinstimmend; unvereinbar

in·con·se·quen·tial unbedeutend

in·con·sid·e·ra·ble unbedeutend

in·con·sid·er·ate unüberlegt; rücksichtslos

in·con·sis·tent unvereinbar; widersprüchlich; inkonsequent

in·con·so·la·ble untröstlich

in·con·spic·u·ous unauffällig

in·con·stant unbeständig, wankelmütig

in·con·test·a·ble unanfechtbar

in·con·ti·nent MED inkontinent

in·con·ve·ni·ence 1. Unbequemlichkeit f; Unannehmlichkeit f, Ungelegenheit f 2. j-m lästig sein; j-m Umstände machen; in·con·ve·ni·ent unbequem; ungelegen, lästig

in·cor·po·rate (sich) vereinigen or zusammenschließen; (mit) einbeziehen; enthalten; eingliedern; Ort eingemeinden; ECON, JUR als Aktiengesellschaft eintragen (lassen)

in·cor·po·rat·ed com·pa·ny ECON Aktiengesellschaft f

in·cor·po·ra·tion Vereinigung f, Zusammenschluss m; Eingliederung f; Eingemeindung f; ECON, JUR Eintragung f als Aktiengesellschaft

in·cor·rect unrichtig, falsch; inkorrekt

in·cor·ri·gi·ble unverbesserlich

in·cor·rup·ti·ble unbestechlich

in·crease 1. zunehmen; (an)wachsen; steigen; vergrößern, vermehren, erhöhen 2. Vergrößerung f, Erhöhung f, Zunahme f, Zuwachs m, (An)Wachsen n, Steigerung f; in·creas·ing·ly immer mehr; ~ **difficult** immer schwieriger

in·cred·i·ble unglaublich

in·cre·du·li·ty Ungläubigkeit f

in·cred·u·lous ungläubig, skeptisch

in·crim·i·nate j-n belasten

in·cu·bate ausbrüten; in·cu·ba·tor Brutapparat m; MED Brutkasten m

in·cur sich et. zuziehen, auf sich laden; Schulden machen; Verluste erleiden

in·cu·ra·ble unheilbar

in·cu·ri·ous nicht neugierig, gleichgültig, uninteressiert

in·cur·sion (feindlicher) Einfall; Eindringen n

in·debt·ed (zu Dank) verpflichtet; ECON verschuldet

in·de·cent unanständig, anstößig; JUR unsittlich, unzüchtig; ~ **assault** JUR Sittlichkeitsverbrechen n

in·de·ci·sion Unentschlossenheit f

in·de·ci·sive unentschlossen; unentschieden; unbestimmt, ungewiss

in·deed 1. adv in der Tat, tatsächlich, wirklich; allerdings; **thank you very much ~!** vielen herzlichen Dank! 2. int ach wirklich?

in·de·fat·i·ga·ble unermüdlich

in·de·fen·si·ble unhaltbar

in·de·fi·na·ble undefinierbar, unbestimmbar

in·def·i·nite unbestimmt; unbegrenzt

in·def·i·nite·ly auf unbestimmte Zeit

in·del·i·cate taktlos; unfein, anstößig

in·dem·ni·fy j-n entschädigen, j-m Schadenersatz leisten (**for** für)

in·dem·ni·ty Entschädigung f

in·dent (ein)kerben, auszacken; PRINT Zeile einrücken

in·de·pen·dence Unabhängigkeit f; Selbstständigkeit f; **Independence Day** Unabhängigkeitstag m

in·de·pen·dent unabhängig; selbstständig

in·de·scri·ba·ble unbeschreiblich

in·de·struc·ti·ble unzerstörbar; unverwüstlich

in·de·ter·mi·nate unbestimmt; unklar, vage

in·dex Index m, (Inhalts-, Namens-, Stichwort)Verzeichnis n, (Sach)Register n; (An)Zeichen n; **cost of living ~** Lebenshaltungsindex m

in·dex card Karteikarte f

in·dex fin·ger ANAT Zeigefinger m

In·di·a Indien n

In·di·an 1. indisch; neg! indianisch, Indianer... 2. Inder(in); **American ~** Indianer(in); ~ **corn** BOT Mais m; ~ **file: in ~** im Gänsemarsch; ~ **sum·mer** Altweibersommer m, Nachsommer m

in·di·a rub·ber Gummi n, m; Radiergummi m

in·di·cate deuten or zeigen auf (acc); TECH anzeigen; MOT blinken; fig hinweisen or hindeuten auf (acc); andeuten; in·di·ca·tion (An)Zeichen n, Hinweis m, Andeutung f, Indiz n

in·dic·a·tive a. ~ **mood** LING Indikativ m

in·di·ca·tor TECH Anzeiger m; MOT Richtungsanzeiger m, Blinker m

in·dict JUR anklagen (**for** wegen)

in·dict·ment JUR Anklage f

in·dif·fer·ence Gleichgültigkeit f

in·dif·fer·ent gleichgültig (**to** gegen);

mittelmäßig

in·di·gent arm

in·di·ges·ti·ble unverdaulich

in·di·ges·tion MED Verdauungsstörung f, Magenverstimmung f

in·dig·nant entrüstet, empört, ungehalten (**about, at, over** über acc)

in·dig·na·tion Entrüstung f, Empörung f (**about, at, over** über acc)

in·dig·ni·ty Demütigung f, unwürdige Behandlung

in·di·rect indirekt; **by ~ means** fig auf Umwegen

in·dis·creet unbesonnen, unbedacht; indiskret; in·dis·cre·tion Unbesonnenheit f; Indiskretion f

in·dis·crim·i·nate kritiklos; wahllos

in·dis·pen·sa·ble unentbehrlich, unerlässlich

in·dis·posed indisponiert, unpässlich; abgeneigt; in·dis·po·si·tion Unpässlichkeit f; Abneigung f (**to do** zu tun)

in·dis·pu·ta·ble unbestreitbar, unstreitig

in·dis·tinct undeutlich; unklar, verschwommen

in·dis·tin·guish·a·ble nicht zu unterscheiden(d) (**from** von)

in·di·vid·u·al **1.** individuell, einzeln, Einzel...; persönlich **2.** Individuum n, Einzelne m, f

in·di·vid·u·al·ism Individualismus m

in·di·vid·u·al·ist Individualist(in)

in·di·vid·u·al·i·ty Individualität f, (persönliche) Note

in·di·vid·u·al·ly einzeln, jede(r, -s) für sich; individuell

in·di·vis·i·ble unteilbar

in·dom·i·ta·ble unbezähmbar, nicht unterzukriegen(d)

in·door Haus..., Zimmer..., Innen..., SPORT Hallen...

in·doors im Haus, drinnen; ins Haus (hinein); SPORT in der Halle

in·dorse → **endorse** etc

in·duce j-n veranlassen; verursachen, bewirken; in·duce·ment Anreiz m

in·duct einführen, -setzen; in·duc·tion Herbeiführung f, Einführung f, Einsetzung f; ELECTR Induktion f

in·dulge nachsichtig sein gegen; e-r Neigung etc nachgeben; **~ in s.th.** sich et. gönnen or leisten; in·dul·gence Nachsicht f; Luxus m; REL Ablass m

in·dul·gent nachsichtig, nachgiebig

in·dus·tri·al industriell, Industrie..., Gewerbe..., Betriebs...

in·dus·tri·al ar·e·a Industriegebiet n

in·dus·tri·al·ist Industrielle m, f

in·dus·tri·al·ize industrialisieren

in·dus·tri·ous fleißig

in·dus·try Industrie(zweig m) f; Gewerbe(zweig m) n; Fleiß m

in·ed·i·ble ungenießbar, nicht essbar

in·ef·fec·tive, in·ef·fec·tu·al unwirksam, wirkungslos; unfähig, untauglich

in·ef·fi·cient ineffizient; unfähig, untauglich; unrationell, unwirtschaftlich

in·el·e·gant unelegant

in·el·i·gi·ble nicht berechtigt

in·ept unpassend; ungeschickt; albern, töricht

in·e·qual·i·ty Ungleichheit f

in·ert PHYS träge (a. fig); inaktiv

in·er·tia PHYS Trägheit f (a. fig)

in·es·cap·a·ble unvermeidlich

in·es·sen·tial unwesentlich, unwichtig (**to** für)

in·es·ti·ma·ble unschätzbar

in·ev·i·ta·ble unvermeidlich

in·ev·i·ta·bly zwangsläufig

in·ex·act ungenau

in·ex·cu·sa·ble unverzeihlich, unentschuldbar

in·ex·haus·ti·ble unerschöpflich; unermüdlich

in·ex·o·ra·ble unerbittlich

in·ex·pe·di·ent unzweckmäßig; nicht ratsam

in·ex·pen·sive billig, preiswert

in·ex·pe·ri·ence Unerfahrenheit f

in·ex·pe·ri·enced unerfahren

in·ex·pert unerfahren; ungeschickt

in·ex·pli·ca·ble unerklärlich

in·ex·pres·si·ble unaussprechlich, unbeschreiblich

in·ex·pres·sive ausdruckslos

in·ex·tri·ca·ble unentwirrbar

in·fal·li·ble unfehlbar

in·fa·mous berüchtigt; schändlich, niederträchtig; in·fa·my Ehrlosigkeit f; Schande f; Niedertracht f

in·fan·cy frühe Kindheit; **be in its ~** fig in den Kinderschuhen stecken

in·fant Säugling m; kleines Kind, Kleinkind n; in·fan·tile kindlich; Kindes..., Kinder...; infantil, kindisch

in·fan·try MIL Infanterie f

in·fat·u·at·ed vernarrt (**with** in *acc*)

in·fect MED *j-n, et.* infizieren, *j-n* anstecken (*a. fig*); verseuchen, verunreinigen; in·fec·tion MED Infektion *f*, Ansteckung *f* (*a. fig*); in·fec·tious MED infektiös, ansteckend (*a. fig*)

in·fer folgern, schließen (**from** aus)

in·fer·ence (Schluss)Folgerung *f*, (Rück)Schluss *m*

in·fe·ri·or 1. untergeordnet (**to** *dat*), niedriger (**to** als); weniger wert (**to** als); minderwertig; *be* ~ **to** *s.o.* j-m untergeordnet sein; j-m unterlegen sein 2. Untergebene *m, f*

in·fe·ri·or·i·ty Unterlegenheit *f*; Minderwertigkeit *f*; ~ com·plex PSYCH Minderwertigkeitskomplex *m*

in·fer·nal höllisch, Höllen...

in·fer·no Inferno *n*, Hölle *f*

in·fer·tile unfruchtbar

in·fest verseuchen, befallen; *fig* überschwemmen (**with** mit)

in·fi·del·i·ty (*esp* eheliche) Untreue

in·fil·trate einsickern in (*acc*); einschleusen (*into* in *acc*); POL unterwandern

in·fi·nite unendlich

in·fin·i·tive *a.* ~ **mood** LING Infinitiv *m*, Nennform *f*

in·fin·i·ty Unendlichkeit *f*

in·firm schwach, gebrechlich

in·fir·ma·ry Krankenhaus *n*; PED *etc* Krankenzimmer *n*

in·fir·mi·ty Schwäche *f*, Gebrechlichkeit *f*

in·flame entflammen (*mst fig*); erregen; *become* ~*d* MED sich entzünden

in·flam·ma·ble brennbar, leicht entzündlich; feuergefährlich

in·flam·ma·tion MED Entzündung *f*

in·flam·ma·to·ry MED entzündlich; *fig* aufrührerisch, Hetz...

in·flate aufpumpen, aufblasen, aufblähen (*a. fig*); ECON *Preise etc* in die Höhe treiben

in·fla·tion ECON Inflation *f*

in·flect LING flektieren, beugen

in·flec·tion LING Flexion *f*, Beugung *f*

in·flex·i·ble unbiegsam, starr (*a. fig*); *fig* inflexibel, unbeweglich, unbeugsam

in·flex·ion *Br* → **inflection**

in·flict (**on**) *Leid, Schaden etc* zufügen (*dat*); *Wunde etc* beibringen (*dat*); *Strafe* auferlegen (*dat*), verhängen (über *acc*); aufbürden, aufdrängen (*dat*)

in·flic·tion Zufügung *f*; Verhängung *f*; Plage *f*

in·flu·ence 1. Einfluss *m* 2. beeinflussen; in·flu·en·tial einflussreich

in·flux Zustrom *m*, Zufluss *m*, (*Waren-*)Zufuhr *f*

in·form benachrichtigen, unterrichten (*of* von), informieren (*of* über *acc*); ~ *against or on s.o.* j-n anzeigen; j-n denunzieren

in·for·mal formlos, zwanglos

in·for·mal·i·ty Formlosigkeit *f*; Ungezwungenheit *f*

in·for·ma·tion Auskunft *f*, Information *f*; Nachricht *f*

in·for·ma·tive informativ; lehrreich; mitteilsam

in·form·er Denunziant(in); Spitzel *m*

in·fra·struc·ture Infrastruktur *f*

in·fre·quent selten

in·fringe ~ **on** *Rechte, Vertrag etc* verletzen, verstoßen gegen

in·fu·ri·ate wütend machen

in·fuse *Tee* aufgießen

in·fu·sion Aufguss *m*; MED Infusion *f*

in·ge·ni·ous genial, einfallsreich; raffiniert; in·ge·nu·i·ty Genialität *f*; Einfallsreichtum *m*

in·gen·u·ous offen, aufrichtig; naiv

in·got (*Gold- etc*)Barren *m*

in·gra·ti·ate ~ *o.s. with s.o.* sich bei j-m beliebt machen

in·grat·i·tude Undankbarkeit *f*

in·gre·di·ent Bestandteil *m*; GASTR Zutat *f*

in·hab·it bewohnen, leben in (*dat*)

in·hab·it·a·ble bewohnbar

in·hab·i·tant Bewohner(in); Einwohner(in)

in·hale einatmen, MED *a.* inhalieren

in·her·ent innewohnend, eigen (*in* *dat*)

in·her·it erben; in·her·i·tance Erbe *n*

in·hib·it hemmen (*a.* PSYCH), (ver)hindern; in·hib·it·ed PSYCH gehemmt; in·hi·bi·tion PSYCH Hemmung *f*

in·hos·pi·ta·ble ungastlich; unwirtlich (*region etc*)

in·hu·man unmenschlich

in·hu·mane inhuman, menschenunwürdig

in·im·i·cal feindselig (**to** gegen); nachteilig (**to** für)

in·im·i·ta·ble unnachahmlich

i·ni·tial 1. anfänglich, Anfangs... 2. Initiale f, (großer) Anfangsbuchstabe

i·ni·tial·ly am or zu Anfang, anfänglich

i·ni·ti·ate in die Wege leiten, ins Leben rufen; einführen

i·ni·ti·a·tion Einführung f

i·ni·tia·tive Initiative f, erster Schritt; **take the ~** die Initiative ergreifen; **on one's own ~** aus eigenem Antrieb

in·ject MED injizieren, einspritzen

in·jec·tion MED Injektion f, Spritze f

in·ju·di·cious unklug, unüberlegt

in·junc·tion JUR gerichtliche Verfügung

in·jure verletzen, verwunden; schaden (dat); kränken; **in·jured 1.** verletzt **2. the ~** die Verletzten pl

in·ju·ri·ous schädlich; **be ~ to** schaden (dat); **~ to health** gesundheitsschädlich

in·ju·ry MED Verletzung f; Kränkung f; **~ time** Br esp soccer: Nachspielzeit f

in·jus·tice Ungerechtigkeit f; Unrecht n; **do s.o. an ~** j-m unrecht tun

ink Tinte f

ink·ling Andeutung f; dunkle or leise Ahnung

ink pad Stempelkissen n

ink·y Tinten…; tinten-, pechschwarz

in·laid eingelegt, Einlege…; **~ work** Einlegearbeit f

in·land **1.** adj inländisch, einheimisch; ECON Binnen… **2.** adv landeinwärts

Inland Rev·e·nue Br Finanzamt n

in·lay Einlegearbeit f; MED (Zahn)Füllung f, Plombe f

in·let GEOGR schmale Bucht; TECH Eingang m, Einlass m

in-line skate Inliner m, Inline Skate m

in·mate Insasse m, Insassin f; Mitbewohner(in)

in·most innerste(r, -s) (a. fig)

inn Gasthaus n, Wirtshaus n

in·nate angeboren

in·ner innere(r, -s); Innen…; verborgen

in·ner·most → inmost

in·nings cricket, baseball: Spielzeit f

inn·keep·er Gastwirt(in)

in·no·cence Unschuld f; Harmlosigkeit f; Naivität f; **in·no·cent** unschuldig; harmlos; arglos, naiv

in·noc·u·ous harmlos

in·no·va·tion Neuerung f

in·nu·en·do (versteckte) Andeutung f

in·nu·mer·a·ble unzählig, zahllos

i·noc·u·late MED impfen

i·noc·u·la·tion MED Impfung f

in·of·fen·sive harmlos

in·op·e·ra·ble MED inoperabel, nicht operierbar; undurchführbar (plan etc)

in·op·por·tune inopportun, unangebracht, ungelegen

in·or·di·nate unmäßig

in·pa·tient MED stationärer Patient, stationäre Patientin

in·put Input m, n, IT a. (Daten)Eingabe f, ELECTR a. Eingangsleistung f

in·quest JUR gerichtliche Untersuchung

in·quire fragen or sich erkundigen (nach); **~ into** et. untersuchen, prüfen

in·quir·ing forschend; wissbegierig

in·quir·y Erkundigung f, Nachfrage f; Untersuchung f; Ermittlung f; **make inquiries** Erkundigungen einziehen

in·qui·si·tion (amtliche) Untersuchung; Verhör n; **Inquisition** REL HIST Inquisition f

in·quis·i·tive neugierig, wissbegierig

in·roads (in[to], on) Eingriff m (in acc), Übergriff m (auf acc)

in·sane geisteskrank, wahnsinnig

in·san·i·ta·ry unhygienisch

in·san·i·ty Geisteskrankheit f, Wahnsinn m

in·sa·tia·ble unersättlich

in·scrip·tion Inschrift f, Aufschrift f; Widmung f

in·scru·ta·ble unerforschlich, unergründlich

in·sect ZO Insekt n; **in·sec·ti·cide** Insektenvertilgungsmittel n, Insektizid n

in·se·cure unsicher; nicht sicher or fest

in·sen·si·ble unempfindlich (**to** gegen); bewusstlos; unempfänglich (**of, to** für); gleichgültig (**of, to** gegen); unmerklich

in·sen·si·tive unempfindlich (**to** gegen); unempfänglich (**of, to** für), gleichgültig (**of, to** gegen)

in·sep·a·ra·ble untrennbar; unzertrennlich

in·sert **1.** einfügen, einsetzen, einführen; (hinein)stecken, Münze einwerfen; inserieren **2.** (Zeitungs)Beilage f, (Buch)Einlage f

in·ser·tion Einfügen n, Einsetzen n, Einführen n, Hineinstecken n; Einfügung f; Einwurf m; Anzeige f, Inserat n

in·sert key IT Einfügetaste f

in·shore an or nahe der Küste; Küsten…

in·side 1. Innenseite *f*; *das* Innere; **turn~ out** umkrempeln; auf den Kopf stellen **2.** *adj* innere(r, -s), Innen…; Insider… **3.** *adv* im Inner(e)n, innen, drinnen; **~ of** F innerhalb (*gen*) **4.** *prp* innerhalb, im Inner(e)n

in·sid·er Insider(in), Eingeweihte *m*, *f*

in·sid·i·ous heimtückisch

in·sight Einsicht *f*, Einblick *m*; Verständnis *n*

in·sig·ni·a Insignien *pl*; Abzeichen *pl*

in·sig·nif·i·cant bedeutungslos; unbedeutend

in·sin·cere unaufrichtig

in·sin·u·ate andeuten, anspielen auf (*acc*); unterstellen; **~ that s.o. …** j-m unterstellen, dass er …

in·sin·u·a·tion Anspielung *f*, Andeutung *f*, Unterstellung *f*

in·sip·id geschmacklos, fad

in·sist bestehen, beharren (**on** auf *dat*)

in·sis·tence Bestehen *n*, Beharren *n*; Beharrlichkeit *f*

in·sis·tent beharrlich, hartnäckig

in·sole Einlegesohle *f*; Brandsohle *f*

in·so·lent unverschämt

in·sol·u·ble unlöslich (*substance etc*); unlösbar (*problem etc*)

in·sol·vent ECON zahlungsunfähig, insolvent

in·som·ni·a Schlaflosigkeit *f*

in·spect untersuchen, prüfen, nachsehen; besichtigen, inspizieren

in·spec·tion Prüfung *f*, Untersuchung *f*, Kontrolle *f*; Inspektion *f*

in·spec·tor Aufsichtsbeamte *m*, Inspektor *m*; (Polizei)Inspektor *m*, (Polizei)Kommissar *m*

in·spi·ra·tion Inspiration *f*, (plötzlicher) Einfall; **in·spire** inspirieren, anregen; *Gefühl etc* auslösen

in·stall TECH installieren, einrichten, aufstellen, einbauen, *Leitung* legen; *j-n in ein Amt etc* einsetzen

in·stal·la·tion TECH Installation *f*, Einrichtung *f*, Einbau *m*; TECH *fertige* Anlage *f*; *fig* Einsetzung *f*, Einführung *f*

in·stall·ment, **in·stal·ment** *Br* ECON Rate *f*; (Teil)Lieferung *f*; Fortsetzung *f*; *radio*, TV Folge *f*

in·stall·ment plan: **buy on the ~** ECON auf Abzahlung *or* Raten kaufen

in·stance Beispiel *n*; (besonderer) Fall; JUR Instanz *f*; **for ~** zum Beispiel

in·stant 1. Moment *m*, Augenblick *m* **2.** sofortig, augenblicklich

in·stan·ta·ne·ous sofortig, augenblicklich; **death was ~** der Tod trat sofort ein

in·stant| cam·e·ra PHOT Sofortbildkamera *f*; **~ cof·fee** GASTR Pulver-, Instantkaffee *m*

in·stant·ly sofort, augenblicklich

in·stead stattdessen, dafür; **~ of** anstelle von, (an)statt

in·step ANAT Spann *m*, Rist *m*

in·sti·gate anstiften; aufhetzen; veranlassen; **in·sti·ga·tor** Anstifter(in); (Auf)Hetzer(in)

in·stil *Br*, **in·still** beibringen, einflößen (*into dat*)

in·stinct Instinkt *m*

in·stinc·tive instinktiv

in·sti·tute Institut *n*

in·sti·tu·tion Institution *f*, Einrichtung *f*; Institut *n*; Anstalt *f*

in·struct unterrichten, -weisen; ausbilden, schulen; informieren; anweisen

in·struc·tion Unterricht *m*; Ausbildung *f*, Schulung *f*, Unterweisung *f*; Anweisung *f*, Instruktion *f*; IT Befehl *m*; **~s for use** Gebrauchsanweisung *f*; **operating ~s** Bedienungsanleitung *f*

in·struc·tive instruktiv, lehrreich

in·struc·tor Lehrer *m*; Ausbilder *m*

in·struc·tress Lehrerin *f*; Ausbilderin *f*

in·stru·ment Instrument *n* (*a.* MUS); Werkzeug *n* (*a. fig*)

in·stru·men·tal MUS Instrumental…; behilflich

in·sub·or·di·nate aufsässig

in·sub·or·di·na·tion Auflehnung *f*, Aufsässigkeit *f*

in·suf·fe·ra·ble unerträglich, unausstehlich

in·suf·fi·cient unzulänglich, ungenügend

in·su·lar Insel…; *fig* engstirnig

in·su·late isolieren; **in·su·la·tion** Isolierung *f*; Isoliermaterial *n*

in·sult 1. Beleidigung *f* **2.** beleidigen

in·sur·ance Versicherung *f*; Versicherungssumme *f*; Absicherung *f* (**against** gegen); **~ com·pa·ny** Versicherungsgesellschaft *f*; **~ pol·i·cy** Versicherungspolice *f*

in·sure versichern (**against** gegen)

in·sured: **the ~** der *or* die Versicherte

in·sur·gent 1. aufständisch **2.** Aufständische *m, f*

in·sur·moun·ta·ble *fig* unüberwindlich

in·sur·rec·tion Aufstand *m*

in·tact intakt, unversehrt, unbeschädigt, ganz

in·take (*Nahrungs- etc*)Aufnahme *f*; (Neu)Aufnahme(n *pl*) *f*, (Neu)Zugänge *pl*; TECH Einlass(öffnung *f*) *m*

in·te·gral ganz, vollständig; wesentlich

in·te·grate (sich) integrieren; zusammenschließen; eingliedern, einbeziehen; **~d circuit** ELECTR integrierter Schaltkreis

in·te·gra·tion Integration *f*

in·teg·ri·ty Integrität *f*; Vollständigkeit *f*; Einheit *f*

in·tel·lect Intellekt *m*, Verstand *m*

in·tel·lec·tual **1.** intellektuell, Verstandes…, geistig **2.** Intellektuelle *m, f*

in·tel·li·gence Intelligenz *f*; nachrichtendienstliche Informationen *pl*

in·tel·li·gent intelligent, klug

in·tel·li·gi·ble verständlich (**to** für)

in·tem·per·ate unmäßig

in·tend beabsichtigen, vorhaben, planen; **~ed for** bestimmt für *or* zu

in·tense intensiv, stark, heftig

in·ten·si·fy intensivieren; (sich) verstärken

in·ten·si·ty Intensität *f*

in·ten·sive intensiv, gründlich; **~ care unit** MED Intensivstation *f*

in·tent **1.** gespannt, aufmerksam; **~ on** fest entschlossen zu (*dat*); konzentriert auf (*acc*) **2.** Absicht *f*, Vorhaben *n*

in·ten·tion Absicht *f*; JUR Vorsatz *m*

in·ten·tion·al absichtlich, vorsätzlich

in·ter bestatten

in·ter… zwischen, Zwischen…; gegenseitig, einander

in·ter·act aufeinander (ein)wirken, sich gegenseitig beeinflussen

in·ter·ac·tion Wechselwirkung *f*

in·ter·cede vermitteln, sich einsetzen (**with** bei; **for** für)

in·ter·cept abfangen

in·ter·ces·sion Fürsprache *f*

in·ter·change **1.** austauschen **2.** Austausch *m*; MOT Autobahnkreuz *n*

in·ter·com Sprechanlage *f*

in·ter·course Verkehr *m*; *a.* **sexual ~** (Geschlechts)Verkehr *m*

in·ter·est **1.** Interesse *n* (**in** an *dat*, für); Wichtigkeit *f*, Bedeutung *f*; Vorteil *m*, Nutzen *m*; ECON Anteil *m*, Beteiligung *f*; ECON Zins(en *pl*) *m*; **take an ~ in** sich interessieren für **2.** interessieren (**in** für *et*); in·ter·est·ed interessiert (**in** an *dat*); **be ~ in** sich interessieren für

in·ter·est·ing interessant

in·terest rate ECON Zinssatz *m*

in·ter·face IT Schnittstelle *f*

in·ter·fere sich einmischen (**with** in *acc*); stören; in·ter·fer·ence Einmischung *f*; Störung *f*

in·te·ri·or **1.** innere(r, -s), Innen…; Binnen…; Inlands… **2.** das Innere; Interieur *n*; POL innere Angelegenheiten *pl*; → *Department of the Interior*; **~ dec·o·ra·tor** Innenarchitekt(in)

in·ter·ject *Bemerkung* einwerfen

in·ter·jec·tion Einwurf *m*; Ausruf *m*; LING Interjektion *f*

in·ter·lace (sich) (ineinander) verflechten

in·ter·lop·er Eindringling *m*

in·ter·lude Zwischenspiel *n*; Pause *f*; **~s of bright weather** zeitweilig schön

in·ter·me·di·a·ry Vermittler(in), Mittelsmann *m*

in·ter·me·di·ate in der Mitte liegend, Mittel…, Zwischen…; PED für fortgeschrittene Anfänger

in·ter·ment Beerdigung *f*, Bestattung *f*

in·ter·mi·na·ble endlos

in·ter·mis·sion Unterbrechung *f*; THEA *etc* Pause *f*

in·ter·mit·tent mit Unterbrechungen, periodisch (auftretend); **~ fever** MED Wechselfieber *n*

in·tern[1] internieren

in·tern[2] Assistenzarzt *m*, -ärztin *f*

in·ter·nal innere(r, -s); einheimisch, Inlands…

in·ter·nal-com·bus·tion en·gine Verbrennungsmotor *m*

in·ter·na·tion·al **1.** international; Auslands… **2.** SPORT Internationale *m, f*, Nationalspieler(in); internationaler Wettkampf; Länderspiel *n*; **~ call** TEL Auslandsgespräch *n*; **~ law** JUR Völkerrecht *n*

In·ter·net Internet *n*; **~ ac·cess** Internetzugang *m*; **~ auc·tion** Internetauktion *f*; **~ caf·é** Internetcafé *n*; **~ con·nec·tion** Internetanschluss *m*

in·tern·ist MED Internist *m*

in·ter·per·son·al zwischenmenschlich

in·ter·pret interpretieren, auslegen, erklären; dolmetschen

in·ter·pre·ta·tion Interpretation f, Auslegung f

in·ter·pret·er Dolmetscher(in)

in·ter·ro·gate verhören, vernehmen; (be)fragen; in·ter·ro·ga·tion Verhör n, Vernehmung f; Frage f

in·ter·rog·a·tive LING Interrogativ..., Frage...

in·ter·rupt unterbrechen

in·ter·rup·tion Unterbrechung f

in·ter·sect (durch)schneiden; sich schneiden or kreuzen; in·ter·sec·tion Schnittpunkt m; (Straßen)Kreuzung f

in·ter·sperse einstreuen, hier und da einfügen

in·ter·state 1. zwischenstaatlich 2. a. ~ highway Autobahn f

in·ter·twine (sich ineinander) verschlingen, sich verflechten

in·ter·val Intervall n (a. MUS), Abstand m; Br Pause f (a. THEA etc); at regular ~s in regelmäßigen Abständen

in·ter·vene eingreifen, einschreiten, intervenieren; dazwischenkommen

in·ter·ven·tion Eingreifen n, Einschreiten n, Intervention f

in·ter·view 1. Interview n; Einstellungsgespräch n 2. interviewen; ein Einstellungsgespräch führen mit

in·ter·view·ee Interviewte m, f

in·ter·view·er Interviewer(in)

in·ter·weave (miteinander) verweben

in·tes·tate: die ~ ohne Hinterlassung e-s Testaments sterben

in·tes·tine ANAT Darm m; pl Eingeweide pl; large ~ Dickdarm m; small ~ Dünndarm m

in·ti·ma·cy Intimität f, Vertrautheit f; (a. plumpe) Vertraulichkeit; intime (sexuelle) Beziehungen pl

in·ti·mate 1. intim (a. sexually); vertraut, eng (friends etc); (a. plump)vertraulich; innerste(r, -s); gründlich, genau (knowledge etc) 2. Vertraute m, f

in·tim·i·date einschüchtern

in·tim·i·da·tion Einschüchterung f

in·to in (acc), in (acc) ... hinein; gegen (acc); MATH in (acc); 4 ~ 20 goes five times 4 geht fünfmal in 20

in·tol·e·ra·ble unerträglich

in·tol·e·rance Intoleranz f, Unduldsamkeit (of gegen)

in·tol·e·rant intolerant, unduldsam (of gegen)

in·to·na·tion MUS Intonation f, LING a. Tonfall m

in·tox·i·cat·ed berauscht, betrunken

in·tox·i·ca·tion Rausch m (a. fig)

in·trac·ta·ble eigensinnig; schwer zu handhaben(d)

in·tran·si·tive LING intransitiv

in·tra·ve·nous MED intravenös

in tray: in the ~ im Posteingang etc

in·trep·id unerschrocken

in·tri·cate verwickelt, kompliziert

in·trigue 1. Intrige f 2. faszinieren, interessieren; intrigieren

in·tro·duce vorstellen (to dat), j-n bekannt machen (to mit); einführen

in·tro·duc·tion Vorstellung f; Einführung f; Einleitung f, Vorwort n; letter of ~ Empfehlungsschreiben n

in·tro·duc·to·ry Einführungs...; einleitend, Einleitungs...

in·tro·spec·tion Selbstbeobachtung f

in·tro·vert PSYCH introvertierter Mensch; in·tro·vert·ed PSYCH introvertiert, in sich gekehrt

in·trude (sich) aufdrängen; stören; am I intruding? störe ich?; in·trud·er Eindringling m, Störenfried m

in·tru·sion Störung f

in·tru·sive aufdringlich

in·tu·i·tion Intuition f

in·tu·i·tive intuitiv

In·u·it a. Innuit Inuit m, Eskimo m

in·un·date überschwemmen, überfluten (a. fig)

in·vade eindringen in (acc), einfallen in (acc), MIL a. einmarschieren in (acc); fig überlaufen, überschwemmen

in·vad·er Eindringling m

in·va·lid[1] 1. krank; invalid(e) 2. Kranke m; f; Invalide m, f

in·val·id[2] (rechts)ungültig

in·val·i·date JUR für ungültig erkären

in·val·u·a·ble fig unschätzbar, unbezahlbar

in·var·i·a·ble unveränderlich

in·var·i·a·bly ausnahmslos

in·va·sion Invasion f (a. MIL), Einfall m, MIL a. Einmarsch m; fig Eingriff m, Verletzung f

in·vec·tive Schmähung(en pl) f, Beschimpfung(en pl) f

in·vent erfinden

in·ven·tion Erfindung f
in·ven·tive erfinderisch; einfallsreich
in·ven·tor Erfinder(in)
in·ven·tory Inventar n, Bestand m; Bestandsliste f; Inventur f
in·verse 1. umgekehrt 2. Umkehrung f, Gegenteil n; in·ver·sion Umkehrung f; LING Inversion f; in·vert umkehren
in·ver·te·brate ZO 1. wirbellos 2. wirbelloses Tier
in·vert·ed com·mas LING Anführungszeichen pl
in·vest ECON investieren, anlegen
in·ves·ti·gate untersuchen; überprüfen; Untersuchungen or Ermittlungen anstellen (**into** über acc), nachforschen
in·ves·ti·ga·tion Untersuchung f; Ermittlung f, Nachforschung f
in·ves·ti·ga·tor: **private ~** Privatdetektiv m
in·vest·ment ECON Investition f, (Kapital)Anlage f
in·ves·tor ECON Anleger m
in·vet·e·rate unverbesserlich; hartnäckig
in·vid·i·ous gehässig, boshaft, gemein
in·vig·o·rate stärken, beleben
in·vin·ci·ble unbesiegbar; unüberwindlich
in·vi·o·la·ble unantastbar
in·vis·i·ble unsichtbar
in·vi·ta·tion Einladung f; Aufforderung f
in·vite einladen; auffordern; Gefahr etc herausfordern; **~ s.o. in** j-n hereinbitten; in·vit·ing einladend, verlockend
in·voice ECON 1. (Waren)Rechnung f 2. in Rechnung stellen, berechnen
in·voke flehen um; Gott etc anrufen; beschwören
in·vol·un·ta·ry unfreiwillig; unabsichtlich; unwillkürlich
in·volve verwickeln, hineinziehen (**in** in acc); j-n, et. angehen, betreffen; zur Folge haben, mit sich bringen
in·volved kompliziert, verworren
in·volve·ment Verwicklung f; Beteiligung f
in·vul·ne·ra·ble unverwundbar; fig unanfechtbar
in·ward 1. adj innere(r, -s), innerlich 2. adv mst **~s** einwärts, nach innen
i·o·dine CHEM Jod n
i·on PHYS Ion n

IOU (= **I owe you**) Schuldschein m
IQ abbr of **intelligence quotient** IQ, Intelligenzquotient m
I·ran Iran m; I·ra·ni·an 1. iranisch 2. Iraner(in); LING Iranisch n
I·raq Irak m; I·ra·qi 1. irakisch 2. Iraker(in); LING Irakisch n
i·ras·ci·ble jähzornig
i·rate zornig, wütend
Ire·land Irland n
ir·i·des·cent schillernd
i·ris ANAT Regenbogenhaut f, Iris f; BOT Schwertlilie f, Iris f
I·rish 1. irisch 2. LING Irisch n; **the ~** die Iren pl
I·rish·man Ire m
I·rish·wom·an Irin f
i·ron 1. Eisen n; Bügeleisen n; **strike while the ~ is hot** fig das Eisen schmieden, solange es heiß ist 2. eisern (a. fig), Eisen...; aus Eisen 3. bügeln; **~ out** ausbügeln
I·ron Cur·tain POL HIST Eiserner Vorhang
i·ron·ic, i·ron·i·cal ironisch, spöttisch
i·ron·ing board Bügelbrett n
i·ron·mon·ger Br Eisenwarenhändler m
i·ron·works TECH Eisenhütte f
i·ro·ny Ironie f
ir·ra·tion·al irrational, unvernünftig
ir·rec·on·ci·la·ble unversöhnlich; unvereinbar
ir·re·cov·e·ra·ble unersetzlich; unwiderbringlich
ir·re·fut·a·ble unwiderlegbar
ir·reg·u·lar unregelmäßig; ungleichmäßig; regelwidrig, vorschriftswidrig
ir·rel·e·vant irrelevant, unerheblich, belanglos (**to** für)
ir·rep·a·ra·ble irreparabel, nicht wieder gutzumachen(d)
ir·re·place·a·ble unersetzlich
ir·re·pres·si·ble nicht zu unterdrücken(d); unbezähmbar
ir·re·proach·a·ble einwandfrei, untadelig
ir·re·sist·i·ble unwiderstehlich
ir·res·o·lute unentschlossen
ir·re·spec·tive: **~ of** ohne Rücksicht auf (acc); unabhängig von
ir·re·spon·si·ble unverantwortlich; verantwortungslos
ir·re·trie·va·ble unwiederbringlich, unersetzlich
ir·rev·e·rent respektlos

ir·rev·o·ca·ble unwiderruflich, endgültig
ir·ri·gate bewässern
ir·ri·ga·tion Bewässerung f
ir·ri·ta·ble reizbar
ir·ri·tant Reizmittel n
ir·ri·tate reizen; (ver)ärgern
ir·ri·tat·ing ärgerlich
ir·ri·ta·tion Reizung f; Verärgerung f; Ärger m (**at** über acc)
is er, sie, es ist
Is·lam der Islam
is·land Insel f; a. **traffic ~** Verkehrsinsel f; **is·land·er** Inselbewohner(in)
isle POET Insel f
i·so·late absondern; isolieren
i·so·lat·ed isoliert, abgeschieden; einzeln; **become ~** vereinsamen
i·so·la·tion Isolierung f, Absonderung f; **~ ward** MED Isolierstation f
Is·rael Israel n
Is·rae·li **1.** israelisch **2.** Israeli m, f
is·sue **1.** Streitfrage f, Streitpunkt m; Ausgabe f; Erscheinen n; JUR Nachkommen(schaft f) pl; fig Ausgang m, Ergebnis n; **be at ~** zur Debatte stehen; **point at ~** strittiger Punkt **2.** v/t Zeitung etc herausgeben; Banknoten etc ausge-

ben; Dokument etc ausstellen; v/i herauskommen, hervorkommen; herausfließen, herausströmen
it es; s.th. previously mentioned: es, er, ihn, sie
I·tal·i·an **1.** italienisch **2.** Italiener(in); LING Italienisch n
i·tal·ics PRINT Kursivschrift f
It·a·ly Italien n
itch **1.** Jucken n, Juckreiz m **2.** jucken, kratzen; **I ~ all over** es juckt mich überall; **be ~ing for s.th.** F et. unbedingt (haben) wollen; **be ~ing to** inf F darauf brennen zu inf
itch·y juckend; kratzend
i·tem Punkt m (on the agenda etc), Posten m (on a list); Artikel m, Gegenstand m; (Presse-, Zeitungs)Notiz f, (a. radio, TV) Nachricht f, Meldung f
i·tem·ize einzeln angeben or aufführen
i·tin·e·ra·ry Reiseweg m, Reiseroute f; Reiseplan m
its sein(e), ihr(e)
it·self sich; sich selbst; selbst; **by ~** (für sich) allein; von selbst; **in ~** an sich
i·vo·ry Elfenbein n
i·vy BOT Efeu m

J

J, j J, j n
jab **1.** (hinein)stechen, (hinein)stoßen **2.** Stich m, Stoß m
jab·ber F (daher)plappern
jack **1.** TECH Hebevorrichtung f; MOT Wagenheber m; cards: Bube m **2. ~ up** Auto aufbocken
jack·al ZO Schakal m
jack·ass ZO Esel m (a. fig)
jack·daw ZO Dohle f
jack·et Jacke f, Jackett n; TECH Mantel m; (Schutz)Umschlag m; (Platten)Hülle f; **~ potatoes, potatoes (boiled) in their ~s** Pellkartoffeln pl
jack knife **1.** Klappmesser n **2.** zusammenklappen, zusammenknicken
jack-of-all-trades Hansdampf m in allen Gassen
jack·pot Jackpot m, Haupttreffer m; **hit the ~** F den Jackpot gewinnen; fig das

große Los ziehen
jade MIN Jade m, f; Jadegrün n
jag Zacken m
jag·ged gezackt, zackig; schartig
jag·u·ar ZO Jaguar m
jail **1.** Gefängnis n **2.** einsperren
jail·bird F Knastbruder m
jail·er Gefängnisaufseher m
jail·house Gefängnis n
jam[1] Konfitüre f, Marmelade f
jam[2] **1.** v/t (hinein)pressen, (hinein)quetschen, (hinein)zwängen, Menschen a. (hinein)pferchen; (ein)klemmen, (ein)quetschen; a. **~ up** blockieren, verstopfen; Funkempfang stören; **~ on the brakes** MOT voll auf die Bremse treten; v/i sich (hinein)drängen or (hinein-) quetschen; TECH sich verklemmen, brake: blockieren **2.** Gedränge n; TECH Blockierung f; Stauung

f, Stockung f; **traffic ~** Verkehrsstau m;
be in a ~ F in der Klemme stecken

jamb (Tür-, Fenster)Pfosten m

jam·bo·ree Jamboree n, Pfadfindertreffen n; Fest n

Jan abbr of **January** Jan., Januar m

jan·gle klimpern or klirren (mit)

jan·i·tor Hausmeister m

Jan·u·a·ry (ABBR of **Jan**) Januar m

Ja·pan Japan n; Jap·a·nese **1.** japanisch **2.** Japaner(in); LING Japanisch n; **the ~** die Japaner pl

jar¹ Gefäß n, Krug m; (Marmelade- etc)-Glas n

jar²: **~ on** wehtun (dat)

jar·gon Jargon m, Fachsprache f

jaun·dice MED Gelbsucht f

jaunt **1.** Ausflug m, MOT Spritztour f **2.** e-n Ausflug or e-e Spritztour machen

jaun·ty unbeschwert, unbekümmert; flott

jav·e·lin SPORT Speer m; **~ (throw)**, **throwing the ~** SPORT Speerwerfen n

jav·e·lin throw·er SPORT Speerwerfer(in)

jaw ANAT Kiefer m; pl ZO Rachen m, Maul n; TECH Backen pl; **lower ~** ANAT Unterkiefer m; **upper ~** ANAT Oberkiefer; **jaw·bone** ANAT Kieferknochen m

jay ZO Eichelhäher m

jay·walk·er unachtsamer Fußgänger

jazz MUS Jazz m

jazz·y F poppig

jeal·ous eifersüchtig (**of** auf acc); neidisch; jeal·ous·y Eifersucht f; Neid m

jeans Jeans pl

jeer **1.** (**at**) höhnische Bemerkung(en) machen (über acc); höhnisch lachen (über acc); **~ (at)** verhöhnen **2.** höhnische Bemerkung; Hohngelächter n

jel·lied GASTR in Aspik, in Sülze

jel·ly Gallert(e f) n; GASTR Gelee n; Aspik m, n, Sülze f; Götterspeise f; **~ ba·by** Br Gummibärchen n; **~ bean** Gummi-, Geleebonbon m, n

jel·ly·fish ZO Qualle f

jeop·ar·dize gefährden

jerk **1.** ruckartig ziehen an (dat); (zusammen)zucken; sich ruckartig bewegen **2.** (plötzlicher) Ruck; Sprung m, Satz m; MED Zuckung f

jerk·y ruckartig; holprig; rüttelnd

jer·sey Pullover m

jest **1.** Scherz m, Spaß m **2.** scherzen, spaßen; jest·er HIST (Hof)Narr m

jet **1.** (Wasser-, Gas- etc)Strahl m; TECH Düse f; AVIAT Jet m **2.** (heraus-, hervor-)schießen (**from** aus); AVIAT F jetten; **~ en·gine** AVIAT Düsen-, Strahltriebwerk n; **~ plane** AVIAT Düsenflugzeug n, Jet m

jet-pro·pelled AVIAT mit Düsenantrieb, Düsen...

jet pro·pul·sion AVIAT Düsen-, Strahlantrieb m

jet·ty MAR (Hafen)Mole f

Jew Jude m, Jüdin f

jew·el Juwel n, m, Edelstein m

jew·el·er, Br jew·el·ler Juwelier m

jew·el·lery Br, jew·el·ry Juwelen pl; Schmuck m

Jew·ess Jüdin f

Jew·ish jüdisch

jif·fy. F **in a ~** im Nu, sofort

jig·saw Laubsäge f; → **jig·saw puz·zle** Puzzle(spiel) n

jin·gle **1.** klimpern (mit), bimmeln (lassen) **2.** Klimpern n, Bimmeln n; Werbesong m, Werbespruch m

jit·ters F **the ~** Bammel m, e-e Heidenangst; jit·ter·y F nervös; ängstlich

job **1.** (einzelne) Arbeit; Beruf m, Beschäftigung f, Stellung f, Stelle f, Arbeit f, Job m (a. IT); Arbeitsplatz m; Aufgabe f, Sache f, Angelegenheit f; a. **~ work** Akkordarbeit f; **by the ~** im Akkord; **out of a ~** arbeitslos **2. ~ around** jobben; **~ ad·ver·tisement** Stellenanzeige f

job·ber Br ECON Börsenspekulant m

job cen·tre Br Arbeitsamt n

job hop·ping häufiger Arbeitsplatzwechsel

job·hunt·ing Arbeitsuche f; **be ~** auf Arbeitsuche sein

job·less arbeitslos

jock·ey Jockei m

jog **1.** stoßen an (acc) or gegen, j-n anstoßen; mst **~ along, ~ on** dahintrotten, dahinzuckeln; SPORT joggen **2.** (leichter) Stoß, Stups m; Trott m; SPORT Trimmtrab m

jog·ger SPORT Jogger(in)

jog·ging SPORT Joggen n, Jogging n

join **1.** v/t verbinden, vereinigen, zusammenfügen; sich anschließen (dat or an acc), sich gesellen zu; eintreten in (acc), beitreten; teilnehmen or sich beteiligen an (dat), mitmachen bei; **~ in** einstimmen in; *v/i* sich vereinigen *or* verbinden; **~ in** teilnehmen *or* sich beteiligen (bei *dat*), mitmachen (bei) **2.** Verbindungsstelle *f*, Naht *f*

join·er Tischler *m*, Schreiner *m*

joint 1. Verbindungs-, Nahtstelle *f*; ANAT, TECH Gelenk *n*; BOT Knoten *m*; *Br* GASTR Braten *m*; F Laden *m*; Bude *f*, Spelunke *f*; *sl* Joint *m*; **out of ~** MED ausgerenkt; *fig* aus den Fugen **2.** gemeinsam, gemeinschaftlich; Mit…

joint·ed gegliedert; Glieder…

joint-stock com·pa·ny *Br* ECON Kapital- *or* Aktiengesellschaft *f*

joint ven·ture ECON Gemeinschaftsunternehmen *n*

joke 1. Witz *m*; Scherz *m*, Spaß *m*; **practical ~** Streich *m*; **play a ~ on s.o.** j-m e-n Streich spielen **2.** scherzen, Witze machen; **jok·er** Spaßvogel *m*, Witzbold *m*; *cards:* Joker *m*

jol·ly 1. *adj* lustig, fröhlich, vergnügt **2.** *adv Br* F ganz schön; **~ good** prima

jolt 1. e-n Ruck *or* Stoß geben; durchrütteln, durchschütteln; rütteln, holpern (*vehicle*); *fig* aufrütteln **2.** Ruck *m*, Stoß *m*; *fig* Schock *m*

joss stick Räucherstäbchen *n*

jos·tle (an)rempeln; dränge(l)n

jot 1. not a ~ keine Spur **2. ~ down** schnell *et.* notieren

joule PHYS Joule *n*

jour·nal Journal *n*; (Fach)Zeitschrift *f*; Tagebuch *n*

jour·nal·ism Journalismus *m*

jour·nal·ist Journalist(in)

jour·ney 1. Reise *f* **2.** reisen

jour·ney·man Geselle *m*

joy Freude *f*; **for ~** vor Freude

joy·ful freudig; erfreut

joy·less freudlos, traurig

joy·stick AVIAT Steuerknüppel *m*; IT Joystick *m*

jub·i·lant jubelnd, überglücklich

ju·bi·lee Jubiläum *n*

judge 1. JUR Richter(in); SPORT Kampf-, Schieds-, Preisrichter(in); *fig* Kenner(in) **2.** JUR *Fall* verhandeln; urteilen, ein Urteil fällen; beurteilen, einschätzen

judg·ment JUR Urteil *n*; Urteilsvermögen *n*; Meinung *f*, Ansicht *f*; göttliches (Straf)Gericht; **the Last Judgment** REL das Jüngste Gericht

Judgment Day *a.* **Day of Judgment** REL Tag *m* des Jüngsten Gerichts, Jüngster Tag

ju·di·cial JUR gerichtlich, Justiz…; richterlich

ju·di·cia·ry JUR Richter *pl*

ju·di·cious klug, weise

ju·do SPORT Judo *n*

jug Krug *m*; Kanne *f*, Kännchen *n*

jug·gle jonglieren (mit); ECON *Bücher etc* frisieren; **jug·gler** Jongleur *m*

juice Saft *m*; MOT F Sprit *m*

juic·y saftig; F pikant (*story etc*); F gepfeffert (*price etc*)

juke·box Musikbox *f*, Musikautomat *m*

Jul *abbr of* **July** Juli *m*

Ju·ly (*abbr* **Jul**) Juli *m*

jum·ble 1. a. ~ together, ~ up durcheinanderbringen *or* durcheinanderwerfen **2.** Durcheinander *n*; **~ sale** *Br* Wohltätigkeitsbasar *m*

jum·bo 1. riesig, Riesen… **2.** AVIAT F Jumbo *m*; **~ jet** AVIAT Jumbo-Jet *m*

jum·bo-sized riesig

jump 1. *v/i* springen; hüpfen; zusammenzucken, -fahren, hochfahren (**at** bei); **~ at the chance** mit beiden Händen zugreifen; **~ to conclusions** voreilige Schlüsse ziehen; *v/t* (hinweg)springen über (*acc*); überspringen; **~ the queue** *Br* sich vordränge(l)n; **~ the lights** bei Rot über die Kreuzung fahren **2.** Sprung *m*

jump·er[1] SPORT (*Hoch- etc*)Springer(in)

jump·er[2] Trägerrock *m*, Trägerkleid *n*; *Br* Pullover *m*

jump·ing jack Hampelmann *m*

jump·y nervös

Jun *abbr of* **June** Juni *m*

junc·tion (Straßen)Kreuzung *f*; RAIL Knotenpunkt *m*

junc·ture: at this ~ zu diesem Zeitpunkt

June (*abbr* **Jun**) Juni *m*

jun·gle Dschungel *m*

ju·ni·or 1. junior; jüngere(r, -s); untergeordnet; SPORT Junioren…, Jugend… **2.** Jüngere *m, f*; **~ school** *Br* Grundschule *f* (*for children aged 7 to 11*)

junk[1] MAR Dschunke *f*

junk[2] F Trödel *m*; Schrott *m*; Abfall *m*; *sl* Stoff *m*

junk food F Junk-Food *n*

junk·ie, junk·y *sl* Junkie *m*, Fixer(in)

junk·yard Schuttabladeplatz   *m*;

Schrottplatz *m*

jur·is·dic·tion JUR Gerichtsbarkeit *f*; Zuständigkeit(sbereich *m*) *f*

ju·ris·pru·dence Rechtswissenschaft *f*

ju·ror JUR Geschworene *m, f*

ju·ry JUR *die* Geschworenen *pl*; SPORT *etc* Jury *f*, Preisrichter *pl*

ju·ry·man JUR Geschworene *m*

ju·ry·wom·an JUR Geschworene *f*

just 1. *adj* gerecht; berechtigt; angemessen **2.** *adv* gerade, (so)eben; genau, eben; gerade (noch), ganz knapp; nur, bloß; **~ about** ungefähr, etwa; **~ like that** einfach so; **~ now** gerade

(jetzt), (so)eben

jus·tice Gerechtigkeit *f*; JUR Richter *m*; **Justice of the Peace** Friedensrichter *m*; **court of ~** Gericht *n*, Gerichtshof *m*

jus·ti·fi·ca·tion Rechtfertigung *f*

jus·ti·fy rechtfertigen

just·ly mit *or* zu Recht

jut: ~ out vorspringen, herausragen

ju·ve·nile 1. jugendlich; Jugend… **2.** Jugendliche *m, f*; **~ court** JUR Jugendgericht *n*; **~ de·lin·quen·cy** JUR Jugendkriminalität *f*; **~ de·lin·quent** JUR straffälliger Jugendlicher, jugendlicher Straftäter

K

K, k K, k *n*

kan·ga·roo ZO Känguru *n*

ka·ra·te SPORT Karate *n*

keel MAR **1.** Kiel *m* **2. ~ over** umschlagen, kentern

keen scharf (*a. fig*); schneidend (*cold*); heftig, stark; lebhaft (*interest*); groß (*appetite etc*); begeistert, leidenschaftlich; **~ on** versessen *or* scharf auf (*acc*)

keep 1. *v/t* (auf-, fest-, zurück)halten; (bei)behalten, bewahren; *Gesetze etc* einhalten, befolgen; *Ware* führen; *Geheimnis* für sich behalten; *Versprechen, Wort* halten; ECON *Buch* führen; aufheben, aufbewahren; abhalten, hindern (**from** von); *Tiere* halten; *Bett* hüten; ernähren, erhalten, unterhalten; **~ early hours** früh zu Bett gehen; **~ one's head** die Ruhe bewahren; **~ one's temper** sich beherrschen; **~ s.o. company** j-m Gesellschaft leisten; **~ s.th. from s.o.** j-m et. vorenthalten *or* verschweigen *or* verheimlichen; **~ time** richtig gehen (*watch*); MUS Takt halten; *v/i* bleiben; sich halten; **~ going** weitergehen; **~ smiling** immer nur lächeln!; **~ (on) talking** weitersprechen; **~ (on) trying** es weiterversuchen, es immer wieder versuchen; **~ s.o. waiting** j-n warten lassen; **~ away** (sich) fernhalten (**from** von); **~ back** zurückhalten (*a. fig*); **~ from doing s.th.** et. nicht tun; **~ in** *Schüler(in)* nachsitzen lassen; **~ off** (sich) fern halten; **~ off!** Betreten

verboten!; **~ on** *Kleidungsstück* anbehalten, anlassen; *Hut* aufbehalten; *Licht* brennen lassen; **keep on doing** fortfahren zu tun; **~ out** nicht hineinor hereinlassen; **~ out!** Zutritt verboten!; **~ to** sich halten an (*acc*); **~ up** *fig* aufrechterhalten; *Mut* nicht sinken lassen; fortfahren mit, weitermachen; **~ s.o. up** j-n nicht schlafen lassen; **~ it up** so weitermachen; **~ up with** Schritt halten mit; **~ up with the Joneses** nicht hinter den Nachbarn zurückstehen (wollen) **2.** (Lebens)Unterhalt *m*; **for ~s** F für immer

keep·er Wärter(in), Wächter(in), Aufseher(in); *mst in cpds*: Inhaber(in), Besitzer(in); **keep·ing** Verwahrung *f*; Obhut *f*; **be in (out of) ~ with …** (nicht) übereinstimmen mit …

keep·sake Andenken *n*

keg Fässchen *n*, kleines Fass

ken·nel Hundehütte *f*; **~s** Hundezwinger *m*; Hundepension *f*

kerb Br → **curb**

ker·chief (Hals-, Kopf)Tuch *n*

ker·nel BOT Kern *m* (*a. fig*)

ker·o·sene Petroleum *n*

ket·tle Kessel *m*

ket·tle·drum MUS (Kessel)Pauke *f*

key 1. Schlüssel *m* (*a. fig*); (*Schreibmaschinen-, Klavier- etc*)Taste *f*; MUS Tonart *f* **2.** Schlüssel… **3.** anpassen (**to** an *acc*); **~ in** IT Daten eingeben; **~ed up** nervös, aufgeregt; überdreht

key·board Tastatur *f*
key·hole Schlüsselloch *n*
key·note Grundton *m*; *fig* Grundgedanke *m*, Tenor *m*
key ring Schlüsselring *m*
key·stone ARCH Schlussstein *m*; *fig* Grundpfeiler *m*
key·word Schlüssel-, Stichwort *n*
kick 1. (mit dem Fuß) stoßen, treten, e-n Tritt geben *or* versetzen (*dat*); *soccer*: schießen, treten, kicken; strampeln; ausschlagen (*horse*); **~ off** von sich schleudern; *soccer*: anstoßen; **~ out** F rausschmeißen; **~ up** hochschleudern; **~ up a fuss** *or* **row** F Krach schlagen **2.** (Fuß)Tritt *m*; Stoß *m*; *soccer*: Schuss *m*; **free ~** MUS Freistoß *m*; **for ~s** F zum Spaß; **they get a ~ out of it** es macht ihnen e-n Riesenspaß
kick·off *soccer*: Anstoß *m*
kick·out *soccer*: Abschlag *m*
kid[1] ZO Zicklein *n*, Kitz *n*; Ziegenleder *n*; F Kind *n*; **~ brother** F kleiner Bruder
kid[2] *v/t* j-n auf den Arm nehmen; **~ s.o.** j-m et. vormachen; *v/i* Spaß machen; **he is only ~ding** er macht ja nur Spaß; **no ~ding!** im Ernst!
kid gloves Glacéhandschuhe *pl* (*a. fig*)
kid·nap entführen, kidnappen
kid·nap·(p)er Entführer(in), Kidnapper(in)
kid·nap·(p)ing Entführung *f*, Kidnapping *n*
kid·ney ANAT Niere *f*; **~ bean** BOT Kidneybohne *f*, rote Bohne; HUNT erlegen, schießen; **ma·chine** MED künstliche Niere
kill töten (*a. fig*), umbringen, ermorden; vernichten; ZO schlachten; HUNT erlegen, schießen; **be ~ed in an accident** tödlich verunglücken; **~ time** die Zeit totschlagen; **~er** Mörder(in), Killer(in); **kill·ing** mörderisch, tödlich
kill·joy Spielverderber *m*
kiln TECH Brennofen *m*
ki·lo F Kilo *n*
kil·o·gram(me) Kilogramm *n*
kil·o·me·ter, *Br* **kil·o·me·tre** Kilometer *m*
kilt Kilt *m*, Schottenrock *m*
kin Verwandtschaft *f*, Verwandte *pl*; **next of ~** der, die nächste Verwandte, die nächsten Angehörigen *pl*
kind[1] freundlich, liebenswürdig, nett; herzlich

kind[2] Art *f*, Sorte *f*; Wesen *n*; **all ~s of** alle möglichen, allerlei; **nothing of the~** nichts dergleichen; **~ of** F ein bisschen
kin·der·gar·ten Kindergarten *m*
kind-heart·ed gütig
kin·dle anzünden, (sich) entzünden; *Interesse etc* wecken
kind·ly 1. *adj* freundlich, liebenswürdig, nett **2.** *adv* → 1; freundlicherweise, liebenswürdigerweise, netterweise
kind·ness Freundlichkeit *f*, Liebenswürdigkeit *f*; Gefälligkeit *f*
kin·dred verwandt; **~ spirits** Gleichgesinnte *pl*
king König *m*
king·dom Königreich *n*; REL Reich *n* Gottes; *fig* Reich *n*; **animal ~** Tierreich *n*; **vegetable ~** Pflanzenreich *n*
king·ly königlich
king-size(d) Riesen…
kink Knick *m*; *fig* Tick *m*, Spleen *m*
kink·y spleenig; pervers
ki·osk Kiosk *m*; *Br* Telefonzelle *f*
kip·per GASTR Räucherhering *m*
kiss 1. Kuss *m* **2.** (sich) küssen
kit Ausrüstung *f*; Arbeitsgerät *n*, Werkzeug(e *pl*) *n*; Werkzeugtasche *f*, -kasten *m*; Bastelsatz *m*; **~ bag** Seesack *m*
kitch·en 1. Küche *f* **2.** Küchen…
kitch·en·ette Kleinküche *f*, Kochnische *f*
kitch·en gar·den Küchen-, Gemüsegarten *m*
kite Drachen *m*; ZO Milan *m*; **fly a ~** e-n Drachen steigen lassen
kit·ten ZO Kätzchen *n*
knack Kniff *m*, Trick *m*, F Dreh *m*; Geschick *n*, Talent *n*
knave *card games*: Bube *m*, Unter *m*
knead kneten; massieren
knee ANAT Knie *n*; TECH Knie(stück) *n*
knee·cap ANAT Kniescheibe *f*
knee-deep knietief, bis an die Knie (reichend)
knee joint ANAT Kniegelenk *n* (*a. TECH*)
kneel knien (**to** vor *dat*)
knee-length knielang
knell Totenglocke *f*
knick·er·bock·ers Knickerbocker *pl*, Kniehosen *pl*
knick·ers *Br* F (Damen)Schlüpfer *m*
knick-knack Nippsache *f*
knife 1. Messer *n* **2.** mit e-m Messer ste-

K

chen *or* verletzen; erstechen
knight 1. Ritter *m; chess:* Springer *m* **2.**
zum Ritter schlagen
knight·hood Ritterwürde *f,* -stand *m*
knit *v/t* stricken; *a.* ~ **together** zusammenfügen, verbinden; ~ **one's brows**
die Stirn runzeln; *v/i* stricken; MED zusammenwachsen
knit·ting 1. Stricken *n;* Strickzeug *n* **2.**
Strick…; ~ **nee·dle** Stricknadel *f*
knit·wear Strickwaren *pl*
knob Knopf *m,* Knauf *m, runder* Griff;
GASTR Stück(chen) *n*
knock 1. schlagen, stoßen; pochen,
klopfen; ~ **at the door** an die Tür klopfen; ~ **about,** ~ **around** herumstoßen; F
sich herumtreiben; F herumliegen; ~
down *Gebäude etc* abreißen; umstoßen, umwerfen; niederschlagen; anfahren, umfahren; überfahren; mit
dem Preis heruntergehen; *auction: et.*
zuschlagen (**to s.o.** j-m); **be ~ed down**
überfahren werden; ~ **off** herunter-, abschlagen; F *et.* hinhauen; F aufhören
(mit); F Feierabend *or* Schluss machen;
~ **out** herausschlagen, -klopfen, *Pfeife*
ausklopfen; *j-n* bewusstlos schlagen;
boxing: k.o. schlagen; *fig* betäuben
(*drug etc*); *fig* F umhauen, schocken;
~ **over** umwerfen, umstoßen; überfahren; **be ~ed over** überfahren werden **2.**
Schlag *m,* Stoß *m;* Klopfen *n;* **there is a**
~ (**on** [*Br* **at**] **the door**) es klopft

knock·er Türklopfer *m*
knock-kneed x-beinig
knock-out *boxing:* K.o. *m*
knoll Hügel *m*
knot 1. Knoten *m;* BOT Astknoten *m;* MAR
Knoten *m,* Seemeile *f* **2.** (ver-)knoten,
(ver)knüpfen; **knot·ty** knotig; knorrig;
fig verwickelt, kompliziert
know wissen; können; kennen; erfahren, erleben; (wieder) erkennen; verstehen; ~ **French** Französisch können;
~ **one's way around** sich auskennen in
(*a place etc*); ~ **all about it** genau Bescheid wissen; **get to** ~ kennenlernen,
~ **one's business,** ~ **the ropes,** ~ **a**
thing or two, ~ **what's what** F sich auskennen, Erfahrung haben; **you** ~ wissen Sie
know-how Know-how *n,* (Sach-, Spezial)Kenntnis(se *pl*) *f*
know·ing klug, gescheit; schlau; verständnisvoll; **know·ing·ly** wissend;
wissentlich, absichtlich, bewusst
knowl·edge Kenntnis(se *pl*) *f;* Wissen *n;*
to my ~ meines Wissens; **have a good** ~
of viel verstehen von, sich gut auskennen in (*dat*)
knowl·edge·a·ble be very ~ **about** viel
verstehen von
knuck·le 1. ANAT (Finger)Knöchel *m* **2.** ~
down to work sich an die Arbeit machen
Krem·lin POL **the** ~ der Kreml

L

L, l L, l *n*
L *abbr of* **large** (**size**) groß
lab F Labor *n*
la·bel 1. Etikett *n,* (Klebe- *etc*)Zettel *m;*
(-)Schild(chen) *n;* (Schall)Plattenfirma *f* **2.** etikettieren, beschriften; *fig* abstempeln als
la·bor 1. (schwere) Arbeit; Mühe *f;* Arbeiter *pl,* Arbeitskräfte *pl;* MED Wehen
pl **2.** (schwer) arbeiten; sich bemühen,
sich abmühen, sich anstrengen
la·bor·a·to·ry Labor(atorium) *n;* ~
assis·tant Laborant(in)
la·bored schwerfällig (*style etc*); mühsam (*breathing etc*)

la·bor·er (*esp* Hilfs)Arbeiter *m*
la·bo·ri·ous mühsam; schwerfällig
la·bor u·ni·on Gewerkschaft *f*
la·bour *Br* → **labor**
Labour *Br* POL die Labour Party
la·boured **la·bour·er** *Br* → **labored, laborer**
La·bour Par·ty *Br* POL Labour Party *f*
lace 1. Spitze *f;* Borte *f;* Schnürsenkel *m*
2. ~ **up** (zu-, zusammen)schnüren;
Schuh zubinden; ~**d with brandy** mit
e-m Schuss Weinbrand
la·ce·rate zerschneiden, zerkratzen,
aufreißen; *j-s Gefühle* verletzen
lack 1. (**of**) Fehlen *n* (von), Mangel *m* (an

dat); **2.** *v/t* nicht haben; *he ~s money* es fehlt ihm an Geld; *v/i* *be ~ing* fehlen; *he is ~ing in courage* ihm fehlt der Mut

lack·lus·ter, *Br* **lack·lus·tre** glanzlos, matt

la·con·ic lakonisch, wortkarg

lac·quer 1. Lack *m*; Haarspray *m*, *n* **2.** lackieren

lad Bursche *m*, Junge *m*

lad·der Leiter *f*; *Br* Laufmasche *f*

lad·der·proof (lauf)maschenfest

la·den (schwer) beladen

la·dle 1. (Schöpf-, Suppen)Kelle *f*, Schöpflöffel *m* **2.** *~ out Suppe* austeilen

la·dy Dame *f*; *Lady* Lady *f*; *~ doctor* Ärztin *f*; *Ladies' room*, *Br* *Ladies(')* Damentoilette *f*

la·dy·bird zo Marienkäfer *m*

la·dy·like damenhaft

lag 1. *mst ~ behind* zurückbleiben **2.** → *time lag*

la·ger Lagerbier *n*

la·goon Lagune *f*

lair zo Lager *n*, Höhle *f*, Bau *m*

la·i·ty Laien *pl*

lake See *m*

lamb zo **1.** Lamm *n* **2.** lammen

lame 1. lahm (*a. fig*) **2.** lähmen

la·ment 1. jammern, (weh)klagen; trauern **2.** Jammer *m*, (Weh)Klage *f*

lam·en·ta·ble beklagenswert; kläglich

lam·en·ta·tion (Weh)Klage *f*

lam·i·nat·ed laminiert, geschichtet, beschichtet; *~ glass* Verbundglas *n*

lamp Lampe *f*; Laterne *f*

lamp·post Laternenpfahl *m*

lamp·shade Lampenschirm *m*

lance Lanze *f*

land 1. Land *n*, AGR *a.* Boden *m*, POL *a.* Staat *m*; *by ~* auf dem Landweg **2.** landen, MAR *a.* anlegen; *Güter* ausladen, MAR *a.* löschen

land a·gent AGR Gutsverwalter *m*

land·ed Land..., Grund...; *~ gentry* Landadel *m*; *~ property* Grundbesitz *m*

land·ing AVIAT Landung *f*, Landen *n*, MAR *a.* Anlegen *n*; Treppenabsatz *m*; *~ field* AVIAT Landeplatz *m*; *~ gear* AVIAT Fahrgestell *n*; *~ stage* MAR Landungsbrücke *f*, -steg *m*; *~ strip* AVIAT Landeplatz *m*

land·la·dy Vermieterin *f*; Wirtin *f*

land·lord Vermieter *m*; Wirt *m*; Grund-

besitzer *m*

land·lub·ber MAR *contp* Landratte *f*

land·mark Wahrzeichen *n*; *fig* Meilenstein *m*

land·own·er Grundbesitzer(in)

land·scape Landschaft *f* (*a. paint*)

land·slide Erdrutsch *m* (*a.* POL); *a ~ victory* POL ein überwältigender Wahlsieg

land·slip (kleiner) Erdrutsch

lane (Feld)Weg *m*; Gasse *f*, Sträßchen *n*; MAR Fahrrinne *f*; AVIAT Flugschneise *f*; SPORT (*einzelne*) Bahn; MOT (Fahr-) Spur *f*; *change ~s* MOT die Spur wechseln; *get in ~* MOT sich einordnen

lan·guage Sprache *f*

lan·guid matt; träg(e)

lank glatt

lank·y schlaksig

lan·tern Laterne *f*

lap¹ Schoß *m*

lap² SPORT **1.** Runde *f*; *~ of hono(u)r* Ehrenrunde *f* **2.** *Gegner* überrunden; e-e Runde zurücklegen

lap³ *v/t:* *~ up* auflecken, aufschlecken; *v/i* plätschern

la·pel Revers *n*, *m*, Aufschlag *m*

lapse 1. Versehen *n*, (kleiner) Fehler *or* Irrtum; Vergehen *n*; Zeitspanne *f*; JUR Verfall *m*; *~ of memory*, *memory ~* Gedächtnislücke *f* **2.** verfallen; JUR verfallen, erlöschen

lar·ce·ny JUR Diebstahl *m*

larch BOT Lärche *f*

lard 1. Schweinefett *n*, Schweineschmalz *n* **2.** *Fleisch* spicken

lar·der Speisekammer *f*, -schrank *m*

large groß; beträchtlich, reichlich; umfassend, weitgehend; *at ~* in Freiheit, auf freiem Fuß; *fig* (sehr) ausführlich; in der Gesamtheit

large·ly großenteils, größtenteils

large-mind·ed aufgeschlossen, tolerant

large·ness Größe *f*

lar·i·at Lasso *n*, *m*

lark¹ zo Lerche *f*

lark² F Jux *m*, Spaß *m*

lark·spur BOT Rittersporn *m*

lar·va zo Larve *f*

lar·yn·gi·tis MED Kehlkopfentzündung *f*; **lar·ynx** ANAT Kehlkopf *m*

las·civ·i·ous geil, lüstern

la·ser PHYS Laser *m*; *~ beam* PHYS Laserstrahl *m*; *~ print·er* ERTT Laserdrucker *m*; *~ tech·nol·o·gy* Lasertechnik *f*

L (marginal tab)

lash 1. Peitschenschnur *f*; (Peitschen-) Hieb *m*; Wimper *f* **2.** peitschen (mit); (fest)binden; schlagen; **~ out** (wild) um sich schlagen

las·so Lasso *n, m*

last¹ 1. *adj* letzte(r, -s); vorige(r, -s); **~ but one** vorletzte(r, -s); **~ night** gestern Abend; letzte Nacht **2.** *adv* zuletzt, an letzter Stelle; **~ but not least** nicht zuletzt, nicht zu vergessen **3.** *der, die, das* Letzte; **at ~** endlich; **to the ~** bis zum Schluss

last² (an-, fort)dauern; (sich) halten; (aus)reichen

last³ (Schuhmacher)Leisten *m*

last·ing dauerhaft; beständig

last·ly zuletzt, zum Schluss

latch 1. Schnappriegel *m*; Schnappschloss *n* **2.** einklinken, zuklinken

latch·key Haus-, Wohnungsschlüssel *m*

late spät; jüngste(r, -s), letzte(r, -s), frühere(r, -s), ehemalig; verstorben; **be ~** zu spät kommen, sich verspäten; RAIL *etc* Verspätung haben; **as ~ as** noch, erst; **of ~** kürzlich; **later on** später

late·ly kürzlich

lath Latte *f*, Leiste *f*

lathe TECH Drehbank *f*

la·ther 1. (Seifen)Schaum *m* **2.** *v/t* einseifen; *v/i* schäumen

Lat·in LING **1.** lateinisch; südländisch **2.** Latein(isch) *n*; **~ A·mer·i·ca** Lateinamerika *n*; **~ A·mer·i·can 1.** lateinamerikanisch **2.** Lateinamerikaner(in)

lat·i·tude GEOGR Breite *f*

lat·ter Letztere(r, -s)

lat·tice Gitter(werk) *n*

lau·da·ble lobenswert

laugh 1. lachen (**at** über *acc*); **~ at s.o.** *a.* j-n auslachen **2.** Lachen *n*, Gelächter *n*

laugh·a·ble lächerlich, lachhaft

laugh·ter Lachen *n*, Gelächter *n*

launch¹ 1. MAR vom Stapel lassen; MIL abschießen, *Rakete a.* starten; *fig Projekt etc* in Gang setzen, starten **2.** MAR Stapellauf *m*; MIL Abschuss *m*, Start *m*

launch² MAR Barkasse *f*

launch·ing → **launch¹ 2.**; **~ pad** Abschussrampe *f*; **~ site** Abschussbasis *f*

launch pad → **launching pad**

laun·der *Wäsche* waschen (und bügeln); F *esp Geld* waschen

laun·der·ette, laun·drette *esp Br*, **laundro·mat®** Waschsalon *m*

laun·dry Wäscherei *f*; Wäsche *f*

laur·el BOT Lorbeer *m* (*a. fig*)

la·va GEOL Lava *f*

lav·a·to·ry Toilette *f*, Klosett *n*; **public ~** Bedürfnisanstalt *f*

lav·en·der BOT Lavendel *m*

lav·ish 1. sehr freigebig, verschwenderisch **2. ~ s.th. on s.o.** j-n mit et. überhäufen *or* überschütten

law Gesetz(e *pl*) *n*; Recht *n*, Rechtssystem *n*; Rechtswissenschaft *f*, Jura; F Bullen *pl* (*police*); F Bulle *m* (*policeman*); Gesetz *n*, Vorschrift *f*; **~ and order** Recht *or* Ruhe und Ordnung

law-a·bid·ing gesetzestreu

law-court Gericht *n*, Gerichtshof *m*

law·ful gesetzlich; rechtmäßig, legitim; rechtsgültig

law·less gesetzlos; gesetzwidrig; zügellos

lawn Rasen *m*

lawn-mow·er Rasenmäher *m*

law·suit JUR Prozess *m*

law·yer JUR (Rechts)Anwalt *m*, (Rechts)Anwältin *f*

lax locker, schlaff; lax, lasch

lax·a·tive MED **1.** abführend **2.** Abführmittel *n*

lay¹ REL weltlich; Laien…

lay² *v/t* legen; *Teppich* verlegen; belegen, auslegen (**with** mit); *Tisch* decken; zo *Eier* legen; vorlegen (**before** *dat*), bringen (**before** vor *acc*); *Schuld etc* zuschreiben, zur Last legen (*dat*); *v/i* zo (Eier) legen; **~ aside** beiseitelegen, zurücklegen; **~ off** *Arbeiter* (*esp* vorübergehend) entlassen; *Arbeit* einstellen; **~ open** darlegen; **~ out** ausbreiten, auslegen; *Garten etc* anlegen; entwerfen, planen; PRINT das Layout (*gen*) machen; **~ up** anhäufen, (an)sammeln; **be laid up** das Bett hüten müssen

lay-by *Br* MOT Parkbucht *f*, Parkstreifen *m*; Parkplatz *m*, Rastplatz *m*

lay·er Lage *f*, Schicht *f*; BOT Ableger *m*

lay·man Laie *m*

lay-off ECON (*esp* vorübergehende) Entlassung

lay·out Grundriss *m*, Lageplan *m*; PRINT Layout *n*, Gestaltung *f*

la·zy faul, träg(e)

LCD *abbr of liquid crystal display* Flüssigkristallanzeige *f*

lead¹ 1. *v/t* führen; (an)führen, leiten; dazu bringen, veranlassen (**to do** zu tun); *v/i* führen; vorangehen; SPORT an der Spitze *or* in Führung liegen; **~ off** anfangen, beginnen; **~ on** j-m et. vormachen *or* weismachen; **~ to** fig führen zu; **~ up to** fig (allmählich) führen zu **2.** Führung *f*; Leitung *f*; Spitzenposition *f*; Vorbild *n*, Beispiel *n*; THEA Hauptrolle *f*; Hauptdarsteller(in); (Hunde)Leine *f*; Hinweis *m*, Tipp *m*, Anhaltspunkt *m*; SPORT *and* fig Führung *f*, Vorsprung *m*; **be in the ~** in Führung sein; **take the ~** in Führung gehen, die Führung übernehmen

lead² CHEM Blei *n*; MAR Lot *n*

lead·ed verbleit, bleihaltig

lead·en bleiern (*a.* fig), Blei...

lead·er (An)Führer(in), Leiter(in); Erste *m*, *f*; *Br* Leitartikel *m*

lead·er·ship Führung *f*, Leitung *f*

lead-free bleifrei

lead·ing leitend; führend; Haupt...

leaf 1. BOT, PRINT Blatt *n*; (*Tür- etc*)Flügel *m*; (*Tisch*)Klappe *f*, Ausziehplatte *f* **2.** **~ through** durchblättern

leaf·let Hand-, Reklamezettel *m*; Prospekt *m*

league POL Bund *m*; SPORT Liga *f*

leak 1. lecken, leck sein; tropfen; **~ out** auslaufen; fig durchsickern **2.** Leck *n*, undichte Stelle (*a.* fig)

leak·age Auslaufen *n*

leak·y leck, undicht

lean¹ (sich) lehnen; (sich) neigen; **~ on** sich verlassen auf (*acc*)

lean² **1.** mager (*a.* fig) **2.** GASTR das Magere; **~ man·age·ment** ECON schlanke Unternehmensstruktur

leap 1. springen; **~ at** fig sich stürzen auf (*acc*) **2.** Sprung *m*

leap·frog Bockspringen *n*

leap year Schaltjahr *n*

learn (er)lernen; erfahren, hören

learn·ed gelehrt

learn·er Anfänger(in); Lernende *m*, *f*; **~ driver** *Br* MOT Fahrschüler(in)

learn·ing Gelehrsamkeit *f*

lease 1. Pacht *f*, Miete *f*; Pacht-, Mietvertrag *m* **2.** pachten, mieten; leasen; **~ out** verpachten, vermieten

leash (Hunde)Leine *f*

least 1. *adj* geringste(r, -s), mindeste(r, -s), wenigste(r, -s) **2.** *adv* am wenigsten; **~ of all** am allerwenigsten **3.** *das* Min-

deste, *das* wenigste; **at ~** wenigstens; **to say the ~** gelinde gesagt

leath·er 1. Leder *n* **2.** ledern; Leder...

leave 1. *v/t* (hinter-, über-, ver-, zurück)lassen, übrig lassen; liegen *or* stehen lassen, vergessen; vermachen, vererben; **be left** übrig bleiben, übrig sein; *v/i* (fort-, weg)gehen, abreisen, abfahren, abfliegen; **~ alone** allein lassen; j-n, et. in Ruhe lassen; **~ behind** zurücklassen; **~ on** anlassen; **~ out** draußen lassen; auslassen, weglassen **2.** Erlaubnis *f*; Urlaub *m*; Abschied *m*; **on ~** auf Urlaub

leav·en Sauerteig *m*

leaves BOT Laub *n*

leav·ings Überreste *pl*

lech·er·ous geil, lüstern

lec·ture 1. UNIV Vorlesung *f* (**über** *acc* on); Vortrag *m*; Strafpredigt *f* **2.** *v/i* UNIV e-e Vorlesung *or* Vorlesungen halten (**über** *acc* on; **vor** *dat* to); e-n Vortrag *or* Vorträge halten; *v/t* j-m e-e Strafpredigt halten

lec·tur·er UNIV Dozent(in); Redner(in)

ledge Leiste *f*, Sims *m*, *n*

leech ZO Blutegel *m*

leek BOT Lauch *m*, Porree *m*

leer 1. anzüglicher *or* lüsterner Seitenblick *m* **2.** anzüglich *or* lüstern blicken *or* schielen (**at** nach)

left¹ **1.** *adj* linke(r, -s), Links... **2.** *adv* links; **turn ~** (sich) nach links wenden; MOT links abbiegen **3.** *die* Linke (*a.* POL, boxing), linke Seite; **on the ~** links, auf der linken Seite; **to the ~** (nach) links; **keep to the ~** sich links halten; links fahren

left² *adj* linke(r, -s)

left-hand linke(r, -s)

left-hand drive MOT Linkssteuerung *f*

left-hand·ed linkshändig; für Linkshänder; **be ~** Linkshänder(in) sein

left lug·gage of·fice *Br* RAIL Gepäckaufbewahrung *f*

left-o·vers (Speise)Reste *pl*

left-wing POL dem linken Flügel angehörend, links..., Links...

leg ANAT Bein *n*; GASTR Keule *f*; MATH Schenkel *m*; **pull s.o.'s ~** F j-n auf den Arm nehmen; **stretch one's ~** sich die Beine vertreten

leg·a·cy fig Vermächtnis *n*, Erbe *n*

le·gal legal, gesetzmäßig; gesetzlich, rechtlich; juristisch, Rechts...

le·gal·i·za·tion Legalisierung f
le·gal·ize legalisieren
le·gal pro·tec·tion Rechtsschutz m
le·ga·tion POL Gesandtschaft f
le·gend Legende f, Sage f
le·gen·da·ry legendär
le·gi·ble leserlich
le·gis·la·tion Gesetzgebung f
le·gis·la·tive POL **1.** gesetzgebend, legislativ **2.** Legislative f, gesetzgebende Gewalt
le·gis·la·tor POL Gesetzgeber m
le·git·i·mate legitim; gesetzmäßig, rechtmäßig; ehelich
lei·sure freie Zeit; Muße f; **at ~** ohne Hast; **~ cen·tre** Br Freizeitzentrum n
lei·sure·ly gemächlich
lei·sure time Freizeit f
lei·sure-time ac·tiv·i·ties Freizeitbeschäftigung f, -gestaltung f
lei·sure·wear Freizeitkleidung f
lem·on BOT **1.** Zitrone f **2.** Zitronen…
lem·on·ade Zitronenlimonade f
lend j-m et. (ver-, aus)leihen
length Länge f; Strecke f; (Zeit)Dauer f; **at ~** ausführlich
length·en verlängern, länger machen; länger werden
length·ways, length·wise der Länge nach
length·y sehr lang
le·ni·ent mild(e), nachsichtig
lens ANAT, PHOT, PHYS Linse f; PHOT Objektiv n
Lent REL Fastenzeit f
len·til BOT Linse f
Le·o ASTR Löwe m; **he (she) is (a) ~** er (sie) ist (ein) Löwe
leop·ard ZO Leopard m
le·o·tard (Tänzer)Trikot n
lep·ro·sy MED Lepra f
les·bi·an **1.** lesbisch **2.** Lesbierin f, F Lesbe f
less **1.** adj and adv kleiner, geringer, weniger **2.** prp weniger, minus, abzüglich
less·en (sich) vermindern or verringern; abnehmen; herabsetzen
less·er kleiner, geringer
les·son Lektion f; (Unterrichts)Stunde f; fig Lehre f; pl Unterricht m
let lassen; esp Br vermieten, verpachten; **~ alone** j-n, et. in Ruhe lassen; geschweige denn; **~ down** hinunterlassen, herunterlassen; Kleider verlän-

gern; j-n im Stich lassen, F j-n sitzen lassen; enttäuschen; **~ go** loslassen; **~ o.s. go** sich gehenlassen; **~'s go** gehen wir!; **~ in** (her)einlassen; **~ o.s. in for s.th.** sich et. einbrocken, sich auf et. einlassen
le·thal tödlich; Todes…
leth·ar·gy Lethargie f
let·ter Buchstabe m; PRINT Type f; Brief m
let·ter·box esp Br Briefkasten m
let·ter car·ri·er Briefträger m
let·tuce BOT (esp Kopf)Salat m
leu·k(a)e·mia MED Leukämie f
lev·el **1.** adj eben; gleich (a. fig); ausgeglichen; **be ~ with** auf gleicher Höhe sein mit; **my ~ best** F mein Möglichstes **2.** Ebene f (a. fig), ebene Fläche; Höhe f (a. GEOGR), (Wasser- etc)Spiegel m, (-)Stand m, (-)Pegel m; Wasserwaage f; fig Niveau n, Stufe f; **sea ~** Meeresspiegel m; **on the ~** F ehrlich, aufrichtig **3.** (ein)ebnen, planieren; dem Erdboden gleichmachen; **~ at** Waffe richten auf (acc); Beschuldigungen erheben gegen (acc) **4.** adv: **~ with** in Höhe (gen)
lev·el cross·ing Br schienengleicher Bahnübergang
lev·el-head·ed vernünftig, nüchtern
le·ver Hebel m
lev·y **1.** Steuer f, Abgabe f **2.** Steuern erheben
lewd geil, lüstern; unanständig, obszön
li·a·bil·i·ty ECON, JUR Verpflichtung f, Verbindlichkeit f; ECON, JUR Haftung f, Haftpflicht f; Neigung f (**to** zu), Anfälligkeit f (**to** für); li·a·ble ECON, JUR haftbar, haftpflichtig; **be ~ for** haften für; **be ~ to** neigen zu, anfällig sein für
li·ar Lügner(in)
li·bel JUR **1.** (schriftliche) Verleumdung or Beleidigung **2.** (schriftlich) verleumden or beleidigen
lib·e·ral **1.** liberal (a. POL), aufgeschlossen; großzügig; reichlich **2.** Liberale m, f (a. POL)
lib·e·rate befreien; lib·e·ra·tion Befreiung f; lib·e·ra·tor Befreier m
lib·er·ty Freiheit f; **take liberties with** sich Freiheiten gegen j-n herausnehmen; willkürlich mit et. umgehen; **be ~ at** frei sein
Li·bra ASTR Waage f; **he (she) is (a) ~** er (sie) ist (eine) Waage

li·brar·i·an Bibliothekar(in)
li·bra·ry Bibliothek f; Bücherei f
li·cence 1. Br → license 1 2. e-e Lizenz or Konzession erteilen (dat); behördlich genehmigen
li·cense 1. Lizenz f, Konzession f; (Führer-, Jagd-, Waffen- etc)Schein m 2. Br → licence 2
li·cense plate MOT Nummernschild n
li·chen BOT Flechte f
lick 1. Lecken n; Salzlecke f 2. v/t ab-, auflecken; F verdreschen, verprügeln; F schlagen, besiegen; v/i lecken; züngeln (flames)
lic·o·rice Lakritze f
lid Deckel m; ANAT (Augen)Lid n
lie¹1. lügen; ~ to s.o. j-n belügen, j-n anlügen 2. Lüge f; tell ~s, tell a ~ lügen; give the ~ to j-n, et. Lügen strafen
lie²1. liegen; let sleeping dogs ~ schlafende Hunde soll man nicht wecken; ~ behind fig dahinter stecken; ~ down sich hinlegen 2. Lage f (a. fig)
lie-down Br F Nickerchen n
lie-in: have a ~ esp Br F sich gründlich ausschlafen
lieu: in ~ of anstelle von (or gen)
lieu·ten·ant MIL Leutnant m
life Leben n; JUR lebenslängliche Freiheitsstrafe; all her ~ ihr ganzes Leben lang; for ~ fürs (ganze) Leben; esp JUR lebenslänglich
life as·sur·ance Br → life insurance
life belt Rettungsgürtel m
life-boat Rettungsboot n
life-guard Bademeister m; Rettungsschwimmer m
life im·pris·on·ment JUR lebenslängliche Freiheitsstrafe
life in·sur·ance Lebensversicherung f
life jack·et Schwimmweste f
life·less leblos; matt, schwung-, lustlos
life·like lebensecht
life·long lebenslang
life pre·serv·er Schwimmweste f; Rettungsgürtel m
life sen·tence JUR lebenslängliche Freiheitsstrafe
life-time Lebenszeit f
lift 1. v/t (hoch-, auf)heben; erheben; Verbot etc aufheben; Gesicht etc liften, straffen; F klauen; v/i sich heben, steigen (a. fog); ~ off starten (rocket), AVIAT abheben 2. (Hoch-, Auf)Heben n;

PHYS, AVIAT Auftrieb m; Br Lift m, Aufzug m, Fahrstuhl m; give s.o. a ~ j-n (im Auto) mitnehmen; F j-n aufmuntern, j-m Auftrieb geben
lift-off Start m, Abheben n
lig·a·ment ANAT Band n
light¹1. Licht n (a. fig); Beleuchtung f; Schein m; Feuer n; fig Aspekt m; Br mst pl (Verkehrs)Ampel f; do you have (Br have you got) a ~? haben Sie Feuer? 2. v/t beleuchten, erleuchten; a. ~ up anzünden; v/i sich entzünden; ~ up fig aufleuchten 3. hell, licht
light²leicht (a. fig); make ~ of s.th. et. leichtnehmen; et. bagatellisieren
light·en¹ v/t erhellen; aufhellen; v/i hell(er) werden, sich aufhellen
light·en²leichter machen or werden; erleichtern
light·er Anzünder m; Feuerzeug n
light-head·ed (leicht) benommen; leichtfertig, töricht
light-heart·ed fröhlich, unbeschwert
light-house Leuchtturm m
light·ing Beleuchtung f
light·ness Leichtheit f; Leichtigkeit f
light·ning Blitz m; like ~ wie der Blitz; (as) quick as ~ blitzschnell
light·ning con·duc·tor Br, ~ rod ELECTR Blitzableiter m
light·weight SPORT Leichtgewicht n, Leichtgewichtler m
like¹1. v/t gernhaben, mögen; I ~ it es gefällt mir; I ~ her ich kann sie gut leiden; how do you ~ it? wie gefällt es dir?, wie findest du es?; I ~ that! iro das hab ich gern!; I should or would ~ to know ich möchte gern wissen; v/i wollen; (just) as you ~ (ganz) wie du willst; if you ~ wenn du willst 2. ~s and dislikes Neigungen und Abneigungen pl
like²1. gleich; wie; ähnlich; ~ that so; feel ~ Lust haben auf (acc) or zu; what is he ~? wie ist er?; that is just ~ him! das sieht ihm ähnlich! 2. der, die, das Gleiche; his ~ seinesgleichen; the ~ dergleichen; the ~s of you Leute wie du
like·li·hood Wahrscheinlichkeit f
like·ly 1. adj wahrscheinlich; geeignet 2. adv wahrscheinlich; not ~! F bestimmt nicht!
like·ness Ähnlichkeit f; Abbild n
like·wise ebenso

L

lik·ing Vorliebe *f*

li·lac 1. lila **2.** BOT Flieder *m*

lil·y BOT Lilie *f*

lil·y of the val·ley BOT Maiglöckchen *n*

limb ANAT (*Körper*)Glied *n*; BOT Ast *m*

lime¹ Kalk *m*

lime² BOT Linde *f*; Limone *f*

lime·light *fig* Rampenlicht *n*

lim·it 1. Limit *n*, Grenze *f*; *within ~s* in Grenzen; *off ~s* Zutritt verboten (*to* für); *that is the ~!* F das ist der Gipfel!, das ist (doch) die Höhe!; *go to the ~* bis zum Äußersten gehen **2.** beschränken (*to* auf *acc*)

lim·i·ta·tion Beschränkung *f*; *fig* Grenze *f*; JUR Verjährung *f*

lim·it·ed beschränkt, begrenzt; *~ (liability) company* Br ECON Gesellschaft *f* mit beschränkter Haftung

lim·it·less grenzenlos

limp¹ 1. hinken, humpeln **2.** Hinken *n*, Humpeln *n*

limp² schlaff, schlapp, F lappig

line¹ 1. Linie *f*, Strich *m*; Zeile *f*; Falte *f*, Runzel *f*; Reihe *f*; (*Menschen-, a.* Auto)Schlange *f*; (*Abstammungs*)Linie *f*; (*Verkehrs-, Eisenbahn- etc*)Linie *f*, Strecke *f*; (*Flug- etc*)Gesellschaft *f*; *esp* TEL Leitung *f*; MIL Linie *f*; Fach *n*, Gebiet *n*, Branche *f*; SPORT (*Ziel- etc*)Linie *f*; Leine *f*; Schnur *f*; Linie *f*, Richtung *f*; *fig* Grenze *f*; *pl* THEA Rolle *f*, Text *m*; *the ~* der Äquator; *draw the ~* Halt machen, die Grenze ziehen (*at* bei); *the ~ is busy or engaged* TEL die Leitung ist besetzt; *hold the ~* TEL bleiben Sie am Apparat; *stand in ~* anstehen, Schlange stehen (*for* um, nach); **2.** lin(i)ieren; *Gesicht* zeichnen, (zer)furchen; *Straße etc* säumen; *~ up* (sich) in e-r Reihe *or* Linie aufstellen, SPORT sich aufstellen; sich anstellen (*for* um, nach)

line² *Kleid etc* füttern; TECH auskleiden, ausschlagen; MOT *Bremsen etc* belegen

lin·e·ar linear; Längen...

lin·en 1. Leinen *n*; (*Bett-, Tisch- etc -*)Wäsche *f* **2.** leinen, Leinen...

lin·en| clos·et, Br *~ cup·board* Wäscheschrank *m*

lin·er MAR Linienschiff *n*; AVIAT Verkehrsflugzeug *n*

lines·man SPORT Linienrichter *m*

lines·wom·an SPORT Linienrichterin *f*

line-up SPORT Aufstellung *f*; Gegenüberstellung *f* (*zur Identifizierung*)

lin·ger verweilen, sich aufhalten; *a. ~ on* dahinsiechen; *~ on* noch dableiben; *fig* fortleben

lin·ge·rie Damenunterwäsche *f*

lin·ing Futter(stoff *m*) *n*; TECH Auskleidung *f*; MOT (*Brems- etc*)Belag *m*

link 1. (*Ketten*)Glied *n*; Manschettenknopf *m*; *fig* (*Binde*)Glied *n*, Verbindung *f* **2.** *a. ~ up* (sich) verbinden

links → *golf links*

link-up Verbindung *f*

lin·seed BOT Leinsamen *m*

lin·seed oil Leinöl *n*

li·on ZO Löwe *m*

li·on·ess ZO Löwin *f*

lip ANAT Lippe *f*; (*Tassen- etc*)Rand *m*; F Unverschämtheit *f*

lip·stick Lippenstift *m*

liq·ue·fy (sich) verflüssigen

liq·uid 1. Flüssigkeit *f* **2.** flüssig; *~ soap* Flüssigseife *f*

liq·ui·date liquidieren (*a.* ECON); *Schulden* tilgen

liq·uid·ize zerkleinern, pürieren

liq·uid·iz·er Mixgerät *n*, Mixer *m*

liq·uor Br alkoholische Getränke *pl*, Alkohol *m*; Schnaps *m*, Spirituosen *pl*

liq·uo·rice Br → *licorice*

lisp 1. lispeln **2.** Lispeln *n*

list¹ Liste *f*, Verzeichnis *n*; MAR Schlagseite *f* **2.** (*in e-e Liste*) eintragen, erfassen; MAR *be ~ing* Schlagseite haben

lis·ten hören; *~ in* Radio hören; *~ in to et.* im Radio (an)hören; *~ in on* Telefongespräch etc abhören *or* mithören; *~ to* anhören (*acc*), zuhören (*dat*); hören auf (*acc*)

lis·ten·er Zuhörer(in); (*Rundfunk*)Hörer(in)

list·less teilnahmslos, lustlos

li·ter Liter *m, n*

lit·e·ral (*wort*)wörtlich; genau; prosaisch

lit·e·ra·ry literarisch, Literatur...

lit·e·ra·ture Literatur *f*

lithe geschmeidig, gelenkig

li·tre Br → *liter*

lit·ter 1. (*esp Papier*)Abfall *m*; AGR Streu *f*; ZO Wurf *m*; Trage *f*; Sänfte *f* **2.** *et.* herumliegen lassen in (*dat*) *or* auf (*dat*); *be ~ed with* übersät sein mit

lit·ter| bas·ket, ~ bin Abfallkorb *m*

lit·tle 1. *adj* klein; wenig; *the ~ ones* die

Kleinen *pl* **2.** *adv* wenig, kaum **3.** Kleinigkeit *f*; **a** ~ ein wenig, ein bisschen; ~ **by** ~ (ganz) allmählich, nach und nach; **not a** ~ nicht wenig

live[1] leben; wohnen (**with** bei); ~ **to see** erleben; ~ **on** leben von; weiterleben; ~ **up to** s-n Grundsätzen *etc* gemäß leben; *Erwartungen etc* entsprechen; ~ **with** mit j-m zusammenleben; mit *et.* leben

live[2] **1.** *adj* lebend, lebendig; richtig, echt; ELECTR Strom führend; *radio*, TV Direkt..., Live-... **2.** *adv* direkt, original, live

live·li·hood (Lebens)Unterhalt *m*

live·li·ness Lebhaftigkeit *f*

live·ly lebhaft, lebendig; aufregend

liv·er ANAT Leber *f* (*a.* GASTR)

liv·e·ry Livree *f*

live·stock Vieh *n*, Viehbestand *m*

liv·id bläulich; F fuchsteufelswild

liv·ing 1. lebend; **the** ~ **image of** das genaue Ebenbild (*gen*) **2.** Leben *n*, Lebensweise *f*; Lebensunterhalt *m*; **the** ~ die Lebenden *pl*; **standard of** ~ Lebensstandard *m*; **earn** *or* **make a** ~ (sich) s-n Lebensunterhalt verdienen

liv·ing room Wohnzimmer *n*

liz·ard ZO Eidechse *f*

load 1. Last *f* (*a. fig*); Ladung *f*; Belastung *f* **2.** *j-n* überhäufen (**with** mit); *Schusswaffe* laden; *a.* ~ **up** (auf-, be-, ein)laden

loaf[1] Laib *m* (Brot); Brot *n*

loaf[2] *a.* ~ **about**, ~ **around** F herumlungern

loaf·er Müßiggänger(in)

loam Lehm *m*; **loam·y** lehmig

loan 1. (Ver)Leihen *n*; ECON Kredit *m*, Darlehen *n*; Leihgabe *f*; **on** ~ leihweise **2.** ~ **s.o. s.th.**, ~ **s.th. to s.o.** j-m *et.* (aus)leihen; *et.* an j-n verleihen

loath: be ~ **to do s.th.** *et.* nur (sehr) ungern tun

loathe verabscheuen, hassen

loath·ing Abscheu *m*

lob *esp tennis*: Lob *m*

lob·by 1. Vorhalle *f*; THEA, *film*: Foyer *n*; Wandelhalle *f*; POL Lobby *f*, Interessengruppe *f* **2.** POL *Abgeordnete etc* beeinflussen

lobe ANAT, BOT Lappen *m*

lob·ster ZO Hummer *m*

lo·cal 1. örtlich, Orts..., lokal, Lokal...

2. Ortsansässige *m*, *f*, Einheimische *m*, *f*; *Br* F Stammkneipe *f*; ~ **call** TEL Ortsgespräch *n*; ~ **e·lec·tions** POL Kommunalwahlen *pl*; ~ **gov·ern·ment** Gemeindeverwaltung *f*; ~ **time** Ortszeit *f*; ~ **traf·fic** Orts-, Nahverkehr *m*

lo·cate ausfindig machen; orten; **be** ~**d** gelegen sein, liegen, sich befinden

lo·ca·tion Lage *f*; Standort *m*; Platz *m* (**for** für); *film*, TV Gelände *n* für Außenaufnahmen; **on** ~ auf Außenaufnahme

lock[1] **1.** (Tür-, Gewehr- *etc*)Schloss *n*; Schleuse(nkammer) *f*; Verschluss *m*; Sperrvorrichtung *f* **2.** *v/t* zu-, verschließen, zu-, versperren (*a.* ~ **up**); umschlingen, umfassen; TECH sperren; *v/i* schließen; abschließbar *or* verschließbar sein; MOT *etc* blockieren; ~ **away** wegschließen, ~ **in** einschließen, einsperren; ~ **out** aussperren; ~ **up** abschließen; wegschließen; einsperren

lock[2] (Haar)Locke *f*

lock·er Spind *m*, Schrank *m*; Schließfach *n*; ~ **room** *esp* SPORT Umkleidekabine *f*, Umkleideraum *m*

lock·et Medaillon *n*

lock·out ECON Aussperrung *f*

lock·smith Schlosser *m*

lock·up Arrestzelle *f*

lo·cust ZO Heuschrecke *f*

lodge 1. Portier-, Pförtnerloge *f*; (*Jagd-, Ski- etc*)Hütte *f*; Sommer-, Gartenhaus *n*; (*Freimaurer*)Loge *f* **2.** *v/i* logieren, (*esp* vorübergehend *or* in Untermiete) wohnen; stecken (bleiben) (*bullet etc*); *v/t* aufnehmen, beherbergen, (für die Nacht) unterbringen; *Beschwerde etc* einreichen; *Berufung*, *Protest* einlegen

lodg·er Untermieter(in); **lodg·ing** Unterkunft *f*; *pl esp* möbliertes Zimmer

loft (Dach)Boden *m*; Heuboden *m*; Empore *f*; (**converted**) ~ Loft *m*, Fabriketage *f*

loft·y hoch; erhaben; stolz, hochmütig

log (Holz)Klotz *m*; (*gefällter*) Baumstamm; (Holz)Scheit *n*; → **log·book** MAR Logbuch *n*; AVIAT Bordbuch *n*; MOT Fahrtenbuch *n*

log cab·in Blockhaus *n*, Blockhütte *f*

log·ger·heads: be at ~ sich streiten, sich in den Haaren liegen (**with** mit)

lo·gic Logik *f*; **lo·gi·cal** logisch

loin GASTR Lende(nstück *n*) *f*; *pl* ANAT Lende *f*

L

loi·ter trödeln; herumlungern

loll hängen (*head*), heraushängen (*tongue*); ~ **around** or **about** F sich rekeln or lümmeln

lol·li·pop GASTR Lutscher *m*; *esp Br* Eis *n* am Stiel; ~ **man** *Br* Schülerlotse *m*; ~ **woman**, ~ **lady** *Br* Schülerlotsin *f*

lol·ly GASTR F Lutscher *m*; **ice~** Eis *n* am Stiel

lone·li·ness Einsamkeit *f*

lone·ly einsam; **become ~** vereinsamen

lone·some einsam

long[1] **1.** adj lang; weit; langfristig **2.** adv lang(e); **as** or **so ~ as** solange wie; vorausgesetzt, dass; ~ **ago** vor langer Zeit **3.** (e-e) lange Zeit; **for ~** lange; **take ~** lange brauchen or dauern

long[2] sich sehnen (**for** nach)

long-dis·tance Fern..., Langstrecken...; ~ **call** TEL Ferngespräch *n*; ~ **run·ner** SPORT Langstreckenläufer(in)

long·hand Schreibschrift *f*

long·ing 1. sehnsüchtig **2.** Sehnsucht *f*, Verlangen *n*

lon·gi·tude GEOGR Länge *f*

long johns lange Unterhose

long jump SPORT Weitsprung *m*

long-life milk *esp Br* H-Milch *f*

long-range MIL, AVIAT Fern..., Langstrecken...; langfristig

long·shore·man Dock-, Hafenarbeiter *m*

long-sight·ed *esp Br* weitsichtig, *fig a.* weitblickend

long-stand·ing seit langer Zeit bestehend; alt

long-term langfristig, auf lange Sicht

long wave ELECTR Langwelle *f*

long-wear·ing strapazierfähig

long-wind·ed langatmig

look 1. sehen, blicken, schauen (**at, on** auf *acc*, nach); nachschauen, nachsehen; *krank etc* aussehen; nach *e-r Richtung* liegen, gehen (*window etc*); ~ **here!** schau mal (her); hör mal (zu)!; ~ **like** aussehen wie; **it ~s as if** es sieht (so) aus, als ob; ~ **after** aufpassen auf (*acc*); sich kümmern um, sorgen für, den *Haushalt etc* versehen; ~ **ahead** nach vorne sehen; *fig* vorausschauen; ~ **around** sich umsehen; ~ **at** ansehen; ~ **back** sich umsehen; *fig* zurückblicken; ~ **down** herab-, heruntersehen (*a. fig* **on s.o.** auf j-n); ~ **for** suchen; ~

forward to sich freuen auf (*acc*); ~ **in** F hereinschauen (**on** bei); ~ **into** untersuchen, prüfen; ~ **on** zusehen, zuschauen (*dat*); betrachten, ansehen (**as** als); ~ **onto** liegen zu, (hinaus)gehen auf (*acc*) (*window etc*); ~ **out** hinaus-, heraussehen; aufpassen, sich vorsehen; ausschauen or Ausschau halten (**for** nach); ~ **over** *et.* durchsehen; *j-n* mustern; ~ **round** sich umsehen; ~ **through** *et.* durchsehen; ~ **up** aufblicken, aufsehen; *et.* nachschlagen; *j-n* aufsuchen **2.** Blick *m*; Miene *f*, (Gesichts)Ausdruck *m*; (**good**) ~**s** gutes Aussehen; **have a ~ at s.th.** sich *et.* ansehen; **I don't like the ~ of it** es gefällt mir nicht

look·ing glass Spiegel *m*

look·out Ausguck *m*; Ausschau *f*; *fig* F Aussicht(en *pl*) *f*; **be on the ~ for** Ausschau halten nach

loom[1] Webstuhl *m*

loom[2] *a.* ~ **up** undeutlich sichtbar werden or auftauchen

loop 1. Schlinge *f*, Schleife *f*; Schlaufe *f*; Öse *f*; AVIAT Looping *m*, *n*; IT Schleife *f* **2.** (sich) schlingen

loop·hole MIL Schießscharte *f*; *fig* Hintertürchen *n*; **a ~ in the law** e-e Gesetzeslücke

loose 1. los(e); locker; weit; frei; **let ~** loslassen; freilassen **2. be on the ~** frei herumlaufen

loos·en (sich) lösen or lockern; ~ **up** SPORT Lockerungsübungen machen

loot 1. Beute *f* **2.** plündern

lop *Baum* beschneiden, stutzen; ~ **off** abhauen, abhacken

lop-sid·ed schief; *fig* einseitig

lord Herr *m*, Gebieter *m*; *Br* Lord *m*; **the Lord** REL Gott *m* (der Herr); **the Lord's Prayer** REL das Vaterunser; **the Lord's Supper** REL das (heilige) Abendmahl; **House of Lords** *Br* POL Oberhaus *n*

Lord Mayor *Br* Oberbürgermeister *m*

lor·ry *Br* MOT Last(kraft)wagen *m*, Lastauto *n*, Laster *m*

lose verlieren; verpassen, versäumen; nachgehen (*watch*); ~ **o.s.** sich verirren; sich verlieren; **los·er** Verlierer(in); **loss** Verlust *m*; Schaden *m*; **at a ~** ECON mit Verlust; **be at a ~** in Verlegenheit sein (**for** um); **lost** verloren; **be ~** sich verirrt haben, sich nicht mehr zurechtfinden (*a. fig*); **be ~ in thought** in Gedanken versunken sein; **get ~** sich verirren; **get ~!** *sl* hau ab!

lost-and-found (of·fice), *Br* **lost prop·er·ty of·fice** Fundbüro *n*

lot Los *n*; Parzelle *f*; Grundstück *n*; ECON Partie *f*, Posten *m*; Gruppe *f*, Gesellschaft *f*; Menge *f*, Haufen *m*; Los *n*, Schicksal *n*; **the ~** alles, das Ganze; **a ~ of** F, **~s of** F viel, e-e Menge; **a bad ~** F ein übler Kerl; **cast** or **draw ~s** losen

loth → **loath**

lo·tion Lotion *f*

lot·te·ry Lotterie *f*

loud laut; *fig* schreiend, grell

loud·mouth *contp* Schwätzer *m*

loud·speak·er Lautsprecher *m*

lounge 1. Wohnzimmer *n*; Aufenthaltsraum *m*, Lounge *f* (*a.* AVIAT); Wartehalle *f* **2.** F *contp* sich flegeln; **~ about, ~ around** herumlungern

louse ZO Laus *f*

lou·sy verlaust; F miserabel, saumäßig

lout Flegel *m*, Lümmel *m*, Rüpel *m*

lov·a·ble liebenswert; reizend

love 1. Liebe *f* (**of, for, to, towards** zu); Liebling *m*, Schatz *m*; *tennis*: null; **be in ~ with** s.o. in j-n verliebt sein; **fall in ~ with** s.o. sich in j-n verlieben; **make ~** sich lieben, miteinander schlafen; **give my ~ to her** grüße sie herzlich von mir; **send one's ~ to** j-n grüßen lassen; **~ from ...** herzliche Grüße von ... **2.** lieben; gern mögen

love af·fair Liebesaffäre *f*

love·ly (wunder)schön; nett, reizend; F prima

lov·er Liebhaber *m*, Geliebte *m*, *f*; (*Musik- etc*) Liebhaber(in), (-)Freund(in); *pl* Liebende *pl*, Liebespaar *n*

lov·ing liebevoll, liebend

low 1. *adj* niedrig (*a. fig*); tief (*a. fig*); knapp (*supplies etc*); gedämpft, schwach (*light*); tief (*sound*); leise (*sound, voice*); *fig* gering(schätzig); ordinär; niedergeschlagen, deprimiert **2.** *adv* niedrig; tief (*a. fig*); leise **3.** METEOR Tief(druckgebiet) *n*; *fig* Tief(punkt *m*) *n*

low·brow F **1.** geistig Anspruchslose *m*, *f*, Unbedarfte *m*, *f* **2.** geistig anspruchslos, unbedarft

low-cal·o·rie kalorienarm, -reduziert

low-e·mis·sion schadstoffarm

low·er 1. niedriger; tiefer; untere(r, -s), Unter... **2.** niedriger machen; herab-, herunterlassen; *Augen, Stimme, Preis etc* senken; *Standard* herabsetzen; *fig* erniedrigen

low-fat fettarm

low-fly·ing plane AVIAT Tiefflieger *m*

low·land Tief-, Flachland *n*

low·ly niedrig

low-necked (tief) ausgeschnitten

low-pitched MUS tief

low-pres·sure METEOR Tiefdruck...; TECH Niederdruck...

low-rise ARCH niedrig (gebaut)

low-spir·it·ed niedergeschlagen

low tide Ebbe *f*

low wa·ter Niedrigwasser *n*

loy·al loyal, treu

loy·al·ty Loyalität *f*, Treue *f*

loz·enge MATH Raute *f*, Rhombus *m*; GASTR Pastille *f*

lu·bri·cant TECH Schmiermittel *n*

lu·bri·cate TECH schmieren, ölen

lu·bri·ca·tion TECH Schmieren *n*, Ölen *n*

lu·cid klar

luck Schicksal *n*; Glück *n*; **bad ~, hard ~, ill ~** Unglück *n*, Pech *n*; **good ~** Glück *n*; **good ~!** viel Glück!; **be in (out of) ~** (kein) Glück haben

luck·i·ly glücklicherweise, zum Glück

luck·y glücklich, Glücks...; **be ~** Glück haben; **~ day** Glückstag *m*; **~ fellow** Glückspilz *m*

lu·cra·tive einträglich, lukrativ

lu·di·crous lächerlich

lug zerren, schleppen

luge SPORT Rennrodeln *n*; Rennrodel *m*, Rennschlitten *m*

lug·gage *esp Br* (Reise)Gepäck *n*; **~ rack** *esp Br* RAIL *etc* Gepäcknetz *n*, Gepäckablage *f*; **~ van** *Br* RAIL Gepäckwagen *m*

luke·warm lau(warm); *fig* lau, mäßig, halbherzig

lull 1. beruhigen; sich legen (*storm*); *mst* **~ to sleep** einlullen **2.** Pause *f*; MAR Flaute *f* (*a. fig*)

lul·la·by Wiegenlied *n*

lum·ba·go MED Hexenschuss *m*

lum·ber¹ schwerfällig gehen; (dahin-) rumpeln (*vehicle*)

lum·ber²1. Bau-, Nutzholz *n*; *esp Br* Gerümpel *n* **2.** *v/t* **~ s.o. with** s.th. *Br* F j-m

L

et. aufhalsen

lum·ber·jack Holzfäller *m*, -arbeiter *m*

lum·ber mill Sägewerk *n*

lum·ber room *esp Br* Rumpelkammer *f*

lum·ber·yard Holzplatz *m*, Holzlager *n*

lu·mi·na·ry *fig* Leuchte *f*, Koryphäe *f*

lu·mi·nous leuchtend, Leucht...

lu·mi·nous di·splay Leuchtanzeige *f*

lu·mi·nous paint Leuchtfarbe *f*

lump 1. Klumpen *m*; Schwellung *f*, Beule *f*; MED Geschwulst *f*, Knoten *m*; GASTR Stück *n*; *in the* ~ in Bausch und Bogen, pauschal **2.** *v/t:* ~ *together fig* zusammenwerfen; in e-n Topf werfen; *v/i* Klumpen bilden, klumpen

lump sug·ar Würfelzucker *m*

lump sum Pauschalsumme *f*

lump·y klumpig

lu·na·cy Wahnsinn *m*

lu·nar ASTR Mond...

lu·nar mod·ule Mond(lande)fähre *f*

lu·na·tic *fig* **1.** wahnsinnig, verrückt **2.** Wahnsinnige *m*, *f*, Verrückte *m*, *f*

lunch, *formal* **lun·cheon 1.** Lunch *m*, Mittagessen *n* **2.** zu Mittag essen

lunch hour, **lunch time** Mittagszeit *f*, Mittagspause *f*

lung ANAT Lungenflügel *m*; *pl* die Lunge

lunge sich stürzen (*at* auf *acc*)

lurch 1. taumeln, torkeln **2.** *leave s.o. in the* ~ j-n im Stich lassen, F j-n sitzen lassen

sen

lure 1. Köder *m*; *fig* Lockung *f* **2.** ködern, (an)locken

lu·rid grell; grässlich, schauerlich

lurk lauern; ~ *about*, ~ *around* herumschleichen

lus·cious köstlich, lecker; üppig; F knackig

lush saftig, üppig

lust 1. sinnliche Begierde, Lust *f*; Gier *f* **2.** ~ *after*, ~ *for* begehren; gierig sein nach

lus·ter, *Br* **lus·tre** Glanz *m*, Schimmer *m*; **lus·trous** glänzend, schimmernd

lust·y kräftig, robust, vital

lute MUS Laute *f*

Lu·ther·an REL lutherisch

lux·u·ri·ant üppig

lux·u·ri·ate schwelgen (*in* in *dat*)

lux·u·ri·ous luxuriös, Luxus...

lux·u·ry 1. Luxus *m*; Komfort *m*; Luxusartikel *m* **2.** Luxus...

lye Lauge *f*

ly·ing lügnerisch, verlogen

lymph MED Lymphe *f*

lynch lynchen; ~ *law* Lynchjustiz *f*

lynx ZO Luchs *m*

lyr·ic 1. lyrisch **2.** lyrisches Gedicht; *pl* Lyrik *f*; (Lied)Text *m*

lyr·i·cal lyrisch, gefühlvoll; schwärmerisch

M

M, m M, m *n*

M *abbr of* **medium (size)** mittelgroß

ma F Mama *f*, Mutti *f*

ma'am → **madam**

ma·cad·am Asphalt *m*

mac·a·ro·ni Makkaroni *pl*

ma·chine 1. Maschine *f* **2.** maschinell herstellen

ma·chine·gun Maschinengewehr *n*

ma·chine-read·a·ble IT maschinenlesbar

ma·chin·e·ry Maschinen *pl*; Maschinerie *f*

ma·chin·ist TECH Maschinist *m*

mach·o *contp* Macho *m*

mack·e·rel ZO Makrele *f*

mac·ro... Makro..., (sehr) groß

mad wahnsinnig, verrückt; VET tollwütig; F wütend; *fig* *be* ~ *about* wild *or* versessen sein auf (*acc*), verrückt sein nach; *drive s.o.* ~ j-n verrückt machen; *go* ~ verrückt werden; *like* ~ wie verrückt

mad·am gnädige Frau

mad·cap verrückt

mad cow dis·ease VET Rinderwahn (-sinn) *m*

mad·den verrückt *or* rasend machen

mad·den·ing unerträglich; verrückt *or* rasend machend

made: ~ *of gold* aus Gold

made-to-meas·ure maßgeschneidert

made-up geschminkt; erfunden

mad·house *fig* F Irrenhaus *n*

mad·ly wie verrückt; F wahnsinnig, schrecklich

mad·man Verrückte *m*

mad·ness Wahnsinn

mad·wom·an Verrückte *f*

mag·a·zine Magazin *n* (*a.* PHOT, MIL), Zeitschrift *f*; Lagerhaus *n*

mag·got ZO Made *f*

Ma·gi: *the* (*three*) ~ die (drei) Weisen aus dem Morgenland, die Heiligen Drei Könige

ma·gic 1. Magie *f*, Zauberei *f*; Zauber *m*; *fig* Wunder *n* **2.** *a.* **magical** magisch, Zauber...

ma·gi·cian Magier *m*, Zauberer *m*; Zauberkünstler *m*

ma·gis·trate (Friedens)Richter(in)

mag·na·nim·i·ty Großmut *f*

mag·nan·i·mous großmütig

mag·net Magnet *m*

mag·net·ic magnetisch, Magnet...

mag·nif·i·cent großartig, prächtig

mag·ni·fy vergrößern

mag·ni·fy·ing glass Vergrößerungsglas *n*, Lupe *f*

mag·ni·tude Größe *f*; Wichtigkeit *f*

mag·pie ZO Elster *f*

ma·hog·a·ny Mahagoni(holz) *n*

maid (Dienst)Mädchen *n*, Hausangestellte *f*; ~ *of hono(u)r* Hofdame *f*; (erste) Brautjungfer

maid·en Jungfern..., Erstlings...

maid·en name Mädchenname *m*

mail 1. Post(sendung) *f*; *by* ~ mit der Post® **2.** mit der Post® (zu)schicken, aufgeben; *Brief* einwerfen

mail·bag Postsack *m*; Posttasche *f*

mail·box Briefkasten *m*

mail car·ri·er, mail·man Briefträger *m*, Postbote *m*

mail or·der Bestellung *f* bei e-m Versandhaus

mail-or·der| firm, ~ **house** Versandhaus *n*

maim verstümmeln

main 1. Haupt..., wichtigste(r, -s); hauptsächlich; *by* ~ *force* mit äußerster Kraft **2.** *mst pl* Hauptleitung *f*, Hauptgas-, Hauptwasser-, Hauptstromleitung *f*; (Strom)Netz *n*; *in the* ~ in der Hauptsache, im Wesentlichen

main·frame IT Großrechner *m*

main·land Festland *n*

main·ly hauptsächlich

main mem·o·ry IT Hauptspeicher *m*; Arbeitsspeicher *m*

main men·u IT Hauptmenü *n*

main road Haupt(verkehrs)straße *f*

main·spring TECH Hauptfeder *f*; *fig* (Haupt)Triebfeder *f*

main·stay *fig* Hauptstütze *f*

main street Hauptstraße *f*

main·tain (aufrecht)erhalten, beibehalten; instand halten, pflegen, TECH *a.* warten; *Familie etc* unterhalten, versorgen; *et.* behaupten

main·te·nance (Aufrecht)Erhaltung *f*; Instandhaltung *f*, Pflege *f*, TECH *a.* Wartung *f*; Unterhalt *m*

maize *esp Br* BOT Mais *m*

ma·jes·tic majestätisch

ma·jes·ty Majestät *f*; *His* (*Her, Your*) *Majesty* Seine (Ihre, Eure) Majestät

ma·jor 1. größere(r, -s), *fig a.* bedeutend, wichtig; JUR volljährig; *C* ~ MUS C-Dur *n* **2.** MIL Major *m*; JUR Volljährige *m, f*; UNIV Hauptfach *n*; MUS Dur *n*; ~ **gen·e·ral** MIL Generalmajor *m*

ma·jor·i·ty Mehrheit *f*, Mehrzahl *f*; JUR Volljährigkeit *f*

ma·jor league *baseball:* oberste Spielklasse

ma·jor road Haupt(verkehrs)straße *f*

make 1. machen; anfertigen, herstellen, erzeugen; (zu)bereiten; (er)schaffen; ergeben, bilden; machen zu; ernennen zu; *Geld* verdienen; sich erweisen als, abgeben (*person*); schätzen auf (*acc*); *Geschwindigkeit* erreichen; *Fehler* machen; *Frieden etc* schließen; *e-e Rede* halten; F *Strecke* zurücklegen; *with inf: j-n* lassen, veranlassen zu, bringen zu, zwingen zu; ~ *it* es schaffen; ~ *do with s.th.* mit et. auskommen, sich mit et. behelfen; *what do you* ~ *of it?* was halten Sie davon?; ~ *believe* vorgeben; ~ *friends with* sich anfreunden mit; ~ *good* wieder gutmachen; *Versprechen etc* halten; ~ *way* Platz machen; ~ *for* zugehen auf (*acc*); sich aufmachen nach; ~ *into* verarbeiten zu; ~ *off* sich davonmachen, sich aus dem Staub machen; ~ *out Rechnung, Scheck etc* ausstellen; ausmachen, erkennen; aus *j-m, e-r Sache* klug werden; ~ *over Eigentum* übertragen; ~ *up* et. zusammenstellen; sich et. ausdenken, *et.* erfinden; (sich) zurechtma-

M

chen *or* schminken; **~ it up** sich versöhnen *or* wieder vertragen (**with** mit); **~ up one's mind** sich entschließen; **be made up of** bestehen aus, sich zusammensetzen aus; **~ up for** nachholen, aufholen; für *et.* entschädigen **2.** Machart f, Bauart f; Fabrikat n, Marke f

make-be·lieve Schein m, Fantasie f

mak·er Hersteller m; **Maker** REL Schöpfer m

make-shift 1. Notbehelf m **2.** behelfsmäßig, Behelfs…

make-up Make-up n, Schminke f; Aufmachung f; Zusammensetzung f

mak·ing Erzeugung f, Herstellung f, Fabrikation f; **be in the ~** noch in Arbeit sein; **have the ~s of** das Zeug haben zu

mal·ad·just·ed nicht angepasst, verhaltensgestört, milieugestört

mal·ad·min·i·stra·tion schlechte Verwaltung; POL Misswirtschaft f

mal·con·tent 1. unzufrieden **2.** Unzufriedene m, f

male 1. männlich **2.** Mann m; ZO Männchen n

male nurse (Kranken)Pfleger m

mal·for·ma·tion Missbildung f

mal·ice Bosheit f; Groll m; JUR böse Absicht, Vorsatz m

ma·li·cious boshaft; böswillig

ma·lign verleumden

ma·lig·nant bösartig (a. MED); boshaft

mall Einkaufszentrum n

mal·le·a·ble TECH verformbar; fig formbar

mal·let Holzhammer m; (Krocket-, Polo)Schläger m

mal·nu·tri·tion Unterernährung f; Fehlernährung f

mal·o·dor·ous übel riechend

mal·prac·tice Vernachlässigung f der beruflichen Sorgfalt; MED falsche Behandlung, (ärztlicher) Kunstfehler

malt Malz n

mal·treat schlecht behandeln; misshandeln

mam·mal ZO Säugetier n

mam·moth 1. ZO Mammut n **2.** Mammut…, Riesen…, riesig

mam·my F Mami f

man 1. Mann m; Mensch(en pl) m; Menschheit f; F (Ehe)Mann m; F Geliebte m; (Schach)Figur f; (Dame)Stein m; **the ~ on** (Br in) **the street** der Mann

auf der Straße **2.** (Raum)Schiff etc bemannen; Büro etc besetzen

man·age v/t Betrieb etc leiten, führen; Künstler, Sportler etc managen; et. zustande bringen; es fertigbringen (**to do** zu tun); umgehen (können) mit; mit j-m, et. fertigwerden; F Arbeit, Essen etc bewältigen, schaffen; v/i auskommen (**with** mit; **without** ohne); F es schaffen, zurechtkommen; F es einrichten, es ermöglichen

man·age·a·ble handlich; lenksam

man·age·ment Verwaltung f; ECON Management n, Unternehmensführung f; Geschäftsleitung f, Direktion f

man·ag·er Verwalter m; ECON Manager m (a. THEA etc); Geschäftsführer m, Leiter m, Direktor m; SPORT (Chef-)Trainer m; **be a good ~** gut or sparsam wirtschaften können

man·a·ge·ri·al ECON geschäftsführend, leitend; **~ position** leitende Stellung; **~ staff** leitende Angestellte pl

man·ag·ing ECON geschäftsführend, leitend; **~ di·rec·tor** Generaldirektor m, leitender Direktor

man·date Mandat n; Auftrag m; Vollmacht f

man·da·to·ry obligatorisch, zwingend

mane ZO Mähne f (a. F)

ma·neu·ver·a. fig **1.** Manöver n **2.** manövrieren

mange VET Räude f

man·ger AGR Krippe f

man·gle 1. (Wäsche)Mangel f **2.** mangeln; j-n übel zurichten, zerfleischen; fig Text verstümmeln

man·gy VET räudig; fig schäbig

man·hood Mannesalter n; Männlichkeit f

ma·ni·a Wahnsinn m; fig (**for**) Sucht f (nach), Leidenschaft f (für), Manie f, Fimmel m; **ma·ni·ac** F Wahnsinnige m, f, Verrückte m, f; fig Fanatiker(in)

man·i·cure Maniküre f, Handpflege f

man·i·fest 1. offenkundig **2.** v/t offenbaren, manifestieren

man·i·fold mannigfaltig, vielfältig

ma·nip·u·late manipulieren; (geschickt) handhaben

ma·nip·u·la·tion Manipulation f

man·kind die Menschheit, die Menschen pl

man·ly männlich

man·made vom Menschen geschaffen, künstlich; **~ fiber** Kunstfaser f

man·ner Art f (und Weise f); Betragen n, Auftreten n; pl Benehmen n, Umgangsformen pl; Manieren pl; Sitten pl

ma·noeu·vre Br → **maneuver**

man·or Br (Land)Gut n; → **man·or house** Herrenhaus n

man·pow·er menschliche Arbeitskraft; Arbeitskräfte pl

man·sion (herrschaftliches) Wohnhaus

man·slaugh·ter JUR Totschlag m, fahrlässige Tötung

man·tel·piece, man·tel·shelf Kaminsims m

man·u·al 1. Hand...; mit der Hand (gemacht) **2.** Handbuch n

man·u·fac·ture 1. erzeugen, herstellen **2.** Herstellung f, Fertigung f; Erzeugnis n, Fabrikat n

man·u·fac·tur·er Hersteller m, Erzeuger m

man·u·fac·tur·ing Herstellungs...

ma·nure AGR **1.** Dünger m, Mist m, Dung m **2.** düngen

man·u·script Manuskript n

man·y 1. viel(e); **~ a** manche(r, -s), manch eine(r, -s); **~ times** oft; **as ~** ebenso viel(e) **2.** viele; **a good ~** ziemlich viel(e); **a great ~** sehr viele

map 1. (Land- etc)Karte f; (Stadt- etc)Plan m **2.** e-e Karte machen von; auf e-r Karte eintragen; **~ out** fig (bis in die Einzelheiten) (voraus)planen

ma·ple BOT Ahorn m

mar beeinträchtigen; verderben

Mar abbr of **March** März m

mar·a·thon SPORT **1.** a. **~ race** Marathonlauf m; **2.** Marathon... (a. fig)

ma·raud plündern

mar·ble 1. Marmor m; Murmel f **2.** marmorn

march 1. marschieren; fig fortschreiten **2.** Marsch m; fig (Fort)Gang m; **the ~ of events** der Lauf der Dinge

March (abbr **Mar**) März m

mare ZO Stute f

mar·ga·rine, Br F **marge** Margarine f

mar·gin Rand m (a. fig); Grenze f (a. fig); fig Spielraum m; (Gewinn-, Verdienst)Spanne f; **by a wide ~** mit großem Vorsprung; **mar·gin·al** Rand...; **~ note** Randbemerkung f

mar·i·hua·na, mar·i·jua·na Marihuana

n

ma·ri·na Boots-, Jachthafen m

ma·rine Marine f; MIL Marineinfanterist m

mar·i·ner Seemann m

mar·i·tal ehelich, Ehe...

mar·i·tal sta·tus Familienstand m

mar·i·time See...; Küsten...; Schifffahrts...

mark¹ 1. Marke f, Markierung f; (Kenn)Zeichen n, Merkmal n; (Körper)Mal n; Ziel n (a. fig); Spur f (a. fig); Fleck m; (Fabrik-, Waren)Zeichen n, (Schutz-, Handels)Marke f; ECON Preisangabe f; PED Note f, Zensur f, Punkt m; SPORT Startlinie f; fig Zeichen n; fig Norm f; **be up to the ~** den Anforderungen gewachsen sein (person) or genügen (performance etc); gesundheitlich auf der Höhe sein; **be wide of the ~** weit danebenschießen; fig sich gewaltig irren; weit danebenliegen (estimate etc); **hit the ~** (das Ziel) treffen; **miss the ~** danebenschießen, das Ziel verfehlen (a. fig) **2.** markieren, anzeichnen; anzeigen; kennzeichnen; Waren auszeichnen; Preis festsetzen; Spuren hinterlassen auf (dat); PED benoten, zensieren; SPORT Gegenspieler decken, markieren; **~ my words** denk an m-e Worte; **to ~ the occasion** zur Feier des Tages; **~ time** auf der Stelle treten (a. fig); **~ down** notieren, vermerken; im Preis herabsetzen; **~ off** abgrenzen; auf e-r Liste abhaken; **~ out** durch Striche etc markieren; bestimmen (**for** für); **~ up** im Preis heraufsetzen

mark² hist (former monetary unit of Germany) (Deutsche) Mark

marked deutlich, ausgeprägt

mark·er Markierstift m; Lesezeichen n; SPORT Bewacher(in)

mar·ket 1. Markt m; Marktplatz m; (Lebensmittel)Geschäft n, Laden m; ECON Absatz m; (**for**) Nachfrage f (nach), Bedarf m (an dat); **on the ~** auf dem Markt or im Handel; **put on the ~** auf den Markt or in den Handel bringen; (zum Verkauf) anbieten **2.** v/t auf den Markt or in den Handel bringen; verkaufen, vertreiben

mar·ket·a·ble ECON marktgängig

mar·ket gar·den *Br* Gemüse- und Obst-gärtnerei *f*

mar·ket·ing ECON Marketing *n*

mark·ing Markierung *f*; zo Zeichnung *f*; SPORT Deckung *f*; **man-to-man ~** Manndeckung *f*

marks·man guter Schütze

mar·ma·lade *esp* Orangenmarmelade *f*

mar·mot zo Murmeltier *n*

ma·roon 1. kastanienbraun **2.** *auf e·r ein·samen Insel* aussetzen **3.** Leuchtrakete *f*

mar·quee Festzelt *n*

mar·quis Marquis *m*

mar·riage Heirat *f*, Hochzeit *f* (**to** mit); Ehe *f*; **civil ~** standesamtliche Trauung

mar·ria·ge·a·ble heiratsfähig

mar·riage cer·tif·i·cate Trauschein *m*, Heiratsurkunde *f*

mar·ried verheiratet; ehelich, Ehe…; ~ **couple** Ehepaar *n*; ~ **life** Ehe(leben *n*) *f*

mar·row ANAT (Knochen)Mark *n*; *fig* Kern *m*, *das* Wesentliche

mar·ry *v/t* heiraten; *Paar* trauen; **be married** verheiratet sein (**to** mit); **get married** heiraten; sich verheiraten (**to** mit); *v/i* heiraten

marsh Sumpf(land *n*) *m*, Marsch *f*

mar·shal 1. MIL Marschall *m*; Bezirkspolizeichef *m* **2.** ordnen; führen

marsh·y sumpfig

mar·ten zo Marder *m*

mar·tial kriegerisch; Kriegs…, Militär…; ~ **arts** asiatische Kampfsportarten *pl*; ~ **law** Kriegsrecht *n*

mar·tyr REL Märtyrer(in) *f* (*a. fig*)

mar·vel 1. Wunder *n* **2.** sich wundern, staunen; **mar·vel·(l)ous** wunderbar; fabelhaft, fantastisch

mar·zi·pan Marzipan *n*, *m*

mas·ca·ra Wimperntusche *f*

mas·cot Maskottchen *n*

mas·cu·line männlich; Männer…; maskulin (*a.* LING)

mash zerdrücken, zerquetschen

mashed po·ta·toes Kartoffelbrei *m*

mask 1. Maske *f* (*a.* IT); **2.** maskieren; *fig* verbergen, verschleiern

masked maskiert; ~ **ball** Maskenball *m*

ma·son Steinmetz *m*; *mst* **Mason** Freimaurer *m*; **ma·son·ry** Mauerwerk *n*

masque THEA HIST Maskenspiel *n*

mas·que·rade 1. Maskerade *f* (*a. fig*);

Verkleidung *f* **2.** sich ausgeben (**as** als, für)

mass 1. Masse *f*; Menge *f*; Mehrzahl *f*; **the ~es** die (breite) Masse **2.** (sich) (an)sammeln *or* (an)häufen **3.** Massen…

Mass REL Messe *f*

mas·sa·cre 1. Massaker *n* **2.** niedermetzeln

mas·sage 1. Massage *f* **2.** massieren

mas·seur Masseur *m*

mas·seuse Masseurin *f*, Masseuse *f*

mas·sif (Gebirgs)Massiv *n*

mas·sive massiv; groß, gewaltig

mass me·di·a Massenmedien *pl*

mass-pro·duce serienmäßig herstellen

mass pro·duc·tion Massen-, Serienproduktion *f*

mast MAR Mast *m*; *Br* ELECTR Sendemast *m*

mas·ter 1. Meister *m* (*a.* PAINT); Herr *m*; *esp Br* Lehrer *m*; Original(kopie *f*) *n*; UNIV Magister *m*; **Master of Arts** (*abbr* **MA**) Magister *m* Artium; ~ **of ceremonies** Conférencier *m* **2.** Meister…; Haupt…; ~ **copy** Originalkopie *f*; ~ **tape** TECH Mastertape *n*, Originaltonband *n* **3.** Herr sein über (*acc*); *Sprache etc* beherrschen; *Aufgabe etc* meistern

mas·ter key Hauptschlüssel *m*

mas·ter·ly meisterhaft, virtuos

mas·ter·piece Meisterstück *n*, -werk *n*

mas·ter·y Herrschaft *f*; Oberhand *f*; Beherrschung *f*

mas·tur·bate masturbieren, onanieren

mat[1] 1. Matte *f*; Untersetzer *m* **2.** sich verfilzen

mat[2] mattiert, matt

match[1] Streichholz *n*, Zündholz *n*

match[2] 1. *der, die, das* Gleiche; (dazu) passende Sache *or* Person, Gegenstück *n*; (*Fußball- etc*)Spiel *n*, (*Box- etc -*) Kampf *m*, (*Tennis- etc*)Match *n*, *m*; Heirat *f*; *gute etc* Partie (*person*); **be a (no) ~ for s.o.** j-m (nicht) gewachsen sein; **find** *or* **meet one's ~** s-n Meister finden **2.** *v/t* j-m, e-r Sache ebenbürtig *or* gewachsen sein, gleichkommen; j-m, e-r Sache entsprechen, passen zu; *v/i* zusammenpassen, übereinstimmen, entsprechen; **gloves to ~** dazu passende Handschuhe

match·box Streichholz-, Zündholzschachtel *f*

M

match·less unvergleichlich, einzigartig
match·mak·er Ehestifter(in)
match point *tennis etc*: Matchball *m*
mate[1] → **checkmate**
mate[2] **1.** (Arbeits)Kamerad *m*, (-)Kollege *m*; ZO Männchen *n*, Weibchen *n*; MAR Maat *m* **2.** ZO (sich) paaren
ma·te·ri·al 1. Material *n*, Stoff *m*; **writing** **~s** Schreibmaterial(ien *pl*) *n* **2.** materiell; leiblich; wesentlich
ma·ter·nal mütterlich, Mutter...; mütterlicherseits
ma·ter·ni·ty 1. Mutterschaft *f* **2.** Schwangerschafts..., Umstands...
ma·ter·ni·ty| leave Mutterschaftsurlaub *m*; **~ ward** Entbindungsstation *f*
math F Mathe *f*
math·e·ma·ti·cian Mathematiker(in)
math·e·mat·ics Mathematik *f*
maths *Br* F Mathe *f*
mat·i·née THEA *etc* Nachmittagsvorstellung *f*
ma·tric·u·late (sich) immatrikulieren
mat·ri·mo·ni·al ehelich, Ehe...
mat·ri·mo·ny Ehe *f*, Ehestand *m*
ma·trix TECH Matrize *f*
ma·tron *Br* MED Oberschwester *f*; Hausmutter *f*; Matrone *f*
mat·ter 1. Materie *f*, Material *n*, Substanz *f*, Stoff *m*; MED Eiter *m*; Sache *f*, Angelegenheit *f*; **printed ~** Drucksache *f*; **what's the ~ (with you)?** was ist los (mit dir)?; **no ~ who** gleichgültig, wer; **for that ~** was das betrifft; **a ~ of course** e-e Selbstverständlichkeit; **a ~ of fact** e-e Tatsache; **as a ~ of fact** tatsächlich, eigentlich; **a ~ of form** e-e Formsache; **a ~ of time** e-e Frage der Zeit **2.** von Bedeutung sein (**to** für); **it doesn't ~** es macht nichts
mat·ter-of-fact sachlich, nüchtern
mat·tress Matratze *f*
ma·ture 1. reif (*a. fig*) **2.** (heran)reifen, reif werden
ma·tu·ri·ty Reife *f* (*a. fig*)
maud·lin rührselig
maul übel zurichten; *fig* verreißen
Maun·dy Thurs·day Gründonnerstag *m*
mauve malvenfarbig, mauve
mawk·ish rührselig
max·i... Maxi..., riesig, Riesen...
max·im Grundsatz *m*
max·i·mum 1. Maximum *n* **2.** maximal, Maximal..., Höchst...

May Mai *m*
may *v/aux ich* kann / mag / darf *etc*, *du* kannst / magst / darfst etc
may·be vielleicht
may·bug ZO Maikäfer *m*
May Day der 1. Mai
may·on·naise Mayonnaise *f*
mayor Bürgermeister(in)
may·pole Maibaum *m*
maze Irrgarten *m*, Labyrinth *n* (*a. fig*)
me mich; mir; F ich
mead·ow Wiese *f*, Weide *f*
mea·ger, *Br* **mea·gre** mager (*a. fig*), dürr; dürftig
meal[1] Mahl(zeit *f*) *n*; Essen *n*
meal[2] Schrotmehl *n*
mean[1] gemein, niederträchtig; geizig, knauserig; schäbig
mean[2] meinen; sagen wollen; bedeuten; beabsichtigen, vorhaben; **be meant for** bestimmt sein für; **~ well (ill)** es gut (schlecht) meinen
mean[3] **1.** Mitte *f*, Mittel *n*, Durchschnitt *m* **2.** mittlere(r, -s), Mittel..., durchschnittlich, Durchschnitts...
mean·ing 1. Sinn *m*, Bedeutung *f* **2.** bedeutungsvoll, bedeutsam
mean·ing·ful bedeutungsvoll; sinnvoll
mean·ing·less sinnlos
means Mittel *n* or *pl*, Weg *m*; ECON Mittel *pl*, Vermögen *n*; **by all ~** auf alle Fälle, unbedingt; **by no ~** keineswegs, auf keinen Fall; **by ~ of** durch, mit
mean·time 1. inzwischen **2.** **in the ~** inzwischen
mean·while inzwischen
mea·sles MED Masern *pl*
mea·sur·a·ble messbar
mea·sure 1. Maß *n* (*a. fig*), TECH Messgerät *n*; MUS Takt *m*; *fig* Maßnahme *f*; **beyond ~** über alle Maßen; **in a great ~** großenteils; **take ~s** Maßnahmen treffen *or* ergreifen **2.** (ab-, aus-, ver)messen; *j-m* Maß nehmen; **~ up to** den Ansprüchen (*gen*) genügen; **measured** gemessen; wohlüberlegt; maßvoll
mea·sure·ment (Ver)Messung *f*; Maß *n*; **~ of ca·pac·i·ty** Hohlmaß *n*
mea·sur·ing tape → **tape measure**
meat GASTR Fleisch *n*; **cold ~** kalter Braten
meat·ball GASTR Fleischklößchen *n*
me·chan·ic Mechaniker(in)

me·chan·i·cal mechanisch; Maschinen...

me·chan·ics PHYS Mechanik f

mech·a·nism Mechanismus m

mech·a·nize mechanisieren

med·al Medaille f; Orden m

med·al·(l)ist SPORT Medaillengewinner(in)

med·dle sich einmischen (**with, in** in acc); med·dle·some aufdringlich

me·di·a Medien pl

med·i·ae·val → **medieval**

me·di·an a. ~ **strip** MOT Mittelstreifen m

me·di·ate vermitteln

me·di·a·tion Vermittlung f

me·di·a·tor Vermittler m

med·ic MIL Sanitäter m

med·i·cal 1. medizinisch, ärztlich 2. ärztliche Untersuchung

med·i·cal cer·tif·i·cate ärztliches Attest

med·i·cat·ed medizinisch

me·dic·i·nal medizinisch, heilkräftig, Heil...

medi·cine Medizin f, a. Arznei f, a. Heilkunde f

med·i·e·val mittelalterlich

me·di·o·cre mittelmäßig

med·i·tate v/i (**on**) nachdenken (über acc); meditieren (über acc); v/t erwägen

med·i·ta·tion Nachdenken n; Meditation f

med·i·ta·tive nachdenklich

Med·i·ter·ra·ne·an Mittelmeer...

me·di·um 1. Mitte f; Mittel n; Medium n 2. mittlere(r, -s), Mittel..., a. mittelmäßig; GASTR medium, halb gar

med·ley Gemisch n; MUS Medley n, Potpourri n

meek sanft(mütig), bescheiden

meet v/t treffen, sich treffen mit; begegnen (dat); j-n kennenlernen; j-n abholen; zusammentreffen mit, stoßen or treffen auf (acc); Wünschen entgegenkommen, entsprechen; e-r Forderung, Verpflichtung nachkommen; v/i zusammenkommen, -treten; sich begegnen, sich treffen; (feindlich) zusammenstoßen; SPORT aufeinandertreffen; sich kennenlernen; ~ **with** zusammentreffen mit; sich treffen mit; stoßen auf (Schwierigkeiten etc); erleben, erleiden

meet·ing Begegnung f, (Zusammen-)Treffen n; Versammlung f, Konferenz f, Tagung f; ~ place Tagungs-, Versammlungsort m; Treffpunkt m

mel·an·chol·y 1. Melancholie f, Schwermut f, Trübsinn m 2. melancholisch, traurig, trübsinnig, wehmütig

mel·low 1. reif, weich; sanft, mild (light); zart (colors); fig gereift (person) 2. reifen (lassen) (a. fig); weich or sanft werden

me·lo·di·ous melodisch

mel·o·dra·mat·ic melodramatisch

mel·o·dy MUS Melodie f

mel·on BOT Melone f

melt (zer)schmelzen; ~ **down** einschmelzen

mem·ber Mitglied n, Angehörige m, f; ANAT Glied n, Gliedmaße f; (männliches) Glied; **Member of Parliament** Br Mitglied n des Unterhauses, Unterhausabgeordnete m, f; mem·ber·ship Mitgliedschaft f; Mitgliederzahl f

mem·brane Membran(e) f

mem·o Memo n

mem·oirs Memoiren pl

mem·o·ra·ble denkwürdig

me·mo·ri·al Denkmal n, Ehrenmal n, Gedenkstätte f (**to** für); Gedenkfeier f (**to** für)

mem·o·rize auswendig lernen, sich et. einprägen

mem·o·ry Gedächtnis n; Erinnerung f; Andenken n; IT Speicher m; **in ~ of** zum Andenken an (acc)

men·ace 1. (be)drohen 2. (Be)Drohung f

mend 1. v/t (ver)bessern; ausbessern, reparieren, flicken; ~ **one's ways** sich bessern; v/i sich bessern 2. ausgebesserte Stelle; **on the ~** auf dem Wege der Bess(e)rung

men·di·cant REL Bettelmönch m

me·ni·al niedrig, untergeordnet

men·in·gi·tis MED Meningitis f, Hirnhautentzündung f

men·o·pause MED Wechseljahre pl

men·stru·ate menstruieren

men·stru·a·tion Menstruation f

men·tal geistig, Geistes...; seelisch, psychisch; ~ a·rith·me·tic Kopfrechnen n; ~ hand·i·cap geistige Behinderung; ~ hos·pi·tal psychiatrische Klinik

men·tal·i·ty Mentalität f

men·tal·ly: ~ **handicapped** geistig behindert; ~ **ill** geisteskrank

men·tion 1. erwähnen; **don't ~ it!** keine

Ursache! **2.** Erwähnung f

men·u Speise(n)karte f; IT Menü n

me·ow ZO miauen

mer·can·tile Handels…

mer·ce·na·ry 1. geldgierig **2.** MIL Söldner m

mer·chan·dise 1. Ware(n pl) f **2.** vermarkten

mer·chan·dis·ing Vermarktung f

mer·chant 1. (Groß)Händler m, (Groß)Kaufmann m **2.** Handels…

mer·ci·ful barmherzig, gnädig

mer·ci·less unbarmherzig, erbarmungslos

mer·cu·ry CHEM Quecksilber n

mer·cy Barmherzigkeit f, Erbarmen f, Gnade f

mere, mere·ly bloß, nur

merge verschmelzen (*into, with* mit); ECON fusionieren

merg·er ECON Fusion f

me·rid·i·an GEOGR Meridian m; fig Gipfel m, Höhepunkt m

mer·it 1. Verdienst n; Wert m; Vorzug m **2.** verdienen

mer·maid Meerjungfrau f, Nixe f

mer·ri·ment Fröhlichkeit f; Gelächter n, Heiterkeit f

mer·ry lustig, fröhlich, ausgelassen; *Merry Christmas!* fröhliche or frohe Weihnachten

mer·ry-go-round Karussell n

mesh 1. Masche f; fig often pl Netz n, Schlingen pl; *be in ~* TECH (ineinander)greifen **2.** TECH (ineinander)greifen; fig passen (*with* zu), zusammenpassen

mess 1. Unordnung f, Durcheinander n; Schmutz m, F Schweinerei f; F Patsche f, Klemme f; MIL Messe f, Kasino n; *make a ~ of* F fig verpfuschen, ruinieren, *Pläne etc* über den Haufen werfen **2.** *~ about, ~ around* F herumspielen, herumbasteln (*with* an dat); herumgammeln; *~ up* in Unordnung bringen, durcheinanderbringen; fig F verpfuschen, ruinieren, *Pläne etc* über den Haufen werfen

mes·sage Mitteilung f, Nachricht f; Anliegen n, Aussage f; *can I take a ~?* kann ich etwas ausrichten?; *get the ~* F kapieren; **mes·sen·ger** Bote m

mess·y unordentlich; unsauber, schmutzig

me·tab·o·lis·m MED Stoffwechsel m

met·al Metall n

me·tal·lic metallisch; Metall…

met·a·mor·pho·sis Metamorphose f, Verwandlung f

met·a·phor Metapher f

me·tas·ta·sis MED Metastase f

me·te·or Meteor m

me·te·or·o·log·i·cal meteorologisch, Wetter…, Witterungs…; *~ of·fice* Wetteramt n

me·te·o·rol·o·gy Meteorologie f, Wetterkunde f

me·ter[1] TECH Messgerät n, Zähler m

me·ter[2] Meter m, n; Versmaß n

meth·od Methode f, Verfahren n; System n; **me·thod·i·cal** methodisch, systematisch, planmäßig

me·tic·u·lous peinlich genau, übergenau

me·tre Br → **meter[2]**

met·ric metrisch; *~ sys·tem* metrisches (Maß- und Gewichts)System

me·trop·o·lis Weltstadt f

met·ro·pol·i·tan … der Hauptstadt

met·tle Eifer m, Mut m, Feuer n

mew ZO miauen

Mex·i·can 1. mexikanisch **2.** Mexikaner(in)

Mex·i·co Mexiko n

mi·aow ZO miauen

mi·cro… Mikro…, (sehr) klein

mi·cro·chip Mikrochip m

mi·cro·e·lec·tron·ics Mikroelektronik f

mi·cro·film Mikrofilm m

mi·cro·or·gan·ism BIOL Mikroorganismus m

mi·cro·phone Mikrofon n

mi·cro·pro·ces·sor Mikroprozessor m

mi·cro·scope Mikroskop n

mi·cro·scop·ic mikroskopisch

mi·cro·wave Mikrowelle f; *~ ov·en* Mikrowellenherd m

mid mittlere(r, -s), Mitt(el)…

mid·air: *in ~* in der Luft

mid·day 1. Mittag m **2.** mittägig, Mittag(s)…

mid·dle 1. mittlere(r, -s), Mittel… **2.** Mitte f

mid·dle-aged mittleren Alters

Mid·dle Ag·es HIST Mittelalter n

mid·dle class(-es) Mittelstand m

mid·dle·man ECON Zwischenhändler m; Mittelsmann m

mid·dle name zweiter Vorname *m*
mid·dle-sized mittelgroß
mid·dle·weight *boxing:* Mittelgewicht *n*, Mittelgewichtler *m*
mid·dling F mittelmäßig, Mittel…; leidlich
mid·field *esp soccer:* Mittelfeld *n*
mid·field·er, mid·field play·er *esp soccer:* Mittelfeldspieler *m*
midge zo Mücke *f*
midg·et Zwerg *m*, Knirps *m*
mid·night Mitternacht *f*; *at ~* um Mitternacht
midst: in the ~ of mitten in (*dat*)
mid·sum·mer Hochsommer *m*; ASTR Sommersonnenwende *f*
mid·way auf halbem Wege
mid·wife Hebamme *f*
mid·win·ter Mitte *f* des Winters; ASTR Wintersonnenwende *f*; *in ~* mitten im Winter
might Macht *f*, Gewalt *f*; Kraft *f*
might·y mächtig, gewaltig
mi·grate (aus)wandern, (fort)ziehen (*a.* zo)
mi·gra·tion Wanderung *f* (*a.* zo)
mi·gra·to·ry Wander…; zo Zug…
mike F Mikrofon *n*
mild mild, sanft, leicht
mil·dew BOT Mehltau *m*
mild·ness Milde *f*
mile Meile *f* (*1,6 km*)
mile·age zurückgelegte Meilenzahl *or* Fahrtstrecke; Meilenstand *m*; *a. ~ al·lowance* Meilengeld *n, appr* Kilometergeld *n*
mile·stone Meilenstein *m* (*a. fig*)
mil·i·tant militant; streitbar, kriegerisch
mil·i·ta·ry 1. militärisch, Militär… **2.** *the ~* das Militär; *~ gov·ern·ment* Militärregierung *f*; *~ po·lice* (*abbr* **MP**) Militärpolizei *f*
mi·li·tia Miliz *f*, Bürgerwehr *f*
milk 1. Milch *f*; *it's no use crying over spilt ~* geschehen ist geschehen **2.** *v/t* melken; *v/i* Milch geben; *~ choc·o·late* Vollmilchschokolade *f*
milk·man Milchmann *m*
milk pow·der Milchpulver *n*, Trockenmilch *f*
milk shake Milchmixgetränk *n*
milk tooth ANAT Milchzahn *m*
milk·y milchig; Milch…
Milky Way ASTR Milchstraße *f*

mill 1. Mühle *f*; Fabrik *f* **2.** *Korn etc* mahlen; *Metall* verarbeiten; *Münze* rändeln
mil·le·pede → **millipede**
mill·er Müller *m*
mil·let BOT Hirse *f*
mil·li·ner Hutmacherin *f*, Putzmacherin *f*, Modistin *f*
mil·lion Million *f*
mil·lion·aire Millionär(in)
mil·lionth 1. millionste(r, -s) **2.** Millionstel *n*
mil·li·pede zo Tausendfüß(l)er *m*
mill·stone Mühlstein *m*; *be a ~ round s.o.'s neck* *fig* j-m ein Klotz am Bein sein
milt zo Milch *f*
mime 1. Pantomime *f*; Pantomime *m* **2.** (panto)mimisch darstellen; mim·ic **1.** mimisch; Schein… **2.** Imitator *m* **3.** nachahmen; nachäffen; **mim·ic·ry** Nachahmung *f*; zo Mimikry *f*
mince 1. *v/t* zerhacken, (zer)schneiden; *he does not ~ matters or his words* er nimmt kein Blatt vor den Mund; *v/i* tänzeln, trippeln **2.** *a. ~d meat* Hackfleisch *n*; **minc·er** Fleischwolf *m*
mind 1. Sinn *m*, Gemüt *n*, Herz *n*; Verstand *m*, Geist *m*; Ansicht *f*, Meinung *f*; Absicht *f*, Neigung *f*, Lust *f*; Erinnerung *f*, Gedächtnis *n*; *be out of one's ~* nicht (recht) bei Sinnen sein; *bear or keep in ~* (immer) denken an (*acc*), *et.* nicht vergessen; *change one's ~* es sich anders überlegen, s-e Meinung ändern; *enter s.o.'s ~* j-m in den Sinn kommen; *give s.o. a piece of one's ~* j-m gründlich die Meinung sagen; *have (half) a ~ to inf* (nicht übel) Lust haben zu *inf*; *lose one's ~* den Verstand verlieren; *make up one's ~* sich entschließen, e-n Entschluss fassen; *to my ~* meiner Ansicht nach **2.** *v/t* achtgeben auf (*acc*); sehen nach, aufpassen auf (*acc*); *et.* haben gegen; *~ the step!* Vorsicht, Stufe!; *~ your own business!* kümmere dich um deine eigenen Angelegenheiten!; *do you ~ if I smoke?, do you ~ my smoking?* haben Sie et. dagegen *or* stört es Sie, wenn ich rauche?; *would you ~ opening the window?* würden Sie bitte das Fenster öffnen?; *would you ~ coming* würden Sie bitte kommen?; *v/i* aufpassen; et. dage-

gen haben; **~ (you)** wohlgemerkt, allerdings; **never ~!** macht nichts!, ist schon gut!; **I don't ~** meinetwegen, von mir aus

mind·less gedankenlos, blind; unbekümmert (*of* um), ohne Rücksicht (*of* auf *acc*)

mine¹ meins; **that's ~** das gehört mir

mine² **1.** Bergwerk *n*, Mine *f*, Zeche *f*, Grube *f*; MIL Mine *f*; *fig* Fundgrube *f* **2.** *v/i* schürfen, graben (*for* nach); *v/t* Erz, Kohle abbauen; MIL verminen

min·er Bergmann *m*, Kumpel *m*

min·e·ral 1. Mineral *n*; *pl Br* Mineralwasser *n* **2.** Mineral...; **~ oil** Mineralöl *n*; **~ wa·ter** Mineralwasser *n*

min·gle *v/t* (ver)mischen; *v/i* sich mischen *or* mengen (**with** unter)

min·i... Mini..., Klein(st)...; → **miniskirt**

min·i·a·ture 1. Miniatur(gemälde *n*) *f* **2.** Miniatur...; Klein...; **~ cam·e·ra** Kleinbildkamera *f*

min·i·mize auf ein Mindestmaß herabsetzen; herunterspielen, bagatellisieren

min·i·mum 1. Minimum *n*, Mindestmaß *n* **2.** minimal, Mindest...

min·ing 1. Bergbau *m* **2.** Berg(bau)..., Bergwerks...; Gruben...

min·i·skirt Minirock *m*

min·is·ter POL Minister(in); Gesandte *m*; REL Geistliche *m*; **min·is·try** POL Ministerium *n*; REL geistliches Amt

mink ZO Nerz *m*

mi·nor 1. kleinere(r, -s), *fig a.* unbedeutend, geringfügig; JUR minderjährig; **A ~** MUS a-Moll *n*; **~ key** MUS Moll(tonart *f*) *n* **2.** JUR Minderjährige *m*, *f*; UNIV Nebenfach *n*; MUS Moll *n*; **mi·nor·i·ty** Minderheit *f*; JUR Minderjährigkeit *f*

min·ster *Br* Münster *n*

mint¹ **1.** Münze *f*, Münzanstalt *f* **2.** prägen

mint² BOT Minze *f*

min·u·et MUS Menuett *n*

mi·nus 1. *prp* minus, weniger; F ohne **2.** *adj* Minus... **3.** Minus *n*, *fig a.* Nachteil *m*

min·ute¹ Minute *f*; Augenblick *m*; **in a ~** sofort; **just a ~!** Moment mal!

mi·nute² winzig; sehr genau

min·utes Protokoll *n*; **take** (*or* **keep**) **the ~** (das) Protokoll führen

mir·a·cle Wunder *n*

mi·rac·u·lous wunderbar

mi·rac·u·lous·ly wie durch ein Wunder

mi·rage Luftspiegelung *f*, Fata Morgana *f*

mire Schlamm *m*; **drag through the ~** *fig* in den Schmutz ziehen

mir·ror 1. Spiegel *m* **2.** (wider)spiegeln (*a. fig*)

mis... miss..., falsch, schlecht

mis·ad·ven·ture Missgeschick *n*; Unglück *n*, Unglücksfall *m*

mis·an·thrope, **mis·an·thro·pist** Menschenfeind(in)

mis·ap·ply falsch an- *or* verwenden

mis·ap·pre·hend missverstehen

mis·ap·pro·pri·ate unterschlagen, veruntreuen

mis·be·have sich schlecht benehmen

mis·cal·cu·late falsch berechnen; sich verrechnen (in *dat*)

mis·car·riage MED Fehlgeburt *f*; Misslingen *n*, Fehlschlag(en *n*) *m*; **~ of justice** JUR Fehlurteil *n*

mis·car·ry MED e-e Fehlgeburt haben; misslingen, scheitern

mis·cel·la·ne·ous gemischt, vermischt; verschiedenartig

mis·cel·la·ny Gemisch *n*; Sammelband *m*

mis·chief Schaden *m*; Unfug *m*; Übermut *m*

mis·chie·vous boshaft, mutwillig; schelmisch

mis·con·ceive falsch auffassen, missverstehen

mis·con·duct schlechtes Benehmen; schlechte Führung; Verfehlung *f*

mis·con·strue falsch auslegen, missdeuten

mis·de·mea·no(u)r JUR Vergehen *n*

mis·di·rect fehlleiten, irreleiten; *Brief etc* falsch adressieren

mise-en-scène THEA Inszenierung *f*

mi·ser Geizhals *m*

mis·e·ra·ble erbärmlich, kläglich, elend; unglücklich

mi·ser·ly geizig, F knick(e)rig

mis·e·ry Elend *n*, Not *f*

mis·fire versagen (*gun*); MOT fehlzünden, aussetzen; *fig* danebengehen

mis·fit Außenseiter(in)

mis·for·tune Unglück *n*, Unglücksfall *m*; Missgeschick *n*

M

mis·giv·ing Befürchtung *f*, Zweifel *m*

mis·guid·ed irregeleitet, irrig, unangebracht

mis·hap Unglück *n*; Missgeschick *n*; *without* ~ ohne Zwischenfälle

mis·in·form falsch unterrichten

mis·in·ter·pret missdeuten, falsch auffassen *or* auslegen

mis·lay *et.* verlegen

mis·lead irreführen, täuschen; verleiten

mis·man·age schlecht verwalten *or* führen *or* handhaben

mis·place *et.* an e-e falsche Stelle legen *or* setzen; *et.* verlegen; ~*d fig* unangebracht, deplatziert

mis·print 1. verdrucken **2.** Druckfehler *m*

mis·read falsch lesen; falsch deuten; missdeuten

mis·rep·re·sent falsch darstellen; entstellen, verdrehen

miss 1. *v/t* verpassen, versäumen, verfehlen; übersehen, nicht bemerken; überhören; nicht verstehen *or* begreifen; vermissen; *a.* ~ *out* auslassen, übergehen, überspringen; *v/i* nicht treffen; missglücken; ~ *out on et.* verpassen **2.** Fehlschuss *m*, Fehlstoß *m*, Fehlwurf *m etc*; Verpassen *n*, Verfehlen *n*

Miss Fräulein *n*

mis·shap·en missgebildet

mis·sile 1. Geschoss *n*; Rakete *f* **2.** Raketen...

miss·ing fehlend; *be* ~ fehlen, verschwunden *or* weg sein; (MIL *a.* ~ *in action*) vermisst; *be* ~ MIL vermisst sein *or* werden

mis·sion (*Militär- etc*)Mission *f*; *esp* POL Auftrag *m*, Mission *f* (*a.* REL); MIL, AVIAT Einsatz *m*

mis·sion·a·ry REL Missionar *m*

mis·spell falsch buchstabieren *or* schreiben

mis·spend falsch verwenden; vergeuden

mist 1. (feiner *or* leichter) Nebel **2.** ~ *over* sich trüben; ~ *up* (sich) beschlagen

mis·take 1. verwechseln (*for* mit); verkennen, sich irren in (*dat*); falsch verstehen, missverstehen **2.** Irrtum *m*, Versehen *n*, Fehler *m*; *by* ~ aus Versehen, irrtümlich; **mis·tak·en** irrig,

falsch (verstanden); *be* ~ sich irren

mis·tle·toe BOT Mistel *f*

mis·tress Herrin *f*; *esp Br* Lehrerin *f*; Geliebte *f*

mis·trust 1. misstrauen (*dat*) **2.** Misstrauen *n* (*of* gegen)

mis·trust·ful misstrauisch

mist·y (leicht) neb(e)lig; *fig* unklar, verschwommen

mis·un·der·stand missverstehen; *j-n* nicht verstehen; **mis·un·der·standing** Missverständnis *n*

mis·use 1. missbrauchen; falsch gebrauchen **2.** Missbrauch *m*

mite ZO Milbe *f*; kleines Ding, Würmchen *n*; *a* ~ F ein bisschen

mi·ter, *Br* **mi·tre** REL Mitra *f*, Bischofsmütze *f*

mitt *baseball*: Fanghandschuh *m*; → **mitten** Fausthandschuh *m*

mix 1. (ver)mischen, vermengen; *Getränke* mixen; sich (ver)mischen; sich mischen lassen; verkehren (*with* mit); ~ *well* kontaktfreudig sein; ~ *up* zusammenmischen, durcheinander mischen; (völlig) durcheinanderbringen; verwechseln (*with* mit); *be* ~*ed up* verwickelt sein *or* werden (*in* in *acc*); (*geistig*) ganz durcheinander sein **2.** Mischung *f*

mixed gemischt (*a. fig*); vermischt, Misch...

mix·er Mixer *m*; TECH Mischmaschine *f*; *radio*, TV *etc*: Mischpult *n*

mix·ture Mischung *f*; Gemisch *n*

mix-up F Verwechs(e)lung *f*

moan 1. Stöhnen *n* **2.** stöhnen

moat (Burg-, Stadt)Graben *m*

mob 1. Mob *m*, Pöbel *m* **2.** herfallen über (*acc*); *j-n* bedrängen, belagern

mo·bile 1. beweglich; MIL mobil, motorisiert; *fig* lebhaft **2.** → *mobile phone or telephone*; ~ *home* Wohnwagen *m*; ~ *phone*, ~ *tel·e·phone* Mobiltelefon *n*, Handy *n*

mo·bil·ize mobilisieren, MIL *a.* mobil machen

moc·ca·sin Mokassin *m*

mock 1. *v/t* verspotten; nachäffen; *v/i* sich lustig machen, spotten (*at* über *acc*); **2.** nachgemacht, Schein...

mock·e·ry Spott *m*, Hohn *m*; Gespött *n*

mock·ing·bird ZO Spottdrossel *f*

mode (Art *f* und) Weise *f*; IT Modus *m*,

Betriebsart *f*

mod·el 1. Modell *n*; Muster *n*; Vorbild *n*; Mannequin *n*; Model *n*, (Foto)Modell *n*; TECH Modell *n*, Typ *m*; *male* ~ Dressman *m* **2.** Modell…, Muster… **3.** *v/t* modellieren, *a. fig* formen; *Kleider etc* vorführen; *v/i* Modell stehen *or* sitzen; als Mannequin *or* (Foto)Modell *or* Dressman arbeiten

mo·dem IT Modem *m*, *n*

mod·e·rate 1. (mittel)mäßig; gemäßigt; vernünftig, angemessen **2.** (sich) mäßigen

mod·e·ra·tion Mäßigung *f*

mod·ern modern, neu

mod·ern·ize modernisieren

mod·est bescheiden

mod·es·ty Bescheidenheit *f*

mod·i·fi·ca·tion (Ab-, Ver)Änderung *f*

mod·i·fy (ab-, ver)ändern

mod·u·late modulieren

mod·ule TECH Modul *n*, ELECTR *a.* Baustein *m*; (*Kommando- etc*)Kapsel *f*

moist feucht

moist·en *v/t* anfeuchten, befeuchten; *v/i* feucht werden

mois·ture Feuchtigkeit *f*

mo·lar ANAT Backenzahn *m*

mo·las·ses Sirup *m*

mold¹ Schimmel *m*; Moder *m*; Humus (-boden) *m*

mold² TECH **1.** (Gieß-, Guss-, Press-) Form *f* **2.** gießen; formen

mol·der *a.* ~ *away* vermodern; zerfallen

mold·y verschimmelt, schimm(e)lig; mod(e)rig

mole¹ ZO Maulwurf *m*

mole² Muttermal *n*, Leberfleck *m*

mole³ Mole *f*, Hafendamm *m*

mol·e·cule Molekül *n*

mole·hill Maulwurfshügel *m*; *make a mountain out of a* ~ aus e-r Mücke e-n Elefanten machen

mo·lest belästigen

mol·li·fy besänftigen, beschwichtigen

mol·lusc *Br*, **mol·lusk** ZO Weichtier *n*

mol·ly·cod·dle F verhätscheln, verzärteln

molt (sich) mausern; *Haare* verlieren

mol·ten geschmolzen

mom F Mami *f*, Mutti *f*

mom-and-pop store Tante-Emma-Laden *m*

mo·ment Moment *m*, Augenblick *m*;

Bedeutung *f*; PHYS Moment *n*

mo·men·ta·ry momentan, augenblicklich

mo·men·tous bedeutsam, folgenschwer

mo·men·tum PHYS Moment *n*; Schwung *m*

Mon *abbr of* **Monday** Mo., Montag *m*

mon·arch Monarch(in), Herrscher(in)

mon·ar·chy Monarchie *f*

mon·as·tery REL (Mönchs)Kloster *n*

Mon·day (*abbr* **Mon**) Montag *m*; *on* ~ (am) Montag; *on* ~*s* montags

mon·e·ta·ry ECON Währungs…; Geld…

mon·ey Geld *n*

mon·ey·box *Br* Sparbüchse *f*

mon·ey·chang·er (Geld)Wechsler *m*; TECH Wechselautomat *m*

mon·ey or·der Post- *or* Zahlungsanweisung *f*

mon·grel ZO Bastard *m*, *esp* Promadenmischung *f*

mon·i·tor 1. Monitor *m*; Kontrollgerät *n*, -schirm *m* **2.** abhören; überwachen

monk REL Mönch *m*

mon·key 1. ZO Affe *m*; F (kleiner) Schlingel; *make a* ~ *(out) of s.o.* F j-n zum Deppen machen **2.** ~ *about*, ~ *around* F (herum)albern; ~ *about or around with* F herumspielen mit *or* an (*dat*) herummurksen an (*dat*); ~ *wrench* TECH Engländer *m*, Franzose *m*; *throw a* ~ *into s.th.* F et. behindern

mon·o 1. Mono *n*; F Monogerät *n* **2.** Mono…

mon·o… ein…, mono…

mon·o·log, *esp Br* **mon·o·logue** Monolog *m*

mo·nop·o·lize monopolisieren; *fig* an sich reißen

mo·nop·o·ly Monopol *n* (*of* auf *acc*)

mo·not·o·nous monoton, eintönig

mo·not·o·ny Monotonie *f*

mon·soon Monsun *m*

mon·ster 1. Monster *n*, Ungeheuer *n* (*a. fig*); Monstrum *n* **2.** Riesen…

mon·stros·i·ty Ungeheuerlichkeit *f*; Monstrum *n*; **mon·strous** ungeheuer; *mst contp* ungeheuerlich; scheußlich

month Monat *m*; **month·ly 1.** monatlich, Monats… **2.** Monatsschrift *f*

mon·u·ment Monument *n*, Denkmal *n*

mon·u·ment·al monumental; F kolossal, Riesen…; Gedenk…

moo ZO muhen

M

mooch F schnorren

mood Stimmung f, Laune f; **be in a good** (**bad**) ~ gute (schlechte) Laune haben, gut (schlecht) aufgelegt sein

mood·y launisch; schlecht gelaunt

moon 1. ASTR Mond m 2. ~ **about, ~ around** F herumtrödeln; F ziellos herumstreichen

moon·light Mondlicht n, -schein m

moon·lit mondhell

moor[1] (Hoch)Moor n

moor[2] MAR vertäuen, festmachen

moor·ings MAR Vertäuung f; Liegeplatz m

moose ZO nordamerikanischer Elch

mop 1. Mopp m; F (Haar)Wust m 2. wischen; ~ **up** aufwischen

mope Trübsal blasen

mo·ped Br MOT Moped n

mor·al 1. moralisch; Moral…, Sitten… 2. Moral f, Lehre f; pl Moral f, Sitten pl

mo·rale Moral f, Stimmung f

mor·al·ize moralisieren (**about, on** über acc)

mor·bid morbid, krankhaft

more 1. adj mehr; noch (mehr); **some ~ tea** noch etwas Tee 2. adv mehr; noch; ~ **and** ~ immer mehr; ~ **or less** mehr oder weniger; **once** ~ noch einmal; **the ~ so because** umso mehr, da; ~ **important** wichtiger; ~ **often** öfter 3. Mehr n (**of** an dat); **a little** ~ etwas mehr

mo·rel BOT Morchel f

more·o·ver außerdem, weiter, ferner

morgue Leichenschauhaus n; F (Zeitungs)Archiv n

morn·ing Morgen m; Vormittag m; **good** ~! guten Morgen!; **in the** ~ morgens, am Morgen; vormittags, am Vormittag; **tomorrow** ~ morgen früh or Vormittag

mo·rose mürrisch, verdrießlich

mor·phi·a, mor·phine PHARM Morphium n

mor·sel Bissen m, Happen m; **a** ~ **of** ein bisschen

mor·tal 1. sterblich; tödlich; Tod(es)… 2. Sterbliche m, f

mor·tal·i·ty Sterblichkeit f

mor·tar[1] Mörtel m

mor·tar[2] Mörser m

mort·gage 1. Hypothek f 2. mit e-r Hypothek belasten, e-e Hypothek aufnehmen auf (acc)

mor·ti·cian Leichenbestatter m

mor·ti·fi·ca·tion Kränkung f; Ärger m, Verdruss m

mor·ti·fy kränken; ärgern, verdrießen

mor·tu·a·ry Leichenhalle f

mo·sa·ic Mosaik n

Mos·lem → **Muslim**

mosque Moschee f

mos·qui·to ZO Moskito m; Stechmücke f

moss BOT Moos n

moss·y BOT moosig, bemoost

most 1. adj meiste(r, -s), größte(r, -s); die meisten; ~ **people** die meisten Leute 2. adv am meisten; ~ **of all** am allermeisten; before adj: höchst, äußerst; **the** ~ **important point** der wichtigste Punkt 3. das meiste, das Höchste; das meiste, der größte Teil; die meisten pl; **at** (**the**) ~ höchstens; **make the** ~ **of** et. nach Kräften ausnutzen, das Beste herausholen aus

most·ly hauptsächlich, meist(ens)

mo·tel Motel n

moth ZO Motte f

moth-eat·en mottenzerfressen

moth·er 1. Mutter f 2. bemuttern

moth·er coun·try Vaterland n, Heimatland n; Mutterland n

moth·er·hood Mutterschaft f

moth·er-in-law Schwiegermutter f

moth·er·ly mütterlich

moth·er-of-pearl Perlmutter f, n, Perlmutt n

moth·er tongue Muttersprache f

mo·tif Motiv n

mo·tion 1. Bewegung f; PARL Antrag m; **in quick** ~ **film**: im Zeitraffer; **in slow** ~ **film**: in Zeitlupe; **put** or **set in** ~ in Gang bringen (a. fig), in Bewegung setzen 2. v/t j-n durch e-n Wink auffordern, j-m ein Zeichen geben; v/i winken

mo·tion·less bewegungslos, unbeweglich

mo·tion pic·ture Film m

mo·ti·vate motivieren, anspornen

mo·ti·va·tion Motivation f, Ansporn m

mo·tive 1. Motiv n, Beweggrund m 2. treibend (a. fig)

mot·ley bunt

mo·to·cross SPORT Motocross m

mo·tor 1. Motor m, fig a. treibende Kraft 2. Motor…

mo·tor·bike Moped n; Br F Motorrad n

mo·tor·boat Motorboot n

mo·tor·cade Auto-, Wagenkolonne f

mo·tor·car Br Kraftfahrzeug n

mo·tor car·a·van Br Wohnmobil n

mo·tor·cy·cle Motorrad n

mo·tor·cy·clist Motorradfahrer(in)

mo·tor home Wohnmobil n

mo·tor·ing Autofahren n; *school of ~* Fahrschule f

mo·tor·ist Autofahrer(in)

mo·tor·ize motorisieren

mo·tor launch Motorbarkasse f

mo·tor·way Br Autobahn f

mot·tled gefleckt, gesprenkelt

mould[1] Br → **mold**[1]

mould[2] Br → **mold**[2]

moul·der Br → **molder**

mould·y Br → **moldy**

moult Br → **molt**

mound Erdhügel m, Erdwall m

mount 1. v/t Pferd etc besteigen, steigen auf (acc); montieren; anbringen, befestigen; Bild etc aufziehen, aufkleben; Edelstein fassen; *~ed police* berittene Polizei; v/i aufsitzen (rider); steigen, fig a. (an)wachsen; *~ up to* sich belaufen auf (acc) 2. Gestell n; Fassung f; Reittier n, Reitpferd n

moun·tain 1. Berg m, pl a. Gebirge n 2. Berg..., Gebirgs...

moun·tain bike Mountainbike n

moun·tain·eer Bergsteiger(in)

moun·tain·eer·ing Bergsteigen n

moun·tain·ous bergig, gebirgig

mourn v/i trauern (*for, over* um); v/t betrauern, trauern um

mourn·er Trauernde m, f

mourn·ful traurig

mourn·ing Trauer f; Trauerkleidung f

mouse zo Maus f (a. IT)

mous·tache → **mustache**

mouth Mund m; zo Maul n, Schnauze f; GEOGR Mündung f; Öffnung f

mouth·ful ein Mundvoll; Bissen m

mouth or·gan F Mundharmonika f

mouth·piece Mundstück n; fig Sprachrohr n

mouth·wash Mundwasser n

mo·va·ble beweglich

move 1. v/t (weg)rücken; transportieren; bewegen, rühren (both a. fig); chess etc: e-n Zug machen mit; PARL beantragen; *~ house* umziehen; *~ heav-*

en and earth Himmel und Hölle in Bewegung setzen; v/i sich (fort)bewegen; sich rühren; umziehen (**to** nach); chess etc: e-n Zug machen; *~ away* weg-, fortziehen; *~ in* einziehen; *~ off* sich in Bewegung setzen; *~ on* weitergehen; *~ out* ausziehen 2. Bewegung f; Umzug m; chess etc: Zug m; fig Schritt m; *on the ~* in Bewegung; auf den Beinen; *get a ~ on!* F Tempo!, mach(t) schon!, los!

move·a·ble → **movable**

move·ment Bewegung f (a. fig); MUS Satz m; TECH Werk n

mov·ie 1. Film m; Kino n 2. Film..., Kino...; *~ cam·e·ra* Filmkamera f; *~ star* Filmstar m; *~ thea·ter* Kino n

mov·ing sich bewegend, beweglich; fig rührend; *~ stair·case* Rolltreppe f; *~ van* Möbelwagen m

mow mähen

mow·er Mähmaschine f, esp Rasenmäher m

MP3 player MP3-Player m

Mr. abbr of **Mister** Herr m

Mrs. Frau f

Ms. Frau f

much 1. adj viel 2. adv sehr; viel; *~ bet·ter* viel besser; *very ~* sehr; *I thought as ~* das habe ich mir gedacht 3. große Sache; *nothing ~* nichts Besonderes; *make ~ of* viel Wesens machen von; *think ~ of* viel halten von; *I am not ~ of a dancer* F ich bin kein großer Tänzer

M

muck F Br AGR Mist m, Dung m; fig Dreck m, Schmutz m; F contp Fraß m

mu·cus (Nasen)Schleim m

mud Schlamm m, Matsch m; Schmutz m (a. fig)

mud·dle 1. Durcheinander n; *be in a ~* durcheinander sein 2. a. *~ up* durcheinanderbringen; *~ through* F sich durchwursteln

mud·dy schlammig, trüb; schmutzig; fig wirr

mud·guard Kotflügel m; Schutzblech n

mues·li Müsli n

muff Muff m

muf·fle Ton etc dämpfen; often *~ up* einhüllen, einwickeln

muf·fler (dicker) Schal; MOT Auspufftopf m

mug[1] Krug m; Becher m; große Tasse; F

Visage *f*; V Fresse *f*

mug² F überfallen und ausrauben

mug·ger F (Straßen)Räuber *m*

mug·ging F Raubüberfall *m, esp* Straßenraub *m*

mug·gy schwül

mul·ber·ry ʙᴏᴛ Maulbeerbaum *m*; Maulbeere *f*

mule ᴢᴏ Maultier *n*; Maulesel *m*

mulled: ~ **wine** Glühwein *m*

mul·li·on ᴀʀᴄʜ Mittelpfosten *m*

mul·ti... viel..., mehr..., Mehrfach..., Multi...

mul·ti·cul·tur·al multikulturell

mul·ti·far·i·ous mannigfaltig, vielfältig

mul·ti·lat·er·al vielseitig; ᴘᴏʟ multilateral, mehrseitig

mul·ti·me·di·a multimedial

mul·ti·na·tion·al ᴇᴄᴏɴ multinationaler Konzern, F Multi *m*

mul·ti·ple 1. vielfach, mehrfach 2. ᴍᴀᴛʜ Vielfache *n*

mul·ti·pli·ca·tion Vermehrung *f*; ᴍᴀᴛʜ Multiplikation *f*; ~ **table** Einmaleins *n*

mul·ti·plic·i·ty Vielfalt *f*; Vielzahl *f*

mul·ti·ply (sich) vermehren, (sich) vervielfachen; ᴍᴀᴛʜ multiplizieren, malnehmen (**by** mit)

mul·ti·pur·pose Mehrzweck...

mul·ti·sto·rey *Br* mehrstöckig; ~ **car park** *Br* Park(hoch)haus *n*

mul·ti·tude Vielzahl *f*

mul·ti·tu·di·nous zahlreich

mum¹ *Br* F Mami *f*, Mutti *f*

mum² 1. *int:* ~ **'s the word** Mund halten!, kein Wort darüber! 2. *adj:* **keep** ~ nichts verraten, den Mund halten

mum·ble murmeln, F nuscheln; mümmeln

mum·mi·fy mumifizieren

mum·my¹ Mumie *f*

mum·my² *Br* F Mami *f*, Mutti *f*

mumps ᴍᴇᴅ Ziegenpeter *m*, Mumps *m*

munch mampfen

mun·dane alltäglich; weltlich

mu·nic·i·pal städtisch, Stadt..., kommunal, Gemeinde...; ~ **council** Stadt-, Gemeinderat *m*

mu·nic·i·pal·i·ty Kommunalbehörde *f*; Stadtverwaltung *f*

mu·ral Wandgemälde *n*

mur·der 1. Mord *m*, Ermordung *f* 2. Mord... 3. ermorden; F verschandeln

mur·der·er Mörder *m*

mur·der·ess Mörderin *f*

mur·der·ous mörderisch

murk·y dunkel, finster

mur·mur 1. Murmeln *n*; Gemurmel *n*; Murren *n* 2. murmeln; murren

mus·cle Muskel *m*

mus·cu·lar Muskel...; muskulös

muse¹ (nach)sinnen, (nach)grübeln (**on, over** über *acc*)

muse² *a.* **Muse** Muse *f*

mu·se·um Museum *n*

mush Brei *m*, Mus *n*; Maisbrei *m*

mush·room 1. ʙᴏᴛ Pilz *m, esp* Champignon *m* 2. rasch wachsen; ~ **up** *fig* (wie Pilze) aus dem Boden schießen

mu·sic Musik *f*; Noten *pl*; **put** *or* **set to** ~ vertonen

mu·si·cal 1. musikalisch; Musik... 2. Musical *n*; ~ **box** *esp Br* Spieldose *f*; ~ **in·stru·ment** Musikinstrument *n*

mu·sic| **box** Spieldose *f*; ~ **cen·ter** (*Br* **cen·tre**) Kompaktanlage *f*; ~ **hall** *Br* Varieté(theater) *n*

mu·si·cian Musiker(in)

mu·sic **stand** Notenständer *m*

musk Moschus *m*

musk·rat ᴢᴏ Bisamratte *f*; Bisampelz *m*

Mus·lim 1. Muslim *m*, Moslem *m* 2. muslimisch, moslemisch

mus·sel ᴢᴏ (Mies)Muschel *f*

must¹ *v/aux* ich muss, *du* musst *etc;* **you** ~ **not** (F **mustn't**) du darfst nicht 2. Muss *n*

must² Most *m*

mus·tache Schnurrbart *m*

mus·tard Senf *m*

mus·ter 1. ~ **up** *s-e* Kraft *etc* aufbieten; *s-n* Mut zusammennehmen 2. **pass** ~ *fig* Zustimmung finden (**with** bei); den Anforderungen genügen

must·y mod(e)rig, muffig

mu·ta·tion Veränderung *f*; ʙɪᴏʟ Mutation *f*

mute 1. stumm 2. Stumme *m, f*; ᴍᴜꜱ Dämpfer *m*

mu·ti·late verstümmeln

mu·ti·la·tion Verstümmelung *f*

mu·ti·neer Meuterer *m*

mu·ti·nous meuternd; rebellisch

mu·ti·ny 1. Meuterei *f* 2. meutern

mut·ter 1. murmeln; murren 2. Murmeln *n*; Murren *n*

mut·ton ɢᴀꜱᴛʀ Hammel-, Schaffleisch *n*; **leg of** ~ Hammelkeule *f*

mut·ton chop GASTR Hammelkotelett n
mu·tu·al gegenseitig; gemeinsam
muz·zle 1. ZO Maul n, Schnauze f; Mündung f (of a gun); Maulkorb m **2.** e-n Maulkorb anlegen (dat), fig a. j-n mundtot machen
my mein(e)
myrrh BOT Myrrhe f
myr·tle BOT Myrte f
my·self ich, mich or mir selbst; mich; mich (selbst); **by ~** allein

mys·te·ri·ous rätselhaft, unerklärlich; geheimnisvoll, mysteriös
mys·te·ry Geheimnis n, Rätsel n; REL Mysterium n; **~ tour** Fahrt f ins Blaue
mys·tic 1. Mystiker(in) **2.** → **mystic·al** mystisch
mys·ti·fy verwirren, vor ein Rätsel stellen; **be mystified** vor e-m Rätsel stehen
myth Mythos m, Sage f
my·thol·o·gy Mythologie f

N

N, n N, n n
nab F schnappen, erwischen
na·dir ASTR Nadir m; fig Tiefpunkt m
nag¹ 1. nörgeln; **~ (at)** herumnörgeln an (dat) **2.** Nörgler(in)
nag² F Gaul m, Klepper m
nail 1. ANAT, TECH Nagel m **2.** (an-)nageln (**to** an acc); **~ pol·ish** Nagellack m; **~ scis·sors** Nagelschere f; **~ var·nish** Br Nagellack m
na·ive, na·ïve naiv (a. art)
na·ked nackt, bloß; kahl; fig ungeschminkt; **nak·ed·ness** Nacktheit f
name 1. Name m; Ruf m; **by ~** mit Namen, namentlich; **by the ~ of ...** namens ...; **what's your ~?** wie heißen Sie?; **call s.o. ~s** j-n beschimpfen **2.** (be)nennen; erwähnen; ernennen zu
name·less namenlos; unbekannt
name·ly nämlich
name·plate Namens-, Tür-, Firmenschild n
name·sake Namensvetter m, Namensschwester f
name tag Namensschild n
nan·ny Kindermädchen n
nan·ny goat ZO Geiß f, Ziege f
nap 1. Schläfchen n; **have** or **take a ~** → **2.** ein Nickerchen machen
nape mst **~ of the neck** ANAT Genick n, Nacken m
nap·kin Serviette f
nap·py Br Windel f
nar·co·sis MED Narkose f
nar·cot·ic 1. narkotisch, betäubend, einschläfernd; Rauschgift...; **~ addiction** Rauschgiftsucht f **2.** Narkotikum n,

Betäubungsmittel n; often pl Rauschgift n; **~s squad** Rauschgiftdezernat n
nar·rate erzählen; berichten, schildern
nar·ra·tion Erzählung f
nar·ra·tive 1. Erzählung f; Bericht m, Schilderung f **2.** erzählend
nar·ra·tor Erzähler(in)
nar·row 1. eng, schmal; beschränkt; knapp **2.** enger or schmäler werden or machen, (sich) verengen; beschränken, einschränken; **nar·row·ly** mit knapper Not; **nar·row-mind·ed** engstirnig, beschränkt; **nar·row·ness** Enge f; Beschränktheit f
na·sal nasal; Nasen...
nas·ty ekelhaft, eklig, widerlich (smell, sight etc); abscheulich (weather etc); böse, schlimm (accident etc); hässlich (character, behavior etc); gemein, fies; schmutzig, zotig (language)
na·tal Geburts...
na·tion Nation f, Volk n
na·tion·al 1. national, National..., Landes..., Volks... **2.** Staatsangehörige m, f; **~ an·them** Nationalhymne f
na·tion·al·i·ty Nationalität f, Staatsangehörigkeit f
na·tion·al·ize ECON verstaatlichen
na·tion·al| park Nationalpark m; **~ so·cial·ism** HIST POL Nationalsozialismus m; **~ so·cial·ist** HIST POL Nationalsozialist m; **~ team** SPORT Nationalmannschaft f
na·tion-wide landesweit
na·tive 1. einheimisch, Landes...; heimatlich, Heimat...; eingeboren, Eingeborenen...; angeboren **2.** Eingebo-

rene *m*, *f*; Einheimische *m*, *f*; ~ language Muttersprache *f*; ~ speak·er Muttersprachler(in)

Na·tiv·i·ty REL die Geburt Christi

nat·ty F schick, *Austrian* fesch

nat·u·ral natürlich; angeboren; Natur...; ~ gas Erdgas *n*

nat·u·ral·ize naturalisieren, einbürgern

nat·u·ral·ly natürlich; von Natur (aus)

nat·u·ral| re·sourc·es Boden- u. Naturschätze *pl*; ~ sci·ence Naturwissenschaft *f*

na·ture Natur *f*; ~ con·ser·va·tion Naturschutz *m*; ~ re·serve Naturschutzgebiet *n*; ~ trail Naturlehrpfad *m*

naugh·ty unartig; unanständig

nau·se·a Übelkeit *f*, Brechreiz *m*

nau·se·ate: ~ s.o. j-m Übelkeit verursachen; *fig* j-n anwidern

nau·se·at·ing ekelerregend, widerlich

nau·ti·cal nautisch, See...

na·val MIL Flotten..., Marine...; See...; ~ base MIL Flottenstützpunkt *m*; ~ officer MIL Marineoffizier *m*; ~ pow·er MIL Seemacht *f*

nave ARCH Mittel-, Hauptschiff *n*

na·vel ANAT Nabel *m* (*a. fig*)

nav·i·ga·ble schiffbar

nav·i·gate MAR befahren; AVIAT, MAR steuern, lenken

nav·i·ga·tion Schifffahrt *f*; AVIAT, MAR Navigation *f*

nav·i·ga·tor AVIAT, MAR Navigator *m*

na·vy (Kriegs)Marine *f*; Kriegsflotte *f*

na·vy blue Marineblau *n*

nay PARL Gegen-, Neinstimme *f*

Na·zi HIST POL *contp* Nazi *m*

Na·zism HIST POL *contp* Nazismus *m*

near 1. *adj* nahe; kurz; nahe (verwandt); *in the ~ future* in naher Zukunft; *be a ~ miss* knapp scheitern 2. *adv* nahe, in der Nähe (*a.* ~ *at hand*); nahe (bevorstehend) (*a.* ~ *at hand*); ~ *the station etc* in der Nähe des Bahnhofs *etc*; ~ *you* in deiner Nähe 3. *prp* nahe (*dat*), in der Nähe von (*or gen*) 4. sich nähern, näher kommen (*dat*)

near·by 1. *adj* nahe (gelegen) 2. *adv* in der Nähe

near·ly beinahe, fast; annähernd

near·sight·ed kurzsichtig

neat ordentlich; sauber; gepflegt; pur (*whisky etc*)

neb·u·lous verschwommen

ne·ces·sar·i·ly notwendigerweise; *not ~* nicht unbedingt

ne·ces·sa·ry notwendig, nötig; unvermeidlich

ne·ces·si·tate *et.* erfordern, verlangen

ne·ces·si·ty Notwendigkeit *f*; (dringendes) Bedürfnis; Not *f*

neck 1. ANAT Hals *m* (*a. of bottle etc*); Genick *n*, Nacken *m*; *be ~ and ~* F Kopf an Kopf liegen (*a. fig*); *be up to one's ~ in debt* F bis zum Hals in Schulden stecken 2. F knutschen, schmusen

neck·er·chief Halstuch *n*

neck·lace Halskette *f*

neck·let Halskettchen *n*

neck·line Ausschnitt *m*

neck·tie Krawatte *f*, Schlips *m*

née: ~ *Smith* geborene Smith

need 1. (*of, for*) (dringendes) Bedürfnis (nach), Bedarf *m* (an *dat*); Notwendigkeit *f*; Mangel *m* (*of, for* an *dat*); Not *f*; *be in ~ of s.th.* *et.* dringend brauchen; *in ~* in Not; *in ~ of help* hilfs-, hilfebedürftig 2. *v/t* benötigen, brauchen; *v/aux* brauchen, müssen

nee·dle 1. Nadel *f* (*a.* BOT, MED); Zeiger *m* 2. F *j-n* aufziehen, hänseln

need·less unnötig, überflüssig

nee·dle·wom·an Näherin *f*

nee·dle·work Handarbeit *f*

need·y bedürftig, arm

ne·ga·tion Verneinung *f*

neg·a·tive 1. negativ; verneinend 2. Verneinung *f*; PHOT Negativ *n*; *answer in the ~* verneinen

ne·glect 1. vernachlässigen; es versäumen (*doing, to do* zu tun); 2. Vernachlässigung *f*; Nachlässigkeit *f*

neg·li·gence Nachlässigkeit *f*, Unachtsamkeit *f*; neg·li·gent nachlässig, unachtsam; lässig, salopp

neg·li·gi·ble unbedeutend

ne·go·ti·ate verhandeln (über *acc*)

ne·go·ti·a·tion Verhandlung *f*

ne·go·ti·a·tor Unterhändler(in)

neigh zo 1. wiehern 2. Wiehern *n*

neigh·bo(u)r Nachbar(in)

neigh·bo(u)r·hood Nachbarschaft *f*, Umgebung *f*

neigh·bo(u)r·ing benachbart, Nachbar..., angrenzend

neigh·bo(u)r·ly (gut)nachbarlich

nei·ther 1. *adj and pron* keine(r, -s) (von beiden) 2. *cj* ~ *...* nor weder ... noch ne·on CHEM Neon *n*; ~ lamp Neonlampe *f*; ~ sign Neon-, Leuchtreklame *f*

neph·ew Neffe *m*

nep·o·tism *contp* Vetternwirtschaft *f*

nerd F Trottel *m*; Computerfreak *m*

nerve Nerv *m*; Mut *m*, Stärke *f*, Selbstbeherrschung *f*; F Frechheit *f*; **get on s.o.'s ~ s ~s** j-m auf die Nerven gehen *or* fallen; **lose one's ~** den Mut *or* die Nerven verlieren; **you've got a ~!** F Sie haben Nerven!; nerve·less kraftlos; mutlos; ohne Nerven, kaltblütig

ner·vous nervös; Nerven...

ner·vous·ness Nervosität *f*

nest 1. Nest *n* 2. nisten

nes·tle (sich) schmiegen *or* kuscheln (**against, on** *an acc*); *a.* ~ **down** sich behaglich niederlassen, es sich bequem machen (**in** *in dat*)

net[1] 1. Netz *n*; ~ **curtain** Store *m* 2. mit e-m Netz fangen *or* abdecken

net[2] 1. netto, Netto..., Rein... 2. netto einbringen

Neth·er·lands die Niederlande *pl*

net·tle 1. BOT Nessel *f* 2. F j-n ärgern

net·work Netz *n* (*a.* IT), Netzwerk *n*; (*Straßen- etc*)Netz *n*; *radio*, TV Sendernetz *n*; **be in the ~** IT am Netz sein

neu·ro·sis MED Neurose *f*; neu·rot·ic MED 1. neurotisch 2. Neurotiker(in)

neu·ter 1. LING sächlich; geschlechtslos 2. LING Neutrum *n*

neu·tral 1. neutral 2. Neutrale *m*, *f*; *a.* ~ **gear** MOT Leerlauf(stellung *f*) *m*

neu·tral·i·ty Neutralität *f*

neu·tral·ize neutralisieren

neu·tron PHYS Neutron *n*

nev·er nie, niemals; nev·er-end·ing endlos, nicht enden wollend, unendlich

nev·er·the·less nichtsdestoweniger, dennoch, trotzdem

new neu; frisch; unerfahren; **nothing ~** nichts Neues

new·born neugeboren

new·com·er Neuankömmling *m*; Neuling *m*

new·ly kürzlich; neu

news Neuigkeit(en *pl*) *f*, Nachricht(en *pl*) *f*

news·a·gent Zeitungshändler(in)

news·boy Zeitungsjunge *m*, Zeitungsausträger *m*

news bul·le·tin Kurznachricht(en *pl*) *f*

news·cast *radio*, TV Nachrichtensendung *f*; news·cast·er *radio*, TV Nachrichtensprecher(in)

news deal·er Zeitungshändler(in)

news·flash *radio*, TV Kurzmeldung *f*

news·let·ter Rundschreiben *n*

news·pa·per Zeitung *f*

news·print Zeitungspapier *n*

news·read·er *esp Br* → **newscaster**

news·reel *film*: Wochenschau *f*

news·room Nachrichtenredaktion *f*

news·stand Zeitungskiosk *m*, -stand *m*

news·ven·dor *esp Br* Zeitungsverkäufer(in)

new year Neujahr *n*, *das* neue Jahr; **New Year's Day** Neujahrstag *m*; **New Year's Eve** Silvester(abend *m*) *m*, *n*

next 1. *adj* nächste(r, -s); (**the**) ~ **day** am nächsten Tag; ~ **door** nebenan; ~ **but one** übernächste(r, -s); ~ **to** gleich neben *or* nach; beinahe, fast *unmöglich etc* 2. *adv* als Nächste(r, -s); demnächst, das nächste Mal 3. *der*, *die*, *das* Nächste; → **kin**

next-door *adj* nebenan

nib·ble *v/i* knabbern (**at** *an dat*); *v/t* Loch *etc* nagen, knabbern (**in** *in acc*)

nice nett, freundlich; hübsch, schön; *fig* fein (*detail etc*)

nice·ly gut, fein; genau, sorgfältig

ni·ce·ty Feinheit *f*; Genauigkeit *f*

niche Nische *f*

nick 1. Kerbe *f* 2. (ein)kerben; *j-n* streifen (*bullet*); *Br* F *et.* klauen; *Br* F *j-n* schnappen

nick·el 1. MIN Nickel *n*; Fünfcentstück *n* 2. TECH vernickeln

nick·el-plate TECH vernickeln

nick-nack → **knick-knack**

nick·name 1. Spitzname *m* 2. *j-m* den Spitznamen ... geben

niece Nichte *f*

nig·gard Geizhals *m*

nig·gard·ly geizig, knaus(e)rig; schäbig, kümmerlich

night Nacht *f*; Abend *m*; **at ~, by ~, in the ~** in der Nacht, nachts

night·cap Schlummertrunk *m*

night·club Nachtklub *m*, Nachtlokal *n*

night·dress (Damen-, Kinder)Nachthemd *n*

night·fall: **at ~** bei Einbruch der Dunkelheit

night·gown → **nightdress**

night·ie F → *nightdress*

night·tin·gale zo Nachtigall *f*

night·ly (all)nächtlich; (all)abendlich; jede Nacht; jeden Abend

night·mare Albtraum *m* (*a. fig*)

night school Abendschule *f*

night shift Nachtschicht *f*

night·shirt (Herren)Nachthemd *n*

night·time: *in the ~, at ~* nachts

night watch·man Nachtwächter *m*

night·y F → *nightdress*

nil Nichts *n*, Null *f*; *our team won two to ~ or by two goals to ~* (*2-0*) unsere Mannschaft gewann zwei zu null (2:0)

nim·ble flink, gewandt; geistig beweglich

nine 1. neun; *~ to five* normale Dienststunden (von 9-5); *a ~-to-five job* e-e (An)Stellung mit geregelter Arbeitszeit **2.** Neun *f*

nine·pins Kegeln *n*

nine·teen 1. neunzehn **2.** Neunzehn *f*

nine·teenth neunzehnte(r, -s)

nine·ti·eth neunzigste(r, -s)

nine·ty 1. neunzig **2.** Neunzig *f*

ninth 1. neunte(r, -s) **2.** Neuntel *n*

ninth·ly neuntens

nip[1] **1.** kneifen, zwicken; F flitzen, sausen; *~ off* F abknipsen; *~ in the bud fig* im Keim ersticken **2.** Kneifen *n*, Zwicken *n*; *it was ~* war ganz knapp; *there's a ~ in the air today* heute ist es ganz schön kalt

nip[2] Schlückchen *n* (*of brandy etc*)

nip·per: (*a pair of*) *~s* (e-e) (Kneif)Zange *f*

nip·ple ANAT Brustwarze *f*; (Gummi-)Sauger *m*; TECH Nippel *m*

ni·ter, *Br* **ni·tre** CHEM Salpeter *m*

ni·tro·gen CHEM Stickstoff *m*

no 1. *adv* nein; nicht **2.** *adj* kein(e); *~ one* keiner, niemand; *in ~ time* im Nu, im Handumdrehen **3.** Nein *n*

no·bil·i·ty (Hoch)Adel *m*; *fig* Adel *m*

no·ble adlig; edel, nobel; prächtig

no·ble·man Adlige *m*

no·ble·wom·an Adlige *f*

no·bod·y 1. niemand, keiner **2.** *fig* Niemand *m*, Null *f*

no·cal·o·rie di·et Nulldiät *f*

noc·tur·nal nächtlich, Nacht...

nod 1. nicken (mit); *~ off* einnicken; *have a ~ding acquaintance with s.o.* j-n flüchtig kennen **2.** Nicken *n*

node BOT, MED Knoten *m*

noise 1. Krach *m*, Lärm *m*; Geräusch *n* **2.** *~ about* (*abroad, around*) Gerücht *etc* verbreiten; **noise·less** geräuschlos; **nois·y** laut, geräuschvoll

no·mad Nomade *m*, Nomadin *f*

nom·i·nal nominell; *~ value* ECON Nennwert *m*

nom·i·nate ernennen; nominieren, (zur Wahl) vorschlagen; **nom·i·na·tion** Ernennung *f*; Nominierung *f*

nom·i·na·tive *a. ~ case* LING Nominativ *m*, erster Fall

nom·i·nee Kandidat(in)

non... nicht..., Nicht..., un...

non·al·co·hol·ic alkoholfrei

non·a·ligned POL blockfrei

non·com·mis·sioned of·fi·cer MIL Unteroffizier *m*

non·com·mit·tal unverbindlich

non·con·duc·tor ELECTR Nichtleiter *m*

non·de·script nichtssagend; unauffällig

none 1. *pron* keine(r, -s), niemand **2.** *adv* in keiner Weise, keineswegs

non·en·ti·ty *fig* Null *f*

none·the·less nichtsdestoweniger, dennoch, trotzdem

non·ex·ist·ence Nichtvorhandensein *n*, Fehlen *n*

non·ex·ist·ent nicht existierend

non·fic·tion Sachbücher *pl*

non·flam·ma·ble, **non·in·flam·ma·ble** nicht brennbar

non·in·ter·fer·ence, **non·in·ter·vention** POL Nichteinmischung *f*

non·i·ron bügelfrei

non·non·sense nüchtern, sachlich

non·par·ti·san POL überparteilich; unparteiisch

non·pay·ment ECON Nicht(be)zahlung *f*

non·plus verblüffen

non·pol·lut·ing umweltfreundlich

non·prof·it, *Br* **non·prof·it·mak·ing** gemeinnützig

non·res·i·dent 1. nicht (orts)ansässig; nicht im Hause wohnend **2.** Nichtansässige *m, f*; nicht im Hause Wohnende *m, f*

non·re·turn·a·ble Einweg...; *~ bot·tle* Einwegflasche *f*

non·sense Unsinn *m*, dummes Zeug

non·skid rutschfest, rutschsicher

non·smok·er Nichtraucher(in)

non·smok·ing Nichtraucher...

non·stick mit Antihaftbeschichtung

non·stop nonstop, ohne Unterbrechung; RAIL durchgehend; AVIAT ohne Zwischenlandung; **~ flight** a. Nonstop-Flug m

non·u·ni·on nicht (gewerkschaftlich) organisiert

non·vi·o·lence (Politik f der) Gewaltlosigkeit f

non·vi·o·lent gewaltlos

noo·dle Nudel f

nook Ecke f, Winkel m

noon Mittag(szeit) f) m; **at ~** um 12 Uhr (mittags)

noose Schlinge f

nope F ne(e), nein

nor → **neither** 2; auch nicht

norm Norm f

nor·mal normal

nor·mal·ize (sich) normalisieren

north 1. Nord, Norden m **2.** adj nördlich, Nord... **3.** adv nach Norden, nordwärts

north·east 1. Nordost, Nordosten m **2.** a. **northeastern** nordöstlich

nor·ther·ly, nor·thern Nord..., nördlich

North Pole Nordpol m

north·ward(s) adv nördlich, nach Norden

north·west 1. Nordwest, Nordwesten m **2.** a. **northwestern** nordwestlich

Nor·way Norwegen n

Nor·we·gian 1. norwegisch **2.** Norweger(in); LING Norwegisch n

nose 1. Nase f; zo Schnauze f; fig Gespür n **2.** Auto etc vorsichtig fahren; a. **~ about, ~ around** fig F herumschnüffeln (in dat) (for nach)

nose·bleed Nasenbluten n; **have a ~** Nasenbluten haben

nose·dive AVIAT Sturzflug m

nos·ey → **nosy**

nos·tal·gia Nostalgie f

nos·tril ANAT Nasenloch n, esp zo Nüster f

nos·y F neugierig

not nicht; **~ a** kein(e)

no·ta·ble bemerkenswert; beachtlich

no·ta·ry mst **~ public** Notar m

notch 1. Kerbe f; GEOL Engpass m **2.** (ein)kerben

note (mst pl) Notiz f, Aufzeichnung f; Anmerkung f; Vermerk m; Briefchen n, Zettel m; (diplomatische) Note; Banknote f, Geldschein m; MUS Note

f; fig Ton m; **take ~s (of)** sich Notizen machen (über acc); **note·book** Notizbuch n; IT Notebook n

not·ed bekannt, berühmt (**for** wegen)

note·pa·per Briefpapier n

note·wor·thy bemerkenswert

noth·ing nichts; **~ but** nichts als, nur; **~ much** F nicht viel; **for ~** umsonst; **to say ~ of** ganz zu schweigen von; **there is ~ like** es geht nichts über (acc)

no·tice 1. Ankündigung f, Bekanntgabe f, Mitteilung f, Anzeige f; Kündigung(sfrist) f; Beachtung f; **give or hand in one's ~** kündigen (**to** bei); **give s.o. ~** j-m kündigen; **give s.o. ~ to quit** j-m kündigen; **at six months' ~** mit halbjährlicher Kündigungsfrist; **take (no) ~ of** (keine) Notiz nehmen von, (nicht) beachten; **at short ~** kurzfristig; **until further ~** bis auf Weiteres; **without ~** fristlos **2.** (es) bemerken; (besonders) beachten or achten auf (acc)

no·tice·a·ble erkennbar, wahrnehmbar; bemerkenswert

no·tice·board Br schwarzes Brett

no·ti·fy et. anzeigen, melden, mitteilen; j-n benachrichtigen

no·tion Begriff m, Vorstellung f; Idee f

no·tions Kurzwaren pl

no·to·ri·ous berüchtigt (**for** für)

not·with·stand·ing trotz (gen)

nought Br: **0.4 (~ point four)** 0,4

noun LING Substantiv n, Hauptwort n

nour·ish (er)nähren; fig hegen

nour·ish·ing nahrhaft

nour·ish·ment Ernährung f; Nahrung f

Nov abbr of **November** Nov., November m

nov·el 1. Roman m **2.** (ganz) neu(artig)

nov·el·ist Romanschriftsteller(in)

no·vel·la Novelle f

nov·el·ty Neuheit f

No·vem·ber (abbr **Nov**) November m

nov·ice Anfänger(in), Neuling m; REL Novize m, Novizin f

now 1. adv nun, jetzt; **~ and again, (every) ~ and then** von Zeit zu Zeit, dann und wann; **by ~** inzwischen; **from ~ (on)** von jetzt an; **just ~** gerade eben **2.** cj a. **~ that** nun da; **now·a·days** heutzutage

no·where nirgends

nox·ious schädlich

noz·zle TECH Schnauze f; Stutzen m; Düse f; Zapfpistole f

N

nu·ance Nuance f

nub springender Punkt

nu·cle·ar Kern..., Atom..., atomar, nuklear, Nuklear...; ~ en·er·gy PHYS Atomenergie f, Kernenergie f; ~ fis·sion PHYS Kernspaltung f

nu·cle·ar-free atomwaffenfrei

nu·cle·ar| fu·sion PHYS Kernfusion f; ~ phys·ics Kernphysik f; ~ pow·er PHYS Atomkraft f, Kernkraft f

nu·cle·ar-pow·ered atomgetrieben

nu·cle·ar| pow·er plant ELECTR Atomkraftwerk n, Kernkraftwerk n; ~ re·ac·tor PHYS Atomreaktor m, Kernreaktor m; ~ war Atomkrieg m; ~ war·head MIL Atomsprengkopf m; ~ waste Atommüll m; ~ weap·ons MIL Atomwaffen pl, Kernwaffen pl

nu·cle·us BIOL, PHYS Kern m (a. fig)

nude 1. nackt 2. art: Akt m

nudge 1. j-n anstoßen, (an)stupsen 2. Stups(er) m

nug·get (esp Gold)Klumpen m

nui·sance Plage f, Ärgernis n; Nervensäge f, Quälgeist m; what a ~! wie ärgerlich!; be a ~ to s.o. j-m lästig fallen, F j-n nerven; make a ~ of o.s. den Leuten auf die Nerven gehen or fallen

nukes F Atom-, Kernwaffen pl

null: ~ and void esp JUR null und nichtig

numb 1. starr (with vor); taub; fig wie betäubt (with vor); 2. starr or taub machen

num·ber 1. Zahl f, Ziffer f; Nummer f; (An)Zahl f; Ausgabe f; (Bus- etc)Linie f; sorry, wrong ~ TEL falsch verbunden! 2. nummerieren; zählen; sich belaufen auf (acc)

num·ber·less zahllos

num·ber·plate esp Br MOT Nummernschild n

nu·me·ral Ziffer f; LING Zahlwort n

nu·me·ra·tor MATH Zähler m

nu·me·rous zahlreich

nun REL Nonne f

nun·ne·ry REL Nonnenkloster n

nurse 1. (Kranken-, Säuglings)Schwester f; Kindermädchen n; (Kranken-)Pflegerin f; → male nurse; a. wet~ Amme f 2. stillen; pflegen; hegen; als Krankenschwester or -pfleger arbeiten; ~ s.o. back to health j-n gesund pflegen

nur·se·ry Tagesheim n, Tagesstätte f; Baum-, Pflanzschule f; ~ rhyme Kinderlied n, Kinderreim m; ~ school Br Vorschule f; ~ slope skiing: F Idiotenhügel m

nurs·ing Stillen n; (Kranken)Pflege f; ~ bot·tle (Saug)Flasche f; ~ home Pflegeheim n

nut BOT Nuss f; TECH (Schrauben)Mutter f; F verrückter Kerl; F Birne f (head)

nut·crack·er(s) Nussknacker m

nut·meg BOT Muskatnuss f

nu·tri·ent 1. Nährstoff m 2. nahrhaft

nu·tri·tion Ernährung f

nu·tri·tious, nu·tri·tive nahrhaft

nut·shell Nussschale f; (to put it) in a ~ F kurz gesagt, mit e-m Wort

nut·ty voller Nüsse, nussig; Nuss...; F verrückt

ny·lon® Nylon® n; ~ stock·ings Nylonstrümpfe® pl

nymph Nymphe f

O

O, o O, o n

o Null f

oaf Lümmel m, Flegel m

oak BOT Eiche f

oar Ruder n

oars·man SPORT Ruderer m

oars·wom·an SPORT Ruderin f

o·a·sis Oase f (a. fig)

oath Eid m, Schwur m; Fluch m; take an ~ e-n Eid leisten or schwören; be on or under ~ JUR unter Eid stehen; take the ~ JUR schwören

oat·meal Hafermehl n, Hafergrütze f

o·be·di·ence Gehorsam m

o·be·di·ent gehorsam

o·bese fett, fettleibig

o·bes·i·ty Fettleibigkeit f

o·bey gehorchen (dat), folgen (dat); Befehl etc befolgen

o·bit·u·a·ry Nachruf m; a. ~ notice Todesanzeige *f*

ob·ject 1. Objekt *n* (*a.* LING); Gegenstand *m*; Ziel *n*, Zweck *m*, Absicht *f* **2.** einwenden; et. dagegen haben

ob·jec·tion Einwand *m*, Einspruch *m* (*a.* JUR); **ob·jec·tion·a·ble** nicht einwandfrei; unangenehm; anstößig

ob·jec·tive 1. objektiv, sachlich **2.** Ziel *n*; **ob·jec·tive·ness** Objektivität *f*

ob·li·ga·tion Verpflichtung *f*; *be under an ~ to s.o.* j-m (zu Dank) verpflichtet sein; *be under an ~ to do* verpflichtet sein, et. zu tun; **ob·lig·a·to·ry** verpflichtend, verbindlich

o·blige nötigen, zwingen; (zu Dank) verpflichten; *~ s.o.* j-m e-n Gefallen tun; *much ~d* besten Dank

o·blig·ing entgegenkommend, gefällig

o·blique schief, schräg; *fig* indirekt

o·blit·er·ate auslöschen; vernichten, völlig zerstören; verdecken

o·bliv·i·on Vergessen(heit *f*) *n*; *fall into ~* in Vergessenheit geraten

o·bliv·i·ous: *be ~ of* or *to s.th.* sich e-r Sache nicht bewusst sein; et. nicht bemerken *or* wahrnehmen

ob·long rechteckig; länglich

ob·nox·ious widerlich

ob·scene obszön, unanständig

ob·scure 1. dunkel, *fig a.* unklar; unbekannt **2.** verdunkeln, verdecken

ob·scu·ri·ty Unbekanntheit *f*; Unklarheit *f*

ob·se·quies Trauerfeier(lichkeiten *pl*) *f*

ob·ser·va·ble wahrnehmbar, merklich; **ob·ser·vance** Beachtung *f*, Befolgung *f*; **ob·ser·vant** aufmerksam; **ob·ser·va·tion** Beobachtung *f*, Überwachung *f*; Bemerkung *f* (*on* über *acc*); **ob·ser·va·to·ry** Observatorium *n*, Sternwarte *f*; **ob·serve** beobachten; überwachen; *Vorschrift etc* beachten, befolgen, einhalten; bemerken, äußern; **ob·serv·er** Beobachter(in)

ob·sess: *be ~ed by* or *with* besessen sein von; **ob·ses·sion** PSYCH Besessenheit *f*, fixe Idee, Zwangsvorstellung *f*; **ob·ses·sive** PSYCH zwanghaft

ob·so·lete veraltet

ob·sta·cle Hindernis *n*

ob·sti·na·cy Starrsinn *m*

ob·sti·nate hartnäckig; halsstarrig, eigensinnig, starrköpfig

ob·struct verstopfen, versperren; blo-

ckieren; behindern

ob·struc·tion Verstopfung *f*; Blockierung *f*; Behinderung *f*

ob·struc·tive blockierend; hinderlich

ob·tain erhalten, bekommen, sich *et.* beschaffen; **ob·tain·a·ble** erhältlich

ob·tru·sive aufdringlich

ob·vi·ous offensichtlich, klar, einleuchtend

oc·ca·sion Gelegenheit *f*; Anlass *m*; Veranlassung *f*; (festliches) Ereignis; *on the ~ of* anlässlich (*gen*)

oc·ca·sion·al gelegentlich; vereinzelt

oc·ca·sion·al·ly gelegentlich, manchmal

Oc·ci·dent *der* Westen, *der* Okzident, *das* Abendland

oc·ci·den·tal abendländisch, westlich

oc·cu·pant Bewohner(in); Insasse *m*, Insassin *f*

oc·cu·pa·tion Beruf *m*; Beschäftigung *f*; MIL, POL Besetzung *f*, Besatzung *f*, Okkupation *f*

oc·cu·py in Besitz nehmen, MIL, POL besetzen; *Raum* einnehmen; in Anspruch nehmen; beschäftigen; *be occupied* bewohnt sein; besetzt sein (*seat*)

oc·cur sich ereignen; vorkommen; *it ~red to me that* es fiel mir ein *or* mir kam der Gedanke, dass

oc·cur·rence Vorkommen *n*; Ereignis *n*; Vorfall *m*

o·cean Ozean *m*, (Welt)Meer *n*

o'clock: (*at*) *five ~* (um) fünf Uhr

Oct *abbr of* **October** Okt., Oktober *m*

Oc·to·ber (*abbr* **Oct**) Oktober *m*

oc·u·lar Augen...

oc·u·list Augenarzt *m*, Augenärztin *f*

OD F *v/i*: *~ on heroin* an e-r Überdosis Heroin sterben

odd sonderbar, seltsam, merkwürdig; einzeln, Einzel...; ungerade (*number*); gelegentlich, Gelegenheits...; *~ jobs* Gelegenheitsarbeiten *pl*; F **30 ~** (et.) über 30, einige 30

odds (Gewinn)Chancen *pl*; *the ~ are 10 to 1* die Chancen stehen 10 zu 1; *the ~ are that* es ist sehr wahrscheinlich, dass; *against all ~* wider Erwarten, entgegen allen Erwartungen; *be at ~* uneins sein (*with* mit); *~ and ends* Krimskrams *m*; **odds-on** hoch, klar (*favorite*), aussichtsreichst (*candidate* *etc)*; F *it's ~ that* es sieht ganz so aus, als ob …

ode Ode *f*

o·do(u)r Geruch *m*

o·do(u)r·less geruchlos

of *prp* von; *origin:* von, aus; *material:* aus; um (*cheat s.o. ~ s.th.* j-n um et. betrügen); *cause:* an (*dat*) (*die~* sterben an); aus (*~ charity* aus Nächstenliebe); vor (*dat*) (*be afraid~* Angst haben vor); auf (*acc*) (*be proud ~* stolz sein auf); über (*acc*) (*be glad~* sich freuen über); nach (*smell ~* riechen nach); von, über (*acc*) (*speak ~ s.th.* von *or* über et. sprechen); an (*acc*) (*think ~ s.th.* an et. denken); *the city ~* London die Stadt London; *the works ~ Dickens* Dickens' Werke; *your letter ~ …* Ihr Schreiben vom *or* …; *five minutes ~ twelve* fünf Minuten vor zwölf

off 1. *adv* fort(…), weg(…); ab(…), abgegangen (*button etc*); weg, entfernt (*3 miles~*); ELECTR *etc* aus(…), aus-, abgeschaltet; TECH zu; aus(gegangen), alle; aus, vorbei; verdorben (*food*); frei; *I must be ~* ich muss gehen *or* weg; *~ with you!* fort mit dir!; *be ~* ausfallen, nicht stattfinden; *10% ~* ECON 10% Nachlass; *~ and on* ab und zu, hin und wieder; *take a day ~* sich e-n Tag freinehmen; *be well* (*badly*) *~* gut (schlecht) d(a)ran *or* gestellt *or* situiert sein **2.** *prp* fort von, weg von, von (…, ab, weg, herunter); abseits von (*or gen*), von … weg; MAR *or der Küste etc*; *be ~ duty* nicht im Dienst sein, dienstfrei haben; *be ~ smoking* nicht mehr rauchen **3.** *adj* frei, arbeits-, dienstfrei; *fig* *have an ~ day* e-n schlechten Tag haben

of·fal GASTR Innereien *pl*

off·col·o(u)r schlüpfrig, zweideutig

of·fence *Br* → *offense*

of·fend beleidigen, kränken; verstoßen (*against* gegen); *of·fend·er* (Übel-, Misse)Täter(in); *first ~* JUR nicht Vorbestrafte *m, f*, Ersttäter(in)

of·fense Vergehen *n*, Verstoß *m*; JUR Straftat *f*; Beleidigung *f*, Kränkung *f*; *take ~* Anstoß nehmen (*at* an *dat*)

of·fen·sive 1. beleidigend, anstößig; widerlich (*smell etc*); MIL Offensiv…, Angriffs… **2.** MIL Offensive *f* (*a. fig*)

of·fer 1. *v/t* anbieten (*a.* ECON); Preis,

Möglichkeit *etc* bieten; Preis, Belohnung aussetzen; sich bereit erklären (*to do* zu tun); *Widerstand* leisten; *v/i* es *or* sich anbieten **2.** Angebot *n*

off·hand 1. *adj* lässig; Stegreif…; *be ~ with s.o.* F mit j-m kurz angebunden sein **2.** *adv* auf Anhieb, so ohne weiteres

of·fice Büro *n*, Geschäftsstelle *f*, (*Anwalts*)Kanzlei *f*; (*esp* öffentliches) Amt, Posten *m*; *mst Office esp Br* Ministerium *n*; *~ block Br*, *~ build·ing* Bürohaus *n*; *~ hours* Dienstzeit *f*; Geschäfts-, Öffnungszeiten *pl*

of·fi·cer MIL Offizier *m*; (*Polizei- etc*)Beamte *m*, (-)Beamtin *f*

of·fi·cial 1. Beamte *m*, Beamtin *f* **2.** offiziell, amtlich, dienstlich

of·fi·ci·ate amtieren

of·fi·cious übereifrig

off·licence *Br* Wein- und Spirituosenhandlung *f*

off·line IT offline, Offline…, rechnerunabhängig

off·peak *~ electricity* Nachtstrom *m*; *~ hours* verkehrsschwache Stunden *pl*

off sea·son Nebensaison *f*

off·set ECON ausgleichen; verrechnen (*against* mit)

off·shoot BOT Ableger *m*, Spross *m*

off·shore vor der Küste

off·side SPORT abseits; *~ position* Abseitsposition *f*, Abseitsstellung *f*; *~ trap* Abseitsfalle *f*

off·spring Nachkomme *m*, Nachkommenschaft *f*

off-the-peg *Br*, **off-the-rack** Konfektions…, … von der Stange

off-the-rec·ord inoffiziell

of·ten oft(mals), häufig

oh *int* oh!

oil 1. Öl *n*; Erdöl *n* **2.** (ein)ölen, schmieren (*a. fig*)

oil change MOT Ölwechsel *m*

oil·cloth Wachstuch *n*

oil·field Ölfeld *n*

oil paint·ing Ölmalerei *f*; Ölgemälde *n*

oil pan MOT Ölwanne *f*

oil plat·form → *oilrig*

oil pol·lu·tion Ölpest *f*

oil-pro·duc·ing coun·try Ölförderland *n*

oil pro·duc·tion Ölförderung *f*

oil re·fin·e·ry Erdölraffinerie *f*

oil·rig (Öl)Bohrinsel *f*
oil·skins Ölzeug *n*
oil slick Ölteppich *m*
oil well Ölquelle *f*
oil·y ölig; *fig* schmierig, schleimig
oint·ment Salbe *f*
OK, o·kay F **1.** *adj and int* okay(!), o.k.(!), in Ordnung(!) **2.** genehmigen, *e-r Sache* zustimmen **3.** Okay *n*, O.K. *n*, Genehmigung *f*, Zustimmung *f*
old **1.** alt **2.** *the ~* die Alten *pl*
old age (hohes) Alter; *~* **pen·sion** Rente *f*, Pension *f*; *~* **pen·sion·er** Rentner(in), Pensionär(in)
old-fash·ioned altmodisch
old·ish ältlich
old peo·ple's home Altersheim *n*, Altenheim *n*
ol·ive BOT Olive *f*; Olivgrün *n*
O·lym·pic Games SPORT Olympische Spiele *pl*
om·i·nous unheilvoll
o·mis·sion Auslassung *f*; Unterlassung *f*; Versäumnis *n*
o·mit auslassen, weglassen; unterlassen
om·nip·o·tent allmächtig
om·nis·ci·ent allwissend
on **1.** *prp* auf (*acc or dat*) (*~ the table* auf dem *or* den Tisch); an (*dat*) (*~ the wall* an der Wand); in (*~ TV* im Fernsehen); *direction, target:* auf (*acc*) … (hin), an (*acc*), nach (*dat*) … (hin); *fig* auf (*acc*) … (hin) (*~ demand* auf Anfrage); *time:* an (*dat*) (*~ Sunday* am Sonntag; *~ the 1st of April* am 1. April); (gleich) nach, bei (*~ his arrival*); gehörig zu, beschäftigt bei (*be ~ a committee* in e-m Ausschuss angehören; *be ~ the „Daily Mail"* bei der "Daily Mail" beschäftigt sein); *state:* in (*dat*), auf (*dat*) (*~ duty* im Dienst; *be ~ fire* in Flammen stehen); *subject:* über (*acc*) (*talk ~ a subject* über ein Thema sprechen); nach (*dat*) (*~ this model* nach diesem Modell); von (*dat*) (*live ~ s.th.* von et. leben); *~ the street* auf der Straße; *~ a train* in e-m Zug; *~ hearing it* als ich *etc* es hörte; *have you any money ~ you?* hast du Geld bei dir? **2.** *adj and adv* an (-geschaltet) (*light etc*), eingeschaltet (*radio etc*), auf (*faucet etc*), (dar)auf(*legen, -schrauben etc*); an(*haben, -ziehen*) (*have a coat ~* e-n Mantel anhaben); auf(*behalten*) (*keep one's hat ~*

den Hut aufbehalten); weiter(*gehen, -sprechen etc*); *and so ~* und so weiter; *~ and ~* immer weiter; *from this day ~* von dem Tage an; *be ~* THEA gegeben werden; *film:* laufen; *radio*, TV gesendet werden; *what's ~?* was ist los?
once **1.** einmal; einst; *~ again, ~ more* noch einmal; *~ in a while* ab und zu, hin und wieder; *~ and for all* ein für alle Mal; *not ~* kein einziges Mal, keinmal; *at ~* sofort; auf einmal, gleichzeitig; *all at ~* plötzlich; *for ~* diesmal, ausnahmsweise; *this ~* dieses eine Mal; *~ upon a time there was …* es war einmal … **2.** sobald
one ein(e); einzig; man; Eins *f*, eins; *~'s* sein(e); *~ day* eines Tages; *~ another* sich (gegenseitig), einander; *~ by ~*, *~ after another*, *~ after the other* e-r nach dem andern; *I for ~* ich zum Beispiel; *the little ~s* die Kleinen *pl*
one-horse town F *contp* Nest *n*
one-self sich (selbst); sich selbst; *(all) by ~* ganz allein; *to ~* ganz für sich (allein)
one-sid·ed einseitig
one-time ehemalig, früher
one-track mind: *have a ~* immer nur dasselbe im Kopf haben
one-two *soccer:* Doppelpass *m*
one-way Einbahn…; *~ street* Einbahnstraße *f*; *~ tick·et* RAIL *etc* einfache Fahrkarte, AVIAT einfaches Ticket; *~ traf·fic* MOT Einbahnverkehr *m*
on·ion BOT Zwiebel *f*
on·line IT online, Online…, rechnerabhängig
on·look·er Zuschauer(in)
on·ly **1.** *adj* einzige(r, -s) **2.** *adv* nur, bloß; erst; *~ yesterday* erst gestern **3.** *cj* F nur, bloß
on·rush Ansturm *m*
on·set Beginn *m*; MED Ausbruch *m*
on·slaught (heftiger) Angriff (*a. fig*)
on·to auf (*acc*)
on·ward(s) *adv* vorwärts, weiter; *from now ~* von nun an
ooze *v/i* sickern; *~ away fig* schwinden; *v/t* absondern; *fig* ausstrahlen, verströmen
o·paque undurchtsichtig; *fig* unverständlich
o·pen **1.** offen, *a.* geöffnet, *a.* frei (*country etc*); öffentlich; *fig* offen, *a.* unentschieden, *a.* freimütig; *fig* zugänglich,

aufgeschlossen (**to** für or dat); **~ all day** durchgehend geöffnet; **in the ~ air** im Freien **2.** golf, tennis: offenes Turnier; **in the~** im Freien; **come out into the~** fig an die Öffentlichkeit treten **3.** v/t öffnen, aufmachen, Buch etc a. aufschlagen; eröffnen; v/i sich öffnen, aufgehen; öffnen, aufmachen (store); anfangen, beginnen; **~ into** führen nach or in (acc); **~ onto** hinausgehen auf (acc)

o·pen-air im Freien

o·pen-end·ed zeitlich unbegrenzt

o·pen·er (Dosen- etc)Öffner m

o·pen-eyed mit großen Augen, staunend

o·pen-hand·ed freigebig, großzügig

o·pen-heart·ed offenherzig

o·pen·ing **1.** Öffnung f; ECON freie Stelle; Eröffnung f, Erschließung f, Einstieg m **2.** Eröffnungs…; Öffnungs…

o·pen-mind·ed aufgeschlossen

o·pen·ness Offenheit f

op·e·ra Oper f; **~ glass·es** Opernglas n; **~ house** Opernhaus n, Oper f

op·e·rate v/i wirksam sein or werden; TECH arbeiten, in Betrieb sein, laufen (machine etc); MED operieren (**on s.o.** j-n); v/t Maschine bedienen, Schalter etc betätigen; Unternehmen, Geschäft betreiben, führen

op·e·rat·ing| room MED Operationssaal m; **~ sys·tem** IT Betriebssystem n; **~ thea·tre** Br MED Operationssaal m

op·e·ra·tion TECH Betrieb m, Lauf m; Bedienung f; ECON Tätigkeit f, Unternehmen n; MED, MIL Operation f; **in ~** TECH in Betrieb; **have an ~** MED operiert werden

op·e·ra·tive TECH wirksam; MED operativ

op·e·ra·tor TECH Bedienungsperson f; IT Operator m; TEL Vermittlung f

o·pin·ion Meinung f, Ansicht f; Gutachten n (**on** über acc); **in my~** meines Erachtens

op·po·nent Gegner(in)

op·por·tune günstig, passend; rechtzeitig

op·por·tu·ni·ty (günstige) Gelegenheit f

op·pose sich widersetzen (dat)

op·posed entgegengesetzt; **be ~ to** gegen … sein

op·po·site **1.** Gegenteil n, Gegensatz m **2.** adj gegenüberliegend; entgegenge-

setzt **3.** adv gegenüber (**to** dat); **4.** prp gegenüber (dat)

op·po·si·tion Widerstand m, Opposition f (a. PARL); Gegensatz m

op·press unterdrücken

op·pres·sion Unterdrückung f

op·pres·sive (be)drückend; hart, grausam; schwül (weather)

op·tic Augen…, Seh…; → op·ti·cal op·tisch; op·ti·cian Optiker(in)

op·ti·mism Optimismus m

op·ti·mist Optimist(in)

op·ti·mis·tic optimistisch

op·tion Wahl f; ECON Option f, Vorkaufsrecht n; MOT Extra n

op·tion·al freiwillig; Wahl…; **be an~ ex·tra** MOT gegen Aufpreis erhältlich sein; **~ sub·ject** PED etc Wahlfach n

or oder; **~ else** sonst

o·ral mündlich; Mund…

or·ange **1.** BOT Orange f, Apfelsine f **2.** orange(farben)

or·ange·ade Orangenlimonade f

o·ra·tion Rede f, Ansprache f

or·a·tor Redner(in)

or·bit **1.** Kreisbahn f, Umlaufbahn f; **get or put into~** in e-e Umlaufbahn gelangen or bringen **2.** v/t die Erde etc umkreisen; v/i die Erde etc umkreisen, sich auf e-r Umlaufbahn bewegen

or·chard Obstgarten m

or·ches·tra MUS Orchester n; THEA Parkett n

or·chid BOT Orchidee f

or·dain: **~ s.o.** (**priest**) j-n zum Priester weihen

or·deal Qual f, Tortur f

or·der **1.** Ordnung f; Reihenfolge f; Befehl m, Anordnung f; ECON Bestellung f, Auftrag m; PARL etc (Geschäfts)Ordnung f; REL etc Orden m; **~ to pay** ECON Zahlungsanweisung f; **in~ to** inf um zu inf; **out of~** TECH nicht in Ordnung, defekt; außer Betrieb; **make to~** auf Bestellung or nach Maß anfertigen **2.** v/t j-m befehlen (**to do** zu tun), et. befehlen, anordnen; j-n schicken, beordern; MED j-m et. verordnen; ECON bestellen; fig ordnen, in Ordnung bringen; v/i bestellen (in restaurant)

or·der·ly **1.** ordentlich; fig gesittet, friedlich **2.** MED Hilfspfleger m

or·di·nal a. **~ number** MATH Ordnungszahl f

or·di·nary üblich, gewöhnlich, normal

ore MIN Erz *n*

or·gan ANAT Organ *n (a. fig)*; MUS Orgel *f*; **~ do·nor** MED Organspender *m*

or·gan·ic organisch

or·gan·ism Organismus *m*

or·gan·i·za·tion Organisation *f*

or·gan·ize organisieren; sich (gewerkschaftlich) organisieren

or·gan·iz·er Organisator(in)

or·gan recip·i·ent MED Organempfänger(in) *m(f)*

or·gasm Orgasmus *m*

o·ri·ent 1. *Orient der* Osten, *der* Orient, *das* Morgenland **2.** orientieren

o·ri·en·tal 1. orientalisch, östlich **2.** *Oriental* Orientale *m*, Orientalin *f*

o·ri·en·tate orientieren

or·i·gin Ursprung *m*, Abstammung *f*, Herkunft *f*

o·rig·i·nal 1. ursprünglich; Original...; originell **2.** Original *n*

o·rig·i·nal·i·ty Originalität *f*

o·rig·i·nal·ly ursprünglich; originell

o·rig·i·nate *v/t* schaffen, ins Leben rufen; *v/i* zurückgehen (*from* auf *acc*), (her)stammen (*from* von, aus)

or·na·ment 1. Ornament(e *pl) n*, Verzierung(en *pl) f*, Schmuck *m*; *fig* Zier(de) *f* (*to* für *or gen*); **2.** verzieren, schmücken (*with* mit)

or·na·men·tal dekorativ, schmückend, Zier...

or·nate *fig* überladen

or·phan 1. Waise *f*, Waisenkind *n* **2.** *be* **~ed** Waise werden

or·phan·age Waisenhaus *n*

or·tho·dox orthodox

os·cil·late PHYS schwingen; *fig* schwanken (*between* zwischen *dat*)

os·prey ZO Fischadler *m*

os·ten·si·ble angeblich, vorgeblich

os·ten·ta·tion (protzige) Zurschaustellung; Protzerei *f*, Prahlerei *f*

os·ten·ta·tious protzend, prahlerisch

os·tra·cize ächten

os·trich ZO Strauß *m*

oth·er andere(r, -s); *the ~ day* neulich; *the ~ morning* neulich morgens; *every* **~ day** jeden zweiten Tag, alle zwei Tage

oth·er·wise anders; sonst

ot·ter ZO Otter *m*

ought *v/aux* ich sollte, *du* solltest *etc*; *you* **~ to have done it** Sie hätten es

tun sollen

ounce Unze *f (28,35 g)*

our unser

ours unsere(r, -s)

our·selves wir *or* uns selbst; uns (selbst)

oust verdrängen, hinauswerfen (*from* aus); *j-n s-s Amtes* entheben

out 1. *adv, adj* aus; hinaus(*gehen, -werfen etc*); heraus(*kommen etc*); aus(*brechen etc*); draußen, im Freien; nicht zu Hause; SPORT aus, draußen; aus, vorbei; aus, erloschen; ausverkauft; F **out**, aus der Mode; **~ of** aus (... heraus); zu ... hinaus; außerhalb von (*or gen*); außer *Reichweite etc*; außer *Atem*, *Übung etc*; (hergestellt) aus; aus *Furcht etc*; *be* **~ of bread** kein Brot mehr haben; *in nine* **~ of ten cases** in neun von zehn Fällen **2.** *prp* F aus (... heraus); zu ... hinaus **3.** outen

out·bal·ance überwiegen

out·bid überbieten

out·board mo·tor Außenbordmotor *m*

out·break MED, MIL Ausbruch *m*

out·build·ing Nebengebäude *n*

out·burst *fig* Ausbruch *m*

out·cast 1. ausgestoßen **2.** Ausgestoßene *m, f*, Verstoßene *m, f*

out·come Ergebnis *n*

out·cry Aufschrei *m*, Schrei *m* der Entrüstung

out·dat·ed überholt, veraltet

out·dis·tance hinter sich lassen

out·do übertreffen

out·door *adj* im Freien, draußen

out·doors *adv* draußen, im Freien

out·er äußere(r, -s)

out·er·most äußerste(r, -s)

out·er space Weltraum *m*

out·fit Ausrüstung *f*, Ausstattung *f*; Kleidung *f*; F (Arbeits)Gruppe *f*

out·fit·ter Ausstatter *m*; *men's* **~** Herrenausstatter *m*

out·go·ing (aus dem Amt) scheidend

out·grow herauswachsen aus (*dat*); *Angewohnheit etc* ablegen; größer werden als

out·house Nebengebäude *n*

out·ing Ausflug *m*; Outing *n*

out·land·ish befremdlich, sonderbar

out·last überdauern, überleben

out·law HIST Geächtete *m, f*

out·lay (Geld)Auslagen *pl*, Ausgaben *pl*

out·let Abfluss *m*, Abzug *m*; *fig* Ventil *n*

out·line 1. Umriss m; Überblick m **2.** umreißen, skizzieren

out·live überleben

out·look (Aus)Blick m, (Aus)Sicht f; Einstellung f, Auffassung f

out·ly·ing abgelegen, entlegen

out·num·ber in der Überzahl sein; **be ~ed by s.o.** j-m zahlenmäßig unterlegen sein

out-of-date veraltet, überholt

out-of-the-way abgelegen, entlegen; fig ungewöhnlich

out·pa·tient MED ambulanter Patient, ambulante Patientin

out·post Vorposten m

out·pour·ing (Gefühls)Erguss m

out·put ECON Output m, Produktion f, Ausstoß m, Ertrag m; IT (Daten)Ausgabe f

out·rage 1. Gewalttat f, Verbrechen n; Empörung f **2.** grob verletzen; j-n empören; **out·ra·geous** abscheulich; empörend, unerhört

out·right 1. adj völlig, gänzlich, glatt (lie etc) **2.** adv auf der Stelle, sofort; ohne Umschweife

out·run schneller laufen als; fig übersteigen, übertreffen

out·set Anfang m, Beginn m

out·shine überstrahlen, fig a. in den Schatten stellen

out·side 1. Außenseite f; SPORT Außenstürmer(in); **at the (very) ~** (aller)höchstens; **~ left (right)** SPORT Linksaußen (Rechtsaußen) m **2.** adj äußere(r, -s), Außen... **3.** adv draußen; heraus, hinaus **4.** prp außerhalb

out·sid·er Außenseiter(in)

out·size 1. Übergröße f **2.** übergroß

out·skirts Stadtrand m, Außenbezirke pl

out·spo·ken offen, freimütig

out·spread ausgestreckt, ausgebreitet

out·stand·ing hervorragend; ECON ausstehend; ungeklärt (problem); unerledigt (work)

out·stay länger bleiben als; → **welcome 4**

out·stretched ausgestreckt

out·strip überholen; fig übertreffen

out tray: in the ~ im Postausgang etc

out·vote überstimmen

out·ward 1. äußere(r, -s); äußerlich **2.** adv mst **outwards** auswärts, nach au-

ßen; **out·ward·ly** äußerlich

out·weigh fig überwiegen

out·wit überlisten, F reinlegen

out·worn veraltet, überholt

o·val 1. oval **2.** Oval n

o·va·tion Ovation f; **give s.o. a standing ~** j-m stehende Ovationen bereiten, j-m stehend Beifall klatschen

ov·en Backofen m, Bratofen m

ov·en-read·y bratfertig

o·ver 1. prp über (acc), über (acc) ... (hin)weg; über (dat), auf der anderen Seite von (or gen); über (acc), mehr als **2.** adv hinüber, herüber (**to** zu); drüben; darüber, mehr; zu Ende, vorüber, vorbei; über..., um...: et. über(geben etc); über(kochen etc); um(fallen, -werfen etc); herum(drehen etc); von Anfang bis Ende, durch(lesen etc); (gründlich) über(legen etc); noch einmal über(legen etc); noch einmal; **all ~** ganz vorbei; **~ and ~ (again)** immer wieder; **~ and above** obendrein, überdies

o·ver·age zu alt

o·ver·all 1. gesamt, Gesamt...; allgemein; insgesamt **2.** Br Arbeitsmantel m, Kittel m; (Br **~s**) Overall m, Arbeitsanzug m; Arbeitshose f

o·ver·awe einschüchtern

o·ver·bal·ance umstoßen, umkippen; das Gleichgewicht verlieren

o·ver·bear·ing anmaßend

o·ver·board MAR über Bord

o·ver·bur·den fig überlasten

o·ver·cast bewölkt, bedeckt

o·ver·charge überlasten, ELECTR a. überladen; ECON j-m zu viel berechnen; Betrag zu viel verlangen

o·ver·coat Mantel m

o·ver·come überwinden, überwältigen; **be ~ with emotion** von s-n Gefühlen übermannt werden

o·ver·crowd·ed überfüllt; überlaufen

o·ver·do übertreiben; GASTR zu lange kochen or braten; **overdone** a. übergar

o·ver·dose Überdosis f

o·ver·draft ECON (Konto)Überziehung f; a. **~ facility** Überziehungskredit m

o·ver·draw ECON Konto überziehen (**by** um)

o·ver·dress (sich) zu fein anziehen; **~ed** overdressed, zu fein angezogen

o·ver·drive MOT Overdrive m, Schongang m

o·ver·due überfällig

o·ver·eat zu viel essen

o·ver·es·ti·mate zu hoch schätzen *or* veranschlagen; *fig* überschätzen

o·ver·ex·pose PHOT überbelichten

o·ver·feed überfüttern

o·ver·flow **1.** *v/t* überfluten, überschwemmen; *v/i* überlaufen, überfließen; überquellen (**with** von); **2.** TECH Überlauf *m*; Überlaufen *n*, -fließen *n*

o·ver·grown BOT überwachsen, überwuchert

o·ver·hang *v/t* über (*dat*) hängen; *v/i* überhängen

o·ver·haul *Maschine* überholen

o·ver·head **1.** *adv* oben, droben **2.** *adj* Hoch..., Ober...; ECON ~ **expenses** *or* **costs** Gemeinkosten *pl*; SPORT Überkopf...; ~ **kick** *soccer:* Fallrückzieher *m* **3.** ECON *esp Br a. pl* Gemeinkosten *pl*

o·ver·hear (zufällig) hören

o·ver·heat·ed überhitzt, überheizt; TECH heiß gelaufen

o·ver·joyed überglücklich

o·ver·lap (sich) überlappen; sich überschneiden

o·ver·leaf umseitig, umstehend

o·ver·load überlasten (*a.* ELECTR), überladen

o·ver·look übersehen; **~ing the sea** mit Blick aufs Meer

o·ver·night **1.** über Nacht; **stay** ~ über Nacht bleiben, übernachten **2.** Nacht..., Übernachtungs...; ~ **bag** Reisetasche *f*

o·ver·pass (Straßen-, Eisenbahn-) Überführung *f*

o·ver·pay zu viel (be)zahlen

o·ver·pop·u·lat·ed übervölkert

o·ver·pow·er überwältigen; **~ing** überwältigend

o·ver·rate überbewerten, überschätzen

o·ver·reach **~ o.s.** sich übernehmen

o·ver·re·act überreagieren, überzogen reagieren (**to** auf *acc*)

o·ver·re·ac·tion Überreaktion *f*, überzogene Reaktion

o·ver·ride sich hinwegsetzen über (*acc*)

o·ver·rule *Entscheidung etc* aufheben, *Einspruch etc* abweisen

o·ver·run länger dauern als vorgesehen; *Signal* überfahren; **be ~ with** wimmeln von

o·ver·seas **1.** *adj* überseeisch, Übersee... **2.** *adv* in *or* nach Übersee

o·ver·see beaufsichtigen, überwachen

o·ver·shad·ow *fig* überschatten, in den Schatten stellen

o·ver·sight Versehen *n*

o·ver·size(d) übergroß, überdimensional, in Übergröße(n)

o·ver·sleep verschlafen

o·ver·staffed (personell) übersetzt

o·ver·state übertreiben

o·ver·state·ment Übertreibung *f*

o·ver·stay länger bleiben als; → **welcome** 4

o·ver·step *fig* überschreiten

o·ver·take überholen; *j-n* überraschen

o·ver·tax zu hoch besteuern; *fig* überbeanspruchen, überfordern

o·ver·throw **1.** *Regierung etc* stürzen **2.** (Um)Sturz *m*

o·ver·time ECON Überstunden *pl*; SPORT (Spiel)Verlängerung *f*; **do ~, work ~** Überstunden machen

o·ver·ture MUS Ouvertüre *f*; Vorspiel *n*

o·ver·turn *v/t* umwerfen, umstoßen; *Regierung etc* stürzen; *v/i* umkippen, MAR kentern

o·ver·view *fig* Überblick *m* (**of** über *acc*)

o·ver·weight **1.** Übergewicht *n* **2.** übergewichtig (*person*), zu schwer (**by** um); **be five pounds ~** fünf Pfund Übergewicht haben

o·ver·whelm überwältigen (*a. fig*)

o·ver·whelm·ing überwältigend

o·ver·work sich überarbeiten; überanstrengen

o·ver·wrought überreizt

o·ver·zeal·ous übereifrig

owe *j-m et.* schulden, schuldig sein; *et.* verdanken

ow·ing ~ **to** infolge, wegen

owl ZO Eule *f*

own **1.** eigen; *my* ~ mein Eigentum; (**all**) **on one's** ~ allein **2.** besitzen; zugeben, (ein)gestehen

own·er Eigentümer(in), Besitzer(in)

own·er·oc·cu·pied *esp Br* eigengenutzt; ~ **flat** Eigentumswohnung *f*

own·er·ship Besitz *m*; Eigentum *n*; Eigentumsrecht *n*

ox ZO Ochse *m*

ox·ide CHEM Oxid *n*, Oxyd *n*

ox·i·dize CHEM oxidieren

ox·y·gen CHEM Sauerstoff *m*; ~ ap·pa·ra-
tus MED Sauerstoffgerät *n*; ~ tent MED
Sauerstoffzelt *n*
oy·ster ZO Auster *f*
o·zone CHEM Ozon *n*

o·zone-friend·ly FCKW-frei, ohne
Treibgas
o·zone| hole Ozonloch *n*; ~ lay·er Ozon-
schicht *f*; ~ lev·els Ozonwerte *pl*; ~
shield Ozonschild *m*

P

P, p P, p *n*
pace 1. Tempo *n*, Geschwindigkeit *f*;
Schritt *m*; Gangart *f* (*of a horse*) 2.
v/t Zimmer etc durchschreiten; *a.* ~
out abschreiten; *v/i* (einher)schreiten;
~ up and down auf und ab gehen
pace·mak·er SPORT Schrittmacher(in);
MED Herzschrittmacher *m*
pace·set·ter SPORT Schrittmacher(in)
Pa·cif·ic *a.* ~ Ocean der Pazifik, der Pa-
zifische *or* Stille Ozean
pac·i·fi·er Schnuller *m*
pac·i·fist Pazifist(in)
pac·i·fy beruhigen, besänftigen
pack 1. Pack(en) *m*, Paket *n*, Bündel *n*;
Packung *f*, Schachtel *f*; ZO Meute *f*; Rudel *n*; *contp* Pack *n*, Bande *f*; MED *etc*
Packung *f*; (Karten)Spiel *n*; a ~ of lies
ein Haufen Lügen 2. *v/t* ein-, zusam-
menpacken, abpacken, verpacken (*a.*
~ up); zusammenpferchen; vollstopfen; *Koffer etc* packen; ~ off F fort-,
wegschicken; *v/i* packen; (sich) drängen (*into* in *acc*); ~ up zusammenpa-
cken; send s.o. ~ing j-n fort- *or* wegja-
gen
pack·age Paket *n*; Packung *f*; software
~ IT Software-, Programmpaket *n*
pack·age| deal F Pauschalangebot *n*,
-arrangement *n*; ~ hol·i·day Pauschal-
urlaub *m*; ~ tour Pauschalreise *f*
pack·et Päckchen *n*; Packung *f*, Schachtel *f*
pack·ing Packen *n*; Verpackung *f*
pact Pakt *m*, POL *a.* Vertrag *m*
pad 1. Polster *n*; SPORT (*Knie- etc*)Schüt-
zer *m*; (*Schreib- etc*)Block *m*; (*Stempel*)Kissen *n*; ZO Ballen *m*; (*Ab-
schuss-*) Rampe *f* 2. (aus)polstern, wat-
tieren
pad·ding Polsterung *f*, Wattierung *f*
pad·dle 1. Paddel *n*; MAR (Rad)Schaufel
f 2. paddeln; plan(t)schen

pad·dock (Pferde)Koppel *f*
pad·lock Vorhängeschloss *n*
pa·gan 1. Heide *m*, Heidin *f* 2. heidnisch
page¹ 1. Seite *f* 2. paginieren
page² 1. (Hotel)Page *m* 2. j-n ausrufen
(lassen)
pag·eant (*a.* historischer) Festzug
pa·gin·ate paginieren
pail Eimer *m*, Kübel *m*
pain 1. Schmerz(en *pl*) *m*; Kummer *m*;
pl Mühe *f*, Bemühungen *pl*; be in
(great) ~ (große) Schmerzen haben;
be a ~ (in the neck) F e-m auf den Wecker gehen; take ~s sich Mühe geben 2.
esp fig schmerzen; pain·ful schmerzhaft, schmerzend; *fig* schmerzlich;
peinlich
pain·kill·er Schmerzmittel *n*
pain·less schmerzlos
pains·tak·ing sorgfältig, gewissenhaft
paint 1. Farbe *f*; Anstrich *m* 2. *v/t* anmalen, bemalen; (an)streichen; *Auto etc*
lackieren; *v/i* malen
paint·box Malkasten *m*
paint·brush (Maler)Pinsel *m*
paint·er (*a.* Kunst)Maler(in), Anstrei-
cher(in)
paint·ing Malerei *f*; Gemälde *n*, Bild *n*
pair 1. Paar *n*; a ~ of ... ein Paar ..., ein(e)
...; a ~ of scissors e-e Schere 2. *v/i* ZO
sich paaren; *a.* ~ off, ~ up Paare bilden;
v/t a. ~ off, ~ up paarweise anordnen; ~
off zwei Leute zusammenbringen, verkuppeln
pa·ja·ma(s) (a pair of) ~s (ein) Schlafanzug *m*, (ein) Pyjama *m*
pal Kamerad *m*, F Kumpel *m*, Spezi *m*
pal·ace Palast *m*, Schloss *n*
pal·a·ta·ble schmackhaft (*a. fig*)
pal·ate ANAT Gaumen *m*; *fig* Geschmack
m
pale¹ 1. blass, *a.* bleich, *a.* hell (*color*) 2.
blass *or* bleich werden

pale² Pfahl *m*; *fig* Grenzen *pl*
pale·ness Blässe *f*
Pal·es·tin·i·an 1. palästinensisch **2.** Palästinenser(in)
pal·ings Lattenzaun *m*
pal·i·sade Palisade *f*; *pl* Steilufer *n*
pal·let TECH Palette *f*
pal·lid blass; **pal·lor** Blässe *f*
palm¹ a. **~ tree** BOT Palme *f*
palm² **1.** ANAT Handfläche *f* **2.** *et.* in der Hand verschwinden lassen; **~ s.th. off on s.o.** F j-m et. andrehen
pal·pa·ble fühlbar, greifbar
pal·pi·tate MED klopfen, pochen
pal·pi·ta·tions MED Herzklopfen *n*
pal·sy MED Lähmung *f*
pal·try armselig
pam·per verwöhnen
pam·phlet Broschüre *f*
pan Pfanne *f*; Topf *m*
pan·a·ce·a Allheilmittel *n*
pan·cake Pfannkuchen *m*
pan·da ZO Panda *m*
pan·da car *Br* (Funk)Streifenwagen *m*
pan·de·mo·ni·um Hölle *f*, Höllenlärm *m*, Tumult *m*, Chaos *n*
pan·der Vorschub leisten (**to** *dat*)
pane (Fenster)Scheibe *f*
pan·el 1. (*Tür*)Füllung *f*, (*Wand*)Täfelung *f*; ELECTR, TECH Instrumentenbrett *n*, (*Schalt-, Kontroll- etc*)Tafel *f*; JUR Liste *f* der Geschworenen; Diskussionsteilnehmer *pl*, Diskussionsrunde *f*; Rateteam *n* **2.** täfeln
pang stechender Schmerz; **~s of hunger** nagender Hunger; **~s of conscience** Gewissensbisse *pl*
pan·han·dle 1. Pfannenstiel *m*; GEOGR schmaler Fortsatz **2.** F betteln
pan·ic 1. panisch **2.** Panik *f* **3.** in Panik versetzen *or* geraten
pan·ick·y: F **be ~** in Panik sein
pan·ic-strick·en von Panik erfasst *or* erfüllt
pan·o·ra·ma Panorama *n*, Ausblick *m*
pan·sy BOT Stiefmütterchen *n*
pant keuchen, schnaufen, nach Luft schnappen
pan·ther ZO Panther *m*; Puma *m*; Jaguar *m*
pan·ties (Damen)Schlüpfer *m*, Slip *m*; Höschen *n*
pan·to·mime THEA Pantomime *f*; *Br* F Weihnachtsspiel *n*

pan·try Speisekammer *f*
pants Hose *f*; *Br* Unterhose *f*; *Br* Schlüpfer *m*
pant·suit *esp MIL* Hosenanzug *m*
pan·ty·hose Strumpfhose *f*
pan·ty·lin·er Slipeinlage *f*
pap Brei *m*
pa·pal päpstlich
pa·per 1. Papier *n*; Zeitung *f*; (Prüfungs)Arbeit *f*; UNIV Klausur(arbeit) *f*; Aufsatz *m*; Referat *n*; Tapete *f*; *pl* (Ausweis)Papiere *pl* **2.** tapezieren
pa·per·back Taschenbuch *n*, Paperback *n*
pa·per bag (Papier)Tüte *f*
pa·per·boy Zeitungsjunge *m*
pa·per clip Büro-, Heftklammer *f*
pa·per cup Pappbecher *m*
pa·per·hang·er Tapezierer *m*
pa·per knife *Br* Brieföffner *m*
pa·per mon·ey Papiergeld *n*
pa·per·weight Briefbeschwerer *m*
par: **at ~** zum Nennwert; **be on a ~ with** gleich *or* ebenbürtig sein (*dat*)
par·a·ble Parabel *f*, Gleichnis *n*
par·a·chute Fallschirm *m*
par·a·chut·ist Fallschirmspringer(in)
pa·rade 1. Umzug *m*, *esp MIL* Parade *f*; *fig* Zurschaustellung *f*; **make a ~ of** *fig* zur Schau stellen **2.** ziehen (**through** *durch*); MIL antreten (lassen), vorbeimarschieren (lassen); zur Schau stellen; **~ (through)** stolzieren durch
par·a·dise Paradies *n*
par·af·fin *Br* Petroleum *n*
par·a·glid·er SPORT Gleitschirm *m*; Gleitschirmflieger(in); **par·a·glid·ing** SPORT Gleitschirmfliegen *n*
par·a·gon Muster *n* (**of** an *dat*)
par·a·graph Absatz *m*, Abschnitt *m*; (Zeitungs)Notiz *f*
par·al·lel 1. parallel (**to, with** zu); **2.** MATH Parallele *f* (*a. fig*); **without ~** ohne Parallele, ohnegleichen **3.** entsprechen (*dat*), gleichkommen (*dat*)
par·a·lyse *Br*, **par·a·lyze** MED lähmen, *fig a.* lahmlegen, zum Erliegen bringen; **~d with** *fig* starr *or* wie gelähmt vor (*dat*)
pa·ral·y·sis MED Lähmung *f*, *fig a.* Lahmlegung *f*
par·a·med·ic MED Sanitäter *m*
par·a·mount größte(r, -s), übergeordnet; **of ~ importance** von (aller)größter

P

Bedeutung *or* Wichtigkeit
par·a·pet Brüstung *f*
par·a·pher·na·li·a (persönliche) Sachen *pl*; Ausrüstung *f*; *esp Br* F Schereien *pl*
par·a·phrase 1. umschreiben **2.** Umschreibung *f*
par·a·site Parasit *m*, Schmarotzer *m*
par·a·troop·er MIL Fallschirmjäger *m*; *pl* Fallschirmjägertruppe *f*
par·boil halb gar kochen, ankochen
par·cel 1. Paket *n*; Parzelle *f* **2. ~ out** aufteilen; **~ up** (als Paket) verpacken
parch ausdörren, austrocknen; vertrocknen
parch·ment Pergament *n*
par·don 1. JUR Begnadigung *f*; *I beg your ~* Entschuldigung!, Verzeihung!; erlauben Sie mal!, ich muss doch sehr bitten!; *a. ~?* F (wie) bitte? **2.** verzeihen; vergeben; JUR begnadigen; *~ me → I beg your pardon*; F (wie) bitte?
par·don·a·ble verzeihlich
pare sich *die Nägel* schneiden; *Apfel etc* schälen
par·ent Elternteil *m*, Vater *m*, Mutter *f*; *pl* Eltern *pl*; **par·ent·age** Abstammung *f*, Herkunft *f*; **pa·ren·tal** elterlich
pa·ren·the·ses (runde) Klammer
par·ents-in-law Schwiegereltern *pl*
par·ent-teach·er meet·ing PED Elternabend *m*
par·ings Schalen *pl*
par·ish REL Gemeinde *f*
par·ish church REL Pfarrkirche *f*
pa·rish·ion·er REL Gemeindemitglied *n*
park 1. Park *m*, (Grün)Anlage(n *pl*) *f* **2.** MOT parken; *look for somewhere to ~ the car* e-n Parkplatz suchen
par·ka Parka *m*, *f*
park·ing MOT Parken *n*; *no ~* Parkverbot, Parken verboten; *~ disk* Parkscheibe *f*; *~ fee* Parkgebühr *f*; *~ garage* Park(hoch)haus *n*; *~ lot* Parkplatz *m*; *~ lot at·tend·ant* Parkwächter *m*; *~ me·ter* Parkuhr *f*; *~ of·fend·er* Parksünder(in); *~ space* Parkplatz *m*, Parklücke *f*; *~ tick·et* Strafzettel *m*
par·ley *esp* MIL Verhandlung *f*
par·lia·ment Parlament *n*
par·lia·men·tar·i·an Parlamentarier(in)
par·lia·men·ta·ry parlamentarisch, Parlaments...
par·lo(u)r *mst in cpds* Salon *m*

pa·ro·chi·al REL Pfarr..., Gemeinde...; *fig* engstirnig, beschränkt
par·o·dy 1. Parodie *f* **2.** parodieren
pa·role JUR **1.** Hafturlaub *m*; bedingte Haftentlassung **2. ~ s.o.** j-m Hafturlaub gewähren; j-n bedingt entlassen
par·quet Parkett *n* (*a.* THEA)
par·quet floor Parkett(fuß)boden *m*
par·rot 1. ZO Papagei *m* (*a. fig*) **2.** *et.* (wie ein Papagei) nachplappern
par·ry abwehren, parieren
par·si·mo·ni·ous geizig
pars·ley BOT Petersilie *f*
par·son REL Pfarrer *m*
par·son·age REL Pfarrhaus *n*
part 1. Teil *m*; TECH Teil *n*, Bau-, Ersatzteil *n*; Anteil *m*; Seite *f*, Partei *f*; THEA, *fig* Rolle *f*; MUS Stimme *f*, Partie *f*; GEOGR Gegend *f*, Teil *m*; (Haar)Scheitel *m*; *for my ~* was mich betrifft; *for the most ~* größtenteils; meistens; *in ~* teilweise, zum Teil; *on the ~ of* von seiten, seitens (*gen*); *on my ~* von m-r Seite; *take ~ in s.th.* an e-r Sache teilnehmen; *take s.th. in good ~* et. nicht übel nehmen **2.** *v/t* trennen; (ab-, zer)teilen; einteilen; *Haar* scheiteln; *~ company* sich trennen (*with* von); *v/i* sich trennen (*with* von); **3.** *adj* Teil... **4.** *adv:* *~ ..., ~* teils ..., teils
par·tial Teil..., teilweise; parteiisch, voreingenommen (*to* für)
par·ti·al·i·ty Parteilichkeit *f*, Voreingenommenheit *f*; Schwäche *f*, besondere Vorliebe (*for* für)
par·tial·ly teilweise, zum Teil
par·tic·i·pant Teilnehmer(in)
par·tic·i·pate teilnehmen, sich beteiligen (*both: in an dat*)
par·tic·i·pa·tion Teilnahme *f*, Beteiligung *f*
par·ti·ci·ple LING Partizip *n*, Mittelwort *n*
par·ti·cle Teilchen *n*
par·tic·u·lar 1. besondere(r, -s), speziell; genau, eigen, wählerisch **2.** Einzelheit *f*; *pl* nähere Umstände *pl or* Angaben *pl*; Personalien *pl*; *in ~* insbesondere; **par·tic·u·lar·ly** besonders
part·ing 1. Trennung *f*, Abschied *m*; *esp Br* (Haar)Scheitel *m* **2.** Abschieds...
par·ti·san 1. Parteigänger(in); MIL Partisan(in) **2.** parteiisch
par·ti·tion 1. Teilung *f*; Trennwand *f* **2. ~**

off abteilen, abtrennen

part·ly teilweise, zum Teil

part·ner Partner(in), ECON *a.* Teilhaber(in); **part·ner·ship** Partnerschaft *f*, ECON *a.* Teilhaberschaft *f*

part-own·er Miteigentümer(in)

par·tridge ZO Rebhuhn *n*

part-time 1. *adj* Teilzeit…, Halbtags…; *~ worker* → **part-timer 2.** *adv* halbtags

part-tim·er F Teilzeitbeschäftigte *m, f*, Halbtagskraft *f*

par·ty Partei *f (a.* POL*)*; *(Arbeits-, Reise-)* Gruppe *f; (Rettungs- etc)*Mannschaft *f*; MIL Kommando *n*, Trupp *m*; Party *f*, Gesellschaft *f*; Teilnehmer(in), Beteiligte *m, f; ~ line* POL Parteilinie *f; ~ pol·i·tics* Parteipolitik *f*

pass 1. *v/i* vorbeigehen, -fahren, -kommen, -ziehen *etc (by* an *dat)*; übergehen *(to* auf *acc)*, fallen *(to* an *acc)*; vergehen *(pain etc, time)*; durchkommen, (die Prüfung) bestehen; gelten *(as, for* als), gehalten werden *(as, for* für) PARL Rechtskraft erlangen; unbeanstandet bleiben; SPORT (den Ball) abspielen *or* passen *(to* zu); *card game:* passen *(a. fig); let s.o. ~* j-n vorbeilassen; *let s.th. ~* et. durchgehen lassen; *v/t* vorbeigehen, -fahren, -fließen, -kommen, -ziehen *etc* an *(dat)*; überholen; *Prüfung* bestehen; *Prüfling* durchkommen lassen; *(mit der Hand)* streichen *(over* über *acc)*; j-m et. reichen, geben, et. weitergeben; SPORT *Ball* abspielen, passen *(to* zu); *Zeit* verbringen; PARL *Gesetz* verabschieden; *Urteil* abgeben, fällen, JUR *a.* sprechen *(on* über *acc); fig* hinausgehen über *(acc)*, übersteigen, übertreffen; *~ away* sterben; *~ off* j-n, et. ausgeben *(as* als); *gut etc* verlaufen; *~ out* ohnmächtig werden **2.** Passierschein *m*; Bestehen *n (examination)*; SPORT Pass *m*, Zuspiel *n; (Gebirgs)*Pass *m; free ~* Frei(fahr)karte *f*; *things have come to such a ~ that* F die Dinge haben sich derart zugespitzt, dass; *make a ~ at* F Annäherungsversuche machen bei

pass·a·ble passierbar, befahrbar; passabel, leidlich

pas·sage Passage *f*, Korridor *m*, Gang *m*; Durchgang *m; (See-, Flug)*Reise *f*; Durchfahrt *f*, Durchreise *f*; Passage *f (a.* MUS*)*, Stelle *f; bird of ~* Zugvogel *m*

pass·book ECON Sparbuch *n*

pas·sen·ger Passagier *m*, Fahrgast *m*, Fluggast *m*, Reisende *m, f*, MOT Insasse *m*, Insassin *f*

pass·er·by Passant(in)

pas·sion Leidenschaft *f*; Wut *f*, Zorn *m*; *Passion* REL Passion *f; ~s ran high* die Erregung schlug hohe Wellen

pas·sion·ate leidenschaftlich

pas·sive passiv; LING passivisch

Pass·o·ver REL Passah(fest) *n*

pass·port (Reise)Pass *m*

pass·word Kennwort *n (a.* IT*)*, MIL *a.* Parole *f*, Losung *f*

past 1. *adj* vergangen; frühere(r, -s); *be ~ a.* vorüber sein; *for some time ~* seit einiger Zeit; *~ tense* LING Vergangenheit *f*, Präteritum *n* **2.** *adv* vorüber, vorbei; *go ~* vorbeigehen **3.** *prp time:* nach, über *(acc)*; über … *(acc)* hinaus; an … *(dat)* vorbei; *half ~ two* halb drei; *~ hope* hoffnungslos **4.** Vergangenheit *f (a.* LING*)*

pas·ta Teigwaren *pl*

paste 1. Paste *f*; Kleister *m*; Teig *m* **2.** kleben *(to, on* an *acc); ~ up* ankleben

paste·board Karton *m*, Pappe *f*

pas·tel Pastell(zeichnung *f) n*

pas·teur·ize pasteurisieren

pas·time Zeitvertreib *m*, Freizeitbeschäftigung *f*

pas·tor REL Pastor *m*, Pfarrer *m*, Seelsorger *m*; **pas·tor·al** REL seelsorgerisch, pastoral; *~ care* Seelsorge *f*

pas·try GASTR *(Blätter-, Mürbe)*Teig *m*; Feingebäck *n; ~ cook* Konditor *m*

pas·ture 1. Weide(land *n) f* **2.** *v/t* weiden (lassen); *v/i* grasen, weiden

pas·ty¹ *esp Br* GASTR (Fleisch)Pastete *f*

past·y² blass, F käsig

pat 1. Klaps *m*; GASTR Portion *f* **2.** tätscheln; klopfen

patch 1. Fleck *m*; Flicken *m*; kleines Stück Land; *in ~es* stellenweise **2.** flicken

pa·tent 1. offenkundig; patentiert; Patent… **2.** Patent *n; take out a ~ for s.th.* (sich) et. patentieren lassen **3.** *et.* patentieren lassen

pa·tent·ee Patentinhaber(in)

pa·tent leath·er Lackleder *n*

pa·ter·nal väterlich; väterlicherseits

pa·ter·ni·ty JUR Vaterschaft *f*

path Pfad *m*; Weg *m*

pa·thet·ic mitleiderregend; kläglich, miserabel

pa·tience Geduld *f; esp Br* Patience *f*

pa·tient¹ geduldig

pa·tient² MED Patient(in)

pat·i·o Terrasse *f;* Innenhof *m,* Patio *m*

pat·ri·ot Patriot(in)

pat·ri·ot·ic patriotisch

pa·trol **1.** Patrouille *f* (a. MIL), Streife *f,* Runde *f;* **on~** auf Patrouille, auf Streife **2.** abpatrouillieren, auf Streife sein in (*dat*), s-e Runde machen in (*dat*)

pa·trol car (Funk)Streifenwagen *m*

pa·trol·man Streifenpolizist *m; Br* motorisierter Pannenhelfer

pa·tron Schirmherr *m;* Gönner *m,* Förderer *m;* (Stamm)Kunde *m;* Stammgast *m;* pat·ron·age Schirmherrschaft *f;* Förderung *f;* pat·ron·ess Schirmherrin *f;* Gönnerin *f,* Förderin *f;* pat·ron·ize fördern; (Stamm)Kunde *or* Stammgast sein bei *or* in (*dat*); gönnerhaft *or* herablassend behandeln

pa·tron saint REL Schutzheilige *m, f*

pat·ter prasseln (*rain*); trappeln (*feet*)

pat·tern **1.** Muster *n* (a. *fig*); Schema *n* **2.** bilden, formen (**after, on** nach)

paunch (dicker) Bauch

pau·per Arme *m, f*

pause **1.** Pause *f* **2.** innehalten, e-e Pause machen

pave pflastern; **~ the way for** *fig* den Weg ebnen für

pave·ment Fahrbahn *f;* Belag *m,* Pflaster *n; Br* Bürgersteig *m,* Gehsteig *m*

pave·ment ca·fé *Br* Straßencafé *n*

paw **1.** ZO Pfote *f,* Tatze *f* **2.** *v/t* Boden scharren; scharren an (*dat*); F betatschen; *v/i* scharren (**at** an *dat*)

pawn¹ *chess:* Bauer *m; fig* Schachfigur *f*

pawn² **1.** verpfänden, versetzen **2. be in ~** verpfändet *or* versetzt sein

pawn·bro·ker Pfandleiher *m*

pawn·shop Leihhaus *n,* Pfandhaus *n*

pay **1.** *v/t et.* (be)zahlen; *j-n* bezahlen; *Aufmerksamkeit* schenken; *Besuch* abstatten; *Kompliment* machen; **~ attention** achtgeben auf (*acc*); PED aufpassen; **~ cash** bar bezahlen; *v/i* zahlen; *fig* sich lohnen; **~ for** (*fig* für) *et.* bezahlen; *fig* büßen; **~ in** einzahlen; **~ into** einzahlen auf (*acc*); **~ off** *et.* ab(be)zahlen; *j-n* auszahlen **2.** Bezahlung *f,* Gehalt *n,* Lohn *m*

pay·a·ble zahlbar, fällig

pay·day Zahltag *m*

pay·ee Zahlungsempfänger(in)

pay en·ve·lope Lohntüte *f*

pay·ing lohnend

pay·mas·ter MIL Zahlmeister *m*

pay·ment (Be)Zahlung *f*

pay pack·et *Br* Lohntüte *f*

pay phone *Br* Münzfernsprecher *m*

pay·roll Lohnliste *f*

pay·slip Lohn-, Gehaltsstreifen *m*

PC *abbr of* **personal computer** PC *m,* Personal Computer *m;* **PC user** PC-Benutzer *m*

pea BOT Erbse *f*

peace Friede(n) *m;* Ruhe *f;* JUR öffentliche Ruhe und Ordnung; **at ~** in Frieden

peace·a·ble friedlich, friedfertig

peace·ful friedlich

peace·lov·ing friedliebend

peace move·ment Friedensbewegung *f*

peace·time Friedenszeiten *pl*

peach BOT Pfirsich(baum) *m*

pea·cock ZO Pfau *m,* Pfauhahn *m*

pea·hen ZO Pfauhenne *f*

peak Spitze *f,* Gipfel *m;* Schirm *m; fig* Höhepunkt *m,* Höchststand *m*

peaked cap Schirmmütze *f*

peak hours Hauptverkehrszeit *f,* Stoßzeit *f;* ELECTR Hauptbelastungszeit *f*

peak| time, **~ viewing hours** *Br* TV Haupteinschaltzeit *f,* Hauptsendezeit *f,* beste Sendezeit

peal **1.** (*Glocken*)Läuten *n;* (*Donner-*) Schlag *m;* **~s of laughter** schallendes Gelächter **2.** a. **~ out** läuten; krachen

pea·nut BOT Erdnuss *f; pl* F lächerliche Summe

pear BOT Birne *f;* Birnbaum *m*

pearl **1.** Perle *f;* Perlmutter *f,* Perlmutt *n* **2.** Perlen...

pearl·y perlenartig, Perlen...

peas·ant Kleinbauer *m*

peat Torf *m*

peb·ble Kiesel(stein) *m*

peck picken, hacken; **~ at one's food** im Essen herumstochern

pe·cu·li·ar eigen, eigentümlich, typisch; eigenartig, seltsam

pe·cu·li·ar·i·ty Eigenheit *f;* Eigentümlichkeit *f*

ped·a·go·gic pädagogisch

ped·al **1.** Pedal *n* **2.** das Pedal treten;

(mit dem Rad) fahren, strampeln
pe·dan·tic pedantisch
ped·es·tal Sockel *m*
pe·des·tri·an 1. Fußgänger(in) **2.** Fußgänger…; ~ **cross·ing** Fußgängerübergang *m*; ~ **mall**, *esp Br* ~ **pre·cinct** Fußgängerzone *f*
ped·i·cure Pediküre *f*
ped·i·gree Stammbaum *m* (*a.* ZO)
ped·lar *Br* → **peddler**
pee F **1.** pinkeln **2. have** (*or* **go for**) **a** ~ pinkeln (gehen)
peek 1. kurz *or* verstohlen gucken (**at** auf *acc*); **2. have** *or* **take a** ~ **at** e-n kurzen *or* verstohlenen Blick werfen auf (*acc*)
peel 1. *v/t* schälen; *a.* ~ **off** abschälen, *Folie, Tapete etc* abziehen, ablösen; *Kleid* abstreifen; *v/i a.* ~ **off** sich lösen (*wallpaper etc*), abblättern (*paint etc*), sich schälen (*skin*) **2.** BOT Schale *f*
peep¹ 1. kurz *or* verstohlen gucken (**at** auf *acc*); *mst* ~ **out** (her)vorschauen **2. take a** ~ **at** e-n kurzen *or* verstohlenen Blick werfen auf (*acc*)
peep² 1. Piep(s)en *n*; F Piepser *m* **2.** piep(s)en
peep·hole Guckloch *n*; (Tür)Spion *m*
peer angestrengt schauen, spähen; ~ **at s.o.** j-n anstarren
peer·less unvergleichlich, einzigartig
peev·ish verdrießlich, gereizt
peg 1. (Holz)Stift *m*, Zapfen *m*, Pflock *m*; (Kleider)Haken *m*; *Br* (Wäsche-)Klammer *f*; (Zelt)Hering *m*; **take s.o. down a** ~ (**or two**) F j-m e-n Dämpfer aufsetzen **2.** anpflocken; *Wäsche* anklammern, festklammern
pel·i·can ZO Pelikan *m*; ~ **cross·ing** *Br* Ampelübergang *m*
pel·let Kügelchen *n*; Schrotkorn *n*
pelt¹ *v/t* bewerfen, *v/i*: **it's** ~**ing** (**down**), *esp Br* **it's** ~**ing with rain** es gießt in Strömen
pelt² ZO Fell *n*, Pelz *m*
pel·vis ANAT Becken *n*
pen¹ (*Schreib*)Feder *f*; Füller *m*; Kugelschreiber *m*
pen²¹. Pferch *m*, (*Schaf*)Hürde *f* **2.** ~ **in**, ~ **up** Tiere einpferchen, *Personen* zusammenpferchen
pe·nal JUR Straf…; strafbar
pe·nal code JUR Strafgesetzbuch *n*
pe·nal·ize bestrafen

pen·al·ty Strafe *f*, SPORT *a.* Strafpunkt *m*; *soccer*: Elfmeter *m*; ~ **ar·e·a**, ~ **box** F *soccer*: Strafraum *m*; ~ **goal** *soccer*: Elfmetertor *n*; ~ **kick** *soccer*: Elfmeter *m*, Strafstoß *m*; ~ **shoot-out** *soccer*: Elfmeterschießen *n*; ~ **spot** *soccer*: Elfmeterpunkt *m*
pen·ance REL Buße *f*
pen·cil 1. Bleistift *m* **2.** (mit Bleistift) markieren *or* schreiben *or* zeichnen; *Augenbrauen* nachziehen
pen·cil case Federmäppchen *n*
pen·cil sharp·en·er Bleistiftspitzer *m*
pen·dant, pen·dent (Schmuck)Anhänger *m*
pend·ing 1. *prp* bis zu **2.** *adj esp* JUR schwebend
pen·du·lum Pendel *n*
pen·e·trate *v/t* eindringen in (*acc*); dringen durch, durchdringen; *v/i* eindringen (**into** in *acc*); **pen·e·trat·ing** durchdringend; *fig* scharf; scharfsinnig; **pen·e·tra·tion** Durchdringen *n*, Eindringen *n*; *fig* Scharfsinn *m*
pen friend *Br* Brieffreund(in)
pen·guin ZO Pinguin *m*
pe·nin·su·la Halbinsel *f*
pe·nis ANAT Penis *m*
pen·i·tence Buße *f*, Reue *f*
pen·i·tent 1. reuig, bußfertig **2.** REL Büßer(in)
pen·i·ten·tia·ry (Staats)Gefängnis *n*, Strafanstalt *f*
pen·knife Taschenmesser *n*
pen name mst name Schriftstellername *m*, Pseudonym *n*
pen·nant Wimpel *m*
pen·ni·less (völlig) mittellos
pen·ny *Br* Penny *m*
pen pal Brieffreund(in)
pen·sion 1. Rente *f*, Pension *f* **2.** ~ **off** pensionieren, in den Ruhestand versetzen
pen·sion·er Rentner(in), Pensionär(in)
pen·sive nachdenklich
pen·tath·lete SPORT Fünfkämpfer(in)
pen·tath·lon SPORT Fünfkampf *m*
Pen·te·cost REL Pfingsten *n*
pent·house Penthouse *n*, Penthaus *n*
pent-up auf-, angestaut (*emotions*)
pe·o·ny BOT Pfingstrose *f*
peo·ple 1. Volk *n*, Nation *f*; die Menschen *pl*, die Leute *pl*; Leute *pl*, Personen *pl*; man; **the** ~ das (*gemeine*) Volk

P

2. besiedeln, bevölkern (**with** mit)

peo·ple's re·pub·lic Volksrepublik *f*

pep F **1.** Pep *m*, Schwung *m* **2.** *mst ~ up* *j-n or et.* in Schwung bringen, aufmöbeln

pep·per 1. Pfeffer *m*; BOT Paprikaschote *f* **2.** pfeffern

pep·per cast·er Pfefferstreuer *m*

pep·per·mint BOT Pfefferminze *f*; Pfefferminz *n*

pep·per·y pfeff(e)rig; *fig* hitzig

pep·pill F Aufputschpille *f*

per per, durch; pro, für, je

per·ceive(be)merken, wahrnehmen; erkennen

per cent, per·cent Prozent *n*

per·cen·tage Prozentsatz *m*; F Prozente *pl*, (An)Teil *m*

per·cep·ti·ble wahrnehmbar, merklich; **per·cep·tion** Wahrnehmung *f*; Auffassung *f*, Auffassungsgabe *f*

perch[1] **1.** (Sitz)Stange *f* **2.** (**on**) sich setzen (auf *acc*), sich niederlassen (auf *acc*, *dat*); F hocken (**on** auf *dat*); ~ *o.s.* F sich hocken (**on** auf *acc*)

perch[2] ZO Barsch *m*

per·co·la·tor Kaffeemaschine *f*

per·cus·sion Schlag *m*; Erschütterung *f*; MUS Schlagzeug *n*; ~ **drill** TECH Schlagbohrer *m*; ~ **in·stru·ment** MUS Schlaginstrument *n*

pe·remp·to·ry herrisch

pe·ren·ni·al ewig, immer während; BOT mehrjährig

per·fect 1. perfekt, vollkommen, vollendet; gänzlich, völlig **2.** vervollkommnen **3.** *a. ~ tense* LING Perfekt *n*

per·fec·tion Vollendung *f*; Vollkommenheit *f*, Perfektion *f*

per·fo·rate durchbohren, -löchern

per·form *v/t* verrichten, durchführen, tun; *Pflicht etc* erfüllen; THEA, MUS aufführen, spielen, vortragen; *v/i* THEA *etc* e-e Vorstellung geben, auftreten, spielen; **per·form·ance** Verrichtung *f*, Durchführung *f*; Leistung *f*; THEA, MUS Aufführung *f*, Vorstellung *f*, Vortrag *m*; **per·form·er** THEA, MUS Darsteller(in), Künstler(in)

per·fume 1. Duft *m*; Parfüm *n* **2.** parfümieren; **per·fum·er·y** Parfümerie *f*

per·haps vielleicht

per·il Gefahr *f*; **per·il·ous** gefährlich

pe·ri·od Periode *f*, Zeit *f*, Zeitdauer *f*,

Zeitraum *m*, Zeitspanne *f*; (Unterrichts)Stunde *f*; MED Periode *f*; LING Punkt *m*; ~ **fur·ni·ture** Stilmöbel *pl*

pe·ri·od·ic periodisch

pe·ri·od·i·cal 1. periodisch **2.** Zeitschrift *f*

pe·riph·e·ral IT Peripheriegerät *n*; ~ **e·quip·ment** IT Peripheriegeräte *pl*

pe·riph·e·ry Peripherie *f*, Rand *m*

per·ish umkommen; GASTR schlecht werden, verderben; TECH verschleißen

per·ish·a·ble leicht verderblich

per·ish·a·bles leicht verderbliche Lebensmittel

per·jure: ~ *o.s.* JUR e-n Meineid leisten

per·ju·ry JUR Meineid *m*; **commit** ~ e-n Meineid leisten

perk ~ **up** *v/i* aufleben, munter werden; *v/t* j-n munter machen, F aufmöbeln

perk·y F munter, lebhaft; keck, selbstbewusst

perm 1. Dauerwelle *f*; **get a** ~ → **2. get one's hair ~ed** sich e-e Dauerwelle machen lassen

per·ma·nent 1. (be)ständig, dauerhaft, Dauer...**2.** *a. ~ wave* Dauerwelle *f*

per·me·a·ble durchlässig (**to** für)

per·me·ate durchdringen; dringen (**into** in *acc*; **through** durch)

per·mis·si·ble zulässig, erlaubt

per·mis·sion Erlaubnis *f*

per·mis·sive liberal; (sexuell) freizügig; ~ **so·ci·e·ty** tabufreie Gesellschaft

per·mit 1. erlauben, gestatten **2.** Genehmigung *f*

per·pen·dic·u·lar senkrecht; rechtwink(e)lig (**to** zu)

per·pet·u·al fortwährend, ständig, ewig

per·plex verwirren

per·plex·i·ty Verwirrung *f*

per·se·cute verfolgen

per·se·cu·tion Verfolgung *f*

per·se·cu·tor Verfolger(in)

per·se·ver·ance Ausdauer *f*, Beharrlichkeit *f*

per·se·vere beharrlich weitermachen

per·sist beharren (**in** auf *dat*); anhalten

per·sis·tence Beharrlichkeit *f*

per·sis·tent beharrlich; anhaltend

per·son Person *f* (*a.* LING)

per·son·al persönlich (*a.* LING); Personal...; Privat...; ~ **com·pu·ter** (*abbr* **PC**) Personal Computer *m*; ~ **da·ta** Personalien *pl*

per·son·al·i·ty Persönlichkeit *f*; *pl* anzügliche *or* persönliche Bemerkungen *pl*

per·son·al| or·ga·ni·zer Notizbuch *n*, Adressbuch *n* und Taschenkalender *m* etc (*in einem*); **~ pro·noun** LING Personalpronomen *n*; **~ ster·e·o** Walkman® *m*

per·son·i·fy personifizieren, verkörpern

per·son·nel Personal *n*, Belegschaft *f*; die Personalabteilung; **~ de·part·ment** Personalabteilung *f*; **~ man·ag·er** Personalchef *m*

per·spec·tive Perspektive *f*; Fernsicht *f*

per·spi·ra·tion Transpirieren *n*, Schwitzen *n*; Schweiß *m*

per·spire transpirieren, schwitzen

per·suade überreden; überzeugen

per·sua·sion Überredung(skunst) *f*; Überzeugung *f*

per·sua·sive überzeugend

pert keck, kess; schnippisch

per·tain: ~ to s.th. et. betreffen

per·ti·nent sachdienlich, relevant, zur Sache gehörig

per·turb beunruhigen

per·vade durchdringen, erfüllen

per·verse pervers; eigensinnig

per·ver·sion Verdrehung *f*; Perversion *f*

per·ver·si·ty Perversität *f*; Eigensinn *m*

per·vert 1. pervertieren; verdrehen **2.** perverser Mensch

pes·sa·ry MED Pessar *n*

pes·si·mism Pessimismus *m*

pes·si·mist Pessimist(in)

pes·si·mis·tic pessimistisch

pest ZO Schädling *m*; F Nervensäge *f*; Plage *f*; **~ con·trol** Schädlingsbekämpfung *f*

pes·ter F *j-n* belästigen, *j-m* keine Ruhe lassen

pes·ti·cide Pestizid *n*, Schädlingsbekämpfungsmittel *n*

pet 1. (zahmes) (Haus)Tier; *often contp* Liebling *m* **2.** Lieblings...; Tier... **3.** streicheln; F Petting machen

pet·al BOT Blütenblatt *n*

pet food Tiernahrung *f*

pe·ti·tion 1. Eingabe *f*, Gesuch *n*, (schriftlicher) Antrag **2.** ersuchen; ein Gesuch einreichen (*for* um), e-n Antrag stellen (*for* auf *acc*)

pet name Kosename *m*

pet·ri·fy versteinern

pet·rol *Br* Benzin *n*

pe·tro·le·um Erdöl *n*, Mineralöl *n*

pet·rol| pump *Br* Zapfsäule *f*; **~ station** *Br* Tankstelle *f*

pet shop Tierhandlung *f*, Zoogeschäft *n*

pet·ti·coat Unterrock *m*

pet·ting F Petting *n*

pet·tish launisch, gereizt

pet·ty belanglos, unbedeutend, JUR *a.* geringfügig; engstirnig; **~ cash** Portokasse *f*; **~ lar·ce·ny** JUR einfacher Diebstahl

pet·u·lant launisch, gereizt

pew (Kirchen)Bank *f*

pew·ter Zinn *n*; *a.* **~ ware** Zinn (-geschirr) *n*

phan·tom Phantom *n*; Geist *m*

phar·ma·cist Apotheker(in)

phar·ma·cy Apotheke *f*

phase Phase *f*

pheas·ant ZO Fasan *m*

phe·nom·e·non Phänomen *n*, Erscheinung *f*

phi·lan·thro·pist Philanthrop(in), Menschenfreund(in)

phil·is·tine F *contp* **1.** Spießer *m* **2.** spießig

phi·lol·o·gist Philologe *m*, Philologin *f*

phi·lol·o·gy Philologie *f*

phi·los·o·pher Philosoph(in)

phi·los·o·phy Philosophie *f*

phlegm MED Schleim *m*

phone 1. Telefon *n*; **answer the~** ans Telefon gehen; **by ~** telefonisch; **on the ~** am Telefon; **be on the ~** Telefon haben; am Telefon sein **2.** telefonieren, anrufen; **~ book** Telefonbuch *n*; **~ booth**, *Br* **~ box** Telefonzelle *f*; **~ call** Anruf *m*, Gespräch *n*

phone-card Telefonkarte *f*

phone-in *radio*, TV Sendung *f* mit telefonischer Zuhörer- *or* Zuschauerbeteiligung

phone num·ber Telefonnummer *f*

pho·net·ics Phonetik *f*

pho·n(e)y F **1.** Fälschung *f*; Schwindler(in) **2.** falsch, gefälscht, unecht; Schein...

phos·pho·rus CHEM Phosphor *m*

pho·to F Foto *n*, Bild *n*; **in the ~** auf dem Foto; **take a ~** ein Foto machen (*of* von)

pho·to·cop·i·er Fotokopiergerät *n*

pho·to·cop·y 1. Fotokopie *f* **2.** fotokopieren

pho·to·graph 1. Fotografie *f* **2.** fotografieren

pho·tog·ra·pher Fotograf(in)

pho·tog·ra·phy Fotografie *f*

phras·al LING Verb *n* mit Adverb (und Präposition)

phrase 1. (Rede)Wendung *f*, Redensart *f*, idiomatischer Ausdruck **2.** ausdrücken; **phrase·book** Sprachführer *m*

phys·i·cal 1. physisch, körperlich; physikalisch; ~**ly handicapped** körperbehindert **2.** ärztliche Untersuchung; ~ **ed·u·ca·tion** Leibeserziehung *f*, Sport *m*; ~ **ex·am·i·na·tion** ärztliche Untersuchung; ~ **hand·i·cap** Körperbehinderung *f*; ~ **train·ing** Leibeserziehung *f*, Sport *m*

phy·si·cian Arzt *m*, Ärztin *f*

phys·i·cist Physiker(in)

phys·ics Physik *f*

phy·sique Körper(bau) *m*, Statur *f*

pi·a·nist MUS Pianist(in)

pi·an·o MUS Klavier *n*

pick 1. (auf)hacken; (auf)picken; auflesen, aufnehmen; pflücken; *Knochen* abnagen; bohren *or* stochern in (*dat*); *F Schloss* knacken; aussuchen, auswählen; ~ **one's nose** in der Nase bohren; ~ **one's teeth** in den Zähnen (herum)stochern; ~ **s.o.'s pocket** j-n bestehlen; **have a bone to** ~ **with s.o.** mit j-m ein Hühnchen zu rupfen haben; ~ **out** (sich) *et.* auswählen; ausmachen, erkennen; ~ **up** aufheben, auflesen, aufnehmen; aufpicken; *Spur* aufnehmen; *j-n* abholen; *Anhalter* mitnehmen; *F Mädchen* aufreißen; *Kenntnisse, Informationen etc* aufschnappen; sich *e-e Krankheit etc* holen; *a.* ~ **up speed** MOT schneller werden **2.** (Spitz)Hacke *f*, Pickel *m*; (Aus)Wahl *f*; **take your** ~ suchen Sie sich etwas aus

pick·a·back huckepack

pick·ax, *Br* **pick·axe** (Spitz)Hacke *f*, Pickel *m*

pick·et Pfahl *m*; Streikposten *m* **2.** Streikposten aufstellen vor (*dat*), mit Streikposten besetzen; Streikposten stehen; ~ **fence** Lattenzaun *m*; ~ **line** Streikpostenkette *f*

pick·le GASTR **1.** Salzlake *f*; Essigsoße *f*; Essig-, Gewürzgurke *f*; *mst pl esp Br* Pickles *pl*; **be in a (pretty)** ~ F (ganz schön) in der Patsche sitzen *or* sein

or stecken **2.** einlegen

pick·lock Einbrecher *m*; TECH Dietrich *m*

pick·pock·et Taschendieb(in)

pick·up Tonabnehmer *m*; Kleintransporter *m*; F (Zufalls)Bekanntschaft *f*

pick·y F wählerisch (**in** *dat* about)

pic·nic 1. Picknick *n* **2.** ein Picknick machen, picknicken

pic·ture 1. Bild *n*; Gemälde *n*; PHOT Aufnahme *f*; Film *m*; *pl esp Br* Kino *n* **2.** darstellen, malen; *fig* sich *j-n, et.* vorstellen; ~ **book** Bilderbuch *n*; ~ **post·card** Ansichtskarte *f*

pic·tur·esque malerisch

pie (*Fleisch- etc*)Pastete *f*; (*mst gedeckter*) (*Apfel- etc*)Kuchen

piece 1. Stück *n*; Teil *n* (*of a machine etc*); Teil *m* (*of a set etc*); *chess*: Figur *f*; *board game*: Stein *m*; (Zeitungs)Artikel *m*, (-)Notiz *f*; **by the** ~ stückweise; **a** ~ **of advice** ein Rat; **a** ~ **of news** e-e Neuigkeit; **give s.o. a** ~ **of one's mind** j-m gründlich die Meinung sagen; **go to** ~**s** F zusammenbrechen; **take to** ~**s** auseinandernehmen **2.** ~ **together** zusammensetzen, zusammenstückeln; *fig* zusammenfügen

piece·meal schrittweise

piece·work Akkordarbeit *f*; **do** ~ im Akkord arbeiten

pier MAR Pier *m*, Landungsbrücke *f*; TECH Pfeiler *m*

pierce durchbohren, durchstechen, durchstoßen; durchdringen

pierc·ing durchdringend, (*Kälte etc a.*) schneidend, (*Schrei a.*) gellend, (*Blick, Schmerz etc a.*) stechend

pi·e·ty Frömmigkeit *f*

pig ZO Schwein *n* (*a.* F); F Ferkel *n*; *sl contp* Bulle *m*

pi·geon ZO Taube *f*

pi·geon·hole 1. Fach *n* **2.** ablegen

pig·gy F Schweinchen *n*

pig·gy·back huckepack

pig·gy bank Sparschwein(chen) *n*

pig·head·ed dickköpfig, stur

pig·let ZO Ferkel *n*

pig·sty Schweinestall *m*, F *contp* Saustall *m*

pig·tail Zopf *m*

pike[1] ZO Hecht *m*

pike[2] → **turnpike**

pile[1] **1.** Stapel *m*, Stoß *m*; F Haufen *m*,

527

pitiable

Menge *f*; **(atomic)** ~ Atommeiler *m* **2.** ~
up (an-, auf)häufen, (auf)stapeln, aufschichten; sich anhäufen; MOT F aufeinander auffahren

pile² Flor *m*

pile³ Pfahl *m*

piles *Br* F MED Hämorrhoiden *pl*

pile-up MOT Massenkarambolage *f*

pil·fer stehlen, klauen

pil·grim Pilger(in)

pil·grim·age Pilgerfahrt *f*, Wallfahrt *f*

pill PHARM Pille *f*; **the** ~ F die (Antibaby)-Pille; **be on the** ~ die Pille nehmen

pil·lar Pfeiler *m*; Säule *f*

pil·li·on MOT Soziussitz *m*

pil·lo·ry **1.** HIST Pranger *m* **2.** fig anprangern

pil·low (Kopf)Kissen *n*

pil·low·case, pil·low slip (Kopf)Kissenbezug *m*

pi·lot **1.** AVIAT Pilot *m*; MAR Lotse *m* **2.** Versuchs…, Pilot… **3.** lotsen; steuern; ~ film TV Pilotfilm *m*; ~ scheme Versuchs-, Pilotprojekt *n*

pimp Zuhälter *m*

pim·ple MED Pickel *m*, Pustel *f*

pin **1.** (Steck)Nadel *f*; (Haar-, Krawatten- etc)Nadel *f*; Brosche *f*; TECH Bolzen *m*, Stift *m*; bowling: Kegel *m*; Pin *m*; (Wäsche)Klammer *f*; *Br* (Reiß)Nagel *m*, (-)Zwecke *f* **2.** (an)heften, anstecken (**to** an *acc*), befestigen (**to** an *dat*); pressen, drücken (**against, to** gegen, an *acc*)

PIN *a.* ~ **number** *abbr of* **personal identification number** PIN, persönliche Geheimzahl

pin·a·fore Schürze *f*

pin·ball Flippern *n*; **play** ~ flippern

pin·ball ma·chine Flipper(automat) *m*

pin·cers (**a pair of** ~ e-e) (Kneif)Zange *f*

pinch **1.** *v/t* kneifen, zwicken; F klauen; *v/i* drücken **2.** Kneifen *n*, Zwicken *n*; Prise *f*; fig Not(lage) *f*

pin·cush·ion Nadelkissen *n*

pine¹ BOT Kiefer *f*, Föhre *f*

pine² sich sehnen (**for** nach)

pine·ap·ple BOT Ananas *f*

pine cone BOT Kiefernzapfen *m*

pine-tree BOT Kiefer *f*, Föhre *f*

pin·ion ZO Schwungfeder *f*

pink **1.** rosa(farben) **2.** Rosa *n*; BOT Nelke *f*

pint Pint *n* (0,47 l, *Br* 0,57 l); *Br* F Halbe *f*

pi·o·neer **1.** Pionier *m* **2.** den Weg bahnen (für)

pi·ous fromm, religiös

pip¹ *Br* (Apfel-, Orangen- etc)Kern *m*

pip² (Piep)Ton *m*

pip³ on cards etc: Auge *n*, Punkt *m*

pipe **1.** TECH Rohr *n*, Röhre *f*; (Tabaks)-Pfeife *f*; MUS (Orgel)Pfeife *f*; *pl Br* F Dudelsack *m* **2.** (durch Rohre) leiten

pipe-line Rohrleitung *f*; Pipeline *f*

pip·er MUS Dudelsackpfeifer *m*

pip·ing **1.** Rohrleitung *f*, Rohrnetz *n* **2.** ~ **hot** kochend heiß, siedend heiß

pi·quant pikant (*a.* fig)

pique **1. in a fit of** ~ gekränkt, verletzt, pikiert **2.** kränken, verletzen; **be** ~**d** *a.* pikiert sein

pi·rate **1.** Pirat *m*, Seeräuber *m* **2.** unerlaubt kopieren *or* nachdrucken *or* nachpressen

pi·rate ra·di·o Piratensender *m or pl*

Pis·ces ASTR Fische *pl*; **he (she) is (a)** ~ er (sie) ist (ein) Fisch

piss V **1.** Pisse *f*; **take the** ~ **out of s.o.** j-n verarschen **2.** pissen; ~ **off!** verpiss dich!

pis·tol Pistole *f*

pis·ton TECH Kolben *m*

pit¹ **1.** Grube *f* (*a.* ANAT), MIN *a.* Zeche *f*; *esp Br* THEA Parkett *n*; *a.* **orchestra** ~ THEA Orchestergraben *m*; MED (esp Pocken)Narbe *f*; car racing: Box *f*; ~ **stop** Boxenstopp *m* **2.** mit Narben bedecken

pit² **1.** BOT Kern *m*, Stein *m* **2.** entkernen, entsteinen

pitch¹ **1.** *v/t* Zelt, Lager aufschlagen; werfen, schleudern; MUS (an)stimmen; *v/i* stürzen, fallen; MAR stampfen; sich neigen (roof etc); ~ **in** F sich ins Zeug legen; kräftig zulangen **2.** *esp Br* SPORT (Spiel)Feld *n*; MUS Tonhöhe *f*; fig Grad *m*, Stufe *f*; *esp Br* Stand(platz) *m*; MAR Stampfen *n*; Neigung *f* (of a roof etc)

pitch² Pech *n*

pitch-black, pitch-dark pechschwarz; stockdunkel

pitch·er¹ Krug *m*

pitch·er² baseball: Werfer *m*

pitch-fork Heugabel *f*, Mistgabel *f*

pit·e·ous kläglich

pit·fall Fallgrube *f*; fig Falle *f*

pith BOT Mark *n*; weiße innere Haut; fig Kern *m*; pith·y markig, prägnant

pit·i·a·ble → **pitiful**

pit·i·ful mitleiderregend, bemitleidenswert; erbärmlich, jämmerlich

pit·i·less unbarmherzig, erbarmungslos

pit·ta bread Fladenbrot n

pit·y1. Mitleid n (**on** mit); *it is a* (**great**) ~ es ist (sehr) schade; *what a* ~! wie schade! **2.** bemitleiden, bedauern

piv·ot 1. TECH Drehzapfen m; fig Dreh- und Angelpunkt m **2.** sich drehen; ~ **on** fig abhängen von

pix·el IT Pixel m

piz·za Pizza f

plac·ard 1. Plakat n; Transparent n **2.** mit Plakaten bekleben

place1. Platz m, Ort m, Stelle f; Stätte f; Haus n, Wohnung f; Wohnort m; (*Arbeits-, Lehr*)Stelle f; *in the first* ~ erstens; *in third* ~ SPORT etc auf dem dritten Platz; *in* ~ *of* anstelle von (or gen); *out of* ~ fehl am Platz; *take* ~ stattfinden; *take s.o.'s* ~ j-s Stelle einnehmen **2.** stellen, legen, setzen; Auftrag erteilen (**with** dat), Bestellung aufgeben (**with** bei); *be* ~*d* SPORT sich platzieren (**second** an zweiter Stelle)

place mat Platzdeckchen n, Set n, m

place·ment test Einstufungsprüfung f

place name Ortsname m

plac·id ruhig; gelassen

pla·gia·rize plagiieren

plague1. Seuche f; Pest f; Plage f **2.** plagen

plaice ZO Scholle f

plaid Plaid n or m

plain 1. adj einfach schlicht; klar (und deutlich); offen (und ehrlich); unscheinbar, wenig anziehend; rein, völlig (*nonsense etc*) **2.** adv F (ganz) einfach **3.** Ebene f, Flachland n

plain choc·olate Br (zart)bittere Schokolade

plain-clothes ... in Zivil

plain-tiff JUR Kläger(in)

plain·tive traurig, klagend

plait esp Br **1.** Zopf m **2.** flechten

plan1. Plan m **2.** planen; beabsichtigen

plane1 Flugzeug n; *by* ~ mit dem Flugzeug; *go by* ~ fliegen

plane²1. flach, eben **2.** MATH Ebene f; fig Stufe f, Niveau n

plane³1. Hobel m **2.** hobeln; ~ *down* abhobeln

plan·et ASTR Planet m

plank Planke f, Bohle f; ~ *bed* Pritsche f

plank·ing Planken pl

plant1. BOT Pflanze f; ECON Werk n, Betrieb m, Fabrik f **2.** (an-, ein)pflanzen; bepflanzen; *Garten etc* anlegen; aufstellen, postieren; ~ *s.th. on s.o* F j-m et. (*Belastendes*) unterschieben

plan·ta·tion Plantage f, Pflanzung f; Schonung f

plant·er Plantagenbesitzer(in), Pflanzer(in); Pflanzmaschine f; Übertopf m

plaque Gedenktafel f; MED Zahnbelag m

plas·ter1. MED Pflaster n; (Ver)Putz m; ~ *of Paris* Gips m; *have one's leg in* ~ MED das Bein in Gips haben **2.** verputzen; bekleben; ~ *cast* Gipsabguss m, Gipsmodell n; MED Gipsverband m

plas·tic 1. plastisch; Plastik... **2.** Plastik n, Kunststoff m; → ~ *mon·ey* F Plastikgeld n, Kreditkarten pl; ~ *wrap* Frischhaltefolie f

plate 1. Teller m; Platte f; (*Namens-, Nummern- etc*)Schild n; (Bild)Tafel f; (Druck)Platte f; Gegenstände pl aus Edelmetall; Doublé n, Dublee n **2.** ~*d with gold, gold-plated* vergoldet

plat·form Plattform f; RAIL Bahnsteig m; (Redner)Tribüne f, Podium n; POL Plattform f; MOT Pritsche f; *party* ~ POL Parteiprogramm n; *election* ~ POL Wahlprogramm n

plat·i·num CHEM Platin n

pla·toon MIL Zug m

plat·ter (Servier)Platte f

plau·si·ble plausibel, glaubhaft

play 1. Spiel n; Schauspiel n, (Theater)Stück n; TECH Spiel n; fig Spielraum m; *at* ~ beim Spiel(en); *in* ~ im Spiel (*ball*); *out of* ~ im Aus (*ball*) **2.** v/i spielen (a. SPORT, THEA etc); v/t Karten, Rolle, Stück etc spielen, SPORT Spiel austragen; ~ *s.o.* SPORT gegen j-n spielen; ~ *the guitar* Gitarre spielen; ~ *a trick on s.o.* j-m e-n Streich spielen; ~ *back* Ball zurückspielen (*to* zu); Tonband abspielen; ~ *s.th. down* verharmlosen, herunterspielen; ~ *off* fig ausspielen (**against** gegen); ~ *on* fig j-s Schwächen ausnutzen

play·back Play-back n, Wiedergabe f, Abspielen n

play·er MUS, SPORT Spieler(in)

play·fel·low Br → **playmate**
play·ful verspielt; scherzhaft
play·go·er Theaterbesucher(in)
play·ground Spielplatz m (a. fig); Schulhof m
play·group Br Spielgruppe f
play·house THEA Schauspielhaus n; Spielhaus n (for children)
play·ing card Spielkarte f
play·ing field Sportplatz m, Spielfeld n
play·mate Spielkamerad(in)
play·pen Laufgitter n, Laufstall m
play·thing Spielzeug n
play·wright Dramatiker(in)
plc, **PLC** Br econ abbr of **public limited company** AG, Aktiengesellschaft f
plea enter a ~ of (**not**) **guilty** JUR sich schuldig bekennen (s-e Unschuld erklären)
plead v/i (dringend) bitten (**for** um); ~ (**not**) **guilty** JUR sich schuldig bekennen (s-e Unschuld erklären); v/t a. JUR zu s-r Verteidigung or Entschuldigung anführen, geltend machen; ~ **s.o.'s case** sich für j-n einsetzen; JUR j-n vertreten
pleas·ant angenehm, erfreulich; freundlich; sympathisch
please 1. j-m gefallen; j-m zusagen, j-n erfreuen; zufriedenstellen; **only to ~ you** nur dir zuliebe; ~ **o.s.** tun, was man will; ~ **yourself!** mach, was du willst! **2.** int bitte; (**yes**,) ~ (ja,) bitte; (oh ja,) gerne; ~ **come in!** bitte, treten Sie ein!
pleased erfreut, zufrieden; **be ~ about** sich freuen über (acc); **be ~ with** zufrieden sein mit; **I am ~ with it** es gefällt mir; **be ~ to do s.th.** et. gern tun; ~ **to meet you!** angenehm!
pleas·ing angenehm
plea·sure Vergnügen n; **at** (**one's**) ~ nach Belieben
pleat (Plissee)Falte f
pleat·ed skirt Faltenrock m
pledge 1. Pfand n; fig Unterpfand n; Versprechen n **2.** versprechen, zusichern
plen·ti·ful reichlich
plen·ty 1. Überfluss m; **in ~** im Überfluss, in Hülle und Fülle; ~ **of** e-e Menge, viel(e), reichlich **2.** F reichlich
pleu·ri·sy MED Brustfell-, Rippenfellentzündung f

pli·a·ble, **pli·ant** biegsam; fig flexibel; fig leicht beeinflussbar
pli·ers (**a pair of** ~ e-e) Beißzange f
plight Not f, Notlage f
plim·soll Br Turnschuh m
plod a. ~ **along** sich dahinschleppen; ~ **away** sich abplagen (**at** mit), schuften
plop F **1.** Plumps m, Platsch m **2.** plumpsen, (ins Wasser) platschen
plot 1. Stück n Land, Parzelle f, Grundstück n; THEA, film etc: Handlung f; Komplott n, Verschwörung f; IT grafische Darstellung f **2.** v/i sich verschwören (**against** gegen); v/t planen; einzeichnen
plot·ter IT Plotter m
plough Br, **plow** AGR **1.** Pflug m **2.** (um)pflügen; **plough·share** Br, **plow·share** AGR Pflugschar f
pluck 1. v/t Geflügel rupfen; mst ~ **out** ausreißen, ausrupfen, auszupfen; MUS Saiten zupfen; ~ **up** (**one's**) **courage** Mut or sich ein Herz fassen; v/i zupfen (**at** an dat); **2.** F Mut m, Schneid m
pluck·y F mutig
plug 1. Stöpsel m; ELECTR Stecker m, F Steckdose f; F MOT (Zünd)Kerze f **2.** v/t F für et. Schleichwerbung machen; a. ~ **up** zustöpseln; zustopfen, verstopfen; ~ **in** ELECTR anschließen, einstecken
plug·ging F Schleichwerbung f
plum BOT Pflaume f; Zwetsch(g)e f
plum·age Gefieder n
plumb 1. (Blei)Lot n **2.** ausloten, fig a. ergründen; ~ **in** esp Br Waschmaschine etc anschließen **3.** adj lotrecht, senkrecht **4.** adv F (haar)genau
plumb·er Klempner m, Installateur m
plumb·ing Klempner-, Installateurarbeit f; Rohre pl, Rohrleitungen pl
plume (Schmuck)Feder f; Federbusch m; (Rauch)Fahne f
plump 1. adj drall, mollig, rund(lich), F pumm(e)lig **2.** ~ **down** fallen or plumpsen (lassen)
plum pud·ding Br Plumpudding m
plun·der 1. plündern **2.** Plünderung f; Beute f
plunge 1. (ein-, unter)tauchen; (sich) stürzen (**into** in acc); **2.** (Kopf)Sprung m; **take the ~** fig das entscheidende Schritt wagen
plu·per·fect a. ~ **tense** LING Plusquam-

perfekt *n*, Vorvergangenheit *f*

plu·ral LING Plural *m*, Mehrzahl *f*

plus 1. *prp* plus, und, *esp* ECON zuzüglich **2.** *adj* Plus…; **~ sign** MATH Plus *n*, Pluszeichen *n* **3.** MATH Plus *n* (*a.* F), Pluszeichen *n*; F Vorteil *m*

plush Plüsch *m*

ply[1] *regelmäßig* verkehren, fahren (*between* zwischen *dat*)

ply[2] *mst in cpds* TECH Lage *f*, Schicht *f*; **three-~** dreifach (*thread etc*); dreifach gewebt (*carpet*)

ply·wood Sperrholz *n*

pm, PM *abbr of* *after noon* (*Latin* *post meridiem*) nachm., nachmittags, abends

pneu·mat·ic Luft…, pneumatisch; TECH Druck…, Pressluft…

pneu·mat·ic drill Pressluftbohrer *m*

pneu·mo·ni·a MED Lungenentzündung *f*

poach[1] GASTR pochieren; **~ed eggs** verlorene Eier *pl*

poach[2] wildern

poach·er Wilddieb *m*, Wilderer *m*

PO Box Postfach *n*; **write to ~ 225** schreiben Sie an Postfach 225

pock MED Pocke *f*, Blatter *f*

pock·et 1. (Hosen- *etc*)Tasche *f* **2.** *adj* Taschen… **3.** einstecken, in die Tasche stecken; *fig* in die eigene Tasche stecken; **pock·et·book** Notizbuch *n*; Brieftasche *f*

pock·et| cal·cu·la·tor Taschenrechner *m*; **~ knife** Taschenmesser *n*; **~ money** Taschengeld *n*

pod BOT Hülse *f*, Schote *f*

po·di·a·trist Fußpfleger(in)

po·em Gedicht *n*

po·et Dichter(in)

po·et·ic dichterisch

po·et·i·cal dichterisch

po·et·ic jus·tice *fig* ausgleichende Gerechtigkeit

po·et·ry Gedichte *pl*; Poesie *f* (*a. fig*), Dichtkunst *f*, Dichtung *f*

poi·gnant schmerzlich; ergreifend

point 1. Spitze *f*; GEOGR Landspitze *f*; LING, MATH, PHYS, SPORT *etc* Punkt *m*; MATH (Dezimal)Punkt *m*; Grad *m*; MAR (*Kompass*)Strich *m*; *fig* Punkt *m*, Stelle *f*, Ort *m*; Zweck *m*; Ziel *n*, Absicht *f*; springender Punkt; Pointe *f*; **two ~ five (2.5)** 2,5; **~ of view** Stand-, Gesichtspunkt *m*; **be on the~ of doing**

s.th. im Begriff sein, et. zu tun; **to the~** zur Sache gehörig; **off** *or* **beside the ~** nicht zur Sache gehörig; **come to the ~** zur Sache kommen; **that's not the ~** darum geht es nicht; **what's the ~?** wozu?; **win on ~s** SPORT nach Punkten gewinnen; **winner on ~s** SPORT Punktsieger *m* **2.** *v/t* (zu)spitzen; *Waffe etc* richten (*at* auf *acc*); **~ one's finger at s.o.** (mit dem Finger) auf j-n zeigen; **~ out** zeigen; *fig* hinweisen *or* aufmerksam machen auf (*acc*); *v/i* (mit dem Finger) zeigen (**at, to** auf *acc*); **~ to** nach e-r Richtung weisen *or* liegen; *fig* hinweisen auf (*acc*)

point·ed spitz; Spitz…; *fig* scharf (*remark etc*); ostentativ

point·er Zeiger *m*; Zeigestock *m*; ZO Pointer *m*, Vorstehhund *m*

point·less sinnlos, zwecklos

points *Br* RAIL Weiche *f*

poise 1. (Körper)Haltung *f*; *fig* Gelassenheit *f* **2.** balancieren; **be ~d** schweben

poi·son 1. Gift *n* **2.** vergiften

poi·son·ous giftig (*a. fig*)

poke 1. *v/t* stoßen; *Feuer* schüren; stecken; *v/i* **~ about, ~ around** F (herum-) stöbern, (-)wühlen (**in** in *dat*); **2.** Stoß *m*

pok·er Schürhaken *m*

pok·y F eng; schäbig

Po·land Polen *n*

po·lar polar; **~ bear** ZO Eisbär *m*

pole[1] GEOGR Pol *m*

pole[2] Stange *f*; Mast *m*; Deichsel *f*; SPORT (Sprung)Stab *m*

Pole Pole *m*, Polin *f*

pole·cat ZO Iltis *m*; F Skunk *m*, Stinktier *n*

po·lem·ic, po·lem·i·cal polemisch

pole star ASTR Polarstern *m*

pole vault SPORT Stabhochsprung *m*, Stabhochspringen *n*

pole-vault SPORT stabhochspringen

pole vault·er SPORT Stabhochspringer(in)

po·lice 1. Polizei *f* **2.** überwachen

po·lice car Polizeiauto *n*

po·lice·man Polizist *m*

po·lice| of·fi·cer Polizeibeamte *m*, -beamtin *f*, Polizist(in); **~ sta·tion** Polizeiwache *f*, Polizeirevier *n*

po·lice·wom·an Polizistin *f*

pol·i·cy Politik f; Taktik f; Klugheit f; (Versicherungs)Police f

po·li·o MED Polio f, Kinderlähmung f

pol·ish 1. polieren; *Schuhe* putzen; **~ up** aufpolieren (*a. fig*) **2.** Politur f; (*Schuh*)Creme f; *fig* Schliff m

Pol·ish 1. polnisch **2.** LING Polnisch n

po·lite höflich

po·lite·ness Höflichkeit f

po·lit·i·cal politisch

pol·i·ti·cian Politiker(in)

pol·i·tics Politik f

pol·ka MUS Polka f

pol·ka-dot gepunktet, getupft

poll 1. (*Meinungs*)Umfrage f; Wahlbeteiligung f; *a. pl* Stimmabgabe f, Wahl f **2.** befragen; *Stimmen* erhalten

pol·len BOT Pollen m, Blütenstaub m

poll·ing Stimmabgabe f; Wahlbeteiligung f; **~ booth** *esp Br* Wahlkabine f; **~ day** Wahltag m; **~ place**, *esp Br* **~ station** Wahllokal n

polls Wahl f; Wahllokal n

poll·ster Demoskop(in), Meinungsforscher(in)

pol·lut·ant Schadstoff m; **pol·lute** beschmutzen, verschmutzen; verunreinigen; **pol·lut·er** a. **environmental ~** Umweltsünder(in); **pol·lu·tion** (*Luft-, Wasser- etc*)Verschmutzung f; Verunreinigung f

po·lo SPORT Polo n

po·lo neck a. **~ sweater** *esp Br* Rollkragenpullover m

pol·yp ZO, MED Polyp m

pol·y·sty·rene® Styropor® n

pom·mel (Sattel- *etc*)Knopf m

pomp Pomp m, Prunk m

pom·pous aufgeblasen, wichtigtuerisch; schwülstig (*speech*)

pond Teich m, Weiher m

pon·der v/i nachdenken (**on, over** über *acc*); v/t überlegen

pon·der·ous schwerfällig; schwer

pon·toon Ponton m

pon·toon bridge Pontonbrücke f

po·ny ZO Pony n

po·ny·tail Pferdeschwanz m

poo·dle ZO Pudel m

pool¹ Teich m, Tümpel m; Pfütze f, (*Blut- etc*)Lache f; (*Schwimm*)Becken n, (*Swimming*)Pool m

pool² **1.** (*Arbeits-, Fahr*)Gemeinschaft f; (*Mitarbeiter- etc*)Stab m; (*Fuhr*)Park m; (*Schreib*)Pool m; ECON Pool m, Kartell n; *card games:* Gesamteinsatz m; Poolbillard n **2.** *Geld, Unternehmen etc* zusammenlegen; *Kräfte etc* vereinen

pool hall, pool-room Billardspielhalle f

pools a. **football ~** *Br* (Fußball)Toto n, m

poor 1. arm; dürftig, mangelhaft, schwach **2. the ~** die Armen pl

poor·ly 1. *adj esp Br* F kränklich, unpässlich **2.** *adv* ärmlich, dürftig, schlecht, schwach

pop¹ 1. v/t zerknallen; F schnell *wohin* tun *or* stecken; v/i knallen; (zer)platzen; **~ in** F auf e-n Sprung vorbeikommen; **~ up** (plötzlich) auftauchen **2.** Knall m; F Limo f

pop² MUS **1.** Pop m **2.** Schlager…; Pop…

pop³ F Paps m, Papa m

pop⁴ *abbr of* **population** Einw., Einwohner pl; Einwohnerzahl f

pop con·cert MUS Popkonzert n

pop·corn Popcorn n, Puffmais m

Pope REL Papst m

pop-eyed F glotzäugig

pop group MUS Popgruppe f

pop·lar BOT Pappel f

pop mu·sic Popmusik f

pop·py BOT Mohn m

pop·u·lar populär, beliebt; volkstümlich; allgemein

pop·u·lar·i·ty Popularität f, Beliebtheit f; Volkstümlichkeit f

pop·u·late bevölkern, besiedeln; bewohnen

pop·u·la·tion Bevölkerung f

pop·u·lous dicht besiedelt, dicht bevölkert

porce·lain Porzellan n

porch überdachter Vorbau; Portal n; Veranda f

por·cu·pine ZO Stachelschwein n

pore¹ Pore f

pore²: **~ over** vertieft sein in (*acc*), *et.* eifrig studieren

pork GASTR Schweinefleisch n

porn F → **porno**

por·no F **1.** Porno m **2.** Porno…

por·nog·ra·phy Pornografie f

po·rous porös

por·poise ZO Tümmler m

por·ridge Porridge m, n, Haferbrei m

port¹ Hafen m; Hafenstadt f

P

port² AVIAT, MAR Backbord n

port³ IT Port m, Anschluss m

port⁴ Portwein m

por·ta·ble tragbar

por·ter (Gepäck)Träger m; esp Br Pförtner m, Portier m; RAIL Schlafwagenschaffner m

port·hole MAR Bullauge n

por·tion 1. (An)Teil m; GASTR Portion f 2. ~ out aufteilen, verteilen (among, between unter acc)

port·ly korpulent

por·trait Porträt n, Bild n, Bildnis n

por·tray porträtieren; darstellen; schildern; por·tray·al THEA Verkörperung f, Darstellung f; Schilderung f

Por·tu·gal Portugal n

Por·tu·guese 1. portugiesisch 2. Portugiese m, Portugiesin f; LING Portugiesisch n; the ~ die Portugiesen pl

pose 1. v/t aufstellen; Problem, Frage aufwerfen, Bedrohung, Gefahr etc darstellen; v/i Modell sitzen or stehen; ~ as sich ausgeben als or für 2. Pose f

posh esp Br F schick, piekfein

po·si·tion 1. Position f, Lage f, Stellung f (a. fig); Stand m; fig Standpunkt m 2. (auf)stellen

pos·i·tive 1. positiv; bestimmt, sicher, eindeutig; greifbar, konkret; konstruktiv 2. PHOT Positiv n

pos·sess besitzen; fig beherrschen

pos·sessed fig besessen

pos·ses·sion Besitz m; fig Besessenheit f

pos·ses·sive besitzergreifend; LING possessiv, besitzanzeigend

pos·si·bil·i·ty Möglichkeit f

pos·si·ble möglich

pos·si·bly möglicherweise, vielleicht; if I ~ can wenn ich irgend kann; I can't ~ do this ich kann das unmöglich tun

post¹ 1. (Tür-, Tor-, Ziel- etc)Pfosten m; Pfahl m 2. a. ~ up Plakat etc anschlagen, ankleben; be ~ed missing AVIAT, MAR als vermisst gemeldet werden

post² esp Br 1. Post® f; Postsendung f; by ~ mit der Post® 2. mit der Post® (zu-)schicken, aufgeben, Brief einwerfen

post³ 1. Stelle f, Job m; Posten m 2. aufstellen, postieren; esp Br versetzen, MIL abkommandieren (to nach)

post... nach..., Nach...

post·age Porto n; ~ stamp Postwertzeichen n, Briefmarke f

post·al postalisch, Post®...; ~ or·der Br ECON Postanweisung f; ~ vote POL Briefwahl f

post·bag esp Br Postsack m

post·box esp Br Briefkasten m

post·card Postkarte f; a. picture ~ Ansichtskarte f

post·code Br Postleitzahl f

post·er Plakat n; Poster n, m

poste res·tante Br 1. Abteilung f für postlagernde Sendungen 2. postlagernd

pos·te·ri·or HUMOR Hinterteil n

pos·ter·i·ty die Nachwelt

post-free esp Br portofrei

post·hu·mous post(h)um

post·man esp Br Briefträger m, Postbote m

post·mark 1. Poststempel m 2. stempeln, abstempeln

post of·fice Post® f; Postamt n, -filiale f

post of·fice box → PO Box

post-paid portofrei

post·pone verschieben, aufschieben

post·pone·ment Verschiebung f, Aufschub m

post·script Postskript(um) n, Nachschrift f

pos·ture 1. (Körper)Haltung f; Stellung f 2. fig sich aufspielen

post·war Nachkriegs...

post·wom·an esp Br Briefträgerin f, Postbotin f

po·sy Sträußchen n

pot 1. Topf m; Kanne f; Kännchen n (Tee etc); SPORT Pokal m 2. Pflanze eintopfen

po·tas·si·um cy·a·nide CHEM Zyankali n

po·ta·to Kartoffel f; → chips, crisps

pot·bel·ly Schmerbauch m

po·ten·cy Stärke f; Wirksamkeit f, Wirkung f; MED Potenz f

po·tent PHARM stark; MED potent

po·ten·tial 1. potenziell, möglich 2. Potenzial n, Leistungsfähigkeit f

pot·hole MOT Schlagloch n

po·tion Trank m

pot·ter¹ Br: ~ about herumwerkeln

pot·ter² Töpfer(in)

pot·ter·y Töpferei f; Töpferware(n pl) f

pouch Beutel m (a. ZO); ZO (Backen)Tasche f

poul·tice MED (warmer) Umschlag *m*
poul·try Geflügel *n*
pounce 1. sich stürzen (**on** auf *acc*); **2.** Satz *m*, Sprung *m*
pound[1] Pfund *n* (453,59 *g*); ~ (**sterling**) (*abbr £*) Pfund *n*
pound[2] Tierheim *n*; Abstellplatz *m* für (polizeilich) abgeschleppte Fahrzeuge
pound[3] *v/t* zerstoßen, zerstampfen; trommeln *or* hämmern auf (*acc*) *or* an (*acc*) *or* gegen (*acc*); *v/i* hämmern (**with** vor *dat*)
pour *v/t* gießen, schütten; ~ **out** ausgießen, ausschütten; *Getränk* eingießen; *v/i* strömen (*a. fig*)
pout *v/t Lippen* schürzen; *v/i* e-n Schmollmund machen; schmollen
pov·er·ty Armut *f*
pow·der 1. Pulver *n*; Puder *m* **2.** pulverisieren; (sich) pudern; ~ **puff** Puderquaste *f*; ~ **room** (Damen)Toilette *f*
pow·er 1. Kraft *f*; Macht *f*; Fähigkeit *f*, Vermögen *n*; Gewalt *f*; JUR Befugnis *f*, Vollmacht *f*; MATH Potenz *f*; ELECTR Strom *m*; **in** ~ POL an der Macht **2.** TECH antreiben; ~ **cut** ELECTR Stromsperre *f*; ~ **fail·ure** ELECTR Stromausfall *m*, Netzausfall *m*
pow·er·ful stark, kräftig; mächtig
pow·er·less kraftlos; machtlos
pow·er| plant Elektrizitäts-, Kraftwerk *n*; ~**pol·i·tics** Machtpolitik *f*; ~**sta·tion** *Br* Elektrizitäts-, Kraftwerk *n*
prac·ti·ca·ble durchführbar
prac·ti·cal praktisch; ~ **joke** Streich *m*
prac·ti·cal·ly so gut wie
prac·tice 1. Praxis *f*; Übung *f*; Gewohnheit *f*, Brauch *m*; **it is common** ~ es ist allgemein üblich; **put into** ~ in die Praxis umsetzen **2.** *v/t* (ein)üben; *als Beruf* ausüben; ~ **law** (**medicine**) als Anwalt (Arzt) praktizieren; *v/i* praktizieren; üben
prac·ticed geübt (**in** in *dat*)
prac·tise *Br* → **practice 2**
prac·tised → **practiced**
prac·ti·tion·er: general ~ praktischer Arzt
prai·rie Prärie *f*
prai·rie schoo·ner HIST Planwagen *m*
praise 1. loben, preisen **2.** Lob *n*
praise·wor·thy lobenswert
pram *Br* Kinderwagen *m*
prance sich aufbäumen, steigen (*horse*);

tänzeln (*horse*); stolzieren
prank Streich *m*
prat·tle: ~ **on** plappern (**about** von)
prawn ZO Garnele *f*
pray beten (**to** zu; **for** für, um)
prayer REL Gebet *n*; *often pl* Andacht *f*; **the Lord's Prayer** das Vaterunser
prayer book REL Gebetbuch *n*
preach predigen (**to** zu, vor *dat*)
preach·er Prediger(in)
pre·am·ble Einleitung *f*
pre·ar·range vorher vereinbaren
pre·car·i·ous prekär, unsicher; gefährlich
pre·cau·tion Vorsichtsmaßnahme *f*; **as a** ~ vorsorglich; **take** ~**s** Vorsichtsmaßnahmen treffen; **pre·cau·tion·a·ry** vorbeugend; vorsorglich
pre·cede voraus-, vorangehen (*dat*)
pre·ce·dence Vorrang *m*
pre·ce·dent Präzedenzfall *m*
pre·cept Regel *f*, Richtlinie *f*
pre·cinct (*Wahl*)Bezirk *m*; (*Polizei*)Revier *n*; *pl* Gelände *n*; *esp Br* (*Einkaufs*)Viertel *n*; (*Fußgänger*)Zone *f*
pre·cious 1. *adj* kostbar, wertvoll; Edel... (*stone etc*) **2.** *adv*: ~ **little** F herzlich wenig
pre·ci·pice Abgrund *m*
pre·cip·i·tate 1. *v/t* (hinunter-, herunter)schleudern; CHEM ausfällen; beschleunigen; stürzen (**into** in *acc*); *v/i* CHEM ausfallen **2.** *adj* überstürzt **3.** CHEM Niederschlag *m*
pre·cip·i·ta·tion CHEM Ausfällung *f*; METEOR Niederschlag *m*; Überstürzung *f*, Hast *f*
pre·cip·i·tous steil (abfallend); überstürzt
pré·cis Zusammenfassung *f*
pre·cise genau, präzis
pre·ci·sion Genauigkeit *f*; Präzision *f*
pre·clude ausschließen
pre·co·cious frühreif; altklug
pre·con·ceived vorgefasst
pre·con·cep·tion vorgefasste Meinung
pre·cur·sor Vorläufer(in)
pred·a·to·ry ZO Raub...
pre·de·ces·sor Vorgänger(in)
pre·des·ti·na·tion Vorherbestimmung *f*; **pre·des·tined** prädestiniert, vorherbestimmt (**to** für, zu)
pre·de·ter·mine vorherbestimmen; vorher vereinbaren

P

pre·dic·a·ment missliche Lage, Zwangslage *f*

pred·i·cate LING Prädikat *n*, Satzaussage *f*; pre·dic·a·tive LING prädikativ

pre·dict vorhersagen, voraussagen

pre·dic·tion Vorhersage *f*, Voraussage *f*; **computer ~** Hochrechnung *f*

pre·dis·pose geneigt machen, einnehmen (**in favor of** für); *esp* MED anfällig machen (**to** für)

pre·dis·po·si·tion: **~ to** Neigung *f* zu, *esp* MED *a*. Anfälligkeit *f* für

pre·dom·i·nant (vor)herrschend, überwiegend

pre·dom·i·nate vorherrschen, überwiegen; die Oberhand haben

pre·em·i·nent hervorragend, überragend

pre·emp·tive ECON Vorkaufs...; MIL Präventiv...

preen ZO *sich or das Gefieder putzen*

pre·fab F Fertighaus *n*

pre·fab·ri·cate vorfabrizieren, vorfertigen; **~d house** Fertighaus *n*

pref·ace **1.** Vorwort *n* (**to** zu); **2.** *Buch, Rede etc* einleiten (**with** mit)

pre·fect *Br* PED Aufsichts-, Vertrauensschüler(in)

pre·fer vorziehen (**to** *dat*), lieber mögen (**to** als), bevorzugen

pref·e·ra·ble: **be ~** (**to**) vorzuziehen sein (*dat*), besser sein (als)

pref·e·ra·bly vorzugsweise, lieber, am liebsten

pref·e·rence Vorliebe *f* (**for** für); Vorzug *m*

pre·fix LING Präfix *n*, Vorsilbe *f*

preg·nan·cy MED Schwangerschaft *f*; ZO Trächtigkeit *f*

preg·nant MED schwanger; ZO trächtig

pre·heat *Backofen etc* vorheizen

pre·judge *j-n* vorverurteilen; vorschnell beurteilen

prej·u·dice **1.** Vorurteil *n*, Voreingenommenheit *f*, Befangenheit *f*; **to the ~ of** zum Nachteil *or* Schaden (*gen*) **2.** einnehmen (**in favo[u]r of** für; **against** gegen); schaden (*dat*), beeinträchtigen

prej·u·diced (vor)eingenommen, befangen

pre·lim·i·na·ry **1.** vorläufig, einleitend, Vor... **2.** *pl* Vorbereitungen *pl*

prel·ude Vorspiel *n* (*a.* MUS)

pre·mar·i·tal vorehelich

pre·ma·ture vorzeitig, verfrüht; *fig* voreilig

pre·med·i·tat·ed JUR vorsätzlich

pre·med·i·ta·tion: **with ~** JUR vorsätzlich

prem·i·er POL Premier(minister) *m*

prem·i·ere, prem·i·ère THEA *etc* Premiere *f*, Ur-, Erstaufführung *f*

prem·is·es Gelände *n*, Grundstück *n*, (Geschäfts)Räume *pl*; **on the ~** an Ort und Stelle, im Haus, im Lokal

pre·mi·um Prämie *f*, Bonus *m*

pre·mi·um (gas·o·line) MOT Super *n*, Superbenzin *n*

pre·mo·ni·tion (böse) Vorahnung

pre·oc·cu·pa·tion Beschäftigung *f* (**with** mit)

pre·oc·cu·pied gedankenverloren, geistesabwesend

pre·oc·cu·py (stark) beschäftigen

prep *Br* F PED Hausaufgabe(n *pl*) *f*

pre·packed. pre·pack·aged abgepackt

pre·paid *post* frankiert, freigemacht; **~ envelope** Freiumschlag *m*

prep·a·ra·tion Vorbereitung *f* (**for** auf *acc*, für); Zubereitung *f*; CHEM, MED Präparat *n*

pre·par·a·to·ry vorbereitend

pre·pare *v/t* vorbereiten; GASTR zubereiten; *v/i:* **~ for** sich vorbereiten auf (*acc*); Vorbereitungen treffen für; sich gefasst machen auf (*acc*)

pre·pared vorbereitet; bereit

prep·o·si·tion LING Präposition *f*, Verhältniswort *n*

pre·pos·sess·ing einnehmend, anziehend

pre·pos·ter·ous absurd; lächerlich, grotesk

pre·pro·gram(me) vorprogrammieren

pre·req·ui·site Vorbedingung *f*, Voraussetzung *f*

pre·rog·a·tive Vorrecht *n*

pre·school Vorschule *f*

pre·scribe *et.* vorschreiben; MED *j-m et.* verschreiben; **pre·scrip·tion** Verordnung *f*, Vorschrift *f*; MED Rezept *n*

pres·ence Gegenwart *f*, Anwesenheit *f*; **~ of mind** Geistesgegenwart *f*

pres·ent[1] Geschenk *n*

pre·sent[2] präsentieren, (über)reichen, (über)bringen, (über)geben; schenken; vorbringen, vorlegen; zeigen, vorführen, THEA *etc* aufführen; schildern, darstellen; *j-n, Produkt etc* vorstellen;

Programm etc moderieren

pres·ent³ 1. anwesend; vorhanden; gegenwärtig, jetzig; laufend; vorliegend (*case etc*); **~ tense** LING Präsens *n*, Gegenwart *f* **2.** Gegenwart *f*, LING *a.* Präsens *n*; **at ~** gegenwärtig, zurzeit; **for the ~** vorerst, vorläufig

pre·sen·ta·tion Präsentation *f*; Überreichung *f*; Vorlage *f*; Vorführung *f*, THEA *etc* Aufführung *f*; Schilderung *f*, Darstellung *f*; Vorstellung *f*; *radio*, TV Moderation *f*

pres·ent-day heutig, gegenwärtig, modern

pre·sent·er *esp Br radio*, TV Moderator(in)

pre·sen·ti·ment (böse) Vorahnung

pres·ent·ly zurzeit, jetzt; *Br* bald

pres·er·va·tion Bewahrung *f*; Erhaltung *f*; GASTR Konservierung *f*

pre·ser·va·tive GASTR Konservierungsmittel *n*

pre·serve 1. bewahren, (be)schützen; erhalten; GASTR konservieren, *Obst etc* einmachen, einkochen **2.** (*Jagd*)Revier *n*; *fig* Ressort *n*, Reich *n*; *mst pl* GASTR *das* Eingemachte

pre·side den Vorsitz haben (**at, over** bei); **pres·i·den·cy** POL Präsidentschaft *f*; Amtszeit *f*; **pres·i·dent** Präsident *m*; ECON Generaldirektor *m*

press 1. *v/t* drücken, pressen; *Frucht* (aus)pressen; drücken auf (*acc*); bügeln; drängen; *j-n* (be)drängen; bestehen auf (*dat*); *v/i* drücken; drängen (*time etc*); (sich) drängen; **~ for** dringen *or* drängen auf (*acc*); **~ on** (zügig) weitermachen **2.** Druck *m* (*a. fig*); (*Wein etc*)Presse *f*; Bügeln *n*; *die* Presse; *a.* **printing ~** Druckerpresse *f*

press a·gen·cy Presseagentur *f*

press box Pressetribüne *f*

press con·fe·rence Pressekonferenz *f*

press·ing dringend

press of·fice Pressebüro *n*, Pressestelle *f*; **press of·fi·cer** Pressereferent(in)

press re·lease Pressemitteilung *f*

press stud *Br* Druckknopf *m*

press-up *esp Br* SPORT Liegestütz *m*

pres·sure PHYS, TECH *etc* Druck *m* (*a. fig*); **~ cook·er** Dampfkochtopf *m*, Schnellkochtopf *m*

pres·tige Prestige *n*, Ansehen *n*

pre·su·ma·bly vermutlich

pre·sume *v/t* annehmen, vermuten; sich erdreisten *or* anmaßen (**to do** zu tun); *v/i* annehmen, vermuten; anmaßend sein; **~ on** et. ausnützen, *et.* missbrauchen

pre·sump·tion Annahme *f*, Vermutung *f*; Anmaßung *f*

pre·sump·tu·ous anmaßend, vermessen

pre·sup·pose voraussetzen

pre·sup·po·si·tion Voraussetzung *f*

pre·tence *Br* → **pretense**; **pre·tend** vortäuschen, vorgeben; sich verstellen; Anspruch erheben (**to** auf *acc*); **she is only ~ing** sie tut nur so; **pre·tend·ed** vorgetäuscht, gespielt; **pre·tense** Verstellung *f*, Vortäuschung *f*; Anspruch *m* (**to** auf *acc*); **pre·ten·sion** Anspruch *m* (**to** auf *acc*); Anmaßung *f*

pre·ter·it(e) LING Präteritum *n*

pre·text Vorwand *m*

pret·ty 1. *adj* hübsch **2.** *adv* ziemlich, ganz schön

pret·zel Brezel *f*

pre·vail vorherrschen, weit verbreitet sein; siegen (**over, against** über *acc*)

pre·vail·ing (vor)herrschend

pre·vent verhindern, verhüten, *e-r Sache* vorbeugen; *j-n* hindern (**from** an *dat*)

pre·ven·tion Verhinderung *f*, Verhütung *f*, Vorbeugung *f*

pre·ven·tive vorbeugend

pre·view *film*, TV Voraufführung *f*; Vorbesichtigung *f*; *film*, TV *etc*: Vorschau *f* (**of** auf *acc*)

pre·vi·ous vorhergehend, vorausgehend, vorherig, vorig; **~ to** bevor, vor (*dat*); **~ knowledge** Vorkenntnisse *pl*

pre·vi·ous·ly vorher, früher

pre-war Vorkriegs...

prey 1. ZO Beute *f*, Opfer *n* (*a. fig*); **be easy ~ for** *or* **to** *fig* e-e leichte Beute sein für **2. ~ on** ZO Jagd machen auf (*acc*); *fig* nagen an (*dat*); **~ on s.o.'s mind** *j-m* keine Ruhe lassen

price 1. Preis *m* **2.** den Preis festsetzen für; auszeichnen (**at** mit)

price·less unbezahlbar

price tag Preisschild *n*

prick 1. Stich *m*; V Schwanz *m*; **~s of conscience** Gewissensbisse *pl* **2.** *v/t* (auf-, durch)stechen, stechen in (*acc*); **her conscience ~ed her** sie hatte Gewissensbisse; **~ up one's ears** die Ohren spitzen; *v/i* stechen

prick·le BOT, ZO Stachel *m*, Dorn *m*

prick·ly stach(e)lig; prickelnd, kribbelnd

pride 1. Stolz *m*; Hochmut *m*; **take (a) ~ in** stolz sein auf (*acc*) **2. ~ o.s. on** stolz sein auf (*acc*)

priest REL Priester *m*

prig Tugendbold *m*

prig·gish tugendhaft

prim steif; prüde

pri·mae·val *esp Br* → **primeval**

pri·ma·ri·ly in erster Linie, vor allem

pri·ma·ry 1. wichtigste(r, -s), Haupt...; grundlegend, elementar, Grund...; Anfangs..., Ur... **2.** POL Vorwahl *f*

pri·ma·ry school *Br* Grundschule *f*

prime 1. MATH Primzahl *f*; *fig* Blüte(zeit) *f*; **in the ~ of life** in der Blüte s-r Jahre; **be past one's ~** s-e besten Jahre hinter sich haben **2.** *adj* erste(r, -s), wichtigste(r, -s), Haupt...; erstklassig **3.** *v/t* TECH grundieren; *j-n* instruieren, vorbereiten; **~ min·is·ter** (*abbr* POL F *PM*) Premierminister(in), Ministerpräsident(in); **~ num·ber** MATH Primzahl *f*

prim·er Fibel *f*, Elementarbuch *n*

prime time TV Haupteinschaltzeit *f*, Hauptsendezeit *f*, beste Sendezeit

pri·me·val urzeitlich, Ur...

prim·i·tive erste(r, -s), ursprünglich, Ur...; primitiv

prim·rose BOT Primel *f*, *esp* Schlüsselblume *f*

prince Fürst *m*; Prinz *m*

prin·cess Fürstin *f*; Prinzessin *f*

prin·ci·pal 1. wichtigste(r, -s), hauptsächlich, Haupt... **2.** PED Direktor(in), Rektor(in); THEA Hauptdarsteller(in); MUS Solist(in)

prin·ci·pal·i·ty Fürstentum *n*

prin·ci·ple Prinzip *n*, Grundsatz *m*; **on ~** grundsätzlich, aus Prinzip

print 1. PRINT Druck *m* (*a. art*); Gedruckte(n); (*Finger- etc*)Abdruck *m*; PHOT Abzug *m*; bedruckter Stoff; **in ~** gedruckt; **out of ~** vergriffen **2.** *v/i* drucken; *v/t* (ab-, auf-, be)drucken; in Druckbuchstaben schreiben; *fig* einprägen (**on** *dat*); *a.* **~ off** PHOT abziehen; **~ out** IT ausdrucken

print·ed mat·ter *post* Drucksache *f*

print·er Drucker *m* (*a.* TECH); **~'s error**

Druckfehler *m*; **~'s ink** Druckerschwärze *f*; **print·ers** Druckerei *f*

print·ing Drucken *n*; Auflage *f*; **~ ink** Druckerschwärze *f*; **~ press** Druckerpresse *f*

print·out IT Ausdruck *m*

pri·or frühere(r, -s); vorrangig

pri·or·i·ty Priorität *f*, Vorrang *m*; MOT Vorfahrt *f*; **give s.th. ~** et. vordringlich behandeln

prise *esp Br* → **prize²**

prism Prisma *n*

pris·on Gefängnis *n*, Strafanstalt *f*

pris·on·er Gefangene *m*, *f*, Häftling *m*; **hold ~**, **keep ~** gefangen halten; **take ~** gefangen nehmen

pri·va·cy Intim-, Privatsphäre *f*; Geheimhaltung *f*

pri·vate 1. privat, Privat...; vertraulich; geheim; **~ parts** Geschlechtsteile *pl* **2.** MIL gemeiner Soldat; **in ~** privat; unter vier Augen

pri·va·tion Entbehrung *f*

priv·i·lege Privileg *n*; Vorrecht *n*

priv·i·leged privilegiert

priv·y: be ~ to eingeweiht sein in (*acc*)

prize¹1. (Sieger-, Sieges)Preis *m*, Prämie *f*, Auszeichnung *f*; (*Lotterie*)Gewinn *m* **2.** preisgekrönt; Preis... **3.** (hoch) schätzen

prize²: ~ open aufbrechen, aufstemmen

prize·win·ner Preisträger(in)

pro¹ F Profi *m*

pro²: the ~s and cons das Pro und Kontra, das Für und Wider

prob·a·bil·i·ty Wahrscheinlichkeit *f*; **in all ~** höchstwahrscheinlich

prob·a·ble *adj* wahrscheinlich

prob·a·bly *adv* wahrscheinlich

pro·ba·tion Probe *f*, Probezeit *f*; JUR Bewährung *f*, Bewährungsfrist *f*

pro·ba·tion of·fi·cer JUR Bewährungshelfer(in)

probe 1. MED, TECH Sonde *f*; *fig* Untersuchung *f* (**into** *gen*); **2.** sondieren; (gründlich) untersuchen

prob·lem Problem *n*; MATH *etc* Aufgabe *f*; **prob·lem·at·ic**, **prob·lem·at·i·cal** problematisch

pro·ce·dure Verfahren *n*, Verfahrensweise *f*, Vorgehen *n*

pro·ceed (weiter)gehen, (weiter)fahren; sich begeben (**to** nach, zu); *fig* weitergehen; *fig* fortfahren; *fig* vorgehen;

~ from kommen or herrühren von; **~ to do s.th.** sich anschicken or daranmachen, et. zu tun

pro·ceed·ing Verfahren n, Vorgehen n

pro·ceed·ings Vorgänge pl, Geschehnisse pl; **start** or **take** (**legal**) **~ against** JUR (gerichtlich) vorgehen gegen

pro·ceeds ECON Erlös m, Ertrag m, Einnahmen pl

pro·cess 1. Prozess m, Verfahren n, Vorgang m; **in the ~** dabei; **be in ~** im Gange sein; **in ~ of construction** im Bau (befindlich) 2. TECH etc bearbeiten, behandeln; IT Daten verarbeiten; PHOT Film entwickeln

pro·ces·sion Prozession f

pro·ces·sor IT Prozessor m; (Wort-, Text)Verarbeitungsgerät n

pro·claim proklamieren, ausrufen

proc·la·ma·tion Proklamation f, Bekanntmachung f

pro·cure (sich) et. beschaffen or besorgen; verkuppeln

prod 1. stoßen; fig anstacheln, anspornen (**into** zu); 2. Stoß m

prod·i·gal 1. verschwenderisch; 2. F Verschwender(in)

pro·di·gious erstaunlich, großartig

prod·i·gy Wunder n; **child ~** Wunderkind n

pro·duce[1] ECON produzieren (a. film, TV), herstellen, erzeugen (a. fig); hervorholen (**from** aus); Ausweis etc (vor)zeigen; Beweise etc vorlegen; Zeugen etc beibringen; Gewinn etc (er)bringen, abwerfen; THEA inszenieren; fig hervorrufen, Wirkung erzielen

prod·uce[2] esp (Agrar)Produkt(e pl) n, (Agrar)Erzeugnis(se pl) n

pro·duc·er Produzent(in) (a. film, TV), Hersteller(in); THEA Regisseur(in)

prod·uct Produkt n, Erzeugnis n

pro·duc·tion ECON Produktion f (a. film, TV), Erzeugung f, Herstellung f; Produkt n, Erzeugnis n; Hervorholen n; Vorzeigen n, Vorlegen n, Beibringung f; THEA Inszenierung f

pro·duc·tive produktiv (a. fig), ergiebig, rentabel; fig schöpferisch

pro·duc·tiv·i·ty Produktivität f

prof F Prof m

pro·fa·na·tion Entweihung f

pro·fane 1. (gottes)lästerlich; profan, weltlich 2. entweihen

pro·fan·i·ty **profanities** Flüche pl, Lästerungen pl

pro·fess vorgeben, vortäuschen; behaupten (**to be** zu sein); erklären

pro·fessed erklärt (enemy etc); angeblich

pro·fes·sion (esp akademischer) Beruf; Berufsstand m

pro·fes·sion·al 1. Berufs..., beruflich; Fach..., fachlich; fachmännisch; professionell 2. Fachmann m, Profi m; Berufsspieler(in), -sportler(in), Profi m

pro·fes·sor Professor(in); Dozent(in)

pro·fi·cien·cy Können n, Tüchtigkeit f

pro·fi·cient tüchtig (**at, in** in dat)

pro·file Profil n; **keep a low ~** Zurückhaltung üben

prof·it 1. Gewinn m, Profit m; Vorteil m, Nutzen m 2. **~ by**, **~ from** Nutzen ziehen aus, profitieren von

prof·it·a·ble gewinnbringend, einträglich; nützlich, vorteilhaft

prof·it·eer contp Profitmacher m, Schieber m

prof·it shar·ing ECON Gewinnbeteiligung f

prof·li·gate verschwenderisch

pro·found fig tief; tiefgründig; profund (knowledge etc)

pro·fuse (über)reich; verschwenderisch; **pro·fu·sion** Überfülle f; **in ~** in Hülle und Fülle

prog·e·ny Nachkommen(schaft f) pl

prog·no·sis MED Prognose f

pro·gram 1. Programm n (a. IT); radio, TV a. Sendung f 2. (vor)programmieren; planen; IT programmieren

pro·gram·er IT Programmierer(in)

pro·gramme Br → program

'pro·gram·mer Br → programer

pro·gress 1. Fortschritt(e pl) m; **make slow ~** (nur) langsam vorankommen; **be in ~** im Gange sein 2. fortschreiten; Fortschritte machen

pro·gres·sive progressiv, fortschreitend; fortschrittlich

pro·hib·it verbieten; verhindern

pro·hi·bi·tion Verbot n

pro·hib·i·tive Schutz... (Zoll etc); unerschwinglich

proj·ect[1] Projekt n, Vorhaben n

pro·ject[2] v/i vorspringen, vorragen, vorstehen; v/t werfen, schleudern; planen; projizieren

pro·jec·tile Projektil n, Geschoss n
pro·jec·tion Vorsprung m, vorspringender Teil; Werfen n, Schleudern n; Planung f; film: Projektion f
pro·jec·tion·ist Filmvorführer m
pro·jec·tor film: Projektor m
pro·le·tar·i·an 1. proletarisch 2. Proletarier(in)
pro·lif·ic fruchtbar
pro·log, esp Br pro·logue Prolog m
pro·long verlängern
prom·e·nade 1. (Strand)Promenade f 2. promenieren
prom·i·nent vorspringend, vorstehend; fig prominent
prom·is·cu·ous sexuell freizügig
prom·ise 1. Versprechen n; fig Aussicht f 2. versprechen
prom·is·ing vielversprechend
prom·on·to·ry GEOGR Vorgebirge n
pro·mote j-n befördern; Schüler versetzen; ECON werben für; Boxkampf, Konzert etc veranstalten; et. fördern; be ~d SPORT esp Br aufsteigen (to in acc)
pro·mot·er Promoter(in), Veranstalter(in); ECON Verkaufsförderer m
pro·mo·tion Beförderung f; PED Versetzung f; SPORT Aufstieg m; ECON Verkaufsförderung f, Werbung f
pro·mo·tion(·al) film Werbefilm m
prompt 1. j-n veranlassen (to do zu tun); führen zu, Gefühle etc wecken; j-m versagen; THEA j-m soufflieren 2. prompt, umgehend, unverzüglich; pünktlich
prompt·er THEA Souffleur m, Souffleuse f
prone auf dem Bauch or mit dem Gesicht nach unten liegend; be ~ to a. MED neigen zu, anfällig sein für
prong Zinke f; (Geweih)Sprosse f
pro·noun LING Pronomen n, Fürwort n
pro·nounce aussprechen; erklären für; JUR Urteil verkünden
pro·nun·ci·a·tion Aussprache f
proof 1. Beweis(e pl) m, Nachweis m; Probe f; PRINT Korrekturfahne f a. PHOT Probeabzug m 2. adj in cpds ...fest, ...beständig, ...dicht, ...sicher; → heatproof, soundproof, waterproof; be ~ against geschützt sein vor (dat) 3. imprägnieren
proof·read PRINT Korrektur lesen
proof·read·er PRINT Korrektor(in)
prop 1. Stütze f (a. fig) 2. a. ~ up stützen;

sich or et. lehnen (against gegen)
prop·a·gate BIOL sich fortpflanzen or vermehren; verbreiten
prop·a·ga·tion Fortpflanzung f, Vermehrung f; Verbreitung f
pro·pel (an)treiben; pro·pel·lant, pro·pel·lent Treibstoff m; Treibgas n
pro·pel·ler AVIAT Propeller m, MAR a. Schraube f
pro·pel·ling pen·cil Drehbleistift m
pro·pen·si·ty fig Neigung f
prop·er richtig, passend, geeignet; anständig, schicklich; echt, wirklich, richtig; eigentlich; (eigentümlich); esp Br F ordentlich, tüchtig, gehörig
prop·er| name, ~ noun Eigenname m
prop·er·ty Eigentum n, Besitz m; Landbesitz m, Grundbesitz m; Grundstück n; fig Eigenschaft f
proph·e·cy Prophezeiung f
proph·e·sy prophezeien
proph·et Prophet m
pro·por·tion 1. Verhältnis n; (An)Teil m; pl Größenverhältnisse pl, Proportionen pl; in ~ to im Verhältnis zu 2. (to) in das richtige Verhältnis bringen (mit, zu); anpassen (dat)
pro·por·tion·al proportional; → proportionate
pro·por·tion·ate (to) im richtigen Verhältnis (zu), entsprechend (dat)
pro·pos·al Vorschlag m; (Heirats)Antrag m; pro·pose v/t vorschlagen; beabsichtigen, vorhaben; Toast ausbringen (to auf acc); ~ s.o.'s health auf j-s Gesundheit trinken; v/i: ~ to j-m e-n (Heirats)Antrag machen
prop·o·si·tion Behauptung f; Vorschlag m, ECON a. Angebot n
pro·pri·e·ta·ry ECON gesetzlich or patentrechtlich geschützt; fig besitzergreifend
pro·pri·e·tor Eigentümer m, Besitzer m, Geschäftsinhaber m
pro·pri·e·tress Eigentümerin f, Besitzerin f, Geschäftsinhaberin f
pro·pri·e·ty Anstand m; Richtigkeit f
pro·pul·sion TECH Antrieb m
pro·sa·ic prosaisch, nüchtern, sachlich
prose Prosa f
pros·e·cute JUR strafrechtlich verfolgen, (gerichtlich) belangen (for wegen)
pros·e·cu·tion JUR strafrechtliche Verfolgung, Strafverfolgung f; the ~ die

Staatsanwaltschaft, die Anklage (-behörde)

pros·e·cu·tor *a.* **public** ~ JUR Staatsanwalt *m*, Staatsanwältin *f*

pros·pect **1.** Aussicht *f* (*a. fig*); Interessent *m*, ECON möglicher Kunde, potenzieller Käufer **2.** ~ *for mining*: schürfen nach; bohren nach

pro·spec·tive voraussichtlich

pro·spec·tus (Werbe)Prospekt *m*

pros·per gedeihen; ECON blühen, florieren; pros·per·i·ty Wohlstand *m*; pros·per·ous ECON erfolgreich, blühend, florierend; wohlhabend

pros·ti·tute Prostituierte *f*, Dirne *f*; **male** ~ Strichjunge *m*

pros·trate **1.** hingestreckt; *fig* am Boden liegend; erschöpft; ~ **with grief** grambeugt **2.** niederwerfen; *fig* erschöpfen; *fig* niederschmettern

pros·y langweilig; weitschweifig

pro·tag·o·nist Vorkämpfer(in), THEA Hauptfigur *f*, Held(in)

pro·tect (be)schützen (**from** vor *dat*; **against** gegen)

pro·tec·tion Schutz *m*; F Schutzgeld *n*; ~ **of animals** Tierschutz; ~ **of endangered species** Artenschutz *m*; ~ money F Schutzgeld *n*; ~ rack·et F Schutzgelderpressung *f*

pro·tec·tive (be)schützend; Schutz...; ~ cloth·ing Schutzkleidung *f*; ~ custody JUR Schutzhaft *f*; ~ du·ty, ~ tar·iff ECON Schutzzoll *m*

pro·tec·tor Beschützer *m*; (*Brust- etc -*)Schutz *m*

pro·tec·to·rate POL Protektorat *n*

pro·test Protest *m*; Einspruch *m* **2.** *v/i* protestieren (**against** gegen); *v/t* protestieren gegen; beteuern

Prot·es·tant REL **1.** protestantisch **2.** Protestant(in)

prot·es·ta·tion Beteuerung *f*; Protest *m* (**against** gegen)

pro·to·col Protokoll *n*

pro·to·type Prototyp *m*

pro·tract in die Länge ziehen, hinziehen

pro·trude herausragen, vorstehen (**from** aus); pro·trud·ing vorstehend (*a. teeth*), vorspringend (*chin*)

proud stolz (**of** auf *acc*)

prove *v/t* be-, er-, nachweisen; *v/i:* ~ (**to be**) sich herausstellen *or* erweisen als

prov·en bewährt

prov·erb Sprichwort *n*

pro·vide *v/t* versehen, versorgen, beliefern; zur Verfügung stellen, bereitstellen; JUR vorsehen, vorschreiben (**that** dass); *v/i:* ~ **against** Vorsorge treffen gegen; JUR verbieten; ~ **for** sorgen für; vorsorgen für; JUR *et.* vorsehen

pro·vid·ed: ~ (**that**) vorausgesetzt(, dass)

pro·vid·er Ernährer(in)

prov·ince Provinz *f*; (Aufgaben-, Wissens)Gebiet *n*; pro·vin·cial **1.** Provinz..., provinziell, *contp* provinzlerisch **2.** *contp* Provinzler(in)

pro·vi·sion Bereitstellung *f*, Beschaffung *f*; Vorkehrung *f*, Vorsorge *f*; Bestimmung *f*, Vorschrift *f*; *pl* Proviant *m*, Verpflegung *f*; **with the** ~ **that** unter der Bedingung, dass

pro·vi·sion·al provisorisch, vorläufig

pro·vi·so Bedingung *f*, Vorbehalt *m*; **with the** ~ **that** unter der Bedingung, dass

prov·o·ca·tion Provokation *f*

pro·voc·a·tive provozierend, (*a. sexually*) aufreizend

pro·voke provozieren, reizen

prowl **1.** *v/i a.* ~ **about**, ~ **around** herumschleichen, herumstreifen; *v/t* durchstreifen **2.** Herumstreifen *n*

prowl car (Funk)Streifenwagen *m*

prox·im·i·ty Nähe *f*

prox·y (Handlungs)Vollmacht *f*; (Stell)Vertreter(in), Bevollmächtigte *m, f*; **by** ~ durch e-n Bevollmächtigten

prude: **be a** ~ prüde sein

pru·dence Klugheit *f*, Vernunft *f*; Besonnenheit *f*

pru·dent klug, vernünftig; besonnen

prud·ish prüde

prune[1] BOT (be)schneiden

prune[2] Backpflaume *f*

prus·sic ac·id CHEM Blausäure *f*

pry[1] neugierig sein; ~ **about** herumschnüffeln; ~ **into** s-e Nase stecken in (*acc*)

pry[2] → **prize**[2]

psalm REL Psalm *m*

pseu·do·nym Pseudonym *n*, Deckname *m*

psy·chi·a·trist Psychiater(in)

psy·chi·a·try Psychiatrie *f*

psy·cho·a·nal·y·sis Psychoanalyse *f*

psy·cho·log·i·cal psychologisch

psy·chol·o·gist Psychologe *m*, Psycho-

login f
psy·chol·o·gy Psychologie f
psy·cho·so·mat·ic psychosomatisch
pub Br Pub n, m, Kneipe f
pu·ber·ty Pubertät f
pu·bic hair Schamhaare pl
pub·lic 1. öffentlich; allgemein bekannt; **make** ~ bekannt machen, an die Öffentlichkeit bringen 2. *die* Öffentlichkeit, *das* Publikum; **in** ~ öffentlich, in aller Öffentlichkeit
pub·li·ca·tion Bekanntgabe f, Bekanntmachung f; Publikation f, Veröffentlichung f
pub·lic| con·ve·ni·ence Br öffentliche Bedürfnisanstalt; ~ **en·e·my** Staatsfeind m; ~ **health** öffentliches Gesundheitswesen; ~ **hol·i·day** gesetzlicher Feiertag
pub·lic·i·ty Publicity f, a. Bekanntheit f, ECON a. Reklame f, Werbung f; ~ **depart·ment** Werbeabteilung f
pub·lic| **li·bra·ry** Leihbücherei f; ~ **rela·tions** (abbr **PR**) Public Relations pl, Öffentlichkeitsarbeit f; ~ **school** staatliche Schule; Br Public School f; ~ **trans·port** esp Br, ~ **trans·por·ta·tion** öffentliche Verkehrsmittel pl
pub·lish bekannt geben or machen; publizieren, veröffentlichen; *Buch etc* verlegen, herausgeben
pub·lish·er Verleger(in), Herausgeber(in); Verlag m, Verlagshaus n
pub·lish·er's. pub·lish·ers. publish·ing house Verlag m, Verlagshaus n
puck·er a. ~ **up** (sich) verziehen, (sich) runzeln
pud·ding Br GASTR Nachspeise f, Nachtisch m; (Reis- etc) Auflauf m; (Art) Fleischpastete f; Pudding m
pud·dle Pfütze f
pu·er·ile infantil, kindisch
puff 1. v/i schnaufen, keuchen; a. ~ **away** paffen (**at** an dat); ~ **up** (an)schwellen; v/t Rauch blasen; ~ **out** Kerze etc ausblasen; Rauch etc ausstoßen; Brust herausdrücken 2. Zug m; (Wind-) Hauch m, (Wind)Stoß m; (Puder)Quaste f; F Puste f
puffed sleeve Puffärmel m
puff pas·try GASTR Blätterteig m
puff·y (an)geschwollen; aufgedunsen
pug ZO Mops m
puke F (aus)kotzen

pull 1. Ziehen n; Zug m, Ruck m; Anstieg m, Steigung f; Zuggriff m, Zugleine f; F Beziehung pl 2. ziehen; ziehen an (dat); zerren; reißen; Pflanze ausreißen; esp Br Bier zapfen; fig anziehen; ~ **ahead of** vorbeiziehen an (dat), MOT überholen (acc); ~ **away** anfahren (bus etc); ~ **down** Gebäude abreißen; ~ **in** einfahren (train); anhalten; ~ **off** et. zustande bringen, schaffen; ~ **out** herausziehen (**of** aus); Tisch ausziehen; RAIL abfahren; MOT ausscheren; fig sich zurückziehen, aussteigen (**of** aus); ~ **over** (s-n Wagen) an die or zur Seite fahren; ~ **round** MED durchbringen; durchkommen; ~ **through** j-n durchbringen; ~ **o.s. together** sich zusammennehmen, F sich zusammenreißen; ~ **up** MOT anhalten; (an)halten; ~ **up to**, ~ **up with** SPORT j-n einholen
pull date Mindesthaltbarkeitsdatum n
pul·ley TECH Flaschenzug m
pull-in Br F Raststätte f, Rasthaus n
pull·o·ver Pullover m
pull-up SPORT Klimmzug m; **do a** ~ e-n Klimmzug machen
pulp 1. Fruchtfleisch n; Brei m 2. Schund...; ~ **novel** Schundroman m
pul·pit Kanzel f
pulp·y breiig
pul·sate pulsieren, vibrieren
pulse Puls m; Pulsschlag m
pul·ver·ize pulverisieren
pu·ma ZO Puma m
pum·mel mit den Fäusten bearbeiten
pump 1. Pumpe f; (Zapf)Säule f 2. pumpen; F j-n aushorchen; ~ **up** aufpumpen; ~ **at·tend·ant** Tankwart m
pump·kin BOT Kürbis m
pun 1. Wortspiel n 2. Wortspiele or ein Wortspiel machen
punch¹ 1. boxen, (mit der Faust) schlagen 2. (Faust)Schlag m
punch² 1. lochen; Loch stanzen (**in** in acc); ~ **in** einstempeln; ~ **out** ausstempeln 2. Locher m; Lochzange f; Locheisen n
punch³ Punsch m
Punch appr Kasper m, Kasperle n, m; **be as pleased** or **proud as** ~ sich freuen wie ein Schneekönig; ~ **and Ju·dy show** Kasperletheater n
punc·tu·al pünktlich
punc·tu·al·i·ty Pünktlichkeit f

punc·tu·ate interpunktieren

punc·tu·a·tion LING Interpunktion *f*; ~ mark LING Satzzeichen *n*

punc·ture 1. (Ein)Stich *m*, Loch *n*; MOT Reifenpanne *f* 2. durchstechen, durchbohren; ein Loch bekommen, platzen; MOT e-n Platten haben

pun·gent scharf, stechend, beißend (*smell, taste*); scharf, bissig (*remark etc*)

pun·ish *j-n* (be)strafen

pun·ish·a·ble strafbar

pun·ish·ment Strafe *f*; Bestrafung *f*

punk Punk *m* (*a.* MUS); Punk(er) *m*

pu·ny schwächlich

pup ZO Welpe *m*, junger Hund

pu·pa ZO Puppe *f*

pu·pil[1] Schüler(in)

pu·pil[2] ANAT Pupille *f*

pup·pet Handpuppe *f*; Marionette *f* (*a. fig*)

pup·pe·teer Puppenspieler(in)

pup·pet show Marionettentheater *n*, Puppenspiel *n*

pup·py ZO Welpe *m*, junger Hund

pur·chase 1. kaufen; *fig* erkaufen 2. Kauf *m*; **make ~s** Einkäufe machen

pur·chas·er Käufer(in)

pure rein; pur

pure·bred ZO reinrassig

pur·ga·tive MED 1. abführend 2. Abführmittel *n*

pur·ga·to·ry REL Fegefeuer *n*

purge 1. *Partei etc* säubern (*of* von); 2. Säuberung *f*, Säuberungsaktion *f*

pu·ri·fy reinigen

pu·ri·tan (HIST *Puritan*) 1. Puritaner(in) 2. puritanisch

pu·ri·ty Reinheit *f*

purl 1. linke Masche 2. links stricken

pur·ple purpurn, purpurrot

pur·pose 1. Absicht *f*, Vorsatz *m*; Zweck *m*, Ziel *n*; Entschlossenheit *f*; **on ~** absichtlich; **to no ~** vergeblich 2. beabsichtigen, vorhaben

pur·pose·ful entschlossen, zielstrebig

pur·pose·less zwecklos; ziellos

pur·pose·ly absichtlich

purr ZO schnurren; MOT summen, surren

purse[1] Geldbeutel *m*, Geldbörse *f*, Portemonnaie *f*; Handtasche *f*; SPORT Siegprämie *f*; *boxing*: Börse *f*

purse[2] ~ **(up) one's lips** die Lippen schürzen

purs·er MAR Zahlmeister *m*

pur·su·ance: *in* (*the*) ~ *of his duty* in Ausübung s-r Pflicht

pur·sue verfolgen; *s-m Studium etc* nachgehen; *Absicht, Politik etc* verfolgen; *Angelegenheit etc* weiterführen

pur·su·er Verfolger(in)

pur·suit Verfolgung *f*; Weiterführung *f*

pur·vey Lebensmittel *etc* liefern

pur·vey·or Lieferant *m*

pus MED Eiter *m*

push 1. stoßen, F schubsen; schieben; *Taste etc* drücken; drängen; (an)treiben; F *Rauschgift* pushen; *fig j-n* drängen (*to do* zu tun); *fig* Reklame machen für; ~ **one's way** sich drängen (*through* durch); ~ **ahead with** *Plan etc* vorantreiben; ~ **along** F sich auf die Socken machen; ~ **around** F herumschubsen; ~ **for** drängen auf (*acc*); ~ **forward with** → **push ahead with**; ~ **o.s. forward** *fig* sich in den Vordergrund drängen *or* schieben; ~ **in** F sich vordrängeln; ~ **off!** F hau ab!; ~ **on with** → **push ahead with**; ~ **out** *fig j-n* hinausdrängen; ~ **through** *et.* durchsetzen; ~ **up** *Preise etc* hochtreiben 2. Stoß *m*, F Schubs *m*; F (Werbe)Kampagne *f*; F Durchsetzungsvermögen *n*, Energie *f*, Tatkraft *f*

push but·ton TECH Druckknopf *m*, Drucktaste *f*

push·chair *Br* Sportwagen *m*

push·er F *contp* Rauschgifthändler *m*

push·o·ver F Kinderspiel *n*

push-up SPORT Liegestütz *m*

puss F ZO Mieze *f*

pus·sy *a.* ~ **cat** F Miezekatze *f*

pus·sy·foot F ~ **about**, ~ **around** leisetreten, sich nicht festlegen wollen

put legen, setzen, stecken, stellen, tun; *j-n in e-e Lage etc*, *et. auf den Markt*, *in Ordnung etc* bringen; *et. in Kraft*, *in Umlauf etc* setzen; SPORT *Kugel* stoßen; unterwerfen, unterziehen (*to dat*); *et.* ausdrücken, *in Worte fassen*; übersetzen (*into German* ins Deutsche); *Schuld* geben (*on dat*); ~ **right** in Ordnung bringen; ~ **s.th. before s.o.** *fig j-m et.* vorlegen; ~ **to bed** ins Bett bringen; ~ **to school** *zur* Schule schicken; ~ **about** *Gerüchte* verbreiten, in Umlauf setzen; ~ **across** *et.* verständlich machen; ~ **ahead** SPORT in Führung bringen; ~ **aside** beiseitelegen; *Ware* zurücklegen; *fig* beiseiteschieben; ~ *away* weglegen, wegtun; auf-, wegräumen; ~ *back* zurücklegen, -stellen, -tun; *Uhr* zurückstellen (*by* um); ~ *by* Geld zurücklegen; ~ *down* v/t hinlegen, niederlegen, hinsetzen, hinstellen; *j-n* absetzen, aussteigen lassen; (auf-, nieder-) schreiben, eintragen; zuschreiben (*to* dat); *Aufstand* niederschlagen; (*a.* v/i) AVIAT landen; ~ *forward Plan etc* vorlegen; *Uhr* vorstellen (*by* um); *fig* vorverlegen (*two days* um zwei Tage; *to* auf acc); ~ *in* v/t hineinlegen, -stecken, -stellen; *Kassette etc* einlegen; installieren; *Gesuch etc* einreichen, *Forderung etc a.* geltend machen; *Antrag stellen; Arbeit, Zeit* verbringen (*on* mit); *Bemerkung* einwerfen; v/i MAR einlaufen (*at* in acc); ~ *off et.* verschieben (*until* auf acc); *j-m* absagen; *j-n* hinhalten (*with* mit), *j-n* vertrösten; *j-n* aus dem Konzept bringen; ~ *on Kleider etc* anziehen, *Hut, Brille* aufsetzen; *Licht, Radio etc* anmachen, einschalten; *Sonderzug* einsetzen; THEA *Stück etc* herausbringen; *et.* vortäuschen; F *j-n* auf den Arm nehmen; ~ *on airs* sich aufspielen; ~ *on weight* zunehmen; ~ *out* v/t hinauslegen, -setzen, -stellen; *Hand etc* ausstrecken; *Feuer* löschen; *Licht, Radio etc* ausmachen (*a. cigarette*), ab-, ausschalten; veröffentlichen, herausgeben; *radio*, TV bringen, senden; *j-n* aus der Fassung bringen; *j-n* verärgern; *j-m* Ungelegenheiten bereiten; *j-m* Um-

stände machen; sich *den Arm etc* verrenken *or* ausrenken; v/i MAR auslaufen; ~ *over* → *put across*; ~ *through* TEL *j-n* verbinden (*to* mit); durch-, ausführen; ~ *together* zusammenbauen, -setzen, -stellen; ~ *up* v/t hinauflegen, -setzen, -stellen; *Hand* (hoch)heben; *Zelt etc* aufstellen; *Gebäude* errichten; *Bild etc* aufhängen; *Plakat, Bekanntmachung etc* anschlagen; *Schirm* aufspannen; *zum Verkauf* anbieten; *Preis* erhöhen; *Widerstand* leisten; *Kampf* liefern; *j-n* unterbringen, (bei sich) aufnehmen; v/i ~ *up at* absteigen in (*dat*); ~ *up with* sich gefallen lassen; sich abfinden mit

pu·tre·fy (ver)faulen, verwesen
pu·trid faul, verfault, verwest; F scheußlich, saumäßig
put·ty 1. Kitt *m* **2.** kitten
put-up job F abgekartetes Spiel
puz·zle 1. Rätsel *n*; Geduld(s)spiel *n* **2.** v/t *j-n* vor ein Rätsel stellen; verwirren; *be* ~*d* vor e-m Rätsel stehen; ~ *out* herausfinden, herausbringen, F austüfteln; v/i sich den Kopf zerbrechen (*about, over* über *dat or* acc)
pyg·my 1. Pygmäe *m*, Pygmäin *f*; Zwerg(in) **2.** *esp zo* Zwerg...
py·ja·mas *Br* → *pajamas*
py·lon TECH Hochspannungsmast *m*
pyr·a·mid Pyramide *f*
pyre Scheiterhaufen *m*
py·thon ZO Python(schlange) *f*
pyx REL Hostienbehälter *m*

Q

Q, q Q, q *n*
quack¹ ZO **1.** quaken **2.** Quaken *n*
quack² *a.* ~ *doctor* Quacksalber *m*, Kurpfuscher *m*; **quack·er·y** Quacksalberei *f*, Kurpfuscherei *f*
quad·ran·gle Viereck *n*
quad·ran·gu·lar viereckig
quad·ra·phon·ic quadrophon(isch)
quad·rat·ic MATH quadratisch
quad·ri·lat·er·al MATH **1.** vierseitig **2.** Viereck *n*
quad·ro·phon·ic → *quadraphonic*

quad·ru·ped ZO Vierfüß(l)er *m*; Vierbeiner *m*
quad·ru·ple 1. vierfach **2.** (sich) vervierfachen
quad·ru·plets Vierlinge *pl*
quads Vierlinge *pl*
quag·mire Morast *m*, Sumpf *m*
quail ZO Wachtel *f*
quaint idyllisch, malerisch
quake 1. zittern, beben (*with, for* vor *dat*; *at* bei); **2.** F Erdbeben *n*
Quak·er REL Quäker(in)

qual·i·fi·ca·tion Qualifikation *f*, Befähigung *f*, Eignung *f* (**for** für, zu); Voraussetzung *f*; Einschränkung *f*

qual·i·fied qualifiziert, geeignet, befähigt (**for** für); berechtigt; bedingt, eingeschränkt; qual·i·fy *v/t* qualifizieren, befähigen (**for** für, zu); berechtigen (**to do** zu tun); einschränken, abschwächen, mildern; *v/i* sich qualifizieren *or* eignen (**for** für; **as** als); SPORT sich qualifizieren (**for** für)

qual·i·ty Qualität *f*; Eigenschaft *f*

qualms Bedenken *pl*, Skrupel *pl*

quan·da·ry: **be in a ~ about what to do** nicht wissen, was man tun soll

quan·ti·ty Quantität *f*, Menge *f*

quan·tum PHYS 1. Quant *n* 2. Quanten…

quar·an·tine 1. Quarantäne *f* 2. unter Quarantäne stellen

quar·rel 1. Streit *m*, Auseinandersetzung *f* 2. (sich) streiten

quar·rel·some streitsüchtig, zänkisch

quar·ry¹ Steinbruch *m*

quar·ry² HUNT Beute *f*, *a. fig* Opfer *n*

quart Quart *n* (*abbr* **qt**) (0,95 *l*, *Br* 1,14 *l*)

quar·ter 1. Viertel *n*, vierter Teil; Quartal *n*, Vierteljahr *n*; Viertelpfund *n*; Vierteldollar *m*; SPORT (Spiel)Viertel *n*; (Himmels)Richtung *f*; Gegend *f*, Teil *m*; (Stadt)Viertel *n*; GASTR (*esp* Hinter)Viertel *n*; Gnade *f*, Pardon *m*; *pl* Quartier *n*, Unterkunft *f* (*a.* MIL); **a ~ of an hour** e-e Viertelstunde; **a ~ of** (*Br* **to**) **five** (ein) Viertel vor fünf (*4.45*); **a ~ after** (*Br* **past**) **five** (ein) Viertel nach fünf (*5.15*); **at close ~s** in *or* aus nächster Nähe; **from official ~s** von amtlicher Seite 2. vierteln; *esp* MIL einquartieren (**on** bei)

quar·ter·deck MAR Achterdeck *n*

quar·ter·fi·nals SPORT Viertelfinale *n*

quar·ter·ly 1. vierteljährlich 2. Vierteljahresschrift *f*

quar·tet(te) MUS Quartett *n*

quartz MIN Quarz *m*; **~ clock** Quarzuhr *f*; **~ watch** Quarz(armband)uhr *f*

qua·ver 1. *v/i* zittern; *v/t et. mit* zitternder Stimme sagen 2. Zittern *n*

quay MAR Kai *m*

quea·sy: **I feel ~** mir ist übel *or* F mulmig

queen Königin *f*; *card game, chess*: Dame *f*; F Schwule *m*, Homo *m*

queen bee ZO Bienenkönigin *f*

queen·ly wie e-e Königin, königlich

queer komisch, seltsam; F wunderlich; F schwul

quench Durst löschen, stillen

quer·u·lous nörglerisch

que·ry 1. Frage *f*; Zweifel *m* 2. infrage stellen, in Zweifel ziehen

quest 1. Suche *f* (**for** nach); **in ~ of** auf der Suche nach 2. suchen (**after, for** nach)

ques·tion 1. Frage *f*, *a.* Problem *n*, *a.* Sache *f*, *a.* Zweifel *m*; **only a ~ of time** nur e-e Frage der Zeit; **this is not the point in ~** darum geht es nicht; **there is no ~ that, it is beyond ~ that** es steht außer Frage, dass; **there is no ~ about this** daran besteht kein Zweifel; **be out of the ~** nicht infrage kommen 2. befragen (**about** über *acc*), JUR vernehmen, verhören (**about** zu); bezweifeln, in Zweifel ziehen, infrage stellen

ques·tion·a·ble fraglich, zweifelhaft; fragwürdig

ques·tion·er Fragesteller(in)

ques·tion| mark Fragezeichen *n*; **~ mas·ter** *esp Br* Quizmaster *m*

ques·tion·naire Fragebogen *m*

queue *esp Br* 1. Schlange *f*; → **jump** 2. *mst* **~ up** Schlange stehen, anstehen, sich anstellen

quib·ble sich herumstreiten (**with** mit; **about, over** wegen)

quick 1. *adj* schnell, rasch; aufbrausend, hitzig (*temper*); **be ~!** mach schnell!, beeil dich! 2. *adv* schnell, rasch 3. **cut s.o. to the ~** *fig* j-n tief verletzen

quick·en (sich) beschleunigen

quick·sand Treibsand *m*

quick-tem·pered aufbrausend, hitzig

quick-wit·ted schlagfertig; geistesgegenwärtig

qui·et 1. ruhig, still; **~, please** Ruhe, bitte; **be ~!** sei still! 2. Ruhe *f*, Stille *f*; **on the ~** F heimlich 3. *v/t a.* **~ down** j-n beruhigen; *v/i a.* **~ down** sich beruhigen

qui·et·en *Br* → **quiet** 3

qui·et·ness Ruhe *f*, Stille *f*

quill ZO (Schwung-, Schwanz)Feder *f*; Stachel *m*

quilt Steppdecke *f*; **quilt·ed** Stepp…

quince BOT Quitte *f*

qui·nine PHARM Chinin *n*

quint F Fünfling *m*

quin·tes·sence Quintessenz *f*; Inbegriff *m*

quin·tet(te) MUS Quintett n
quin·tu·ple 1. fünffach **2.** (sich) verfünf-
fachen
quin·tu·plets Fünflinge pl
quip 1. geistreiche or witzige Bemerkung **2.** witzeln, spötteln
quirk Eigenart f, Schrulle f; **by some ~
of fate** durch e-e Laune des Schicksals,
durch e-n verrückten Zufall
quit F v/t aufhören mit; **~ one's job** kündigen; v/i aufhören; kündigen
quite ganz, völlig; ziemlich; **~ a few**
ziemlich viele; **~ nice** ganz nett, recht
nett; **~ (so)!** esp Br genau, ganz recht;
be ~ right völlig recht haben; **she's ~ a
beauty** sie ist e-e wirkliche Schönheit
quits F quitt (**with** mit); **call it ~** es gut

sein lassen
quit·ter: F **be a ~** schnell aufgeben
quiv·er¹ zittern (**with** vor dat; **at** bei)
quiv·er² Köcher m
quiz 1. Quiz n; Prüfung f, Test m **2.** aus-
fragen (**about** über acc)
quiz·mas·ter Quizmaster m
quiz·zi·cal spöttisch-fragend
quo·ta Quote f, Kontingent n
quo·ta·tion Zitat n; ECON Notierung f;
Kostenvoranschlag m; **~ marks** LING
Anführungszeichen pl
quote zitieren; Beispiel etc anführen;
Preis nennen; **be ~d at** ECON notieren
mit
quo·tient MATH Quotient m

R

R, r R, r n
rab·bi REL Rabbiner m
rab·bit ZO Kaninchen n
rab·ble Pöbel m, Mob m
rab·ble-rous·ing Hetz..., aufwiegle-
risch
rab·id VET tollwütig; fig fanatisch
ra·bies VET Tollwut f
rac·coon ZO Waschbär m
race¹ Rasse f, Rassenzugehörigkeit f;
(Menschen)Geschlecht n
race² 1. (Wett)Rennen n, (Wett)Lauf m
2. v/i an (e-m) Rennen teilnehmen; um
die Wette laufen or fahren etc; rasen,
rennen; MOT durchdrehen; v/t um die
Wette laufen or fahren etc mit; rasen
mit
race car MOT Rennwagen m
race·course Rennbahn f
race·horse Rennpferd n
rac·er Rennpferd n; Rennrad n, Rennwagen m
race ri·ots Rassenunruhen pl
race·track Rennbahn f
ra·cial rassisch, Rassen...
rac·ing 1. Rennsport m **2.** Renn...
rac·ing car Br MOT Rennwagen m
rac·ism Rassismus m
rac·ist 1. Rassist(in) **2.** rassistisch
rack 1. Gestell n, (Geschirr-, Zeitungs-
etc)Ständer m, RAIL (Gepäck)Netz n,

MOT (Dach)Gepäckständer m; HIST
Folter(bank) f **2. be ~ed by** or **with** geplagt or gequält werden von; **~ one's
brains** sich das Hirn zermartern, sich
den Kopf zerbrechen
rack·et¹ tennis etc: Schläger m
rack·et² F Krach m, Lärm m; Schwindel
m, Gaunerei f; (Drogen- etc)Geschäft
n; organisierte Erpressung
rack·et·eer Gauner m; Erpresser m
ra·coon → **raccoon**
rac·y spritzig, lebendig; gewagt (joke)
ra·dar TECH Radar m, n; **~ screen** Radar-
schirm m; **~ speed check** MOT Radarkontrolle f; **~ sta·tion** Radarstation f; **~
trap** MOT Radarkontrolle f
ra·di·al 1. radial, Radial..., strahlenförmig **2.** MOT Gürtelreifen m
ra·di·al¦ tire, Br ~ tyre → **radial** 2
ra·di·ant strahlend, leuchtend (a. fig
with vor dat)
ra·di·ate ausstrahlen; strahlenförmig
ausgehen (**from** von)
ra·di·a·tion Ausstrahlung f
ra·di·a·tor Heizkörper m; MOT Kühler m
rad·i·cal 1. radikal (a. POL); MATH Wurzel... **2.** POL Radikale m, f
ra·di·o 1. Radio(apparat m) n; Funk m;
Funkgerät n; **by ~** über Funk; **on the ~**
im Radio **2.** funken
ra·di·o·ac·tive radioaktiv; **~ waste**

Atommüll *m*, radioaktiver Abfall

ra·di·o·ac·tiv·i·ty Radioaktivität *f*

ra·di·o| **ham** Funkamateur *m*; ~ **play** Hörspiel *n*; ~ **set** Radioapparat *m*; ~ **sta·tion** Funkstation *f*; Rundfunksender *m*, -station *f*; ~**ther·a·py** MED Strahlentherapie *f*, Röntgentherapie *f*; ~**tow·er** Funkturm *m*

rad·ish BOT Rettich *m*; Radieschen *n*

ra·di·us MATH Radius *m*

raf·fle 1. Tombola *f* **2.** *a.* ~ *off* verlosen

raft Floß *n*

raf·ter (Dach)Sparren *m*

rag Lumpen *m*, Fetzen *m*; Lappen *m*; *in* ~*s* zerlumpt

rage 1. Wut *f*, Zorn *m*; *fly into a* ~ wütend werden; *the latest* ~ *f* der letzte Schrei; *be all the* ~ F große Mode sein **2.** wettern (*against, at* gegen); wüten, toben

rag·ged zerlumpt; struppig; *fig* stümperhaft

raid 1. (*on*) Überfall *m* (auf *acc*), MIL *a.* Angriff *m* (gegen); Razzia *f* (in *dat*); **2.** überfallen, MIL *a.* angreifen; e-e Razzia machen in (*dat*)

rail 1. Geländer *n*; Stange *f*; (Handtuch)Halter *m*; (Eisen)Bahn *f*; RAIL Schiene *f*, *pl a.* Gleis *n*; *by* ~ mit der Bahn **2.** ~ *in* einzäunen; ~ *off* abzäunen

rail·ing *often pl* (Gitter)Zaun *m*

rail·road Eisenbahn *f*; ~**line** Bahnlinie *f*; ~**sta·tion** Bahnhof *m*

rail·way *Br* → *railroad*

rain 1. Regen *m*, *pl* Regenfälle *pl*; *the* ~*s* die Regenzeit **2.** regnen; *it never* ~*s but it pours* es kommt immer gleich knüppeldick, ein Unglück kommt selten allein

rain·bow Regenbogen *m*

rain·coat Regenmantel *m*

rain·fall Niederschlag(smenge *f*) *m*

rain for·est GEOGR Regenwald *m*

rain·proof regendicht, wasserdicht

rain·y regnerisch, verregnet, Regen...

raise 1. heben; hochziehen; erheben; *Denkmal etc* errichten; *Staub etc* aufwirbeln; *Gehalt, Miete etc* erhöhen; *Geld* zusammenbringen, beschaffen; *Kinder* aufziehen, großziehen; *Tiere* züchten; *Getreide etc* anbauen; *Frage* aufwerfen, *et.* zur Sprache bringen; *Blockade etc*, *a. Verbot* aufheben **2.** Lohn- *or* Gehaltserhöhung *f*

rai·sin Rosine *f*

rake 1. Rechen *m*, Harke *f* **2.** *v/t:* ~ (*up*) (zusammen)rechen, (zusammen)harken; F ~ *in* scheffeln; *v/i:* ~ *about,* ~ *around* herumstöbern

rak·ish flott, keck, verwegen

ral·ly 1. (sich) (wieder) sammeln; sich erholen (*from* von) (*a.* ECON); ~ *round* sich scharen um **2.** Kundgebung *f*, (Massen)Versammlung *f*; MOT Rallye *f*; *tennis etc:* Ballwechsel *m*

ram 1. ZO Widder *m*, Schafbock *m*; TECH Ramme *f* **2.** rammen

ram·ble 1. wandern, umherstreifen; abschweifen **2.** Wanderung *f*; **ram·bler** Wanderer *m*; BOT Kletterrose *f*

ram·bling weitschweifig; weitläufig; ~ **rose** BOT Kletterrose *f*

ramp Rampe *f*; MOT (Autobahn)Auffahrt *f*; (Autobahn)Ausfahrt *f*

ram·page 1. ~ *through* (wild *or* aufgeregt) trampeln durch (*elephant etc*); → **2.** *go on the* ~ *through* randalierend ziehen durch

ram·pant *be* ~ wuchern (*plant*); grassieren (*in* in *dat*)

ram·shack·le baufällig (*building*); klapp(e)rig (*vehicle*)

ranch Ranch *f*; (Geflügel- *etc*)Farm *f*

ranch·er Rancher *m*; (Geflügel- *etc*) Züchter *m*

ran·cid ranzig

ran·co(u)r Groll *m*, Erbitterung *f*

ran·dom 1. *adj* ziellos, wahllos; zufällig, Zufalls...; ~ *sample* Stichprobe *f* **2.** *at* ~ aufs Geratewohl

range 1. Reich-, Schuss-, Tragweite *f*; Entfernung *f*; *fig* Bereich *m*, *a.* Spielraum *m*, *a.* Gebiet *n*; (Schieß)Stand *m*, (-)Platz *m*; (Berg)Kette *f*; offenes Weidegebiet; ECON Kollektion *f*, Sortiment *n*; Küchenherd *m*; *at close* ~ aus nächster Nähe; *within* ~ *of vision* in Sichtweite; *a wide* ~ *of* ... eine große Auswahl an ... (*dat*) **2.** *v/i:* ~ *from* ... *to* ..., ~ *between* ... *and* ... sich zwischen ... und ... bewegen (*prices etc*); *v/t* aufstellen, anordnen

range find·er PHOT Entfernungsmesser *m*

rang·er Förster *m*; Ranger *m*

rank[1] 1. Rang *m* (*a.* MIL), (soziale) Stellung; Reihe *f*; (Taxi)Stand *m*; *of the first* ~ *fig* erstklassig; *the* ~ *and file* *fig* die Basis; **the ~s** *fig* das Heer, die Masse **2.** *v/t* rechnen, zählen (**among** zu); stellen (**above** über *acc*); *v/i* zählen, gehören (**among** zu); gelten (**as** als)

rank² BOT (üppig) wuchernd; übel riechend, übel schmeckend; *fig* krass (*outsider*), blutig (*beginner*)

ran·kle *fig* nagen, wehtun, F wurmen

ran·sack durchwühlen, durchsuchen; plündern

ran·som 1. Lösegeld *n* **2.** freikaufen, auslösen

rap 1. Klopfen *n*; Klaps *m* **2.** klopfen (an *acc*, auf *acc*)

ra·pa·cious habgierig

rape¹ 1. vergewaltigen **2.** Vergewaltigung *f*

rape² BOT Raps *m*

rap·id schnell, rasch

ra·pid·i·ty Schnelligkeit *f*

rap·ids GEOGR Stromschnellen *pl*

rapt: with ~ attention mit gespannter Aufmerksamkeit

rap·ture Entzücken *n*, Verzückung *f*; **go into ~s** in Verzückung geraten

rare¹ selten, rar; dünn (*air*); F Mords...

rare² GASTR blutig (*steak*)

rar·e·fied dünn (*air*)

rar·i·ty Seltenheit *f*; Rarität *f*

ras·cal Schlingel *m*

rash¹ voreilig, vorschnell, unbesonnen

rash² MED (Haut)Ausschlag *m*

rash·er dünne Speckscheibe

rasp 1. raspeln; kratzen **2.** Raspel *f*; Kratzen *n*

rasp·ber·ry BOT Himbeere *f*

rat ZO Ratte *f* (*a. contp*); F **smell a ~** Lunte *or* den Braten riechen

rate 1. Quote *f*, Rate *f*, (Geburten-, Sterbe)Ziffer *f*; (Steuer-, Zins- *etc*)Satz *m*; (Wechsel)Kurs *m*; Geschwindigkeit *f*, Tempo *n*; **at any ~** auf jeden Fall **2.** einschätzen, halten (**as** für); *Lob etc* verdienen; **be ~d as** gelten als

rate of ex·change ECON (Umrechnungs-, Wechsel)Kurs *m*

rate of in·terest ECON Zinssatz *m*

ra·ther ziemlich; eher, vielmehr, besser gesagt; **~!** *esp Br* F und ob!; **I would** *or* **had ~ go** ich möchte lieber gehen

rat·i·fy POL ratifizieren

rat·ing Einschätzung *f*; *radio*, TV Einschaltquote *f*

ra·ti·o MATH Verhältnis *n*

ra·tion 1. Ration *f* **2.** *et.* rationieren; **~ out** zuteilen (**to** *dat*)

ra·tion·al rational; vernunftbegabt; vernünftig; verstandesmäßig

ra·tion·al·i·ty Vernunft *f*

ra·tion·al·ize rational erklären; ECON rationalisieren

rat race F endloser Konkurrenzkampf

rat·tle 1. klappern; rasseln *or* klimpern (mit); prasseln (**on** auf *acc*) (*rain etc*); rattern, knattern (*vehicle*); rütteln an (*dat*); F *j-n* verunsichern; **~ at** rütteln an (*dat*); **~ off** F *Gedicht etc* herunterrasseln; F **~ on** quasseln (**about** über *acc*); F **~ through** *Rede etc* herunterrasseln **2.** Klappern *n* (*etc* → 1); Rassel *f*, Klapper *f*

rat·tle·snake ZO Klapperschlange *f*

rau·cous heiser, rau

rav·age verwüsten

rav·ag·es Verwüstungen *pl*, *a. fig* verheerende Auswirkungen *pl*

rave fantasieren, irrereden; toben; wettern (**against, at** gegen); schwärmen (**about** von)

rav·el (sich) verwickeln *or* verwirren

ra·ven ZO Rabe *m*

rav·e·nous ausgehungert, heißhungrig

ra·vine Schlucht *f*, Klamm *f*

rav·ing mad tobsüchtig

rav·ings irres Gerede, Delirien *pl*

rav·ish·ing *fig* hinreißend

raw GASTR roh, ECON, TECH *a.* Roh...; MED wund; METEOR nasskalt; *fig* unerfahren; **~ vegetables and fruit** Rohkost *f*

raw-boned knochig, hager

raw·hide Rohleder *n*

raw ma·te·ri·al Rohstoff *m*

ray Strahl *m*; *fig* Schimmer *m*

ray·on Kunstseide *f*

ra·zor Rasiermesser *n*; Rasierapparat *m*; **electric ~** Elektrorasierer *m*

ra·zor blade Rasierklinge *f*

ra·zor('s) edge *fig* kritische Lage; **be on a ~** auf des Messers Schneide stehen

re... wieder, noch einmal, neu

reach 1. *v/t* erreichen; reichen *or* gehen bis an (*acc*) *or* zu; **~ down** hinunterreichen (**from** von); **~ out** Arm *etc* ausstrecken; *v/i* reichen, gehen, sich erstrecken; *a.* **~ out** greifen, langen (**for** nach); **~ out** die Hand ausstrecken **2.** Reichweite *f*; **within** (**out of**) **~** in (außer) Reichweite; **within easy ~** leicht erreichbar

re·act reagieren (**to** auf *acc*; CHEM **with** mit); re·ac·tion Reaktion *f* (*a.* CHEM)

re·ac·tor PHYS Reaktor *m*

read lesen; TECH (an)zeigen; *Zähler etc* ablesen; UNIV studieren; deuten, verstehen (**as** als); sich *gut etc* lesen (lassen); lauten; ~ (**s.th.**) **to s.o.** j-m (et.) vorlesen

read·a·ble lesbar; leserlich; lesenswert

read·er Leser(in); Lektor(in); Lesebuch *n*

read·i·ly bereitwillig, gern; leicht, ohne weiteres

read·i·ness Bereitschaft *f*

read·ing **1.** Lesen *n*; Lesung *f* (*a.* PARL); TECH Anzeige *f*, (*Thermometer- etc* -) Stand *m*; Auslegung *f* **2.** Lese...; ~ *matter* Lesestoff *m*

re·ad·just TECH nachstellen, korrigieren; ~ (**o.s.**) **to** sich wieder anpassen (*dat*) *or* an (*acc*), sich wieder einstellen auf (*acc*)

read·y bereit, fertig; bereitwillig; im Begriff (**to do** zu tun); schnell, schlagfertig; ~ **for use** gebrauchsfertig; **get ~** (sich) fertig machen

read·y cash → **ready money**

read·y-made Konfektions...

read·y meal Fertiggericht *n*

read·y mon·ey Bargeld *m*

real echt; wirklich, tatsächlich, real; F **for ~** echt, im Ernst

real es·tate Grundbesitz *m*, Immobilien *pl*; ~ a·gent Grundstücks-, Immobilienmakler *m*

re·al·ism Realismus *m*

re·al·ist Realist(in)

re·al·is·tic realistisch

re·al·i·ty Realität *f*, Wirklichkeit *f*

re·al·i·za·tion Erkenntnis *f*; Realisierung *f* (*a.* ECON), Verwirklichung *f*

re·al·ize sich klarmachen, erkennen, begreifen, einsehen; realisieren (*a.* ECON), verwirklichen

real·ly wirklich, tatsächlich; **well, ~!** ich muss schon sagen!; ~**?** im Ernst?

realm Königreich *n*; *fig* Reich *n*

real·tor Grundstücks-, Immobilienmakler *m*

reap *Getreide etc* schneiden; *Feld* abernten; *fig* ernten

re·ap·pear wieder erscheinen

rear **1.** *v/t Kind, Tier* aufziehen, großziehen; *Kopf* heben; *v/i* sich aufbäumen (*horse*) **2.** Rückseite *f*, Hinterseite *f*, MOT Heck *n*; **in** (*Br* **at**) **the ~ of** hinter (*dat*); **bring up the ~** die Nachhut bilden **3.** hinter, Hinter..., Rück..., MOT *a.* Heck...

rear-end col·li·sion MOT Auffahrunfall *m*

rear·guard MIL Nachhut *f*

rear light MIL Rücklicht *n*

re·arm MIL (wieder) aufrüsten

re·ar·ma·ment MIL (Wieder)Aufrüstung *f*

rear·most hinterste(r, -s)

rear·view mir·ror MOT Rückspiegel *m*

rear·ward **1.** *adj* hintere(r, -s), rückwärtig **2.** *adv a.* **rearwards** rückwärts

rear-wheel drive MOT Hinterradantrieb *m*

rear win·dow MOT Heckscheibe *f*

rea·son **1.** Grund *m*; Verstand *m*; Vernunft *f*; **by ~ of** wegen; **for this ~** aus diesem Grund; **it stands to ~ that** es leuchtet ein, dass **2.** *v/i* vernünftig *or* logisch denken; vernünftig reden (**with** mit); *v/t* folgern, schließen (**that** dass); ~ **s.o. into** (**out of**) **s.th.** j-m et. einreden (ausreden); **rea·son·a·ble** vernünftig; günstig (*price*); ganz gut, nicht schlecht

re·as·sure beruhigen

re·bate ECON Rabatt *m*, (Preis)Nachlass *m*; Rückzahlung *f*

reb·el[1] **1.** Rebell(in); Aufständische *m*, *f* **2.** aufständisch

re·bel[2] rebellieren, sich auflehnen (**against** gegen)

re·bel·lion Rebellion *f*, Aufstand *m*

re·bel·lious rebellisch, aufständisch

re·birth Wiedergeburt *f*

re·bound **1.** abprallen, zurückprallen (**from** von); *fig* zurückfallen (**on** auf *acc.*); **2.** SPORT Abpraller *m*

re·buff **1.** schroffe Abweisung, Abfuhr *f* **2.** schroff abweisen

re·build wieder aufbauen (*a. fig*)

re·buke **1.** rügen, tadeln **2.** Rüge *f*, Tadel *m*

re·call **1.** zurückrufen, abberufen; MOT (in die Werkstatt) zurückrufen; sich erinnern an (*acc*); erinnern an (*acc*) **2.** Zurückrufung *f*, Abberufung *f*; Rückrufaktion *f*; **have total ~** das absolute Gedächtnis haben; **beyond ~, past ~** unwiederbringlich *or* unwiderruflich vorbei

re·ca·pit·u·late rekapitulieren, (kurz) zusammenfassen

re·cap·ture wieder einfangen (*a. fig*); *Häftling* wieder fassen; MIL zurückerobern

re·cast TECH umgießen; umformen, neu gestalten; THEA *etc* umbesetzen, neu besetzen

re·cede schwinden; **receding chin** fliehendes Kinn

re·ceipt *esp* ECON Empfang *m*, Eingang *m*; Quittung *f*; *pl* Einnahmen *pl*

re·ceive bekommen, erhalten; empfangen; *j-n* aufnehmen (**into** in *acc*); *radio*, TV empfangen; **re·ceiv·er** Empfänger(in); TEL Hörer *m*; JUR Hehler(in); *a.* **official ~** *Br* JUR Konkursverwalter *m*

re·cent neuere(r, -s); jüngste(r, -s)

re·cent·ly kürzlich, vor kurzem

re·cep·tion Empfang *m*; Aufnahme *f* (**into** in *acc*); *radio*, TV Empfang *m*; *a.* **~ desk** *hotel*: Rezeption *f*, Empfang *m*

re·cep·tion·ist Empfangsdame *f*, -chef *m*; MED Sprechstundenhilfe *f*

re·cep·tive aufnahmefähig; empfänglich (**to** für)

re·cess Unterbrechung *f*, (Schul)Pause *f*; PARL, JUR Ferien *pl*; Nische *f*

re·ces·sion ECON Rezession *f*

re·ci·pe (Koch)Rezept *n*

re·cip·i·ent Empfänger(in)

re·cip·ro·cal wechselseitig, gegenseitig

re·cip·ro·cate *v/i* TECH sich hin- und herbewegen; sich revanchieren; *v/t* *Einladung etc* erwidern

re·cit·al Vortrag *m*, (*Klavier- etc*)Konzert *n*, (*Lieder*)Abend *m*; Schilderung *f*; re·ci·ta·tion Aufsagen *n*, Hersagen *n*; Vortrag *m*; **re·cite** aufsagen, hersagen; vortragen; aufzählen

reck·less rücksichtslos

reck·on *v/t* (aus-, be)rechnen; glauben, schätzen; **~ up** zusammenrechnen; *v/i*: **~ on** rechnen mit; **~ with** rechnen mit; **~ without** nicht rechnen mit

reck·on·ing (Be)Rechnung *f*; **be out in one's ~** sich verrechnet haben

re·claim zurückfordern; *Gepäck etc* abholen; *dem Meer etc Land* abgewinnen; TECH wiedergewinnen

re·cline sich zurücklehnen

re·cluse Einsiedler(in)

rec·og·ni·tion (Wieder)Erkennen *n*; Anerkennung *f*

rec·og·nize (wieder) erkennen; anerkennen; zugeben, eingestehen

re·coil 1. zurückschrecken (**from** vor *dat*); 2. Rückstoß *m*

rec·ol·lect sich erinnern an (*acc*)

rec·ol·lec·tion Erinnerung *f* (**of** an *acc*)

rec·om·mend empfehlen (**as** als; **for** für)

rec·om·men·da·tion Empfehlung *f*

rec·om·pense 1. entschädigen (**for** für); 2. Entschädigung *f*

rec·on·cile versöhnen, aussöhnen; in Einklang bringen (**with** mit)

rec·on·cil·i·a·tion Versöhnung *f*, Aussöhnung *f* (**between** zwischen *dat*; **with** mit)

re·con·di·tion TECH (general)überholen

re·con·nais·sance MIL Aufklärung *f*, Erkundung *f*

re·con·noi·ter, *Br* re·con·noi·tre MIL erkunden, auskundschaften

re·con·sid·er noch einmal überdenken

re·con·struct wieder aufbauen (*a. fig*); *Verbrechen etc* rekonstruieren

re·con·struc·tion Wiederaufbau *m*; Rekonstruktion *f*

rec·ord¹ Aufzeichnung *f*; JUR Protokoll *n*; Akte *f*; (Schall)Platte *f*; SPORT Rekord *m*; **off the ~** inoffiziell; **have a criminal ~** vorbestraft sein

re·cord² aufzeichnen, aufschreiben, schriftlich niederlegen; JUR protokollieren, zu Protokoll nehmen; *auf Schallplatte, Tonband etc* aufnehmen; *Sendung a.* aufzeichnen, mitschneiden

re·cord·er (*Kassetten*)Rekorder *m*; (*Tonband*)Gerät *n*; MUS Blockflöte *f*

re·cord·ing Aufnahme *f*, Aufzeichnung *f*, Mitschnitt *f*

rec·ord play·er Plattenspieler *m*

re·count erzählen

re·cov·er *v/t* wiedererlangen, wiederbekommen, wieder finden; *Kosten etc* wiedereinbringen; *Fahrzeug, Verunglückten etc* bergen; **~ consciousness** MED wieder zu sich kommen, das Bewusstsein wiedererlangen; *v/i* sich erholen (**from** von); **re·cov·er·y** Wiedererlangen *n*; Wiederfinden *n*; Bergung *f*; Genesung *f*; Erholung *f*

rec·re·a·tion Entspannung *f*; Unterhal-

tung *f*, Freizeitbeschäftigung *f*
re·cruit 1. MIL Rekrut *m*; Neue *m*, *f*, neues Mitglied **2.** MIL rekrutieren; *Personal* einstellen; *Mitglieder* werben
rec·tan·gle MATH Rechteck *n*
rec·tan·gu·lar rechteckig
rec·ti·fy ELECTR gleichrichten
rec·tor REL Pfarrer *m*
rec·to·ry REL Pfarrhaus *n*
re·cu·pe·rate sich erholen (***from*** von) (*a. fig*)
re·cur wiederkehren, wieder auftreten
re·cur·rence Wiederkehr *f*
re·cur·rent wiederkehrend
re·cy·cla·ble TECH recycelbar, wiederverwertbar; **re·cy·cle** TECH *Abfälle* recyceln, wieder verwerten; **~d paper** Recyclingpapier *n*, Umwelt(schutz)-papier *n*; **re·cy·cling** TECH Recycling *n*, Wiederverwertung *f*
red 1. rot **2.** Rot *n*; **be in the~** ECON in den roten Zahlen sein
red·breast → **robin**
Red Cres·cent Roter Halbmond
Red Cross Rotes Kreuz
red·cur·rant BOT Rote Johannisbeere
red·den röten; rot färben; rot werden
red·dish rötlich
re·dec·o·rate *Zimmer etc* neu streichen *or* tapezieren
re·deem *Pfand, Versprechen etc* einlösen; REL erlösen
Re·deem·er REL Erlöser *m*, Heiland *m*
re·demp·tion Einlösung *f*; REL Erlösung *f*
re·de·vel·op *Gebäude, Stadtteil* sanieren
red-faced verlegen, mit rotem Kopf
red-hand·ed: catch s.o. ~ j-n auf frischer Tat ertappen
red·head F Rotschopf *m*, Rothaarige *f*
red-head·ed rothaarig
red her·ring *fig* falsche Fährte *or* Spur
red-hot rot glühend; *fig* glühend; F brandaktuell (*news etc*)
Red In·di·an *contp* Indianer(in)
red-let·ter day Freuden-, Glückstag *m*
red·ness Röte *f*
re·dou·ble verdoppeln
red tape Bürokratismus *m*, F Amtsschimmel *m*
re·duce verkleinern; *Geschwindigkeit, Risiko etc* verringern, *Steuern etc* senken, *Preis, Waren etc* herabsetzen, reduzieren (***from ... to*** von ... auf *acc*),

Gehalt etc kürzen; verwandeln (**to** in *acc*), machen (**to** zu); reduzieren, zurückführen (**to** auf *acc*); **re·duc·tion** Verkleinerung *f*; Verringerung *f*, Senkung *f*, Herabsetzung *f*, Reduzierung *f*, Kürzung *f*
re·dun·dant überflüssig
reed BOT Schilf(rohr) *n*
re·ed·u·cate umerziehen
re·ed·u·ca·tion Umerziehung *f*
reef (Felsen)Riff *n*
reek 1. Gestank *m* **2.** stinken (**of** nach)
reel¹ 1. Rolle *f*, Spule *f* **2. ~ off** abrollen, abspulen; *fig* herunterrasseln
reel² sich drehen; (sch)wanken, taumeln, torkeln; *my head ~ed* mir drehte sich alles
re·e·lect wieder wählen
re·en·ter wieder eintreten in (*acc*), wieder betreten; **re·en·try** Wiedereintreten *n*, Wiedereintritt *m*
ref F SPORT Schiri *m*
re·fer: ~ to verweisen *or* hinweisen auf (*acc*); *j-n* verweisen an (*acc*); sich beziehen auf (*acc*); anspielen auf (*acc*); erwähnen (*acc*); nachschlagen in (*dat*)
ref·er·ee SPORT Schiedsrichter *m*, Unparteiische *m*; *boxing*: Ringrichter *m*
ref·er·ence Verweis *m*, Hinweis *m* (**to** auf *acc*); Verweisstelle *f*; Referenz *f*, Empfehlung *f*, Zeugnis *n*; Bezugnahme *f* (**to** auf *acc*); Anspielung *f* (**to** auf *acc*); Erwähnung *f* (**to** gen); Nachschlagen *n* (**to** in *dat*); *list of* **~s** Quellenangabe *f*; **~ book** Nachschlagewerk *n*; **~ li·bra·ry** Handbibliothek *f*; **~ number** Aktenzeichen *n*
ref·er·en·dum POL Referendum *n*, Volksentscheid *m*
re·fill 1. wieder füllen, nachfüllen, auffüllen **2.** (*Ersatz*)Mine *f*; (*Ersatz*)Patrone *f*
re·fine TECH raffinieren; *fig* verfeinern, kultivieren; **~ on** verbessern, verfeinern
re·fined TECH raffiniert; *fig* kultiviert, vornehm
re·fine·ment TECH Raffinierung *f*; *fig* Verbess(e)rung *f*, Verfeinerung *f*; Kultiviertheit *f*, Vornehmheit *f*
re·fin·e·ry TECH Raffinerie *f*
re·flect *v/t* reflektieren, zurückwerfen, -strahlen, (wider)spiegeln; **be ~ed in** sich (wider)spiegeln in (*dat*) (*a. fig*);

v/i nachdenken (**on** über *acc*); ~ (**badly**)
on sich nachteilig auswirken auf (*acc*);
ein schlechtes Licht werfen auf (*acc*)

re·flec·tion Reflexion *f*, Zurückwerfung
f, -strahlung *f*, (Wider)Spiegelung *f* (*a.
fig*); Spiegelbild *n*; Überlegung *f*; Betrachtung *f*; **on** ~ nach einigem Nachdenken

re·flec·tive reflektierend; nachdenklich

re·flex Reflex *m*; ~ **ac·tion** Reflexhand-
lung *f*; ~ **cam·e·ra** PHOT Spiegelreflex-
kamera *f*

re·flex·ive LING reflexiv, rückbezüglich

re·form 1. reformieren, verbessern; sich
bessern **2.** Reform *f* (*a.* POL), Besserung
f; **ref·or·ma·tion** Reformierung *f*; Besserung *f*; **the Reformation** REL die Reformation; **re·form·er** *esp* POL Reformer *m*; REL Reformator *m*

re·fract *Strahlen etc* brechen

re·frac·tion (*Strahlen- etc*)Brechung *f*

re·frain¹: ~ **from** sich enthalten (*gen*),
unterlassen (*acc*)

re·frain² Kehrreim *m*, Refrain *m*

re·fresh (**o.s.**) sich erfrischen, stärken;
Gedächtnis auffrischen

re·fresh·ing erfrischend (*a. fig*)

re·fresh·ment Erfrischung *f*

re·frig·er·ate TECH kühlen

re·frig·er·a·tor Kühlschrank *m*

re·fu·el auftanken

ref·uge Zuflucht *f*, Zufluchtsstätte *f*; *Br*
Verkehrsinsel *f*

ref·u·gee Flüchtling *m*

ref·u·gee camp Flüchtlingslager *n*

re·fund 1. Rückzahlung *f*, Rückerstattung *f* **2.** *Geld* zurückzahlen, zurücker-
statten; *Auslagen* ersetzen

re·fur·bish aufpolieren (*a. fig*), renovieren

re·fus·al Ablehnung *f*; Weigerung *f*;
Verweigerung *f*

re·fuse¹ *v/t* ablehnen; verweigern; sich
weigern, es ablehnen (**to do** zu tun);
v/i ablehnen; sich weigern

ref·use² Abfall *m*, Abfälle *pl*, Müll *m*

ref·use dump Müllabladeplatz *m*

re·fute widerlegen

re·gain wieder-, zurückgewinnen

re·gale: ~ **s.o. with s.th.** j-n mit et. erfreuen *or* ergötzen

re·gard 1. Achtung *f*; Rücksicht *f*; *pl*
Grüße *pl*; **in this** ~ in dieser Hinsicht;
with ~ **to** im Hinblick auf (*acc*); hin-

sichtlich (*gen*); **with kind** ~**s** mit
freundlichen Grüßen **2.** betrachten
(*a. fig*), ansehen; ~ **as** betrachten als,
halten für; **as** ~ **s** ... was ... betrifft

re·gard·ing bezüglich, hinsichtlich (*gen*)

re·gard·less: ~ **of** ohne Rücksicht auf
(*acc*), ungeachtet (*gen*)

regd *abbr of* **registered** ECON eingetra-
gen; *post* eingeschrieben

re·gen·e·rate (sich) erneuern *or* regene-
rieren

re·gent Regent(in)

re·gi·ment 1. MIL Regiment *n*, *fig a.*
Schar *f* **2.** reglementieren, bevormun-
den

re·gion Gegend *f*, Gebiet *n*, Region *f*

re·gion·al regional, örtlich, Orts...

re·gis·ter 1. Register *n*, Verzeichnis *n*,
(*Wähler- etc*)Liste *f* **2.** *v/t* registrieren,
eintragen (lassen); *Meßwerte* anzei-
gen; *Brief etc* einschreiben lassen; *v/i*
sich eintragen (lassen)

re·gis·tered let·ter Einschreib(e)brief
m, Einschreiben *n*

re·gis·tra·tion Registrierung *f*, Eintragung *f*; MOT Zulassung *f*; ~ **fee** Anmel-
degebühr *f*; ~ **num·ber** MOT (polizeili-
ches) Kennzeichen

re·gis·try Registratur *f*

re·gis·try of·fice *esp Br* Standesamt *f*

re·gret 1. bedauern; bereuen **2.** Bedauern *n*; Reue *f*; **re·gret·ful** bedauernd;
re·gret·ta·ble bedauerlich

reg·u·lar 1. regelmäßig; geregelt, geord-
net; richtig; normal; MIL Berufs...; ~
gas (*Br* **petrol**) MOT Normalbenzin *n*
2. F Stammkunde *m*, Stammkundin
f; Stammgast *m*; SPORT Stammspie-
ler(in); MIL Berufssoldat *m*; MOT
Normal(-benzin) *n*

reg·u·lar·i·ty Regelmäßigkeit *f*

reg·u·late regeln, regulieren; TECH einstellen, regulieren

reg·u·la·tion Reg(e)lung *f*, Regulierung
f; TECH Einstellung *f*; Vorschrift *f*

reg·u·la·tor TECH Regler *m*

re·hears·al MUS, THEA Probe *f*

re·hearse MUS, THEA proben

reign 1. Regierung *f*, *a. fig* Herrschaft *f*
2. herrschen, regieren

re·im·burse *Auslagen* erstatten, vergüten

rein 1. Zügel *m* **2.** ~ **in** *Pferd etc* zügeln;
fig bremsen

R

rein·deer ZO Ren *n*, Rentier *n*

re·in·force verstärken

re·in·force·ment Verstärkung *f*

re·in·state *j-n* wieder einstellen (*as* als; *in* in *dat*)

re·in·sure rückversichern

re·it·e·rate (ständig) wiederholen

re·ject *j-n, et.* ablehnen, *Bitte* abschlagen, *Plan etc* verwerfen; *j-n* ab-, zurückweisen; MED *Organ etc* abstoßen

re·jec·tion Ablehnung *f*; Verwerfung *f*; Zurückweisung *f*; MED Abstoßung *f*

re·joice sich freuen, jubeln (*at, over* über *acc*); **re·joic·ing(s)** Jubel *m*

re·join[1] wieder zusammenfügen; wieder zurückkehren zu

re·join[2] erwidern

re·ju·ve·nate verjüngen

re·kin·dle *Feuer* wieder anzünden; *fig* wieder entfachen

re·lapse 1. zurückfallen, wieder verfallen (*into* in *acc*); rückfällig werden; MED e-n Rückfall bekommen **2.** Rückfall *m*

re·late *v/t* erzählen, berichten; in Verbindung *or* Zusammenhang bringen (*to* mit); *v/i* sich beziehen (*to* auf *acc*); zusammenhängen (*to* mit)

re·lat·ed verwandt (*to* mit)

re·la·tion Verwandte *m, f*; Beziehung *f* (*between* zwischen *dat*; *to* zu); *pl* diplomatische, *geschäftliche* Beziehungen *pl*; *in* or *with* ~ *to* in Bezug auf (*acc*)

re·la·tion·ship Verwandtschaft *f*; Beziehung *f*, Verhältnis *n*

rel·a·tive[1] Verwandte *m, f*

rel·a·tive[2] relativ, verhältnismäßig; bezüglich (*to* gen); LING Relativ...; bezüglich

rel·a·tive pro·noun LING Relativpronomen *n*, bezügliches Fürwort

re·lax *v/t Muskeln etc* entspannen; *Griff etc* lockern; *fig* nachlassen in (*dat*); *v/i* sich entspannen, *fig a.* ausspannen; sich lockern

re·lax·a·tion Entspannung *f*; Erholung *f*; Lockerung *f*

re·laxed entspannt, zwanglos

re·lay[1] **1.** Ablösung *f*, SPORT Staffel *f*; *radio*, TV Übertragung *f*; ELECTR Relais *n* **2.** *radio*, TV übertragen

re·lay[2] *Kabel, Teppich* neu verlegen

re·lay race SPORT Staffel *f*

re·lease 1. entlassen, freilassen; loslas-

sen; freigeben, herausbringen, veröffentlichen; MOT *Handbremse* lösen; *fig* befreien, erlösen **2.** Entlassung *f*, Freilassung *f*; Befreiung *f*; Freigabe *f*; Veröffentlichung *f*; PHOT Auslöser *m*; *film: often* **first** ~ Uraufführung *f*

rel·e·gate verbannen; **be** ~**d** SPORT absteigen (*to* in *acc*)

re·lent nachgeben; nachlassen

re·lent·less unbarmherzig; anhaltend

rel·e·vant relevant, erheblich, wichtig; sachdienlich, zutreffend

re·li·a·bil·i·ty Zuverlässigkeit *f*

re·li·a·ble zuverlässig

re·li·ance Vertrauen *n*; Abhängigkeit *f* (*on* von)

rel·ic Relikt *n*, Überrest *m*; REL Reliquie *f*

re·lief Erleichterung *f*; Unterstützung *f*, Hilfe *f*; Sozialhilfe *f*; Ablösung *f*; Relief *n*; ~ **map** GEOGR Reliefkarte *f*

re·lieve *Schmerz, Not* lindern, *j-n, Gewissen* erleichtern; *j-n* ablösen

re·li·gion Religion *f*

re·li·gious Religions...; religiös; gewissenhaft

rel·ish 1. *fig* Gefallen *m*, Geschmack *m* (*for* an *dat*); GASTR Würze *f*, Soße *f*; *with* ~ mit Genuss **2.** genießen, sich *et.* schmecken lassen; Geschmack *or* Gefallen finden an (*dat*)

re·luc·tance Widerstreben *n*; *with* ~ widerwillig, ungern

re·luc·tant widerstrebend, widerwillig

re·ly: ~ **on** sich verlassen auf (*acc*)

re·main 1. (ver)bleiben; übrig bleiben **2.** *pl* (Über)Reste *pl*

re·main·der Rest *m*; Restbetrag *m*

re·make 1. wieder *or* neu machen **2.** Remake *n*, Neuverfilmung *f*

re·mand JUR **1. be** ~**d in custody** in Untersuchungshaft bleiben **2. be on** ~ in Untersuchungshaft sein; *prisoner on* ~ Untersuchungsgefangene *m, f*

re·mark 1. *v/t* bemerken, äußern; *v/i* sich äußern (*on* über *acc*, zu); **2.** Bemerkung *f*

re·mark·a·ble bemerkenswert; außergewöhnlich

rem·e·dy 1. (Heil-, Hilfs-, Gegen)Mittel *n*; (Ab)Hilfe *f* **2.** *Schaden etc* beheben; *Missstand* abstellen; *Situation* bereinigen

R

re·mem·ber sich erinnern an (*acc*); denken an (*acc*); **please ~ me to her** grüße sie bitte von mir

re·mem·brance Erinnerung *f*; **in ~ of** zur Erinnerung an (*acc*)

re·mind erinnern (**of** an *acc*)

re·mind·er Mahnung *f*

rem·i·nis·cences Erinnerungen *pl* (**of** an *acc*); **rem·i·nis·cent: be ~ of** erinnern an (*acc*)

re·mit Schulden, *Strafe* erlassen; *Sünden* vergeben; *Geld* überweisen (**to** dat or an *acc*); **re·mit·tance** ECON Überweisung *f* (**to** an *acc*)

rem·nant (Über)Rest *m*

re·mod·el umformen, umgestalten

re·morse Gewissensbisse *pl*, Reue *f* (**über** *acc* for)

re·morse·ful zerknirscht, reumütig

re·morse·less unbarmherzig

re·mote fern, entfernt; abgelegen, entlegen; **~ con·trol** TECH Fernlenkung *f*, Fernsteuerung *f*; Fernbedienung *f*

re·mov·al Entfernung *f*; Umzug *m*

re·mov·al van Möbelwagen *m*

re·move *v/t* entfernen (**from** von); *Hut, Deckel etc* abnehmen; *Kleidung* ablegen; beseitigen, aus dem Weg räumen; *v/i/i* (um)ziehen (**from** von; **to** nach)

re·mov·er (*Flecken- etc*)Entferner *m*

Re·nais·sance die Renaissance

ren·der berühmt, schwierig, möglich etc machen; *Dienst* erweisen; *Gedicht, Musikstück* vortragen; übersetzen, übertragen (**into** in *acc*); *mst ~ down* *Fett* auslassen

ren·der·ing *esp Br* → **rendition**

ren·di·tion MUS *etc* Vortrag *m*; Übersetzung *f*, Übertragung *f*

re·new erneuern; *Gespräch etc* wieder aufnehmen; *Kraft etc* wiedererlangen; *Vertrag, Pass* verlängern (lassen)

re·new·al Erneuerung *f*; Verlängerung *f*

re·nounce verzichten auf (*acc*); *s-m Glauben etc* abschwören

ren·o·vate renovieren

re·nown Ruhm *m*; **re·nowned** berühmt (**as** als; **for** wegen, für)

rent¹ 1. Miete *f*; Pacht *f*; Leihgebühr *f*; **for ~** zu vermieten, zu verleihen **2.** mieten, pachten (**from** von); *a.* **~ out** vermieten, verpachten (**to** an *acc*); **~ed car** Miet-, Leihwagen *m*

rent² Riss *m*

rent·al Miete *f*; Pacht *f*; Leihgebühr *f*; **~ car** Miet-, Leihwagen *m*

re·nun·ci·a·tion Verzicht *m* (**of** auf *acc*); Abschwören *n*

re·pair 1. reparieren, ausbessern; *fig* wieder gutmachen **2.** Reparatur *f*; Ausbesserung *f*; *pl* Instandsetzungsarbeiten *pl*; **beyond ~** nicht mehr zu reparieren; **in good** (**bad**) **~** in gutem (schlechtem) Zustand; **be under ~** in Reparatur sein; **the road is under ~** an der Straße wird gerade gearbeitet

rep·a·ra·tion Wiedergutmachung *f*; Entschädigung *f*; *pl* POL Reparationen *pl*

rep·ar·tee Schlagfertigkeit *f*; schlagfertige Antwort(en *pl*) *f*

re·pay *et.* zurückzahlen; *Besuch* erwidern; *et.* vergelten; *j-n* entschädigen

re·pay·ment Rückzahlung *f*

re·peal *Gesetz etc* aufheben

re·peat 1. *v/t* wiederholen; nachsprechen; **~ o.s.** sich wiederholen; *v/i* F aufstoßen (**on** *s.o.* j-m) (*food*) **2.** *radio*, TV Wiederholung *f*; **re·peat·ed** wiederholt; **re·peat·ed·ly** verschiedentlich

re·pel *Angriff, Feind* zurückschlagen; *Wasser etc, fig j-n* abstoßen

re·pel·lent abstoßend

re·pent bereuen

re·pent·ance Reue *f* (**for** über *acc*)

re·pen·tant reuig, reumütig

re·per·cus·sion *mst pl* Auswirkungen *pl* (**on** auf *acc*)

rep·er·toire THEA *etc* Repertoire *n*

rep·er·to·ry the·a·ter (*Br* **the·a·tre**) Repertoiretheater *n*

rep·e·ti·tion Wiederholung *f*

re·place an *j-s* Stelle treten, *j-n*, *et.* ersetzen; TECH austauschen, ersetzen

re·place·ment TECH Austausch *m*; Ersatz *m*

re·plant umpflanzen

re·play 1. SPORT *Spiel* wiederholen; *Tonband-, Videoaufname etc* abspielen **2.** SPORT Wiederholung *f*

re·plen·ish (wieder) auffüllen

re·plete satt; angefüllt, ausgestattet (**with** mit)

rep·li·ca *art:* Originalkopie *f*; Kopie *f*, Nachbildung *f*

re·ply 1. antworten, erwidern (**to** auf *acc*); **2.** Antwort *f*, Erwiderung *f* (**to** auf *acc*); **in ~ to** (als Antwort) auf (*acc*)

re·ply cou·pon Rückantwortschein *m*

re·ply-paid en·ve·lope Freiumschlag *m*

re·port 1. Bericht *m*; Meldung *f*, Nachricht *f*; Gerücht *n*; Knall *m*; **~ card** PED Zeugnis *n* **2.** berichten (über *acc*); (sich) melden; anzeigen; *it is ~ed that* es heißt, dass; *~ed speech* LING indirekte Rede; **re·port·er** Reporter(in), Berichterstatter(in)

re·pose Ruhe *f*; Gelassenheit *f*

re·pos·i·to·ry (Waren)Lager *n*; *fig* Fundgrube *f*, Quelle *f*

rep·re·sent *j-n, Wahlbezirk* vertreten; darstellen; hinstellen (*as, to be* als)

rep·re·sen·ta·tion Vertretung *f*; Darstellung *f*

rep·re·sen·ta·tive 1. repräsentativ (*a.* POL), typisch (*of* für); **2.** (Stell)Vertreter(in); ECON (Handels)Vertreter(in); PARL Abgeordnete *m, f*; *House of Representatives* Repräsentantenhaus *n*

re·press unterdrücken; PSYCH verdrängen; **re·pres·sion** Unterdrückung *f*; PSYCH Verdrängung *f*

re·prieve JUR **1.** *he was ~d* er wurde begnadigt; s-e Urteilsvollstreckung wurde ausgesetzt **2.** Begnadigung *f*; Vollstreckungsaufschub *m*

rep·ri·mand 1. rügen, tadeln (*for* wegen); **2.** Rüge *f*, Tadel *m*, Verweis *m*

re·print 1. neu auflegen *or* drucken, nachdrucken **2.** Neuauflage *f*, Nachdruck *m*

re·pri·sal Repressalie *f*, Vergeltungsmaßnahme *f*

re·proach 1. Vorwurf *m* **2.** vorwerfen (*s.o. with s.th.* j-m et.); Vorwürfe machen; **re·proach·ful** vorwurfsvoll

rep·ro·bate verkommenes Subjekt

re·pro·cess NUCL wieder aufbereiten

re·pro·cess·ing TECH Wiederaufbereitung *f*; **~ plant** TECH Wiederaufbereitungsanlage *f*

re·pro·duce *v/t Ton etc* wiedergeben; *Bild etc* reproduzieren; *~ o.s.* → *v/i* BIOL sich fortpflanzen, sich vermehren

re·pro·duc·tion BIOL Fortpflanzung *f*; Reproduktion *f*; Wiedergabe *f*; PED Nacherzählung *f*

re·pro·duc·tive BIOL Fortpflanzungs...

re·proof Rüge *f*, Tadel *m*

re·prove rügen, tadeln (*for* wegen)

rep·tile ZO Reptil *n*

re·pub·lic Republik *f*

re·pub·li·can 1. republikanisch **2.** Republikaner(in)

re·pug·nant widerlich, abstoßend

re·pulse 1. *j-n, Angebot etc* zurückweisen; MIL *Angriff* zurückschlagen **2.** MIL Zurückschlagen *n*; Zurückweisung *f*

re·pul·sion Abscheu *m*, Widerwille *m*; PHYS Abstoßung *f*

re·pul·sive abstoßend, widerlich, widerwärtig; PHYS abstoßend

rep·u·ta·ble angesehen

rep·u·ta·tion (guter) Ruf, Ansehen *n*

re·pute (guter) Ruf

re·put·ed angeblich

re·quest 1. (*for*) Bitte *f* (um), Wunsch *m* (nach); *at the ~ of s.o., at s.o.'s ~* auf j-s Bitte hin; *on ~* auf Wunsch **2.** um *et.* bitten *or* ersuchen; *j-n* bitten, ersuchen (*to do* zu tun)

re·quest stop *Br* Bedarfshaltestelle *f*

re·quire erfordern; benötigen, brauchen; verlangen; *if ~d* wenn nötig

re·quire·ment Erfordernis *n*, Bedürfnis *n*; Anforderung *f*

req·ui·site 1. erforderlich **2.** *mst pl* Artikel *pl*

req·ui·si·tion 1. Anforderung *f*; MIL Requisition *f*, Beschlagnahme *f*; *make a ~ for et.* anfordern **2.** anfordern; MIL requirieren, beschlagnahmen

re·sale Wieder-, Weiterverkauf *m*

re·scind JUR *Gesetz, Urteil etc* aufheben

res·cue 1. retten (*from* aus, vor *dat*); **2.** Rettung *f*; Hilfe *f* **3.** Rettungs...

re·search 1. Forschung *f* **2.** forschen; *et.* erforschen

re·search·er Forscher(in)

re·sem·blance Ähnlichkeit *f* (*to* mit; *between* zwischen *dat*)

re·sem·ble ähnlich sein, ähneln (*both: dat*)

re·sent übel nehmen, sich ärgern über (*acc*); **re·sent·ful** ärgerlich (*of, at* über *acc*); **re·sent·ment** Ärger *m* (*against, at* über *acc*)

res·er·va·tion Reservierung *f*, Vorbestellung *f*; Vorbehalt *m*; (*Indianer*)Reservat(ion *f*) *n*; (*Wild*)Reservat *n*

re·serve 1. (sich) *et.* aufsparen (*for* für); sich vorbehalten; reservieren (lassen), vorbestellen **2.** Reserve *f* (*a.* MIL); Vorrat *m*; (*Naturschutz-, Wild*)Reservat *n*; SPORT Reservespieler(in); Reserviertheit *f*, Zurückhaltung *f*

re·served zurückhaltend, reserviert

res·er·voir Reservoir *n* (*a. fig* **of** an *dat*)

re·set *Uhr* umstellen; *Zeiger etc* zurückstellen (**to** auf *acc*)

re·set·tle umsiedeln

re·side wohnen, ansässig sein, s-n Wohnsitz haben

res·i·dence Wohnsitz *m*, Wohnort *m*; Aufenthalt *m*; Residenz *f*; *official* ~ Amtssitz *m*; ~ per·mit Aufenthaltsgenehmigung *f*, -erlaubnis *f*

res·i·dent 1. wohnhaft, ansässig **2.** Bewohner(in), *in a town etc a.* Einwohner(in); (Hotel)Gast *m*; MOT Anlieger(in)

res·i·den·tial Wohn…; ~ar·e·a Wohngebiet *n*, Wohngegend *f*

res·id·u·al übrig (geblieben), restlich, Rest…; ~ pol·lu·tion Altlasten *pl*

res·i·due Rest *m*, CHEM a. Rückstand *m*

re·sign *v/i* zurücktreten (**from** von); *v/t Amt etc* niederlegen; aufgeben; verzichten auf (*acc*); ~ o.s. to sich fügen in (*acc*), sich abfinden mit

res·ig·na·tion Rücktritt *m*; Resignation *f*

re·signed ergeben, resigniert

re·sil·i·ence Elastizität *f*; *fig* Zähigkeit *f*; **re·sil·i·ent** elastisch; *fig* zäh

res·in Harz *n*

re·sist widerstehen (*dat*); Widerstand leisten, sich widersetzen (*both: dat*)

re·sist·ance Widerstand *m* (*a.* ELECTR); MED Widerstandskraft *f*; (Hitze- etc -)Beständigkeit *f*, (Stoß- etc)Festigkeit *f*

re·sist·ant widerstandsfähig; (hitze- etc)beständig, (stoß- etc)fest

res·o·lute resolut, entschlossen

res·o·lu·tion Beschluss *m*, PARL etc a. Resolution *f*; Vorsatz *m*; Entschlossenheit *f*; Lösung *f*

re·solve 1. beschließen; *Problem etc* lösen; (sich) auflösen; ~ on sich entschließen zu **2.** Vorsatz *m*; Entschlossenheit *f*

res·o·nance Resonanz *f*; voller Klang

res·o·nant voll(tönend); widerhallend

re·sort 1. Erholungsort *m*, Urlaubsort *m*; **have** ~ to → **2.** ~ to Zuflucht nehmen zu

re·sound widerhallen (**with** von)

re·source Mittel *n*, Zuflucht *f*; Ausweg *m*; Einfallsreichtum *m*; *pl* Mittel *pl*;

(*natürliche*) Reichtümer *pl*, (Boden-, Natur)Schätze *pl*

re·source·ful einfallsreich, findig

re·spect 1. Achtung *f*, Respekt *m* (*both:* **for** vor *dat*); Rücksicht *f* (**for** auf *acc*); Beziehung *f*, Hinsicht *f*; **with** ~ **to** … was … anbelangt *or* betrifft; **in this** ~ in dieser Hinsicht; *give my* ~**s to** … e-e Empfehlung an … (*acc*) **2.** *v/t* respektieren, *a.* achten, *a.* berücksichtigen, beachten

re·spect·a·ble ehrbar, anständig, geachtet; F ansehnlich, beachtlich

re·spect·ful respektvoll, ehrerbietig

re·spec·tive jeweilig; *we went to our* ~ *places* jeder ging zu seinem Platz

re·spec·tive·ly beziehungsweise

res·pi·ra·tion Atmung *f*

res·pi·ra·tor Atemschutzgerät *n*

re·spite Pause *f*; Aufschub *m*, Frist *f*; **without** ~ ohne Unterbrechung

re·splen·dent glänzend, strahlend

re·spond antworten, erwidern (**to** auf *acc*; **that** dass); reagieren, MED *a.* ansprechen (**to** auf *acc*)

re·sponse Antwort *f*, Erwiderung *f* (**to** auf *acc*); *fig* Reaktion *f* (**to** auf *acc*)

re·spon·si·bil·i·ty Verantwortung *f*; **on one's own** ~ auf eigene Verantwortung; **sense of** ~ Verantwortungsgefühl *n*; **take** (**full**) ~ **for** die (volle) Verantwortung übernehmen für

re·spon·si·ble verantwortlich; verantwortungsbewusst; verantwortungsvoll

rest¹ 1. Ruhe(pause) *f*; Erholung *f*; TECH Stütze *f*; (Telefon)Gabel *f*; **have** *or* **take** **a** ~ sich ausruhen; **set s.o.'s mind at** ~ j-n beruhigen **2.** *v/i* ruhen; sich ausruhen; lehnen (**against**, **on** an *dat*); **let** **s.th.** ~ et. auf sich beruhen lassen; ~ **on** ruhen auf (*dat*) (*a. fig*); *fig* beruhen auf (*dat*); *v/t* (aus)ruhen (lassen); lehnen (**against** gegen; **on** an *acc*)

rest² Rest *m*; **all the** ~ **of them** alle Übrigen; **for the** ~ im Übrigen

rest ar·e·a MOT Rastplatz *m*

res·tau·rant Restaurant *n*, Gaststätte *f*

rest·ful ruhig, erholsam

rest home Altenpflegeheim *n*; Erholungsheim *n*

res·ti·tu·tion ECON Rückgabe *f*, Rückerstattung *f*

res·tive unruhig, nervös

rest·less ruhelos, rastlos; unruhig

res·to·ra·tion Wiederherstellung *f*; Restaurierung *f*; Rückgabe *f*, Rückerstattung *f*; **re·store** wiederherstellen; restaurieren; zurückgeben, -erstatten; *be ~d (to health)* wieder gesund sein

re·strain (from) zurückhalten (von), hindern an (*dat*); *I had to ~ myself* ich musste mich beherrschen (*from doing s.th.* um nicht et. zu tun)

re·strained beherrscht; dezent (*color*)

re·straint Beherrschung *f*, Zurückhaltung *f*; ECON Be-, Einschränkung *f*

re·strict ECON beschränken (**to** auf *acc*), einschränken

re·stric·tion ECON Be-, Einschränkung *f*; *without ~s* uneingeschränkt

rest room Toilette *f*

re·struc·ture umstrukturieren

re·sult 1. Ergebnis *n*, Resultat *n*; Folge *f*; *as a ~ of* als Folge von (*or gen*); *without ~* ergebnislos **2.** folgen, sich ergeben (*from* aus); *~ in* zur Folge haben (*acc*), führen zu

re·sume wieder aufnehmen; fortsetzen; *Platz* wieder einnehmen

re·sump·tion Wiederaufnahme *f*; Fortsetzung *f*

Res·ur·rec·tion REL Auferstehung *f*

re·sus·ci·tate MED wieder beleben

re·sus·ci·ta·tion MED Wiederbelebung *f*

re·tail ECON **1.** Einzelhandel *m*; *by ~* im Einzelhandel **2.** Einzelhandels... **3.** *adv* im Einzelhandel **4.** *v/t* im Einzelhandel verkaufen (*at, for* für); *v/i* im Einzelhandel verkauft werden (*at, for* für); **re·tail·er** ECON Einzelhändler(in)

re·tain (be)halten, bewahren; *Wasser, Wärme* speichern

re·tal·i·ate Vergeltung üben, sich revanchieren; **re·tal·i·a·tion** Vergeltung *f*, Vergeltungsmaßnahmen *pl*

re·tard verzögern, aufhalten, hemmen; (*mentally*) *~ed* (geistig) zurückgeblieben

retch würgen

re·tell nacherzählen

re·think *et.* noch einmal überdenken

re·ti·cent schweigsam, zurückhaltend

ret·i·nue Gefolge *n*

re·tire *v/i* in Rente *or* Pension gehen, sich pensionieren lassen; sich zurückziehen; *~ from business* sich zur Ruhe setzen; *v/t* in den Ruhestand versetzen,

pensionieren; **re·tired** pensioniert, im Ruhestand (lebend); *be ~ a.* in Rente *or* Pension sein; **re·tire·ment** Pensionierung *f*, Ruhestand *m*

re·tir·ing zurückhaltend

re·tort 1. (scharf) entgegnen *or* erwidern **2.** (scharfe) Entgegnung *or* Erwiderung

re·touch PHOT retuschieren

re·trace *Tathergang etc* rekonstruieren; *~ one's steps* denselben Weg zurückgehen

re·tract *v/t Angebot* zurückziehen; *Behauptung* zurücknehmen; *Geständnis* widerrufen; TECH, ZO einziehen; *v/i* TECH, ZO eingezogen werden

re·train umschulen

re·tread MOT **1.** *Reifen* runderneuern **2.** runderneuerter Reifen

re·treat 1. MIL Rückzug *m*; Zufluchtsort *m* **2.** sich zurückziehen; zurückweichen (*from* vor *dat*)

ret·ri·bu·tion Vergeltung *f*

re·trieve zurückholen, wiederbekommen; *Fehler, Verlust etc* wieder gutmachen; HUNT apportieren

ret·ro·ac·tive JUR rückwirkend

ret·ro·grade rückschrittlich

ret·ro·spect: *in ~* im Rückblick

ret·ro·spec·tive rückblickend; JUR rückwirkend

re·try JUR *Fall* erneut verhandeln; neu verhandeln gegen *j-n*

re·turn 1. *v/i* zurückkehren, zurückkommen; zurückgehen; *~ to* auf *ein Thema etc* zurückkommen; in *e-e Gewohnheit etc* zurückfallen; in *e-n Zustand etc* zurückkehren; *v/t* zurückgeben (**to** *dat*); zurückbringen (**to** *dat*); zurückschicken, -senden (**to** *dat or an acc*); zurücklegen, -stellen; erwidern; *Gewinn etc* abwerfen; → *verdict* **2.** Rückkehr *f*; *fig* Wiederauftreten *n*; Rückgabe *f*; Zurückbringen *n*; Zurückschicken *n*, -senden *n*; Zurücklegen *n*, -stellen *n*; Erwiderung *f*; (*Steuer*)Erklärung *f*; *tennis etc*: Return *m*, Rückschlag *m*; ECON *a. pl* Gewinn *m*; *Br* → *return ticket*; *Br many happy ~s (of the day)* herzlichen Glückwunsch zum Geburtstag; *by ~ (of post)* umgehend, postwendend; *in ~ for* (als Gegenleistung) für **3.** *adj* Rück...

re·turn·a·ble *in cpds* Mehrweg...; *~ bot-*

R

tie Pfandflasche *f*

return| game, ~ **match** SPORT Rückspiel *n*; re·turn key IT Eingabetaste *f*; ~ **tick·et** *Br* RAIL Rückfahrkarte *f*; AVIAT Rückflugticket *n*

re·u·ni·fi·ca·tion POL Wiedervereinigung *f*

re·un·ion Treffen *n*, Wiedersehensfeier *f*; Wiedervereinigung *f*

re·us·a·ble wieder verwendbar

rev F MOT **1.** Umdrehung *f*; ~ **counter** Drehzahlmesser *m* **2.** *a.* ~ **up** aufheulen (lassen)

re·val·ue ECON *Währung* aufwerten

re·veal den Blick freigeben auf (*acc*), zeigen; *Geheimnis etc* enthüllen, aufdecken; **re·veal·ing** aufschlussreich (*remark etc*); offenherzig (*dress etc*)

rev·el: ~ **in** schwelgen in (*dat*); sich weiden an (*dat*)

rev·e·la·tion Enthüllung *f*; REL Offenbarung *f*

re·venge 1. Rache *f*; *esp* SPORT Revanche *f*; **in** ~ **for** aus Rache für; **take** ~ **on s.o. for s.th.** sich an j-m für et. rächen **2.** rächen; **re·venge·ful** rachsüchtig

re·ve·nue Staatseinkünfte *pl*, Staatseinnahmen *pl*

re·ver·be·rate nach-, widerhallen

re·vere (ver)ehren; **rev·e·rence** Verehrung *f*; Ehrfurcht *f* (**for** vor *dat*)

Rev·e·rend REL Hochwürden *m*

rev·e·rent ehrfürchtig, ehrfurchtsvoll

rev·er·ie (Tag)Träumerei *f*

re·vers·al Umkehrung *f*; Rückschlag *m*

re·verse 1. *adj* umgekehrt; **in** ~ **order** in umgekehrter Reihenfolge **2.** *Wagen* im Rückwärtsgang fahren *or* rückwärtsfahren; *Reihenfolge etc* umkehren; *Urteil etc* aufheben; *Entscheidung etc* umstoßen **3.** Gegenteil *n*; MOT Rückwärtsgang *m*; Rückseite *f*, Kehrseite *f* (*of a coin*); Rückschlag *m*; ~ **gear** MOT Rückwärtsgang *m*; ~ **side** linke (*Stoff*)Seite *f*

re·vers·i·ble doppelseitig (tragbar)

re·vert: ~ **to** in e-n Zustand zurückkehren; in *e-e Gewohnheit etc* zurückfallen; auf *ein Thema* zurückkommen

re·view 1. Überprüfung *f*, Besprechung *f*, Kritik *f*, Rezension *f*; MIL Parade *f*; PED (*Stoff*)Wiederholung *f* (**for** für *e-e Prüfung*); **2.** überprüfen; besprechen, rezensieren; MIL besichtigen, inspizieren; PED *Stoff* wiederholen (**for** für *e-e Prüfung*)

re·view·er Kritiker(in), Rezensent(in)

re·vise revidieren, *Ansicht* ändern, *Buch etc* überarbeiten; *Br* PED *Stoff* wiederholen (**for** für *e-e Prüfung*)

re·vi·sion Revision *f*, Überarbeitung *f*; überarbeitete Ausgabe; *Br* PED (*Stoff-*) Wiederholung *f* (**for** für *e-e Prüfung*)

re·viv·al Wiederbelebung *f*; Wiederaufleben *n*

re·vive wieder beleben; wieder aufleben (lassen); *Erinnerungen* wachrufen; MED wieder zu sich kommen; sich erholen

re·voke widerrufen, zurücknehmen, rückgängig machen

re·volt 1. *v/i* sich auflehnen, revoltieren (**against** gegen); Abscheu empfinden, empört sein (**against, at, from** über *acc*); *v/t* mit Abscheu erfüllen, abstoßen **2.** Revolte *f*, Aufstand *m*

re·volt·ing abscheulich, abstoßend

rev·o·lu·tion Revolution *f*, Umwälzung *f*; ASTR Umlauf *m* (**round** um); TECH Umdrehung *f*; **number of** ~**s** Drehzahl *f*; ~ **counter** Drehzahlmesser *m*; **rev·o·lu·tion·a·ry 1.** revolutionär; Revolutions... **2.** POL Revolutionär(in)

rev·o·lu·tion·ize revolutionieren

re·volve sich drehen (**on, round** um); ~ **around** *fig* sich drehen um

re·volv·er Revolver *m*

re·volv·ing Dreh...; ~ **door(s)** Drehtür *f*

re·vue THEA Revue *f*, Kabarett *n*

re·vul·sion Abscheu *m*

re·ward 1. Belohnung *f* **2.** belohnen

re·ward·ing lohnend

re·write neu schreiben, umschreiben

rhap·so·dy MUS Rhapsodie *f*

rhe·to·ric Rhetorik *f*

rheu·ma·tism MED Rheumatismus *m*, F Rheuma *n*

rhi·no F, **rhi·no·ce·ros** ZO Rhinozeros *n*, Nashorn *n*

rhu·barb BOT Rhabarber *m*

rhyme 1. Reim *m*; Vers *m*

rhyth·m Rhythmus *m*

rhyth·mic, rhyth·mi·cal rhythmisch

rib ANAT Rippe *f*

rib·bon (*a.* Farb-, Ordens)Band *n*; Streifen *m*; Fetzen *m*

rib cage ANAT Brustkorb *m*

rice BOT Reis *m*

ripple

rice pud·ding GASTR Milchreis *m*
rich 1. reich (*in* an *dat*); prächtig, kostbar; GASTR schwer; AGR fruchtbar, fett (*soil*); voll (*sound*); satt (*color*); ~ (*in calories*) kalorienreich **2. the ~** die Reichen *pl*
rick (Stroh-, Heu)Schober *m*
rick·ets MED Rachitis *f*
rick·et·y F *fig* gebrechlich; wack(e)lig
rid befreien (*of* von); **get ~ of** loswerden
rid·den in *cpds* geplagt von
rid·dle[1] Rätsel *n*
rid·dle[2] **1.** grobes Sieb, Schüttelsieb *n* **2.** sieben; durchlöchern, durchsieben
ride 1. *v/i* reiten; fahren (*on* auf e-m *Fahrrad etc*; *on or Br in* in e-m *Bus etc*); *v/t* reiten (auf *dat*); Fahrrad, Motorrad fahren, fahren auf (*dat*) **2.** Ritt *m*; Fahrt *f*; **rid·er** Reiter(in); (*Motorrad-, Rad*)Fahrer(in)
ridge GEOGR (*Gebirgs*)Kamm *m*, Grat *m*; ARCH (*Dach*)First *m*
rid·i·cule 1. Spott *m* **2.** lächerlich machen, spotten über (*acc*), verspotten
ri·dic·u·lous lächerlich
rid·ing Reit…
ri·fle[1] Gewehr *n*
ri·fle[2] durchwühlen
rift Spalt *m*, Spalte *f*; *fig* Riss *m*
rig 1. Schiff auftakeln; ~ *out* j-n ausstaffieren; ~ *up* F (behelfsmäßig) zusammenbauen (*from* aus); **2.** MAR Takelage *f*; TECH Bohrinsel *f*; F Aufmachung *f*
rig·ging MAR Takelage *f*
right 1. *adj* recht; richtig; rechte(r, -s), Rechts…; *all ~!* in Ordnung!, gut!; *that's all ~!* das macht nichts!, schon gut!, bitte!; *that's ~!* richtig!, ganz recht!, stimmt!; *be ~* recht haben; *put ~*, *set ~* in Ordnung bringen; berichtigen, korrigieren **2.** *adv* (nach) rechts; richtig; genau; gerade (-wegs); direkt; ganz; völlig; *~ away* sofort; ~ *now* im Moment; sofort; ~ *on* geradeaus; *turn ~* (sich) nach rechts wenden; MOT rechts abbiegen **3.** Recht *n*; *die* Rechte (*a.* POL, *boxing*), rechte Seite *f*; *on the ~* rechts, auf der rechten Seite; *to the ~* (nach) rechts; *keep to the ~* sich rechts halten; MOT rechts fahren **4.** aufrichten; *et.* wieder gutmachen; in Ordnung bringen
right an·gle MATH rechter Winkel
right-an·gled MATH rechtwink(e)lig

right·eous gerecht (*anger etc*)
right·ful rechtmäßig
right-hand rechte(r, -s); ~ *drive* MOT Rechtssteuerung *f*
right-hand·ed rechtshändig; für Rechtshänder; *be ~* Rechtshänder(in) sein
right·ly richtig; mit Recht
right of way MOT Vorfahrt *f*, Vorfahrtsrecht *n*; Durchgangsrecht *n*
right-wing POL dem rechten Flügel angehörend, Rechts…
rig·id starr, steif; *fig* streng, strikt
rig·or·ous streng; genau
rig·o(u)r Strenge *f*, Härte *f*
rile F ärgern, reizen
rim Rand *m*; TECH Felge *f*
rim·less randlos
rind (*Zitronen- etc*)Schale *f*; (*Käse*)Rinde *f*; (*Speck*)Schwarte *f*
ring[1] **1.** Ring *m*; Kreis *m*; Manege *f*; (*Box*)Ring *m*; (*Spionage- etc*)Ring *m* **2.** umringen, umstellen; *Vogel* beringen
ring[2] **1.** läuten; klingeln; klingen (*a. fig*); *Br* TEL anrufen; *the bell is ~ing* es läutet *or* klingelt; ~ *the bell* läuten, klingeln; ~ *back Br* TEL zurückrufen; ~ *for* nach j-m, *et.* läuten; *Arzt etc* rufen; ~ *off Br* TEL (den Hörer) auflegen, Schluss machen; ~ *s.o.* (*up*) j-n *or* bei j-m anrufen **2.** Läuten *n*, Klingeln *n*; *fig* Klang *m*; *Br* TEL Anruf *m*; F *give s.o. a ~* j-n anrufen
ring bind·er Ringbuch *n*
ring fin·ger Ringfinger *m*
ring·lead·er Rädelsführer(in)
ring·let (Ringel)Löckchen *n*
ring road *Br* Umgehungsstraße *f*; Ringstraße *f*
ring·side: at the ~ *boxing*: am Ring
rink (Kunst)Eisbahn *f*; Rollschuhbahn *f*
rinse *a.* ~ *out* (aus)spülen
ri·ot 1. Aufruhr *m*; Krawall *m*; *run ~* randalieren; *run ~ through* randalierend ziehen durch **2.** Krawall machen, randalieren; **ri·ot·er** Aufrührer(in); Randalierer(in); **ri·ot·ous** aufrührerisch; randalierend; ausgelassen, wild
rip 1. *a.* ~ *up* zerreißen; ~ *open* aufreißen; F ~ *s.o. off* j-n neppen **2.** Riss *m*
ripe reif; **rip·en** reifen (lassen)
rip-off F Nepp *m*
rip·ple 1. (sich) kräuseln; plätschern, rie-

seln **2.** kleine Welle; Kräuselung *f*;
Plätschern *n*, Rieseln *n*

rise 1. aufstehen, sich erheben; REL auferstehen; aufsteigen (*smoke etc*); sich
heben (*curtain, spirits*); ansteigen
(*road, river etc*), anschwellen (*river
etc*); (an)steigen (*temperature etc*), *prices etc*: *a.* anziehen; stärker werden
(*wind etc*); aufgehen (*sun etc, bread
etc*); entspringen (*river etc*); *fig* aufsteigen; *fig* entstehen (**from, out of** aus); *a.*
~ up sich erheben (**against** gegen); **~ to
the occasion** sich der Lage gewachsen
zeigen **2.** (An)Steigen *n*; Steigung *f*;
Anhöhe *f*; ASTR Aufgang *m*; *Br* Lohn-
or Gehaltserhöhung *f*; *fig* Anstieg *m*;
Aufstieg *m*; **give~to** verursachen, führen zu

ris·er: *early* **~** Frühaufsteher(in)

ris·ing 1. Aufstand *m* **2.** aufstrebend

risk 1. Gefahr *f*, Risiko *n*; *at one's own* **~**
auf eigene Gefahr; *at the* **~** *of doing
s.th.* auf die Gefahr hin, et.. zu tun;
be at **~** gefährdet sein; *run the* **~** *of doing s.th.* Gefahr laufen, et. zu tun; *run
a* **~**, *take a* **~** ein Risiko eingehen **2.** wagen, riskieren; **risk·y** riskant

rite Ritus *m*; Zeremonie *f*

rit·u·al 1. rituell; Ritual… **2.** Ritual *n*

ri·val 1. Rivale *m*, Rivalin *f*, Konkur-
rent(in) **2.** Konkurrenz…, rivalisierend
3. rivalisieren *or* konkurrieren mit; **ri-
val·ry** Rivalität *f*; Konkurrenz *f*; Konkurrenzkampf *m*

riv·er Fluss *m*; Strom *m*; **riv·er·side**
Flussufer *m*; *by the* **~** am Fluss

riv·et 1. TECH Niet *m, n*, Niete *f* **2.** TECH
(ver)nieten; *fig* Aufmerksamkeit,
Blick richten (**on** auf *acc*)

road (Auto-, Land)Straße *f*; *fig* Weg *m*;
on the **~** auf der Straße; unterwegs;
THEA auf Tournee

road ac·ci·dent Verkehrsunfall *m*

road·block Straßensperre *f*

road hog F Verkehrsrowdy *m*

road map Straßenkarte *f*

road safe·ty Verkehrssicherheit *f*

road·side Straßenrand *m*; *at the* **~**, *by
the* **~** am Straßenrand

road toll Straßenbenutzungsgebühr *f*

road·way Fahrbahn *f*

road works Straßenarbeiten *pl*

road·wor·thi·ness Verkehrssicherheit *f*;
road·wor·thy verkehrssicher

roam *v/i* (umher)streifen, (-)wandern;
v/t streifen *or* wandern durch

roar 1. Brüllen *n*, Gebrüll *n*; Brausen *n*,
Krachen *n*, Donnern *n*; **~s of laughter**
brüllendes Gelächter **2.** brüllen; brausen; donnern (*truck, gun etc*)

roast GASTR **1.** *v/t* braten (*a. v/i*); *Kaffee
etc* rösten **2.** Braten *m* **3.** *adj* gebraten

roast beef GASTR Rinderbraten *m*

rob *Bank etc* überfallen; *j-n* berauben

rob·ber Räuber *m*

rob·ber·y Raubüberfall *m*, (*Bank-*)
Raub *m*, (*Bank*)Überfall *m*

robe *a. pl* Robe *f*, Talar *m*

rob·in ZO Rotkehlchen *n*

ro·bot Roboter *m*

ro·bust robust, kräftig

rock¹ schaukeln, wiegen; erschüttern (*a.
fig*)

rock² Fels(en) *m*; Felsen *pl*; GEOL Gestein *n*; Felsbrocken *m*; Stein *m*; *Br*
Zuckerstange *f*, *pl* Klippen *pl*; F *on
the* **~s** in ernsten Schwierigkeiten
(*business etc*); kaputt (*marriage etc*);
GASTR mit Eis

rock³ *a.* **~ music** Rock(musik *f*) *m*; →
rock 'n' roll

rock·er Kufe *f*; Schaukelstuhl *m*; *Br* Ro-
cker *m*; *off one's* **~** F übergeschnappt

rock·et 1. Rakete *f* **2.** rasen, schießen; *a.*
~ up hochschnellen, in die Höhe schießen (*prices*)

rocking chair Schaukelstuhl *m*

rocking horse Schaukelpferd *n*

rock 'n' roll MUS Rock 'n' Roll *m*

rock·y felsig; steinhart

rod Rute *f*; TECH Stab *m*, Stange *f*

ro·dent ZO Nagetier *n*

ro·de·o Rodeo *m, n*

roe ZO *a.* **hard~** Rogen *m*; *a.* **soft~** Milch
f

roe·buck ZO Rehbock *m*

roe deer ZO Reh *n*

rogue Schurke *m*, Gauner *m*; Schlingel
m, Spitzbube *m*

ro·guish schelmisch, spitzbübisch

role THEA Rolle *f* (*a. fig*)

roll 1. *v/i* rollen; sich wälzen; fahren; MAR
schlingern; (g)rollen (*thunder*); *v/t et.*
rollen; auf-, zusammenrollen; *Zigarette* drehen; **~ down** *Ärmel* herunter-
krempeln; MOT *Fenster* herunterkur-
beln; **~ out** ausrollen; **~ up** aufrollen;
(sich) zusammenrollen; *Ärmel* hoch-

krempeln; MOT *Fenster* hochkurbeln **2.**
Rolle *f*; GASTR Brötchen *n*, Semmel *f*;
Namens-,   Anwesenheitsliste   *f*;
(G)Rollen *n* (*of thunder*); (*Trommel*)-
Wirbel *m*; MAR Schlingern *n*

roll call Namensaufruf *m*
roll·er (Locken)Wickler *m*; TECH Rolle *f*,
Walze *f*

roll·er coast·er Achterbahn *f*
roll·er skate Rollschuh *m*
roll·er·skate Rollschuh laufen
roll·er·skat·ing Rollschuhlaufen *n*
roll·er tow·el Rollhandtuch *n*
roll·ing pin Nudelholz *n*
roll-on Deoroller *m*
Ro·man **1.** römisch **2.** Römer(in)
ro·mance Abenteuer-, Liebesroman *m*;
Romanze *f*; Romantik *f*
Ro·mance LING romanisch
Ro·ma·ni·a Rumänien *n*
Ro·ma·ni·an **1.** rumänisch **2.** Rumäne *m*,
Rumänin *f*; LING Rumänisch *n*
ro·man·tic **1.** romantisch **2.** Romanti-
ker(in)
ro·man·ti·cism Romantik *f*
romp *a.* ~ **about**, ~ **around** herumtollen,
herumtoben
romp·ers Spielanzug *m*
roof **1.** Dach *n*; MOT Verdeck *n* **2.** mit e-m
Dach versehen; ~ **in**, ~ **over** überda-
chen
roof·ing felt Dachpappe *f*
roof-rack MOT Dachgepäckträger *m*
rook[1] ZO Saatkrähe *f*
rook[2] chess: Turm *m*
rook[3] F *j-n* betrügen (**of** um)
room **1.** Raum *m*, *a.* Zimmer *n*, *a.* Platz
m; *fig* Spielraum *m* **2.** wohnen
room·er Untermieter(in)
room·ing·house Fremdenheim *n*, Pension *f*
room·mate Zimmergenosse *m*, -genos-
sin *f*
room ser·vice Zimmerservice *m*
room·y geräumig
roost **1.** (Hühner)Stange *f*; ZO Schlaf-
platz *m* **2.** auf der Stange *etc* sitzen
or schlafen
roost·er ZO (Haus)Hahn *m*
root **1.** Wurzel *f*; **take** ~ Wurzeln schlagen (*a. fig*) **2.** *v/i* Wurzeln schlagen;
wühlen (**for** nach); ~ **about** herumwühlen (**among** in *dat*); *v/t* ~ **out** *fig* ausrotten; ~ **up** mit der Wurzel ausreißen

root·ed: **deeply** ~ *fig* tief verwurzelt;
stand ~ **to the spot** wie angewurzelt
dastehen
rope **1.** Seil *n*; MAR Tau *n*; Strick *m*; (*Per-
len- etc*)Schnur *f*; **give s.o. plenty of** ~
j-m viel Freiheit *or* Spielraum lassen;
know the ~**s** F sich auskennen; **show
s.o. the** ~**s** F j-n einarbeiten **2.** festbinden (**to** an *dat or acc*); ~ **off** (durch ein
Seil) absperren *or* abgrenzen; ~ ladder Strickleiter *f*
ro·sa·ry REL Rosenkranz *m*
rose **1.** BOT Rose *f*; Brause *f* **2.** rosarot,
rosenrot
ros·trum Redner-, Dirigentenpult *n*
ros·y rosig (*a. fig*)
rot **1.** *v/t* (ver)faulen *or* verrotten lassen;
v/i a. ~ **away** (ver)faulen, verrotten,
morsch werden **2.** Fäulnis *f*
ro·ta·ry rotierend, sich drehend; Rotati-
ons…, Dreh…; ro·tate rotieren (lassen), (sich) drehen; turnusmäßig (aus-
-) wechseln; ro·ta·tion Rotation *f*, Drehung *f*; Wechsel *m*
ro·tor TECH Rotor *m*
rot·ten verfault, faul; verrottet, morsch;
fig miserabel; gemein; **feel** ~ F sich
mies fühlen
ro·tund rund und dick
rough **1.** *adj* rau; uneben (*road etc*); stürmisch (*sea, crossing, weather*); grob;
barsch; hart; grob, ungefähr (*estimate
etc*); roh, Roh… **2.** *adv* **sleep** ~ im Frei-
en übernachten; **play** ~ SPORT hart spielen **3.** *golf*: Rough *n*; **write it out in** ~
first zuerst ins Unreine schreiben **4.**
~ **it** F primitiv *or* anspruchslos leben;
~ **out** entwerfen, skizzieren; ~ **up** F
j-n zusammenschlagen
rough·age MED Ballaststoffe *pl*
rough·cast ARCH Rauputz *m*
rough| cop·y Rohentwurf *m*, Konzept
n; ~ draft Rohfassung *f*
rough·en rau werden; rau machen, an-
rauen, aufrauen
rough·ly grob, *fig a.* ungefähr
rough·neck F Schläger *m*
rough·shod: **ride** ~ **over** *j-n* rücksichtslos behandeln; sich rücksichtslos über
et. hinwegsetzen
round **1.** *adj* rund; **a** ~ **dozen** ein rundes
Dutzend; **in** ~ **figures** aufgerundet, ab-
gerundet, rund(e) … **2.** *adv* rund(her)-
um, rings(her)um; überall, auf *or* von

R

or nach allen Seiten; **turn** ~ sich umdrehen; **invite s.o.** ~ j-n zu sich einladen; ~ **about** F ungefähr; **all** (**the**) **year** ~ das ganze Jahr hindurch *or* über; **the other way** ~ umgekehrt **3.** *prp* (rund) um, um (*acc* ... herum); in *or* auf (*dat*) ... herum; **trip** ~ **the world** Weltreise *f* **4.** Run-de *f, a.* Rundgang *m*, MED Visite *f, a.* Lage *f* (*beer etc*); Schuss *m*; *esp Br* Scheibe *f* (*bread etc*); MUS Kanon *m* **5.** rund machen, (ab)runden, *Lippen* spitzen; umfahren, fahren um, *Kurve* nehmen; ~ **down** *Zahl etc* abrunden (**to** auf *acc*); ~ **off** *Essen etc* abrunden, beschließen (**with** mit); *Zahl etc* auf- *or* abrunden (**to** auf *acc*); ~ **up** *Vieh* zusammentreiben; *Leute etc* zusammentrommeln; *Zahl etc* aufrunden (**to** auf *acc*)

round·a·bout 1. *Br* MOT Kreisverkehr *m*; *Br* Karussell *n* **2. take a ~ route** e-n Umweg machen; **in a ~ way** *fig* auf Umwegen

round trip Hin- und Rückfahrt *f*; Hin- und Rückflug *m*

round-trip tick·et Rückfahrkarte *f*; Rückflugticket *n*

round-up Razzia *f*

rouse *j-n* wecken; *fig j-n* aufrütteln, wach rütteln; *j-n* erzürnen, reizen

route Route *f*, Strecke *f*, Weg *m*, (*Bus-etc*)Linie *f*

rou·tine 1. Routine *f*; **the same old** (**dai-ly**) ~ das (tägliche) ewige Einerlei **2.** üblich, routinemäßig, Routine...

rove (umher)streifen, (umher)wandern

row¹ Reihe *f*

row²1. rudern **2.** Kahnfahrt *f*

row³ *Br* F **1.** Krach *m*; (lauter) Streit **2.** (sich) streiten

row·boat Ruderboot *n*

row·er Ruderer *m*, Ruderin *f*

row house Reihenhaus *n*

row·ing boat *Br* Ruderboot *n*

roy·al königlich, Königs...

roy·al·ty die königliche Familie; Tantieme *f* (**on** auf *acc*)

rub 1. *v/t* reiben; abreiben; polieren; ~ **dry** trocken reiben; ~ **it in** *fig* F darauf herumreiten; ~ **shoulders with** F verkehren mit; *v/i* reiben, scheuern (**against, on** an *dat*); ~ **down** abreiben, trocken reiben; abschmirgeln, abschleifen; ~ **off** abreiben; abgehen (*paint etc*); ~ **off on**(**to**) *fig* abfärben

auf (*acc*); ~ **out** *Br* ausradieren **2. give s.th. a** ~ et. abreiben *or* polieren

rub·ber Gummi *n, m*; *esp Br* Radier-gummi *m*; Wischtuch *n*; F Gummi *m*

rub·ber band Gummiband *n*

rub·ber din·ghy Schlauchboot *n*

rub·ber·neck F **1.** neugierig gaffen **2.** *a.* **rubbernecker** Gaffer(in), Schaulusti-ge *m, f*

rub·ber·y gummiartig; zäh

rub·bish *Br* Abfall *m*, Abfälle *pl*, Müll *m*; F Schund *m*; Quatsch *m*, Blödsinn *m*; ~ **bin** *Br* Mülleimer *m*; ~ **chute** *Br* Müllschlucker *m*

rub·ble Schutt *m*; Trümmer *pl*

ru·by Rubin *m*; Rubinrot *n*

ruck·sack *esp Br* Rucksack *m*

rud·der AVIAT, MAR Ruder *n*

rud·dy frisch, gesund

rude unhöflich, grob; unanständig (*joke etc*); bös (*shock etc*)

ru·di·men·ta·ry elementar, Anfangs...; primitiv

ru·di·ments Anfangsgründe *pl*

rue·ful reuevoll, reumütig

ruff Halskrause *f* (*a.* zo)

ruf·fle 1. kräuseln; *Haar* zerzausen; *Federn* sträuben; ~ **s.o.'s composure** *j*-n aus der Fassung bringen **2.** Rüsche *f*

rug Vorleger *m*, Brücke *f*; *esp Br* dicke Wolldecke

rug·by *a.* ~ **football** SPORT Rugby *n*

rug·ged GEOGR zerklüftet, schroff; TECH robust, stabil; zerfurcht (*face*)

ru·in 1. Ruin *m*; *mst pl* Ruine(n *pl*) *f*, Trümmer *pl* **2.** ruinieren, zerstören

ru·in·ous ruinös

rule 1. Regel *f*; Spielregel *f*; Vorschrift *f*; Herrschaft *f*; Lineal *n*; **against the** ~**s** regelwidrig; verboten; **as a** ~ in der Re-gel; **as a** ~ **of thumb** als Faustregel; **work to** ~ Dienst nach Vorschrift tun **2.** *v/t* herrschen über (*acc*); *esp* JUR ent-scheiden; *Papier* lin(i)ieren; *Linie* zie-hen; **be** ~**d by** *fig* sich leiten lassen von; beherrscht werden von; ~ **out** et. aus-schließen; *v/i* herrschen (**over** über *acc*); *esp* JUR entscheiden

rul·er Herrscher(in); Lineal *n*

rum Rum *m*

rum·ble rumpeln (*vehicle*); (g)rollen (*thunder*); knurren (*stomach*)

ru·mi·nant zo Wiederkäuer *m*

ru·mi·nate ZO wiederkäuen

rum·mage F 1. *a.* ~ *about* herumstöbern, herumwühlen (*among, in, through* in *dat*); 2. Ramsch *m*; ~ *sale* Wohltätigkeitsbasar *m*

ru·mo(u)r F 1. Gerücht *n*; ~ *has it that* es geht das Gerücht, dass 2. *it is* ~*ed that* es geht das Gerücht, dass; *he is* ~*ed to be* ... man munkelt, er sei ...

rump F Hinterteil *n*

rum·ple zerknittern, zerknüllen, zerwühlen; *Haar* zerzausen

run 1. *v/i* laufen (*a.* SPORT), rennen; fahren, verkehren, gehen (*train, bus etc*); laufen, fließen, zerfließen, zerlaufen (*butter, paint etc*); TECH laufen (*engine*), in Betrieb *or* Gang sein; verlaufen (*road etc*); *esp* JUR laufen, laufen (*for one year* ein Jahr); THEA *etc* laufen (*for three months* drei Monate lang); lauten (*text*); gehen (*melody*); POL kandidieren (*for* für); ~ *dry* austrocknen; ~ *low* knapp werden; ~ *short* knapp werden; ~ *short of gas* (*Br petrol*) kein Benzin mehr haben; *v/t Strecke, Rennen* laufen; *Zug, Bus* fahren *or* verkehren lassen; *Wasser, Maschine etc* laufen lassen; *Geschäft, Hotel etc* führen, leiten; *Zeitungsartikel etc* abdrucken, bringen; → *s.o. home* F j-n nach Hause bringen *or* fahren; → *errand*; ~ *across* j-n zufällig treffen; stoßen auf (*acc*); ~ *after* hinterherlaufen, nachlaufen (*dat*); ~ *along!* F ab mit dir!; ~ *away* davonlaufen (*from* vor *dat*); ~ *away with* durchbrennen mit; durchgehen mit (*feelings etc*); ~ *down* MOT anfahren, umfahren; F schlechtmachen; ausfindig machen; ablaufen (*watch*); leer werden (*battery*); ~ *in* Wagen *etc* einfahren; F *Verbrecher* schnappen; ~ *into* laufen *or* fahren gegen; j-n zufällig treffen; *fig* geraten in (*acc*); *fig* sich belaufen auf (*acc*); ~ *off with* → *run away with*; ~ *on* weitergehen, sich hinziehen (*until* bis); F unaufhörlich reden (*about* über *acc*, von); ~ *out* ablaufen (*time etc*); ausgehen, zu Ende gehen (*supplies etc*); ~ *out of gas* (*Br petrol*) kein Benzin mehr haben; ~ *over* MOT überfahren; überlaufen, überfließen; ~ *through* überfliegen, durchgehen, durchlesen; ~ *up Flagge* hissen; *hohe Rechnung, Schulden* machen; ~ *up*

against stoßen auf (*acc*) 2. Lauf *m* (*a.* SPORT); Fahrt *f*; Spazierfahrt *f*; Ansturm *m*, ECON *a.* Run *m* (*on* auf *acc*); THEA *etc* Laufzeit *f*; Laufmasche *f*; Gehege *n*; Auslauf *m*, (*Hühner*)Hof *m*; SPORT (*Bob-, Rodel-*) Bahn *f*; (*Ski-*) Hang *m*; ~ *of good* (*bad*) *luck* Glückssträhne *f* (Pechsträhne *f*); *in the long* ~ auf die Dauer; *in the short* ~ zunächst; *on the* ~ auf der Flucht

run·a·bout F MOT Stadt-, Kleinwagen *m*

run·a·way Ausreißer(in)

rung Sprosse *f*

run·ner SPORT Läufer(in); Rennpferd *n*; *mst in cpds* Schmuggler(in); (*Schlitten-, Schlittschuh*)Kufe *f*; Tischläufer *m*; TECH (*Gleit*)Schiene *f*; BOT Ausläufer *m*; ~ *bean Br* BOT grüne Bohne

run·ning 1. Laufen *n*, Rennen *n*; Führung *f*, Leitung *f* 2. fließend; SPORT Lauf...; *two days* ~ zwei Tage hintereinander; ~ *costs* ECON Betriebskosten *pl*, laufende Kosten *pl*

run·ny F flüssig; laufend (*nose*), tränend (*eyes*)

run-off POL Stichwahl *f*

run-up SPORT Zweite *m*, *f*, Vizemeister(in)

run·way AVIAT Start- und Landebahn *f*, Rollbahn *f*, Piste *f*

rup·ture 1. Bruch *m* (*a.* MED *and fig*), Riss *m* 2. bersten, platzen; (zer)reißen; ~ *o.s.* MED sich e-n Bruch heben *or* zuziehen

ru·ral ländlich

ruse List *f*, Trick *m*

rush¹ 1. *v/i* hasten, hetzen, stürmen, rasen; ~ *at* losstürzen *or* sich stürzen auf (*acc*); ~ *in* hineinstürzen, hineinstürmen, hereinstürzen, hereinstürmen; ~ *into fig* sich stürzen in (*acc*); *et.* überstürzen; *v/t* antreiben, drängen, hetzen; schnell bringen; *Essen* hinunterschlingen; losstürmen auf (*acc*); *don't* ~ *it* lass dir Zeit dabei 2. Ansturm *m*; Hast *f*, Hetze *f*; Hochbetrieb *m*; ECON stürmische Nachfrage; *what's all the* ~*?* wozu diese Eile *or* Hetze?

rush² BOT Binse *f*

rush hour Rushhour *f*, Hauptverkehrszeit *f*, Stoßzeit *f*

rush-hour traf·fic Stoßverkehr *m*

rusk *esp Br* Zwieback *m*

Rus·sia Russland *n*

R

Rus·sian 1. russisch **2.** Russe *m*, Russin *f*; LING Russisch *n*

rust 1. Rost *m* **2.** *v/t* (ein-, ver)rosten lassen; *v/i* (ein-, ver)rosten

rus·tic ländlich, bäuerlich; rustikal

rus·tle 1. rascheln (mit), knistern; *Vieh* stehlen **2.** Rascheln *n*

rust·proof rostfrei, nicht rostend

rust·y rostig; *fig* eingerostet

rut¹ 1. (Rad)Spur *f*, Furche *f*; *fig* (alter) Trott; *the daily* ~ das tägliche Einerlei **2.** furchen; *rutted* ausgefahren

rut² ZO Brunft *f*, Brunst *f*

ruth·less unbarmherzig; rücksichtslos, skrupellos

rye BOT Roggen *m*

S

S, s S, s *n*

S *abbr of* **small** (**size**) klein

sa·ber, *Br* **sa·bre** Säbel *m*

sa·ble ZO Zobel *m*; Zobelpelz *m*

sab·o·tage 1. Sabotage *f* **2.** sabotieren

sack 1. Sack *m*; *get the* ~ *Br* F rausgeschmissen werden; *give s.o. the* ~ *Br* F j-n rausschmeißen; *hit the* ~ F sich in die Falle *or* Klappe hauen **2.** in Säcke füllen, einsacken; *Br* F j-n rausschmeißen

sack·cloth, sack·ing Sackleinen *n*

sac·ra·ment REL Sakrament *n*

sa·cred geistlich (*music etc*); heilig

sac·ri·fice 1. Opfer *n* **2.** opfern

sac·ri·lege REL Sakrileg *n*; Frevel *m*

sac·ris·ty REL Sakristei *f*

sad traurig; schmerzlich; schlimm

sad·dle 1. Sattel *m* **2.** satteln

sa·dism Sadismus *m*

sa·dist Sadist(in)

sa·dis·tic sadistisch

sad·ness Traurigkeit *f*

sa·fa·ri Safari *f*; ~ *park* Safaripark *m*

safe 1. sicher **2.** Safe *m*, *n*, Tresor *m*, Geldschrank *m*

safe con·duct freies Geleit

safe de·pos·it Tresor *m*

safe-de·pos·it box Schließfach *n*

safe·guard 1. Schutz *m* (*against* gegen, vor *dat*); **2.** schützen (*against, from* gegen, vor *dat*)

safe·keep·ing sichere Verwahrung

safe·ty 1. Sicherheit *f* **2.** Sicherheits...; ~ *belt* → *seat belt*; ~ *is·land* Verkehrsinsel *f*; ~ *lock* Sicherheitsschloss *n*; ~ *mea·sure* Sicherheitsmaßnahme *f*; ~ *pin* Sicherheitsnadel *f*

sag sich senken, absacken; durchhängen; (herab)hängen (*shoulders*); *fig*

sinken (*morale*); nachlassen (*interest etc*)

sa·ga·cious scharfsinnig

sa·gac·i·ty Scharfsinn *m*

sage BOT Salbei *m*, *f*

Sa·git·tar·i·us ASTR Schütze *m*; *he* (*she*) *is* (*a*) ~ er (sie) ist (ein) Schütze

sail 1. Segel *n*; Segelfahrt *f*; (*Windmühlen*)Flügel *m*; *set* ~ auslaufen (*for* nach); *go for a* ~ segeln gehen **2.** *v/i* MAR segeln, fahren; auslaufen (*for* nach); gleiten, schweben; *go* ~*ing* segeln gehen; *v/t* MAR befahren; *Schiff* steuern, *Boot* segeln

sail·board Surfbrett *n*

sail·boat Segelboot *n*

sail·ing Segeln *n*; Segelsport *m*; *when is the next* ~ *to …?* wann fährt das nächste Schiff nach …?; ~ *boat* *Br* Segelboot *n*; ~ *ship* Segelschiff *n*

sail·or Seemann *m*, Matrose *m*; *be a good* (*bad*) ~ (nicht) seefest sein

sail·plane Segelflugzeug *n*

saint Heilige *m*, *f*

saint·ly heilig, fromm

sake: *for the* ~ *of …* um … (*gen*) willen; *for my* ~ meinetwegen; *for God's* ~ F um Gottes willen

sal·a·ble verkäuflich

sal·ad Salat *m*; ~ *dress·ing* Dressing *n*, Salatsoße *f*

sal·a·ried: ~ *employee* Angestellte *m*, *f*, Gehaltsempfänger(in)

sal·a·ry Gehalt *n*

sale Verkauf *m*; Absatz *m*, Umsatz *m*; (Saison)Schlussverkauf *m*; Auktion *f*, Versteigerung *f*; *for* ~ zu verkaufen; *not for* ~ unverkäuflich; *be on* ~ verkauft werden, erhältlich sein

sale·a·ble → *salable*

sales·clerk (Laden)Verkäufer(in)
sales·girl (Laden)Verkäuferin f
sales·man Verkäufer m; (Handels-)
Vertreter m
sales rep·re·sen·ta·tive Handlungsrei-
sende m, f; (Handels)Vertreter(in)
sales slip ECON Quittung f
sales tax ECON Umsatzsteuer f
sales·wom·an Verkäuferin f; (Handels)Vertreterin f
sa·line salzig, Salz…
sa·li·va Speichel m
sal·low gelblich
salm·on ZO Lachs m
sal·on (Schönheits- etc)Salon m
sa·loon Br MOT Limousine f; HIST Saloon
m; MAR Salon m
sa·loon car Br MOT Limousine f
salt 1. Salz n **2.** salzen; (ein)pökeln, ein-
salzen (a. ~ **down**); Straße etc (mit Salz)
streuen **3.** Salz…; gepökelt; salzig, gesalzen
salt·cel·lar Br Salzstreuer m
salt·pe·ter, esp Br **salt·pe·tre** CHEM Salpeter m
salt shak·er Salzstreuer m
salt wa·ter Salzwasser n
salt·y salzig
sal·u·ta·tion Gruß m, Begrüßung f; Anrede f; **sa·lute 1.** MIL salutieren; (be)-
grüßen **2.** Gruß m; MIL Ehrenbezeu-
gung f; Salut m
sal·vage 1. Bergung f; Bergungsgut n **2.**
bergen (**from** aus); retten (a. fig)
sal·va·tion Rettung f; REL Erlösung f;
(Seelen)Heil n
Sal·va·tion Ar·my Heilsarmee f
salve (Heil)Salbe f
same: the ~ derselbe, dieselbe, dasselbe; **all the ~** trotzdem; **it is all the ~**
to me es ist mir ganz egal
sam·ple 1. Muster n, Probe f **2.** kosten,
probieren
san·a·to·ri·um Sanatorium n
sanc·ti·fy heiligen
sanc·tion 1. Billigung f, Zustimmung f;
mst pl Sanktionen pl **2.** billigen, sank-
tionieren
sanc·ti·ty Heiligkeit f
sanc·tu·a·ry Zuflucht f, Asyl n; ZO
Schutzgebiet n
sand 1. Sand m; pl Sandfläche f **2.** Straße
etc mit Sand (be)streuen; TECH schmir-
geln

san·dal Sandale f
sand·bag Sandsack m
sand·bank GEOGR Sandbank f
sand·box Sandkasten m
sand·cas·tle Sandburg f
sand·man Sandmännchen n
sand·pa·per Sand-, Schmirgelpapier n
sand·pip·er ZO Strandläufer m
sand·pit Br Sandkasten m; Sandgrube f
sand·stone GEOL Sandstein m
sand·storm Sandsturm m
sand·wich 1. Sandwich n **2. be ~ed be-**
tween eingekeilt sein zwischen (dat); ~
s.th. in between fig et. einschieben
zwischen (acc or dat)
sand·y sandig; rotblond
sane geistig gesund; JUR zurechnungsfähig; vernünftig
san·i·tar·i·um → **sanatorium**
san·i·ta·ry hygienisch; Gesundheits…; ~
nap·kin, Br ~ **tow·el** (Damen)Binde f
san·i·ta·tion sanitäre Einrichtungen pl;
Kanalisation f
san·i·ty geistige Gesundheit f; JUR Zurechnungsfähigkeit f
San·ta Claus der Weihnachtsmann, der
Nikolaus
sap¹ BOT Saft m
sap² schwächen
sap·phire Saphir m
sar·casm Sarkasmus m
sar·cas·tic sarkastisch
sar·dine ZO Sardine f
sash¹ Schärpe f
sash² Fensterrahmen m
sash win·dow Schiebefenster n
sas·sy frech
Sat abbr of **Saturday** Sa., Samstag m,
Sonnabend m
Sa·tan der Satan
satch·el (Schul)Ranzen m; Schultasche
f
sat·ed fig übersättigt
sat·el·lite Satellit m; **by** or **via ~** über
Satellit **2.** Satelliten…; ~ **dish** F Satel-
litenschüssel f
sat·in Satin m
sat·ire Satire f
sat·ir·ic, **sat·ir·i·cal** satirisch
sat·i·rist Satiriker(in)
sat·ir·ize verspotten
sat·is·fac·tion Befriedigung f; Genug-
tuung f, Zufriedenheit f
sat·is·fac·to·ry befriedigend, zufrieden-

stellend

sat·is·fy befriedigen, zufrieden stellen; überzeugen; *be satisfied that* davon überzeugt sein, dass

sat·u·rate (durch)tränken (*with* mit); CHEM sättigen (*a. fig*)

Sat·ur·day Sonnabend *m*, Samstag *m*; *on* ~ (am) Sonnabend *or* Samstag; *on* ~s sonnabends, samstags

sauce Soße *f*

sauce·pan Kochtopf *m*

sau·cer Untertasse *f*

sauc·y *Br* frech

saun·ter bummeln, schlendern

saus·age Wurst *f*; *a. small* ~ Würstchen *n*

sav·age 1. wild; unzivilisiert **2.** Wilde *m, f*; **sav·ag·e·ry** Wildheit *f*; Rohheit *f*, Grausamkeit *f*

save 1. retten (*from* vor *dat*); Geld, Zeit *etc* (ein)sparen; *et.* aufheben, aufsparen (*for* für); *j-m et.* ersparen; IT (ab)speichern, sichern; SPORT *Schuss* halten, parieren, *Tor* verhindern **2.** SPORT Parade *f*

sav·er Retter(in); ECON Sparer(in)

sav·ings ECON Ersparnisse *pl*; ~ *account* Sparkonto *n*; ~ *bank* Sparkasse *f*; ~ *de·pos·it* Spareinlage *f*

sa·vio(u)r Retter(in); *the Savio(u)r* REL der Erlöser, der Heiland

sa·vo(u)r mit Genuss essen *or* trinken; ~ *of fig* e-n Beigeschmack haben von

sa·vo(u)r·y schmackhaft

saw Säge *f* **2.** sägen

saw·dust Sägemehl *n*, Sägespäne *pl*

saw·mill Sägewerk *n*

Sax·on 1. (Angel)Sachse *m*, (Angel-)Sächsin *f* **2.** (angel)sächsisch

say 1. sagen; aufsagen; *Gebet* sprechen, *Vaterunser* beten; ~ *grace* das Tischgebet sprechen; *what does your watch* ~*?* wie spät ist es auf deiner Uhr?; *he is said to be* ... er soll ... sein; *it* ~*s* es lautet (*letter etc*); *it* ~*s here* hier heißt es; *it goes without* ~*ing* es versteht sich von selbst; *no sooner said than done* gesagt, getan; *that is to* ~ das heißt; *(and) that's* ~*ing s.th.* (und) das will was heißen; *you said it* du sagst es; *you can* ~ *that again!* das kannst du laut sagen!; *I* ~ sag(en Sie) mal!; ich muss schon sagen!; *I can't* ~ das kann ich nicht sagen **2.** Mitspra-

cherecht *n* (*in* bei); *have one's* ~ s-e Meinung äußern, zu Wort kommen; *he always has to have his* ~ er muss immer mitreden

say·ing Sprichwort *n*, Redensart *f*; *as the* ~ *goes* wie man so (schön) sagt

scab MED, BOT Schorf *m*; *contp* Streikbrecher(in)

scaf·fold (Bau)Gerüst *n*; Schafott *n*

scaf·fold·ing (Bau)Gerüst *n*

scald 1. sich *die Zunge etc* verbrühen; *Milch* abkochen; ~*ing hot* kochend heiß **2.** MED Verbrühung *f*

scale[1] Skala *f* (*a. fig*), Grad- *or* Maßeinteilung *f*; MATH, TECH Maßstab *m* (*a. fig*); Waage *f*; MUS Skala *f*, Tonleiter *f*; *fig* Ausmaß *n*, Umfang *m* **2.** erklettern; ~ *down* fig verringern; ~ *up* fig erhöhen

scale[2] Waagschale *f*; (*a pair of*) ~*s* (e-e) Waage

scale[3] **1.** ZO Schuppe *f*; TECH Kesselstein *m*; *the* ~*s fell from my eyes* es fiel mir wie Schuppen von den Augen **2.** *Fisch* (ab)schuppen

scal·lop ZO Kammmuschel *f*

scalp 1. Kopfhaut *f*; Skalp *m* **2.** skalpieren

scal·y ZO schuppig (*a. fig*)

scamp F Schlingel *m*, (kleiner) Strolch

scam·per trippeln; huschen

scan 1. *et.* absuchen (*for* nach); *Zeitung etc* überfliegen; IT, *radar*, TV abtasten, scannen **2.** MED *etc* Scanning *n*

scan·dal Skandal *m*; Klatsch *m*

scan·dal·ize: *be* ~*d at s.th.* über et. empört *or* entrüstet sein

scan·dal·ous skandalös; *be* ~ *a.* ein Skandal sein (*that* dass)

Scan·di·na·vi·a Skandinavien *n*

Scan·di·na·vi·an 1. skandinavisch **2.** Skandinavier(in)

scan·ner TECH Scanner *m*

scant dürftig, gering

scant·y dürftig, kärglich, knapp

scape·goat Sündenbock *m*

scar MED **1.** Narbe *f* (*a. fig*) **2.** e-e Narbe *or* Narben hinterlassen auf (*dat*) *or* fig bei *j-m*; ~ *over* vernarben

scarce knapp (*food etc*); selten; *be* ~ Mangelware sein (*a. fig*); **scarce·ly** kaum; **scar·ci·ty** Mangel *m*, Knappheit *f* (*of* an *dat*)

scare 1. erschrecken; *be* ~*d* Angst ha-

ben (**of** vor *dat*); ~ **away**, ~ **off** verjagen,
-scheuchen **2.** Schreck(en) *m*; Panik *f*
scare·crow Vogelscheuche *f* (*a. fig*)
scarf Schal *m*; Hals-, Kopf-, Schulter-
tuch *n*
scar·let scharlachrot; ~ **fe·ver** MED
Scharlach *m*
scarred narbig
scath·ing bissig (*remark etc*); vernichtend (*criticism etc*)
scat·ter (sich) zerstreuen (*crowd*); ausstreuen, verstreuen; auseinanderstie-
ben (*birds etc*)
scat·ter·brained F schusselig, schusslig
scat·tered verstreut; vereinzelt
scav·enge ~ **on** ZO leben von; ~ **for** suchen (nach)
scene Szene *f*; Schauplatz *m*; *pl* THEA
Kulissen *pl*
sce·ne·ry Landschaft *f*, Gegend *f*; THEA
Bühnenbild *n*, Kulissen *pl*
scent 1. Duft *m*, Geruch *m*; *esp Br* Parfüm *n*; HUNT Witterung *f*; Fährte *f*, Spur
f (*a. fig*) **2.** wittern; *esp Br* parfümieren;
scent·less geruchlos
scep·ter, *Br* **scep·tre** Zepter *n*
scep·tic, **scep·ti·cal** *Br* → **skeptic** *etc*
sched·ule 1. Aufstellung *f*, Verzeichnis
n; (*Arbeits-, Stunden-, Zeit- etc*)Plan
m; Fahr-, Flugplan *m*; **ahead of** ~
dem Zeitplan voraus, früher als vorgesehen; **be behind** ~ Verspätung haben;
im Verzug or Rückstand sein; **on** ~
(fahr-) planmäßig, pünktlich **2. the
meeting is** ~**d for Monday** die Sitzung
ist für Montag angesetzt; **it is** ~**d to
take place tomorrow** es soll morgen
stattfinden
sched·uled **de·par·ture** (fahr)planmä-
ßige Abfahrt; ~ **flight** Linienflug *m*
scheme 1. *esp Br* Programm *n*, Projekt
n; Schema *n*, System *n*; Intrige *f*, Ma-
chenschaft *f* **2.** intrigieren
schmaltz·y F schnulzig
schnit·zel GASTR Wiener Schnitzel *n*
schol·ar Gelehrte *m*, *f*; UNIV Stipen-
diat(in); **schol·ar·ly** gelehrt
schol·ar·ship Gelehrsamkeit *f*; UNIV
Stipendium *n*
school¹ 1. Schule *f* (*a. fig*); UNIV Fakultät
f; Hochschule *f*; **at** ~ auf *or* in der Schule; **go to** ~ in die *or* zur Schule gehen **2.**
j-n schulen, unterrichten; *Tier* dressieren

school² ZO Schule *f*, Schwarm *m*
school·bag Schultasche *f*
school·boy Schüler *m*
school·child Schulkind *n*
school·fel·low → **schoolmate**
school·girl Schülerin *f*
school·ing (Schul)Ausbildung *f*
school·mate Mitschüler(in), Schulka-
merad(in)
school·teach·er (Schul)Lehrer(in)
school·yard Schulhof *m*
schoo·ner MAR Schoner *m*
sci·ence Wissenschaft *f*; *a.* **natural** ~ Na-
turwissenschaft(en *pl*) *f*; ~ **fic·tion**
(*abbr* **SF**) Sciencefiction *f*
sci·en·tif·ic (natur)wissenschaftlich; exakt, systematisch
sci·en·tist (Natur)Wissenschaftler(in)
sci-fi F Sciencefiction *f*
scis·sors (**a pair of** ~ e-e) Schere *f*
scoff 1. spotten (**at** über *acc*) **2.** spöttische Bemerkung
scold schimpfen (mit)
scoop 1. Schöpfkelle *f*; (*Mehl- etc* -)
Schaufel *f*; (*Eis- etc*)Portionierer *m*;
Kugel *f* (*icecream*); *newspaper*, *radio*,
TV Exklusivmeldung *f*, F Knüller *m* **2.**
schöpfen, schaufeln; ~ **up** aufheben,
hochheben
scoot·er (Kinder)Roller *m*; (*Motor-*)
Roller *m*
scope Bereich *m*; Spielraum *m*
scorch *v/t* ansengen, versengen, verbrennen; ausdörren; *v/i Br* MOT F rasen
score 1. SPORT (Spiel)Stand *m*, (-)Ergeb-
nis *n*; MUS Partitur *f*; Musik *f*; 20
(Stück); *a.* ~ **mark** Kerbe *f*, Rille *f*; **what
is the** ~? wie steht es *or* das Spiel?; **the
~ stood at** *or* **was 3-2** das Spiel stand
3:2; **keep** (**the**) ~ anschreiben; ~**s of**
e-e Menge; **four** ~ **and ten** neunzig;
on that ~ deshalb, in dieser Hinsicht;
have a ~ **to settle with s.o.** e-e alte
Rechnung mit *j-m* zu begleichen haben
2. *v/t* SPORT *Punkte, Treffer* erzielen,
Tor a. schießen; *Erfolg, Sieg* erringen;
MUS instrumentieren; die Musik
schreiben zu *or* für; einkerben; *v/i*
SPORT e-n Treffer *etc* erzielen, ein Tor
schießen; erfolgreich sein
score·board SPORT Anzeigetafel *f*
scor·er SPORT Torschütze *m*, Torschützin
f; Anschreiber(in)
scorn Verachtung *f*

S

scorn·ful verächtlich

Scor·pi·o ASTR Skorpion m; **he (she) is (a) ~** er (sie) ist (ein) Skorpion

Scot Schotte m, Schottin f

Scotch **1.** schottisch **2.** Scotch m

scot-free: F **get off ~** ungeschoren davonkommen

Scot·land Schottland n

Scots schottisch; Scotsman Schotte m; Scots·wom·an Schottin f

Scot·tish schottisch

scoun·drel Schurke m

scour¹ scheuern, schrubben

scour² Gegend absuchen, durchkämmen (**for** nach)

scourge **1.** Geißel f (a. fig) **2.** geißeln, fig a. heimsuchen

scout **1.** esp MIL Kundschafter m; Br motorisierter Pannenhelfer; a. **boy ~** Pfadfinder m; a. **girl ~** Pfadfinderin f; a. **talent ~** Talentsucher(in) **2. ~ about, ~ around** sich umsehen (**for** nach); a. **~ out** MIL auskundschaften

scowl **1.** finsteres Gesicht **2.** finster blicken; **~ at s.o.** j-n böse or finster anschauen

scram·ble **1.** klettern; sich drängeln (**for** zu); **2.** Kletterei f; Drängelei f

scram·bled eggs Rührei(er pl) n

scrap¹ **1.** Stückchen n, Fetzen m; Altmaterial n; Schrott m; pl Abfall m, Speisereste pl **2.** verschrotten; ausrangieren; Plan etc aufgeben, fallen lassen

scrap² F **1.** Streiterei f; Balgerei f **2.** sich streiten; sich balgen

scrap·book Sammelalbum n

scrape **1.** (ab)kratzen, (ab)schaben; sich die Knie etc aufschürfen; Wagen etc ankratzen; scheuern (**against** an dat); (entlang)streifen; scharren **2.** Kratzen n; Kratzer m, Schramme f; fig Klemme f

scrap heap Schrotthaufen m

scrap met·al Altmetall n, Schrott m

scrap pa·per esp Br Schmierpapier n

scrap val·ue Schrottwert m

scrap·yard Schrottplatz m

scratch **1.** (zer)kratzen; abkratzen; s-n Namen etc einkratzen; (sich) kratzen; scharren **2.** Kratzer m, Kratzen n; Gekratze n; Kratzen n; **from ~** F ganz von vorn **3.** (bunt) zusammengewürfelt

scratch·pad Notiz-, Schmierblock m

scratch pa·per Schmierpapier n

scrawl **1.** kritzeln **2.** Gekritzel n

scraw·ny dürr

scream **1.** schreien (**with** vor dat); a. **~ out** schreien; **~ with laughter** vor Lachen brüllen **2.** Schrei m; **~s of laughter** brüllendes Gelächter; **be a ~** F zum Schreien (komisch) sein

screech **1.** kreischen (a. fig), (gellend) schreien **2.** Kreischen n; (gellender) Schrei

screen **1.** Wand-, Ofen-, Schutzschirm m; film: Leinwand f; radar, TV, IT Bildschirm m; Fliegenfenster n, -gitter n; fig Tarnung f **2.** abschirmen; film zeigen, Fernsehprogramm a. senden; fig j-n decken; fig j-n überprüfen; **~ off** abtrennen

screen·play Drehbuch n

screen sav·er IT Bildschirmschoner m

screw **1.** TECH Schraube f; **he has a ~ loose** F bei ihm ist e-e Schraube locker **2.** (an)schrauben (**to** an acc); V bumsen, vögeln; **~ up** Gesicht verziehen; Augen zusammenkneifen; **~ up one's courage** sich ein Herz fassen

screw·ball F Spinner(in)

screw·driv·er Schraubenzieher m

screw top Schraubverschluss m

scrib·ble **1.** (hin)kritzeln **2.** Gekritzel n

scrimp: **~ and save** jeden Cent zweimal umdrehen

script Manuskript n; film, TV Drehbuch n, Skript n; THEA Text m, Textbuch n; Schrift(zeichen pl) f; Br UNIV (schriftliche) Prüfungsarbeit

Scrip·ture a. **the ~s** REL die Heilige Schrift

scroll **1.** Schriftrolle f **2. ~ down (up)** IT zurückrollen (vorrollen)

scro·tum ANAT Hodensack m

scrub¹ **1.** schrubben, scheuern **2.** Schrubben n, Scheuern n

scrub² Gebüsch n, Gestrüpp n

scru·ple **1.** Skrupel m, Zweifel m, Bedenken pl **2.** Bedenken haben

scru·pu·lous gewissenhaft

scru·ti·nize genau prüfen; mustern

scru·ti·ny genaue Prüfung; prüfender Blick

scu·ba div·ing (Sport)Tauchen n

scuf·fle **1.** Handgemenge n, Rauferei f **2.** sich raufen

scull **1.** Skull n; Skullboot n **2.** rudern, skullen

sculp·tor Bildhauer *m*

sculp·ture 1. Bildhauerei *f*; Skulptur *f*, Plastik *f* **2.** hauen, meißeln, formen

scum Schaum *m*; *fig* Abschaum *m*

scurf (Kopf)Schuppen *pl*

scur·ri·lous beleidigend; verleumderisch

scur·ry huschen; trippeln

scur·vy MED Skorbut *m*

scut·tle: ~ *away*, ~ *off* davonhuschen

scythe Sense *f*

sea Meer *n* (*a. fig*), See *f*; *at*~ auf See; *by* ~ auf dem Seeweg; *by the* ~ am Meer

sea·food GASTR Meeresfrüchte *pl*

sea·gull ZO Seemöwe *f*

seal[1] ZO Robbe *f*, Seehund *m*

seal[2] **1.** Siegel *n*; TECH Plombe *f*; TECH Dichtung *f* **2.** (ver)siegeln; TECH plombieren; abdichten; *fig* besiegeln; *~ed envelope* verschlossener Briefumschlag; ~ *off* Gegend *etc* abriegeln

sea lev·el: *above* (*below*) ~ über (unter) dem Meeresspiegel

seal·ing wax Siegellack *m*

seam Naht *f*; Fuge *f*; GEOL Flöz *n*

sea·man Seemann *m*

seam·stress Näherin *f*

sea·plane Wasserflugzeug *n*

sea·port Seehafen *m*; Hafenstadt *f*

sea pow·er Seemacht *f*

search 1. *v/i* suchen (*for* nach); ~ *through* durchsuchen; *v/t* j-n, *et.* durchsuchen (*for* nach) **2.** Suche *f* (*for* nach); Fahndung *f* (*for* nach); Durchsuchung *f*; *in* ~ *of* auf der Suche nach; **search·ing** prüfend (*look*); eingehend (*examination*)

search·light (Such)Scheinwerfer *m*

search par·ty Suchmannschaft *f*

search war·rant JUR Haussuchungs-, Durchsuchungsbefehl *m*

sea·shore Meeresküste *f*

sea·sick seekrank

sea·side: *at or by the* ~ am Meer; *go to the* ~ ans Meer fahren

sea·side re·sort Seebad *n*

sea·son[1] Jahreszeit *f*; Saison *f*, THEA *etc a.* Spielzeit *f*, (*Jagd-*, *Urlaubs- etc*)Zeit *f*; *in* (*out of*) ~ in (außerhalb der (Hoch)Saison; *cherries are now in* ~ jetzt ist Kirschenzeit; *Season's Greetings!* Frohe Weihnachten!; *with the compliments of the* ~ mit den besten Wünschen zum Fest

sea·son[2] *Speise* würzen (*with* mit); *Holz* ablagern

sea·son·al saisonbedingt, Saison...

sea·son·ing GASTR Gewürz *n*

sea·son tick·et RAIL *etc* Dauer-, Zeitkarte *f*; THEA Abonnement *n*

seat 1. Sitz(gelegenheit *f*) *m*; (Sitz)Platz *m*; Sitz(fläche *f*) *m*; Hosenboden *m*; Hinterteil *n*; (*Geschäfts-*, *Regierungs- etc*)Sitz *m*; PARL Sitz *m*; *take a* ~ Platz nehmen; *take one's* ~ s-n Platz einnehmen **2.** *j-n* setzen; Sitzplätze bieten für; *be* ~*ed* sitzen; *please be* ~*ed* bitte nehmen Sie Platz; *remain* ~*ed* sitzen bleiben

seat belt AVIAT, MOT Sicherheitsgurt *m*; *fasten one's* ~ sich anschnallen

sea ur·chin ZO Seeigel *m*

sea·ward(s) seewärts

sea·weed BOT (See)Tang *m*

sea·wor·thy seetüchtig

sec F Augenblick *m*, Sekunde *f*; *just a* ~ Augenblick(, bitte)!

se·cede sich abspalten (*from* von)

se·ces·sion Abspaltung *f*, Sezession *f* (*from* von)

se·clud·ed abgelegen, abgeschieden (*place*); zurückgezogen (*life*)

se·clu·sion Abgeschiedenheit *f*; Zurückgezogenheit *f*

sec·ond[1] **1.** *adj* zweite(r, -s); *every* ~ *day* jeden zweiten Tag, alle zwei Tage; ~ *to none* unerreicht, unübertroffen; *but on* ~ *thoughts* (*Br thought*) aber wenn ich es mir so überlege **2.** *adv* als Zweite(r, -s) **3.** *der, die, das* Zweite; MOT zweiter Gang; Sekundant *m*; *pl* F ECON Waren *pl* zweiter Wahl **4.** *Antrag etc* unterstützen

sec·ond[2] Sekunde *f*; *fig* Augenblick *m*, Sekunde *f*; *just a* ~ Augenblick(, bitte)!

sec·ond·a·ry sekundär, zweitrangig; PED höher

sec·ond-best zweitbeste(r, -s)

sec·ond class RAIL *etc* zweiter Klasse

sec·ond-class zweitklassig

sec·ond floor erster (*Br* zweiter) Stock

sec·ond hand Sekundenzeiger *m*

sec·ond-hand aus zweiter Hand; gebraucht; antiquarisch

sec·ond·ly zweitens

sec·ond-rate zweitklassig

se·cre·cy Verschwiegenheit *f*; Geheimhaltung *f*

S

se·cret 1. geheim, Geheim…; heimlich; verschwiegen **2.** Geheimnis *n*; **in ~** heimlich, im Geheimen; **keep s.th. a ~** et. geheim halten (**from** vor *dat*); **can you keep a ~?** kannst du schweigen?

se·cret a·gent Geheimagent(in)

sec·re·ta·ry Sekretär(in); POL Minister(in)

Sec·re·ta·ry of State POL Außenminister(in); *Br* Minister(in)

se·crete MED absondern; **se·cre·tion** MED Sekret *n*; Absonderung *f*

se·cre·tive verschlossen

se·cret·ly heimlich

se·cret ser·vice Geheimdienst *m*

sec·tion Teil *m*; Abschnitt *m*; JUR Paragraf *m*; Abteilung *f*; MATH, TECH Schnitt *m*

sec·tor Sektor *m*, Bereich *m*

sec·u·lar weltlich

se·cure 1. sicher (**against, from** vor *dat*) **2.** Tür *etc* fest verschließen; *et.* sichern (**against, from** vor *dat*)

se·cu·ri·ty Sicherheit *f*; *pl* ECON Wertpapiere *pl*; **~ check** Sicherheitskontrolle *f*; **~ mea·sure** Sicherheitsmaßnahme *f*; **~ risk** Sicherheitsrisiko *n*

se·dan MOT Limousine *f*

se·date ruhig, gelassen

sed·a·tive *mst* MED **1.** beruhigend **2.** Beruhigungsmittel *n*

sed·i·ment (Boden)Satz *m*

se·duce verführen

se·duc·er Verführer(in)

se·duc·tion Verführung *f*

se·duc·tive verführerisch

see¹ *v/i* sehen; nachsehen; **I~!** (ich) verstehe!, ach so!; **you~** weißt du; **let me~** warte mal, lass mich überlegen; **we'll~** mal sehen; *v/t* sehen; besuchen; *j-n* aufsuchen, *j-n* konsultieren; **~ s.o. home** *j-n* nach Hause bringen *or* begleiten; **~ you!** bis dann!, auf bald!; **~ about** sehen nach, sich kümmern um; **~ off** *j-n* verabschieden (**at** *am* Bahnhof *etc*); **~ out** *j-n* hinausbringen, hinausbegleiten; **~ through** *j-n*, *et.* durchschauen; *j-m* hinweghelfen über (*acc*); **~ to it that** dafür sorgen, dass

see² REL Bistum *n*, Diözese *f*; **Holy See** der Heilige Stuhl

seed 1. BOT Same(n) *m*; AGR Saat *f*, Saatgut *n*; (*Apfel- etc*)Kern *m*; SPORT gesetzter Spieler, gesetzte Spielerin; **go** *or* **run to ~** BOT schießen; **go to ~** F herunterkommen, verkommen **2.** *v/t* besäen; entkernen; SPORT *Spieler* setzen; *v/i* BOT in Samen schießen

seed·less BOT kernlos

seed·y F heruntergekommen

seek *Schutz*, *Wahrheit etc* suchen

seem scheinen; **seem·ing** scheinbar

seep sickern

see·saw Wippe *f*, Wippschaukel *f*

seethe schäumen (*a. fig*); *fig* kochen

see-through durchsichtig

seg·ment Teil *m*, *n*; Stück *n*; Abschnitt *m*; Segment *n*

seg·re·gate trennen

seg·re·ga·tion Rassentrennung *f*

seize *j-n*, *et.* packen, ergreifen; *Macht etc* an sich reißen; *et.* beschlagnahmen; *et.* pfänden; **sei·zure** Beschlagnahme *f*; Pfändung *f*; MED Anfall *m*

sel·dom *adv* selten

se·lect 1. (aus)wählen **2.** ausgewählt; exklusiv; **se·lec·tion** (Aus)Wahl *f*; ECON Auswahl *f* (**of** an *dat*)

self Ich *n*, Selbst *n*

self-as·sured selbstbewusst, -sicher

self-cen·tered, *Br* **self-cen·tred** egozentrisch

self-col·o(u)red einfarbig

self-con·fi·dence Selbstbewusstsein *n*, Selbstvertrauen *n*

self-con·fi·dent selbstbewusst

self-con·scious befangen, gehemmt, unsicher

self-con·tained (in sich) abgeschlossen; *fig* verschlossen; **~ flat** *Br* abgeschlossene Wohnung

self-con·trol Selbstbeherrschung *f*

self-crit·i·cal selbstkritisch

self-de·fence *Br*, **self-de·fense** Selbstverteidigung *f*; **in ~** in *or* aus Notwehr

self-de·ter·mi·na·tion POL Selbstbestimmung *f*

self-em·ployed selbstständig

self-es·teem Selbstachtung *f*

self-ev·i·dent selbstverständlich; offensichtlich

self-gov·ern·ment POL Selbstverwaltung *f*

self-help Selbsthilfe *f*; **~ group** Selbsthilfegruppe *f*

self-im·por·tant überheblich

self-in·dul·gent nachgiebig gegen sich

selbst; zügellos

self·in·terest Eigennutz *m*

self·ish selbstsüchtig, egoistisch

self·knowl·edge Selbsterkenntnis *f*

self·pit·y Selbstmitleid *n*

self·por·trait Selbstporträt *n*

self·pos·sessed selbstbeherrscht

self·re·li·ant selbstständig

self·re·spect Selbstachtung *f*

self·right·eous selbstgerecht

self·sat·is·fied selbstzufrieden

self·serv·ice 1. mit Selbstbedienung, Selbstbedienungs... **2.** Selbstbedienung *f*

self·stud·y Selbststudium *n*

self·suf·fi·cient ECON autark

self·sup·port·ing finanziell unabhängig

self·willed eigensinnig, eigenwillig

sell *v/t* verkaufen; *v/i* verkauft werden (*at, for* für); sich *gut etc* verkaufen (lassen), gehen; *~ by ...* mindestens haltbar bis ...; *~ off* (*esp* billig) abstoßen; *~ out* ausverkaufen; *be sold out* ausverkauft sein; *~ up esp Br* sein *Geschäft etc* verkaufen; **sell-by date** Mindesthaltbarkeitsdatum *n*; **sell·er** Verkäufer(in); *good ~* ECON gut gehender Artikel

sem·blance Anschein *m* (*of* von)

se·men MED Samen(flüssigkeit *f*) *m*, Sperma *n*

se·mes·ter UNIV Semester *n*

sem·i... halb..., Halb...

sem·i·cir·cle Halbkreis *m*

sem·i·co·lon LING Semikolon *n*, Strichpunkt *m*

sem·i·con·duc·tor ELECTR Halbleiter *m*

sem·i·de·tached (**house**) *Br* Doppelhaushälfte *f*

sem·i·fi·nals SPORT Semi-, Halbfinale *n*

sem·i·nar·y Priesterseminar *n*

sem·i·pre·cious: *~ stone* Halbedelstein *m*

sem·i·skilled angelernt

sem·o·li·na Grieß *m*

sen·ate POL Senat *m*

sen·a·tor POL Senator *m*

send *et., a.* Grüße, Hilfe etc senden, schicken (**to** dat or an acc); Ware etc senden, verschicken (**to** an acc); *j-n* schicken (**to** ins Bett etc); with adj or pp: machen; *~ word to s.o.* j-m Nachricht geben; *~ away* fort-, wegschicken; Brief etc absenden, abschicken; *~*

down Preise etc fallen lassen; *~ for* nach *j-m* schicken, *j-n* kommen lassen; sich *et.* kommen lassen, *et.* anfordern; *~ in* einsenden, einschicken, einreichen; *~ off* fort-, wegschicken; Brief etc absenden, abschicken; SPORT *j-n* vom Platz stellen; *~ on Brief etc* nachsenden, nachschicken (**to** an *acc*); Gepäck etc vorausschicken; *~ out* hinausschicken; Einladungen etc verschicken; *~ up Preise etc* steigen lassen

send·er Absender(in)

se·nile senil; **se·nil·i·ty** Senilität *f*

se·ni·or 1. senior; älter (**to** als); dienstälter; rangälter; Ober... **2.** Ältere *m, f*; UNIV Student(in) im letzten Jahr; *he is my ~ by a year* er ist ein Jahr älter als ich; *~ cit·i·zens* ältere Mitbürger *pl*, Senioren *pl*

se·ni·or·i·ty (höheres) Alter; (höheres) Dienstalter; (höherer) Rang

se·ni·or part·ner ECON Seniorpartner *m*

sen·sa·tion Empfindung *f*; Gefühl *n*; Sensation *f*

sen·sa·tion·al F großartig, fantastisch; sensationell, Sensations...

sense 1. Sinn *m*; Verstand *m*; Vernunft *f*; Gefühl *n*; Bedeutung *f*; *bring s.o. to his ~s* j-n zur Besinnung or Vernunft bringen; *come to one's ~s* zur Besinnung or Vernunft kommen; *in a ~* in gewisser Hinsicht; *make ~* e-n Sinn ergeben; vernünftig sein; *~ of duty* Pflichtgefühl *n*; *~ of security* Gefühl *n* der Sicherheit **2.** fühlen, spüren

sense·less bewusstlos; sinnlos

sen·si·bil·i·ty Empfindlichkeit *f*; *a. pl* Empfindsamkeit *f*, Zartgefühl *n*

sen·si·ble vernünftig; spürbar, merklich; *esp Br* praktisch (*clothes etc*)

sen·si·tive empfindlich; sensibel, empfindsam, feinfühlig

sen·sor TECH Sensor *m*

sen·su·al sinnlich

sen·su·ous sinnlich

sen·tence 1. LING Satz *m*; JUR Strafe *f*, Urteil *n*; *pass or pronounce ~* das Urteil fällen (**on** über *acc*); **2.** JUR verurteilen (**to** zu)

sen·ti·ment Gefühle *pl*; Sentimentalität *f*; *a. pl* Ansicht *f*, Meinung *f*

sen·ti·men·tal sentimental; gefühlvoll

sen·ti·men·tal·i·ty Sentimentalität *f*

sen·try MIL Wache *f*, (Wach[t])Posten *m*

S

sep·a·ra·ble trennbar; sep·a·rate 1. (sich) trennen; (auf-, ein-, zer)teilen (*into* in *acc*); 2. getrennt, separat; einzeln; sep·a·ra·tion Trennung *f*; (Auf-, Ein-, Zer)Teilung *f*

Sept *abbr of* **September** Sept., September *m*

Sep·tem·ber September *m*

sep·tic MED vereitert, septisch

se·quel Nachfolgeroman *m*, -film *m*, Fortsetzung *f; fig* Folge *f;* Nachspiel *n*

se·quence (Aufeinander-, Reihen)Folge *f; film*, TV Sequenz *f*, Szene *f;* **~ of tenses** LING Zeitenfolge *f*

ser·e·nade MUS 1. Serenade *f*, Ständchen *n* 2. *j-m* ein Ständchen bringen

se·rene klar; heiter; gelassen

ser·geant MIL Feldwebel *m*; (Polizei-)Wachtmeister *m*

se·ri·al 1. Fortsetzungsroman *m*; (*Rundfunk-*, *Fernseh*)Serie *f* 2. serienmäßig, Serien..., Fortsetzungs...

se·ries Serie *f*, Reihe *f*, Folge *f*; (*Buch-*)Reihe *f*, (*Rundfunk-*, *Fernseh*)Serie *f*, Sendereihe *f*

se·ri·ous ernst, ernsthaft; ernstlich; schwer (*illness, damage, crime etc*); **be ~** es ernst meinen (*about* mit)

se·ri·ous·ness Ernst *m*, Ernsthaftigkeit *f*; Schwere *f*

ser·mon REL Predigt *f*; F Moral-, Strafpredigt *f*

ser·pen·tine gewunden, kurvenreich

ser·rat·ed zackig, gezackt

se·rum MED Serum *n*

ser·vant Diener(in) (*a. fig*); Dienstmädchen *n*; → **civil servant**

serve 1. *v/t j-m, s-m* Land *etc* dienen; *Dienstzeit* (*a.* MIL) ableisten, *Amtszeit etc* durchlaufen; *j-n, et.* versorgen (*with* mit); *Essen* servieren; *Alkohol* ausschenken; *j-n* (*im Laden*) bedienen; JUR *Strafe* verbüßen; *e-m Zweck* dienen; *e-n Zweck* erfüllen; JUR *Vorladung etc* zustellen (**on s.o.** *j-m*); *tennis etc:* aufschlagen; **are you being ~d?** werden Sie schon bedient?; (**it**) **~s him right** F (das) geschieht ihm ganz recht; *v/i esp* MIL dienen; servieren; dienen (**as, for** als); *tennis etc:* aufschlagen; **XY to ~** *tennis etc:* Aufschlag XY; **~ on a committee** e-m Ausschuss angehören 2. *tennis etc:* Aufschlag *m*

serv·er *tennis etc:* Aufschläger(in);

GASTR Servierlöffel *m*

ser·vice 1. Dienst *m* (**to** an *dat*); Dienstleistung *f*; (*Post-, Staats-, Telefon- etc*-)Dienst *m*; (*Zug- etc*)Verkehr *m*; ECON Service *m*, Kundendienst *m*; Bedienung *f*; Betrieb *m*; REL Gottesdienst *m*; TECH Wartung *f*, MOT *a.* Inspektion *f*; (*Tee- etc*)Service *n*; JUR Zustellung *f* (*e-r Vorladung*); *tennis etc:* Aufschlag *m*; *pl* MIL Streitkräfte *pl* 2. TECH warten

ser·vice·a·ble brauchbar; strapazierfähig

ser·vice| ar·e·a MOT (Autobahn)Raststätte *f;* **~ charge** Bedienung *f*, Bedienungszuschlag *m;* **~ sta·tion** Tankstelle *f;* (*Reparatur*)Werkstatt *f*

ser·vi·ette *esp Br* Serviette *f*

ser·vile sklavisch (*a. fig*); servil, unterwürfig

serv·ing Portion *f*

ser·vi·tude Knechtschaft *f*; Sklaverei *f*

ses·sion Sitzung *f*; Sitzungsperiode *f*; **be in ~** JUR, PARL tagen

set 1. *v/t* setzen, stellen, legen; *in e-n Zustand* versetzen; veranlassen (**doing** zu tun); TECH einstellen, *Uhr* stellen (**by** nach), *Wecker* stellen (**for** auf *acc*); *Tisch* decken; *Preis, Termin etc* festsetzen, festlegen; *Rekord* aufstellen; *Edelstein* fassen (**in** in *dat*); *Ring etc* besetzen (**with** mit); *Flüssigkeit* erstarren lassen; *Haar* legen; *Knochen* einrenken, einrichten; MUS vertonen; PRINT absetzen; *Aufgabe, Frage* stellen; **~ at ease** beruhigen; **~ an example** ein Beispiel geben; **~ s.o. free** j-n freilassen; **~ going** in Gang setzen; **~ s.o. thinking** j-m zu denken geben; **~ one's hopes on** s-e Hoffnung setzen auf (*acc*); **~ s.o.'s mind at rest** j-n beruhigen; **~ great (little) store by** großen (geringen) Wert legen auf (*acc*); **the novel is ~ in** der Roman spielt in (*dat*); *v/i* ASTR untergehen; fest werden, erstarren; HUNT vorstehen; **~ about doing s.th.** sich daranmachen, et. zu tun; **~ about s.o.** F über j-n herfallen; **~ aside** beiseitelegen; JUR *Urteil etc* aufheben; **~ back** verzögern; *j-n, et.* zurückwerfen (**by two months** um zwei Monate); **~ in** einsetzen; **~ off** aufbrechen, sich aufmachen; hervorheben, betonen; *et.* auslösen; **~ out** arrangieren, herrichten; aufbrechen, sich aufmachen; **~**

out to do s.th. sich daranmachen, et. zu tun; **~ up** errichten; *Gerät etc* aufbauen; *Firma etc* gründen; *et.* auslösen, verursachen; *j-n* versorgen (**with** mit); sich niederlassen; **~ o.s. up as** sich ausgeben für **2.** *adj* festgesetzt, festgelegt; F bereit, fertig; starr (*smile etc*); **~ lunch** *or* **meal** *Br* Menü *n*; **~ phrase** feststehender Ausdruck; **be ~ on doing s.th.** (fest) entschlossen sein, et. zu tun; **be all ~** F startklar sein **3.** Satz *m*; (*Möbel- etc*)Garnitur *f*, (*Tee- etc*)Service *n*; (*Fernseh-, Rundfunk-*)Apparat *m*, (-)Gerät *n*; THEA Bühnenbild *n*; *film*, TV Set *n*, *m*; *tennis etc*: Satz *m*; (Personen)Kreis *m*, Clique *f*; (*Kopf- etc*)Haltung *f*; **have a shampoo and ~** sich die Haare waschen und legen lassen
set·back Rückschlag *m* (**to** für)
set·square *Br* Winkel *m*, Zeichendreieck *n*
set·tee Sofa *n*
set the·o·ry MATH Mengenlehre *f*
set·ting ASTR Untergang *m*; TECH Einstellung *f*; Umgebung *f*; *film etc*: Schauplatz *m*; (*Gold- etc*)Fassung *f*
set·ting lo·tion Haarfestiger *m*
set·tle *v/i* sich niederlassen (**on** auf *acc or dat*), sich setzen (**on** auf *acc*) (*a. ~ down*); sich niederlassen (**in** in *dat*); sich legen (*dust*); sich setzen (*coffee etc*); sich senken (*building etc*); sich beruhigen (*person, stomach etc*), sich legen (*a. ~ down*); sich einigen; *v/t j-n*, *Nerven etc* beruhigen; vereinbaren; *Frage etc* klären, entscheiden; *Streit etc* beilegen; *Land* besiedeln; *Leute* ansiedeln; *Rechnung* begleichen, bezahlen; *Konto* ausgleichen; *Schaden* regulieren; *s-e Angelegenheiten* in Ordnung bringen; **~ o.s.** sich niederlassen (**on** auf *acc or dat*), sich setzen (**on** auf *acc*); **that's ~s it** damit ist der Fall erledigt; **that's ~d then** das ist also klar; **~ back** sich (gemütlich) zurücklehnen; **~ down** *v/i* sesshaft werden; **~ down to** sich widmen (*dat*); **~ for** sich zufriedengeben *or* begnügen mit; **~ in** sich einleben *or* eingewöhnen; **~ on** sich einigen auf (*acc*); **~ up** (be)zahlen; abrechnen (**with** mit)
set·tled fest (*ideas etc*); geregelt (*life*); beständig (*weather*)
set·tle·ment Vereinbarung *f*; Klärung *f*;

Beilegung *f*; Einigung *f*; Siedlung *f*; Besiedlung *f*; Begleichung *f*, Bezahlung *f*; **reach a ~** sich einigen
set·tler Siedler(in)
sev·en 1. sieben **2.** Sieben *f*
sev·en·teen 1. siebzehn **2.** Siebzehn *f*
sev·en·teenth siebzehnte(r, -s)
sev·enth 1. siebente(r, -s), siebte(r, -s) **2.** Siebentel *n*, Siebtel *n*
sev·enth·ly siebentens, siebtens
sev·en·ti·eth siebzigste(r, -s)
sev·en·ty 1. siebzig **2.** Siebzig *f*
sev·er durchtrennen; abtrennen; *Beziehungen* abbrechen; (zer)reißen
sev·er·al mehrere
sev·er·al·ly einzeln, getrennt
se·vere schwer (*injuries, setback etc*); stark (*pain*); hart, streng (*winter*); streng (*person, discipline etc*); scharf (*criticism etc*); **se·ver·i·ty** Schwere *f*; Stärke *f*; Härte *f*; Strenge *f*; Schärfe *f*
sew nähen
sew·age Abwasser *n*
sew·age works Kläranlage *f*
sew·er Abwasserkanal *m*
sew·er·age Kanalisation *f*
sew·ing 1. Nähen *n*; Näharbeit *f* **2.** Näh...; **~ ma·chine** Nähmaschine *f*
sex Geschlecht *n*; Sexualität *f*; Sex *m*; Geschlechtsverkehr *m*
sex·ism Sexismus *m*
sex·ist 1. sexistisch **2.** Sexist(in)
sex·ton Küster *m* (und Totengräber *m*)
sex·u·al sexuell, Sexual..., geschlechtlich, Geschlechts...; **~ ha·rass·ment** sexuelle Belästigung; **~ in·ter·course** Geschlechtsverkehr *m*
sex·u·al·i·ty Sexualität *f*
sex·y F sexy, aufreizend
shab·by schäbig
shack Hütte *f*, Bude *f*; F *contp* Schuppen *m*
shack·les Fesseln *pl*, Ketten *pl* (*both a. fig*)
shade 1. Schatten *m* (*a. fig*); (*Lampen-*)Schirm *m*; Schattierung *f*; Rouleau *n*; *fig* Nuance *f*; **a ~** *fig* ein kleines bisschen, e-e Spur **2.** abschirmen (**from** gegen); schattieren; **~ off** allmählich übergehen (**into** in *acc*)
shad·ow 1. Schatten *m* (*a. fig*); **there's not a** *or* **the ~ of a doubt about it** daran besteht nicht der geringste Zweifel **2.** *j-n* beschatten

shad·ow·y schattig, dunkel; verschwommen, vage, schemenhaft

shad·y schattig; Schatten spendend; F zwielichtig, fragwürdig

shaft (*Pfeil- etc*)Schaft *m*; (*Hammer- etc*)Stiel *m*; TECH Welle *f*; (*Aufzugs-, Bergwerks- etc*)Schacht *m*; (*Sonnen- etc*)Strahl *m*

shag·gy zottig, struppig

shake 1. *v/t* schütteln; rütteln an (*dat*); erschüttern; ~ *hands* sich die Hand geben *or* schütteln; *v/i* zittern, beben, wackeln (*with* vor *dat*); ~ *down* herunterschütteln; durchsuchen, F filzen; *Br* F kampieren; ~ *off* abschütteln; *Erkältung etc* loswerden; ~ *up* Kissen *etc* aufschütteln; *Flasche, Flüssigkeit* (durch-) schütteln; *fig* erschüttern **2.** Schütteln *n*; F Milchshake *m*; ~ *of the head* Kopfschütteln *n*

shake·down F Erpressung *f*; Durchsuchung *f*, Filzung *f*; *Br* (Not)Lager *n*

shak·en *a.* ~ *up* erschüttert

shak·y wack(e)lig; zitt(e)rig

shall *v/aux* future: ich werde, wir werden; *in questions:* soll ich …?, sollen wir …?; ~ *we go?* gehen wir?

shal·low seicht, flach, *fig a.* oberflächlich; **shal·lows** seichte *or* flache Stelle, Untiefe *f*

sham 1. Farce *f*; Heuchelei *f* **2.** unecht, falsch; vorgetäuscht, geheuchelt **3.** *v/t Mitgefühl etc* vortäuschen, heucheln; *Krankheit etc* simulieren; *sich* verstellen, heucheln; *he's only* ~*ming* er tut nur so

sham·bles F Schlachtfeld *n*, wüstes Durcheinander, Chaos *n*

shame 1. Scham *f*, Schamgefühl *n*; Schande *f*; ~*!* pfui!; ~ *on you!* pfui!; schäm dich!; *put to* ~ → **2.** beschämen; Schande machen (*dat*)

shame·faced betreten, verlegen

shame·ful beschämend; schändlich

shame·less schamlos

sham·poo 1. Shampoo *n*, Schampon *n*, Schampun *n*; Haarwäsche *f*; → *set 3* **2.** *Haare* waschen; *j-m* die Haare waschen; *Teppich etc* schamponieren

shank TECH Schaft *m*; GASTR Hachse *f*

shan·ty¹ Hütte *f*, Bude *f*

shan·ty² Shanty *n*, Seemannslied *n*

shan·ty·town Elendsviertel *n*

shape 1. Form *f*; Gestalt *f*; Verfassung *f*, Zustand *m*; *in good* (*bad*) ~ in gutem (schlechten) Zustand; (*in* (*out of*) ~ SPORT (nicht) gut in Form; *take* ~ *fig* Gestalt annehmen **2.** *v/t* formen; gestalten; *v/i a.* ~ *up* sich *gut* etc machen

shape·less formlos; ausgebeult

shape·ly wohlgeformt

share 1. Anteil *m* (*in, of* an *dat*); *esp Br* ECON Aktie *f*; *go* ~*s* teilen; *have a* (*no*) ~ *in* (nicht) beteiligt sein an (*dat*) **2.** *v/t* (sich) *et.* teilen (*with* mit); *a.* ~ *out* verteilen (*among, between* an *acc*, unter *acc*); *v/i* teilen; ~ *in* sich teilen in (*acc*)

share·hold·er *esp Br* ECON Aktionär(in)

shark ZO Hai(fisch) *m*

sharp 1. *adj* scharf (*a. fig*); spitz; abrupt; schneidend (*wind, frost, command, voice, etc*); beißend (*cold, smell etc*); stechend, heftig (*pain*); gescheit; MUS (*um e-n Halbton*) erhöht; *C* ~ MUS Cis *n* **2.** *adv* scharf, abrupt; MUS zu hoch; pünktlich, genau; *at eight o'clock* ~ Punkt 8 (Uhr)

sharp·en *Messer etc* schärfen, schleifen; *Bleistift etc* spitzen

sharp·en·er (*Messer- etc*)Schärfer *m*; (*Bleistift*)Spitzer *m*

sharp·ness Schärfe *f* (*a. fig*)

sharp·shoot·er Scharfschütze *m*

sharp·sight·ed scharfsichtig

sharp·wit·ted scharfsinnig

shat·ter *v/t* zerschmettern, zerschlagen; *Hoffnungen etc* zerstören; *v/i* zerspringen, zersplittern

shat·ter·ing vernichtend; erschütternd

shat·ter·proof splitterfrei

shave 1. (sich) rasieren; (glatt) hobeln; *j-n, et.* streifen **2.** Rasur *f*; *have a* ~ sich rasieren; *that was a close* ~ das war knapp, das ist gerade noch einmal gut gegangen!; **shav·en** kahl geschoren

shav·er (*esp* elektrischer) Rasierapparat *m*

shav·ing 1. Rasieren *n* **2.** Rasier…; ~ *bag* Kulturbeutel *m*; ~ *brush* Rasierpinsel *m*; ~ *cream* Rasiercreme *f*

shav·ings Späne *pl*

shawl Umhängetuch *n*; Kopftuch *n*

she 1. *pron* sie **2.** Sie *f*; ZO Weibchen *n* **3.** *adj in cpds* ZO …weibchen *n*; ~*bear* Bärin *f*

sheaf Bündel *n*; AGR Garbe *f*

shear 1. scheren **2.** (*a pair of*) ~*s* (e-e)

große Schere

sheath (*Schwert- etc*)Scheide *f*; Hülle *f*; *Br* Kondom *n*, *m*; **sheathe** *Schwert etc* in die Scheide stecken; TECH umhüllen, verkleiden, ummanteln

shed[1] Schuppen *m*; Stall *m*

shed[2] *Tränen etc* vergießen; *Blätter etc* verlieren; *fig Hemmungen etc* ablegen; *~ its skin* sich häuten; *a few pounds* ein paar Pfund abnehmen

sheen Glanz *m*

sheep ZO Schaf *n*

sheep-dog ZO Schäferhund *m*

sheep-ish verlegen

sheep-skin Schaffell *n*

sheer rein, bloß; steil, (fast) senkrecht; hauchdünn

sheet Betttuch *n*, (Bett)Laken *n*, Leintuch *n*; (*Glas-, Metall- etc*)Platte *f*; Blatt *n*, Bogen *m*; weite (*Eis- etc*)Fläche; *the rain was coming down in ~s* es regnete in Strömen

sheet light-ning Wetterleuchten *n*

shelf (*Bücher-, Wand- etc*)Brett *n*, (-)Bord *n*; GEOGR Riff *n*; *pl* Regal *n*; *off the ~* gleich zum Mitnehmen

shell 1. (*Austern-, Eier-, Nuss- etc*) Schale *f*; BOT (*Erbsen- etc*)Hülse *f*; ZO Muschel *f*; (*Schnecken*)Haus *n*; ZO Panzer *m*; MIL Granate *f*; (Geschoss-, Patronen)Hülse *f*; Patrone *f*; TECH Rumpf *m*, Gerippe *n*, ARCH *a.* Rohbau *m* 2. schälen, enthülsen; mit Granaten beschießen

shell-fish ZO Schal(en)tier *n*

shel-ter 1. Zuflucht *f*, Schutz *m*; Unterkunft *f*, Obdach *n*; MIL Unterstand *m*; *run for ~* Schutz suchen; *take ~* bei j-m unterstellen (*under* unter *dat*); *bus ~* Wartehäuschen *n* 2. *v/t* schützen (*from* vor *dat*); *v/i* sich unterstellen

shelve *v/t Bücher* in ein Regal stellen; *Plan etc* aufschieben, zurückstellen; *v/i* sanft abfallen (*garden etc*)

shep-herd 1. Schäfer *m*, Hirt *m* 2. j-n führen

sher-iff Sheriff *m*

shield 1. Schild *m* 2. j-n (be)schützen (*from* vor *dat*); j-n decken

shift 1. *v/t et.* bewegen, schieben, *Möbelstück a.* (ver)rücken; *Schuld etc* (ab-)schieben (*onto* auf *acc*); *~ gear*(s) MOT schalten; *v/i* sich bewegen; umspringen (*wind*); *fig* sich verlagern or

verschieben *or* wandeln; MOT schalten (*into, to* in *acc*); *~ from one foot to the other* von e-m Fuß auf den anderen treten; *~ on one's chair* auf s-m Stuhl *ungeduldig etc* hin und her rutschen 2. *fig* Verlagerung *f*, Verschiebung *f*, Wandel *m*; ECON Schicht *f*; *~ key* TECH Umschalttaste *f*; *~ work-er* Schichtarbeiter(in)

shift-y F verschlagen

shim-mer schimmern; flimmern

shin 1. *a. ~bone* ANAT Schienbein *n* 2. *~ up* hinaufklettern; *~ down* herunterklettern

shine 1. *v/i* scheinen; leuchten; glänzen (*a. fig*); *v/t Schuhe etc* polieren 2. Glanz *m*

shin-gle[1] grober Strandkies

shin-gle[2] (Dach)Schindel *f*

shin-gles MED Gürtelrose *f*

shin-y blank, glänzend

ship 1. Schiff *n* 2. verschiffen; ECON verfrachten, versenden

ship-ment ECON Ladung *f*; Verschiffung *f*, Verfrachtung *f*, Versand *m*

ship-own-er Reeder *m*; Schiffseigner *m*

ship-ping Schifffahrt *f*; Schiffsbestand *m*; ECON Verschiffung *f*, Verfrachtung *f*, Versand *m*

ship-wreck Schiffbruch *m*

ship-wrecked 1. *be ~* Schiffbruch erleiden 2. schiffbrüchig

ship-yard (Schiffs)Werft *f*

shirk sich drücken (vor *dat*)

shirk-er Drückeberger(in)

shirt Hemd *n*

shirt-sleeve 1. Hemdsärmel *m*; *in (one's) ~s* in Hemdsärmeln, hemdsärmelig 2. hemdsärmelig

shish ke-bab GASTR Schaschlik *m*, *n*

shit V 1. Scheiße *f* (*a. fig*); *fig* Scheiß *m* 2. (voll)scheißen

shiv-er 1. zittern (*with vor dat*); 2. Schauer *m*; *pl* MED F Schüttelfrost *m*; *the sight sent ~s (up and) down my spine* bei dem Anblick überlief es mich eiskalt

shoal[1] Untiefe *f*; Sandbank *f*

shoal[2] ZO Schwarm *m*

shock[1] 1. Schock *m* (*a. MED*); Wucht *f*; ELECTR Schlag *m*, (*a. MED* Elektro-) Schock *m*; *be in* (*a state of*) *~* unter Schock stehen 2. schockieren, empören; j-m e-n Schock versetzen

shock² (~ **of hair** Haar)Schopf *m*

shock ab·sorb·er TECH Stoßdämpfer *m*

shock·ing schockierend, empörend, anstößig; F scheußlich

shod·dy minderwertig (*goods*); gemein, schäbig (*trick etc*)

shoe 1. Schuh *m*; Hufeisen *n* **2.** *Pferd* beschlagen

shoe·horn Schuhanzieher *m*, -löffel *m*

shoe·lace Schnürsenkel *m*

shoe·mak·er Schuhmacher *m*, Schuster *m*

shoe·shine boy Schuhputzer *m*

shoe store (*Br* shop) Schuhgeschäft *n*

shoe·string Schnürsenkel *m*

shoot 1. *v/t* schießen, HUNT *a.* erlegen; abfeuern, abschießen; erschießen; *Riegel* vorschieben; *j-n* fotografieren, aufnehmen, *Film* drehen; *Heroin etc* spritzen; ~ **the lights** MOT bei Rot fahren; *v/i* schießen (*at* auf *acc*); jagen; Fig schießen, rasen; *film*, TV drehen, filmen; BOT sprießen, treiben **2.** BOT Trieb *m*; Jagd *f*; Jagdrevier *n*

shoot·er F Schießeisen *n*

shoot·ing 1. Schießen *n*; Schießerei *f*; Erschießung *f*; Anschlag *m*; Jagd *f*; *film*, TV Dreharbeiten *pl*, Aufnahmen *pl* **2.** stechend (*pain*); ~ **gal·le·ry** Schießbude *f*; ~ **range** Schießstand *m*; ~ **star** ASTR Sternschnuppe *f*

shop 1. *Br* Laden *m*, Geschäft *n*; Werkstatt *f*; Betrieb *m*; *talk* ~ fachsimpeln **2.** *mst* **go shopping** einkaufen gehen

shop as·sis·tant *Br* Verkäufer(in)

shop·keep·er *Br* Ladenbesitzer(in), Ladeninhaber(in)

shop·lift·er Ladendieb(in)

shop·lift·ing Ladendiebstahl *m*

shop·per Käufer(in)

shop·ping 1. Einkauf *m*, Einkaufen *n*; Einkäufe *pl* (*items bought*); **do one's** ~ *Br* einkaufen, (s-e) Einkäufe machen **2.** Einkaufs…; ~ **bag** Einkaufsbeutel *m*, -tasche *f*; ~ **cart** Einkaufswagen *m*; ~ **cen·ter** (*Br* cen·tre) Einkaufszentrum *n*; ~ **list** Einkaufsliste *f*, -zettel *m*; ~ **mall** Einkaufszentrum *n*; ~ **precinct** *Br* Fußgängerzone *f*; ~ **street** Geschäfts-, Ladenstraße *f*

shop stew·ard ECON gewerkschaftlicher Vertrauensmann

shop·walk·er *Br* Aufsicht(sperson) *f*

shop win·dow Schaufenster *n*

shore¹ Küste *f*; (*See*)Ufer *n*; **on** ~ an Land

shore²: ~ **up** (ab)stützen

short 1. *adj* kurz; klein (*person*); kurz angebunden, barsch, schroff (*with* zu); GASTR mürbe; **be** ~ **for** die Kurzform sein von; **be** ~ **of** … nicht genügend … haben **2.** *adv* plötzlich, abrupt; ~ **of** außer; **cut** ~ plötzlich unterbrechen; **fall** ~ **of** *et.* nicht erreichen; **stop** ~ plötzlich innehalten, stutzen; **stop** ~ **of** *or* **at** zurückschrecken vor (*dat*); → **run** *I* **3.** F Kurzfilm *m*; ELECTR Kurze *m*; **called** … **for** ~ kurz … genannt; **in** ~ kurz(um)

short·age Knappheit *f*, Mangel *m* (**of** an *dat*)

short·com·ings Unzulänglichkeiten *pl*, Mängel *pl*, Fehler *pl*

short cut Abkürzung *f*; **take a** ~ (den Weg) abkürzen

short·en *v/t* (ab-, ver)kürzen; *v/i* kürzer werden

short·hand Kurzschrift *f*, Stenografie *f*

short·ly bald; barsch, schroff; mit wenigen Worten

short·ness Kürze *f*; Schroffheit *f*

shorts *a.* **pair of** ~ Shorts *pl*; (Herren)Unterhose *f*

short·sight·ed *esp Br* kurzsichtig (*a. fig*)

short sto·ry Kurzgeschichte *f*

short-tem·pered aufbrausend, hitzig

short-term ECON kurzfristig

short time ECON Kurzarbeit *f*

short wave ELECTR Kurzwelle *f*

short-wind·ed kurzatmig

shot Schuss *m*; Schrot(kugeln *pl*) *m*, *n*; SPORT Kugel *f*; *guter etc* Schütze *m*; *soccer etc*: Schuss *m*; *basketball etc*: Wurf *m*; *tennis*, *golf*: Schlag *m*; PHOT Schnappschuss *m*, Aufnahme *f*; *film*, TV Aufnahme *f*, Einstellung *f*; MED F Spritze *f*; F Schuss *m* (*of drugs*); *fig* F Versuch *m*; **a** ~ **of rum** ein Schluck Rum; **I'll have a** ~ **at it** ich probier's mal; **not by a long** ~ F noch lange nicht; → **big shot**

shot·gun Schrotflinte *f*

shot·gun wed·ding F Mussheirat *f*

shot put SPORT Kugelstoßen *n*

shot put·ter SPORT Kugelstoßer(in)

shoul·der 1. ANAT Schulter *f*; MOT Standspur *f*; Bankett *n* **2.** schultern; *Kosten, Verantwortung etc* übernehmen; (mit der Schulter) stoßen; ~ **bag** Schulter-, Umhängetasche *f*; ~ **blade** ANAT Schulterblatt *n*; ~ **strap** Träger *m*; Tragriemen *m*

shout 1. *v/i* rufen, schreien (**for** nach; **for help** um Hilfe); ~ **at s.o.** j-n anschreien; *v/t* rufen, schreien **2.** Ruf *m*, Schrei *m*

shove 1. stoßen, F schubsen; *et.* schieben, stopfen **2.** Stoß *m*, F Schubs *m*

shov·el 1. Schaufel *f* **2.** schaufeln

show 1. *v/t* zeigen, vorzeigen, anzeigen; *j-n* bringen, führen (**to** zu); zeigen, *film etc a.* vorführen, TV *a.* bringen; *v/i* zu sehen sein; **be ~ing** gezeigt werden, laufen; ~ **around** herumführen; ~ **in** herein-, hineinführen, herein-, hineinbringen; ~ **off** angeben *or* protzen (mit); vorteilhaft zur Geltung bringen; ~ **out** heraus-, hinausführen, heraus-, hinausbringen; ~ **round** herumführen; ~ **up** *v/t* herauf-, hinaufführen, herauf-, hinaufbringen; sichtbar machen; *j-n* entlarven, bloßstellen; *et.* aufdecken; *j-n* in Verlegenheit bringen; *v/i* zu sehen sein; F aufkreuzen, auftauchen **2.** THEA *etc* Vorstellung *f*, Show *f*; *radio*, TV Sendung *f*; Ausstellung *f*; Zurschaustellung *f*, Demonstration *f*; *fig* leerer Schein; **be on** ~ ausgestellt *or* zu besichtigen sein; **steal the ~ from s.o.** *fig* j-m die Schau stehlen; **make a ~ of** *Anteilnahme, Interesse etc* heucheln; **put up a poor** ~ F e-e schwache Leistung zeigen; **be in charge of the whole** ~ F den ganzen Laden schmeißen **3.** Muster...

show·biz F, **show busi·ness** Showbusiness *n*, Showgeschäft *n*, Unterhaltungsindustrie *f*

show·case Schaukasten *m*, Vitrine *f*

show·down Kraft-, Machtprobe *f*

show·er 1. (Regen- *etc*)Schauer *m*; (*Funken*)Regen *m*; (*Wasser-, Wort-etc*)Schwall *m*; Dusche *f*; (Geschenk-) Party *f*; **have** *or* **take a** ~ duschen **2.** *v/t* j-n mit *et.* überschütten *or* überhäufen; *v/i* duschen; ~ **down** niederprasseln

show jump·er SPORT Springreiter(in)

show jump·ing SPORT Springreiten *n*

show-off F Angeber(in)

show·room Ausstellungsraum *m*

show tri·al JUR Schauprozess *m*

show·y auffallend

shred 1. Fetzen *m* **2.** zerfetzen; in (schmale) Streifen schneiden, schnitzeln, schnetzeln; in den Papier- *or* Reißwolf geben; **shred·der** Schnitzelmaschine *f*; Papier-, Reißwolf *m*

shrewd scharfsinnig; schlau

shriek 1. (gellend) aufschreien; ~ **with laughter** vor Lachen kreischen **2.** (schriller) Schrei

shrill schrill; *fig* heftig, scharf, lautstark

shrimp ZO Garnele *f*; *fig contp* Knirps *m*

shrine Schrein *m*

shrink 1. (ein-, zusammen)schrumpfen (lassen); einlaufen; *fig* abnehmen **2.** F Klapsdoktor *m*

shrink·age Schrumpfung *f*; Einlaufen *n*; *fig* Abnahme *f*

shrink-wrap einschweißen

shriv·el schrumpfen (lassen); runz(e)lig werden (lassen)

shroud 1. Leichentuch *n* **2.** *fig* hüllen

Shrove Tues·day Fastnachts-, Faschingsdienstag *m*

shrub Strauch *m*, Busch *m*

shrub·ber·y BOT Strauch-, Buschwerk *n*, Gebüsch *n*

shrug 1. *a.* ~ **one's shoulders** mit den Achseln *or* Schultern zucken **2.** Achselzucken *n*, Schulterzucken *n*

shuck BOT **1.** Hülse *f*, Schote *f*; Schale *f* **2.** enthülsen; schälen

shud·der 1. schaudern **2.** Schauder *m*

shuf·fle 1. *v/t* Karten mischen; *Papiere etc* umordnen, hierhin oder dorthin legen; ~ **one's feet** schlurfen; *v/i* schlurfen; *Karten* mischen **2.** Schlurfen *n*, schlurfender Gang; Mischen *n*

shun *j-n, et.* meiden

shunt *Zug etc* rangieren, verschieben; *a.* ~ **off** F *j-n* abschieben (**to** in *acc*, nach)

shut (sich) schließen; zumachen; ~ **down** *Fabrik etc* schließen; ~ **off** *Wasser, Gas, Maschine etc* abstellen; ~ **up** einschließlich; einsperren; *Geschäft* schließen; ~ **up!** F halt die Klappe!

shut·ter Fensterladen *m*; PHOT Verschluss *m*

shut·tle 1. Pendelverkehr *m*; (*Raum-*) Fähre *f*, (-)Transporter *m*; TECH Schiffchen *n* **2.** hin- und herbefördern

shut·tle·cock SPORT Federball *m*

shut·tle ser·vice Pendelverkehr *m*

shy 1. scheu; schüchtern **2.** scheuen (**at** vor *dat*); ~ **away from** *fig* zurückschrecken vor (*dat*)

shy·ness Scheu f; Schüchternheit f

sick 1. krank; *be ~ esp Br* sich übergeben; *she was or felt ~* ihr war schlecht; *get ~* krank werden; *be off ~* krank (geschrieben) sein; *report ~* sich krank melden; *be ~ of s.th.* F et. satthaben; *it makes me ~* F mir wird schlecht davon, *a. fig* es ekelt *or* widert mich an **2.** *the ~* die Kranken *pl*

sick·bed Krankenlager n

sick·en v/t j-n anekeln, anwidern; v/i *esp Br* krank werden

sick·le ['sɪkl] Sichel f

sick leave: *be on ~* krank (geschrieben) sein, wegen Krankheit fehlen

sick·ly kränklich; ungesund; matt; widerlich (*smell etc*)

sick·ness Krankheit f; Übelkeit f; ~ ben·e·fit *Br* Krankengeld n

side 1. Seite f; *esp Br* SPORT Mannschaft f; *~ by ~* nebeneinander; *take ~s* Partei ergreifen (*with* für; *against* gegen) **2.** Seiten...; Neben... **3.** Partei ergreifen (*with* für; *against* gegen)

side·board Anrichte f, Sideboard n

side·car MOT Bei-, Seitenwagen m

side dish GASTR Beilage f

side·long seitlich; Seiten...; ~ **glance** Seitenblick m

side street Nebenstraße f

side·swipe Seitenhieb m

side·track j-n ablenken; F et. abbiegen; RAIL *etc* rangieren, verschieben

side·walk Bürgersteig m, Gehsteig m

side·walk ca·fé Straßencafé n

side·ways seitlich; seitwärts, nach der *or* zur Seite

sid·ing RAIL Nebengleis n

si·dle: *~ up to s.o.* sich an j-n heranschleichen

siege MIL Belagerung f; *lay ~ to* belagern (*a. fig*)

sieve 1. Sieb n **2.** (durch)sieben

sift (durch)sieben; *a. ~ through fig* sichten, durchsehen, prüfen

sigh 1. seufzen **2.** Seufzer m

sight 1. Sehvermögen n, Sehkraft f, Augenlicht n; Anblick m; Sicht(weite) f; *pl* Visier n; Sehenswürdigkeiten f; *at ~, on ~* sofort; *at first ~* auf den ersten Blick von (*or gen*); *at first ~* auf den ersten Blick; *catch ~ of* erblicken; *know by ~* vom Sehen kennen; *lose ~ of* aus den Augen verlieren; *be (with)in*

~ *in Sicht sein* (*a. fig*) **2.** sichten

sight-read MUS vom Blatt singen *or* spielen

sight·see·ing Sightseeing n, Besichtigung f von Sehenswürdigkeiten; *go ~* sich die Sehenswürdigkeiten anschauen; ~ **tour** Sightseeingtour f, Besichtigungstour f, (Stadt)Rundfahrt f

sight·se·er Tourist(in)

sight test Sehtest m

sign 1. Zeichen n; (*Hinweis-, Warn- etc*)Schild n; *fig* (An)Zeichen n **2.** unterschreiben, unterzeichnen; *Scheck* ausstellen; ~ *in* sich eintragen; ~ *out* sich austragen

sig·nal 1. Signal n (*a. fig*); Zeichen n (*a. fig*) **2.** (ein) Zeichen geben; signalisieren

sig·na·to·ry Unterzeichner(in)

sig·na·ture Unterschrift f; Signatur f; ~ **tune** *radio*, TV Kennmelodie f

sign·board (Aushänge)Schild n

sign·er Unterzeichnete m, f

sig·net Siegel n

sig·nif·i·cance Bedeutung f, Wichtigkeit f; **sig·nif·i·cant** bedeutend, bedeutsam, wichtig; bezeichnend

sig·ni·fy bedeuten; andeuten

sign·post Wegweiser m

si·lence 1. Stille f; Schweigen n; ~*!* Ruhe!; *in ~* schweigend; *reduce to ~ → 2.* zum Schweigen bringen

si·lenc·er TECH Schalldämpfer m; *Br* MOT Auspufftopf m

si·lent still; schweigend; schweigsam; stumm; ~ **part·ner** ECON stiller Teilhaber

sil·i·con CHEM Silizium n

sil·i·cone CHEM Silikon n

silk 1. Seide f **2.** Seiden...

silk·worm ZO Seidenraupe f

silk·y seidig; samtig (*voice*)

sill (*Fenster*)Brett n

sil·ly 1. albern, töricht, dumm **2.** F Dummchen n

sil·ver 1. Silber n **2.** silbern, Silber... **3.** versilbern

sil·ver-plat·ed versilbert

sil·ver·ware Tafelsilber n

sil·ver·y silberglänzend; *fig* silberhell

sim·i·lar ähnlich (*to dat*)

sim·i·lar·i·ty Ähnlichkeit f

sim·i·le Gleichnis n, Vergleich m

sim·mer leicht kochen, köcheln; ~ *with*

fig kochen vor (*rage etc*), fiebern vor (*excitement etc*); **~ down** F sich beruhigen, F sich abregen

sim·per albern *or* affektiert lächeln

sim·ple einfach, schlicht; leicht; dumm, einfältig; naiv; **the ~ fact is that ...** es ist einfach e-e Tatsache, dass ...

sim·ple-mind·ed dumm; naiv

sim·pli·ci·ty Einfachheit *f*, Schlichtheit *f*; Dummheit *f*; Naivität *f*

sim·pli·fi·ca·tion Vereinfachung *f*

sim·pli·fy vereinfachen

sim·ply einfach; bloß, nur

sim·u·late vortäuschen; MIL, TECH simulieren

sim·ul·ta·ne·ous simultan, gleichzeitig

sin 1. Sünde *f* **2.** sündigen

since 1. *adv a.* **ever ~** seitdem, seither **2.** *prp* (*dat*) seit(dem); da **3.** *cj* seit(dem); da

sin·cere aufrichtig, ehrlich, offen

sin·cer·i·ty Aufrichtigkeit *f*; Offenheit *f*

sin·ew ANAT Sehne *f*

sin·ew·y sehnig; *fig* kraftvoll

sin·ful sündig, sündhaft

sing singen; **~ s.th. to s.o.** j-m et. vorsingen

singe (sich et.) ansengen *or* versengen

sing·er Sänger(in)

sing·ing Singen *n*, Gesang *m*

sin·gle 1. einzig; einzeln, Einzel...; einfach; ledig, unverheiratet; **~ in ~ file** im Gänsemarsch **2.** Br RAIL *etc* einfache Fahrkarte, AVIAT einfaches Ticket (*both a.* **~ ticket**); Single *f*; Single *m*, Unverheiratete *m*, *f* **3.** **~ out** sich herausgreifen

sin·gle-breast·ed einreihig

sin·gle-en·gined AVIAT einmotorig

sin·gle fam·i·ly home Einfamilienhaus *n*

sin·gle fa·ther allein erziehender Vater

sin·gle-hand·ed eigenhändig, allein

sin·gle-lane MOT einspurig

sin·gle-mind·ed zielstrebig, -bewusst

sin·gle moth·er allein erziehende Mutter

sin·gle pa·rent Alleinerziehende *m*, *f*

sin·gle room Einzelzimmer *n*

sin·gles *esp tennis*: Einzel *n*; **a ~ match** ein Einzel; **men's ~** Herreneinzel *n*; **women's ~** Dameneinzel *n*

sin·glet Br ärmelloses Unterhemd *or* Trikot

sin·gle-track eingleisig, einspurig

sin·gu·lar 1. einzigartig, einmalig **2.** LING Singular *m*, Einzahl *f*

sin·is·ter finster, unheimlich

sink 1. *v/i* sinken, untergehen; sich senken; **~ in** eindringen (*a. fig*); *v/t* versenken; Brunnen *etc* bohren; Zähne *etc* vergraben (**into** in *acc*); **2.** Spülbecken *n*, Spüle *f*; Waschbecken *n*

sin·ner Sünder(in)

sip 1. Schlückchen *n* **2.** *v/t* nippen an (*dat*) *or* von; schlückchenweise trinken; *v/i* nippen (**at** an *dat or* von)

sir mein Herr; **Dear Sir or Madam** Sehr geehrte Damen und Herren (*address in letters*)

sire ZO Vater *m*, Vatertier *n*

si·ren Sirene *f*

sis·sy F Weichling *m*

sis·ter Schwester *f*; Br MED Oberschwester *f*; REL (Ordens)Schwester *f*

sis·ter·hood Schwesternschaft *f*

sis·ter-in-law Schwägerin *f*

sis·ter·ly schwesterlich

sit *v/i* sitzen; sich setzen; tagen; *v/t* j-n setzen; *esp* Br Prüfung ablegen, machen; **~ down** sich setzen; **~ for** Br Prüfung ablegen, machen; **~ in** ein Sit-in veranstalten; an e-m Sit-in teilnehmen; **~ in for** j-n vertreten; **~ in on** als Zuhörer teilnehmen an (*dat*); **~ on** sitzen auf (*dat*) (*a. fig*); **~ on a committee** e-m Ausschuss angehören; **~ out** das Ende (*gen*) abwarten; Krise *etc* aussitzen; **~ up** sich *or* j-n aufrichten *or* aufsetzen; aufrecht sitzen; aufbleiben

sit·com → situation comedy

sit-down *a.* **~ strike** Sitzstreik *m*; *a.* **~ demonstration** *or* F **demo** Sitzblockade *f*

site Platz *m*, Ort *m*, Stelle *f*; (*Ausgrabungs*)Stätte *f*; Baustelle *f*

sit-in Sit-in *n*, Sitzstreik *m*

sit·ting Sitzung *f*

sit·ting room *esp* Br Wohnzimmer *n*

sit·u·at·ed be ~ liegen, gelegen sein

sit·u·a·tion Lage *f*, Situation *f*; **~ com·e·dy** TV *etc* Situationskomödie *f*

six 1. sechs **2.** Sechs *f*

six·teen 1. sechzehn **2.** Sechzehn *f*

six·teenth sechzehnte(r, -s)

sixth 1. sechste(r, -s) **2.** Sechstel *n*

sixth·ly sechstens

six·ti·eth sechzigste(r, -s)

S

six·ty 1. sechzig **2.** Sechzig *f*

size 1. Größe *f, fig a.* Ausmaß *n*, Umfang *m* **2.** ~ **up** F abschätzen

siz(e)·a·ble beträchtlich

siz·zle brutzeln

skate 1. Schlittschuh *m*; Rollschuh *m* **2.** Schlittschuh laufen, eislaufen; Rollschuh laufen

skate·board Skateboard *n*

skat·er Eisläufer(in), Schlittschuhläufer(in); Rollschuhläufer(in)

skat·ing Eislaufen *n*, Schlittschuhlaufen *n*; **free** ~ Kür *f*, Kürlauf *m*; ~ **rink** (Kunst)Eisbahn *f*; Rollschuhbahn *f*

skel·e·ton Skelett *n*, Gerippe *n*

skep·tic Skeptiker(in)

skep·ti·cal skeptisch

sketch 1. Skizze *f*; THEA *etc* Sketch **2.** skizzieren

skew·er 1. (Brat)Spieß *m* **2.** (auf)spießen

ski 1. Ski *m* **2.** Ski… **3.** Ski fahren *or* laufen

skid 1. MOT rutschen, schleudern **2.** MOT Rutschen *n*, Schleudern *n*; TECH Kufe *f*

skid mark(s) MOT Bremsspur *f*

ski·er Skifahrer(in), Skiläufer(in)

ski goggles Skibrille *f*

ski·ing Skifahren *n*, Skilaufen *n*, Skisport *m*

ski jump (Sprung)Schanze *f*

ski jump·er Skispringer *m*

ski jump·ing Skispringen *n*

skil·ful *Br* → **skillful**

ski lift Skilift *m*

skill Geschicklichkeit *f*, Fertigkeit *f*

skilled geschickt (**at, in** in *dat*)

skilled work·er Facharbeiter(in)

skill·ful geschickt

skim *Fett etc* abschöpfen (*a.* ~ *off*); *Milch* entrahmen; (hin)gleiten über (*acc*); *a.* ~ *over*, ~ *through Bericht etc* überfliegen

skim(med) milk Magermilch *f*

skimp *a.* ~ *on* sparen an (*dat*)

skimp·y dürftig; knapp

skin 1. ANAT Haut *f*; ZO Fell *n*; BOT Schale *f* **2.** *Tier* abhäuten; *Zwiebel etc* schälen; sich *das Knie etc* aufschürfen

skin-deep (nur) oberflächlich

skin div·ing Sporttauchen *n*

skin-flint Geizhals *m*

skin·ny F dürr, mager

skin·ny-dip F nackt baden

skip 1. *v/i* hüpfen, springen; seilhüpfen, seilspringen; *v/t et.* überspringen, auslassen **2.** Hüpfer *m*

skip·per MAR, SPORT Kapitän *m*

skir·mish Geplänkel *n*

skirt 1. Rock *m* **2.** *a.* ~ (**a**)**round** umgeben; *Problem etc* umgehen

skirt·ing board *Br* Scheuerleiste *f*

ski| run Skipiste *f*; ~ **tow** Schlepplift *m*

skit·tle Kegel *m*

skulk sich herumdrücken, herumschleichen

skull ANAT Schädel *m*

skul(l)·dug·ger·y F fauler Zauber

skunk ZO Skunk *m*, Stinktier *n*

sky *a.* **skies** Himmel *m*

sky·jack *Flugzeug* entführen

sky·jack·er Flugzeugentführer(in)

sky·lark ZO Feldlerche *f*

sky·light Dachfenster *n*

sky·line Skyline *f*, Silhouette *f*

sky·rock·et F hochschnellen, in die Höhe schießen

sky·scrap·er Wolkenkratzer *m*

slab (*Stein- etc*)Platte *f*; dickes Stück

slack 1. locker; ECON flau; *fig* lax, lasch, nachlässig **2.** bummeln; ~ **off**, ~ **up** *fig* nachlassen, (*person a.*) abbauen

slack·en *v/t* lockern; verringern; ~ **speed** langsamer werden; *v/i* locker werden; *a.* ~ **off** nachlassen

slacks F Hose *f*

slag TECH Schlacke *f*

sla·lom SPORT Slalom *m*

slam 1. *a.* ~ **shut** zuschlagen, F zuknallen; *a.* ~ **down** F *et.* knallen (**on** auf *acc*); ~ **on the brakes** F MOT auf die Bremse steigen **2.** Zuschlagen *n*; Knall *m*

slan·der 1. Verleumdung *f* **2.** verleumden; **slan·der·ous** verleumderisch

slang 1. Slang *m*; Jargon *m* **2.** *esp Br* F *j-n* wüst beschimpfen

slant 1. schräg legen *or* liegen; sich neigen **2.** schräge Fläche; Abhang *m*; *fig* Einstellung *f*; **at** *or* **on a** ~ schräg

slant·ing schräg

slap 1. Klaps *m*, Schlag *m* **2.** e-n Klaps geben (*dat*); schlagen; klatschen (**down on** auf *acc*; **against** gegen)

slap·stick THEA Slapstick *m*, Klamauk *m*; ~ **com·e·dy** Slapstickkomödie *f*

slash 1. auf-, zerschlitzen; *Preise* drastisch herabsetzen; *Ausgaben etc* dras tisch kürzen; **~ at** schlagen nach **2.** Hieb *m*; Schlitz *m*

slate 1. Schiefer *m*; Schiefertafel *f*; POL Kandidatenliste *f* **2.** mit Schiefer decken; *j-n* vorschlagen (**for, to be** als); *et.* planen (**for** für)

slaugh·ter 1. Schlachten *n*; *fig* Blutbad *n*, Gemetzel *n* **2.** schlachten; *fig* niedermetzeln; **slaugh·ter·house** Schlachthaus *n*, Schlachthof *m*

Slav 1. Slawe *m*, Slawin *f* **2.** slawisch

slave 1. Sklave *m*, Sklavin *f* (*a. fig*) **2.** *a.* **~ away** sich abplagen, F schuften

slav·er geifern, sabbern

sla·ve·ry Sklaverei *f*

slav·ish sklavisch

sleaze unsaubere Machenschaften; Kumpanei *f*; F POL Filz *m*

slea·zy schäbig, heruntergekommen; anrüchig

sled 1. (*a.* Rodel)Schlitten *m* **2.** Schlitten fahren, rodeln

sledge *Br* → **sled**

sledge·ham·mer TECH Vorschlaghammer *m*

sleek 1. glatt, glänzend; geschmeidig; MOT schnittig **2.** glätten

sleep 1. Schlaf *m*; *I couldn't get to* **~** ich konnte nicht einschlafen; *go to* **~** einschlafen (F *a. leg etc*); *put to* **~** Tier einschläfern **2.** *v/i* schlafen; **~ late** lang *or* länger schlafen; **~ on** *Problem etc* überschlafen; **~ with s.o.** mit j-m schlafen; *v/t* Schlafgelegenheit bieten für

sleep·er Schlafende *m*, *f*, Schläfer(in); *Br* RAIL Schwelle *f*; RAIL Schlafwagen *m*

sleep·ing bag Schlafsack *m*

Sleep·ing Beau·ty Dornröschen *n*

sleep·ing| car RAIL Schlafwagen *m*; **~ part·ner** *Br* ECON stiller Teilhaber; **~ pill** PHARM Schlaftablette *f*, -mittel *n*; **~ sick·ness** MED Schlafkrankheit *f*

sleep·less schlaflos

sleep·walk·er Schlafwandler(in)

sleep·y schläfrig, müde; verschlafen

sleep·y·head F Schlafmütze *f*

sleet 1. Schneeregen *m*; Graupelschauer *m* **2.** *it's* **~ing** es gibt Schneeregen; es graupelt

sleeve Ärmel *m*; TECH Manschette *f*, Muffe *f*; *esp Br* (Platten)Hülle *f*

sleeve·less ärmellos

sleigh (*esp* Pferde)Schlitten *m*

sleight of hand Fingerfertigkeit *f*; *fig* (Taschenspieler)Trick *m*

slen·der schlank; *fig* mager, dürftig; schwach (*hope etc*)

slice 1. Scheibe *f*, Stück *n*; *fig* Anteil *m* (*of* an *dat*); **2.** *a.* **~ up** in Scheiben *or* Stücke schneiden; **~ off** *Stück* abschneiden (**from** von)

slick 1. gekonnt; geschickt, raffiniert; glatt (*road etc*) **2.** F (*Öl*)Teppich *m* **3.** **~ down** *Haar* glätten, F anklatschen

slick·er Regenmantel *m*

slide 1. gleiten (lassen); rutschen; schlüpfen; schieben; *let things* **~** *fig* die Dinge schleiffenlassen **2.** Gleiten *n*, Rutschen *n*; Rutsche *f*, Rutschbahn *f*; TECH Schieber *m*; PHOT Dia *n*; Objektträger *m*; (*Erd- etc*)Rutsch *m*; *Br* (*Haar*)Spange *f*; **~ rule** Rechenschieber *m*; **~ tack·le** *soccer*: Grätsche *f*

slid·ing door Schiebetür *f*

slight 1. leicht, gering(fügig), unbedeutend **2.** beleidigen, kränken **3.** Beleidigung *f*, Kränkung *f*

slim 1. schlank; *fig* gering **2.** *a.* **be slimming, be on a slimming diet** e-e Schlankheitskur machen, abnehmen

slime Schleim *m*

slim·y schleimig (*a. fig*)

sling 1. aufhängen; F schleudern **2.** Schlinge *f*; Tragriemen *m*; Tragetuch *n*; Schleuder *f*

slip¹ 1. *v/i* rutschen, schlittern; ausgleiten, ausrutschen; schlüpfen; *v/t* sich losreißen von; **~ s.th. into s.o.'s hand** j-m et. in die Hand schieben; **~ s.o. s.th.** j-m et. zuschieben; **~ s.o.'s attention** j-m *or* j-s Aufmerksamkeit entgehen; **~ s.o.'s mind** j-m entfallen; *she has* **~ped** *a disk* MED sie hat e-n Bandscheibenvorfall; **~ by, ~ past** verstreichen (*time*); **~ off, ~ out of** schlüpfen aus; **~ on** überstreifen, schlüpfen in (*acc*) **2.** Ausgleiten *n*, (Aus)Rutschen *n*; Versehen *n*; Unterrock *m*; (*Kissen*)Bezug *m*; **~ of the tongue** Versprecher *m*; *give s.o. the* **~** F j-m entwischen

slip² *a.* **~ of paper** Zettel *m*

slip-case Schuber *m*

slip-on 1. *adj* **~ shoe** → **2.** Slipper *m*

slipped disk MED Bandscheibenvorfall *m*

slip·per Hausschuh *m*, Pantoffel *m*

slip·per·y glatt, rutschig, glitschig

slip road *Br* MOT → **ramp**

S

slip·shod schlampig

slit 1. Schlitz *m* 2. schlitzen; **~ open** aufschlitzen

slith·er gleiten, rutschen

sliv·er (*Glas- etc*) Splitter *m*

slob·ber sabbern

slo·gan Slogan *m*

sloop MAR Schaluppe *f*

slop 1. *v/t* verschütten; *v/i* überschwappen; schwappen (**over** über *acc*); 2. *a. pl* schlabb(e)riges Zeug; (*Tee-, Kaffee-*) Rest(-e *pl*) *m*; *esp Br* Schmutzwasser *n*

slope 1. (Ab)Hang *m*; Neigung *f*, Gefälle *n* 2. sich neigen, abfallen

slop·py schlampig; F gammelig; F rührselig

slot Schlitz *m*, (Münz)Einwurf *m*; IT Steckplatz *m*

sloth ZO Faultier *n*

slot ma·chine (Waren-, Spiel)Automat *m*

slouch 1. krumme Haltung; F latschiger Gang 2. krumm dasitzen *or* dastehen; F latschen

slough¹: **~ off** *Haut* abstreifen, ZO sich häuten

slough² Sumpf *m*, Sumpfloch *n*

Slo·vak 1. slowakisch 2. Slowake *m*, Slowakin *f*; LING Slowakisch *n*

Slo·va·ki·a Slowakei *f*

slov·en·ly schlampig

slow 1. *adj* langsam; begriffsstutzig; ECON schleppend; **be (ten minutes) ~** (zehn Minuten) nachgehen 2. *adv* langsam 3. *v/t often* **~ down, ~ up** *Geschwindigkeit* verringern; *v/i often* **~ down, ~ up** langsamer fahren *or* gehen *or* werden

slow·coach *Br* → **slowpoke**

slow·down ECON Bummelstreik *m*

slow lane MOT Kriechspur *f*

slow mo·tion Zeitlupe *f*

slow-mov·ing kriechend (*traffic*)

slow·poke Langweiler(in)

slow·worm ZO Blindschleiche *f*

sludge Schlamm *m*

slug¹ ZO Nacktschnecke *f*

slug²F (*Gewehr- etc*) Kugel *f*; Schluck *m* (*whisky etc*)

slug³F *j-m* e-n Faustschlag versetzen

slug·gish träge; ECON schleppend

sluice TECH Schleuse *f*

slum *a. pl* Slums *pl*, Elendsviertel *n or pl*

slum·ber POET 1. schlummern 2. *a. pl*

Schlummer *m*

slump 1. ECON stürzen (*prices*), stark zurückgehen (*sales etc*); **sit ~ed over** zusammengesunken sitzen über (*dat*); **~ into a chair** sich in e-n Sessel fallen lassen 2. ECON starker Konjunkturrückgang; **~ in prices** Preissturz *m*

slur¹ 1. MUS *Töne* binden; **~ one's speech** undeutlich sprechen; lallen 2. undeutliche Aussprache

slur² 1. verleumden 2. **~ on s.o.'s reputation** Rufschädigung *f*

slurp F schlürfen

slush Schneematsch *m*; F Kitsch *m*

slush·y F kitschig

slut Schlampe *f*; Nutte *f*

sly gerissen, schlau, listig; **on the ~** heimlich

smack¹ 1. *j-m* e-n Klaps geben; **~ one's lips** sich (geräuschvoll) die Lippen lecken; **~ down** F et. hinklatschen 2. klatschendes Geräusch, Knall *m*; F Schmatz *m* (*kiss*); F Klaps *m*

smack² **~ of** *fig* schmecken *or* riechen nach

small 1. *adj and adv* klein; **~ wonder** (**that**) kein Wunder, dass; **feel ~** *fig* sich klein (und hässlich) vorkommen 2. **~ of the back** ANAT Kreuz *n*; **~ ad** Kleinanzeige *f*; **~ arms** Handfeuerwaffen *pl*; **~ change** Kleingeld *n*; **~ hours: in the ~** in den frühen Morgenstunden

small-mind·ed engstirnig; kleinlich

small·pox MED Pocken *pl*

small print *das* Kleingedruckte

small talk Small Talk *m, n*, oberflächliche Konversation; **make ~** plaudern

small-time F klein, unbedeutend; *in cpds* Schmalspur…

small town Kleinstadt *f*

smart 1. schick, fesch; smart, schlau, clever 2. wehtun; brennen 3. (brennender) Schmerz; **~ al·eck** F Besserwisser(in), Klugscheißer(in)

smart·ness Schick *m*; Schlauheit *f*, Cleverness *f*

smash 1. *v/t* zerschlagen (*a.* **~ up**); schmettern (*a. tennis etc*); *Aufstand etc* niederschlagen, *Drogenring etc* zerschlagen; **~ up one's car** s-n Wagen zu Schrott fahren; *v/i* zerspringen; **~ into** prallen an (*acc*) *or* gegen, krachen gegen 2. Schlag *m*; *tennis etc*: Schmetterball *m*; → **smash hit, smash-up**

smash hit Hit *m*

smash-up MOT, RAIL schwerer Unfall

smear 1. Fleck *m*; MED Abstrich *m*; Verleumdung *f* **2.** (ein-, ver)schmieren; (sich) verwischen; verleumden

smell 1. *v/i* riechen (*at* an *dat*); duften; stinken; *v/t* riechen (an *dat*); **2.** Geruch *m*; Gestank *m*; Duft *m*

smell·y übel riechend, stinkend

smelt *Erz* schmelzen

smile 1. Lächeln *n* **2.** lächeln; *~ at j-n* anlächeln, *j-m* zulächeln; *j-n, et.* belächeln, lächeln über (*acc*); *~* **to o.s.** schmunzeln

smiley Smiley *n*

smirk (selbstgefällig *or* schadenfroh) grinsen

smith Schmied *m*

smith·e·reens: smash (in)to ~ F in tausend Stücke schlagen *or* zerspringen

smith·y Schmiede *f*

smit·ten verliebt, F verknallt (**with** in *acc*); *be~by or with fig* gepackt werden von

smock Kittel *m*

smog Smog *m*

smoke 1. Rauch *m*; *have a ~* eine rauchen **2.** rauchen; räuchern

smok·er Raucher(in); RAIL Raucher *m*, Raucherabteil *n*

smoke-stack Schornstein *m*

smok·ing Rauchen *n*; *no ~* Rauchen verboten; *~* **com·part·ment** RAIL Raucher *m*, Raucherabteil *n*

smok·y rauchig; verräuchert

smooch F schmusen

smooth 1. glatt (*a. fig*); ruhig (*a. journey etc*); mild (*wine*); *fig* (aal)glatt **2.** *a. ~ out* glätten, glatt streichen; *~away Falten etc* glätten; *Schwierigkeiten etc* aus dem Weg räumen; *~ down* glatt streichen

smoth·er ersticken

smo(u)l·der glimmen, schwelen

smudge 1. Schmutzfleck *m* **2.** (be-, ver)schmieren; (sich) verwischen

smug selbstgefällig

smug·gle schmuggeln (*into* nach; in *acc*); **smug·gler** Schmuggler(in)

smut Rußflocke *f*; Schmutz *m* (*a. fig*)

smut·ty *fig* schmutzig

snack Snack *m*, Imbiss *m*; *have a ~* e-e Kleinigkeit essen

snack bar Snackbar *f*, Imbissstube *f*

snag 1. *fig* Haken *m* **2.** mit *et.* hängen bleiben (*on* an *dat*)

snail ZO Schnecke *f*

snake ZO Schlange *f*

snap 1. *v/i* (zer)brechen, (zer)reißen; *a. ~ shut* zuschnappen; *~ at* schnappen nach; *j-n* anschnauzen; *~ out of it!* F Kopf hoch!, komm, komm!; *~ to it!* mach fix!; *v/t* zerbrechen; PHOT F knipsen; *~ one's fingers* mit den Fingern schnalzen; *~ one's fingers at fig* keinen Respekt haben vor (*dat*), sich hinwegsetzen über (*acc*); *~ off* abbrechen; *~ up et.* schnell entschlossen kaufen; *~ it up!* mach fix! **2.** Krachen *n*, Knacken *n*, Knall *m*; PHOT F Schnappschuss *m*; Druckknopf *m*; F Schwung *m*; *cold ~* Kälteeinbruch *m*

snap fas·ten·er Druckknopf *m*

snap·pish *fig* bissig

snap·py modisch, schick; *make it ~!* F mach fix!

snap·shot PHOT Schnappschuss *m*

snare 1. Schlinge *f*, Falle *f* (*a. fig*) **2.** in der Schlinge fangen; F *et.* ergattern

snarl 1. knurren; *~ at s.o.* j-n anknurren **2.** Knurren *n*

snatch 1. *v/t et.* packen; *Gelegenheit* ergreifen; *ein paar Stunden Schlaf etc* ergattern; *~ s.o.'s handbag* j-m die Handtasche entreißen; *v/i ~ at* (schnell) greifen nach; *Gelegenheit* ergreifen **2.** *make a ~ at* (schnell) greifen nach; *~ of conversation* Gesprächsfetzen *m*

sneak 1. *v/i* (sich) schleichen; *Br* F petzen; *v/t* F stibitzen **2.** *Br* F Petze *f*

sneak·er Turnschuh *m*

sneer 1. höhnisch *or* spöttisch grinsen (*at* über *acc*); spotten (*at* über *acc*); **2.** höhnisches *or* spöttisches Grinsen; höhnische *or* spöttische Bemerkung

sneeze 1. niesen **2.** Niesen *n*

snick·er kichern (*at* über *acc*)

sniff 1. *v/i* schniefen; schnüffeln (*at* an *dat*); *~ at fig* die Nase rümpfen über (*acc*); *v/t Klebstoff etc* schnüffeln, *Kokain etc* schnupfen **2.** Schniefen *n*

snif·fle 1. schniefen **2.** Schniefen *n*; *she's got the ~s* F ihr läuft dauernd die Nase

snig·ger *esp Br* → **snicker**

snip 1. Schnitt *m* **2.** durchschnippeln; *~ off* abschnippeln snipe¹ ZO Schnepfe f

snipe² aus dem Hinterhalt schießen (**at** auf acc)

snip·er Heckenschütze m

sniv·el greinen, jammern

snob Snob m; snob·bish versnobt

snoop: ~ **about**, ~ **around** F herumschnüffeln

snoop·er F Schnüffler(in)

snooze F **1.** ein Nickerchen machen **2.** Nickerchen n

snore **1.** schnarchen **2.** Schnarchen n

snor·kel **1.** Schnorchel m **2.** schnorcheln

snort **1.** schnauben **2.** Schnauben n

snot·ty nose F Rotznase f

snout ZO Schnauze f, Rüssel m

snow **1.** Schnee m (a. sl cocaine) **2.** schneien; **be ~ed in** or **up** eingeschneit sein

snow·ball Schneeball m; ~ **fight** Schneeballschlacht f

snow·board Snowboard n; ~**ing** Snowboardfahren n

snow·bound eingeschneit

snow·capped schneebedeckt

snow·drift Schneewehe f

snow·drop BOT Schneeglöckchen n

snow·fall Schneefall m

snow·flake Schneeflocke f

snow line Schneegrenze f

snow·man Schneemann m

snow·mo·bile Schneemobil n

snow·plough Br, snow·plow Schneepflug m

snow·storm Schneesturm m

snow-white schneeweiß

Snow White Schneewittchen n

snow·y schneereich; verschneit

snub j-n brüskieren; j-n vor den Kopf stoßen

snub nose Stupsnase f

snuff¹ Schnupftabak m

snuff² Kerze ausdrücken, löschen; ~ **out** Leben auslöschen

snuf·fle schnüffeln, schniefen

snug gemütlich, behaglich; clothing: gut sitzend; eng (anliegend)

snug·gle: ~ **up to s.o.** sich an j-n kuscheln; ~ **down in bed** sich ins Bett kuscheln

so so; deshalb; → **hope** 2, **think**; **is that ~?** wirklich?; **an hour or ~** etwa e-e Stunde; **she is tired ~ am I** sie ist müde - ich auch; ~ **far** bisher

soak v/t einweichen (**in** in dat); durchnässen; ~ **up** aufsaugen; v/i sickern

soak·ing a. ~ **wet** völlig durchnässt, F klatschnass

soap **1.** Seife f; F → **soap opera 2.** (sich) einseifen

soap op·e·ra radio, TV Seifenoper f

soap·y Seifen...; seifig; fig F schmeichlerisch

soar (hoch)aufsteigen; hochragen; ZO, AVIAT segeln, gleiten; fig in die Höhe schnellen (prices etc)

sob **1.** schluchzen **2.** Schluchzen n

so·ber **1.** nüchtern (a. fig) **2.** ernüchtern; ~ **up** nüchtern machen or werden

so-called sogenannt

soc·cer Fußball m

soc·cer hoo·li·gan Fußballrowdy m

so·cia·ble gesellig

so·cial sozial, Sozial...; gesellschaftlich, Gesellschafts...; ZO gesellig; ~ **dem·ocrat** POL Sozialdemokrat(in); ~ **insurance** Sozialversicherung f

so·cial·ism Sozialismus m

so·cial·ist **1.** Sozialist(in) **2.** sozialistisch

so·cial·ize v/i gesellschaftlich verkehren (**with** mit); v/t sozialisieren

so·cial| sci·ence Sozialwissenschaft f; ~ **se·cu·ri·ty** Br Sozialhilfe f; **be on** ~ Sozialhilfe beziehen; ~ **ser·vic·es** esp Br Sozialeinrichtungen; ~ **work** Sozialarbeit f; ~ **work·er** Sozialarbeiter(in)

so·ci·e·ty Gesellschaft f; Verein m

so·ci·ol·o·gy Soziologie f

sock Socke f

sock·et ELECTR Steckdose f; Fassung f; (Anschluss)Buchse f; ANAT (Augen-) Höhle f

so·da Soda(wasser) n; (Orangen- etc)Limonade f

sod·den aufgeweicht (ground); durchweicht (clothes)

so·fa Sofa n

soft weich; sanft; leise; gedämpft (light etc); F leicht, angenehm, ruhig (job etc); alkoholfrei (drink); F verweichlicht

soft drink Soft Drink m, alkoholfreies Getränk

soft·en v/t weich machen; Wasser enthärten; Ton, Licht, Stimme etc dämpfen; ~ **up** F j-n weich machen; v/i weich(er) or sanft(er) or mild(er) werden

soft·heart·ed weichherzig

soft land·ing weiche Landung

soft·ware IT Software *f*; ~ **pack·age** IT Softwarepaket *n*

soft·y F Softie *m*, Weichling *m*

sog·gy aufgeweicht, matschig

soil[1] Boden *m*, Erde *f*

soil[2] beschmutzen, schmutzig machen

so·lar Sonnen…;~ **en·er·gy** Solar-, Sonnenenergie *f*;~ **pan·el** Sonnenkollektor *m*;~ **sys·tem** Sonnensystem *n*

sol·der TECH (ver)löten

sol·dier Soldat *m*

sole[1] **1.** (Fuß-, Schuh)Sohle *f* **2.** besohlen

sole[2] ZO Seezunge *f*

sole[3] einzig; alleinig, Allein…

sole·ly (einzig und) allein, ausschließlich

sol·emn feierlich; ernst

so·lic·it bitten um

so·lic·i·tous besorgt (*about, for* um)

sol·id 1. fest; stabil; massiv; MATH körperlich; gewichtig, triftig (*reason etc*); stichhaltig (*argument etc*); solid(e), gründlich (*work etc*); einmütig, geschlossen; *a* ~ *hour* F e-e geschlagene Stunde **2.** MATH Körper *m*; *pl* feste Nahrung

sol·i·dar·i·ty Solidarität *f*

so·lid·i·fy fest werden (lassen); *fig* (sich) festigen

so·lil·o·quy Selbstgespräch *n*, *esp* THEA Monolog *m*

sol·i·taire Solitär *m*; Patience *f*

sol·i·ta·ry einsam, (*Leben a.*) zurückgezogen, (*Ort etc a.*) abgelegen; einzig; ~ **con·fine·ment** JUR Einzelhaft *f*

so·lo MUS Solo *n*; AVIAT Alleinflug *m*

so·lo·ist MUS Solist(in)

sol·u·ble CHEM löslich; *fig* lösbar

so·lu·tion CHEM Lösung *f*; *fig* (Auf)Lösung *f*

solve *Fall etc* lösen

sol·vent 1. ECON zahlungsfähig **2.** CHEM Lösungsmittel *n*

som·ber, *Br* **som·bre** düster, trüb(e); *fig* trübsinnig

some (irgend)ein; *pl* einige, ein paar; manche; etwas, ein wenig, ein bisschen; ungefähr; ~ *20 miles* etwa 20 Meilen; ~ *more cake* noch ein Stück Kuchen; *to* ~ *extent* bis zu e-m gewissen Grade

some·bod·y jemand

some·day eines Tages

some·how irgendwie

some·one jemand

some·place irgendwo, irgendwohin

som·er·sault 1. Salto *m*; Purzelbaum *m*; *turn a* ~ → **2.** e-n Salto machen; e-n Purzelbaum schlagen

some·thing etwas; ~ *like* ungefähr

some·time irgendwann

some·times manchmal

some·what ein bisschen, ein wenig

some·where irgendwo(hin)

son Sohn *m*; ~ *of a bitch* V Scheißkerl *m*

so·na·ta MUS Sonate *f*

song MUS Lied *n*; Gesang *m*

song·bird ZO Singvogel *m*

son·ic Schall…; ~ *bang* *Br*, ~ *boom* Überschallknall *m*

son-in-law Schwiegersohn *m*

son·net Sonett *n*

so·no·rous sonor, volltönend

soon bald; *as* ~ *as* sobald; *as* ~ *as possible* so bald wie möglich

soon·er eher, früher; ~ *or later* früher oder später; *the* ~ *the better* je eher, desto besser; *no* ~ *… than* kaum … als; *no* ~ *said than done* gesagt, getan

soot Ruß *m*

soothe beruhigen, beschwichtigen (*a.* ~ *down*); *Schmerzen* lindern, mildern

sooth·ing beruhigend; lindernd

soot·y rußig

sop[1] Beschwichtigungsmittel *n* (*to* für)

sop[2]: ~ *up* aufsaugen

so·phis·ti·cat·ed anspruchsvoll, kultiviert; intellektuell; TECH raffiniert, hoch entwickelt

soph·o·more Student(in) im zweiten Jahr

sop·o·rif·ic einschläfernd

sop·ping *a.* ~ *wet* F klatschnass

sor·cer·er Zauberer *m*, Hexenmeister *m*, Hexer *m*

sor·cer·ess Zauberin *f*, Hexe *f*

sor·cer·y Zauberei *f*, Hexerei *f*

sor·did schmutzig; schäbig

sore 1. weh, wund (*a. fig*); entzündet; F *fig* sauer; *I'm* ~ *all over* mir tut alles weh; ~ *throat* Halsentzündung *f*; *have a* ~ *throat a.* Halsschmerzen haben **2.** wunde Stelle, Wunde *f*

sor·rel[1] BOT Sauerampfer *m*

sor·rel[2] **1.** ZO Fuchs *m* (*horse*) **2.** rotbraun

sor·row Kummer *m*, Leid *n*, Schmerz *m*, Trauer *f*

sor·row·ful traurig, betrübt

sor·ry **1.** *adj* traurig, jämmerlich; *be or feel ~ for s.o.* j-n bedauern *or* bemitleiden; *I'm ~ for her* sie tut mir leid; *I am ~ to say* ich muss leider sagen; *I'm ~* → **2.** *int* (es) tut mir leid!; Entschuldigung!, Verzeihung!; *~? esp Br* wie bitte?

sort **1.** Sorte *f*, Art *f*; ~ *of* F irgendwie (*of a ~, of ~s* F so etwas Ähnliches wie; *all ~s of things* alles Mögliche; *nothing of the ~* nichts dergleichen; *what ~ of (a) man is he?* wie ist er?; *be out of ~s* F nicht auf der Höhe *or* auf dem Damm sein; *be completely out of ~s* SPORT F völlig außer Form sein **2.** sortieren; *~ out* aussortieren; *Problem etc* lösen, *Frage etc* klären

SOS SOS *n*; *send an ~* ein SOS funken; *~ call or message* SOS-Ruf *m*

soul Seele *f* (*a. fig*); MUS Soul *m*

sound¹ **1.** Geräusch *n*; Laut *m*; PHYS Schall *m*; *radio*, TV Ton *m*; MUS Klang *m*, Sound *m* **2.** *v/i* (er)klingen, (er)tönen; *sich gut etc* anhören; *v/t* LING (aus)-sprechen; MAR (aus)loten; MED abhorchen; *~ one's horn* MOT hupen

sound² gesund; intakt, in Ordnung; solid(e), stabil, sicher; klug, vernünftig (*person, advice etc*); gründlich (*training etc*); gehörig (*beating*); vernichtend (*defeat*); fest, tief (*sleep*)

sound| bar·ri·er Schallgrenze *f*, Schallmauer *f*; *~ film* Tonfilm *m*

sound·less lautlos

sound·proof schalldicht

sound·track Filmmusik *f*; Tonspur *f*

sound wave Schallwelle *f*

soup **1.** Suppe *f* **2.** *~ up* F *Motor* frisieren

sour **1.** sauer; *fig* mürrisch **2.** sauer werden (lassen); *fig* trüben, verbittern

source Quelle *f*, *fig a.* Ursache *f*, Ursprung *m*

south **1.** Süd, Süden *m* **2.** *adj* südlich, Süd… **3.** *adv* nach Süden, südwärts

south·east **1.** Südost, Südosten *m* **2.** *a.* south·east·ern südöstlich

south·er·ly, south·ern südlich, Süd…

south·ern·most südlichste(r, -s)

South Pole Südpol *m*

south·ward(s) südlich, nach Süden

south·west **1.** Südwest, Südwesten *m* **2.** *a.* south·west·ern südwestlich

sou·ve·nir Souvenir *n*, Andenken *n* (*of* an *acc*)

sove·reign **1.** Monarch(in), Landesherr(in) **2.** POL souverän

sove·reign·ty Souveränität *f*

So·vi·et HIST POL sowjetisch, Sowjet…

sow¹ (aus)säen

sow² ZO Sau *f*

soy bean BOT Sojabohne *f*

spa (Heil)Bad *n*

space **1.** Raum *m*, Platz *m*; (Welt)-Raum *m*; Zwischenraum *m*; Zeitraum *m* **2.** *a. ~ out* in Abständen anordnen; PRINT sperren

space age Weltraumzeitalter *n*

space bar TECH Leertaste *f*

space cap·sule Raumkapsel *f*

space cen·ter (*Br* cen·tre) Raumfahrtzentrum *n*

space·craft (Welt)Raumfahrzeug *n*

space flight (Welt)Raumflug *m*

space·lab Raumlabor *n*

space·man F Raumfahrer *m*; Außerirdische *m*

space probe (Welt)Raumsonde *f*

space re·search (Welt)Raumforschung *f*

space·ship Raumschiff *n*

space shut·tle Raumfähre *f*, Raumtransporter *m*

space sta·tion (Welt)Raumstation *f*

space·suit Raumanzug *m*

space walk Weltraumspaziergang *m*

space·wom·an F (Welt)Raumfahrerin *f*; Außerirdische *f*

spa·cious geräumig

spade Spaten *m*; *card game*: Pik *n*, Grün *n*; *king of ~s* Pikkönig *m*; *call a ~ a ~* das Kind beim (rechten) Namen nennen

Spain Spanien *n*

span **1.** Spanne *f*; Spannweite *f* **2.** *Fluss etc* überspannen; *fig* sich erstrecken über (*acc*)

span·gle **1.** Flitter *m*, Paillette *f* **2.** mit Flitter *or* Pailletten besetzen; *fig* übersäen (*with* mit)

Span·iard Spanier(in)

span·iel ZO Spaniel *m*

Span·ish **1.** spanisch **2.** LING Spanisch *n*; *the ~* die Spanier *pl*

spank j-m den Hintern versohlen

spank·ing Tracht *f* Prügel

span·ner *esp Br* Schraubenschlüssel *m*; *put or throw a ~ in the works* F j-m in die Quere kommen

spar *boxing*: sparren (**with** mit); *fig* sich ein Wortgefecht liefern (**with** mit)

spare **1.** *j-n, et.* entbehren; *Geld, Zeit etc* übrig haben; *keine Kosten, Mühen etc* scheuen; **~ s.o. s.th.** j-m et. ersparen **2.** Ersatz..., Reserve...; überschüssig **3.** MOT Ersatz-, Reservereifen *m*; *esp Br* → **~ part** TECH Ersatzteil *n, m*

spare room Gästezimmer *n*

spare time Freizeit *f*

spar·ing sparsam; *use ~ly* sparsam umgehen mit

spark **1.** Funke(n) *m* (*a. fig*) **2.** Funken sprühen

spark·ing plug *Br* → **spark plug**

spar·kle **1.** funkeln, blitzen (**with** vor *dat*); perlen (*drink*) **2.** Funkeln *n*, Blitzen *n*; spar·kling funkelnd, blitzend; (geist)sprühend, spritzig; **~ wine** Sekt *m*, Schaumwein *m*

spark plug MOT Zündkerze *f*

spar·row ZO Spatz *m*, Sperling *m*

spar·row·hawk ZO Sperber *m*

sparse spärlich, dünn

spasm MED Krampf *m*; Anfall *m*

spas·mod·ic MED krampfartig; *fig* sporadisch, unregelmäßig

spas·tic MED **1.** spastisch **2.** Spastiker(in)

spa·tial räumlich

spat·ter (be)spritzen

spawn **1.** ZO laichen; *fig* hervorbringen **2.** ZO Laich *m*

speak *v/i* sprechen, reden (**to, with** mit; **about** über *acc*); sprechen (**to** vor *dat*; **about, on** über *acc*); **so to ~** sozusagen; **speaking!** TEL am Apparat!; **~ up** lauter sprechen; *v/t* sprechen, sagen; *Sprache* sprechen

speak·er Sprecher(in), Redner(in)

spear **1.** Speer *m* **2.** aufspießen; durchbohren

spear·head Speerspitze *f*; MIL Angriffsspitze *f*; SPORT (Sturm-, Angriffs)Spitze *f*

spear·mint BOT Grüne Minze

spe·cial **1.** besondere(r, -s); speziell; Sonder...; Spezial... **2.** Sonderbus *m*, Sonderzug *m*; *radio, TV* Sondersendung *f*; ECON F Sonderangebot *n*; **be on ~** ECON im Angebot sein

spe·cial·ist Spezialist(in), MED a. Facharzt *m*, Fachärztin *f* (**in** für)

spe·ci·al·i·ty *Br* → **specialty**

spe·cial·ize sich spezialisieren (**in** auf *acc*)

spe·cial·ty Spezialgebiet *n*; GASTR Spezialität *f*

spe·cies Art *f*, Spezies *f*

spe·cif·ic konkret, präzis; spezifisch, speziell, besondere(r, -s); eigen (**to** *dat*)

spe·ci·fy genau beschreiben *or* angeben *or* festlegen

spe·ci·men Exemplar *n*; Probe *f*, Muster *n*

speck kleiner Fleck, (*Staub*)Korn *n*; Punkt *m* (**on the horizon** am Horizont)

speck·led gefleckt, gesprenkelt

spec·ta·cle Schauspiel *n*; Anblick *m*; (**a pair of**) **~s** (e-e) Brille

spec·tac·u·lar **1.** spektakulär **2.** große (*Fernseh- etc*)Show

spec·ta·tor Zuschauer(in)

spec·ter (*fig a. Schreck*)Gespenst *n*

spec·tral geisterhaft, gespenstisch

spec·tre *Br* → **specter**

spec·u·late spekulieren, Vermutungen anstellen (**about, on** über *acc*); ECON spekulieren (**in** mit); spec·u·la·tion Spekulation *f* (*a. ECON*), Vermutung *f*; spec·u·la·tive spekulativ, ECON a. Spekulations...; spec·u·la·tor ECON Spekulant(in)

speech Sprache *f*; Rede *f*, Ansprache *f*; **make a ~** e-e Rede halten

speech day *Br* PED (Jahres)Schlussfeier *f*

speech·less sprachlos (**with** vor *dat*)

speed **1.** Geschwindigkeit *f*, Tempo *n*, Schnelligkeit *f*; TECH Drehzahl *f*; PHOT Lichtempfindlichkeit *f*; *sl* Speed *n*; MOT *etc* Gang *m*; **five-speed gearbox** Fünfganggetriebe *n*; **at a ~ of** mit e-r Geschwindigkeit von; **at full** *or* **top ~** mit Höchstgeschwindigkeit **2.** *v/i* rasen; **be ~ing** MOT zu schnell fahren; **~ up** beschleunigen, schneller werden; *v/t* rasch bringen *or* befördern; **~ up** *et.* beschleunigen

speed·boat Rennboot *n*

speed·ing MOT zu schnelles Fahren, Geschwindigkeitsüberschreitung *f*

speed lim·it MOT Geschwindigkeitsbegrenzung *f*, Tempolimit *n*

speed·om·e·ter MOT Tachometer *m, f*

speed trap MOT Radarfalle *f*

speed·y schnell, (*reply etc a.*) prompt

spell **1.** *a.* **~ out** buchstabieren; (*orthographisch richtig*) schreiben

spell² Weile f; (Husten- etc)Anfall m; *for a ~* e-e Zeit lang; *a ~ of fine weather* e-e Schönwetterperiode; *hot ~* Hitzewelle f

spell³ Zauber m (a. fig)

spell·bound wie gebannt

spell·er IT Speller m, Rechtschreibsystem n; *be a good (bad) ~* in Rechtschreibung gut (schlecht) sein

spell·ing Buchstabieren n; Rechtschreibung f; Schreibung f, Schreibweise f;~ **mis·take** (Recht)Schreibfehler m

spend Geld ausgeben (*on* für); Urlaub, Zeit verbringen

spend·ing Ausgaben pl

spend·thrift Verschwender(in)

spent verbraucht

sperm BIOL Sperma n, Samen m

sphere Kugel f; fig (Einfluss- etc)Sphäre f, (Einfluss- etc)Bereich m, Gebiet n

spher·i·cal kugelförmig

spice 1. Gewürz n; fig Würze f 2. würzen

spick-and-span blitzsauber

spic·y gut gewürzt, würzig; fig pikant

spi·der ZO Spinne f

spike 1. Spitze f; Dorn m; Stachel m; SPORT Spike m, Dorn m; pl Spikes pl, Rennschuhe pl 2. aufspießen

spill 1. v/t ausschütten, verschütten; ~ **the beans** F alles ausplaudern, singen; → **milk** 1; v/i fig strömen (*out of* aus); ~ **over** überlaufen; fig übergreifen (*into* auf acc); 2. F Sturz m

spin 1. v/t drehen; Wäsche schleudern; Münze hochwerfen; Fäden, Wolle etc spinnen; ~ **out** Arbeit etc in die Länge ziehen; Geld etc strecken; v/i sich drehen; spinnen; *my head was ~ning* mir drehte sich alles; ~ **along** MOT dahinrasen; ~ **round** herumwirbeln 2. (schnelle) Drehung; SPORT Effet m; TECH Schleudern n; AVIAT Trudeln n; *be in a (flat) ~* esp Br F am Rotieren sein; *go for a ~* MOT F e-e Spritztour machen

spin·ach BOT Spinat m

spin·al ANAT Rückgrat...; ~ **col·umn** ANAT Wirbelsäule f, Rückgrat n;~ **cord**, ~ **mar·row** ANAT Rückenmark n

spin·dle Spindel f

spin-dri·er (Wäsche)Schleuder f

spin-dry Wäsche schleudern

spin-dry·er → **spin-drier**

spine ANAT Wirbelsäule f, Rückgrat n; ZO Stachel m; BOT a. Dorn m; (Buch-)

-) Rücken m

spin·ning| mill TECH Spinnerei f; ~ **top** Kreisel m; ~ **wheel** Spinnrad n

spin·ster ältere unverheiratete Frau, contp alte Jungfer, spätes Mädchen

spin·y ZO stach(e)lig, BOT a. dornig

spi·ral 1. spiralförmig, Spiral... 2. (a. ECON Preis- etc)Spirale f

spi·ral stair·case Wendeltreppe f

spire (Kirch)Turmspitze f

spir·it Geist m; Stimmung f, Einstellung f; Schwung m; Elan m; CHEM Spiritus m; mst pl Spirituosen pl

spir·it·ed energisch; erregt (debate etc)

spir·it·less temperamentlos; mutlos

spir·its Laune f, Stimmung f; *be in high ~* in Hochstimmung sein; ausgelassen or übermütig sein; *be in low ~* niedergeschlagen sein

spir·i·tu·al 1. geistig; geistlich 2. MUS Spiritual n

spit¹ 1. spucken; knistern (fire), brutzeln (meat etc); a. ~ **out** ausspucken; ~ **at s.o.** j-n anspucken; *it is ~ting (with rain)* es tröpfelt 2. Spucke f

spit² (Brat)Spieß m; GEOGR Landzunge f

spite 1. Bosheit f, Gehässigkeit f; *out of or from pure ~* aus reiner Bosheit; *in ~ of* trotz (gen) 2. j-n ärgern

spite·ful boshaft, gehässig

spit·ting im·age Ebenbild n; *she is the ~ of her mother* sie ist ihrer Mutter wie aus dem Gesicht geschnitten

spit·tle Speichel m, Spucke f

splash 1. (be)spritzen; klatschen; plan(t)schen; platschen; ~ **down** wassern 2. Klatschen n, Platschen n; Spritzer m, Spritzfleck m; esp Br GASTR Spritzer m, Schuss m

splash·down Wasserung f

splay a. ~ **out** Finger, Zehen spreizen

spleen ANAT Milz f

splen·did großartig, herrlich, prächtig

splen·do(u)r Pracht f

splice miteinander verbinden, Film etc (zusammen)kleben

splint MED Schiene f; *put in a ~*, *put in ~s* schienen

splin·ter 1. Splitter m 2. (zer)splittern; ~ **off** absplittern; fig sich abspalten (*from* von)

split 1. v/t (zer)spalten; zerreißen; a. ~ **up** aufteilen (*between* unter acc; *into* in acc); sich et. teilen; ~ **hairs** Haarspalterei treiben; **~ one's sides** F sich vor Lachen biegen; v/i sich spalten; zerreißen; sich teilen (**into** in acc); a. **~ up (with)** Schluss machen (mit), sich trennen (von) **2.** Riss m; Spalt m; Aufteilung f; fig Bruch m; fig Spaltung f

split·ting heftig, rasend (headache etc)

splut·ter stottern (a. MOT); zischen

spoil 1. v/t verderben; ruinieren; j-n verwöhnen, Kind a. verziehen; v/i verderben, schlecht werden **2.** mst pl Beute f

spoil·er MOT Spoiler m

spoil·sport F Spielverderber(in)

spoke TECH Speiche f

spokes·man Sprecher m

spokes·wom·an Sprecherin f

sponge 1. Schwamm m; Schnorrer(in); Br → **sponge cake 2.** v/t a. **~ down** (mit e-m Schwamm) abwaschen; **~ off** weg-, abwischen; **~ (up)** aufsaugen, aufwischen (**from** von); et. schnorren (**from, off, on** von, bei); v/i schnorren (**from, off, on** bei)

sponge cake Biskuitkuchen m

spong·er Schnorrer(in)

spong·y schwammig; weich

spon·sor 1. Bürge m, Bürgin f; Sponsor(in), Geldgeber(in); Spender(in) **2.** bürgen für; sponsern

spon·ta·ne·ous spontan

spook F Geist m

spook·y F gespenstisch, unheimlich

spool Spule f; **~ of thread** Garnrolle f

spoon 1. Löffel m **2.** löffeln

spoon-feed Kind etc füttern

spoon·ful (ein) Löffel (voll)

spo·rad·ic sporadisch, gelegentlich

spore BOT Spore f

sport 1. Sport m; Sportart f; F feiner Kerl; pl Sport m **2.** herumlaufen mit; protzen mit

sports Sport...; **~ car** MOT Sportwagen m; **~ cen·ter** (Br cen·tre) Sportzentrum n

sports·man Sportler m

sports·wear Sportkleidung f

sports·wom·an Sportlerin f

spot 1. Punkt m, Tupfen m; Fleck m; MED Pickel m; Ort m, Platz m, Stelle f; radio, TV (Werbe)Spot m; F Spot m; **a ~ of** Br F ein bisschen; **on the ~** auf der Stelle, sofort; zur Stelle; an Ort und Stelle, vor Ort; auf der Stelle; **soft~** fig Schwäche f (**for** für); **tender~**

empfindliche Stelle; **weak~** schwacher Punkt; Schwäche f **2.** entdecken, sehen

spot check Stichprobe f

spot·less tadellos sauber; fig untad(e)lig

spot·light Spotlight n, Scheinwerfer m; Scheinwerferlicht n

spot·ted getüpfelt; fleckig

spot·ter Beobachter m

spot·ty pick(e)lig

spouse Gatte m, Gattin f, Gemahl(in)

spout 1. v/t Wasser etc (heraus)spritzen; v/i spritzen (**from** aus); **2.** Schnauze f, Tülle f; (Wasser- etc)Strahl m

sprain MED **1.** sich et. verstauchen **2.** Verstauchung f

sprat ZO Sprotte f

sprawl ausgestreckt liegen or sitzen (a. **~ out**); sich ausbreiten

spray 1. (be)sprühen; spritzen; sich die Haare sprayen; Parfüm etc versprühen, zerstäuben **2.** Sprühnebel m; Gischt m, f; Spray m, n; → **sprayer**

spray can → **spray·er** Sprüh-, Spraydose f, Zerstäuber m

spread 1. v/t ausbreiten, Arme a. ausstrecken, Finger etc spreizen (all a. **~ out**); Furcht, Krankheit, Nachricht etc verbreiten, Gerücht a. ausstreuen; Butter etc streichen (**on** auf acc); Brot etc (be)streichen (**with** mit); v/i sich ausbreiten (a. **~ out**); sich erstrecken (**over** über acc); sich verbreiten, übergreifen (**to** auf acc); sich streichen lassen (butter etc) **2.** Ausbreitung f, Verbreitung f; Ausdehnung f; Spannweite f; GASTR Aufstrich m

spread·sheet IT Tabellenkalkulation f, Tabellenkalkulationsprogramm n

spree: **go(out)on a ~** F e-e Saoftour machen; **go on a buying** (or **shopping, spending**) **~** wie verrückt einkaufen

sprig BOT kleiner Zweig

spright·ly lebhaft; rüstig

spring 1. v/i springen; **~ from** herrühren von; **~ up** aufkommen (wind); aus dem Boden schießen (building etc); v/t: **~ a leak** ein Leck bekommen; **~ a surprise on s.o.** j-n überraschen **2.** Frühling m, Frühjahr n; Quelle f; TECH Feder f; Elastizität f; Federung f; Sprung m, Satz m; **in (the)** ~ im Frühling

spring·board Sprungbrett n

spring-clean gründlich putzen, Früh-

jahrsputz machen (in *dat*)
spring tide Springflut *f*
spring-time Frühling *m*, Frühlingszeit *f*, Frühjahr *n*
spring-y elastisch, federnd
sprin-kle 1. *Wasser etc* sprengen (**on** auf *acc*); *Salz etc* streuen (**on** auf *acc*); *et.* (be)sprengen *or* bestreuen (**with** mit); *it is sprinkling* es tröpfelt **2.** Sprühregen *m*
sprin-kler (*Rasen*)Sprenger *m*; Sprinkler *m*, Berieselungsanlage *f*
sprin-kling: *a* ~ *of* ein bisschen, ein paar
sprint SPORT **1.** sprinten; spurten **2.** Sprint *m*; Spurt *m*
sprint-er SPORT Sprinter(in)
sprite Kobold *m*
sprout BOT **1.** sprießen (*a. fig*), keimen; wachsen lassen **2.** Spross *m*; (*Brussels*) ~**s** Rosenkohl *m*
spruce[1] BOT Fichte *f*; Rottanne *f*
spruce[2] adrett
spry rüstig, lebhaft
spur 1. Sporn *m* (*a.* zo); *fig* Ansporn *m* (**to** zu); *on the* ~ *of the moment* spontan **2.** *e-m Pferd* die Sporen geben; *often* ~ *on fig* anspornen (**to** zu)
spurt[1] **1.** spurten, sprinten **2.** plötzliche Aktivität, (*Arbeits*)Anfall *m*; Spurt *m*, Sprint *m*
spurt[2] **1.** spritzen (**from** aus); **2.** (*Wasser etc*)Strahl *m*
sput-ter stottern (*a.* MOT); zischen
spy 1. Spion(in) **2.** spionieren, Spionage treiben (**for** für); ~ *into fig* herumspionieren in (*dat*); ~ *on* j-m nachspionieren
spy-hole (Tür)Spion *m*
squab-ble (sich) streiten (**about, over** um, wegen)
squad Mannschaft *f*, Trupp *m*; (*Überfall- etc*)Kommando *n*; Dezernat *n*
squad car (Funk)Streifenwagen *m*
squad-ron MIL, AVIAT Staffel *f*; MAR Geschwader *n*
squal-id schmutzig, verwahrlost, verkommen, armselig
squall Bö *f*
squan-der *Geld, Zeit etc* verschwenden, *Chance* vertun
square 1. Quadrat *n*; Viereck *n*; *öffentlicher* Platz; MATH Quadrat(zahl *f*) *n*; *board game:* Feld *n*; TECH Winkel(maß *n*) *m* **2.** quadratisch, Quadrat...; vier-

eckig; rechtwink(e)lig; eckig (*shoulders etc*); *fig* fair, gerecht; *be* (*all*) ~ quitt sein **3.** quadratisch *or* rechtwink(e)lig machen (*a.* ~ *off or up*); in Quadrate einteilen (*a.* ~ *off*); MATH *Zahl* ins Quadrat erheben; *Schultern* straffen; *Konto* ausgleichen; *Schulden* begleichen; *fig* in Einklang bringen *or* stehen (**with** mit); ~ *up* F abrechnen; ~ *up to* sich j-m, e-m *Problem etc* stellen
square root MATH Quadratwurzel *f*
squash[1] **1.** zerdrücken, zerquetschen; quetschen, zwängen (**into** in *acc*); ~ *flat* flach drücken, F platt walzen **2.** Gedränge *n*; SPORT Squash *n*
squash[2] BOT Kürbis *m*
squat 1. hocken, kauern; *leer stehendes Haus* besetzen; ~ *down* sich (hin)kauern *or* (hin)hocken **2.** gedrungen, untersetzt; **squat-ter** Hausbesetzer(in)
squaw Squaw *f*
squawk kreischen, schreien; F lautstark protestieren (**about** gegen)
squeak 1. piep(s)en (*mouse etc*); quietschen (*door etc*) **2.** Piep(s)en *n*; Piep(s) *m*; Quietschen *n*; **squeak-y** piepsig (*voice*); quietschend (*door etc*)
squeal 1. kreischen (**with** vor *dat*); ~ *on s.o. fig* F j-n verpfeifen **2.** Kreischen *n*; Schrei *m*
squeam-ish empfindlich, zart besaitet
squeeze 1. drücken; auspressen, ausquetschen; (sich) quetschen *or* zwängen (**into** in *acc*); **2.** Druck *m*; GASTR Spritzer *m*; Gedränge *n*
squeez-er (*Frucht*)Presse *f*
squid ZO Tintenfisch *m*
squint schielen; blinzeln
squirm sich winden
squir-rel ZO Eichhörnchen *n*
squirt 1. (be)spritzen **2.** Strahl *m*
stab 1. *v/t* niederstechen; *be ~bed in the arm* e-n Stich in den Arm bekommen; *v/i* stechen (**at** nach); **2.** Stich *m*
sta-bil-i-ty Stabilität *f*; *fig* Dauerhaftigkeit *f*; Ausgeglichenheit *f*
sta-bil-ize (sich) stabilisieren
sta-ble[1] stabil; *fig* dauerhaft; ausgeglichen
sta-ble[2] Stall *m*
stack 1. Stapel *m*, Stoß *m*; ~*s of*, *a* ~ *of* F jede Menge *Arbeit etc* **2.** stapeln; voll stapeln (**with** mit); ~ *up* aufstapeln
sta-di-um SPORT Stadion *n*

staff 1. Stab *m*; Mitarbeiter(stab *m*) *pl*; Personal *n*, Belegschaft *f*; Lehrkörper *m*; MIL Stab *m* **2.** besetzen (**with** mit)

staff room Lehrerzimmer *n*

stag ZO Hirsch *m*

stage 1. THEA Bühne *f* (*a. fig*); Etappe *f* (*a. fig*), (Reise)Abschnitt *m*; Teilstrecke *f*, Fahrzone *f* (*bus etc*); *fig* Stufe *f*, Stadium *n*, Phase *f* **2.** THEA inszenieren; veranstalten

stage-coach Postkutsche *f*

stage|di·rec·tion THEA Regieanweisung *f*; ~ **fright** Lampenfieber *n*; ~ **man·ag·er** THEA Inspizient *m*

stag·ger 1. *v/i* (sch)wanken, taumeln, torkeln; *v/t j-n* sprachlos machen, F umhauen; *Arbeitszeit etc* staffeln **2.** Wanken *n*, Schwanken *n*, Taumeln *n*

stag·nant stehend (*water*); *esp* ECON stagnierend

stag·nate *esp* ECON stagnieren

stain 1. *v/t* beflecken; (ein)färben; *Holz* beizen; *Glas* bemalen; *v/i* Flecken bekommen, schmutzen **2.** Fleck *m*; TECH Färbemittel *n*; (*Holz*)Beize *f*; Makel *m*

stained glass Bunt-, Farbglas *n*

stain·less nicht rostend, rostfrei

stair (Treppen)Stufe *f*; *pl* Treppe *f*

stair·case, stair·way Treppe *f*; Treppenhaus *n*

stake¹ 1. Pfahl *m*, Pfosten *m*; HIST Marterpfahl *m* **2.** ~ **off,** ~ **out** abstecken

stake² 1. Anteil *m*, Beteiligung *f* (**in** an *dat*) (*a.* ECON); (*Wett- etc*)Einsatz *m*; **be at** ~ *fig* auf dem Spiel stehen **2.** *Geld etc* setzen (**on** auf *acc*); *Ruf etc* riskieren, aufs Spiel setzen

stale al(t)backen; abgestanden, *beer etc*: *a.* schal, *air etc*: *a.* verbraucht

stalk¹ BOT Stängel *m*, Stiel *m*, Halm *m*

stalk² *v/t* sich heranpirschen an (*acc*); verfolgen, hinter *j-m, et.* herschleichen; *v/i* stolzieren

stall¹ 1. (*Obst- etc*)Stand *m*, (*Markt- etc*)Bude *f*; AGR Box *f*; *pl* REL Chorgestühl *n*; *Br* THEA Parkett *n* **2.** *v/t Motor* abwürgen; *v/i* MOT absterben

stall² *v/i* Ausflüchte machen; Zeit schinden; *v/t j-n* hinhalten; *et.* hinauszögern

stal·li·on ZO (Zucht)Hengst *m*

stal·wart kräftig, robust; *esp* POL treu

stam·i·na Ausdauer *f*; Durchhaltevermögen *n*, Kondition *f*

stam·mer 1. stottern, stammeln **2.** Stottern *n*, Stammeln *n*

stamp 1. *v/i* sta(m)pfen, trampeln; *v/t Pass etc* (ab)stempeln; *Datum etc* aufstempeln (**on** auf *acc*); *Brief etc* frankieren; *fig j-n* abstempeln (**as** als, zu); ~ **one's foot** aufstampfen; ~ **out** *Feuer* austreten; TECH ausstanzen **2.** (Brief-) Marke *f*, (*Steuer- etc*)Marke *f*; Stempel *m*; **~ed addressed envelope** Freiumschlag *m*

stam·pede 1. ZO wilde Flucht; wilder Ansturm, Massenansturm *m* (**for** auf *acc*); **2.** *v/i* zu durchgehen; *v/t* in Panik versetzen

stanch treu, zuverlässig

stand 1. *v/i* stehen; aufstehen; *fig fest etc* bleiben; ~ **still** still stehen; *v/t* stellen (**on** auf *acc*); aushalten, ertragen; *e-r Prüfung etc* standhalten; *Probe* bestehen; *Chance* haben; *Drink etc* spendieren; **I can't ~ him** (*or it*) ich kann ihn (*or* das) nicht ausstehen *or* leiden; ~ **around** herum|stehen; ~ **back** zurücktreten; ~ **by** danebenstehen; *fig* zu *j-m* halten; zu *et.* stehen; ~ **idly by** tatenlos zusehen; ~ **down** verzichten; zurücktreten; JUR den Zeugenstand verlassen; ~ **for** stehen für, bedeuten; sich *et.* gefallen lassen, *et.* dulden; *esp Br* kandidieren für; ~ **in** einspringen (**for** für); ~ **in for s.o.** *a. j-n* vertreten; ~ **on** (*fig* be)stehen auf (*dat*); ~ **out** hervorstechen; sich abheben (**against** gegen, von); ~ **over** überwachen, aufpassen auf (*acc*); ~ **together** zusammenhalten, -stehen; ~ **up** aufstehen, sich erheben; ~ **up for** eintreten *or* sich einsetzen für; ~ **up to** *j-m* mutig gegenübertreten, *j-m* die Stirn bieten **2.** (*Obst-, Messe- etc*)Stand *m*; (*Schirm-, Noten-etc*)Ständer *m*; SPORT *etc* Tribüne *f*; (*Taxi*)Stand(platz) *m*; JUR Zeugenstand *m*; **take a ~** *fig* Position beziehen (**on** zu)

stan·dard¹ 1. Norm *f*, Maßstab *m*; Standard *m*, Niveau *n*; ~ **of living, living** ~ Lebensstandard *m* **2.** normal, Normal...; durchschnittlich, Durchschnitts...; Standard...

stan·dard² Standarte *f*; MOT Stander *m*; HIST Banner *n*

stan·dard·ize vereinheitlichen, *esp* TECH standardisieren, normen

stan·dard lamp *Br* Stehlampe *f*

stand·by 1. Reserve *f*; AVIAT Stand-by *n*; **be on~** in Bereitschaft stehen **2.** Reserve…, Not…; AVIAT Stand-by…

stand-in *film*, TV Double *n*; Ersatzmann *m*; Vertreter(in)

stand·ing 1. stehend; *fig* ständig; → **ova·tion 2.** Rang *m*, Stellung *f*; Ansehen *n*, Ruf *m*; Dauer *f*; **of long ~** alt, seit langem bestehend; **~ or·der** ECON Dauerauftrag *m*; **~ room:** **~ only** nur noch Stehplätze

stand·off·ish F (sehr) ablehnend, hochnäsig

stand·point *fig* Standpunkt *m*

stand·still Stillstand *m*; **be at a ~** stehen (*car etc*); stillstehen (*production etc*); **bring to a ~** Auto etc zum Stehen bringen; *Produktion etc* zum Erliegen bringen

stand-up Steh…; **~ fight** Schlägerei *f*

stan·za Strophe *f*

sta·ple¹ 1. Hauptnahrungsmittel *n*; ECON Haupterzeugnis *n* **2.** Haupt…; üblich

sta·ple² 1. Heftklammer *f*; Krampe *f* **2.** heften

sta·pler TECH (Draht)Hefter *m*

star 1. ASTR Stern *m*; PRINT Sternchen *n*; THEA, SPORT *etc* Star *m* **2.** *v/t* PRINT mit e-m Sternchen kennzeichnen; **~ring…** in der Hauptrolle *or* in den Hauptrollen…; **a film ~ring…** ein Film mit … in der Hauptrolle *or* den Hauptrollen; *v/i* die *or* e-e Hauptrolle spielen (**in** in *dat*)

star·board AVIAT, MAR Steuerbord *n*

starch 1. (*Kartoffel- etc*)Stärke *f*; stärkereiches Nahrungsmittel; (*Wäsche-*) Stärke *f* **2.** Wäsche stärken

stare 1. starren; **~ at** *j-n* anstarren **2.** (starrer) Blick, Starren *n*

stark 1. *adj fig* nackt; **be in ~ contrast to** in krassem Gegensatz stehen zu **2.** *adv*: F **~ naked** splitternackt; **~ raving mad**, **~ staring mad** total verrückt

star·light ASTR Sternenlicht *n*

star·ling ZO Star *m*

star·lit stern(en)klar

star·ry Stern…, Sternen…

star·ry-eyed F blauäugig, naiv

start 1. *v/i* anfangen, beginnen (*a.* **~ off**); aufbrechen (**for** nach) (*a.* **~ off**, **~ out**); RAIL *etc* abfahren; MAR ablegen; AVIAT abfliegen, starten; MOT anspringen; TECH anlaufen; SPORT starten; zusammenfahren, -zucken (**at** bei); **to ~ with** zusammen…

anfangs, zunächst; erstens; **~ from scratch** ganz von vorn anfangen; *v/t* anfangen, beginnen (*a.* **~ off**); in Gang setzen *or* bringen, *Motor etc a.* anlassen, starten **2.** Anfang *m*, Beginn *m*, (*esp* PRINT) Start *m*; Aufbruch *m*; Auffahren *n*, Aufschrecken *n*; **at the ~** am Anfang; SPORT am Start; **for a ~** erstens; **from ~ to finish** von Anfang bis Ende

start·er SPORT Starter(in); MOT Anlasser *m*, Starter *m*; *esp Br* GASTR F Vorspeise *f*; **for ~s** zunächst einmal

start·le erschrecken; überraschen, bestürzen

starv·a·tion Hungern *n*; **die of ~** verhungern; **~ diet** F Fasten-, Hungerkur *f*, Nulldiät *f*

starve hungern (lassen); **~ (to death)** verhungern (lassen); **I'm starving!** *Br* F, **I'm ~d!** F ich komme um vor Hunger!

state 1. Zustand *m*; Stand *m*, Lage *f*; POL (Bundes-, Einzel)Staat *m*; *often* **State** POL Staat *m* **2.** Staats…, staatlich **3.** angeben, nennen; erklären; JUR aussagen (**that** dass); festlegen, festsetzen

State De·part·ment POL Außenministerium *n*

state·ly gemessen, würdevoll; prächtig

state·ment Statement *n*, Erklärung *f*; Angabe *f*; JUR Aussage *f*; ECON (*Bank-, Konto*)Auszug *m*; **make a ~** e-e Erklärung abgeben

state-of-the-art TECH neuest, modernst

states·man POL Staatsmann *m*

stat·ic statisch

sta·tion 1. (*a. Bus-, U-*)Bahnhof *m*, Station *f*; (*Forschungs-, Rettungs- etc*)Station *f*; Tankstelle *f*; (*Feuer*)Wache *f*; (*Polizei*)Revier *m*; (*Wahl*)Lokal *n*; *radio*, TV Sender *m*, Station *f* **2.** aufstellen, postieren; MIL stationieren

sta·tion·ar·y stehend

sta·tion·er Schreibwarenhändler(in); **sta·tion·er's** (**shop**) Schreibwarenhandlung *f*; **sta·tion·er·y** Schreibwaren *pl*; Briefpapier *n*

sta·tion·mas·ter RAIL Stations-, Bahnhofsvorsteher *m*

sta·tion wag·on MOT Kombiwagen *m*

sta·tis·ti·cal statistisch

sta·tis·ti·cian Statistiker *m*

sta·tis·tics Statistik(en *pl*) *f*

stat·ue Statue *f*, Standbild *n*

sta·tus Status *m*, Rechtsstellung *f*; (*Fa-*

milien)Stand *m*; Stellung *f*, Rang *m*, Status *m*; ~ line IT Statuszeile *f*

stat·ute Gesetz *n*; Statut *n*, Satzung *f*

stat·ute of lim·i·ta·tions JUR Verjährungsfrist *f*; *come under the* ~ verjähren

staunch[1] *Br* → **stanch**

staunch[2] *Blutung* stillen

stay 1. bleiben (*with s.o.* bei j-m); wohnen (*at* in *dat*; *with s.o.* bei j-m); ~ *put* sich nicht (vom Fleck) rühren; ~ *away* wegbleiben, sich fernhalten (*from* von); ~ *up* aufbleiben **2.** Aufenthalt *m*; JUR Aussetzung *f*, Aufschub *m*

stead·fast treu, zuverlässig; fest

stead·y 1. *adj* fest; stabil; ruhig (*hand*), gut (*nerves*); gleichmäßig **2.** (sich) beruhigen **3.** *int a.* ~ *on!* Br F Vorsicht! **4.** *adv*: *go* ~ *with s.o.* (fest) mit j-m gehen **5.** feste Freundin, fester Freund

steak GASTR Steak *n*; (*Fisch*)Filet *n*

steal stehlen (*a. fig*); sich stehlen, (sich) schleichen (*out of* aus)

stealth: *by* ~ heimlich, verstohlen

stealth·y heimlich, verstohlen

steam 1. Dampf *m*; Dunst *m*; *let off* ~ Dampf ablassen, *fig a.* sich Luft machen **2.** Dampf… **3.** *v/i* dampfen; ~ *up* beschlagen (*mirror etc*); *v/t* GASTR dünsten, dämpfen

steam·boat Dampfboot *n*, Dampfer *m*

steam·er Dampfer *m*, Dampfschiff *n*; Dampf-, Schnellkochtopf *m*

steam·ship Dampfer *m*, Dampfschiff *n*

steel 1. Stahl *m* **2.** ~ *o.s. for* sich wappnen gegen

steel·work·er Stahlarbeiter *m*

steel·works Stahlwerk *n*

steep[1] steil; *fig* stark (*rise etc*); F happig

steep[2] eintauchen (*in* in *acc*); *Wäsche* (ein)weichen

stee·ple Kirchturm *m*

stee·ple·chase *horse racing*: Hindernisrennen *n*; SPORT Hindernislauf *m*

steer[1] ZO (junger) Ochse

steer[2] steuern, lenken

steer·ing col·umn MOT Lenksäule *f*

steer·ing wheel MOT Lenkrad *n*, *a.* MAR Steuerrad *n*

stein Maßkrug *m*

stem 1. BOT Stiel *m* (*a. of a wine glass etc*), Stängel *m*; LING Stamm *m* **2.** ~ *from* stammen *or* herrühren von

stench Gestank *m*

sten·cil Schablone *f*; PRINT Matrize *f*

ste·nog·ra·pher Stenotypistin *f*

step 1. Schritt *m* (*a. fig*); Stufe *f*; Sprosse *f*; (*a pair of*) ~s (e-e) Tritt- *or* Stufenleiter; *mind the* ~! Vorsicht, Stufe!; ~ *by* ~ Schritt für Schritt; *take* ~s Schritte *or* et. unternehmen **2.** gehen; treten (*in* in *acc*; *on* auf *acc*); ~ *on it*, ~ *on the gas* MOT F Gas geben, auf die Tube drücken; ~ *aside* zur Seite treten; *fig* Platz machen; ~ *down* *fig* Platz machen; ~ *up* Produktion *etc* steigern

step-by-step *fig* schrittweise

step·fa·ther Stiefvater *m*

step·lad·der Tritt-, Stufenleiter *f*

step·moth·er Stiefmutter *f*

steppes GEOGR Steppe *f*

step·ping-stone *fig* Sprungbrett *n* (*to* für)

ster·e·o 1. Stereo *n*; Stereogerät *n*, Stereoanlage *f* **2.** Stereo…; ~ *sys·tem* MUS Kompaktanlage *f*

ster·ile steril (*a. fig*), *a.* unfruchtbar, MED *a.* keimfrei

ste·ril·i·ty Sterilität *f* (*a. fig*), Unfruchtbarkeit *f*

ster·il·ize MED sterilisieren

ster·ling das Pfund Sterling

stern[1] streng

stern[2] MAR Heck *n*

stew 1. *Fleisch, Gemüse* schmoren, *Obst* dünsten; ~*ed apples* Apfelkompott *n* **2.** Eintopf *m*; *be in a* ~ in heller Aufregung sein

stew·ard Ordner *m*; AVIAT, MAR Steward *m*

stew·ard·ess AVIAT, MAR Stewardess *f*

stick[1] trockener Zweig; Stock *m*; ([*Eis*]*Hockey*)Schläger *m*; (*Besen- etc-*) Stiel *m*; AVIAT (*Steuer*)Knüppel *m*; Stück *n*, Stange *f*, (*Lippen- etc*)Stift *m*, Stäbchen *n*

stick[2] *v/t* mit *e-r* Nadel *etc* stechen (*into* in *acc*); *et.* kleben (*on* auf, an *acc*); an-, festkleben (*with* mit); stecken; F tun, stellen, setzen, legen; *I can't* ~ *him* (*or it*) *esp Br* F ich kann ihn (*or das*) nicht ausstehen *or* leiden; *v/i* kleben; kleben bleiben (*to* an *dat*); stecken bleiben; ~ *at nothing* vor nichts zurückschrecken; ~ *by* F bleiben bei; F zu j-m halten; ~ *out* vorstehen; abstehen; *et.* ausstrecken *or* vorstrecken; ~ *to* bleiben bei

S

stick·er Aufkleber *m*

stick·ing plas·ter *Br* Heftpflaster *n*

stick·y klebrig (**with** von); F heikel, unangenehm

stiff 1. *adj* steif; F stark (*drink etc*); schwer, hart (*task, penalty etc*); hartnäckig (*resistance*); F happig, gepfeffert, gesalzen (*price*); **keep a ~ upper lip** *fig* Haltung bewahren **2.** *adv* äußerst; höchst; **be bored ~** F sich zu Tode langweilen; **be scared ~** e-e wahnsinnige Angst haben; **be worried ~** sich furchtbare Sorgen machen

stiff·en *v/t* Wäsche stärken; versteifen; verstärken; *v/i* steif werden; sich verhärten *or* versteifen

sti·fle ersticken; *fig* unterdrücken

stile Zauntritt *m*

sti·let·to Stilett *n*; **~ heel** Bleistift-, Pfennigabsatz *m*

still¹ 1. *adv* (immer) noch, noch immer; *with comparative*: noch **2.** *cj* dennoch, trotzdem

still² 1. *adj* still; ruhig; GASTR ohne Kohlensäure **2.** *film*, TV Standfoto *n*

still·born MED tot geboren

still life PAINT Stillleben *n*

stilt Stelze *f*; **stilt·ed** *fig* gestelzt

stim·u·lant MED Stimulans *n*, Anregungs-, Aufputschmittel *n*; *fig* Anreiz *m*, Ansporn *m* (**to** für)

stim·u·late stimulieren (*a. fig*), anregen, *fig a.* anspornen

stim·u·lus Reiz *m*; *fig* Anreiz *m*, Ansporn *m* (**to** für)

sting 1. stechen (*insect*); brennen (auf *or* in *dat*); **2.** Stachel *m*; Stich *m*; Brennen *n*, brennender Schmerz

stin·gy F knaus(e)rig, knick(e)rig (*person*); mick(e)rig (*meal etc*)

stink 1. stinken (**of** nach); **~ up** (*Br* **out**) verpesten **2.** Gestank *m*

stint: ~ o.s. (**of** *s.th.*) sich einschränken (mit et.); **~** (**on**) *s.th.* sparen mit et.

stip·u·late zur Bedingung machen; festsetzen, vereinbaren; **stip·u·la·tion** Bedingung *f*; Vereinbarung *f*

stir 1. (um)rühren; (sich) rühren *or* bewegen; *j-n* aufwühlen; **~ up** *Unruhe* stiften; *Streit* entfachen; *Erinnerungen* wachrufen **2.** **give** *s.th.* **a ~** et. umrühren; **cause** (*or* **create**) **a ~** für Aufsehen sorgen

stir·rup Steigbügel *m*

stitch 1. Stich *m*; Masche *f*; MED Seitenstechen *n* **2.** zunähen, *Wunde* nähen (*a.* **~ up**); heften

stock 1. Vorrat *m* (**of** an *dat*); GASTR Brühe *f*; *a.* **live~** Viehbestand *m*; (*Gewehr*)Schaft *m*; *fig* Abstammung *f*, Herkunft *f*; ECON Aktie(n *pl*) *f*; *pl* Aktien *pl*, Wertpapiere *pl*; **have** *s.th.* **in ~** ECON et. vorrätig *or* auf Lager haben; **take ~** ECON Inventur machen; **take ~ of** *fig* sich klar werden über (*acc*) **2.** ECON *Ware* vorrätig haben, führen; **~ up** sich eindecken *or* versorgen (**on**, **with** mit); **3.** Serien…; Standard…; stereotyp

stock·breed·er AGR Viehzüchter *m*

stock·breed·ing AGR Viehzucht *f*

stock·brok·er ECON Börsenmakler *m*

stock ex·change ECON Börse *f*

stock·hold·er ECON Aktionär(in)

stock·ing Strumpf *m*

stock mar·ket ECON Börse *f*

stock·pile 1. Vorrat *m* (**of** an *dat*); **2.** e-n Vorrat anlegen an (*dat*)

stock·still regungslos

stock·tak·ing ECON Inventur *f*; *fig* Bestandsaufnahme *f*

stock·y stämmig, untersetzt

stol·id gleichmütig

stom·ach 1. ANAT Magen *m*; Bauch *m*; *fig* Appetit *m* (**for** auf *acc*); **2.** vertragen (*a. fig*)

stom·ach·ache MED Magenschmerzen *pl*, Bauchschmerzen *pl*, Bauchweh *n*

stom·ach up·set MED Magenverstimmung *f*

stone 1. Stein *m*, BOT *a.* Kern *m*; (*Hagel*)Korn *n* **2.** mit Steinen bewerfen; steinigen; entkernen, entsteinen

stone·ma·son Steinmetz *m*

stone·ware Steingut *n*

ston·y steinig; steinern (*face etc*), eisig (*silence*)

stool Hocker *m*, Schemel *m*; MED Stuhl *m*, Stuhlgang *m*

stool·pi·geon F (Polizei)Spitzel *m*

stoop 1. *v/i* sich bücken (*a.* **~ down**); gebeugt gehen; **~ to** *fig* sich herablassen *or* hergeben zu **2.** gebeugte Haltung

stop 1. *v/i* (an)halten, stehen bleiben (*a. watch etc*), stoppen; aufhören; *esp Br* bleiben; **~ dead** plötzlich *or* abrupt stehen bleiben; **~ at nothing** vor nichts zurückschrecken; **~ short of** doing, **~**

short at s.th. zurückschrecken vor (*dat*); *v/t* anhalten, stoppen; aufhören mit; ein Ende machen *or* setzen (*dat*); *Blutung* stillen; *Arbeiten, Verkehr etc* zum Erliegen bringen; *et.* verhindern; *j-n* abhalten (***from*** von), hindern (***from*** an *dat*); *Rohr etc* verstopfen (*a.* **~ up**); *Zahn* füllen, plombieren; *Scheck* sperren (lassen); **~ by** vorbeischauen; **~ in** vorbeischauen (***at*** bei); **~ off** F kurz Halt machen; **~ over** kurz Halt machen; Zwischenstation machen **2.** Halt *m*; (*Bus*)Haltestelle *f*; PHOT *mst* Blende *f*; *mst* LING Punkt *m*

stop·gap Notbehelf *m*

stop·light MOT Bremslicht *n*; rotes Licht

stop·o·ver Zwischenstation *f*; AVIAT Zwischenlandung *f*

stop·page Unterbrechung *f*, Stopp *m*; Verstopfung *f*; Streik *m*; Br (Gehalts-, Lohn)Abzug *m*

stop·per Stöpsel *m*

stop sign MOT Stoppschild *n*

stop·watch Stoppuhr *f*

stor·age ECON Lagerung *f*; Lagergeld *n*; IT Speicher *m*

store 1. (ein)lagern; *Energie* speichern; IT (ab)speichern, sichern; *a.* **~ up** sich e-n Vorrat anlegen an (*dat*) **2.** Vorrat *m*; Lager *n*, Lagerhalle *f*, Lagerhaus *n*; Laden *m*, Geschäft *n*, *esp* Br Kaufhaus *n*, Warenhaus *n*

store·house Lagerhaus *n*; *fig* Fundgrube *f*

store·keep·er Ladenbesitzer(in)

store·room Lagerraum *m*

sto·rey Br → **story²**

...**sto·reyed** Br, ...**sto·ried** mit ... Stockwerken, ...stöckig

stork ZO Storch *m*

storm 1. Unwetter *n*; Gewitter *n*; Sturm *m* **2.** *v/t* MIL *etc* stürmen; *v/i* stürmen, stürzen; **storm·y** stürmisch

sto·ry¹ Geschichte *f*; Märchen *n* (*a. fig*); Story *f*, *a.* Handlung *f*, *a.* Bericht *m* (***on*** über *acc*)

sto·ry² Stock *m*, Stockwerk *n*, Etage *f*

stout korpulent, vollschlank; *fig* unerschrocken; entschieden

stove Ofen *m*, Herd *m*

stow *a.* **~ away** verstauen

stow·a·way AVIAT, MAR blinder Passagier

strad·dle rittlings sitzen auf (*dat*)

strag·gle verstreut liegen *or* stehen; BOT *etc* wuchern; **~ in** F einzeln eintrudeln

strag·gler Nachzügler(in)

strag·gly verstreut (liegend); BOT *etc* wuchernd; struppig (*mustache etc*)

straight 1. *adj* gerade; glatt (*hair*); pur (*whisky etc*); aufrichtig, offen, ehrlich; *sl* hetero(*sexuell*); *sl* clean, sauber; **put ~** in Ordnung bringen **2.** *adv* gerade; genau, direkt; klar; ehrlich, anständig; **~ ahead** geradeaus; **~ off** F sofort; **~ on** geradeaus; **~ out** F offen, rundheraus **3.** SPORT (*Gegen-, Ziel*)Gerade *f*

straight·en *v/t* gerade machen, (gerade) richten; **~ out** in Ordnung bringen; *v/i a.* **~ out** gerade werden; **~ up** sich aufrichten

straight·for·ward aufrichtig; einfach

strain 1. *v/t* Seil etc (an)spannen; *sich, Augen etc* überanstrengen; sich *e-n Muskel etc* zerren; *Gemüse, Tee etc* abgießen; *v/i* sich anstrengen; **~ at** zerren *or* ziehen an (*dat*) **2.** Spannung *f*; Anspannung *f*; Strapaze *f*; *fig* Belastung *f*; MED Zerrung *f*; **strained** MED gezerrt; gezwungen (*smile etc*); gespannt (*relations*); **look ~** abgespannt aussehen

strain·er Sieb *n*

strait GEOGR Meerenge *f*, Straße *f*; *pl fig* Notlage *f*

strait·ened **live in ~ circumstances** in beschränkten Verhältnissen leben

strand Strang *m*; Faden *m*; (*Kabel-*) Draht *m*; (*Haar*)Strähne *f*

strand·ed **be ~** MAR gestrandet sein; **be (left) ~** *fig* festsitzen (***in*** in *dat*)

strange merkwürdig, seltsam, sonderbar; fremd; **strang·er** Fremde *m*, *f*

stran·gle erwürgen

strap 1. Riemen *m*, Gurt *m*; (*Uhr*)Armband *n*; Träger *m* **2.** festschnallen; anschnallen

stra·te·gic strategisch

strat·e·gy Strategie *f*

stra·tum GEOL Schicht *f* (*a. fig*)

straw Stroh *n*; Strohhalm *m*

straw·ber·ry BOT Erdbeere *f*

stray 1. (herum)streunen; sich verirren; *fig* abschweifen (***from*** von); **2.** verirrtes *or* streunendes Tier **3.** verirrt (*bullet, dog etc*); streunend (*dog etc*); vereinzelt

streak 1. Streifen *m*; Strähne *f*; (*Charakter*)Zug *m*; **a ~ of lightning** ein Blitz; **lucky ~** Glückssträhne *f* **2.** flitzen;

streifen

streak·y streifig; GASTR durchwachsen

stream 1. Bach *m*; Strömung *f*; *fig* Strom *m* **2.** strömen; flattern, wehen

stream·er Luft-, Papierschlange *f*; Wimpel *m*; IT Streamer *m*

street 1. Straße *f*; *on* (*esp Br in*) *the* ~ auf der Straße **2.** Straßen…

street·car Straßenbahn(wagen *m*) *f*

street sweep·er Straßenkehrer *m*

strength Stärke *f*, Kraft *f*, Kräfte *pl*

strength·en *v/t* (ver)stärken; *v/i* stärker werden

stren·u·ous anstrengend, strapaziös; unermüdlich

stress 1. *fig* Stress *m*; PHYS, TECH Beanspruchung *f*, Belastung *f*, Druck *m*; LING Betonung *f*; *fig* Nachdruck *m* **2.** betonen

stress·ful stressig, aufreibend

stretch 1. *v/t* strecken; (aus)weiten, dehnen; spannen; *fig* es nicht allzu genau nehmen mit; ~ *out* ausstrecken; *be fully* ~*ed fig* richtig gefordert werden; voll ausgelastet sein; *v/i* sich dehnen, *a.* länger *or* weiter werden; sich dehnen *or* recken *or* strecken; sich erstrecken; ~ *out* sich ausstrecken **2.** Dehnbarkeit *f*, Elastizität *f*; Strecke *f*; SPORT (Gegen-, Ziel)Gerade *f*; Zeit *f*, Zeitraum *m*, Zeitspanne *f*; *have a* ~ sich dehnen *or* recken *or* strecken

stretch·er Trage *f*

strick·en schwer betroffen; ~ *with* befallen *or* ergriffen von

strict streng, strikt; genau; ~*ly* (*speaking*) genau genommen

strict·ness Strenge *f*

stride 1. schreiten, mit großen Schritten gehen **2.** großer Schritt

strife Streit *m*

strike 1. *v/t* schlagen; treffen; einschlagen in (*acc*) (*lightning*); Streichholz anzünden; MAR auflaufen auf (*acc*); streichen (*from, off* aus *dat*, von); stoßen auf (*acc*); *j-n* beeindrucken; *j-m* einfallen, in den Sinn kommen; *Münze* prägen; *Saite etc* anschlagen; *Lager, Zelt* abbrechen; *Flagge, Segel* streichen; ~ *out* (aus)streichen; ~ *up Lied etc* anstimmen; *Freundschaft etc* schließen; *v/i* streiken; streichen; ECON streiken; ~ (*out*) *at s.o.* auf *j-n* einschlagen **2.** ECON Streik *m*; (*Öl- etc*)Fund *m*; MIL

Angriff *m*; *soccer*: Schuss *m*; *be on* ~ streiken; *go on* ~ streiken, in den Streik treten; *a lucky* ~ ein Glückstreffer

strik·er ECON Streikende *m*, *f*; *soccer*: Stürmer(in)

strik·ing apart; auffallend

string 1. Schnur *f*, Bindfaden *m*; (*Schürzen-, Schuh-etc*)Band *n*; (*Puppenspiel*) Faden *m*, Draht *m*; (*Perlen- etc*)Schnur *f*; MUS, SPORT Saite *f*; (*Bogen*)Sehne *f*; BOT Faser *f*; IT Zeichenfolge *f*; *fig* Reihe *f*, Serie *f*; *the* ~*s* MUS die Streichinstrumente *pl*, die Streicher *pl*; *pull a few* ~*s fig* ein paar Beziehungen spielen lassen; *with no* ~*s attached fig* ohne Bedingungen **2.** *Perlen etc* aufreihen; *Gitarre etc* besaiten, *Tennisschläger etc* bespannen; *Bohnen* abziehen **3.** MUS Streich…; *string bean* BOT grüne Bohne

strin·gent streng

string·y fas(e)rig

strip 1. *v/i*: *a.* ~ *off* sich ausziehen (*to* bis auf *acc*); *v/t* ausziehen; *Farbe etc* abkratzen, *Tapete etc* abreißen (*from, off* von); *a.* ~ *down* TECH zerlegen, auseinandernehmen; ~ *s.o. of s.th.* j-m et. rauben *or* wegnehmen **2.** (*Land-, Papier- etc*)Streifen *m*; Strip *m*

stripe Streifen *m*; *striped* gestreift

strive: ~ *for or after* streben nach

stroke 1. streicheln; streichen über (*acc*) **2.** Schlag *m* (*a.* SPORT); MED Schlag (-anfall) *m*; (*Pinsel*)Strich *m*; *swimming*: Zug *m*; TECH Hub *m*; → *four--stroke engine*; ~ *of lightning* Blitzschlag *m*; *a.* ~ *of luck fig* ein glücklicher Zufall, ein Glücksfall

stroll 1. bummeln, spazieren **2.** Bummel *m*, Spaziergang *m*

stroll·er Bummler(in), Spaziergänger(in); Sportwagen *m*

strong stark (*a.* GASTR, PHARM); kräftig; mächtig; stabil; fest; robust

strong·box (Geld-, Stahl)Kassette *f*

strong·hold Festung *f*; Stützpunkt *m*; *fig* Hochburg *f*

strong-mind·ed willensstark

strong room Tresor(raum) *m*

struc·ture Struktur *f*; (Auf)Bau *m*, Gliederung *f*; Bau *m*, Konstruktion *f*

strug·gle 1. kämpfen, ringen (*with* mit; *for* um); sich abmühen; sich winden, zappeln; ~ *against* sich sträuben gegen

S

2. Kampf *m*

strum klimpern auf (*dat*) (*or* **on** auf *dat*)

strut[1] stolzieren

strut[2] TECH Strebe *f*; Stütze *f*

stub 1. (*Bleistift-, Zigaretten- etc*)Stummel *m*; Kontrollabschnitt *m* **2.** sich *die Zehe* anstoßen; ~ **out** *Zigarette* ausdrücken

stub·ble Stoppeln *pl*

stub·bly stoppelig

stub·born eigensinnig, stur; hartnäckig

stub·born·ness Starrsinn *m*

stuck-up F hochnäsig

stud[1] **1.** (*Kragen-, Manschetten*)Knopf *m*; *soccer:* Stollen *m*; Beschlagnagel *m*; Ziernagel *m*; *pl* MOT Spikes *pl* **2. be** ~**ded with** besetzt sein mit; übersät sein mit; ~**ded tires** Spikesreifen *pl*

stud[2] Gestüt *n*

stu·dent Student(in); Schüler(in)

stud farm Gestüt *n*

stud horse ZO Zuchthengst *m*

stud·ied wohlüberlegt; gesucht

stu·di·o Studio *n*; Atelier *n*; *a.* ~ **apartment**, *Br* ~ **flat** Studio *n*, Einzimmerappartement *n*; ~ **couch** Schlafcouch *f*

stu·di·ous fleißig

stud·y 1. Studium *n*; Studie *f*, Untersuchung *f*; Arbeitszimmer *n*; *pl* Studium *n* **2.** studieren; lernen (**for** für)

stuff 1. Zeug *n* **2.** (aus)stopfen, stopfen, vollstopfen; füllen (*a.* GASTR); ~ **o.s.** F sich vollstopfen; **stuff·ing** Füllung *f* (*a.* GASTR)

stuff·y stickig; spießig; prüde

stum·ble 1. stolpern (**on, over,** *fig* **at, over** über *acc*); ~ **across,** ~ **on** stoßen auf (*acc*) **2.** Stolpern *n*

stump 1. Stumpf *m*; Stummel *m* **2.** stampfen, stapfen

stump·y F kurz und dick

stun betäuben; *fig* sprachlos machen

stun·ning fantastisch; unglaublich

stunt[1] (das *Wachstum gen*) hemmen; ~**ed** BIOL verkümmert; **become** ~**ed** BIOL verkümmern

stunt[2] (*Film*)Stunt *m*; (*gefährliches*) Kunststück; (*Reklame*)Gag *m*

stunt|man *film,* TV Stuntman *m*, Double *n*; ~**wom·an** *film,* TV Stuntwoman *f*, Double *n*

stu·pid dumm; F blöd

stu·pid·i·ty Dummheit *f*

stu·por Betäubung *f*; **in a drunken** ~ im

Vollrausch

stur·dy kräftig, stämmig; *fig* entschlossen, hartnäckig

stut·ter 1. stottern (*a.* MOT); stammeln **2.** Stottern *n*, Stammeln *n*

sty[1] → **pigsty**

sty[2], **stye** MED Gerstenkorn *n*

style 1. Stil *m*; Ausführung *f*; Mode *f* **2.** entwerfen; gestalten

styl·ish stilvoll; modisch, elegant

styl·ist Stilist(in)

Sty·ro·foam® Styropor® *n*

suave verbindlich

sub·con·scious Unterbewusstsein *n*; ~**ly** im Unterbewusstsein

sub·di·vi·sion Unterteilung *f*; Unterabteilung *f*

sub·due unterwerfen; *Ärger etc* unterdrücken; **sub·dued** gedämpft (*light, voice etc*); ruhig, still (*person*)

sub·ject 1. Thema *n*; PED, UNIV Fach *n*; LING Subjekt *n*, Satzgegenstand *m*; Untertan(in); Staatsangehörige *m, f,* -bürger(in) **2.** *adj:* **to** ~ anfällig für; **be** ~ **to** *a.* neigen zu; **be** ~ **to** unterliegen (*dat*); abhängen von; **prices** ~ **to change** Preisänderungen vorbehalten **3.** unterwerfen; ~ **to** *e-m Test etc* unterziehen; *der Kritik etc* aussetzen

sub·jec·tion Unterwerfung *f*, Abhängigkeit *f* (**to** von)

sub·ju·gate unterjochen, unterwerfen

sub·junc·tive LING *a.* ~ **mood** Konjunktiv *m*

sub·lease, sub·let untervermieten, weitervermieten

sub·lime großartig; *fig* total

sub·ma·chine gun Maschinenpistole *f*

sub·ma·rine 1. unterseeisch **2.** Unterseeboot *n*, U-Boot *n*

sub·merge tauchen; (ein)tauchen (**in** in *acc*)

sub·mis·sion Einreichung *f*; *boxing etc:* Aufgabe *f*; Unterwerfung *f* (**to** unter);

sub·mis·sive unterwürfig

sub·mit *Gesuch etc* einreichen (**to** *dat or* bei); sich fügen (**to** *dat or in acc*); *boxing etc:* aufgeben

sub·or·di·nate 1. untergeordnet (**to** *dat*); **2.** Untergebene *m, f* **3.** ~ **to** unterordnen (*dat*), zurückstellen (hinter *acc*); ~ **clause** LING Nebensatz *m*

sub·scribe *v/t Geld* gegen, spenden (**to** für); *v/i:* ~ **to** *Zeitung etc* abonnieren;

sub·scrib·er Abonnent(in); TEL Teilnehmer(in); sub·scrip·tion Abonnement n; (Mitglieds)Beitrag m

sub·se·quent später

sub·side sich senken (building, road etc); zurückgehen (flood, demand etc), sich legen (storm, anger etc)

sub·si·di·a·ry 1. Neben...; ~ question Zusatzfrage f 2. ECON Tochtergesellschaft f

sub·si·dize subventionieren

sub·si·dy Subvention f

sub·sist leben, existieren (on von)

sub·sis·tence Existenz f

sub·stance Substanz f (a. fig), Stoff m; das Wesentliche, Kern m

sub·stan·dard minderwertig

sub·stan·tial solid (furniture etc); beträchtlich (salary etc), (changes etc a.) wesentlich; reichlich, kräftig (meal)

sub·stan·ti·ate beweisen

sub·stan·tive LING Substantiv n, Hauptwort n

sub·sti·tute 1. Ersatz m; Stellvertreter(in), Vertretung f; SPORT Auswechselspieler(in), Ersatzspieler(in) 2. ~ s.th. for s.th. et. durch et. ersetzen, et. gegen et. austauschen or auswechseln; ~ for einspringen für, j-n vertreten sub·sti·tu·tion Ersatz m; SPORT Austausch m, Auswechslung f

sub·ter·fuge List f

sub·ter·ra·ne·an unterirdisch

sub·ti·tle Untertitel m

sub·tle fein (differences etc); raffiniert (plan etc); scharf (mind); scharfsinnig

sub·tract MATH abziehen, subtrahieren (from von); sub·trac·tion MATH Abziehen n, Subtraktion f

sub·trop·i·cal subtropisch

sub·urb Vorort m, Vorstadt f

sub·ur·ban Vorort..., vorstädtisch, Vorstadt...

sub·ver·sive umstürzlerisch, subversiv

sub·way Unterführung f; U-Bahn f

suc·ceed v/i Erfolg haben, erfolgreich sein, (plan etc a.) gelingen; ~ to in e-m Amt nachfolgen; ~ to the throne auf dem Thron folgen; v/t: ~ s.o. as j-s Nachfolger werden als

suc·cess Erfolg m

suc·cess·ful erfolgreich

suc·ces·sion Folge f; Erb-, Nach-, Thronfolge f; five times in ~ fünfmal

hintereinander; in quick ~ in rascher Folge; suc·ces·sive aufeinanderfolgend; suc·ces·sor Nachfolger(in); Thronfolger(in)

suc·cu·lent GASTR saftig

such solche(r, -s); derartige(r, -s); so; derart; ~ a so ein(e)

suck 1. v/t saugen; lutschen (an dat); v/i saugen (at an dat); 2. have or take a ~ at saugen or lutschen an (dat)

suck·er zo Saugnapf m, Saugorgan n; TECH Saugfuß m; BOT Wurzelschössling m, Wurzelspross m; F Trottel m, Simpel m; Lutscher m

suck·le säugen, stillen

suc·tion (An)Saugen n; Saugwirkung f; ~ pump TECH Saugpumpe f

sud·den plötzlich, unvermittelt; all of a ~ F ganz plötzlich

sud·den·ly plötzlich

suds Seifenschaum m

sue JUR j-n verklagen (for auf acc, wegen); klagen (for auf acc)

suede, suède Wildleder n, Velours (-leder) n

su·et GASTR Nierenfett n, Talg m

suf·fer v/i leiden (from an dat, unter dat); darunter leiden; v/t erleiden; Folgen tragen; suf·fer·er Leidende m, f; suf·fer·ing Leiden n; Leid n

suf·fi·cient genügend, genug, ausreichend; be ~ reichen, (aus)reichen

suf·fix LING Suffix n, Nachsilbe f

suf·fo·cate ersticken

suf·frage POL Wahl-, Stimmrecht n

suf·fuse durchfluten (light etc); überziehen (color etc)

sug·ar 1. Zucker m 2. zuckern

sug·ar beet BOT Zuckerrübe f

sug·ar bowl Zuckerdose f

sug·ar·cane BOT Zuckerrohr n

sug·ar tongs Zuckerzange f

sug·ar·y süß; fig süßlich

sug·gest vorschlagen, anregen; hindeuten or hinweisen auf (acc), schließen lassen auf (acc); andeuten

sug·ges·tion Vorschlag m, Anregung f; Anflug m, Spur f; Andeutung f; PSYCH Suggestion f

sug·ges·tive zweideutig (remark etc), vielsagend (look etc)

su·i·cide Selbstmord m; Selbstmörder(in); commit ~ Selbstmord begehen

suit 1. Anzug m; Kostüm n; card game:

Farbe f; JUR Prozess m; **follow ~** fig dem Beispiel folgen, dasselbe tun **2.** v/t j-m passen (date etc); j-n kleiden, j-m stehen; et. anpassen (**to** dat); **~ s.th., be ~ed to s.th.** geeignet sein or sich eignen für; **~ yourself!** mach, was du willst!

sui·ta·ble passend, geeignet (**for, to** für)

suit·case Koffer m

suite (Möbel-, Sitz)Garnitur f; Suite f, Zimmerflucht f; MUS Suite f; Gefolge n

sul·fur CHEM Schwefel m

sul·fu·ric ac·id CHEM Schwefelsäure f

sulk schmollen, F eingeschnappt sein

sulk·y schmollend, F eingeschnappt

sul·len mürrisch, verdrossen

sul·phur Br → **sulfur**

sul·phu·ric ac·id Br → **sulfuric acid**

sul·try schwül; aufreizend (look etc)

sum 1. Summe f; Betrag m; (einfache) Rechenaufgabe; **do ~s** rechnen **2. ~ up** zusammenfassen; j-n, et. abschätzen

sum·mar·ize zusammenfassen

sum·ma·ry Zusammenfassung f, (kurze) Inhaltsangabe

sum·mer Sommer m; **in (the) ~** im Sommer; **~ camp** Ferienlager n; **~ holi·days** Br Sommerferien pl; **~ school** Ferienkurs m

sum·mer·time Sommer m, Sommerszeit f; **in (the) ~** im Sommer

sum·mer| time esp Br Sommerzeit f; **~ va·ca·tion** Sommerferien pl

sum·mer·y sommerlich, Sommer…

sum·mit Gipfel m (a. ECON, POL, fig); **~ con·fe·rence** POL Gipfelkonferenz f; **~ meet·ing** POL Gipfeltreffen n

sum·mon auffordern; Versammlung etc einberufen; JUR vorladen; **~ up** Kraft, Mut etc zusammennehmen

sum·mons JUR Vorladung f

sump Br MOT Ölwanne f

sump·tu·ous luxuriös, aufwändig

sun 1. Sonne f **2.** Sonnen… **3. ~ o.s.** sich sonnen

Sun abbr of **Sunday** So., Sonntag m

sun·bathe sich sonnen, ein Sonnenbad nehmen

sun·beam Sonnenstrahl m

sun·bed Sonnenbank f

sun·burn Sonnenbrand m

sun cream Sonnencreme f

sun·dae GASTR Eisbecher m

Sun·day (abbr **Sun**) Sonntag m; **on ~** (am) Sonntag; **on ~s** sonntags

sun·dial Sonnenuhr f

sun·dries Diverses, Verschiedenes

sun·dry diverse, verschiedene

sun·glass·es (**a pair of ~** e-e) Sonnenbrille f

sunk·en MAR gesunken, versunken; versenkt; tief liegend; eingefallen (cheeks), (a. eyes) eingesunken

sun·light Sonnenlicht n

sun·lit sonnenbeschienen

sun·ny sonnig

sun·rise Sonnenaufgang m; **at ~** bei Sonnenaufgang

sun·roof Dachterrasse f; MOT Schiebedach n

sun·set Sonnenuntergang m; **at ~** bei Sonnenuntergang

sun·shade Sonnenschirm m

sun·shine Sonnenschein m

sun·stroke MED Sonnenstich m

sun·tan (Sonnen)Bräune f; **~ lo·tion** Sonnenschutz m, Sonnencreme f; **~ oil** Sonnenöl n

su·per F super, spitze, klasse

su·per… Über…, über…

su·per·a·bun·dant überreichlich

su·per·an·nu·at·ed pensioniert, im Ruhestand

su·perb ausgezeichnet

su·per·charg·er MOT Kompressor m

su·per·cil·i·ous hochmütig, F hochnäsig

su·per·fi·cial oberflächlich

su·per·flu·ous überflüssig

su·per·hu·man übermenschlich

su·per·im·pose überlagern; Bild etc einblenden (**on** in acc)

su·per·in·tend die (Ober)Aufsicht haben über (acc), überwachen; leiten

su·per·in·tend·ent Aufsicht f, Aufsichtsbeamter m, -beamtin f; Br Kriminalrat m

su·pe·ri·or 1. ranghöher (**to** als); überlegen (**to** dat), besser (**to** als); ausgezeichnet, hervorragend; überheblich, überlegen; **Father Superior** REL Superior m; **Mother Superior** REL Oberin f **2.** Vorgesetzte m, f; **su·pe·ri·or·i·ty** Überlegenheit f (**over** gegenüber)

su·per·la·tive 1. höchste(r, -s), überragend **2.** a. **~ degree** LING Superlativ m

su·per·mar·ket Supermarkt m

su·per·nat·u·ral übernatürlich

S

su·per·nu·me·ra·ry zusätzlich

su·per·sede ablösen, ersetzen, verdrängen

su·per·son·ic AVIAT, PHYS Überschall...

su·per·sti·tion Aberglaube *m*

su·per·sti·tious abergläubisch

su·per·store Großmarkt *m*

su·per·vene dazwischenkommen

su·per·vise beaufsichtigen, überwachen; **su·per·vi·sion** Beaufsichtigung *f*, Überwachung *f*; *under s.o.'s ~* unter j-s Aufsicht; **su·per·vi·sor** Aufseher(in), Aufsicht *f*

sup·per Abendessen *n*; *have ~* zu Abend essen; → *lord*

sup·plant verdrängen

sup·ple gelenkig, geschmeidig, biegsam

sup·ple·ment 1. Ergänzung *f*; Nachtrag *m*, Anhang *m*; Ergänzungsband *m*; (*Zeitungs- etc*)Beilage *f* **2.** ergänzen; **sup·ple·men·ta·ry** ergänzend, zusätzlich

sup·pli·er ECON Lieferant(in), *a. pl* Lieferfirma *f*

sup·ply 1. liefern; stellen, sorgen für; *j-n*, *et.* versorgen, ECON beliefern (*with* mit); **2.** Lieferung *f* (*to* an *acc*); Versorgung *f*, ECON Angebot *n*; *mst pl* Vorrat *m* (*of* an *dat*), *a.* Proviant *m*, MIL Nachschub *m*; *~ and demand* ECON Angebot und Nachfrage

sup·port 1. (ab)stützen, *Gewicht etc* tragen; *Währung* stützen; unterstützen; unterhalten, sorgen für **2.** Stütze *f*; TECH Träger *m*; *fig* Unterstützung *f*

sup·port·er Anhänger(in) (*a.* SPORT), Befürworter(in)

sup·pose 1. annehmen, vermuten; *be ~d to ...* sollen; *what is that ~d to mean?* was soll denn das?; *I ~ so* ich nehme es an, vermutlich **2.** *cj* angenommen; wie wäre es, wenn

sup·posed angeblich, vermeintlich

sup·pos·ing → *suppose 2*

sup·po·si·tion Annahme *f*, Vermutung *f*

sup·pos·i·to·ry PHARM Zäpfchen *n*

sup·press unterdrücken

sup·pres·sion Unterdrückung *f*

sup·pu·rate MED eitern

su·prem·a·cy Vormachtstellung *f*

su·preme höchste(r, -s), oberste(r, -s), Ober...; größte(r, -s)

sur·charge 1. Nachporto *or* e-n Zuschlag erheben (*on* auf *acc*) **2.** Auf-

schlag *m*, Zuschlag *m* (*on* auf *acc*); Nach-, Strafporto *n* (*on* auf *acc*)

sure 1. *adj* sicher; *~ of o.s.* selbstsicher; *~ of winning* siegessicher; *~ thing!* F (aber) klar!; *be or feel ~* sicher sein; *be ~ to ...* vergiss nicht zu ...; *for ~* ganz sicher *or* bestimmt; *make ~ that* sich (davon) überzeugen, dass; *to be ~* sicher(lich) **2.** *adv* F sicher, klar; *~ enough* tatsächlich

sure·ly sicher(lich)

sure·ty JUR Bürge *m*, Bürgin *f*; Bürgschaft *f*, Sicherheit *f*; *stand ~ for s.o.* für j-n bürgen

surf 1. Brandung *f* **2.** SPORT surfen

sur·face 1. Oberfläche *f*; (*Straßen*)Belag *m* **2.** auftauchen; *Straße* mit e-m Belag versehen **3.** Oberflächen...; *fig* oberflächlich; *~ mail* gewöhnliche Post

surf·board Surfboard *n*, Surfbrett *n*

surf·er Surfer(in), Wellenreiter(in)

surf·ing Surfen *n*, Wellenreiten *n* (*f*)

surge 1. *fig* Welle *f*, Woge *f*, (*Gefühls*)Aufwallung *f* **2.** (vorwärts-)drängen; *~ (up)* aufwallen

sur·geon MED Chirurg(in)

sur·ge·ry MED Chirurgie *f*; operativer Eingriff, Operation *f*; *Br* Sprechzimmer *n*; *Br* Sprechstunde *f*; *a. doctor's ~* Arztpraxis *f*; *~ hours* MED *Br* Sprechstunde(n *pl*) *f*

sur·gi·cal MED chirurgisch

sur·ly mürrisch, unwirsch

sur·name Familienname *m*, Nachname *m*, Zuname *m*

sur·pass *Erwartungen etc* übertreffen

sur·plus 1. Überschuss *m* (*of* an *dat*) **2.** überschüssig

sur·prise 1. Überraschung *f*, Verwunderung *f*; *take s.o. by* j-n überraschen **2.** überraschen; *be ~d at or by* überrascht sein über (*acc*)

sur·ren·der 1. *v/i ~ to* MIL, *a. fig* sich ergeben (*dat*), kapitulieren vor (*dat*); *~ to the police* sich der Polizei stellen; *v/t et.* übergeben, ausliefern (*to dat*); aufgeben, verzichten auf (*acc*); *~ o.s. to the police* sich der Polizei stellen **2.** MIL Kapitulation *f* (*a. fig*); Aufgabe *f*, Verzicht *m*

sur·ro·gate Ersatz *m*

sur·ro·gate moth·er Leihmutter *f*

sur·round umgeben; umstellen

sur·round·ing umliegend

sur·round·ings Umgebung *f*

sur·vey 1. (sich) *et.* betrachten (*a. fig*); *Haus etc* begutachten; *Land* vermessen **2.** Umfrage *f*; Überblick *m* (*of* über *acc*); Begutachtung *f*; Vermessung *f*

sur·vey·or Gutachter *m*; Land(ver)messer *m*

sur·viv·al Überleben *n* (*a. fig*); Überbleibsel *n*; ~ **in·stinct** Selbsterhaltungstrieb *m*; ~ **kit** Überlebensausrüstung *f*; ~ **train·ing** Überlebenstraining *n*

sur·vive überleben; *Feuer etc* überstehen; erhalten bleiben *or* sein

sur·vi·vor Überlebende *m*, *f* (*from*, *of gen*)

sus·cep·ti·ble empfänglich, anfällig (*both*: **to** für)

sus·pect 1. *j-n* verdächtigen (*of gen*); *et.* vermuten; *et.* anzweifeln, *et.* bezweifeln **2.** Verdächtige *m*, *f* **3.** verdächtig, suspekt

sus·pend *Verkauf, Zahlungen etc* (vorübergehend) einstellen; JUR *Verfahren, Urteil* aussetzen; *Strafe* zur Bewährung aussetzen; *j-n* suspendieren; vorübergehend ausschließen (*from* aus); SPORT *j-n* sperren; (auf)hängen; **be ~ed** schweben; **sus·pend·er** *Br* Strumpfhalter *m*, Straps *m*; Sockenhalter *m*; (*a.* **a pair of**) ~**s** Hosenträger *pl*

sus·pense Spannung *f*; **in** ~ gespannt, voller Spannung

sus·pen·sion (vorübergehende) Einstellung; Suspendierung *f*; vorübergehender Ausschluss; SPORT Sperre *f*; MOT *etc* Aufhängung *f*; ~ **bridge** Hängebrücke *f*; ~ **rail·way** *esp Br* Schwebebahn *f*

sus·pi·cion Verdacht *m*; Verdächtigung *f*; Argwohn *m*, Misstrauen *n*; *fig* Hauch *m*, Spur *f*; **sus·pi·cious** verdächtig; argwöhnisch, misstrauisch; **become** ~ Verdacht schöpfen

sus·tain *j-n* stärken; *Interesse etc* aufrechterhalten; *Schaden, Verlust* erleiden; JUR *e-m Einspruch etc* stattgeben

swab MED **1.** Tupfer *m*; Abstrich *m* **2.** *Wunde* abtupfen

swad·dle *Baby* wickeln

swag·ger stolzieren

swal·low¹ 1. schlucken (*a.* F); hinunterschlucken; ~ **up** *fig* schlucken, verschlingen **2.** Schluck *m*

swal·low² ZO Schwalbe *f*

swamp 1. Sumpf *m* **2.** überschwemmen; **be ~ed with** *fig* überschwemmt werden mit; **swamp·y** sumpfig

swan ZO Schwan *m*

swank 1. F *esp Br* angeben **2.** F *esp Br* Angeber(in); Angabe *f* **3.** F piekfein

swank·y F piekfein; *esp Br* angeberisch

swap F **1.** (ein)tauschen **2.** Tausch *m*

swarm 1. ZO Schwarm *m* (*a. fig*) **2.** ZO schwärmen; *fig a.* strömen; *a. fig* wimmeln (**with** von)

swar·thy dunkel (*skin*), dunkelhäutig (*person*)

swas·ti·ka Hakenkreuz *n*

swat *Fliege etc* totschlagen

sway 1. *v/i* sich wiegen, schaukeln; ~ **be·tween** *fig* schwanken zwischen (*dat*); *v/t* hin- und herbewegen, schwenken, *s-n Körper* wiegen; beeinflussen **2.** Schwanken *n*, Schaukeln *n*

swear fluchen; schwören; ~ **at s.o.** *j-n* wüst beschimpfen; ~ **by** *fig* schwören auf (*acc*); ~ **s.o. in** JUR *j-n* vereidigen

sweat 1. *v/i* schwitzen (**with** vor *dat*); *v/t*: ~ **out** *Krankheit* ausschwitzen; ~ **blood** F sich abrackern (**over** mit) **2.** Schweiß *m*; F Schufterei *f*; **get in(to) a** ~ *fig* F ins Schwitzen geraten *or* kommen

sweat·er Pullover *m*

sweat-shirt Sweatshirt *n*

sweat·y schweißig, verschwitzt; nach Schweiß riechend, Schweiß...; schweißtreibend

Swede Schwede *m*, Schwedin *f*

Swe·den Schweden *n*

Swe·dish 1. schwedisch **2.** LING Schwedisch *n*

sweep 1. *v/t* kehren, fegen; *fig* fegen über (*acc*) (*storm etc*); *Horizont etc* absuchen (**for** nach); *fig Land etc* überschwemmen; ~ **along** mitreißen; *v/i* kehren, fegen; rauschen (*person*) **2.** Kehren *n*, Fegen *n*; Hieb *m*, Schlag *m*; F Schornsteinfeger *m*, Kaminkehrer *m*; **give the floor a good** ~ den Boden gründlich kehren *or* fegen; **make a clean** ~ gründlich aufräumen; SPORT gründlich abräumen

sweep·er (*Straßen*)Kehrer *m*; Kehrmaschine *f*; *soccer*: Libero *m*

sweep·ing durchgreifend (*changes etc*); pauschal, zu allgemein

sweep·ings Kehricht *m*

sweet 1. süß (*a. fig*); lieblich; lieb; ~ **nothings** Zärtlichkeiten *pl*; **have a ~ tooth** gern naschen **2.** *Br* Süßigkeit *f*, Bonbon *m, n*; *Br* Nachtisch *m*; ~ **corn** *esp Br* BOT Zuckermais *m*

sweet·en süßen

sweet·heart Schatz *m*, Liebste *m, f*

sweet pea BOT Gartenwicke *f*

sweet shop *esp Br* Süßwarengeschäft *n*

swell 1. *v/i a.* ~ **up** MED (an)schwellen; *a.* ~ **out** sich blähen; *v/t fig* Zahl *etc* anwachsen lassen; *a.* ~ **out** Segel blähen **2.** MAR Dünung *f* **3.** F klasse

swell·ing MED Schwellung *f*

swel·ter vor Hitze fast umkommen

swerve 1. schwenken (**to the left** nach links), e-n Schwenk machen; *fig* abweichen (**from** von); **2.** Schwenk *m*, Schwenkung *f*, MOT *etc a.* Schlenker *m*

swift schnell

swim 1. *v/i* schwimmen; *fig* verschwimmen; **my head was ~ming** mir drehte sich alles; *v/t* Strecke schwimmen; *Fluss etc* durchschwimmen **2.** Schwimmen *n*; **go for a ~** schwimmen gehen

swim·mer Schwimmer(in)

swim·ming Schwimmen *n*; ~ **bath(s)** *Br* Schwimmbad *n*, *esp* Hallenbad *n*; ~ **cap** Badekappe *f*, Bademütze *f*; ~ **cos·tume** Badeanzug *m*; ~ **gear** Badezeug *n*; ~ **pool** Swimmingpool *m*, Schwimmbecken *n*; ~ **things** Badesachen *pl*; ~ **trunks** Badehose *f*

swim·suit Badeanzug *m*

swin·dle 1. *j-n* beschwindeln (**out of** um); **2.** Schwindel *m*

swine ZO Schwein *n* (*a.* F *fig*)

swing 1. *v/i* (hin- und her)schwingen; sich schwingen; einbiegen, -schwenken (**into** in *acc*); MUS schwungvoll spielen (*band etc*); Schwung haben (*music*); ~ **round** sich ruckartig umdrehen; ~ **shut** zuschlagen (*door etc*); *v/t et.*, *die Arme etc* schwingen **2.** Schwingen *n*; Schaukel *f*; *fig* Schwung *m*; *fig* Umschwung *m*; **in full ~** in vollem Gang

swing door Pendeltür *f*

swin·ish ekelhaft

swipe 1. Schlag *m* **2.** schlagen (**at** nach)

swirl 1. wirbeln **2.** Wirbel *m*

swish¹ *v/i* sausen, zischen; rascheln (*silk etc*); *v/t* mit *dem Schwanz* schlagen **2.** Sausen *n*, Zischen *n*; Rascheln *n*;

Schlagen *n*

swish² *Br* feudal, schick

Swiss 1. schweizerisch, eidgenössisch, Schweizer... **2.** Schweizer(in); **the ~** die Schweizer *pl*

switch 1. ELECTR, TECH Schalter *m*; RAIL Weiche *f*; Gerte *f*, Rute *f*; *fig* Umstellung *f* **2.** ELECTR, TECH (um)schalten (*a.* ~ **over**) (**to** auf *acc*); RAIL rangieren; wechseln (**to** zu); ~ **off** abschalten, ausschalten; ~ **on** anschalten, einschalten

switch·board ELECTR Schalttafel *f*; (Telefon)Zentrale *f*

Swit·zer·land die Schweiz

swiv·el (sich) drehen

swiv·el chair Drehstuhl *m*

swoon in Ohnmacht fallen

swoop 1. *fig* F zuschlagen (*police etc*); *a.* ~ **down** ZO herabstoßen (**on** auf *acc*); ~ **on** F herfallen über (*acc*) **2.** Razzia *f*

swop F → **swap**

sword Schwert *n*

syc·a·more BOT Bergahorn *m*; Platane *f*

syl·la·ble Silbe *f*

syl·la·bus PED, UNIV Lehrplan *m*

sym·bol Symbol *n*

sym·bol·ic symbolisch

sym·bol·is·m Symbolik *f*

sym·bol·ize symbolisieren

sym·met·ri·cal symmetrisch

sym·me·try Symmetrie *f*

sym·pa·thet·ic mitfühlend; verständnisvoll; wohlwollend

sym·pa·thize mitfühlen; sympathisieren

sym·pa·thiz·er Sympathisant(in)

sym·pa·thy Mitgefühl *n*; Verständnis *n*

sym·pho·ny MUS Sinfonie *f*; ~ **orchestra** MUS Sinfonieorchester *n*

symp·tom Symptom *n*

syn·chro·nize *v/t* aufeinander abstimmen; *Uhren, Film* synchronisieren; *v/i* synchron gehen *or* sein

syn·o·nym Synonym *n*

sy·non·y·mous synonym; gleichbedeutend

syn·tax LING Syntax *f*, Satzlehre *f*

syn·the·sis Synthese *f*

syn·thet·ic CHEM synthetisch; ~ **fi·ber** (*Br* **fi·bre**) Kunstfaser *f*

Syr·i·a Syrien *n*

sy·ringe MED Spritze *f*

syr·up Sirup *m*

sys·tem System *n*; (*Straßen- etc*)Netz *n*; Organismus *m*

sys·te·mat·ic systematisch
sys·tem er·ror IT Systemfehler *m*

T

T, t T, t *n*
tab Aufhänger *m*, Schlaufe *f*; Lasche *f*; Etikett *n*, Schildchen *n*; Reiter *m*; F Rechnung *f*
ta·ble 1. Tisch *m*; (*Tisch*)Runde *f*; Tabelle *f*, Verzeichnis *n*; MATH Einmaleins *n*; **at ~** bei Tisch; **at the ~** am Tisch; **turn the ~s (on s.o.)** *fig* den Spieß umdrehen **2.** *fig* auf den Tisch legen; *esp fig* zurückstellen
ta·ble·cloth Tischdecke *f*, Tischtuch *n*
ta·ble·land GEOGR Tafelland *n*, Plateau *n*, Hochebene *f*
ta·ble lin·en Tischwäsche *f*
ta·ble·mat Untersetzer *m*
ta·ble·spoon Esslöffel *m*
tab·let PHARM Tablette *f*; Stück *n*; (*Stein- etc*)Tafel *f*
ta·ble ten·nis SPORT Tischtennis *n*
ta·ble·top Tischplatte *f*
ta·ble·ware Geschirr *n* und Besteck *n*
tab·loid Boulevardblatt *n*, -zeitung *f*
tab·loid press Boulevardpresse *f*
ta·boo 1. tabu **2.** Tabu *n*
tab·u·lar tabellarisch
tab·u·late tabellarisch (an)ordnen
tab·u·la·tor Tabulator *m*
tach·o·graph MOT Fahrtenschreiber *m*
ta·chom·e·ter MOT Drehzahlmesser *m*
tac·it stillschweigend
ta·ci·turn schweigsam, wortkarg
tack 1. Stift *m*, (Reiß)Zwecke *f*; Heftstich *m* **2.** heften (**to** an *acc*); **~ on** anfügen (**to** *dat*)
tack·le 1. *Problem etc* angehen; *soccer etc: ballführenden Gegner* angreifen; *j-n* zur Rede stellen (**about** wegen); **2.** TECH Flaschenzug *m*; (*Angel*)Gerät(e *pl*) *n*; *soccer etc:* Angriff *m*
tack·y klebrig; F schäbig
tact Takt *m*, Feingefühl *n*
tact·ful taktvoll
tac·tics Taktik *f*
tact·less taktlos
tad·pole ZO Kaulquappe *f*
taf·fe·ta Taft *m*

taf·fy Sahnebonbon *m*, *n*, Toffee *n*
tag 1. Etikett *n*; (*Namens-, Preis*)Schild *n*; (*Schnürsenkel*)Stift *m*; stehende Redensart *f*; *a.* **question ~** LING Frageanhängsel *n* **2.** etikettieren; *Waren* auszeichnen; anhängen; **~ along** F mitgehen, mitkommen; **~ along behind s.o.** F hinter j-m hertrotten
tail 1. Schwanz *m*; Schweif *m*; hinterer Teil; F Schatten *m*, Beschatter(in); *pl* Rück-, Kehrseite *f*; Frack *m*; **put a ~ on j-n** beschatten lassen; **turn ~** *fig* sich auf dem Absatz umdrehen; **with one's ~ between one's legs** *fig* mit eingezogenem Schwanz **2.** F *j-n* beschatten; **~ back** *esp Br* MOT sich stauen (**to** bis zu); **~ off** schwächer werden, abnehmen, nachlassen
tail·back *esp Br* MOT Rückstau *m*
tail·coat Frack *m*
tail end Ende *n*, Schluss *m*
tail·light MOT Rücklicht *n*
tai·lor 1. Schneider *m* **2.** schneidern
tai·lor-made Maß...; maßgeschneidert (*a. fig*)
tail pipe TECH Auspuffrohr *n*
tail·wind Rückenwind *m*
taint·ed GASTR verdorben
take 1. *v/t* nehmen; (weg)nehmen; mitnehmen; bringen; MIL, MED einnehmen; *chess etc: Figur, Stein* schlagen; *Gefangene, Prüfung etc* machen; UNIV studieren; *Preis etc* erringen; *Scheck etc* (an)nehmen; *Rat* annehmen; *et.* hinnehmen; fassen, Platz bieten für; *et.* aushalten, ertragen; PHOT *et.* aufnehmen, *Aufnahme* machen; *Temperatur* messen; *Notiz* machen, niederschreiben; *ein Bad, Zug, Bus, Weg etc* nehmen; *Gelegenheit, Maßnahmen* ergreifen; *Mut* fassen; *Zeit, Geduld etc* erfordern, brauchen; *Zeit* dauern; **it took her four hours** sie brauchte vier Stunden; **I ~ it that** ich nehme an, dass; **~ it or leave it** F mach, was du willst; **~ all in all** im Großen (und) Ganzen; **this seat**

is ~*n* dieser Platz ist besetzt; *be* ~*n by or with* angetan sein von; *be* ~*n ill or sick* erkranken, krank werden; ~ *to bits or pieces et.* auseinandernehmen, zerlegen; ~ *the blame* die Schuld auf sich nehmen; ~ *care* vorsichtig sein, aufpassen; ~ *care!* F mach's gut!; ~ *care 1*; ~ *hold of* ergreifen; ~ *part* teilnehmen (*in* an *dat*); → *part 1*; ~ *pity on* Mitleid haben mit; ~ *a walk* e-n Spaziergang machen; ~ *my word for it* verlass dich drauf; → *advice, bath 1, break 1, lead*[1] 2, *message, oath, offense, place 1, prisoner, risk 1, seat 1, step 1, trouble 1, turn 2, etc*; *v/i* MED wirken, anschlagen; ~ *after* j-m nachschlagen, ähneln; *jemandem* ähnlich sehen; ~ *along* mitnehmen; ~ *apart* auseinandernehmen (*a. fig* F), zerlegen; ~ *away* wegnehmen (*from s.o.* j-m); ... ~ *away Br* ... zum Mitnehmen; ~ *back* zurückbringen; zurücknehmen; bei j-m Erinnerungen wachrufen; j-n zurückversetzen (*to* in *acc*); ~ *down* herunternehmen, abnehmen; *Hose* herunterlassen; auseinandernehmen, zerlegen; (sich) *et.* aufschreiben *or* notieren; sich *Notizen* machen; *what do you* ~ *me for?* wofür hältst du mich eigentlich?; ~ *from* j-m *et.* wegnehmen, MATH abziehen von; ~ *in* j-n (bei sich) aufnehmen; *fig et.* einschließen; *Kleidungsstück* enger machen; *et.* begreifen; j-n hereinlegen, F j-n aufs Kreuz legen; *be* ~*n in by* hereinfallen auf (*acc*); ~ *off* *Kleidungsstück* ablegen, ausziehen, *Hut etc* abnehmen; *et.* ab-, wegnehmen; abziehen, AVIAT abheben; SPORT abspringen; F sich davonmachen; ~ *a day off* sich e-n Tag freinehmen; ~ *on* j-n einstellen; *Arbeit etc* annehmen, übernehmen; *Farbe, Ausdruck etc* annehmen; sich anlegen mit; ~ *out* herausnehmen, *Zahn* ziehen; j-n ausführen, ausgehen mit j-m; *Versicherung* abschließen; *s-n Frust etc* auslassen (*on* an *dat*); ~ *over Amt, Macht, Verantwortung etc* übernehmen; die Macht übernehmen; ~ *to* Gefallen finden an (*dat*); ~ *to doing s.th.* anfangen, et. zu tun; ~ *up Vorschlag etc* aufgreifen; *Zeit etc* in Anspruch nehmen, *Platz einnehmen; Erzählung etc* aufnehmen; ~ *up doing s.th.* anfangen, sich

mit et. zu beschäftigen; ~ *up with* sich einlassen mit 2. *film*, TV Einstellung *f*; F Einnahmen *pl*

take-a-way *Br* 1. Essen *n* zum Mitnehmen 2. Restaurant *n* mit Straßenverkauf

take-off AVIAT Abheben *n*, Start *m*; SPORT Absprung *m*

tak-ings Einnahmen *pl*

tale Erzählung *f*; Geschichte *f*; Lüge *f*, Lügengeschichte *f*, Märchen *n*; *tell* ~*s* petzen

tal-ent Talent *n*, Begabung *f*

tal-ent-ed talentiert, begabt

tal-is-man Talisman *m*

talk 1. *v/i* reden, sprechen, sich unterhalten (*to, with* mit; *about* über *acc*; *of* von); ~ *about s.th. a.* et. besprechen; *s.o. to* ~ *to* Ansprechpartner(in); *v/t Unsinn etc* reden; reden *or* sprechen *or* sich unterhalten über (*acc*); ~ *s.o. into s.th.* j-n zu et. überreden; ~ *s.o. out of s.th.* j-m et. ausreden; ~ *s.th. over Problem etc* besprechen (*with* mit); ~ *round* j-n bekehren (*to* zu), umstimmen 2. Gespräch *n*, Unterhaltung *f* (*with* mit; *about* über *acc*); Vortrag *m*; Sprache *f*, Sprechweise *f*; Gerede *n*, Geschwätz *n*; *give a* ~ e-n Vortrag halten (*to* vor *dat*; *about, on* über *acc*); *be the* ~ *of the town* Stadtgespräch sein; *baby* ~ Babysprache *f*, kindliches Gebabbel; → *small talk*

talk-a-tive gesprächig, redselig

talk-er: *be a good* ~ gut reden können

talk-ing-to F Standpauke *f*; *give s.o. a* ~ j-m e-e Standpauke halten

talk show TV Talkshow *f*

talk-show host TV Talkmaster *m*

tall groß (*person*), hoch (*building etc*)

tal-low Talg *m*

tal-ly[1] SPORT *etc* Stand *m*; *keep a* ~ *of* Buch führen über (*acc*)

tal-ly[2] übereinstimmen (*with* mit); *a.* ~ *up* zusammenrechnen, -zählen

tal-on ZO Kralle *f*, Klaue *f*

tame 1. ZO zahm; *fig* fad(e), lahm 2. ZO zähmen (*a. fig*)

tam-per: ~ *with* sich zu schaffen machen an (*dat*)

tam-pon MED Tampon *m*

tan 1. *Fell* gerben; bräunen; braun werden 2. Gelbbraun *n*; (Sonnen)Bräune *f* 3. gelbbraun

T

tang (scharfer) Geruch *or* Geschmack

tan·gent MATH Tangente *f*; *fly or* **go off at a ~** plötzlich (vom Thema) abschweifen

tan·ge·rine BOT Mandarine *f*

tan·gi·ble greifbar, *fig a.* handfest, klar

tan·gle **1.** (sich) verwirren *or* verheddern, durcheinanderbringen; durcheinanderkommen **2.** Gewirr *n*, *fig a.* Wirrwarr *m*, Durcheinander *n*

tank MOT *etc* Tank *m*; MIL Panzer *m*

tank·ard (Bier)Humpen *m*

tank·er MAR Tanker *m*, Tankschiff *n*; AVIAT Tankflugzeug *n*; MOT Tankwagen *m*

tan·ner Gerber *m*

tan·ne·ry Gerberei *f*

tan·ta·lize *j-n* aufreizen

tan·ta·liz·ing verlockend

tan·ta·mount: **be ~ to** gleichbedeutend sein mit, hinauslaufen auf (*acc*)

tan·trum Wut-, Tobsuchtsanfall *m*

tap[1] **1.** TECH Hahn *m*; **beer on ~** Bier *n* vom Fass **2.** *Naturschätze etc* erschließen; *Vorräte etc* angreifen; *Telefon* (-*leitung*) abhören, F anzapfen; *Fass* anzapfen, anstechen

tap[2] **1.** mit *den Fingern, Füßen* klopfen, mit *den Fingern* trommeln (**on** *auf acc*); antippen; **~ s.o. on the shoulder** j-m auf die Schulter klopfen; **~ on** (leicht) klopfen an (*acc*) *or auf* (*acc*) *or gegen* **2.** (leichtes) Klopfen; Klaps *m*

tap dance Stepptanz *m*

tape **1.** (schmales) Band; Kleb(e)streifen *m*; (Magnet-, Video-, Ton)Band *n*; (*Video- etc*)Kassette *f*; (Band)Aufnahme *f*; TV Aufzeichnung *f*; SPORT Zielband *n*; → **red tape 2.** (auf Band) aufnehmen; TV aufzeichnen; *a.* **~ up** (mit Klebeband) zukleben

tape deck Tapedeck *n*

tape meas·ure Bandmaß *n*, Maßband *n*, Messband *n*

ta·per *a.* **~ off** spitz zulaufen, sich verjüngen; *fig* langsam nachlassen

tape re·cord·er Tonbandgerät *n*

tape re·cord·ing Tonbandaufnahme *f*

ta·pes·try Gobelin *m*, Wandteppich *m*

tape·worm ZO Bandwurm *m*

taps MIL Zapfenstreich *m*

tap wa·ter Leitungswasser *n*

tar **1.** Teer *m* **2.** teeren

tare ECON Tara *f*

tar·get (Schieß-, Ziel)Scheibe *f*; MIL Ziel *n* (*a. fig*), ECON *a.* Soll *n*; *fig* Zielscheibe *f*; **~ ar·e·a** MIL Zielbereich *m*; **~ group** Zielgruppe *f*

tar·iff ECON Zoll(tarif) *m*; *esp Br* Preisverzeichnis *n*

tar·mac Asphalt *m*; AVIAT Rollfeld *n*, Rollbahn *f*

tar·nish *v/i* anlaufen; *v/t* Ansehen *etc* beflecken

tart[1] *esp Br* Obstkuchen *m*; Obsttörtchen *n*; F Flittchen *n*, *sl* Nutte *f*

tart[2] herb, sauer; scharf (*a. fig*)

tar·tan Tartan *m*; Schottenstoff *m*; Schottenmuster *n*

tar·tar MED Zahnstein *m*; CHEM Weinstein *m*

task Aufgabe *f*; **take s.o. to ~** *fig* j-n zurechtweisen (**for** wegen); **~ force** MIL *etc* Sonder-, Spezialeinheit *f*

tas·sel Troddel *f*, Quaste *f*

taste **1.** Geschmack *m* (*a. fig*), Geschmackssinn *m*; Kostprobe *f*; Vorliebe *f* (**for** für); **2.** *v/t* kosten, probieren; schmecken; *v/i* schmecken (**of** nach)

taste·ful *fig* geschmackvoll

taste·less geschmacklos (*a. fig*)

tast·y schmackhaft

tat·tered zerlumpt

tat·ters Fetzen *pl*; **in ~** zerfetzt, in Fetzen; *fig* ruiniert

tat·too[1] **1.** Tätowierung *f* **2.** (ein)tätowieren

tat·too[2] MIL Zapfenstreich *m*

taunt **1.** verhöhnen, verspotten **2.** höhnische *or* spöttische Bemerkung

Tau·rus ASTR Stier *m*; **he (she) is (a) ~** er (sie) ist (ein) Stier

taut straff; *fig* angespannt

taw·dry (billig und) geschmacklos

taw·ny gelbbraun

tax **1.** Steuer *f* (**on** *auf acc*); **2.** besteuern; *j-s Geduld etc* strapazieren

tax·a·ble steuerpflichtig

tax·a·tion Besteuerung *f*

tax e·va·sion Steuerhinterziehung *f*

tax·i **1.** Taxi *n*, Taxe *f* **2.** AVIAT rollen

tax·i driv·er Taxifahrer(in)

tax·i rank, tax·i stand Taxistand *m*

tax of·fi·cer Finanzbeamte *m*

tax·pay·er Steuerzahler(in)

tax re·duc·tion Steuersenkung *f*

tax re·turn Steuererklärung *f*

T-bar Bügel *m*; *a.* **~ lift** Schlepplift *m*

tea Tee *m*; *have a cup of* ~ e-n Tee trinken; *make some* ~ e-n Tee machen *or* kochen

tea·bag Teebeutel *m*, Aufgussbeutel *m*

teach lehren, unterrichten (in *dat*); *j-m et.* beibringen; unterrichten (*at* an *dat*)

teach·er Lehrer(in)

tea co·sy Teewärmer *m*

tea·cup Teetasse *f*; *a storm in a* ~ *fig* ein Sturm im Wasserglas

team Team *n*, *a.* Arbeitsgruppe *f*, SPORT *a.* Mannschaft *f*, *soccer: a.* Elf *f*

team·ster MOT LKW-Fahrer *m*

team·work Zusammenarbeit *f*, Teamwork *n*; Zusammenspiel *n*

tea·pot Teekanne *f*

tear[1] Träne *f*; *in* ~*s* weinend, in Tränen (aufgelöst)

tear[2] **1.** *v/t* zerreißen; sich *et.* zerreißen (*on* an *dat*); weg-, losreißen (*from* von); *v/i* (zer)reißen; F rasen, sausen; ~ *down* Plakat *etc* herunterreißen; *Haus etc* abreißen; ~ *off* abreißen; sich *Kleidung* vom Leib reißen; ~ *out* (her)ausreißen; ~ *up* aufreißen; zerreißen **2.** Riss *m*

tear·drop Träne *f*

tear·ful weinend; tränenreich

tear·jerk·er F Schnulze *f*

tea·room Teestube *f*

tease necken, hänseln; ärgern

tea·spoon Teelöffel *m*

teat zo Zitze *f*; *Br* (Gummi)Sauger *m*

tech·ni·cal technisch; fachlich, Fach…

tech·ni·cal·i·ty technische Einzelheit; reine Formsache

tech·ni·cian Techniker(in)

tech·nique Technik *f*, Verfahren *n*

tech·nol·o·gy Technologie *f*; Technik *f*

ted·dy bear Teddybär *m*

te·di·ous langweilig, ermüdend

teem: ~ *with* wimmeln von, strotzen von *or* vor (*dat*)

teen·age(d) im Teenageralter; für Teenager; **teen·ag·er** Teenager *m*

teens: *be in one's* ~ im Teenageralter sein

tee·ny(-**wee·ny**) F klitzeklein, winzig

tee shirt → *T-shirt*

teethe zahnen

tee·to·tal·(l)er Abstinenzler(in)

tel·e·cast Fernsehsendung *f*

tel·e·com·mu·ni·ca·tions Telekommunikation *f*, Fernmeldewesen *n*

tel·e·gram Telegramm *n*

tel·e·graph 1. *by* ~ telegrafisch **2.** telegrafieren

tel·e·graph·ic telegrafisch

te·leg·ra·phy Telegrafie *f*

tel·e·phone 1. Telefon *n* **2.** telefonieren; anrufen; ~ *booth*, ~ *box Br* Telefonzelle *f*, Fernsprechzelle *f*; ~ *call* Telefonanruf *n*, Telefongespräch *n*; ~ *di·rec·to·ry* → *phone book*; ~ *number* Telefonnummer *f*

te·leph·o·nist *esp Br* Telefonist(in)

tel·e·pho·to lens PHOT Teleobjektiv *n*

tel·e·print·er Fernschreiber *m*

tel·e·scope Teleskop *n*, Fernrohr *n*

tel·e·text Teletext *m*, Videotext *m*

tel·e·type·writ·er Fernschreiber *m*

tel·e·vise im Fernsehen übertragen *or* bringen; **tel·e·vi·sion 1.** Fernsehen *n*; *a.* ~ *set* Fernsehapparat *m*, -gerät *n*, F Fernseher *m*; *on* ~ im Fernsehen; *watch* ~ fernsehen **2.** Fernseh…

tel·ex 1. Telex *n*, Fernschreiben *n* **2.** telexen (*to* an *acc*), ein Telex schicken (*dat*)

tell *v/t* sagen; erzählen; erkennen (*by* an *dat*); *Namen etc* nennen; *et.* anzeigen; *j-m* sagen, befehlen (*to do* zu tun); *I can't* ~ *one from the other*, *I can't* ~ *them apart* ich kann sie nicht auseinanderhalten; *v/i* sich auswirken (*on* bei, auf *acc*), sich bemerkbar machen; *who can* ~? wer weiß?; *you can never* ~, *you never can* ~ man kann nie wissen; ~ *against* sprechen gegen; von Nachteil sein für; ~ *s.o. off* F mit j-m schimpfen (*for* wegen); ~ *on s.o.* j-n verpetzen *or* verraten

tell·er Kassierer(in)

tell·ing aufschlussreich

tell·tale 1. verräterisch **2.** F Petze *f*

tel·ly *Br* F Fernseher *m*

te·mer·i·ty Frechheit *f*, Kühnheit *f*

tem·per 1. Temperament *n*, Wesen *n*, Wesensart *f*; Laune *f*, Stimmung *f*; TECH Härte(grad *m*) *f*; *keep one's* ~ sich beherrschen, ruhig bleiben; *lose one's* ~ die Beherrschung verlieren **2.** TECH *Stahl* härten

tem·pe·ra·ment Temperament *n*, Naturell *n*, Wesen *n*, Wesensart *f*

tem·pe·ra·men·tal launisch; von Natur aus

tem·pe·rate gemäßigt (*climate*, *region*)

tem·pe·ra·ture Temperatur f; *have a ~* MED erhöhte Temperatur or Fieber haben

tem·pest POET (heftiger) Sturm

tem·ple[1] Tempel m

tem·ple[2] ANAT Schläfe f

tem·po·ral weltlich; LING temporal, der Zeit

tem·po·ra·ry vorübergehend, zeitweilig

tempt/-*n* in Versuchung führen; *j-n* verführen (*to* zu); **temp·ta·tion** Versuchung f, Verführung f; **tempt·ing** verführerisch

ten 1. zehn **2.** Zehn f

ten·a·ble *fig* haltbar

te·na·cious hartnäckig, zäh

ten·ant Pächter(in), Mieter(in)

tend neigen, tendieren (*to* zu); *~ upwards* e-e steigende Tendenz haben

ten·den·cy Tendenz f; Neigung f

ten·der[1] empfindlich, *fig a.* heikel; GASTR zart, weich; sanft, zart, zärtlich

ten·der[2] RAIL, MAR Tender m

ten·der[3] ECON **1.** Angebot n; *legal ~* gesetzliches Zahlungsmittel **2.** ein Angebot machen (*for* für)

ten·der·foot F Neuling m, Anfänger m

ten·der·loin GASTR zartes Lendenstück

ten·der·ness Zartheit f; Zärtlichkeit f

ten·don ANAT Sehne f

ten·dril BOT Ranke f

ten·e·ment Mietshaus n, *contp* Mietskaserne f

ten·nis Tennis n; *~ court* Tennisplatz m; *~ play·er* Tennisspieler(in)

ten·or MUS, JUR Tenor m, JUR *a.* Wortlaut m, Sinn m; Verlauf m

tense[1] LING Zeit(form) f, Tempus n

tense[2] gespannt, straff (*rope etc*), (an)gespannt (*a. fig*); (über)nervös, verkrampft (*person*)

ten·sion Spannung f (*a.* ELECTR)

tent Zelt n

ten·ta·cle ZO Tentakel m, n, Fangarm m

ten·ta·tive vorläufig; vorsichtig, zaghaft

tenth 1. zehnte(r, -s) **2.** Zehntel n

tenth·ly zehntens

ten·u·ous *fig* lose (*link, relationship etc*)

ten·ure Besitz m, Besitzdauer f; *~ of office* Amtsdauer f, Dienstzeit f

tep·id lau(warm)

term 1. Zeit f, Zeitraum m, Dauer f; JUR Laufzeit f; PED, UNIV Semester n, *esp Br* Trimester n; Ausdruck m, Bezeich-

nung f; *~ of office* Amtsdauer f, Amtsperiode f, Amtszeit f; *pl* Bedingungen *pl*; *be on good* (*bad*) *~s with* gut (schlecht) auskommen mit; *they are not on speaking ~s* sie sprechen nicht (mehr) miteinander; *come to ~s* sich einigen (*with* mit); **2.** nennen, bezeichnen als

ter·mi·nal 1. End...; letzte(r, -s); MED unheilbar; im Endstadium; *~ly ill* unheilbar krank **2.** RAIL *etc* Endstation f; Terminal m, n; ELECTR Pol m; IT Terminal n, Datenendstation f

ter·mi·nate v/t beenden; *Vertrag* kündigen, lösen; MED *Schwangerschaft* unterbrechen; v/i enden; ablaufen (*contract*)

ter·mi·na·tion Beendigung f; Kündigung f, Lösung f; Ende n; Ablauf m

ter·mi·nus RAIL *etc* Endstation f

ter·race Terrasse f; Häuserreihe f; *mst pl esp Br* SPORT Ränge *pl*

ter·raced house *Br* Reihenhaus n

ter·res·tri·al irdisch; Erd...; *esp* BOT, ZO Land...

ter·ri·ble schrecklich

ter·rif·ic F toll, fantastisch; irre (*speed, heat etc*)

ter·ri·fy/-*m* schreckliche Angst einjagen

ter·ri·to·ri·al territorial, Gebiets...

ter·ri·to·ry Territorium n, (*a.* Hoheits-, Staats)Gebiet n

ter·ror Entsetzen n; Schrecken m; POL Terror m; F Landplage f; *in ~* in panischer Angst

ter·ror·is·m Terrorismus m

ter·ror·ist Terrorist(in)

ter·ror·ize terrorisieren

terse *fig* knapp, kurz (und bündig)

test 1. Test m, Prüfung f; Probe f **2.** testen, prüfen; probieren; *j-s Geduld etc* auf e-e harte Probe stellen

tes·ta·ment *last will and ~* JUR Letzter Wille, Testament n

test an·i·mal Versuchstier n

test card TV Testbild n

test drive MOT Probefahrt f

tes·ti·cle ANAT Hoden m

tes·ti·fy JUR aussagen

tes·ti·mo·ni·al Referenz f

tes·ti·mo·ny JUR Aussage f; Beweis m

test pi·lot AVIAT Testpilot m

test tube CHEM Reagenzglas n

tes·ty gereizt

tet·a·nus MED Tetanus *m*, Wundstarrkrampf *m*

teth·er 1. Strick *m*; Kette *f*; *at the end of one's ~* *fig* mit s-n Kräften *or* Nerven am Ende sein **2.** *Tier* anbinden; anketten

text 1. Text *m*; TEL SMS *f*; Kurzmitteilung *f* **2.** eine SMS schicken / schreiben; *I'll ~ you* ich schicke dir eine SMS

text·book Lehrbuch *n*

tex·tile 1. Stoff *m*, *pl* Textilien *pl* **2.** Textil...

text message TEL SMS *f*; Kurzmitteilung *f*; *I'll send you a ~* ich schicke dir eine SMS

tex·ture Textur *f*, Gewebe *n*; Beschaffenheit *f*; Struktur *f*

than als

thank 1. *j-m* danken, sich bei *j-m* bedanken (*for* für); *~ you* danke; *~ you very much* vielen Dank; *no, ~ you* nein, danke; (*yes,*) *~ you* ja, bitte **2.** *~s* Dank *m*; *~s* (schön); *no, ~s* nein, danke; *~s to* dank (*gen*), wegen (*gen*)

thank·ful dankbar

thank·less undankbar

that 1. *pron and adj* das; jene(r, -s), der, die, das, derjenige, diejenige, dasjenige **2.** *relative pron* der, die, das, welche(r, -s) **3.** *cj* dass **4.** *adv* F so, dermaßen; *it's ~ simple* so einfach ist das

thatch 1. mit Stroh *or* Reet decken **2.** (Dach)Stroh *n*, Reet *n*; Strohdach *n*, Reetdach *n*

thaw 1. (auf)tauen **2.** Tauwetter *n*; (Auf)Tauen *n*

the 1. der, die, das, *pl* die **2.** *adv*: *~ ... ~ ...* je ... desto ...; *~ sooner ~ better* je eher, desto besser

the·a·ter Theater *n*; UNIV (*Hör*)Saal *m*; MIL (Kriegs)Schauplatz *m*

the·a·ter·go·er Theaterbesucher(in)

the·a·tre *Br* → *theater*; MED Operationssaal *m*

the·at·ri·cal Theater...; *fig* theatralisch

theft Diebstahl *m*

their ihr(e)

theirs der (die, das) ihrige *or* ihre

them sie (*acc pl*); ihnen (*dat*)

theme Thema *n*

them·selves sie (*acc pl*) selbst; sich (selbst)

then 1. *adv* dann; da; damals; *by ~* bis dahin; *from ~ on* von da an; → *every,*

now 1, there 2. adj damalig

the·o·lo·gian Theologe *m*, Theologin *f*

the·ol·o·gy Theologie *f*

the·o·ret·i·cal theoretisch

the·o·rist Theoretiker *m*

the·o·ry Theorie *f*

ther·a·peu·tic therapeutisch; F wohltuend; gesund

ther·a·pist Therapeut(in)

ther·a·py Therapie *f*

there 1. da, dort; (da-, dort)hin; *~ is, ~ are* es gibt, es ist, *pl* es sind; *~ and then* auf der Stelle; *~ you are* hier bitte; siehst du!, na also! **2.** *int* so; siehst du!, na also!; *~, ~* ist ja gut!

there·a·bout(s) so ungefähr

there·af·ter danach

there·by dadurch

there·fore deshalb, daher; folglich

there·up·on darauf(hin)

ther·mal 1. thermisch, Thermo..., Wärme... **2.** Thermik *f*

ther·mom·e·ter Thermometer *n*

ther·mos® Thermosflasche® *f*

the·sis These *f*; UNIV Dissertation *f*, Doktorarbeit *f*

they sie *pl*; man

thick 1. *adj* dick, (*fog etc a.*) dicht; F dumm; F dick befreundet; *be ~ with* wimmeln von; *~ with smoke* verräuchert; *that's a bit ~!* *esp Br* F das ist ein starkes Stück! **2.** *adv* dick, dicht; *lay it on ~* F dick auftragen **3.** *in the ~ of* mitten in (*dat*); *through ~ and thin* durch dick und dünn; thick·en dicker werden, (*fog etc a.*) dichter werden; GASTR eindicken, binden

thick·et Dickicht *n*

thick·head·ed F strohdumm

thick·ness Dicke *f*; Lage *f*, Schicht *f*

thick·set gedrungen, untersetzt

thick-skinned *fig* dickfellig

thief Dieb(in)

thigh ANAT (Ober)Schenkel *m*

thim·ble Fingerhut *m*

thin 1. *adj* dünn; dürr; spärlich, dürftig; schütter (*hair*); schwach, (*excuse etc a.*) fadenscheinig **2.** *adv* dünn **3.** verdünnen; dünner werden, (*fog, hair a.*) sich lichten

thing Ding *n*; Sache *f*; *pl* Sachen *pl*, Zeug *n*; *fig* Dinge *pl*, Lage *f*, Umstände *pl*; *I couldn't see a ~* ich konnte überhaupt nichts sehen; *another ~* et. anderes; *the right* ~ das Richtige

thing·a·ma·jig F Dings(bums) *m, f, n*

think *v/i* denken (*of* an *acc*); nachdenken (*about* über *acc*); *I* ~ *so* ich glaube *or* denke schon; *I'll* ~ *about it* ich überlege es mir; ~ *of* sich erinnern an (*acc*); ~ *of doing s.th.* beabsichtigen *or* daran denken, et. zu tun; *what do you* ~ *of or about ...?* was halten Sie von ...?; *v/t* denken, glauben, meinen; j-n, et. halten für; ~ *over* nachdenken über (*acc*), sich et. überlegen; ~ *up* sich et. ausdenken

think tank Beraterstab *m*, Sachverständigenstab *m*, Denkfabrik *f*

third 1. dritte(r, -s) 2. Drittel *n*

third·ly drittens

third-rate drittklassig

Third World Dritte Welt

thirst Durst *m*

thirst·y durstig; *be* ~ Durst haben, durstig sein

thir·teen 1. dreizehn 2. Dreizehn *f*

thir·teenth dreizehnte(r, -s)

thir·ti·eth dreißigste(r, -s)

thir·ty 1. dreißig 2. Dreißig *f*

this diese(r, -s); ~ *morning* heute Morgen; ~ *is John speaking* TEL hier (spricht) John

this·tle BOT Distel *f*

thong (Leder)Riemen *m*

thorn Dorn *m*

thorn·y dornig; *fig* schwierig, heikel

thor·ough gründlich, genau; fürchterlich (*mess etc*)

thor·ough·bred ZO Vollblüter *m*

thor·ough·fare Hauptverkehrsstraße *f*; *no* ~*!* Durchfahrt verboten!

though 1. *cj* obwohl; (je)doch; *as* ~ als ob 2. *adv* dennoch, trotzdem

thought Denken *n*; Gedanke *m* (*of* an *acc*); *on second* ~ wenn ich es mir (recht) überlege

thought·ful nachdenklich; rücksichtsvoll, aufmerksam

thought·les gedankenlos; rücksichtslos

thou·sand 1. tausend 2. Tausend *n*

thou·sandth 1. tausendste(r, -s) 2. Tausendstel *n*

thrash verdreschen, verprügeln; SPORT F j-m e-e Abfuhr erteilen; ~ *about*, ~ *around* sich *im Bett etc* hin und her werfen; um sich schlagen; zappeln (*fish*); ~ *out* Problem etc ausdiskutie-

ren

thrash·ing Dresche *f*, Tracht *f* Prügel

thread 1. Faden *m* (*a. fig*); Garn *n*; TECH Gewinde *n* 2. Nadel einfädeln; *Perlen etc* auffädeln, aufreihen

thread-bare abgewetzt, abgetragen; *fig* abgedroschen

threat Drohung *f*; Bedrohung *f*, Gefahr *f* (*to* gen *or* für)

threat·en (be)drohen

threat·en·ing drohend

three 1. drei 2. Drei *f*

three·fold dreifach

three-ply → *ply²*

three-score sechzig

three-stage dreistufig

thresh AGR dreschen

thresh·ing ma·chine AGR Dreschmaschine *f*

thresh·old Schwelle *f*

thrift Sparsamkeit *f*

thrift·y sparsam

thrill 1. prickelndes Gefühl; Nervenkitzel *m*; aufregendes Erlebnis 2. *v/t be* ~*ed* (ganz) hingerissen sein (*at, about* von)

thrill·er Thriller *m*, F Reißer *m*

thrill·ing spannend, fesselnd, packend

thrive gedeihen; *fig* blühen, florieren

throat ANAT Kehle *f*, Gurgel *f*; Rachen *m*; Hals *m*; *clear one's* ~ sich räuspern; → *sore* 1

throb 1. hämmern (*machine*), (*heart etc a.*) pochen, schlagen; pulsieren (*pain*) 2. Hämmern *n*, Pochen *n*, Schlagen *n*

throm·bo·sis MED Thrombose *f*

throne Thron *m*

throng 1. Schar *f*, Menschenmenge *f* 2. sich drängen (*in dat*)

throt·tle 1. erdrosseln; ~ *down* MOT, TECH drosseln, Gas wegnehmen 2. TECH Drosselklappe *f*

through 1. *prp* durch (*acc*); bis (einschließlich); *Monday* ~ *Friday* von Montag bis Freitag 2. *adv* durch; ~ *and* ~ durch und durch; *put s.o.* ~ *to* TEL j-n verbinden mit; *wet* ~ völlig durchnässt 3. *adj* durchgehend (*train etc*); Durchgangs...

through·out 1. *prp*: ~ *the night* die ganze Nacht hindurch; ~ *the country* im ganzen Land, überall im Land 2. *adv* ganz, überall; die ganze Zeit (hindurch)

through traf·fic Durchgangsverkehr *m*

through·way *Br* → **thruway**

throw 1. werfen; *Hebel etc* betätigen; *Reiter* abwerfen; *Party* geben, F schmeißen; **~ a four** e-e Vier würfeln; **~ off** *Jacke etc* abwerfen; *Verfolger* abschütteln; *Krankheit* loswerden; **~ on** sich *e-e Jacke etc* (hastig) überwerfen; **~ out** hinauswerfen; wegwerfen; **~ up** *v/t* hochwerfen; F *Job* hinschmeißen; F (er)brechen; *v/i* F (sich er)brechen **2.** Wurf *m*

throw·a·way Wegwerf...; Einweg...; **~ pack** Einwegpackung *f*

throw·in *soccer:* Einwurf *m*

thru F → **through**

thrum → **strum**

thrush zo Drossel *f*

thrust 1. *j-n, et.* stoßen (*into in acc*); *et.* stecken, schieben (*into in acc*); **~ at** stoßen nach; **~ s.th. upon s.o.** j-m et. aufdrängen **2.** Stoß *m*; MIL Vorstoß *m*; PHYS Schub *m*, Schubkraft *f*

thru·way Schnellstraße *f*

thud 1. dumpfes Geräusch, Plumps *m* **2.** plumpsen

thug Verbrecher *m*, Schläger *m*

thumb 1. ANAT Daumen *m* **2.** **~ a lift or ride** per Anhalter fahren, trampen (*to nach*); **~ through a book** ein Buch durchblättern; **well-thumbed** abgegriffen

thumb·tack Reißzwecke *f*, Reißnagel *m*, Heftzwecke *f*

thump 1. *v/t* j-m e-n Schlag versetzen; **~ out** *Melodie* herunterhämmern (**on the piano** auf dem Klavier); *v/i* (heftig) schlagen *or* hämmern *or* pochen (*a. heart*); plumpsen; trampeln **2.** dumpfes Geräusch, Plumps *m*; Schlag *m*

thun·der 1. Donner *m*, Donnern *n* **2.** donnern

thun·der·bolt Blitz *m* und Donner *m*

thun·der·clap Donnerschlag *m*

thun·der·cloud Gewitterwolke *f*

thun·der·ous donnernd (*applause*)

thun·der·storm Gewitter *n*, Unwetter *n*

thun·der·struck wie vom Donner gerührt

Thur(s) *abbr of* **Thursday** Do., Donnerstag *m*

Thurs·day (*abbr* **Thur**, **Thurs**) Donnerstag *m*; **on ~** (am) Donnerstag; **on ~s** donnerstags

thus so, auf diese Weise; folglich, somit; **~ far** bisher

thwart durchkreuzen, vereiteln

thyme BOT Thymian *m*

thy·roid (gland) ANAT Schilddrüse *f*

tick¹ 1. Ticken *n*; Haken *m*, Häkchen *n* **2.** *v/i* ticken; *v/t* mst **~ off** ab-, anhaken

tick² zo Zecke *f*

tick³ **on ~** *Br* F auf Pump

tick·er·tape pa·rade Konfettiparade *f*

tick·et 1. Fahrkarte *f*, Fahrschein *m*; Flugkarte *f*, Flugschein *m*, Ticket *n*; (*Eintritts-, Theater- etc*)Karte *f*; (*Gepäck*)Schein *m*; Etikett *n*, (*Preis- etc* -) Schild *n*; POL Wahl-, Kandidatenliste *f*; (*a.* **parking~**) MOT Strafzettel *m* **2.** etikettieren; bestimmen, vorsehen (**for** für)

tick·et·can·cel·(l)ing ma·chine (Fahrschein)Entwerter *m*

tick·et col·lec·tor (Bahnsteig)Schaffner(in); **~ machine** Fahrkartenautomat *m*; **~ of·fice** RAIL Fahrkartenschalter *m*

tick·ing Inlett *n*; Matratzenbezug *m*

tick·le kitzeln

tick·lish kitz(e)lig, *fig a.* heikel

tid·al wave Flutwelle *f*

tid·bit Leckerbissen *m*

tide 1. Gezeiten *pl*; Flut *f*; *fig* Strömung *f*, Trend *m*; **high~** Flut *f*; **low~** Ebbe *f* **2.** **~ over** *fig a.* j-n hinweghelfen über (*acc*); j-n über Wasser halten

ti·dy 1. sauber, ordentlich, aufgeräumt; F hübsch, beträchtlich (*Sum etc*) **2.** (*a.* **~ up** in Ordnung bringen, (*Zimmer a.*) aufräumen; **~ away** wegräumen, aufräumen

tie 1. Krawatte *f*, Schlips *m*; Band *n*; Schnur *f*; Stimmengleichheit *f*; SPORT Unentschieden *n*; (*Pokal*)Spiel *n*; RAIL Schwelle *f*; mst *pl fig* Bande *pl* **2.** *v/t* an-, festbinden; (sich) *Krawatte etc* binden; *fig* verbinden; **the game was ~d** SPORT das Spiel ging unentschieden aus; *v/i:* **they ~d for second place** SPORT etc sie belegten gemeinsam den zweiten Platz; **~ down** *fig* (an)binden; j-n festlegen (**to** auf *acc*); **~ in with** übereinstimmen mit, passen zu; verbinden *or* koppeln mit; **~ up** *Paket etc* verschnüren; *et.* in Verbindung bringen (**with** mit); *Verkehr etc* lahmlegen; **be ~d up** ECON fest angelegt sein (**in** in *dat*)

tie·break(·**er**) *tennis*: Tie-Break *m, n*
tie-in (enge) Verbindung, (enger) Zusammenhang; ECON Kopplungsgeschäft *n*; **a book movie~** *appr* das Buch zum Film
tie-on Anhänge…
tie-pin Krawattennadel *f*
tier (Sitz)Reihe *f*; Lage *f*, Schicht *f*; *fig* Stufe *f*
tie-up (enge) Verbindung, (enger) Zusammenhang; ECON Fusion *f*
ti·ger ZO Tiger *m*
tight 1. *adj* fest (sitzend), fest angezogen; straff (*rope etc*); eng (*a. dress etc*); knapp (*a. fig*); F knick(e)rig; F blau; **be in a ~ corner** in der Klemme sein *or* sitzen *or* stecken **2.** *adv* fest; F gut; **hold~** festhalten; **sleep~!** F schlaf gut!
tight·en festziehen, anziehen; *Seil etc* straffen; **~ one's belt** *fig* den Gürtel enger schnallen; **~ up (on)** *Gesetz etc* verschärfen
tight-fist·ed F knick(e)rig
tights (*Tänzer-, Artisten*)Trikot *n*; *esp Br* Strumpfhose *f*
ti·gress ZO Tigerin *f*
tile 1. (Dach)Ziegel *m*; Fliese *f*, Kachel *f* **2.** (mit Ziegeln) decken; fliesen, kacheln
til·er Dachdecker *m*; Fliesenleger *m*
till[1] → **until**
till[2] (Laden)Kasse *f*
tilt 1. kippen; sich neigen **2.** Kippen *n*; **at a~** schief, schräg; (**at**) *full~* F mit Volldampf
tim·ber *Br* Bau-, Nutzholz *n*; Baumbestand *m*, Bäume *pl*; Balken *m*
time 1. Zeit *f*; Uhrzeit *f*; MUS Takt *m*; Mal *n*; **~ after ~**, **~ and again** immer wieder; **every ~ I …** jedes Mal, wenn ich …; **how many ~s?** wie oft?; **next ~** nächstes Mal; **this ~** diesmal; **three ~s** dreimal; **three ~s four equals** *or* **is twelve** drei mal vier ist zwölf; **what's the ~?** wie spät ist es?; **what ~?** um wie viel Uhr?; **all the ~** die ganze Zeit; **at all ~s, at any ~** jederzeit; **at the ~** damals; **at the same ~** gleichzeitig; **at ~s** manchmal; **by the ~** wenn; als; **for a ~** e-e Zeit lang; **for the ~ being** vorläufig, fürs Erste; **from ~ to ~** von Zeit zu Zeit; **have a good ~** sich gut unterhalten *or* amüsieren; **in ~** rechtzeitig; **in no**

~ (at all) im Nu; **on~** pünktlich; **some~ ago** vor einiger Zeit; **to pass the~** zum Zeitvertreib; **take one's~** sich Zeit lassen **2.** *et.* timen (*a.* SPORT); (ab)stoppen; zeitlich abstimmen, den richtigen Zeitpunkt wählen *or* bestimmen für
time| card Stechkarte *f*; **~ clock** Stechuhr *f*; **~ lag** Zeitdifferenz *f*
time-lapse *film*: Zeitraffer…
time·less immer während, ewig; zeitlos
time lim·it Frist *f*
time·ly (recht)zeitig
time sheet Stechkarte *f*
time sig·nal *radio*: Zeitzeichen *n*
time·ta·ble *Br* Fahrplan *m*, Flugplan *m*; Stundenplan *m*; Zeitplan *m*
tim·id ängstlich, furchtsam, zaghaft
tim·ing Timing *n*
tin 1. Zinn *n*; *Br* (Blech-, Konserven)Dose *f*, (-)Büchse *f* **2.** verzinnen; *Br* einmachen, eindosen
tinc·ture Tinktur *f*
tin-foil Stanniol(papier) *n*; Alufolie *f*
tinge 1. tönen; **be~d with** *fig* e-n Anflug haben von **2.** Tönung *f*; *fig* Anflug *m*, Spur *f* (**of** von)
tin·gle prickeln, kribbeln
tink·er herumpfuschen, herumbasteln (**at** an *dat*)
tin·kle bimmeln; klirren
tinned *Br* Dosen…, Büchsen…
tinned fruit *Br* Obstkonserven *pl*
tin o·pen·er *Br* Dosenöffner *m*, Büchsenöffner *m*
tin·sel Lametta *n*; Flitter *m*
tint 1. (Farb)Ton *m*, Tönung *f* **2.** tönen
ti·ny winzig
tip[1] **1.** Spitze *f*; Filter *m*; **it's on the ~ of my tongue** *fig* es liegt mir auf der Zunge **2.** mit e-r Spitze versehen
tip[2] **1.** *esp Br* (aus)kippen, schütten; kippen; **~ over** umkippen **2.** *esp Br* (*Schutt- etc*)Abladeplatz *m*, (-)Halde *f*; *Br fig* F Saustall *m*
tip[3] **1.** Trinkgeld *n* **2.** *j-m* ein Trinkgeld geben
tip[4] **1.** Tipp *m*, Rat(schlag) *m* **2.** tippen auf (*acc*) (**as** als); **~ s.o. off** j-m e-n Tipp *or* Wink geben
tip·sy angeheitert
tip·toe 1. on~ auf Zehenspitzen **2.** auf Zehenspitzen gehen
tire[1] MOT Reifen *m*
tire[2] ermüden, müde machen *or* werden

tired müde; **be ~ of** j-n, et. satt haben

tire·less unermüdlich

tire·some ermüdend; lästig

tis·sue BIOL Gewebe n; Papier(taschen)-tuch n; → **~ pa·per** Seidenpapier n

tit¹ F contp Titte f

tit² ZO Meise f

tit·bit esp Br → **tidbit**

tit·il·late j-n (sexuell) anregen

ti·tle Titel m; JUR (Rechts)Anspruch m (**to** auf acc)

ti·tle-hold·er SPORT Titelhalter(in)

ti·tle page Titelseite f

ti·tle role THEA etc Titelrolle f

tit·mouse ZO Meise f

tit·ter 1. kichern 2. Kichern n

to 1. prp zu; an (acc), für, in (acc), in (dat), nach; (im Verhältnis or im Vergleich) zu, gegen(über); extent, limit, degree: bis, (bis) zu, (bis) an (acc); time: bis, bis zu, bis gegen, vor (dat); **from Monday ~ Friday** von Montag bis Freitag; **a quarter ~ one** (ein) Viertel vor eins, drei viertel eins; **go ~ Italy** nach Italien fahren; **go ~ school** in die or zur Schule gehen; **have you ever been ~ Rome?** bist du schon einmal in Rom gewesen?; **~ me** etc mir etc; **here's ~ you!** auf Ihr Wohl!, prosit! 2. adv zu; **pull ~** Tür etc zuziehen; **come ~** (wieder) zu sich kommen; **~ and fro** hin und her, auf und ab 3. with infinitive: zu; intention, aim: um zu; **~ go** gehen; **easy ~ learn** leicht zu lernen; **... ~ earn money** ... um Geld zu verdienen

toad ZO Kröte f, Unke f

toad·stool BOT ungenießbarer Pilz; Giftpilz m

toad·y 1. Kriecher(in) 2. **~ to s.o.** fig vor j-m kriechen

toast¹ 1. Toast m 2. toasten; rösten

toast² 1. Toast m, Trinkspruch m 2. auf j-n or j-s Wohl trinken

toast·er TECH Toaster m

to·bac·co Tabak m; **to·bac·co·nist** Tabak(waren)händler(in)

to·bog·gan 1. (Rodel)Schlitten m 2. Schlitten fahren, rodeln

to·day 1. adv heute; heutzutage; **a week ~, ~ week** heute in e-r Woche, heute in acht Tagen 2. **~'s paper** die heutige Zeitung, die Zeitung von heute; **of ~, ~'s** von heute, heutig

tod·dle auf wack(e)ligen or unsicheren

Beinen gehen

to-do F fig Theater n

toe ANAT Zehe f; Spitze f

toe·nail ANAT Zehennagel m

tof·fee, tof·fy Sahnebonbon m, n, Toffee n

to·geth·er zusammen; gleichzeitig

toi·let Toilette f; **~ pa·per** Toilettenpapier n; **~ roll** esp Br Rolle f Toilettenpapier

to·ken Zeichen n; **as a ~, in ~ of** als or zum Zeichen (gen); zum Andenken an (acc); **~ strike** Warnstreik m

tol·e·ra·ble erträglich

tol·e·rance Toleranz f; Nachsicht f

tol·e·rant tolerant (**of**, **towards** gegenüber)

tol·e·rate tolerieren, dulden; ertragen

toll¹ Benutzungsgebühr f, Maut f; **heavy death ~** große Zahl an Todesopfern; **take its ~ (on)** fig s-n Tribut fordern (von); s-e Spuren hinterlassen (bei)

toll² läuten

toll-free TEL gebührenfrei

toll road gebührenpflichtige Straße, Mautstraße f

tom F → **tomcat**

to·ma·to BOT Tomate f

tomb Grab n; Grabmal n; Gruft f

tom·boy Wildfang m

tomb·stone Grabstein m

tom·cat ZO Kater m

tom·fool·e·ry Unsinn m

to·mor·row 1. adv morgen; **a week ~, ~ week** morgen in e-r Woche, morgen in acht Tagen; **~ morning** morgen früh; **~ night** morgen Abend 2. **the day after ~** übermorgen; **of ~, ~'s** von morgen

ton (abbr **t**, **tn**) Tonne f

tone 1. Ton m; Klang m; (Farb)Ton m; MUS Note f; MED Tonus m; fig Niveau n 2. **~ down** abschwächen; **~ up** Muskeln etc kräftigen

ton·er for cleansing the face Gesichtswasser n; PRINT Toner m

tongs (**a pair of ~** e-e) Zange f

tongue ANAT, TECH Zunge f; (Mutter)-Sprache f; Klöppel m (e-r Glocke); **hold one's ~** den Mund halten

ton·ic Tonikum n, Stärkungsmittel n; Tonic n; MUS Grundton m

to·night heute Abend or Nacht

ton·sil ANAT Mandel f

ton·sil·li·tis MED Mandelentzündung f; Angina f

too zu; zu, sehr; auch (noch)

tool Werkzeug n, Gerät n; ~ **bag** Werkzeugtasche f; ~ **box** Werkzeugkasten m; ~ **kit** Werkzeug n

tool·mak·er Werkzeugmacher m

tool·shed Geräteschuppen m

toot esp MOT hupen

tooth Zahn m

tooth·ache Zahnschmerzen pl, Zahnweh n

tooth·brush Zahnbürste f

tooth·less zahnlos

tooth·paste Zahncreme f, Zahnpasta f

tooth·pick Zahnstocher m

top¹ 1. oberer Teil; GEOGR Gipfel m, Spitze f; BOT Krone f, Wipfel m; Kopfende n, oberes Ende; Oberteil n; Oberfläche f; Deckel m; Verschluss m; MOT Verdeck n; MOT höchster Gang; **at the ~ of the page** oben auf der Seite; **at the ~ of one's voice** aus vollem Hals; **on ~** oben(auf); darauf, F drauf; **on ~ of** (oben) auf (dat or acc), über (dat or acc) **2.** oberste (-r, -s); Höchst..., Spitzen...; Top... **3.** bedecken (**with** mit); fig übersteigen, übertreffen; ~ **up** Tank etc auffüllen; F j-m nachschenken

top² Kreisel m (toy)

top hat Zylinder m

top-heav·y kopflastig (a. fig)

top·ic Thema n; **top·ic·al** aktuell

top·ple: mst ~ **over** umkippen; ~ **the government** die Regierung stürzen

top·sy-tur·vy in e-r heillosen Unordnung

torch Br Taschenlampe f; Fackel f

torch·light Fackelschein m; ~ **procession** Fackelzug m

tor·ment 1. Qual f **2.** quälen, peinigen, plagen

tor·na·do Tornado m, Wirbelsturm m

tor·pe·do MIL **1.** Torpedo m **2.** torpedieren (a. fig)

tor·rent reißender Strom; fig Schwall m

tor·ren·tial: ~ **rain** sintflutartige Regenfälle pl

tor·toise ZO Schildkröte f

tor·tu·ous gewunden

tor·ture 1. Folter f, Folterung f; fig Qual f, Tortur f **2.** foltern; fig quälen

toss 1. v/t werfen; Münze hochwerfen; GASTR schwenken; ~ **off** F Bild etc hinhauen; v/i a. ~ **about**, ~ **and turn** sich im Schlaf hin und her werfen; a. ~ **up** e-e Münze hochwerfen; ~ **for s.th.** um et. losen; ~ **one's head** den Kopf zurückwerfen **2.** Wurf m; Zurückwerfen n; Hochwerfen n

tot F Knirps m

to·tal 1. völlig, total; ganz, gesamt, Gesamt... **2.** Gesamtbetrag m, -menge f **3.** sich belaufen auf (acc); ~ **up** zusammenrechnen, -zählen

tot·ter schwanken, wanken

touch 1. (sich) berühren; anfassen; Essen etc anrühren; fig herankommen an (acc); fig rühren; ~ **wood!** toi, toi, toi!; ~ **down** AVIAT aufsetzen; ~ **up** ausbessern; PHOT retuschieren **2.** Tastempfindung f; Berührung f, MUS etc Anschlag m; (Pinsel- etc)Strich m; GASTR Spur f; Verbindung f, Kontakt m; fig Note f; fig Anflug m; **a ~ of flu** e-e leichte Grippe; **get in ~ with s.o.** sich mit j-m in Verbindung setzen

touch-and-go F kritisch, riskant, prekär; **it was ~ whether** es stand auf des Messers Schneide, ob

touch·down AVIAT Aufsetzen n, Landung f

touched gerührt; F leicht verrückt

touch·ing rührend

touch·line soccer: Seitenlinie f

touch·stone Prüfstein m (**of** für)

touch·y empfindlich; heikel (subject etc)

tough zäh; widerstandsfähig; fig hart; schwierig (problem, negotiations etc)

tough·en a. ~ **up** hart or zäh machen or werden

tour 1. Tour f (**of** durch), (Rund)Reise f, (Rund)Fahrt f; Ausflug m; Rundgang m (**of** durch); THEA Tournee f (a. SPORT); **go on ~** auf Tournee gehen; ~ **conduct** 2 2. bereisen, reisen durch

tour·is·m Tourismus m, Fremdenverkehr m

tour·ist 1. Tourist(in) **2.** Touristen...; ~ **class** AVIAT, MAR Touristenklasse f; ~ **in·dus·try** Tourismusgeschäft n; ~ **in·for·ma·tion of·fice**, ~ **of·fice** Verkehrsverein m; ~ **sea·son** Reisesaison f, Reisezeit f

tour·na·ment Turnier n

tou·sled zerzaust

tow 1. Boot etc schleppen, Auto etc a. abschleppen **2.** **give s.o. a ~** j-n abschleppen; **take in** ~ Auto etc abschleppen

to·ward, esp Br **to·wards** auf (acc) ... zu, (in) Richtung, zu; time: gegen; fig gegenüber

tow·el 1. Handtuch n, (Bade- etc)Tuch n **2.** (mit e-m Handtuch) abtrocknen oder abreiben

tow·er 1. Turm m **2.** ~ **above**, ~ **over** überragen; ~ **block** Br Hochhaus n

tow·er·ing turmhoch; fig überragend; **in a ~ rage** wütend vor Zorn

town Stadt f; Kleinstadt f; **go into** ~ in die Stadt gehen; ~ **cen·tre** Br Innenstadt f, City f; ~ **coun·cil** Br Stadtrat m; ~ **coun·ci(l)·lor** Br Stadtrat m, Stadträtin f; ~ **hall** Rathaus n

town·ie F Städter(in), Stadtmensch m

town|plan·ner Stadtplaner(in); ~ **planning** Stadtplanung f

towns·peo·ple Städter pl, Stadtbevölkerung f

tow·rope MOT Abschleppseil n

tox·ic toxisch, giftig; Gift...

tox·ic waste Giftmüll m

tox·ic waste dump Giftmülldeponie f

toy 1. Spielzeug n, pl a. Spielsachen pl, ECON Spielwaren pl **2.** Spielzeug...; Miniatur...; Zwerg... **3.** ~ **with** spielen mit (a. fig)

trace 1. (durch)pausen; j-n, et. ausfindig machen, aufspüren; et. finden; a. ~ **back** et. zurückverfolgen (**to** bis zu); ~ **s.th. to** et. zurückführen auf (acc) **2.** Spur f (a. fig)

track 1. Spur f (a. fig), Fährte f; Pfad m, Weg m; RAIL Gleis n, Geleise n; TECH Raupe f, Raupenkette f; SPORT (Renn-, Aschen)Bahn f, (Renn)Strecke f; tape etc: Spur f; Nummer f (on an LP etc) **2.** verfolgen; ~ **down** aufspüren; auftreiben

track and field SPORT Leichtathletik f

track e·vent SPORT Laufdisziplin f

track·ing sta·tion Bodenstation f

track·suit Trainingsanzug m

tract Fläche f, Gebiet n; ANAT (Verdauungs)Trakt m, (Atem)Wege pl

trac·tion Ziehen n, Zug m

trac·tion en·gine Zugmaschine f

trac·tor Traktor m, Trecker m

trade 1. Handel m; Branche f, Gewerbe n; (esp Handwerks)Beruf m **2.** Handel treiben, handeln; ~ **on** ausnutzen; ~ **a·gree·ment** Handelsabkommen n

trade·mark Warenzeichen n

trade name Markenname m, Handelsbezeichnung f

trade price Großhandelspreis m

trad·er Händler(in)

trades·man (Einzel)Händler m; Ladeninhaber m; Lieferant m

trade(Br **trades**)| u·nion Gewerkschaft f; ~ u·nion·ist Gewerkschaftler(in)

tra·di·tion Tradition f; Überlieferung f

tra·di·tion·al traditionell

traf·fic 1. Verkehr m; (esp illegaler) Handel (**in** mit); **2.** (esp illegal) handeln (**in** mit); ~ **cir·cle** MOT Kreisverkehr m; ~ **in·struc·tion** Verkehrsunterricht m; ~ **is·land** Verkehrsinsel f; ~ **jam** (Verkehrs)Stau m, Verkehrsstockung f; ~ **light**(s) Verkehrsampel f; ~ **of·fend·er** Verkehrssünder(in); ~ **of·fense** (Br **offence**) Verkehrsdelikt n; ~ **reg·u·la·tions** Straßenverkehrsordnung f; ~ **sign** Verkehrszeichen n, -schild n; ~ **sig·nal** → **traffic light**(s); ~ **war·den** Br Parküberwacher(in), Politesse f

tra·ge·dy Tragödie f

tra·gic tragisch

trail 1. v/t et. nachschleifen lassen; verfolgen; SPORT zurückliegen hinter (dat) (**by** um); v/i sich schleppen; BOT kriechen; SPORT zurückliegen (**by 3-0** 0:3); ~ (**along**) **behind s.o.** hinter j-m herschleifen **2.** Spur f (a. fig), Fährte f; Pfad m, Weg m; ~ **of blood** Blutspur f; ~ **of dust** Staubwolke f

trail·er MOT Anhänger m; Wohnwagen m, Caravan m; film, TV Trailer m, Vorschau f; ~ **park** Standplatz m für Wohnwagen

train 1. RAIL Zug m; Kolonne f, Schlange f; Schleppe f; fig Folge f, Kette f; **by** ~ mit der Bahn, mit dem Zug; ~ **of thought** Gedankengang m **2.** v/t j-n ausbilden (**as** als, zum), schulen; SPORT trainieren; Tier abrichten, dressieren; Kamera etc richten (**on** auf acc); v/i ausgebildet werden (**as** als, zum); SPORT trainieren (**for** für)

train·ee Auszubildende m, f

train·er Ausbilder(in); ZO Abrichter(in), Dompteur m, Dompteuse f; SPORT Trainer(in); Br Turnschuh m

train·ing Ausbildung f, Schulung f; Abrichten n, Dressur f; SPORT Training n

trait (Charakter)Zug m

trai·tor Verräter *m*

tram *Br* Straßenbahn(wagen *m*) *f*

tram·car *Br* Straßenbahnwagen *m*

tramp **1.** sta(m)pfen *or* trampeln (durch) **2.** Tramp *m*, Landstreicher *m*, Vagabund *m*; Wanderung *f*; Flittchen *n*; tram·ple (zer)trampeln

trance Trance *f*

tran·quil ruhig, friedlich

tran·quil·(l)i·ty Ruhe *f*, Frieden *m*

tran·quil·(l)ize beruhigen

tran·quil·(l)iz·er PHARM Beruhigungsmittel *n*

trans·act *Geschäft* abwickeln, *Handel* abschließen

trans·ac·tion Abwicklung *f*, Abschluss *m*; Geschäft *n*, Transaktion *f*

trans·at·lan·tic transatlantisch, Transatlantik…, Übersee…

tran·scribe abschreiben, kopieren; *Stenogramm etc* übertragen

tran·script Abschrift *f*, Kopie *f*

tran·scrip·tion Umschreibung *f*, Umschrift *f*; Abschrift *f*, Kopie *f*

trans·fer **1.** *v/t* (**to**) *Betrieb etc* verlegen (nach); *j-n* versetzen (nach); SPORT *Spieler* transferieren (zu); abgeben (an *acc*); *Geld* überweisen (an *acc*, auf *acc*); JUR *Eigentum*, *Recht* übertragen (auf *acc*); *v/i* SPORT wechseln (**to** zu); umsteigen (**from … to …** von … auf … *acc*); **2.** Verlegung *f*, Versetzung *f*; SPORT Transfer *m*, Wechsel *m*; ECON Überweisung *f*; JUR Übertragung *f*; Umsteige(fahr)karte *f*

trans·fer·a·ble übertragbar

trans·fixed *fig* versteinert, starr

trans·form umwandeln, verwandeln

trans·for·ma·tion Umwandlung *f*, Verwandlung *f*

trans·form·er ELECTR Transformator *m*

trans·fu·sion MED Bluttransfusion *f*, Blutübertragung *f*

trans·gress verletzen, verstoßen gegen

tran·sient flüchtig, vergänglich

tran·sis·tor Transistor *m*

tran·sit Transit-, Durchgangsverkehr *m*; ECON Transport *m*; **in ~** unterwegs, auf dem Transport

tran·si·tion Übergang *m*

tran·si·tive LING transitiv

tran·si·to·ry → *transient*

trans·late übersetzen (**from English into German** aus dem Englischen ins

Deutsche)

trans·la·tion Übersetzung *f*

trans·la·tor Übersetzer(in)

trans·lu·cent lichtdurchlässig

trans·mis·sion MED Übertragung *f*; *radio*, TV Sendung *f*; MOT Getriebe *n*

trans·mit *Signale* (aus)senden; *radio*, TV senden; PHYS *Wärme etc* leiten; *Licht etc* durchlassen; MED *Krankheit* übertragen

trans·mit·ter Sender *m*

trans·par·en·cy Durchsichtigkeit *f* (*a. fig*); *fig* Durchschaubarkeit *f*; Dia (-positiv) *n*; Folie *f*; trans·par·ent durchsichtig (*a. fig*); *fig* durchschaubar

tran·spire transpirieren, schwitzen; *fig* durchsickern; F passieren

trans·plant **1.** umpflanzen, verpflanzen (*a. MED*); MED transplantieren **2.** MED Transplantation *f*, Verpflanzung *f*; Transplantat *n*

trans·port **1.** Transport *m*, Beförderung *f*; Beförderungs-, Verkehrsmittel *n or pl*; MIL Transportschiff *n*, -flugzeug *n*, (*Truppen*)Transporter *m* **2.** transportieren, befördern

trans·port·a·ble transportabel, transportfähig

trans·por·ta·tion Transport *m*, Beförderung *f*

trap **1.** Falle *f* (*a. fig*); **set a ~ for s.o.** j-m e-e Falle stellen; **shut one's ~, keep one's ~ shut** F die Schnauze halten **2.** (in *or* mit e-r Falle) fangen; *fig* in e-e Falle locken; **be ~ped** eingeschlossen sein

trap·door Falltür *f*; THEA Versenkung *f*

tra·peze Trapez *n*

trap·per Trapper *m*, Fallensteller *m*, Pelztierjäger *m*

trap·pings Rangabzeichen *pl*; *fig* Drum und Dran *n*

trash F Schund *m*; Quatsch *m*, Unsinn *m*; Abfall *m*, Abfälle *pl*, Müll *m*; Gesindel *n*

trash·can Abfall-, Mülleimer *m*; Abfall-, Mülltonne *f*

trash·y Schund…

trav·el **1.** *v/i* reisen; fahren; TECH *etc* sich bewegen; *fig* sich verbreiten; *fig* schweifen, wandern; *v/t* bereisen; *Strecke* zurücklegen, fahren **2.** Reisen *n*; *pl* (*esp* Auslands)Reisen *pl*; **~ a·gen·cy** Reisebüro *n*; **~ a·gent** Reisebüroinha-

ber(in); Angestellte *m, f* in e-m Reisebüro; ~ a·gent's, ~ bu·reau Reisebüro
n

trav·el·(l)er Reisende *m, f*

trav·el·(l)er's check (*Br* cheque) Rei-
se-, Travellerscheck *m*

trav·el·(l)ing| bag Reisetasche *f;* ~
ex·pens·es Reisekosten *pl*

trav·el sick·ness Reisekrankheit *f*

trav·es·ty Zerrbild *n*

trawl **1.** Schleppnetz *n* **2.** mit dem
Schleppnetz fischen

trawl·er MAR Trawler *m*

tray Tablett *n*; Ablagekorb *m*

treach·er·ous verräterisch; tückisch

treach·er·y Verrat *m*

trea·cle *esp Br* Sirup *m*

tread **1.** treten (**on** auf *acc*; in *acc*); *Pfad
etc* treten **2.** Gang *m*; Schritt(e *pl*) *m*;
(Reifen)Profil *n*

tread·mill Tretmühle *f* (*a. fig*)

trea·son Landesverrat *m*

trea·sure **1.** Schatz *m* **2.** sehr schätzen; in
Ehren halten

trea·sur·er Schatzmeister(in)

trea·sure trove Schatzfund *m*

Trea·su·ry *Br,* ~ De·part·ment Finanz-
ministerium *n*

treat **1.** *j-n, et.* behandeln; umgehen mit;
et. ansehen, betrachten (*as* als); MED
j-n behandeln (*for* gegen); *j-n* einladen
(*to* zu); ~ *o.s. to s.th. a.* sich et. spendieren; ~ *o.s. to s.th.* sich et. leisten *or*
gönnen; *be* ~*ed for* MED in ärztlicher
Behandlung sein wegen **2.** (besondere)
Freude *or* Überraschung; *this is my* ~
das geht auf meine Rechnung, ich lade
dich *etc* ein

trea·tise Abhandlung *f*

treat·ment Behandlung *f*

treat·y Vertrag *m*

tre·ble¹ **1.** dreifach **2.** (sich) verdreifachen

tre·ble² MUS Knabensopran *m*; *radio:*
(Ton)Höhe *f*

tree BOT Baum *m*

tre·foil BOT Klee *m*

trel·lis BOT Spalier *n*

trem·ble zittern (*with* vor *dat*)

tre·men·dous gewaltig, enorm; F klasse,
toll

trem·or Zittern *n*; Beben *n*

trench Graben *m*; MIL Schützengraben
m

trend Trend *m*, Entwicklung *f*, Tendenz
f; Mode *f*

trend·y F **1.** modern, modisch; *be* ~ als
schick gelten, in sein **2.** *esp Br contp*
Schickimicki *m*

tres·pass **1.** ~ *on Grundstück etc* unbefugt betreten; *j-s Zeit etc* über Gebühr
in Anspruch nehmen; *no* ~*ing* Betreten verboten! **2.** unbefugtes Betreten

tres·pass·er: ~*s will be prosecuted* Betreten bei Strafe verboten!

tres·tle Bock *m*, Gestell *n*

tri·al **1.** JUR Prozess *m*, (Gerichts)Ver-
handlung *f*, (-)Verfahren *n*; Erprobung
f, Probe *f*, Prüfung *f*, Test *m*; Plage *f*; *on*
~ auf *or* zur Probe; *be on* ~ erprobt *or*
getestet werden; *be on* ~, *stand* ~ vor
Gericht stehen (*for* wegen); *by way of* ~
versuchsweise **2.** Versuchs..., Probe...

tri·an·gle Dreieck *n*; Winkel *m*, Zeichendreieck *n*

tri·an·gu·lar dreieckig

tri·ath·lon SPORT Triathlon *n, m*, Drei-
kampf *m*

trib·al Stammes...

tribe (Volks)Stamm *m*

tri·bu·nal JUR Gericht(shof *m*) *n*

trib·u·ta·ry GEOGR Nebenfluss *m*

trib·ute: *be a* ~ *to j-m* Ehre machen; *pay*
~ *to j-m* Anerkennung zollen

trick **1.** Trick *m*; (*Karten- etc*)Kunststück
n; Streich *m*; *card game:* Stich *m*;
(merkwürdige) Angewohnheit, Eigenart *f*; *play a* ~ *on s.o. j-m* e-n Streich
spielen **2.** Trick...; ~ *question* Fangfra-
ge *f* **3.** überlisten, F reinlegen

trick·e·ry Tricks *pl*

trick·le **1.** tröpfeln; rieseln **2.** Tröpfeln *n*;
Rinnsal *n*

trick·ster Betrüger(in), Schwindler(in)

trick·y heikel, schwierig; durchtrieben,
raffiniert

tri·cy·cle Dreirad *n*

tri·dent Dreizack *m*

tri·fle **1.** Kleinigkeit *f*; Lappalie *f*; *a* ~ ein
bisschen, etwas **2.** ~ *with fig* spielen
mit; *he is not to be* ~*d with* er lässt
nicht mit sich spaßen

tri·fling geringfügig, unbedeutend

trig·ger Abzug *m*; *pull the* ~ abdrücken

trig·ger-hap·py F schießwütig

trill **1.** Triller *m* **2.** trillern

trim **1.** *Hecke etc* stutzen, beschneiden,
sich *den Bart etc* stutzen; *Kleidungs-*

stück besetzen (*with* mit); **~med with fur** pelzbesetzt, mit Pelzbesatz; **~ off** abschneiden **2. give s.th. a ~** et. stutzen, et. (be)schneiden; **be in good ~** F gut in Form sein **3.** gepflegt

trim·mings Besatz *m*; GASTR Beilagen *pl*

Trin·i·ty REL Dreieinigkeit *f*

trin·ket (*esp* billiges) Schmuckstück

trip 1. *v/i* stolpern (**over** über *acc*); (e-n) Fehler machen; *v/t a.* **~ up** j-m ein Bein stellen (*a. fig*) **2.** (kurze) Reise; Ausflug *m*, Trip *m* (*a. sl*); Stolpern *n*, Fallen *n*

tripe GASTR Kaldaunen *pl*, Kutteln *pl*

trip·le 1. dreifach **2.** verdreifachen

trip·le jump SPORT Dreisprung *m*

trip·lets Drillinge *pl*

trip·li·cate 1. dreifach **2. in ~** in dreifacher Ausfertigung

tri·pod PHOT Stativ *n*

trip·per *esp Br* (*esp Tages*) Ausflügler(in)

trite abgedroschen, banal

tri·umph 1. Triumph *m*, *fig* Sieg *m* (**over** über *acc*); **2.** triumphieren (**over** über *acc*)

tri·um·phal Triumph...

tri·um·phant triumphierend

triv·i·al unbedeutend, bedeutungslos; trivial, alltäglich

trol·ley *esp Br* Einkaufswagen *m*; Gepäckwagen *m*, Kofferkuli *m*; (*Tee- etc*) Wagen *m*; (**supermarket**) **~** Einkaufswagen *m*; **shopping ~** Einkaufsroller *m*

trol·ley·bus Oberleitungsbus *m*, Obus *m*

trom·bone MUS Posaune *f*

troop 1. Schar *f*; *pl* MIL Truppen *pl* **2.** (*herein- etc*) strömen; **~ the colour** *Br* MIL e-e Fahnenparade abhalten

troop·er MIL Kavallerist *m*; Panzerjäger *m*; Polizist *m*

tro·phy Trophäe *f*

trop·ic ASTR, GEOGR Wendekreis *m*; **the~ of Cancer** der Wendekreis des Krebses; **the~ of Capricorn** der Wendekreis des Steinbocks

trop·i·cal tropisch, Tropen...

trop·ics Tropen *pl*

trot 1. Trab *m*; Trott *m* **2.** traben (lassen); **~ along** F losziehen

trou·ble 1. Schwierigkeit *f*, Problem *n*, Ärger *m*; Mühe *f*; MED Beschwerden *pl*; *a. pl* POL Unruhen *pl*; *pl* Unannehmlichkeiten *pl*; **be in ~** in Schwierigkei-

ten sein; **get into ~** Schwierigkeiten *or* Ärger bekommen; *j-n* in Schwierigkeiten bringen; **get** *or* **run into ~** in Schwierigkeiten geraten; **have ~ with** Schwierigkeiten *or* Ärger haben mit; **put s.o. to ~** j-m Mühe *or* Umstände machen; **take the ~ to do s.th.** sich die Mühe machen, et. zu tun **2.** *v/t* j-n beunruhigen; j-m Mühe *or* Umstände machen; j-n bemühen (**for** um), bitten (**for** um; **to do** zu tun); **be ~d by** geplagt werden von, leiden an (*dat*); *v/i* sich bemühen (**to do** zu tun), sich Umstände machen (**about** wegen)

trou·ble·mak·er Störenfried *m*, Unruhestifter(in)

trou·ble·some lästig

trouble spot *esp* POL Krisenherd *m*

trough Trog *m*; Wellental *n*

trounce SPORT haushoch besiegen

troupe THEA Truppe *f*

trou·ser: (**a pair of**) **~s** (e-e) Hose *f*

trou·ser suit *Br* Hosenanzug *m*

trous·seau Aussteuer *f*

trout *zo* Forelle *f*

trow·el (Maurer)Kelle *f*

tru·ant Schulschwänzer(in); **play ~** *Br* (die Schule) schwänzen

truce MIL Waffenstillstand *m* (*a. fig*)

truck 1. MOT Lastwagen *m*; Fernlaster *m*; *Br* RAIL (offener) Güterwagen; Transportkarren *m* **2.** auf *or* mit Lastwagen transportieren

truck driv·er, truck·er MOT Lastwagenfahrer *m*; Fernfahrer *m*

truck farm ECON Gemüse- und Obstgärtnerei *f*

trudge (mühsam) stapfen

true wahr; echt, wirklich; treu (**to** *dat*); **be~** wahr sein, stimmen; **come ~** in Erfüllung gehen; wahr werden; **~ to life** lebensecht

tru·ly wahrheitsgemäß; wirklich, wahrhaft; aufrichtig

trump 1. Trumpf(karte *f*) *m*; *pl* Trumpf *m* **2.** mit e-m Trumpf stechen; **~ up** erfinden

trum·pet 1. MUS Trompete *f* **2.** trompeten; *fig* ausposaunen

trun·cheon (Gummi)Knüppel *m*, Schlagstock *m*

trun·dle *Karren etc* ziehen

trunk (Baum)Stamm *m*; Schrankkoffer *m*; *zo* Rüssel *m*; ANAT Rumpf *m*; MOT

T

Kofferraum *m*; ~ road *Br* Fernstraße *f*

trunks (*a. a pair of* ~ e-e) (*Bade*)Hose *f*; SPORT Shorts *pl*

truss 1. *a.* ~ *up j-n* fesseln; GASTR *Geflügel etc* dressieren **2.** MED Bruchband *n*

trust 1. Vertrauen *n* (*in* zu); JUR Treuhand *f*; ECON Trust *m*; Großkonzern *m*; **hold s.th. in** ~ et. treuhänderisch verwalten (*for* für); **place s.th. in s.o.'s** ~ *j-m* et. anvertrauen **2.** *v/t* (ver)trauen (*dat*); sich verlassen auf (*acc*); (zuversichtlich) hoffen; ~ **him!** das sieht ihm ähnlich!; *v/i:* ~ **in** vertrauen auf (*acc*); ~ **to** sich verlassen auf (*acc*)

trust·ee JUR Treuhänder(in); Sachverwalter(in)

trust·ful, **trust·ing** vertrauensvoll

trust·wor·thy vertrauenswürdig, zuverlässig

truth Wahrheit *f*

truth·ful wahr; wahrheitsliebend

try 1. *v/t* versuchen; *et.* (aus)probieren; JUR (über) *e-e Sache* verhandeln; *j-m* den Prozess machen (*for* wegen); *j-n, j-s* Geduld, Nerven *etc* auf *e-e* harte Probe stellen; ~ *s.th.* **on** Kleid etc anprobieren; ~ *s.th.* **out** et. ausprobieren; *v/i* es versuchen; ~ **for** *Br*, ~ **out for** sich bemühen um **2.** Versuch *m*; **give** *s.o.*, *s.th. a* ~ es mit *j-m*, et. versuchen; **have a** ~ es versuchen; **try·ing** anstrengend

tsar HIST Zar *m*

T-shirt T-Shirt *n*

tub Bottich *m*, Zuber *m*, Tonne *f*; Becher *m*; F (*Bade*)Wanne *f*

tub·by F pumm(e)lig

tube Röhre *f* (*a.* ANAT), Rohr *n*; Schlauch *m*; Tube *f*; *Br* F U-Bahn *f* (*in London*); F Röhre *f*, Glotze *f*

tube·less schlauchlos

tu·ber BOT Knolle *f*

tu·ber·cu·lo·sis MED Tuberkulose *f*

tu·bu·lar röhrenförmig

tuck 1. stecken; ~ **away** F wegstecken; ~ **in** *esp Br* F reinhauen, zulangen; ~ **up** (**in bed**) *Kind* ins Bett packen **2.** Biese *f*; Saum *m*; Abnäher *m*

Tue(s) *abbr of* **Tuesday** Di., Dienstag *m*

Tues·day (*abbr* **Tue, Tues**) Dienstag *m*; **on** ~ (am) Dienstag; **on** ~**s** dienstags

tuft (*Gras-*, *Haar- etc*)Büschel *n*

tug 1. zerren *or* ziehen (*an dat or* **at** *an dat*); **2. give** *s.th. a* ~ zerren *or* ziehen an (*dat*)

tug-of-war SPORT Tauziehen *n* (*a. fig*)

tu·i·tion Unterricht *m*; Unterrichtsgebühr(en *pl*) *f*

tu·lip BOT Tulpe *f*

tum·ble 1. fallen, stürzen; purzeln (*a. fig*) **2.** Fall *m*, Sturz *m*

tum·ble-down baufällig

tum·bler (*Trink*)Glas *n*

tu·mid MED geschwollen

tum·my F Bauch *m*, Bäuchlein *n*

tu·mo(u)r MED Tumor *m*

tu·mult Tumult *m*

tu·mul·tu·ous tumultartig, (*applause etc*) stürmisch

tu·na ZO Thunfisch *m*

tune 1. MUS Melodie *f*; **be out of** ~ verstimmt sein **2.** *v/t mst* ~ **in** Radio etc einstellen (*to* auf *acc*); *a.* ~ **up** MUS stimmen; *a.* ~ **up** Motor tunen; *v/i:* ~ **in** (das Radio *etc*) einschalten; ~ **up** MUS (die Instrumente) stimmen

tune·ful melodisch

tune·less unmelodisch

tun·er radio, TV Tuner *m*

tun·nel 1. Tunnel *m* **2.** Berg durchtunneln; Fluss etc untertunneln

tun·ny ZO Thunfisch *m*

tur·ban Turban *m*

tur·bid trüb (*water*); dick, dicht (*smoke etc*); *fig* verworren, wirr

tur·bine TECH Turbine *f*

tur·bo F, **tur·bo-charg·er** MOT Turbolader *m*

tur·bot ZO Steinbutt *m*

tur·bu·lent turbulent

tu·reen (*Suppen*)Terrine *f*

turf 1. Rasen *m*; Sode *f*, Rasenstück *n*; **the** ~ die (Pferde)Rennbahn; der Pferderennsport **2.** mit Rasen bedecken

tur·gid MED geschwollen

Turk Türke *m*, Türkin *f*

Tur·key die Türkei

tur·key ZO Truthahn *m*, Truthenne *f*, Pute *f*, Puter *m*; **talk** ~ F offen *or* sachlich reden

Turk·ish 1. türkisch **2.** LING Türkisch *n*

tur·moil Aufruhr *m*

turn 1. *v/t* drehen, herum-, umdrehen; (um)wenden; *Seite* umblättern; *Schlauch etc* richten (*on* auf *acc*); *Antenne* ausrichten (*toward[s]* auf *acc*); *Aufmerksamkeit* zuwenden (*to* dat); verwandeln (*into* in *acc*); *Laub etc* färben; *Milch* sauer werden lassen; TECH

formen, drechseln; **~ the corner** um
die Ecke biegen; **~ loose** los-, freilassen; **~ s.o.'s stomach** j-m den Magen
umdrehen; → **inside** 1, **upside down,
somersault** 1; *v/i* sich (um)drehen; abbiegen (**onto** auf *acc*; **into** in
acc); MOT wenden; *blass, sauer etc* werden; sich verwandeln, *fig a*. umschla-
gen (**into, to** in *acc*); → **left** 2, **righ** 2;
~ against j-n aufbringen *or* aufhetzen
gegen; *fig* sich wenden gegen; **~ away**
(sich) abwenden (**from** von); *j-n* abweisen, wegschicken; **~ back** umkehren;
j-n zurückschicken; *Uhr* zurückstellen;
~ down *Radio etc* leiser stellen; *Gas etc*
klein(er) stellen; *Heizung etc* runter-
schalten; *j-n, Angebot etc* ablehnen;
Kragen umschlagen; *Bettdecke* zurückschlagen; **~ in** *v/t* zurückgeben; *Gewinn etc* erzielen, abgeben; **~ o.s. in** sich
einreichen, abgeben; **~ o.s. in** sich stellen;
v/i F sich aufs Ohr legen; **~ off** *v/t Gas,
Wasser etc* abdrehen; *Licht, Radio etc*
ausmachen, ausschalten; *Motor* abstellen; F *j-n* anwidern; F *j-m* die Lust
nehmen; *v/i* abbiegen; **~ on** *Gas, Wasser etc* aufdrehen; *Gerät* anstellen;
Licht, Radio etc anmachen, an-, einschalten; F *j-n* antörnen; anmachen;
~ out *v/t Licht* ausmachen, ausschalten; *j-n* hinauswerfen; F *Waren* ausstos-
sen; *Tasche etc* (aus)leeren; *v/i* it kommen (**for** zu); sich erweisen *or* herausstellen als; **~ over** (sich) umdrehen;
Seite umblättern; wenden; *et*. umkippen; sich *et*. überlegen; *j-n, et*. übergeben (**to** *dat*); *Waren* umsetzen; **~ round**
sich umdrehen; **~ one's car round**
wenden; **~ to** sich an *j-n* wenden; sich
zuwenden (*dat*); **~ up** *Kragen* hoch-
schlagen; *Ärmel, Saum etc* umschlagen; *Radio etc* lauter stellen; *Gas etc*
aufdrehen; *fig* auftauchen **2.** (Um-)
Drehung *f*; Biegung *f*, Kurve *f*, Kehre
f; Abzweigung *f*; *fig* Wende *f*, Wendung *f*; **at every ~** auf Schritt und Tritt;
by ~s abwechselnd; **in ~** der Reihe
nach; abwechselnd; **it is my ~** ich bin
an der Reihe *or* F dran; **make a left
~** (nach) links abbiegen; **take ~s** sich
abwechseln (**at** bei); **take a ~ for the
better** (**worse**) sich bessern (sich verschlimmern); **do s.o. a good** (**bad**) **~**
j-m e-n guten (schlechten) Dienst er-

weisen
turn-coat Abtrünnige *m*, *f*, Überläu-
fer(in); (**political**) **~** F Wendehals *m*
turn-er Drechsler *m*; Dreher *m*
turn-ing *esp Br* Abzweigung *f*
turn-ing cir-cle MOT Wendekreis *m*
turn-ing point *fig* Wendepunkt *m*
tur-nip BOT Rübe *f*
turn-off Abzweigung *f*
turn-out Besucher(zahl *f*) *pl*, Beteiligung *f*; Wahlbeteiligung *f*; F Aufmachung *f*
turn-o-ver ECON Umsatz *m*; Personal-
wechsel *m*, Fluktuation *f*
turn-pike (**road**) gebührenpflichtige
Schnellstraße
turn-stile Drehkreuz *n*
turn-ta-ble Plattenteller *m*
turn-up *Br* (Hosen)Aufschlag *m*
tur-pen-tine CHEM Terpentin *n*
tur-quoise MIN Türkis *m*
tur-ret ARCH Ecktürmchen *n*; MIL (Panzer)Turm *m*; MAR Gefechtsturm *m*, Ge-
schützturm *m*
tur-tle ZO (See)Schildkröte *f*
tur-tle-dove ZO Turteltaube *f*
tur-tle-neck Rollkragen(pullover) *m*
tusk ZO Stoßzahn *m*; Hauer *m*
tus-sle F Gerangel *n*
tus-sock Grasbüschel *n*
tu-te-lage (An)Leitung *f*; JUR Vormundschaft *f*
tu-tor Privat-, Hauslehrer(in); *Br* UNIV
Tutor(in), Studienleiter(in)
tu-to-ri-al *Br* UNIV Tutorenkurs *m*
tux-e-do Smoking *m*
TV 1. TV *n*, Fernsehen *n*; Fernsehgerät
n, F Fernseher *m*; **on ~** im Fernsehen;
watch ~ fernsehen **2.** Fernseh…
twang 1. Schwirren *n*; *mst* **nasal ~** nä-
selnde Aussprache **2.** schwirren (lassen)
tweak F zwicken, kneifen
tweet ZO piep(s)en
tweez-ers (**a pair of ~** e-e) Pinzette *f*
twelfth 1. zwölfte(r, -s) **2.** Zwölftel *n*
twelve 1. zwölf **2.** Zwölf *f*
twen-ti-eth zwanzigste(r, -s)
twen-ty 1. zwanzig **2.** Zwanzig *f*
twice zweimal
twid-dle (herum)spielen mit (*or* **with**
mit); **~ one's thumbs** Däumchen drehen
twig BOT dünner Zweig, Ästchen *n*

twi·light (*esp* Abend)Dämmerung *f*; Zwielicht *n*, Dämmerlicht *n*

twin 1. Zwilling *m*; *pl* Zwillinge *pl* **2.** Zwillings…; doppelt **3.** *be ~ned with* die Partnerstadt sein von

twin-bed·ded room Zweibettzimmer *n*

twin beds zwei Einzelbetten

twin broth·er Zwillingsbruder *m*

twine 1. Bindfaden *m*, Schnur *f* **2.** (sich) schlingen *or* winden (*round* um); *a. ~ together* zusammendrehen

twin-en·gined AVIAT zweimotorig

twinge stechender Schmerz, Stechen *n*; *a ~ of conscience* Gewissensbisse *pl*

twin·kle 1. glitzern (*stars*), (*a.* eyes) funkeln (*with* vor *dat*); **2.** Glitzern *n*, Funkeln *n*; *with a ~ in one's eye* augenzwinkernd

twin sis·ter Zwillingsschwester *f*

twin town Partnerstadt *f*

twirl 1. (herum)wirbeln; wirbeln (*round* über *acc*); **2.** Wirbel *m*

twist 1. *v/t* drehen; wickeln (*round* um); *fig* verdrehen; *~ off* abdrehen, *Deckel* abschrauben; *~ one's ankle* (mit dem Fuß) umknicken, sich den Fuß vertreten; *her face was ~ed with pain* ihr Gesicht war schmerzverzerrt; *v/i* sich winden, (*river etc a.*) sich schlängeln **2.** Drehung *f*; Biegung *f*; (*überraschende*) Wendung; MUS Twist *m*

twitch 1. *v/t* zucken (mit); *v/i* zucken (*with* vor); zupfen (*at* an *dat*); **2.** Zucken *n*; Zuckung *f*

twit·ter 1. zwitschern **2.** Zwitschern *n*, Gezwitscher *n*; *be all of a ~* F ganz aufgeregt sein

two 1. zwei; *the ~ cars* die beiden Autos; *the ~ of us* wir beide; *in ~s* zu zweit,

paarweise; *cut in ~* in zwei Teile schneiden; *put ~ and ~ together* zwei und zwei zusammenzählen **2.** Zwei *f*

two-edged zweischneidig

two-faced falsch, heuchlerisch

two·fold zweifach

two·pence *Br* zwei Pence *pl*

two-pen·ny *Br* für zwei Pence

two-piece zweiteilig; *~ dress* Jackenkleid *n*

two-seat·er AVIAT, MOT Zweisitzer *m*

two-sid·ed zweiseitig

two-sto·ried, *Br* **two-sto·rey** zweistöckig

two-way traf·fic MOT Gegenverkehr *m*

ty·coon (*Industrie- etc*)Magnat *m*

type 1. Art *f*, Sorte *f*; Typ *m*; PRINT Type *f*, Buchstabe *m* **2.** *v/t et.* mit der Maschine schreiben, tippen; *v/i* Maschine schreiben, tippen

type·writ·er Schreibmaschine *f*

type·writ·ten maschine(n)geschrieben

ty·phoid (fe·ver) MED Typhus *m*

ty·phoon Taifun *m*

ty·phus MED Flecktyphus *m*, -fieber *n*

typ·i·cal typisch, bezeichnend (*of* für)

typ·i·fy typisch sein für, kennzeichnen; verkörpern

typ·ing er·ror Tippfehler *m*

typ·ing pool ECON Schreibzentrale *f*

typ·ist Schreibkraft *f*; Maschinenschreiber(in)

ty·ran·ni·cal tyrannisch

tyr·an·nize tyrannisieren

tyr·an·ny Tyrannei *f*

tyr·ant Tyrann(in)

tyre *Br* → **tire**[1]

tzar → **tsar**

U

U, u U, u *n*

ud·der ZO Euter *n*

ug·ly hässlich (*a. fig*); bös(e), schlimm (*wound etc*)

ul·cer MED Geschwür *n*

ul·te·ri·or: *~ motive* Hintergedanke *m*

ul·ti·mate letzte(r, -s), End…; höchste(r, -s)

ul·ti·mate·ly letztlich; schließlich

ul·ti·ma·tum Ultimatum *n*; *deliver an ~ to s.o.* j-m ein Ultimatum stellen

ul·tra·high fre·quen·cy ELECTR Ultrakurzwelle *f*

ul·tra·ma·rine ultramarin

ul·tra·son·ic Ultraschall…

ul·tra·sound PHYS Ultraschall *m*

ul·tra·vi·o·let ultraviolett

um·bil·i·cal cord ANAT Nabelschnur *f*

um·brel·la (Regen)Schirm *m*; *fig* Schutz *m*

um·pire SPORT **1.** Schiedsrichter(in) **2.** als Schiedsrichter(in) fungieren (bei)

un·a·bashed unverfroren

un·a·bat·ed unvermindert

un·a·ble unfähig, außerstande, nicht in der Lage

un·ac·cept·a·ble unzumutbar

un·ac·count·a·ble unerklärlich

un·ac·cus·tomed ungewohnt

un·ac·quaint·ed: *be ~ with s.th.* et. nicht kennen, mit e-r Sache nicht vertraut sein

un·ad·vised unbesonnen, unüberlegt

un·af·fect·ed natürlich, ungekünstelt; *be ~ by* nicht betroffen sein von

un·aid·ed ohne Unterstützung, (ganz) allein

un·al·ter·a·ble unabänderlich

u·nan·i·mous einmütig; einstimmig

un·an·nounced unangemeldet

un·an·swer·a·ble unwiderlegbar; nicht zu beantworten(d)

un·ap·pe·tiz·ing unappetitlich

un·ap·proach·a·ble unnahbar

un·armed unbewaffnet

un·asked ungestellt (*question*); unaufgefordert, ungebeten (*guest etc*)

un·as·sist·ed ohne (fremde) Hilfe, (ganz) allein

un·as·sum·ing bescheiden

un·at·tached ungebunden, frei

un·at·tend·ed unbeaufsichtigt

un·at·trac·tive unattraktiv, wenig anziehend, reizlos

un·au·thor·ized unberechtigt, unbefugt

un·a·void·a·ble unvermeidlich

un·a·ware: *be ~ of s.th.* sich e-r Sache nicht bewusst sein, et. nicht bemerken

un·a·wares: *catch or take s.o.* ~ j-n überraschen

un·bal·ance *j-n* aus dem (seelischen) Gleichgewicht bringen

un·bal·anced unausgeglichen, labil

un·bar aufriegeln, entriegeln

un·bear·a·ble unerträglich; *person:* unausstehlich

un·beat·a·ble unschlagbar

un·beat·en ungeschlagen, unbesiegt

un·be·com·ing unvorteilhaft

un·be·known(st): ~ *to s.o.* ohne j-s Wissen

un·be·liev·a·ble unglaublich

un·bend gerade biegen; sich aufrichten; *fig* aus sich herausgehen, auftauen

un·bend·ing unbeugsam

un·bi·as(s)ed unvoreingenommen, JUR unbefangen

un·bind losbinden

un·blem·ished makellos

un·born ungeboren

un·break·a·ble unzerbrechlich

un·bri·dled *fig* ungezügelt, zügellos; ~ *tongue* lose Zunge

un·bro·ken ununterbrochen; heil, unversehrt; nicht zugeritten (*horse*)

un·buck·le aufschnallen, losschnallen

un·bur·den: ~ *o.s. to s.o.* j-m sein Herz ausschütten

un·but·ton aufknöpfen

un·called-for ungerechtfertigt; unnötig; unpassend

un·can·ny unheimlich

un·cared-for vernachlässigt

un·ceas·ing unaufhörlich

un·cer·e·mo·ni·ous brüsk, unhöflich; überstürzt

un·cer·tain unsicher, ungewiss, unbestimmt; vage; METEOR unbeständig

un·cer·tain·ty Unsicherheit *f*, Ungewissheit *f*

un·chain losketten

un·changed unverändert

un·chang·ing unveränderlich

un·char·i·ta·ble unfair

un·checked ungehindert; ungeprüft

un·chris·tian unchristlich

un·civ·il unhöflich

un·civ·i·lized unzivilisiert

un·cle Onkel *m*

un·com·fort·a·ble unbequem; *feel ~* sich unbehaglich fühlen

un·com·mon ungewöhnlich

un·com·mu·ni·ca·tive wortkarg, verschlossen

un·com·pre·hend·ing verständnislos

un·com·pro·mis·ing kompromisslos

un·con·cerned: *be ~ about* sich keine Gedanken *or* Sorgen machen über (*acc*); *be ~ with* uninteressiert sein an (*dat*)

un·con·di·tion·al bedingungslos

un·con·firmed unbestätigt

un·con·scious unbewusst; unbeabsichtigt; MED bewusstlos; *be ~ of* sich e-r Sache nicht bewusst sein, nicht bemerken; un·con·scious·ness MED Bewusstlosigkeit f

un·con·sti·tu·tion·al verfassungswidrig

un·con·trol·la·ble unkontrollierbar; nicht zu bändigen(d); unbändig (*rage etc*); un·con·trolled unkontrolliert

un·con·ven·tion·al unkonventionell

un·con·vinced: *be* ~ nicht überzeugt sein (*about* von)

un·con·vinc·ing nicht überzeugend

un·cooked ungekocht, roh

un·cork entkorken

un·count·a·ble unzählbar

un·coup·le abkoppeln

un·couth *fig* ungehobelt

un·cov·er aufdecken, *fig a.* enthüllen

un·crit·i·cal unkritisch; *be* ~ *of s.th.* e-r Sache unkritisch gegenüberstehen

unc·tion REL Salbung f

unc·tu·ous salbungsvoll

un·cut ungekürzt (*film, novel etc*); ungeschliffen (*diamond etc*)

un·dam·aged unbeschädigt, unversehrt, heil

un·dat·ed undatiert, ohne Datum

un·daunt·ed unerschrocken, furchtlos

un·de·cid·ed unentschieden, offen; unentschlossen

un·de·mon·stra·tive zurückhaltend, reserviert

un·de·ni·a·ble unbestreitbar

un·der 1. *prp* unter (*dat or acc*) 2. *adv* unten; darunter

un·der·age minderjährig

un·der·bid unterbieten

un·der·brush → *undergrowth*

un·der·car·riage AVIAT Fahrwerk *n*, Fahrgestell *n*

un·der·charge zu wenig berechnen; zu wenig verlangen

un·der·clothes, un·der·cloth·ing → *underwear*

un·der·coat Grundierung f

un·der·cov·er: ~ *agent* verdeckter Ermittler

un·der·cut *j-n* (im Preis) unterbieten

un·der·de·vel·oped unterentwickelt; ~ *country* Entwicklungsland *n*

un·der·dog Benachteiligte *m, f*

un·der·done nicht durchgebraten

un·der·es·ti·mate zu niedrig schätzen *or* veranschlagen; *fig* unterschätzen

un·der·ex·pose PHOT unterbelichten

un·der·fed unterernährt

un·der·go erleben, durchmachen; MED

sich *e-r Operation etc* unterziehen

un·der·grad F, un·der·grad·u·ate Student(in)

un·der·ground 1. *adv* unterirdisch, unter der Erde 2. *adj* unterirdisch; *fig* Untergrund... 3. *esp Br* Untergrundbahn *f*, U-Bahn *f*; *by* ~ mit der U-Bahn

un·der·growth Unterholz *n*

un·der·hand, un·der·hand·ed heimlich; hinterhältig

un·der·line unterstreichen (*a. fig*)

un·der·ling *contp* Untergebene *m, f*

un·der·ly·ing zugrunde liegend

un·der·mine unterspülen; *fig* untergraben, unterminieren

un·der·neath 1. *prp* unter (*dat or acc*) 2. *adv* darunter

un·der·nour·ished unterernährt

un·der·pants Unterhose f

un·der·pass Unterführung f

un·der·pay *j-m* zu wenig bezahlen, *j-n* unterbezahlen

un·der·priv·i·leged unterprivilegiert, benachteiligt

un·der·rate unterbewerten, -schätzen

un·der·sec·re·ta·ry POL Staatssekretär *m*

un·der·sell ECON *Ware* verschleudern, unter Wert verkaufen; ~ *o.s.* *fig* sich schlecht verkaufen

un·der·shirt Unterhemd *n*

un·der·side Unterseite f

un·der·signed: *the* ~ der *or* die Unterzeichnete, die Unterzeichneten *pl*

un·der·size(d) zu klein

un·der·staffed (personell) unterbesetzt

un·der·stand verstehen; erfahren *or* gehört haben (*that* dass); *make o.s. understood* sich verständlich machen; *am I to* ~ *that* soll das heißen, dass; *give s.o. to* ~ *that* *j-m* zu verstehen geben, dass

un·der·stand·a·ble verständlich

un·der·stand·ing 1. Verstand *m*; Verständnis *n*; Abmachung *f*; Verständigung *f*; *come to an* ~ e-e Abmachung treffen (*with* mit); *on the* ~ *that* unter der Voraussetzung, dass 2. verständnisvoll

un·der·state untertreiben, untertrieben darstellen; un·der·state·ment Understatement *n*, Untertreibung *f*

un·der·take *v/t.* übernehmen; sich verpflichten (*to do* zu tun) un·der·tak·er Leichenbestatter *m*; Beerdigungs-, Bestattungsinstitut *n*

un·der·tak·ing Unternehmen *n*; Zusicherung *f*

un·der·tone *fig* Unterton *m*; *in an* ~ mit gedämpfter Stimme

un·der·val·ue unterbewerten

un·der·wa·ter **1.** *adj* Unterwasser... **2.** *adv* unter Wasser

un·der·wear Unterwäsche *f*

un·der·weight **1.** Untergewicht *n* **2.** untergewichtig, zu leicht (*by* um); *she is five pounds* ~ sie hat fünf Pfund Untergewicht

un·der·world Unterwelt *f*

un·de·served unverdient

un·de·sir·a·ble unerwünscht

un·de·vel·oped unerschlossen (*area*); unentwickelt

un·dies F (Damen)Unterwäsche *f*

un·dig·ni·fied würdelos

un·di·min·ished unvermindert

un·dis·ci·plined undiszipliniert

un·dis·cov·ered unentdeckt

un·dis·guised unverhohlen

un·dis·put·ed unbestritten

un·dis·turbed ungestört

un·di·vid·ed ungeteilt

un·do aufmachen, öffnen; *fig* zunichtemachen; un·do·ing *be s.o.'s* ~ j-s Ruin *or* Verderben sein; un·done unerledigt; offen; *come* ~ aufgehen

un·doubt·ed unbestritten

un·doubt·ed·ly zweifellos, ohne (jeden) Zweifel

un·dreamed-of, un·dreamt-of ungeahnt

un·dress sich ausziehen; *j-n* ausziehen

un·due übermäßig

un·du·lat·ing sanft (*hills*)

un·dy·ing ewig

un·earned *fig* unverdient

un·earth ausgraben, *fig a.* ausfindig machen, aufstöbern

un·earth·ly überirdisch; unheimlich; *at an* ~ *hour* F zu e-r unchristlichen Zeit

un·eas·i·ness Unbehagen *n*

un·eas·y unruhig (*sleep*); unsicher (*peace*); *feel* ~ sich unbehaglich fühlen; *I'm* ~ *about* mir ist nicht wohl bei

un·e·co·nom·ic unwirtschaftlich

un·ed·u·cat·ed ungebildet

un·e·mo·tion·al leidenschaftslos, kühl, beherrscht

un·em·ployed **1.** arbeitslos **2.** *the* ~ die Arbeitslosen *pl*

un·em·ploy·ment Arbeitslosigkeit *f*; ~ a·gen·cy *Am* Arbeitsagentur *f*; ~ bene·fit *Br*, ~ com·pen·sa·tion Arbeitslosengeld *n*

un·end·ing endlos

un·en·dur·a·ble unerträglich

un·en·vi·a·ble wenig beneidenswert

un·e·qual ungleich (*a. fig*), unterschiedlich; *fig* einseitig; *be* ~ *to* e-r Aufgabe *etc* nicht gewachsen sein

un·e·qual(l)ed unerreicht, unübertroffen

un·er·ring unfehlbar

un·e·ven uneben; ungleich(mäßig); ungerade (*number*)

un·e·vent·ful ereignislos

un·ex·am·pled beispiellos

un·ex·pec·ted unerwartet

un·ex·posed *phot* unbelichtet

un·fail·ing unerschöpflich; nie versagend

un·fair unfair, ungerecht

un·faith·ful untreu (*to dat*)

un·fa·mil·i·ar ungewohnt; unbekannt; nicht vertraut (*with* mit)

un·fas·ten aufmachen, öffnen; losbinden

un·fa·vo(u)r·a·ble ungünstig; unvorteilhaft (*for, to* für); negativ, ablehnend

un·feel·ing gefühllos, herzlos

un·fin·ished unvollendet; unfertig; unerledigt

un·fit nicht fit, nicht in Form; ungeeignet, untauglich; unfähig

un·flag·ging unermüdlich, unentwegt

un·flap·pa·ble F nicht aus der Ruhe zu bringen(d)

un·fold auffalten, auseinanderfalten; darlegen, enthüllen; sich entfalten

un·fore·seen unvorhergesehen, unerwartet

un·for·get·ta·ble unvergesslich

un·for·got·ten unvergessen

un·for·tu·nate unglücklich; unglückselig; bedauerlich

un·for·tu·nate·ly leider

un·found·ed unbegründet

un·friend·ly unfreundlich (*to, towards* zu)

un·furl *Fahne* aufrollen, entrollen, *Segel* losmachen

un·fur·nished unmöbliert

un·gain·ly linkisch, unbeholfen

un·god·ly gottlos; *at an ~ hour* F zu e-r unchristlichen Zeit

un·gra·cious ungnädig; unfreundlich

un·grate·ful undankbar

un·guard·ed unbewacht; unbedacht, unüberlegt

un·hap·pi·ly unglücklicherweise, leider; un·hap·py unglücklich

un·harmed unversehrt

un·health·y kränklich, nicht gesund; ungesund; *contp* krankhaft, unnatürlich

un·heard: *go ~* keine Beachtung finden, unbeachtet bleiben; un·heard-of noch nie da gewesen, beispiellos

un·hinge: *~ s.o.('s mind) fig* j-n völlig aus dem Gleichgewicht bringen

un·ho·ly F furchtbar, schrecklich

un·hoped-for unverhofft, unerwartet

un·hurt unverletzt

u·ni·corn Einhorn *n*

un·i·den·ti·fied unbekannt, nicht identifiziert

u·ni·fi·ca·tion Vereinigung *f*

u·ni·form **1.** Uniform *f* **2.** gleichmäßig; einheitlich

u·ni·form·i·ty Einheitlichkeit *f*

u·ni·fy verein(ig)en; vereinheitlichen

u·ni·lat·e·ral *fig* einseitig

un·i·ma·gin·a·ble unvorstellbar

un·i·ma·gin·a·tive fantasielos, einfallslos

un·im·por·tant unwichtig

un·im·pressed: *remain ~* unbeeindruckt bleiben (*by* von)

un·in·formed nicht unterrichtet *or* eingeweiht

un·in·hab·it·a·ble unbewohnbar

un·in·hab·it·ed unbewohnt

un·in·jured unverletzt

un·in·tel·li·gi·ble unverständlich

un·in·ten·tion·al unabsichtlich, unbeabsichtigt

un·in·terest·ed uninteressiert (*in* an *dat*); *be ~ in* a. sich nicht interessieren für; un·in·terest·ing uninteressant

un·in·ter·rupt·ed ununterbrochen

u·nion Vereinigung *f*; Union *f*; Gewerkschaft *f*; u·nion·ist Gewerkschaftler(in); u·nion·ize (sich) gewerkschaftlich organisieren

u·nique einzigartig; einmalig

u·ni·son: *in ~* gemeinsam

u·nit Einheit *f*; *PED* Unit *f*, Lehreinheit *f*;

MATH Einer *m*; TECH (Anbau)Element *n*, Teil *n*; *~ furniture* Anbaumöbel *pl*

u·nite verbinden, vereinigen; sich vereinigen *or* zusammentun

u·nit·ed vereinigt, vereint

U·nit·ed King·dom *das* Vereinigte Königreich (*England, Scotland, Wales and Northern Ireland*)

U·nit·ed States of A·mer·i·ca *die* Vereinigten Staaten von Amerika

u·ni·ty Einheit *f*; MATH Eins *f*

u·ni·ver·sal allgemein; universal, universell; Welt...

u·ni·verse Universum *n*, Weltall *n*

u·ni·ver·si·ty Universität *f*, Hochschule *f*; *~ grad·u·ate* Akademiker(in)

un·just ungerecht

un·kempt ungekämmt (*hair*); ungepflegt (*clothes etc*)

un·kind unfreundlich

un·known **1.** unbekannt (*to dat*); **2.** *der, die, das* Unbekannte; *~ quan·ti·ty* MATH unbekannte Größe (*a. fig*), Unbekannte *f*

un·law·ful ungesetzlich, gesetzwidrig

un·lead·ed bleifrei

un·learn *Ansichten etc* ablegen, aufgeben

un·less wenn ... nicht, außer wenn ..., es sei denn ...

un·like *prp* im Gegensatz zu; *he is very ~ his father* er ist ganz anders als sein Vater; *that is very ~ him* das sieht ihm gar nicht ähnlich

un·like·ly unwahrscheinlich

un·lim·it·ed unbegrenzt

un·list·ed: *be ~* nicht im Telefonbuch stehen; *~ num·ber* TEL Geheimnummer *f*

un·load entladen, abladen, ausladen; MAR *Ladung* löschen

un·lock aufschließen

un·loos·en losmachen; lockern; lösen

un·loved ungeliebt

un·luck·y unglücklich; *be ~* Pech haben

un·made ungemacht

un·manned unbemannt

un·marked nicht gekennzeichnet; SPORT ungedeckt, frei

un·mar·ried unverheiratet, ledig

un·mask *fig* entlarven

un·matched unübertroffen, unvergleichlich

un·men·tio·na·ble Tabu...; *be ~* tabu

sein

un·mis·tak·a·ble unverkennbar, unverwechselbar, untrüglich

un·mo·lest·ed unbehelligt

un·moved ungerührt; *she remained ~ by it* es ließ sie kalt

un·mu·si·cal unmusikalisch

un·named ungenannt

un·nat·u·ral unnatürlich; widernatürlich

un·nec·es·sa·ry unnötig

un·nerve entnerven

un·no·ticed unbemerkt

un·num·bered unnummeriert

un·ob·tru·sive unauffällig, unaufdringlich

un·oc·cu·pied leer (stehend), unbewohnt; unbeschäftigt

un·of·fi·cial inoffiziell

un·pack auspacken

un·paid unbezahlt; *post* unfrei

un·par·al·leled einmalig, beispiellos

un·par·don·a·ble unverzeihlich

un·per·turbed gelassen, ruhig

un·pick *Naht etc* auftrennen

un·placed: *be ~* SPORT sich nicht platzieren können

un·play·a·ble SPORT unbespielbar

un·pleas·ant unangenehm, unerfreulich; unfreundlich

un·plug den Stecker (*gen*) herausziehen

un·pol·ished unpoliert; *fig* ungehobelt

un·pol·lut·ed sauber, unverschmutzt

un·pop·u·lar unpopulär, unbeliebt

un·pop·u·lar·i·ty Unbeliebtheit *f*

un·prac·ti·cal unpraktisch

un·prac·ticed, *Br* un·prac·tised ungeübt

un·pre·ce·dent·ed beispiellos, noch nie da gewesen

un·pre·dict·a·ble unvorhersehbar; unberechenbar (*person*)

un·prej·u·diced unvoreingenommen; JUR unbefangen

un·pre·med·i·tat·ed nicht vorsätzlich; unüberlegt

un·pre·pared unvorbereitet

un·pre·ten·tious bescheiden, einfach, schlicht

un·prin·ci·pled skrupellos, gewissenlos

un·prin·ta·ble nicht druckfähig *or* druckreif

un·pro·duc·tive unproduktiv, unergiebig

un·pro·fes·sion·al unprofessionell; unfachmännisch

un·prof·it·a·ble unrentabel

un·pro·nounce·a·ble unaussprechbar

un·pro·tect·ed ungeschützt

un·proved, un·prov·en unbewiesen

un·pro·voked grundlos

un·pun·ished unbestraft, ungestraft; *go ~* straflos bleiben

un·qual·i·fied unqualifiziert, ungeeignet (*for* für); uneingeschränkt

un·ques·tion·a·ble unbestritten

un·ques·tion·ing bedingungslos

un·quote: *quote ... ~* Zitat ... Zitat Ende

un·rav·el (sich) auftrennen (*pullover etc*); entwirren

un·read·a·ble nicht lesenswert, unlesbar, *a.* unleserlich

un·re·al unwirklich

un·rea·lis·tic unrealistisch

un·rea·son·a·ble unvernünftig; übertrieben, unzumutbar

un·rec·og·niz·a·ble nicht wieder zu erkennen(d)

un·re·lat·ed: *be ~* in keinem Zusammenhang stehen (*to* mit)

un·re·lent·ing unvermindert

un·re·li·a·ble unzuverlässig

un·re·lieved ununterbrochen, ständig

un·re·mit·ting unablässig, unaufhörlich

un·re·quit·ed: *~ love* unerwiderte Liebe

un·re·served uneingeschränkt; nicht reserviert

un·rest POL *etc* Unruhen *pl*

un·re·strained hemmungslos, ungezügelt

un·re·strict·ed uneingeschränkt

un·ripe unreif

un·ri·val(l)ed unerreicht, unübertroffen, einzigartig

un·roll (sich) aufrollen *or* entrollen; sich entfalten

un·ruf·fled gelassen, ruhig

un·ru·ly ungebärdig, wild; widerspenstig (*hair*)

un·sad·dle *Pferd* absatteln; *Reiter* abwerfen

un·safe unsicher, nicht sicher

un·said unausgesprochen

un·sal(e)·a·ble unverkäuflich

un·salt·ed ungesalzen

un·san·i·tar·y unhygienisch

un·sat·is·fac·to·ry unbefriedigend

un·sat·u·rat·ed CHEM ungesättigt
un·sa·vo(u)r·y anrüchig, unerfreulich
un·scathed unversehrt, unverletzt
un·screw abschrauben, losschrauben
un·scru·pu·lous skrupellos, gewissenlos
un·seat *Reiter* abwerfen; *j-n s-s* Amtes entheben
un·seem·ly ungebührlich
un·self·ish selbstlos, uneigennützig
un·set·tle durcheinanderbringen; beunruhigen; aufregen
un·set·tled ungeklärt, offen (*question etc*); unsicher (*situation etc*); METEOR unbeständig
un·shak(e)·a·ble unerschütterlich
un·shav·en unrasiert
un·shrink·a·ble nicht eingehend *or* einlaufend
un·sight·ly unansehnlich; hässlich
un·skilled **~ worker** ungelernter Arbeiter
un·so·cia·ble ungesellig
un·so·cial **work ~ hours** außerhalb der normalen Arbeitszeit arbeiten
un·so·lic·it·ed unaufgefordert ein- *or* zugesandt, ECON *a.* unbestellt
un·solved ungelöst (*problem etc*)
un·so·phis·ti·cat·ed einfach, schlicht; TECH unkompliziert
un·sound nicht gesund; nicht in Ordnung; morsch; unsicher, schwach; nicht stichhaltig (*argument etc*); **of ~ mind** unzurechnungsfähig
un·spar·ing großzügig, freigebig, verschwenderisch; schonungslos, unbarmherzig
un·speak·a·ble unbeschreiblich, entsetzlich
un·spoiled, un·spoilt unverdorben; nicht verwöhnt *or* verzogen
un·sta·ble instabil; unsicher, schwankend; labil (*person*)
un·stead·y wack(e)lig, schwankend, unsicher; unbeständig; ungleichmäßig, unregelmäßig
un·stop *Abfluss etc* frei machen; *Flasche* entstöpseln
un·stressed LING unbetont
un·stuck **come ~** abgehen, sich lösen; *fig* scheitern
un·stud·ied ungekünstelt, natürlich
un·suc·cess·ful erfolglos, ohne Erfolg; vergeblich

un·suit·a·ble unpassend, ungeeignet; unangemessen
un·sure unsicher; **~ of o.s.** unsicher
un·sur·passed unübertroffen
un·sus·pect·ed unverdächtig; unvermutet; un·sus·pect·ing nichts ahnend, ahnungslos
un·sus·pi·cious arglos; unverdächtig, harmlos
un·sweet·ened ungesüßt
un·swerv·ing unbeirrbar, unerschütterlich
un·tan·gle entwirren (*a. fig*)
un·tapped unerschlossen (*resource etc*)
un·teach·a·ble unbelehrbar (*person*); nicht lehrbar
un·ten·a·ble unhaltbar (*theory etc*)
un·think·a·ble undenkbar, unvorstellbar; un·think·ing gedankenlos
un·ti·dy unordentlich
un·tie aufknoten, *Knoten etc* lösen; losbinden
un·til *prp, cj* bis; **not ~** erst; erst wenn, nicht bevor
un·time·ly vorzeitig, verfrüht; unpassend, ungelegen
un·tir·ing unermüdlich
un·told *fig* unermesslich
un·touched unberührt, unangetastet
un·true unwahr, falsch
un·trust·wor·thy unzuverlässig, nicht vertrauenswürdig
un·used[1] unbenutzt, ungebraucht
un·used[2] **be ~ to s.th.** an et. nicht gewöhnt sein, et. nicht gewohnt sein; **be ~ to doing s.th.** es nicht gewohnt sein, et. zu tun
un·u·su·al ungewöhnlich
un·var·nished *fig* ungeschminkt
un·var·y·ing unveränderlich, gleichbleibend
un·veil *Denkmal etc* enthüllen
un·versed unbewandert, unerfahren (**in** in *dat*)
un·voiced unausgesprochen
un·want·ed unerwünscht, ungewollt
un·war·rant·ed ungerechtfertigt
un·washed ungewaschen
un·wel·come unwillkommen
un·well **be or feel ~** sich unwohl fühlen *or* nicht wohlfühlen
un·whole·some ungesund (*a. fig*)
un·wield·y unhandlich, sperrig
un·will·ing widerwillig; ungern; **be ~ to**

do s.th. et. nicht tun wollen

un·wind (sich) abwickeln; F abschalten, sich entspannen

un·wise unklug

un·wit·ting unwissentlich; unbeabsichtigt

un·wor·thy unwürdig; *he (she) is ~ of it* er (sie) verdient es nicht, er (sie) ist es nicht wert

un·wrap auswickeln, auspacken

un·writ·ten ungeschrieben

un·yield·ing unnachgiebig

un·zip den Reißverschluss (*gen*) aufmachen

up 1. *adv* herauf, hinauf, aufwärts, nach oben, hoch, in die Höhe; oben; *~ there* dort oben; *jump ~ and down* hüpfen; *walk ~ and down* auf und ab gehen, hin und her gehen; *~ to* bis zu; *be ~ to s.th.* F et. vorhaben, et. im Schilde führen; *not to be ~ to s.th.* e-r Sache nicht gewachsen sein; *it's ~ to you* das liegt bei dir **2.** *prp* herauf, hinauf; oben auf (*dat*); *~ the river* flussaufwärts **3.** *adj* nach oben (gerichtet), Aufwärts…; ASTR aufgegangen; ECON gestiegen; *time:* abgelaufen, um; aufgestanden, F auf; *the ~ train* der Zug nach London; *be ~ and about* F wieder auf den Beinen sein; *what's ~?* F was ist los? **4.** F *v/t* Angebot, *Preis etc* erhöhen **5.** *the ~s and downs* F die Höhen und Tiefen *pl* (*of life* des Lebens)

up-and-com·ing aufstrebend, vielversprechend

up·bring·ing Erziehung *f*

up·com·ing bevorstehend

up·coun·try landeinwärts; im Landesinneren

up·date 1. auf den neuesten Stand bringen; aktualisieren **2.** Lagebericht *m*

up·end hochkant stellen

up·grade *j-n* befördern

up·heav·al *fig* Umwälzung *f*

up·hill aufwärts, bergan; bergauf führend; *fig* mühsam

up·hold *Rechte etc* schützen, wahren; JUR *Urteil* bestätigen

up·hol·ster *Möbel* polstern

up·hol·ster·er Polsterer *m*

up·hol·ster·y Polsterung *f*; Bezug *m*; Polsterei *f*

up·keep Instandhaltung(skosten *pl*) *f*; Unterhalt(ungskosten *pl*) *m*

up·land *mst pl* Hochland *n*

up·lift 1. *j-n* aufrichten, *j-m* Auftrieb geben **2.** Auftrieb *m*

up·on → *on, once 1*

up·per obere(r, -s), Ober…;

up·per·most 1. *adj* oberste(r, -s), größte(r, -s), höchste(r, -s); *be ~* oben sein; *fig* an erster Stelle stehen **2.** *adv* nach oben

up·right aufrecht, *a.* gerade, *fig a.* rechtschaffen

up·ris·ing Aufstand *m*

up·roar Aufruhr *m*; **up·roar·i·ous** lärmend, laut; schallend (*laughter*)

up·root ausreißen, entwurzeln; *fig j-n* herausreißen (*from* aus)

up·set umkippen, umstoßen, umwerfen; *Pläne etc* durcheinanderbringen, stören; *j-n* aus der Fassung bringen; *the fish has ~ me or my stomach* ich habe mir durch den Fisch den Magen verdorben; *be ~* aufgeregt sein; aus der Fassung *or* durcheinander sein; gekränkt *or* verletzt sein

up·shot Ergebnis *n*

up·side down verkehrt herum; *fig* drunter und drüber; *turn ~* umdrehen, *a. fig* auf den Kopf stellen

up·stairs 1. die Treppe herauf *or* hinauf, nach oben; oben **2.** im oberen Stockwerk (gelegen), obere(r, -s)

up·start Emporkömmling *m*

up·state im Norden (e-s Bundesstaats)

up·stream fluss-, stromaufwärts

up·take: F *be quick (slow) on the ~* schnell begreifen (schwer von Begriff sein)

up-to-date modern; aktuell, auf dem neuesten Stand

up·town in den Wohnvierteln; in die Wohnviertel

up·turn Aufschwung *m*

up·ward(s) aufwärts, nach oben

u·ra·ni·um CHEM Uran *n*

ur·ban städtisch, Stadt…

ur·ban·i·za·tion Verstädterung *f*

ur·chin Bengel *m*

urge 1. *j-n* drängen (*to do* zu tun); drängen auf (*acc*); *a. ~ on j-n* drängen, antreiben **2.** Drang *m*, Verlangen *n*

ur·gen·cy Dringlichkeit *f*

ur·gent dringend; *be ~ a.* eilen

u·ri·nate urinieren; **u·rine** Urin *m*

urn Urne *f*

us uns; *all of* ~ wir alle; *both of* ~ wir beide

us·age Sprachgebrauch *m*; Behandlung *f*; Verwendung *f*, Gebrauch *m*

USB flash drive IT USB-Stick *m*

use 1. *v/t* benutzen, gebrauchen, anwenden, verwenden; (ver)brauchen; ~ *up* auf-, verbrauchen; *v/i*: *I* ~*d to live here* ich habe früher hier gewohnt **2.** Benutzung *f*, Gebrauch *m*, Verwendung *f*; Nutzen *m*; *be of* ~ nützlich *or* von Nutzen sein (*to* für); *it's no* ~ *doing* es ist nutzlos *or* zwecklos *zu inf*; → *milk 1*

used[1]: *be* ~ *to s.th.* an et. gewöhnt sein, et. gewohnt sein; *be* ~ *to doing s.th.* es gewohnt sein, et. zu tun

used[2] gebraucht; ~ *car* Gebrauchtwagen *m*;~ *car deal·er* Gebrauchtwagenhändler(in)

use·ful nützlich

use·less nutzlos, zwecklos

us·er Benutzer(in); Verbraucher(in)

us·er-friend·ly benutzer- *or* verbraucherfreundlich

us·er in·ter·face IT Benutzeroberfläche *f*

ush·er 1. Platzanweiser *m*; Gerichtsdiener *m* **2.** *j-n* führen, geleiten (*into* in *acc*; *to* zu)

ush·er·ette Platzanweiserin *f*

u·su·al gewöhnlich, üblich

u·su·al·ly (für) gewöhnlich, normalerweise

u·sur·er Wucherer *m*

u·su·ry Wucher *m*

u·ten·sil Gerät *n*

u·te·rus ANAT Gebärmutter *f*

u·til·i·ty Nutzen *m*; *pl* Leistungen *pl* der öffentlichen Versorgungsbetriebe

u·til·ize nutzen

ut·most äußerste(r, -s), größte(r, -s), höchste(r, -s)

u·to·pi·an utopisch

ut·ter[1] total, völlig

ut·ter[2] äußern, *Seufzer etc* ausstoßen, *Wort* sagen

U-turn MOT Wende *f*; *fig* Kehrtwendung *f*

u·vu·la ANAT (Gaumen)Zäpfchen *n*

V

V, v V, v *n*

va·can·cy freie *or* offene Stelle; *vacancies* Zimmer frei; *no vacancies* belegt

va·cant leer stehend, unbewohnt; frei (*seat etc*); frei, offen (*job*); *fig* leer (*expression, stare etc*)

va·cate *Hotelzimmer* räumen; *Stelle etc* aufgeben

va·ca·tion 1. Ferien *pl*, Urlaub *m*; *esp Br* UNIV Semesterferien *pl*; JUR Gerichtsferien *pl*; *be on* ~ im Urlaub sein, Urlaub machen **2.** Urlaub machen, die Ferien verbringen

va·ca·tion·er, **va·ca·tion·ist** Urlauber(in)

vac·cin·ate MED impfen

vac·cin·a·tion MED (Schutz)Impfung *f*

vac·cine MED Impfstoff *m*

vac·il·late *fig* schwanken

vac·u·um 1. PHYS Vakuum *n* **2.** F *Teppich, Zimmer etc* saugen;~ *bot·tle* Thermosflasche® *f*;~ *clean·er* Staubsauger *m*;~ *flask Br* Thermosflasche® *f*;~*packed* vakuumverpackt

vag·a·bond Vagabund *m*, Landstreicher(in)

va·ga·ry *mst pl* Laune *f*; wunderlicher Einfall

va·gi·na ANAT Vagina *f*, Scheide *f*

va·gi·nal ANAT vaginal, Scheiden…

va·grant Nichtsesshafte *m*, *f*, Landstreicher(in)

vague verschwommen; vage; unklar

vain eingebildet, eitel; vergeblich; *in* ~ vergebens, vergeblich

va·le·ri·an BOT, PHARM Baldrian *m*

val·et (Kammer)Diener *m*

val·id stichhaltig, triftig; gültig (*for two weeks* zwei Wochen); JUR rechtsgültig, rechtskräftig; *be* ~ gelten

va·lid·i·ty (JUR Rechts)Gültigkeit *f*; Stichhaltigkeit *f*, Triftigkeit *f*

val·ley Tal *n*

val·u·a·ble 1. wertvoll **2.** *pl* Wertgegenstände *pl*, Wertsachen *pl*

val·u·a·tion Schätzung *f*; Schätzwert *m* (*on gen*)

val·ue 1. Wert *m*; *be of ~* wertvoll sein (*to* für); *get ~ for money* reell bedient werden **2.** *Haus etc* schätzen (*at* auf *acc*); *j-n, j-s Rat etc* schätzen

val·ue-ad·ded tax *Br* ECON (*abbr* **VAT**) Mehrwertsteuer *f*

val·ue·less wertlos

valve TECH, MUS Ventil *n*; ANAT (*Herz- etc*)Klappe *f*

vam·pire Vampir *m*

van MOT Lieferwagen *m*, Transporter *m*; *Br* RAIL (geschlossener) Güterwagen

van·dal Wandale *m*, Vandale *m*

van·dal·ism Wandalismus *m*, Vandalismus *m*

van·dal·ize mutwillig beschädigen *or* zerstören

vane TECH (*Propeller- etc*)Flügel *m*; (*Wetter*)Fahne *f*

van·guard MIL Vorhut *f*

va·nil·la Vanille *f*

van·ish verschwinden

van·i·ty Eitelkeit *f*; *~ bag* Kosmetiktäschchen *n*; *~ case* Kosmetikkoffer *m*

va·por·ize verdampfen; verdunsten (lassen)

va·po(u)r Dampf *m*, Dunst *m*; *~ trail* AVIAT Kondensstreifen *m*

var·i·a·ble 1. variabel, veränderlich; unbeständig, wechselhaft; TECH einstellbar, regulierbar **2.** MATH, PHYS Variable *f*, veränderliche Größe (*both a. fig*)

var·i·ance: *be at ~ with* im Gegensatz *or* Widerspruch stehen zu

var·i·ant 1. abweichend, verschieden **2.** Variante *f*; *var·i·a·tion* Abweichung *f*; Schwankung *f*; MUS Variation *f*

var·i·cose veins MED Krampfadern *pl*

var·ied unterschiedlich; abwechslungsreich

va·ri·e·ty Abwechslung *f*; Vielfalt *f*; ECON Auswahl *f*, Sortiment *n* (*of an dat*); BOT, ZO Art *f*; Varietee *n*; *for a ~ of reasons* aus den verschiedensten Gründen

var·i·ous verschieden; mehrere, verschiedene

var·nish 1. Lack *m* **2.** lackieren

var·si·ty team SPORT Universitäts-, College-, Schulmannschaft *f*

var·y *v/i* sich (ver)ändern; variieren, auseinandergehen (*opinions etc*) (*on*

über *acc*); *~ in size* verschieden groß sein; *v/t* (ver)ändern; variieren

vase Vase *f*

vast gewaltig, riesig, (*area a.*) ausgedehnt, weit; *vast·ly* gewaltig, weitaus

vat (großes) Fass, Bottich *m*

VAT *abbr of* *value-added tax* ECON Mehrwertsteuer *f*

vau·de·ville Varietee(theater) *n*

vault[1] ARCH Gewölbe *n*; *a. pl* Stahlkammer *f*, Tresorraum *m*; (Keller)Gewölbe *n*; Gruft *f*

vault[2] **1.** *~ (over)* springen über (*acc*) **2.** *esp* SPORT Sprung *m*

vault·ing horse *gymnastics*: Pferd *n*; *~ pole* SPORT Sprungstab *m*

VCR *abbr of* *video cassette recorder* Videorekorder *m*, Videogerät *n*

veal GASTR Kalbfleisch *n*; *~ chop* Kalbskotelett *n*; *~ cutlet* Kalbsschnitzel *n*; *~ roast* Kalbsbraten *m*

veer (sich) drehen; MOT ausscheren; *~ to the right* das Steuer nach rechts reißen

veg·e·ta·ble 1. *mst pl* Gemüse *n* **2.** Gemüse…; Pflanzen…

veg·e·tar·i·an 1. Vegetarier(in) **2.** vegetarisch

veg·e·tate (dahin)vegetieren

veg·e·ta·tion Vegetation *f*

ve·he·mence Vehemenz *f*, Heftigkeit *f*; **ve·he·ment** vehement, heftig

ve·hi·cle Fahrzeug *n*; *fig* Medium *n*

veil 1. Schleier *m* **2.** verschleiern (*a. fig*)

vein ANAT Vene *f*, Ader *f* (*a.* BOT, GEOL, *fig*); *fig* (*Charakter*)Zug *m*; Stimmung *f*

ve·loc·i·ty TECH Geschwindigkeit *f*

ve·lour(s) Velours *m*

vel·vet Samt *m*; **vel·vet·y** samtig

vend·er → *vendor*

vend·ing ma·chine (Verkaufs-, Waren-)Automat *m*

vend·or (*Straßen*)Händler(in), (*Zeitungs- etc*)Verkäufer(in)

ve·neer 1. Furnier *n*; *fig* Fassade *f* **2.** furnieren

ven·e·ra·ble ehrwürdig

ven·e·rate verehren

ven·e·ra·tion Verehrung *f*

ve·ne·re·al dis·ease MED Geschlechtskrankheit *f*

Ve·ne·tian 1. Venezianer(in) **2.** venezianisch; *~ blind* (Stab)Jalousie *f*

ven·geance Rache *f*; *take ~ on* sich rä-

V

chen an (*dat*); **with a ~** mächtig, F wie
verrückt

ve·ni·al entschuldbar, verzeihlich; REL
lässlich

ven·i·son GASTR Wildbret *n*

ven·om ZO Gift *n, fig a.* Gehässigkeit *f*

ven·om·ous giftig, *fig a.* gehässig

ve·nous MED venös

vent 1. *v/t s-m* Zorn *etc* Luft machen, *s-e
Wut etc* auslassen, abreagieren (**on** an
dat); **2.** Schlitz *m* (*in a coat etc*); TECH
(Abzugs)Öffnung *f*; **give ~ to** *s-m* Ärger *etc* Luft machen

ven·ti·late (be)lüften; *fig* äußern

ven·ti·la·tion (Be)Lüftung *f*, Ventilation
f

ven·ti·la·tor Ventilator *m*

ven·tri·cle ANAT Herzkammer *f*

ven·tril·o·quist Bauchredner(in)

ven·ture 1. *esp* ECON Wagnis *n*, Risiko *n*;
ECON Unternehmen *n*; → **joint venture
2.** sich wagen; riskieren

ven·ue SPORT Austragungsort *m*

verb LING Verb *n*, Zeitwort *n*

verb·al mündlich; wörtlich, Wort…

ver·dict JUR (Urteils)Spruch *m*; *fig* Urteil *n*; **bring in** *or* **return a ~ of (not)
guilty** JUR auf (nicht) schuldig erkennen

ver·di·gris Grünspan *m*

verge 1. Rand *m* (*a. fig*); **be on the ~ of**
kurz vor (*dat*) stehen; **be on the ~ of
despair** (**tears**) der Verzweiflung
(den Tränen) nahe sein **2. ~ on** *fig* grenzen an (*acc*)

ver·i·fy bestätigen; nachweisen; (über-)
prüfen

ver·i·ta·ble wahr

ver·mi·cel·li Fadennudeln *pl*

ver·mi·form ap·pen·dix ANAT Wurmfortsatz *m*, Blinddarm *m*

ver·mil·i·on 1. zinnoberrot **2.** Zinnoberrot *n*

ver·min Ungeziefer *n*; Schädlinge *pl*; *fig*
Gesindel *n*, Pack *n*

ver·min·ous voller Ungeziefer

ver·nac·u·lar Dialekt *m*, Mundart *f*; *in
the ~* im Volksmund

ver·sa·tile vielseitig; vielseitig verwendbar

verse Verdichtung *f*; Vers *m*; Strophe *f*

versed: **be** (**well**) **~ in** beschlagen *or* be-
wandert sein in (*dat*)

ver·sion Version *f*; TECH Ausführung *f*;

Darstellung *f* (*of an event*); Fassung *f*
(*of a film etc*); Übersetzung *f*

ver·sus (*abbr* **v., vs.**) SPORT, JUR gegen

ver·te·bra ANAT Wirbel *m*

ver·te·brate ZO Wirbeltier *n*

ver·ti·cal vertikal, senkrecht

ver·ti·go MED Schwindel *m*; **suffer from
~** an *or* unter Schwindel leiden

verve Elan *m*, Schwung *m*

ver·y 1. *adv* sehr; aller…; *I ~ much hope
that* ich hoffe sehr, dass; **the ~ best** das
Allerbeste; **for the ~ last time** zum al-
lerletzten Mal **2.** *adj* **the ~** genau der *or*
die *or* das; **the ~ opposite** genau das
Gegenteil; **the ~ thing** genau das Richtige; **the ~ thought of** schon der *or* der
bloße Gedanke an (*acc*)

ves·i·cle MED Bläschen *n*

ves·sel ANAT, BOT Gefäß *n*; Schiff *n*

vest Weste *f*; *Br* Unterhemd *n*; *kugelsi-
chere* Weste

ves·ti·bule (Vor)Halle *f*

ves·tige *fig* Spur *f*

vest·ment Ornat *n*, Gewand *n*, Robe *f*

ves·try REL Sakristei *f*

vet¹ F Tierarzt *m*, Tierärztin *f*

vet² *esp Br* F überprüfen

vet³ MIL F Veteran *m*

vet·e·ran 1. MIL Veteran *m* (*a. fig*) **2.** alt-
gedient; erfahren; **~ car** *Br* Oldtimer *m*
(*built before 1905*)

vet·e·ri·nar·i·an Tierarzt *m*, -ärztin *f*

vet·e·ri·na·ry tierärztlich; **~ sur·geon** *Br*
Tierarzt *m*, Tierärztin *f*

ve·to 1. Veto *n* **2.** sein Veto einlegen gegen

vexed ques·tion leidige Frage

vi·a über (*acc*), via

vi·a·duct Viadukt *m*, *n*

vi·al (*esp* Arznei)Fläschchen *n*

vibes F Atmosphäre *f*

vi·brant kräftig (*color etc*); pulsierend
(*city etc*)

vi·brate *v/i* vibrieren, zittern; flimmern;
fig pulsieren; *v/t* in Schwingungen versetzen; **vi·bra·tion** Vibrieren *n*, Zittern
n; *pl* F Atmosphäre *f*

vic·ar REL Pfarrer *m*

vic·ar·age Pfarrhaus *n*

vice¹ Laster *n*

vice² *esp Br* Schraubstock *m*

vice… Vize…, stellvertretend

vice squad Sittendezernat *n*, Sittenpo-
lizei *f*; Rauschgiftdezernat *n*

vi·ce ver·sa: *and* ~ und umgekehrt

vi·cin·i·ty Nähe *f*; Nachbarschaft *f*

vi·cious brutal; bösartig

vi·cis·si·tudes *das* Auf und Ab, *die* Wechselfälle *pl*

vic·tim Opfer *n*

vic·tim·ize (ungerechterweise) bestrafen, ungerecht behandeln; schikanieren

vic·to·ri·ous siegreich

vic·to·ry Sieg *m*

vid·e·o 1. Video *n*; Videokassette *f*; F Videoband *n*; *esp Br* Videorekorder *m*, Videogerät *n*; **on** ~ auf Video **2.** Video... **3.** *esp Br* auf Video aufnehmen, aufzeichnen; ~ **cam·e·ra** Videokamera *f*; ~ **cas·sette** Videokassette *f*; ~ **cas·sette re·cord·er** → *video recorder*; ~ **clip** Videoclip *m*

vid·e·o·disk Bildplatte *f*

vid·e·o| game Videospiel *n*; ~ **li·brary** Videothek *f*; ~ **re·cord·er** Videorekorder *m*, Videogerät *n*; ~ **re·cord·ing** Videoaufnahme *f*, Videoaufzeichnung *f*; ~ **shop** *Br*, ~ **store** Videothek *f*

vid·e·o·tape 1. Videokassette *f*; Videoband *n* **2.** auf Video aufnehmen, aufzeichnen

vid·e·o·text Bildschirmtext *m*

vie wetteifern (*with* mit; *for* um)

Vi·en·nese 1. Wiener(in) **2.** wienerisch, Wiener...

view 1. Sicht *f* (*of* auf *acc*); Aussicht *f*, (Aus)Blick *m* (*of* auf *acc*); Ansicht *f* (*a.* PHOT), Meinung *f* (*about, on* über *acc*); *fig* Überblick *m* (*of* über *acc*); *a room with a* ~ ein Zimmer mit schöner Aussicht; *be on* ~ ausgestellt *or* zu besichtigen sein; *be hidden from* ~ nicht zu sehen sein; *come into* ~ in Sicht kommen; *in full* ~ *of* direkt vor *j-s* Augen; *in* ~ *of fig* angesichts (*gen*); *in my* ~ m-r Ansicht nach; *keep in* ~ et. im Auge behalten; *with a* ~ *to fig* mit Blick auf (*acc*) **2.** *v/t* Haus *etc* besichtigen; *fig* betrachten (*as* als); *v/i* fernsehen

view·da·ta Bildschirmtext *m*

view·er Fernsehzuschauer(in), F Fernseher(in); TECH (*Dia*)Betrachter *m*

view·find·er PHOT Sucher *m*

view·point Gesichts-, Standpunkt *m*

vig·il (Nacht)Wache *f*

vig·i·lance Wachsamkeit *f*

vig·i·lant wachsam

vig·or·ous energisch; kräftig

vig·o(u)r Energie *f*

Vi·king Wikinger *m* **2.** Wikinger...

vile gemein, niederträchtig; F scheußlich

vil·lage Dorf *n*; ~ **green** Dorfanger *m*

vil·lag·er Dorfbewohner(in)

vil·lain Bösewicht *m*, Schurke *m*; *Br* F Ganove *m*

vin·di·cate *j-n* rehabilitieren; *et.* rechtfertigen; *et.* Bestätigen

vin·dic·tive rachsüchtig, nachtragend

vine BOT (Wein)Rebe *f*; Kletterpflanze *f*

vin·e·gar Essig *m*

vine·grow·er Winzer *m*

vine·yard Weinberg *m*

vin·tage 1. Weinernte *f*, Weinlese *f*; GASTR Jahrgang *m* **2.** GASTR Jahrgangs...; *fig* hervorragend, glänzend; *a 1999* ~ ein 1999er Jahrgang *or* Wein

vin·tage car *esp Br* Oldtimer *m* (*built between 1919 and 1930*)

vi·o·la MUS Bratsche *f*

vi·o·late *Vertrag etc* verletzen, *a.* *Versprechen* brechen, *Gesetz etc* übertreten; *Ruhe etc* stören; *Grab etc* schänden; **vi·o·la·tion** Verletzung *f*, Bruch *m*, Übertretung *f*

vi·o·lence Gewalt *f*; Gewalttätigkeit *f*; Ausschreitungen *pl*; Heftigkeit *f*

vi·o·lent gewalttätig; gewaltsam; heftig

vi·o·let 1. BOT Veilchen *n* **2.** violett

vi·o·lin MUS Geige *f*, Violine *f*

vi·o·lin·ist Geiger(in), Violinist(in)

VIP *abbr of very important person* VIP *f*

vi·per ZO Viper *f*, Natter *f*

VIP lounge AVIAT *etc* VIP-Lounge *f*; SPORT Ehrentribüne *f*

vir·gin 1. Jungfrau *f* **2.** jungfräulich, unberührt (*both a. fig*)

Vir·go ASTR Jungfrau *f*; *he (she) is (a)* ~ er (sie) ist Jungfrau

vir·ile männlich; potent

vi·ril·i·ty Männlichkeit *f*; Potenz *f*

vir·tu·al eigentlich, praktisch

vir·tu·al·ly praktisch, so gut wie

vir·tu·al re·al·i·ty IT virtuelle Realität

vir·tue Tugend *f*; Vorzug *m*, Vorteil *m*; *by* **or** *in* ~ *of* aufgrund (*gen*), kraft (*gen*); *make a* ~ *of necessity* aus der Not e-e Tugend machen

vir·tu·ous tugendhaft

vir·u·lent MED (akut und) bösartig;

schnell wirkend (*poison*); *fig* bösartig, gehässig

vi·rus MED Virus *n, m*

vi·sa Visum *n*, Sichtvermerk *m*

vis·cose Viskose *f*

vis·cous dickflüssig, zähflüssig

vise TECH Schraubstock *m*

vis·i·bil·i·ty Sicht *f*, Sichtverhältnisse *pl*, Sichtweite *f*

vis·i·ble sichtbar; (er)sichtlich

vi·sion Sehkraft *f*; Weitblick *m*; Vision *f*

vi·sion·a·ry 1. weitblickend; eingebildet, unwirklich **2.** Fantast(in), Träumer(in); Seher(in)

vis·it 1. *v/t j-n* besuchen, *Schloss etc a.* besichtigen; *et.* inspizieren; *v/i:* **be ~ing** auf Besuch sein (**with** bei) **2.** Besuch *m*, Besichtigung *f* (**to** gen); Plauderei *f*, **for** *or* **on a ~** auf Besuch; **have a ~ from** Besuch haben von; **pay a ~ to** *j-n* besuchen, *j-m* e-n Besuch abstatten; *Arzt* aufsuchen

vis·it·ing hours MED Besuchszeit *f*

vis·it·or Besucher(in), Gast *m*

vi·sor Visier *n*; Schirm *m*; MOT (Sonnen-)Blende *f*

vis·u·al Seh...; visuell; **~ aids** PED Anschauungsmaterial *n*, Lehrmittel *pl*; **~ dis·play u·nit** IT Bildschirmgerät *n*, Datensichtgerät *n*; **~ in·struc·tion** PED Anschauungsunterricht *m*

vis·u·al·ize sich *et.* vorstellen

vi·tal vital, Lebens...; lebenswichtig; unbedingt notwendig; **of ~ importance** von größter Wichtigkeit

vi·tal·i·ty Vitalität *f*

vit·a·min Vitamin *n*; **~ de·fi·cien·cy** Vitaminmangel *m*

vit·re·ous Glas...

vi·va·cious lebhaft, temperamentvoll

viv·id hell (*light*); kräftig, leuchtend (*color*); anschaulich (*description*); lebhaft (*imagination*)

vix·en co Füchsin *f*

V-neck V-Ausschnitt *m*

V-necked mit V-Ausschnitt

vo·cab·u·la·ry Vokabular *n*, Wortschatz *m*; Wörterverzeichnis *n*

vo·cal Stimm...; F lautstark; MUS Vokal..., Gesang...; **~ cords** ANAT Stimmbänder *pl*

vo·cal·ist Sänger(in)

vo·ca·tion Begabung *f* (**for** für); Berufung *f*

vo·ca·tion·al Berufs...; **~ ed·u·ca·tion** Berufsausbildung *f*; **~ guid·ance** Berufsberatung *f*; **~ train·ing** Berufsausbildung *f*

vogue Mode *f*; **be in ~** Mode sein

voice 1. Stimme *f*; **active ~** LING Aktiv *n*; **passive ~** LING Passiv *n* **2.** zum Ausdruck bringen; LING (stimmhaft) aussprechen; **voiced** LING stimmhaft; **voice·less** LING stimmlos

void 1. leer; JUR ungültig; **~ of** ohne **2.** (Gefühl *n* der) Leere *f*

vol *abbr of* **volume** Bd., Band *m*

vol·a·tile cholerisch (*person*); explosiv (*situation etc*); CHEM flüchtig

vol·ca·no Vulkan *m*

vol·ley 1. Salve *f*; (*Geschoss- etc*)Hagel *m* (*a. fig*); *tennis:* Volley *m*, Flugball *m*; *soccer:* Volleyschuss *m* **2.** *Ball* volley schießen

vol·ley·ball SPORT Volleyball *m*

volt ELECTR Volt *n*

volt·age ELECTR Spannung *f*

vol·u·ble redselig; wortreich

vol·ume Band *m*; Volumen *n*, Rauminhalt *m*; Umfang *m*, große Menge; Lautstärke *f*

vo·lu·mi·nous bauschig (*dress etc*); geräumig; umfangreich (*notes etc*)

vol·un·ta·ry freiwillig; unbezahlt

vol·un·teer 1. *v/i* sich freiwillig melden (**for** zu) (*a.* MIL); *v/t Hilfe etc* anbieten; *et.* von sich aus sagen, F herausrücken mit **2.** Freiwillige *m, f*; freiwilliger Helfer

vo·lup·tu·ous sinnlich (*lips etc*); aufreizend (*gesture etc*); üppig (*body etc*); kurvenreich (*woman*)

vom·it 1. *v/t* erbrechen; *v/i* (sich er)brechen, sich übergeben **2.** Erbrochene *n*

vo·ra·cious unersättlich (*appetite etc*)

vote 1. Abstimmung *f* (**about, on** über *acc*); (Wahl)Stimme *f*; Stimmzettel *m*; *a. pl* Wahlrecht *n*; **~ of no confidence** Misstrauensvotum *n*; **take a ~ on s.th.** über et. abstimmen **2.** *v/i* wählen; **~ for** (**against**) stimmen für (gegen); **~ on** abstimmen über (*acc*); *v/t* wählen; *et.* bewilligen; **~ out of office** abwählen

vot·er Wähler(in)

vot·ing booth Wahlkabine *f*

vouch: ~ for (sich ver)bürgen für

vouch·er Gutschein *m*, Kupon *m*

vow 1. Gelöbnis *n*; Gelübde *n*; *take a ~*, *make a ~* ein Gelöbnis *or* Gelübde ablegen **2.** geloben, schwören (*to do* zu tun)

vow·el LING Vokal *m*, Selbstlaut *m*

voy·age (See)Reise *f*

vul·gar vulgär, ordinär; geschmacklos

vul·ne·ra·ble *fig* verletzbar, verwundbar; verletzlich; anfällig (*to* für)

vul·ture ZO Geier *m*

W

W, w W, w *n*

wad (*Watte- etc*)Bausch *m*; Bündel *n*; (*Papier- etc*)Knäuel *m*, *n*

wad·ding Einlage *f*, Füllmaterial *n*

wad·dle watscheln

wade *v/i* waten; *~ through* waten durch; F sich durchkämpfen durch, *et.* durchackern; *v/t* durchwaten

wa·fer (*esp* Eis)Waffel *f*; Oblate *f*; REL Hostie *f*

waf·fle¹ Waffel *f*

waf·fle² *Br* F schwafeln

waft *v/i* ziehen (*smell etc*); *v/t* wehen

wag 1. wedeln (mit) **2.** *with a ~ of its tail* schwanzwedelnd

wage¹ *mst pl* (Arbeits)Lohn *m*

wage²: *~ (a) war against or on* MIL Krieg führen gegen; *fig* e-n Feldzug führen gegen

wage| earn·er Lohnempfänger(in); Verdiener(in); *~ freeze* Lohnstopp *m*; *~ ne·go·ti·a·tions* Tarifverhandlungen *pl*

wa·ger Wette *f*

wage rise Lohnerhöhung *f*

wag·gle F wackeln (mit)

wag·gon *Br* → **wag·on** Fuhrwerk *n*, Wagen *m*; *Br* RAIL (offener) Güterwagen; (*Tee- etc*)Wagen *m*

wag·tail ZO Bachstelze *f*

wail 1. jammern; heulen (*siren, wind*) **2.** Jammern *n*; Heulen *n*

wain·scot (Wand)Täfelung *f*

waist Taille *f*

waist·coat *esp Br* Weste *f*

waist·line Taille *f*

wait 1. *v/i* warten (*for, on* auf *acc*); *~ for s.o.* j-n erwarten; *keep s.o. ~ing* j-n warten lassen; *~ and see!* warte es ab!; *~ on s.o.* j-n bedienen; *~ up* F aufbleiben (*for* wegen); *v/t*: *~ one's chance* auf e-e günstige Gelegenheit warten (*to do* zu tun); *~ one's turn* warten,

bis man an der Reihe ist **2.** Wartezeit *f*; *have a long ~* lange warten müssen; *lie in ~ for s.o.* j-m auflauern

wait·er Kellner *m*, Ober *m*; *~, the check* (*Br* bill), *please!* (Herr) Ober, bitte zahlen!

wait·ing Warten *n*; *no ~* MOT Halt(e)verbot *n*; *~ list* Warteliste *f*; *~ room* MED *etc* Wartezimmer *n*; RAIL Wartesaal *m*

wait·ress Kellnerin *f*, Bedienung *f*; *~, the check* (*Br* bill), *please!* Fräulein, bitte zahlen!

wake¹ *v/i a. ~ up* aufwachen, wach werden; *v/t a. ~ up* (auf)wecken; *fig* wachrufen, wecken

wake² MAR Kielwasser *n*; *follow in the ~ of fig* folgen auf (*acc*)

wake·ful schlaflos

wak·en *v/i a. ~ up* aufwachen, wach werden; *v/t a. ~ up* (auf)wecken

walk 1. *v/i* (zu Fuß) gehen, laufen; spazieren gehen; wandern; *v/t* Strecke gehen, laufen; *j-n* bringen (*to* zu; *home* nach Hause); *Hund* ausführen; *Pferd* im Schritt gehen lassen; *~ away → walk off*; *~ in* hineingehen, hereinkommen; *~ off* fort-, weggehen; *~ off with* F abhauen mit; F *Preis etc* locker gewinnen; *~ out* hinausgehen; (*unter* Protest) den Saal *etc* verlassen; ECON streiken, in (den) Streik treten; *~ out on s.o.* F j-n verlassen, j-n im Stich lassen; *~ up* hinaufgehen, heraufkommen; *~ up to s.o.* auf j-n zugehen; *~ up!* treten Sie näher! **2.** Spaziergang *m*; Wanderung *f*; Spazier-, Wanderweg *m*; *go for a ~*, *take a ~* e-n Spaziergang machen, spazieren gehen; *an hour's ~* e-e Stunde Fußweg *or* zu Fuß; *from all ~s of life* Leute aus allen Berufen *or* Schichten

walk·a·way F Spaziergang *m*, leichter Sieg

walk·er Spaziergänger(in); Wanderer *m*, Wand(r)erin *f*; SPORT Geher(in); *be a good ~* gut zu Fuß sein

walk·ie-talk·ie Walkie-Talkie *n*, tragbares Funksprechgerät

walk·ing Gehen *n*, Laufen *n*; Spazierengehen *n*; Wandern *n*; *~ pa·pers: get one's ~* F den Laufpass bekommen; *~ shoes* Wanderschuhe *pl*; *~ stick* Spazierstock *m*; *~ tour* Wanderung *f*

Walk·man® Walkman® *m*

walk·out Auszug *m* (*by, of* e-r Delegation etc); ECON Ausstand *m*, Streik *m*

walk·over → *walkaway*

walk-up F (Miets)Haus *n* ohne Fahrstuhl; Wohnung *f* or Büro *n* etc in e-m Haus ohne Fahrstuhl

wall 1. Wand *f*; Mauer *f* **2.** *a. ~ in* mit e-r Mauer umgeben; *~ up* zumauern

wall cal·en·dar Wandkalender *m*

wall-chart Wandkarte *f*

wal·let Brieftasche *f*

wall·flow·er F Mauerblümchen *n*

wal·lop F *j-m* ein Ding verpassen; SPORT *j-n* erledigen, vernichten (*at* in *dat*)

wal·low sich wälzen; *fig* schwelgen, sich baden (*in* in *dat*)

wall·pa·per 1. Tapete *f* **2.** tapezieren

wall-to-wall: *~ carpet(ing)* Spannteppich *m*, Teppichboden *m*

wal·nut BOT Walnuss(baum *m*) *f*

wal·rus ZO Walross *n*

waltz 1. Walzer *m* **2.** Walzer tanzen

wand (*Zauber*)Stab *m*

wan·der (herum)wandern, herumlaufen, umherstreifen; *fig* abschweifen; fantasieren

wane 1. ASTR abnehmen; *fig* schwinden **2.** *be on the ~ fig* im Schwinden begriffen sein

wan·gle F deichseln, hinkriegen; *~ s.th. out of s.o.* j-m et. abluchsen; *~ one's way out of* sich herauswinden aus

want 1. *v/t* et. wollen; *j-n* brauchen; *j-n* sprechen wollen; F et. brauchen, nötig haben; *be ~ed* (*polizeilich*) gesucht werden (*for* wegen); *v/i* wollen; *I don't ~ to* ich will nicht; *he does not ~ for anything* es fehlt ihm an nichts **2.** Mangel *m* (*of* an *dat*); Bedürfnis *n*, Wunsch *m*; Not *f*; *~ ad* Kleinanzeige *f*

want·ed (*polizeilich*) gesucht

wan·ton mutwillig

war Krieg *m* (*a. fig*); *fig* Kampf *m*
(*against* gegen)

war·ble ZO trillern

ward 1. MED Station *f*; Br POL Stadtbezirk *m*; JUR Mündel *n* **2.** *~ off* Schlag etc abwehren, *Gefahr* etc abwenden

war·den Aufseher(in); Heimleiter(in); (Gefängnis)Direktor(in)

ward·er Br Aufsichtsbeamte *m*, -beamtin *f*

war·drobe Kleiderschrank *m*; Garderobe *f*

ware·house Lager(haus) *n*

war·fare Krieg *m*; Kriegführung *f*

war·head MIL Spreng-, Gefechtskopf *m*

war·like kriegerisch; Kriegs...

warm 1. *adj* warm, *fig a.* herzlich; *I am ~, I feel ~* mir ist warm **2.** *v/t a. ~ up* wärmen, sich *die Hände* etc wärmen; *Motor* warm laufen lassen; *v/i a. ~ up* warm or wärmer werden, sich erwärmen; **warmth** Wärme *f*

warm-up SPORT Aufwärmen *n*

warn warnen (*against, of* vor *dat*); *j-n* verständigen

warn·ing Warnung *f* (*of* vor *dat*); Verwarnung *f*; *without ~* ohne Vorwarnung; *~ sig·nal* Warnsignal *n*

warp sich verziehen *or* werfen

war·rant 1. JUR (Durchsuchungs-, Haft-etc)Befehl *m* **2.** *et.* rechtfertigen; *~ of ar·rest* JUR Haftbefehl *m*

war·ran·ty ECON Garantie(erklärung) *f*; *it's still under ~* darauf ist noch Garantie

war·ri·or Krieger *m*

war·ship Kriegsschiff *n*

wart MED Warze *f*

war·y vorsichtig

was *ich, er, sie, es* war; *passive: ich, er, sie, es* wurde

wash *v/t* waschen, sich *die Hände* etc waschen; *v/i* sich waschen; sich *gut* etc waschen (lassen); *~ up v/i Br* abwaschen, (das) Geschirr spülen; *v/t* anschwemmen, anspülen; *~ one's dirty linen* schmutzige Wäsche waschen **2.** Wäsche *f*, MOT Waschanlage *f*, Waschstraße *f*; *be in the ~* in der Wäsche sein; *give s.th. a ~* et. waschen; *have a ~* sich waschen

wash·a·ble (ab)waschbar

wash-and-wear bügelfrei; pflegeleicht

wash·ba·sin Br, **wash·bowl** Waschbecken *n*

wash·cloth Waschlappen *m*

wash·er Waschmaschine *f*; TECH Unterlegscheibe *f*

wash·ing 1. Wäsche *f* **2.** Wasch...

wash·ing| ma·chine Waschmaschine *f*; **~ pow·der** Waschpulver *n*, -mittel *n*

washing-up *Br* Abwasch *m*; **do the ~** den Abwasch machen

wash·room Toilette *f*

wasp ZO Wespe *f*

waste 1. Verschwendung *f*; Abfall *m*; Müll *m*; **~ of time** Zeitverschwendung *f*; **hazardous ~**, **special toxic ~** Sondermüll *m*; **special ~ dump** Sondermülldeponie *f* **2.** *v/t* verschwenden, vergeuden; *j-n* auszehren; *v/i* **~ away** immer schwächer werden (*person*) **3.** überschüssig; Abfall...; brachliegend, öde; **lay ~** verwüsten

waste dis·pos·al Abfall-, Müllbeseitigung *f*; Entsorgung *f*; **~ site** Deponie *f*

waste·ful verschwenderisch

waste| gas Abgas *n*; **~ pa·per** Abfallpapier *n*; Altpapier *n*

waste·pa·per bas·ket Papierkorb *m*

waste pipe Abflussrohr *n*

watch 1. *v/i* zuschauen; **~ for** warten auf (*acc*); **~ out!** pass auf!, Vorsicht!; **~ out for** Ausschau halten nach; sich in Acht nehmen vor (*dat*); *v/t* beobachten; zuschauen bei, sich *et.* ansehen; → **television 2.** (*Armband-, Taschen*)Uhr *f*; Wache *f*; **keep ~** Wache halten, wachen (**over** über *acc*); **be on the ~ for** Ausschau halten nach; auf der Hut sein vor (*dat*); **keep (a) careful** or **close ~ on** genau beobachten, scharf im Auge behalten

watch·dog Wachhund *m*

watch·ful wachsam

watch·mak·er Uhrmacher(in)

watch·man Wachmann *m*, Wächter *m*

watch·tow·er Wach(t)turm *m*

wa·ter 1. Wasser *n* **2.** *v/t Blumen* gießen, *Rasen etc* sprengen; *Vieh* tränken; **~ down** verdünnen, verwässern; *fig* abschwächen; *v/i* tränen (*eyes*); **make s.o.'s mouth ~** *j-m* den Mund wässerig machen

wa·ter bird ZO Wasservogel *m*

wa·ter·col·o(u)r Wasser-, Aquarellfarbe *f*; Aquarellmalerei *f*; Aquarell *n*

wa·ter·course Wasserlauf *m*

wa·ter·cress BOT Brunnenkresse *f*

wa·ter·fall Wasserfall *m*

wa·ter·front Hafenviertel *n*; **along the ~** am Wasser entlang

wa·ter·hole Wasserloch *n*

wa·ter·ing can Gießkanne *f*

wa·ter jump SPORT Wassergraben *m*

wa·ter lev·el Wasserstand *m*

wa·ter lil·y BOT Seerose *f*

wa·ter·mark Wasserzeichen *n*

wa·ter·mel·on BOT Wassermelone *f*

wa·ter| pol·lu·tion Wasserverschmutzung *f*; **~ po·lo** SPORT Wasserball(spiel *n*) *m*

wa·ter·proof 1. wasserdicht **2.** *Br* Regenmantel *m* **3.** imprägnieren

wa·ters Gewässer *pl*; Wasser *pl*

wa·ter·shed GEOGR Wasserscheide *f*; *fig* Wendepunkt *m*

wa·ter·side Ufer *n*

wa·ter ski·ing SPORT Wasserskilaufen *n*

wa·ter·tight wasserdicht, *fig a.* hieb- und stichfest

wa·ter·way Wasserstraße *f*

wa·ter·works Wasserwerk *n*; **turn on the ~** F zu heulen anfangen

wa·ter·y wäss(e)rig

watt ELECTR Watt *n*

wave 1. *v/t* schwenken; winken mit; *Haar* wellen, in Wellen legen; **~ one's hand** winken; **~ s.o. aside** *j-n* beiseitewinken; *v/i* winken; wehen (*flag etc*); sich wellen (*hair*); **~ at s.o.**, **~ to s.o.** *j-m* zuwinken **2.** Welle *f* (*a. fig*); Winken *n*

wave·length PHYS Wellenlänge *f* (*a. fig*)

wa·ver flackern; schwanken

wav·y wellig, gewellt

wax¹ 1. Wachs *n*; (*Ohren*)Schmalz *n* **2.** wachsen; bohnern

wax² ASTR zunehmen

wax·en wächsern

wax·works Wachsfigurenkabinett *n*

wax·y wächsern

way 1. Weg *m*; Richtung *f*, Seite *f*; Entfernung *f*, Strecke *f*; Art *f*, Weise *f*; **~s and means** Mittel und Wege *pl*; **~ back** Rückweg *m*, Rückfahrt *f*; **~ home** Heimweg *m*; **~ in** Eingang *m*; **~ out** Ausgang *m*; **be on the ~ to**, **be on one's ~ to** unterwegs sein nach; **by ~ of** über (*acc*), via; *esp Br* statt; **by the ~** übrigens; **give ~** nachgeben; *Br* MOT die Vorfahrt lassen; **in a ~** in gewisser Hinsicht; **in no ~** in keiner Weise;

lead the ~ vorangehen; **let s.o. have his (own)** ~ j-m s-n Willen lassen; **lose one's** ~ sich verlaufen *or* verirren; **make** ~ Platz machen (**for** für); **no** ~! F kommt überhaupt nicht in Frage!; **out of the** ~ ungewöhnlich; **this** ~ hierher; hier entlang **2.** *adv* weit

way·bill ECON Frachtbrief *m*

way·lay j-m auflauern; j-n abfangen, abpassen

way·ward eigensinnig, launisch

we wir *pl*

weak schwach (**at, in** in *dat*), GASTR *a.* dünn; **weak·en** *v/t* schwächen (*a.* *fig*); *v/i* schwächer werden; *fig* nachgeben; **weak·ling** Schwächling *m*, F Schlappschwanz *m*; **weak·ness** Schwäche *f*

weal Striemen *m*

wealth Reichtum *m*; *fig* Fülle *f* (**of** von)

wealth·y reich

wean entwöhnen; ~ **s.o. from** *or* **off s.th.** j-m et. abgewöhnen

weap·on Waffe *f* (*a.* *fig*)

wear 1. *v/t* Bart, Brille, Schmuck etc tragen, Mantel etc *a.* anhaben, Hut etc *a.* aufhaben; abnutzen, abtragen; ~ **an angry expression** verärgert dreinschauen; *v/i* sich abnutzen, verschleißen; sich gut *etc* halten; **s.th. to** ~ et. zum Anziehen; ~ **away** (sich) abtragen *or* abschleifen; ~ **down** (sich) abtreten (*stairs*), (sich) ablaufen (*heels*), (sich) abfahren (*tires*); abschleifen; j-n zermürben; ~ **off** nachlassen (*pain etc*); ~ **on** sich hinziehen (**all day** über den ganzen Tag); ~ **out** (sich) abnutzen *or* abtragen; *fig* j-n erschöpfen **2.** *often* in *cpds* Kleidung *f*; *a.* ~ **and tear** Abnutzung *f*, Verschleiß *m*; **the worse for** ~ abgenutzt, verschlissen; F lädiert

wear·i·some ermüdend; langweilig; lästig

wear·y erschöpft, müde; ermüdend, anstrengend; **be** ~ **of s.th.** F et. satthaben

wea·sel ZO Wiesel *n*

weath·er 1. Wetter *n*; Witterung *f* **2.** *v/t* dem Wetter aussetzen; *fig* Krise etc überstehen; *v/i* verwittern

weath·er-beat·en verwittert

weath·er|·chart METEOR Wetterkarte *f*; ~ **fore·cast** METEOR Wettervorhersage *f*; Wetterbericht *m*

weath·er·man *radio*, TV Wetteransager *m*

weath·er·proof 1. wetterfest **2.** wetterfest machen

weath·er| re·port METEOR Wetterbericht *m*; ~ **sta·tion** METEOR Wetterwarte *f*; ~ **vane** Wetterfahne *f*

weave weben; *Netz* spinnen; *Korb* flechten; ~ **one's way through** sich schlängeln durch; **weav·er** Weber(in)

web Netz *n* (*a.* *fig*), Gewebe *n*; ZO Schwimmhaut *f*

wed heiraten

Wed(s) *abbr of* **Wednesday** Mi., Mittwoch *m*

wed·ding 1. Hochzeit *f* **2.** Hochzeits..., Braut..., Ehe..., Trau...

wed·ding ring Ehering *m*, Trauring *m*

wedge 1. Keil *m* **2.** verkeilen, mit e-m Keil festklemmen; ~ **in** einkeilen, einzwängen

Wednes·day (*abbr* **Wed, Weds**) Mittwoch *m*; **on** ~ (am) Mittwoch; **on** ~**s** mittwochs

wee[1] ~ klein, winzig; **a** ~ **bit** ein (kleines) bisschen

wee[2] F **1.** Pipi machen **2. do** *or* **have a** ~ Pipi machen

weed 1. Unkraut *n* **2.** jäten

weed·kill·er Unkrautvertilgungsmittel *n*

weed·y voll Unkraut; F schmächtig; F rückgratlos

week Woche *f*; ~ **after** ~ Woche um Woche; **a** ~ **today, today** ~ heute in e-r Woche *or* in acht Tagen; **every other** ~ jede zweite Woche; **for** ~**s** wochenlang; **four times a** ~ viermal die Woche; **in a** ~**('s time)** in e-r Woche

week·day Wochentag *m*

week·end Wochenende *n*; **on** (*Br* **at**) **the** ~ am Wochenende; **week·end·er** Wochenendausflügler(in)

week·ly 1. Wochen...; wöchentlich **2.** Wochenblatt *n*, Wochen(zeit)schrift *f*, Wochenzeitung *f*

weep weinen (**for** um j-n; **over** über *acc*); MED nässen

weep·ing wil·low BOT Trauerweide *f*

weep·y F weinerlich; rührselig

wee-wee F → **wee**[2]

weigh *v/t* (ab)wiegen; *fig* abwägen (**against** gegen); ~ **anchor** MAR den Anker lichten; **be** ~**ed down with** *fig* niedergedrückt werden von; *v/i* ... Kilo etc wiegen; ~ **on** *fig* lasten auf (*dat*)

weight 1. Gewicht *n*; Last *f* (*a. fig*); *fig* Bedeutung *f*; *gain ~, put on ~* zunehmen; *lose ~* abnehmen **2.** beschweren
weight·less schwerelos
weight·less·ness Schwerelosigkeit *f*
weight lift·er SPORT Gewichtheber *m*
weight lift·ing SPORT Gewichtheben *n*
weight·y schwer; *fig* schwerwiegend
weir Wehr *n*
weird unheimlich; F sonderbar, verrückt
wel·come 1. *int ~ back!, ~ home!* willkommen zu Hause!; *~ to England!* willkommen in England! **2.** *v/t* begrüßen (*a. fig*), willkommen heißen **3.** *adj* willkommen; *you are ~ to do it* Sie können es gerne tun; *you're ~!* nichts zu danken!, keine Ursache!, bitte sehr! **4.** Empfang *m*, Willkommen *n*; *outstay or overstay one's ~* j-s Gastfreundschaft überstrapazieren *or* zu lange in Anspruch nehmen
weld TECH schweißen
wel·fare Wohl(ergehen) *n*; Sozialhilfe *f*; *be on ~* Sozalhilfe beziehen; *~ state* Wohlfahrtsstaat *m*; *~ work* Sozialarbeit *f*; *~ work·er* Sozialarbeiter(in)
well[1] **1.** *adv* gut; gründlich; *as ~* ebenso, auch; *as ~ as ...* sowohl ... als auch ...; nicht nur ..., sondern auch ...; *very ~* also gut, na gut; *~ done!* bravo!; → *off I* **2.** *int* nun, also; *~, ~!* na so was! **3.** *adj* gesund; *feel ~* sich wohlfühlen
well[2] **1.** Brunnen *m*; (*Öl*)Quelle *f*; (*Aufzugs- etc*)Schacht *m* **2.** *a. ~ out* quellen (*from* aus); *tears ~ed (up) in their eyes* die Tränen stiegen ihnen in die Augen
well-bal·anced ausgeglichen (*person*); ausgewogen (*diet*)
well-be·haved artig, gut erzogen
well-be·ing Wohl(befinden) *n*
well-dis·posed: be ~ towards s.o. j-m wohlgesinnt sein
well-done GASTR durchgebraten
well-earned wohlverdient
well-fed gut genährt
well-found·ed (wohl) begründet
well-in·formed gut unterrichtet; gebildet
well-known (wohl) bekannt
well-mean·ing wohlmeinend, gut gemeint; **well-meant** gut gemeint
well-off 1. wohlhabend, vermögend, bessergestellt; *be ~ for* gut versorgt

sein mit **2.** *the ~* die Wohlhabenden *pl*
well-read belesen
well-timed (zeitlich) günstig, im richtigen Augenblick
well-to-do wohlhabend, reich
well-worn abgetragen; *fig* abgedroschen
Welsh 1. walisisch **2.** LING Walisisch *n*; *the ~* die Waliser *pl*
welt Striemen *m*
wel·ter Wirrwarr *m*, Durcheinander *n*
wel·ter·weight SPORT Weltergewicht *n*; Weltergewichtler *m*
were *du* warst, *Sie* waren, *sie* waren, *ihr* wart
west 1. West, Westen *m*; *the West* POL der Westen; die Weststaaten *pl* **2.** *adj* westlich, West... **3.** *adv* nach Westen, westwärts; *west·er·ly* West..., westlich; *west·ern* **1.** westlich, West... **2.** Western *m*; *west·ward(s)* westlich, nach Westen
wet 1. nass, feucht **2.** Nässe *f* **3.** nass machen, anfeuchten
weth·er ZO Hammel *m*
wet nurse Amme *f*
whack (knallender) Schlag; F Anteil *m*
whacked F fertig, erledigt
whack·ing 1. *Br F* Mords... **2.** (Tracht *f*) Prügel *pl*
whale ZO Wal *m*
wharf Kai *m*
what 1. *pron* was; *~ about ...?* wie wärs mit ...?; *~ for?* wozu?; *so ~?* na und?; *know ~'s ~* F wissen, was Sache ist **2.** *adj* was für ein(e), welche(r, -s); alle, die; alles, was
what-cha-ma-call-it F → *whatsit*
what·ev·er 1. *pron* was (auch immer); alles, was; egal, was **2.** *adj* welche(r, -s) ... auch (immer); *no ... ~* überhaupt kein(e) ...
whats·it F Dings(bums, -da) *m, f, n*
what·so·ev·er → *whatever*
wheat BOT Weizen *m*
whee·dle beschwatzen; *~ s.th. out of s.o.* j-m et. abschwatzen
wheel 1. Rad *n*; MOT, MAR Steuer *n* **2.** schieben, rollen; kreisen; *~ about, ~ (a)round* herumfahren, herumwirbeln
wheel·bar·row Schubkarre(n *m*) *f*
wheel·chair Rollstuhl *m*
wheel clamp MOT Parkkralle *f*
wheeled mit Rädern; fahrbar; *in cpds*

W

…räd(e)rig

wheeze keuchen, pfeifend atmen

whelp zo Welpe *m*, Junge *n*

when wann; als; wenn; obwohl; *since ~?* seit wann?

when·ev·er wann auch (immer); jedes Mal, wenn

where·so; wohin; *~ … (from)?* woher?; *~ … (to)?* wohin?; *where·a·bouts* **1.** *adv* wo etwa **2.** Verbleib *m*; Aufenthalt *m*, Aufenthaltsort *m*

where·as während, wohingegen

where·by wodurch, womit; wonach

where·u·pon worauf, woraufhin

wher·ev·er wo *or* wohin auch (immer); ganz gleich wo *or* wohin

whet *Messer etc* schärfen; *fig Appetit* anregen

wheth·er ob

whey Molke *f*

which welche(r, -s); der, die, das; was; *~ of you?* wer von euch?

which·ev·er welche(r, -s) auch (immer); ganz gleich, welche(r, -s)

whiff Luftzug *m*; Hauch *m* (*a. fig of* von); Duft *m*, Duftwolke *f*

while 1. Weile *f*; *for a ~* e-e Zeit lang **2.** *cj* während; obwohl **3.** *mst ~ away* sich *die Zeit* vertreiben (*by doing s.th.* mit et.)

whim Laune *f*

whim·per 1. wimmern; zo winseln **2.** Wimmern *n*; zo Winseln *n*

whim·si·cal wunderlich; launisch

whine 1. zo jaulen; jammern (*about* über *acc*) **2.** zo Jaulen *n*; Gejammer *n*

whin·ny zo **1.** wiehern **2.** Wiehern *n*

whip 1. Peitsche *f*; GASTR Creme *f* **2.** *v/t* (aus)peitschen; GASTR schlagen; *v/i* sausen, flitzen, (*wind*) fegen

whipped| cream Schlagsahne *f*, Schlagrahm *m*; *~ eggs* Eischnee *m*

whip·ping (Tracht *f*) Prügel *pl*

whip·ping boy Prügelknabe *m*

whip·ping cream Schlagsahne *f*, Schlagrahm *m*

whir → **whirr**

whirl 1. wirbeln; *my head is ~ing* mir schwirrt der Kopf **2.** Wirbeln *n*; Wirbel *m* (*a. fig*); *my head's in a ~* mir schwirrt der Kopf

whirl·pool Strudel *m*; Whirlpool *m*

whirl·wind Wirbelsturm *m*

whirr schwirren

whisk 1. schnelle Bewegung; Wedel *m*;

GASTR Schneebesen *m* **2.** GASTR schlagen; *~ its tail* zo mit dem Schwanz schlagen; *~ away* Fliegen etc verscheuchen *or* wegscheuchen; *et.* schnell verschwinden lassen *or* wegnehmen

whis·ker zo Schnurr- *or* Barthaar *n*; *pl* Backenbart *m*

whis·k(e)y Whisky *m*

whis·per 1. flüstern **2.** Flüstern *n*; *say s.th. in a ~* et. im Flüsterton sagen

whis·tle 1. Pfeife *f*; Pfiff *m* **2.** pfeifen

white 1. weiß **2.** Weiß(e) *n*; Weiße *m, f*; Eiweiß *n*; *~ bread* Weißbrot *n*; *~ coffee Br* Milchkaffee *m*, Kaffee *m* mit Milch

white-col·lar work·er (Büro)Angestellte *m, f*

white lie Notlüge *f*

whit·en weiß machen *or* werden

white·wash 1. Tünche *f* **2.** tünchen, anstreichen; weißen; *fig* beschönigen

whit·ish weißlich

Whit·sun Pfingstsonntag *m*; Pfingsten *n or pl*

Whit Sunday Pfingstsonntag *m*

Whit·sun·tide Pfingsten *n or pl*

whiz(z) F **1.** *~ by, ~ past* vorbeizischen, vorbeidüsen **2.** Ass *n*, Kanone *f* (*at* in *dat*); *~ kid* F Senkrechtstarter(in)

who wer; wen; wem; welche(r, -s); der, die, das

who·dun·(n)it F Krimi *m*

who·ev·er wer *or* wen *or* wem auch (immer); egal, wer *or* wen *or* wem

whole 1. *adj* ganz **2.** *das* Ganze; *the ~ of London* ganz London; *on the ~* im Großen (und) Ganzen

whole-heart·ed ungeteilt (*attention*), voll (*support*), ernsthaft (*effort etc*)

whole-heart·ed·ly uneingeschränkt, voll und ganz

whole·meal Vollkorn…; *~ bread* Vollkornbrot *n*

whole·sale ECON **1.** Großhandel *m* **2.** Großhandels…; *~ mar·ket* ECON Großmarkt *m*

whole·sal·er ECON Großhändler *m*

whole·some gesund

whole wheat → **wholemeal**

whol·ly gänzlich, völlig

whoop 1. schreien, *esp* jauchzen; *~ it up* F auf den Putz hauen **2.** (*esp* Freuden)-

Schrei m

whoop·ee: F *make~* auf den Putz hauen

whoop·ing cough MED Keuchhusten m

whore Hure f

why warum, weshalb; *that's* ~ deshalb

wick Docht m

wick·ed gemein, niederträchtig

wick·er·work Korbwaren pl

wick·et *cricket:* Tor n

wide 1. *adj* breit; weit offen, aufgerissen (*eyes*); *fig* umfangreich (*knowledge etc*), vielfältig (*interests etc*) **2.** *adv* weit; *go* ~ danebengehen; *go* ~ *of the goal* SPORT am Tor vorbeigehen

wide-an·gle lens PHOT Weitwinkelobjektiv n

wide-a·wake hellwach; *fig* aufgeweckt, wach

wide-eyed mit großen *or* aufgerissenen Augen; naiv

wid·en verbreitern; breiter werden

wide-o·pen weit offen, aufgerissen (*eyes*)

wide·spread weit verbreitet

wid·ow Witwe f

wid·owed verwitwet; *be* ~ verwitwet sein; Witwe(r) werden

wid·ow·er Witwer m

width Breite f; Bahn f

wield Einfluss etc ausüben

wife (Ehe)Frau f, Gattin f

wig Perücke f

wild 1. *adj* wild; stürmisch (*wind, applause etc*); außer sich (*with* vor dat); verrückt (*idea etc*); *make a* ~ *guess* einfach drauflosraten; *be* ~ *about* (ganz) verrückt sein nach **2.** *adv:* *go* ~ ausflippen **3.** *in the* ~ in freier Wildbahn; *the* ~s die Wildnis

wild·cat ZO Wildkatze f

wild·cat strike ECON wilder Streik

wil·der·ness Wildnis f

wild·fire: *spread like* ~ sich wie ein Lauffeuer verbreiten

wild·life Tier- und Pflanzenwelt f

wil·ful Br → *willful*

will¹ *v/aux* ich, du will(st) etc; ich werde … etc

will² Wille m; Testament n; *of one's own free* ~ aus freien Stücken

will³ durch Willenskraft erzwingen; JUR vermachen

will·ful eigensinnig; absichtlich, *esp* JUR vorsätzlich

will·ing bereit (*to do* zu tun); (bereit)willig

will-o'-the-wisp Irrlicht n

wil·low BOT Weide f

wil·low·y *fig* gertenschlank

will-pow·er Willenskraft f

wil·ly-nil·ly wohl oder übel

wilt verwelken, welk werden

wi·ly gerissen, raffiniert

wimp F Schlappschwanz m

win 1. *v/t* gewinnen; ~ *s.o. over or round to* j-n gewinnen für; *v/i* gewinnen, siegen; *OK, you* ~ okay, du hast gewonnen **2.** *esp* SPORT Sieg m

wince zusammenzucken (*at* bei)

winch TECH Winde f

wind¹ 1. Wind m; Atem m, Luft f; MED Blähungen pl; *the* ~ MUS die Bläser pl **2.** *j-m* den Atem nehmen *or* verschlagen; HUNT wittern

wind² 1. *v/t* drehen (an dat); Uhr etc aufziehen; wickeln (*round* um); *v/i* sich winden *or* schlängeln; ~ *down* Autofenster etc herunterdrehen, -kurbeln; Produktion etc reduzieren; sich entspannen; ~ *up* v/t Autofenster etc hochdrehen, -kurbeln; Uhr etc aufziehen; Versammlung etc schließen (*with* mit); Unternehmen liquidieren, auflösen; v/i F enden, landen; (*esp* s-e Rede) schließen (*by saying* mit den Worten); **2.** Umdrehung f

wind·bag F Schwätzer(in)

wind·fall BOT Fallobst n; unverhofftes Geschenk; unverhoffter Gewinn

wind·ing gewunden

wind·ing stairs Wendeltreppe f

wind in·stru·ment MUS Blasinstrument n

wind·lass TECH Winde f

wind·mill Windmühle f

win·dow Fenster n; Schaufenster n; Schalter m; ~ *clean·er* Fensterputzer m; ~ *dress·er* Schaufensterdekorateur(in); ~ *dress·ing* Schaufensterdekoration f; *fig* F Mache f

win·dow·pane Fensterscheibe f

win·dow seat Fensterplatz m

win·dow shade Rouleau n

win·dow-shop: *go window-shopping* e-n Schaufensterbummel machen

win·dow·sill Fensterbank f, -brett n

wind·pipe ANAT Luftröhre f

wind·screen Br MOT Windschutzscheibe f; ~ **wip·er** Br MOT Scheibenwischer m

wind·shield MOT Windschutzscheibe f; ~ **wip·er** MOT Scheibenwischer m

wind·surf·ing SPORT Windsurfing n, Windsurfen n

wind·y windig; MED blähend

wine Wein m; ~ **cel·lar** Weinkeller m; ~ **list** Weinkarte f; ~ **mer·chant** Weinhändler m

win·er·y Weinkellerei f

wine tast·ing Weinprobe f

wing ZO Flügel m, Schwinge f; Br MOT Kotflügel m; AVIAT Tragfläche f; AVIAT MIL Geschwader n; pl THEA Seitenkulisse f

wing·er SPORT Außenstürmer(in), Flügelstürmer(in)

wink 1. zwinkern; ~ **at** j-m zuzwinkern; et. geflissentlich übersehen; ~ **one's lights** Br MOT blinken **2.** Zwinkern n; *I didn't get a ~ of sleep last night, I didn't sleep a ~ last night* ich habe letzte Nacht kein Auge zugetan; → **for·ty** 1

win·ner Gewinner(in), esp SPORT Sieger(in)

win·ning 1. einnehmend, gewinnend **2.** pl Gewinn m

win·ter 1. Winter m; **in (the)** ~ im Winter **2.** überwintern; den Winter verbringen; ~ **sports** Wintersport m

win·ter·time Winter m; Winterzeit f; **in (the)** ~ im Winter

win·try winterlich; fig frostig

wipe (ab-, auf)wischen; ~ **off** ab-, wegwischen; ~ **out** auswischen; auslöschen, ausrotten; ~ **up** aufwischen

wip·er MOT (Scheiben)Wischer m

wire 1. Draht m; ELECTR Leitung f; Telegramm n **2.** Leitungen verlegen in (dat) (a. ~ **up**); j-m ein Telegramm schicken; j-m et. telegrafieren

wire·less drahtlos, Funk…

wire net·ting Maschendraht m

wire·tap j-n, j-s Telefon abhören

wir·y fig drahtig

wis·dom Weisheit f, Klugheit f

wis·dom tooth Weisheitszahn m

wise weise, klug

wise·crack F **1.** Witzelei f **2.** witzeln

wise guy F Klugscheißer m

wish 1. wünschen; wollen; ~ **s.o. well** j-m alles Gute wünschen; *if you* ~ *(to)* wenn du willst; ~ **for s.th.** sich et. wünschen **2.** Wunsch m **(for** nach)

wish·ful think·ing Wunschdenken n

wish·y-wash·y F labb(e)rig, wäss(e)rig; fig lasch (person); verschwommen

wisp (Gras-, Haar)Büschel n

wist·ful wehmütig

wit Geist m, Witz m; geistreicher Mensch; a. pl Verstand m; **be at one's ~s' end** mit s-r Weisheit am Ende sein

witch Hexe f

witch·craft Hexerei f

with mit; bei; vor (dat)

with·draw v/t Geld abheben **(from** von); Angebot etc zurückziehen, Anschuldigung etc zurücknehmen; MIL Truppen zurückziehen, abziehen; v/i sich zurückziehen; zurücktreten **(from** von)

with·draw·al Rücknahme f; esp MIL Abzug m, Rückzug m; Rücktritt m **(from** von), Ausstieg m **(from** aus); MED Entziehung f, Entzug m; **make a ~** Geld abheben **(from** von); ~ **cure** MED Entziehungskur f; ~ **symp·toms** MED Entzugserscheinungen pl

with·er eingehen or verdorren or (ver)welken (lassen)

with·hold zurückhalten; ~ **s.th. from s.o.** j-m et. vorenthalten

with·in innerhalb (gen)

with·out ohne (acc)

with·stand e-m Angriff etc standhalten; Beanspruchung etc aushalten

wit·ness 1. Zeuge m, Zeugin f; ~ **for the defense** (Br **defence**) JUR Entlastungszeuge m, -zeugin f; ~ **for the prosecution** JUR Belastungszeuge m, -zeugin f **2.** Zeuge sein von et.; et. bezeugen, Unterschrift beglaubigen; ~ **box** Br, ~ **stand** JUR Zeugenstand m

wit·ti·cis·m geistreiche or witzige Bemerkung; **wit·ty** geistreich, witzig

wiz·ard Zauberer m; fig Genie n **(at** in dat)

wiz·ened verhutzelt

wob·ble v/i wackeln, zittern (a. voice), schwabbeln; MOT flattern; fig schwanken; v/t wackeln an (dat)

woe·ful traurig; bedauerlich

wolf 1. ZO Wolf m; **lone** ~ fig Einzelgänger(in) **2.** a. ~ **down** F Essen hinunterschlingen

wom·an Frau f; ~ **doc·tor** Ärztin f; ~ **driv·er** Frau f am Steuer

W

wom·an·ish weibisch

wom·an·ly fraulich; weiblich

womb ANAT Gebärmutter f

women's| lib·ber F Emanze f; **~** movement Frauenbewegung f; **~ ref·uge** Br, **~ shel·ter** Frauenhaus n

won·der 1. neugierig or gespannt sein, gern wissen mögen; sich fragen, überlegen; sich wundern, erstaunt sein (**about** über acc); **I ~ if you could help me** vielleicht können Sie mir helfen **2.** Staunen n, Verwunderung f; Wunder n; **do** or **work ~s** wahre Wunder vollbringen; Wunder wirken (**for** bei)

won·der·ful wunderbar, wundervoll

wont 1. be~ to do s.th. et. zu tun pflegen **2. as was his ~** wie es s-e Gewohnheit war

woo umwerben, werben um

wood 1. Holz n; Holzfass n; a. pl Wald m, Gehölz n; **touch ~!** unberufen!, toi, toi, toi!; **he can't see the ~ for the trees** er sieht den Wald vor lauter Bäumen nicht

wood·cut Holzschnitt m

wood·cut·ter Holzfäller m

wood·ed bewaldet

wood·en hölzern (a. fig), aus Holz, Holz…

wood·peck·er ZO Specht m

wood·wind 1. ~ MUS die Holzblasinstrumente pl, die Holzbläser pl; **~ in·strument** Holzblasinstrument n

wood·work Holzarbeit f

wood·y waldig; BOT holzig

wool Wolle f

wool·(l)en 1. wollen, Woll… **2.** pl Wollsachen pl, Wollkleidung f

wool·(l)y 1. wollig; fig schwammig **2.** pl F Wollsachen pl

word 1. Wort n; Nachricht f; Losung f, Losungswort n; Versprechen n; Befehl m; pl MUS etc Text m; **have a ~** or **a few ~s with s.o.** mit j-m sprechen **2.** et. ausdrücken, Text abfassen, formulieren; **word·ing** Wortlaut m

word| or·der LING Wortstellung f; **~ pro·cess·ing** IT Textverarbeitung f; **~ pro·ces·sor** IT Textverarbeitungsgerät n

word·y wortreich, langatmig

work 1. Arbeit f; Werk n; pl TECH Werk n, Getriebe n; ECON Fabrik f; **at ~** bei der Arbeit; **be in ~** Arbeit haben; **be out of ~** arbeitslos sein; **go** or **set to ~** an die Arbeit gehen **2.** v/i arbeiten (**at, on** an dat); TECH funktionieren (a. fig); wirken; **~ to rule** Dienst nach Vorschrift tun; v/t j-n arbeiten lassen; Maschine etc bedienen, et. betätigen; et. bearbeiten; bewirken, herbeiführen; **~ one's way** sich durcharbeiten or durchkämpfen; **~ off** Schulden abarbeiten; Wut etc abreagieren; **~ out** v/t ausrechnen; Aufgabe lösen; Plan etc ausarbeiten; fig sich et. zusammenreimen; v/i gut gehen, F klappen; aufgehen; F SPORT trainieren; **~ up** Zuhörer etc aufpeitschen, aufwühlen; et. ausarbeiten (**into** zu); **be ~ed up** aufgeregt or nervös sein (**about** wegen)

work·a·ble formbar; fig durchführbar

work·a·day Alltags…

work·a·hol·ic F Arbeitssüchtige m, f

work·bench TECH Werkbank f

work·book PED Arbeitsheft n

work·day Arbeitstag m; Werktag m; **on ~s** werktags

work·er Arbeiter(in); Angestellte m, f

work ex·pe·ri·ence Erfahrung f

work·ing werktätig; Arbeits…; **~ knowl·edge** Grundkenntnisse pl; **in ~ order** in betriebsfähigem Zustand; **~ class** Arbeiterklasse f; **~ day** → **workday**; **~ hours** Arbeitszeit f

work·ings Arbeits-, Funktionsweise f

work·man Handwerker m

work·man·like fachmännisch

work·man·ship fachmännische Arbeit

work of art Kunstwerk n

work·out F SPORT Training n

work·place Arbeitsplatz m; **at the ~** am Arbeitsplatz

works coun·cil Betriebsrat m

work·sheet PED etc Arbeitsblatt n

work·shop Werkstatt f; Workshop m

work·shy arbeitsscheu

work·sta·tion IT Bildschirmarbeitsplatz m

work-to-rule Br Dienst m nach Vorschrift

world 1. Welt f; **all over the ~** in der ganzen Welt; **bring into the ~** auf die Welt bringen; **do s.o. a** or **the ~ of good** j-m unwahrscheinlich guttun; **mean all the ~ to s.o.** j-m alles bedeuten; **they are ~s apart** zwischen ihnen liegen Welten; **think the ~ of** große Stücke halten von; **what in the ~ …?** was um alles in der Welt ...? **2.** Welt...; **~ cham·pi·on** SPORT Weltmeister *m*; **~ cham·pi·onship** SPORT Weltmeisterschaft *f*

World Cup Fußballweltmeisterschaft *f*; *skiing:* Weltcup *m*

world-fa·mous weltberühmt

world lit·er·a·ture Weltliteratur *f*

world·ly weltlich; irdisch

world·ly-wise weltklug

world| mar·ket ECON Weltmarkt *m*; **~ pow·er** POL Weltmacht *f*; **~ rec·ord** SPORT Weltrekord *m*; **~ trip** Weltreise *f*; **~ war** Weltkrieg *m*

world·wide weltweit; auf der ganzen Welt

worm 1. ZO Wurm *m* **2.** *Hund etc* entwurmen; **~ one's way through** sich schlängeln *or* zwängen durch; **~ o.s. into s.o.'s confidence** sich in j-s Vertrauen einschleichen; **~ s.th. out of s.o.** j-m et. entlocken

worm-eat·en wurmstichig

worm's-eye view Froschperspektive *f*

worn-out abgenutzt, abgetragen; *fig* erschöpft

wor·ried besorgt, beunruhigt

wor·ry 1. beunruhigen; (sich) Sorgen machen; **don't ~!** keine Angst!, keine Sorge! **2.** Sorge *f*

worse schlechter, schlimmer; **~ still** was noch schlimmer ist; **to make matters ~** zu allem Übel

wors·en schlechter machen *or* werden, (sich) verschlechtern

wor·ship 1. Verehrung *f*; Gottesdienst *m* **2.** *v/t* anbeten, verehren; *v/i* den Gottesdienst besuchen

wor·ship·(p)er Anbeter(in), Verehrer(in); Kirchgänger(in)

worst 1. *adj* schlechteste(r, -s), schlimmste(r, -s) **2.** *adv* am schlechtesten, am schlimmsten **3.** *der, die, das* Schlechteste *or* Schlimmste; **at (the) ~** schlimmstenfalls

wor·sted Kammgarn *n*

worth 1. wert; **~ reading** lesenswert **2.** Wert *m*; **worth·less** wertlos

worth·y würdig

would-be Möchtegern...

wound 1. Wunde *f*, Verletzung *f* **2.** verwunden, verletzen

wow *int* F wow!, Mensch!, toll!

wran·gle 1. (sich) streiten **2.** Streit *m*

wrap 1. *v/t a.* **~ up** (ein)packen, (ein)wickeln (*in* in *dat*); et. wickeln ([a]round um); *v/i:* **~ up** sich warm anziehen **2.** Umhang *m*

wrap·per (Schutz)Umschlag *m*

wrap·ping Verpackung *f*; **~ pa·per** Einwickel-, Pack-, Geschenkpapier *n*

wrath Zorn *m*

wreath Kranz *m*

wreck 1. MAR Wrack *n* (*a. fig*) **2.** *Pläne etc* zunichtemachen; **be ~ed** MAR zerschellen; Schiffbruch erleiden

wreck·age Trümmer *pl* (*a. fig*), Wrackteile *pl*

wreck·er MOT Abschleppwagen *m*

wreck·ing| com·pa·ny Abbruchfirma *f*; **~ ser·vice** MOT Abschleppdienst *m*

wren ZO Zaunkönig *m*

wrench 1. MED sich *das Knie etc* verrenken; **~ s.th. from** *or* **out of s.o.'s hands** j-m et. aus den Händen winden, j-m et. entwinden; **~ off** et. mit e-m Ruck abreißen *or* wegreißen; **~ open** aufreißen **2.** Ruck *m*; MED Verrenkung *f*; *Br* TECH Schraubenschlüssel *m*

wrest: ~ s.th. from *or* **out of s.o.'s hands** j-m et. aus den Händen reißen, j-m et. entreißen *or* entwinden

wres·tle *v/i* SPORT ringen (**with** mit), *fig a.* kämpfen (**with** mit); *v/t* SPORT ringen gegen; **wres·tler** SPORT Ringer *m*; **wres·tling** SPORT Ringen *n*

wretch *often* HUMOR Schuft *m*, Wicht *m*

wretch·ed elend; (tod)unglücklich; scheußlich; verdammt, verflixt

wrig·gle *v/i* sich winden; zappeln; **~ out of** *fig* F sich herauswinden aus; sich drücken vor (*dat*); *v/t* mit den Zehen wackeln

wring *j-m die Hand* drücken; *die Hände* ringen; *den Hals* umdrehen; **~ out** *Wäsche etc* auswringen; **~ s.o.'s heart** j-m zu Herzen gehen

wrin·kle 1. Falte *f*, Runzel *f* **2.** runzeln; *Nase* krausziehen, rümpfen; faltig *or* runz(e)lig werden

wrist ANAT Handgelenk *n*

wrist·band Bündchen *n*, (Hemd)Manschette *f*; Armband *n*

wrist·watch Armbanduhr *f*

writ JUR Befehl *m*, Verfügung *f*

write schreiben; **~ down** auf-, niederschreiben; **~ off** *j-n*, ECON *et.* abschreiben; **~ out** *Namen etc* ausschreiben;

Bericht etc ausarbeiten; *j-m e-e Quittung etc* ausstellen; **~ pro·tec·tion** IT Schreibschutz *m*

writ·er Schreiber(in), Verfasser(in), Autor(in); Schriftsteller(in)

writhe sich krümmen *or* winden (*in, with* vor *dat*)

writ·ing 1. Schreiben *n*; (Hand)Schrift *f*; Schriftstück *n*; *pl* Werke *pl*; *in* ~ schriftlich **2.** Schreib...; **~ case** Schreibmappe *f*; **~ desk** Schreibtisch *m*; **~ pad** Schreibblock *m*; **~ pa·per** Briefpapier *n*, Schreibpapier *n*

writ·ten schriftlich

wrong 1. *adj* falsch; unrecht; *be* ~ falsch sein, nicht stimmen; unrecht haben; falsch gehen (*watch*); **be on the** ~ **side of forty** über 40 (Jahre alt) sein; *is anything* ~*?* ist et. nicht in Ordnung?; *what's* ~ *with her?* was ist los mit

ihr?, was hat sie? **2.** *adv* falsch; *get* ~ *j-n, et.* falsch verstehen; *go* ~ e-n Fehler machen; kaputtgehen; *fig* F schiefgehen **3.** Unrecht *n*; *be in the* ~ im Unrecht sein **4.** *j-m* unrecht tun

wrong·ful ungerechtfertigt; gesetzwidrig

wrong-way driv·er MOT F Geisterfahrer(in)

wrought i·ron Schmiedeeisen *n*

wrought-i·ron schmiedeeisern

wry süßsauer (*smile*); ironisch, sarkastisch (*humor etc*)

wt *abbr of* **weight** Gew., Gewicht *n*

WWF *abbr of* **World Wide Fund for Nature** WWF *m*

WYSIWYG *abbr of* **what you see is what you get** IT was du (*auf dem Bildschirm*) siehst, bekommst du (*auch ausgedruckt*)

X

X, x X, x *n*

xen·o·pho·bi·a Fremdenhass *m*; Ausländerfeindlichkeit *f*

XL *abbr of* **extra large** (**size**) extragroß

X·mas F → **Christmas**

X-ray MED **1.** röntgen **2.** Röntgenstrahl *m*; Röntgenaufnahme *f*, -bild *n*; Röntgenuntersuchung *f*

xy·lo·phone MUS Xylophon *n*

Y

Y, y Y, y *n*

yacht MAR **1.** (Segel)Boot *n*; Jacht *f* **2.** segeln; *go* ~*ing* segeln gehen

yacht club Segelklub *m*, Jachtklub *m*

yacht·ing Segeln *n*, Segelsport *m*

Yan·kee F Yankee *m*, Ami *m*

yap kläffen; F quasseln

yard[1] (*abbr* **yd**) Yard *n* (91, 44 cm)

yard[2] Hof *m*; (*Bau-, Stapel- etc*)Platz *m*; Garten *m*

yard·stick *fig* Maßstab *m*

yarn Garn *n*

yawn 1. gähnen **2.** Gähnen *n*

yeah F ja

year Jahr *n*; *all the* ~ *round* das ganze Jahr hindurch; ~ *after* ~ Jahr für Jahr; ~ *in* ~ *out* jahraus, jahrein; *this* ~ dieses

Jahr; *this* ~*'s* diesjährige(r, -s)

year·ly jährlich

yearn sich sehnen (*for* nach; *to do* danach, zu tun); **yearn·ing 1.** Sehnsucht *f* **2.** sehnsüchtig

yeast Hefe *f*

yell 1. schreien, brüllen (*with* vor *dat*); ~ *at s.o.* j-n anschreien *or* anbrüllen; ~ (*out*) *et.* schreien, brüllen **2.** Schrei *m*

yel·low 1. gelb; F feig(e) **2.** Gelb *n*; *at* ~ MOT bei Gelb **3.** (sich) gelb färben; gelb werden; vergilben

yel·low fe·ver MED Gelbfieber *n*

yel·low·ish gelblich

Yel·low Pag·es® TEL *die* Gelben Seiten *pl*, Branchenverzeichnis *n*

yel·low press Sensationspresse *f*

yelp 1. (auf)jaulen; aufschreien **2.** (Auf)Jaulen *n*; Aufschrei *m*

yes 1. ja; doch **2.** Ja *n*

yes·ter·day gestern; **~ morning** (**afternoon**) gestern Morgen (Nachmittag); **the day before ~** vorgestern

yet 1. *adv in questions:* schon; noch; (doch) noch; doch, aber; **as ~** bis jetzt, bisher; **not~** noch nicht **2.** *cj* aber, doch

yew BOT Eibe *f*

yield *v/t* Früchte tragen; *Gewinn* abwerfen; *Resultat etc* ergeben, liefern; *v/i* nachgeben; **~ to** MOT *j*-m die Vorfahrt lassen **2.** Ertrag *m*

yip·pee *int* F hurra!

yo·del 1. jodeln **2.** Jodler *m*

yo·ga Yoga *m*, *n*, Yoga *m*, *n*

yog·h(o)urt, yog·urt Jog(h)urt *m*, *n*

yoke Joch *n* (*a. fig*)

yolk (Ei)Dotter *m*, *n*, Eigelb *n*

you du, ihr, Sie; (*dat*) dir, euch, Ihnen; (*acc*) dich, euch, Sie; man

young 1. jung **2.** ZO Junge *pl*; **with ~** ZO trächtig; **the ~** die jungen Leute *pl*, die Jugend

young·ster Junge *m*

your dein(e); *pl* euer, eure; Ihr(e) (*a. pl*)

yours deine(r, -s); *pl* euer eure(s); Ihre(r, -s) (*a. pl*); **a friend of ~** ein Freund von dir; **Yours, Bill** Dein Bill

your·self selbst; dir, dich, sich; **by ~** allein

youth Jugend *f*; Jugendliche *m*

youth club Jugendklub *m*

youth·ful jugendlich

youth hos·tel Jugendherberge *f*

yuck·y *contp* scheußlich

Yu·go·slav HIST **1.** jugoslawisch **2.** Jugoslawe *m*, Jugoslawin *f*; **Yu·go·sla·vi·a** HIST Jugoslawien *n*

yup·pie, yup·py *abbr of* **young upwardly-mobile** *or* **urban professional** junger, aufstrebender *or* städtischer Karrieremensch, Yuppie *m*

Z

Z, z Z, z *n*

zap F *esp computer game etc:* abknallen, fertigmachen; MOT beschleunigen (**from ... to ...** von ... auf *acc* ...); jagen, hetzen; TV *Fernbedienung* bedienen; TV zappen, umschalten; **~ off** abzischen; **~ to** düsen *or* jagen *or* hetzen nach

zap·per TV F Fernbedienung *f*

zap·py *Br* F voller Pep, schmissig, fetzig

zeal Eifer *m*

zeal·ot Fanatiker(in), Eiferer *m*, Eiferin *f*; **zeal·ous** eifrig; **be ~ to do s.th.** eifrig darum bemüht sein, et. zu tun

ze·bra ZO Zebra *n*

ze·bra cross·ing *Br* Zebrastreifen *m*

zen·ith Zenit *m* (*a. fig*)

ze·ro Null *f*; Nullpunkt *m*; **20 degrees below ~** 20 Grad unter Null **2.** Null...;~ **growth** Nullwachstum *n*;~ **op·tion** POL Nulllösung *f*

zest *fig* Würze *f*; Begeisterung *f*; **~ for life** Lebensfreude *f*

zig·zag 1. Zickzack *m* **2.** Zickzack... **3.** im Zickzack fahren, laufen *etc*, zick-

zackförmig verlaufen

zinc CHEM Zink *n*

zip¹ 1. Reißverschluss *m* **2. ~ the bag open** (**shut**) den Reißverschluss der Tasche aufmachen (zumachen); **~ s.o. up** *j*-m den Reißverschluss zumachen

zip² 1. Zischen *n*, Schwirren *n*; F Schwung *m* **2.** zischen; schwirren; **~ by, ~ past** vorbeiflitzen

zip code Postleitzahl *f*

zip fas·ten·er *esp Br* → **zipper**

zip·per Reißverschluss *m*

zo·di·ac ASTR Tierkreis *m*; **signs of the ~** Tierkreiszeichen *pl*

zone Zone *f*

zoo Zoo *m*, Tierpark *m*

zo·o·log·i·cal zoologisch; **~ gar·dens** Tierpark *m*, zoologischer Garten

zo·ol·o·gist Zoologe *m*, Zoologin *f*

zo·ol·o·gy Zoologie *f*

zoom 1. surren; F sausen; F *fig* in die Höhe schnellen; PHOT zoomen; **~ by, ~ past** F vorbeisausen; **~ in on** PHOT *et.* heranholen **2.** Surren *n*; *a.* **~ lens** PHOT Zoom *n*, Zoomobjektiv *n*

APPENDICES

States of the
Federal Republic of Germany

Baden-Württemberg ['baːdən'vʏrtəmberk] Baden-Württemberg
Bayern ['baɪɐn] Bavaria
Berlin [bɛr'liːn] Berlin
Brandenburg ['brandənburk] Brandenburg
Bremen ['breːmən] Bremen
Hamburg ['hamburk] Hamburg
Hessen ['hɛsən] Hesse
Mecklenburg-Vorpommern ['meːklənburk'foːɐpɔmɐn] Mecklenburg-Western Pomerania
Niedersachsen ['niːdɐzaksən] Lower Saxony
Nordrhein-Westfalen ['nɔrtraɪnvɛst'faːlən] North Rhine-Westphalia
Rheinland-Pfalz ['raɪnlant'pfalts] Rhineland-Palatinate
Saarland ['zaːɐlant]: *das ~* the Saarland
Sachsen ['zaksən] Saxony
Sachsen-Anhalt ['zaksən'anhalt] Saxony-Anhalt
Schleswig-Holstein ['ʃleːsvɪç'hɔlʃtaɪn] Schleswig-Holstein
Thüringen ['tyːrɪŋən] Thuringia

States of the Republic of Austria

Burgenland ['burgənlant]: *das ~* the Burgenland
Kärnten ['kɛrntən] Carinthia
Niederösterreich ['niːdɐˀøːstəraɪç] Lower Austria
Oberösterreich ['oːbɐˀøːstəraɪç] Upper Austria
Salzburg ['zaltsburk] Salzburg
Steiermark ['ʃtaɪɐmark]: *die ~* Styria
Tirol [ti'roːl] Tyrol
Vorarlberg ['foːɐˀarlbɛrk] Vorarlberg
Wien [viːn] Vienna

Cantons of the Swiss Confederation

Aargau ['aːrgaʊ]: *der ~* the Aargau
Appenzell [apən'tsɛl] Appenzell
Basel ['baːzəl] Basel, Basle
Bern [bɛrn] Bern(e)
Freiburg ['fraɪburk], *French* **Fribourg** [fri'buːr] Fribourg
Genf [gɛnf], *French* **Genève** [ʒə'nɛːv] Geneva
Glarus ['glaːrʊs] Glarus
Graubünden [graʊ'bʏndən] Graubünden, Grisons
Jura ['juːra]: *der ~* the Jura
Luzern [lu'tsɛrn] Lucerne
Neuenburg ['nɔʏənburk], *French* **Neuchâtel** [nøʃa'tɛl] Neuchâtel
St. Gallen [zaŋkt 'galən] St Gallen, St Gall
Schaffhausen [ʃaf'haʊzən] Schaffhausen
Schwyz [ʃviːts] Schwyz
Solothurn ['zoːloturn] Solothurn
Tessin [tɛ'siːn]: *der ~* the Ticino, *Italian* **Ticino** [ti'tʃiːno]: *das ~* the Ticino
Thurgau ['tuːrgaʊ]: *der ~* the Thurgau
Unterwalden ['ʊntɐvaldən] Unterwalden
Uri ['uːri] Uri
Waadt [va(ː)t], *French* **Vaud** [vo] Vaud
Wallis ['valɪs], *French* **Valais** [va'lɛ]: *das ~* the Valais, Wallis
Zug [tsuːk] Zug
Zürich ['tsyːrɪç] Zurich

European currency

Germany and Austria

1 euro (€) = 100 cent (ct)

coins

1 ct
2 ct
5 ct
10 ct
20 ct
50 ct
€ 1
€ 2

bills (*Br* bank notes)

€ 5
€ 10
€ 20
€ 50
€ 100
€ 200
€ 500

Switzerland

1 Swiss franc (Sfr) = 100 Rappen (Rp) / centimes (c)

coins

1 Rp
5 Rp
10 Rp
20 Rp
½ Sfr (50 Rp)
1 Sfr
2 Sfr
5 Sfr

bills (*Br* bank notes)

10 Sfr
20 Sfr
50 Sfr
100 Sfr
200 Sfr
1000 Sfr

Numbers

Cardinal numbers

0	null *nought, zero*	51	einundfünfzig *fifty-one*
1	eins *one*	60	sechzig *sixty*
2	zwei *two*	61	einundsechzig *sixty-one*
3	drei *three*	70	siebzig *seventy*
4	vier *four*	71	einundsiebzig *seventy-one*
5	fünf *five*	80	achtzig *eighty*
6	sechs *six*	81	einundachtzig *eighty-one*
7	sieben *seven*	90	neunzig *ninety*
8	acht *eight*	91	einundneunzig *ninety-one*
9	neun *nine*	100	hundert *a* or *one hundred*
10	zehn *ten*	101	hunderteins *a hundred and one*
11	elf *eleven*	200	zweihundert *two hundred*
12	zwölf *twelve*	300	dreihundert *three hundred*
13	dreizehn *thirteen*	572	fünfhundertzweiundsiebzig *five hundred and seventy-two*
14	vierzehn *fourteen*		
15	fünfzehn *fifteen*	1000	tausend *a* / *one thousand*
16	sechzehn *sixteen*	1999	neunzehnhundertneunundneunzig *nineteen (hundred and) ninety-nine*
17	siebzehn *seventeen*		
18	achtzehn *eighteen*		
19	neunzehn *nineteen*	2000	zweitausend *two thousand*
20	zwanzig *twenty*	2010	*as year:* zweitausendzehn *two thousand (and) ten*
21	einundzwanzig *twenty-one*		
22	zweiundzwanzig *twenty-two*	5044	TEL fünfzig vierundvierzig *five O (or zero) double four*
30	dreißig *thirty*		
31	einunddreißig *thirty-one*	1,000,000	eine Million *one million*
40	vierzig *forty*	2,000,000	zwei Millionen *two million*
41	einundvierzig *forty-one*	1,000,000,000	eine Milliarde *a* / *one billion*
50	fünfzig *fifty*		

Ordinal numbers

1. erste *first* *(1st)*
2. zweite *second* *(2nd)*
3. dritte *third* *(3rd)*
4. vierte *fourth* *(4th)*
5. fünfte *fifth* *(5th) etc* .
6. sechste *sixth*
7. siebente *seventh*
8. achte *eighth*
9. neunte *ninth*
10. zehnte *tenth*
11. elfte *eleventh*
12. zwölfte *twelfth*
13. dreizehnte *thirteenth*
14. vierzehnte *fourteenth*
15. fünfzehnte *fifteenth*
16. sechzehnte *sixteenth*
17. siebzehnte *seventeenth*
18. achtzehnte *eighteenth*
19. neunzehnte *nineteenth*
20. zwanzigste *twentieth*
21. einundzwanzigste *twenty-first*
22. zweiundzwanzigste *twenty-second*
23. dreiundzwanzigste *twenty-third*
30. dreißigste *thirtieth*
31. einunddreißigste *thirty-first*

40. vierzigste *fortieth*
41. einundvierzigste *forty-first*
50. fünfzigste *fiftieth*
51. einundfünfzigste *fifty-first*
60. sechzigste *sixtieth*
61. einundsechzigste *sixty-first*
70. siebzigste *seventieth*
71. einundsiebzigste *seventy-first*
80. achtzigste *eightieth*
81. einundachtzigste *eighty-first*
90. neunzigste *ninetieth*
100. hundertste *(one) hundredth*
101. hundert(und)erste *(one) hundred and first*
200. zweihundertste *two hundredth*
300. dreihundertste *three hundredth*
572. fünfhundert(und)zweiundsiebzigste *five hundred and seventy-second*
1000. tausendste *(one) thousandth*
1970. neunzehnhundert(und)siebzigste *nineteen hundred and seventieth*
500 000. fünfhunderttausendste *five hundred thousandth*
1 000 000. millionste *(one) millionth*

649

Fractions, decimals and mathematical calculation methods

$^1/_2$ halb *one / a half*
$^1/_2$ eine halbe Meile *half a mile*
$1^1/_2$ anderthalb / eineinhalb *one and a half*
$2^1/_2$ zweieinhalb *two and a half*
$^1/_3$ ein Drittel *one / a third*
$^2/_3$ zwei Drittel *two thirds*
$^1/_4$ ein Viertel *one fourth, one / a quarter*
$^3/_4$ drei Viertel *three fourths, three quarters*
$1^1/_4$ ein und eine viertel Stunde *one hour and a quarter*
$^1/_5$ ein Fünftel *one / a fifth*
$3^4/_5$ drei vier Fünftel *three and four fifths*
0,4 null Komma vier *point four (.4)*
2,5 zwei Komma fünf *two point five (2.5)*

einfach *single*
    zweifach *double, twofold*
    dreifach *threefold, treble, triple*
    vierfach *fourfold, quadruple*
    fünffach *fivefold, quintuple*

einmal *once*
    zweimal *twice*
    dreimal *three times*
    viermal *four times*
    fünfmal *five times*
    zweimal so viel (so viele) *twice as much (many)*

erstens *first(ly), in the first place*
zweitens *secondly; in the second place*
drittens *thirdly; in the third place*

$2 \times 3 = 6$ zwei mal drei ist sechs, zwei multipliziert mit drei ist sechs *two threes are six, two multiplied by three is six*

$7 + 8 = 15$ sieben plus acht ist fünfzehn *seven plus eight is fifteen*

$10 - 3 = 7$ zehn minus drei ist sieben *ten minus three is seven*

$20 : 5 = 4$ zwanzig (dividiert) durch fünf ist vier *twenty divided by five is four*

German weights and measures

I linear measure

1 mm   *Millimeter* millimeter, *Br* millimetre
= $^1/_{1000}$ meter (*Br* metre)
= 0.003 feet
= 0.039 inches

1 cm   *Zentimeter* centimeter, *Br* centimetre
= $^1/_{100}$ meter (*Br* metre)
= 0.39 inches

1 dm   *Dezimeter* decimeter, *Br* decimetre
= $^1/_{10}$ meter (*Br* metre)
= 3.94 inches

1 m   *Meter* meter, *Br* metre
= 1.094 yards
= 3.28 feet
= 39.37 inches

1 km   *Kilometer* kilometer, *Br* kilometre
= 1,000 meters (*Br* metres)
= 1,093.637 yards
= 0.621 (statute) miles

1 sm   *Seemeile* nautical mile
= 1,852 meters (*Br* metres)

II square measure

1 mm²   *Quadratmillimeter* square millimeter (*Br* millimetre)
= 0.0015 square inches

1 cm²   *Quadratzentimeter* square centimeter (*Br* centimetre)
= 0.155 square inches

1 m²   *Quadratmeter* square meter (*Br* metre)
= 1.195 square yards
= 10.76 square feet

1 a   *Ar* are
= 100 square meters (*Br* metres)
= 119.59 square yards
= 1,076.40 square feet

1 ha   *Hektar* hectare
= 100 ares
= 10,000 square meters (*Br* metres)
= 11,959.90 square yards
= 2.47 acres

1 km²   *Quadratkilometer* square kilometer (*Br* kilometre)
= 100 hectares
= 1,000,000 square meters (*Br* metres)
= 247.11 acres
= 0.386 square miles

III cubic measure

1 cm³   *Kubikzentimeter* cubic centimeter (*Br* centimetre)
= 1,000 cubic millimeters (*Br* millimetres)
= 0.061 cubic inches

1 dm³   *Kubikdezimeter* cubic decimeter (*Br* decimetre)
= 1,000 cubic centimeters (*Br* centimetres)
= 61.025 cubic inches

1 m³   *Kubikmeter*
1 rm   *Raummeter*   } cubic meter (*Br* metre)
1 fm   *Festmeter*
= 1,000 cubic decimeters (*Br* decimetres)
= 1.307 cubic yards
= 35.31 cubic feet

1 RT   *Registertonne* register ton
= 2.832 m³
= 100 cubic feet

IV measure of capacity

1 l   *Liter* liter, *Br* litre
= 10 deciliters (*Br* decilitres)
= 2.11 pints (*Am*)
= 8.45 gills (*Am*)
= 1.06 quarts (*Am*)
= 0.26 gallons (*Am*)
= 1.76 pints (*Br*)
= 7.04 gills (*Br*)
= 0.88 quarts (*Br*)
= 0.22 gallons (*Br*)

1 hl   *Hektoliter* hectoliter, *Br* hectolitre
= 100 liters (*Br* litres)
= 26.42 gallons (*Am*)
= 2.84 bushels (*Am*)
= 22.009 gallons (*Br*)
= 2.75 bushels (*Br*)

V weight

1 mg   *Milligramm* milligram(me)
= $\frac{1}{1000}$ gram(me)
= 0.015 grains

1 g   *Gramm* gram(me)
= $\frac{1}{1000}$ kilogram(me)
= 15.43 grains

1 Pfd   *Pfund* pound (German)
= $\frac{1}{2}$ kilogram(me)
= 500 gram(me)s
= 1.102 pounds (1b)

1 kg   *Kilogramm*, *Kilo* kilogram(me)
= 1,000 gram(me)s
= 2.204 pounds (1b)

1 Ztr.   *Zentner* centner
= 100 pounds (German)
= 50 kilogram(me)s
= 110.23 pounds (1b)
= 1.102 US hundredweights
= 0.98 British hundredweights

1 t   *Tonne* ton
= 1,000 kilogram(me)s
= 1.102 US tons
= 0.984 British tons

Conversion tables for temperatures

°C (Celsius)	°F (Fahrenheit)
100	212
95	203
90	194
85	185
80	176
75	167
70	158
65	149
60	140
55	131
50	122
45	113
40	104
35	95
30	86
25	77
20	68
15	59
10	50
5	41
0	32
− 5	23
−10	14
−15	5
−17.8	0
−20	− 4
−25	−13
−30	−22
−35	−31
−40	−40
−45	−49
−50	−58

Clinical thermometer

°C (Celsius)	°F (Fahrenheit)
42.0	107.6
41.8	107.2
41.6	106.9
41.4	106.5
41.2	106.2
41.0	105.8
40.8	105.4
40.6	105.1
40.4	104.7
40.2	104.4
40.0	104.0
39.8	103.6
39.6	103.3
39.4	102.9
39.2	102.6
39.0	102.2
38.8	101.8
38.6	101.5
38.4	101.1
38.2	100.8
38.0	100.4
37.8	100.0
37.6	99.7
37.4	99.3
37.2	99.0
37.0	98.6
36.8	98.2
36.6	97.9

How to convert Celsius into Fahrenheit and vice versa

To convert Celsius into Fahrenheit multiply by 9, divide by 5 and add 32.

To convert Fahrenheit into Celsius subtract 32, multiply by 5 and divide by 9.

German irregular verbs

infinitive – 3rd person singular – past tense – past participle

backen – backt/bäckt – backte – gebacken

bedingen – bedingt – bedang (bedingte) – bedungen (*conditional*: bedingt)

befehlen – befiehlt – befahl – befohlen

beginnen – beginnt – begann – begonnen

beißen – beißt – biss – gebissen

bergen – birgt – barg – geborgen

bersten – birst – barst – geborsten

bewegen – bewegt – bewog – bewogen

biegen – biegt – bog – gebogen

bieten – bietet – bot – geboten

binden – bindet – band – gebunden

bitten – bittet – bat – gebeten

blasen – bläst – blies – geblasen

bleiben – bleibt – blieb – geblieben

bleichen – bleicht – blich – geblichen

braten – brät – briet – gebraten

brauchen – braucht – brauchte – gebraucht (*v/aux* brauchen)

brechen – bricht – brach – gebrochen

brennen – brennt – brannte – gebrannt

bringen – bringt – brachte – gebracht

denken – denkt – dachte – gedacht

dreschen – drischt – drosch – gedroschen

dringen – dringt – drang – gedrungen

dürfen – darf – durfte – gedurft (*v/aux* dürfen)

empfangen – empfängt – empfing – empfangen

empfehlen – empfiehlt – empfahl – empfohlen

empfinden – empfindet – empfand – empfunden

erlöschen – erlischt – erlosch – erloschen

erschrecken – erschrickt – erschrak – erschrocken

essen – isst – aß – gegessen

fahren – fährt – fuhr – gefahren

fallen – fällt – fiel – gefallen

fangen – fängt – fing – gefangen

fechten – ficht – focht – gefochten

finden – findet – fand – gefunden

flechten – flicht – flocht – geflochten

fliegen – fliegt – flog – geflogen

fliehen – flieht – floh – geflohen

fließen – fließt – floss – geflossen

fressen – frisst – fraß – gefressen

frieren – friert – fror – gefroren

gären – gärt – gor (*esp fig* gärte) – gegoren (*esp fig* gegärt)

gebären – gebärt (gebiert) – gebar – geboren

geben – gibt – gab – gegeben

gedeihen – gedeiht – gedieh – gediehen

gehen – geht – ging – gegangen

gelingen – gelingt – gelang – gelungen

gelten – gilt – galt – gegolten

genesen – genest – genas – genesen

genießen – genießt – genoss – genossen

geschehen – geschieht – geschah – geschehen

gewinnen – gewinnt – gewann – gewonnen

gießen – gießt – goss – gegossen

gleichen – gleicht – glich – geglichen

gleiten – gleitet – glitt – geglitten

glimmen – glimmt – glomm – geglommen

graben – gräbt – grub – gegraben

greifen – greift – griff – gegriffen

haben – hat – hatte – gehabt

halten – hält – hielt – gehalten

hängen – hängt – hing – gehangen

hauen – haut – haute (hieb) – gehauen

heben – hebt – hob – gehoben

heißen – heißt – hieß – geheißen

helfen – hilft – half – geholfen

kennen – kennt – kannte – gekannt

klingen – klingt – klang – geklungen

kneifen – kneift – kniff – gekniffen

kommen – kommt – kam – gekommen

können – kann – konnte – gekonnt (*v/aux* können)

kriechen – kriecht – kroch – gekrochen

laden – lädt – lud – geladen

lassen – lässt – ließ – gelassen (*v/aux* lassen)

laufen – läuft – lief – gelaufen

leiden – leidet – litt – gelitten

leihen – leiht – lieh – geliehen

lesen – liest – las – gelesen
liegen – liegt – lag – gelegen
lügen – lügt – log – gelogen
mahlen – mahlt – mahlte – gemahlen
meiden – meidet – mied – gemieden
melken – melkt – melkte (molk) – gemolken (gemelkt)
messen – misst – maß – gemessen
misslingen – misslingt – misslang –
misslungen
mögen – mag – mochte – gemocht
(v/aux mögen)
müssen – muss – musste – gemusst
(v/aux müssen)
nehmen – nimmt – nahm – genommen
nennen – nennt – nannte – genannt
pfeifen – pfeift – pfiff – gepfiffen
preisen – preist – pries – gepriesen
quellen – quillt – quoll – gequollen
raten – rät – riet – geraten
reiben – reibt – rieb – gerieben
reißen – reißt – riss – gerissen
reiten – reitet – ritt – geritten
rennen – rennt – rannte – gerannt
riechen – riecht – roch – gerochen
ringen – ringt – rang – gerungen
rinnen – rinnt – rann – geronnen
rufen – ruft – rief – gerufen
salzen – salzt – salzte – gesalzen (ge-
salzt)
saufen – säuft – soff – gesoffen
saugen – saugt – sog – gesogen
schaffen – schafft – schuf – geschaffen
schallen – schallt – schallte (scholl) –
geschallt (for **erschallen** a. erschollen)
scheiden – scheidet – schied – geschieden
scheinen – scheint – schien – geschienen
scheißen – scheißt – schiss – geschissen
scheren – schert – schor – geschoren
schieben – schiebt – schob – geschoben
schießen – schießt – schoss – geschos-
sen
schinden – schindet – schund –
geschunden
schlafen – schläft – schlief – geschlafen
schlagen – schlägt – schlug – geschlagen
schleichen – schleicht – schlich – geschlichen
schleifen – schleift – schliff – geschliffen
schließen – schließt – schloss – geschlossen

schlingen – schlingt – schlang – geschlungen
schmeißen – schmeißt – schmiss –
geschmissen
schmelzen – schmilzt – schmolz –
geschmolzen
schneiden – schneidet – schnitt –
geschnitten
schreiben – schreibt – schrieb – geschrieben
schreien – schreit – schrie – ge-
schrie(e)n
schreiten – schreitet – schritt – geschritten
schweigen – schweigt – schwieg –
geschwiegen
schwellen – schwillt – schwoll – geschwollen
schwimmen – schwimmt – schwamm –
geschwommen
schwinden – schwindet – schwand –
geschwunden
schwingen – schwingt – schwang –
geschwungen
schwören – schwört – schwor – geschworen
sehen – sieht – sah – gesehen
sein – ist – war – gewesen
senden – sendet – sandte – gesandt
sieden – siedet – sott – gesotten
singen – singt – sang – gesungen
sinken – sinkt – sank – gesunken
sinnen – sinnt – sann – gesonnen
sitzen – sitzt – saß – gesessen
sollen – soll – sollte – gesollt (v/aux
sollen)
spalten – spaltet – spaltete – gespalten
(gespaltet)
speien – speit – spie – gespie(e)n
spinnen – spinnt – spann – gesponnen
sprechen – spricht – sprach – gesprochen
sprießen – sprießt – spross – gesprossen
springen – springt – sprang – gesprungen
stechen – sticht – stach – gestochen
stecken – steckt – steckte (stak) – ge-
steckt
stehen – steht – stand – gestanden
stehlen – stiehlt – stahl – gestohlen
steigen – steigt – stieg – gestiegen
sterben – stirbt – starb – gestorben
stinken – stinkt – stank – gestunken

stoßen – stößt – stieß – gestoßen

streichen – streicht – strich – gestrichen

streiten – streitet – stritt – gestritten

tragen – trägt – trug – getragen

treffen – trifft – traf – getroffen

treiben – treibt – trieb – getrieben

treten – tritt – trat – getreten

trinken – trinkt – trank – getrunken

trügen – trügt – trog – getrogen

tun – tut – tat – getan

überwinden – überwindet – überwand – überwunden

verderben – verdirbt – verdarb – verdorben

verdrießen – verdrießt – verdross – verdrossen

vergessen – vergisst – vergaß – vergessen

verlieren – verliert – verlor – verloren

verschleißen – verschleißt – verschliss – verschlissen

verschwinden – verschwindet – verschwand – verschwunden

verzeihen – verzeiht – verzieh – verziehen

wachsen – wächst – wuchs – gewachsen

wägen – wägt – wog (*rare* wägte) – gewogen (*rare* gewägt)

waschen – wäscht – wusch – gewaschen

weben – webt – wob – gewoben

weichen – weicht – wich – gewichen

weisen – weist – wies – gewiesen

wenden – wendet – wandte – gewandt

werben – wirbt – warb – geworben

werden – wird – wurde – geworden (worden*)

werfen – wirft – warf – geworfen

wiegen – wiegt – wog – gewogen

winden – windet – wand – gewunden

wissen – weiß – wusste – gewusst

wollen – will – wollte – gewollt (v/*aux* wollen)

wringen – wringt – wrang – gewrungen

ziehen – zieht – zog – gezogen

zwingen – zwingt – zwang – gezwungen

---

* only in connection with the past participles of other verbs, *e.g.* **er ist gesehen worden** he has been seen.

English irregular verbs

infinitive – past tense – past participle

arise – arose – arisen
awake – awoke – awoke*
be – was – been
bear – bore – *getragen*: borne – *geboren*: born
beat – beat – beaten, beat
become – became – become
beget – begot – begotten
begin – began – begun
bend – bent – bent
bereave – bereft* – bereft*
beseech – besought – besought
bet – bet * – bet*
bid – bade, bid – bidden, bid
bide – bode* – bided
bind – bound – bound
bite – bit – bitten
bleed – bled – bled
bless – blest* – blest*
blow – blew – blown
break – broke – broken
breed – bred – bred
bring – brought – brought
build – built – built
burn – burnt* – burnt*
burst – burst – burst
buy – bought – bought
cast – cast – cast
catch – caught – caught
choose – chose – chosen
cleave – cleft, clove* – cleft, cloven*
cling – clung – clung
clothe – clad* – clad*
come – came – come
cost – cost – cost
creep – crept – crept
crow – crew* – crowed
cut – cut – cut
deal – dealt – dealt
dig – dug – dug
dive – dived, *a.* dove – dived
do – did – done
draw – drew – drawn
dream – dreamt* – dreamt*
drink – drank – drunk
drive – drove – driven
dwell – dwelt* – dwelt*
eat – ate – eaten

fall – fell – fallen
feed – fed – fed
feel – felt – felt
fight – fought – fought
find – found – found
fit – fitted, *a.* fit – fitted, *a.* fit
flee – fled – fled
fling – flung – flung
fly – flew – flown
forbid – forbade – forbidden
forget – forgot – forgotten
forsake – forsook – forsaken
freeze – froze – frozen
get – got – got, *a.* gotten
give – gave – given
go – went – gone
grind – ground – ground
grow – grew – grown
hang – hung – hung
have – had – had
hear – heard – heard
heave – hove* – hove*
hew – hewed – hewn*
hide – hid – hidden
hit – hit – hit
hold – held – held
hurt – hurt – hurt
keep – kept – kept
kneel – knelt* – knelt*
knit – knit* – knit*
know – knew – known
lay – laid – laid
lead – led – led
lean – leant* – leant*
leap – leapt* – leapt*
learn – learnt* – learnt*
leave – left – left
lend – lent – lent
let – let – let
lie – lay – lain
light – lit* – lit*
lose – lost – lost
make – made – made
mean – meant – meant
meet – met – met
mow – mowed – mown*
pay – paid – paid
plead – pleaded, *a.* pled – pleaded, *a.* pled

put – put – put	**spin** – spun – spun
read – read – read	**spit** – spat – spat
rid – rid – rid	**split** – split – split
ride – rode – ridden	**spoil** – spoilt* – spoilt*
ring – rang – rung	**spread** – spread – spread
rise – rose – risen	**spring** – sprang, *a.* sprung – sprung
run – ran – run	**stand** – stood – stood
saw – sawed – sawn*	**stave** – stove* – stove*
say – said – said	**steal** – stole – stolen
see – saw – seen	**stick** – stuck – stuck
seek – sought – sought	**sting** – stung – stung
sell – sold – sold	**stink** – stank, stunk – stunk
send – sent – sent	**strew** – strewed – strewn*
set – set – set	**stride** – strode – stridden
sew – sewed – sewn*	**strike** – struck – struck
shake – shook – shaken	**string** – strung – strung
shave – shaved – shaven*	**strive** – strove – striven
shear – sheared – shorn	**swear** – swore – sworn
shed – shed – shed	**sweat** – sweat* – sweat*
shine – shone – shone	**sweep** – swept – swept
shit – shit – shit	**swell** – swelled – swollen
shoe – shod – shod	**swim** – swam – swum
shoot – shot – shot	**swing** – swung – swung
show – showed – shown*	**take** – took – taken
shrink – shrank – shrunk	**teach** – taught – taught
shut – shut – shut	**tear** – tore – torn
sing – sang – sung	**tell** – told – told
sink – sank – sunk	**think** – thought – thought
sit – sat – sat	**thrive** – throve* – thriven*
slay – slew – slain	**throw** – threw – thrown
sleep – slept – slept	**thrust** – thrust – thrust
slide – slid – slid	**tread** – trod – trodden, trod
sling – slung – slung	**wake** – woke* – woke(n)*
slink – slunk – slunk	**wear** – wore – worn
slit – slit – slit	**weave** – wove – woven
smell – smelt* – smelt*	**wed** – wedded, wed – wedded, wed
sow – sowed – sown*	**weep** – wept – wept
speak – spoke – spoken	**wet** – wet* – wet*
speed – sped* – sped*	**win** – won – won
spell – spelt* – spelt*	**wind** – wound – wound
spend – spent – spent	**wring** – wrung – wrung
spill – spilt* – spilt*	**write** – wrote – written

Irregular forms marked with asterisks (*)
can be exchanged for the regular forms.

German declension and conjugation

A. Declension

Order of cases: *nom, gen, dat, acc, sg* and *pl.* – Compound nouns and adjectives (e.g. *Eisbär, Ausgang, abfällig* etc.) inflect like their last elements (*Bär, Gang, fällig*). *dem* = demonstrative, *imp* = imperative, *ind* = indicative, *perf* = perfect, *pres* = present, *pres p* = present participle, *rel* = relative, *su* = substantive.

I. Nouns

1 Bild ~(e)s[1] ~(e) ~
Bilder[2] ~ ~n ~

[1] **es only:** Geist, Geistes.
[2] **a, o, u > ä, ö, ü:** Rand, Ränder; Haupt, Häupter; Dorf, Dörfer; Wurm, Würmer.

---

2 Reis* ~es ['-zəs] ~(e) ~
Reiser[1] ['-zɐ] ~ ~n ~

[1] **a, o > ä, ö:** Glas, Gläser ['glɛːzɐ]; Haus, Häuser ['hɔyzɐ]; Fass, Fässer; Schloss, Schlösser.

* Fass, Fasse(s).

---

3 Arm ~(e)s[1,2] ~(e)[1] ~
Arme[3] ~ ~n ~

[1] **without e:** Billard, Billard(s).
[2] **es only:** Maß, Maßes.
[3] **a, o, u > ä, ö, ü:** Gang, Gänge; Saal, Säle; Gebrauch, Gebräuche [gə'brɔʏçə]; Sohn, Söhne; Hut, Hüte.

---

4 Greis[1]* ~es ['-zəs] ~(e) ~
Greise[2] ['-zə] ~ ~n ~

[1] **s > ss:** Kürbis, Kürbisse(s).
[2] **a, o, u > ä, ö, ü:** Hals, Hälse; Bass, Bässe; Schoß, Schöße; Fuchs, Füchse; Schuss, Schüsse.

* Ross, Rosse(s).

---

5 Strahl ~(e)s[1,2] ~(e)[2] ~
Strahlen[3] ~ ~ ~

[1] **es only:** Schmerz, Schmerzes.
[2] **without e:** Juwel, Juwel(s).
[3] Sporn, Sporen.

---

6 Lappen ~s ~ ~*
Lappen[1] ~ ~ ~

[1] **a, o > ä, ö:** Graben, Gräben; Boden, Böden.

* *Infinitives used as nouns have no pl* : Geschehen, Befinden etc.

---

7 Maler ~s ~ ~
Maler[1] ~ ~n ~

[1] **a, o, u > ä, ö, ü:** Vater, Väter; Kloster, Klöster; Bruder, Brüder.

---

8 Untertan ~s ~ ~
Untertanen[1,2] ~ ~ ~

[1] **with change of accent:** Pro'fessor, Profes'soren [-'soːrən]; 'Dämon ['dɛːmɔn], Dä'monen [dɛ'moːnən].

[2] *pl* **ien** [-jən]: Kolleg, Kollegien [-'leːgjən]; Mineral, Mineralien.

---

9 Studium ~ ~ ~
Studien[1,2] ['-djən] ~ ~ ~

[1] **a and o(n) > en:** Drama, Dramen; Stadion, Stadien.

[2] **on and um > a:** Lexikon, Lexika; Neutrum, Neutra.

10 Auge ~s ~ ~
Augen ~ ~ ~

11 Genie ~s[1]* ~ ~
Genies[2]* ~ ~ ~

[1] **without inflection:** Bouillon etc.

[2] pl **s** or **ta:** Komma, Kommas or Kommata; **but:** 'Klima, Klimate [kli'maːtə] (3).

* **s** is pronounced: [ʒeˈniːs].

12 Bär* ~en[1] ~en[1] ~en[1]
Bären ~ ~ ~

[1] Herr, sg mst Herrn; Herz, gen Herzens, acc Herz.

* ...'log as well as ... 'loge (13), e.g. Biolog(e).

13 Knabe ~n[1] ~n ~n
Knaben ~ ~ ~

[1] ns: Name, Namens.

14 Trübsal ~ ~ ~
Trübsale[1,2,3] ~ ~n ~

[1] **a, o, u > ä, ö, ü:** Hand, Hände;

Braut, Bräute; Not, Nöte; Luft, Lüfte; Nuss, Nüsse; **without e:** Tochter, Töchter; Mutter, Mütter.

[2] **s > ss:** Kenntnis, Kenntnisse; Nimbus, Nimbusse.

[3] **is** or **us > e:** Kultus, Kulte; **with change of accent:** Diˈakonus, Diaˈkone [-ˈkoːnə].

15 Blume ~ ~ ~
Blumen ~ ~ ~

...**ee:** eː, pl eːən, e.g. Iˈdee, Iˈdeen.

...**ie** { **stressed syllable:** iː, pl iːən, e.g. Batteˈrie(n).
{ **unstressed syllable:** jə, pl jən, e.g. Arˈterie(n).

16 Frau ~ ~ ~
Frauen[1,2,3] ~ ~ ~

[1] **in > innen:** Freundin, Freundinnen.

[2] **a, is, os** and **us > en:** Firma, Firmen; Krisis, Krisen; Epos, Epen; Genius, Genien; **with change of accent:** ˈHeros, Heˈroen [heˈroːən]; Diˈakonus, Diaˈkonen [-ˈkoːnən].

[3] **s > ss:** Kirmes, Kirmessen.

II. Proper nouns

17 In general proper nouns have no pl.

The following form the gen sg with **s:**

1. **Proper nouns without a definite article:** Friedrichs, Paulas, (Friedrich von) Schillers, Deutschlands, Berlins;

2. **Proper nouns, masculine and neuter** (except the names of countries) **with a definite article and an adjective:** des braven Friedrichs Bruder, des jungen Deutschlands (Söhne).

After **s, sch, ß, tz, x,** and **z** the gen sg ends in **-ens** or **'** (instead of **'** it is

more advisable to use the definite article or von), e.g. die Werke des [or von] Sokrates, Voß or Sokrates', Voß' [**not** Sokratessens, **seldom** Vossens] Werke; **but:** die Umgebung von Mainz.

Feminine names ending in a consonant or the vowel e form the gen sg with **(en)s** or **(n)s;** in the dat and acc sg such names may end in **(e)n** (pl = **a**).

If a proper noun is followed by a title, only the following forms are inflected:

1. **the title when used** with a definite article:
der Kaiser Karl (der Große)
des ~s ~ (des ~n)
etc.

2. *the (last) name when used with – out an article:*

Kaiser Karl (der Große)
~ ~s (des ~n) etc.
(*but*: Herrn Lehmanns Brief).

III. Adjectives and participles
(also used as nouns*), pronouns, etc.

18

	m	f	n	pl

a) gut
$$\begin{cases} er^{1,2} & \sim e & \sim es & \sim e° \\ en^{**} & \sim er & \sim en^{**} & \sim er \\ em & \sim er & \sim em & \sim en \\ en & \sim e & \sim es & \sim e \end{cases}$$
without article, after prepositions, personal pronouns, and invariables

b) gut
$$\begin{cases} e^{1,2} & \sim e & \sim e & \sim en \\ en & \sim en & \sim en & \sim en \\ en & \sim en & \sim en & \sim en \\ en & \sim e & \sim e & \sim en \end{cases}$$
with definite article (22) or with pronoun (21)

c) gut
$$\begin{cases} er^{1,2} & \sim e & \sim es & \sim en \\ en & \sim en & \sim en & \sim en \\ en & \sim en & \sim en & \sim en \\ en & \sim e & \sim es & \sim en \end{cases}$$
with indefinite article or with pronoun (20)

[1] krass, krasse(r, ~s, ~st etc.).
[2] **a, o, u > ä, ö, ü** *when forming the comp and sup:* alt, älter(e, ~es etc.), ältest (der ~e, am ~en); grob, gröber(e, ~es etc.), gröbst (der ~e, am ~en); kurz, kürzer(e, ~es etc.), kürzest (der ~e, am ~en).

* e.g. Böse(r) *su:* der (die, eine) Böse, ein Böser; Böse(s) *n:* das Böse, *without*

article Böses; *in the same way* Abgesandte(r) *su*, Angestellte(r) *su* etc.; *in some cases the use varies.*

** *Sometimes the gen sg ends in ~es instead of ~en:* gutes (*or* guten) Mutes sein.

° *In* böse, böse(r, ~s, ~st etc.) *one* e *is dropped.*

The grades of comparison

The endings of the comparative *and* superlative *are:*

	reich	schön
comp	reicher	schöner
sup	reichst	schönst

inflected according to (18²).

After vowels (except [18°]) *and after* d, s, sch, ß, st, t, tz, x, y, z *the* sup *ends in* ~est, *but in unstressed syllables after* d, sch *and* t *generally in* ~st: blau, 'blauest; rund, 'rundest; rasch, 'raschest etc.; *but*: 'dringend, 'dringendst; 'närrisch, 'närrischst; ge'eignet, ge'eignetst.

Note. – *The adjectives ending in* ~el, ~en (*except* ~nen) *and* ~er (e.g. dunkel, eben, heiter), *and also the possessive adjectives* unser *and* euer *generally drop* e.

Inflection:

	~e	~em	~en	~er	~es, and
~el >	~le	~lem*	~len*	~ler	~les
~en >	~(e)ne	~(e)nem	~(e)nen	~(e)ner°	~(e)nes
~er >	~(e)re	~rem*	~ren*	~(e)rer°	~(e)res

* *or* ~elm, ~eln, ~erm, ~ern; e.g. **dunk|el:** ~le, ~lem (*or* ~elm), ~len (*or* ~eln), ~ler, ~les; **eb|en:** ~(e)ne, ~(e)nem etc.; **heit|er:** ~(e)re, ~rem (*or* ~erm) etc.

° *The inflected comp ends in* ~ner *and* ~rer *only:* eben, ebnere(r, ~s etc.); heiter, heitrere(r, ~s etc.); *but sup* ebenst, heiterst.

19

	1st pers. *m, f, n*	2nd pers. *m, f, n*	3rd pers. *m*	*f*	*n*
sg	ich	du	er	sie	es
	meiner*	deiner*	seiner*	ihrer	seiner*
	mir	dir	ihm	ihr	ihm°
	mich	dich	ihn	sie	es°
pl	wir	ihr	sie		(Sie)
	unser	euer	ihrer		(Ihrer)
	uns	euch	ihnen		(Ihnen)°
	uns	euch	sie		(Sie)°

* *In poetry sometimes without inflection:* gedenke mein!; *also* es *instead of* seiner *n* (= *e-r Sache*): ich bin es überdrüssig.

° *Reflexive form:* sich.

20

	m	f	n	pl
mein		~e	~	~e*
dein	es	~er	~es	~er
sein	em	~er	~em	~en
(k)ein	en	~e	~	~e

* *The indefinite article* ein *has no* pl. – *In poetry* mein, dein *and* sein *may stand behind the* su *without inflection:* die Mutter (Kinder) mein, *or as predicate:* der Hut [die Tasche, das Buch] ist mein; *without su:* meiner *m*, meine *f*, mein(e)s *n*, meine *pl* etc.: wem gehört der Hut [die Tasche, das Buch]? es ist meiner (meine, mein[e]s); *or with definite article:* der (die, das) meine, *pl* die meinen (18b). *Regarding* unser *and* euer *see note* (18).

¹ **welche(r, s)** *as rel pron:* gen sg dessen, deren, *gen pl* deren, *dat pl* denen (23).

* *Used as su*, dies *is preferable to* dieses.

** manch, solch, welch *frequently are uninflected:*

manch	guter	(ein guter)	Mann
solch	~en	(~es ~en)	~es
welch	~em	(~em ~en)	~e
		etc. (18)	

Similarly all:

all	der	(dieser,	mein	) Schmerz	
~	des	(~es,	~es)		~es

21

	m	f	n	pl
dies	er	~e	~es*	~e**¹
jen	es	~er	~es	~er¹
manch	em	~er	~em	~en¹
welch	en	~e	~es*	~e

22

m	f	n	pl	
der	die	das	die¹	
des	der	des	der	**definite**
dem	der	dem	den	**article**
den	die	das	die	

¹ derjenige, derselbe – desjenigen, demjenigen, desselben, demselben etc. (18b).

¹ **also** derer, **when used as** dem pron

* **also** des.

---

23 *Relative pronoun*

m	f	n	pl
der	die	das	die
dessen*	deren	dessen*	deren¹
dem	der	dem	denen
den	die	das	die

24

wer	was	jemand, niemand
wessen*	wessen	~(e)s
wem	–	~(em°)
wen	was	~(en°)

* **also** wes.

° **preferably without inflection.**

B. Conjugation

In the conjugation tables (25–30) only the simple verbs may be found; in the alphabetical list of the German irregular verbs compound verbs are only included when no simple verb exists (e.g. **beginnen**; *ginnen* does not exist). In order to find the conjugation of any compound verb (with separable or inseparable prefix, regular or irregular) look up the respective simple verb.

Verbs with separable and stressed prefixes such as **'ab-, 'an-, 'auf-, 'aus-, 'bei-, be'vor-, 'dar-, 'ein-, em'por-, ent'gegen-, 'fort-, 'her-, he'rab-** etc. and also *'klar-[legen], 'los-[schießen], 'sitzen [bleiben], über'hand [nehmen]* etc. (but not the verbs derived from compound nouns as *be'antragen* or *be'ratschlagen* from *Antrag* and *Ratschlag* etc.) take the preposition **zu** (in the *inf* and the *pres p*) and the syllable **ge** (in the *pp* and in the passive voice) between the stressed prefix and their root.

Verbs with inseparable and unstressed prefixes such as **be-, emp-, ent-, er-, ge-, ver-, zer-** and generally **miss-** (in spite of its being stressed) take the preposition **zu** before the prefix and drop the syllable **ge** in the *pp* and in the passive voice. The prefixes **durch-, hinter-, über-, um-, unter-, voll-,**

wi(e)der- are separable when stressed and inseparable when unstressed, e.g.

geben: *zu geben, zu gebend; gegeben; ich gebe, du gibst* etc.;

'abgeben: *'abzugeben, 'abzugebend; 'abgegeben; ich gebe (du gibst etc.) ab;*

ver'geben: *zu ver'geben, zu ver'gebend; ver'geben; ich ver'gebe, du ver'gibst* etc.;

'umgehen: *'umzugehen, 'umzugehend; 'umgegangen; ich gehe (du gehst etc.) um;*

um'gehen: *zu um'gehen, zu um'gehend; um'gangen; ich um'gehe, du um'gehst* etc.

The same rules apply to verbs with two prefixes, e.g.

zu'rückbehalten [see *halten*]: *zu'rück-zubehalten, zu'rückzubehaltend; zu-'rückbehalten; ich behalte (du be-hältst etc.) zurück;*

wieder 'aufheben [see *heben*]: *wieder 'aufzuheben, wieder 'aufzuhebend; wieder 'aufgehoben; ich hebe (du hebst etc.) wieder auf.*

The forms in parentheses ( ) follow the same rules.

a) 'Weak' conjugation

25   loben

pres ind
$\begin{cases} \text{lobe} & \text{lobst} & \text{lobt} \\ \text{loben} & \text{lobt} & \text{loben} \end{cases}$

pres subj
$\begin{cases} \text{lobe} & \text{lobest} & \text{lobe} \\ \text{loben} & \text{lobet} & \text{loben} \end{cases}$

pret ind
and *subj*
$\begin{cases} \text{lobte} & \text{lobtest} & \text{lobte} \\ \text{lobten} & \text{lobtet} & \text{lobten} \end{cases}$

imp sg lob(e), *pl* lob(e)t, loben Sie;
inf pres loben; *inf perf* gelobt haben;
pres p lobend; *pp* gelobt (18; 29**).

26   reden

pres ind
$\begin{cases} \text{rede} & \text{redest} & \text{redet} \\ \text{reden} & \text{redet} & \text{reden} \end{cases}$

pres subj
$\begin{cases} \text{rede} & \text{redest} & \text{rede} \\ \text{reden} & \text{redet} & \text{reden} \end{cases}$

pret ind
and *subj*
$\begin{cases} \text{redete} & \text{redetest} & \text{redete} \\ \text{redeten} & \text{redetet} & \text{redeten} \end{cases}$

imp sg rede, *pl* redet, reden Sie;
inf pres reden; *inf perf* geredet haben;
pres p redend; *pp* geredet (18; 29**).

27   reisen

pres ind
$\begin{cases} \text{reise} & \text{rei(se)st*} & \text{reist} \\ \text{reisen} & \text{reist} & \text{reisen} \end{cases}$

pres subj
$\begin{cases} \text{reise} & \text{reisest} & \text{reise} \\ \text{reisen} & \text{reiset} & \text{reisen} \end{cases}$

pret ind
and *subj*
$\begin{cases} \text{reiste} & \text{reistest} & \text{reisten} \\ \text{reisten} & \text{reistet} & \text{reisten} \end{cases}$

imp sg reise, *pl* reist, reisen Sie;
inf pres reisen; *inf perf* gereist sein *or now
rare* haben; *pres p* reisend; *pp* gereist
(18; 29**).

    * **sch:** naschen, nasch(e)st; **ß:** spa-
ßen, spaßt (spaßest); **tz:** ritzen, ritzt (rit-
zest); **x:** hexen, hext (hexest); **z:** reizen,
reizt (reizest); faulenzen, faulenzt (fau-
lenzest).

28   fassen

pres ind
$\begin{cases} \text{fasse} & \text{fasst (fassest)fasst} \\ \text{fassen} & \text{fasst} & \text{fassen} \end{cases}$

pres subj
$\begin{cases} \text{fasse} & \text{fassest} & \text{fasse} \\ \text{fassen} & \text{fasset} & \text{fassen} \end{cases}$

pret ind
and *subj*
$\begin{cases} \text{fasste} & \text{fasstest} & \text{fasste} \\ \text{fassten} & \text{fasstet} & \text{fassten} \end{cases}$

imp sg fasse (fass), *pl* fasst, fassen Sie;
inf pres fassen; *inf perf* gefasst haben;
pres p fassend; *pp* gefasst (18; 29**).

29   handeln

pres ind

handle*	handelst	handelt
handeln	handelt	handeln

pres subj

handle*	handelst	handle*
handeln	handelt	handeln

pret ind and *subj*

handelte	handeltest	handelte
handelten	handeltet	handelten

imp sg handle, *pl* handelt, handeln Sie;
inf pres handeln; *inf perf* gehandelt haben; *pres p* handelnd; *pp* gehandelt (18).

    * *Also* handele; wandern, wand(e)re;
bessern, bessere (bessre); donnern, don-
nere.

    ** *Without ge, when the first syllable
is unstressed,* e.g. be'grüßen, be'grüßt;
ent'stehen, ent'standen; stu'dieren,
studiert (*not* gestudiert); trom'peten,
trom'petet (*also when preceded by a
stressed prefix:* 'austrompeten, 'aus-
trompetet, *not* 'ausgetrompetet). *In
some weak verbs the pp ends in en in instead of t,* e.g. mahlen, gemahlen. *With
the verbs* brauchen, dürfen, heißen, helfen, hören, können, lassen, lehren, lernen, machen, mögen, müssen, sehen, sollen, wollen *the pp is replaced by inf
(without* ge), *when used in connection
with another inf,* e.g. ich habe ihn singen
hören, du hättest es tun können, er hat gehen müssen, ich hätte ihn laufen lassen
sollen.

b) 'Strong' conjugation

30 fahren

pres ind	fahre	fährst	fährt
	fahren	fahrt	fahren

pres subj	fahre	fahrest	fahre
	fahren	fahret	fahren

pret ind	fuhr	fuhr(e)st	fuhr
	fuhren	fuhrt	fuhren

pres subj	führe	führest	führe
	führen	führet	führen

imp sg fahr(e), *pl* fahr(e)t, fahren Sie;
inf pres fahren; *inf perf* gefahren haben
or sein;
pres p fahrend; *pp* gefahren (18; 29**).

Proper names

Aachen ['aːxən] Aachen, Aix-la-Cha – pelle
Adler ['aːdlɐ] *Austrian psychologist*
Adria ['aːdria] *die* ~ the Adriatic (Sea)
Afrika ['aːfrika] Africa
Ägäis [ɛˈgɛːɪs] *die* ~ the Aegean (Sea)
Ägypten [ɛˈgʏptən] Egypt
Albanien [alˈbaːnjən] Albania
Algerien [alˈgeːrjən] Algeria
Algier ['alʒiːɐ] Algiers
Allgäu ['algɔʏ]: *das* ~ the Al(l)gäu (*region of Bavaria, Germany*)
Alpen ['alpən]: *die* ~ *pl* the Alps
Amerika [aˈmeːrika] America
Anden ['andən]: *die* ~ *pl* the Andes
Antillen [anˈtɪlən]: *die* ~ *pl* the Antilles
Antwerpen [antˈvɛrpən] Antwerp
Apenninen [apeˈniːnən]: *die* ~ *pl* the Apennines
Argentinien [argɛnˈtiːnjən] Argentina, the Argentine
Ärmelkanal ['ɛrməlkanaːl]: *der* ~ the English Channel, the Channel
Asien ['aːzjən] Asia
Athen [aˈteːn] Athens
Äthiopien [ɛˈtjoːpjən] Ethiopia
Atlantik [atˈlantɪk]: *der* ~ the Atlantic (Ocean)
Australien [aʊsˈtraːljən] Australia

Bach [bax] *German composer*
Barlach ['barlax] *German sculptor*
Basel ['baːzəl] Basel, Basle
Bayern ['baɪɐn] Bavaria
Beethoven ['beːthoːfən] *German composer*
Belgien ['bɛlgjən] Belgium
Berlin [bɛrˈliːn] *German city*
Bern [bɛrn] Bern(e)
Bloch [blɔx] *German philosopher*
Böcklin ['bœkliːn] *German painter*
Bodensee ['boːdənzeː]: *der* ~ Lake Constance
Böhm [bøːm] *Austrian conductor*
Böhmen ['bøːmən] *hist* Bohemia
Böll [bœl] *German author*
Bonn [bɔn] *German city*
Brahms [braːms] *German composer*
Brasilien [braˈziːljən] Brazil

Braunschweig ['braʊnʃvaɪk] Braun – schweig, Brunswick
Brecht [brɛçt] *German dramatist*
Bremen ['breːmən] *German city*
Bruckner ['brʊknɐ] *Austrian composer*
Brüssel ['brʏsəl] Brussels
Budapest ['buːdapɛst] *Hungarian city*
Bukarest ['buːkarɛst] Bucharest
Bulgarien [bʊlˈgaːrjən] Bulgaria

Calais [kaˈlɛː]: *die Straße von* ~ the Straits of Dover
Calvin [kalˈviːn] *Swiss religious reform – er*
Chile ['tʃiːle] Chile
China ['çiːna] China

Daimler ['daɪmlɐ] *German inventor*
Dänemark ['dɛːnəmark] Denmark
Deutschland ['dɔʏtʃlant] Germany
Diesel ['diːzəl] *German inventor*
Döblin ['døːbliːn] *German author*
Dolomiten [doloˈmiːtən]: *die* ~ *pl* the Dolomites
Donau ['doːnaʊ]: *die* ~ the Danube
Dortmund ['dɔrtmʊnt] *German city*
Dresden ['dreːsdən] *German city*
Dünkirchen ['dyːnkɪrçən] Dunkirk
Dürer ['dyːrɐ] *German painter*
Dürrenmatt ['dʏrənmat] *Swiss dramatist*
Düsseldorf ['dʏsəldɔrf] *German city*

Egk [ɛk] *German composer*
Eichendorff ['aɪçəndɔrf] *German poet*
Eiger ['aɪgɐ] *Swiss mountain*
Einstein ['aɪnʃtaɪn] *German physicist*
Elbe ['ɛlbə]: *die* ~ (*German river*)
Elsass ['ɛlzas]: *das* ~ Alsace
England ['ɛŋlant] England
Essen ['ɛsən] *German city*
Europa [ɔʏˈroːpa] Europe

Finnland ['fɪnlant] Finland
Florenz [floˈrɛnts] Florence
Fontane [fɔnˈtaːnə] *German author*
Franken ['fraŋkən] Franconia
Frankfurt am Main ['fraŋkfʊrt am 'maɪn] Frankfurt on the Main
Frankfurt an der Oder ['fraŋkfʊrt an

deːʀ 'oːdɐ] Frankfurt on the Oder
Frankreich ['fraŋkraiç] France
Freud [frɔyt] *Austrian psychologist*
Frisch [frɪʃ] *Swiss author*

Garmisch ['garmɪʃ] *health resort in Bavaria, Germany*
Genf [gɛnf] Geneva; **~er See** Lake Geneva
Genua ['geːnua] Genoa
Goethe [gøːtə] *German poet*
Grass [gras] *German author*
Griechenland ['griːçənlant] Greece
Grillparzer ['grɪlpartsɐ] *Austrian dramatist*
Grönland ['grøːnlant] Greenland
Gropius ['groːpjʊs] *German architect*
Großbritannien [groːsbri'tanjən] (Great) Britain
Großglockner ['groːsglɔknɐ]: **der ~** (*Austrian mountain*)
Grünewald ['gryːnəvalt] *German painter*

Haag [haːk]: **Den ~** The Hague
Hahn [haːn] *German chemist*
Hamburg ['hamburk] *German city*
Händel ['hɛndəl] Handel (*German composer*)
Hannover [ha'noːfɐ] Hanover
Harz [haːɐts]: **der ~** the Harz (Mountains)
Hauptmann ['hauptman] *German dramatist*
Haydn ['haidən] *Austrian composer*
Hegel ['heːgəl] *German philosopher*
Heidegger ['haidɛgɐ] *German philosopher*
Heidelberg ['haidəlbɛrk] *German city*
Heine ['hainə] *German poet*
Heisenberg ['haizənbɛrk] *German physicist*
Heißenbüttel ['haisənbytəl] *German poet*
Helgoland ['hɛlgolant] Hel(i)goland
Helsinki ['hɛlzɪŋki] *Finnish city*
Hesse ['hɛsə] *German poet*
Hindemith ['hɪndəmɪt] *German composer*
Hölderlin ['hœldəliːn] *German poet*
Holland ['hɔlant] Holland

Indien ['ɪndjən] India
Inn [ɪn]: **der ~** (*affluent of the Danube*)

Innsbruck ['ɪnsbrʊk] *Austrian city*
Irak [i'raːk]: **der ~** Iraq
Iran [i'raːn]: **der ~** Iran
Irland ['ɪrlant] Ireland
Island ['iːslant] Iceland
Israel ['ɪsrael] Israel
Italien [i'taːljən] Italy

Japan ['jaːpan] Japan
Jaspers ['jaspɐs] *German philosopher*
Jordanien [jɔr'daːnjən] Jordan
Jung [jʊŋ] *Swiss psychologist*
Jungfrau ['jʊŋfrau]: **die ~** (*Swiss mountain*)

Kafka ['kafka] *Czech author*
Kanada ['kanada] Canada
Kant [kant] *German philosopher*
Karlsruhe ['karlsruːə] *German city*
Kärnten ['kɛrntən] Carinthia
Kästner ['kɛstnɐ] *German author*
Kiel [kiːl] *German city*
Klee [kleː] *Swiss-born painter*
Kleist [klaist] *German poet*
Koblenz ['koːblɛnts] Koblenz, Coblenz
Kokoschka [ko'kɔʃka] *Austrian painter*
Köln [kœln] Cologne
Kolumbien [ko'lʊmbjən] Colombia
Kolumbus [ko'lʊmbʊs] Columbus
Konstanz ['kɔnstants] Constance
Kopenhagen [ko:pən'haːgən] Copenhagen
Kordilleren [kɔrdɪl'jeːrən]: **die ~ pl** the Cordilleras
Kreml ['kreːməl]: **der ~** the Kremlin

Leibniz ['laibnɪts] *German philosopher*
Leipzig ['laiptsɪç] Leipzig, Leipsic
Lessing ['lɛsɪŋ] *German poet*
Libanon ['liːbanɔn]: **der ~** (the) Lebanon
Liebig ['liːbɪç] *German chemist*
Lissabon ['lɪsabɔn] Lisbon
London ['lɔndɔn] London
Lothringen ['loːtrɪŋən] Lorraine
Lübeck ['lyːbɛk] *German city*
Luther ['lʊtɐ] *German religious reformer*
Luxemburg ['lʊksəmburk] Luxemb(o)urg
Luzern [lu'tsɛrn] Lucerne

Maas [maːs]: **die ~** the Meuse, the Maas
Madrid [ma'drɪt] Madrid
Mahler ['maːlɐ] *Austrian composer*

Mailand ['maɪlant] Milan
Main [maɪn]: **der** ~ (*German river*)
Mainz [maɪnts] *German city*
Mann [man] *name of three German authors*
Marokko [ma'rɔko] Morocco
Matterhorn ['matɐhɔrn]: **das** ~ (*Swiss mountain*)
Meißen ['maɪsən] Meissen
Menzel ['mɛntsəl] *German painter*
Mexiko ['mɛksiko] Mexico
Mies van der Rohe ['miːs fan deːɐ 'roːə] *German architect*
Mittelmeer ['mɪtalmeːɐ]: **das** ~ the Mediterranean (Sea)
Moldau ['mɔldaʊ]: **die** ~ the Vltava; *hist* the Moldau (*Bohemian river*)
Mörike ['møːrɪkə] *German poet*
Mosel ['moːzəl]: **die** ~ the Moselle
Mössbauer ['mœsbaʊɐ] *German physicist*
Moskau ['mɔskaʊ] Moscow
Mozart ['moːtsart] *Austrian composer*
München ['mʏnçən] Munich

Neapel [ne'aːpəl] Naples
Neiße ['naɪsə]: **die** ~ (*German river*)
Neufundland [nɔy'fʊntlant] Newfoundland
Neuseeland [nɔy'zeːlant] New Zealand
Niederlande ['niːdəlandə]: **die** ~ *pl* the Netherlands
Nietzsche ['niːtʃə] *German philosopher*
Nil [niːl]: **der** ~ the Nile
Nordamerika ['nɔrt?a'meːrika] North America
Nordsee ['nɔrtzeː]: **die** ~ the North Sea
Normandie [nɔrman'diː]: **die** ~ Normandy
Norwegen ['nɔrveːgən] Norway
Nürnberg ['nʏrnbɛrk] Nuremberg

Oder ['oːdɐ]: **die** ~ (*German river*)
Orff [ɔrf] *German composer*
Oslo ['ɔslo] Oslo
Ostende [ɔst'?ɛndə] Ostend
Österreich ['øːstəraɪç] Austria
Ostsee ['ɔstzeː]: **die** ~ the Baltic (Sea)

Palästina [palɛs'tiːna] Palestine
Paris [pa'riːs] Paris
Pfalz [pfalts]: **die** ~ the Palatinate
Philippinen [fɪlɪ'piːnən]: **die** ~ *pl* the Philippines
Planck [plaŋk] *German physicist*
Polen ['poːlən] Poland
Porsche ['pɔrʃə] *German inventor*
Portugal ['pɔrtugal] Portugal
Prag [praːk] Prague
Preußen ['prɔysən] *hist* Prussia
Pyrenäen [pyre'nɛːən]: **die** ~ *pl* the Pyrenees

Rhein [raɪn]: **der** ~ the Rhine
Rilke ['rɪlkə] *Austrian poet*
Rom [roːm] Rome
Röntgen ['rœntgən] *German physicist*
Ruhr [ruːɐ]: **die** ~ (*German river*); **Ruhrgebiet** ['ruːɐgəbiːt]: **das** ~ (*industrial center of Germany*)
Rumänien [ru'mɛːnjən] Rumania, Ro(u)mania
Russland ['rʊslant] Russia

Saale ['zaːlə]: **die** ~ (*German river*)
Saar [zaːɐ]: **die** ~ (*affluent of the Moselle*)
Salzburg ['zaltsbʊrk] *Austrian city*
Schiller ['ʃɪlɐ] *German poet*
Schönberg ['ʃøːnbɛrk] *Austrian composer*
Schottland ['ʃɔtlant] Scotland
Schubert ['ʃuːbɐt] *Austrian composer*
Schumann ['ʃuːman] *German composer*
Schwaben ['ʃvaːbən] Swabia
Schwarzwald ['ʃvartsvalt]: **der** ~ the Black Forest
Schweden ['ʃveːdən] Sweden
Schweiz [ʃvaɪts]: **die** ~ Switzerland
Sibirien [zi'biːrjən] Siberia
Siemens ['ziːməns] *German inventor*
Sizilien [zi'tsiːljən] Sicily
Skandinavien [skandi'naːvjən] Scandinavia
Slowakei [slova'kaɪ]: **die** ~ Slovakia
Sofia ['zɔfja] Sofia
Spanien ['ʃpaːnjən] Spain
Spitzweg ['ʃpɪtsveːk] *German painter*
Spranger ['ʃpraŋɐ] *German philosopher*
Stifter ['ʃtɪftɐ] *Austrian author*
Stockholm ['ʃtɔkhɔlm] Stockholm
Storm [ʃtɔrm] *German poet*
Straßburg ['ʃtraːsbʊrk] Strasbourg
Strauß [ʃtraʊs] *Austrian composer*
Strauss [ʃtraʊs] *German composer*
Südamerika ['zyːt?a'meːrika] South America

Syrien ['zy:rjən] Syria

Themse ['tɛmzə]: *die* ~ the Thames
Tirol [ti'ro:l] (the) Tyrol
Tschechien ['tʃɛçjən] Czech Republic
Türkei [tyr'kaɪ]: *die* ~ Turkey

Ungarn ['ʊŋgarn] Hungary
Ural [u'ra:l]: *der* ~ the Urals

Venedig [ve'ne:dɪç] Venice
Vereinigte Staaten (von Amerika)
[fɛr'''aɪnɪçtə 'ʃta:tən (fɔn a'me:rɪka)]:
die Vereinigten Staaten (von Amerika) the United States (of America)
Vierwaldstätter See [fi:rə'valtʃtɛtə

'ze:]: *der* ~ Lake Lucerne **Wagner** ['va:-gnɐ] *German composer*
Wankel ['vaŋkəl] *German inventor*
Warschau ['varʃaʊ] Warsaw
Weichsel ['vaɪksəl]: *die* ~ the Vistula
Weiß [vaɪs] *German dramatist*
Werfel ['vɛrfəl] *Austrian author*
Weser ['ve:zə]: *die* ~ (*German river*)
Wien [vi:n] Vienna
Wiesbaden ['vi:sba:dən] *German city*

Zuckmayer ['tsʊkmaɪɐ] *German dramatist*
Zweig [tsvaɪk] *Austrian author*
Zürich ['tsy:rɪç] Zurich
Zypern ['tsy:pɐn] Cyprus

German abbreviations

Abb. *Abbildung* illustration

Abf. *Abfahrt* departure, *abbr* dep.

Abt. *Abteilung* department, *abbr* dept.

a. D. *außer Dienst* retired

ADAC *Allgemeiner Deutscher Automobil-Club* General German Automobile Association

AG *Aktiengesellschaft* (stock) corporation, joint-stock company

allg. *allgemein* general

Ank. *Ankunft* arrival

atü *Atmosphärenüberdruck* atmospheric excess pressure

Bd. *Band* volume, *abbr* vol.; **Bde. Bände** volumes, *abbr* vols.

Betr. *Betreff, betrifft* letter : subject, re

BRD *Bundesrepublik Deutschland* Federal Republic of Germany

CDU *Christlich-Demokratische Union* Christian Democratic Union

CSU *Christlich-Soziale Union* Christian Social Union

DB *Deutsche Bahn* *Germany's main railway operator*

DDR *hist Deutsche Demokratische Republik* German Demoratic Republic

DGB *Deutscher Gewerkschaftsbund* Federation of German Trade Unions

d. h. *das heißt* that is, *abbr* i. e.

DIN *Deutsche Industrie-Norm(en)* German Industrial Standards

DM *hist Deutsche Mark* German Mark(s)

dpa *Deutsche Presse-Agentur* German Press Agency

Dr. *Doktor* Doctor, *abbr* Dr.

DRK *Deutsches Rotes Kreuz* German Red Cross

EDV *Elektronische Datenverarbeitung* electronic data processing, *abbr* EDP

EM *Europameisterschaft* European championship(s)

EU *Europäische Union* European Union, *abbr* EU

e. V. *eingetragener Verein* registered association, incorporated, *abbr* inc.

FDP *Freie Demokratische Partei* Liberal Democratic Party

Forts. *Fortsetzung* continuation

geb. *geboren* born; **geborene ...** née; *gebunden* bound

Ges. *Gesellschaft* association, company; society

gez. *gezeichnet* signed, *abbr* sgd

GmbH *Gesellschaft mit beschränkter Haftung* private limited liability company

h. c. *honoris causa* = ehrenhalber; *academic title* : honorary

Hrsg. *Herausgeber* editor, *abbr* ed.

i. A. *im Auftrage* for, by order, under instruction

Ing. *Ingenieur* engineer

Inh. *Inhaber* proprietor

inkl. *inklusive, einschließlich* inclusive

Interpol *Internationale Kriminalpolizeiliche Organisation* International Criminal Police Commission

IOK *Internationales Olympisches Komitee* International Olympic Committee, *abbr* IOC

ISBN *Internationale Standardbuchnummer* international standard book number, *abbr* ISBN

i. V. *in Vertretung* by proxy, as a substitute

jr., jun. *junior, der Jüngere* junior *abbr* jr, jun.

Kat *Katalysator* catalytic converter, catalyst, *abbr* cat.

Kfz. *Kraftfahrzeug* motor vehicle

KG *Kommanditgesellschaft* limited

partnership

Kl. *Klasse* class; *school*: form

'Kripo *Kriminalpolizei* Criminal Investigation Department, *abbr* CID

Kto. *Konto* account, *abbr* a/c

lfd. *laufend* current, running

Lfg., Lfrg. *Lieferung* delivery; instal(l)-ment, part

Lkw, LKW *Lastkraftwagen* truck, lorry

lt. *laut* according to

MdB *Mitglied des Bundestages* Member of the Bundestag

MEZ *mitteleuropäische Zeit* Central European Time

MS, Ms. *Manuskript* manuscript, *abbr* MS, ms.

mtl. *monatlich* monthly

n. Chr. *nach Christus* after Christ, *abbr* AD

No., Nr. *Numero, Nummer* number, *abbr* No., no

o. B. *ohne Befund* MED without findings

OEZ *osteuropäische Zeit* Eastern European Time, *abbr* EET

PDS *hist Partei des Demokratischen Sozialismus* Party of Democratic Socialism

Pf *hist Pfennig former German coin* : pfennig

Pfd. *Pfund German weight* : pound

PKW, Pkw *Personenkraftwagen* car

PLZ *Postleitzahl* zip code, *Br* post – code

Prof. *Professor* professor

PS *Pferdestärke(n)* horse-power, *abbr* HP, h.p.; *postscriptum, Nachschrift* postscript, *abbr* PS

Rel. *Religion* religion

S. *Seite* page

s. *siehe* see, *abbr* v., vid. (= vide)

Sa. *Summa, Summe* sum, total

sen. *senior, der Ältere* senior

s. o. *siehe oben* see above

sog. *so genannt* so-called

SPD *Sozialdemokratische Partei Deutschlands* Social Democratic Party of Germany

St. *Stück* piece; *Sankt* Saint

Std. *Stunde* hour, *abbr* h

Str. *Straße* street, *abbr* St.

StVO *Straßenverkehrsordnung* (road) traffic regulations, *in GB* : Highway Code

s. u. *siehe unten* see below

tägl. *täglich* daily, per day

Tel. *Telefon* telephone

TH *Technische Hochschule* college *or* institute of technology

TU *Technische Universität* technical university; college *or* institute of technology

TÜV *Technischer Überwachungs – Verein* safety standards authority

u. a. *und andere(s)* and others; *unter anderem or anderen* among other things, inter alia

UKW *Ultrakurzwelle* ultra-short wave, very high frequency, *abbr* VHF

V *Volt* volt; *Volumen* volume

v. Chr. *vor Christus* before Christ, *abbr* BC

vgl. *vergleiche* confer, *abbr* cf.

WAA *Wiederaufbereitungsanlage* reprocessing plant

WEZ *westeuropäische Zeit* Greenwich Mean Time, *abbr* GMT

WG *Wohngemeinschaft* flat share, flat sharing (community)

WM *Weltmeisterschaft* world championship(s); *soccer*: World Cup

z. B. *zum Beispiel* for instance, *abbr* e.g.

z. H(d). *zu Händen* attention of, to be delivered to, care of, *abbr* c/o

z. T. *zum Teil* partly

zus. *zusammen* together

z. Z(t). *zur Zeit* at the time, at present, for the time being